AA Lifestyle Guides in association with
Corus and Regal

CW01560713

30 re✓axing le
in 6 Free Prize D

see overleaf for terms & condition.

Whether you are looking for a short romantic interlude, a family holiday, an active weekend or just a relaxing break away - you'll feel right at home at Corus and Regal hotels.

Make your choice from historic coaching inns, elegant country houses and city centre hotels. Or maybe you'd prefer a traditional seaside resort. With over 100 hotels throughout the UK, we're sure to have somewhere to suit you.

The Rose & Crown Hotel, Salisbury, Wiltshire

Corus and Regal hotels

For more information on Corus and Regal hotels and for your complimentary copy of their 'Leisure Times' brochure call: 01905 730370 quoting 'AA Lifestyle Guides'

HOW TO ENTER

Just complete (in capitals please) and send off this card or alternatively, send your name and address on a **stamped** postcard to the address overleaf (no purchase required). Entries limited to one per household and to residents of the UK and Republic of Ireland over the age of 18. This card will require a stamp if posted in the Republic of Ireland. **Closing date 30th October 2000**

MR/MRS/MISS/MS/OTHER, PLEASE STATE:

NAME:

ADDRESS:

POSTCODE: TEL. NO:

Are you an AA Member? Yes/No   Have you bought this or any other AA Lifestyle Guide before? Yes/No
If yes, please indicate the year of the last edition you bought:

The AA Hotel Guide	19____	**AA Camping and Caravanning (Europe)**	19____
AA Best Restaurants	19____	**AA Hotels in France**	19____
AA Bed and Breakfast Guide	19____	**AA Bed & Breakfast in France**	19____
AA Camping & Caravanning (Britain & Ireland)	19____	**AA Best Pubs & Inns**	19____

If you do not wish to receive further information or special offers from
AA Publishing ☐   Corus and Regal hotels ☐   please tick the box(es)   BR00

CHRISTMAS CASH BACK OFFER   Offer closes 31 January 2000.

Buy any two of the following AA 2000 Lifestyle Guides, return the cash back vouchers and we'll send you a cheque to the value of the two vouchers up to a maximum of £5.

The Hotel Guide (£2.50 voucher) The Restaurant Guide (£2.50 voucher) Best Pubs & Inns (£1.50 voucher) Bed & Breakfast Guide (£1.50 voucher) The Britain Guide (£1.50 voucher).

HOW TO PARTICIPATE See overleaf for full terms and conditions.

Detach vouchers from books and post them, together with a stamped self-addressed envelope, to AA Lifestyle Guides Cash Back, Fanum House (4), Basing View, Basingstoke, Hants RG21 4EA.

CASH BACK
£2.50
R

Terms and Conditions

1. Five winners will be drawn for each of the six prize draws to take place on 31st December, 1999, 29 February, 28 April, 30 June, 31 August, 31 October, 2000.

2. Closing date for receipt of entries is midday on the relevant draw date. Final close date for receipt of entries is 30 October 2000.

3. Entries received after any draw date other than the final one will go forward into the next available draw. Entries will be placed in one draw only. Only one entry per household accepted.

4. Winners will be notified by post within 14 days of the relevant draw date. Prizes must be booked within 3 months of the relevant draw date. Prizes are not transferable and there will be no cash alternative.

5. This offer cannot be used in conjunction with any other discount, promotion or special offer.

6. Each prize consists of two nights' accommodation, full traditional breakfast and a complimentary bottle of wine on arrival, for two adults sharing a standard twin/double room at participating Corus and Regal hotels. Supplements may be charged for feature and family rooms. All offers of accommodation are made subject to availablity.

7. All hotel accommodation, services and facilities are provided by Corus and Regal hotels and AA Publishing is not party to your agreement with Corus & Regal hotels in this regard.

8. The prize draw is open to anyone resident in the UK or the Republic of Ireland over the age of 18 other than employees of the Automobile Association or Corus and Regal hotels, their subsidiary companies, their families or agents.

9. For a list of winners, please send a stamped, self-addressed envelope to AA Lifestyle Guides Winners, Publishing Admin, Fanum House, Basing View, Basingstoke, Hants, RG21 4EA.

10. If this card is posted in the Republic of Ireland it must have a stamp.

BUSINESS REPLY SERVICE
Licence No BZ 343

PLEASE NOTE: Requires a stamp if posted in Republic of Ireland

AA Lifestyle Guide 2000 Prize Draw

AA PUBLISHING
FANUM HOUSE
BASING VIEW
BASINGSTOKE
HANTS RG21 4EA

CASH BACK £2·50

CHRISTMAS CASH BACK TERMS & CONDITIONS

1. This offer is open only to residents of the UK and Republic of Ireland.

2. Only original vouchers will be accepted and no responsibility will be accepted for vouchers lost or damaged in the post or illegible applications.

3. You may make any number of applications provided two AA Lifestyle Guides 2000 are purchased in each instance.

4. Each application must be accompanied by a clearly legible stamped self-addressed envelope.

5. **Closing date for receipt of vouchers is 31 January 2000.**

Restaurants

How to use *this guide*

1   The Guide's entries are divided into sections. London restaurants are listed alphabetically by name. There is also a London postcode index on page 739. In the rest of Britain, establishments are listed in country and county order, by town, and then alphabetically within that town. There is also an index by establishment name.

2   indicates an entry new to the Guide this year.

3   indicates an establishment which responded '50% or more' when asked what percentage of their ingredients are organically sourced.

4   is the Guide's rosette award for cooking quality. Every restaurant included has been awarded one or more rosettes, up to a maximum of five. See below for a clear explanation of how they are graded.

5   Directions are given wherever they have been supplied by the proprietor.

6   The establishment's address and postcode.

7   The map number. In the London section, each restaurant has a map reference number to help locate its approximate position on the Central or Greater London maps on page 736. In the remainder of the Guide, the map references refer to the 16 pages of maps of Britain starting on page 719. First is the map page number, followed by the National Grid Reference. To find the location, read the first figure across and the second figure vertically within the lettered square.

8   The establishment's telephone and fax numbers, including STD code.

9   The names of the chef(s) and owner(s) (entries of two rosettes and above only). These are as up-to-date as we could make them at the time of going to press, but changes in personnel often occur, and may affect both the style and the quality of the restaurant.

10 *Alc* is the cost of a meal for one person, including coffee and service but not wine. Set-price lunch and dinner menus come next. If these meals have more or less than three courses we have indicated this. The cost of the house wine or one of the cheaper wines on the list follows. Prices quoted are a guide only, and are subject to change without notice. ☺ indicates where restaurants have told us they offer dinner for under £25 a head (excluding wine).

2

1   BRISTOL, The Restaurant NEW

5   **Directions**: City centre

6   The Street XY21 1AB

7   **Map 3**: ST57

8   **Tel**: 0111 2345678
    Fax: 0111 3456789

9   **Chef**: John Brown
    Owner: John & Mary Brown

10 **Cost**: *Alc* £26.50, set-price L £11.50 (2 courses)/D £22. H/wine £9.75. ☺

11 **Times**: Noon-last L 2pm/7pm-last D 10pm. Closed L Sat, Sun, Mon, 1 wk Easter, 1 wk summer, 10 days Xmas, Bhs

12 **Additional**: Bar meals; Sunday L; Children welcome; ⑥ dishes

13 **Seats**: 40. Private dining room 26. Jacket & tie preferred

14 **Smoking**: No smoking in dining room

15 **Accommodation**: 3 en suite ★ ★ ★

16 **Credit cards**: none taken

11 The times of the first and last orders for meals, and the days of the week the restaurant is closed, together with seasonal closures. Note that opening times are liable to change without notice. It is always a good idea to telephone any establishment which you are intending to visit to avoid disappointment.

12 In addition to meals in the restaurant, bar meals are served at lunch and/or dinner; Sunday lunch is served; Children are welcome, any age limitations are specified; ✿ indicates where a vegetarian choice is always offered on a menu. Almost all restaurants featured will prepare a vegetarian dish or accommodate a special diet if given prior notice, but even where a symbol appears by an entry it is wise to check with the establishment first.

13 The number of seats in the restaurant. Not all restaurants will take private parties, the number given is for the maximum number of people in a party. Jacket and tie are compulsory in a few restaurants, and this is specified.

14 Establishments that do not allow smoking in the dining room may allow it elsewhere, in a lounge or bar, for instance. If you are a smoker, it is worth checking beforehand.

15 Accommodation is also available. If a hotel belongs to the AA Hotel scheme, then its star rating also appears here.

16 All establishments take major credit cards, except where we specify otherwise.

Telephone for directions appears where an establishment has not supplied us with current details.

Signature dishes appear at the end of the main entry and are supplied by chefs from establishments who have three or more Rosettes. Some entries do not show signature dishes either because the chef has chosen not to give them, or the establishment was a late appointment.

How the AA Assesses Restaurants for Rosette Awards

The AA's rosette award scheme is the only home-grown, nation-wide scheme for assessing the quality of food served by restaurants and hotels. The rosette scheme is an award scheme, not a classification scheme and although there is necessarily an element of subjectivity when it comes to assessing taste, we aim for a consistent approach to our awards throughout the UK. It is important, however, to remember that many places serve enjoyable food but do not qualify for an AA award.

Our awards are made solely on the basis of a meal visit or visits by one or more of our hotel and restaurant inspectors who have an unrivalled breadth and depth of experience in assessing quality. They award rosettes annually on a rising scale of one to five.

Recommendations from users of the guides are always welcome and will be passed on to the inspectors on merit for their consideration, but we do not guarantee a meal visit or an entry in the guide. Rosette awards are made or withdrawn only on the basis of our own inspectors' meal visits.

So What Makes A Restaurant Worthy of a Rosette Award?

For our inspectors, frequently eating alone, the top and bottom line is the food. They are not swayed by a fashionable or luxurious setting, by the friendliness or immaculate uniforms of the staff, by fussy, over-elaborate presentation, or even by the size of the bill. The taste of the food is what counts for them, and whether the dish successfully delivers to the diner what the menu promises. A restaurant is only as good as its worst meal.

Although presentation and competent service should be appropriate to the style of the restaurant and the quality of the food, they cannot affect the rosette assessment as such, either up or down.

The following summaries attempt to explain what our inspectors look for, but are intended only as guidelines. The AA is constantly reviewing its award criteria and competition usually results in an all-round improvement in standards, so it becomes increasingly difficult for restaurants to reach award level.

One rosette

At the simplest level, one rosette, the chef should display a mastery of basic techniques and be able to produce dishes of sound quality and clarity of flavours, using good, fresh ingredients:

Summary
* Fresh ingredients
* Sound quality
* Basic technical skills - e.g. pastry, sauce-making
* Home-made desserts, stocks, sauces
* Clarity of flavours
* Simple, uncomplicated dishes
* Food served at correct temperature

Two rosettes

To gain two rosettes, the chef must show greater technical skill, more consistency and judgement in combining and balancing ingredients and a clear ambition to achieve high standards. Inspectors will look for evidence of innovation to test the dedication of the kitchen brigade, and the use of seasonal ingredients sourced from quality suppliers.

Summary
* Dedicated approach
* Sound technical skills, both classical and modern
* Seasonal, high quality ingredients
* Clear, well defined flavours
* Consistency throughout all courses
* Side dishes matched to main ingredients
* Some innovative dishes
* Balanced, harmonious combinations
* More sophisticated and appropriate garnishes

Three rosettes

This award takes a restaurant into the big league, and, in a typical year, fewer than 10 per cent of restaurants in our scheme achieve this distinction. Expectations of the kitchen are high, and inspectors find little room for inconsistencies. Exact technique, flair and imagination will come through in every dish, and balance and depth of flavour are all-important.

Summary
* No inconsistencies
* Extra quality checks made

* Ancillaries (e.g. appetisers, bread, garnishes, petits fours), if provided, should contribute to the meal, not merely be padding
* The diner's high expectations should be fully met
* Higher technical skills successfully executed
* Vegetables, as a general rule, an integral part of main dish
* Depth of flavour in stocks and sauces
* Flair and imaginative combinations of ingredients
* Specialist, high quality suppliers

Four rosettes

This is an exciting award because, at this level, not only should all technical skills be exemplary, but there should also be daring ideas, and they must work. There is no room for disappointment. Flavours should be accurate and vibrant.

Summary
* No disappointments and few faults
* Ingredients from suppliers of international repute
* All items made in-house
* Thorough grounding in classical techniques
* Repertoire equally at home in traditional and modern dishes
* Evolving ideas and concepts, with an element of excitement and daring

Five rosettes

This award is the ultimate awarded only when the cooking is at the pinnacle of achievement. Technique should be of such perfection that flavours, combinations and textures show a faultless sense of balance, giving each dish an extra dimension. The sort of cooking that never falters and always strives to give diners a truly memorable taste experience.

Summary
* Faultless presentation
* Perfection in every element at every inspection visit
* Attention to detail throughout
* Intense, exciting flavours
* Harmonious marriage of ingredients
* Skilful use of luxury ingredients
* Secret ingredients giving an extra dimension to a dish
* All culinary skills come to fruition together

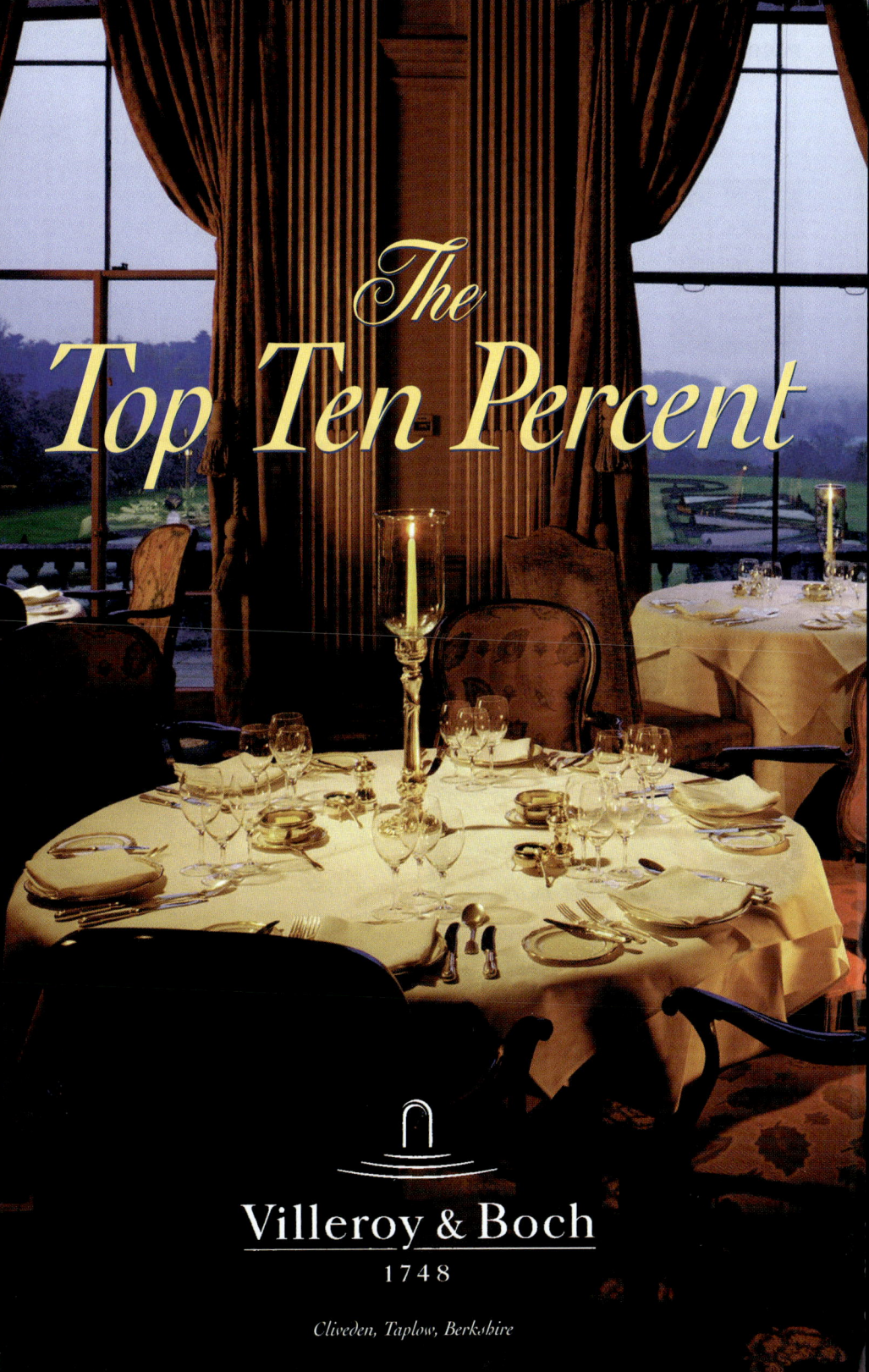

Founded in 1748, Villeroy & Boch is one of Europe's oldest and largest family owned industrial enterprises. Started by François Boch and three of his sons, the business now owns 20 production plants and employs over 10,000 personnel, many of whom come from families that have worked for the company for generations.

Switch Coffee House

Villeroy & Boch

Raymond Blanc

Ivoire

Totally devoted to the production of quality ranges including ceramics, Villeroy & Boch has, from the very start, been at the forefront of technical innovation within the industry. Innovations that revolutionised manufacturing processes and set industry standards during the early 1800s, and which today continue to push back the boundaries of ceramic manufacturing.

Artistic expertise is another cornerstone of the company and Villeroy & Boch has a well deserved reputation for creating beautiful and aspirational products. This is based on the skill of its in-house craftsmen, and frequent collaborations with renowned designers such as Paloma Picasso. The company portfolio now includes many award-winning designs, and one current tableware best-seller, Vieux Luxembourg, was first created in 1760.

The Villeroy & Boch products illustrating this section are a small indication of the variety and versatility for which the company is known, they are used in many of the better restaurants around the UK and are also available to the consumer at leading department stores, specialist shops, or from The House of Villeroy & Boch shop at Bluewater, Kent.

If you would like a brochure and stockist list, telephone 0181 875 6060 (24 hrs)

✿✿✿✿ LONDON

Chez Nico,
At Ninety Park Lane, W1
0171 409 1290
Le Gavroche,
43 Upper Brook Street, W1
0171 408 0881
Le Meridien Piccadilly,
Marco Pierre White,
The Oak Room 21 Piccadilly, W1
0171 437 0202
Restaurant Gordon Ramsay,
68 Royal Hospital Road, SW3
0171 352 6045
La Tante Claire,
The Berkeley, Wilton Place, SW1
0171 823 2003

ENGLAND

BERKSHIRE
L'Ortolan, Church Lane, Shinfield
0118 9883783

DEVON
Gidleigh Park, Chagford
01647 432367

OXFORDSHIRE
Le Manoir Aux Quat' Saisons,
Great Milton
01844 278881

SCOTLAND

HIGHLAND
Altnaharrie Inn, Ullapool
01854 633230

✿✿✿✿ LONDON

Pied à Terre,
34 Charlotte Street, W1
0171 636 1178
Mandarin Oriental Hyde Park,
66 Knightsbridge, SW1
0171 235 2000
The Square,
6, Bruton Street,W1
0171 495 7100

ENGLAND

BERKSHIRE
The Fat Duck, High Street, Bray
01628 580333
Waterside Inn, Ferry Road, Bray
01628 620691

CUMBRIA
Michael's Nook, Grasmere,
015394 35496

GLOUCESTERSHIRE
Le Champignon Sauvage,
24, Suffolk Road, Cheltenham
01242 573449

LINCOLNSHIRE
Winteringham Fields,
Winteringham
01724 733096

RUTLAND
Hambleton Hall, Oakham
01572 756991

SOMERSET
Restaurant Lettonie,
35, Kelston Road, Bath
01225 446676

REPUBLIC OF IRELAND

DUBLIN
Thornton's Restaurant,
1, Portobello Road, Dublin 8
01 4549067

✿✿✿ LONDON

EC4
City Rhodes, 1, New Street Square
0171 583 1313

NW1
Landmark Hotel,
222 Marylebone Road
0171 631 8000

SW1
Le Caprice,
Arlington House, Arlington Street
0171 629 2239
The Halkin Hotel, Halkin Street
0171 333 1000
The Lanesborough,
Hyde Park Corner
0171 259 5599
Roussillon,
16, St Barnabas Street,
0171 730 5550
Sheraton Park Tower,
101 Knightsbridge
0171 235 8050
Zafferano, 15, Lowndes Street
0171 235 5800

SW3
Bibendum, Michelin House,
0171 581 5817
The Capital,
Basil Street, Knightsbridge,
0171 589 5171
Floriana,
15 Beauchamp Place,
0171 838 1500
Zaika,
257-259 Fulham Road,
0171 351 7823

SW6
755 Fulham Road,
755 Fulham Road
0171 371 0755

SW7
Hilaire, 68, Old Brompton Road
0171 584 8993

SW10
Aubergine,
11 Park Walk, SW10
0171 352 3449
The Canteen,
Harbour Yard, Chelsea Harbour
0171 351 7330

SW13
Riva Restaurant,
169, Church Road, Barnes
0181 748 0434

SW14
Petrus, 33 St James Street
0171 930 4272

SW17
Chez Bruce, 2, Bellevue Road
0181 672 0114

W1
Alastair Little Restaurant,
49 Frith Street
0171 734 5183
The Dorchester, The Oriental,
Park Lane
0171 317 6328
**The London Hilton On Park
Lane,** 22 Park Lane
0171 493 8000
Hotel Inter-Continental,
1, Hamilton Place, Hyde Park
0171 409 3131
Lindsay House, 21 Romilly Street
0171 439 0450
Mirabelle, 56 Curzon Street
0171 499 4636
Mortons,
28 Berkeley Square,
0171 493 7171
L'Odeon, 65, Regent Street
0171 287 1400
Orrery,
55-57 Marylebone High Street
0171 616 8000
Quo Vadis, 26-29 Dean Street
0171 437 9585

W6
River Café, Thames Wharf Studios,
Hammersmith
0171 381 8824

W8
Royal Garden Hotel,
2-24 Kensington High Street
0171 937 8000

W11
Halcyon Hotel, 81, Holland Park
0171 727 7288
Leith's, 92, Kensington Park Road
0171 229 4481

W14

Chinon, 23, Richmond Way
0171 602 5968

WC2

The Ivy,
1, West Street, Covent Garden
0171 836 4751
The Savoy, River Restaurant,
The Strand
0171 836 4343

ENGLAND

BEDFORDSHIRE

Flitwick Manor,
Church Road, Flitwick
01525 712242

BERKSHIRE

Fredrick's Hotel,
Shoppenhangers Road, Maidenhead
01628 635934
The Vineyard at Stockcross,
Stockcross, Newbury
01635 528770
Royal Oak Hotel,
The Square, Yattendon
01635 201325

BRISTOL

Harveys Restaurant,
12, Denmark Street, Bristol
0117 927 5034

BUCKINGHAMSHIRE

Hartwell House,
Oxford Road, Aylesbury
01296 747444

CAMBRIDGESHIRE

The Pink Geranium,
Station Road, Melbourn
01763 260215

CHESHIRE

Crabwall Manor,
Parkgate Road, Mollington, Chester
01244 851666
The Chester Grosvenor,
Eastgate, Chester
01244 324024
Nunsmere Hall,
Tarporley Road, Oakmere, Sandiway
01606 889100

CORNWALL & ISLES OF SCILLY

Pennypots,
Maenporth Beach, Falmouth
01326 250251
Well House Hotel,
St Keyne, Liskeard
01579 342001
The Seafood Restaurant,
Riverside, Padstow
01841 532485

St Martin's On The Isle,
Lower Town, St Martin's
01720 422092
Hotel Tresanton,
Lower Castle Road, St Mawes
01326 270055

CUMBRIA

Sharrow Bay, Howtown
017684 86301
Underscar Manor,
Applethwaite, Keswick
017687 75000
Rampsbeck Country House Hotel,
Watermillock
017684 86442
Holbeck Ghyll,
Holbeck Lane, Windermere
015394 32375

DERBYSHIRE

Fischer's Baslow Hall,
Calver Road, Baslow
01246 583259
The Old Vicarage,
Ridgeway Moor, Ridgeway
0114 2475814

DEVON

Holne Chase Hotel,
Two Bridges Road, Ashburton
01364 631471
The Horn Of Plenty, Gulworthy
01822 832528
Arundell Arms, Lifton
01566 784666
Chez Nous,
13, Frankfurt Gate, Plymouth
01752 266793
Whitechapel Manor, South Molton
01769 573377
Pophams, Castle Street, Winkleigh
01837 83767

Jardin d'Alsace

DORSET

Summer Lodge, Evershot
01935 83424
Stock Hill Country House Hotel,
Stock Hill, Gillingham
01747 823626

GLOUCESTERSHIRE

Buckland Manor,
Buckland, Broadway
01386 852626
The Greenway,
Shurdington, Cheltenham
01242 862352
Lower Slaughter Manor,
Lower Slaughter
01451 820456
The Close Hotel,
8 Long Street, Tetbury
01666 502272
Lords Of The Manor,
Upper Slaughter
01451 820243

GREATER LONDON

Chapter One, Farnborough
Common, Locksbottom, Bromley
01689 854848

GREATER MANCHESTER

Juniper,
21, The Downs, Altrincham
0161 929 4008

HAMPSHIRE

Le Poussin,
The Courtyard, Brockenhurst
01590 623063
36 On The Quay,
47 South Street, Emsworth
01243 375592
The Three Lions,
Stuckton, Fordingbridge
01425 652489

Hollington Country House,
Woolton Hill, Highclere
01635 255100
Chewton Glen Hotel,
Christchurch Road, New Milton
01425 275341
Old Manor House,
21, Palmerston Street, Romsey
01794 517353

HERTFORDSHIRE
Edgwarebury Hotel,
Barnet Lane, Elstree
0181 953 8227
Marriott Hanbury Manor, Ware
01920 487722

KENT
Eastwell Manor,
Boughton Lees, Ashford
01233 219955
Read's Restaurant,
Painters Forstal Faversham
01795 535344
Sandgate Hotel,
The Esplanade, Folkestone
01303 220444

LANCASHIRE
Northcote Manor, Langho
01254 240555
Paul Heathcote's Restaurant,
104-106 Higher Road, Longridge
01772 784969

LINCOLNSHIRE
Harry's Place, 17, High Street,
Great Gonerby, Grantham
01476 561780

NORFOLK
Morston Hall, Blakeney
01263 741041
Adlard's Restaurant,
79, Upper Giles Street, Norwich
01603 633522

NOTTINGHAMSHIRE
Hart's Restaurant,
1 Standard Court, Nottingham
0115 911 0666

OXFORDSHIRE
Chavignol,
7, Horsefair, Chipping Norton
01608 644490
Beetle & Wedge,
Ferry Lane, Moulsford
01491 651381
Feathers Hotel, Market Street,
Woodstock 01993 812291

SHROPSHIRE
Merchant House,
62, Lower Corve Street, Ludlow
01584 875438

Mr Underhill's Restaurant,
Dinham Weir, Ludlow
01584 874431
Oaks Restaurant,
17 Corve Street, Ludlow
01584 872325
Overton Grange,
Hereford Road, Ludlow
01584 873500
Sol Restaurant,
82, Wyle Cop, Shrewsbury
01743 340560
Old Vicarage Hotel,
Worfield
01746 716497

SOMERSET
Bath Priory, Weston Road, Bath
01225 331922
Royal Crescent,
16, Royal Crescent, Bath
01225 823333
Homewood Park,
Hinton Charterhouse
01225 723731
Hunstrete House Hotel,
Hunstrete
01761 490490
Charlton House Hotel,
Charlton Road, Shepton Mallet
01749 342008
White House Hotel,
Long Street, Williton
01984 632306

SUFFOLK
Hintlesham Hall, Hintlesham
01473 652334

SURREY
Pennyhill Park,
London Road, Bagshot
01276 471774
Michels', 13, High Street, Ripley
01483 224777

SUSSEX, EAST
Röser's Restaurant, 64, Eversfield
Place, St Leonards-On-Sea
01424 712218

SUSSEX, WEST
Gravetye Manor, East Grinstead
01342 810567
South Lodge Hotel,
Brighton Road, Lower Beeding
01403 891711

TYNE & WEAR
21 Queen Street,
Quayside, Newcastle Upon Tyne
0191 222 0755

WARWICKSHIRE
Mallory Court Hotel,
Harbury Lane, Bishop's Tachbrook,
Royal Leamington Spa
01926 330214

ISLE OF WIGHT
George Hotel,
Quay Street, Yarmouth
01983 760331

WILTSHIRE
Manor House Hotel, Castle Combe
01249 782206
Lucknam Park, Colerne
01225 742777
London House Restaurant,
Market Place, Pewsey
01672 564775
Howard's House Hotel,
Teffont Evias, Salisbury
01722 716392

WORCESTERSHIRE
The Lygon Arms, Broadway
01386 852255
Brockencote Hall,
Chaddesley Corbett
01562 777876
Croque-En-Bouche,
221, Wells Road, Malvern
01684 565612

YORKSHIRE, NORTH
Middlethorpe Hall,
Bishopthorpe Road, York
01904 641241

YORKSHIRE, SOUTH
Smith's Of Sheffield,
34, Sandygate Road, Sheffield
01142 666 096

YORKSHIRE, WEST
Box Tree Restaurant,
35-37, Church Street, Ilkley
01943 608484
Pool Court At 42,
44, The Calls, Leeds
0113 244 4242
Rascasse, Canal Wharf, Leeds
0113 244 6611

CHANNEL ISLANDS
JERSEY
Longueville Manor, St Saviour
01534 25501

SCOTLAND
ABERDEENSHIRE
Darroch Learg,
Braemar Road, Ballater
013397 55443

ARGYLL & BUTE
Isle Of Eriska, Eriska
01631 720371
Kilfinan Hotel, Kilfinan
01700 821201
Airds Hotel, Port Appin
01631 730236

AYRSHIRE, SOUTH
Lochgreen House, Troon
01292 313343

Switch Coffee House

DUMFRIES & GALLOWAY
Kirroughtree House,
Minnigaff, Newton Stewart
01671 402141
Knockinaam Lodge, Portpatrick
01776 810471

DUNBARTONSHIRE, WEST
Cameron House Hotel, Balloch
01389 755565

EDINBURGH, CITY OF
Atrium,
Cambridge Street, Edinburgh
0131 228 8882
The Sheraton Grand Hotel,
1, Festival Square, Edinburgh
0131 229 9131

FIFE
Cellar Restaurant,
24, East Green, Anstruther
01333 310378
Ostlers Close, Bonnygate, Cupar
01334 655574
The Peat Inn, Peat Inn
01334 840206

GLASGOW, CITY OF
One Devonshire Gardens, Glasgow
0141 339 2001

HIGHLAND
Arisaig House, Beasdale, Arisaig
01687 450622
Inverlochy Castle,
Torlundy, Fort William
01397 702177
The Cross,
Tweed Mill Brae, Kingussie
01540 661166

LOTHIAN, EAST
La Potinière, Main Street, Gullane
01620 843214

PERTH & KINROSS
Kinloch House, Blairgowrie
01250 884237
Kinnaird, Dunkeld
01796 482440

STIRLING
Roman Camp Hotel, Callander
01877 330003

WALES

CARDIFF
St David's Hotel & Spa,
Havannah Street, Cardiff Bay
029 20454045

CEREDIGION
Ynyshir Hall, Eglwysfach
01654 781209

CONWY
Tan-Y-Foel,
Capel Garmon, Betws-Y-Coed
01690 710507
The Old Rectory, Llansanffraid
Glan Conwy, Conwy
01492 580611
Bodysgallen Hall, Llandudno
01492 584466
St Tudno, Promenade, Llandudno
01492 874411

DENBIGHSHIRE
Tyddyn Llan, Llandrillo
01490 440264

GWYNEDD
Plas Bodegroes,
Nefyn Road, Pwllheli
01758 612363

MONMOUTHSHIRE
Walnut Tree Inn, Llanddewi Skyrrid
01873 852797
Crown At Whitebrook, Whitebrook
01600 860254

POWYS
Carlton House,
Dolycoed Road, Llanwrtyd Wells
01591 610248
Llangoed Hall, Llyswen
01874 754525

SWANSEA
Fairyhill,
Reynoldston
01792 390139

NORTHERN IRELAND

BELFAST
Deanes,
38-40, Howard Street, Belfast
01232 560000

DOWN
Shanks, The Blackwood,
Crawfordsburn Road, Bangor
01247 853313

REPUBLIC OF IRELAND

CORK
Longueville House Hotel,
Mallow
022 47156

DONEGAL
Harvey's Point Country Hotel,
Lough Eske, Donegal
073 22208

DUBLIN
Hibernian Hotel, Eastmoreland
Place, Ballsbridge, Dublin
01 6687666
The Clarence,
6-8 Wellington Quay, Dublin
01 6709000
The Merrion Hotel,
Upper Merrion Street, Dublin
01 6030600

KERRY
Park Hotel Kenmare,
Kenmare
064 41200
Agadoe Heights Hotel,
Killarney
064 31766

KILDARE
The Kildare Hotel, Straffan
01 6017200

LIMERICK
Dunraven Arms Hotel,
Adare
061 396633

the top ten percent

AA Hotel Services

The AA Hotel Booking Service - Now you have a free, simple way to reserve a place to stay for a week, weekend, or a one-night stopover.

Do you want to book somewhere in the Lake District that has leisure facilities; a city-centre hotel in Glasgow with parking facilities, or do you need accommodation near Dover which is handy for the Eurotunnel? The AA Booking Service can take the hassle out of booking the right place for you.

If you are touring round the UK or Ireland, simply give the AA Hotel Booking Service your list of overnight stops, and from one phone call all your accommodation can be booked for you.

Telephone 0870 5050505

Office hours
Monday - Friday 9am - 6pm
Saturday 9am - 1pm
The service is not available
Sundays or Bank Holidays

Full listings of AA recognised accommodation available through the Hotel Booking Service can be found and booked at the AA's Internet Site:

http://www.theaa.co.uk/hotels

Chefs' Chef
of the year

Who will be the AA Chefs' Chef to take us into the millennium?

It was an extraordinary result. In the past, when we've asked the 1,800 AA Rosetted chefs to nominate one of their peers for the prestigious Chefs' Chef of the Year, there has always been a huge response and a clear winner. But the millennium vote was different: a huge response with six highly regarded but very different chefs polling the same number of votes:

Raymond Blanc	*Le Manoir Aux Quat' Saisons*
Michael Caines	*Gidleigh Park*
Peter Gordon	*The Sugar Club*
Philip Howard	*The Square*
Rick Stein	*Seafood Restaurant*
Marco Pierre White	*The Oak Room*

So out went 1,800 more nomination forms. This time we asked everyone to pick just one of the six. And they did - with a vengeance. We polled more votes the second time around. It was still a tight call, but the finalists for the year 2000 are as follows, listed alphabetically.

Raymond Blanc,
Le Manoir Aux Quat' Saisons

Raymond Blanc arrived in England in 1972, at the age of 23, to work as a waiter at the Rose Revived, near Witney in Oxfordshire. When the chef became ill, he took over, and the rest, they say, is history. Today, Blanc is acknowledged as one of the finest chefs in the world, noted not just for his sense of imagination and adventure with food, but for his intelligent approach to it. In 1984 he fulfilled a personal ambition when he opened Le Manoir Aux Quat' Saisons in Great Milton in Oxfordshire. Many would have been satisfied with that, but Blanc is not the sort of person to stand still. In 1991, Le Manoir's Ecole de Cuisine was set up to offer non-professional cooks the opportunity to develop their skills, and the now famed two acre organic kitchen garden took shape. In 1996, Blanc opened the first of his brasserie-style operations in Oxford; Le Petit Blanc has gone on to be replicated at Cheltenham. And for the millennium, the 15th-century Le Manoir has just undergone a multi-million pound refurbishment. And he still cooks.

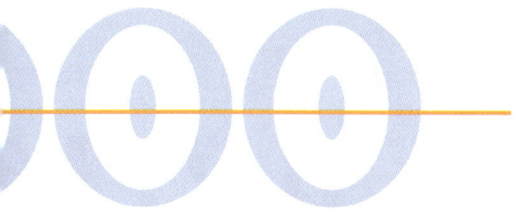

OOOO

Rick Stein,
The Seafood Restaurant, Padstow
❀ ❀ ❀

Michael Caines,
Gidleigh Park, Chagford
❀ ❀ ❀ ❀ ❀

The youngest of our nominated chefs was shortlisted last year for Chefs' Chef of the Year, an impressive achievement for a young man no one had heard of five years ago. When Shaun Hill quit the kitchens of Gidleigh Park, Michael Caines was appointed to take over - an unknown 25 year old with an impressive CV that took in the kitchens of Raymond Blanc in Oxfordshire, Joël Robuchon in Paris and Bernard Loiseau in Salieu in Burgundy. It was an act of impressive talent spotting on the part of Gidleigh Park owner, Paul Henderson. Shaun Hill was a hard act to follow and it says something about Caines that he has matched Gidleigh Park perfectly, his own ambition and achievement ensuring that he is currently the youngest chef to hold the AA's top accolade of five Rosettes. He works hard at his craft, his French training forming the backbone of his ideas, the regional and local produce inspiring his menus, and his outlook young, sharp and to the point. Taste and flavour are paramount, accuracy is everything - hard lessons learnt in France and given the incisive but potent Caines twist.

Rick Stein remains a popular chef's choice; shortlisted for the 1999 award, he is once again a hot contender for the Chefs' Chef 2000 award. He has been an inspiration to many, both in showing how far a completely self-taught chef can go, and as a passionate advocate of fish cookery. An Oxford graduate, Stein has successfully married sheer enthusiasm for food with a thoughtful, considered manner; a combination that has enabled him to develop a world-class seafood restaurant. He has always claimed he opened his restaurant out of desperation - the site had previously been a night-club which the police had closed down. Whatever, it was a shrewd move, as was the idea to cook the locally-caught fish at a time when fish was usually regarded with dread by generations raised on Friday fish at school. Through his popular TV series, and through his cookery books, Stein has single handedly raised the profile of fish cookery in this country. He has put Padstow on the map, opening cheaper, more accessible versions of his style - St Petroc Hotel and Rick Stein's Café - in the wake of his fame.

AA wine

From an entry of close on 850 of the restaurants featured in the 1999 Restaurant Guide, our panel of assessors sat down to appraise some of the country's most interesting wine lists.

Reaching decisions was even more difficult than in our first year, but after about 20 hours of painful deliberations, agreement was reached among our three assessors on the best 120 which were to be invited to go through to Round Two.

The questionnaire for Round Two, in similar vein to last year, asked contestants to match wine to food. Firstly on a fixed menu, no expense spared, we asked contestants to make the choice appropriate not only to each dish, but also to follow a balanced progression through the menu as a whole. As a second part of this section we asked for wines with a price ceiling of £30 to partner individual dishes.

This was the most serious part of our questionnaire, but in lighter vein we also gave an example of a wine list displaying a range of faults, which had been commonly found on the wine lists our assessors had been looking at, to help them to separate sheep from goats in this second stage.

These common faults were:

- Split vintages
- Simple spelling mistakes
- Giving no provenance for a wine
- Offering wines all from a single grower or négociant, and that is not necessarily the best
- Stocking only 'standard' lines
- Badly organised and difficult for the customer to work through
- Lists not revised to remove 'out of stock' or 'unavailable' bins
- Confusing wines of one region with those of another: for example, Rhone/Burgundy; Beaujolais/Loire

Two other faults also helped eliminate some contestants:

- Only completing side one of our questionnaire
- Not giving any name or address

awards

Willi Opitz, award-winning dessert winemaker (left) with Paul Richardson, of The Old Bridge Hotel, Huntingdon, winner of the Automobile Association Wine Award 1999

LONDON
Atlantic Bar
Café du Jardin
Chez Nico
Four Seasons
Leith's Restaurant
Odette's
Pied à Terre
Ransome's Dock

ENGLAND
Harvey's, Bristol
Bell Inn, Aston Clinton
Three Horseshoes, Madingley
Corisande Manor, Newquay
Crosby Lodge, Carlisle
Callow Hall, Ashbourne
Fischer's, Baslow
Corse Lawn, Corse Lawn
Vistro, Crawley

36 on the Quay, Emsworth
Chewton Glen, New Milton
Sandgate Hotel, Folkestone
Northcote Manor, Langho
Winteringham Fields, Winteringham
Adlard's Restaurant, Norwich
French Partridge, Horton
Sir Charles Napier, Chinnor
Chavignol, Chipping Norton
Hintlesham Hall, Hintlesham
Ashdown Park Hotel, Forest Row
George and Dragon, Rowde
Cottage in the Woods, Malvern Wells
Meltons, York

CHANNEL ISLANDS
Suma's Restaurant, Gorey, Jersey

SCOTLAND
Kinloch House, Blairgowrie
Knockinaam Lodge, Portpatrick
Greywalls, Gullane
Witchery by the Castle, Edinburgh

WALES
St Tudno, Llandudno
Llangoed Hall, Llyswen
St David's Park, Ewloe
Fairyhill, Reynoldston

The AA Wine Award is sponsored by  **T&W Wines** of Thetford, Norfolk

*Last year's winner, **The Old Bridge** at Huntingdon, generously did not enter this year, but their entry and that of Scotland's winner, **Kinnaird** at Dunkeld are also highlighted as holders of the Wine Award.*

Organic
MATTERS

BSE turned us all into food experts. It made us ask where our food came from. Then, just as we were learning to live without beef, along came E-coli and other food-related scares. But it was the mother of all monsters, genetically modified foods, that finally put the boot in. Enough, enough, we shrieked, desperately reading the small print on every item of food we bought. Is it any wonder that organic food products are so widely available in Britain today; that major supermarkets are rapidly reversing out of the genetically modified road they had greedily rushed down, in order to jump on the growing fleet of organic bandwagons.

But we have only ourselves to blame. The public demand for cheap food products created the situation where feeding cattle dead carcasses was an obvious money-saving solution. After all, it's cheap protein! We may shudder now, but only after the awful consequences have been made all too apparent.

The huge public outcry against genetically modified foods has its roots in the BSE scandal. As the Greenpeace True Food Campaign so forcefully states - 'genetic engineering transfers genes from one species to another - in ways that could never happen in nature... Genes have been transferred from a fish into a strawberry, and from a human into a sheep.' And we don't like the sound of it, let alone want to eat it!

With public confidence already shaken and with big commercial food producers viewed as not having our best interests at heart - driven by profit, with loyalty only to their shareholders - the consensus is that we have had enough of agri-businesses mucking around with the things

we eat; enough of being human guinea pigs. Is it too much to want to eat eggs from chickens that have been free to roam in the fresh air, eat meat from animals who have been humanely reared, taste vegetables free from the pesticides, herbicides, and preservatives that keep them supermarket fresh? There is a direct link between the food we eat and good health - BSE and the E-coli outbreaks proved that forcefully.

But what about when we go out to eat. How can we be sure that the food restaurateurs serve us is as carefully considered as the food we eat at home? How do restaurateurs shape up to a food-safety conscious public?

In particular, what are the views of the 1,900 establishments listed in *The Restaurant Guide?* With this in mind we asked all the AA Rosetted hotels and restaurants just what their buying policy was - how much food was locally sourced, how much organic.

It is obviously a subject close to many restaurateurs' hearts; the response was tremendous. Raymond Blanc's two acre organic kitchen garden may have been well documented in the media, but it appears many country properties quietly make the most of their gardens and surrounding countryside. And what an industrious lot they are: growing vegetables, fruit, herbs and flowers, going out and collecting seasonal wild foods such as wild garlic, sea beet, sorrel, samphire, elderflowers, ceps, wood blewits. As for sourcing, the buying philosophy of many was summed up by Beechwood Hotel, North Walsham, Norfolk, when they wrote - 'we are strongly opposed to intensive livestock production including battery farm eggs.'

Scotland's natural larder is a rich resource. Fouters Bistro in Ayr, are strong supporters of organic smallholdings and producers 'buying when produce is in season, which our menus reflect.' And, like all catering establishments recognised by The Taste of Scotland, Fouters have a mission statement that includes offering guests 'as much as possible of locally sourced produce'. Guests at Creagan House, Strathyre are assured that eggs are 'truly free-range from a local farm - over the mountain visible from the dining room.' A statement endorsed by The Cross at Kingussie who make a valid point: '...we would rather know where the food originates from than buy blind just because it says organic.' Adding, for good measure, that genetically modified foods will never knowingly find their way into their kitchen.
Genetic engineering gets short shrift.
'P.S. I am also very anti genetic engineering', from Mrs Day of The Edgemoor Hotel in Devon, is typical of many comments made to us. And it is good to learn that Greenpeace UK have picked up on this general mood with their Chefs against GE campaign, launched in the spring of 1999 with eighteen top chefs in support. Chefs will be invited to sign a well publicised anti-genetic engineering statement, adhere to a 4-point pledge on how to go GE free, and be provided with a draft letter to send out to suppliers. A prominently displayed sticker will act as a badge of reassurance for customers.
For many, buying organic food is the only safe

bet. 'I would love to run a purely organic restaurant and over the last few years have experimented in various ways', remarks Veronica Shaw, of Veronica's Restaurant in Bayswater, London. But the inconsistency of supply, fluctuations in pricing, with meat still being excessively high, and government inertia regarding funding, present real stumbling blocks for such restaurateurs.

But it is predicted that in the first decade of the new millennium, the organic sector will grow by a further 30 per cent. As we went to press, the Soil Association was finalising the criteria required to gain its Organic Restaurant Certificate. Thus far, three restaurants have been awarded the Certificate on the grounds of their strong organic commitment. For the consumer this provides a much needed assurance that the restaurant is sourcing properly and that it has been properly inspected by the Soil Association.

And that list looks set to grow. The informal all-day café, Sauce, in London's Camden High Street, is just one such place looking to apply for the Soil Association Certificate; 95 per cent of its produce is already organic.

From our research it is obvious that of the restaurants listed in *The Restaurant Guide,* the majority make a sincere effort to buy locally produced ingredients and carefully check the provenance of produce from further afield. This did not surprise us - it is a message that has been coming through in inspectors' reports for the last few years. However, when we asked establishments how much of their produce was organically sourced, we honestly had no idea what the response would be.
So much so, when we started to identify the places that would carry our special organic symbol, we realised that, such was the response, we had to raise our standard from 25 per cent to 50 per cent organic produce. Restaurateurs are making a very clear statement- they care about what they are feeding us.

The start of a new millennium appeared to be the perfect time to introduce a new AA award, that of Restaurant of the Year. However, in the spirit of devolution, with the forming of the Scottish Parliament and Welsh Assembly, it seemed appropriate to introduce four national winners: one each for England, Republic of Ireland, Scotland and Wales. We asked all our inspectors to nominate restaurants that had particularly impressed them in the research for the millennium edition of The Restaurant Guide *and a fierce debate ensued; the contenders were strong and passionately argued for. Here are our four Restaurants of the Year for the year 2000:*

Restaurant
of the year

Club Gascon,
57 West Smithfield, London EC1
❀ ❀

When Vincent Labeyrie and chef Pascal Aussignac teamed up to open a restaurant specialising in the cooking of the south-west region of France, they had no idea of the effect it would have on the London eating scene. The wait for a table is 2-3 weeks, and cancellations are hotly fought over. Nearly everyone involved in Club Gascon is a native of that part of France; indeed Vincent Labeyrie jokes that they are the south-west embassy. Pascal Aussignac's training with Alain Dutournier is all too apparent in dishes that are pure classics. The restaurant showcases the produce and cooking of the south west, not reinvents it. Thus foie gras (an entire section of the menu), duck confit, cassoulet, garbure appear on a menu that is almost revolutionary in concept, designed around small portions so that you can make up your own tasting menu, usually of about six or seven courses - staff explain the concept clearly. They use connections to import all their fresh ingredients directly, cutting out the middleman and passing the benefit onto the customer.

Braidwoods
Dalry, North Ayrshire
❀ ❀

'We're literally stuck in the middle of a field surrounded by cows and sheep', observes Keith Braidwood when asked to describe his restaurant. The small, whitewashed 200 year-old cottage has a comfortable, almost homely appeal and is the setting for some astonishing cooking. Both Keith and Nicola Braidwood cook, and their CVs read like a culinary tour of Scotland's finest - The Peat Inn, Inverlochy Castle, Murrayshall Hotel - but when they realised their dream and opened Braidwoods five years ago, Nicola opted to run front of house. It's very much their place, help is part-time, and the tremendous effort they both put into the restaurant pays dividends. It's all very time consuming, especially when you consider that from a menu of three choices per course, some 80-90 dishes might be sent out in one evening, all cooked to order. They make everything from the puff pastry to the hand-made chocolates (the latter the result of a week spent in Holland learning the process), rely on good suppliers 'it's getting better all the time', offer a seasonally driven menu and consciously keep their style simple.

2000

Le Gallois
6-8 Romilly Crescent, Cardiff
❀ ❀

The light, modern split-level restaurant exudes vitality, and the food has certainly hit a spot with the natives of Cardiff. When Le Gallois opened in the spring of 1998 it hit the ground running - full at lunch and packed at dinner. It's a family affair. Padrig Jones in the kitchen takes centre stage, but mum and dad do accounts and marketing, sister Elan and brother-in-law Francis run front of house overseen by restaurant manager, fiancé Karen. Padrig's high profile London influences come through clearly in his cooking - especially the time spent with Marco Pierre White. Padrig's approach is to do simple food properly, slowly building, introducing ideas and techniques, working on a first things first basis. However, the love of handling quality fresh ingredients is frustrated by the problems of sourcing such items. Wales has some of the best raw materials in Britain - but much is exported. Thus fish can be local, but it can also come from Devon and Cornwall. What Padrig would like to see is more chefs coming to Cardiff to open restaurants. He has shown the way and is reaping visible rewards - and there's nothing like a little healthy competition.

Thornton's Restaurant
1 Portobello Road, Dublin
❀ ❀ ❀ ❀

The canal side location may be tricky to find, but perseverance is rewarded by an accommodating ground-floor bar and elegant restaurant upstairs. Since out first visit three years ago, we've noted an extra confidence in the cooking and this is reflected in the maturity and assurance required to offer a successful wide repertoire. Kevin Thornton remains down to earth, very likeable and with pure philosophies on food that ensures only the best raw produce is used in the kitchen. Of a stunning dish of plump, lightly seared scallops served with great coral jus and a rough pea purée to give texture and depth, he shrugged and commented 'the scallops were still pumping as they hit the pan'. This is serious food, reminiscent of Tom Atkins style at London's Pied à Terre, but overall it retains it's own identity combined with classical technique and sticks to firm Irish roots. Roast loin of suckling pig, for example, slow cooked, sticky, and set on maxim potatoes, the accompanying stuffed trotter light and flavoursome, with a simple garnish of turnip and garlic is served with a separate dish of new potatoes - a nod to the traditional Dublin diner.

Telephone number *changes*

From 22 April 2000 there will be new dialling codes beginning with 02 in London, Cardiff, Coventry, Portsmouth, Southampton and right across Northern Ireland. At the same time, all local numbers in these areas will become eight-digit numbers.

Portsmouth Area Telephone Number Changes

From the 22 April 2000, all dialling codes listed as (01705) will change to (023), followed by an eight-digit local number, starting with 92. For example, (01705) 123456 will become (023) 9212 3456.

Southampton Area Telephone Number Changes

From 22 April 2000, all dialling codes listed as (01703) will change to (023), followed by an eight-digit local number, starting with 80. For example, (01703) 123456 will become (023) 8012 3456.

Coventry Area Telephone Number Changes

From the 22 April 2000, all dialling codes listed as (01203) will change to (024), followed by an eight-digit local number. starting with 76. For example, (01203) 123456 will become (024) 7612 3456.

Cardiff Area Telephone Number Changes

From the 22 April 2000, all dialling codes listed as (01222) will change to (029), followed by an eight-digit local number, starting with 20. For example, (01222) 123456 will become (029) 2012 3456.

London Telephone Number Changes

From the 22 April 2000, the dialling code for the whole of London will be (020), followed by an eight-digit local number. For example, (0171) 123 4567 will become (020) 7123 4567, (0181) 123 4567 will become (020) 8123 4567.

Northern Ireland Telephone Number Changes

From the 22 April 2000, the dialling code for the whole of Northern Ireland will be (028), followed by an eight-digit local number. For example, (01232) 123456 will become (028) 9012 3456, (012477) 123456 will become (028) 4271 2345.

In case of difficulties, please consult directory enquiries.

LONDON

Abingdon

A former pub, attractively renovated, with casual, well-informed service from a team said to be a delight to deal with. Coupled with a menu that takes in crispy duck salad with sweet-and-sour dressing, smoked haddock with bubble-and-squeak and a poached egg, or grilled corn-fed chicken breast stuffed with herby couscous with a red pepper coulis, it all adds up to a seductive, successful formula. Our inspector started with faultless leek and potato soup, went on to fresh, perfectly cooked sea bass with chive butter sauce, roasted fennel and 'the best mash in ages', and finished with an excellent, deep lemon tart. Equally, you could choose marinated calamari with olive and tomato salsa, roasted rump of lamb with a mint jus, and tarte Tatin with vanilla ice cream. Breads are 'just great', side orders are generous, and the short, snappy wine list has nine by the glass.

Directions: ⊖ High Street Kensington

54 Abingdon Road W8 6AP
Map GtL: C3
Tel: 0171 9373339
Fax: 0171 7956388
Chef: Tom Lander
Owners: Peter Staples,
Susannah Staples
Cost: *Alc* £25, set-price L £9.95 (2 courses). ☺ H/wine £9.75
Times: 12.30-2.30pm/6.30-10.45pm. Closed 3 days Xmas
Additional: Bar food; Sunday L; Children welcome; ◑ dishes
Seats: 48
Smoking: No pipes & cigars; Air conditioning

The Academy

Converted into a splendid hotel from five Georgian terraced houses and recently substantially refurbished. The restaurant is on the lower ground floor and has a contemporary feel: walls are enlivened by three large mural works, there are direct spotlights onto bare tables, plain wood floors, and the staff are dressed in black. The menu features a selection of Mediterranean (predominantly Italian) dishes along the lines of goats' cheese tart, various kinds of pasta, lamb with tabouleh, squid with chilli, and chicken with polenta. We found a variation on a classic gazpacho to be very good, veal layered and wrapped in Parma ham and sage leaves excellent, served with good saffron risotto and plum crumble tart had a crisp pastry, with some delicious ice cream served alongside. Music is played on a regular basis.

Directions: Five minutes walk from Oxford St. ⊖ Tottenham Court Road, Goodge St

17-21 Gower Street WC1E 6HG
Map: D4
Tel: 0171 6367612
Fax: 0171 6363442
Chef: John O'Riordan
Owner: Alan Rivers
Cost: *Alc* £22, set-price L & D £10 (2 courses). ☺ H/wine £9.95
Times: Noon-3pm/4-11pm. Closed Sat, Sun
Additional: Bar food; Children welcome; ◑ dishes
Seats: 48. Private dining room 6-20
Smoking: No-smoking area; Air conditioning
Accommodation: 48 en suite ★★★

Adams Café

Small North African café-cum-restaurant run by a friendly team. Expect good value Tunisian and Moroccan dishes and sample one of the aromatic tagine dishes cooked in traditional pots, including lamb with prunes, almonds and sultanas.

Smoking: No pipes & cigars

Directions: ⊖ Shepherd's Bush, Hammersmith

77 Askew Road W12 9AH
Map GtL: C2
Tel/Fax: 0181 7430572
Cost: *Alc* £16.95. ☺ H/wine £7.50
Times: D only, 7-11pm. Closed 1wk Xmas, 1 wk end Aug
Additional: Children welcome; ◑ dishes

Alastair Little W11

There's a relaxed, informal feel to this busy 'shop-front' restaurant just off Ladbroke Grove. Simplicity drives the thinking behind Alastair Little's second restaurant, from the

136a Lancaster Road W11 1QU
Map: C2
Tel: 0171 2432220
Fax: 0171 7924504
Chef: Edwin Lewis

straightforward no-frills decor to the Italian-influenced menu. We loved the home-made focaccia with rock salt crust; just out of the oven it was the best we had ever tasted. Equally impressive was a roast pigeon breast served on salsa with broad beans, tomato and plenty of olive oil. Fresh home-salted cod came next, a nice dish served with baby artichoke. Dessert was a perfect pannacotta, rich with vanilla – it was 'shiny and firm and gorgeously creamy' and tasted delicious when scooped up with the accompanying plump blueberries.

Directions: ⊖ Ladbroke Grove. From tube turn R, Lancaster Road is 1st R

Owners: Alastair Little, Kirsten Tormod Pedersen, Mercedes André-Vega
Cost: *Alc* £22, set-price D £27.50. H/wine £13
Times: 12.30-2.30pm (3pm Sat)/7-11pm. Closed Sun, Bhs
Additional: Children welcome; ⑤ dishes
Seats: 40
Smoking: Air conditioning

Alastair Little Soho

'Modern, functional' is how the Soho landmark describes itself. Alastair Little was ahead of the times when he conceived the place on minimalist lines. However, sixteen years later 'this is one of the more dated (in appearance) of the Soho restaurants', and that's from a staunch supporter. It is the cooking that draws the attention, majoring on the quality of ingredients and the utter simplicity of its approach. Staff fit the bill well, casually dressed in jeans, shirts and long aprons and pleasant with it. The short menu changes twice daily, owes a lot to the Mediterranean in general and Italy in particular, and is good value; the terse descriptions – minestrone of broccoli, potatoes and borlotti beans, or truffled breast of chicken with stewed leeks – emphasising the simple technique. Our spring meal opened with asparagus baked with balsamic and topped with shaved Pecorino, went on to a good Mediterranean-style dish of bourride of salt cod, squid and prawns in a 'soup' of saffron and chilli, and finished with a startling 'not like anything I'd had before and more enjoyable' tiramisu (layers of chocolate sponge with Mascarpone and a rich espresso cutting the sweetness). There are about 50 wines on the wine list, well-balanced between Europe and the New World and ranging between £16 and £95, but the majority are under £30.

49 Frith Street W1V 5TE
Map: D4
Tel: 0171 7345183
Fax: 0171 7924504
Chef: Alastair Little
Owners: Alastair Little, Kirsten Tormod Pedersen, Mercedes André-Vega
Cost: Set-price L £25/D £33. H/wine £14
Times: Noon-3pm/6-11pm. Closed L Sat, all Sun, Bhs
Additional: Children welcome; ⑤ dishes
Seats: 55. Private dining room 20
Smoking: Air conditioning

Directions: ⊖ Leicester Square, Tottenham Court Road

Alba Restaurant

A short walk from the Barbican, this bright, modern restaurant is popular with the local business community. The modern Italian menu is sensibly short encouraging some serious cooking on the part of the kitchen. At our last test meal this was exemplified by a starter of beetroot ravioli in olive oil with Pecorino cheese and poppy seeds that was just bursting with flavour. Main dishes could range from poached monkfish with citrus fruit sauce and spinach salad, to a Trentino lamb stew or classic pollo cacciatore made with corn-fed chicken. Finish with the likes of spiced apple strudel from the southern Tyrol or tiramisu. The helpfully annotated wine list is an impressive tour of the best Italian vineyards.

Directions: ⊖ Barbican

107 Whitecross Street EC1 8JD
Map: F4
Tel: 0171 5881798
Fax: 0171 6385793
Chef: Renzo Geminiani
Owner: R Venerandi
Cost: *Alc* £27, set-price D £11.90 (2 courses). ☺ H/wine £10.50
Times: Noon-3pm/6-11pm. Closed Sat, Sun, 10 days Xmas, Bhs
Additional: Bar food; Children welcome; ⑤ dishes
Seats: 55. Private dining room 30
Smoking: No pipes & cigars; Air conditioning

Alfred

Cheerful eaterie. Expect honest, consistent cooking of uncomplicated dishes from a menu with a distinctly British slant. Nearly two dozen

245 Shaftesbury Avenue WC2 8EH
Map: D3
Tel: 0171 2402566
Fax: 0171 4970672

wines come by the glass and there's an exceptional choice of bottled beers.

Seats: 45. Private dining room 16
Smoking: No pipes & cigars; Air conditioning

Directions: Close to Shaftesbury Theatre

Cost: *Alc* £27, set-price L & D £15.90. ☺ H/wine £11.75
Times: Noon-3.30pm/6-11.30pm. Closed L Sat, all Sun, Xmas, Bhs
Additional: Children welcome; 🍽 dishes

Al San Vincenzo

There are few really good restaurants west of Marble Arch and north of Hyde Park that could be counted as proper neighbourhood establishments, but Al San Vincenzo is just such a place. It's small, serving just twenty-four, plainly decorated with bare boards, black and white photographs on plain white walls, yet with a surprisingly warm and intimate atmosphere. This is due to the husband and wife team of Vincenzo and Elaine Borgonzolo: he in the kitchen, she directing the floor. The menus, hand-written, change regularly and offer decent, rustic, original cooking. Several meals taken this year have highly endorsed pan-fried prawns with chilli and cracked pepper, and Puy lentils, pigeon and cabbage (real depth of flavour). The puddings are mostly straightforward and delicious. The short wine list complements the concise menu.

30 Connaught Street W2 2AF
Map: B3
Tel: 0171 2629623
Chef: Vincenzo Borgonzolo
Owners: Elaine & Vincenzo Borgonzolo
Cost: *Alc* £35. H/wine £13
Times: 12.30-1.45pm/7-9.45pm. Closed L Sat, all Sun, Xmas
Additional: Children 13+
Seats: 24
Smoking: No pipes and cigars

Directions: 2nd left in Edgware Road, from Marble Arch

Anglesea Arms

Lively London village gastro-pub with great twists including a log-burning spit roaster fired-up outdoors. Arrive early to beat the crowds, and try robust, up-to-date cooking that takes in the likes of calves' liver on mash with back bacon and red wine jus.

Directions: Off Goldhawk Road. ⊖ Goldhawk Road, Ravenscourt Park

35 Wingate Road W6 0UR
Map GtL: C3
Tel: 0181 7491291
Fax: 0181 7491254
Telephone for further details

Anna's Place

Small, pretty restaurant with a glassed in sun terrace and known for its Swedish food. Try Scandinavian specialities – gravad lax, raw herrings – or opt for other European dishes followed by home-made desserts.

Directions: Left off Balls Pond Road into Mildmay Park. On the corner of Newington Green, Bus 73, 171, 141 to Newington Green

90 Mildmay Park N1 4PR
Map GtL: D3
Tel: 0171 2499379
Cost: *Alc* £20. ☺ H/wine £9.95.
Times: Noon-2.15pm/7-11pm. Closed L Mon, all Sun
Additional: Children welcome; 🍽 dishes
Credit cards: None

Apprentice Restaurant 🌸

Physically part of Conran's Gastrodome, but a separate entity – the eating outlet of the Butler's Wharf Chef School, with the upbeat modern cooking and service provided by students. Our experience is that a meal here can sometimes exceed the restaurant's rating. Both prices and decor are modest.

Additional: Children welcome; 🍽 dishes
Smoking: No-smoking area, No pipes & cigars

Directions: On S side of river, 2 minutes from Tower Bridge. ⊖ Tower Hill, London Bridge

Cardamon Building 31 Shad Thames SE1 2YR
Map: G3
Tel: 0171 2340254
Fax: 0171 4032638
Cost: *Alc* £22.50, set-price L £12.50/D £17.50. ☺ H/wine £10.25
Times: Noon-1.30pm/6.30-8.30pm. Closed Sat, Sun, Bhs

Aroma II

Bright and spacious Chinese offering speciality noodle and dumpling dishes on the light-lunch menu and more unusual Peking and Cantonese in the evening, Look out for pig's crackling with turnips and chives, pork knuckle with jellyfish, crispy shredded duck and, for dessert, deliciously light black bean puffs.

Directions: Telephone for directions

118 Shaftesbury Avenue W1V 7DJ
Map: D3
Tel: 0207 4370370/0377
Fax: 0207 4370377
Cost: Alc £15
Times: Noon-11.30pm (10.30pm Sun)
Additional: Bar food; Sunday L;
Children welcome; 🍴 dishes
Smoking: No-smoking area; Air conditioning

Assaggi

Italian restaurant with warm Mediterranean decor located over a pub. Assaggi pasta loaf is a cross between ravioli and lasagne, and other options are venison and fish of the day.

Smoking: No pipes & cigars; Air conditioning

Directions: ⊖ Westbourne Grove

39 Chepstow Place W2 4TS
Map GtL: C3
Tel: 0171 7925501
Cost: Alc £30. ☺ H/wine £10.95
Times: 12.30-2.30pm/7.30-11pm.
Closed Sun, Xmas
Additional: Children welcome;
🍴 dishes

Les Associés ✻✻

Set back from the main road, this little neighbourhood restaurant has a terrace at the front; within walls are strewn with big paintings and charcoal drawings. The hand-written *carte* is in French and supplemented by daily specials, offering four first courses, two fish and four meat main courses. Our pan-fried brill served with a seafood sauce was 'beautifully fresh and plump', and was teamed with first-class vegetables and an excellent pommes Anna. Tarte Tatin was also well-executed and served with a light crème anglaise. Excellent espresso comes with Whittakers mints. The entirely French wine list is well chosen and diners are encouraged to be adventurous in selecting a bottle. The service is directed by the charming patron.

Directions: ⊖ Finsbury Park

172 Park Road N8 8JT
Map: B5
Tel/Fax: 0181 3488944
Chef: Marc Spindler
Owners: Dominique Chéhère,
Marc Spindler
Cost: Alc £25, set-price L £10.50 (2 courses). H/wine £9.80
Times: 12.30-3pm/7.30-10pm. Closed L Sat, D Sun, all Mon, 15 Aug-1 Sep, 1st 2 wks Jan
Additional: Sunday L
Seats: 35

Athenaeum Hotel ✻

Stylish contemporary restaurant with Jerusalem stone floor and natural lighting. Brasserie-type menu reflecting international influences with some Cajun, Thai and Italian dishes.

116 Piccadilly W1V 0BJ
Map: C3
Tel: 0171 4703333
Fax: 0171 4931860
Cost: Alc £31. H/wine £13.95
Times: 12.30-2.30pm/6-11pm. Closed L Sat & Sun
Additional: Children welcome;
🍴 dishes
Smoking: No-smoking area; Air conditioning
Accommodation: 157 en suite
★ ★ ★ ★

Directions: ⊖ Hyde Park Corner, Green Park

Atlantic Bar and Grill

This restaurant, located on a back street behind Piccadilly, shares its vast basement with a notable cocktail bar. In the evenings it becomes a bustling, chaotic and shamelessly fashionable venue, although in recent years, it has suffered in the fashion stakes from stiff competition from neighbours. . There are *carte,* bar, set lunch and pre-theatre menus. All the dishes change frequently and, in style and influence, come from all over the world. First courses include Nashi pear and chargrilled haloumi salad, which sits beside more homely dishes such as woodland mushroom risotto and dill-cured salmon. Main courses are categorised by fish or meat with five choices in each. Where the produce comes from is frequently noted in the description, e.g. crisp Newlyn cod, or free-range Pinney farm chicken breast. All these are served with a variety of accompaniments: the grilled Hebridean salmon with creamed champagne, sorrel, lobster torpedo mash and crisp pancetta. Desserts are kept fairly simple and the service can be slow.

20 Glasshouse Street W1R 5RQ
Map: D3
Tel: 0171 7344888
Fax: 0171 7343609
Chef: Richard Sawyer
Owner: Oliver Peyton
Cost: *Alc* £32, set-price L £14.50/D £16.50 (pre-theatre). ☺ H/wine £12.50
Times: Noon-3pm/6pm-12.30am (7-10.30pm Sun). Closed L Sat & Sun, Bhs
Additional: Bar food; Children welcome; ⓥ dishes
Seats: 180. Private dining room 70
Smoking: Air conditioning

Directions: Just off Piccadilly Circus.
⊖ Piccadilly Circus
**Shortlisted for the AA Wine Award –
see p16**

Aubergine

Last year we reported on the early promise of William Drabble who had just taken over at Michael's Nook in Grasmere (see entry, Cumbria). The ink had not dried on that edition when Drabble moved to London, to take over the premises so loudly vacated by Gordon Ramsay. A hard act to follow, but we can confirm that our initial impressions in Cumbria were well founded and Drabble is now firmly at home in this small Chelsea street. Imagination there is in plenty with luxuries in abundance, but there is proper thought for techniques which coax brilliant flavours from such prime raw materials. A meal taken one Monday evening when the place was packed and remained buzzing all night with satisfied customers sums it all up. It included a germiny of lobster with new potatoes and mint, some seared scallops with a vibrant pea purée, and roasted red mullet with a goats' cheese and basil tortellini, which all showed the kitchen's enjoyment of fish cookery. Intelligence and technique came through in a 'subtle in flavour but sublime in texture' mousse of foie gras with leeks and morels, as well as in an organic fillet of beef with celeriac purée and Madeira jus. Desserts have been extolled to the heavens, especially a mille-feuille of caramelised pineapple, coconut ice cream and vanilla butter

11 Park Walk SW10
Map: A1
Tel: 0171 3523449
Fax: 0171 3511770
Chef: William Drabble
Owners: A to Z Restaurant
Cost: Set-price L £15 (2 courses)/D £39.50. H/wine £15
Times: Noon-2.30pm/6.45-10.45pm. Closed L Sat, all Sun, 2 wks Aug, Xmas, New Year, Bhs
Additional: Children welcome; ⓥ dishes
Seats: 50
Smoking: No pipes & cigars; Air conditioning

Directions: Fulham Road. Heading west, 2nd road L after MGM cinema

sauce, and petits fours – an assortment of superb chocolates, jellies and tiny tartlets. The lengthy wine list offers a good, broad selection and plenty of choice by the glass. The liqueur trolley is serious business too, with more fine Armagnac and brandies than anything else.

Signature dishes: boudin of pigeon with foie gras, caramelised turnips, morels and truffle jus; tranche of sea bass with bouillabaisse potatoes, sweet pepper and tomato bouillon; mille-feuille of caramelised pineapple with coconut ice cream and vanilla butter sauce.

The Avenue

Bright, modern glass-fronted restaurant in St James. A brasserie-style menu draws the crowds, offering choices such as a smoked haddock fishcake with Welsh rarebit and chocolate orange tart.

7-9 St James's Street SW1
Map: C3
Tel: 0171 321 2111
Fax: 0171 321 2500
Telephone for further details

Directions: ⊖ Green Park. R past The Ritz, R into St. James's St

Babur Brasserie

119 Brockley Rise Forest Hill
SE23 1JP
Map GtL: D2
Tel: 0181 2912400/4881
Fax: 0181 2914881
Chef: Enam Rahman
Cost: *Alc* £16. ☺ H/wine £7.95
Times: Noon-2pm/6-11pm. Closed L Fri, 25, 26 Dec
Additional: Sunday L; Children welcome; ● dishes
Seats: 56
Smoking: No-smoking area; Air conditioning

A life-size model tiger leaps out from above the doorway at this renowned Indian just off the South Circular. The menu of around a dozen main dishes is serious, far removed from the standard curry house formula, and the emphasis is on regional dishes. The cooking is also notable for freshness and distinct spicing. A well-reported meal included bite-sized pieces of battered saithi fish with fresh coriander dip, 'murgh kofti' – deep-fried cakes of spiced shredded chicken bound with mashed potato, and 'baingan badaml' – split baby aubergine roasted with mustard, garlic, onion and tamarind and served in a creamy peanut sauce. There's a good choice of desserts too: try 'Viceroy's banana pie' – a banana and apricot flan topped with flaked roast almonds, or 'rasmalai' – curd cheese with cream and pistachios. Also worth a try is 'mango lassi', a thirst-quenching drink made from rose water, yogurt and fresh mango.

Directions: 5 mins walk from Honor Oak BR Station, where parking is available

Bank Restaurant

Always jam-packed with a dynamic atmosphere and fast turnaround. Vibrant 'liberated French' and English cooking

1 Kingsway WC2B 6XF
Map: E4
Tel: 0171 3799797
Fax: 0171 3799014

weakened by inconsistencies. Ultra-modern design with a great sense of space and American-style cocktail bar. Brilliant for breakfast and weekend brunch too.

Additional: Bar food; Sat/Sun Brunch (11.30am-3.30pm); Children welcome; ◑ dishes
Smoking: Air conditioning

Directions: ⊖ Holborn. On Aldwych opposite Bush House

Cost: Alc £35, set-price L & D £17.50. ☺
Times: Noon-3pm/5.30-11.30pm (10pm Sun)

Basil Street Hotel ✿

Traditional-style restaurant on the first floor of this historic, splendidly old-fashioned hotel. The menu includes home-made soups and pâtés, with main courses such as liver and bacon, and roast cod.

Smoking: No-smoking area; No pipes & cigars; Jacket & tie preferred
Accommodation: 80 en suite ★ ★ ★

Directions: ⊖ Knightsbridge

Basil Street Knightsbridge SW3 1AH
Map: C3
Tel: 0171 5813311
Fax: 0171 5813693
Cost: Alc £19.50, set-price L £10 (2 courses)/D £21. ☺ H/wine £13.75
Times: 12.30-2.30pm/6.30-10pm
Additional: Bar food L; Sunday L; Children welcome; ◑ dishes

Belair House ✿✿

Gallery Road SE21 7AB
Map GtL: D2
Tel: 0181 2999788
Fax: 0171 2996793

Chef: Colin Barnett
Owner: Gary & Jayne Cady
Cost: Alc £30, set-price L £17.50/D £24.95. ☺ H/wine £15
Times: Noon-2.30pm/7-10.30pm
Additional: Sunday L; Children welcome; ◑ dishes
Seats: 60. Private dining room 14
Smoking: No pipes & cigars

This Palladian Georgian-style mansion is set in Blair Park, a municipal park. The whole building has been lovingly restored but the only original part of the house is the 18th-century spiral staircase, the rest is a 20th-century pastiche. The interior is decorated with bright yellows and blues, the windows are large and the restaurant is light and airy. The menu is written daily and lists seven first courses and main courses. The kitchen's inspiration is firmly placed in Europe. Beetroot consommé comes with a foie gras and wild mushroom dumpling, potted vanilla tarragon lobster with a mango salsa. The main courses are marginally more pedestrian: rack of lamb, olive oil and basil mash, aubergine, haricots verts, although a fillet of salmon with asparagus was 'lifted by a scallop soufflé'. There is a competent, if uninspiring, wine list with only two half-bottles.

Directions: From Brixton: Gallery Road is the 1st turning off the South Circular after passing West Dulwich train station. From Catford: 1st turning off South Circular after Dulwich College

Belvedere

An Edwardian building situated in the midst of Holland Park. The restaurant, on two floors, is both bright and modern yet with a classic touch. Waiters are dressed formally and there's a modern European menu. There's a choice of set-menu and *carte* at both lunch and dinner, with a number of tempting dishes on offer. Home-made sultana and white rolls precede first courses such as a wafer thin carpaccio of venison brushed with olive oil, marinated enoki mushrooms and herb tuile, and nicely executed main dishes like tournedos of chargrilled salmon on polenta with a light carrot and sorrel purée with bouillabaisse dressing. Desserts are good. A well-balanced wine list accompanies the menu.

Directions: On Kensington High Street side of Holland Park. ⊖ Holland Park

Abbotsbury Road Holland Park
W8 6LU
Map GtL: C3
Tel: 0171 6021238
Fax: 0171 6104382
Chef: Marc Brown
Owner: Caledonian Heritable
Cost: *Alc* £30, set-price L £16.50 (2 courses). H/wine £13.50
Times: Noon-2.30pm/7-10.30pm. Closed D Sun, 25 Dec, 1 Jan
Additional: Sunday L; Children welcome; 🍃 dishes
Seats: 130
Smoking: Air conditioning

Bengal Clipper

Spacious, modern Indian set in the old cardamom warehouse at Butlers Wharf. The menu's strength are its Bengali and Goan dishes: try golda chingri pardanashin' – giant prawns served in the shell of a baby coconut.

Butlers Wharf SE1 2YE
Map GtL: D3
Tel: 0171 3579001
Fax: 0171 3579002
Cost: *Alc* £25, set-price L £10/D £25. ☺ H/wine £8.95
Times: Noon-2.45pm/6-11.30pm
Additional: Sunday L; Children welcome; 🍃 dishes
Smoking: Air conditioning

Directions: By Tower Bridge. ⊖ Tower Hill

Bentley's

Bentley's has been synonymous with seafood since it opened its doors in the middle of the First World War. Eat in the Oyster Bar or in the old-fashioned surroundings of the first-

11-15 Swallow Street W1R 7HD
Map: C3
Tel: 0171 7344756
Fax: 0171 2872972
Chef: Jamie Kimm
Owner: Oscar Owide
Cost: *Alc* £35, set-price L & D £19.50. ☺ H/wine £16.50
Additional: Bar food; Sunday L; Children welcome; 🍃 dishes
Seats: 80. Private dining room 16
Smoking: Air conditioning

Directions: ⊖ Piccadilly Circus. Swallow Street links Regent St & Piccadilly and is opposite St James's Church on Piccadilly

floor restaurant with its comfortable booth seating and foodie stills and period caricature prints hanging on the walls. This is a place where the traditional and the modern sit side by side: starters of dressed crab, half a lobster with mayonnaise, moules marinière, crab risotto with saffron and red peppers, and sashimi of tuna and salmon. Main courses range from the plain roasted brill with seasonal Jersey Royals and asparagus with hollandaise, through cod and chips with tartare sauce, to salmon and haddock fishcake with a poached egg, or roasted John Dory with a velouté of peas and foie gras. Only the freshest produce from sea and river finds its way into the kitchen, meat devotees are not entirely overlooked, and incidentals like salads, vegetables and puddings of perhaps lemon tart with 'nice thin pastry' get mentioned in dispatches. Perhaps surprisingly, red wines are a strong point on the wine list, which features a section of bottles from the 'Old Colonies' (including the USA).

Bibendum

Michelin House 81 Fulham Road SW3 6RD
Map: A1
Tel: 0171 5815817
Fax: 0171 8237925
Chef: Matthew Harris
Owners: Sir Terence Conran, Lord Hamlyn, Simon Hopkinson, Graham Williams
Cost: Set-price L £29. H/wine £12
Times: Noon-2.30pm/7-11.30pm. Closed 25-27 Dec
Additional: Sunday L; Children welcome
Seats: 72
Smoking: No pipes; Air conditioning

Conran flagship in a landmark building. It's now over a decade since Sir Terence Conran and his partners converted the Art Deco Michelin building into ground-floor oyster bar and first-floor restaurant. Forget Eurostarring to Paris – this is the place for fried frogs' legs with warm potato purée and black truffles, calves' brains en persillade with red wine sauce, escargots de Bourgogne and jambon persillé with sauce gribiche. On the other hand, you could start with a tasty dish of duck confit cleverly put together as part of a deep potato cake, creamy and soupy pea and mint risotto, or artichoke soup spiced with sage and pesto. Artichoke, this time puréed, and pesto could also appear as a foil to main-course scallops, and sage used to flavour roast pigeon with rich Mascarpone polenta to produce a 'perfectly enjoyable' dish. The high spot of our meal was a huge wedge of 'divine' chocolate tart, its excellent crisp pastry containing a deep filling, with sumptuous pistachio ice cream, and melt-in-the-mouth chocolate truffles with coffee are equally enjoyable. The wine list must be one of the best in the land, if pricy, but there are plenty of more approachable bottles too.
   Signature dishes: sautéed scallops with shellfish ravioli and chives; grilled entrecôte with onion and mustard crust; pithiviers au chocolat.

Directions: ⊖ South Kensington

Bice ❀❀

Downstairs from DKNY, a fashionable, expensive Italian restaurant. It's worth a visit for a mix of clientele that ranges from fashion victim, through business suits to comfort-clad American tourists. The service has that direct American-style no-nonsense approach – a warm welcome and really means business. For the area, the quality and simplicity of the food is hard to beat. The star of our test meal was undoubtedly lamb cutlets, fresh and well prepared, steeped in fennel oil and lightly grilled, but a satisfying risotto alla milanese came a close second. Interesting all-Italian wine list but few bottles under £20.

Directions: Off Piccadilly, near Old Bond Street. ⊖ Green Park

13 Albemarle Street W1X 3HA
Map: C3
Tel: 0171 4091011
Fax: 0171 4930081
Chef: Antonello Tagliabue
Owners: Mr R Ruggeri & Mr S Frittella
Cost: *Alc* £31, set-price L £20 (2 courses)/D £25. ☺ H/wine £14
Times: Noon-2.30pm/6-10.30pm. Closed L Sat, Sun, Easter, Xmas, Bhs
Additional: Children welcome; ❂ dishes
Seats: 105. Private dining room 20
Smoking: Air conditioning

The Big Chef ❀❀

The 150 seater beneath a large circular glass dome, is decorated in shades of yellow, with mock Art Deco features. The Big Chef takes pride of place at the top of an escalator, lording it above floors of shops and offices in Canary Wharf; it's all rather reminiscent of a swish US shopping mall, especially when you note that it shares the top floor with a number of other 'eateries', which are mainly of the large chain variety. The main menu is predominantly French, frequently employing terms like 'ravigote' and 'beurre maitre d'hôtel', and the cooking is good, well-presented and looks pretty on the plate. We found a mosaique of ham and parsley with sauce gribiche to be meaty and well matched, and enjoyed a salmon fishcake set on spinach and topped with a poached egg and slightly frothed hollandaise speckled with finely chopped sorrel. The wine list is reasonably priced and not dominated by Grand Crus, as one might expect; the staff are predominantly French.

Second Floor Cabot Place East Canary Wharf E14 4QT
Map GtL: E3
Tel: 0171 5130513
Fax: 0171 5130557
Telephone for further details

Directions: Docklands Railway; main shopping mall of Canary Wharf

The Birdcage of Fitzrovia ❀❀

110 Whitfield Street W1P 5RU
Map: C3
Tel: 0171 3239655
Chef: Michael Von Hruschka
Owners: Michael Von Hruschka, Caroline Faulkner
Cost: *Alc* £26.50, set-price L £19.50/D £38.50. H/wine £16
Times: Noon-2.30pm/6-11.15pm. Closed L Sat, all Sun

This little restaurant is situated in Whitfield Street, an unremarkable street running parallel to Tottenham Court Road. A small iron railing around the front and a tall arch distinguishes it from the rest of the buildings. The restaurant is small and decorated with French 18th-century bird cages, eastern ephemera, feathers and a large mirrored glass dragon, the ambience is not unlike a private dining room. The menu is a fusion of many different influences. The set-menu lists sushi with mussel ceviche on the same list of first courses as coconut and foie gras soup and flying fish roe on quail egg omelette. A vegetarian and a fish option are included in the five main courses. Typical dishes are grilled mackerel with Peruvian mash, Indian risotto with plantain and lotus root and birdcage sweetbreads with jasmine-infused polenta. The desserts are very pretty. An interesting, shortish wine list is made into an origami bird and includes an organic champagne.

Additional: dishes
Seats: 28
Smoking: Smoking restricted (2 tables)

Directions: ⊖ Warren Street. Opposite the University

Bistro 190, Fish Restaurant at 190 ✿✿

190 Queen's Gate SW7 5EU
Map: A1
Tel: 0171 5815666
Fax: 0171 5818172
Chef: Simon North
Owner: Simpsons of Cornhill
Cost: Alc £32 (Fish). Set-price D £25 (Fish). H/wine £11
Times: Noon-last D 11.30pm. Fish D only, 6-11pm. Closed Sun, Bhs (Fish), 25 Dec
Additional: Sunday L; Children welcome; dishes
Seats: 40 (Fish) 60 (Bistro)

Two very different restaurants under one roof. The immensely popular Bistro 190 occupies the ground floor of the Gore Hotel. It's a light, high-ceilinged room with huge windows overlooking Queensgate, walls strewn with old prints and large mirrors, and a tremendously laid-back atmosphere – the informality sitting well with the decor and service. A basket of fresh, crusty bread with some olive oil to dip, then mussels potent with garlic, crisp-skinned duck leg, the meat falling off the bone, served with pak choi, and raspberry cheesecake gives the style. To reach Fish at 190 you need to pass through the clamorous bar opposite the bistro 'a great place to people watch', and head downstairs where the atmosphere becomes more discreet, the tone that of a gentleman's club – especially given that the decor is all dark panelled walls with well-spaced tables covered by brilliant white table cloths spotlit from above. The menu is, of course, predominantly fish, with langoustine, lobster, scallops, sea bass making appearances, as well as the likes of bouillabaise. Plenty of room and comfortable seating means that one is lured into a sense of timelessness. The wine list is the usual selection of worldwide choices.

Directions: Next to Gore Hotel on Queensgate. ⊖ South Kensington

Bluebird ✿✿

350 King's Road SW3 5UU
Map: B1
Tel: 0171 5591000
Fax: 0171 5591111
Chef: Andrew Sargent
Owner: Sir Terence Conran
Cost: Alc £35, set-price L & D £15.75. ☺ H/wine £12.75
Times: Noon-3.30pm (11am-4pm Sat & Sun)/6-11.30pm (10.30pm Sun)
Additional: Sun brunch; Children welcome; dishes
Seats: 240. Private dining room 32
Smoking: Air conditioning

As alive as ever, with the flower shop, street café, kitchen shop and posh supermarket all busy. Overlooking all of this is the vast, hugely popular restaurant, all neutral tones, natural light, soaring Bluebird giant kites overhead, and prompt staff. Andrew Sargent moved here from Le Pont de la Tour at the beginning of 1999, but apart from a little refocusing the menu remains pretty much the same. Sensibly, given the numbers that pass through each day, the kitchen is produce led (and prime raw materials at that). Crustacea feature and it's quite something to see people dwarfed at table by platters of shellfish – for a brief moment you could be in France. Other must-haves are classics such as sirloin with béarnaise or Chateaubriand (for two) with perfect matchstick fries. Rare tuna with pickled ginger, cucumber and wasabi, and a wonderfully tender five-spice duck with bok choi and plum sauce are examples of the oriental side of the menu. However retro-dishes such as prawn cocktail and chicken Kiev are best left alone. Desserts are stellar with champagne jelly, chocolate marquise and even the Bluebird selection of sorbets fighting it out for pole position.

Directions: ⊖ Sloane Square

Blue Print Café

Conran bistro/brasserie on the first floor of the Design Museum. Short ambitious menu belts out tagliatelle with asparagus, roast cod with saffron potatoes, and raspberry shortcake.

Additional: Sunday L; Children welcome; dishes

Directions: SE of Tower Bridge, on mezzanine of the Design Museum

The Design Museum Shad Thames Street SE1 2YD
Map: G3
Tel: 0171 3787031
Fax: 0171 3578810
Cost: *Alc* £25. ☺ H/wine £14.50
Times: Noon-3pm/6-11pm. Closed D Sun

Boisdale ❀❀ NEW

Upmarket Scottish restaurant with deep red walls, lots of pictures and bistro-type tables and chairs. The best place for haggis in London. Cock-a-leekie soup is the traditional rendition with prunes, leeks and a strong, clear broth; smoked Highland venison salad simply lets the superb main ingredient speak for itself. Potted lobster, rocket salad and warm toasted brioche is rich and well made, and beef fillet is tender and full of flavour, served with home-made chips. Other main courses might include fishcakes (made from cod), smoked haddock and Orkney salmon or game in season. Desserts, even raspberry cranachan, are the weakest section, but a wide range of savouries make a welcome addition to the menu. A back tobacco bar, strong on cigars, suits the Sloaney, cashmere-Crombie-clad clientele down to the ground. Service is good, if at times bordering on the condescending.

15 Eccleston Street SW1W 9LX
Tel: 0171 7306922
Fax: 0171 7300548
Chef: Lenny Walcott
Owners: Ranald & Kate Macdonald
Cost: *Alc* £35, set-price L&D £16.90.
H/wine £12.50
Times: Noon-2.30pm/7-10.30pm
Additional: Bar food; Sat & Sun brunch; Children welcome
Seats: 40. Private dining room 20
Smoking: Air conditioning

Directions: ⊖ Victoria

Bombay Bicycle Club ❀

Bentwood chairs, flowers, palms by the large windows and murals on the walls are the setting for Indian fare of crispy vegetable samosas, cod curry, gosht kata masala (curried lamb with cardamom), Bombay mushrooms and top-drawer naan. Finish with ice cream.

Additional: Children welcome; dishes

Directions: ⊖ Clapham South

95 Nightingale Lane SW12 8NX
Map: G3
Tel: 0181 6736217
Fax: 0181 6739100
Cost: *Alc* £25
Times: D only, 7-11pm. Closed Sun, 25 Dec, Bhs

The Brackenbury ❀❀

If only every part of residential London could have a local restaurant like this one. Set in so-called Brackenbury Village, this is a small, bustling restaurant that has been converted from two former shops, with a bar at the back and outdoor dining on the pavement in summer. The menu changes daily and offers seven choices at every stage. Cooking is honest, robust and uses the freshest ingredients. Cream of mussel and saffron soup came with plenty of mussels, crab cakes with fennel and lime salad was full of flavour with a nice friable golden coating. Leek, goats' cheese and artichoke tart with rocket salad had 'a soft creamy filling, nice pastry and was clearly freshly baked'. Mascarpone and orange sorbet was 'good with a zesty orange flavour , mocha zabaglione parfait with raspberry sauce was 'pleasantly flavoured'. Good espresso coffee and an excellent choice of wines by the glass. Friendly service.

129-131 Brackenbury Road W6 0BQ
Map GtL: C3

Tel: 0181 7480107
Fax: 0181 7410905
Chef: Marcia Chang-Hong
Owners: Place Restaurants
Cost: *Alc* £20, set-price L £9.50 (2 courses). ☺ H/wine £9.50
Times: 12.30-2.45pm/7-10.45pm.
Closed L Sat, D Sun, 25 Dec, 1 Jan
Additional: Children welcome; dishes
Seats: 50
Smoking: No pipes & cigars

Directions: Off Goldhawk Road.
⊖ Hammersmith & Goldhawk Road

Brown's, 1837

Albemarle Street Mayfair W1X 4BP
Map: C3
Tel: 0171 4081837
Fax: 0171 4081838
Cost: *Alc* £45, set-price L
£24/D £45. H/wine £18
Times: 12.30-2pm/7-10.30pm. Closed
L Sat, all Sun
Additional: Bar food; Children
welcome; ❹ dishes
Seats: 88. Private dining room 12
Smoking: No-smoking area; Air
conditioning
Accommodation: 118 en suite
★★★★

Directions: Main entrance in
Albemarle Street, off Piccadilly.
❺ Piccadilly Circus, Green Park

*Brown's Hotel has become a famous Mayfair institution,
and rightly so.* Renowned for its wonderful afternoon teas, it
is now promoting its restaurant to a wider audience. The
walls are oak-panelled and the restaurant will seat up to
ninety people in grand style. Although there are elements of
contemporary cooking to be found on the menu, the
repertoire is, by and large, a classical French one, with an
emphasis on gracious dining. The set-menu is accompanied by
a 'Menu Dégustation' written in French with an English
translation, including coquilles St Jacques à la vapeur, soufflé
au Roquefort and ananas flambé. 'Well-flavoured' chicken
and truffle consommé, accurately prepared sweetbreads,
served with a sound potato galette, nicely crisped braised
leeks and a well-flavoured Meaux mustard sauce, were the
components of one inspection meal. The hot chocolate soufflé
was short in flavour but nicely presented. The wine list is
impressive with some great vintages, but
at a price.

Buchan's

62-64 Battersea Bridge Road
SW11 3AG
Map GtL: C2
Tel: 020 72280888
Fax: 020 79241718
Chef: Moray Fergusson
Owner: Anthony Brown
Cost: *Alc* £21.50, set-price L £8.50.
☺ H/wine £10.50

A spacious wine bar, backed by a light, bright restaurant.
Throughout the 70s and 80s Battersea saw a number of
restaurants opening, and though it has become less fashionable
to open a new establishment, the owners of Buchan's have
been in business only since 1996. In that time they have
managed to develop a restaurant serving modern British
cooking, with a heavy accent on Scottish, that is popular with

the locals. Neeps, tatties, a wee dram, Scotch broth and Angus fillet feature beside sun-dried risotto, coulibiac of Mediterranean vegetables and Mozzarella, pan-fried guinea fowl laid over a potato, prune and pear compote with ribbons of vegetables, and roast fillet of monkfish set on a slice of Jerusalem artichoke with a lime tomato and parsley nut butter. The ingredients used by the kitchen are obviously well chosen, particularly the meats. The vegetables are served separately. Four desserts are offered with a selection of British cheeses.

Directions: 200 yds S of Battersea Bridge.

Butlers Wharf Chop House

The Butlers Wharf Building
36e Shad Thames SE1 2YE

Part of Sir Terence Conran's 'Gastrodome' at Butlers Wharf, within sight of Tower Bridge. The restaurant is divided into a bar, which serves simple dishes, a restaurant, and a terrace which is only used in fine weather. The menu pays homage to the 'best' of British cooking. The set-price lunch menu offers two or three courses, with a *carte* offered at dinner. First-class ingredients are used in a variety of straightforward dishes: Dorset crab mayonnaise, fish and chips, and steak-and-kidney pudding, and roast rump of lamb, served more adventurously with a beetroot mash and mint cream. Nine desserts, ice creams and sorbets are safe yet uninspiring. The wine list is supplemented by good beers.

Map: D3
Tel: 0171 4033403
Fax: 0171 4033414
Chef: David Hollins
Owner: Sir Terence Conran
Cost: *Alc* £30, set-price L £22.75. ☺
H/wine from £13.95
Times: Noon-3pm/6-11pm. Closed L Sat, D Sun
Additional: Bar food; Sunday L; Children welcome; ✿ dishes
Seats: 115

Times: Noon-2.45pm/7-10.45pm. Closed 26 Dec, 1 Jan, Good Fri, Easter Mon
Additional: Bar food; Sunday L; Children welcome; ✿ dishes
Seats: 70. Private dining room 45
Smoking: Air conditioning

Directions: On river front, on SE side of Tower Bridge

Byron's Restaurant

3a Downshire Hill Hampstead
NW3 1NR

Informal restaurant in a quiet side street off Hampstead High Street, with striking slate-blue paintwork. Inside are bare boards, banquette-style seating and bentwood chairs, with crisp white linen, good glassware and cutlery giving a feeling of sophistication. Around eight starters and main courses see the likes of first-class saffron and chilli risotto with prawns, or nicely flavoured salmon and smoked haddock fishcake, then well-timed pan-fried calves' liver on wilted spinach with rich sage-flavoured gravy, or shank of lamb with mash and candied shallots. Seared tuna, served pink, with guacamole and tomato salsa might be among the fish options. Although enjoyable, we felt the addition of strawberry coulis, berries and chocolate sauce to bread-and-butter pudding with vanilla ice cream was gilding the lily somewhat. The wine list is fairly short but interesting, with some less common French bottles.

Map GtL: C4
Tel/Fax: 0171 4353544
Chef: Jonathan Coxon
Owners: Richard Horwood, Tim Keenes
Cost: *Alc* £25, set-price L £10 (2 courses). ☺
Times: Noon-3.30pm/7-11pm. 25-26 Dec
Additional: Sunday L; Children 9+; ✿ dishes
Smoking: No-smoking area; Air conditioning

Directions: ⊖ Hampstead, Belsize Park

Cadogan Hotel

75 Sloane Street
SW1X 9SG

This so called Pont Street Dutch corner building overlooks the well-kept gardens of Cadogan Square. The formal Edwardian restaurant has leaded windows, intricate plasterwork and a variety of decorative plates, mirrors and paintings adorn the cream-painted walls. The restaurant offers both set menus and a *carte* at lunch and dinner with the kitchen working in the modern British style, but with a strong classical base: pan-fried foie gras on a potato galette with a

Map: B2
Tel: 0171 2357141
Fax: 0171 2450994
Chef: Graham Thompson
Owner: Historic House Hotels Ltd
Cost: *Alc* £39, set-price L £18.90/D £27. H/wine £13.50

Sancerre and grape butter; roast tronçon of turbot with girolles, garlic confit and red wine fume. True Brit classics include Loch Fyne oak-smoked salmon, a delicious grilled Dover sole, and seared cannon of English lamb. Desserts include lemon soufflé and roasted baby pineapple with vanilla and ginger. The wine list is comprehensive and features a good selection of half-bottles.

Directions: Sloane Square, Knightsbridge

Café du Jardin

Popular Theatreland brasserie with a lively roll-call of dishes such as grilled swordfish steak on baby plum tomatoes in a turmeric and basil oil dressing.

Additional: Children welcome; 🍴 dishes.
Smoking: Air conditioning

Directions: On the corner of Wellington Street and Tavistock Street. Covent Garden

Le Café du Marché

Inviting French restaurant in a quiet mews close to the Barbican. Saddle of rabbit wrapped in smoked ham and served with a robust sauce, followed by a fine Bakewell tart, are recommended.

Smoking: No pipes & cigars; Air conditioning

Directions: Barbican

Café Fish

Bustling two-storey seafooder just off Shaftesbury Avenue, with a simple approach from the kitchen, backed up by friendly service. The crustacea is ever popular.

Directions: Piccadilly Circus. Off the Haymarket

Cadogan Hotel

Times: 12.30-2pm/5.30-9.45pm.
Closed L Sat
Additional: Bar food; Sunday L;
Children 10+; 🍴 dishes
Seats: 36. Private dining room 32.
Jacket & tie preferred at D
Smoking: No pipes & cigars; Air conditioning
Accommodation: 65 en suite

28 Wellington Street WC2E 7BD
Map: D3
Tel: 0171 8368769
Fax: 0171 8364123
Cost: *Alc* £25, set-price L & D £13.50. ☺ H/wine £9.50
Times: Noon-3pm/5.30-midnight.
Closed 24, 25 Dec

Shortlisted for the AA Wine Award –
see p16

Charterhouse Mews Charterhouse
Square EC1M 6AH
Map: E5
Tel: 0171 6081609
Fax: 0171 3367055
Cost: *Alc* £23.95, set-price D £23.95.
☺ H/wine £12
Times: Noon-2.30pm/6-10pm. Closed
L Sat, all Sun

36-40 Rupert Street W1
Map: D3
Tel: 0171 930 3999
Fax: 0171 839 4880
Telephone for further details

Cambio de Tercio ❀

Abstracts based on bullfighting themes adorn the walls of this small, bustling Spanish restaurant. An impressive range of sherries and good-value tapas give way to the likes of seafood and chicken paella, suckling pig Segovian-style and beef fillet with port wine.

Additional: Children 1+; ❹ dishes

Directions: Close to junction with Drayton Gdns.
⊖ Gloucester Rd

163 Old Brompton Road SW5 0LJ
Map: A1
Tel: 0171 244 8970
Fax: 0171 3738817
Cost: Alc £30. ☺
Times: 12.30-2.30pm/7-11.30pm.
Closed 10 days Xmas

Cannizaro House ❀❀

West Side Wimbledon Common
SW19 4UE
Map GtL: C2
Tel: 0181 8791464
Fax: 0181 8797338
Chef: Pascal Vallée
Owner: Thistle Hotels
Cost: Alc £35, set-price L £23.75/D
£28 75. H/wine £16.95
Times: Noon-2pm/7-10.30pm
Additional: Sunday L; Children 8+;
❹ dishes
Seats: 48. Private dining rooms 8/100.
Jacket & tie preferred
Smoking: No-smoking area; No pipes
& cigars
Accommodation: 45 en suite ★★★★

Well-loved historical landmark that is a haven of peace and quiet. Richly decorated public rooms are comfortable and well-endowed with oil paintings, murals and massive fireplaces. Cocktails on the terrace are a great summer pastime. The staff are dedicated to the task of making guests feel well looked after, and a driver is even available at times to assist in short journeys. Classical French cuisine is given a modern interpretation; seared scallops of foie gras are served upon an apple and potato rösti with Calvados scented jus, and braised shin of veal with root vegetables is enhanced by a rich braising liquor with a sage and asparagus soufflé. Dover sole meunière is there for anyone who finds the 'casserole of fish with lobster and scallops with ribbons of carrot and courgette served with an orange scented sauce upon sea pickle' simply too much of a mouthful to take.

Directions: From A3 (London Rd) Tibbets Corner, take A219 (Parkside) right into Cannizaro Rd, then R into West Side

The Canteen ❀❀❀

This could be Marbella if the sun were shining and the temperature higher. The conservatory-style front section of the Canteen is the best for watching the boats and bustle of Chelsea Harbour's marina. The restaurant's cool, elegant decor of pale yellow and parquet floor is broken up by the playing-card motif, which is just as prevalent as ever. Smoked bresaola with crispy potatoes and celeriac remoulade, then main courses of perhaps lobster tempura with Chinese noodles, or roast fillet of lamb with garlic mash, and a pudding of chocolate soufflé show the hand the kitchen is dealing.

Harbour Yard Chelsea Harbour
SW10 0XD
Map GtL: C2
Tel: 0171 3517330
Fax: 0171 3516189
Chef: Raymond Brown
Owners: Claudio Pulze,
Michael Caine
Cost: Alc £30, set-price L £19.50.
H/wine £14
Times: Noon-3pm/6.30-11pm. Closed
L Sat, all Sun, Xmas, Bhs

The Canteen

Additional: Children welcome;
 dishes
Seats: 120
Smoking: Air conditioning

Directions: Off Lots Road, Chelsea.
⊖ Fulham Broadway

Ravioli of salmon with sweet wine shallots and oyster velouté turns out to be a mousseline encased in pasta, a warm and tender oyster atop, the whole thing tasting sublime. Accurately timed roast saddle of rabbit comes with crisp, freshly made polenta and an interesting contrast in mushrooms à la grecque, tangy with vinegar. Skill with puddings shows up in the chef's assiette of perfectly smooth crème caramel, tangy sorbets sitting on tiny meringues, and chocolate mousse on sponge wrapped in a dark and shiny chocolate ribbon.

Cantina del Ponte ✿

Less pricey, informal Conran Gastrodome eaterie with a riverside location and an Italian-inspired menu offering pizza, pasta or risotto, as well as roast rump of lamb, grilled tuna, and pannacotta with raspberries and grappa. Portions on the whole are generous.

Additional: Sunday L; Children welcome; dishes

Directions: SE side of Tower Bridge, by riverfront

The Butlers Wharf Building
36c Shad Thames SE1 2YE
Map GtL: G3
Tel: 0171 4035403
Fax: 0171 4030267
Cost: *Alc* £25, set-price L £12.50 (2 courses). ☺ H/wine £11.95
Times: Noon-3pm/6-11pm. Closed D Sun

The Capital ✿✿✿

Basil Street Knightsbridge SW3 1AT
Map: B2
Tel: 0171 5895171
Fax: 0171 2250011
Chef: Eric Chavot
Owner: David Levin
Cost: *Alc* £60, set-price L £21.50/D £60 (7 courses). H/wine £14.50

When we visited, it was still early days for the newly arrived Eric Chavot, but he had already made his mark and the future promises well in the skilful hands of a chef capable of the sort of great cooking that stays long in the memory. Confidence and clarity are the words that come to mind when

describing Chavot's cooking. Chilled tomato consommé with red mullet was a study on the themes of hot and cold – the fillet sitting on a circle of warm potato in the centre of the plate, all elements packed with flavour. More striking tastes and textures with a main course of pan-fried brill with fèves and petit pois, lightly doused in a frothy mushroom flavoured sauce and a few dots of highly flavoured basil oil. Warm chocolate marbre with coconut sorbet was a skilled version of this increasingly popular gooey dessert cake. The dining room was due for some refurbishment at the time of writing, but the great chandeliers and mirrored walls are, we're glad to say, there to stay.

Times: 12.30-2.30pm/7-11.15pm.
Closed D 25 Dec
Additional: Children welcome;
dishes
Seats: 35. Private dining room 24
Smoking: No pipes & cigars; Air conditioning
Accommodation: 48 en suite ★ ★ ★ ★

Directions: Between Harrods and Sloane Street. ⊖ Knightsbridge

Le Caprice

Arlington Street SW1A 1RT
Map: C3
Tel: 0171 6292239
Fax: 0171 4939040
Chefs: Elliot Ketley, Mark Hix
Owners: Jeremy King, Christopher Corbin
Cost: *Alc* £40. H/wine £11.25
Times: Noon-3pm/5.30-midnight.
Closed 25, 26 Dec, 1 Jan, Aug Bh
Additional: Sunday brunch; Children welcome; dishes
Seats: 70
Smoking: No pipes; Air conditioning

Directions: ⊖ Green Park. Arlington St runs beside The Ritz, Le Caprice is at the end

London classic with exemplary service – a place to see and be seen. Restaurants come and go but Le Caprice sails on as strongly as ever, thronged with the capital's chattering classes. The stark black and white decor might have something of retro chic to it, but here it feels like a design classic when in lesser places it would just seem dated. To say that the menu has evolved hardly at all is no criticism, as the whole style is pretty timeless; the old classics still there in the form of Caesar salad, dressed crab, eggs Benedict and salmon fishcakes. Red mullet soup with fiery rouille is spot on, with tuna sashimi no less a successful starter. Chargrilled squid with crispy pancetta and a rocket and red pepper salsa shows the kitchen working in modern idiom, all components tasting as they should and harmoniously matched, or there might be beef braised in stout with mashed parsnips and caramelised onions, and deep-fried plaice with minty pea purée and chips. A simple pudding of chilled red berries with a jug of warm chocolate sauce has been described as an 'inspired dish', and baked Alaska, or cappuccino crème brûlée might be there too. Pitchers of Buck's Fizz show up on the popular Sunday brunch menu, and there's a decent choice of wines by the glass.

Caraffini

61-63 Lower Sloane Street
SW1W 8DH
Map: B2
Tel: 0171 2590235
Fax: 0171 2590236
Chefs: John Patino, Serafino Ramalhoto
Owners: Frank di Rienzo, Paolo Caraffini
Cost: *Alc* £25. ☺
Times: 12.30-2.30pm/6.30-11.30pm.
Closed Sun, Bhs
Seats: 70
Smoking: No pipes & cigars; Air conditioning

Sloane Square's local neighbourhood Italian. Caraffini has lots to commend it: fresh and prettily decked out in pale blues and yellows, flower filled, and stage-managed by Italian waiters in pale-blue shirts who play to the audience; regulars are greeted by name and made much of. The long menu lists mostly trattoria-style dishes (fritto misto mare, saltimbocca alla romana, piccata al limone) but does include some simple chargrills such as the very good monkfish with fresh herbs and olive oil that we tried at inspection. That meal also took in gutsy mixed wild mushrooms with grilled polenta, and the 'best tiramisu to be tasted this year'. The wine list is reasonably priced.

Directions: ⊖ Sloane Square

The Cavendish St James's

81 Jermyn Street
SW1Y 6JF
Map: D3
Tel: 0171 9302111
Fax: 0171 8392125

Large, modern hotel with a good range of amenities that includes the smart 81 Restaurant. Here a Med-style menu with strong Spanish flavours also takes in the likes of mussels with garlic cream, wild

boar cutlet with chive and leek mash, Puy lentils and port sauce, and cod fillet with pepper sauce.

Caviar House

Sea-blue and sand colours, crystal mosaics covering mirror frames , waterfalls mounted in picture frames form a striking, fresh, light backdrop. Apart from caviar, scallops, smoked salmon, oysters and lobster are available at both courses, and courses are interchangeable. Excellent-quality raw materials are used, and beautifully presented Japanese-style, in small, rich portions. Pâté de foie gras comes as a starter with a 'heavenly' fresh, warm brioche, and a main-course platter de gourmet provides the opportunity to try langoustines, scallops, duck and foie gras all dressed with caviar. Sablé of strawberries and raspberries with eau de vie and cardamom ice cream is a 'delicious confection' of a dessert. Don't forget you can buy some caviar to take away from the shop at the front.

Chapter One

Boldly confident modern restaurant yet offering reassuring standards of comfort and service. This distinctive Tudor-style building with a large car park (exactly what's needed given its out-of-town setting and popularity) has been a restaurant since 1937, and a 1996 makeover provides the current clean and stylish look of blond wood, warm, sunny colours, deep blue chairs and wooden stained-glass partitions. The bar-brasserie is worth recognition in its own right – expect chicken Caesar salad, and grilled salmon with warm potato salad, French beans

The Cavendish St James's

Cost: *Alc* £22, set-price L & D £19.50. ☺ H/wine £12
Times: Noon-2.30pm/6-10pm. Closed L Sat
Additional: Bar food; Children welcome; 🍴 dishes
Smoking: No-smoking area; No pipes & cigars; Air conditioning
Accommodation: 251 en suite
★★★★

Directions: ⊖ Green Park, Piccadilly Circus

161 Piccadilly W1V 9DF
Map: C3
Tel: 0171 4090445
Fax: 0171 4931667
Chef: Masayuki Hari
Cost: *Alc* £40, set-price L & D £22.50 (2 courses). H/wine £12.95
Times: Noon-3pm/7-9.30pm. Closed Sun, Bhs
Additional: Bar food; Children welcome
Seats: 35
Smoking: Air conditioning

Directions: ⊖ Green Park

Locksbottom Farnborough Common BR6 8NF
Map GtL: E1
Tel: 01689 854848
Fax: 01689 858439
Chef: John Wood
Owner: Selective Restaurants Group
Cost: *Alc* £26, set-price L £19.50. H/wine £11
Times: Noon-2.30pm/6.30-11pm
Additional: Bar food L; Sunday L; Children welcome; 🍴 dishes

and black olives – but it's the restaurant that earns the place its rosettes. A starter described tersely as 'oriental duck confit with sweet-and-sour cabbage' has been on the menu since John Wood took over the restaurant, and rightly so as it turns out to be a circle of textbook confit on a bed of Japanese-style, lightly pickled cabbage, just warmed through and heady with notes of ginger, chilli and cumin. Eastern influences might surface again in a main course of oriental salmon with basil couscous, but the repertoire also extends to chump of pork with braised pig's cheek sauce and caramelised apple mash, and praiseworthy fillet of cod on seafood risotto – clams, mussels and squid – spiked with saffron broth. The kitchen's perfect timing also shows up in passion fruit soufflé with 'blindingly good' yogurt sorbet. Follow that with excellent espresso and petits fours and go for one of the impressive array of pudding wines or digestifs.

Seats: 120. Private dining room 55
Smoking: No pipes & cigars; Air conditioning

Directions: At junction of A21 and A232

Chapter Two NEW

Chapter Two, younger sibling of Chapter One (see entry above), located in a parade of shops overlooking the green expanse of Blackheath. Restaurant chic rules with pale wood, firm use of colour, abstracts on the wall and the menu brings us bang up-to-date with a range of traditional ideas and dishes given a modern spin. Grilled tuna, caramelised onions and sauce vierge made a brilliant start to the meal; a deeply satisfying main course braised shank of lamb with roasted root vegetables was just pipped to the post by some stunning grilled smoked haddock with superb curried saffron risotto and baby spinach – a kedgeree for our times. Desserts are typically well thought out. Try the baked chocolate cheesecake with plum compote or the crème caramel, roast pear and Armagnac ice cream. Dinner is particularly good value – if only every neighbourhood had a local like this, the Chapters might become a Volume.

43-45 Montpelier Vale
Blackheath Village SE3 0TJ
Map GtL: E3
Tel: 0181 3332666
Fax: 0181 3558399
Chef: Adrian Jones
Owner: Selective Restaurants Group
Cost: *Alc* £24, set-price L £19.50/D £22.50. ☺ H/wine £13
Times: Noon-2.30pm/6.30-10.30pm
Additional: Sunday L; Children welcome; ✦ dishes
Seats: 80
Smoking: No pipes & cigars; Air conditioning

Directions: In centre of Blackheath village

Chelsea Village Hotel NEW

A must for Chelsea football fans – hard by the stadium! Kings Brasserie has a striking modern look and a menu full of global influences. In other words, dishes range from beef, mushroom and stout pie to seared tuna teriyaki.

Smoking: No-smoking area; No pipes & cigars; Air conditioning
Accommodation: 160 en suite ★ ★ ★ ★

Directions: ⊖ Fulham Broadway. Next to Chelsea Football Stadium

Stamford Bridge Fulham Road
SW6 1HS
Map: A1
Tel: 0171 5651400
Fax: 0171 5651450
Cost: *Alc* £ 30. ☺ H/wine £12.50
Times: Noon-3pm/6-11pm
Additional: Bar food; Sunday L; Children welcome; ✦ dishes

The Chesterfield Hotel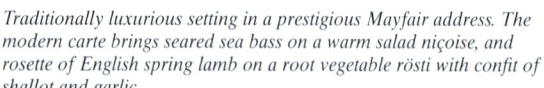

Traditionally luxurious setting in a prestigious Mayfair address. The modern carte brings seared sea bass on a warm salad niçoise, and rosette of English spring lamb on a root vegetable rösti with confit of shallot and garlic.

Smoking: Air conditioning
Accommodation: 110 en suite ★ ★ ★ ★

Directions: ⊖ Green Park. Bottom of Berkeley Square, on corner of Charles Street & Queen Street

35 Charles Street Mayfair W1X 8LX
Map: C3
Tel: 0171 4912622
Fax: 0171 4914793
Cost: *Alc* £27.50, set-price L £10.50/D £15.50. ☺ H/wine £14
Times: Noon-2pm/6-10pm
Additional: Bar food; Sunday L; Children welcome; ✦ dishes

Chez Bruce

Upscale modern restaurant with service to match. Putty-coloured walls, fresh flowers, modern lighting, white-clothed tables with serious glasses (wines by the glass feature quite well, as do half-bottles), and staff who make guests feel at home, all help to produce a good atmosphere chez Bruce Poole. He describes his style as 'mainly classical French with 30 per cent of whatever we feel like': Mozzarella and pimento crostini with balsamico and pesto, or osso bucco with risotto milanese falling into the latter category, plaice goujons with tartare sauce and steamed red mullet with a bourride sauce and provençale tart in the former. Veal and ham terrine studded with gherkins – meaty, with a hint of tarragon, and 'a pretty picture' – with beetroot remoulade and half a soft-boiled egg is as authentic as they come, and there might be deep-fried pig's trotter with sauce gribiche, or steamed scallop mousseline with buttered cockles and mussels. Praise has been heaped on a main course of roasted John Dory, perfectly cooked, mildly crunchy balsamic-tasting braised chicory on top, accompanied by white bean purée that's as smooth as silk and hinting of garlic, as well as grilled calves' kidneys with gratin dauphinoise and poivrade sauce – a dish that 'looked delicious'. Rhubarb compote with rhubarb sorbet is a popular pudding, and orange and almond cake hits the button but takes off with its additional smooth, perfectly balanced lemon-yogurt ice cream.

2 Bellevue Road
Wandsworth Common SW17 7EG
Map GtL: C2
Tel: 0181 6720114
Fax: 0181 7676648
Chef: Bruce Poole
Owners: Bruce Poole,
Nigel Platts-Martin
Cost: Set-price D £25. H/wine £11
Times: Noon-2pm/7-10.30pm. Closed
D Sun, 1 wk Xmas, Bh Mon
Additional: Sunday L; Children at L
only
Seats: 70. Private dining room 18
Smoking: No pipes & cigars; Air
conditioning

Directions: 2 mins walk from
Wandsworth Common (BR).
⊖ Balham (5 mins)

Chez Max

Bistro-style atmosphere with attentive and knowledgeable service. The French cooking is both imaginative and good; attention to detail shows in home-marinated olives, baked olive-oil bread and super Charentais butter. Bourgeoise classics include terrine de jambon persillé, blanquette de veau, and pigeon d'Anjou roti aux raisins de Muscat confit et aux morilles. A starter of galette de Picandou à basilic was a delicious combination of distinctive goats' cheese, tomato with real taste and a high-baked base with melt-in-the-mouth consistency. Main course of seared cod with smoked streaky bacon and fennel effectively balanced delicate fish with strong flavour. Flat white beans and perfect gaufrette potatoes rounded off the whole experience. Tarte au citron was up amongst the greats, 'reminiscent of the Roux recipe with a sharp flavour and perfect base'.

168 Ifield Road SW10 9AF
Map: C2
Tel: 0171 8350874
Fax: 0171 2440618
Chef: Zak el Hamdou
Owners: Graham Thomson,
Steven Smith
Cost: Set-price L £14.50 (2 courses)/D
£27.50. H/wine £12
Times: Noon-2.30pm/7-11pm. Closed
L Sat, all Sun & Mon, Xmas, Aug, Bhs
Additional: Children welcome
Seats: 50
Smoking: No-smoking area; No pipes
& cigars

Directions: Turn off the Fulham Road into Ifield Road,
restaurant is 500 yds on the L

Chez Moi ❁❁

A well-loved restaurant on the north-side of Holland Park, established for over thirty years. The interior, with its deep-red walls hung with elaborate gilt-framed mirrors, has barely changed since it opened, and couldn't be further from the minimal style that is currently so popular; most inspectors are in agreement that this is one of the most romantic, intimate restaurants in the capital. Broadly speaking, the cooking is French, but many other influences have, over the years, been incorporated into the repertoire. Japanese-style scallops are seared with a touch of sesame oil and served with slices of

1 Addison Avenue W11 4QS
Map GtL: C3
Tel: 0171 6038267
Fax: 0171 6033898
Chef: Richard Walton
Owners: Richard Walton, Colin Smith
Cost: *Alc* £30, set-price L £15. ☺
H/wine £10.75
Times: 12.30-1.45pm/7-10.45pm.
Closed L Sat, all Sun, Bhs
Additional: Children welcome (no
small babies); ♨ dishes

futo-maki roll (nori, wasabi, sticky rice, gravad lax, avocado, spring onion and cucumber). Nine main courses include a Moroccan lamb tagine, and Thai chicken, but there is also rack of lamb à la diable, and sautéed Dutch veal kidneys in mustard sauce. The restaurant makes superior desserts and both the service and the wine list is polished.

Directions: N side of Holland Park Avenue, opposite Kensington Hilton. ⊖ Holland Park

Seats: 45
Smoking: No pipes & cigars; Air conditioning

Chez Nico
at Ninety Park Lane ⚜⚜⚜⚜⚜

A grand restaurant offering space and comfort within the Grosvenor House Hotel, but very much its own boss. Nico Ladenis' place remains immaculate in every sense with great, albeit formal, staff, but with touches of personality from the more senior – the sommelier is particularly good. And the stylish, understated room is an antidote to the minimalism of so many newer openings in the capital – here tables are wide and well-spaced, seats comfortably padded, floor-length tablecloths, carpets and drapes absorb any hard-edged noise. The *carte* offers an haute cuisine-dominated selection of dishes: two foie gras starters, as well as guesting in two main courses, scallops are billed twice, and there are a lot of truffles. But there is some broadening out as we noted in a super dish of noisettes of pig's trotter with celeriac – the pig's trotter Koffmann-style, stuffed with chic mousse and sweetbreads, sliced with thin pasta-like layers of celeriac above and below and a spot-on truffley meat jus. There's a directness to Paul Rhodes' cooking, no matter how sophisticated it may be, and his ability lies in eliciting intense flavours through careful technique and a recognition that taste matters. A case in point was another spot-on starter – risotto with black truffle purée and top-notch Parmesan, as well as a great chunky fillet of seared sea bass, caramelised without and tender within, with a pungent basil-flavoured pomme purée and confit of fennel. Desserts are classics: for example chocolate negus with pistachio sauce or the thin apple tarte with vanilla ice cream. All the ancillaries are determinedly good: great breads, *amuse-bouche*, impressive petits fours, monolithic wine list.
Signature dishes: seared escalope of fresh foie gras with brioche and caramelised oranges; grilled milk-fed veal cutlet with roast garlic, rosemary butter sauce and pomme purée; tulipe with vanilla ice cream and red berries in Armagnac.

90 Park Lane W1A 3AA
Map: B3
Tel: 0171 4091290
Fax: 0171 3554877
Chefs: Paul Rhodes, Nico Ladenis
Owners: Nico & Dinah-Jane Ladenis
Cost: *Alc* £70, set-price L £25 & £40/D £75 (10 course gastronomic). H/wine £18.50
Times: Noon-2pm/7-11pm. Closed L Sat, all Sun, 10 days Xmas, 4 days Easter, Bhs
Additional: Children 10+
Seats: 75. Private dining room 20
Smoking: No pipes; Air conditioning

Directions: Part of Grosvenor House Hotel

AA Shortlisted for Wine Award-see page 16

Chinon Restaurant ⚜⚜⚜

Chinon, in an unremarkable parade of shops, is a long, thin room with a patio garden at the back and some tables for fine-weather eating. This might be west London, but some of the dishes are straight out of provincial France. How about a simple but effective 'great' starter of ham with pickles and country bread, or duck rillettes garnished with leaves, followed by calves' liver with mustard sauce and fondant potatoes? But Jonathon Hayes shows a reluctance to be pigeonholed, also turning out tempura prawns with lemon and raisin chutney, duck breast with swede purée and Savoy cabbage cooked with bacon and orange sauce, and fried squid with spaghetti. Crab ravioli is something of a signature dish: two sheets of the 'thinnest, most ethereal' pasta sandwiching a huge mound of

23 Richmond Way W14 0AS
Map GtL: C3
Tel: 0171 6025968
Fax: 0171 6024082
Chef: Jonathon Hayes
Owners: Barbara Deane, Jonathon Hayes
Cost: *Alc* £35. ☺ H/wine £14
Seats: 30
Smoking: No pipes & cigars; Air conditioning

Directions: ⊖ Shepherd's Bush. Off Blythe Road which is off Shepherd's Bush Road

sweet, full-flavoured white crab in a smooth beurre blanc dotted with pesto. Roast rack of new season's English lamb, 'herby and delicious', served with garlic cream sauce, asparagus and morels brought a breath of spring to one diner, who finished with a thick slice of caramelised pineapple hinting of spices with vanilla ice cream filling the cored-out centre. Hayes has a way with other fruity puddings, too, as in passion fruit sorbet with a fruit brûlée, chilled fruit soup, and lemon tart.

The Chiswick

Popular neighbourhood restaurant with bare wooden tables and casual Mediterranean bistro-style setting. Menu choices include onion and rosemary soup, whole devilled quail with tortilla, and a good traditional roast beef withYorkshire pudding for Sunday lunch.

Directions: On Chiswick High Road close to junction with Turnham Green Terrace. ⊖ Turnham Green (3 mins)

131-133 Chiswick High Road W4
Map: B3
Tel: 0181 9946887
Fax: 0181 9945504
Telephone for further details

Chor Bizarre

16 Albemarle Street W1X 3HA
Map: C2
Tel: 0171 6299802/6298542
Fax: 0171 4937756
Cost: *Alc* £28, set-price L £14.95/D £28. ☺ H/wine £13.75
Times: Noon-2.30pm/6-11.30pm
Additional: Children welcome; ﴾ dishes
Smoking: No-smoking area; Air conditioning

Directions: ⊖ Green Park

Cluttered with unusual artefacts and offering a broad range of regional Indian dishes, research is thorough and it pays to be adventurous. More conservative tastes are satisfied with familiar tandooris, tikkas and pakoras. Wines are matched to the food.

Christopher's

Victorian building on three floors with a stone spiral staircase. All-American menu of bold flavours: Maryland crab cakes with red pepper mayo, and blackened salmon with paprika oil.

Additional: Bar food; Sunday L; Children welcome
Smoking: Air conditioning; Jacket & tie preferred

Directions: 100 yds from the Royal Opera House. ⊖ Covent Garden

18 Wellington Street WC2E 7DD
Map: E3
Tel: 0171 2404222
Fax: 0171 8363506
Cost: *Alc* £32. H/wine £11.50
Times: Noon-3pm/6-11pm. Closed D Sun, Xmas

Churchill Inter-Continental

Clementines is the flagship restaurant of this luxury hotel.
Executive Chef Idris Caldora is one of the country's most respected professionals, and his cooking is always basically simple, stylish and fresh. Nonetheless, the menu at Clementine's

30 Portman Square
W1A 4ZX
Map: B4
Tel: 0171 4865800
Fax: 0171 4861255
Chef: Idris Caldora

reads like a railway time table with symbols identifying dishes suitable for good bone health, dishes for vegetarians and signature dishes, sometimes in various combinations. We were pleased to find roasted onion and garlic soup with goats' cheese croûtons good for bones and vegetarians. Signature terrine of foie gras, celeriac and duck confit with herb salad won't help either bones or veggies; grilled yellow fin tuna with Mediterranean vegetable, ragout and tomato dressing is only for bones. Still, to be fair, the cause is a good one and money from each dish ordered will be donated to the National Osteoporosis Society, although the menu does not make it clear whether that means from every dish or only from bone-friendly dishes. Perhaps there should be a symbol of explanation.

Directions: Close to Marble Arch, just off Oxford Street

Cost: *Alc* £35, set-price L £18 (2 courses). H/wine £14.50
Times: 12.30-2.55pm/6-10.55pm. Closed L Sat
Additional: Sunday L; Children welcome; ✿ dishes
Seats: 102
Smoking: No-smoking area; Air conditioning
Accommodation: 440 en suite
★★★★★

Chutney Mary Restaurant

A stylish Indian evoking the comfortable days of the British Raj. The bright menus take you on a trail-blazing tour of the Indian regions: try a medium-spiced roast duck curry from Kerala, an earthy rogan josh from Kashmir, or a fiery prawn curry from Mangalore.

535 King's Road Chelsea SW10 0SZ
Map GtL: C2
Tel: 0171 3513113/7658
Fax: 0171 3517694
Cost: *Alc* £25, set-price L £12.50 (2 courses). ☺ H/wine £11.50
Times: 12.30-2.30pm /6.30-11.15pm. Closed D 25 Dec, 26 Dec
Additional: Sunday L; Children welcome; ✿ dishes
Smoking: No-smoking area; No pipes & cigars; Air conditioning

Directions: On corner of King's Road and Lots Road; 2 mins from Chelsea Harbour. ⊖ Fulham Broadway

Cibo ✿✿

A bright and cheerful shop fronted restaurant close to Olympia with much to please in the way of decor. Striking paintings of nudes and a 3-D sculpture, crisp white-clothed tables and a bar which provides the main focal point, all entice the would be diner. Choose from a traditional Italian menu, with a few specialities, that offers fresh and satisfying cooking. Our most recent meal brought delightful, locally made ciabatta and focaccia, huge black olives and thin slices of pizza to start, then perfectly cooked asparagus with Parmesan and grilled polenta. Our main courses featured a piping hot plate of sauté of seafood and shellfish (langoustines, prawns, mussels, clams, squid, baby octopus) in a white wine, tomato and herb liquor. Finish with a delicious pannacotta-like chocolate cream – silky smooth with a rich chocolate flavour.

3 Russell Gardens W14 8EZ
Map GtL: C3
Tel: 0171 3712085
Fax: 0171 6021371
Telephone for further details

Directions: Russell Gardens is a residential area off Holland Road. ⊖ Kensington (Olympia), Shepherd's Bush

City Rhodes Restaurant

Youthful staff are charming, enthusiastic and superbly trained. City Rhodes is a nightmare to find, but perseverance will be handsomely rewarded. Entrance is via a ground floor

1 New Street Square EC4A 3JB
Map: E4
Tel: 0171 5831313
Fax: 0171 5831662

City Rhodes Restaurant

Chefs: Gary Rhodes, Michael Bedford
Owners: Gardner Merchant
Cost: *Alc* £55. H/wine £12.50
Times: Noon-2.30pm/6-9pm. Closed Sat, Sun, Bhs
Additional: Children welcome; dishes
Seats: 100. Private dining room 12
Smoking: No pipes & cigars; Air conditioning

Directions: Off Shoe Lane, behind International Press Centre

lobby done up as a sort of shrine to Gary Rhodes, then up a circular staircase into the habitat not of telly Gary or frozen meals Gary, but of Gary the serious chef (although day-to-day cooking is in the capable hands of Michael Bedford). The first-floor room is sleek, well-groomed, and minimalist in style and the cooking is good enough to silence the sceptics. A pressed tomato cake with peppered goats' cheese was stunning in its simplicity; caramelised shallot and cep tart with red wine butter reached even greater heights. The Rhodes approach is to rework old, and occasionally stodgy sounding classics, by giving them a much lighter touch; roast calves' liver and kidney with sweet red wine carrots and rosemary butter sauce was much lighter than the description implied, and red wine beef lasagne with wild mushroom cream sauce, made with tender slow-cooked meat, was a clever take on the familiar. Desserts are pure joy – lemon curd with caramelised figs and almond crisps and baked egg custard tart both are on their way to becoming new signature dishes.

Claridges

Gloriously grand hotel finally resurfacing from a period of refurbishment. Claridge's Restaurant and The Orangery remain as elegant as ever, though subtle changes have been made. There is now a 'Claridge's Centenary' menu available at lunch in addition to the *carte*, and a 'Menu Sonata' in the evenings, a four-course affair with 'a fragrance of wild herbs and spices', split into nine so-called 'preludes', four fish and shellfish, four grills and roasts, and seven entrees. Classical British with a strong French accent sums up the style: a trio of foie gras with elderflower sauce and aromatic spiced bread; baked filet of turbot with onion soubise; Chateaubriand and sautéed mignon of veal with morels. The desserts continue in the same vein with a white chocolate dome and chocolate truffle centre with raspberry coulis. An orchestra entertains dinner-dance guests on Friday and Saturday nights.

Directions: At the corner of Brook & Davies Street

Brook Street W1A 2JQ
Map: C3
Tel: 0171 6298860
Fax: 0171 4992210
Chef: John Williams
Owner: The Savoy Group
Cost: *Alc* £55, set-price L £29.50/D £39
Times: 12.30pm-2.45pm/7-10.45pm
Additional: Bar food; Sunday L: Children welcome; dishes
Seats: 120. Private dining rooms. Jacket & tie preferred
Smoking: No-smoking area; No pipes & cigars; Air conditioning
Accommodation: 197 en suite
★ ★ ★ ★ ★

Clarke's

Lovely, idiosyncratic restaurant that continues to attract the Kensington locals as well as foreigners. The ground-floor, double-frontage is split in half, with Clarke's shop on one side

124 Kensington Church Street
W8 4BH
Map GtL: C3
Tel: 0171 2219225
Fax: 0171 2294564

and the restaurant on the other; however, in the light and airy basement, the restaurant extends over both. The lunch menu consists of four starters, three main courses and three desserts – each course one price. In the evening there is a set menu, with no choices, that changes once a week. A typical example might be buffalo Mozzarella with a salad of grapes, black olives, capers and wild rocket with herbed foccacia, followed by chargrilled breast of free-range duck with crackling, red wine, Seville orange and sage glaze, roasted desirée potatoes, herbed carrots and leaf spinach, then cheese with oatmeal biscuits and apple, with a warm buckwheat pancake with lemon curd, caramelised lemon and Yorkshire rhubarb to finish. There is an impressive wine list which includes many of California's best wines. Home-made breads, chocolate truffles, and other delicacies are for sale in the next door shop.

Chefs: Sally Clarke, Elizabeth Payne
Owner: Sally Clarke
Cost: Set-price L £29/D £42
Times: 12.30-2pm/7-10pm. Closed Sat, Sun, 10 days Xmas, 2wks summer
Additional: Children welcome
Seats: 90
Smoking: No-smoking area; No pipes & cigars; Air conditioning

Directions: ⊖ Notting Hill Gate

Club Gascon

NEW

Crowded, clamorous restaurant where reservations well in advance are recommended. Your standard three-course format this is not. Based on south-west France and the Basque region, the menu is divided into sections such as 'la route du sel' (Bayonne ham, spicy Basque pâté, for example), 'les pâturages' (venison cooked on the embers of vine shoots, carpaccio of duck breast), and, most important, 'les foies gras'. The idea is to order six or seven little dishes to make your own tasting menu. Luckily, waiters are in bountiful supply to explain both the concept and the unfamiliar terms (zipister sauce, anyone? Or roast millas – actually a type of polenta – with baby corn?). Cassoulet is good, foie gras – both duck and goose – comes every which way, even sushi-style, crispy smoked eel is served with horseradish cream, Perennial cheese is accompanied by herb salad and tomato confit, and chips are the thick-cut sort. A former Lyons Tea House with a striking blue and dark marble decor, with cramped tables, a large bar and an exclusively French wine list, is where it's all happening. Winner of the AA Restaurant of the Year Award. See page 20.

57 West Smithfield EC1
Map: F4
Tel: 0171 7960600
Fax: 0171 7960601
Chef: Pascal Aussignac
Owners: Vincent Labeyrie, Mourad Mazouz
Cost: *Alc* £25, set-price L & D £30 (5 courses). ☺ H/wine £10.50
Times: Noon-2pm/7-10pm. Closed L Sat, all Sun, Xmas-New Year
Additional: Children welcome; ♨ dishes
Seats: 60
Smoking: Air conditioning

Directions: ⊖ Barbican. Opposite Smithfield Market

Coast Restaurant

On the trendy side of modern, but not so avant-garde as to frighten off anyone dressed in M&S. Bright, light and airy with pale green walls, although the wooden chairs with citrus yellow inserts are not the most comfy for those endowed with well-upholstered posteriors. Several deep-green booths are dotted around the room. Very child friendly (on Saturday and Sunday lunchtimes) assuming you have offspring who actually enjoy courgette flower tempura with lemon oil. In with all the fancy stuff, however, there are also traditional dishes, such as ham, egg and chips, albeit given a designer twist in the presentation. Chocolate torte with vanilla ice cream and light caramel sauce is always a crowd pleaser. Wines aren't cheap but there is plenty by the glass.

Albemarle Street W1
Map: C3
Tel: 0171 4955999
Fax: 0171 4952999
Times: Noon-2.45pm (3.30pm Sat)/6-11.45pm. Closed Sun
Telephone for further details

Directions: ⊖ Green Park

The Collection

Former fashion warehouse is home to a lively ground-floor bar and mezzanine restaurant. Interesting menus include exotic dishes such

264 Brompton Road SW3
Map: B1
Tel: 0171 2251212
Fax: 0171 2251050

as steamed foie gras, pork dumplings with chilli honey dip on the mezzanine; simple noodle and salad dishes on the ground floor.

The Collection

Telephone for further details

Directions: ⊖ South Kensington

The Connaught ❀❀

The service is from the top drawer in this traditional, formal restaurant. Times may be changing, but not at The Connaught where, for a few brief hours, one can be forgiven for thinking the old world remains. It is fitting that Michel Bourdin's style and menu are just so, so classical, and that this is a kitchen that remains proudly and solidly steeped in the past (turn of the century to be exact). The main menu (the same in the restaurant and the grill room) is 'dedicated' to the traditions of Escoffier and had he eaten here, we doubt whether Bourdin would have been reproached. A signature terrine Connaught was unfortunately foiled by its cold temperature, but better were the noisettes d'agneau Edward VII, perfectly timed and seasoned, with foie gras and a slice of black truffle. The accompanying 'légumes printaniers' were spot-on, as were the boiled new potatoes. (Gratin daupinoise was requested at the outset but the kitchen couldn't oblige.) The sweet trolley is a grand production, groaning under the weight of choice, although a crème brûlée had reached room temperature, which marred the texture, but the flavour was fine. Coffee and petits fours were from the same school.

Carlos Place W1Y 6AL
Map: C3
Tel: 0171 4990888
Fax: 0171 4953262
Chef: Michel Bourdin
Owners: The Savoy Group
Cost: *Alc* £40, set-price L £27.50/D £37.50. H/wine £22
Times: 12.30-2.30pm/6-10.45pm
Additional: Sunday L; Children welcome; ✿ dishes
Seats: 70 (Grill Room 35). Private dining room 22. Jacket & tie preferred
Smoking: Air conditioning
Accommodation: 90 en suite
★ ★ ★ ★ ★

Directions: On corner of Mount Street and Carlos Place. ⊖ Bond Street/ Green Park

Conrad International ❀

Mediterranean-style views over the marina set this hotel restaurant apart. Vibrant dishes range from Caesar salad and baked oysters 'Muscovite', to spiced duck with red cabbage, chargrilled lamb with herb and mustard jus and, for pudding, warm raspberry tart.

Chelsea Harbour SW10 0XG
Map GtL: C2
Tel: 0171 8233000
Fax: 0171 3516525
Telephone for further details

Directions: ⊖ Fulham Broadway, Earls Court

The Cook House

Minimalist restaurant with a terracotta floor and the menu written on glass over the open-plan kitchen, with options like fish stew, pot-roasted rabbit, and ribeye of Angus beef.

Additional: Children welcome
Smoking: No-smoking area; No pipes & cigars, Air conditioning

Directions: ⊖ Putney Bridge

56 Lower Richmond Road Putney
SW15 1JT
Map GtL: C2
Tel: 0181 7852300
Cost: Alc £24.50. ☺ Unlicensed
Times: D only, 7-11pm. Closed Sun, Mon

Copthorne Tara

French-style brasserie with a choice of menus. International favourites include balti chicken tikka masala, Thai sea bass, and tagliatelle Don Alfredo with prawns and mushrooms.

Smoking: No-smoking area; Air conditioning
Accommodation: 825 en suite ★ ★ ★ ★

Directions: ⊖ High Street Kensington

Scarsdale Place Wrights Lane W8 5SR
Map GtL: C3
Tel: 0171 9377211
Fax: 0171 9377100
Cost: Alc £35, set-price L & D £19.
☺ H/wine £12.10
Times: Noon-2.30pm/5-10.45pm
Additional: Bar food; ✿ dishes

Coulsdon Manor

Vegetarians are offered their own multi-choice menu, featuring innovative ideas such as savoury layers of pancake and vegetable purées with garlic cream sauce. On the main *carte*, first courses set the tone for upmarket, country house cooking – terrine of morel mushroom and truffle with sherry and caramelised shallot dressing, for example. Optional middle courses include a basket of poached quails' eggs glazed with Hollandaise sauce. Well-honed kitchen skills and industry are demonstrated in a typical main course of charred and steamed supreme of salmon placed onto lobster mash with a beetroot jus and carrot spaghetti, and in labour-intensive desserts such as baked Alaska filled by a liquid cranberry centre with a clementine coulis. More mainstream dishes include roasted marinated rump of lamb, dauphinoise potato and courgette, tian of provençale vegetables. All dishes on the *carte* carry a suggestion for a recommended wine from the extensive cellar.

Directions: M23 N until road becomes A23. After 2.5 miles, R after Coulsdon S Railway Station onto B2030 (Purley). Follow uphill 1 mile, L past pond, 0.5 mile, and turn R into Coulsdon Court Rd

Coulsdon Court Road Croydon
CR5 2LL
Map GtL: D1
Tel: 0181 6680414
Fax: 0181 6683118
Chef: Neil Bradshaw
Owner: Marston Hotels
Cost: Alc £30, set-price L £17/D £25.
☺ H/wine £12.40
Times: 12.30-2pm/7-9.30pm. Closed L Sat
Additional: Bar food; Sunday L; Children welcome; ✿ dishes
Seats: 140. Private dining room 120
Smoking: No smoking in dining room; Air conditioning
Accommodation: 35 en suite ★ ★ ★ ★

The Cow Dining Room

The restaurant is set above a busy and successful pub and has the atmosphere of a private dining room. The pub downstairs serves quality ales and wonderfully fresh shellfish including langoustines and oysters – all simply served. Upstairs, the restaurant walls are strikingly adorned with Francis Bacon prints and the daily changing set-menu (sometimes even twice daily as they do use only the freshest ingredients) offers nine starters and eight main courses. This is modern British cooking with a twist; the kitchen understands how to make the most of a wide range of ingredients, offering such varied dishes as Borscht soup, a fabulous carpaccio of beef, avocado and

89 Westbourne Park Road W2 5QH
Map GtL: C3
Tel: 0171 2210021
Chef: Caroline Perry
Owner: Tom Conran
Cost: Set-price D £19.50. ☺ H/wine £12.95
Times: D only, 7-10.45pm
Additional: Bar food; Sunday L; Children welcome; ✿ dishes
Seats: 32
Smoking: No pipes

pepper nori rolls with wasabi and soy dipping sauce, Thai monkfish curry and a mezze plate of baba ghanoush, falafel, tabouleh, flat breads and harissa yogurt. Plus an excellent beer-battered cod and flat chips, and some successfully executed French regional dishes: various terrines, and pigeon with peas. Six desserts are offered, plus Neal's Yard cheeses.

Directions: ⊖ Royal Oak, Westbourne Park, Queensway. 5 mins from Portobello Market

The Crescent

*See **The Montcalm-Hotel Nikko London***

The Criterion

224 Piccadilly W1V 9LB
Map: C3
Tel: 0171 9300488
Fax: 0171 9308380
Chef: Tim Payne
Owners: Marco Pierre White, Jimmy Lahoud & Granada
Cost: *Alc* £28, set-price L & D £17.95. ☺ H/wine £13
Times: Noon-2.15pm/6-11.30pm (10.15pm Sun). Closed L Sun, Xmas
Additional: Children welcome; ⓭ dishes
Seats: 175

Directions: ⊖ Piccadilly Circus

*A **great place for people-watching.*** 'This is such an impressive venue, the decor is stunning and fascinates me every time I see it; and the place just heaves from 5.30pm til late', comments an inspector on Marco Pierre White's opulent restaurant at the heart of Piccadilly Circus. A gold mosaic ceiling glitters down the entire length of the 45 metre long room; semi-precious stones stud the walls. However, the rather menacing likeness of the famous proprietor that dominates the menu and wine list, also bears the legend 'To know how to eat well one must first know how to wait!'. Not in our experience. Service is, shall we say, very rapid, perhaps necessarily so for the volume of business The Criterion is doing. During our visit a group of 20 theatregoers left at 7.30pm to be replaced by a party of 75. Our own meal, served at the gallop, brought tarte Tatin of endives topped with grilled scallops, nicely balanced by fine-diced onion and beetroot in balsamic vinegar; confit of duck with colcannon and a port and plum jus which rather missed the mark; and warm plum and almond tart with milk ice cream, which raised standards again.

Crowne Plaza London – Heathrow ✿

Smart restaurant from the Simply Nico chain serving modern British food (seared tuna, with lime and chilli, and rump of lamb with Tatin provençale) and a fairly serious choice of wines.

Stockley Road UB7 9NA
Map GtL: A2
Tel: 01895 445555
Fax: 01895 445122
Telephone for further details

Directions: 2 miles N of M4 J4/A408

Crowthers Restaurant

Neighbourhood restaurant noted for attentive service and modern Anglo-French cooking. The kitchen makes good use of fresh produce. Begin with grilled aubergine with tomato, Feta and pesto and follow, perhaps, with herb-crusted lamb with rosemary jus.

Additional: Children welcome; 🍴 dishes
Smoking: Air conditioning

Directions: Train to Mortlake; train or tube to Richmond. Between junction of Sheen Lane & Clifford Ave

481 Upper Richmond Road West East Sheen SW14 7PU
Map GtL: B2
Tel/Fax: 0181 8766372
Cost: Set-price D £23.50. H/wine £9.75
Times: L by arrangement, D only, 7-10pm. Closed Sun, Mon, 1 wk Xmas, 2 wks Aug

Cucina

45a South End Road NW3 2QB
Map GtL: C4
Tel: 0171 4357814
Fax: 0171 4357815
Chefs: Stephen Baker, Andy Poole
Owners: V Mascarenhas, A Poole, S Baker
Cost: *Alc* £22.50, set-price L £10 (2 courses)/D £16.95. ☺ H/wine £10.95
Times: Noon-2.30pm/7-10.30pm(11pm Fri, Sat). Closed D Sun, Easter, Bhs
Additional: Sunday L; Children welcome; 🍴 dishes
Seats: 65. Pivate dining room 30
Smoking: No pipes & cigars; Air conditioning

Busy, modern restaurant, simply decked out in warm Mediterranean colours. The spacious colourful room is enhanced by lots of different artwork, and offset by a sharp, snappy menu that nods towards the Sugar Club in style. Thus one can expect Pacific rim dishes along the lines of hot-and-sour tiger prawn laksa with coconut and lime gremolata, chargrilled mahi mahi with Cajun-spiced sweetcorn and pepper 'succotash'. However, the more classic twice-baked goats' cheese soufflé, braised lamb shank with goats' cheese and rosemary mash, and chargrilled rib of beef with frites sit just as happily on the menu. Warm lemon cake with crème fraîche is well made. The one side of A4 that represents the wine list is punchy, modern and to the point with prices, on the whole, below the £20 mark.

Directions: Opposite Hampstead BR station. ⊖ Belsize Park, Hampstead

Dakota

NEW

Large airy former pub with log stockades hinting at the cooking's provenance in America's south-west. Rajas salsa and guajillo carnita seem a revelation for those who have rejected TexMex. Pecan-smoked rabbit, and roasted plums with liquorice ice cream are a must.

Additional: Sunday L; Children welcome; 🍴 dishes
Smoking: Air conditioning

Directions: ⊖ Notting Hill Gate or Westbourne Park

127 Ledbury Road W11 2AQ
Map GtL: C3
Tel: 0171 7929191
Fax: 0171 7929090
Cost: *Alc* £30, set-price L £11.95 (2 courses). ☺ H/wine £10.95
Times: Noon-3.30pm/7-11pm. Closed 25, 26 Dec, wknd of Notting Hill Carnival

Dan's Restaurant

Something of a place to be seen where the proprietor, the eponymous Dan Whitehead, personally greets his regulars. Look out for the excellent value set lunch menu.

Directions: At Kings Road end of Sydney Street. ⊖ S. Kensington

119 Sydney Street SW3 6NR
Map: B1
Tel: 0171 3522718
Fax: 0171 3523265
Telephone for further details

Daphne's

110-112 Draycott Avenue SW3 3AE
Map: B1
Tel: 0171 5894257
Fax: 0171 5812232
Chef: Lee Purcell
Cost: *Alc* £30. H/wine £13
Times: Noon-3pm/7-10.30pm. Closed Xmas

Directions: Jnc of Draycott Avenue & Walton Street. ⊖ South Kensington

Chic Chelsea hang-out. The long restaurant splits into three dining rooms and each has a slightly different atmosphere. The conservatory at the back, for example, has a retractable roof, and the front room looks out on to Draycott Avenue. The 'designed' strong Mediterranean look matches the modern Italian menu. Linguine with clams, risotto with summer truffle and zucchia, roast duck with trevisano and lentils, and vanilla pannacotta with pear compôte are substantial enough to satisfy more than the ladies-who-lunch who are loyal customers.

The Depot Waterfront Brasserie

A room with a view, right on the banks of the Thames. The old parquet floor, white walls with a bit of brick showing through and generally simple decor suits the easy atmosphere. Fishcakes are a constant fixture on the menu, perhaps salmon and sorrel or cod and crab with cucumber and lemon crème fraîche. In hot weather, gazpacho with basil cream has the original addition of a cube of frozen olive oil. Desserts are more conventional – treacle tart, poached pear and vanilla ice cream, chocolate mousse. There is a wine list of 50 popular bins, with plenty to choose from by the glass. Prices, for both food and wine, are reasonable.

Tideway Yard Mortlake High Street SW14 8SN
Map GtL: C2
Tel: 0181 8789462
Fax: 0181 3921361
Telephone for further details

Directions: Between Barnes Bridge and Mortlake train stations

The Dorchester, Grill Room

Grand hotel with style and service to match. The Grill keeps the flag flying with traditional British food and gentleman's club power-dining on a grand scale. The decor is thoroughly opulent with gold leaf and leather aplenty, staff are immaculate in every sense and there are trolleys for just about everything. The majority of diners come for the Cornish dressed crab, steak and kidney pie or roast Angus beef with Yorkshire

Park Lane W1A 2HJ
Map: C3
Tel: 0171 3176336
Fax: 0171 3176464
Chef: Willi Elsener
Cost: *Alc* £45, set price L £29.50/D £39.50 (4 courses). H/wine £22
Times: 12.30-2.30pm/6-11pm (7-10.30pm Sun & Bhs)

The Dorchester, Grill Room

Additional: Sunday L; Children welcome; ✿ dishes
Seats: 81
Smoking: Air conditioning
Accommodation: 248 en suite
★ ★ ★ ★ ★

Directions: Two-thirds of the way down Park Lane, fronting a small island garden. ✆ Hyde Park Corner

pudding, and this is the essence of the place. Chef Willi Elsener, however, also offers a more innovative style of cooking with dishes such as salad of pan-fried warm scallops on a confit of tomatoes flavoured with coriander and oven-baked sea bass with black bean sauce and spring onions served on stir-fried vegetables. The groaning edifice that is the sweet trolley is probably not bettered anywhere. Anachronism or classic tradition? Debate over brandy and cigars.

The Dorchester, The Oriental

Park Lane W1A 2HJ
Map: C3
Tel: 0171 3176328
Fax: 0171 4090114
Chefs: Willi Elsener, Kenneth Poon
Cost: *Alc* £47, set-price L £25 (4 courses)/D £47 (5 courses). H/wine £22
Times: Noon-2.30pm/7pm-11pm. Closed L Sat, all Sun, Aug
Additional: Children welcome; ✿ dishes
Seats: 51. Private dining rooms 5-16
Smoking: Air conditioning
Accommodation: 248 en suite
★ ★ ★ ★ ★

Directions: See Dorchester Grill Room (previous entry)

Great Cantonese cooking served impeccably by tail-coated waiters in first-class, stylishly understated surroundings. The staff are true Dorchester professionals and conduct themselves with the utmost discretion and skill, but without sacrificing any sense of hospitality. As well as the *carte,* there are several set menus, a page of vegetarian dishes and special chef's recommendations – and it is worth spending some time discussing with your waiter how best to construct a balanced meal – their advice is spot-on. One of the most striking thing about the cooking is the absence of *wei fen* (MSG), thus allowing flavours to ring true. A hot starter of honey-cured barbecue pork garnished with exquisitely sculpted carrot was all it promised to be; cold shredded duck and chicken with fresh apricot and onions in peanut sauce was equally excellent. A sublime hot-and-sour soup was perfectly balanced. Braised minced pork with silky tofu and sea-spiced sauce was an effective combination, but the star turn, for our inspector at least, was fragrant stir-fried beef with lemon grass and black pepper. He ended his report pleading to be sent back.

Drones of Pont Street

Decor is cool and chic, as befits any Knightsbridge eaterie, with apricot walls and wrought iron chairs. Pan-Mediterranean cooking, with an emphasis on Italian, and lunch and dinner menus that differ little apart from price. In the past we have enjoyed dishes such as spinach gnocchi with a buttery sauce, roasted walnuts and Parmesan shavings, as well as new season's lamb fillet coated with a mustard crust with an aromatic courgette and basil purée and charlotte of ratatouille-type vegetables. Before you hit the excellent espresso, there may be delicately poached pears with sabayon and honey ice cream. Even if you don't sport the obligatory designer accessories and are without a mobile phone, staff are friendly enough not to make you feel like a hick.

1 Pont Street SW1X 9EJ
Map: B2
Tel: 0171 2596166
Fax: 0171 2596177
Telephone for further details

Directions: ⊖ Knightsbridge and Sloane Square

The Eagle

Roaringly successful media pub on Farringdon Road known for its huge platefuls of robust Mediterranean-style food, perhaps marinated anchovies with slow-roasted tomatoes on rocket and toasted ciabatta.

Directions: N end of Farringdon Road close to Mount Pleasant. ⊖ Farringdon

159 Farringdon Road EC1R 3AL
Map GtL: E5
Tel: 0171 8371353
Credit cards: None
Telephone for further details

Ellington's

Duke is the Ellington of the restaurant's name, whose picture appears around the split-level room; there is also a pleasant patio area. The menu is modern, eclectic and seasonal.

Directions: Opposite Chingford railway station

140 Station Road Chingford E4 6AN
Map GtL: E5
Tel: 0181 5245544
Fax: 0181 5594993
Telephone for further details

English Garden Restaurant

10 Lincoln Street SW3 2TS
Map: B1
Tel: 0171 5847272
Fax: 0171 5812848
Chef: Barry Scarborough
Owner: Roger Wren
Cost: *Alc* £28, set-price L £17. ☺
H/wine £11
Times: 12.30-2.30pm/7.30-9.30pm
Additional: Sunday L; Children welcome; 🍴 dishes
Seats: 70. Private dining room 30
Smoking: Air conditioning

Directions: ⊖ Sloane Square

Long-established and tucked away in a quiet, terraced side street off the King's Road. Stylishly converted from a typical Chelsea townhouse, the restaurant is made up of two connecting dining rooms: one at the front, decorated with faux marble walls, and a 'conservatory' at the back, with white painted brick walls, large mirrors and a domed skylight. The menu changes seasonally, and most dishes are quite straightforward. First courses on the spring menu could include cream of lobster soup with garlic croûtons, and chicken livers on toasted brioche. We chose grilled scallops with slow-roasted shallots, a simple saffron jus and crisped sage leaves, then roast ham on a mound of English mustard mash, then warm banana cake with hot fudge sauce. Other desserts include lemon, orange and ginger curd tart, served with clotted cream and blueberry coulis.

The English House ❀❀

A period English house in a quiet terraced street at the back of Sloane Square. The ground-floor dining room is decorated in classical Georgian style with masses of chintz, and three private dining rooms on the upper floors are all similarly decorated. Six first, and seven main courses are offered on a straightforward *carte*, which changes with the seasons. First courses range from smoked chicken, or devilled crab cakes, to prawn and mussel terrine with champagne. Main courses are equally conservative – roast fillet of beef with a horseradish crust and Yorkshire pudding, calves' liver and bacon, and fish pie are all staples. The delicious desserts are also English, and the coffee comes with Yorkshire fudge. The predominantly French wine list is well chosen and reasonably priced.

Directions: ⊖ South Kensington, Sloane Square

3 Milner Street SW3 2QA
Map: B1
Tel: 0171 5843002
Fax: 0171 5812848
Chef: Danny Leahy
Owner: Roger Wren
Cost: *Alc* £32, set-price L £15.75. ☺
H/wine £11
Times: 12.30-2.30pm (2pm Sun)/7.30-11.30pm (10pm Sun). Closed 26 Dec
Additional: Sunday L; Children welcome; ◑ dishes
Seats: 26. Private dining room 14
Smoking: No-smoking area; No pipes and cigars

L'Escargot –
The Ground Floor Restaurant ❀❀

48 Greek Street W1V 5LQ
Map: D4

Established in 1927, this Soho landmark maintains a buzzy atmosphere and attentive, mainly French staff. The old lady of Greek Street wears her age well. The Ground Floor is a strong room where black banquettes contrast with crisp white linen, colour is injected by coloured glass vases filled with bright modern flower arrangements and by a dramatic art collection, notably the works of the Spanish painter Miro. In keeping with such a setting, the punchy menu marries modern ideas with classic techniques. Roasted scallops are partnered with langoustines and served with curried lentils, and a super dish of braised pork cheeks and crisp belly is successfully paired with celeriac fondant. Dishes such as feuilleté of snails, bacon, button onions, morels and herb purée, and calves' liver with Alsace bacon are in keeping with the brasserie feel. The lengthy wine list is well balanced and offers a good range under £25 (also a fair few over £1,000).

Times: 12.15-2.15pm/6-11.30pm. Closed L Sat, all Sun, Xmas
Additional: Children welcome; ◑ dishes
Seats: 150. Private dining rooms 25-60
Smoking: No pipes & cigars; Air conditioning
Directions: ⊖ Tottenham Court Rd, Leicester Sq

Tel: 0171 4397474
Fax: 0171 4370790
Chef: Andrew Thompson
Owner: Jimmy Lahoud
Cost: *Alc* £28, set-price L & pre-theatre D £17.95. H/wine £13

L'Escargot –
The Picasso Room ❀❀ NEW

48 Greek Street W1V 5LQ
Map: D4
Tel: 0171 4397474
Fax: 0171 4370790
Chef: Brendan Fyldes

The Picasso Room is the upstairs restaurant at L'Escargot, distinct from its ground floor counterpart by a discreet, intimate setting, and an amazing collection of original Picasso

L'Escargot – The Picasso Room

Owner: Jimmy Lahoud
Cost: Set-price L £27.50/D £42.
H/wine £14
Times: 12.15-2.15pm/7-11pm. Closed
L Sat, all Sun & Mon, 25, 26 Dec, 1
Jan, Aug
Additional: Children welcome;
❹ dishes
Seats: 30
Smoking: Air conditioning

Directions: ➡ Tottenham Court Rd,
Leicester Sq

ceramics, prints, drawings. The approach here is more formal, the appointments comfortable and expensive, with smart leather tub chairs, crisp linen and Villeroy and Boch plates. The kitchen delivers classic French, cooking based on a concise *menu du jour* with two choices per course, plus a heftier *carte.* Starters take in tartlet of escargots, wild mushrooms, and a well-timed red wine poached egg, or the chef's signature chilled bouillon of tomato and basil, goats' cheese ravioli, spring onions and courgettes. Our main course was roast cod with deftly prepared basil and Parmesan beignets and sauce vierge. For dessert, a savarin of red fruit compote was excellent, with individual flavours standing out. Take time over the enormous wine list with its many Burgundy and Bordeaux heavyweights.

Fifth Floor Restaurant ❀❀

Harvey Nichols Knightsbridge
SW1X 7RJ
Map: B2
Tel: 0171 2355250
Fax: 0171 8232209
Chef: Henry Harris
Owner: Harvey Nichols Ltd
Times: Noon-3pm (3.30pm Sat,
Sun)/6.30-11.30pm. Closed D Sun,
25, 26 Dec
Additional: Bar food L; Sunday L;
Children welcome; ❹ dishes
Seats: 120
Smoking: No pipes; Air conditioning

Directions: ➡ Knightsbridge. Entrance
on Sloane Street

Busy, buzzy restaurant sharing the fifth floor of Harvey Nicks with a food and wine shop, café and sushi bar. Beyond a sizeable bar (bar meals at lunch, snacks at night) the vaulted restaurant offers a fixed-price lunch and slightly longer evening *carte.* Foodwise the style is mainstream modern without eccentricity. Good herbed olives and an excellent bread basket made a good beginning to our test meal. Then a well-conceived starter of accurately cooked brill fillet on a bed of fennel and spinach purée with chervil vinaigrette kept up the pace, which was maintained by two generous slices of first-rate rare sirloin with two sauces, a meaty bordelaise and a tarragon-rich béarnaise. To finish a fresh plum and ginger tartlet came topped with a pistachio sprinkled quenelle of crème fraîche and gingery plum coulis.

Fish!

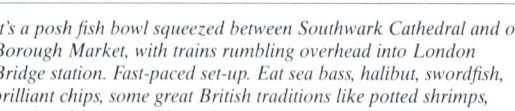

It's a posh fish bowl squeezed between Southwark Cathedral and old Borough Market, with trains rumbling overhead into London Bridge station. Fast-paced set-up. Eat sea bass, halibut, swordfish, brilliant chips, some great British traditions like potted shrimps, bread-and-butter pudding. Go.

Smoking: Air conditioning

Directions: ⊖ London Bridge

Cathedral Street Borough Market
SE1 9AL
Map: F3
Tel: 0171 8363236
Cost: Alc £25. ☺ H/wine £9.90
Times: 11.30am-3pm/5.30-11pm.
Closed Sun, Bhs
Additional: Children welcome

Floriana

Chic, fashionable restaurant attracting more than the* Hello! *crowd. Fabio Trabocchi is a chef to watch, with a brilliant style of new Italian cooking that is as different from the River Café as that is, in turn, from check-clothed trattorias. His background with the legendary Gualtiero Marchesi shows in the way he daringly takes ingredients and techniques further and further down a complex, modernist path without losing sight of home base. A starter of Scottish lobster salad with a cold tomato soup was made with superbly good ingredients; home-made tagliatelle verdi with porcini and walnut sauce described as 'simply stunning'. Spicy roasted Challandais duck with roast endive and pears in a deep port sauce was a bravura exploration of great flavour contrasts, a pickled plum adding another sparkling dimension. Hard to pick out other dishes from the fount of ideas, but specialities include sea bass steamed in lettuce, seaweed with oysters, potato fondant in Champagne sauce with chives. Then there's steam-roasted free-range chicken in a thyme and mustard seed consommé with vegetables and quails' eggs served with salsa verde, plus a dessert of marinated pineapple carpaccio with basil sorbet. The setting is Knightsbridge cool; the food makes the flash bulbs pop.

15 Beauchamp Place SW3 1NQ
Map: C3
Tel: 0171 8381500
Fax: 0171 5841464
Chef: Fabio Trabocchi
Owners: Sammy Hawa,
Ricardo Mazzucchelli
Cost: Alc £45, set-price L £19.50.
H/wine £16
Times: 12.30-3pm/7-11pm. Closed
Sun, 15-31 Aug
Additional: Children welcome;
🍴 dishes
Seats: 90. Private dining room 30
Smoking: Air conditioning

Directions: ⊖ Knightsbridge

Foundation

Harvey Nichols Seville Street
Knightsbridge SW1X 7RJ
Map: C3
Tel: 0171 2018000
Fax: 0171 2018080
Owners: Harvey Nichols
Restaurants Ltd
Telephone for further details

Stylish eaterie, clamorous bar, located in the basement of Harvey Nichols. A continuous flowing water wall with green and silver lighting running the length of the bar provides the focal point and a sense of glacial cool in this modern interior, which is simply furnished with plain wood and steel-framed chairs. The overall cooking style is Mediterranean with light lunches (no division indicated between first and main courses). However, the cooking shifts up a gear in the evening, although most dishes appear at both times of day. Marinated squid comes with Puy lentils and a rocket salad, baked egg with spinach and salmon 'caviar' with nicely glazed hollandaise, and pan-fried chicken teams up with a potato pancake and morel cream sauce.

Directions: ↔ Knightsbridge. Entrance off Seville Street opposite The Sheraton Hotel

The Four Seasons Hotel

The grand foyer is an elegant introduction to the wood-panelled Lanes Restaurant. Now strikingly revamped in shades of midnight blue, bottle green and deep cranberry, with a stunning array of glass artwork, a magnificent glass and marble central buffet plus side views of Park Lane. Contemporary, cosmopolitan menus are matched with a polished but easy style of service. Seared quail breast on autumn leaves with a grape and coconut sauce, excellent quality brill and shellfish stew, scented delicately with cardamom, that sort of thing. At lunch the menu tends to be lighter; dinner has a more refined style. Both menus include a pasta section – pappardelle with slow-cooked rabbit and baby onion, for example – and traditional specialities such as grilled Dover sole. Desserts tempt with apple mille-feuille with caraway parfait and quince sauce, and the intriguing crispy chocolate feuille de brick, pearl barley and chestnut compôte.

Directions: ↔ Hyde Park Corner, Green Park. Set back from Park Lane in Hamilton Place

Hamilton Place Park Lane W1A 1AZ
Map: C3
Tel: 0171 4990888
Fax: 0171 4931895
Chef: Eric Deblonde, Shaun Whatling
Cost: Alc £45, set-price L £32/D £30.50. H/wine £16
Times: Noon-2.30pm/6-11pm (6.30-10.30pm Sun)
Additional: Bar food; Sunday L; Children welcome; ⑤ dishes
Seats: 90. Private dining rooms 4-400
Smoking: No-smoking area; Air conditioning
Accommodation: 220 en suite
★ ★ ★ ★ ★

Shortlisted for AA Wine Award – see p16

The Fox Reformed

Wine bar at the heart of community life, with its own reading circle, backgammon club, and tutored wine tastings. Wholesome cooking is offered from regular and specials menus.

Directions: Opposite the junction with Woodlea Road

176 Stoke Newington Church Street N16 0JL
Map GtL: D4
Tel/Fax: 0171 254 5975
Telephone for further details

Frederick's Restaurant

Comfortable restaurant of long standing. In its 30 years Frederick's has seen off quite a few of the newer boys, and it's still seen as an oasis to some people, who appreciate the comfort of the interior, with its mix of the traditional and the innovative, attentive and skilled service. An added bonus is the good-value set lunch and pre-theatre menus of, say, smoked tomato soup with basil oil, and Lancashire hotpot. The full *carte* is a long affair, wide in scope: foie gras baked in brioche with leeks and truffle oil, or half a lobster sesame-roasted with pak choi and soy, with main courses of smoked haddock tortilla with tomato salad, or pan-fried veal chop with roast pepper stuffed with risotto. An inspector came away happy after lobster tortellini with Thai dressing, a generous portion of beef ragout, tender and tasty, with smooth parsnip mash, and passion fruit crème brûlée. Note that children have their own separate set menu on Saturday lunchtimes.

Directions: ↔ Angel – 2 mins walk to Camden Passage. Restaurant amongst the antique shops

Camden Passage Islington N1 8EG
Map GtL: D3
Tel: 0171 3592888
Fax: 0171 3595173
Chef: Andrew Jeffs
Owner: Louis Segal
Cost: Alc £28, set-price D £12 (2 courses). H/wine £10.95
Times: Noon-2.30pm/5.45-11.30pm. Closed Sun, Xmas, New Year
Additional: Bar food; Children welcome; ⑤ dishes
Seats: 130. Private dining rooms 20, 32
Smoking: No-smoking area; Air conditioning

French House Dining Room

First-floor dining room over renowned Soho pub. The daily menu offers an imaginative choice of robust fare along the lines of crisp pigs' tails with watercress, and rabbit saddle with beetroot.

Additional: Bar food; Children welcome; 🍴 dishes

Directions: Above the French House pub. ⊖ Leicester Square, Piccadilly Circus

49 Dean Street W1V 5HL
Tel: 0171 4372477
Fax: 0171 2879109
Cost: Alc £22. ☺ H/wine £9.95
Times: Noon-3pm/6-11.15pm. Closed Sun, Xmas-New Year, Bhs

Friends Restaurant

Tudor building with oak beams and open fireplaces in a semi-rural location. Dishes might include hot vichyssoise with Welsh rarebit, and pan-fried pollock fillet with a crab crust.

11 High Street Pinner
HA5 5PJ
Map GtL: A4
Tel/Fax: 0181 8660286
Cost: Alc £27, set-price L £16.50/D £21.50. ☺ H/wine £11-£16
Times: Noon-2pm/6.30-10pm. Closed D Sun, Bhs
Additional: Sunday L; Children welcome; 🍴 dishes
Smoking: No-smoking area; No pipes & cigars

Directions: Follow A404 from Harrow. In the centre of Pinner. ⊖ Pinner (2 min walk)

Fung Shing

Friendly Cantonese restaurant where approachable staff are willing to advise and recommend dishes. Regarded as one of the best, though not the cheapest, restaurants in Chinatown – a great help when it comes to considering which of the dozens of dishes to order. Will it be whole squid stuffed with seafood, or 'meltingly tender' braised suckling pig subtly spiced with a touch of star anise? The answer is probably to go with as many people as possible, and order as much of the menu as possible. But look out for lightly battered shell crab served with slivers of deep-fried garlic and tiny rings of red-hot chilli, fresh steamed scallop in a black bean sauce, and braised shark's fin in a 'nest' of prawn and pork mince bound together with egg white.

Directions: ⊖ Leicester Square. Behind Empire Cinema

15 Lisle Street WC2H 7BE
Map: D3
Tel: 0171 4371539
Fax: 0171 7340284
Chef: Mr T X Lye
Cost: Alc £15, set-price D £18 (2 courses). ☺ H/wine £12
Times: Noon-11.30pm. Closed 24-26 Dec
Additional: Sunday L; Children welcome; 🍴 dishes
Seats: 125. Private dining room 25
Smoking: No pipes & cigars; Air conditioning

The Gate

This vegetarian restaurant, which has been open nine years, is hidden away at the back of Hammersmith, near Hammersmith Bridge. But those who do find it remain hugely enthusiastic. Located on the first floor of an old artists' studio, the restaurant is flooded with light from the large north-facing windows. The *carte* lists seven first, and six main courses, listing dishes that are varied, interesting, and intelligently assembled – high marks for presentation. Globe artichokes are topped with

51 Queen Caroline Street W6 9QL
Map GtL: C3
Tel: 0181 7486932
Fax: 0181 5631719
Chefs: Richard Whitting, Adrian Daniel
Owners: M & A Daniel
Cost: Alc £20, set-price L & D £18.50. ☺ H/wine £8.90
Times: Noon-2.30pm/6-10.30pm.

a poached egg served with oyster mushrooms and glazed with a hollandaise sauce, for example, and baked goats' cheese is coated in pistachio nuts and served on a bed of mustard leaves. Main courses include a daily pasta, a 'tricolore' ravioli, Mexican tortilla and a delicious rocket salad with balsamic vinegar dressing. Vegan options are offered. Freshly made lemonade and other fruit juices and some organic wines are to be found on the drinks list.

Directions: Telephone for directions

Gaudi Restaurante

Colourful tiles, mirrors, stained glass and much wrought iron give a Gaudi-esque feeling. The staff, professional and friendly, are as Spanish as the menus. Gazpacho sounds familiar enough, but here it's enhanced by cured ham (one of the rare occasions when meat turns up among starters), or steamed lobster. Roasted peppers are stuffed with salt-cod mousse and served with a nest of leeks and courgettes with green bean sauce, and razor clams are partnered with sweetbreads, 'salmorejo' and sherry vinegar. That the kitchen is clearly steeped in the cuisine shows through what are often complex main courses: roast duck leg with deep-fried breast stuffed with foie gras, cinnamon and sesame sauce and wild mushrooms in a potato nest, or baby squid stuffed with spinach, pine nuts and sultanas, grilled, then placed on squid-ink-soaked saffron rice. A dab hand at timing and seasoning is behind a ragout of goose, beautifully tender, in a rich sauce hinting of cinnamon with a dish of 'superb' stir-fried vegetables. Desserts might run to Manchego cheese mousse with quince, walnuts and honey, or a gratin of raspberries and figs with a Pacheron-flavoured sabayon. Nibbles (perhaps fried chorizo) are moreish, breads are decent, and the exclusively Spanish wine list has some interesting regional wines and rarer classics, all at reasonable prices.

63 Clerkenwell Road EC1M 5PT
Map: E4
Tel: 0171 6083220
Fax: 0171 2501057
Chef: Nacho Martinez
Owner: John Newman
Cost: *Alc* £35, set-price L £15. ☺
H/wine £11.50
Times: Noon-2.30pm/6-10.30pm.
Closed Sat, Sun, Xmas, Easter, Bhs
Additional: Children welcome;
❸ dishes
Seats: 45. Private dining room 30
Smoking: No-smoking area; No pipes
& cigars; Air conditioning

Directions:❺ Farringdon. Corner of Turnmill St and Clerkenwell Road

Le Gavroche Restaurant

The feel of a discreet, English gentleman's club with lots of service to match. The setting is comfortable, although the tables may be a little too close together. However our lunch visit saw the dining room full and buzzing. Michel Roux has really made his mark here. 'I had fricassée de homard et pied de cochon farci: lobster and stuffed pigs trotter precise, and balance spot on, accompanying onion, caper and gherkin sauce well-timed and perfect for the main ingredients. Côte de veau sur mousseline d'haricots blancs et sauce verte: the rib of veal was very good quality, the purée delightfully smooth with great clarity to flavour, and a vibrant herb sauce. Assiette of dessert included raspberry mille-feuille, mango parfait, vanilla ice cream in a brandy snap basket, mini rum baba, mini chocolate delice with gold leaf, and a chocolate cup filled with white chocolate mousse.' Quite a lunch, considering it is topped and tailed by canapés, breads and petits fours, but one showing marks of skill and discretion at most turns, and exact technique. Roux's enthusiasm for grouping elements of a dish, instanced above, manifests itself in items offered on the excellent value set lunch. Dishes such as gratin of crab with penne and Parmesan, or a supreme of chicken teamed with a cep-flavoured risotto. Service from an all French team, while

Closed L Sat, all Sun, Bhs
Additional: Children welcome;
❸ dishes
Seats: 50
Smoking: No pipes & cigars

43 Upper Brook Street
W1Y 1PF
Map: B3
Tel: 0171 4080881/4991826
Fax: 0171 4090939/4914387
Chef: Michel A Roux
Cost: *Alc* £100, set-price L £37/D £78
(7 courses)
Times: Noon-2pm/7pm-11pm. Closed
Sat, Sun, Xmas, New Year, Bhs
Seats: 60. Private dining room 8-20.
Jacket & tie preferred
Smoking: No pipes, cigars in lounge
only; Air conditioning

Directions: From Park Lane, into
Upper Brook Street (one way),
restaurant is on R.❺ Marble Arch

well staffed, lacked the expected care and attention normally associated at this level. The lengthy wine list remains rooted in France and is not cheap, but don't despair – the sommelier is excellent and will give good advice on what to drink with your meal. Indeed, there are a few bins under £20.

Gay Hussar ✿

A Soho fixture, largely unchanged since the 50s with its red banquettes and carpets. Perennial favourites are wild cherry soup, and roast duck with red cabbage, potatoes and apple sauce.

Additional: Children welcome; ♨ dishes
Smoking: Air conditioning

Directions: Off Soho Square. ⊖ Tottenham Court Road

2 Greek Street W1V 6NB
Map: D4
Tel: 0171 4370973
Fax: 0171 4374631
Cost: *Alc* £25, set-price L £18. ☺
H/wine £10.50
Times: 12.15-2.45pm/5.30-10.45pm.
Closed Sun, Bhs

Gilbey's ✿✿

77 The Grove Ealing W5 5LL
Map GtL: B3
Tel: 0181 8407568
Fax: 0181 8401905
Chef: Stephen Spooner
Owners: The Gilbey Family
Cost: *Alc* £21.15, set-price L & D
£10.50. ☺ H/wine £5.65
Times: Noon-2.30pm/7-10pm. Closed
Bh Mon
Additional: Sunday L; Children
welcome; ♨ dishes
Seats: 50. Private dining for 25
Smoking: No pipes & cigars

Locals vie for tables with travellers on the nearby M4, M40 and North Circular. The kitchen cooks well, offering dishes that are tersely described: mussels braised in saffron with squid ink risotto; Parma ham and radiccio salad with sage and olive oil dressing. Main courses range from pork and leek sausages with creamy mash and onion gravy, and knuckle of pork, to braised lamb shank on mushroom polenta with rosemary. The desserts are mostly classics, such as lemon tart, baked ginger pudding and home-made ice creams. The wines are impressive and include wine from Gilbey's own English vineyard. The restaurant is particularly proud of its reputedly unique policy of selling French wines that are imported directly and sold at shop prices.

Directions: ⊖ Ealing Broadway (3 mins)

Gladwins Restaurant ✿✿

The basement restaurant has the current style points: light wood, bright colours. Modern British dishes co-habit with Eastern ones on a menu which avoids fusion confusion. There are global influences certainly, but middle and far-eastern spices are integral, with the odd Caribbean slant to starters and main courses and puddings firmly rooted in Europe. Oriental king scallop and ginger on pak choi, triple breast of game with

Minster Court Mark Lane EC3R 7AA
Tel: 0171 4440004
Fax: 0171 4440001
Cost: *Alc* £35. H/wine £12.50
Times: L only, noon-2.30pm. Closed
Sat, Sun
Additional: ♨ dishes
Smoking: No pipes; Air conditioning

Fino sherry sauce on rösti pancakes, and lemon tart are typical of the style.

Directions: Opposite Fenchurch Station, between Fenchurch Street & Eastcheap. ✚ Bank, Monument

The Glasshouse ❁❁

Appealing neighbourhood restaurant from the people who brought you The Square and Chez Bruce. Situated in the prettiest part of Kew, with its etched glass windows and contemporary art, The Glasshouse creates a positive first impression. Its pleasant appearance and locale, bright, breezy menu and style of service, not to mention good cooking, have made it a favourite amongst Kew residents and booking is essential. Seasonal ingredients are given pride of place and the kitchen delivers gutsy cooking with flavours very much to the fore, as noted in the baked sardines with baby squid, tomato, garlic and butter beans tried at inspection. The daily changing set-menu also brings deep-fried truffled egg, oyster and salmon ragout, assiette of pork with sauerkraut, and a particularly satisfying braised leg of rabbit with ribbon vegetables, noodles and sage. Desserts such as caramelised apple tart with clotted cream, cheesecake with griottine cherries and Kirsch, or savarin of blueberries with lemon chiboust maintain standards to the very end.

14 Station Road TW9 3PZ
Map GtL: B2
Tel: 0181 9406777
Fax: 0181 9403833
Chef: Anthony Boyd
Owners: Nigel Platts-Martin, Bruce Poole
Cost: Set-price L £17.50/D £23.50. H/wine £13.50
Times: Noon-2.15pm/7-10.30pm. Closed D Sun, Xmas, Bhs
Additional: Sunday L; Children 3+; ◑ dishes
Seats: 65
Smoking: No pipes & cigars; Air conditioning

Directions: Telephone for directions

Globe ❁

Eclectic modern cooking in a lively atmosphere. An abundance of glass and bright blue and yellow decor will cheer up any dull day. Enthusiastic and friendly staff.

Additional: Sunday L; ◑ dishes
Smoking: No-smoking area; Air conditioning

Directions: At the end of Eton Avenue. ✚ Swiss Cottage

100 Avenue Road Swiss Cottage NW3 3HF
Map:
Tel: 0171 7227200
Fax: 0171 7222772
Cost: *Alc* £22, set-price L £13 (2 courses). ☺ H/wine £9.95
Times: Noon-3pm/6-11pm (7pm Sun). Closed L Sat, 25 Dec

Goring Hotel ❁❁

Beeston Place Grosvenor Gardens SW1W 0JW
Map: C2
Tel: 0171 3969000
Fax: 0171 8344393
Chef: Derek Quelch
Owner: George Goring
Cost: Set-price L £27.50/D £35. H/wine £18.50
Times: 12.30-2.30pm/6-10pm. Closed L Sat
Additional: Bar food; Sunday L; Children welcome; ◑ dishes
Seats: 60. Private dining rooms 4-50
Smoking: Air conditioning
Accommodation: 75 en suite ★★★★

Personally run by the Goring family since 1910, a superb example of the true British tradition of hotel-keeping and hospitality. The Dining Room, with a highly regarded wine list, proffers many old favourites such as grilled Dover sole and lobster Thermidor alongside more contemporary choices. Large carver chairs accommodate the most ample and staff bustle around attending to every whim. Goring hors d'oeuvres might include tuna with caramelised red onion, potted shrimps and asparagus in chive and tomato dressing. A main course of John Dory with spinach was enlivened by a mild curry sauce; steaks come from the Buccleuch Estate. Straightforward vegetables have a healthy sousing in butter (nothing PC here, thank you – and you'll have to switch off that mobile phone as well). The lunchtime dessert trolley, another nostalgic sight, carries a grand choice including bread-and-butter pudding, lemon tart and traditional fresh fruit salad.

Directions: ⊖ Victoria – onto Victoria Street, turn L into Grosvenor Gdns, cross Buckingham Palace Road, 75 yds turn L into Beeston Place

Goring Hotel

Granita ❀❀

Minimalist restaurant for Islington's chattering classes. Seven years on and Granita is still going strong, its decor simple and stark – bold turquoise walls, tightly packed maple tables and bare floorboards. But when the crowd is in, the noise levels are high and the atmosphere is charged; this is a lively, exciting place to enjoy some great global cooking. The short menu reads like a shopping list of ingredients – starters include smoked salmon, wilted red chard, smoked potatoes, mustard, and wok-seared squid, tamarind, chilli, garlic, Chinese watercress. That doesn't mean it's all just thrown together, serious thought goes into the creation of these dishes. Simple but exact techniques came through in a well reported chump of lamb with marinated chargrilled aubergine, chilli, yogurt and rocket, also chargrilled tuna with black beans, red pepper and grilled new potatoes. A short list of modern wines hits the spot, both in taste and price.

Directions: ⊖ Highbury & Islington, Angel. Opposite St Mary's Church

127 Upper Street Islington N1 1QP
Map GtL: D3
Tel: 0171 2263222
Fax: 0171 2264833
Chef: Ahmed Kharshoum
Owners: Vikki Leffman & Ahmed Kharshoum
Cost: *Alc* £25, set-price L £11.95 (2 courses). ☺ H/wine £10.50
Times: 12.30-2.30pm/6.30-10.30pm. Closed L Tue, all Mon, 10 days Xmas, 1 wk Easter, 2 wks Aug
Additional: Sunday L; ⓭ dishes
Seats: 70
Smoking: No pipes & cigars; Air conditioning

Green Olive ❀❀

Hard by the canals of Little Venice, a delightful, friendly, busy modern Italian restaurant. Exposed brick walls and waxed floorboards contrast with the crisp damask-clothed tables at which guests tuck into the likes of Tuscan bean and vegetable soup, followed perhaps by grilled swordfish with a warm potato, red onion and green bean salad in black olive sauce, or prosciutto-wrapped rabbit on wilted spinach with polenta and rosemary jus. Finish with warm chocolate brownies with vanilla gelato and citrus cheesecake or perhaps take in the selection of Italian cheeses. Apart from the fizz, the good selection of wines is exclusively Italian. Lunch is a *carte* while the evening menu comes priced for two, three or four courses.

Directions: ⊖ Warwick Avenue

5 Warwick Place W9 2PX
Map GtL: C3
Tel: 0171 2892469
Fax: 0171 2894178
Chef: Stefano Savio
Owner: Bijan Behzadi
Cost: Set-price D £23.50. ☺ H/wine £12.50
Times: 12.30-2.15pm/7-10.30pm. Closed L Mon-Fri, Xmas, Easter, Bhs
Additional: Sunday L; Children 14+; ⓭ dishes
Seats: 52. Private dining room 15
Smoking: No pipes & cigars; Air conditioning

The Greenhouse Restaurant ❀❀

Formal, but still a relaxing atmosphere, with natural light from large picture windows. Approached through a pretty garden at the back of Berkeley Square, this restaurant has seen

27a Hay's Mews W1X 7RJ
Map: C3
Tel: 0171 4993331
Fax: 0171 4995368
Chef: Jeff Galvin

The Greenhouse Restaurant

Owner: David Levin
Cost: Alc £30, set-price L £21.50.
H/wine £12
Times: 12.30-2.30pm/6.30-11.15pm.
Closed L Sat, 26-31 Dec, Bhs
Additional: Sunday L; Children
welcome; ⓐ dishes
Seats: 95
Smoking: No pipes; Air conditioning

Directions: Behind Dorchester Hotel
just off Hill St, nr Berkeley Sq

a few personnel changes over the years but it remains popular among the established crowd who either frequent or live in Mayfair. There is both a *carte* and a set menu offered at lunch, the former only in the evenings. The emphasis is probably more modern European than it used to be: celeriac and pumpkin soups, rillettes of salmon, pressed terrine of pork, smoked haddock risotto, fillet of beef bourguignonne with parsnips, and red mullet with couscous all appear, but traditionally English dishes, such as an exemplary dressed Cornish crab, are also available. The service is professional and unobtrusive.

Green's Restaurant
& Oyster Bar ✿✿

36 Duke Street SW1Y 6DF
Map: C3
Tel: 0171 9304566
Fax: 0171 4917463
Chef: Philomena Frealey
Owner: Simon Parker-Bowles
Cost: Alc £37.50, set-price D £40. ☺
H/wine £12
Times: Noon-2.30pm/6-11pm. Closed
Sun 1 May-31Aug
Additional: Bar food; Sunday L;
Children welcome; ⓐ dishes
Seats: 64. Private dining room 36
Smoking: No pipes; Air conditioning

Directions: Opposite the Cavendish
Hotel

A long-established restaurant with the feel of an exclusive dining club. The style is modern without going over the top – expect dishes along the lines of black leg chicken breast with wild mushrooms and pan-fried sea bass with herb polenta, as well as simple offerings such as corned beef hash with fried egg. As you'd expect, fish and shellfish make a strong appearance: smoked eel salad, and potted shrimps with toast, for example while main dishes range from roast halibut with mussel stew to whole Canadian lobster, served cold. Our inspection meal took in a 'perfect' tart of roasted peppers and goats' cheese, and an 'unbeatable' seared wild salmon, served on a bed of soft wild mushrooms and 'superb' spinach. Dessert was a very rich chocolate and orange soufflé.

Halcyon Hotel

Town-house hotel decorated in country-house mode. Huge floppy sofas in the bar are a temptation to linger before moving on to 'The Room', a litotes for a comfortable restaurant where contemporary art provides splashes of colour to white walls and the floors are of blond wood. This is the scene for some forward-thinking cooking: sautéed foie gras with caramelised orange salad; grilled fillet of sea bass with a soup of red mullet and basil. Indeed, fish and seafood make a strong showing with seared scallops, slightly acidulated with lime, set in individual baskets of pastry, topped with a fine spaghetti of leeks and set on an intense, earthy cep sauce – described by one inspector as 'stunning'. Foie gras might appear among main courses, alongside roast Bresse pigeon with potato purée, and cropping up with wild mushrooms and breast of corn-fed chicken with white pudding. Skill with pastry comes to the fore in desserts of a tulip basket of outstanding orange ice cream with superb warm chocolate mousse containing chunks of chocolate, and caramelised lemon tart with blackcurrant sorbet. Staff bring a discreet yet friendly and unstuffy approach.

81 Holland Park W11 3RZ
Map GtL: C3
Tel: 0171 7277288
Fax: 0171 2298516
Chef: Martin Hadden
Owners: The Khanna Family
Cost: *Alc* £45.50, set-price L £23/D £43. H/wine £17.50
Times: Noon-2.30pm/7-10.30pm (11pm Fri, Sat). Closed L Sat, Bhs
Additional: Bar food; Sunday L; Children welcome; 🍴 dishes
Seats: 45. Private dining room 12
Smoking: Air conditioning
Accommodation: 42 en suite ★ ★ ★ ★

Directions: 200 metres up Holland Park Ave from Shepherds Bush roundabout. ⊖ Holland Park (2 mins)

The Halkin Hotel, Stefano Cavallini at The Halkin

The dining room of this super-smart hotel is serene and cool, the staff dressed in Armani. This is not just modern Italian cooking, it is 'La Cucina Essenziale', derived from research into ancient Italian culinary traditions but reinterpreted in the

Halkin Street Belgravia SW1X 7DJ
Map GtL: C2
Tel: 0171 3331000
Fax: 0171 3331100
Chef: Stefano Cavallini
Owner: Como Holdings
Cost: *Alc* £55, set-price L £25/D £50 (5 courses). H/wine £19
Times: 12.30-2.30pm/7.30-11pm. Closed L Sat & Sun, 25 Dec, some Bhs
Additional: Bar food; Children welcome; 🍴 dishes
Seats: 45. Private dining room 30
Smoking: No-smoking area; No pipes & cigars; Air conditioning
Accommodation: 41 en suite ★ ★ ★ ★

Directions: Between Belgrave Square & Grosvenor Place. Access via Chapel St into Headfort Place and L into Halkin St

light of today's taste and way of life. Stefano Cavallini seeks to replace heavy sauces, fats and cream, with vegetable broth, olive oil and other more suitable elements, and cooking styles are chosen to preserve nutrients and essential flavours. Well, that's what the blurb says, and, remarkably, the actual cooking, as sampled in the menu degustazione, lives up to the billing. Pan-fried foie gras with Castelluccio lentils was beautifully seasoned and timed to the second; pheasant tortellini with cauliflower sauce and black truffle equally impressive. Sweet-and-sour flavours gave edge to a sauce served with lightly battered, deep-fried mixed fish. Classical skills underpinned a rich red wine sauce with shredded Savoy cabbage and noisettes of pink, tender venison. Poached fruit with champagne sorbet was designer-elegant. On our visit the service at first appeared cool, but soon mellowed out to become, well, more authentically Italian. There is a serious wine operation under the guidance of a well-informed and helpful sommelier.

Hamiltons Restaurant

Settle into this elegant Parisienne bistro-style restaurant tucked into the quiet area of St Margarets. There's a convivial atmosphere and contemporary dishes along the lines of seared red mullet fillet on a rich tomato fondue.

43 Crown Road St Margaret's Twickenham TW1 3EJ
Map GtL: B2
Tel: 0181 8923949
Fax: 0181 8915448
Cost: *Alc* £23, set-price L £10.95 (2 courses)/D £17.95. ☺ H/wine £11.50
Times: Noon-2.30pm/7-10.30pm. Closed L Sat, D Sun, Bhs
Additional: Sunday L; Children 5+; ✿ dishes
Smoking: Air conditioning

Directions: From London follow A316 over Twickenham Bridge, L at 1st roundabout. After 400yds fork R into Crown Road

Heather's

Authentic vegetarian and vegan cooking in a relaxed and spacious setting with a garden and roof terrace as well. An eat-as-much-as-you-like buffet is excellent value and may feature corn and bean chowder, Hungarian pepper stew and imaginative salads and dips.

74 Macmillan Street SE8 3HA
Map GtL: D3
Tel: 0181 6916665
Fax: 0181 6923263
Cost: Set-price D £12. ☺ H/wine £7.50
Times: D only, 7-10.30pm. Closed Mon
Additional: Sunday L (12.30-3pm); Children welcome; ✿ dishes
Smoking: No smoking in dining room
Credit cards: None

Directions: 400 mtrs from Deptford railway station on the Thames Path Walk opposite St Nicholas' Church

Hilaire ✿✿✿

68 Old Brompton Road SW7 3LQ
Map: A1
Tel: 0171 5848993
Fax: 0171 5812949
Chef/Owner: Bryan Webb
Cost: *Alc* £37, set-price L £18.50 (2 courses)/D £33. H/wine £14
Times: 12.15-2.30pm/6.30-11.30pm. Closed L Sat, all Sun, 2 wks Aug, 10 days Xmas
Additional: Children welcome; ◑ dishes
Seats: 56. Private dining room 20
Smoking: No pipes & cigars; Air conditioning

Directions: On N side of Old Brompton Rd. ↔ South Kensington. Half way between tube and junction with Queensgate

Well-established restaurant with polished service. The shop-fronted restaurant is quite deceptive. You enter a small, cosy dining room warmed by lemon colours, but a visit to the downstairs cloakroom reveals a small bar and another half-a-dozen tables. In keeping with the intimacy of the place, staff go about their business in a friendly, relaxed manner, decidedly unfussy, which is just what is needed. Bryan Webb's hand-written menu offers around eight choices at each course with descriptions taking the direct approach, for example, breast of duck, potato pancake, cider and apple sauce. This may seem a tad understated, but the flavour combinations in gently sautéed lambs' sweetbreads with peas, onions and mint, and a cracking fillet of turbot with brown shrimps and vibrant dill and cress sauce are arresting in their simplicity. Desserts play it safe with the likes of a well-made caramelised lemon and banana tart with caramel ice cream. The wine list is well balanced, lots at reasonable prices and good offerings by the glass.
   Signature dishes: smoked eel with new potato salad and bacon; chargrilled wild salmon, asparagus salad 'beurre blanc'; roast pheasant with chestnuts, onions and potato fondant; whimberry crème brûlée with whimberry sorbet.

The Hogarth ✿

33 Hogarth Road Kensington SW5 0QQ
Map GtL: C3
Tel: 0171 3706831
Fax: 0171 3736179
Cost: *Alc* £17, set-price L £13/D £17. ☺ H/wine £12.40
Times: 10am-10pm
Additional: Bar food; Sunday L; Children welcome; ◑ dishes
Smoking: No-smoking area; Air conditioning
Accommodation: 85 en suite ★★★

Directions: ↔ Earl's Court

Purpose built hotel off the Earl's Court Road. The Terrace Bistro and Bar offers all day service from sandwiches to crispy chilly squid, Oriental salmon, or ribeye beef.

Hotel Inter-Continental London – Le Soufflé

In a prime site on Hyde Park Corner, the Inter-Continental is everything expected of a large, modern, international hotel. Le Soufflé is decorated in pale colours, with upholstered chairs and plenty of elbowroom. There are a number of menus to choose between, from a two-course business lunch, or an innovative set-price organic menu, to the pinnacle of a no-choice eight-course 'Gourmet Menu' at nearly £100, the sommelier's selection of wines thrown in, for those who want to scale the heights. The repertoire is wide-ranging and shows an up-to-the-minute approach with the kitchen brigade a hive of industry. Crab and avocado go into full-flavoured ravioli with a light bisque and cucumber 'spaghetti', langoustines, shiitaki mushrooms and celeriac are the partners in a fricassée, and pan-fried foie gras comes with a salad of artichokes, endive, beans and radish. For main courses, fillet of Scottish salmon, oven-roasted and served on a bed of paella, is finished off with a subdued watercress sauce and garnished with grilled asparagus, and herb dumplings are the accompaniment for roast venison with braised celery and Savoy cabbage. Those wishing to ignore the Healthy Heart symbol set against certain dishes on the menu could have a soufflé at each course, from one of Cheddar with pumpkin chutney to Grand Marnier with chocolate. Service, from a mainly young French team, is impeccable, and even those not on expenses will find much of interest on the wine list.

Signature dishes: truffled scallop and lobster tartlet with watercress vinaigrette; laki-spiced duck with foie gras and rösti; marbled pear and bitter chocolate soufflé.

1 Hamilton Place Hyde Park Corner
W1V 0QY
Map: C2
Tel: 0171 3188577
Fax: 0171 4910926
Chef: Peter Kromberg
Owner: Bass Hotels, Inter-Continental Hotels
Cost: *Alc* £47, set-price L £29.50/D £39. H/wine £16
Times: 12.30-3pm/7-10.30pm (11.15pm Sat). Closed L Sat, D Sun, all Mon, Xmas, Bhs
Additional: Bar food; Sunday L; ✤ dishes
Seats: 80
Smoking: No pipes; Air conditioning
Accommodation: 460 en suite
★ ★ ★ ★ ★

Directions: On Hyde Park Corner. ⊖ Hyde Park Corner

The Hothouse ✤

Warehouse conversion bar/restaurant near Tower Bridge. The menu has a classic French base but incorporates mainstream modern British and North African influences in say, fish soup provençale or lamb fillet on hot tabouleh couscous.

78-80 Wapping Lane E1 9NF
Map GtL: D3
Tel: 0171 4884797
Fax: 0171 4889500
Telephone for further details

Directions: ⊖ Tower Bridge, Wapping

Hyatt Carlton Tower Hotel, Grissini ✤✤

Subtly lit, modern and comfortable and done out in natural colours, with a teak floor and lavender banquettes. Conservatory-style windows give views over the gardens of Cadogan Place, and a domed glass roof creates an alfresco atmosphere. The menus might convert sterling to the Euro, but modern Italian is the currency the kitchen deals in, from tuna carpaccio with aged balsamic, olives and Parmesan shavings, through pumpkin risotto with asparagus, to pan-fried duck breast glazed with vin santo. Start with perhaps a pair of terrines – duck and chicken – with apple marmalade and sultana croûtons, and go on to pan-fried fillet of turbot with grilled zucchini, San Marzano tomatoes and oregano coulis. Main courses are divided equally between meat and fish, the former typified by osso bucco, or rack of lamb roasted with tarragon served with candied onions and broad beans.

Cadogan Place SW1X 9PY
Map: B2
Tel: 0171 8587171
Fax: 0171 2359129
Chef: Giuseppe Lavarra
Cost: *Alc* £26, set-price L £19.50 (2 courses)/D £28.50. H/wine £19
Times: 12.30-2.45pm/6.30-10.45pm. Closed L Sat, D Sun
Additional: Sunday L; Children welcome; ✤ dishes
Seats: 80. Private dining room 50
Smoking: No-smoking area; Air conditioning
Accommodation: 220 en suite
★ ★ ★ ★ ★

Tiramisu, made with chestnut purée, is 'fantastic', and the selection of Italian cheeses includes Montasio and Caprino. You have to ask to see the list of non-Italian wines, but why bother when virtually every Italian region is represented among over 80 bottles?

Directions: ⊖ Knightsbridge, Sloane Sq

Ikkyu

Casual, smoky basement restaurant offering a rough and ready but very edible style of Japanese food. Prices are reasonable, service friendly, laid-back but not very fluent, and the Japanese menu only gives basic English translations. Go with a sense of adventure and you will be well rewarded.

Directions: ⊖ Goodge Street

67a Tottenham Court Road W1P 9PA
Map: C3
Tel: 0171 6369286
Cost: H/wine £9.50
Times: Noon-2.30pm/6-10.30pm.
Closed Sat, L Sun, Xmas, Easter
Additional: Children welcome
Smoking: No-smoking area

The Ivy ❀❀❀

Stars are drawn to The Ivy like small boys to a jar of Nutella, to the extent there is an unspoken sense of outrage should the celebrity count fall below par. What? Only Parkinson and Helvin? Ho hum, it still remains one of the best addresses in town (as long as you can get in). The original decor has been sympathetically updated; oak panels, dark green leather banquettes, flattering lighting and modern art on the walls help keep the atmosphere convivial and relaxed. The menu is eclectic and slightly eccentric, one for all comers, which in theory should not work as well as it does in practice. It is divided into many sections from hors d'oeuvre through to coffees and teas (Ethiopian full roast and Fauchon tisanes, of course). Salads, for instance, include west coast-style salad of grilled pumpkin with rocket and polenta croûtons, as well as crispy duck and watercress. Retro shepherd's pie and braised beef in Guinness demand to be eaten with the honeyed parsnips and bubble-and-squeak. Roast mallard with foie gras, fondant potato and truffled Savoy cabbage goes for the big flavour; Thai baked sea bass with fragrant rice and soy dip is more of a starlet's lunch. Little can beat the roast poulet des Landes with truffle jus and dauphin potato – for two, so share it with your bank manager, agent or lover.

1 West Street Covent Garden WC2H 9NE
Map: D3
Tel: 0171 8364751
Fax: 0171 2409333
Chefs: Des McDonald, Aian Bird
Owners: Jeremy King, Christopher Corbin
Cost: *Alc* £42. H/wine £11.25
Times: Noon-3pm/5.30-midnight.
Closed 25, 26 Dec, 1 Jan, Aug Bh
Additional: Sunday L; Children welcome; ◑ dishes
Seats: 100. Private dining room min 25
Smoking: No pipes; Air conditioning

Directions: ⊖ Leicester Square, Covent Garden

J. Sheekey ❀❀

NEW

Now part of the Ivy and Caprice stable, with a revamp that has updated but kept the individual look of the place.
Original 1890's wood panelling, little rooms off a corridor and black and white photos of thespians remind us this is theatreland, but modern lighting and a general fresh new look make all the difference. Tables are small and cramped, but the high standard of service soon help you cease to notice. Star billing still goes to fish and seafood – classics in the repertoire include Morecambe Bay potted shrimps, fish pie, and perfect salmon fishcake with sautéed spinach and sorrel sauce. Strong support comes from a brilliant salad playing Caesar, and a good fettucine with cockles and parsley. Whole sea bream hogs the limelight, in a complete ensemble performance with head, tail and béarnaise sauce. Rice pudding with raspberry jam and treacle tart both deserve an encore. The place simply buzzes with life again – it's good to have it back on form.

28-32 St Martin's Court WC2N 4AL
Map: D3
Tel: 0171 2402565
Fax: 0171 2408114
Chef: Tim Hughes
Owners: Jeremy King, Christopher Corbin
Cost: *Alc* £38, set-price L £13.50. ☺ H/wine £11.25
Times: Noon-3pm/5.30-midnight.
Closed Bhs
Additional: Sunday L; Children welcome; ◑ dishes
Seats: 105
Smoking: No cigars; Air conditioning

Directions: ⊖ Leicester Square

Justin de Blanc

Brasserie-style restaurant with big windows, bright decor and a spiral staircase to the basement. Options might include braised lamb shank with parsnip purée and there's always fish of the day.

Additional: Children welcome; dishes

Directions: In the bend of Old Marylebone Lane after turning off Marylebone High Street. ⊖ Bond Street

120 Marylebone Lane W1M 5FZ
Map: C3
Tel: 0171 4865250
Fax: 0171 9354046
Cost: *Alc* £20, set-price L £9.75 (2 courses). ☺ H/wine £9.50
Times: Noon-3pm/6-10.30pm. Closed Sat, Sun, Bhs

Kai Mayfair

65 South Audley Street W1Y 5FD
Map: C3
Tel: 0171 4938988
Fax: 0171 4931456
Chef: Qo Ly
Owner: Bernard Yeoh
Cost: *Alc* £40. H/wine £16
Times: Noon-2.30pm/6.30-11.15pm. Closed Xmas, New Year
Additional: Children welcome;  dishes
Seats: 100. Private dining rooms 6, 12
Smoking: Air conditioning

Eating alone is no way to enjoy Chinese food – and our inspector regretted there were no others to share the splendid meal, and to order more dishes to sample 'probably the best Chinese meal I've had all year'. The menu of this elegant, pricy restaurant is more adventurous than most, as well as delightfully descriptive. The Enrichment of the Surprised Piglet – steamed pork dumplings to you and me – paved the way for Hokkien Opium, a clear soup of salted mustard leaves and beancurd. Claypot duck, sliced duck in a casserole with vegetables, glass noodles and a thick dark sauce encouraged further helpings, although there were still some smashing stir-fried spicy aubergines with black beans and garlic to get through. The waiter tried to put our intrepid reporter off ordering a dish of fried rice with deep-fried salted fish and unsalted anchovies, but she went ahead fearlessly: 'It was really good, if you like aged fish, which I do'. Mmm.

Directions: Marble Arch onto Park Lane, situated behind Dorchester, or Oxford St into N Audley St, past American Embassy into S Audley St

Kastoori

Bright, spacious 'pure vegetarian' Indian. The menu is laden with strong Gujerati and Indo-African influences. Various thalis are a good introduction to the style, but if you can't decide, try one of the Thanki 'family specials'.

Smoking: Air conditioning

Directions: ⊖ Tooting Bec, Tooting Broadway (between the two)

188 Upper Tooting Road SW17 7EJ
Map GtL: C2
Tel/Fax: 0181 7677027
Cost: ☺ H/wine £7.50
Times: 12.30-2.30pm/6-10.30pm. Closed L Mon & Tue, 1 wk mid Jan
Additional: Sunday L; Children welcome; dishes

Kensington Place

201/205 Kensington Church Street
W8 7LX
Map GtL: C3
Tel: 0171 7273184
Fax: 0171 2292025
Chef: Rowley Leigh
Owners: Place Restaurants
Cost: Alc £27.50, set-price L £14.50.
☺ H/wine £10.50
Times: Noon-3pm (3.30pm Sat &
Sun)/6.30-11.45pm (10.15pm Sun).
Closed Xmas
Additional: Sunday L; Children
welcome; ✿ dishes
Seats: 135
Smoking: No pipes; Air conditioning

Directions: 150 yds before junction of
Kensington Church St & Notting Hill
Gate

Close-packed, high-volume, and still refusing to slow down.
Still crazy after all these years, Kensington Place continues to
pull in the crowds – even on a frosty February lunchtime.
Buzzing and humming, it's a fun place and the food is good.
The style is modern, with a fresh simplicity noted in starters
such as speckled endive, russet apple and walnut salad, and
Jerusalem artichoke soup with hazelnuts. Our lone inspector
decided on a rich treat: griddled foie gras with sweetcorn
pancakes, followed by sautéed fillets of Dover sole in a cream
sauce. But noisettes of venison with pickled quince and pine
kernels, or sea bass with rhubarb, chilli and ginger are equally
typical. Desserts range from bread-and-butter pudding made
with quince jam, to pancakes with orange and Grand Marnier.

Laicram Thai

Good cooking, with a restrained chilli quotient, from a menu
that's sensibly not over-long. Starters are all freshly cooked –
minced pork dumplings in garlic and soya sauce, deep-fried
prawns with sweet chilli sauce, mini crab and coriander cakes,
beef and chicken satay, vegetables deep-fried in crisp batter
are amongst the selections. A roast duck curry, a speciality of
the house, however, disappointed with dry meat, although the
sauce, made with coconut, kaffir lime leaf, garlic and pea
aubergines, was spot-on. Whole prawns fried with garlic,
pepper and spring onions, and stir-fried mixed vegetables were
well up to the mark. Desserts shed a new light on a part of the
menu usually best avoided – try the mango mousse or mini-
selection of sticky rice, coconut milk pudding and sweet baked
cake, all wrapped in vine leaves, and be prepared to be won
over.

1 Blackheath Grove
Blackheath SE3
Map GtL: E2
Tel: 0181 8524710
Chef/Owner: Mrs S Dhirabutra
Cost: Alc £20. ☺ H/wine £9.50
Times: Noon-2.30pm/6-11pm. Closed
Mon, Bhs
Additional: Children welcome;
✿ dishes
Seats: 50
Smoking: Air conditioning

Directions: Off the main shopping
street, in a side road near the Post
Office. Opposite the station

Landmark Hotel,
The Dining Room

Built in 1899 and now restored to its original style, the
Landmark was designed around a glass-roofed atrium. Light
meals and teas are served in here among the tall palms, with
the panelled Cellars another eating option, while the Dining
Room, an impressive room with high moulded ceiling,
chandeliers and spectacular flower displays, is the main venue.
This is the setting for dishes in the modern European idiom:

222 Marylebone Road NW1 6JQ
Map: E4
Tel: 0171 6318230
Fax: 0171 6318011
Chef: Andrew McLeish
Cost: Alc £45, set-price L £26/D £42.
☺ H/wine £18.50
Times: Noon-2.30pm/7-10.30pm.
Closed L Sat, D Sun

Landmark Hotel,
The Dining Room

Additional: Sunday L; Children
welcome; ✿ dishes
Seats: 80
Smoking: No-smoking area; Air
conditioning
Accommodation: 298 en suite
★ ★ ★ ★ ★

Directions: ⊖ Marylebone – directly
opposite

tortellini of wild mushrooms, truffles and chicken velouté, roast
saddle of lamb with caramelised kidneys and sweetbreads in a
sauce of tomatoes, olives and basil, then mango and coconut
rice pudding. An *amuse-bouche*, foie gras terrine with
caramelised fig, say, arrives before starters of perhaps chicken
confit with truffled green beans and Muscat grapes, or a simple
dish of roast langoustine tails, cooked to perfection, in a light
yet full-flavoured bouillon with whole vine tomatoes. At
inspection the star of the show was a main course of rabbit
feuilleté, minced rabbit and root vegetables in a light puff
pastry basket alongside tiny rabbit cutlets, liver and saddle,
with a pool of well-balanced, glossy sauce hinting of thyme.
Baked zander with a potato and truffle soufflé and creamed
spinach could be a fish option, and the kitchen's skill with
pastrywork shines through properly caramelised tarte Tatin
with a caramel ice cream. Don't miss out on the petits fours
with coffee, either.

The Lanesborough

Hyde Park Corner SW1X 7TA
Map: C3
Tel: 0171 2595599
Fax: 0171 2595606
Chef: Paul Gayler
Owner: Rosewood Hotels & Resorts
Cost: *Alc* £48.50, set-price L
£24.50/D £29.50. H/wine £17.50
Times: Noon-2.30pm/6.30-midnight
Additional: Bar food; Sunday L;
Children welcome; ✿ dishes
Seats: 106. Private dining rooms.
Jacket & tie preferred
Smoking: Air conditioning
Accommodation: 95 en suite
★ ★ ★ ★ ★

Directions: On Hyde Park Corner

The Conservatory restaurant is all chinoiserie. Huge palms
sprout under the oriental trappings, with fountains adding who
knows what to the atmosphere. The hotel, built in 1828 and
named after a country house that once stood on the site, has
been meticulously and expensively restored to its original
grandeur. But it's a setting appropriate for a menu that takes
in tempura vegetables with sticky rice, plum and watercress,
Thai-inspired shrimp risotto, and Szechuan pepper-crusted
duck with lime and ginger. Not that the kitchen is stuck out
East, for the menu encompasses Moroccan carrot soup with

chermoula, gremolata sea bass with scallops and thyme-infused grilled vegetables, and rosette of venison with red cabbage, chestnuts and wild mushrooms. And, as befits a chef who's at the cutting edge of vegetarian cooking, there's an exclusively vegetarian menu with, at lunchtime, an 'express' menu that includes a glass of wine. The kitchen is a busy place, producing exemplary hand-made pasta and breads, and shows a light touch with pastries – witness a quince tart with balsamic and orange caramel ice cream.

Launceston Place

1a Launceston Place W8 5RL
Map: A2
Tel: 0171 9376912
Fax: 0171 9382412
Chefs: Philip Reed
Owners: Place Restaurants
Cost: *Alc* £28.50, set-price L £17.50.
☺ H/wine £10.75
Times: 12.30-2.45pm/7-11.30pm.
Closed L Sat, D Sun, Bhs
Additional: Sunday L; Children welcome; ⬤ dishes
Seats: 75. Private dining room 12, 28
Smoking: No pipes; Air conditioning

Neighbourhood restaurant with smart clientele and sound service. Few restaurants manage the consistently high standard of cooking that Launceston Place achieves. Decorated in pastel country house shades, it is favoured by both Kensington shoppers and enlightened local diners. A starter of twice-baked goats' cheese soufflé with poached pears and a watercress salad was a model of lightness and subtle flavour. Roast pigeon is rarely served as moist as here – a delight to eat with a robust sauce, melt-in-the-mouth onion tart, red cabbage and château potatoes. Our inspector enthused equally about a crème brûlée with eggshell caramel and near perfect consistency. It is also notable that the set menu is in no way a poor relation to the *carte*. A team of smart, informed waitresses are skilful and attentive to detail without displaying the least servility. A wine list of some ninety bins offers some real bargains, especially within the Burgundies.

Directions: Just south of Kensington Palace. ⊖ Gloucester Road, High Street Kensington

Lawn

1 Lawn Terrace Blackheath SE3 9LJ
Map GtL: D3
Tel: 0181 3790724
Fax: 0181 3799014
Cost: *Alc* £35, set-price L & D £15.50(Mon-Fri 6-7pm). ☺ H/wine £13.50
Times: Noon-3pm/6-11pm. Closed D Sun, L Mon

Formerly One Lawn Terrace, a contemporary first-floor restaurant now owned by the Bank group. Dishes in the Bank style include Parmesan risotto and wild rocket, and duck confit with wok vegetables and plum sauce.

Additional: Sunday L; Children welcome; ⬤ dishes
Smoking: Air conditioning

Directions: Turn R out of Blackheath BR station, up the hill & first rd on R

Leith's Restaurant

A sense of comfort permeates Leith's and service is equally accommodating. Semicircular blue armchairs are arranged at well-set tables, pale ochre walls are hung with mirrors and paintings, and subdued lighting dictates the atmosphere. Leith's first opened its doors 30 years ago, but life moves on, and so do menus that incorporate tartare of sea trout with crispy Serrano ham, tempura oyster and caviar crème fraîche. But an element of the security blanket is strong, grilled loin of pork with sweetbread and chicken galette, or pot-roast guinea fowl with morels and smoked lentils mingling with the likes of steamed fillet of tuna with ginger and beanshoots, shallot purée and herb sauce. A starter of sautéed red mullet with avocado and a vinaigrette of yellow and red peppers delivers a gusty combination of flavours, but better balance showed through in a main-course marriage of salmon, celery butter sauce and saffron risotto. Desserts reach a high note in the shape of poached pear with raspberries accompanied by intense-tasting Poire William sorbet, warm raspberry cream and a well-judged slick of caramel. Wine lovers will have a high old time with the wine list, while the hard-pressed could opt for a bottle from the house selection.

92 Kensington Park Road W11 2PN
Map GtL: C3
Tel: 0171 2294481
Fax: 0171 2211246
Chef: Alastair Ross
Owners: Christopher Bland, Caroline Waldegrave, Alex Floyd, Nick Tarayan
Cost: *Alc* £47, set-price L £17.50/D £29.50 (both 2 courses). H/wine £16.50
Times: 12.15-2.15pm/7-11.30pm. Closed L Sat & Mon, all Sun, 2 wks Xmas, Bhs
Additional: Children 7+; 🌢 dishes
Seats: 75. Private dining rooms 4-36
Smoking: No-smoking area; No pipes & cigars; Air conditioning

Directions: 500 yds north of Notting Hill Gate. ⊖ Notting Hill Gate

**Shortlisted for the AA Wine Award –
see p16**

Leith's Soho 🌸

Sleek, modern and crisp – that goes for both interior and food. Saddle of venison, choucroute, liver timbale and caramelised parsnips is a gusty main course to follow Leith's classic prawn cocktail.

41 Beak Street W1R 3LE
Map: D4
Tel: 0171 2872057
Fax: 0171 2871767
Cost: *Alc* £35, fixed-price L & D £19.50. ☺ H/wine £11.75
Times: Noon-2.30pm/6-11.15pm. Closed L Sat, all Sun, 2 wks Xmas-New Year, Bhs
Additional: Children welcome; 🌢 dishes
Smoking: Air conditioning

Directions: ⊖ Piccadilly Circus

Lemonia

A Mediterranean air at this bustling Greek restaurant. From good mezze the menu extends to traditional moussaka, deep-fried baby squid, lamb baked in lemon, spices and herbs, and delicious, honey-soaked baklava.

Smoking: No cigars & pipes; Air conditioning

Directions: ⊖ Chalk Farm. 200 metres from Primrose Hill Park

89 Regent's Park Road NW1 8UY
Map GtL: C3
Tel: 0171 5867454
Fax: 0171 4832630
Cost: *Alc* £18.50, set-price L £7.95/D £12.25. ☺ H/wine £11
Times: Noon-3pm/6-11.30pm. Closed L Sat, D Sun, 25, 26 Dec
Additional: Sunday L; Children welcome; ▲ dishes

Lexington

Fun restaurant with a live jazz pianist three nights a week. Dishes have a Mediterranean influence, and there is a popular two choice, two course menu at £11.95.

Directions: ⊖ Oxford Circus, Tottenham Court Road, Piccadilly Circus

45 Lexington Street W1R 3LG
Map: D3
Tel: 0171 434 3401
Fax: 0171 287 2997
Telephone for further details

Lindsay House

21 Romilly Street W1V 5TG
Map: D3
Tel: 0171 4390450
Fax: 0171 4377349
Chef/Owner: Richard Corrigan
Cost: *Alc* £60, set-price L £23/D £42. H/wine £14
Times: Noon-3pm/6-11pm. Closed L Sat, all Sun, 2 wks Aug, Bhs
Additional: Children welcome; ▲ dishes
Seats: 50. Private dining rooms 18, 40
Smoking: Air conditioning

Directions: ⊖ Leicester Square

You have to ring the bell to be admitted to this Soho house. One of the affable staff opens it promptly and shows you to a table on the ground or first-floor dining room (other rooms, spread over three floors, are for private parties). In an area awash with trend-setters (and trend-followers, come to that), Richard Corrigan is his own man, cooking from the heart in a style rooted in the great British (and Irish) traditions. Shoulder and belly of pork with crubeens and choucroute might feature alongside saddle of rabbit stuffed with black pudding, and pigeon en croûte with Savoy cabbage and wild mushrooms, bold, gutsy-sounding dishes that none the less show restraint in the handling to produce even delicate combinations of flavours. Fine slivers of tender ox-tongue come as a cold starter with sweet beetroot salad and salsa verde, or there might be lobster and langoustine with melon and sweet potato, or sautéed lambs' sweetbreads with broad beans. Sweetbreads could also show up as a main course with roast rib of beef with a sauce of garlic, rosemary and Madeira, while suckling pig appears in ravioli with foie gras, leek and tarragon, and as 'well-seasoned, with a piece of young crunchy skin' main course with mustard and tarragon sauce. Raspberry sorbet might accompany chocolate tart in precisely cooked pastry, or the same fruit could go into its own tart and appear with passion fruit ice cream.

Livebait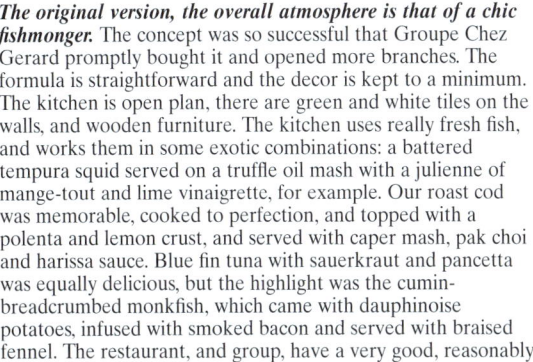

The original version, the overall atmosphere is that of a chic fishmonger. The concept was so successful that Groupe Chez Gerard promptly bought it and opened more branches. The formula is straightforward and the decor is kept to a minimum. The kitchen is open plan, there are green and white tiles on the walls, and wooden furniture. The kitchen uses really fresh fish, and works them in some exotic combinations: a battered tempura squid served on a truffle oil mash with a julienne of mange-tout and lime vinaigrette, for example. Our roast cod was memorable, cooked to perfection, and topped with a polenta and lemon crust, and served with caper mash, pak choi and harissa sauce. Blue fin tuna with sauerkraut and pancetta was equally delicious, but the highlight was the cumin-breadcrumbed monkfish, which came with dauphinoise potatoes, infused with smoked bacon and served with braised fennel. The restaurant, and group, have a very good, reasonably priced wine list. The branch at 21 Wellington Street WC2, tel 0171 8367161, is also recommended.

43 The Cut SE1 8LF
Map: E3
Tel: 0171 9287211
Fax: 0171 9282279
Owner: Groupe Chez Gerard
Telephone for further details

Directions: Near Old Vic Theatre

Lola's

A light and airy space with the feeling of a conservatory about it. Lola's is on the first floor of what was a tram shed and convenient for the antique dealers of Islington's celebrated Camden Passage. This is the setting for the sort of cooking Italians would be at home with: risotto; tagliatelle with ceps, truffle sauce and rocket salad; monkfish 'osso bucco' with gremolata and olive oil mash; even pizza. On the other hand, the kitchen shows some latitude as regards nationality, turning out starters of crab and prawn bisque, followed by slow-cooked pigeon with lightly textured black pudding, braised white beans and spinach. Caesar salad might make an appearance on the 'express' set-price lunch menu alongside a main-course risotto of chicory, fennel, lemon and Parmesan. Cheeses are British, leaving chocaholics to go for truffle cake. Italy heads up the wine list, where around a dozen bottles are also sold by the glass.

359 Upper Street Islington N1 2UD
Map GtL: D3
Tel: 0171 3591932
Fax: 0171 3592209
Chef: Juliet Peston
Owners: Carol George,
Morfudd Richards
Cost: *Alc* £22, set-price L £10 (2 courses). ☺
Times: Noon-2.30pm (3pm Sat & Sun)/6.30-11pm (10pm Sun). Closed some Bhs
Additional: Sunday L; Children welcome; ✤ dishes
Seats: 80
Smoking: Air conditioning

Directions: ⊖ Angel

London Hilton on Park Lane

The top-floor Windows Restaurant, with its sweeping views, is the place to head for at the London Hilton. Business lunches see a weekly-rotating joint of meat carved at table from a trolley: roast rib of beef with mustard sauce on Monday, provençale-style roast leg of lamb on Friday, for instance. The *carte* itself is based firmly in Jacques Rolancy's homeland, the style described as 'French cuisine bourgeoise'. Pan-fried langoustines with thyme-scented courgettes and wild mushroom fricassée might not be everyone's idea of bourgeois, but while other luxury items crop up – foie gras, for instance, as a starter with date purée or going into a sauce to partner main-course roasted sole with stir-fried vegetables – this is a considered menu with a kitchen focused on satisfying people's palates. Simple but none the less appreciated starters have included a salad of fresh herbs and croquant vegetables, and scallops marinated in lemon juice and Alba oil on celeriac mash. Tournedos of salmon with a bean salad and balsamic

22 Park Lane W1Y 4BE
Map: C3
Tel: 0171 4938000
Fax: 0171 2084142
Chef: Jacques Rolancy
Owner: Ladbroke Hotels
Cost: *Alc* £60, set-price L £39.50/D £44 (5 courses). H/wine £15.50
Times: 12.30-2.30pm/7-10.30pm. Closed L Sat, D Sun
Additional: Bar food; Sunday brunch; Children welcome; ✤ dishes
Seats: 90. Jacket & tie preferred at D
Smoking: No pipes; Air conditioning
Accommodation: 446 en suite

Directions: ⊖ Hyde Park Corner. Restaurant on 28th floor of hotel

vinaigrette, fillet of venison in a parsley and truffle crust with potato galette, and snail-stuffed roast chicken breast with glazed potatoes show a similar approach to main courses. Typical of puddings are lavender-scented crème brûlée, and pear tarte Tatin with liquorice toffee and a light vanilla cream.

Signature dishes: wild mushroom risotto with a morel and asparagus sauce; rack of lamb with vegetables en cocotte; monkfish pot-roasted with potatoes, artichokes, baby onions and bacon.

London Marriott
County Hall ❀❀

A great historic site but beg river view tables in the formal restaurant. The setting is quite special with the erstwhile seat of London government brought back to life as a grand hotel. The restaurant takes what advantage in can of views of the river down towards the Houses of Parliament, but even if a window table is unavailable, the rest of the light, bright room is well-spaced and comfortable. Despite the rather formal setting, the kitchen has adopted a brasserie style with punchy flavours to the fore. The brigade delivers well, cucumber and asparagus spring rolls with chilli dipping, daube of pork with cabbage stuffed with bacon and served with mini chateau potatoes, and pistachio soufflé with bitter chocolate sauce showing the range admirably.

The County Hall SE1 7PB
Tel: 020 79285200
Fax: 0171 9285300
Chef: David Ali
Cost: *Alc* £25, set-price L & D £19.50. ☺ H/wine £13.50
Times: Noon-11.45pm
Additional: Bar food; Children welcome; ⚘ dishes
Seats: 80
Smoking: No-smoking area; Air conditioning
Accommodation: 200 en suite
★ ★ ★ ★ ★

Directions: ⊖ Westminster, Waterloo

London Marriott
Grosvenor Square Hotel ❀❀

Grosvenor Square W1A 4AW
Map: C3
Tel: 0171 4931232
Fax: 0171 4913201
Chef: Nick Hawkes
Cost: *Alc* £28, set-price L £20.50/D £12.95. ☺ H/wine £16.50
Times: Noon-10.30pm. Closed L Sat, 1 Jan
Additional: Bar food; Sunday L; Children welcome; ⚘ dishes
Seats: 72. Private dining room 40
Smoking: No-smoking area; Air conditioning
Accommodation: 221 en suite
★ ★ ★ ★

Directions: ⊖ Bond Street. Hotel entrance is on Duke St, off Oxford St

Popular smart hotel restaurant in the heart of Mayfair. A late summer meal in the smart wood-panelled Diplomat restaurant opened with a simple dish of Cornish crab with pickled ginger, sesame wafers and saffron aïoli. The main course of duck breast with caramelised sweetbreads contrasted nicely with some dark mushrooms and a well-reduced jus. Desserts come from the trolley, backed up by a selection of British farmhouse cheeses. The wine list is comprehensive, with plenty by the glass. If you're after a bargain, try the pre-theatre four course menu for just £12.95 – if you wish you can save dessert and coffee until after the performance.

The Lowndes Hyatt Hotel

21 Lowndes Street SW1X 9ES
Map: B2
Tel: 0171 8231234
Fax: 0171 2351154
Telephone for further details

Directions: ⊖ Knightsbridge. From
Sloane Street take first L into Lowndes
Square, located on the bottom right
hand corner

*Open all day, offering a quiet alternative to the bustle of
Knightsbridge. Sample healthy breakfasts and freshly pressed juices,
as well as corn-fed breast of chicken with sun-dried tomato farce
and oregano jus.*

Maison Novelli,
Novelli EC1

It looks as if it were created on a shoe-string (it was). But
change is in the air, and Jean-Christophe Novelli was planning
a revamp of the entire Clerkenwell premises as we went to
press. He may be temporarily out of the kitchen, but the
kitchen team deliver with the usual Novelli flourishes. One
inspector noted that a pressed terrine of rabbit, duck and
Toulouse sausage was a meaty, gutsy creation – its white bean
and scallion vinaigrette adding more oomph. Roast sea bass,
wonderfully seasoned, was served atop tagliatelli mixed with a
robust pesto; oyster froth underlined the sea element.
Another meal saw more sea bass, this time served with
roasted tomatoes, olives, aubergine caviar and chorizo in a
splendid marriage of robust flavours. Dishes indeed have that
depth of flavour which is trumpeted by the height of the
constructions on the plate – built up by the kitchen and
knocked down by eager appetites in the dining room. Hot
chocolate fondant was timed to a T and served on a white
chocolate sauce that was all creamy richness and delight,
lemon tart was sharp yet delicate, offset by an intense
raspberry sorbet. Service is attentive and occasionally smiling.
Adjoining is Novelli EC1, tel 0171 2516606, a light, airy
brasserie with closely packed tables, a lively atmosphere and a
generous *carte* of modern French food.

29 Clerkenwell Green EC1R 0DU
Map GtL: D3
Tel: 0171 2516606
Fax: 0171 4901083
Chefs: Michael Bird, Jean-Christophe
Novelli
Owner: Jean-Christophe Novelli
Cost: *Alc* £45
Times: Noon-3.30pm/6.30-11.15pm.
Closed Sat, Sun
Additional: ⑤ dishes
Seats: 60. Private dining room 30
Smoking: Air conditioning

Directions: ⊖ Farringdon

Mandarin Kitchen

*Spacious and busy modern Chinese restaurant. Fish is a speciality
and live lobsters and crabs are a particular feature, served baked or
steamed with a variety of sauces.*

Additional: ⑤ dishes
Smoking: Air conditioning

Directions: ⊖ Queensway (opposite), Bayswater

14 Queensway W2 3RX
Map: C3
Tel: 0171 727 9012/9468
Fax: 0171 7279468
Cost: *Alc* £20, set-price L & D £9.90
(2 courses). ☺ H/wine £10.50
Times: Noon-11.30pm

Mandarin Oriental Hyde Park, The Park Restaurant

Grand hotel dining room with high ceilings, chandeliers and formal staff. David Nicholls has certainly found his feet since moving on from The Ritz and a superlative-strewn report from one inspector said it all. 'I started with a dish that made me remember why I enjoyed Nicholls' food so much the last time I ate it: simple concept, clean, fresh, bags of taste, executed immaculately.' The dish in question was sweet grilled scallops with haricot vert and herb salad, anchovies, piles of ripe tomato concasse with a chiffonade of basil and a few olive pieces. Delicious. The centrepiece of the meal was a plate of signature pot-roast pork: tongue, temple, cheek, all meltingly gelatinous with a piece of brain giving creamy soft velvet notes, with buttered iceberg lettuce, asparagus, and a ravioli of wild mushroom; a twist on that modern classic by Richard Neat. Time spent by Nicholls' pastry chef in the kitchens of Alain Ducasse showed through in a real tour de force assiette of chocolate desserts: tiny fondant with a piece of banana inside, mini bitter chocolate tart with the added temptations of nuts and orange, a ball of the bitterest, cleanest chocolate sorbet and, almost as an afterthought, a tiny quenelle of mousse with dots of an almost black, intense chocolate sauce garnished with gold leaf. After this, petits fours still managed to be as good as they can ever get.

Signature dishes: ravioli of scallops, Dublin Bay prawns, morels, leeks and fennel cream; pot-roast pork, buttered iceberg lettuce, ravioli of wild mushroom and asparagus; hot chocolate fondant, mille-feuille of pear sorbet.

66 Knightsbridge SW1X 7LA
Map: B2
Tel: 0171 2352000
Fax: 0171 2354552
Chef: David Nicholls
Cost: Alc £34.50, set-price L £23.50/D £32. H/wine £17.50
Times: Noon-2.30pm/6.30-10.30pm
Additional: Bar food; Sunday L; Children welcome; ✿ dishes
Seats: 76. Private dining room 30
Smoking: No-smoking area; Air conditioning
Accommodation: 200 en suite
★ ★ ★ ★ ★

Directions: ⊖ Knightsbridge

Mas Café

Happening place for an arty clientele with a large bar area and music to enhance the atmosphere. Service is friendly, the cooking accurate, and the food full of flavour.

Directions: ⊖ Ladbroke Grove, Westbourne Park. Parallel to Portobello Road

6-8 All Saints Road W11 1HA
Map Gtl: C3
Tel/Fax: 0171 2430969
Telephone for further details

Mash

Popular bar-cum-micro brewery with an upstairs restaurant. Decent service and an appealing weekend atmosphere for kids when American-style brunch comes into its own. Pizzas are from the wood-fired oven, and there's a range of up-to-date Med-inspired dishes with a few oriental twists.

Directions: ⊖ Oxford Circus. At the Oxford Street end of Great Portland Street

19-20 Great Portland Street W1 5DB
Map: C3
Tel: 0171 6375555
Fax: 0171 6377333
Times: Noon-3pm (4pm Sat) 6-11.30pm
Telephone for further details

Matsuri ✿✿

The chic surroundings make a good starting point for an introduction to Japanese cuisine. Matsuri means festival in Japanese and lots of touches around the dining room are related to the various (usually religious) festivals held throughout the year in Japan. Staff are particularly helpful and pleased to guide newcomers around the menu. The centre

15 Bury Street SW1Y 6AL
Map: D3
Tel: 0171 8391101
Fax: 0171 9307010
Chef: Kanehiro Takase
Owner: JRK (UK) Ltd
Cost: Alc £40, set-price L £20/D £35.
☺ H/wine £18

piece of any meal here, and the primary raison d'être of the restaurant, is teppanyaki, with lobster and assorted seafood, steaks, duck, chicken and pork on offer. Great tempura, good sashimi and sushi, and that holy trinity of Japanese meals, miso soup, steamed rice and mixed pickles, more or less complete the picture.

Directions: ⊖ Green Park. Walk towards Piccadilly Circus, turn right into St James', 1st left into Jermyn St. 1st right is Bury St

Times: Noon-2.30pm/6-10.30pm. Closed Sun, Bhs
Additional: Children welcome; ⏰ dishes
Seats: 120. Private dining rooms 7-18
Smoking: No-smoking area; No pipes & cigars; Air conditioning

McClements' Restaurant

Small, local restaurant near Twickenham Station, with candles and fresh flowers on the table. The menu is short and the wine list reasonably priced, with a few wine 'greats' at somewhat prohibitive prices at the back. Amongst the plate of hors d'oeuvre there may be foie gras, hot quail in pastry, pan-fried bass fillet, salmon on rösti, scallops with chicory and quail in pastry. Past dishes enjoyed also include roast monkfish and scallops with saffron and vegetable jus, and a splendid assiette of desserts: lemon mousse, crème brûlée, chocolate tart, raspberry sorbet, praline parfait and coconut ice cream on apple tart – an impressive performance given the restricted size of the kitchen. Chez Clements, 108 Heath Road, Twickenham, tel, 0181 891 0008 is a recent addition, offering larger premises and a more mainstream version of the McClements' style

2 Whitton Road Twickenham
Map GtL: B2
Tel: 0181 7449598
Chef/Owner: John McClements
Telephone for further details

Directions: In a small parade of shops next to Twickenham station

Memories of China Restaurant

Comfortable wicker armchairs in the bar area, screens acting as partitions, solicitous and efficient staff are what you'll find at this upmarket Chinese. A number of fixed-price menus are on offer, from a quick executive luncheon to an imperial Mandarin-style banquet. The latter starts with steamed lobster in spicy ma-la sauce, and takes in, among others, Peking duck, steamed cabbage and crab rolls, shark's fin soup, Yellow River sweet-and-sour whole fish, and ends with chilled lotus nut soup and an assortment of fresh fruit. Mix-and-match according to taste from the *carte:* Shanghai fish and crab soup, or spare ribs to start, then perhaps Cantonese sweet-and-sour prawns, Szechuan hot fried shredded beef, Peking quick-fried lamb with garlic and spring onions, spicy beancurd casserole and Yangchow fried rice (with shrimps, chicken and peas). The wine list is a round-the-world affair. Those who don't want wine could wash it all down with saké (also sold by the quarter- and half-bottle) or Tsingtao beer.

67 Ebury Street SW1W 0NZ
Map: C2
Tel: 0171 7307734/4276
Fax: 0171 7302992
Chef: Kam Po But
Owners: A-Z Group
Cost: *Alc* £35, set-price L £20.50/D £21.50. ☺ H/wine £13.50
Times: Noon-2.15pm/7-11pm. Closed L Sun, Bhs
Additional: Children welcome; ⏰ dishes
Seats: 80. Private dining room 20
Smoking: Air conditioning

Directions: At the junction of Ebury Street and Eccleston Street. ⊖ Sloane Square, Victoria

Le Meridien Piccadilly – The Oak Room, Marco Pierre White

This premier-division restaurant is run on the drive, ambition and brilliance of one man – Marco Pierre White. The grand-scale room is a fitting setting, with enough gilt, chandeliers, spotlit art, and broad, well-spaced tables to dedicate it as a temple to haute cuisine – only the lovely oak panelling adds

21 Piccadilly W1V 0BH
Map: D3
Tel: 0171 4370202
Fax: 0171 4373574
Chef/Owner: Marco Pierre White
Cost: *Alc* £80, set-price L £37.50/D £55

warmth. Staff are formal, the tone hushed and discreet. This is complex cooking, standards are impressive, as they might be at the price (though the set-lunch remains a satisfactory bargain), with impact coming through an extraordinary ability to coax the last nuance of flavour out of these, the very best raw materials. A summer lunch (from the *carte*) that included a terrine of leeks with truffle en gelée and vinaigrette of truffle, which was made of the tenderest, youngest leeks and was bright, fresh and simple, but perfect, also took in a stunning pigeon de Bresse that was tender, full of flavour and beautifully pink, partnered by an astonishing timbale of intensely flavoured foie gras mousse topped with a slice of truffle; and a feuillantine of raspberries of the very finest crisp pastry layered with 'about a pound of superb plump raspberries that tasted divine'. The set-price lunch brings labour and effort, as well as taste and flavour, for your money – it is without doubt, the best value in town. Steak tartare, for example, is just perfect, properly prepared with the right degree of spicing, a lightly boiled, shelled quails egg on top, and served with the very best pommes allumettes and salad. A simply described goujons of sole proved to be chunky pieces of fish in an intensely flavoured lobster bouillon alongside a delicate lobster mousse ('heavenly'), and two quenelles of the lightest crab mousse. Pear Tatin with vanilla ice had excellent pear flavour and text-book caramelised pastry. A half-bottle of wine is included in the set-price – an excellent Macon Solutre 97 (Denuziller), or Givry Premier Cru 97 (Laborbe Juillot) on our visit. We found petits fours in the shape of a tray of friandises containing tuiles, palmiers, madelines, mini baba, lemon tart, raspberry tart, a further tray of hand-made chocolates, as well as *amuse-bouche* (a brilliant gravad lax) and pre-dessert (a quivering mini crème caramel) to be tip-top.

Times: Noon-2.15pm/7-11pm. Closed L Sat, all Sun, 2 wks Aug, Bhs
Additional: Children welcome; 🍴 dishes
Seats: 80. Private dining room 80
Smoking: No pipes & cigars; Air conditioning

Directions: At Piccadilly Circus end of Piccadilly. ⊖ Piccadilly Circus

Le Meridien Piccadilly – La Terrace ❀❀

Revamped conservatory-style restaurant in grand hotel. 'Wonderfully bright and airy by day' notes our inspector on the smart new-look La Terrace, now overseen by the pneumatically charged, Parisian-based chef Michel Rostang. His protégé, Pascal Even, interprets Rostang's style in an unashamedly French manner. Initial reports suggest that the new regime needs time to settle in and establish their own identity; the rich, robust country fare sits uneasily in such a modern setting, especially in a city where many kitchens are striving for a lighter touch. Our meal took in warm artichoke and Beaufort terrine (rather heavy on the cheese), an unremarkable quails' breasts and baby spinach 'kebabed' on rosemary stalks with gratin dauphinoise, and a 'sensual' chocolate fondant.

Directions: ⊖ Piccadilly Circus

Le Meridien Piccadilly 21 Piccadilly W1V 0BH
Map: D3
Tel: 0870 4008400
Fax: 0171 4651616
Chef: Pascal Even
Cost: *Alc* £35, set-price L & D £23.50. ☺ H/wine £19
Times: Noon-2pm/6-10.45pm
Additional: Children welcome; 🍴 dishes
Seats: 122
Smoking: No-smoking area; Air conditioning
Accommodation: 266 en suite
★★★★★

Le Meridien Waldorf ❀❀

A historic hotel complete with its famous Palm Court Lounge. This is one of the most romantic settings in town for dinner: high ceilings brushed by Kentia palm trees, gold leaf, natural light, columns, harpist in the afternoon and a piano at night. The menu revolves around a bistro-style theme and

Aldwych WC2B 4DD
Map: E4
Tel: 0171 8362400
Fax: 0171 8367244
Chef: Christophe Clevely
Cost: *Alc* £50, set-price L & D £26.50. ☺ H/wine £23

there's also an informal all-day brasserie. Our test meal took in a well-timed quail breast in a rose lentil soup with celeriac purée, Mediterranean grouper with coco beans, lemon and pommes Pont-Neuf, and cardamom parfait for dessert. There are regular jazz evenings and the Palm Court afternoon tea dances are a weekend institution.

Directions: Covent Garden

Times: Noon-2.30pm/6-11.15pm. Closed L Sat
Additional: Bar food; Children welcome; dishes
Seats: 90. Private dining room 20
Smoking: No-smoking area; Air conditioning
Accommodation: 292 en suite
★ ★ ★ ★ ★

Mezzo

One of the largest restaurants in Europe, divided into an upper level brasserie, and a more formal restaurant in the basement. On entering, one is immediately struck by the dramatic double height space, and a massive wall of glass that descends through both floors and separates the restaurants from their respective kitchens. The upstairs brasserie is modern in style, with aluminium chairs, sycamore tables and taupe-upholstered banquettes along the wall. The food comes unerringly quickly from the kitchen, and includes a combination of Mediterranean and Asian dishes. Downstairs, in the more traditional restaurant, the array of set menus is overwhelming and the style basically European. Simple, classic grills and crustacea are to be found alongside more complex dishes such as terrine of foie gras and leek, truffle vinaigrette, pumpkin ravioli, and fillet of beef Wellington. The cooking is assured, but sometimes lacks character. The wine list is impressive though safe, and the service is efficient but charmless. However the restaurant and staff alike are immaculately presented.

100 Wardour Street W1V 3LE
Map: D3
Tel: 0171 3144000
Fax: 0171 3144040
Chef: Tom Meenaghan
Owner: Sir Terence Conran
Cost: Alc £25, set-price L £12.50 (2 courses)/D £14. H/wine £12.50
Times: Noon-3pm/6-12.30am. Closed L Sat
Additional: Bar food; Sunday L; Children welcome; dishes
Seats: 350. Private dining room 44
Smoking: Air conditioning

Directions: Piccadilly Circus & Leicester Square

Millennium Baileys Hotel

The modern-look Olives restaurant sits comfortably alongside 19th-century architectural features. Modern British dishes include roast duck breast with braised cabbage, bacon and cherry sauce.

Smoking: Air conditioning
Accommodation: 212 en suite ★ ★ ★ ★

Directions: Gloucester Road. Opposite Tube Station

140 Gloucester Road SW7 4QH
Map: A2
Tel: 0171 3736000
Fax: 0171 3703760
Cost: Alc £16.50; set-price D £12.75 (2 courses). H/wine £9.95
Times: D only, 5.30-10.30pm
Additional: Bar food; Children welcome; dishes

Millennium Britannia Mayfair

Well-managed Mayfair hotel that is going from strength to strength. With its well-equipped 24 hour business centre and fitness room, it is perhaps not surprising that the hotel's restaurant, Shogun, offers Japanese fare. However, at our spring test meal the clientele appeared to be a mixture of local businesses and curious visitors of mixed nationalities. Endorsed at that meal were clean, fresh appetisers of thin crab noodles and sesame-coated prawns, roast duck with teriyaki, and mixed tempura. A plate of tasty-looking sushi delivered to another table got the thumbs up for presentation.

Directions: Bond Street, Green Park

Grosvenor Square W1A 3AN
Map: C3
Tel: 0171 6299400
Fax: 0171 6298168
Chef: Neil Gray
Cost: Alc £30, set-price L £21.50.
H/wine £15
Times: Noon-3pm/6-10.30pm
Additional: Bar food; Sunday L; Children welcome; dishes
Seats: 98. Private dining room 70
Smoking: No-smoking area; Air conditioning
Accommodation: 336 en suite
★ ★ ★ ★

Millennium Chelsea

Upscale setting for a cosmo crowd. The blending of Sloane
Street prices and European food with an Asian influence is
impressive. Kitchen skills are evident but on our visit they had
seemed to lose the plot where taste is concerned. Mushroom
and chilli roll with oriental salad was as exotic as a supermarket
takeaway; salmon with herb risotto, though carefully prepared,
sat on a bed of green rice which tasted of pesto. The menu
contains some interesting and ambitious ideas along the lines of
lobster tail on aubergine moutabel with red wine syrup and
capsicum fritter, or supreme of duckling with thyme and wild
cranberries. Pear charlotte on butterscotch sauce is one of the
simpler desserts, otherwise expect the likes of mango mousse,
sesame cream and sweet fruit spring roll with berry compote.
Non-English speaking staff cruise the room.

17 Sloane Street Knightsbridge
SW1X 9NU
Map: B2
Tel: 0171 2354377
Fax: 0171 2353705
Chef: Paul C Bates
Owner: Millennium & Copthorne
Group of Hotels
Cost: *Alc* £35, set-price L £16.50/D
£26.50 (5 courses). H/wine £14.80
Times: Noon-2.30pm/7-10.15pm.
Closed Sun
Additional: Bar food; Children
welcome; 🍃 dishes
Seats: 90. Private dining room 100
Smoking: No-smoking area; No pipes
& cigars; Air conditioning
Accommodation: 222 en suite
★ ★ ★ ★

Directions: ⊖ Knightsbridge

Millennium Gloucester

*The South West 7 Restaurant, with light-wood panelling, hardwood
floors and original artwork, offers an Italian menu with pasta dishes,
pizza and a selection of meat and fish.*

4-18 Harrington Gardens SW7 4LH
Tel: 0171 3736030
Fax: 0171 3316131
Cost: *Alc* £15. ☺ H/wine £10.50
Times: D only, 5.30-10.15pm. Closed
Sun
Additional: Children welcome;
🍃 dishes
Smoking: No-smoking area; Air
conditioning
Accommodation: 610 en suite
★ ★ ★ ★

Directions: ⊖ Gloucester Road

Mims

***A black-painted etched-glass-fronted restaurant next to a
filling station and a newsagent's.*** Inside, there are black-
topped tables, a tiled floor and limey-yellow walls in the front
area. The daily-changing menus are hand-written, the cooking
techniques are simple – grilling, pan-frying, steaming and

63 East Barnet Road
EN4 8RN
Map GtL: C4
Tel/Fax: 0181 4492974
Chef/Owner: Mr A Al-Sersy
Cost: Set-price L £10.50 (2 courses)/D
£14 (2 courses). ☺ H/wine £9.50

roasting – show skill, jazzed up with intelligent combinations, garnishings and flavoured oils. Start with crab sausage, and go on to roast rump of lamb with roast vegetables. A brochette of chicken with courgettes, ceps, onion and potatoes hit the spot for us, as did main-course red mullet, grilled, with Pernod cream sauce and basil mash. Banana ice cream with caramel sauce, or perhaps a tart – pear and almond, say – round things off. Breads are made in-house and served with flavoured butters of perhaps tomato and garlic, and a short wine list manages to pack in quite a lot of interest.

Directions: On East Barnet Road, next to garage and almost opposite Sainsbury's

Times: Noon-2.30pm/6.30-10.30pm (Sat noon-11pm). Closed Mon
Seats: 45
Smoking: No-smoking area; No pipes & cigars

Mirabelle

56 Curzon Street W1Y 8DL
Map: C3
Tel: 0171 4994636
Fax: 0171 4995449
Chef: Charlie Rushton
Owners: Marco Pierre White, Jimmy Lahoud
Cost: Alc £35, set-price L £17.95. H/wine £14.50
Times: Noon-2.30pm (3pm Sun)/6-11.30pm (10.30pm Sun)
Additional: Sunday L; Children welcome; ⚙ dishes
Seats: 110. Private dining rooms 36, 48
Smoking: Air conditioning

Classical 1930s decor is the setting; 'affordable glamour' is the theme. Marco Pierre White scores brilliantly once again. Great boulevardier dishes such as omelette Arnold Bennett and smoked haddock, bubble-and-squeak, beurre blanc sit alongside MPW signatures such as foie gras parfait en gélée with toasted Poilâne bread, and daube of Aberdeen Angus à l'ancienne. The menu is a textbook of British and French classics – calves' liver with bacon and sage and shallot gravy; potted shrimps 'Mirabelle'; grilled lemon sole, tartare sauce; pot au feu of young chicken with herbs; choucroute of pork chop 'alsacienne' – all confidently done with great panache and without unnecessary fripperies. Best desserts sampled have been glacé prune and Armagnac, and tarte sablé of bitter chocolate. Lunch is an undoubted bargain, perhaps soup au pistou, followed by nage of salmon and sea scallops and French farmhouse cheeses. The wine list is a doorstopper, and although it would be easy to break the bank, there are some good-value bottles at the more accessible end. Brilliant Sunday brunch includes kedgeree, corned beef hash and fried eggs (plus HP sauce), Cumberland sausages and home-made baked beans, and devilled kidneys and bacon.

Directions: ⊖ Green Park

Mitsukoshi

Dorland House 14-20
Lower Regent Street SW1Y 4PH
Map: C3
Tel: 0171 9300317
Fax: 0171 8391167
Chef: Yoshihiro Motohashi
Cost: Alc £30, set-price L & D £35 (6 courses). H/wine £17
Times: Noon-2pm/6-9.30pm. Closed Sun, Xmas, Easter
Additional: Children welcome
Seats: 56. Private dining rooms 12, 22
Smoking: No pipes & cigars; Air conditioning

Mitsukoshi is decorated in the standard decor of blond wood, white walls and massive twig arrangements – all very simple, very clean. 'Ninety per cent of our customers are Japanese,' writes the restaurant, which is set in the basement of a Japanese department store. A number of set-price menus will deliver the (authentic) goods to the hesitant: from one, an appetiser, then sashimi, tempura, sukiyaki, rice, miso and pickles, and finally fruit. An inspector started with natto – fermented soya bean – went on to light, delicately textured steamed egg custard with chicken, shrimp and vegetables, and then sushi of salmon, tuna and eel ('fresh, clear flavours and a pungent hit of wasabi'), and finally 'exactly cooked' grilled salmon with teriyaki. Excellent miso soup, of superb flavour, and good, slightly sticky boiled rice finished the savouries before a serving of fruit. Service is charming and helpful, and prices on a rudimentary wine list soon soar into the stratosphere – drink saké.

Directions: ⊖ Piccadilly Circus

Miyama, City Miyama

Tucked away, dimunitive Japanese restaurant that offers a good deal for lunch in an area that can be expensive and booked up at that time of day. Expect all the usual characters: miso soup, tempura, sushi, sashimi and teriyaki, and yakitori. Sister restaurant, City Miyami, opposite St Paul's in the Nikko building in Godliman Street EC4, tel 0171 4891937 also offers a good set-lunch and give-away weekend prices.

Smoking: Air conditioning

Directions: ⊖ Green Park

38 Clarges Street W1Y 7PJ
Map: C3
Tel: 0171 4992443
Fax: 0171 4931573
Cost: *Alc* £24, set-price L £18 (4 courses)/D £34 (7 courses). ☺ H/wine £10
Times: Noon-2.30pm/6-10.30pm. Closed L Sat & Sun
Additional: Bar food; Children welcome; ⓐ dishes

Momo

Tiny, unpretentious neighbourhood restaurant serving Ealing's large Japanese community. There are few of the usual hallmarks, although tempura, teriyaki and sushi make appearances, the interest lies in the more unusual dishes on offer. Very friendly staff.

Additional: Bar food; Children welcome; ⓐ dishes

Directions: ⊖ North Ealing (opposite)

14 Queens Parade W5 3HU
Map GtL: B3
Tel: 0181 9970206/0306
Fax: 0181 9970206
Cost: *Alc* £25, set-price L from £16/D from £25 (4 courses). ☺ H/wine £9
Times: Noon-2.30pm/6-10pm. Closed Sun, 1 wk Aug, 1 wk after Xmas

Monkey's ❀❀

A neighbourhood restaurant of long-standing. Indeed, nothing much has changed since it opened. The combination of the monkey-themed decor and highly attentive service makes this an ideal eating place for both business suits and Chelsea locals, and it succeeds in being 'all things to all people', with reasonable variety and scope to be found within the two set-price menus. We enjoyed perfectly cooked scallops served on a bed of lentils, rack of lamb, roasted pink and accompanied by a slightly spicy, mint sauce, and a good tarte au citron. Seasonal menus and specials are worth following. The coffee is excellent, as are the petits fours. 'Very enjoyable it was too'. There is a reasonable wine list and knowledgeable service.

1 Cale Street Chelsea Green SW3 3QT
Map: B1
Tel: 0171 3524711
Telephone for further details

Directions: Corner of Cale St & Markhay St. ⊖ Sloane Square (5 mins)

Mon Plaisir ❀❀

Authentic French atmosphere at tightly spaced tables in cosy picture-lined rooms. Mon Plaisir has been feeding the capital's Francophiles since the 1940s, and the place still hums with people casually tucking into such bistro staples as entrecôte grillée avec allumettes, poulet rôti chasseur and steak tartare. But a new English chef adds another dimension to the repertoire, so alongside duck à l'orange might be confit of quail with a ravioli of pea purée and pearl barley with tarragon vinaigrette, cassoulet of mussels with chilli and ginger, and calves' liver in a lime crust. An inspector left perfectly happy after a meal of chicken liver parfait, and a generous portion of guinea fowl cooked in a rich wild mushroom liquor served with dauphinoise potatoes and garlicky green beans. Pudding, chosen from a range of tartes, Tatins, mousses, brûlées and sorbets, was walnut tart, of excellent nutty flavour, with good vanilla cream and ice cream. Staff are all French, and the wine list offers good, mainly French, quality.

21 Monmouth Street WC2H 9DD
Map: D4
Tel: 0171 8367243
Fax: 0171 2404774
Chef: Patrick Smith
Owner: Alain Lhermitte
Cost: *Alc* £34, set-price L £14.95
Times: Noon-2.15pm/5.50-11.15pm. Closed L Sat, all Sun, 10 days Xmas, 4 days Easter
Additional: Children welcome; ⓐ dishes
Seats: 96. Private dining room 28
Smoking: Air conditioning

Directions: ⊖ Leicester Square. Off Seven Dials

Monsieur Max

Monsieur Max continues its transformation into a rustic French eaterie. Wooden floors, tiled walls and assorted mirrors can be espied through the curtain-free front window that looks onto the busy High Street. French bourgeois food is served by predominantly French staff, all knowledgeable and quietly efficient. Bread arrives as you sit down, no side plate so it's onto the table with gusto. Then rillettes of pork and duck, haricots verts, pear chutney and toasted pain Poilâne, followed by roasted lemon sole with girolles, braised Puy lentils, grilled pancetta and champagne sauce. Or, two can share a whole poulet de Bresse, simply roasted with gratin dauphinoise and morel cream sauce, the leg with mixed leaf salad and truffle jus. Terrines, ballotines, duck confit, salad lyonnaise, coq au vin, and choucroute are amongst dishes that gladden the heart of Francophiles.

Directions: On E side of Bushy Park

133 High Street Hampton Hill
TW12 1NJ
Map: C2
Tel: 0181 9795546
Fax: 0181 9793747
Chefs: Max Renzland, Alex Bentley, Morgan Meunier
Owner: Max Renzland
Cost: Set-price L £14 (Mon-Fri)/D £19.50. ☺ H/wine £9.50
Times: Noon-2.30pm/7-10.30pm. Closed L Sat, D 25 Dec, all 26 Dec
Additional: Sunday L; Children welcome; ✍ dishes
Seats: 80. Private dining room 20
Smoking: No pipes & cigars; Air conditioning

The Montcalm-Hotel Nikko London

Great Cumberland Place W1A 2LF
Map: B4
Tel: 0171 4024288
Fax: 0171 7249180
Chef: Stephen Whitney
Cost: *Alc* £24, set-price L £19 (2 courses)/D £24. ☺
Times: 12.30-2.30pm/6.30-10pm. Closed L Sat & Sun
Additional: Bar food; ✍ dishes
Seats: 65. Private dining room 16-60
Smoking: No-smoking area; No pipes & cigars; Air conditioning
Accommodation: 120 en suite
★ ★ ★ ★

Fresh-looking conservatory-style restaurant with lion's head fountain, trompe l'oeil floral cornucopias and landscape mural. Lengthy menus are frequently a warning sign of poor kitchen ability but, for once, the broad choice contains some splendid, original ideas: marinated swordfish, yellow wax beans, sauce vierge; calamari and shellfish laksa with rice soup noodles; salad of roast partridge, beetroot and Parmesan chips. A dozen main courses and, seemingly, a dozen good choices – we would be hard put to decide between poached native lobster with roast Thai spices or salmon schnitzel with goats' cheese, spring onions and broad beans. Some dishes have an almost Catalan slant, note poached breast of chicken with shellfish served with saffron potatoes in bouillabaisse stew, but the modern American influence is the most exciting one with maple glazed breast of duck, sweetcorn and butternut pancake, pecan and Bourbon jus a typical example. Sorbets quatre épices (rosemary, cinnamon, clove and bay leaf) suggest a kitchen that's willing to take risks and takes nothing for granted.

Directions: From Marble Arch tube turn L then 1st L (Great Cumberland Place). After traffic lights hotel is a crescent on R

Moro

Lively, often full-to-bursting restaurant with Spanish-North African-influenced cooking. Bare decor (who notices), brilliant long bar serving tapas, great bread, as well as crab brik with cumin, coriander and harissa, and chargrilled marinated leg of lamb with foul (a white bean dish) and braised chard.

Additional: Bar food; Children welcome; ✿ dishes
Seats: 75

Directions: Exmouth Market is on the corner of Rosebery Avenue and Farringdon Road

34-36 Exmouth Market EC1R 4QE
Map: E5
Tel: 0171 8338336
Fax: 0171 8339338
Chefs: Samuel Clark, Samantha Clark
Owners: Samuel Clark, Samantha Clark, Mark Sainsbury
Cost: *Alc* £30
Times: 12.30-2.30pm/7-10.30pm. Closed Sat, Sun, Xmas, Easter, Bhs

Mortens NEW

Mortens is a private club which has opened its lovely first-floor restaurant to the public. It's the chance to see behind hitherto closed doors that adds a dash of spice to the experience. It's a lovely room with good views over Berkeley Square, especially if you are fortunate enough to secure a window table. Garry Hollihead left Mortons shortly after setting up the brigade but, by chance, our initial inspection visit coincided with his day off, and we were impressed by the cooking of sous chef Philip Reynolds. Reynolds has now taken over and has clearly adopted a different tack. All produce continues to be purchased fresh every day, but the overall style is now simpler and more direct. Dishes are described with brevity: salad escabeche, red mullet pepper confit; potato and aubergine terrine, goats' cheese fondant; maize fed chicken, wild mushroom ravioli. Another dinner in mid July showed great touches of style in concepts such as an *amuse-bouche* of artichoke and potato soup, some perfectly plump, sweet scallops with a lovely intense ginger purée and some lemon vinaigrette providing just the right level of acidity, and light crisp banana beignets that were offered with a tuile basket filled with 'really good' rum and raisin ice cream. The wine list features very little under £20. The clientele are of the sort that used to run the country.

28 Berkeley Square W1X 5HA
Map: C3
Tel: 0171 4937171
Fax: 0171 4953160
Chef: Philip Reynolds
Owners: Simon Lowe, Andrew Leeman, Howard Malin
Cost: *Alc* £45, set-price L £22.50/D £29.50. H/wine £18
Times: Noon-2.30pm/7-11.30pm. Closed L Sat, all Sun, Bhs
Additional: Children welcome; ✿ dishes
Seats: 60

Directions:⊖ Bond Street. On northern side of Berkeley Sq

Mulligan's of Mayfair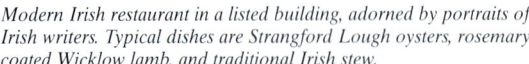

Modern Irish restaurant in a listed building, adorned by portraits of Irish writers. Typical dishes are Strangford Lough oysters, rosemary coated Wicklow lamb, and traditional Irish stew.

Additional: Bar food; Children 14+; ✿ dishes

Directions: Cork Street is between Burlington Gardens and Clifford Street

13-14 Cork Street W1X 1PF
Map: C3
Tel: 0171 4091370
Fax: 0171 4092732
Cost: *Alc* £26.50, set-price L & D £17.50. ☺ H/wine £10.50
Times: Noon-3pm/last D 9.30pm. Closed L Sat, all Sun, 25 Dec, Bhs

Museum Street Café

A clean-cut, minimalist decor with some good modern art and views of St George's church through the skylight. Quality shines at this modern deli-style café-cum-restaurant specialising in upbeat Italian vegetarian food. It's a popular venue for lunch. We thoroughly enjoyed a basket of freshly sliced bread – light wholemeal and nutty walnut – a vivid orange carrot and shallot soup, parsnip pancakes (crisply

47 Museum Street WC1A 1LY
Map: D4
Tel/Fax: 0171 4053211
Chefs/Owners: Gail Koerber, Mark Nathan
Cost: *Alc* £18.75. H/wine £10.50
Times: L only, Noon-3pm. Closed Sun
Additional: Children welcome; ✿ dishes.

caramelised on the outside, squidgy inside) that came with roasted field mushrooms, 'perfect' al dente purple sprouting broccoli, and a chive crème fraîche quenelle. All this was washed down with a tall glass of freshly squeezed carrot and ginger juice (if you fancy something a bit stronger, the short wine list offers a punchy selection of popular vintages). Desserts include Valrhona chocolate cake, home-made caramel ice cream and cheeses from Neal's Yard Dairy.

Seats: 40
Smoking: No smoking in dining room

Directions: Off Bloomsbury Way, near British Museum

Neal Street Restaurant

The interior has become something of a period piece, designed by Sir Terence Conran in the 70s. It is still possible to see many of his design trademarks: painted brick walls, quarry tiles, service stations, and lots of chrome and marble. Though the paintings have changed and the walls are now white, the menu graphic, designed by David Hockney, remains the same, unlike the style of cooking which owner Antonio Carluccio has gradually evolved over the years. However, the entirely Italian repertoire is still more old-fashioned and more formally presented than in many of the new wave Italian restaurants. Carluccio is famous for his mushrooms, and they feature heavily on the *carte*. In winter, when truffles are in season, a memorable home-made tagliatelle is served with lashings of white truffle grated in front of the customer. Simpler dishes, such as a 'ragu' of Sicilian spring vegetables with peas, broad beans and artichokes flavoured with capers in a thin broth-thickened polenta work the best. Desserts are excellent, the formal service is attentive, and the predominantly Italian wine list, including some special bottles from the Ricasoli Estate, is a treat.

26 Neal Street WC2H 9PS
Map: D4
Tel: 0171 8368368
Fax: 0171 8362740
Chef: Kirk Vincent
Owner: Antonio Carluccio
Cost: *Alc* £40. H/wine £13
Times: 12.30-2.30pm/6-11pm. Closed Sun, 25 Dec-1 Jan, Bhs
Additional: Children welcome; dishes
Seats: 60. Private dining room 24
Smoking: Air conditioning

Directions: ⊖ Covent Garden (2 mins)

New World

Close your eyes, listen and smell and you could be transported to Hong Kong. This is a typically jumbo-size Hong Kong-style restaurant, seating 700 on several floors, and decorated in the traditional 'lucky' colours of red and gold. It's one of the best places in Chinatown for the Sunday dim sum ritual; pace yourself, however, otherwise overload settles in early despite the tiny portions, each marked on a slip and totalised at the end of the meal. Other times, choose house specialities such as sesame sautéed chicken with bamboo shoots and carrots, fried squid cake with mincemeat and quick-fried scallops with hot spicy sauce. Stuffed green pepper, beancurd and aubergines are amongst a selection of hot-pan dishes; hotpot ones include braised brisket of beef with bean sauce and belly pork and yam. There are also some unusual lamb and venison specials.

1 Gerrard Place W1V 7LL
Map: D3
Tel: 0171 4342508
Fax: 0171 2873994
Chef: Lap Diep
Owner: Cho Shun Ng
Cost: Set-price L & D £7.50 (2 courses). ☺ H/wine £8.50
Times: 11.30am-11.30pm. Closed 25, 26 Dec
Additional: Sunday L; Children welcome; dishes
Seats: 600. Private dining room 400
Smoking: No-smoking area; Air conditioning

Directions: In Chinatown, just south of Shaftesbury Avenue

Nico Central

With the BBC and Oxford Circus just a block away, it is wise to book for lunch at this smart, well-established restaurant. Sunflower yellow walls (sporting Picasso-style prints), pale-wood flooring and colourful seating create a bright, airy environment in which to enjoy good mainstream French cooking. Tuck into excellent country-style bread and olives

35 Great Portland Street W1N 5DD
Map: C4
Tel: 0171 4368846
Fax: 0171 4363455
Chef: JP Patruno
Owner: The Restaurant Partnership
Cost: Set-price L £23.50/D £25.50. H/wine £15

while choosing from starters like watercress soup, provençal vegetable tart and goats' cheese terrine with peppers, and main dishes such as our well-presented seared cod with lentils. Vegetables were simply cooked then tossed in butter with nutmeg and black pepper. Desserts included a perfectly executed crème caramel served with a compote of fresh figs, pears and kiwi fruit in a cinnamon-flavoured syrup, their famous chocolate marquise and a super-looking lemon tart. Good coffee and truffles round things off.

Times: Noon-2pm/7-11pm. Closed L Sat, all Sun
Additional: Children 7+; ✿ dishes
Seats: 50. Private dining room 12
Smoking: No pipes & cigars; Air conditioning

Directions: Oxford St end of Portland St. ⊖ Oxford Circus

Nicole's

Nicole's is a fashionable Bond Street watering hole of impeccable taste. With a design as beautifully understated as the clothes, all tan leather upholstery, stainless steel and oak wood floor and food that is equally classy, with a light touch that makes even dieting pleasurable. Watercress, red chicory, fennel and blood orange salad, or marinated seafood with lime, coriander and flat bread, and grilled tuna with cannellini beans, roast pepper and onion, caper and fennel relish show the style exactly. Only slightly more naughty are roast lamb rump with braised lentils and salsa verde, and grilled chicken with potato and Feta gratin, black olive, lemon and parsley relish. There's slim line wannabe-a-model fresh fruit salad, but mums whose age and hips will never meet again can compensate with baked date and toffee pudding with crème fraîche or hot chocolate soufflé with dark chocolate sauce. Or maybe that's for the sugar daddies.

158 New Bond Street W1 9PA
Map: D4
Tel: 0171 4998408
Fax: 0171 4090381
Chef: Annie Wayte
Owner: Stephen Marks
Cost: *Alc* £33. H/wine £11.95
Times: Noon-3.30pm/6.30-10.45pm. Closed D Sat, all Sun, Bhs
Additional: Bar food L; Children welcome; ✿ dishes
Seats: 65
Smoking: No-smoking area; No pipes & cigars; Air conditioning

Directions: ⊖ Green Park, Bond St

Nobu

Nobu is a fashion statement in itself. The London branch of this ground-breaking New York restaurant is sited on the first-floor of that A-list playground, the starkly minimalist Metropolitan Hotel (whose lobby can, on arrival, present an impenetrable face to the unknown diner who merely wants to eat modern Japanese). Do not be startled by a curious cry staff emit as you are led to your table – this is to alert the waiters to your arrival (we think) and, with luck, might summon one as helpful and spot-on in her advice as we had: top marks here. The food is astonishing and, without question, some of the most imaginative in town. The quality of the ingredients is impeccably high but such freshness dictates equally sky-high prices. Shellfish is particularly good – oysters with choice of sauce, sweet shrimp new-style sashimi – and seafood toban yaki was made memorable by its precision and delicacy. Sushi of fresh salmon, yellow tail and, particularly, sea eel, also found favour, as did some brilliantly light tempura – sweet potato is a must try – but dessert just missed the mark: a chocolate bento box with goma ice cream that contrasted heavily with the lightness that went before. A punchy, modern wine list complements the food exactly.

Metropolitan Hotel 19 Old Park Lane W1Y 4LB
Map: C3
Tel: 0171 4474747
Fax: 0171 4474749
Chef: Mark Edwards
Owners: Nobu Matsuhisa, Drew Nieporent, Robert de Niro, Mr & Mrs Ong
Cost: *Alc* £65, set-price L £25/D £60 (7 courses). H/wine £15
Times: Noon-2.15pm/6-10.15pm. Closed L Sat & Sun
Additional: Bar food D; Children welcome; ✿ dishes
Seats: 150. Private dining rooms 12-40
Smoking: No-smoking area; Air conditioning

Directions: ⊖ Hyde Park, Green Park

Noho ✿

Thai-inspired food served by an international coterie of staff – testament to the global cooking and eating styles. The large selection of noodle dishes, curries, tempura and stir-fries reflect this in a trendy setting in the heart of ad-land.

32 Charlotte Street W1P 1HP
Tel: 0171 6364445
Telephone for further details

Directions: Telephone for directions

Novelli W8

More bistro than restaurant, with the Novelli signature blue walls and young casual staff. The budget decor is already showing signs of wear and tear but, given the relaxed style, we thought our lunch good value. A mix of classic French and Mediterranean flavours defines the style and the cooking carries enough punch to make an impact. Our test meal brought blackened carpaccio of venison with an onion confit tart and rocket salad, poached salmon with Spanish white bean and parsley sauce with fried risotto rice balls with Mozzarella and fresh tomato sauce, and crème cibouste with poached pear and caramel. Not the most comfortable seating for those over 40, however!

Directions: ⊖ Notting Hill Gate

122 Palace Gardens Terrace W8 4RT
Map GtL: C3
Tel: 0171 2294024
Fax: 0171 2431826
Chefs: Jason Ward,
Jean-Christophe Novelli
Owner: Jean-Christophe Novelli
Cost: *Alc* £35, set-price L £15. ☺
Times: 12.30-3.30pm/6-10.30pm.
Closed Sun, Mon
Additional: ❸ dishes
Seats: 60
Smoking: Air conditioning

L'Odéon

Fabulous views over Regent Street and Piccadilly Circus make this one of the best vantage points in town. L'Odeon has gone through several head chefs since it opened; the current incumbent is Colin Layfield. His menu takes in many modern British ideas – pan-fried crab cakes, pak choi, parsley sauce; saddle of rabbit wrapped in Parma ham, sweet potato purée, Pommery mustard sauce; seared tuna on lime pickled potatoes, tomato and orange jus. The usual suspects are there – confits and risottos, pestos and raviolis, marmalades, lobster oil and truffle dressing – but there are also some more classic leanings with pot-roasted veal sweetbreads with marjoram root vegetables and grilled Dover sole, green vegetables and beurre noisette. Desserts lapse into the experimental with soft caramel with pistachio and salted peanuts and vanilla ice cream, and coconut and lime rice pudding, pineapple glazed with star anise and gingerbread ice cream. The proof of the pudding, however, remains an open question.

65 Regent Street W1R 7HH
Map: C3
Tel: 0171 2871400
Fax: 0171 2871300
Chef: Colin Layfield
Owners: Pierre & Kathleen Condou
Cost: *Alc* £35, set-price L/D £19
Times: Noon-2.45pm/5.30-11.30pm.
Closed Sun, Bhs
Seats: 250. Private dining room 20
Smoking: No-smoking area; No pipes & cigars; Air conditioning

Directions: Piccadilly Circus, entrance in Air Street, opposite Café Royal

Odettes

Elegant neighbourhood restaurant with charming service. In the heart of Primrose Hill, this is a feel-good restaurant reflecting the cosmopolitan bustle all around. The upper restaurant is lined with mirrors of all shapes and sizes, ideal for the vain and voyeurs alike. Large French-style flower arrangements abound, the linen is crisp and white. Good

130 Regents Park Road NW1 8XL
Map: C4
Tel: 0171 5865486/8766
Fax: 0171 5862575
Chef: Simon Bradley
Owner: Simone Green
Cost: *Alc* £26.25, set-price L £10. ☺
H/wine £10.95

cheese straws might precede a tartlet of asparagus with warm new potato and chive sauce, or warm rabbit salad with pancetta, kidney and liver. Herb roasted black leg chicken with summer vegetables was a well-flavoured dish; other choices might include veal chop with wild mushrooms and rosemary or baked salmon with caramelised salsify and toasted almonds. Some dishes are simply classics, peppered fillet of beef with creamed spinach and 'pont-neuf' potatoes fried in duck fat, for example; others take a simple idea and add an unusual element, as in cod with baby squid, coco beans and oven-dried tomatoes, or potted Agen prunes in saffron custard.

Times: 12.30-2.30pm/7-11pm. Closed (rest) L Sat , D Sun, 1 wk Xmas, Bhs
Additional: Wine bar; Sunday L; Children welcome; ✿ dishes
Seats: 60. Private dining rooms 8, 30
Smoking: No pipes & cigars; Air conditioning
Directions: By Primrose Hill. ⊖ Chalk Farm
**Shortlisted for the AA Wine Award –
see p16**

Offshore

Bright, glass-fronted restaurant specialising in that particular French-Mauritian seafood Sylvain Ho Wing Cheong is renowned for – French in sytle with a spicy oriental twist. We heavily endorse the delightfully named 'Picky-Picky' surprise degustation menu.

Additional: Sunday L; Children welcome; ✿ dishes
Smoking: Air conditioning

Directions: ⊖ Holland Park

148 Holland Park Avenue W11 4UE
Tel: 0171 2216090
Fax: 0171 3139700
Cost: *Alc* £40, set-price L £18/D £26.50 (degustation menu). ☺
H/wine £12.50
Times: Noon-3pm/6.30-11pm. 25, 26 Dec, some Bhs

Olivo

Striking Italian swathed in Med sand and azure blue tones. Dishes veer towards rustic, displaying a marked Sardinian influence: chargrilled stuffed baby squid with sweet plum tomatoes and basil, say, or lamb casserole with wild fennel and mash.

Additional: Children welcome; ✿ dishes
Smoking: No pipes & cigars; Air conditioning

Directions: From Buckingham Palace Road, opposite Victoria Station, turn into Eccleston Street. Olivo is on L

21 Eccleston Street SW1W 9LX
Map: C3
Tel: 0171 7302505
Fax: 0171 8248190
Cost: *Alc* £27, set-price L £17. H/wine £10.50
Times: Noon-2.30pm/7-11pm. Closed L Sat & Sun, Bhs

One Aldwych – Axis, Indigo

Part of the magnificent new hotel, once the home of the Morning Post newspaper, two restaurants offer a contrast of styles: light and airy Indigo on the gallery overlooking the cocktail bar, and Axis, the 'serious' venue, with its stark, dramatic look. At Indigo, thoughtfully, the efficient and friendly staff allocate 'ringside' seats to single diners first. The gently muted greys and neutrals which feature throughout the hotel, are broken up by stunning splashes of colour from the dramatic flower and vegetable displays. Pleasantly surprised by the reasonable prices for high-standard brasserie-style cooking, we enjoyed a well-timed, creamy lobster risotto, followed by a richly flavoured, tender duck confit with nicely crisped skin. Raspberry shortcake made a simple but good pudding, followed by coffee and chocolate truffles. It's open all day for breakfast, lunch, afternoon tea and dinner. Axis, on the other hand, presents a stark, dramatic look – the white washed walls are broken up by big, bold red and black artwork. Here, the ambitious kitchen tries hard, has an up-to-date outlook, with fish a favourite, as well as a predilection for

1 Aldwych WC2B 4BZ
Tel: 020 73000300
Fax: 020 73000301
Chefs: Julian Jenkins (Indigo), Mark Gregory (Axis)
Cost: *Alc* £30 (Indigo) £35 (Axis), set-price L £19.75 (Sat-Indigo only)/D £19.75 (pre & post-theatre). H/wine £17.50
Times: 11.30am-3pm (noon Axis)/6-11.15pm. Axis closed L Sat, all Sun, Bhs
Additional: Children welcome; ✿ dishes
Seats: 62 (Indigo) 117 (Axis). Private dining room 48 (Indigo)
Smoking: No pipes & cigars; Air conditioning
Accommodation: 105 en suite
★★★★★

taking traditional dishes and giving them a modern spin: in the case of our jugged hare, taking it off the bone and serving packed into a ball, with some fine-diced beetroot. Flavours are sound, as is technique, which we noted in our smoked haddock and cheese soufflé tart, and simple chocolate tart.

Directions: ⊖ Covent Garden, Charing Cross

One Lombard Street, The Brasserie ✿✿

NEW

A swanky high-ceilinged restaurant occupying a former banking hall. The Brasserie at One Lombard Street has a neo-classical interior, bare white walls and domed skylights – all of which helps to create a buzzy atmosphere. The pan-European menu is simple and to the point with six or seven choices for each course, including four different caviars, with main courses split according to ingredients: pasta, fish, meat, crustacea. We went for a sound poached skate wing with capers, parsley and black butter, but other options were seared scallops with roast tomatoes, saffron and Pernod, a classic Cumberland sausage with grain mustard mash, and blackened wood pigeon with caramelised parsnips and carrots. Desserts range from pineapple and mango salad with coconut sorbet to bitter chocolate tart.

1 Lombard Street EC3V 9AA
Map GtL: G3
Tel: 0171 9296611
Fax: 0171 9296622
Chef: Herbert Berger
Owner: Soren Jessen
Cost: Alc £30. H/wine £13.50
Times: 11.30-2.45pm/6-9.45pm. Closed Sat, Sun, Bhs
Seats: 150. Private dining room 40
Smoking: Air conditioning

Directions: Telephone for directions

Opus 70 ✿

Opus 70 is part of the Mayfair Inter-Continental Hotel, but with its own street entrance. It's a contemporary restaurant providing a thoroughly cosmopolitan setting for dishes from the Far East, America, and Britain.

The Mayfair Inter-Continental Hotel
Stratton Street W1A 2AN
Map: C3
Tel: 0171 3447070
Fax: 0171 3447071
Cost: Alc £30, set-price L £20. H/wine £12
Times: Noon-2.30pm/6-11pm. Closed L Sat, L Bhs
Additional: Bar food; Sunday L; Children welcome; ✿ dishes
Smoking: No-smoking area; Air conditioning
Accommodation: 287 en suite
★ ★ ★ ★ ★

Directions: From Hyde Park Corner, turn L off Piccadilly just below Green Park tube station

L'Oranger ✿✿

Stylish modern restaurant in an upscale Mayfair street. Natural light streams into the restaurant through a skylight, creating a bright, warm setting. The modern *carte* kicks off with starters ranging from braised Swiss chard in veal broth, to ravioli of beef Monegasque with Parmesan. We enjoyed a mid-winter meal that started with a crisp tartlet of fresh salted cod and potato served with finely chopped shallots and tomato. 'Succulent' roasted loin of veal followed, wrapped in bacon and sage and served with creamy wild mushrooms on a bed of spinach. The meal ended on a high – spiced sablé with 'fruity' pineapple sorbet. On warm summer evenings a small number

5 St James's Street SW1A 1EF
Map: C3
Tel: 0171 8393774
Fax: 0171 8394330
Chef: Kamel Benamar
Owner: Giuliano Lotto
Cost: Alc £35.50, set-price L £23.50/D £33.50. H/wine £16
Times: Noon-3pm/6-11pm. Closed L Sat, all Sun
Additional: Children welcome; ✿ dishes
Seats: 55. Private dining room 20

L'Oranger

Smoking: No pipes & cigars; Air conditioning

Directions: ⊖ Green Park. St James's Street is accessible by car via Pall Mall

of tables are set outside in the courtyard. The wine list is focused on the old world, and is particularly strong in its selection from Burgundy.

Orrery

55-57 Marylebone High Street
W1M 3AE
Map: B4
Tel: 0171 6168000
Fax: 0171 6168080
Chef: Chris Galvin
Owner: Conran Restaurants
Cost: *Alc* £50, set-price L £23.50/D £45 (5 courses). H/wine £13
Times: Noon-3pm/7-11pm. Closed Good Fri
Additional: Bar food; Sunday L; Children welcome; ⑤ dishes
Seats: 80
Smoking: No pipes

Directions: ⊖ Baker Street. At very northern end of Marylebone High Street

Smart, modern decor for the smallest in the Conran gastro-empire. 'This allows for better control and consistency' is the opinion of one who was delighted with the whole set up. Clever menus, for instance, are short and to the point and the kitchen doesn't stumble around the solar system (Orrery: a mechanical model of the solar system) trying to fuse Martian ingredients with Jupiter's herbs. It's also a very smart setting, carved out of old stables at the leafier end of Marylebone High Street, with good modern design (of course), tasteful modern table touches, and nippy, attentive soigné service. A tome of a wine list too, save time to study it. There's also a small, cosy, corner bar and for summer evenings, the adjoining food shop's terrace opens up to bar customers. Menus are slightly shorter at lunch. From a choice of leek and potato soup with flaked haddock and poached egg, vine tomato and buffalo Mozzarella tart, and pressed pork hock and foie gras with green tomato and fennel chutney, we chose the latter – chunky meat with gaps filled in by the liver and an astringent chutney. Good. Epigramme of sole with sauce antiboise was perfectly timed and delicate, a signature bitter chocolate terrine with pistachio sauce was all smooth richness. Spot on espresso came with exact petits fours.
Signature dishes: terrine of foie gras with Sauternes jelly, toasted brioche; lobster tagine; canard au sang with braised endive and potato galette.

Orsino

Popular Italian eaterie, buzzy atmosphere. Imaginative pizzas, unusual pasta dishes as well as roast John Dory with white beans, tomato and wild garlic, or veal escalopes with asparagus, lemon and butter. Good Italian wine list.

Smoking: No-smoking area; No pipes & cigars; Air conditioning

Directions: ⊖ Holland Park

119 Portland Road W11 4LN
Map GtL: C3
Tel: 0171 2213299
Fax: 0171 2299414
Cost: *Alc* £28.50, set-price L £15.50.
☺ H/wine £11.50
Times: Noon-11.30pm. Closed 25, 26 Dec
Additional: Children welcome; 🍴 dishes

Orso Restaurant

A well-kept secret with welcoming atmosphere, informal and jolly. This distinctly Italian old-timer keeps well up to date, offering robust modern cooking based on good quality produce. The informality works well with the cooking style and there's a studied casualness about the place that belies well-timed service. Lots of pre-theatre diners, for example, are handled with exact precision; no missing the curtain call here. A winter meal that opened with roast spicy sausage with a light shallot and red wine sauce with soft polenta, went on to chargrilled marinated lamb fillet in tomato, black olive and rosemary sauce, and finished with warn apricot and almond tart accompanied by Mascarpone, scored top marks for flavour, technique and satisfaction. Good Italian wine list with half the 70 bins under £20.

Directions: ⊖ Covent Garden. 1 block in from The Strand, 2 blocks down from Royal Opera House

27 Wellington Street WC2E 7DA
Map: D3
Tel: 0171 2405269
Fax: 0171 4972148
Chef: Martin Wilson
Cost: *Alc* £30, set-price L (Sat & Sun only) £16/pre-theatre (to 6.45pm) £15. H/wine £11.50
Times: Noon-12.45am. Closed 24, 25 Dec
Additional: Sunday L; Children welcome; 🍴 dishes
Seats: 110
Smoking: No-smoking area; No pipes & cigars; Air conditioning

Osteria Antica Bologna

Rustic Italian osteria with bare wooden floors and wrought iron work. This is a great place for simple, unusual regional dishes such as Sicilian goat stew with almond pesto and grilled pollinate, and potato and barley gnocchi with wild mushrooms and tomato sauce.

Directions: Off Battersea Rise, between Wandsworth and Clapham Commons

23 Northcote Road SW11 1NG
Map GtL: C2
Tel/Fax: 0171 9784771
Cost: *Alc* £17, set-price L £8.50 (2 courses). ☺ H/wine £7.90
Times: Noon-3pm/6-11pm (open all day Sat & Sun)
Additional: Sunday L; Children welcome; 🍴 dishes
Smoking: Air conditioning

Oxo Tower Restaurant

8th Floor Oxo Tower Wharf Barge House Street SE1 9PH
Map: E3
Tel: 0171 8033888
Fax: 0171 8033812

Oxo is not the easiest place to find, despite the trademark tower acting as a beacon on the South Bank skyline. But once

whisked up to this eighth floor restaurant and brasserie, you will marvel at one of the best views in London, overlooking the Thames, St Paul's Cathedral and down river to the Houses of Parliament. This large, modern, light, airy and fashionable restaurant offers a set menu at lunch and a rather pricier *carte* in the evenings. We dined on a raviolo of sweetcorn with girolles and Parmesan set on a bed of spinach, then roast pork (a fat slice of loin with a single bone attached) with a prune tart and cinnamon jus. Chocolate and black cherry mousse 'en cadeau', however, was 'poor'. It seems a shame that such a wonderful setting should not be matched by equally good service – there may be plenty of staff but it can be difficult to attract their attention.

Owners: Harvey Nichols Restaurants Ltd
Telephone for further details

Directions: Blackfriars. In between Blackfriars Bridge and Waterloo Bridge

The Peasant

Ornate corner pub with a traditional feel downstairs and a modern restaurant upstairs. The same rustic Mediterranean menu is offered throughout, so choose your atmosphere.

Directions: Farringdon, Angel

24 St John Street EC1 4PH
Map: E4
Tel: 0171 3367726
Fax: 0171 2514476
Telephone for further details

The People's Palace

South Bank mega-eaterie whose major attractions are views over the Thames, the extended opening hours and the facility to pre-order meals. Plus contemporary food with a nod to British tradition in dishes such as haunch of venison with braised red cabbage and mulled wine jus.

Additional: Sunday L; Children welcome; ⛛ dishes
Smoking: No-smoking area; Air conditioning

Directions: Level 3 of the Royal Festival Hall

Royal Festival Hall Belvedere Road SE1 8XX
Map: E3
Tel: 0171 9289999
Fax: 0171 9282355
Cost: Alc £25, set-price L £12.50 (2 courses)/D £15.50 (2 courses, btw 5.30-7pm). ☺ H/wine £11.50
Times: Noon-3pm/5.30-11pm. Closed Bhs

Pétrus NEW

Pétrus is a long, high-ceilinged room with massive moody oil reproductions of food still lifes on the walls, round tables clothed in oatmeal and white (no garish colours here), and seating comfortable enough to while away a couple of hours watching the movers-and-shakers who frequent the place. Wines are kept in a 'cellar' that's visible, the list concentrating on the eponymous Château Pétrus at prices that corroborate that this is one of the costliest wines in the world; house wines, very drinkable and full of character, are more easily attainable. This is an ambitious enterprise, with a kitchen that's strong on precision and presentation delivering food that's big on flavour. Typical of the currency are rabbit terrine with cabbage, pickled onions and sliced leeks, halibut braised with asparagus and lettuce served with Sauternes sauce and grapefruit, and pan-fried sweetbreads on sautéed ceps in a light veal jus. Duck confit ravioli comes in a flying saucer shape of wafer-thin pasta on a bed of spinach dribbled with a soy-based sauce and makes a tasty starter. The 'winner' for an inspector was a main course of chunks of John Dory on red pepper confit in mussel and tomato sauce garnished with crisply fried aubergine, all a happy marriage and a pretty sight. Puddings are a masterstroke too, as in a thinnest of thin pastry tart filled with tangy, trembling passion fruit coupled with a 'smooth and sexy' orange sorbet in a brandy snap.

33 St James's Street SW1 1HD
Map: D3
Tel: 0171 9304272
Fax: 0171 9309702
Chef/Owner: Marcus Wareing
Cost: Alc £30.50, set-price L £19.50/D £28. H/wine £15
Times: Noon-2.45pm/6.45-11pm. Closed L Sat, all Sun, Xmas, Bhs
Additional: Children welcome; ⛛ dishes
Seats: 55
Smoking: No pipes & cigars; Air conditioning

Directions: Green Park

Pharmacy Restaurant

Trustafarian hang-out designed by Damien Hirst. The ground floor bar is for drinks and snacks, the first-floor restaurant serves mod-Euro dishes such as papardelle with chicken livers and rocket, and chargrilled scallops with leeks and button mushrooms. Weekends are popular.

Smoking: Air conditioning

Directions: ⊖ Notting Hill Gate

150 Notting Hill Gate W11 3QG
Map GtL: C3
Tel: 0171 2212442
Fax: 0171 2432345
Cost: *Alc* £40, set-price L £15.50 (2 courses)/D £40. ☺
H/wine £9
Times: Noon-2.45pm/6.45-10.45pm
Additional: Bar food; Sunday L; Children welcome; ⚫ dishes

Pied à Terre 🌸🌸🌸🌸

Stylish, simple, a Web site and e-mail address on the menu, Pied à Terre is at the cutting edge of modern cooking. Tom Aikens proves he has the courage of his convictions by presenting braised pig's head with steamed trotter, deep-fried brains and ears and celery purée as one of his most outstanding and challenging dishes. Once the order is taken a plethora of bread is offered ('I watched one diner polish off eight rolls,' comments an inspector, impressed). Terrines are prominent among starters with ham hock, sweetbreads, white beans and rosemary vinaigrette enjoyed for its taste and strong visual appeal. Otherwise there might be a warm salad of pigeon and beetroot with loads of colour and height. Roasting is a favoured treatment of main-course meats and fish: sea bass with red pepper sauce and braised fennel, or lamb fillet with garlic and rocket salad and olive sauce. Saucing itself is seen as one of the kitchen's greatest accomplishments, as in a 'delicious' red wine sauce, vaguely sweet but acidic, garnet-coloured with a high gloss, and not too overpowering for the brill fillet, ceps and roasted asparagus that came with it. There can be no better example of the kitchen's industry than a pudding of chocolate soufflé with chocolate and cherry mille-feuille, white chocolate ice cream and white chocolate parfait, or silky-textured mango sorbet with vanilla-flavoured mango jelly and whipped coconut cream. And as much care is lavished on the petits fours served with coffee. The budget-conscious should stick to the 'suggested wines' on the wine list; those prepared to pay can drink one of France's greatest.

Signature dishes: Boudin of guinea fowl with asparagus, French bean salad and cep vinaigrette; roasted turbot fillets with caramelised endive, red wine sauce and roasted queen scallops; raspberry brûlée and sablé with raspberry parfait and sauce.

34 Charlotte Street W1P 1HJ
Map: C4
Tel: 0171 6361178
Fax: 0171 9161171
Chef: Thomas Aikens
Owners: Thomas Aikens, David Moore
Cost: *Alc* £50, set-price L £23/D £35. H/wine £17
Times: 12.15-2.30pm/7-10.45pm. Closed L Sat, all Sun, last 2 wks Aug, 2 wks Xmas & New Year
Additional: Children welcome; ⚫ dishes
Seats: 40. Private dining room 14
Smoking: Air conditioning

Directions: ⊖ Goodge Street. S of BT Tower

Shortlisted for AA Wine Award-see page 16

Le Pont de la Tour

The centre of Conranland. Impeccably stylish, with a high-flying atmosphere, the cooking is steeped in the classical mould, deft in touch and confident in execution. The menu reads like a dream: whole roast buttered lobster with herbs; grilled veal chop with a sauté of ceps, roast shallot and Armagnac purée. Roast breast of wood pigeon, tender to an extreme and cooked a delicious pink, was served with a beetroot and lentil sauce in a meaty jus given further depth by foie gras. A hearty Dijon mustard sauce gave extra lift to a baked leg of rabbit with pancetta and girolles. Wonderful St Emilion au chocolat pays full tribute to the sensual delights of rich cocoa. The wine list rises to the occasion with a long and interesting list, ably supported by knowledgeable staff.

Directions: SE side of Tower Bridge

The Butlers Wharf Building
36d Shad Thames SE1 2NQ
Map: G3
Tel: 0171 4038403
Fax: 0171 4030267
Chef: David Burke
Owner: Sir Terence Conran
Cost: *Alc* £40. H/wine £11.95
Times: Noon-3pm/6-11.30pm. Closed L Sat
Additional: Bar food; Sunday L; Children welcome; 🍴 dishes
Seats: 130. Private dining room 20

The Popeseye

A simple, successful formula prevails here: steaks and nothing but, from grass-eating Aberdeen Angus cattle, fillet, sirloin and popeseye (the Scottish name for rump), all served with great chips by cheerful staff.

Directions:⊖ Hammersmith. Restaurant located behind Olympia

108 Blythe Road W14 0HD
Map GtL: C3
Tel: 0171 6104578
Fax: 0171 3521279
Cost: ☺ H/wine £11.50
Times: D only, 6.30-10.30pm. Closed Sun, Aug
Additional: Children welcome
Credit cards: None

La Porte des Indes

Stylish Indian on two impressive floors with a 40ft-high marble waterfall cascading down between carved stone balustrades. At lunch there's a brilliant great value buffet: dishes range from battered aubergine, to 'smoky' tandoori chicken. Not your average curry house.

Additional: Sunday L; Children welcome; 🍴 dishes
Smoking: Air conditioning

Directions:⊖ Marble Arch. Behind Cumberland Hotel

32 Bryanston Street W1H 7AE
Map: D4
Tel: 0171 2240055
Fax: 0171 2241144
Cost: *Alc* £35, set-price L £15/D £33. H/wine £10.50.
Times: Noon-2.30pm (3pm Sun)/7-midnight (Sun 6-10.30pm). Closed L Sat

Purple Sage

Stylish modern Italian close to Selfridges featuring authentic pizzas from the brick oven, salads, pasta and risottos, including a fine, saffron flavoured shellfish risotto ai profumi di mare. Try too the yogurt sorbet and excellent espresso.

Additional: Children welcome; 🍴 dishes
Smoking: No pipes & cigars; Air conditioning

Directions:⊖ Bond Street

92 Wigmore Street W1H 9DR
Map: C3
Tel: 0171 4861912
Fax: 0171 4861913
Cost: *Alc* £22. ☺ H/wine £9.50
Times: Noon-2.30pm/6-10.30pm. Closed Sun

Putney Bridge

'Great meal, great setting' summed up an inspector after a visit to this award-winning, strikingly modern building beside the Thames. A long glass frontage in the upstairs restaurant gives wide views over the water; downstairs is the bar. A new chef brings a change in direction, with menus based squarely

The Embankment
SW15 1LB
Map GtL: C2
Tel: 0181 7801811
Fax: 0181 7801211
Chef: Anthony Demetre
Owner: Gerald Davidson

on France with the rest of Europe getting a look in too. If 'terrine of foie gras with pears and celeriac, quatre épices and pain Poilâne' sounds a bit pidgin, it's none the less a wonderful innovation on the classic, the flavours blending perfectly. Crab remoulade, ravioli of duck confit with mushrooms, and pithiviers of snails with two sauces could also be starter choices, with main courses split equally between fish and meat. Roast sea bass with wild mushroom risotto is enhanced by a velouté of ceps and Jerusalem artichokes to make the dish 'a great success', a seasonal stew of peas, broad beans and carrots might partner an assiette of rabbit, while loin of lamb is roasted and poached and served with couscous provençale. Warm Valrhona chocolate moelleux with almond milk sorbet, or exotic fruit croustillant round things off. The long wine list, strongest in France, has a fair range by the glass.

Cost: Alc £40, set-price L £17/D £37.50. H/wine £13.50
Times: Noon-2.15pm/7-10.45pm. Closed D Sun
Additional: Sunday L; Children welcome; 🍃 dishes
Seats: 120
Smoking: Air conditioning

Directions: ⊖ Putney Bridge. Walk out of station and across bridge. Restaurant is the first building on R, facing onto river

Quaglino's

Landmark restaurant with great sense of style. The emphasis is on enjoyment, and there are plenty of taste sensations on the easy-reading menu – pan-fried foie gras with spiced pear and rocket, followed by sea bream saltimbocca with lemon and sage.

Seats: 267. Private dining room 40
Smoking: Air conditioning

Directions: Bury St is off Jermyn St, ⊖ Green Park

16 Bury Street St James's SW1Y 6AL
Map: C3
Tel: 0171 9306767
Fax: 0171 8392866
Cost: Alc £26, set-price L & D £15. ☺ H/wine £12.50
Times: Noon-3pm/5.30-midnight(1am Fri-Sat, 11pm Sun)
Additional: Bar food; Children 14+ in bar only; 🍃 dishes

Quality Chop House

Mahogany booths and etched mirrors maintain the 19th-century atmosphere of this unfussy, relaxed restaurant. The menu is eclectic: from jellied eels to Beluga caviar, and calves' liver, to eggs, bacon and chips, all tastes and budgets are catered for. The fish repertoire has been extended by knocking through to next door and opening the Quality Fish House.

Additional: Sunday L; 🍃 dishes
Smoking: No-smoking area; Air conditioning

Directions: On the south side of Farringdon Road, from its junction with Rosebery Avenue. ⊖ Farringdon

94 Farringdon Road EC1 3EA
Map: E4
Tel: 0171 8375093
Cost: Alc £24
Times: Noon-2.55pm (3.55pm Sun)/6.30-11.25pm (Sun from 7pm). Closed L Sat

Quincy's Restaurant

Quincy's well deserves the popular local following it has built up over the years. It is the sort of cosy, informal little restaurant all neighbourhoods should have. Monthly-changing menu with daily soup and fish dishes. The choice is short, but thoughtfully constructed, with cooking that is judicious and well-tempered. Dishes are concisely described – seared chicken with chickpea salsa, soy and chilli; pigeon breast with sweet potato, foie gras and pear confit; calves' liver, shallot purée and sherry vinegar sauce. Vegetarian choice is well balanced – leek and Gruyère flan with grilled mushrooms, red onion and port dressing, on one sample menu, followed by baked squash, haricot cassoulet and truffle oil. Desserts, such as coconut and lemon grass fritters with roast pineapple and frozen ginger yogurt have bright, fresh flavours. Dinner only, but it's a bonus to find somewhere so good open on Sunday night.

675 Finchley Road NW2 2JP
Map GtL: C4
Tel: 0171 7948499
Chef: David Philpott
Owner: David Wardle
Cost: Set-price D £25. H/wine £10
Times: D only, 7-11pm
Additional: Children welcome; 🍃 dishes
Seats: 30
Smoking: No pipes & cigars; Air conditioning

Directions: Situated between Hendon Way & Cricklewood Lane on the Finchley Road

Quo Vadis

Exemplary service, as with all Marco Pierre White places.
Newly refurbished, with crisp table linen, hallmarked silver, extra banquette seating and rich brown leather upholstery; all classically smart, despite the MPW masterpeices, such as lizard skeletons on the ceiling and a framed chicken head with solitary egg. Well, at least this challenging chef's debut in the art world provides a talking point. Our meal, taken a week after reopening ('still painting outside') went down well. Simple, rustic French bread in huge chunks came with lovely unsalted butter, and from a menu that interpersed good old-fashioned items with more up-to-date dishes, we chose one from the former category – a well-composed Caesar salad with fresh anchovies, crisp slivers of pancetta and croûtons, though dressed with more of a mustard than classic dressing. A more modern approach defined a restrained salmon and fennel ravioli with Emmenthal glaze, which was teamed with a tomato sauce, and duck confit (two legs) were matched with pak choi, chargrilled carrots and a bitter-sweet sauce. Pannacotta with champagne poached strawberries was, sadly, a poor note on which to end the meal.

26-29 Dean St W1V 6LL
Map: D4
Tel: 0171 4379585
Fax: 0171 4349972
Chef: Philip Cooper
Owners: Marco Pierre White, Jimmy Lahoud
Cost: *Alc* £40, set-price L & D £17.95 (pre-theatre). ☺ H/wine £12.50
Times: Noon-2.15pm/6-11.15pm. Closed L Sat & Sun, 25, 26 Dec, 1 Jan
Additional: Children welcome early evening; ⏂ dishes
Seats: 80. Private dining room 12/30
Smoking: Air conditioning

Directions: ⊖ Leicester Square

Radisson Edwardian Berkshire Hotel

Hidden oasis of calm amidst the hustle and bustle of Oxford Street. The hotel's Ascot's Restaurant is smart, wood-panelled and offers distinctly modern British cooking, with those tell-tale influences from around the world evident in dishes such as chargrilled honey and lemon chicken with coriander and rocket, and pan-fried fillet of beef with smoked bacon, shallots and red wine. A summer lunch might start with warmed focaccia and a delicate chicken and leek terrine with fennel and foie gras, followed perhaps by tempura of lemon sole and mange tout salad. Desserts range from banana pizza with honey and ginger ice cream, to praline parfait with griottine cherries.

Directions: ⊖ Bond Street (opposite)

Oxford Street W1N 0BY
Map: C3
Tel: 0171 6297474
Fax: 0171 4951686
Chef: Dorian Breakspear-Coyle
Owner: Radisson Edwardian Hotels
Cost: *Alc* £30, set-price L & D £18.50 (2 courses). ☺ H/wine £14.75
Times: 12.30-2.30pm/5.30-10.30pm. Closed L Sat, L Sun, L Bhs
Additional: Bar food; Children welcome; ⏂ dishes
Seats: 50. Private dining room 16
Smoking: No-smoking area; Air conditioning
Accommodation: 147 en suite
★ ★ ★ ★

Radisson Edwardian Hampshire Hotel

Stylish, period Leicester Square hotel. Contemporary British cooking takes in roast fillet of salmon with braised bok choi and herb broth, or curried crab and spring onion risotto.

Smoking: No-smoking area; Air-conditioning
Accommodation: 124 en suite ★ ★ ★ ★

Directions: S side of Leicester Square on corner with St Martin's Street

Leicester Square WC2H 7LH
Map: C3
Tel: 0171 6660902
Fax: 0171 9308122
Cost: *Alc* £30, set-price L & D £25. H/wine £14.25
Times: 12.30-2.30pm/6-11pm
Additional: Bar food; Sunday L; Children welcome; ⏂ dishes

Radisson Edwardian Mountbatten Hotel

Consistency is the key to the cooking. Our meal of baked goats' cheese with girolles, salmon with chorizo oil and crab ravioli, and

Monmouth Street WC2H 9HD
Map: E3
Tel: 0171 8364300
Fax: 0171 2403540

white chocolate tart should have played to a larger house than the poor one it got the night we were there. That's theatreland for you.

Smoking: No-smoking area; Air conditioning
Accommodation: 127 en suite ★ ★ ★ ★

Directions: ⊖ Leicester Square

The Radisson
SAS Portman Hotel

Modern international cooking for modern international travellers. The Portman Corner offers a lunch buffet Monday to Friday with a supplement if a main course, such as confit of rabbit leg with red onion parcel and herb oil dressing or thyme-infused rump of lamb with spinach and cranberries, is taken from the *carte*. There are some interesting ideas such as cayenne spiced sweetbread with onion and sesame tuiles and apple jus reduction, or saltimbocca of monkfish with sage leaves and red and yellow sauces. Side dishes get welcome extra attention, and chicory and sweet mustard salad, green beans with red chillies, Mascarpone and garlic risotto all add extra interest to this neglected section. Nor is the kitchen a slouch when it comes to dessert, willing to think big with the likes of tarte Tatin of sweet pear, roasted pecans and black pepper ice cream.

Directions: Off Oxford St. Close to Marble Arch. ⊖ Marble Arch

22 Portman Square W1H 9FL
Map: B3
Tel: 0171 2086137
Fax: 0171 2244928
Chef: Brian Kerr
Cost: *Alc* £26.90, set-price L & D £23.95. H/wine £13.50
Times: 12.30-11pm. Closed L Sat
Additional: Bar food; Sunday L; Children welcome; ✿ dishes
Seats: 85. Private dining room 18
Smoking: No-smoking area; Air conditioning
Accommodation: 280 en suite ★ ★ ★ ★

Cost: *Alc* £26, set-price L & D £22.50. ☺ H/wine £14.75
Times: 12.30-2.30pm/5.30-11pm. Closed L Sat & Sun, Bhs
Additional: Bar food; Children welcome; ✿ dishes

Rain

NEW

A restaurant that describes itself as 'rustic but funky'. You walk into a heady den with low-lying plump cushions set before a disproportionately large bar before going into the restaurant itself: scratched walls of green and blue, oriental artefacts, organza drapes. It also defines the style as new Asian, or oriental fusion food. Tamarind, wasabi, peanut sauce, Japanese seven spice, lemongrass, oyster sauce, coconut milk and sesame are just some of the seasonings used in the modestly described dishes that deliver more than is promised by the menu. A subtle, clever and well-timed starter of wok-seared tuna coated in cracked peppers is served warm with a cream of wasabi and sesame, while a main course of tamarind-spiced duck with fried sweet potato and noodles is commended for the accuracy of its cooking and for that tamarind sauce boosted by garlic, lemon and soy. Vegetables spiced with kim-chee are covered in a hot, sweet tomato sauce, and East meets West in puddings like coconut and ginger tiramisu. Staff are diligently well-informed to deal with customers' queries, and the wine list is a deliberate attempt to marry grapes with food.

303 Portobello Road W10 5TD
Map GtL: C3
Tel: 0181 9682001
Chef/Owner: Sameer Vaswani
Cost: *Alc* £32, set-price L £12 (2 courses). ☺ H/wine £11
Times: Noon-2.45pm/7-10.30pm. Closed D Sun, L Mon, Xmas
Additional: Bar food; Sunday L; Children welcome; ✿ dishes
Seats: 47
Smoking: No-smoking area; No pipes & cigars; Air conditioning

Directions: ⊖ Ladbroke Grove. N end of Portobello Road

The Raj Vogue

The most traditional of Indian restaurants, comfortable with red plush chairs. The menu offers favourite dishes from every region of the sub-continent, including tandoori specialities.

Directions: ⊖ Archway. Opposite the Whittington Hospital

34 Highgate Hill N19 5NL
Map GtL: C4
Tel: 0171 2729091
Fax: 0171 2811485
Telephone for further details

Rani ✿

Renowned Indian vegetarian, comfortably furnished and adorned with photos of rural India. Gujerati dishes, samosas and parathas, are enhanced by excellent home-made chutneys and exceptional breads. Pleasant service.

Additional: Sunday L (12.15-6pm); Children welcome; ⚘ dishes
Smoking: No-smoking area; No pipes & cigars

Directions: 5 min walk from Finchley Central Station

7 Long Lane Finchley N3 2PR
Map GtL: C4
Tel/Fax: 0181 3494386
Cost: *Alc* £16.75, set-price D £12.45
(2 courses). ☺ H/wine £9.70
Times: D only, 6-10.30pm. Closed
25, 31 Dec

Ransome's Dock ✿✿

The restaurant, tucked away on the south of the Thames, overlooks an undistinguished dry dock with no view of the river. But this small restaurant is stylish, its walls painted a bold blue and hung with good contemporary art. The kitchen is keen on sourcing first-class ingredients, with some of the meats being identified, such as Shorthorn beef, Tyrolean bacon and Trelough duck, and the cooking has a strong, modern European feel. The monthly-changing *carte* is supplemented by a set-menu at lunch and by specials in the evening. The range of dishes takes in starters of penne with Fontina and Parmesan cheeses, Joselito black pig chorizo with Spanish olives, and Morecambe bay potted shrimps, with Dutch calves' liver, and filo turnovers with spinach, and Feta cheese among the main courses. Desserts are up to the mark with crème brûlée and baked banana both popular. There is a very good wine list, a popular weekend brunch menu, and the service is friendly and courteous.

35-37 Parkgate Road Battersea
SW11 4NP
Map GtL: C2
Tel: 0171 2231611
Fax: 0171 9242614
Chef: Martin Lam
Owners: Martin & Vanessa Lam
Cost: *Alc* £25, set-price L £11.50 (2
courses). ☺ H/wine £13.50
Times: Noon-5pm/6-11pm. Closed D
Sun, Xmas
Additional: Sunday L; Children
welcome; ⚘ dishes
Seats: 55
Smoking: No pipes; Air conditioning

Directions: Between Albert and
Battersea Bridges

**Shortlisted for the AA Wine Award –
see p16**

Rasa ✿✿

Pass the shrine to Krishna and take a seat at one of the metal-framed chairs in the bright and cheerful surroundings. Walls are rag-rolled in pink and hung with decorative brass pieces, classical Indian music playing in the background. This is the original Rasa, dedicated to the vegetarian cuisine of Kerala, and plenty of friendly, helpful staff, plus an informative menu describing the backgrounds of the dishes and how they are normally served in their homeland, make the experience rewarding. Clear flavours and subtle combinations of herbs and spices are the kitchen's stock in trade. Start with Mysore bonda – potato croquettes with ginger, coriander, mustard seed and curry and served with creamy coconut chutney – and go on to masala dosai – a huge, paper-thin pancake folded over a soft potato filling with a lentil and vegetable sauce, with perhaps a dish of okra stir-fried with chillies and coconut to accompany. Our meal finished on a high note with rice-powder dumplings with banana and coconut in cashew-flavoured cream.

55 Stoke Newington Church Street
N16 0AR
Map GtL: D4
Tel: 0171 2490344
Fax: 0171 2498748
Chef: Rajan Karajtic
Owner: Sivadas Sreedharan
Cost: *Alc* £15, set-price L & D £15.
☺ H/wine £9.50
Times: Noon-2pm/6-10.45pm. Closed
L Mon-Fri, 25, 26 Dec
Additional: Children welcome;
⚘ dishes
Seats: 45
Smoking: No smoking in dining room;
Air conditioning

Directions: BR from Liverpool St to
Stoke Newington High St

Rasa Sumudra ✿✿

Lively, successful Indian seafooder with charming service.
Das Sreedharan hails from Kerala and his delicate Keralian
vegetarian food has already established a reputation at Stoke

5 Charlotte Street
W1P 1HD
Map: C4
Tel: 0171 6370222
Fax: 0171 6370224

Newington (Rasa) and, more recently, in the west end at Rasa W1 (see entries above and below). This latest addition concentrates on seafood, although the tried-and-tested vegetarian menu common to the other two is threaded through, and the popular pre-meal snacks and chutneys are offered alongside new additions of fish and prawn chutneys ('prawn good, but fish an acquired taste'). The best dishes we tried were koonthal fry (squid rings of remarkable tenderness, stir-fried with onions, chilli and mustard seeds), and nilam padungi charu (lemon sole of such incredible freshness and timing). Meen manga curry (king fish cooked in a powerful chilli-based sauce) we decided was another acquired taste. Accompanying vegetable curries were good. Desserts do attempt to be more interesting than in most Indian restaurants; although gulab jaman and kulfi appear, there's more imagination at work.

Chefs: Anil Narayan, Pramod Pillai, Ajil Kumar
Owner: Sivadas Sreedharan
Cost: *Alc* £30, set-price L £14.95. ☺ H/wine £10.50
Times: Noon-3.15pm/6-11pm. Closed Sun, Bhs
Additional: Children welcome; 🍴 dishes
Seats: 110. Private dining rooms 10, 30
Smoking: No-smoking area; Air conditioning

Directions: ⊖ Tottenham Court Road, Goodge Street

Rasa W1 ❀❀

Bright, friendly Keralan restaurant that is far removed from your average curry house. Das Sreedharan's second vegetarian restaurant in the more accessible Oxford Street area. It's similar to the Stoke Newington outpost (see entry) – outstanding Indian regional cooking, pleasant staff and a garish pink colour scheme. What is on offer is some of the best Indian food in the capital, imaginative, impressive quality, with vibrant flavours through imaginative spicing. Our meal opened with pre-meal snacks – basically Keralan street food – crisp, deep-fried takes on the pappadom, served with a range of home-made chutneys, then a complimentary coconut dosa, which was moreish. Banana boli is battered plantain (with black sesame seeds and turmeric) served with a smooth, comforting peanut and ginger sauce. Main course curries included beet cheera pachadi (beetroot in a sauce of yogurt, roasted coconut, mustard seeds and curry leaves); the accompanying lemon rice was excellent. This place has hardly drawn breath since it opened – booking is essential.

6 Dering Street, W1R 9AB
Map: C4
Tel: 0171 6291326
Fax: 0171 4919540
Chef: R S Binuraj
Owner: Das Sreedharan
Cost: *Alc* £18, set-price L £22.50 (5 courses)
Times: Noon-2.30pm/6-10.30pm. Closed L Sun, 24 Dec-4 Jan
Additional: Children welcome; 🍴 dishes only
Seats: 90
Smoking: No smoking in dining room; Air conditioning

Directions: ⊖ Bond Street

Redmond's ❀❀

In a row of shops in a prosperous south London residential area. Redmond's is a quiet lunch-time venue (with the exception of Sunday lunch), but comes alive at night when the menu is marginally more expensive. It's a bright open setting with plain walls adorned with zany, colourful avant-garde paintings. Redmond Hayward's evolving menu reads like many these days: modern English with the odd nod towards somewhere else, on our visit Japan and the Mahgreb. That lunch included tuna tartare with hints of ginger and mirin, and a roast mallard that was the business – slightly gamey flavour coming through the tender breast – with caramelised roots vegetables and black pudding that fitted their parts beautifully. White chocolate tart was cleverly supported by a contrasting fuller dark chocolate sorbet and a token amount of passion fruit sauce. The wine list is very helpfully annotated and written for enjoyment with a special section for halves, magnums and dessert.

170 Upper Richmond Road West SW14 8AW
Map GtL: B2
Tel: 0181 8781922
Fax: 0181 8781133
Chef: Redmond Hayward
Owners: Redmond & Pippa Hayward
Cost: Set-price D £24.50. H/wine £12.50
Times: Noon-2pm/7-10.30pm. Closed L Sat, D Sun, 4 days Xmas, Bhs (ex Good Fri)
Additional: Sunday L; Children welcome; 🍴 dishes
Seats: 54
Smoking: No pipes & cigars; Air conditioning

Directions: Located half-way between Putney and Richmond on the South Circular Road at the Barnes end of Sheen

The Red Pepper

Lively Italian-style restaurant with a relaxed atmosphere. Freshly-prepared pizzas emerge tantalisingly from the wood-fired brick oven, while more traditional Med dishes include smoked swordfish carpaccio and linguine with new potatoes, green beans and pesto sauce.

Smoking: No pipes & cigars; Air conditioning

Directions: ⊖ Warwick Ave

8 Formosa Street W9 1EE
Map: C4
Tel: 0171 2662708
Fax: 0171 2665522
Cost: Alc £20. ☺ H/wine £9
Times: 12.30-2.30pm/6.30-10.45pm.
Closed L Mon-Fri, 25, 26 Dec, 1 Jan
Additional: Sunday L; Children
welcome; ⚫ dishes

Restaurant
Gordon Ramsay ✿✿✿✿✿✿ NEW

For anyone just tuning in, the old Tante Claire premises have been updated, with panels of opaque glass and cappuccino (how apt!) beige suede seats creating a more spacious, lighter effect. It is sometimes hard to separate Ramsay the Chef from Ramsay the Notorious, but perhaps only those with huge talent can get away with such publicity – and no one doubts Ramsay is well endowed with the right stuff. Spotlights enable diners to visually savour every last item on the plate. The three-course menu is interspersed by morsels of delicious things, so to commence there may be a little pot of jellied foie gras mousse, melting over the tongue to enable flavour sensations to be maximised. More than adequate compensation for surprisingly ordinary bread rolls and little cups of rather dull pumpkin soup with girolles and Parmesan topping. First courses, however, banished all doubts with a full-scale serving of roasted scallops with cauliflower purée and mini-florets deep-fried in crunchy batter, played off against a tangy white raisin vinaigrette. Another starter, frogs' legs in a curry batter and Jerusalem artichoke sauce, however, was a tad less successful despite a vibrant, clear-flavoured sauce with velvety texture. Both main courses sampled proved total winners – red mullet on caramelised endive with langoustine beignets and red pepper vinaigrette, and Bresse pigeon, poached and grilled with foie gras pizza, celeriac and truffle sauce, a brilliant combination of perfect ingredients, technique and timing. Just to keep you going before the dessert, all guests are offered a painter's palette of tiny cornets filled with passion fruit cream, a tiny glass of ice cream and a mini lemon balm brûlée. Then come the real desserts – superb chocolate fondant with a biscuity exterior and melted centre, perhaps, or a trio of orange desserts (sorbet, tart and soufflé in a wee copper pan). Coffee and sweetmeats continue the binge to its memorable close. The sommelier has a charmingly unpretentious manner, and although young, possesses an encyclopaedic knowledge of his subject.

66 Royal Hospital Road SW3 4HP
Map: B1
Tel: 0171 3524441
Fax: 0171 3523334
Chef/Owner: Gordon Ramsay
Cost: Alc £50, set-price L £28/D £65
(7 courses). H/wine £15
Times: Noon-2.45pm/6.45-11pm.
Closed Sat, Sun, Xmas, New Year,
Bhs
Seats: 45
Smoking: No pipes & cigars; Air
conditioning

Rhodes in the Square ✿✿

Everything adds up to a relaxed and comfortable environment, with armchair-type chairs 'great for slouching'. White-clothed tables, their china and cutlery shining, stand out amid the predominantly dark blue colour scheme at Gary Rhodes' Pimlico branch, with oblong blocks of colour on some walls. Lobster omelette Thermidor is now something of a signature dish, sharing first-course billing with a typical Rhodes' dish of rich pigeon faggot on a potato cake with

Dolphin Square Chichester Street
SW1V 3LX
Map: D1
Tel: 0171 7986767
Fax: 0171 7985685
Chef: Gary Rhodes
Owner: Gardner Merchant &
Gary Rhodes
Cost: Alc £50, set-price L £19.50. ☺
H/wine £15.95

Rhodes in the Square

Times: Noon-2.15pm/7-9.45pm.
Closed L Sat, D Sun
Additional: Sunday L, Children
welcome; dishes
Seats: 90
Smoking: No pipes & cigars; Air
conditioning

Directions: ⊖ Pimlico

mustard cabbage, or perhaps fillet of trout on a bed of potatoes
zapped up with lime pickle. Roast meats turn up among main
courses in the shape of beef with bitter onions, and loin of
pork, perfectly cooked and most tender, with crackling, sage-
sautéed onions, apple, and mashed potatoes as smooth as silk,
with perhaps tuna steak au poivre among fish dishes. Jaffa-cake
pudding, dense of texture and flavour, comes drizzled with
strong chocolate sauce hinting of Grand Marnier, and lovers of
bread-and-butter pudding will be pleased to find it on the
menu too. The wine list runs to around four pages, with some
serious offerings.

Richmond Gate Hotel ✿✿

Richmond Hill Richmond-upon-
Thames TW10 6RP
Map GtL: B2
Tel: 0181 9400061
Fax: 0181 3320354
Cost: Set-price L £19.25/D £26.75.
H/wine £14.95
Times: 12.30-2.30pm/7-9.30pm.
Closed L Sat
Additional: Sunday L; Children
welcome; ⑨ dishes
Seats: 30. Private dining room 50
Smoking: No smoking in dining room;
Air conditioning
Accommodation: 66 en suite ★★★★

Directions: At top of Richmond Hill
opposite Star & Garter & just outside
Richmond Park

*Gates on the Park is small enough for guests to feel they're
not in a hotel at all.* Yellow, sage green and white are the
main colours, and comfortable chairs, linen-covered tables,
candles and fresh flowers add to the air of quality. The menu
picks up ideas from here, there and everywhere: tuna spring
roll; walnut and potato gnocchi with asparagus and rocket;
pig's trotter and black pudding; red mullet provençale. Chicken
and lobster cannelloni, the meat layered with basil and sage on
a sauce of sweetcorn and saffron, was the star of one meal. It
was followed by nicely flavoured loin of lamb stuffed with
garlic mousse with a spinach gâteau, Swiss chard, parsnip
purée and caramelised carrots. Puddings are no less
accomplished: witness a plate of strawberry soufflé, a brandy
snap of strawberry sorbet and a crisp tart of strawberries in
vanilla cream. Breads are good, a superb eye for detail
oversees petits fours. The wine list runs to five or so pages.

Ristorante L'Incontro ❀❀

It shows how quickly fashions change when one hears that this restaurant is undergoing major refurbishment as we went to press. It was only a few years ago that the decor of chrome, black and white seemed to be the height of modern sophistication, but now Lord Linley has been commissioned to update the party room of this ultra-fashionable establishment, and the colour schemes are all set to change. However, the food remains the same. There is a reasonable set lunch, but when the action takes off in the evenings, prices rocket accordingly. The menu has a strong Venetian theme, and the strength lies in flavour rather than presentation. Carpaccio alla rucola is the only meat dish in the antipasti section, the others are mainly fish. The flavour of 'baccala mantecato' was stunning and came with a good, grainy polenta. Equally delicious was the poached sea bass served on rosemary and accompanied by a small amount of olive oil, balsamic vinegar and fresh herbs. Desserts do not disappoint: we found home-made almond tart to be excellent. The wine list is predominantly, but not entirely, Italian, and extremely expensive.

87 Pimlico Road SW1W 8PH
Map: C1
Tel: 0171 7303663/6327
Fax: 0171 7305062
Chef: Simone Rettore
Owner: Santin Group Ltd
Cost: *Alc* £38.50, set-price L £20.50.
☺ H/wine £15.75
Times: 12.30-2.30pm/7-11.30pm
(10.30pm Sun). Closed L Sat & Sun,
25-26 Dec, some Bhs
Additional: Children welcome;
🍴 dishes
Seats: 65. Private dining room 35.
Jacket & tie preferred
Smoking: No pipes; Air conditioning

Directions: From Lower Sloane Street,
left into Pimlico Road, restaurant is on
R. ⊖ Sloane Square

The Ritz ❀❀

150 Piccadilly W1V 9DG
Map: C3
Tel: 0171 4938181
Fax: 0171 4932687
Chef: Giles Thompson
Cost: *Alc* £55, set-price L £35/ D £45.
H/wine £19.50
Times: 12.30-2.30pm/6-11pm
Additional: Palm Court; Sunday L;
Children welcome; 🍴 dishes
Seats: 120. Private dining rooms 65.
Jacket & tie preferred
Smoking: No pipes; Air conditioning
Accommodation: 131 en suite
★ ★ ★ ★ ★

Directions: ⊖ Green Park

A legend among great metropolitan hotels and the byword for magnificent style and decor. The Ritz is one of London's most famous landmarks and occupies a prime position on Piccadilly overlooking Green Park. The dining room is grandiose, sumptuously furnished, full of gilt and chintz, with polished silver, striking flower arrangements and a giant trompe l'oeil that sweeps across the ornate ceiling. Smart and highly efficient staff tend to your every need, offering either an evening *carte* of international dishes or, by contrast, a lunch menu featuring more traditional items, including grills and roasts from the trolley. Dishes sampled at inspection included a well-made langoustine risotto with saffron, followed by a perfectly timed and well-flavoured loin of veal with sweetbreads and kidney, with a rhubarb and green peppercorn nage compote with savarin and crème fraîche ice cream for dessert.

Riva Restaurant ❀❀❀

Simple, understated decor is offset by big mirrors and cathedral-sized arrangements of flowers. Tables, however, are small and close, yet the spot-on service – no fuss, no intrusion,

169 Church Road Barnes SW13 9HR
Map GtL: C3
Tel/Fax: 0181 7480434
Chef: Francesco Zanchetta
Owner: Andrea Riva

no rush – is a major plus. A short menu features northern
Italian cooking, but the food comes with a difference – at its
base is a good use of fresh herbs and excellent quality primary
ingredients, at the heart a perfect understanding of flavour and
texture contrasts. Pasta is unusual, whether teamed with
roasted chestnuts, mushrooms and Mascarpone, or with
mussels, clams and bottarga, and risotto gets the treatment in a
signature fresh water cray fish, peppers, curry, paprika and
garlic. Beautifully fresh breads of carrot, olive and ciabatta set
the tone for the meal to come. In our case superb grilled squid
with wild herbs, then the centrepiece, an excellent quality pan-
fried calves' liver with garlic-flavoured polenta and wild
mushrooms. An alcoholic tiramisu was chosen from a list of
classic Italian desserts given a modern twist; zabaglione, for
example, served with poached pears, vanilla ice cream and
nocello. The all Italian wine list offers about thirty bins with
prices ranging from £9.50 to £40.

Signature dishes: creamy salt cod on polenta; sturgeon fillets
in a prosecco sauce, black truffles, juniper berries with buck
wheat pasta; roast quails, acacia honey, balsamic vinegar sauce
with mashed potatoes; sbrisolona – maize and almond crumble
soaked in vin santo with Mascarpone

Cost: *Alc* £30. H/wine £9.95
Times: Noon-2.30pm/7-11pm. Closed
L Sat, Xmas, Easter, last 2 wks Aug
Additional: Children welcome;
🍴 dishes
Seats: 50
Smoking: No pipes & cigars; Air
conditioning

Directions: Junction of Church Rd
with Castelnau Rd. ⊖ Hammersmith

River Café

**Simple modern decor, stainless steel and not a lot of room
between tables at this riverside restaurant.** Famously
dedicated to Italian country cooking with an all-Italian wine
list, coarse Tuscan bread arrives with thick, unctuous olive oil
and menus are littered with pasta, risotto, bruschetta and
salads. Vegetables and herbs play an important part in each
dish, and marinades are used to good effect – anchovies in vin
santo served with a flavour-bursting salad of buffalo
Mozzarella, courgettes, mint, basil, Parmesan and marjoram
bruschetta, for instance. The favoured cooking vehicles are the
chargrill and the wood-fired oven, the former to produce
scallops with red chillies, borlotti beans, rocket and red wine
vinegar, the latter loin of organic pork stuffed with porcini,
thyme, lemon zest and prosciutto fat served with broad beans
braised in milk. Sardines might be simply wood-baked with
parsley, breadcrumbs, chilli and lemon zest and served with
dandelion leaves and pine nuts to make a well-balanced
starter, while simplicity and exemplary ingredients show up in
insalata of summer leaves, aged Pecorino and balsamic vinegar.
An inspector wrote rapturously of 'tender' wood-roasted
Bresse pigeon full of gamey flavour accompanied by mixed
roast vegetables with a smattering of herbs, and of wobbly,
silky, grappa-infused pannacotta sprinkled with vanilla seeds
with caramelised blood oranges, concluding 'I was having such
a good time I couldn't leave well alone and had Gorgonzola
and more bread to finish off'.

Thames Wharf Studios Rainville Road
W6 9HA
Map GtL: C3
Tel: 0171 3818824
Fax: 0171 3816217
Chefs/Owners: Rose Gray,
Ruth Rogers
Cost: *Alc* £63. H/wine £9.50
Times: 12.30-3pm/7-9.45pm. Closed
D Sun, Bhs
Additional: Sunday L; Children
welcome; 🍴 dishes
Seats: 90
Smoking: No pipes & cigars

Directions: Off Fulham Palace Rd.
Junction of Rainville Road and
Bowfell Road. ⊖ Hammersmith

R.K. Stanleys

*British bangers are the speciality of this upmarket, child-friendly
diner near Oxford Circus – try game, Thai and Caribbean-style
varieties plus daily specials such as calves' liver and bacon.*

Smoking: No-smoking area; Air conditioning

Directions: ⊖ Oxford Circus

6 Little Portland Street W1N 5AG
Map: B3
Tel: 0171 4620099
Fax: 0171 4620088
Times: Noon-11.30pm.
Closed Sun
Additional: Children welcome;
🍴 dishes

Roussillon

Anyone feeling world-weary about the London restaurant scene should book a table at Roussillon. It is rare to find somewhere so truly original in this age of camp followers and overworked trends. Alexis Gaulthier comes with an impressive pedigree, via Alain Ducasse and Chez Panisse, but is blazing his own path. Menus are strictly seasonal, even the covers depict the appropriate seasonal plants; the vegetarian 'Garden' menu that included, in spring, Kentish dandelion, wild rocket and baby red chard in balsamic vinegar dressing, and chrysanthemum soufflé with oven roasted leaves, might be the best in London. Ingredients are wonderful – organic Ross chicken, organic Scottish beef, Welsh lamb, Blue Bembridge lobster – and cooked in exciting ways to extract maximum flavour. Monkfish is pot-roasted in chicken jus with country bacon, girolles, button onions and braised lettuce; grilled pigeon is served with large slices of potato and foie gras. A dessert of confit beetroot and ginger tartlet with lemon aromatic cream challenges preconceptions, as does a main course of grilled sea bass with raw and cooked purple artichoke, carrot and radish leaves. Gaulthier, however, does not lack a sense of humour: note his spicy, soft-boiled organic Red House Farm egg, with gingerbread fingers and a maple infusion. Boiled egg and soldiers for the chattering classes. Brilliant.

16 St Barnabas Street SW1W 8PB
Map: C1
Tel: 0171 7305550
Fax: 0171 8248617
Chef: Alexis Gauthier
Owners: James & Andrew Palmer, Alexis Gauthier
Cost: Alc £28, set-price L £16/D £18 (2 courses). ☺ H/wine £12.50
Times: Noon-2.15pm/7-10.15pm. Closed Sun, 15-28 Aug, 24 Dec-5 Jan
Additional: Children 12+; ◑ dishes
Seats: 50. Private dining room 25
Smoking: No-smoking area; No pipes & cigars; Air conditioning

Directions: ⊖ Sloane Square. Off Pimlico Road

Royal China W2 & SW15

Hugely popular Chinese restaurant. Expect an extensive menu of mainly Szechuan and Cantonese dishes, along with a few unexpected specialities. Stewed eggplant with minced pork in spicy black bean sauce in a clay pot and grilled dumplings go down a treat. The sister branch at 3 Chelverton Road, Putney, tel 0181 788 0907, also comes highly commended.

13 Queensway W2 4QJ
Map: A3
Tel/Fax: 0171 221 2535
Telephone for further details

Directions: ⊖ Queensway, Bayswater

Royal Garden Hotel

2-24 Kensington High Street W8 4PT
Map GtL: C3
Tel: 0171 9378000
Fax: 0171 3611991
Chef: Derek Baker
Cost: Alc £40, set-price L £21. H/wine £13.25
Times: Noon-2.30pm/5.30-11pm.

Take the lift from the marble-floored lobby at this tall, modern hotel, get out at the tenth floor and take a table in the contemporary, bright, smart restaurant and gasp at the views over Kensington Gardens and Hyde Park. With its base in the classical repertoire, the kitchen grabs modern idea, often from the East, and produces zappy dishes of vibrant flavours: seared scallops on sweet-and-sour chicory with sauce vierge, galantine of oriental chicken and tuna with ravigote dressing, and main courses of roasted sea bass with braised leeks and a caramelised onion bhajia, or pan-fried calves' liver with blue cheese gnocchi à l'alsacienne. An inspector started with wild mushroom soufflé, full of fungus flavour, tipped on a neat pile of crisp pear finished off with watercress salad and blobs of truffle mayonnaise, and then enjoyed a main course of flaky fillet of cod with tomato risotto and olives. Puddings end a 'fun and enjoyable experience' on an upbeat note in the shape of banana soufflé with sweet-and-sour lychee ice cream, or a spot-on bitter redcurrant tart with orange sorbet.

Closed L Sat, all Sun
Additional: ✿ dishes
Seats: 100
Smoking: No-smoking area
Accommodation: 400 en suite
★ ★ ★ ★ ★

Directions: Next door to Kensington Palace. ⊖ High Street Kensington

Royal Lancaster Hotel, Nipa Thai ✿✿

Elegant oriental-style dining room and efficient service from some of the friendliest staff we have ever encountered. There are strong Thai links as The Royal Lancaster is a sister to the Landmark in Bangkok. An all-female team runs the kitchen with staff in traditional dress out front. The menu is sensibly less extensive than is the norm, and offers a good selection of expected dishes such as curries, salads, and pan-fried dishes. We tried a delicious kao krieb pak moh (steamed minced chicken with peanuts in a Thai flour crêpe), kaeng kiew warn kai (green chicken curry authentically produced with tiny Thai aubergines, basil leaves and coconut milk), and phad kraprao kung (stir-fried prawns with basil leaves) and fragrant jasmine rice. A selection of traditional Thai puddings are offered, but these are an acquired taste.

Lancaster Terrace W2 2TY
Map GtL: C3
Tel: 0171 2626737
Fax: 0171 7243191
Chef: Nongyao Thoopchoi
Cost: *Alc* £26, set-price L & D £23/£26. ☺ H/wine £17
Times: Noon-2pm/6.30-10.30pm. Closed L Sat, all Sun
Additional: Children welcome; ✿ dishes.
Seats: 55
Smoking: Air conditioning
Accommodation: 416 en suite
★ ★ ★ ★

Directions: Opposite Hyde Park on the Bayswater Road. On 1st floor of hotel. ⊖ Lancaster Gate

Royal Lancaster Hotel, Park Restaurant ✿✿

Some of the best view across Hyde Park and Kensington Gardens can be had from the upper floors of this 18-storey hotel. And considering it is hard against Lancaster Gate Tube station – giving easy access to the rest of the capital – the location couldn't be bettered. Mediterranean in style, The Pavement caters for all-day snacking and grazing, but it's in the smart Park Restaurant that serious cooking takes place with

Lancaster Terrace W2 2TY
Map GtL: C3
Tel: 0171 2626737
Fax: 0171 7243191
Chef: Nigel Blatchford
Cost: Set-price L & D £23.50. ☺ H/wine £17
Times: 12.30-2.30pm/6.30-10.30pm. Closed L Sat, all Sun

**Royal Lancaster Hotel,
Park Restaurant**

Additional: Children welcome;
🍴 dishes
Seats: 60. Private dining room 6.
Jacket & tie preferred
Smoking: Air conditioning
Accommodation: 416 en suite
★ ★ ★ ★

Directions: Opposite Hyde Park on
the Bayswater Road. On 1st floor of
hotel. ⊖ Lancaster Gate

foie gras and duck liver parfait, lobster, tiger prawns,
langoustines, monkfish and mussels in a Thermidor sauce, and
an excellent lemon tart, chosen from the dessert trolley,
showing the range of modern British cooking.

RSJ, The Restaurant on the South Bank

13a Coin Street SE1 8YQ
Map: E3
Tel: 0171 6330881
Fax: 0171 4012455
Owner: Nigel Wilkinson
Telephone for further details

*Comfortable restaurant, a short walk from the South Bank
Centre.* The interior, designed by Julian Wykeham, is a joy
with its bright yellows and silver-grey and white paintwork.
The restaurant is spread over three floors with the kitchen on
the ground floor. The cooking style has kept up with fashion
with fish dishes being particularly good. We came for lunch and
chose from the keenly priced lunch menu – wild mushroom
risotto, then tenderloin of pork with slices of black pudding
celeriac and carrot purées, and a delicious caramelised apple
and Calvados sauce. The menu is supported by a daily
changing selection of specials such as guinea fowl and foie gras
sausage with petit pois and roast beetroot stuffed with goats'
cheese, mushrooms, tofu and crispy carrots. The wine list is
justly famous and includes a particularly interesting selection
of Loire wines.

Directions: On the corner of Coin St
and Stamford St; near National
Theatre and LWT studios

Rules 🌸🌸

35 Maiden Lane Covent Garden
WC2E 7LB
Map: D3
Tel: 0171 8365314
Fax: 0171 4971081
Chef: David Chambers
Owner: John Mayhew
Cost: *Alc* £31, pre-theatre D (3-6pm)
£18.95 (2 courses). H/wine £12.50
Times: Open all day, noon-11.30pm.
Closed 4 days Xmas
Additional: Sunday L
Seats: 140. Private dining rooms 65
Smoking: Air conditioning

*Rules was described by the late Sir John Betjeman as 'unique
and irreplaceable, part of literary and theatrical London',
and as the century closes, will have been serving its clientele
through four centuries.* The modernisation of Rules has been
seamless. There has been no makeover as at J Sheeky's, the
interior has the patina of age, with black-painted woodwork
and the nicotine-coloured walls crammed with pictures,
cartoons and prints. The menu relies on safe English classics
like Morecambe Bay potted brown shrimps in spiced lobster
butter. A twice-baked mushroom and goats' cheese soufflé is
about the most adventurous starter. The main courses include
freshwater and sea fish (four choices), prime Aberdeen Angus
beef (five choices), lamb (two) and their signature dishes of
feathered and furred game (there are eight – with a number of
birds served in season). Seasonal birds are provided by the
owners' country estate. Thirty-seven wines are listed.

Directions: ⊖ Covent Garden

Sabras

Charming old timer with twenty-five years under its belt. The atmosphere at this family-run restaurant is comfortable, with upholstered chairs, and functional Formica-topped tables. The menu is entirely vegetarian, covering mumbai specialities from Bombay, south Indian pancakes, north Indian dal-subji dishes, and some offerings from the owner's home region, Gujarat. Starters include delicious farassan, which come with suitable chutneys and patra, consisting of yam leaves spread with flour batters, garlic, tamarind, sesame seeds and spices then rolled, steamed, sliced and fried. Our inspection chickpea curry from the Punjab proved to be 'the best I have ever had – containing not only cucumber and carrot but home-made curd and spices', and puri was nicely puffed-up without being too crisp. Basudi, a creamy milk-based dessert flavoured with almonds, pistachios and cardamoms, was served refreshingly chilled. The restaurant does offer some wines and beers, but it is well worth trying their excellent lassi or the freshly pressed apple and carrot juice.

Willesden High Road NW10 2RX
Map GtL: C3
Tel: 0181 4590340
Credit cards: None
Telephone for further details

Directions: ⊖ Willesden Green

St John

Converted smoke-house with large paper-clad wooden tables. Minimalist menu offers 'nose-to-tail' eating such as tripe, fennel and butter bean soup, pot-roasted Gloucester Old Spot, and cods roe, bacon and spinach.

Additional: Bar food; Children welcome; ⚬ dishes
Smoking: Air conditioning

26 St John Street EC1M 4AY
Map: F5
Tel: 0171 2510848
Fax: 0171 2514090
Cost: Alc £25
Times: Noon-3pm/6-11.30pm. Closed L Sat, all Sun, Xmas

Directions: ⊖ Farringdon. 100 metres from Smithfield Market on N side

St Quentin Brasserie

Slick, professional French brasserie with all the expected buzz. Burgundy snails with asparagus, ceps and tarragon in puff pastry, roast monkfish with pancetta, basil and tomato butter sauce, and calves' liver with caramelised shallots, bacon and creamed potatoes have been well reported.

243 Brompton Road SW3 2EP
Map: B2
Tel: 0171 5898005
Fax: 0171 5846064
Owner: Groupe Chez Gerard
Telephone for further details

Directions: ⊖ South Kensington. Opposite Brompton Oratory

Salloos

Long established family-run Pakistani restaurant in an old mews house. We enjoyed a good chicken shish kebab, and the palak gosht – a mildly spiced dish of lamb and spinach – was excellent.

Additional: Children 8+, ⚬ dishes
Smoking: No pipes & cigars; Air conditioning

62-64 Kinnerton Street
SW1X 8ER
Map: B2
Tel: 0171 2354444
Fax: 0171 2595703
Cost: Alc £30, set-price L £16. ☺
Times: Closed Sun

Directions: Nr. Hyde Park Corner – take 1st L into Wilton Place, 1st R opposite Berkeley Hotel. ⊖ Knightsbridge

Santini

A smart Italian restaurant with a welcoming atmosphere. The cooking emphasises its Venetian roots – try scallops sautéed in wine, butter and olive oil followed by tagliatelle with porcini mushrooms. Finish with an Italian pastry and a great heart-stopping espresso.

Smoking: No pipes; Air conditioning

Directions: On corner of Ebury Street and Lower Belgrave Street. ↔ Victoria

29 Ebury Street SW1W 0NZ
Map: C1
Tel: 0171 7304094
Fax: 0171 7300544
Cost: *Alc* £37.50, set-price L £19.75. ☺ H/wine £15.75
Times: 12.30-2.30pm/7-11.30pm (10.30pm Sun). Closed L Sat, L Sun, 25, 26 Dec, some Bhs
Additional: Children welcome; ⌕ dishes

Sartoria ⊛⊛

Given the Saville Row address, no Conran restaurant could fail to take advantage of the thematic inspiration. It is, however, done stylishly and wittily with 'safari-suit' beige marble floor, 'business-suit' grey walls, chairs and banquettes, 'shirt-white' table linen - although two obese tailors dummies at the entrance are a little off-putting. Antimacassars sport a silver-grey needle and thread motif, and there are framed, folded shirts and ties on the wall. A slick team of staff wear the traditional black and white with long aprons, and there is a smart cocktail bar with over twenty grappas on the list. Sophisticated school of River Café cooking includes rabbit risotto with borlotti beans and rosemary, and pan-fried scallops with fresh broad beans, peas and mint. Green tomato tart with zabaglione proved surprisingly good, the seeded tomatoes tasting like delicate apricots. Espresso is served with Amaretti di Saronno.

20 Saville Row W1X 1AE
Map: D3
Tel: 0171 5347000
Fax: 0171 5347070
Chef: Darren Simpson
Owner: Sir Terence Conran
Cost: *Alc* £40. ☺ £14
Times: Noon-3.15pm/6.30-10.45pm. Closed L Sun, 25 Dec, Bhs
Additional: Bar food; Children welcome; ⌕ dishes
Seats: 120. Private dining rooms 16-32
Smoking: Air conditioning

Directions: ↔ Piccadilly Circus, Oxford Circus. Corner of New Burlington Street & Saville Row, off Regent Street

Sauce ⊛   NEW

Brightly coloured modern diner. Ingredients are 95% organic, and include all day brunch, salads, main plates ranging from veggie burger to braised saffron lamb, and that millennium version of the sandwich – wraps.

Smoking: No pipes & cigars; Air conditioning

Directions: Telephone for directions

214 Camden High Street NW1 8QR
Map GtL: C3
Tel: 0171 4820777
Cost: *Alc* £25
Times: Noon-11pm. Closed D Sun, 25, 26 Dec
Additional: Bar food; Sunday L; Children welcome; ⌕ dishes

Savoy Grill ⊛⊛

Often regarded as the place where men, as opposed to ladies, lunch. Indeed, many regard the Savoy Grill as their private club, but it is equally accessible to all who wish to experience a real British institution. The room is dominated by the yew-wood panelling and there are a series of private booths. The menu is dominated by the regular daily items: Lancashire hotpot on Mondays, roast rib of beef on Thursdays, and so on, but some marginally more interesting dishes are offered on the *carte*. Much enjoyed by our reporter was a delicious shallot tarte Tatin with Mascarpone and rocket salad – featured under the specialities of the chef, and a main course of wood pigeon, peas enveloped in ravioli and bacon with a good reduced sauce. From the sweet trolley came a wide selection, notably pecan pie, crème brûlée, profiteroles and tiramisu, but the extremely impressive cheese board might hold more attraction here. The service is both professional and solicitous.

Strand WC2R 0EU
Map: E3
Tel: 0171 8364343
Fax: 0171 2406040
Chef: Simon Scott
Owner: The Savoy Group plc
Cost: *Alc* £55, pre-theatre D £29.75. H/wine £19
Times: 12.30-2.30pm/6-11.15pm. Closed L Sat, all Sun, Aug
Additional: Children 12+; ⌕ dishes
Seats: 85. Jacket & tie preferred
Smoking: No pipes; Air conditioning
Accommodation: 207 en suite
★ ★ ★ ★ ★

Directions: ↔ Embankment. Walk E through riverside gardens to hotel

The Savoy,
River Restaurant ✿✿✿

Everyone wants to sit beside the window, so it's a privilege to secure one of the coveted tables. The setting generates a sense of keen anticipation and the atmosphere is relaxed in the best European way, despite the formality of the smoked salmon and dessert trolleys and silver cloches. Luxury ingredients are part of the style – home-made goose liver pâté is served with duck confit and truffle salad, and Beluga caviar with buckwheat blinis is there for the big deal-signing moment. A seasonal menu, matched with wines from the Savoy Cellars, might be centred around roast milk-fed lamb filled with its farce, with new Jersey potatoes baked with onions and melted Parmesan tomatoes. Our meal began with creamy chilled celeriac and pea soup adorned with a swirl of truffle oil, and followed by Scottish salmon rosette set in a cucumber jelly. Light and delicious, it was just the thing for an early summer meal. Halibut with aubergines was tip-top, but devilled kidneys needed better trimming and crispier herb beignets. Anton Edelmann keeps a sharp eye on trends, but uses new ideas with discretion, thus he updates organic fillet of Welsh lamb with braised fennel and tamarillo chutney, and adds a touch of class to pine nut soufflé with a red wine ice cream.

Strand WC2R 0EU
Map: E3
Tel: 0171 8361533
Fax: 0171 4202576
Chef: Anton Edelmann
Owner: The Savoy Group plc
Cost: Alc £56, set-price L £29.75/D £39.50 (£43.50 Sat & Sun). H/wine £19
Times: 12.30-2.30pm/6-11.30pm
Additional: Bar food; Sunday L; Children welcome; ✿ dishes
Seats: 150. Private rooms 200-250. Jacket & tie preferred
Smoking: No-smoking area; Air conditioning
Accommodation: 207 en suite
★ ★ ★ ★ ★

Directions: ⊖ Embankment. Walk E through riverside gardens to hotel

Scotts ✿

Purple and gold, with the look of a 1930s ocean liner, Scotts sails through a splendid fish and seafood carte in a style that befits its ritzy Mayfair address.

Additional: Bar food; Sunday L; Children welcome; ✿ dishes
Smoking: No-smoking area; Air conditioning

Directions: Mount St runs between Park Lane and Berkeley Sq. ⊖ Green Park

20 Mount Street W1Y 6HE
Map: C3
Tel: 0171 6295248
Fax: 0171 4998246
Cost: Alc £45, set-price L £24.50. H/wine £12
Times: Noon-3pm/6-11pm

Searcy's Brasserie ✿

Library Floor Barbican Centre Silk Street EC2Y 8DS
Map: F4
Tel: 0171 5883008
Fax: 0171 3827247
Cost: Alc £32.50, set-price L & D £21.50. ☺ H/wine £10.95
Times: Noon-2.30pm/5-10.30pm (till 6.30 Sun). Closed L Sat, 2 days Xmas
Additional: Sunday L; Children welcome; ✿ dishes
Seats: 100
Smoking: No-smoking area; Air conditioning

Modern brasserie in the Barbican Centre that comes into its own when combined with a concert or play. Strong Med influences in carpaccio of scallops with red pepper purée, and cannon of lamb with aubergine and pine kernel caviar.

Directions: ⊖ Barbican, Moorgate

Selsden Park Hotel

The vast restaurant is quite grand in the 'old' sense, overseen by a willing team of professional staff. The menu is adventurous, and the presentation of dishes, at times, is stunning. There is serious intent and commitment towards full-flavoured, honest-tasting dishes with an underlying theme of simplicity. Cappuccino of brown shrimps and scallops was served with a spoonful of the thinnest, deep-fried onion rings; penne with ham, spring peas and sorrel possessed a balance of accurate flavours. Well-thought out main courses range from salmon roasted pink with French beans and harissa crème fraîche to daube of beef with black olives, Italian parsley and horseradish croûtons. Our inspector almost thought a flying saucer had landed on the plate, with the arrival of a lemon meringue mille-feuille composed of whimsical, wafer-thin biscuits.

Directions: 3m SE of Croydon off A2022

Addington Road Sanderstead South
Croydon CR2 8YA
Map 4: TQ36
Tel: 0181 6578811
Fax: 0181 6516171
Chef: Stephen Cane
Cost: Alc £37.50, set-price D £24.95
(4 courses). ☺ H/wine £12.95
Times: 12.30-2pm/7-9.30pm
Additional: Bar food; Sunday L;
Children welcome; ✦ dishes
Seats: 280. Private dining room 40.
Jacket & tie preferred
Smoking: No smoking in dining room;
Air conditioning
Accommodation: 205 en suite
★ ★ ★ ★

755 Fulham Road

755 Fulham Road SW6 5UU
Map: A1
Tel: 0171 3710755
Fax: 0171 3710695
Chef: Alan Thompson
Owners: Alan & Georgina Thompson
Cost: Alc £32, set-price L £12.50/D
£18 (both 2 courses). ☺ H/wine
£12.50
Times: 12.30-2.30pm/7-11pm. Closed
D Sun, all Mon, 10 days Xmas, 2 wks
summer, Bhs
Additional: Sunday L (noon-4pm);
Children welcome on Sun; ✦ dishes
Seats: 45. Private dining room 35
Smoking: Air conditioning

Two creamy-coloured floors with two small, narrow rooms, but a menu that is big in scope. Service by smartly uniformed staff is professional and attentive, overseen by Georgina Thompson who manages front of house, whilst husband Alan goes from strength to strength behind the scenes. Strong flavours predominate – roast oxtail with sweet potato and red onion fondue; braised pig's trotter with sweetbreads and truffle potato purée; roast and confit mallard with rösti potato and sweetcorn purée. Griddled foie gras with Yorkshire pudding and Madeira is offered with an optional glass of Monbazillac. Fish is no exception to the big, bold style, both seared Cajun mackerel with aubergine caviar and endive salad, and bouillabaisse of monkfish with green lip mussels and vermicelli are vibrant and confident ideas. Rabbit and pine nut terrine with beetroot and balsamic salad was a perfect match of ideas and execution. Precisely timed, crisp-skinned pan-fried sea bream was given textural contrast and a touch of acidity with creamy cauliflower brandade and sautéed artichokes. Warm prune and Armagnac beignets filled with ice cream are the test of any kitchen's capabilities – here, they are not to be missed.

Directions: ⊖ Parsons Green

Shepherds

It takes someone of the stature of Richard Shepherd to develop this site into a profitable restaurant and succeed where others have failed. Shepherds works to a tried-and-tested formula – one which certainly finds favour with the inhabitants of Pimlico and Westminster. Touchingly, Peter Langan who died in 1990, is still featured on the menu alongside Shepherd and co-owner Michael Caine. Neither the decor nor the menu are follow current fashion trends – the latter being rather long by today's standards with seventeen starters, eighteen main courses and twelve desserts – but it is thoroughly British in the old-fashioned sense. Steak and kidney pudding, roast beef and Yorkshire pudding, haunch of venison with chestnuts and port sauce, and grilled plaice with parsley butter are typical, although there is a sprinkling of more exotic dishes, such as spinach and ricotta dumplings with a red pepper sauce. The wine list is very assured.

Directions: Near Tate Gallery and Westminster Hospital.
⊖ Pimlico

Marsham Court Marsham Street
SW1P 4LA
Map: D2
Tel: 0171 8349552
Fax: 0171 2336047
Chef: Jeremy Stent
Owners: Richard Shepherd & Michael Caine
Cost: Set-price L £22.95 (2 courses)/D £24.95. H/wine £11.50
Times: 12.30-2.45pm/6.30-11pm. Closed Sat, Sun, Bhs
Additional: Bar food; Children welcome; ✿ dishes
Seats: 90. Private dining room 32
Smoking: No-smoking area; Air conditioning

Sheraton Park Tower, Restaurant One-O-One

Light nautical colours blend in with some colourful food prints and there is a welcome sense of spaciousness. Window tables look down over the heavy traffic and busy shoppers of Knightsbridge. Pascal Proyart's 'cuisine de la mer' fits the setting well and includes scallops and sea bass cooked in half a dozen different ways, especially the latter baked whole in a crust of Brittany rock sea salt (for two). The foundation is French from the Dover sole with sauce dijonnaise to the pan-seared John Dory with forestière potato and beurre piment à l'ail doux. The choice is extensive, an embarrassment of riches perhaps, with starters such as mouclade de moules marinière, soupe de poisson with grilled flaked red mullet or sea-scallops and cep mushroom Parmesan risotto, not to mention around seventeen main courses on the *carte*. Our inspector finally opted for great flavoured, slow-roasted salmon tournedos and foie gras with its own jus and sauce périgourdine, the fish moulded into a boneless circle with excellent saucing. There are some non-piscatorial inclusions such as Scottish fillet of beef roasted in mustard and parsley with red Burgundy sauce. One of the most intriguing desserts is pear and goats' cheese honey-crusted parcel with ginger ice cream.

Directions: ⊖ Knightsbridge. E, just after Harvey Nichols

101 Knightsbridge SW1X 7RN
Map: B2
Tel: 0171 2907101
Fax: 0171 2356196
Chef: Pascal Proyart
Owner: Starwood Sheraton Hotels
Cost: *Alc* £40, set-price L £24/D £49 (4 courses). H/wine £17.95
Times: Noon-2.30pm/7-10.30pm
Additional: Children welcome
Seats: 86
Smoking: Air conditioning
Accommodation: 289 en suite
★★★★★

Sheraton Skyline

Airport hotel offering formal service from genuine and fun staff, innovative and daring combinations from the kitchen, with spicy crab broth, and a smooth chocolate and rosemary tart wowing us at inspection.

Directions: Telephone for directions

Bath Road Hayes UB3 5BP
Tel: 020 87592535
Fax: 020 87509150
Telephone for further details

Simply Nico

This, the original Simply Nico, is the pick of a bunch of a chain owned by the Restaurant Partnership; it remains closest to the precept laid down by Nico Ladenis. 'They've got everything pretty much right here', comments our inspector on the pleasant setting, slick, friendly staff, straightforward (and good-value) pricing, and sound, uncomplicated French cooking that largely sticks to tried-and-trusted combinations. This translates as mushroom and artichoke tartlet with poached egg and hollandaise, corn-fed chicken with spinach and morel sauce, shank of lamb with roast parsnip and rosemary jus. Two dishes, grilled goats' cheese with red pepper and basil oil, and foie gras with caramelised oranges are fixtures, by popular demand, otherwise the menu changes gradually over time. Puddings fit the mould with a pear and frangipane tart with caramel ice cream going down nicely.

48a Rochester Row SW1P 1JU
Map: D2
Tel: 0171 6308061
Fax: 0171 8288541
Chef: Richard Hugill
Owner: The Restaurant Partnership
Cost: Set-price D £28.50. H/wine £13.50
Times: Closed L Sat, all Sun
Additional: Children 10+; 🍴 dishes
Seats: 45
Smoking: No pipes & cigars; Air conditioning

Directions: ⊖ Victoria

Singapore Garden

Situated in a shopping parade: two former shop units, one with a bar and counter. Cream walls, plain wood floors, with tables laid with wipeable paper squares, paper napkins and fresh carnations add up to unremarkable decor. There is a long *carte* which is primarily Chinese, with a section of Singapore and Malaysian dishes; it is from these two latter areas that the dishes are of particular note. We found Singaporean laska to be a substantial creamy soup with a gentle curry flavour and containing rice vermicelli and bean sprouts, a fish cake was very moreish with its tangy coriander taste, and lemongrass chicken may have lacked lemongrass, but it did have a potent chilli flavour and the chicken was succulent. That dish came with spring onion tops, straw mushrooms with seasonal greens , including some perfectly-cooked broccoli florets. Singapore Garden has been open for sixteen years, with a sister restaurant in Gloucester Place, NW1.

83/83a Fairfax Road NW6 4DY
Map GtL: C4
Tel: 0171 3285314
Fax: 0171 6240656
Chef/Owner: Siam Kiang Lim
Cost: *Alc* £20, set-price L £8/D £17.50 (5 courses). ☺ H/wine £10.95
Times: Noon-2.45pm/6-10.45pm (11.15pm Fri & Sat). Closed 1 wk Xmas
Additional: Sunday L; Children welcome; 🍴 dishes
Seats: 100
Smoking: No pipes & cigars; Air conditioning

Directions: Off Finchley Road, on R before Belsize Park roundabout. ⊖ Swiss Cottage, Finchley Road. No parking restrictions

Snows-on-the-Green

Bright decor bring a hint of the Mediterranean to this double-fronted restaurant. The menu gives more than a nod towards the Med too. Tuscan bean, sausage and cabbage soup with sun-dried tomatoes and pesto crostini, a carpaccio of venison, or risotto of smoked haddock, Cheddar and saffron (full of flavour, with all the ingredients shining through) were among the starters on a winter menu. Robust coq au vin on a bed of 'superb' mash, baked cod in a herb crust with lyonnaise potatoes, braised pig's trotters with sweetbreads, chorizo, apples and mash are what you can expect for main courses, with spicy vegetable roulade with a mango, lime and cucumber salsa among the vegetarian choices. Tarte Tatin was described as 'delicious'.

166 Shepherd's Bush Road Hammersmith W6 7PB
Map GtL: C3
Tel: 0171 6032142
Fax: 0171 6027553
Chef/Owner: Sebastian Snow
Cost: *Alc* £25, set-price L £16.50. ☺ H/wine £10.50
Times: Noon-3pm/6-11pm. Closed Sat L, D Sun, Bh Mon
Additional: Sunday L; Children welcome; 🍴 dishes
Seats: 100. Private dining room 25
Smoking: No-smoking area; Air conditioning

Directions: ⊖ Hammersmith, Goldhawk Road. Opposite Brook Green

Sonny's Restaurant

Restaurant, café and small delicatessen rolled into one.
Sonny's has been totally refurbished, extended towards the
rear in a bright, modern style, with a specially commissioned
fireplace in the back wall. At inspection, a main course of roast
partridge on braised red cabbage with a glazed pear and five
spice sauce 'did justice to both season and seasoning'.
Otherwise, there might be dishes such as grilled monkfish with
a risotto of lemon and ginger and coriander essence. A starter
of black pasta with pan-fried calamari and scallops is as
attractively presented as it can be, while the more robust
appetite could opt for pig's trotters with grain mustard dressing
and Jerusalem artichoke crisps. Ginger and cardamom brûlée
tart with vanilla tuiles makes a tempting dessert. The set two-
course lunch is so popular that service can become stretched.
The two-page wine list is helpfully annotated, with a decent
choice by the glass.

Directions: From Castlenau end of Church Road, on left by
shops. ⊖ Hammersmith

94 Church Road Barnes SW13 0DQ
Map: C3
Tel: 0181 7480393
Fax: 0181 7482698
Chef: Leigh Diggins
Owner: Rebecca Mascarenhas
Cost: *Alc* £22.50, set-price L £12 (2
courses). ☺ H/wine £9.50
Times: 12.30-2.30pm/7.30-11pm.
Closed D Sun, Bhs
Additional: Bar food L; Sunday L;
Children welcome; ⌀ dishes
Seats: 100. Private dining room 24
Smoking: No pipes & cigars; Air
conditioning

Sotheby's, The Café

*Great little restaurant which spills out into the main corridor
of the world-famous auctioneers.* Chef Caroline Crumby has
been here since the place opened, and there's no doubting her
enthusiasm and commitment to organic produce. The daily-
changing menu offers a small choice at each course, the style is
modern brasserie: leek and pancetta tartlet with a poached egg
and hollandaise, grilled fillet of red mullet nicely set off by an
anchovy and rosemary dressing with braised fennel with rocket
salad, and fig ice cream with blackcurrant sauce show what the
kitchen's about. Service is swift – as it needs to be during busy
lunchtimes – friendly and helpful, and Sotheby's wine
department has had a hand in the carefully compiled, short list.
Note that The Café is also open for breakfast and afternoon
tea.

34 Bond Street W1A 2AA
Map: D4
Tel: 0171 2935077
Fax: 0171 2955920
Chef: Caroline Crumby
Cost: *Alc* £22
Times: L only, noon-3pm. Closed Sat,
Sun, Xmas, New Year, last 2 wks Aug
Additional: ⌀ dishes
Seats: 46
Smoking: No smoking in dining room;
Air conditioning

Directions: ⊖ Bond Street

Spiga

*Busy, informal Italian from the Giorgio Locatelli stable. Strong line
in pizzas from a wood-fired oven, but pasta, rabbit with polenta and
grilled radicchio, or braised cod with cherry tomatoes, black olives
and basil, make a strong showing.*

Additional: Children welcome; ⌀ dishes
Smoking: No pipes & cigars; Air conditioning

Directions: At the Shaftesbury Avenue end of Wardour Street

84-86 Wardour Street W1V 3LF
Map: D4
Tel: 0171 7343444
Fax: 0171 7343332
Cost: *Alc* £23. ☺ H/wine £10.50
Times: Noon-3pm/6-midnight (11pm
Sun, Mon, Tue)

La Spighetta

*Italian restaurant with an open wood-burning oven producing a
great range of pizzas. Dishes sampled have included chargrilled
mushrooms with polenta, and pan-fried calves' liver with mash.*

Directions: Half way down Baker St towards Oxford St turn L
into Blandford St. ⊖ Baker St

43 Blandford Street W1H 3AE
Map: B4
Tel/Fax: 0171 4867340
Telephone for further details

The Square

Huge etched windows, a parquet floor, abstracts on the walls and well-spaced tables all add up to a contemporary, sophisticated restaurant. Philip Howard is one of London's finest, an innovative, inspired chef whose cooking draws an appreciative crowd – The Square is one of the most booked-up restaurants in town. Herb risotto with oysters, salmon, caviar and champagne, roast Bresse pigeon with stuffed Savoy cabbage, crusted brill with leeks, noodles and truffles and tournedos Rossini show the sort of things the kitchen deals in – an understated modern classicism that revels in contrasts of texture and flavour. An *amuse-bouche* of, say, frothy mushroom soup arrives first, and then a terrine – of foie gras with duck confit and truffles – or crisp red mullet with anchovy blinis, fennel and tapenade. Loin of venison, perfect of timing and texture, makes a fine main course, served with celeriac purée and caramelised vegetables arranged in a tower, or there might be fillet of salmon with root vegetables and red wine, or daube de boeuf of a size that 'would have satisfied any French front-row forward'. As a finale, a classic tarte Tatin with rum ice cream, or soft, intense prune and Armagnac soufflé. Breads are good, and petits fours make coffee something special. Service can be stretched at busy times but staff are knowledgeable about food and wine – as they need to be with a list running to around 40 pages (although a page of the sommelier's selection eases choice).

Directions: Bond Street

6 Bruton Street W1X 7AG
Map: C3
Tel: 0171 4957100
Fax: 0171 4957150
Chef: Philip Howard
Owners: Philip Howard & Nigel Platts-Martin
Cost: Alc £48, set-price D £45. H/wine £18.50
Times: Noon-2.45pm/7-11pm. Closed L Sat & Sun, 25-26 Dec, 1 Jan
Additional: Children 10+; ✿ dishes
Seats: 70. Private dining room 18
Smoking: No pipes & cigars; Air conditioning

The Stafford ✿✿

Luxury is the trademark of this 18th-century town-house hotel. The restaurant, strong on the comfort factor, occupies a large, well-proportioned room with a muralled ceiling, chandelier, sconces, silver carvery trolleys and big glasses waiting for big vintages to be poured into them. The kitchen weaves its own distinctive course between the traditional, the classical and the fashionable, from roast chicken with roast potatoes, cabbage and chopped carrots, through Dover sole meunière, to roast veal cutlet topped with tomato, Parma ham and a Parmesan biscuit with fried polenta and chargrilled marinated aubergine. An inspector started with shellfish bisque bursting with flavour, continued with lamb cutlet minced with red pepper and basil, then pan-fried and served with a meaty

16-18 St James's Place SW1A 1NJ
Map: D4
Tel: 0171 4930111
Fax: 0171 4937121
Chef: Chris Oakes
Owner: Shire Inns Ltd
Cost: Alc £43, set-price L £22 (2 courses)/D £29. H/wine £17.50
Times: 12.30-2.30pm/6-10.30pm. Closed L Sat
Additional: Bar food; Sunday L; Children 8+; ✿ dishes
Seats: 50. Private room 44. Jacket & tie preferred
Smoking: No pipes & cigars; Air conditioning
Accommodation: 81 en suite ★ ★ ★ ★

Directions: Green Park. 5 mins St James's Palace

jus, cubed breadcrumbed potatoes and spring greens, and finished with Sussex pond pudding, its plate drizzled with custard, although chocolate and orange bread-and-butter pudding could be an option too. Incidentals like breads and petits fours are first-rate, and staff are friendly, unstuffy and helpful.

Stephen Bull Restaurant

Stephen Bull's premier restaurant – the interior has modern but undramatic styling. Plain grey walls, a few pieces of modern art, some illuminated glass shelves of bottles and simple black leather chairs serve to concentrate the attention on tables covered with white paper squares over white cloths. The daily changing menu has enough variety to make choice difficult, but our inspector selected well with Jerusalem artichoke soup, then seared scallops, truffle oil and chives followed by peppered monkfish, fricassee of wild mushrooms, shallot purée and red wine sauce, and a spiced plum crumble tart with mulled red wine ice cream to finish. Despite the many elements, each was good in itself. Earthy, robust flavours predominate.

Directions: Off Marylebone High St, 75 yards down on L.
⊖ Bond Street

5-7 Blandford Street W1H 3AA
Map: B4
Tel: 0171 4869696
Fax: 0171 2240324
Chef: Robert Jones
Owner: Stephen Bull
Cost: *Alc* £29, set-price D £27.50.
H/wine £11.50
Times: Noon-2.30pm/6-10.30pm.
Closed L Sat, all Sun, 1 wk Xmas, Bhs
Additional: Children welcome;
🌢 dishes
Seats: 53
Smoking: No pipes & cigars; Air conditioning

Stephen Bull Smithfield

Stephen Bull in informal mode – spacious with strong colours, black unadorned tables and wooden floors. The nicely varied menu lists simply described dishes that are built around balance and flavour. Starters such as baby Caesar salad, marinated quail with basil, and roast haggis with potatoes and turnips are typical of the style. A sample meal started with freshly-made terrine of corn-fed chicken and foie gras, served with clementine chutney. Peppered monk fish set on a bed of spinach and chunky slices of crispy leeks was a another good choice, accompanied by nothing more than a simple brandy cream sauce. For dessert, an apple charlotte stack was decorated with ribbons of chocolate and caramel. Wines are listed by style, and there's a good choice by the glass and half-bottle.

Directions: Halfway between Clerkenwell Rd & Smithfield Market

71 St John Street EC1 4AN
Map: E5
Tel: 0171 4901750
Fax: 0171 4903128
Chef: Danny Lewis
Owner: Stephen Bull
Cost: *Alc* £23
Times: Noon-2.30pm/6-10.30pm.
Closed L Sat, all Sun, 1 wk Xmas, Bhs
Additional: Children welcome;
🌢 dishes
Seats: 110
Smoking: No-smoking area; No pipes & cigars; Air conditioning

The Stepping Stone

Minimalist decor with stone-tiled floor, moulded wooden seats, modern art (for sale) and a relaxed atmosphere. The urban rustic menu changes daily and the cooking is modern and straightforward, although dishes tend to be more combinations of complementary elements than well-integrated wholes. Not that it makes the choice any less difficult when there's Trelough duck breast with Puy lentils and braised chicory with orange on the menu, as well as roast halibut with mussels, saffron mash, leeks and crème fraîche. Starters might include beetroot soup with horseradish cream, or pork and rabbit terrine with home-made pickles and chutney. All meat dishes, such as rack of spring lamb with vegetable rotoli and

123 Queenstown Road SW8 3RH
Map GtL: C2
Tel: 0171 6220555
Fax: 0171 6224230
Chef: Matthew Owsley-Brown
Owners: Gary & Emer Levy
Cost: *Alc* £23, set-price L
£11.75/early D £10 (both 2 courses).
☺ H/wine £11
Times: Noon-2.30pm (3pm Sun)/7-11pm (10pm Mon). Closed L Sat, D Sun, Bh Mon
Additional: Sunday L; Children welcome; 🌢 dishes

spinach, are cooked medium unless otherwise requested. As well as cheese from Neal's Yard, there may be iced caramel mousse with roast apples, or prune and Armagnac tart. Weekday 'Early Bird' dinners (tables vacated by 8.45) are particularly good value.

Directions: Clapham Common. From Lavender Hill/Wandsworth Road crossroads, head up Queenstown Road towards Chelsea Bridge. Restaurant on L after 0.5 mile

Seats: 70. Private dining room 30
Smoking: No-smoking area; No pipes & cigars; Air conditioning

Stratfords ✿

7 Stratford Road W8 6RF
Map GtL: C3
Tel: 0171 9376388
Fax: 0171 9383435
Telephone for further details

Directions: High Street Kensington

Beach-hut blues and yellows enliven this attractive restaurant and set the tone for the menu's seafood theme. Start perhaps with grilled prawns with a touch of garlic, followed by lightly fried lemon sole served simply with parsley butter.

The Sugar Club ✿✿

A popular haunt for Soho's media folk. The Sugar Club comes with typical late-nineties metropolitan restaurant décor (pale colours, blond wood) and ultra-cool staff who nevertheless remain approachable and friendly. That the restaurant started life in the mid 1980s in New Zealand gives a clue to the attractive Pacific-rim based fusion menu, perhaps the best of its kind in London at the moment. Dishes such as crispy duck ravioli with daikon (Japanese white radish), pickled ginger and dipping sauce, roast lamb chump with braised cardoons, saffron potatoes and anchovy-herb paste, and breast of Trelough duck on vanilla scented flageolet beans with wok-fried bok choi show the range of global influences. There's no lack of imagination among the desserts with goats' curd and vanilla cream with saffron peach and plantain crisps, and white chocolate mousse with yuzu roast plum and black sesame praline sharing the *carte* with a more prosaic sticky toffee pudding.

21 Warwick Street W1
Map GtL: C3
Tel: 0171 4377776
Fax: 0171 4377778
Chef: Peter Gordon
Owners: Ashley Sumner, Vivienne Hayman
Cost: *Alc* £28.50. ☺ H/wine £10.50
Times: Noon-2.30pm/6-10.45pm. Closed 25, 26 Dec, 1 Jan
Additional: Sunday L; Children 7+; ♨ dishes
Seats: 140. Private dining room 60
Smoking: No-smoking area; No pipes & cigars; Air conditioning

Directions: Oxford Circus

Suntory Restaurant ✿✿

The oldest Japanese restaurant in London. Now entering its twenty fourth year, Suntory has built up quite a fan base. They offer some of the most reasonably priced Japanese food in London, especially at lunch, but the sky can also be the limit, so choose conservatively to stay within budget. There are two dining rooms, the shabu-shabu room and the teppanyaki grill room, and the menu also offers the familiar tempura, teriyaki,

72 St James's Street SW1A 1PH
Map: C3
Tel: 0171 4090201
Fax: 0171 4990208
Telephone for further details

Directions: At the bottom of St James's Street. Green Park

sashimi, sushi. The cooking is good, saké is worth ordering – 'it has real character'. There are now sixteen restaurants world-wide to this chain.

Supan Thai Restaurant

Neighbourhood restaurant with a loyal following. Traditionally clad Thai ladies serve a wide range of dishes: stir-fried rice noodles with prawns and black bean sauce, perhaps, or chargrilled marinated chicken with spicy chilli sauce.

Directions: At Harrow Road end of Fernhead Road, at its junction with Elgin Avenue

4 Fernhead Road W9 3ET
Map: B3
Tel: 0181 9699387
Cost: *Alc* £11.90. ☺ H/wine £7.50
Times: D only, 6.30-10.55pm. Closed Mon, 25, 26 Dec, Notting Hill Carnival
Additional: Children welcome; ➋ dishes
Smoking: No pipes & cigars

Swallow International Hotel

One of the few London hotels with its own car park. The hotel's restaurant is hidden away at the back with piano music drifting through from the cocktail bar. Plenty of choice with some traditional, some ambitious dishes: ribeye steaks; baked cod with pancetta.

Directions: ⊖ Gloucester Road, Earls Court

Cromwell Road SW5 0TH
Map: A2
Tel: 0171 9731000
Fax: 0171 2448194
Accommodation: 421 en suite
★ ★ ★ ★
Telephone for further details

Tajine NEW

Small room packed with tables and heady with aromatic scents wafting out of steaming tagine pots placed in front of a mixed bag of customers. The North African food is homely and lovingly prepared – must-haves include merguez, couscous and tagines, of course. Harissa is not served unless requested, but does add an extra layer of flavour. Fresh bread is encrusted in sesame seeds, and the Moroccan rosé makes a suitable accompaniment, although the mint tea is particularly refreshing. Service is solicitous and very friendly. One of the best new ethnic restaurants this year.

7a Dorset Street W1
Tel/Fax: 0171 9351545
Telephone for further details

Directions: Telephone for directions

Tamarind

20 Queen Street W1X 7PJ
Map: C3
Tel: 0171 6293561
Fax: 0171 4995034
Chef: Atul Kochhar
Owner: Indian Cuisine Ltd

The Mayfair address sends the right signals – an up-market Indian restaurant with formal service. Glass-fronted with designer interior, strip-wood floor and arty steel and tan

leather chairs, that's Tamarind, and prices do reflect the upscale location. Basically the cooking is Punjabi with the menu offering a mix of the familiar and the unusual. From the latter there's 'murg kaleji masala' – chicken livers fried in onions, cumin and coriander, or 'hari machchi' – John Dory with crispy spinach. We went for the good-value set-price lunch which began with pappadoms and three good chutneys. After that, a trio of starters on a single plate: roasted vegetables, prawns in mango pickle sauce, and sago cakes flavoured with ginger. Then lemon sole served with a gentle yogurt-based sauce and fresh coriander, and tender lamb with spinach purée. Desserts are simple and include rasmalai and kulfi.

Directions: ⊖ Green Park. Head for Hyde Park, and turn 4th R into Half Moon St and walk to end (Curzon St). Turn L, and Queen St is 1st R

Cost: *Alc* £30, set-price L £16.50/D £22.50 (pre-theatre). ☺ H/wine £13.50
Times: Noon-3pm/6-11.30pm. Closed L Sat, 25-26 Dec
Additional: Sunday L; Children welcome; ✿ dishes
Seats: 90. Jacket & tie preferred
Smoking: Air conditioning

La Tante Claire

A famous chef in a new setting of muted purples, greens and blues, with a turquoise carpet, white linen and fabulous glasses. It could not have been easy for Pierre Koffmann to move from a much-loved Chelsea home to a new location in a corner of The Berkeley Hotel, but any transitional pains were smoothed out by the time we visited. One of London's most respected chefs, he has the knack of positively inspiring his staff to welcome and respect all who come to dine chez Koffmann, with the result that the almost expected holier-than-thou attitude oft found in places of this stature is thankfully missing. The decor has been brought up to date but on the *carte* all the Koffmann classics, such as pieds de cochon farcis aux morilles, are reassuringly still in place. A wee amuse-bouche fillet of marinated red mullet with dressed leaves, saffron and pickled vegetables and shades of exotic spicing, was Koffmann's quietly considered play on fusion food and a good prelude to the triumphal first course – coquille Saint Jacques roties a l'encre – superb sweet scallops with a black-as-night ink sauce artfully dribbled with red and yellow swirls. Daube de joue de boeuf grandmère was a stroll down the lane of culinary nostalgia, with beef cheeks of the most succulent tenderness, sweet and sticky, and a simply sublime garnish of bacon, onion and mushroom. Dependent on long, involved and highly refined cooking techniques, this is one dish which is truly a test of cooking skills ('If only my grandmother could cook like this', our inspector practically sobbed into his sauce). Details remain outstanding and include some of the best bread in London. Koffmann still hits the heights and it proves a change of address need mean no loss of excellence.

Berkeley Hotel Wilton Place Knightsbridge SW1X 7RL
Map: B2
Tel: 0171 8232003
Fax: 0171 8232001
Chef: Pierre Koffmann
Owner: The Savoy Group Plc
Cost: *Alc* £80, set-price L £28
Times: 12.30-2pm/7.30-11pm. Closed L Sat, all Sun, 24 Dec-2 Jan
Additional: Children 12+; ✿ dishes
Seats: 70. Private dining room 14
Smoking: No pipes & cigars; Air conditioning

Directions: 300 metres along Knightsbridge from Hyde Park Corner. ⊖ Hyde Park Corner

Tatsuso Restaurant ✿✿

A pricy Japanese popular with city folk and probably best visited for lunch when the area is in full swing. There's a tepanyaki bar on the entrance floor, where you can watch the chef at work, while downstairs the traditionally-styled restaurant features blond wood, pale colours and silk paintings. The set menus are recommended for simplicity: a typical selection will include sashimi, tempura, Japanese clear soup and toban yaki (sliced beef served in a casserole). Our inspector tried chicken teriyaki ('decent flavours'), prawn,

32 Broadgate Circle EC1M 6BT
Map: G4
Tel: 0171 6385863
Fax: 0171 6385864
Chef: Nobuyuki Yamanaka
Owner: Terutoshi Fujii
Cost: *Alc* £40, set-price L £34/D £58 (6 courses). H/wine £14
Times: 11.30am-2.45pm/6-10pm. Closed Sat, Sun
Additional: Children 10+; ✿ dishes

salmon and vegetable tempura ('light and up to the mark'), and vegetable and seaweed salad. Sushi is considered excellent. All in all, this is a stylish Japanese – but make sure your wallet's stuffed before booking a table.

Directions: Ground floor of Broadgate Circle. ⊖ Liverpool St

Seats: 140. Private dining room 10
Smoking: No pipes & cigars; Air conditioning

Teatro

Very design conscious. Teatro is a slick, well-run operation that continues to pull in the punters. That the menu is printed in a sans-serif typeface with not a capital letter in sight is testament to the modishness of the kitchen's style. A starter of 'risotto of ceps with truffle oil' is an understatement for what was described as 'all heart, gusto and fungus' given a lift by the oil. The kitchen manages to tease all the flavours out of the ingredients in a main course of poulet noir with thyme jus and crisp shallots on Parmesan risotto. Roasted fillet of sea bass in a herb crust with braised salsify and a subdued basil vinaigrette 'a picture on the plate' might be among the fish dishes, and pheasant breast stuffed with quince and cranberry among the meat. Pear tarte Tatin comes with Jersey cream, and breads are good.

Directions: ⊖ Leicester Square, Piccadilly Circus

93-107 Shaftesbury Avenue W1V 8BT
Map: C3
Tel: 0171 4943040
Fax: 0171 4943050
Chef: Stuart Gillies
Owners: Lee Chapman, Leslie Ash
Cost: *Alc* £35, set-price L & D £18. ☺ H/wine £12
Times: Noon-2.45pm/6-11.30pm. Closed Sat L, all Sun, Xmas, Bhs
Additional: Children welcome; ✤ dishes
Seats: 90
Smoking: No pipes; Air conditioning

Teca NEW

Once a betting shop, now a minimalist restaurant. The centre of the room is occupied by a large bar, smartly but simply decorated with wood and leather, there's subdued lighting plus a fair amount of noise when busy. A quick glance at the short, sharp menu shows that this is cooking from the modern Italian school: saffron risotto, carpaccio of sea bass on spinach, roasted John Dory in rosemary sauce with chard and cannellini, and chicken breast stuffed with confit of lemon with braised radicchio and sautéed potatoes. At inspection, pumpkin ravioli with sage butter was precisely cooked, and ricotta gnocchi a good, humble foil for a perfectly seared slice of foie gras – 'a delight'. Monkfish, partridge, fillet of beef and turbot could all be principals among main courses, or tender, pink saddle of venison in a rich gravy boosted by blueberries, with cheesy fried polenta a good match. Vanilla mille-feuille is said to float off the fork, and there might be tiramisu or chocolate mousse with raspberry sauce. Background notes on the wine list make interesting reading, with quality the keynote, not least among the six house wines.

54 Brook Mews W1Y 2NY
Map: C3
Tel: 0171 4954774
Fax: 0171 4913545
Chef: Marco Torri
Owner: Marco Bacchetta
Cost: *Alc* £30, set-price L £19. H/wine £12
Times: Noon-2.30pm/7-10.30pm. Closed Sun, Bhs
Additional: Children welcome; ✤ dishes
Seats: 75
Smoking: No-smoking area; Air conditioning

Directions: ⊖ Bond Street

The Thai Garden

Close to the heart of Bethnal Green, a simple vegetarian and fish Thai eaterie that offers good-value set menus and a keenly priced carte. Expect deep-fried curried seafood, pomfret fish topped with chilli sauce, and Thai aubergines and mixed vegetable curry with coconut cream.

Smoking: No-smoking area; Air conditioning

Directions: 2nd left off Roman Road (1-way street); ⊖ Bethnal Green

249 Globe Road E2 0JD
Map GtL: D3
Tel: 0181 9815748
Cost: *Alc* £18, set-price L & D £7.50 (2 courses). ☺ H/wine £7.50
Times: Noon-2.45pm/6-10.45pm. Closed L Sat & Sun, Bhs
Additional: Children welcome; ✤ dishes

Thailand

Informal Thai restaurant on a small scale – just like eating in some one's home. Chicken curry with coconut may be standard in all Thai restaurants, but this one is the sweetest, roundest of them all, fragrant with sweet basil, lemongrass, galangal and kaffir lime leaves.

Directions: Opposite Goldsmiths' College. New Cross, New Cross Gate

15 Lewisham Way SE14 6PP
Map GtL: D3
Tel: 0181 6914040
Telephone for further details

The Thistle Tower

Elegant riverside hotel restaurant blessed with wonderful views. A contemporary menu with imaginatively crafted dishes includes roasted cannon of lamb with grain mustard polenta, and warm plum tart with elderflower sorbet.

Additional: Children welcome; 🍴 dishes
Smoking: No-smoking area; No pipes & cigars; Air conditioning
Accommodation: 800 en suite ★ ★ ★ ★

Directions: Adjacent to Tower of London and Tower Bridge on N bank of River Thames

St Katharine's Way E1 9LD
Map: G3
Tel: 0171 4812575
Fax: 0171 4884106
Cost: £38. H/wine £16.75
Times: D only, 7-10.30pm. Closed Sun, 26 Dec-10 Jan

Titanic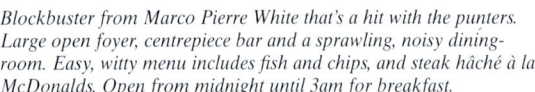

Blockbuster from Marco Pierre White that's a hit with the punters. Large open foyer, centrepiece bar and a sprawling, noisy dining-room. Easy, witty menu includes fish and chips, and steak hâché à la McDonalds. Open from midnight until 3am for breakfast.

Additional: Bar food; Children welcome; 🍴 dishes
Smoking: Air conditioning

Directions: Piccadilly Circus

81 Brewer Street W1R 3FH
Map: D3
Tel: 0171 4371912
Fax: 0171 4394747
Cost: *Alc* £30, set-price L £13.50. ☺
Times: Noon-2.30pm/5.30pm-midnight (until 3am for breakfast). Closed L Sat, all Sun

Turners Restaurant

Celebrity chef Brian Turner is very much the attentive host in his intimate and welcoming restaurant. A varied choice of around nine starters, ten main courses and seven desserts provides plenty to choose from. Amongst starters, worth trying is a well-made duck confit with foie gras terrine, displaying sound culinary skills. Otherwise, try perhaps the carpaccio of tuna with pickled vegetables, or crab with sour cream and a spiced cucumber salsa. Main courses could involve panaché of monkfish and langoustine tails with a rich and creamy saffron beurre blanc, roast of English lamb in rosemary and herb crust, or calves' kidneys with celeriac timbale and a Pommery cream sauce. To finish, choose white chocolate and raspberry mouse, or apple and almond cake with caramelised apples.

Directions: South Kensington, Knightsbridge. Behind Harrods

87-89 Walton Street SW3 2HP
Map: A1
Tel: 0171 5846711
Fax: 0171 5844441
Chef: J Lucas
Owner: Brian Turner
Cost: *Alc* £45, set-price L £15/D £29.50. H/wine £15.50
Times: 12.30-last L 2.30pm/7.30-last D 11.15pm. Closed L Sat, Bhs, 1 wk Xmas
Additional: Sunday L; Children welcome at L
Seats: 56. Private dining room 6
Smoking: Air conditioning

Two Four Two

Under-the-railway-arches-style wine bar-cum-restaurant near Waterloo Station. Brian Turner (not the TV celeb one) used to cook at the English Garden in Chelsea. Changing to this less fashionable, but very up-and-coming area (the new Tate Gallery is down the road), has proved an inspired move for a chef who has not lost his touch in the process. More or less solo in the kitchen when we visited, Turner's menu is a simple affair – and all the better for it. Fresh, vibrant, seasonal, we enjoyed smoked haddock on a warm spinach tart with poached egg, as well as a lively watercress, walnut and raspberry salad. A filled chicken breast with Brie and Jarlsberg with roasted baby leeks and cream was a blast-from-the-past 80s kind of dish, but a lightness of touch kept it well in the modern idiom. Baked loin of cod with warm tomato concasse and coriander crust, served with curly kale, was also excellent. Desserts don't slow the pace down, as we saw in an absolutely fabulous blueberry and vanilla meringue, and hot cinnamon pancakes with sloe gin plums (lovely) and crème fraîche. Keenly priced, wide-ranging wine list.

Directions: ⊖ Blackfriars, Waterloo

242 Blackfriars Road SE1 9UF
Map: F3
Tel: 0171 9288689
Fax: 0171 9284447
Chef: Brian Turner
Owner: Peter D B McKinley
Cost: Set-price L £18.95. ☺ H/wine £8.95
Times: Noon-2.30pm/D by prior arrangement. Closed Sat & Sun, Xmas, Bhs
Additional: Bar food L; ✤ dishes
Seats: 28. Private dining room 8
Smoking: No-smoking area; Air conditioning

Vama

A smart Indian restaurant specialising in cooking from the North West Frontier. Tandoori dishes and game feature strongly – we enjoyed mushrooms stuffed with home-made cheese and pomegranate, and duck marinated in garlic and ginger.

Directions: ⊖ Sloane Square. Telephone for directions

438 King's Road SW10 0LJ
Map: C3
Tel: 0171 3514118
Fax: 0171 5658501
Cost: *Alc* £30. ☺ H/wine £9.95
Times: Noon-2.30pm/6.30-11pm. Closed 25, 26 Dec, 1 Jan
Additional: Sunday L; Children welcome; ✤ dishes
Smoking: No-smoking area; No pipes & cigars; Air conditioning

Vasco & Piero's Pavilion

Much-loved by politicians and music types, this charming Soho Italian is as popular as ever. Typical starters from the short carte include carpaccio of tuna, rucola, and tomato, and thinly sliced roast pork with radicchio and Pecorino cheese.

Additional: Children 6+; ✤ dishes
Smoking: No pipes; Air conditioning

Directions: On corner of Great Marlborough Street & Noel Street. ⊖ Oxford Circus

15 Poland Street W1V 3DE
Map GtL: D4
Tel: 0171 4378774
Fax: 0171 4370467
Cost: *Alc* £32, set-price D £18.50. ☺ H/wine £9.95
Times: Noon-3pm/6-11pm (from 7pm Sat). Closed L Sat, all Sun, Bhs

The Veeraswamy Restaurant ✿

99-101 Regent Street W1R 8RS
Map: C3
Tel: 0171 7341401
Telephone for further details

Directions: Entrance near junction of Swallow St & Regent St, located in Victory House. Entrance in Swallow Street.

Britain's oldest Indian restaurant, dating from 1927, now under same ownership as Chutney Mary with bold modern decor. Food is Southern Indian with some northern 'court' dishes.

La Ventura ✿

NEW

28 Crouch Hill N4 4AU
Map GtL: D4
Tel: 0171 2815811
Cost: *Alc* £19.50. ☺ H/wine £8.50
Times: 11am-4pm/6-11pm

A simple, neighbourhood restaurant/bar decked out in chic 1920's decor. The food is modern European with the emphasis on Italy. Expect the likes of roast leg of rabbit wrapped in Parma ham, and ravioli with spiced aubergine, mizuna and chilli mayonnaise.

Additional: Bar food; Sunday L; Children welcome; ✤ dishes
Smoking: No-smoking area

Directions: ⊖ Finsbury Park, At junction of Crouch Hill and Japan Crescent

Veronica's ✿✿

3 Hereford Road
W2 4AB
Map GtL: C3
Tel: 0171 2295079/2291452
Fax: 0171 2291210
Chefs: Antonio Feliccio, Veronica Shaw
Owners: Veronica & Philip Shaw
Cost: *Alc* £28, set-price L & D £16.50. ☺

Cheerful neighbourhood restaurant with historical leanings.
The kitchen deals exclusively with British historical dishes and the menu gives a potted history of each one. Around 10 main courses are divided almost equally between meat, fish and vegetarian. Pan-fried fillet of plaice, fresh and well-timed, comes with a butter of anchovy, mint and lime on wilted spinach, fillet of beef is chargrilled and then 'finished' between

smoking planks of oak before joining creamed potato on the plate, while 'funges and beans' turns out to be crushed red beans with leeks, mushrooms and almonds. Finish with sweet spinach tart with rosewater.

Directions: ⊖ Bayswater, Queensway. Hereford Rd runs parallel to Queensway in between Bayswater Rd and Westbourne Grove

Times: Noon-2.30pm/6-11.30pm. Closed L Sat, all Sun, Bhs
Additional: Children welcome; ✤ dishes
Seats: 70. Private dining room 35

Villandry

Sparsely styled, with simple wooden tables and chairs, the open-plan restaurant fits easily into the rear of one of the most tempting food stores in London. It is a natural partnership – you eat and buy, or buy and eat carefully sourced produce of the highest quality. The menu changes twice daily to reflect market freshness. Typically, start with fish soup with rouille croûton or smoked herring, watercress and beetroot salad with horseradish, then choose from organic rib of beef with champ potato cake and wild mushrooms, or grilled fillet of mullet with anchovy rostini, cherry tomatoes and spinach. Vegetarian dishes include pumpkin and sage risotto with crème fraîche. Phillipe Olivier cheeses are hard to pass on, but there's also moist chocolate cake or pear Tatin. A changing selection of beers makes an interesting alternative to the short wine list. Note that evening access is via Bolsover Street.

170 Great Portland Street W1N 5TB
Map: C4
Tel: 0171 6313131
Fax: 0171 6313030
Chef: Roz Carrarini
Owner: Jean-Charles Carrarini
Cost: *Alc* £30. ☺ H/wine £11
Times: Noon-2.45pm/7-9.45pm. Closed D Sun, 25 Dec, 1 Jan, 1 May
Additional: Sunday L; Children welcome; ✤ dishes
Seats: 100. Private dining room 20
Smoking: No smoking in dining room; Air conditioning

Directions: ⊖ Great Portland Street. Restaurant entrance at 91 Bolsover St

Vong

Merging of France and the Orient in the discreet confines of the Berkeley Hotel. Vong is decorated in rich Indonesian hues, reflecting the vivid colours of the oriental spices on display, offset by the use of natural stone, timbers and white orchids. The menu is an inventory of fusion dishes of the sort which all too often excite on paper more than on the palate. Prices, too, might make some blanch. Although pretty on the eye, several dishes sampled fell short of the mark – chicken and coconut milk soup and crab spring roll with tamarind ketchup were both subdued in flavour. Crisp squab with chilli onion compote, corn pancake and foie gras made more of an impact, the bird just bloody and well hung. The accompaniments worked well except for a fatty pancake; along with the richness of the goose liver, this was overkill. Mostly French, plentiful and well-meaning, staff are under the guidance of a US Vongster from the mother Vong in New York.

Directions: ⊖ Hyde Park Corner, Knightsbridge

The Berkeley Hotel Wilton Place Knightsbridge SW1X 7RL
Map: B2
Tel: 0171 2351010
Fax: 0171 2351011
Chef: Shaun Gilmore
Owners: Savoy Group
Cost: *Alc* £40, set-price L £20/D £45 (7 courses). ☺ (pre-theatre). H/wine £19
Times: Noon-2.30pm (from 11.30am Sat & Sun)/6-11.30pm. Closed Xmas
Additional: Bar food L; Sunday Brunch; Children 12+; ✤ dishes
Seats: 130
Smoking: No-smoking area; Air conditioning

The Washington Mayfair Hotel

Spacious modern restaurant with strong blue colours. Dishes range from battered cod with chips and pea purée to lamb noisette on flageolet beans scented with ginger and rosemary.

Smoking: No-smoking area; Air conditioning
Accommodation: 173 en suite ★★★★

Directions: ⊖ Green Park

5-7 Curzon Street W1Y 8DT
Map: C3
Tel: 0171 4997000
Fax: 0171 4956172
Cost: *Alc* £25, set-price L £9.95/D £17.95. ☺ H/wine £12.95
Times: Noon-2.30pm/5.30-10pm
Additional: Bar food; Children welcome; ✤ dishes

Westbury Hotel ❀❀

Bond Street W1A 4UH
Map: C3
Tel: 0171 6297755
Fax: 0171 4951163
Chef: Jon McCann
Cost: *Alc* £30, set-price L £19.50/D £21.50. ☺ H/wine £15.50
Times: Noon-2.30pm/6-10pm. Closed L Sat & Sun
Additional: Bar food; Children welcome; ❹ dishes
Seats: 46. Private dining rooms 12-80
Smoking: No-smoking area
Accommodation: 150 en suite
★ ★ ★ ★

Directions: ⊖ Oxford Circus, Piccadilly Circus, Bond Street

Top-drawer hotel restaurant in a prime Bond Street site. The room is light, airy, and relaxing, with upholstered dining chairs, large, well-spaced tables, quality linen and tableware. Luxury items of course, lobster, crab and foie gras – the latter as a terrine with asparagus and leeks – but the kitchen goes into contemporary mode with carpaccio of salmon and tuna with an oriental dressing, and glazed goats' cheese with bruschetta and rocket. Main courses offer seared duck breast with pak choi, glazed apples and sesame jus, and tiger prawns sautéed with saffron, chilli and tomatoes. At inspection, sea bream, served simply with a herb butter, French beans and lyonnaise potatoes, came a close second to the sticky toffee pudding with its light texture and dense caramel flavour 'one of the best I've had'. The set-price menus are good value, petits fours are served with coffee, and the wine list is typical of this style of operation.

The White House Hotel ❀❀

Albany Street NW1 3UP
Map: D4
Tel: 0171 3871200
Fax: 0171 3880091
Chef: Colin Norman
Cost: *Alc* £28.85, set-price L £23.75/D £24.50. ☺ H/wine £12.50
Times: 12.30-2.15pm/D from 6.30pm. Closed D Sat, all Sun
Additional: Children 6+; ❹ dishes
Seats: 105. Private dining room 110
Smoking: Air conditioning
Accommodation: 582 en suite
★ ★ ★ ★

Directions: ⊖ Great Portland Street

The White House was formerly an exclusive block of flats. This eight-storey hotel stands next to Regents Park and is geared mainly to the business executive. The rather formal restaurant offers both a set-menu and a *carte*, featuring traditional dishes – including the odd flambéed item and a dessert trolley. However there is a good level of consistency from the kitchen. A starter of fresh pea and bacon soup had 'a lovely colour and was delicious', the roast goats' cheese with plum tomatoes and rosemary was 'spot on'. The lobster

Thermidor risotto was ' one of the best risottos I have had anywhere'. All desserts, including floating islands and caramelised apple meringue were appealing. The hotel has a good selection of wines by the glass and the staff are well trained, interested and helpful.

White Onion

Fashionable Islington eatery with simple, understated decor and considerable charm. Part of a steadily growing collection of good-value modern restaurants owned by Bijan Behzadi, the White Onion is, in our opinion, one of the best. A conclusion Islington's finest (and Kathy Burke) appear to agree with considering the number of people turned away when we visited. Booking is essential. Eric Guignard can cook and he offers a short, punchy menu with strong Mediterranean overtones. Wild mushroom risotto had full, well-rounded flavours, a deliciously crisp-skinned magret of duck came on a bed of spinach with a tart, luminous but rich orange butter sauce, and chocolate brownie with white chocolate ice cream was just perfect. The sixty bin wine list offers good quality and covers most of Europe with a few New World.

Directions: ⊖ Angel/Highbury & Islington (midway between two). Close to Almeida St

297 Upper Street N1 2TU
Map GtL: D3
Tel/Fax: 0171 3593533
Chef: Eric Guignard
Owner: Bijan Behzadi
Cost: *Alc* £24.30, set-price L £10 (2 courses). ☺ H/wine £9.50
Times: Noon-2.15pm/6.30-11pm. Closed L Mon-Fri, 25, 26 Dec
Additional: Sunday L, Children welcome
Seats: 63
Smoking: No pipes & cigars; Air conditioning

Wilson's

One of the best kept secrets in Brook Green. A charming, unassuming *restaurant du quartier* that has been providing satisfying food in a pleasant and relaxed atmosphere for almost two years. With its wheelback chairs, punkas overhead and tartan curtains there's a partly Scottish accent that takes in a kilted proprietor who presides over the service and can, on occasion, be persuaded to play the bagpipes. The main menu, roughly ten choices per course, does not change much, but a short set-price menu has also been introduced. Dishes are straightforward, but not without interest: Finnan haddock pudding with a spinach and bacon salad, perhaps, or a kedgeree mould with a light curry flavour, and grilled lamb cutlets served with a redcurrant and mustard sauce. Desserts are notably good, particularly the raspberry queen of puddings.

Directions: ⊖ Hammersmith

236 Blythe Road W14 0HJ
Map GtL: C3
Tel: 0171 6037267
Fax: 0171 6029018
Chef: Robert Hilton
Owners: Robert Hilton, Robert Wilson
Cost: *Alc* £23.50. ☺ H/wine £10.50
Times: D only, 7-10pm. Closed Sun, Xmas, Bhs
Additional: Sunday L; Children welcome; ⊕ dishes
Seats: 42
Smoking: Air conditioning

Wiltons

The plush green interior is in keeping with the St James location. A series of connected rooms with secluded booth seating provides a discreet atmosphere in which Wilton habitués can talk business, conduct affairs of state or swop shooting stories. Traditional British cooking rules OK, with raw ingredients that are second to none. The emphasis is on fish and game, although there are also steaks, sausages and grilled lambs' kidneys. The menu remains doggedly in clubland format with cold buffet, hors d'oeuvre, omelettes and savoury sections, and features classics such as whitebait, lobster cocktail, omelette Arnold Bennett and anchovies on toast. In season there are gulls' eggs, asparagus and fresh raspberries. Most fish

55 Jermyn Street SW1Y 6LX
Map: C3
Tel: 0171 6299955
Fax: 0171 4956233
Chef: Ross Hayden
Owners: Rupert Hambro & Partners
Cost: *Alc* £55. ☺ H/wine £17.50
Times: Noon-2.30pm/6-10.30pm. Closed Sat, Bhs
Additional: Sunday L; Children 12+
Seats: 90. Private dining room 18. Jacket & tie preferred
Smoking: Air conditioning

Wiltons

Directions: Opposite Turnbull & Asser (shirtmakers), near Piccadilly Circus & Ritz Hotel. ⊖ Green Park

dishes are simply cooked – poached turbot, grilled halibut, cold Spey salmon – and even when dressed up a bit – baked fillet of lemon sole with chive and lemon dressing, for example – they retain an essential simplicity.

Yas

7 Hammersmith Road W14 8XJ
Map Gtl: C3
Tel: 0171 6039148
Fax: 0171 6033320
Cost: *Alc* £20, set-price D £15. ☺
H/wine £8
Times: Noon-5am

Expect friendly service and simple, freshly cooked food at this Iranian eaterie. Super flat bread comes straight from the tandoor to go with chicken stew with saffron rice, or halibut cooked with herbs, chillis, garlic and tamarind. Plenty of familiar kebabs for the less adventurous.

Additional: Bar food; Sunday L; Children welcome; dishes
Smoking: No-smoking area

Directions: ⊖ Kensington (Olympia)

YMing ✿✿

35-36 Greek Street W1V 5LN
Map: D4
Tel: 0171 7342721
Fax: 0171 4370292
Chef: Hung Lim
Owner: Christine Yau
Cost: *Alc* £15, set-price L £10/D £20. ☺ H/wine £9.20
Times: Noon-11.45pm. Closed Sun, 25-26 Dec
Additional: Children welcome; ◑ dishes
Seats: 50. Private dining room 25
Smoking: No-smoking area; Air conditioning

Directions: Off Shaftesbury Ave, behind Palace Theatre

This restaurant, on the corner of Greek Street is painted an unusual, pretty green and is a rather original Chinese restaurant, quite unlike most other Chinese establishments in Soho. The food is described as northern Chinese, but there are many other regional specials to be found on the various menus. Four set menus includes one that's entirely vegetarian, the carte is an extensive list but includes many home-made additions such as pickles and dumplings. Look out for old favourites such as home-made prawn cakes, double-braised pork hotpot and duck breast slices with orange and spices, and aubergine delight with bacon. There are six types of lobster dishes, the most interesting being the dry lobster with spiced salt. The wine list is well-matched to the menu.

Yumi Restaurant

One of the nicer Japanese restaurants in London with great atmosphere and staff. The ambience is that of a neighbourhood restaurant unlike, say, Suntory or Tatsuso, where the clientele is 99% business suits. The decor is typically minimalist, with a sushi bar and some private rooms on the ground floor (given an element of authenticity with their tatami mat floors), and the main restaurant and yet more private dining rooms in the basement. The food is straightforward Japanese with some curious chef's recommendations, Camembert and smoked salmon tempura, for example, or maguro burger of minced tuna with a home-made sauce. Otherwise it is all pretty familiar with miso soup, sushi, sashimi and the likes of tempura udon built around fillet of grilled beef or grilled chicken with teriyaki sauce.

Directions: A few yards east of the junction of George Street and Gloucester Place. ⊖ Marble Arch

110 George Street W1H 5RL
Map: B4
Tel: 0171 9358320
Fax: 0171 2240917
Chef: M Sato
Owners: Miss Y Fujii, Mr T Osumi
Cost: *Alc* £40, set-price D £38 (7 courses). ☺ H/wine £12.90
Times: D only, 5.30-10.30pm
Additional: Children 10+; ◑ dishes
Seats: 70. Private dining room 16
Smoking: No pipes & cigars; Air conditioning

Zafferano

The discreet, stylish Belgravia restaurant always plays to a full, cosmopolitan house. Decor is simple with textile wall hangings and some dramatically arranged flowers, but the food is the thing here – Giorgio Locatelli's modern Italian menu still outclasses most of the rest. Dishes that remain in the memory are pork fillet with black cabbage and cannellini beams, flat spaghetti with sweet chilli, garlic and crab, and chargrilled eels with herbs. Other dishes in the rather rustic repertoire include sweet-and-sour skate salade, minced pork wrapped in Savoy cabbage leaves with pan-fried risotto, and cannoli siciliani. Ciabatta comes with the now statutory pool of olive oil, but what stands out throughout a meal here is the sheer quality of the ingredients. Hand-made buffalo mozzarella, for example, when served with baked aubergine, is left dramatically whole. As our inspector said 'not a chicken cacciatore in sight'.

15 Lowndes Street SW1X 9EY
Map: B2
Tel: 0171 2355800
Fax: 0171 2351971
Chef/Owner: Giorgio Locatelli
Cost: *Alc* £35, set-price L £20.50/D £32.50. H/wine £11
Times: Noon-2.25pm/7-10.45pm. Closed Sun, Xmas, New Year
Additional: Children welcome; ◑ dishes
Seats: 55
Smoking: Air conditioning

Directions: Off Knightsbridge – around corner from The Sheraton Park Tower Hotel. ⊖ Knightsbridge

Zaika NEW

Indian restaurant of immense style. The Fulham Road address has been home to a number of talented chefs, but the combination of restaurateur Claudio Pulze and Indian chef Vineet Bhatia has hit the ground running. Pulze's ambition is to own a group of restaurants – under the title Cuisine's Collection – each dedicated to one great world cuisine; this is his homage to the Indian sub continent. It is hard to pigeon-hole Bhatia's cooking, however, because no other Indian chef in the country cooks as he does. He is ambitious and imaginative, his food based on respect for prime quality ingredients and long-established technique. The menu deliberately stays short to ensure quality and extends well beyond the familiar boundaries of Anglo-Indian food. Bhatia also introduces a welcome lightness of touch,

257-259 Fulham Road SW3 6HY
Map: A1
Tel: 0171 3517823
Fax: 0171 3764971
Chef: Vineet Bhatia
Owner: Cuisine's Collection
Cost: *Alc* £20, set-price L £9.95 (2 courses)/D £20 (5 courses). H/wine £12.50
Times: Noon-2.45pm/6.30-10.45pm. Closed L Sat, all Sun, Bhs
Additional: Children welcome; ◑ dishes
Seats: 70. Private dining room 12
Smoking: No pipes & cigars; Air conditioning

which is the defining characteristic of his skilful team. Tandoori home-smoked salmon flavoured with mustard and dill can be described by one word – stunning. Indian risotto with red onion and coriander topped by a crispy prawn is a deft, successful take on fusion. Stellar main courses have included herb-marinated sea bass baked in banana leaf and served with coconut rice and lentils, and a classic Kashmiri rogan josh cooked with lamb shanks (on the bone) in a rich onion and tomato sauce. Desserts try hard, but are perhaps the least successful; tandoori-baked fruits and kulfi are the best bets.

Directions: ⊖ South Kensington

Zen Central, Garden, ZENW3 ✿

Sleek, upmarket group of Chinese restaurants in unfussy designer-modern black and white. Grilled Peking dumplings, steamed scallops with a 'punchy' black bean sauce and deep-fried shell crab with peppercorn salt show the style. Zen Garden, 15-16 Berkeley Street W1X 5AE, tel 0171 4931381, and ZENW3, 83 Hampstead High Street NW3 1RE, tel 0171 7947863, are also recommended.

Additional: Sunday L; Children welcome; ◑ dishes
Smoking: No pipes & cigars; Air conditioning

Directions: Off Curzon Street, near Curzon Cinema, and behind London Hilton/Dorchester hotels. ⊖ Green Park

20-22 Queen Street W1X 7PJ
Map: C3
Tel: 0171 6298103/8089
Fax: 0171 4936181
Cost: *Alc* £20, set-price D £28. ☺ H/wine £15
Times: 12.15-2.30pm/6.30-11.15pm. Closed 24-25 Dec

ENGLAND
BEDFORDSHIRE

ASPLEY GUISE,

Moore Place Hotel ❀❀

Attractive Georgian mansion in its own grounds in the centre of the village. Inside is a small lounge area, a cosy bar and the Greenhouse Restaurant, which has large picture windows looking out over a courtyard complete with waterfall and fishpond. One menu is designed for guests with special dietary needs, so vegans could start with a tartlet of roasted vegetables with balsamic-dressed salad, while the rest of us could go for pan-fried lambs' kidneys, or smoked duck breast. Mainstream dishes encompass medallions of pork fillet, tender and full of flavour, on rösti, and grilled fillet of cod in mustardy breadcrumbs with thyme sauce. Cheddar and walnut cheesecake, with apple and raisin compote, makes an unusual pudding, or ask if liquorice ripple ice cream is on offer and go for that.

The Square MK17 8DW
Map 4: SP93
Tel: 01908 282000
Fax: 01908 281888
Chef: Clive Southgate
Owners: The Vickers Family
Cost: *Alc* £26.50, set-price L £14.50/D £22.95. ☺ H/wine £11.50
Times: 12.30-2pm/7.30-9.45pm. Closed L Sat
Additional: Bar food; Sunday L; Children welcome; ❹ dishes
Seats: 80. Private dining room 20
Smoking: No smoking in dining room; Air conditioning
Accommodation: 54 en suite ★ ★ ★

Directions: On border with Buckinghamshire – in centre of village; nr M1/J13

BEDFORD, Knife & Cleaver ❀

Victorian-style conservatory with lots of flowering plants. Expect exuberant cooking from an extensive menu, supported by a good wine list with plenty by the carafe or glass.

The Grove Houghton Conquest MK45 3LA
Map 5: TL04
Tel: 01234 740387
Fax: 01234 740900
Cost: *Alc* £27, set-price L £11.95 (2 courses)/D £20. ☺ H/wine £10.50
Times: Noon-2.30pm/7-9.30pm. Closed L Sat, D Sun, 27-30 Dec
Additional: Bar food; Sunday L; Children welcome; ❹ dishes
Smoking: No smoking in dining room; Air conditioning
Accommodation: 9 en suite ★ ★

Directions: M1/J12/13, between A6 & B530. 2m N of Ampthill, 5m S of Bedford

BEDFORD,
Woodlands Manor Hotel

Green Lane Clapham MK41 6EP
Map 5: TL04
Tel: 01234 363281
Fax: 01234 272390
Cost: *Alc* £25.95, set-price L
£14.95. H/wine £11.75
Times: 12.30-2pm/7.30-9.30pm.
Closed L Sat
Additional: Bar Food; Sunday L;
Children welcome; ❹ dishes
Smoking: No smoking in dining room
Accommodation: 33 en suite ★ ★ ★

Directions: 2 miles N of Bedford, in
Kettering direction on A6

*Period manor house with welcoming open fires and views over
mature gardens. An imaginative menu with some fairly ambitious
dishes keeps pace with modern trends.*

DUNSTABLE,
Old Palace Lodge Hotel

*Listed hotel building with a traditionally styled restaurant. A typical
meal could be galantine of duck, chicken and pheasant followed by
marinated loin of venison.*

Smoking: Air conditioning
Accommodation: 68 en suite ★ ★ ★

Directions: From M1/J11 take Dunstable exit at roundabout.
After 2 miles road passes under bridge. Hotel on R opposite
church

Church Street LU5 4RT
Map 4: TL02
Tel: 01582 662201
Fax: 01582 696422
Cost: *Alc* £30, set-price L £12.95/D
£19.95. ☺ H/wine £10.95
Times: 12.30-1.45pm/7-9.45pm.
Closed L Sat
Additional: Sunday L; Children
welcome; ❹ dishes

FLITWICK, # Flitwick Manor

Church Road MK45 1AE
Map 4: TL03
Tel: 01525 712242
Fax: 01525 718753
Chef: Richard Salt
Owner: Menzies Hotels
Cost: *Alc* £37.50. H/wine £18
Times: Noon-1.30pm/7-9.30pm

A classic country-house hotel surrounded by open parkland.
The restaurant lives up to expectations: heavily draped
windows, fresh flowers on clothed tables, stylish chinaware and
a soothing atmosphere. Risotto of garden herbs with pan-fried
scallops and rocket pesto is a good illustration of the kitchen's

style, along with a 'super' starter of wild mushroom tortellini with foie gras and a rich jus made from Agen prunes. Duck breast is glazed with honey and cracked black peppercorns before being roasted and served with a sauce of red wine and blackcurrants, pan-fried medallions of venison come with Burgundy sauce, and a full-bodied red onion dopiaza accompanies baked fillet of salmon. Workmanship with pastry comes to the fore in puddings of lemon tarte Tatin, good, crisp and buttery, with a 'thin, crunchy caramel crust', served with figs poached in red wine, and treacle tart accompanied by Bailey's ice cream. Vegetarians get a good deal, with their own menu, and six house wines kick off the wine list.

Signature dishes: noisettes of spring lamb with morels; John Dory and lobster sautéed with ginger; medallions of venison with fig and walnut ravioli.

Additional: Sunday L; Children welcome; dishes
Seats: 55. Private dining rooms 8, 16. Jacket & tie preferred
Smoking: No smoking in dining room
Accommodation: 17 en suite ★ ★ ★

Directions: On A5120, 2 miles from M1/J12

WOBURN,

Paris House Restaurant ❀❀

Woburn Park MK17 9QP
Map 4: SP93
Tel: 01525 290692
Fax: 01525 290471
Chef/Owner: Peter Chandler
Cost: *Alc* £45, set-price L £26/D £48 (5 courses). H/wine £13
Times: Noon-1.45pm/7-9.45pm. Closed D Sun, all Mon, Feb
Additional: Sunday L; Children welcome, dishes
Seats: 45. Private dining room 14
Smoking: No pipes & cigars

Directions: On A4012, 1.5 miles out of Woburn towards Hockcliffe, through huge archway

Few restaurants have such an impressive approach. Turn off the main road through an elaborate archway and up the long, winding drive that dissects the Duke of Bedford's deer park at Woburn. The mock-Tudor building was built for the Paris Exhibition of 1878 and makes an ideal restaurant. There's a comfy bar, and walls are strewn with pictures of chef-patron Peter Chandler's race horses. The menu sticks to a tried-and-tested formula and makes the best of local and seasonal produce. Ballotine of duck with redcurrant relish, well-timed monkfish 'Beaujolais', and an accurately cooked, subtle hot raspberry soufflé are fairly typical of the range. As well as the *carte*, there's a daily changing gastronomique menu, as well as a set lunch. Breads, canapés and petits fours show attention to detail. The wine list is soundly based, a well-considered, carefully annotated exploration of the French vineyards.

BERKSHIRE

BRACKNELL,

Coppid Beech Hotel

The hotel is built in Alpine style to match the ski slope and ice rink adjacent. It's rather disappointing not to find vin chaud and fondue on the menu. Still, there are compensations in the form of classy, bold modern British dishes. Steamed rod-caught sea bass and seared scallops are served with Pernod and vanilla butter, and pavé of lamb 'hot-pot style' comes with baby carrots and stuffed cabbage. Fricassée of baby vegetables with watercress soufflé and a light buttered nage makes for imaginative vegetarian eating. Oriental flavourings are explored in roast breast of Gressingham duck with bok-choi, potato galette and black pepper and pineapple jus, as well as chicken broth with char-sui pork and shiitake mushrooms. There is a grill section for those who like their steaks plain and simple, but three cheers for a kitchen that includes local rabbit with home-made linguine, salsify, asparagus and a rich red wine butter in their repertoire.

John Nike Way RG12 8TF
Map 4: SU86
Tel: 01344 303333
Fax: 01344 301200
Chef: Neil Thrift
Owners: Nike Group Hotels
Cost: *Alc* £25, set-price L £17.50/D £22.95. ☺ H/wine £12.50
Times: Noon-2pm/7-10pm. Closed L Sat
Additional: Bar food; Sunday L; Children welcome; ✿ dishes
Seats: 100
Smoking: No-smoking area; Air conditioning
Accommodation: 205 en suite ★ ★ ★ ★

Directions: From M4/J10, follow A329 (M) to 1st exit. At roundabout take 1st exit to Binfield; hotel 300 metres on R

BRACKNELL,

Stirrups Country House

Dating from the 17th century, Stirrups is now a modern hotel with first-class hospitality and service. Anglo/French dishes are served in the Tudor-style beamed restaurant.

Maidens Green RG42 6LD
Map 4: SU86
Tel: 01344 882284
Fax: 01344 882300
Cost: Set-price L & D £18.25. ☺ H/wine £9.50
Times: Noon-2pm/7-10pm (9pm Sun)
Additional: Bar food; Sunday L; Children welcome; ✿ dishes
Smoking: No smoking in dining room
Accommodation: 24 en suite ★ ★ ★

Directions: 3m N of Bracknell on B3022 towards Windsor

BRAY, **Chauntry House**

18th-century country house whose public rooms have an air of exquisite charm and comfort. In winter, enjoy an aperitif in front of the open fire in the drawing room before going on to choose perhaps sherry-infused game consommé with vegetables, followed by crisply skinned duck breast with lightly sautéed duck livers of superb flavour plus a blackberry and red wine sauce, and then mincemeat tart. Spring might see a starter of crab risotto with lobster bisque, then roast loin of lamb with spinach mousse, and a dessert of chocolate mousse, a good example of a classic. Bread rolls are commended, staff are prolific and pleasant and the wine list is a well-thought-out, informative selection of fairly priced bottles, with house Sauvignon Blanc more than acceptable.

Directions: From M4/J8/9 take A308M, then A308 (Windsor). L on B3028. Into Bray & hotel 100yds on R

SL6 2AB
Map 4: SU97
Tel: 01628 673991
Fax: 01628 773089
Chef: Chris Hope
Owners: Alan Moxon, Luis Carvalho
Cost: _Alc_ £30. ☺ H/wine £12.50
Times: Noon-2pm/7-9pm. Closed Sun, Xmas, New Year, Bhs
Additional: Children welcome; dishes
Seats: 40. Private dining room 20
Smoking: No smoking in dining room
Accommodation: 15 en suite ★ ★ ★

BRAY, **The Fat Duck**

Something of an eye-opener. 'How Heston Blumenthal has developed since I first ate here a couple of years ago, when his steak and chips was an example of how a simple dish can be outstanding.' remarks an inspector of this cutting-edge restaurant. Much has been made of the rather off-beat cooking techniques, the bizarre (to some) combinations and the obsessive nature of Blumenthal himself, but the many months of research that go into each dish is evident, as is the sheer technique and skill. Witness a cuttlefish cannelloni of duck and maple syrup – a remarkable construction, with chopped confit flavoured with syrup contained within a wafer-thin 'pasta' of cuttlefish, sliced when frozen, and served in a fresh, pungent flat parsley broth garnished with white turnip. Unlikely combinations work well, as in a roast spiced cod with braised cockscombs, lentils (cooked in Badoit) with a brunoise of vegetables including cucumber, a lovely smooth pea purée and a rich jus further enriched with sweet wine. That meal also took in an appetiser of a demi-tasse of really intense and frothy butternut squash soup with a 'surprise' seafood raviolo, a crab feuillantine with roast foie gras, a slice of excellent marinated salmon, crystallised seaweed and a light oyster juice dressing, and an unusual pastilla of pigeon. Bavarois of butternut squash, goats' milk ice cream was nothing less than brilliant. Service is attentive, casual and informed. Big changes are planned in terms of decor and kitchen – one source of

High Street Maidenhead SL6 2AQ
Map 4: SU97
Tel: 01628 580333
Fax: 01628 776188
Chef: Heston Blumenthal
Owners: Mr & Mrs H Blumenthal
Cost: _Alc_ £55, set-price L £23.50. H/wine £16
Times: Noon-2pm/7-9.30pm. Closed D Sun, all Mon, 2 wks from 23 Dec
Additional: Children welcome
Seats: 45
Smoking: No pipes & cigars

Directions: M4 J8/9 (Maidenhead), take A308 towards Windsor. turn L into Bray. Restaurant in centre of village on L

amazement is how such astonishing food can come out of such a small space – and an extended kitchen will also provide the impetus for an extended range on the menu, with pre-dessert and petits fours already coming under scrutiny.

Signature dishes: lasagne of langoustines, pig's trotter and truffles; veal sweetbread roast in salt crust with hay, confit parsnips, cockles à la plancha, lettuce and truffle cream; chocolate coulant, milk ice cream.

BRAY, Monkey Island Hotel ❀❀

SL6 2EE
Map 4: SU97
Tel: 01628 623400
Fax: 01628 784732
Chef: Chris Coubrough
Owner: NGH Properties Ltd
Cost: *Alc* £34.50, set-price L £21/D £29.50. H/wine £14.50
Times: 12.30-2.30pm/7.30-9.30pm. Closed L Sat, 26 Dec-15 Jan
Additional: Bar food; Sunday L; Children welcome; ❧ dishes
Seats: 90. Private dining rooms 120. Jacket & tie preferred
Smoking: No-smoking area
Accommodation: 26 en suite ★ ★ ★ ★

Directions: M4/J8/9, A308 (M) (Windsor) 1st L to Bray, 1st R into Old Mill Lane, hotel at end

Terrific staff for whom service and guest care count. The hotel is on a private island in the Thames with the Pavilion Restaurant sited on the narrowest tip. Colours are muted, french doors open riverside, the tall ceiling and Art Deco lighting add a quality touch, and although the place seats around a hundred, it is not in any way cramped. Our inspector was impressed by the deftness of the cooking. Her meal took in trio of sushi with pickled ginger and soy, a classic breast of chicken, the skin nicely seared, with Puy lentils, slow roast garlic and red wine jus, and a good banana custard tart. These come from a menu that takes a catholic, relaxed approach to what tastes good. Thus seafood ravioli with tomato pesto sauce, or clear Thai fish soup with glass noodles, and venison with blue cheese mousse appear on the same menu.

BRAY, Waterside Inn ❀❀❀❀

The setting is stunning: river views, flotillas of passing ducks, a weeping willow strung with fairy lights. This is one of the few restaurants in Britain where one comes close to the experience of dining in true French *haute cuisine* style, highly proper but with an essential, underlying simplicity. The discreet, well-judged service also helps create a more relaxed atmosphere than one might expect, so that even when very busy, one feels unpressured and well-cared for. Michel Roux and head chef Mark Dodson ensure the cooking is an impressive combination of highly accurate flavours and exemplary technical execution. The uncompromising quality of produce is shown to greatest effect in dishes such as a cassolette of langoustines and scallops with wild mushrooms and a light juniper nage. Fruit adds an interesting dimension – pan-fried escalopes of foie gras were perfectly partnered by rhubarb and pear and further enhanced by the accompanying bitter-sweet sauce; a beautifully balanced mandarin sauce

Ferry Road SL6 2AT
Map 4: SU97
Tel: 01628 620691
Fax: 01628 784710
Chefs: Michel Roux, Mark Dodson
Owner: Michel Roux
Cost: *Alc* £80, set-price L £29.50 (£44 Sun)/D £68 (5 courses). H/wine £25
Times: Noon-2pm (2.30pm Sun)/7-10pm. Closed L Tue, D Sun (1 Oct-30 Apr), all Mon, 26 Dec-27 Jan, 24-27 Apr
Additional: Sunday L; Children 12+; ❧ dishes
Smoking: No pipes & cigars
Seats: 75. Private dining room 8
Accommodation: 9 en suite

injected vibrancy into fillets of sole filled with langoustine mousse. The appetites of the bourgeoisie are welcomed here, summoned to table with a splendidly hearty and succulent dish of pan-fried veal chop served on a ragout of white beans and tongue, garnished with calves' sweetbread and a rich truffle sauce. A fine roll-call of classic desserts include warm golden plum soufflé, and raspberry and lemon gratin with orange and Grand Marnier sauce. There is also a wide selection of French and English unpasteurised farm cheeses. From canapés to petits fours, everything is of the highest order. The large wine list is rooted in France and predictably includes some real classic vintages and producers; less predictably, a page is dedicated to new young producers, and although prices are generally high, there are also some good value bottles to be found.

Directions: M4/J8/9. On A3089 towards Windsor, turn L before M/way overpass for Bray. Restaurant clearly signposted

BURCHETT'S GREEN, **The Crown**

SL6 6QZ
Map 4: SU88
Tel: 01628 822844
Cost: *Alc* £25. ☺ H/wine £8.95
Times: Noon-1.45pm/7-9.45pm
Additional: Bar Food L; Sunday L; Children 12+ in bar; dishes

Converted village pub that has a winning formula of delicious home cooking and a relaxed informal atmosphere. Slow cooked hock of lamb with root vegetables, and calves' liver with crispy bacon and bubble-and-squeak draws appreciative crowds.

Directions: From M4/J8/9 take A404(M) take exit signposted Henley & Burchett's Green

COOKHAM DEAN,
The Inn on the Green

The Old Cricket Common SL6 9NZ
Map 4: SU88
Tel: 01628 482638
Fax: 01628 487474
Cost: *Alc* £30, set-price L & D £15.95. ☺ H/wine £9.50
Times: Noon-2.30pm/7.30-10pm
Additional: Bar food L; Sunday L; Children welcome; dishes
Accommodation: 8 en suite

Directions: From A404 towards Marlow High St. Cross bridge towards Bisham. 1st L into Quarry Wood Rd, R into Hills Lane, R at memorial cross

Olde worlde inn with modern additions and up-to-date food. Dishes encompass monkfish tails wrapped in filo with wild rice, marinated ostrich steak, and venison with red cabbage and blackcurrant sauce.

MAIDENHEAD,
Fredrick's Hotel

An air of opulence and luxury, with panelled walls, chandeliers and spotlights, cabinets of china, and an abundance of fresh flowers. 'Joan Collins would be at home here,' noted an inspector. Luxuries turn up on the menu too, in the shape of warm salad of langoustines, oysters and mussels in saffron and coriander dressing, and foie gras with Sauternes and apple jelly, although the kitchen is equally at home with

Shoppenhangers Road
SL6 2PZ
Map 4: SU88
Tel: 01628 581000
Fax: 01628 771054
Chef: Brian Cutler
Owner: Fredrick W Lösel
Cost: *Alc* £50, set-price L £25.50/D £35.50. H/wine £15

Fredrick's Hotel

Times: Noon-2pm/7-9.45pm. Closed
L Sat, 24 Dec-3 Jan
Additional: Bar food; Sunday L;
Children welcome; 🍴 dishes
Seats: 60. Private dining room 130
Smoking: No cigars & pipes; Air
conditioning
Accommodation: 37 en suite ★ ★ ★ ★

fried calves' sweetbreads with chicken livers, saddle and
ballotine of rabbit, and skate meunière. Canapés set the ball
rolling before warm crispy duck salad with a sweet oriental
dressing. We were impressed with the care that went into a
main course of assorted seafood – white fish, scallops and
mussels – each component retaining its own distinct flavour, in
a clear herb-scented, slightly peppery broth garnished with
asparagus and samphire. Chocolate and banana tart hinting of
rum makes a rich ending, pear mousse with a matching sorbet
perhaps a more refreshing one, before as many as six kinds of
petits fours with coffee.

Directions: From M4/J8/9 take A404(M), then turning for Cox
Green/White Waltham. L into Shoppenhangers Lane. Restaurant
on R

MAIDENHEAD,
Ye Olde Bell Hotel

*Historic hotel dating from 1135, with an oak-panelled restaurant
overlooking landscaped gardens. Expect traditional Chateaubriand
for two, magret of duck, and roast rack of lamb.*

Accommodation: 47 en suite ★ ★ ★

Directions: Take A4130 to Henley, at East Arms pub turn R into
Hurley village. Hotel 800 yds down road

Hurley SL6 5LX
Map 4: SU88
Tel: 01628 825881
Fax: 01628 825939
Cost: *Alc* £35, set-price L £17.95/D
£23.50. H/wine £12.95
Times: 12.30-1.45pm/7.30-9.30pm.
Additional: Bar food; Sunday L;
Children welcome; 🍴 dishes

NEWBURY,
Donnington Valley Hotel ✿✿

Guests cannot fail to be impressed by this exceptional hotel.
The smart galleried restaurant has an almost Mediterranean
feel to it – part tiled floor, dark wood furniture, high-backed
chairs, crisp white linen and good glassware, backed up by
attentive, professional service. The Med theme runs through
the menu with dishes such as risotto of smoked mussels and
crab, or layered marinated peppers with red onion confit and
fried leaves of filo. We found seared scallops to be well-timed,
served with tiny blobs of herb purée, a light bouillon plus
spring onions and coriander dressing; roasted fillet of sea bass
came with sweet potato purée and a sun-dried tomato pickle
that worked very well. Peach and Sauternes soupière makes a

Old Oxford Road Donnington
RG14 3AG
Map 4: SU46
Tel: 01635 551199
Fax: 01635 551123
Chef: Kelvin Johnson
Owner: Sir Peter Michael
Cost: *Alc* £31.50, set-price L £15/D
£23.50 (4 courses). ☺ H /wine £11
Times: Noon-2pm/7-10pm
Additional: Bar food; Sunday L;
Children welcome; 🍴 dishes
Seats: 85. Private dining rooms 30.
Jacket & tie preferred

Donnington Valley Hotel

Smoking: No smoking in dining room
Accommodation: 58 en suite ★ ★ ★ ★

Directions: Exit M4/J13, take A34
S/bound and exit Donnington Castle.
Turn R over bridge then L

refreshing and intriguing dessert choice. The wine list is impressive but expensive with a vast representation from California, where owner Sir Peter Michael has a vineyard.

NEWBURY,

Hollington Country House

See Highclere, Hampshire

NEWBURY, **Regency Park Hotel**

Popular conference venue (within easy reach of the M3, M4) set in five acres of peaceful grounds. The new Watermark Restaurant is a spacious room resplendent in green and golden yellow with great views of the gardens. The kitchen offers a modern menu with fine chicken liver parfait and plum jam, or smoked duck salad with raspberries and a lemon and ginger dressing typical first course choices. The theme is continued with pan-fried guinea fowl carved onto an asparagus mash with sherry cream sauce, or seared slithers of salmon with black pepper and a rich chive and tomato butter. For dessert, red wine jelly layered with red berries and natural yogurt is a hit.

Directions: From Thatcham A4, towards Newbury, turn R into Northfield Road, then L at mini roundabout. Hotel is on R

Bowling Green Road Thatcham
RG18 3RP
Map 4: SU46
Tel: 01635 871555
Fax: 01635 871571
Chef: Paul Green
Cost: *Alc* £28, set-price L £14.75/D £22. ☺ H/wine £12.75
Times: Noon-1.50pm/7-9.20pm
Additional: Bar food; Sunday L; Children welcome; ✿ dishes
Seats: 100. Private dining room 40
Smoking: No smoking in dining room; Air conditioning
Accommodation: 45 en suite ★ ★ ★ ★

NEWBURY,

The Vineyard at Stockcross

The Vineyard at Stockcross was beautifully restored and refurbished in 1998. The hotel is set in immaculate grounds that centres on a pond dramatically lit by flaming torches. The split-level restaurant has an elegant Portland stone floor, a fine steel balustrade depicting a grapevine that winds its way throughout the room, and fine silver cutlery, crockery and glasses. The carte is, in essence, a modern interpretation of French classics, but with hints of west-coast American discernible in some dishes. Clean and precise flavours came through in an amuse-bouche of asparagus soup flavoured with truffle oil, and first-rate scalded sea scallops accompanied by a sauce vierge and croquant of fennel. Next came 'carre' of lamb – three cutlets served perfectly pink, sitting on a bed of

Stockcross RG20 8JU
Map 4: SU46
Tel: 01635 528770
Fax: 01635 528398
Chef: Billy Reid
Cost: Alc £50, set-price L £20/D £39
Times: Noon-1.45pm/7-9.45pm
Additional: Sunday L; ✿ dishes
Seats: 50. Private dining room 30-40
Smoking: No-smoking area; No pipes & cigars; Air conditioning
Accommodation: 33 en suite ★ ★ ★ ★

The Vineyard at Stockcross

Directions: Take A34 Newbury by-pass to A4 Bath Road interchange, then take B4000 to Stockcross, hotel on R

creamed spinach and mushrooms, with a rosemary dauphinoise, and its counterpart, Goosnargh duckling, was accurately cooked, sliced thick and served with delicious, crisp baby vegetables and a light port jus. Desserts included a good lemongrass parfait, and a clever chocolate fondant with white chocolate sauce. This all comes with lots of service and it is outstanding. There is an extremely impressive wine list with a notable selection of Californian wines.

NEWBURY, The Water Rat NEW

Attractive brick-and-thatch pub in a tiny hamlet off the A4 and just a short stroll from the Kennet & Avon Canal. Smiling and neatly attired young staff offer casual yet efficient service and daily changing menus are sensibly short. Fans will remember Carole Evans from her days at the Roebuck in Brimfield (see entry, Shropshire), and pleased to learn that she is still cooking well. Her style is simple, light and modern but can also take in hearty steak and kidney pie to please the traditionalists. We tried a robust smoked chicken terrine studded with raisins and accompanied by mango and orange chutney and crisp leaves drizzled with lemon oil; a beautifully crisp duck confit with good red cabbage – the sweet-and-sour element successfully enhanced by an orange cider sauce; and a sublime lemon tart. The wine list offers good reading with useful short tasting notes and sourced from a variety of suppliers, tapping into the strengths of each for the best selection.

Marsh Benham RG20 8LY
Map 4: SU46
Tel: 01635 582017
Fax: 01635 37338
Chef: Carole Evans
Cost: *Alc* £20, set-price D £25. ☺ H/wine £9.50
Times: Noon-2pm/7-9pm. Closed D Sun & Mon, 25 Dec, 31 Dec
Additional: Bar food; Sunday L; Children welcome; ♨ dishes
Seats: 36. Private dining room 25
Smoking: No-smoking area; No pipes

Directions: 5 miles from Hungerford; 3 miles from Newbury – just 400yds off A4

PANGBOURNE, Copper Inn

Church Road RG8 7AR
Map 4: SU67
Tel: 0118 9842244
Fax: 0118 9845542
Chef: Stuart Shepherd
Owner: Michel Rosso
Cost: *Alc* £26, set-price L £13.95 (2 courses)/D £21.95. ☺ H/wine £12.95
Times: Noon-2.30pm/7-9.30pm (10pm Fri & Sat, 9pm Sun)
Additional: Bar food L; Sunday L; Children welcome; ♨ dishes
Seats: 65. Private dining rooms 8, 30
Smoking: No-smoking area; No pipes
Accommodation: 22 en suite ★ ★ ★

An atmosphere of calm and comfort at this 19th-century coaching inn. Warm colours, well-spaced tables, tapestries, Mediterranean plates and oil-paintings on the walls, all create a striking impression in the restaurant. Lamb shank braised with vegetables, Puy lentils and smoked bacon makes a hearty, warming main course in winter, and horseradish mash brings a burst of complementary flavour to roasted fillet of sea bass with clams marinière. Otherwise, there might be osso buco of monkfish with gremolata linguine, or chicken breast with pesto risotto. For the finale, go for cappuccino brûlée, local farmhouse cheeses, or, if you remember to order in advance, chocolate fondant soufflé. Two pages of a 'sélection du patron' head up the wine list, and a good mixed bag they are too.

Directions: 5 miles from M4/J12, at junction of A329 Reading/Oxford and A340; next to parish church

Copper Inn

SHINFIELD, L'Ortolan

A smartly appointed bar adjoins a fair-sized conservatory, and the dining room has a warm, light decor. A range of menus is offered, including a 'menu gourmand' for two, a brace of 'menu du jour' at £26 and £44 respectively, and quite an extensive *carte*. Choice from all these seems a little too complex and due to the total number of dishes there is some obvious duplication of ingredients; foie gras, for example, crops up in a number of dishes on the *carte*, and is dotted around the various menus. However, John Burton-Race's cooking abilities are as sound as they ever were, as could be noted in a spring lunch taken by a duo of inspectors. Canapés showed much effort and took in cod beignets with mustard, curried chicken (satay-style), spring rolls with a chilli dip, and a salmon mousse en croûte topped with some caviar. Tortellini of fresh Cornish crab spiked with ginger and coriander had a fresh seasonal appeal, a layered terrine of foie gras, ham and lentils was a classic. Poussin gourmand comprised four components: a tender breast scented with Marc de Bourgogne and stuffed with a light mousse; a creamy morel sauce; a slice of beautifully pan-fried foie gras served on some baby spinach with a Sauternes sauce; and a puff pastry case lined with leek mousse and topped with asparagus spears. Exquisite. Tiare of salmon (marinated and roasted) came with foie gras wrapped in spinach and a well-judged sweet-and-sour port sauce. Chocolate fondant with caramelised bananas, frothy crème anglaise and a banana ice cream was truly first-class. Service, from an all-French team, is highly professional. The wine list has its roots in France with good quality throughout, as well as variety of vintages and producers for each wine.

Church Lane RG2 9BY
Map 4: SU73
Tel: 0118 9883783
Fax: 0118 9885391
Chef/Owner: John W Burton-Race
Cost: *Alc* £70, set-price L £26/D £44. H/wine £14
Times: Noon-2.15pm/7-10pm. Closed D Sun, all Mon, 1st 5 days Jan
Additional: Sunday L; Children welcome; ✿ dishes
Seats: 60. Private dining room 30
Smoking: No pipes & cigars; Air conditioning

Directions: From M4/J11, take A33 (Basingstoke). At roundabout L to Three Mile Cross, L towards Shinfield, R opposite The Hungry Horse pub. Restaurant on L, 1 mile

SONNING, The French Horn

Superbly located hotel on the banks of the Thames. From the restaurant guests can watch the passing river life while enjoying some sound French cooking. Start with a classic – pan-fried slice of goose foie gras served with apple slices and Calvados sauce, or pan-fried scallops laced with ginger dressing. There's a good selection of seafood (we recommend the deep-fried Dublin Bay prawns), as well as a substantial choice of meat dishes: roasted saddle of marinated hare; roasted chump of lamb with provençale vegetables; and the restaurant's signature dish – half a duck, spit-roasted in front

RG4 6TN
Map 4: SU77
Tel: 0118 9692204
Fax: 0118 9442210
Chef: Gille Company
Owners: The Emmanuel Family
Cost: *Alc* £45, set-price L £19.50/D £32. H/wine £13
Times: Noon-2pm/7-9.30pm. Closed Good Fri
Additional: Sunday L; Children welcome; ✿ dishes

The French Horn

Seats: 70. Private dining room 24
Smoking: No pipes & cigars in dining room
Accommodation: 20 en suite ★ ★ ★

of the fire in the bar and carved at the table. Lunch is a simpler affair; expect dishes such as steak and kidney pudding, whole trout roasted with almonds, and grilled lambs kidneys and bacon.

Directions: M4/J8/9 & A4, village centre, on the river

STREATLEY,
Swan Diplomat Hotel ✿✿

High Street RG8 9HR
Map 4: SU58
Tel: 01491 878800
Fax: 01491 872554
Chef: Damian Bradley
Cost: *Alc* £37, set-price L £25/D £32. H/wine £9.50
Times: D only, 7-10pm
Additional: Bar food; Sunday L (Noon-2pm); Children welcome; ✍ dishes
Seats: 70. Private dining room 20
Smoking: No pipes & cigars
Accommodation: 46 en suite ★ ★ ★ ★

Directions: Follow A329 from Pangbourne, on entering Streatley turn R at traffic lights. The hotel is on L before bridge

Great location backed up by sound service. The restaurant of this perfectly sited hotel (on the banks of the Thames) continues serenely on its way, continuing to please by its consistency. Simplicity is not scorned here: a warm salad of partridge breast is accompanied by pancetta, roast garlic and Puy lentils; roast rack of English lamb is cooked with thyme and served with roasted winter vegetables, potato purée and a redcurrant jus. Yet there's a sense of adventure carried through at the same time, with a pan-fried foie gras served on a celeriac galette and backed up by buttered spinach, seared mango and orange truffle dressing. The Club Room lets old England live on, with lunchtime offerings of braised beef and stout pie and grilled Cumberland sausage ring and spring onion mash, in amongst the risotto of tomato and black olive, and black and white linguini with pesto.

WINDSOR,

Aurora Garden Hotel

Elegant conservatory-style restaurant overlooking floodlit water gardens and terrace. Typical dishes are roast pork with apple sauce, and grilled salmon fillet with garlic butter.

Smoking: No smoking in dining room; Air conditioning
Accommodation: 19 en suite ★ ★

Directions: From M4 take A308 (Staines); at 3rd roundabout take 3rd exit (Bolton Ave). Hotel is 500yds on R

Bolton Avenue SL4 3JF
Map 4: SU97
Tel: 01753 868686
Fax: 01753 831394
Cost: *Alc* £8.95, set-price L £8.95/D £12.95. ☺ H/wine £9.50
Times: Noon-2.30pm/7-9.30pm. Closed L Sat
Additional: Bar food; Sunday L; Children welcome; ⚫ dishes

WINDSOR, **The Castle Hotel** ✿✿

High Street SL4 1LJ
Map 4: SU97
Tel: 01753 851011
Fax: 01753 830244
Chef: Andrew Barrass
Owner: Forte Hotels
Cost: *Alc* 32.50, set-price L £10 (2 courses)/D £24. ☺ H/wine £12.50
Times: Noon-2pm/7-10pm.
Additional: Bar food; Sunday L
Seats: 60. Private dining room 25
Smoking: No smoking in dining room
Accommodation: 111 en suite ★ ★ ★

Directions: In town centre, opposite Guildhall

Popular tourist and conference hotel located in the shadow of Windsor Castle. The elegant main restaurant, with crisp white cloths and topiary decorations, serves British cooking; there is also a less formal café for bistro meals and snacks. A good-value business lunch might feature chicken Caesar salad and supreme of chicken in rich red wine jus. The main, seasonal menu is bang up to date with dishes such as Thai scented seafood bisque, griddled swordfish steak with tomato fondue served with red onion and garlic mashed potatoes, and pan-fried guinea fowl with caramelised apples and wild mushroom and herb risotto. Scallops with pancetta and basil were successful in their simplicity, but deep-fried brie with sun-dried tomatoes in filo parcels less so, although clearly home-made.

WINDSOR,

Oakley Court Hotel ✿✿

Divided restaurant in Gothic Victorian hotel – once the location for Hammer horrors. The proximity to Heathrow means that the hotel attracts quite a few conference guests. The setting is suitably smart with attentive service and a pleasant atmosphere. A short *carte* keeps up with metropolitan trends with starters such as tartare of smoked haddock and Cornish crab with caviar and lime and 'chevrill' vierge, or seared foie gras on a brioche croûte with caramelised oranges and a warm truffle butter sauce, as well as rack of lamb with haricot beans, tomato and garlic plus roast black pudding among main courses, with a lavender honey tuile bringing up the rear.

Windsor Road Water Oakley SL4 5UR
Map 4: SU97
Tel: 01753 609988
Fax: 01628 637011
Chef: Charles Cooper
Cost: *Alc* £40. H/wine £14.95
Times: 12.30-1.45pm/7.30-9.45pm
Additional: Bar food; Sunday L; Children welcome; ⚫ dishes
Seats: 70. Private dining room 200. Jacket & tie preferred
Smoking: No smoking in dining room

Oakley Court Hotel

Accommodation: 115 en suite
★ ★ ★ ★

Directions: From London M4.J6 onto
A308 to Maidenhead or from Reading
M4 J8/9 onto A308. Hotel beside the
Thames off A308

WINDSOR,

Sir Christopher Wren's House Hotel ❀❀

Thames Street SL4 1PX
Map 4: SU97
Tel: 01753 861354
Fax: 01753 860172
Telephone for further details

Refurbishment of this historical landmark on Eton Bridge has brought this hotel bang up to date. 'The Sir Christopher Wren is sheer pleasure, especially at lunchtime when one can watch the Thames flow past and remember a calmer way of life', comments an inspector on the tranquil nature of this pleasant place. The style is fairly opulent without too much excess, and the dining room and bar both offer the luxury of space; staff are old school and courteous. Our test meal revealed real ambition in the kitchen. We took in mille-feuille of scallops with piccalilli baby leeks and sauce nero, chargrilled breast of duck with a pithiviers of celeriac and wild mushrooms flavoured with fresh liver boudin, and glazed lemon tart with citrus sorbet and raspberry purée. Breads are made in house and are excellent.

WINKFIELD, **Rose & Crown** ❀

Woodside Windsor Forest SL4 2DP
Map 4: SU97
Tel: 01344 882051
Fax: 01344 885346
Cost: *Alc* £20. ☺ H/wine £8.75
Times: Noon-2.30pm/7-9.30pm.
Closed D Sun & Mon
Additional: Bar food; Sunday L;
Children 10+; ✿ dishes
Smoking: No pipes & cigars

A traditional pub run in a relaxed manner by the Morris family. A serious approach to food, apparent in dishes such as pavé of sea bass with pesto risotto, and medallions of beef with shallot confit and red wine sauce.

Accommodation: 2 rooms

Directions: M3/J3 from Ascot racecourse on A332, take 2nd exit from Heatherwood Hospital rdbt, then 2nd L

YATTENDON, **Royal Oak** ❀❀❀

The Square RG18 0UG
Map 4: SU57
Tel: 01635 201325
Fax: 01635 201926
Chef: Robbie Macrae
Owner: The Restaurant Partnership
Cost: Set-price D £32.50. H/wine £9.95
Times: Noon-2.30pm/7-9.30pm.
Closed L Sat, D Sun, 1 Jan
Additional: Bar food (Brasserie);

Idiosyncratic country inn with civilized service. Robbie Macrae, from the Marco Pierre White stable, has learnt his trade well and offers a style of cooking that concentrates on matching big flavours with lovely, brave ideas such as oysters with scrambled eggs, chive velouté and Keta caviar, and tartlet of lambs fillet with sweetbreads and Parma ham. Fashion is turned on its head with tournedos Rossini, confit shallots and baby vegetables, as well as the welcome inclusion of sauerkraut in a dish of roast loin of venison with wild mushrooms and

Royal Oak

Sunday L; Children welcome
Seats: 24. Private dining room 10.
Jacket & tie preferred
Smoking: No smoking in dining room
Accommodation: 5 en suite ★ ★

sauce veneur. French-influenced desserts include hot chocolate
fondant with griottine cherries and hazelnut parfait with Kirsch
cream. The bar menu has a brasserie slant with dishes such as
confit of Barbary duck leg with honey-roast vegetables and
gratin potatoes, or chargrilled tuna with crushed new potatoes
and pesto. It all adds a cosmopolitan touch to the popular
17th-century inn, deep in the Berkshire countryside. The
dining room is light and bright, full of fresh flowers, plants and
pictures and, although away from the river, there is a beautiful
garden for outside dining in the summer.

Directions: M4/J12 follow signs towards Pangbourne, turn L for
Yattendon; in centre of the village

BRISTOL

BRISTOL, **Aztec Hotel** ✿

*Quarterjacks, the bright, modern, bustling restaurant at this Bristol
hotel, offers a Med-inspired menu that takes in sweet seared scallops
with yellow pepper risotto, and pan-fried chicken breast with
crunchy asparagus and saffron sauce.*

Directions: On Aztec West Business Park at interchange of
M4/M5

Aztec West Business Park
Almondsbury BS12 4TS
Map 3: ST57
Tel: 01454 201090
Fax: 01454 201593
Telephone for further details

BRISTOL, **Bells Diner** ✿

*Quiet backstreet setting with a relaxed and trendy atmosphere. There
are Moroccan and African influences set alongside a more familiar
repertoire of goats' cheese soufflé and seared sea bass.*

Additional: Sunday L (ex May-Sep); Children welcome;
 dishes
Smoking: No smoking in dining room

Directions: Corner premises in York Road, Montpellier

1 York Road BS6 5QB
Map 3: ST57
Tel: 0117 9240357
Fax: 0117 9244280
Cost: *Alc* £18. ☺ H/wine £9.95
Times: Noon-2.30pm/7-10.15pm.
Closed L Sat & Mon, D Sun, 24-30
Dec, last wk Aug

BRISTOL, **Berkeley Square Hotel**

The hotel is set in a Georgian terrace forming part of an elegant square. However, the restaurant interior is modern, as are the interesting dishes offered from a choice of menus.

Accommodation: 41 en suite ★ ★ ★

Directions: Top of Park Street turn L at traffic lights into Berkeley Square, hotel on R

15 Berkeley Square Clifton BS8 1HB
Map 3: ST57
Tel: 0117 9254000
Fax: 0117 9252970
Cost: *Alc* £22. ☺ H/wine £8.95
Times: Noon-2pm/7-10.30pm. Closed L Sun
Additional: Children welcome; 🍴 dishes

BRISTOL, **Blue Goose**

Vibrant restaurant in blue – a lively setting for dishes such as Toulouse sausage in brioche with Bavarian cumin seed cabbage, and pan-fried salmon with colcannon and chive sauce.

Smoking: No-smoking area; Air conditioning

Directions: From city centre, A38 N (Stokes Croft) approx 2 miles to Horefield. On L, corner of Ash & Gloucester Rds

344 Gloucester Road Horfield BS7 8UR
Map 3: ST57
Tel: 0117 9420940
Fax: 0117 9444033
Cost: *Alc* £17
Times: D only, 7-10pm. Closed Sun, Mon
Additional: Children 5+; 🍴 dishes

BRISTOL,
Bristol Marriott Hotel

Le Château is a splendid restaurant in a modern hotel, where wood panelling, upholstered chairs, floor length curtains, and well spaced, candlelit tables set the scene for Anglo-French cooking.

Smoking: No-smoking area; Air conditioning
Accommodation: 289 en suite ★ ★ ★ ★

Directions: Close to Bristol city centre, at the Old Market, opposite castle ruins

Lower Castle Street BS1 3AD
Map 3: ST57
Tel: 0117 9294281
Fax: 0117 9276377
Cost: *Alc* £17.50
Times: D only, 7-10.30pm. Closed Sun, Xmas wk
Additional: Children welcome; 🍴 dishes

BRISTOL,
Glass Boat Restaurant

Welsh Back
BS1 4SB
Map 3: ST57
Tel: 0117 9290704
Fax: 0117 9297338
Chef: Michel Lemoin
Owner: Arne Ringner

Slick and professional service without being formal.
Permanently moored in the rejuvenated Bristol Dock, the Glass Boat Restaurant provides quite a setting for that power lunch or romantic candlelit dinner. The cooking is modern

British with Mediterranean influences. The latter is evident in the likes of chargrilled Mediterranean-vegetable tartlet with provençale herb salad, warm goats' cheese on a garlic crouton with a tomato and basil salad, and provençale-style braised beef with an orange and olive compote. It was the dessert list that provided the highlight of our most recent meal; a delicious chocolate pudding concealing a liquid, bitter chocolate centre. Both old and New World wines appear on a list that has something to suit most pockets.

Directions: By Bristol Bridge in the old centre of Bristol

Cost: *Alc* £24, set-price L £12 (2 courses)/D £17.50. ☺ H/wine £9.75
Times: Noon-2pm/6.30-11pm. Closed L Sat, all Sun
Additional: Children welcome; 🍴 dishes
Seats: 100. Private dining room 40
Smoking: No-smoking area; No pipes & cigars; Air conditioning

BRISTOL, **Harveys**

12 Denmark Street BS1 5DQ
Map 3: ST57
Tel: 0117 9275034
Fax: 0117 9275001
Chef: Daniel Galmiche
Owners: John Harvey & Sons
Cost: Set-price L £17.95/D £39.95. ☺ H/wine £14
Times: Noon-1.30pm/7-9.30pm. Closed L Sat, all Sun, 3rd wk Feb, 2 wks Aug
Additional: Children welcome; 🍴 dishes
Seats: 60. Private dining room 40
Smoking: Air conditioning

Harveys of Bristol must be a household name. The medieval cellars that house the elegant Conran-designed restaurant, were once used to bottle its Bristol Cream sherry. Indeed, take the chance to wander through the cellars and examine the unique and fascinating exhibits on show. As befits a wine merchant, the wine list runs to over 300 bins. 'Modern French' is how the kitchen describes its style, which extends to carpaccio of Scottish beef with pesto, rocket and Parmesan, and loin of lamb with rosemary jus on herb risotto. Pedigree ingredients are handled with imaginative flair by Daniel Galmiche, to produce starters of perhaps herby consommé of quail, three breast slices, crisped and of excellent flavour, with foie gras toast, or a terrine of duck with pistachio nuts, 'just as a terrine should be', served with a chutney of winter fruits tasting of cinnamon. An understanding of textures and combinations shines through a main course of Scottish beef pan-fried with sage and garlic accompanied by Chinese cabbage and caramelised shallots, the beef itself accurately cooked with a wee crust to hold in its juices, or fillet of turbot baked in a langoustine bouillon served with wild mushrooms, asparagus and truffle. Desserts might include classics of 'wonderfully light' crème brûlée with Harveys ice cream, or pistachio soufflé with vanilla ice cream.
Signature dishes: warm potato and truffle salad with roasted Scottish scallop and balsamic dressing; pan-roast farm pigeon with sautéed new potatoes with sea salt and herbs; warm bitter chocolate tart with a salad of citrus fruits and zest.

AA Wine Award see page 16
Shortlisted for

Directions: City centre off Unity Street at bottom of Park Street, opposite City Hall and Cathedral; follow signs for Harveys Wine Museum

BRISTOL, **Howards Restaurant**

1a-2a Avon Crescent Hotwells
BS1 6XQ
Map 3: ST57
Tel: 0117 9262921
Fax: 0117 9255585
Chef: David Short
Owner: Christopher Howard
Cost: *Alc* £25, set-price L £15/D
£16.50. ☺ H/wine £8.95
Times: Noon-2pm/7-11pm. Closed L
Sat, all Sun, Bhs
Additional: Children welcome;
🌢 dishes
Seats: 60. Private dining room 27
Smoking: No-smoking area

Directions: 5 minutes from city centre
following signs for M5/Avonmouth,
On the dockside over a small bridge,
close to SS Great Britain.

Check directions unless you know your way around Bristol.
The burgundy-fronted bistro-style restaurant is nicely decked
out: wood panelling, striped wallpaper, small bar area on
entering and attracts a loyal clientele. The *carte* is
supplemented by vegetarian blackboard specials and by set
lunch and dinner menus, all of which are changed regularly to
take advantage of seasonal produce. Game terrine
accompanied by a tomato and chilli chutney, or warm bacon
and scallop salad with tarragon dressing are typical starters,
followed perhaps by loin of lamb topped by herb mousse and
served with basil and tomato sauce. Desserts include a super
chocolate truffle torte with crème fraîche and raspberry sauce.
The wine list is in line with the food, and selected half-bottles
are offered on a blackboard.

BRISTOL,
Hunt's Restaurant

26 Broad Street BS1 2HG
Map 3: ST57
Tel/Fax: 0117 9265580
Chef: Andrew Hunt
Owners: Andrew & Anne Hunt
Cost: *Alc* £30, set-price L £13.90 (2
courses). ☺ H/wine £9.95
Times: Noon-2pm/7-10pm. Closed L
Sat, all Sun & Mon, 1 wk Easter, 2
wks Aug, 10 days Xmas
Additional: Children welcome;
🌢 dishes
Seats: 40. Private dining room 26

Directions: City centre, 25 yds from
St John's Arch

A city-centre restaurant pleasing for its simplicity combined
with a certain elegance. Starched tablecloths, fresh flowers,
smart but relaxed staff sums it up. Andrew Hunt is an
accomplished chef with a good pedigree and his interpretation
of modern British cooking is some of the best in the city. An
expressive and inventive Mediterranean seam runs through the
menu, most creative when it comes to fish cookery: this yields
such dishes as roast Cornish turbot with a hazelnut pesto and
tomato, or smoked haddock Monte Carlo with parsley, tomato,
poached egg and new potatoes. Some items defy simple
pigeonholes and are the better for it: local pheasant with
celery, port and wild thyme, or medallions of venison with
sweet dill gherkins, sour cream and tarragon, for example.
Desserts do not disappoint, whether a fine chocolate marquise
with coffee bean sauce, or a walnut and treacle tart with fresh
figs and Pernod.

BRISTOL, **Markwicks**

43 Corn Street BS1 1HT
Map 3: ST57
Tel/Fax: 0117 9262658
Chef: Stephen Markwick
Owners: Stephen & Judy Markwick
Cost: *Alc* £29.50, set-price L
£17.50/D £25.50. H/wine £12.50

Elegant city-centre restaurant in what was once a bank vault.
Stephen Markwick has a strong following for cooking that
offers an assured, confident modern style based on sound
classical technique allied to good raw materials. Both the set
lunch and dinner menus are a bargain. From the short, hand-

Markwicks

Times: Noon-2pm/7-10pm. Closed L Sat, all Sun
Additional: Children welcome; 🍷 dishes
Seats: 45. Private dining rooms 6-20

Directions: Top end of Corn Street beneath Commercial Rooms

written carte comes grilled pigeon breast with pancetta and butter bean purée, followed by calves' liver with onion and thyme purée with Puy lentils and Sauternes sauce. Fish is a strength with an unusual but very successful scallop tart accompanied by pak choi and ginger beurre blanc, or a perfectly timed pan-fried fillet of sea bass with roasted fennel and red pepper sauce showing what can be done. Chocoholic inspectors have praised the hot chocolate fondant with sauce anglaise.

BRISTOL, Red Snapper ✿

1 Chandos Road Redland
BS6 6PG
Map 3: ST57
Tel: 0117 9737999
Fax: 0117 9247316
Cost: *Alc* D £22.50, set-price L £12.
☺ H/wine £9.50
Times: Noon-1.45pm/7.30-9.45pm.
Closed D Sun, L Mon, 1 wk after Xmas
Additional: Sunday L; Children welcome
Smoking: No pipes & cigars

Directions: Telephone for directions

Fresh, simple and stylish, with red table tops and walls and a stripped wooden floor. Fish figures prominently: zander fillet with capers and fennel; sole meunière.

BRISTOL, Riverstation ✿✿

Very avant garde for Bristol: contemporary, light, 'transparent' building, converted from a dock-side river police station. The first-floor restaurant has a terrace looking over the water for alfresco dining (weather permitting), and there's a deli and café downstairs – where there is also a small outside deck. The interior is defined by clean lines and high quality materials: glass, marble, steel, zinc and wood. The food blends distinctive combinations with innovative ideas. The Mediterranean is a strong influence: pancetta, risotto, pesto, chorizo, salsa rossa, balsamic are buzz words that leap out from the menu, but things oriental are not neglected. Deep-fried crab cakes with sweet chilli sauce and pickled papaya, and

The Grove BS1 4RB
Map 3: ST57
Tel: 0117 9144434
Fax: 0117 9349990
Chef: Peter Taylor
Owners: Shirley Anne Bell, Peter Taylor, John Payne
Cost: *Alc* £22, set-price L £10.50/D £12.95 (both 2 courses). ☺ H/wine £9.50
Times: Noon-2.30pm/6-10.30pm.
Closed L Sat, 25-28 Dec
Additional: Sunday L; Children welcome; 🍷 dishes

rare-roast duck breast with braised tofu, pak choi and black bean sauce are interesting ideas that work well, mainly because the kitchen prefers not to mess around too much with things on the plate. Rum baba with coffee ice cream is an up-to-date dessert. Strong selection of wines by the glass.

Seats: 130
Smoking: No-smoking area; No pipes & cigars

Directions: Telephone for directions

BRISTOL,
Swallow Royal Hotel ✿✿

College Green BS1 5TA
Map 3: ST57
Tel: 0117 9255100
Fax: 0117 9304740
Chef: Giles Stonehouse
Cost: *Alc* £27, set-price L & D £22.
☺ H/wine £13.20
Times: 12.30-2.30pm/ 7-10.30pm
Additional: Bar food; Sunday L; Children welcome; ♨ dishes
Seats: 150
Smoking: No-smoking area; Air conditioning
Accommodation: 242 en suite
★ ★ ★ ★

Directions: City centre, next to cathedral

Restored mid-Victorian landmark building next to the cathedral. The original Palm Court (lofty stained-glass ceiling, statues, Bath-stone columns) creates a stunning backdrop for the smart dinner-only restaurant that takes its name. In such a setting the correct, formal service seems quite appropriate and is matched by a stylish French-inspired menu. Begin with the likes of pan-fried foie gras with Calvados apple compote and toasted brioche, or perhaps langoustine tails on tomato and red pepper relish with crustace oil before moving on to flambé of duck magret with a five-spice and oyster jus, or a roast loin and braised shoulder of lamb with a couscous pithiviers and mint basil jus. Desserts range from Bramley apple crumble with cinnamon custard to almond nougat terrine and crêpes flambé. The hotel's Terrace restaurant provides a less formal eating option.

BUCKINGHAMSHIRE

ASTON CLINTON, **The Bell Inn**

Beautiful gardens and roses around the door add to the charm of this 17th-century former coaching inn. Once inside choose between the mellow flagstoned-floored bar or elegant pine-panelled lounge for pre-prandial drinks before moving into the spacious restaurant whose walls are covered with murals representing the four seasons. The classy menu is full of interest with starters such as boudin of rabbit with confit of the thigh on tomato and braised lettuce, and main courses of grilled medallions of monkfish on a mussel fritter with

Aylesbury
HP22 5HP
Map 4: SP81
Tel: 01296 630252
Fax: 01296 631250
Chef: Colin Woodward
Owners: Michael D G Harris, G W Botley, G Le Roux
Cost: *Alc* £35, set-price L £14.50. ☺ H/wine £13
Times: Noon-2pm/7-9.30pm

'spaghetti' vegetables and a chilli and soy jus, and locally shot pheasant with a shepherd's pie of the leg and ginger wine sauce. Look out too for the Bell's famous Aylesbury Duckling, bred especially for them by Richard Waller. The comprehensive wine list is evidence of owner Michael Harris' passion for, and deep knowledge of, the subject.

Directions: In the centre of the village on the A41, 4 miles from Aylesbury. 10 mins M25/J20

The Bell Inn

Additional: Bar food L; Sunday L; Children welcome; dishes
Seats: 90. Private dining room 20
Smoking: No smoking in dining room
Accommodation: 20 en suite ★ ★ ★

Shortlisted for the AA Wine Award – see page 16

ASTON CLINTON,

West Lodge Hotel ❀❀

Originally built as a house for a member of the Rothschild family. Hot-air balloons grace the walls of the Victorian-style Mongolfier Restaurant and are used as a logo on the menus, reflecting the fact that the owners run a commercial flight balloon business from the hotel. The set-price menu changes weekly and offers four starters, four main courses and four desserts. The style of cooking is best described as modern classical French: puff pastry filled with scrambled egg and truffle; fillet of beef and pork with a red wine and tarragon mustard sauce; crème brûlée with forest fruits. The wine list is entirely French and in some places limited. For example, there is only one white Burgundy and that is a Grand Cru. The reds are a better bet. The restaurant is only open to the public on Fridays and Saturdays.

Directions: On A41 between Aylesbury and Hemel Hempstead.

London Road Nr Aylesbury
HP22 5HL
Map 4: SP81
Tel: 01296 630362
Fax: 01296 630151
Chef: Philippe Brillant
Owners: Irene & Jeff Burlinson
Cost: *Alc* £36.75, set-price D £30. H/wine £15
Times: D only, 7.30-9pm. Only open Fri & Sat D
Additional: Bar food D; Children 12+; dishes
Seats: 26
Smoking: No smoking in dining room; Air conditioning
Accommodation: 7 en suite ★ ★

AYLESBURY, Hartwell House

Oxford Road HP17 8NL
Map 4: SP81
Tel: 01296 747444
Fax: 01296 747450
Chef: Roger Barstow
Owner: Historic House Hotels Ltd
Cost: *Alc* £29, set-price L £29/D £44.
H/wine £12.90
Times: 12.30-1.45pm/7.30-9.40pm.
Additional: Sunday L; Children 8+;
👍 dishes
Seats: 70. Private dining rooms 18/30.
Jacket & tie preferred at D
Smoking: No smoking in dining room
Accommodation: 46 en suite ★ ★ ★ ★

Directions: 2 miles from Aylesbury on
A418 (Oxford)

Grand country mansion with service to match. The grandness
of the public rooms is carried through to the dining room –
well-spaced tables that are smartly appointed and a subtle
lemon decor add up to a stunning, elegant setting. Roger
Barstow displays exact timing as well as direct flavours on a
lengthy fixed-price menu that is no stranger to the richest of
ingredients: foie gras accompanies both roasted fillet of halibut
and breast of Aylesbury duckling, but the repertoire also covers
a lot of territory and bristles with ideas. There is, for example, a
trio of marinated tuna, baby squid and oyster on a sesame seed
and wasabi dressing, or pan-fried sea scallops and Dover sole
with a parsley purée, black noodles and Noilly Prat sauce. An
early spring lunch ('very quiet – dinner is more the thing here'),
impressed with its sound skill and quality ingredients. Note a
superb layered terrine of salmon, sole and king prawn with
saffron dressing, roast chump of lamb, accompanied by pesto
crushed potatoes, Jerusalem artichokes and garlic jus, and a trio
of apple desserts: mini mille-feuille of apple sorbet with apple
crisps, a light apple parfait garnished with a julienne of apple,
and a little apple tarte Tatin. The wine list, as might be
expected, is quite large but is surprisingly lacking in depth
considering the clientele the place must attract.

BUCKINGHAM, Villiers Hotel

3 Castle Street MK18 1BS
Map 4: SP63
Tel: 01280 822444
Fax: 01280 822113
Chef: Paul Stopps
Owners: Tom Scrase, Henry Scrase,
Nicholas Pattie
Cost: *Alc* £28, set-price D £19.75. 😊
H/wine £11.95
Times: D only, 7-10pm (L by
arrangement). Closed D Sun. 26 Dec,
1 Jan
Additional: Bar food L; Sunday L;
Children welcome; 👍 dishes
Seats: 55. Private dining room 16
Smoking: Air conditioning
Accommodation: 38 en suite ★ ★ ★

*Well equipped hotel with spacious bedrooms and excellent
conference facilities.* Oliver Cromwell billeted his troops at
this old coaching inn in 1643, and some 350 years later, Villiers

is still welcoming guests. Two restaurants and a stone-flagged pub compete for attention. We dined in Henry's Restaurant, which overlooks the cobbled courtyard. A well-flavoured fishcake with coriander and spicy mustard dressing got the meal under way, followed by a first-class saddle of venison, tender and pink, served with a raspberry sauce and roasted Med vegetables. Dessert was an excellent fig and raspberry tart, while good filter coffee and a handful of truffle and praline petits fours rounded the meal off.

Directions: Town centre – Castle Street is to R of Town Hall near main square.

BURNHAM,
Burnham Beeches Hotel

18th-century royal hunting lodge, built in what was once part of Windsor Park. The menu encompasses roast saddle of lamb, sauté of wild duck, and tempura of red mullet.

Smoking: No smoking in dining room
Accommodation: 82 en suite ★ ★ ★

Directions: Off A355 via Farnham Royal roundabout

Grove Road SL1 8DP
Map 4: SU98
Tel: 01628 429955
Fax: 01628 603994
Cost: *Alc* £22.50, set-price L £17.50
Times: 12.30-2pm/7-10pm. Closed L Sat
Additional: Bar Food; Sunday L; Children welcome; ✿ dishes

BURNHAM BEECHES,
Grovefield Hotel

Close to Heathrow and Windsor, Grovefield is set in spacious grounds. Totally refurbished, rooms are brightly decorated and comfortable. Fine dining in the restaurant.

Directions: Telephone for directions

Taplow Common Road SL1 8LP
Tel: 01628 603131
Fax: 01628 668078
Telephone for further details

CHENIES,
Bedford Arms Chenies

Peaceful 19th-century country inn just minutes from the M25 serving Anglo-French food: chicken liver parfait with Melba toast; pigeon and blueberry salad with raspberry dressing.

WD3 6EQ
Map 4: TQ09
Tel: 01923 283301
Fax: 01923 284825
Cost: *Alc* £30, set-price L £18.50/D £23. ☺ H/wine £12.55
Times: 12.30-2pm/7.30-10pm. Closed Sat L
Additional: Bar food; Sunday L; Children welcome; ✿ dishes
Smoking: No pipes & cigars
Accommodation: 10 en suite ★ ★ ★

Directions: M25, J18/A404 towards Amersham, turn R to Latimer/Chenies, hotel is visible 200yds

DINTON, La Chouette

A relaxed, informal restaurant at the end of a quiet road.
Frédéric Desmette runs a one-man band. The extrovert chef
and owner somehow manages to handle the bar, kitchen and
front of house single handedly The style of cooking reflects
Belgian roots, but many dishes have a French ring – fillet of
brill in a champagne sauce, for example, or wild duck with
woodland mushrooms. For something truly Belgian go for
pheasant with chicory. On a crisp February evening we kicked
off, however, with purée of prawns folded in a béchamel sauce
topped with breadcrumbs. Then an 'earthy winter dish' of
rabbit cooked in brown beer with carrots, mushrooms, lardons
and prunes. For dessert, a 'very good' fresh fruit sabayon.

Westlington Green Nr Aylesbury
HP17 8UW
Map 4: SP71
Tel/Fax: 01296 747422
Chef/Owner: Frédéric Desmette
Cost: *Alc* £35, set-price L £11/D
£27.50 (4 courses). H/wine £10.50
Times: Noon-2pm/7-9pm. Closed L
Sat, all Sun
Additional: Children welcome
Seats: 40
Smoking: No pipes & cigars

Directions: On A418 at Dinton

HADDENHAM,
The Green Dragon

8 Churchway Haddenham HP17 8AA
Map 4: SP70
Tel: 01844 291403
Cost: *Alc* £23. ☺ H/wine £10.95
Times: Noon-2pm/7-9pm. Closed D
Sun
Additional: Bar food L; Sunday L;
Children 6+; ☙ dishes

Directions: From M40 take A329
towards Thame, then A418. Turn 1st
R after entering Haddenham

*A small, cheery pub restaurant near the village green. Expect
modern British dishes with the odd Mediterranean twist – try seared
tuna steak with ginger and lemon grass.*

IVINGHOE,
The King's Head ✿

LU7 9EB
Map 4: SP91
Tel: 01296 668388/668264
Fax: 01296 668107
Telephone for further details

Directions: From M25/J20. Take the
A41(M) towards Tring. Turn R, B488
(Ivinghoe). Hotel on R at the junction
with B489

*Traditional restaurant with some of the atmosphere of an exclusive
club, including some smooth and skilled service. Expect chicken
liver pâté, Cajun salmon on spinach with lemon butter sauce, and
raspberry cheesecake from the dessert trolley.*

MARLOW,

The Compleat Angler

Marlow Bridge SL7 1RG
Map 4: SU88
Tel: 01628 484444
Fax: 01628 486388
Cost: *Alc* £50, set-price L £17.95 (2
courses)/D £33.50. H/wine £15
Times: 12.30-2pm/7-9.45pm
Additional: Bar food; Sunday L;
Children welcome; ✿ dishes
Accommodation: 65 en suite ★ ★ ★ ★

Directions: From M4/J8/9 or M40/J4
take A404; hotel is on S bank of river
by bridge

*Well-known hotel on the banks of the Thames with the smart
Riverside Restaurant overlooking the rushing waters of Marlow
weir. Modern ideas influence the likes of pan-fried goose liver with
broken potatoes and olives.*

MARLOW,

Danesfield House ✿✿

Henley Road SL7 2EY
Map 4: SU88
Tel: 01628 891010
Fax: 01628 890408
Chef: Michael Macdonald
Cost: *Alc* £45, set-price L £25.50/D
£35.50 (4 courses). H/wine £19.50
Times: Noon-2.30pm/7-10pm
Additional: Bar food (brasserie);
Sunday L; Children welcome;
✿ dishes
Seats: 45. Private dining room up to
110
Smoking: No smoking in dining room
Accommodation: 87 en suite ★ ★ ★ ★

Directions: M40/J4, A404 to Marlow,
then A4155 to Henley. Hotel 2 miles
on L

Grand building, grand service. It's difficult to believe that this
grand Tudor/Gothic pile, complete with crenellations and acres
of formal gardens, was actually built as late as 1899. Imposing
public rooms include the Oak Room restaurant where mellow
panelling and a fine, ornate plaster ceiling are matched by
elegantly appointed tables and courteous, willing service. The
stylish menu reflects the seasons and has its roots in classical
French cuisine. Note ravioli of lobster sauce amèricaine, and
goats' cheese soufflé with poached pears and walnut dressing,
or the likes of roasted sea bass with black olive crust and pesto,
and medallion of Suffolk venison with 'sauce au chocolate
amer et vinaigre de framboise'. Some 20 or so champagnes
head an impressive wine list.

TAPLOW,

Cliveden Hotel, Waldo's Restaurant

Maidenhead SL6 0JF
Map 4: SU98
Tel: 01628 668561
Fax: 01628 661837
Cost: Set-price D £58. H/wine £19
Times: Waldo's D only, 7.30-9.15pm.
Closed Sun, Mon, 24 Dec-17 Jan
Smoking: No smoking in dining room;
Air conditioning
Accommodation: 38 en suite ★★★★★

No rosettes awarded this year, for as we went to press we learnt that chef Gary Jones was leaving Cliveden's premier restaurant, the four AA Rosetted Waldo's. John Wood (formerly Chapter One, see entry, London) has been appointed executive chef.

Directions: On B476, 2 miles N of Taplow

CAMBRIDGESHIRE

BYTHORN, Bennett's Restaurant

Delightful rural inn with pretty restaurant and bustling bar. Anglo-French dishes include salmon terrine with watercress sauce, and sautéed calves' liver and venison with wild mushrooms.

Directions: Between Kettering & Huntingdon on A14

The White Hart Huntingdon
PE18 0QN
Map 4: TL07
Tel/Fax: 01832 710226
Telephone for further details

CAMBRIDGE, Arundel House

Chesterton Road CB4 3AN
Map 5: TL45
Tel: 01223 367701
Fax: 01223 367721
Cost: *Alc* £22, set-lunch £11.95/D
£15.95. ☺ H/wine £9.75
Times: 12.15-1.45pm/6.30-9.30pm.
Closed 25-26 Dec
Additional: Bar food; Sunday L;
Children welcome; ✿ dishes
Smoking: No smoking in dining room;
Air conditioning
Accommodation: 102 en suite ★★

Directions: On A1303, overlooking
River Cam

Menus at both the informal conservatory brasserie and the elegant restaurant cover a wide choice of cuisines. Although on the city centre ring road, the hotel is close to the River Cam and has views over Jesus Green.

CAMBRIDGE,

Cambridge Garden House
Moat House

Purpose-built hotel in a peaceful setting overlooking the River Cam. The stylish restaurant has a contemporary look matched by a menu offering Cullen skink, or pan-fried chicken with wild mushrooms and a rich port jus.

Directions: City centre, from Trumpington Street past Fitzwilliam Museum, L into Mill Lane

Granta Place Mill Lane CB2 1RT
Map 5: TL45
Tel: 01223 259988
Fax: 01223 316605
Telephone for further details

CAMBRIDGE,

Midsummer House

Stylish setting with good service. In summer, the upper dining-room is the place to dine, overlooking the Cam awash with rowers and punts. Otherwise the large conservatory and smaller adjoining salon make a smart but simply styled backdrop for cooking with a pronounced French flavour. Typical dishes include tortellini of sweetbreads and morels, braised cos lettuce, parsley and hazelnut butter, and roast squab pigeon, pommes Anna, tarte Tatin of onion, caramelised endive, jus of morels. Hot prune and Armagnac soufflé with prune and Armagnac ice cream makes for a suitably Gallic ending. Note that the lovely little house is on the Common – but you can only get there on foot.

Directions: Park in Pretoria Road, off Chesterton Road, then walk across footbridge to restaurant

Midsummer Common CB4 1HA
Map 5: TL45
Tel: 01223 369299
Fax: 01223 302672
Chef: Daniel Clifford
Owner: Russell Morgan
Cost: *Alc* £43.50, set-price L £19.50/D £39.50. H/wine £11.95
Times: Noon-1.45pm/7-9.45pm. Closed L Sat, D Sun, all Mon
Additional: Sunday L; Children welcome; ❹ dishes
Seats: 30. Private dining room 16

CAMBRIDGE,

22 Chesterton Road ❁❁ ⟪NEW⟫

Smart, relaxed surroundings – like walking into somebody's house. To the point modern English cooking with a French classical base is the idiom for this sound restaurant just on the outer rim of the city centre. Chinese-style pork with mooli and bok choi brings an oriental twist, but the Mediterranean, in the guise of ratatouille tart with plum tomatoes, basil and olive oil could also feature. A main course of roast poussin with herbs and breadcrumbs, served with spring vegetables has been well reported, as has baked lemon cheesecake with a rich chocolate sauce. Guinness bread is very, very good. There's a wide-ranging wine list with over 80 to choose from, all at keen prices.

Directions: Telephone for directions

22 Chesterton Road CB4 3AX
Map 5: TL45
Tel: 01223 351880
Fax: 01223 323814
Chef: Ian Rheinhardt
Owner: David Carter
Cost: *Alc* £23.50. H/wine £9.25
Times: L by arrangement/ D to 9.30pm. Closed Sun, Mon, 1 wk Xmas-New Year
Additional: Children 10+; ❹ dishes
Seats: 28. Private dining room 12
Smoking: No pipes & cigars; Air conditioning

DUXFORD,

Duxford Lodge Hotel ❁❁

Compact, turn of the century red-brick country house hotel. The charmingly decorated restaurant, Le Paradis, still gains approval for straightforward smooth duck liver and

Ickleton Road CB2 4RU
Map 5: TL44
Tel: 01223 836444
Fax: 01223 832271
Chef: Kevin Bingham

Duxford Lodge Hotel

Owners: Ronald & Suzanne Craddock
Cost: *Alc* £26, set-price L £13.99/D
£20.50. ☺ H/wine £9.95
Times: Noon-2pm/7-9.30pm. Closed
L Sat, 25 Dec-3 Jan
Additional: Sunday L; Children
welcome; ✦ dishes
Seats: 40. Private dining rooms 24
Smoking: No-smoking area; No pipes
& cigars; Air conditioning
Accommodation: 15 en suite ★ ★ ★

Armagnac parfait with a walnut, pear and celery chutney, poached breast of chicken with truffle and fresh herb dumplings and a rich port sauce, as well as medallions of venison with buttered spinach, red wine jelly and caramelised chestnuts. Hot figs cooked in mulled wine and topped with a raspberry sabayon vies for attention with orange and Grand Marnier pancake soufflé. The light lunch menu is excellent value.

Directions: M11/J10, take A505 E then 1st R to Duxford; take R fork at T-junction, entrance 70 yards on L

ELY, Lamb Hotel

Pleasant, centrally located hotel where traditional dishes such as cauliflower soup and summer pudding are balanced with modern British ideas such as fillet of pork with cranberry and orange jus.

Directions: Follow A10 to Ely, then city centre signs. Hotel on corner of High St adjacent cathedral

2 Lynn Road CB7 4EJ
Map 5: TL58
Tel: 01353 663574
Fax: 01353 662023
Telephone for further details

ELY,
Old Fire Engine House

Lovage soup, pigeon pie, Norfolk marsh samphire and jugged hare are amongst some of the seasonally changing dishes at this friendly 18th-century restaurant-cum-art gallery. Equally traditional English puds may include syllabub, apple pie or treacle tart.

Smoking: No smoking in dining room.

Directions: Facing St Mary's Church in town centre

25 St Mary's Street
CB7 4ER
Map 5: TL58
Tel: 01353 662582
Cost: *Alc* £23. ☺ H/wine £8.
Times: 12.15-2pm/7.15-9pm. Closed
D Sun, 2 wks from 24 Dec, Bhs
Additional: Children welcome;
✦ dishes

FOWLMERE,
The Chequers Inn

Ambitious cooking, with just one menu offered in the restaurant and bar (supplemented by daily blackboard specials) of this civilized 16th-century inn with Samuel Pepys connections. There is an upbeat Mediterranean flavour to many of the dishes.

Royston SG8 7SR
Map 5: TL44
Tel: 01763 208369
Fax: 01763 208944
Cost: *Alc* £17.70. ☺ H/wine £4.65
Times: Noon-2pm/7-10pm. Closed 25
Dec

The Chequers Inn

Smoking: No smoking in dining room

Directions: Between Royston & Cambridge, B1368 turn off the A10

HUNTINGDON,
Old Bridge Hotel

Stylish, extremely popular hotel from the excellent Huntsbridge stable. Consistency is the buzzword with a sharply focused menu that owes a lot to the Mediterranean. The Huntsbridge ethos of making good food accessible to all works well here. There's a Conranesque brasserie feel combined with the welcome informality of various eating areas and styles of service. There is, for example, a weekday lunchtime buffet that is excellent value. Otherwise expect duck liver parfait with chestnut salad and red wine vinaigrette, baked sea bass with saffron risotto and ratatouille sauce, or calves' liver with creamed leeks, rösti potato, mushroom, pearl barley and red wine sauce. Desserts range from hot praline soufflé with Chantilly cream to sunken chocolate cake with white chocolate ice cream. Winner of our Wine Award last year, the outstanding wine list includes a good range of halves and wines by the glass, as well as a wonderful selection of producers and countries.

1 High Street PE18 6TQ
Map 4: TL27
Tel: 01480 452681
Fax: 01480 411017
Chefs: Nick Steiger, Martin Russell
Owner: Huntsbridge Ltd
Cost: *Alc* £24. ☺ H/wine £9.75
Times: Noon-2.30pm/6.30-10.30pm. Closed D 25 Dec
Additional: Sunday L; Children welcome; 🍴 dishes
Seats: 32 + 70. Private dining room 28
Smoking: No smoking in dining room
Accommodation: 25 en suite ★ ★ ★

Directions: Off A1 near junction with A1-M1 link and A604/M11

KEYSTON, **Pheasant Inn**

Huntingdon PE18 0RE
Map 4: TL07
Tel: 01832 710241
Fax: 01832 710340
Chef: Martin Lee
Owner: John Hoskins (Huntsbridge Ltd)
Cost: *Alc* £25
Times: Noon-2pm/6.30-10pm (6-9pm Sat/7-9.30pm Sun)
Additional: Bar food L; Sunday L; Children welcome; 🍴 dishes
Seats: 120.
Smoking: No smoking in dining room

Directions: In the village centre, clearly signposted off A14

Picture-postcard village inn with white walls and thatched roof. The interior is no less idyllic, with open fires, oak beams, lots of pictures and historical farm machinery, stuffed animals and seating areas that vary from scrubbed tables to tablecloths and carpeting. Order as much or as little as you like and sit where you will. The kitchen is as comfortable in Italy as it is in

England, with garlic polenta accompanying corn-fed Goosnargh chicken, and olive oil mash and sun-dried tomato tapenade served with grilled fillet of salmon. More traditionally, roast pheasant breast comes with bread sauce and roast potatoes. Warm chicken liver mousse with shiitaki mushrooms and a rich tomato and port sauce has made an impressive starter, and was enjoyed as much as the chocolate fondant – a freshly baked, light chocolate sponge with a runny centre – served with Jersey cream. Good bread rolls, praiseworthy coffee, real ales and an excellent wine list complete the picture.

MADINGLEY,
Three Horseshoes ❁❁

Reassuringly old period pub with eager, youthful service. The Three Horseshoes is one of a group of individual inns owned by the pioneering Huntsbridge Ltd. Each is run by a chef-patron under the management of Master of Wine, John Hoskins, who is responsible for the serious wine list, which blends a good value mix of top-class modern producers with lots of exciting wines by the glass. Richard Stokes is the main man here, offering a robust cuisine that has a cosmopolitan, gutsy edge to it with busy Pacific rim and Mediterranean influences. The one menu is served informally in the bar, with more style in the restaurant. This is seriously good cooking. Cured duck breast salad comes with pickled vegetables, salsa verde and Mostardo di Cremona, pan-fried turbot with chickpea, chilli, mint and olive salad with humous and black olive sauce. Or there could be a punchy chargrilled chicken tikka with pickled okra, tomato and herb salad, dahl and coriander yogurt. Sunday lunch delivers the business with a perfect roast sirloin of beef with roast potatoes, roast root vegetables and red wine and onion gravy.

High Street CB3 8AB
Map 5: TL36
Tel: 01954 210221
Fax: 01594 212043
Chef: Richard Stokes
Owner: Huntsbridge
Cost: *Alc* £23 ☺
Times: Noon-2pm/6.30-9.30pm
Additional: Children welcome; 🍴 dishes
Seats: 55
Smoking: No smoking in dining room

Directions: 1.5 m from M11/J13, 2 miles W of Cambridge

Shortlisted for AA Wine Award – see page 16

MELBOURN,
The Pink Geranium ❁❁❁

The feeling is very country house: it's a comfortable place to eat with lots of lounge seating and a formality of approach. 'Chintz has been commented on here, but it is not nearly as offensive as I would have expected' comments one inspector of Steven Saunders's well-regarded restaurant. The place was heaving when we visited, amazing in a location which is miles from anywhere, but it says a lot about the food. A mosaic of roasted rabbit loin with duck confit and braised duck gizzard, and an intermediate course of steamed tranche of turbot with almond and cauliflower purée, bok choi and coconut and fennel emulsion punched above their weight in terms of flavour and spoke reams of the time chef Mark Jordan spent with Jean-Christophe Novelli. However, the tower of food presentation style, which looks great but is impossible to eat without making a mess of the dish, holds sway here. The next dish was a well-judged collection of classic flavours: a cutlet of venison with great braised red cabbage, pomme fondant, garlic confit and a fumé of ceps – all great, earthy, wintry flavours enhanced by a superb sauce and the carefully judged sweet-sour balance in the cabbage. The restaurant manager is excellent and does the whole menu and wine list monty very well.

Station Road SG8 6DX
Map 5: TL34
Tel: 01763 260215
Fax: 01763 262110
Chefs: Mark Jordan, Steven Saunders
Owners: Sally & Steven Saunders
Cost: *Alc* £40, set-price L £14 (2 courses)/D £30. H/wine £12
Times: Noon-2pm/7-9.30pm. Closed Sun, Mon
Additional: 🍴 dishes
Seats: 60. Private dining room 18. Jacket & tie preferred
Smoking: No smoking in dining room

Directions: On A10 between Royston and Cambridge. In centre of the village, opposite the church

MELBOURN, **Sheene Mill**

Station Road SG8 6DX
Map 5: TL34
Tel: 01763 261393
Fax: 01763 261376
Chefs: Steven Saunders, Alex Williams
Owners: Steven & Sally Saunders
Cost: Alc £25, set-price L £10 (2 courses). ☺ H/wine £10
Times: Noon-2pm/7-10pm. Closed D Sun
Additional: Bar food; Sunday L; Children welcome; 🍴 dishes
Seats: 110
Smoking: No-smoking area; No pipes & cigars
Accommodation: 9 en suite

Modern British meets Pacific rim in a historic watermill that has been given a vibrant, contemporary makeover. Owned by Steven Saunders from The Pink Geranium just down the road (see previous entry), the concept takes wing with dishes such as smoked duck fajita with spicy tomato chutney; barbecued loin of rabbit with mizuno leaf and mirin dressing; lobster and crab risotto with coriander and papaya coulis; rack of lamb with sweet potato hash, shiitake mushroom and ginger jus. Not everything flirts with the exotic, there's also beef fillet burger with spicy tomato relish and fries, steamed haddock with onion mash and parsley sauce, and classic French onion soup, although the kitchen can't resist jazzing up the venison sausages with tomato and jalapeño mash. Desserts are less exploratory, but are no less appealing for that – hot plum soufflé, Sussex lemon pond pudding, pecan pie with white chocolate ice cream show the style.

Directions: Take 2nd exit from A10 Melbourn by-pass signed Melbourn. Sheene Mill is 300yds down Station Road on R

PETERBOROUGH, **Orton Hall**

Orton Longueville PE2 7DN
Map 4: TL19
Tel: 01733 391111
Fax: 01733 231912
Cost: Alc £29.70, set-price D £19.50. ☺ H/wine £11.50
Times: Noon-2pm/7-9pm. Closed L Sat & Sun, Bhs
Additional: 🍴 dishes
Smoking: No smoking in dining room
Accommodation: 63 en suite ★ ★ ★

Historic, rambling country house, popular for weddings. Clever modern additions and fine oak panelling complement the enthusiastic cooking in the elegant Huntley restaurant.

Directions: Off A605 (East) opposite Orton Mere

STILTON, **Bell Inn Hotel** ✿

Great North Road PE7 3RA
Map 5: TL18
Tel: 01733 241066
Fax: 01733 245173
Cost: Set-price L&D £19.95. ☺
H/wine £9.95
Times: Noon-2pm/7-9.30pm. Closed
L Sat, 25 Dec
Additional: Sunday L; Children 8+;
❸ dishes
Smoking: No-smoking area
Accommodation: 19 en suite ★ ★ ★

Directions: From A1(M)/J16 follow
signs to Stilton. Hotel on High Street
in centre of village

*Olde-worlde galleried restaurant with cooking that mixes modern
and traditional influences to good effect: pan-fried baby chicken,
onion risotto and confit of root vegetables. Long Clawson Stilton is
served with home-baked plum bread.*

WANSFORD, **Haycock Hotel** ✿

PE8 6JA
Map 4: TL09
Tel: 01780 782223
Fax: 01780 783508
Chef: Neil Smith
Telephone for further details

Directions: In village centre between
A1 & A47

*Superior 17th-century pit stop on the A1 with restaurant and
informal brasserie-cum-conservatory. Roasts from the carving
trolley plus more vibrant, cosmopolitan dishes.*

WISBECH, **Crown Lodge Hotel**

*Light, modern and relaxing hotel restaurant offering a wide choice.
Roast saddle of rabbit, or baked fillet of Lowestoft cod with blue
cheese and orange crust are typical examples.*

Smoking: Air conditioning
Accommodation: 10 en suite ★ ★

Directions: 5 miles SE of Wisbech on A1122 close to junction
with A1101

Downham Road Outwell PE14 8SE
Map 5: TF40
Tel: 01945 773391
Fax: 01945 772668
Cost: *Alc* £19.75, set-price L & D
£15.75. ☺ H/wine £8.35
Times: Noon-2pm/6.30-10pm. Closed
25, 26 Dec, 1 Jan
Additional: Bar food; Sunday L;
Children welcome; ❸ dishes

CHESHIRE

ALDERLEY EDGE,

Alderley Edge Hotel

Macclesfield Road SK9 7BJ
Map 7: SJ87
Tel: 01625 583033
Fax: 01625 586343
Chef: Nicholas J Walton
Owner: J W Lees (Brewers) Ltd
Cost: Alc £40, set-price L £14.50/D
£23.95. ☺ H/wine £12.95
Times: Noon-2pm/7-10pm
Additional: Bar food L; Sunday L;
Children welcome; ● dishes
Seats: 80. Private dining rooms 18,
25. Jacket & tie preferred
Smoking: No pipes; Air conditioning
Accommodation: 46 en suite ★ ★ ★

Originally home to a Victorian cotton baron, the scale is still sumptuous. The location in the big-bucks north Cheshire stockbroker belt ensures the 500 strong wine list, 100 champagnes and notable collection of Cognacs, Armagnacs and single malts are well sampled. Eclectic is the word: potted tuna served in a savoury sesame tuile with lime and pickled ginger salsa, and gateau of foie gras and chicken liver 'rolled in morel powder' arranged on an orange and thyme marmalade and accompanied by a butter brioche, set the tone. Verbosity is the second word: ballotine of pheasant filled with a farci of its own leg laced with spiced pears sliced around a Lancashire pudding enhanced with a dark scrumpy and tarragon jus. Desserts are an oasis of welcome simplicity – an orange tart with caramel ice cream was a credit to the chef pâtissier.

Directions: A538 to Alderley Edge, then B5087 Macclesfield road

ALSAGER,

Manor House Hotel NEW

Audley Road ST7 2QQ
Map 7: SJ75
Tel: 01270 884000
Fax: 01270 882483
Chef: David Green
Owner: Compass Hotels
Cost: Alc £25, set-price L £13.50/D
£21 (4 courses). ☺ H/wine £10.95
Times: 12.30-2.30pm/7.15-9.30pm.
Closed L Sat
Additional: Bar food; Sunday L;
Children welcome; ● dishes
Seats: 100. Private dining room 30
Smoking: No-smoking area
Accommodation: 57 en suite ★ ★ ★

The restaurant still features the original oak beams of the old farm, around which the modern hotel has grown up. An extensive menu caters for a wide range of local tastes. Starters include Highland game terrine with toasted saffron brioche and spiced pear chutney, as well as tandoori roasted chicken fillet with naan bread and cucumber and mint yogurt. Several classic dishes such as tournedos Rossini, fillet of lamb en croûte, and veal Cordon Bleu are among the main courses; a flambée section includes steak Diane and medalions of pork normande. The traditional wins hands-down, though, when it comes to desserts: iced strawberry parfait; tulip basket with summer berries and Chantilly cream; vanilla crème brûlée.

Directions: Take A500 towards Stoke-on-Trent. After 0.5 mile take 1st slip road, Alsager, L at top, hotel on L before village

BOLLINGTON,
Mauro's Restaurant

Friendly proprietor-run village restaurant with a relaxed Mediterranean feel. Vincenzo Mauro is enthusiastic about food and is happy to share his knowledge with guests. Daily specials, recited at the table, complement a fairly extensive *carte* of largely mainstream Italian dishes. Our inspection meal got off to a good start with a thick bean and veal soup, which set our inspector's 'pulses' racing. This was followed by a 'brilliantly fresh' halibut, matched superbly by a dill and lime sauce. Dessert was a very light home-made pannacotta with a rich blackcurrant base. The Italy-dominated wine list includes a few bargains.

Directions: Situated on the main street of the village, at the Pott Shrigley end

88 Palmerston Street SK10 5PW
Map 7: SJ97
Tel: 01625 573898
Chef/Owner: Vincenzo Mauro
Cost: *Alc* £21, set-price L/D £11.95.
☺ H/wine £10
Times: Noon-1.45pm/6.45-10pm.
Closed Sun, all Mon, L Sat
Additional: Bar food L; Children welcome; ✿ dishes
Seats: 49
Smoking: No pipes and cigars in dining room

BROXTON, # Broxton Hall Hotel

Half-timbered Tudor hall with an extensive French-style carte – paupiettes of lemon sole stuffed with mushrooms and braised fennel with lemon and butter sauce, and crêpes with Cointreau and orange sauce are evergreen favourites.

Accommodation: 10 en suite ★ ★ ★

Directions: On A41 halfway between Whitchurch and Chester, at Broxton roundabout

Whitchurch Road CH3 9JS
Map 7: SJ45
Tel: 01829 782321
Fax: 01829 782330
Cost: Set-price L £16.50/ D £25.50 (4 courses). ☺ H/wine £12
Times: Noon-2pm/7-9.30pm Closed 25-26 Dec, 1 Jan
Additional: Bar Food L; Sunday L; Children welcome; ✿ dishes
Smoking: No smoking in dining room

CHESTER,
The Chester Grosvenor

Eastgate CH1 1LT
Map 7: SJ46
Tel: 01244 324024
Fax: 01244 313246
Chef: Simon Radley
Cost: *Alc* £52.50, set-price L £25/D £45 (5 courses). H/wine £12
Times: Noon-2.30pm/7-9.30pm. Closed D Sun, L Mon, 25 Dec-2 Jan
Additional: Sunday L; Children welcome; ✿ dishes
Seats: 46. Private dining room 20

The Grosvenor is 'the smartest place in town,' with grandeur and opulence are its hallmarks. Guests are chaperoned to the library bar, where menus and wine list are presented for perusal by knowledgeable staff who have the knack of making everyone feel relaxed and are happy to chat about any dish you care to mention. Meals are taken in the classic-style restaurant amid mahogany tables, silk drapes and a glass atrium with a large orange tree set below. The bread trolley is an adventure in itself, but it's the arrival of an amuse-bouche that sets excitement levels soaring: perhaps a cushion of veal

sweetbreads topped with a roasted langoustine on buttered spinach, 'totally harmonious, robust and yet refined'. Luxury ingredients abound, as in a composition of foie gras, truffles and minutely turned root vegetables tossed in truffle oil, a courgette flower stuffed with light chicken and foie gras mousse also appearing on the plate. A main course was roast tail of monkfish with Italian ham and a cassoulet of cannellini beans, well-presented, the disparate elements fusing into a unified whole, and cooked to perfection. Puddings of perhaps honey-roasted pear with a buttery almond biscuit may be outshone by the excellent petits fours served with coffee, among them light, creamy fudge and a sponge soaked in brandy.

Smoking: No smoking in dining room; Air conditioning
Accommodation: 85 en suite
★★★★★

Directions: City centre adjacent to the Eastgate Clock and Roman Walls

CHESTER,

Crabwall Manor Hotel

Parkgate Road Mollington CH1 6NE
Map 7: SJ46
Tel: 01244 851666
Fax: 01244 851400
Chefs: Kate Cook, Michael Truelove
Owners: Carl Lewis, John Henley, Michael Truelove
Cost: *Alc* £30. H/wine £13.50
Times: Noon-2pm/7-9.30pm
Additional: Sunday L; Children welcome; 🍴 dishes
Seats: 100. Private dining room 90. Jacket & tie preferred
Accommodation: 48 en suite ★★★

Directions: From A56 take A5117 then A540. Set back from A540

History and style with service to match. A rebuilt 17th-century manor house notable for its flamboyant castellations. (The original building was mentioned in the Domesday Book.) Food is at the centre of things and whilst the chef of many years, Michael Truelove, is now the general manager, he still has input in the kitchen. The menu is pretty much classic country house with the odd Mediterranean intervention. Fish is well represented and some sweet seared scallops with a Sauterne sauce were the highlight of one inspection lunch. Succulent corn-fed chicken comes in a simple combination with baby fennel and a well judged chicken stock jus. On the dessert front there are offerings such as roasted peach served with a peach parfait or an accurate version of classic lemon tart. The wine list is wide ranging and mark-ups are sensible.

CHESTER, Curzon Hotel

Swiss chef/proprietor at this small hotel (15-minute walk from the centre) offers zürigeschnetzeltes, strips of pork in white wine sauce accompanied by rösti. But there may also be beef mexicaine, or chicken breast in mustard sauce.

52-54 Hough Green CH4 8JQ
Map 7: SJ46
Tel: 01244 678581
Fax: 01244 680866
Cost: *Alc* £17.50, set-price L & D £16. ☺ H/wine £9
Times: D only, 7-9pm

Additional: Children welcome; 🍴 dishes
Smoking: No smoking in dining room
Accommodation: 16 en suite ★★

Directions: From M53 take A483 R towards Chester. At 3rd roundabout 2nd L onto A5104. Hotel 500yds on R.

CHESTER,
Gateway To Wales Hotel ✿✿

Welsh Road Deeside CH5 2HX
Map 7: SJ46
Tel: 01244 830332
Fax: 01244 836190
Chef: Chris Thompson
Owner: Mrs DK Harford-Corbett
Cost: *Alc* £29.93, set-price L £11.95
(2 courses)/D £17.95 (5 courses). ☺
H/wine £9.95
Times: Noon-2.30pm (Sun noon-9pm)/7-9.30pm
Additional: Bar food; Sunday L;
Children welcome; ✿ dishes
Seats: 40. Private dining room 12
Smoking: No smoking in dining room
Accommodation: 39 en suite ★ ★ ★

Popular hotel of modern construction but traditional values.
As the name implies, The Regency Room is ornately decorated
in that period style, with a dress code to match – no 'loud T-
shirts and training shoes after 7pm'. Dishes are presented with
some flair and evident technique, but well-defined core
flavours were lacking in a first course of 'oven-baked beef
mushrooms with goats' cheese and rosemary set on a bed of
French leaves topped with asparagus basil oil and garnished
with garlic scented croûtons'. The same caveat applied to a
main course of 'medallions of venison layered with parsnip
purée draped over a raspberry and burgundy jus garnished
with roasted garlic'. A wide selection of fresh vegetables,
presented in a side dish, however were all precisely cooked
and true of taste. Orange and brandy syllabub with home-
made shortbread scored highly for texture and again indicated
hardwork behind the scenes.

Directions: From Chester follow signs
for Deeside/Queensferry taking A548.
Turn R at roundabout, to 2nd
roundabout, where hotel can be seen.
Near RAF Sealand

CHESTER,
Mollington Banastre Hotel ✿

Parkgate Road CH1 6NN
Map 7: SJ46
Tel: 01244 851471
Fax: 01244 851165
Telephone for further details

Directions: Bear L at end of M56 onto
A5117, L at roundabout onto A540,
the hotel is 2 miles on R

*Decorated in mellow yellow, the Garden Room offers an interesting
carte. We dined well, however, on the menu du jour – leek and
potato soup, brill with mushrooms and hazelnut parfait.*

HANDFORTH, **Belfry Hotel** ✿

Stanley Road SK9 3LD
Map 7: SJ88
Tel: 0161 4370511
Fax: 0161 4990597
Telephone for further details

*New management and ongoing renovations but still the same
traditional, service and range of tried and trusted dishes including
game terrine, poached fillets of halibut with langoustines and rice
pudding.*

Directions: A34 to Handforth, at end of village

KNUTSFORD, **Belle Époque** ✿✿

Built in 1907, the unique architecture of the Belle Époque is
matched by a flamboyant art nouveau interior. An Anglo/French
menu ranges from duck confit via mustard-glazed salmon to loin of
organic pork with black pudding, Bramley apples and Calvados.

Smoking: No-smoking area; No pipes & cigars
Accommodation: 6 en suite

Directions: 2 miles off A50. 2 miles from M6/J19

60 King Street WA16 6DT
Map 7: SJ77
Tel: 01565 633060
Fax: 01565 634150
Cost: *Alc* £20, set-price L £6.95.
☺ H/wine £9.95
Times: Noon-2pm/7-10pm. Closed L
Sat, all Sun, Bhs
Additional: Children welcome;
🥕 dishes

KNUTSFORD, **Cottons Hotel** ✿

*Cooking with a Cajun influence gives a lift to the busy commercial
hotel restaurant. Grilled Bay shrimp and crab cake and seafood
risotto are amongst the extensive choices.*

Directions: From M6 J19/A556 (Stockport). Turn R at lights (A50
to Knutsford). Hotel 1.5 miles on R

Manchester Road WA16 0SU
Map 7: SJ77
Tel: 01565 650333
Fax: 01565 755351
Telephone for further details

KNUTSFORD, **Dick Willetts** ✿

*Exclusively vegetarian and no smoking restaurant at the Toft Hotel.
Dishes include 'burrito refritto' with salsa and guacamole, asparagus
and herb strudel, as well as almond and sesame roast.*

Additional: Children 12+; 🥕 dishes only
Smoking: No smoking in dining room
Accommodation: 10 en suite ★★

Directions: One mile S of Knutsford on A50

Toft Hotel Toft Road WA16 9EH
Map 7: SJ77
Tel: 01565 634443
Fax: 01565 632603
Cost: Set-price D £21.75. ☺ H/wine
£9.50
Times: D only, 7.15-9.30pm. Closed
Sun-Thu, Xmas

KNUTSFORD, **Longview Hotel**

55 Manchester Road WA16 0LX
Map 7: SJ77
Tel: 01565 632119
Fax: 01565 652402
Cost: *Alc* £20. ☺ H/wine £9.25
Times: D only, 6.30-9pm. Closed
Sun, 24 Dec-3 Jan
Additional: Bar food D; Children
welcome; ✿ dishes
Smoking: No smoking in dining room
Accommodation: 23 en suite ★ ★

Directions: From M6/J19, A556
(Chester, Northwich). Turn L at lights
(Knutsford), L again at roundabout,
A50. Hotel 200yds on R

*Victorian hotel overlooking Knutsford Heath. Fresh local produce is
used to good effect in modern British dishes such as roast chicken
breast flamed in Calvados and served with morel mushrooms.*

NANTWICH, **Rookery Hall**

Worleston CW5 6DQ
Map 7: SJ65
Tel: 01270 610016
Fax: 01270 626027
Chef: Craig Grant
Cost: *Alc* £18.50, set-price D £39.50
(5 courses). ☺ H/wine £16
Times: Noon-2pm/7-9.30pm. Closed
L Sat
Additional: Bar food; Sunday L;
Children welcome; ✿ dishes
Seats: 36. Private dining room 66.
Jacket & tie preferred
Smoking: No smoking in dining room
Accommodation: 45 en suite ★ ★ ★

Directions: On B5074 north of
Nantwich; situated 1.5 miles on right
towards Worleston village

**Built in 1816 and subsequently modified, Rookery Hall is a
two-storey building of mellowed sandstone under a
balustraded roof in 38 acres of gardens and wooded
parkland.** Inside are well-proportioned rooms, a notable oak
staircase, wood panelling and the occasional ghost or two. Fish
and shellfish are strong points, as in a starter of prawns with
provençale vegetables bound together with a rich tomato
sauce, or brochette of salmon, monkfish and red snapper subtly
flavoured with lemongrass on a julienne of courgettes with a
fennel and watercress dressing. Rump of lamb might be one of
the meat dishes, served on a bed of bubble-and-squeak with
ratatouille and a herb jus, with a terrine of ham hock with Puy
lentils and pickled oyster mushrooms among starters. The
kitchen's talents extend into puddings of an attractive-looking
tuile cage of berries and passion fruit coulis, or white peach
soufflé with schnapps ice cream. The interesting wine list
includes a good selection by the glass.

PRESTBURY,
White House Restaurant

Ryland and Judith Wakeham's attractive 18th-century farmhouse continues to please. You can eat well and cheaply off the lunch menu and bar snack choices (a mix of tradition with roast English sirloin of beef and Yorkshire pudding appearing on the former, or a more modish ciabatta bread steak sandwich on the latter). In the evening an extensive carte kicks in, offering a menu that's completely in the modern idiom. Consider this: to begin, terrine of smoked salmon, champagne and crème fraîche on cucumber cappuccino, then whole Dover sole grilled with lime gremolata, or hoisin-glazed Cheshire lamb shank on sweet potato mash accompanied by a selection of vegetables. To finish, warm blueberry frangipane with lemon curd ice cream. Some menu choices are marked as low in reduced oil, butter and cream.

Directions: Village centre on A538 N of Macclesfield

SK10 4DG
Map 7: SJ87
Tel: 01625 829376
Fax: 01625 828627
Chefs: Ryland Wakeham,
Mark Cunniffe
Owners: Ryland & Judith Wakeham
Cost: *Alc* £27, set-price L £12.95/D
£17.95. ☺ H/wine £12.95
Times: Noon-2pm/7-10pm. Closed D
Sun, L Mon, 25 Dec
Additional: Bar food L; Sunday L;
Children welcome; ✍ dishes
Seats: 70. Private dining room 40
Smoking: No pipes & cigars
Accommodation: 11 en suite

PUDDINGTON, Craxton Wood

Parkgate Road L66 9PB
Map 7: SJ37
Tel: 0151 3394717
Fax: 0151 3391740
Chef: James Minnis
Owner: Macdonald Hotels plc
Cost: *Alc* £30, set-price L £16.85 (5
courses)/D £25.85 (5 courses). ☺
H/wine £15.85
Times: Noon-2pm/7-9.45pm
Additional: Bar food; Sunday L;
Children welcome; ✍ dishes
Seats: 120. Private dining room 30.
Jacket & tie preferred
Smoking: No smoking in dining room
Accommodation: 72 en suite ★★★

The large house set in its own attractive wooded ground has seen some major changes since the last edition of **Best Restaurants,** *with refurbishment adding 60 bedrooms.* Althought the menu is in French, with English subtitles, the seasonally changing menus have more than a streak of modern British ideas threaded through. Keeping up with the times are the likes of medallions of pan-fried monkfish served with vegetables, soy sauce and sushi nori from the *carte,* or slices of pan-fried game garnished with fruits and a rich game sauce, served with small dumplings from the 'menu du mois'.

Directions: From end of M56 (direction N Wales) take A5117 (Queensferry). R at 1st roundabout onto A540 (Hoylake). Hotel 200 yds after next traffic lights.

SANDIWAY,
Nunsmere Hall Hotel

Turn of the century mansion built for a shipping magnate, set on a mini-peninsula surrounded on three sides by a 60-acre lake. It still has the air of a past era, with open fires and

Tarporley Road Oakmere CW8 2ES
Map 7: SJ67
Tel: 01606 889100
Fax: 01606 889055
Chef: Wayne Vickerage

Nunsmere Hall Hotel

Owners: Julie & Malcolm McHardy
Cost: *Alc* £37, set-price L £19.25 (2 courses). H/wine £15.50
Times: Noon-1.45pm/7-9.45pm
Additional: Bar food L; Sunday L; Children 10+ at L; dishes
Seats: 50. Private dining room 45. Jacket & tie preferred
Smoking: No smoking in dining room
Accommodation: 36 en suite ★ ★ ★

Directions: From M6/J19 take A56 for 9 miles. Turn L onto A49 towards Tarporley, hotel 1 mile on L

elegant rooms of comfortable solidity, while the Crystal Restaurant overlooks the sunken Italian garden. A new chef took over the stoves in early 1999, bringing with him a cosmopolitan awareness and a desire to let the finest ingredients do the talking, eschewing unnecessary complexities in the process. Smoked haddock and basil soup, or quail salad with lentils, celeriac purée and a truffled jus might precede braised chump of lamb with roasted vegetables and parsnip purée, or roast sea bass with queen scallops and essence of red pepper. We were impressed as much by canapés and bread as by a simple, harmonious starter of warm duck confit with caper dressing sitting as a tower atop shaved celeriac. Simple is the word used to describe a red wine sauce with a main course of halibut with pommes persillées, but the workmanship that went into turning out a veal stock-based sauce, rich yet light, to produce such 'astonishing flavours' was impressive. Vegetarians are particularly well looked after, and sweet lovers won't be disappointed either, with perhaps bitter chocolate truffle cake with raspberry coulis, or apple crème brûlée to go for. The long wine list befits its grand surroundings but kicks off with a page of cellarman's choices by the glass and bottle.

TARPORLEY, **The Wild Boar** ❀

Striking 17th-century black-and-white timbered building (now a hotel). Sound English cooking along the lines of rabbit and venison sausage and roasted fillet of salmon served on tangy laverbread with beurre blanc.

Directions: Two miles from Tarporley on A49 towards Whitchurch

Whitchurch Road Beeston CW6 9NW
Map 7: SJ56
Tel: 01829 260309
Fax: 01829 261081
Telephone for further details

WARRINGTON,
Daresbury Park Hotel ❀❀

Large, modern hotel with extensive conference and leisure facilities. Inspectors have been impressed by the cooking in the Terrace Restaurant. Traditionally decorated in earthy tones of tangerine and burnt orange, it has its own private lounge away from the hullabaloo of the busy hotel, and staff are friendly yet professional. At inspection, everything was worthy of note – from seven types of bread to cappuccino. A starter of toasted brioche topped with a poached egg, covered in home-smoked salmon, lightly glazed with hollandaise and topped off

Daresbury WA4 4BB
Map 7: SJ68
Tel: 01925 267331
Fax: 01925 265615
Chef: David Chapman
Owner: De Vere Hotels Ltd
Cost: *Alc* £30
Times: D only, 7.15-10pm. Closed Sun, Bhs
Additional: Bar food; Sunday L; Children welcome; ⌀ dishes

with Sevruga caviar was 'a very successful dish'; then came main courses of tuna steak 'served deliciously and bravely pink' in a sesame crust with tomato salsa, and a superbly seasoned, tender fillet of beef with buttered spinach, spot-on polenta and ratatouille in a light Madeira jus; banana tarte Tatin was misnamed – a tower of sliced banana on a pastry base covered in butterscotch sauce – it was, however, enjoyable despite the name. Plans are afoot to refurbish, enlarge and rename the restaurant in early 2000.

WARRINGTON,

Park Royal International

An extensive menu catering for a wide ranging clientele. Dishes might include rack of lamb with herb crust, and chocolate and Amaretto mousse with wild berry sauce.

WARRINGTON, Rockfield Hotel

Anglo-Swiss cooking is served in the attractively furnished restaurant at this former Edwardian gentleman's residence. Fondue is a feature, along with Swiss wines and speciality coffees.

Smoking: No smoking in dining room
Accommodation: 12 en suite ★★

Directions: From M6/J20 take A50 (Warrington) to fork with A56 (1.50 miles). Turn L into Victoria Rd. Alexandra Rd is 60 yds on R.

Daresbury Park Hotel

Smoking: No-smoking area; Air conditioning
Accommodation: 183 en suite
★ ★ ★ ★

Directions: M56/J11 onto A56 to Warrington. Just on L off roundabout

---

Stretton Road Stretton WA4 4NS
Map 7: SJ68
Tel: 01925 730706
Fax: 01925 730740
Cost: *Alc* £25, set-price L £12.95/D £17.95. ☺ H/wine £9.95
Times: Noon-2pm/7-10pm
Additional: Bar Food; Sunday L; Children welcome; ✇ dishes
Smoking: No-smoking area; Air conditioning
Accommodation: 140 en suite
★ ★ ★ ★

Directions: M56/J10, follow A49 signed Warrington, R towards Appleton Thorn at 1st lights; hotel 200 yds on R

Alexandra Road Grappenhall WA4 2EL
Map 7: SJ68
Tel: 01925 262898
Fax: 01925 263343
Cost: *Alc* £25, set-price L £11.95 (4 courses)/D £16.50 (4 courses). ☺ H/wine £9.95
Times: D only, 7-9pm. Closed D Sun, Easter
Additional: Sunday L (Noon-2pm); Children welcome; ✇ dishes

WILMSLOW, **Bank Square** ✿✿

4-6 Bank Square SK9 1AN
Map 7: SJ88
Tel: 01625 539754
Chef: Michael Dodds
Owners: David & Janet Rivett
Cost: *Alc* £26, set-price L £9.95 (2 courses)/D £10.95 (2 courses). ☺
H/wine £12.50
Times: Noon-2.30pm/6.30-10.30pm. Closed Sun
Additional: Bar food L; Children welcome; ❹ dishes
Seats: 50
Smoking: No pipes & cigars; Air conditioning

Directions: Telephone for directions

First-floor restaurant in former bank premises, featuring a lively ground-floor bar. The restaurant, despite the century-old building, wears a bright modern look with wooden floors, and plain rough-cast walls in blue and white, and there's an eye for quality in the choice of table appointments. Our winter inspection meal revealed a generous kitchen big on flavours but with a need to keep an eye on timing and technique. A rather large canapé 'big enough for a starter' was a well-made and full-flavoured game pâté, served with toast and apple and pear chutney. Home-cured salmon in juniper and thyme had lovely texture and flavour, and duck breast with orange sauce went well, although a bulky selection of overly al dente vegetables did nothing for the finesse of the dish. Cinder toffee parfait, light and studded with chocolate-coated honeycomb brought back childhood memories, described in one word – 'yummy'.

WILMSLOW,
Stanneylands Hotel ✿✿

Stanneylands Road SK9 4EY
Map 7: SJ88
Tel: 01625 525225
Fax: 01625 537282
Chef: James Lally
Owner: Gordon Beech
Cost: *Alc* £35, set-price L £13.50/D £32 (6 courses). H/wine £12
Times: 12.30-2.45pm/7-10pm. Closed D Sun
Additional: Sunday L; Children welcome; ❹ dishes
Seats: 80. Private dining room 60
Smoking: Air conditioning
Accommodation: 31 en suite ★★★

Directions: From M56/J5 follow Wilmslow/Moss Nook. At traffic lights R, through Styal, L at Handforth sign – follow into Stanneylands Rd

Edwardian country house hotel handy for the airport and motorway system. The place is very professionally run and the sense of teamwork infectious. The kitchen attempts a marriage between fashion (charred tuna, wok-fried vegetables, crab and ginger spring roll) and classic cooking (steamed Goosnargh chicken, truffle-buttered young leeks and chestnuts with fondant potatoes), and the general consensus is that the balance between cost, style, friendliness and service is just right. Highlights of meals taken this year include mille-feuille of roasted sea scallops and langoustine with ginger dressing, open ravioli of crab and spring onion with lemon sole fillets, and Valhrona chocolate tart with alpine strawberries. The wide global influence of the wine list provides interest, includes 13 house wines, and an interesting selection for those who wish to splash out and be adventurous.

WILMSLOW,
Thistle Manchester Airport

Hotel handy for the airport. Dinner might include fish terrine wrapped in crêpes with a tangy lime and coriander tartare, herbed pork collops in a sun-dried tomato, basil and wine sauce and lemon meringue pie.

180 Wilmslow Road SK9 3LG
Map 7: SJ88
Tel: 01625 529211
Fax: 01625 536812
Telephone for further details

Directions: 3 miles from M56/J5 turn off A34 onto B5358 towards Wilmslow. Hotel on L before Handforth Station

CORNWALL & ISLES OF SCILLY

ALTARNUN, Penhallow Manor

The listed Georgian rectory featured in Daphne du Maurier's 'Jamaica Inn'. The set-price menu is supplemented by seasonal and fresh fish dishes from the daily specials blackboard.

Smoking: No smoking in dining room
Accommodation: 6 en suite ★★

Directions: From Launceston A30 8 miles; 1 mile after B3257 take slip road to Altarnun, hotel near church

Launceston PL15 7SJ
Map 2: SX28
Tel: 01566 86206
Fax: 01566 86179
Cost: Set-price D £21.50 (4 courses).
☺ H/wine £8.50
Times: 12.30-2.30pm/7.30-8.45pm.
Closed Jan, Feb
Additional: Bar food L; Children 12+; dishes

BRYHER, Hell Bay Hotel

Small hotel located on the smallest of the inhabited islands. Local produce is a feature, and dishes might include seafood bisque, and whole grilled plaice filled with a glazed banana.

Smoking: No smoking in dining room
Accommodation: 14 en suite ★★★

Directions: By boat from main island of St Mary's

Isles of Scilly TR23 0PR
Map 2: SW17
Tel: 01720 422947
Fax: 01720 423004
Cost: Set-price D £23 (4 courses). ☺
H/wine £12
Times: D only, 7.15-8.30pm. Closed Nov-Mar
Additional: Bar food L; Children 5+; ☙ dishes

BUDE, Atlantic Hotel

From a superb position overlooking the beach, town and downs, the restaurant offers modern English cooking featuring dishes such as rack of lamb or sweet-and-sour halibut steaks.

Smoking: No smoking in dining room
Accommodation: 13 en suite ★★

Directions: From M5/J31, follow A30 past Okehampton. Then A386 (Bude) to join A3072 (Holsworthy & Bude)

17-18 Summerleaze Crescent EX23 8HJ
Map 2: SS20
Tel: 01288 352451
Fax: 01288 356666
Cost: Set-price D £14.80. ☺ H/wine £7.40
Times: D only, 7-8pm. Closed Nov-Mar
Additional: Bar Food L; Children welcome; ☙ dishes

CALLINGTON,
Thyme and Plaice ❀❀

Natural cream colours, wooden beams and an open log fire give a warm and welcoming feel to the cottagey listed building. The cooking is modern British but includes nothing too outlandish, and the six-course dinners offer remarkable value for money. Start with leek and potato soup with white truffle oil, followed perhaps by roast breast of pigeon with spring leaves and Caesar dressing. The fish course might be the lovely sounding trio of salmons with fresh dill sauce, before a choice of fillet of Cornish beef with wild mushroom and Madeira sauce or best end of English lamb with parsnip purée and simple jus. A selection of cheeses, and then it's into the last lap with hot chocolate and Grand Marnier soufflé with orange ice cream, freshly brewed coffee and petits fours.

Directions: Follow signs to Callington. Turn L at traffic lights and R into Church St

3 Church Street PL17 7RE
Map 2: SX36
Tel/Fax: 01579 384933
Chef: Matthew Dixon
Owners: Matthew Dixon & Alison Britchford
Cost: Set-price D £19.95 (6 courses). ☺ H/wine £7.95
Times: D only, 7-9.30pm. Closed Sun-Wed, Jan
Additional: Children 8+; ❦ dishes
Seats: 20
Smoking: No smoking in dining room

CONSTANTINE,
Trengilly Wartha Inn ❀❀

Originally a small farmhouse, the inn nestles in a wooded valley, surrounded by six acres of gardens and meadows. The country-style restaurant offers a range of locally produced meats and game, such as Cornish lamb cutlet and noisette with tarragon mousse, red wine and mushroom sauce, or locally smoked chicken and pigeon breast terrine served with home-made damson chutney. Fish and shellfish come from local waters: Falmouth Bay scallops are served in a modern classic way with Puy lentils and coriander in a soy vinaigrette; thick fillets of John Dory with caramelised onion and balsamic vinegar sauce. Desserts are richly imaginative. Up to 20 wines are featured by the glass and there's a selection of over 200 bottles, many drawn from their own merchant business 'Les Caves du Cochonnet' based in the old piggery!

Directions: In Constantine village turn L at top of hill, follow signs for Gweek, one mile out of village turn L, follow signposts to hotel.

Nancenoy TR11 5RP
Map 2: SW87
Tel/Fax: 01326 340332
Chef: Mike Maguire, Nick Tyler
Owners: Mike & Helen Maguire, Nigel & Isabel Logan
Cost: Set-price D £22.50. ☺ H/wine £9
Times: D only, 7.30-9.30pm. Closed 25 Dec
Additional: Bar food; Children welcome; ❦ dishes
Seats: 28
Accommodation: 8 rooms (7 en suite) ★ ★

CONSTANTINE BAY,
Treglos Hotel ❀

An imaginative menu of well presented dishes might include breast of pigeon encased in game terrine, and sea bass with sautéed fennel and yellow peppers on a Pernod scented fumet.

Smoking: No smoking in dining room; Air conditioning; Jacket & tie preferred
Accommodation: 44 en suite ★ ★ ★

Directions: Take B3276 (Constantine Bay). At village stores turn R, hotel is 50 yards on L

Padstow PL28 8JH
Map 2: SW87
Tel: 01841 520727
Fax: 01841 521163
Cost: *Alc* £28, set-price L £12.50/D £23 (5 courses). ☺ H/wine £10.50
Times: Noon-2.15pm/7.30-9pm
Additional: Bar food L; Sunday L; Children 7+; ❦ dishes

FALMOUTH,

Falmouth Beach Resort Hotel

Seafront hotel overlooking Falmouth Bay. Options include the fresh local fish of the day, sirloin or fillet steak au poivre, and roast Barbary duck with piquant orange sauce.

Smoking: No smoking in dining room
Accommodation: 125 en suite ★ ★ ★

Directions: From A39 to Falmouth follow signs to seafront and Gyllyngvase Beach. Hotel opposite Gyllyngvase Beach

Gyllyngvase Beach TR11 4NA
Map 2: SW83
Tel: 01326 318084
Fax: 01326 319147
Cost: Alc £27, set-price L £13. ☺ H/wine £8.60
Times: 12.30-2pm/7-9pm
Additional: Bar food; Sunday L; Children 7+; ◑ dishes

FALMOUTH, Greenbank Hotel

Harbourside hotel offering superb views from the attractive cane-furnished restaurant. There is a good choice of fish, grills, and dishes cooked at the table, including flambés.

Smoking: No smoking in dining room
Accommodation: 75 en suite ★ ★ ★

Directions: 500yds past Falmouth Marina overlooking the water

Harbourside TR11 2SR
Map 2: SW83
Tel: 01326 312440
Fax: 01326 211362
Cost: Alc £22.50, set-price L £11/D £19.95. ☺ H/wine £7.95
Times: Noon-2pm/7-midnight
Additional: Bar Food; Sunday L; Children welcome; ◑ dishes

FALMOUTH, Penmere Manor

Mongleath Road TR11 4PN
Map 2: SW83
Tel: 01326 211411
Fax: 01326 317588
Chef: Martin Jones
Owners: Andrew Pope, Elizabeth Rose
Cost: Set-price D £16.50 (2 courses). ☺ H/wine £8.50
Times: D only, 7-9pm. Closed 23-28 Dec
Additional: Children welcome; ◑ dishes
Seats: 60
Smoking: No smoking in dining room; Air conditioning
Accommodation: 37 en suite ★ ★ ★

Hotel with a range of leisure activities. Don't worry about accumulating calories at Penmere Manor: you can work them off in the Fountains Leisure Club or in an outdoor woodland fitness trail and swimming pool amid the five acres of subtropical gardens. Bolitho's Restaurant is the place to eat. Seared scallops, perfectly cooked, are garnished with bacon and walnuts and served in a tarragon cream sauce, whilst leg of rabbit is boned and stuffed with wild mushrooms and herbs, baked and surrounded by a Madeira-infused jus. Main courses could include grilled escalope of pork artistically garnished with roasted peppers and cherry tomatoes on a tomato and onion sauce, and pan-fried sirloin steak in a rich red wine sauce with herb-flavoured mash. Cheeses are quite rightly from the West Country. Many of the bins on the wine list are also offered by the glass and half-bottle.

Directions: Turn L into Mongleath Road off A39 1 mile after Hill Head roundabout

FALMOUTH,

Pennypots Restaurant

Maenporth Beach TR11 5HN
Map 2: SW83
Tel: 01326 250251
Fax: 01326 251040
Chef/Owner: Kevin Viner
Cost: Set-price D £33.50. H/wine £9.50
Times: D only, 7-9.30pm. Closed Sun, Mon, 4 wks winter
Additional: Bar food; Sunday L (Oceans Bar); Children welcome
Seats: 40
Smoking: Air conditioning

Directions: 3 miles S of Falmouth, follow signs for Maenporth

Pennypots is Maenporth Beach, dominating the hinterland with its slightly incongruous modern styling. The teddy bears have been thinned out somewhat since our last inspection, to be replaced with various carefully chosen objects. Given the magnificence of the view, the interior design is almost an insignificance, but actual decor is clean and uncluttered, mostly blue hues and cane-backed chairs. Jane Viner is very much in charge front of house and has an utterly unpretentious and engaging manner, nothing starchy here, whilst Kevin holds sway in the kitchen. Our meal opened on a high note and never faltered. A terrine of chicken livers and foie gras, served with toasted brioche was 'wonderful' with strong, gutsy flavour. Roast turbot, tiger prawns and squid on a lemon and thyme veal jus was a superb piece of sea-fresh turbot, roasted on the bone and perfectly cooked. Roast potatoes, beautiful sweet carrots, courgettes and a side plate of new potatoes in skins, full of earthy flavour, were well-chosen accompaniments. A palette cleansing apple and basil sorbet was a marriage made in heaven, perfect judgement of flavours, an example of a combination that really does work extremely well. For dessert, a chocolate temptation of chocolate, orange and Grand Marnier flavoured crème fraîche served on a Kirsch and white chocolate base with a black cherry coulis. Bliss. Canapés, breads, and petits fours are all exemplary. The contemporary wine list has a good showing from around the globe, excellent choice of half-bottles, all reasonably priced. The bistro-style downstairs operation is called Oceans Beach Bar and Grill.

FALMOUTH, **Powell's Cellars**

29 High Street TR11 3AD
Map 2: SW83
Tel: 01326 311212
Fax: 01326 311805
Cost: *Alc* £28, set-price D £14.95. ☺ H/wine £8.95
Times: D only from 7pm. Closed Mon, 25, 26 Dec, 1 Jan, D Sun in Jan & Feb
Additional: Children welcome; ♨ dishes
Smoking: No-smoking area; No pipes

Former cheese and wine cellar with low arched ceilings, redecorated in Art Deco style. Our inspector enjoyed hot tartlet of chicken breast and asparagus with a creamy lobster sauce, lemon sole fillet wrapped around a salmon and prawn mousse with a sun-dried tomato concasse, and iced blackcurrant and schnapps soufflé accompanied by a blackcurrant and passion fruit coulis. There's a range of steaks, and dishes such as roast goose breast with honey-glazed shallots. Modest wine list with just three available by the glass.

Directions: Follow signs to 'Town Centre' and park in 'The Moor' car park. Short walk along Webber St to High St – turn L and look for signs

FALMOUTH, **Royal Duchy Hotel** ❀❀

Cliff Road TR11 4NX
Map 2: SW83
Tel: 01326 313042
Fax: 01326 319420
Chef: Des Turland
Owner: P R Brend & Sons, Hoteliers Ltd
Cost: *Alc* £27, set-price L £9.95 (4 courses)/D £22 (5 courses). ☺ H/wine £8.50
Times: 12.30-2pm/7-9pm
Additional: Bar food L; Sunday L; Children welcome; ♨ dishes

Dinner plays a major part in the daily schedule of guests at this popular resort hotel. The kitchen endeavours to make each meal something of an occasion. Although there's always chilled fruit juice and soup (minted green pea or tomato), more adventurous first courses might include prawn tartare with sour cream and lemon chervil dressing, or honey roast quail with bacon potato cake and rosemary jus. Then a choice of sorbet or consommé, after which decisions have to be made between the roast fillet of Cornish haddock on egg noodles with lime-scented beurre blanc or roast honey gammon with crushed olive oil potatoes and shallot Madeira gravy. Great

British tradition is maintained on Sundays with roast sirloin of
Scotch beef and Yorkshire pudding. To finish, there's fresh
fruit salad with Cornish clotted cream or you can throw
caution to the winds with an iced cappuccino parfait served in
a chocolate cup surrounded by pineapple caramel sauce.

FOWEY, Food For Thought

The Quay PL23 1AT
Map 2: SX15
Tel: 01726 832221
Fax: 01726 832077
Chef/Owner: Martin Billingsley
Times: D only, 7-9.30pm. Closed
Sun, Jan, Feb
Additional: Children 12+; 🍴 dishes
Seats: 40

Directions: Walk down to the quay
from the town centre car park

'Parking can be a nightmare, especially from May to
September when there is no parking immediately outside the
restaurant', notes an inspector of this charming quayside place.
However, he found the walk well worth the effort. The
beamed, soundly appointed restaurant has been run by Martin
and Caroline Billingsley for twenty years, and they play the
hosts with enthusiasm, he in the kitchen, she out front
supervising a young team. The cooking is quite simple
although the skill underlying it is worth stressing; the food here
has character and is by no means out of touch with
metropolitan thinking. Sliced seared fillet of tender beef,
spiked with slivers of fresh ginger and doused in a peppery
Szechuan dressing, then a fat tranche of cod, cooked to a
delicate perfection, generously topped with fine brioche
crumbs and white crab meat, and accompanied by a robust
lobster cream sauce, had star billing on one superlative strewn
report. Good materials and really fresh vegetables are two
more components for success. Individual sticky toffee pudding
has a timeless appeal, especially when served on a toffee sauce
with a scoop of home-made liquorice ice cream, plus a dollop
of clotted cream. There's a comprehensive wine list, including
a few half-bottles and some New World wines.

FOWEY, Fowey Hall

Hanson Drive PL23 1ET
Map 2: SX15
Tel: 01726 833866
Fax: 01726 834100
Chef: Tony Duce
Cost: Set-price D £29.50. H/wine £14
Times: Noon-2pm/7.30-9.30pm
Additional: Bar food; Sunday L;
Children welcome; 🍴 dishes
Accommodation: 25 en suite ★ ★ ★

*A very child-friendly hotel (although not permitted in the
dining room), run by a young, eager team.* The dining room is
a stunning wood-panelled room, candle-lit at night, with lofty
ceilings, plasterwork and pillars. The cooking observes current
trends and takes note of the location and seasons. Our
inspection meal included a rustic pressed rabbit and duck
terrine came with date chutney, fillet of salmon with crab
dumplings and herb butter (an understated description that
tasted better than it read), and a delicate toasted raspberry
marshmallow with vanilla ice cream. The almost exclusively
French wine list is written in an enthusiastic and de-mystifying
style with a good range starting around £10 for house wine.

FOWEY, Fowey Hotel

Grand hotel perched above the estuary with marvellous river and marina views. Public rooms include a spacious bar, elegant restaurant and smart drawing room. The set-price menu offers five or six choices at each stage with ideas built around local supplies and a willingness on the part of the kitchen to impart boldness with modern recipes. Thus a cannon of Cornish lamb is oven-cooked with sage and partnered by marmalade mash potato and a Marsala sauce, or medallions of monkfish are served on a sweet potato purée with a smoked fish sauce. Starters can range from cream of mushroom and fennel soup to a timbale of poached salmon, white crab meat and smoked salmon. The likes of warm blackcherry soufflé with blueberry ice cream, a savoury Welsh rarebit, or locally made cheeses form the backbone of the dessert choices.

Directions: From A390 take B3269 for approx 5 miles, follow signs for Fowey & continue along Pavillion Road for 0.75 mile. 2nd R

The Esplanade PL23 1HX
Map 2: SX15
Tel: 01726 832551
Fax: 01726 832125
Chef: David Swade
Owner: Mr E K Richardson
Cost: Set-price D £23.95 (4 courses).
☺ H/wine £11.50
Times: Noon-2.30pm/7-9.15pm
Additional: Bar food; Sunday L; Children welcome; ♨ dishes
Seats: 70.
Smoking: No smoking in dining room
Accommodation: 21 en suite ★★★

FOWEY, Marina Hotel

Commanding spectacular views over the Fowey Estuary, the Waterside Restaurant excels in local seafood such as lobster or poached lemon sole stuffed with crab. Cornish lamb with herb crust provides an alternative for meat-eaters.

Accommodation: 11 en suite ★★

Directions: From A38 Dobwalls take A390 to St Austell. At Lostwithiel take B3269 to Fowey

Esplanade PL23 1HY
Map 2: SX15
Tel: 01726 833315
Fax: 01726 832779
Cost: *Alc* £25, set-price D £18. ☺ H/wine £9.95
Times: D only, 7-8.30pm. Closed mid Dec-end Feb
Additional: Children 12+; ♨ dishes
Smoking: No smoking in dining room

GILLAN, Tregildry Hotel

Country hotel with spectacular sea and river views. The dining room makes the most of the wonderful views as much as the menu relies on fresh local produce with Cornish fish, creams, ice creams and West Country farmhouse cheeses heading the list. Our test meal included a competent caramelised onion and tomato tart, fillet of pork medallions with a honeyed sauce and timbale of rice containing red peppers and sultanas, and sticky toffee pudding with caramel sauce and locally-made fudge ice cream.

Directions: A3083 from Helston (Lizard Road), take 1st L for St Keverne. Follow signs for Manaccan and Gillan

TR12 6HG
Map 2: SW52
Tel: 01326 231378
Fax: 01326 231561
Chef: Huw Phillips
Owners: Huw & Lynne Phillips
Cost: Set-price D £23.50 (4 courses).
☺ H/wine £10.25
Times: D only, 7-8.45pm. Closed Nov-Feb
Additional: Children 8+; ♨ dishes
Seats: 30
Smoking: No smoking in dining room
Accommodation: 10 en suite ★★

GOLANT, Cormorant Hotel

Local produce, particularly fresh seafood, features on the French inspired menu at this delightful hotel above the fishing village of Golant. Splendid views over the Fowey estuary are an added attraction.

Smoking: No smoking in restaurant
Accommodation: 11 en suite ★★

Directions: Turn from A390 St Austell Rd onto B3269 to Fowey. Turn L to Golant. Go to end (almost to water's edge), entrance on R

Fowey PL23 1LL
Map 2: SX15
Tel/Fax: 01726 833426
Cost: *Alc* £27.50, set-price D £19 (4 courses). ☺ H/wine £9.50
Times: Noon-1.55pm/7-8.55pm
Additional: Bar food L; ♨ dishes

HELSTON, **Nansloe Manor**

A perfect Georgian manor at the end of a tree-lined drive.
Cornish fish and seafood are given prominence on the menu.
Fish soup is enriched with tomatoes as well as olive oil and
topped with a deep-fried saffron beignet, and Cornish crab and
gazpacho couscous salad is layered with Parmesan crisps and
circled by a basil dressing. The cooking contains some lively
ideas – baked spiced cod fillet with chilli squash mash,
marinated pimentos and frothy coriander sauce; seared fresh
scallops with home-made Angel Hair pasta and bittersweet
lemon and olive oil relish; passion fruit, lychee and
Mascarpone cheesecake set on smooth mango and Galliano
sauce. Meat selections include griddled beef with deep-fried
crispy aubergines and wilted spinach stack set on a tomato
essence and juniper dressing.

Meneage Road TR13 0SB
Map 2: SW62
Tel: 01326 574691
Fax: 01326 564680
Chef: Howard Ridden
Owners: The Ridden Family
Cost: *Alc* £27, set-price L £15. ☺
H/wine £10.80
Times: D only, 7-8.30pm
Additional: Sunday L (noon-1.30pm);
Children 10+; ❹ dishes
Seats: 40. Jacket & tie preferred
Smoking: No smoking in dining room
Accommodation: 7 en suite ★★

Directions: 300yds from junction of
A394 and A3083 down a well-signed
drive

LAUNCESTON,
Percy's at Coombeshead

A special place, not least in terms of location. The short
menu is constructed on a simple pattern. There is usually a
lightly spiced fish chowder to begin, goats' cheese served,
perhaps, with pan-fried polenta and spicy sauce, or chicken
livers sautéed with smoked bacon and balsamic vinaigrette.
Percy's mixed salad memorably includes anything from nettles
to watercress and nasturtiums. Breast of wild duck is cooked
pink with a juniper glaze, but oven-roast bacon-wrapped
partridge needs no more than good game jus. Puddings tend to

Virginstow EX21 5EA
Map 2: SX38
Tel: 01409 211236
Fax: 01409 211275
Chef: Tina Bricknell-Webb
Owners: Tony & Tina Bricknell-Webb
Cost: Set-price D £24. ☺ H/wine
£9.95
Times: D only, 6.30-9.30pm. Closed
Nov
Additional: Children 12+; ❹ dishes
Seats: 34. Private dining room 14

the cumbersome in terms of flavour and texture combinations – hazelnut shortcake was heavy going although the accompanying lemon geranium ice cream impressed. Still, there was nothing but praise for a steamed chocolate and Grand Marnier truffle pudding with orange marmalade ice cream and a smooth, bitter dark chocolate sauce.

Directions: Follow signs to restaurant from Gridley Corner A388 (St Giles on the Heath) or at Metherell Cross, B3218 (Okehampton-Bude)

LISKEARD,
Well House Hotel ❀❀❀

Charming small hotel offering a personal level of hospitality. The valley setting between Liskeard and Looe offers the sort of tranquility that makes for a relaxing break. Cameron Brown has now departed and has been replaced by John Lyons; early reports suggest a successful takeover. Local and regional produce drives the menu, so that Cornish fish soup with garlic croûtons and aïoli, pan-fried brill with parsnip purée and a casserole of spring vegetables, and West Country cheeses appear on the daily changing set-price menu. Metropolitan influences are readily adopted: ballotine of ham shank and foie gras with onion Tatin and sherry caramel, roast fillet of beef with peppercorn risotto and Madeira sauce, and apple crème brûlée with apple sorbet reveals a chef well up on the latest trends.

Directions: At St Keyne Church follow signs to St Keyne Well, the restaurant is 0.5 mile further

Smoking: No smoking in dining room
Accommodation: 8 en suite

St Keyne PL14 4RN
Map 2: SX26
Tel: 01579 342001
Fax: 01579 343891
Chef: John Lyons
Owners: Nick Wainford, Ione Nurdin
Cost: Set-price L £21.95 (2 courses)/D £26.95. H/wine £9.95
Times: 12.30-1.30pm/7.15-8.45pm
Additional: Sunday L; Children 8+ at D; ❹ dishes
Seats: 32
Smoking: No-smoking area; No pipes & cigars
Accommodation: 9 en suite ★★

MARAZION, **Mount Haven Hotel** ❀

Split-level restaurant in an old coaching house. Local fish is featured, with dishes such as poached fillet of John Dory with scallops, served in a saffron cream scented sauce.

Turnpike Road TR17 0DQ
Map 2: SW53
Tel: 01736 710249
Fax: 01736 711658
Cost: *Alc* £21, set-price D £19.50. ☺ H/wine £9
Times: D only, 7-9pm (8.30pm Oct-Apr)
Additional: Bar food D; Sunday L (noon-1.30pm); Children welcome; ❹ dishes
Smoking: No smoking in dining room
Accommodation: 17 en suite ★★

Directions: Through village to end of built-up area

MAWNAN SMITH, **Budock Vean** ❀❀

Impressive hotel with health spa and extensive leisure facilities. The sixty five acres of mature grounds stretch down to the foreshore of the Helford River – a setting that sees much repeat visitors. The menu takes in a lot of local

Falmouth TR11 5LG
Map 2: SW72
Tel: 01326 252100
Fax: 01326 250892
Chef: Darren Kelly
Owners: The Barlow Family

specialities including lobsters and Helford oysters, and the kitchen industriously makes good bread and canapés. A typical meal would take in warm king prawn and monkfish salad with lemongrass, pan-fried seared loin of lamb with port wine and balsamic jus (accompanied by fresh mint, caramelised baby onions and celeriac dauphinoise), and spicy apple and raisin parcels with brandied sauce anglaise and parisienne of apples.

Directions: Three miles S of Falmouth. Straight on at Mawnan Smith for 1.5 miles. Hotel on L

Cost: *Alc* £25, set-price D £23.50. ☺
Times: Noon-2.30pm/7.30-9.30pm. Closed Jan
Additional: Bar food L; Sunday L; Children 10+; 🍴 dishes
Seats: 120. Private dining room 40. Jacket & tie preferred at D
Smoking: No smoking in dining room
Accommodation: 58 en suite ★ ★ ★ ★

MAWNAN SMITH, Meudon Hotel ✿

Dine beneath a fruiting vine in a conservatory restaurant where the garden sweeps down to the sea. Local seafood is a speciality of the set-price menu.

Falmouth TR11 5HT
Map 2: SW72
Tel: 01326 250541
Fax: 01326 250543
Cost: Set-price D £25 (5 courses). ☺ H/wine £11
Times: 12.30-2pm/7.30-9pm. Closed Nov-Feb
Additional: Bar food L; Sunday L; Children welcome; 🍴 dishes
Accommodation: 29 en suite ★ ★ ★

Directions: From Truro take A39 towards Falmouth. At 'Hillhead' roundabout turn R. Hotel 4m on L

MAWNAN SMITH,
Trelawne Hotel ✿✿

Privately-owned hotel in stunning surroundings. Hutches, the hotel's restaurant looks over gardens to the sea with views of Falmouth and St Mawes. there's a good-value set-price menu, offering about six choices at each course, plus daily specials. The kitchen grasps current fashion, but given the more mature clientele, handles it with restraint. Thus smoked mackerel tartlets on a crab and dill sabyon were light, fluffy and tasted exactly as they should, cappuccino of mushroom soup was also clear flavoured. The supreme of cod that followed was served

TR11 5HS
Map 2: SW72
Tel: 01326 250226
Fax: 01326 250909
Chef: Nigel Woodland
Owners: G P Gibbons & D D Gibbons
Cost: *Alc* £19.50, set-price D £19.50. ☺ H/wine £8.90
Times: D only, 7-8.45pm
Additional: Bar food L; Children 7+; 🍴 dishes

on a bed of sweet potato champ with smoked haddock and
chive beurre blanc. Dessert proved to be an excellent
chocolate teardrop filled with white chocolate and Mascarpone
cream with Morello cherries in a Marsala wine syrup.

Directions: From Truro take A39 towards Falmouth. R at
Hillhead rdbt, take exit signed Maenporth. 3 miles, past
Maenporth beach, hotel on top of hill on L

Seats: 30
Smoking: No smoking in dining room
Accommodation: 14 en suite ★ ★ ★

MOUSEHOLE, Cornish Range

*Small, plainly attired, but serious about seafood. The short menu
gets straight to the point with parcels of smoked salmon and crab,
and creamy fish pie filled with chunks of Newlyn fish and prawns.
Booking advisable.*

Smoking: No-smoking area

Directions: Mousehole is 3 miles from Penzance, via Newlyn

6 Chapel Street TR19 6SB
Map 2: SW42
Tel: 01736 731488
Fax: 01736 732173
Cost: *Alc* £20. ☺ H/wine £9.95
Times: D only, 7-9.30pm. Closed Jan
Additional: Sunday L winter only
(12.30-2pm); ♨ dishes

MOUSEHOLE, Old Coastguard Inn

Attentive staff lift this old inn above the ordinary. The open-
plan bar leads into the restaurant fronted by a long, stylish
conservatory with views over the gardens to the sea. Wooden
floors and bare wood polished tables sum up the informal,
friendly brasserie-style atmosphere and the place attracts a
good showing of locals as well as tourists. The kitchen displays
ample evidence of cooking skills, displaying clear flavours and
not a little style. Note our meal that opened with delicate crab
cakes lifted by Thai spices and cooled by guacamole, a mixed
fish grill that took in perfectly cooked tranches of salmon,
monkfish and mackerel offset by samphire and herbs.
Chocolate torte was just right too,

Directions: From Penzance to Newlyn. Inn 1st large building on
L, just after public car park

The Parade TR19 6PR
Map 2: SW42
Tel: 01736 731222
Fax: 01736 731720
Chefs: Freddie Wood, Keith Terry,
Mary Kitchen
Owners: Bill Trelcar, Peter Wood
Cost: Set-price D £19. ☺ H/wine £8
Times: Noon-2.30pm/6-9.30pm
Additional: Bar food; Children
welcome; ♨ dishes
Seats: 50
Smoking: No smoking in dining room
Accommodation: 24 en suite ★ ★

NEWQUAY, Corisande Manor

*The hotel, built for an Austrian count in Black Forest style, offers a
short choice of carefully prepared dishes including succulent chicken
supreme with bacon and coriander cream sauce.*

Accommodation: 12 en suite ★ ★

Directions: Off the main road down the Pentire headland, left at
Newquay Nursing Home into Pentire Crescent, then R into
Riverside Avenue

Riverside Avenue Pentire TR7 1PL
Map 2: SW86
Tel: 01637 872042
Fax: 01637 874557
Cost: Set-price D £19.50 (4 courses).
☺ H/wine £9.75
Times: D only at 8pm
Additional: Children welcome
Smoking: No smoking in dining room
**Shortlisted for AA Wine Award – see
page 16**

NEWQUAY, Porth Veor Manor

*A Victorian manor house with fine views over Porth beach. The
simple menu lists a good selection; try smoked mackerel mousse,
lamb with sherry and mushroom sauce, and some excellent local
cheeses.*

Directions: Leave Newquay on A3058. After 1 mile turn L onto
B3276 (Padstow Coast Rd). Hotel is on L at bottom of hill

Porth Way TR7 3LW
Map 2: SW86
Tel: 01637 873274
Fax: 01637 851690
Telephone for further details

PADSTOW, **Brocks**

The Strand PL28 8AJ
Map 2: SW97
Tel: 01841 532565
Chefs: Sylvain Lesenne, Rupert Patrick
Owners: Tim & Hazel Brocklebank
Cost: *Alc* £27, set-price D £21. ☺
H/wine £10.95
Times: 12.15-1.50pm/7-9.15pm
(10pm Fri, Sat). Closed Sun, Mon
Additional: Children welcome;
✤ dishes
Seats: 40
Smoking: No smoking in dining room

Casual, upbeat restaurant that's a hit with visitors and locals alike. Slap bang in the centre of town, Brocks has been doing a roaring trade since it opened in early 1998. The short menu offers a mixture of strong rustic flavours and classic styles: pan-fried scallops with roasted red pepper dressing, and baked fillet of curried cod with vegetable tagliatelle are typical examples. Basil gnocchi with finely shaved Parmesan and tomato sauce kicked of a late autumn meal that was followed by a nicely seared breast of chicken, served with Ricotta tartlet, spinach, and crisp strips of deep-fried parsnip. To finish, banana fritters with vanilla ice cream and ginger biscuits proved to be a good combination. The short wine list offers a limited selection of bottles for under £20, with just a couple of wines by the glass.

Directions: Follow one way around harbour. Just past bandstand on L

PADSTOW,
Old Custom House Inn

South Quay PL28 8ED
Map 2: SW97
Tel: 01841 532359
Fax: 01841 533372
Telephone for further details

Charming harbour-side hotel with lovely sea views. The bar is popular with locals and visitors, and the restaurant offers good-value dishes along the lines of crab and smoked salmon risotto drizzled with pesto, and roasted cannon of lamb.

Directions: From Wadebridge take A389 (Padstow). Second turning on R after Padstow school, go round sharp bend at bottom of hill. Restaurant is opposite entrance to harbour car park

PADSTOW, **St Petroc's House**

4 New Street PL28 8EA
Map 2: SW97
Tel: 01841 532700
Fax: 01841 532942
Chef: David Pope
Owner: Rick & Jill Stein
Cost: Set-price L & D £19.95. ☺
H/wine £12.95
Times: 12.30-2pm/7-9.30pm. Closed
Mon, 19-27 Dec
Additional: Children welcome
Seats: 35. Private dining room 12
Smoking: No smoking in restaurant;
Air conditioning
Accommodation: 13 en suite

The younger sibling of Rick Stein's destination restaurant is a relaxed, child-friendly, bistro sort of place. It serves simple, rustic Italian and French dishes and offers good value. Fish, naturally enough, takes centre stage. Mackerel is pan-fried with tomato salad and olive tapenade, grilled cod served on braised Savoy cabbage with bacon and beer. Whole grilled scored lemon sole with sea salt and lemon needs no further elaboration, and pan-fried salmon with white wine, parsley and butter sauce and new potatoes is about as fancy as it gets. Starters are equally simple with filling soups (lentil, potato and lemon, for example) or lightly grilled goats' cheese with beetroot salad. There's also chargrilled sirloin steak. Puddings are tried and tested versions of sticky toffee pudding, bread-and-butter pudding and crème brûlée.

Directions: Follow one-way around harbour, take 1st L, situated on the R

PADSTOW,
The Seafood Restaurant

Riverside PL28 8BY
Map 2: SW97
Tel: 01841 532700
Fax: 01841 532942
Chef: Rick Stein

'It is good to see everyone tucking into fruits de mer with such gusto and delight', comments an inspector, who judged the quality of the fish and the timing at Rick Stein's renowned seafooder as perfect. The big room is light, bright, modern with a terrific buzz that must be constant these days as advance booking is essential to ensure a table. TV fame may have spread the word far and wide, but it is a credit to Stein that he maintains standards under such pressure. This is fish cookery that is simplicity itself, it eschews heavy sauces and takes notice of the seasons. A fat fillet of haddock, for example, requires little more than some haricot beans, tarragon, capers and warm mayonnaise, whilst a fleshy wing of skate gets the classic tried-and-tested treatment: black butter and capers. Modern ideas are there aplenty. Among the starters squid is sautéed and served in a salad with chilli, mint, coriander and roasted rice, hot shellfish is teamed with olive oil, garlic and lemon juice, or there's a delicious baked crab and Gruyère tart. Goan fish curry with raita and kachumber reflects Stein's willingness to explore fish cookery globally. Some imaginative desserts move away from the standard pudding format of modern British restaurants – note ricotta drop scone with blackcurrant compote, and a moist orange and almond cake with bitter chocolate sauce and kumquats.

Owners: Mr & Mrs C R Stein
Cost: *Alc* £45, set-price L £28/D £34. H/wine £12.95
Times: Noon-2pm/7-10pm. Closed Sun, Xmas wk
Additional: Children 4+; dishes
Seats: 100
Smoking: No pipes & cigars; Air conditioning
Accommodation: 13 en suite ★ ★

Directions: Situated on South Quay

PENZANCE,
Harris' Restaurant

Hidden away, tiny, with a pleasant atmosphere and a modern British cooking style. The emphasis is on fish, but venison with wild mushrooms, beetroot, caraway and red wine sauce was just as successful.

Directions: Telephone for directions

46 New Street PL18 2LZ
Map 2: SW43
Tel: 01736 364408
Telephone for further details

POLPERRO, The Kitchen

Cosy pine-furnished restaurant where international influences are reflected in the extensive menu. There is plenty of fresh seafood, including local crab, and a good choice for vegetarians.

Smoking: No smoking in dining room

Directions: Between the harbour and the car park

The Coombes PL13 2RQ
Map 2: SX25
Tel: 01503 272780
Cost: *Alc* £20. ☺ H/wine £9
Times: D only, 7-9.30pm. Closed Oct-Easter
Additional: Children 12+; dishes

POLZEATH,
Cornish Cottage Hotel

The Faulkners run this delightful small hotel to a high standard. A set dinner menu offers some four choices at each course with local ingredients playing a major role. Cornish lobster, for example, is available at 24 hours' notice, but otherwise there could be poached halibut steak with roasted tomatoes and buttered noodles, or chargrilled fillet of beef with chateau potatoes and a shallot Tatin. Starters take in braised leg of guinea fowl with a puffed ravioli of mushrooms, or cream of asparagus soup, and desserts include a honey-roasted fruit salad with a white wine sabayon. Wines are treated with respect.

Directions: From Wadebridge/Camelford pass the 'Bee Centre' and take the R fork. The hotel is 300 yds on R.

New Polzeath Nr Rock PL27 6UF
Map 2: SW97
Tel: 01208 862213
Fax: 01208 862259
Chef: John Lyons
Owners: Mr & Mrs D Faulkner
Cost: *Alc* £29.50, set-price D £27.50 (6 courses). H/wine £11
Times: D only, 7-9pm
Additional: Children 12+
Seats: 32
Smoking: No smoking in dining room
Accommodation: 12 en suite ★ ★

PORT GAVERNE,
Port Gaverne Hotel

Port Isaac PL29 3SQ
Map 2: SX08
Tel: 01208 880244
Fax: 01208 880151
Cost: *Alc* £22.50. ☺ H/wine £7.60
Times: D only, 7-9.30pm. Closed
early Jan-mid Feb
Additional: Sunday L (12-2pm)
Smoking: No smoking in dining room
Accommodation: 17 en suite ★ ★

Directions: Signposted from B3314, 2
miles from Delabole

*Flagstones, beams and steep stairways are what you might expect at
an ancient seaside inn. Fish figures prominently on the restaurant
menu, ranging from whole grilled plaice with prawns and
mushrooms to monkfish with orange and ginger sauce.*

PORT ISAAC,
The Castle Rock Hotel

*There's a panoramic view of Port Isaac Bay from this hotel
restaurant. Pan-fried Megrim sole is a locally landed speciality,
along with Port Isaac lobster or crab, or balti-style mussels.*

Accommodation: 17 en suite ★ ★

Directions: From A39 take B3314 then B3267 to top of Port
Isaac village

4 New Road PL29 3SB
Map 2: SW98
Tel: 01208 880300
Fax: 01208 880219
Cost: *Alc* £20, set-price D £16.
☺ H/wine £7.50
Times: Noon-2pm/6.30-9pm
Additional: Bar food L; Children 5+;
🍴 dishes
Smoking: No smoking in dining room

PORTHLEVEN,
Critchards Seafood Restaurant

*Fresh, locally caught seafood is the mainstay of this charming
harbourside restaurant. Cantonese-style scallops, and monkfish New
Orleans style show the kitchen's adventurous disposition.*

Accommodation: 2 en suite

Directions: Overlooking the harbour

The Harbour Head TR13 9JA
Map 2: SW62
Tel: 01326 562407
Fax: 01326 564444
Cost: *Alc* £25
Times: D only, 6.30-9.30pm. Closed
Sun, Jan
Additional: Children 6+; 🍴 dishes
Smoking: No smoking in dining room

PORTREATH,
Tabb's Restaurant

**To spot 'hoggs pudding' with onion gravy and chopped apple
salad on a charmingly hand-drawn menu is a sight to
gladden the heart of anyone wishing to celebrate some of the
overlooked glories of British regional cooking.** Pot-roasted
wild rabbit with cumin seeds, garlic and onions is also a
welcome sight, but most of the menu follows the more
mainstream modern British idiom: goats' cheese and avocado

Railway Terrace TR16 4LD
Map 2: SW64
Tel/Fax: 01209 842488
Chef: Nigel Tabb
Owners: Nigel & Melanie Tabb
Cost: *Alc* £20, set-price D £14.50. ☺
H/wine £8.95
Times: D only, 7-9pm. Closed Tue, 2
wks Jan, Nov

timbale with pine nuts and mixed leaves; steamed fillet of hake with leeks, mushrooms and white wine butter sauce; pan-fried slices of duck breast on shredded celeriac with dry sherry and green peppercorn sauce. Several dishes have a touch of the Med about them such as grilled fillet of turbot with a garlic crust and a pepper and tomato vinaigrette.

Directions: At the centre of the village, under the viaduct

Additional: Sunday L (12.15-1.45pm); Children welcome; dishes
Seats: 35
Smoking: No pipes & cigars

PORTSCATHO,
Rosevine Hotel ❀❀

Porthcurnick Beach St Mawes
TR2 5EW
Map 2: SW83
Tel: 01872 580206
Fax: 01872 580230
Chef: Keith S Makepeace
Owners: The Makepeace Family
Cost: *Alc* L £20, set-price D £34. H/wine £13.50
Times: Noon-2.30pm/7.15-9pm. Closed Nov-Feb
Additional: Bar food L; Sunday L; Children welcome; dishes
Seats: 50
Smoking: No smoking in dining room
Accommodation: 17 en suite ★ ★ ★

Directions: Off A3078, hotel signed on R, 2 miles after Ruan High Lanes

The dining room overlooks the garden and out to sea. The Georgian country house is splendidly run by the Makepeace family with a blend of formal style but without (as our inspector put it) 'going down the cut crystal route'. The cooking is not flamboyant, but takes a sound, unified approach to all the output, from scones to petits fours. Confidence is growing as could be seen in our test meal that took in sauté of local scallops with fresh pea purée and tarragon-infused jus, pan-fried breast of Gressingham duck accompanied by braised red cabbage, fondant potatoes and a lemongrass and coriander jus, and lemon crème brûlée. Small details also came up trumps: home-made breads of walnut and apricot, olive oil and tomato, and cheese and bacon; an appetiser of a frothy cup of lobster cappuccino bisque; own fudge and chocolate truffles. The wine list majors in French heavyweights augmented by a smattering of other European/New World producers.

REDRUTH,
Basset Count House ❀❀

In the middle of nowhere. This splendid granite house is named after the tin-mining count house it once was. It's warm and cosy, with big log fires, squishy sofas and three separate dining areas, all very classy. Ann Long brings her own individual approach to her menus, from a starter of a high pile of smoked salmon in a kedgeree cake with a quail's egg at its centre, to moist chicken breast rolled in a rich chicken mousse, roasted and sliced and accompanied by al dente pasta with walnuts, parsley and Stilton. Parsnip, ginger and coconut soup, thick and creamy, successfully walks the tightrope of flavours,

Carnkie TR16 6RZ
Map 2: SW64
Tel: 01209 215181
Chef: Ann Long
Owner: John Milan
Cost: *Alc* £23, set-price L £12.50 (4 courses). ☺ H/wine £9.50
Times: Noon-2pm/7-9pm. Closed D Sun, all Mon, Tue
Additonal: Sunday L; Children 8+
Seats: 36. Private dining room 12. Jacket & tie preferred

Smoking: No smoking in dining room

and crab tartlet is made with fine, crisp pastry. Loads of vegetables are placed in the middle of the table, family-style, for main courses: snowy-white roast cod fillet under a good foil of a crust of Parmesan, parsley and garlic, 'a lovely piece' of pink best end of lamb wrapped in puff pastry with mint pesto and a clear, shiny, dense red wine sauce, or caramelised duck breast flavoured with lavender and coriander served with a berry sauce. Creamy puddings end on a rich note – pannacotta, or a signature dish of 'truly yummy' raspberry oatmeal meringue, like a posh version of Eton mess, with perhaps fresh fruit salad for the more health-conscious. Care goes into incidentals like breads and home-made Turkish delight, and the serviceable wine list is fairly priced.

Directions: 2 miles W of Redruth off B3297

REDRUTH,

Penventon Hotel

TR15 1TE
Map 2: SW64
Tel: 01209 203000
Fax: 01209 203001
Cost: *Alc* £20, set-price L £ 10 (2 courses)/D £14. ☺ H/wine £9
Additional: Bar food L; Sunday L; Children welcome; 🍴 dishes
Smoking: No-smoking area; No pipes & cigars
Accommodation: 55 en suite ★ ★ ★

A pianist plays in the restaurant of this extended Georgian mansion where a lively, international rendition of the likes of sliced supreme of chicken with a light mango sauce, and scampi flambéed in brandy is on offer.

Directions: On Redruth intersection of A30, 1 mile S of town centre

RUAN HIGH LANES,

The Hundred House Hotel

TR2 5JR
Map 2: SW93
Tel: 01872 501336
Fax: 01872 501151
Cost: Set-price D £24 (4 courses). ☺
H/wine £7.50
Times: D only, 7.30-8pm. Closed Nov
– Feb
Smoking: No smoking in dining room;
Air conditioning
Accommodation: 10 en suite ★ ★

Directions: On A3078 4 miles after
Tregony on R

Family pictures and fine antiques fill the Edwardian country house. The daily-changing dinner menu is essentially English in style: roast loin of pork with port and redcurrant cream sauce, meringues with clotted cream and hot fudge sauce and West Country cheeses.

ST AUSTELL,

Boscundle Manor Hotel

Personally run manor house with a daily menu featuring good, fresh produce. In traditional style could be crab Mornay, roast duck with cherry and brandy sauce, fillet of pork Normandy. Superior wine list of surprising length.

Accommodation: 10 en suite ★ ★

Directions: 2 miles E of St Austell, off A390 on road signposted Tregrehan

Tregrehan PL25 3RL
Map 2: SX05
Tel: 01726 813557
Fax: 01726 814997
Cost: Set-price D £20 (4 courses). ☺
H/wine £9.50
Times: D only, 7.30-8pm. Closed Sun
Additional: Children welcome
Smoking: No smoking in dining room

ST AUSTELL, Carlyon Bay Hotel

Sea Road Carlyon Bay PL25 3RD
Map 2: SX05
Tel: 01726 812304
Fax: 01726 814938
Telephone for further details

Directions: A390 towards St Austell;
from town follow Charlestown then
Carlyon Bay/Crinnis. Hotel at end of
Sea Road near Cornwall Coliseum

Enjoy stunning sea views from cliff-top walks before returning for dinner at this friendly hotel. There's a strong Thai influence in some of the dishes, crab soup spiced with ginger and lemon grass, for example, but there's also plenty of traditional English fare.

ST IVES,

Carbis Bay Hotel

Carbis Bay TR26 2NP
Map 2: SW54
Tel: 01736 795311
Fax: 01736 797677
Telephone for further details

Family-owned hotel overlooking its own sandy beach. Traditional atmosphere in the dining room is offset by up-to-date dishes of terrine of salmon with sweet peppers, and beef and veal fillets with mushroom duxelle and hollandaise.

Directions: Telephone for directions

ST IVES, Chy-an-Dour Hotel

Trelyon Avenue TR26 2AD
Map 2: SW54
Tel: 01736 796436
Fax: 01736 795772
Cost: Set-price D £17. ☺ H/wine £5.75
Times: D only, 7-8pm. Closed Dec-Feb
Additional: Children 5+; ✿ dishes

Enjoy the views over beach and sea from vast dining room windows. Satisfy both traditional and adventurous tastes with onion soup, and chicken breast in coconut with mango and pineapple sauce, and raspberry Charlotte.

Smoking: No smoking in dining room
Accommodation: 23 en suite ★★

Directions: Hotel on main road into St Ives, A3074

ST IVES, Garrack Hotel ✿✿

Burthallan Lane Higher Ayr
TR26 3AA
Map 2: SW54
Tel: 01736 796199
Fax: 01736 798955
Chef: Ben Reeve
Owners: Frances, Michael & Stephen Kilby
Cost: Alc £26.15, set-price D £22.50 (4 courses). ☺ H/wine £8.14
Times: D only, 7-9pm
Additional: Bar food; Children welcome; ✿ dishes
Seats: 48
Smoking: No smoking in dining room
Accommodation: 16 en suite ★★★

Directions: Follow signs for 'Porthmeor Beach and Car Parks'

Run by the same family for over 30 years. The Garrack is set in extensive grounds and has wonderful views over Porthmeor beach. Lobster, landed in the town or at Newlyn, is something of a house speciality, sautéed and tossed in pasta with fennel and pesto, or cold with a mixed-leaf salad, and locally sourced fish might run to 'delicious, succulent' grilled fillet of turbot. Cornish lamb is rolled in mustard and chives, roasted, and served with mead jus, and fillet of beef, organically reared, might be marinated in soy and ginger and accompanied by a wild mushroom wun-tun. Starters are well-reported too, as in deep-fried fillets of plaice in Parmesan with wasabi aïoli and garlic and horseradish dressing, or local goats' cheese, grilled and accompanied by pickled pears. Skill with pastrywork comes to the fore in puddings of perhaps a light and flavoursome chocolate and pecan tart. Breads – sage and rosemary, say – are made in-house, and the widely ranging wine list supports Cornish vineyards by offering no fewer than seven bottles.

ST IVES,

Mermaid Seafood Restaurant

21 Fish Street TR26 1LT
Map 2: SW54
Tel: 01736 796816
Fax: 01736 799099
Cost: *Alc* £18, set-price L £8.95/D £12.50. ☺ H/wine £7.95
Times: Noon-2pm/6-10pm. Closed Sun
Additional: Children welcome; ♨ dishes
Smoking: No smoking in dining room

Directions: Along Harbour Street towards the Sloop Inn, turn L. Restaurant is at top of street on R.

Cornish lobster and Dover sole are top choices at this well-established seafood restaurant located in an atmospheric former sail loft in the appropriately named Fish Street.

ST IVES, **Pig 'n' Fish**

The bare wooden floor can be rather clattery, but service, from French waiters, is friendly. A feature of this light and airy first-floor restaurant is the high-beamed ceiling, from which fishing nets would have hung when pilchards were the town's main catch, and paintings by local artists hanging on the walls. Fish is the main business here, from a clear crab soup with rouille and Parmesan 'highly successful, marvellous,' enthused an inspector, to succulent roast spiced cod with Puy lentils. Fillet of turbot with leeks and sorrel and tarragon butter could be an alternative main course, an Eastern influence showing up in fillets of lemon sole with ginger, spring onions and soya butter, with breast of Gressingham duck with chicory and balsamic vinegar the sole meat offering. An inspector judged chocolate marquise both technically perfect and wholly delicious. Home-made breads are wonderful. As you'd expect with a preponderance of fish, the wine list is biased towards whites.

Norway Lane TR26 1LZ
Map 2: SW54
Tel: 01736 794204
Chef: Paul Sellars
Owners: Debby & Paul Sellars
Cost: *Alc* £25, set-price L £15.50/ D £21.50. ☺ H/wine £10
Times: 12.30-2.30pm/7-9pm. Closed Sun, D Mon, Nov-mid Mar
Additional: Children 2+
Seats: 30
Smoking: No smoking in dining room

Directions: 300 yards from St Ives Tate Gallery

ST IVES, **Skidden House**

Skidden Hill TR26 2DU
Map 2: SW54
Tel: 01736 796899
Fax: 01736 798619
Telephone for further details

Directions: A30 to St Erth roundabout, then A3074 to St Ives; follow to railway/coach station, then first R. Hotel is 30 metres on R

Charming old hotel in the centre of town. Dinner is served in the intimate bistro-style restaurant where fresh local produce is used to good effect – try blast-from-the-past beef Stroganoff. The selection of Cornish cheeses is excellent.

ST KEYNE,

Old Rectory House Hotel ❀❀

Liskeard PL14 4RL
Map 2: SX26
Tel: 01579 342617
Fax: 01579 342293
Chef: Glen Gatland
Owners: Mr & Mrs J Minifie
Cost: *Alc* £23, set-price D £21.50. ☺
Times: D only, 7-8.30pm. Closed D Sun
Additional: Children 12+; 🍂 dishes
Seats: 18
Smoking: No smoking in dining room
Accommodation: 8 en suite ★★

Beautifully furnished dining room in a charming country hotel. The size of the Old Rectory is one of the plus points to a stay here, as is the relaxed and considerate style of service. There are, for instance, a limited number of tables, so if all residents are dining in, there is little extra room for outside guests. Simple, uncluttered presentation allows the clear flavours of good, fresh ingredients to come through. Peppered chicken livers on a garlic croûton, noisettes of lamb served on fried slices of aubergine with a good jus, and chocolate brownies with almonds are typical of a menu that is short but well balanced.

Directions: 3 miles from Liskeard on B3254

ST MARTIN'S,

St Martin's on the Isle ❀❀❀

TR25 0QW
Map 2: SW28
Tel: 01720 422092
Fax: 01720 422298
Chef: Patrick Pierre Tweedie
Owner: Mr Peter Sykes
Cost: Set-price D £25. ☺ H/wine £14
Times: D only, 7-9.30pm. Closed Nov-Feb
Additional: Bar meals L; Children 12+; 🍂 dishes

The island hideaway is ideal for those looking for peace and tranquillity. The hotel has its own beach, jetty and yacht and enjoys an unrivalled panorama of sea and surrounding islands. A better setting for dinner could hardly be found, and as if this were not satisfaction enough, the cooking simply gets better and better, under the direction of chef Patrick Pierre Tweedie. Sweet, tender, locally caught scallops are seared and served with tomatoes, almost confit-like in sweetness and texture, and balsamic vinegar dressing. There was a surf''n'turf element to excellent fillet of beef with celeriac purée, potato galette and crab ravioli served with baby carrots. The four main courses on the short, daily changing menu divide equally between meat and fish – a sample menu offered roasted swordfish medallion with tapenade jus; braised silver sea bream and fennel pot au feu; rump of lamb, niçoise style; guinea fowl with 'morille farce', fettucine pasta. Presentation can be visually exciting, managing to avoid the contrived 'how do I eat it?' look of some tower blocks. Desserts are equally spot-on – chocolate fondant with rice pudding ice cream made a brilliant finish. A bargain, even if you do have to cross water to get there.

Seats: 60
Smoking: No smoking in dining room
Accommodation: 30 en suite ★ ★ ★

Directions: 28 miles from Penzance via helicopter, steamship or aircraft, then 20-minute launch boat ride to Isles of Scilly

ST MARY'S, Star Castle Hotel

Built in 1593 as a defensive fortress, now a remarkably comfortable hotel with high levels of attentive service. An elevated position gives panoramic views of the surrounding islands, The hotel's main restaurant is a highly atmospheric, dungeon-style room that attracts a loyal following; when we visited the place was packed. The menu is presented in a scroll tied with ribbon – in keeping with the medieval-style of the castle. However, despite a few retro-dishes such as chicken Kiev and beef Stroganoff, the kitchen shows plenty of awareness of modern trends. Both our chunky fish soup, and pork saltimbocca (wrapped in fresh sage and procuitto) and served with an excellent pimento flavoured sauce with roasted vegetables had a strong Mediterranean feel, and dark chocolate cup with fresh raspberry coulis was well made with sound flavour. Good home-made breads.

The Garrison TR21 0JA
Map 2: SW28
Tel/Fax: 01720 423342
Chef: Christopher Evans
Owners: John & Mary Nicholls
Cost: Set-price D £24 (5 courses). ☺
H/wine £8.95
Times: D only, 6.30-8.30pm. Closed Nov-Feb
Additional: Bar food L; Children 5+; 🍲 dishes
Seats: 40
Smoking: No smoking in dining room
Accommodation: 34 en suite ★ ★ ★

Directions: Flights available from Lands End, Plymouth, Exeter, Bristol & Southampton. Helicopter or ferry from Penzance. Hotel taxi meets all guests from airport or quay

ST MAWES,
Hotel Tresanton NEW

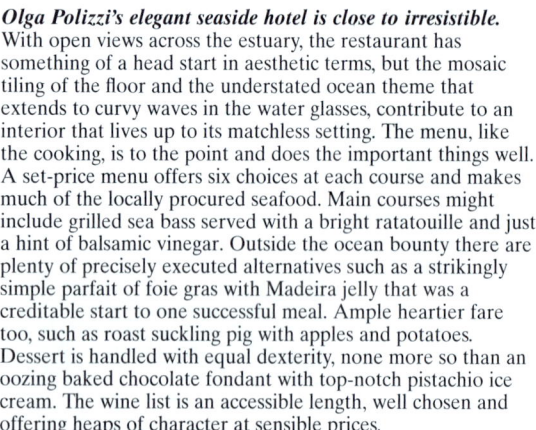

Olga Polizzi's elegant seaside hotel is close to irresistible. With open views across the estuary, the restaurant has something of a head start in aesthetic terms, but the mosaic tiling of the floor and the understated ocean theme that extends to curvy waves in the water glasses, contribute to an interior that lives up to its matchless setting. The menu, like the cooking, is to the point and does the important things well. A set-price menu offers six choices at each course and makes much of the locally procured seafood. Main courses might include grilled sea bass served with a bright ratatouille and just a hint of balsamic vinegar. Outside the ocean bounty there are plenty of precisely executed alternatives such as a strikingly simple parfait of foie gras with Madeira jelly that was a creditable start to one successful meal. Ample heartier fare too, such as roast suckling pig with apples and potatoes. Dessert is handled with equal dexterity, none more so than an oozing baked chocolate fondant with top-notch pistachio ice cream. The wine list is an accessible length, well chosen and offering heaps of character at sensible prices.

Lower Castle Road TR2 5DR
Map 2: SW83
Tel: 01326 270055
Fax: 01326 270053
Chef: Barry Zonfrillo
Owner: Olga Polizzi
Cost: Alc £30, set-price L £15 (2 courses)/D £30. H/wine £11
Times: 12.30-2.30pm/7-10.30pm. Closed 4 Jan-11 Feb
Additional: Bar food L; Sunday L; Children welcome
Seats: 48. Private dining room 60
Smoking: No-smoking area
Accommodation: 26 en suite

Directions: Telephone for directions

ST MAWES,

Idle Rocks Hotel ✿✿

Harbour Side TR2 5AN
Map 2: SW83
Tel: 01326 270771
Fax: 01326 270062
Chef: Alan Vickops
Owners: Mr & Mrs E K Richardson
Cost: Set-price D £24.50. ☺ H/wine
£10.75
Times: Noon-3pm/7-9.15pm
Additional: Bar food L; Children 7+;
🍴 dishes
Seats: 60
Smoking: No smoking in dining room
Accommodation: 28 en suite ★★★

If 'location, location, location', to quote Conrad Hilton, are the three most important attributes to a hotel's success, the Idle Rocks must be the envy of his late eye: it's right on the waterfront, looking over the yachts bobbing away in the harbour. The terrace is understandably popular for bar lunches of perhaps salmon and cod fishcakes with salad. Glass panels in the nautically themed restaurant make the most of the views too, but you can turn your back on the sea, menu-wise, and go for glazed guinea fowl sausage flecked with mushrooms and served with a rosemary and port sauce, or a main course pan-fried calves' liver with wild mushroom salad and a honey and grain mustard sauce. A soup is recommended as a starter, creamy tomato, for instance, good-quality stock accounting for its full flavour and, this being Cornwall, who could resist a pudding with clotted cream, like a zesty lemon tart?

Directions: Take A3078 to St Mawes. Hotel is on L as you enter the village, at water's edge

ST MAWES, **Rising Sun Hotel** ✿

Truro TR2 5DJ
Map 2: SW83
Tel: 01326 270233
Fax: 01326 270198
Telephone for further details

Imaginative cooking and fresh local seafood are one feature of this harbour-side hotel. Another is the bar – a focal point of village life. Look out for succulent supreme of chicken with a white wine and grape sauce, and grilled salmon served with lemon-flavoured spaghetti.

Directions: On harbour front

ST MELLION,

St Mellion International ✿

Saltash PL12 6SD
Map 2: SX36
Tel: 01579 351351
Fax: 01579 350537
Cost: Alc £25.75, set-price D £23. ☺
H/wine £10.70
Times: D only, 7-9.30pm
Additional: Sunday L (12.30-2pm);
Children welcome; dishes

A combination of time-share, hotel and golf and sporting centre, the restaurant offers tried and tested dishes of warm duck breast salad, beef fillet with wild mushroom sauce, and crème brûlée.

Smoking: No smoking in dining room; Air conditioning
Accommodation: 24 en suite ★★★

Directions: On A388 about 4 miles N of Saltash

ST WENN, Wenn Manor

A convivial atmosphere permeates this former parsonage with its 'country house meets pub' style. Cooking is straightforward and reliable – expect salmon with dill mayonnaise, or venison with port and blackberry sauce.

Smoking: No-smoking area; No pipes & cigars; Air conditioning
Accommodation: 3 en suite

Directions: Halfway between A30/A39, next to church in village

Bodmin PL30 5PS
Map 2: SW96
Tel: 01726 890240
Fax: 01726 890680
Cost: Alc £21. H/wine £9.50
Times: Noon-2pm/7-9pm. Closed Xmas 10 days
Additional: Bar food; Sunday L; Children 10+; 🍴 dishes

TALLAND BAY, Talland Bay Hotel

Trad English country house, delightful sea views, and a strong emphasis on seafood – try seared local scallops with black linguini. Roast loin of pork with an apple and Calvados sauce for meat lovers.

Smoking: No smoking in dining room
Accommodation: 19 en suite ★ ★ ★

Directions: Follow A387 Polperro road from Looe, hotel signed from crossroads

Nr Looe PL13 2JB
Map 2: SX25
Tel: 01503 272667
Fax: 01503 272940
Cost: Set-price D £22. ☺ H/wine £10.50
Times: D only, 7.30-9pm. Closed Jan, part Feb
Additional: Bar food L; Children 5+; 🍴 dishes

TINTAGEL, Trebrea Lodge

An elevated position, stunning views, an ideal place to stay. Dinner in the panelled dining-room offers a simple set menu. Cheese soufflé with mixed leaf salad, roasted cod fillet with beurre blanc, sautéed apples with orange caramel sauce and local cheese lit up a dark December night.

Smoking: No smoking in dining room
Accommodation: 7 en suite ★ ★

Directions: From Camelford (A39) follow signs to Tintagel. 1 mile before village turn R for Trenale

Trenale PL34 0HR
Map 2: SX08
Tel: 01840 770410
Fax: 01840 770092
Cost: Set-price D £22 (4 courses). ☺ H/wine £9.50
Times: D only at 8pm. Closed Jan-mid Feb
Additional: Children 12+; 🍴 dishes

TRESCO, The Island Hotel

No traffic, no crowds – probably one of the most idyllically sited hotels in Britain. The magnificent island setting and stunning gardens are only the first impressions as guests are met at the heliport or pier and transported by tractor and trailer. The hotel itself is constantly upgrading and improving, with lounges and dining room making the most of stunning sea views. Local fish and shellfish are staples of the daily changing menus, noted in dishes such as poached Tresco lobster ravioli with wilted spinach and a shellfish sauce, or baked fillet of sea bass with saffron cream potato with seared scallops and a balsamic reduction. But equally enticing are the likes of pan-fried breast of corn-fed chicken with dauphinoise potatoes and tarragon creamed sauce, or roast noisettes of English lamb served on rösti potato with Puy lentils, baby carrots and a rosemary jus.

Directions: Situated on north-eastern tip of island

Isles of Scilly TR24 0PU
Map 2: SW17
Tel: 01720 422883
Fax: 01720 423008
Chef: Peter Hingston
Owner: Robert Dorrien-Smith
Times: Noon-2.15pm/6.45-9.30pm. Closed Nov-Mar
Additional: Bar food L; Children welcome; 🍴 dishes
Seats: 110. Private dining room 20
Smoking: No pipes & cigars
Accommodation: 48 en suite ★ ★ ★

TRESCO, **New Inn**

The focal point of social life on this enchanting island. Food has a strong Mediterranean feel, especially in the use of fresh local fish: fillet of Newlyn monkfish with hot pepper marmalade, and poached John Dory with a tomato and shallot salsa.

Smoking: No smoking in dining room
Accommodation: 14 en suite ★★

Directions: 250 yds from the harbour (private island, contact hotel for details)

Isles of Scilly TR24 0QQ
Map 2: SW17
Tel: 01720 422844
Fax: 01720 423200
Cost: Set-price D £22.50. ☺ H/wine £8.95
Times: Noon-2pm/7-9pm
Additional: Bar food; Sunday L; Children 14+; ◑ dishes

TRURO, **Alverton Manor**

Impressive sandstone property standing proudly in six acres of elegant grounds with service to match. The former convent (the chapel is now used for weddings), draws visitors for some sound cooking. The dining room is candlelit at night and forms a soothing backdrop to good regional produce: pan-fried Cornish king scallops with fresh coriander perhaps, or locally-caught turbot served with a seafood ravioli. The highlight of our meal was pheasant and duck terrine with wild mushrooms, pistachio nuts, and toasted brioche, all complemented by an 'excellent' orange, cranberry and juniper chutney. At all times staff are polite, formal and smartly dressed.

Directions: From the Truro by-pass, take A39 to St Austell. Just past the church on L

Tregolls Road TR1 1ZQ
Map 2: SW84
Tel: 01872 276633
Fax: 01872 222989
Chefs: Nick Cassidy, Robert Brandreth
Owner: Mr M Sagin
Cost: *Alc* £25.55, set-price L £16.25/D £21.50. ☺ H/wine £9.95
Times: Noon-1.45pm/7-9.30pm
Additional: Bar food; Sunday L; Children welcome; ◑ dishes
Seats: 50. Private dining room 50. Jacket & tie preferred
Smoking: No smoking in dining room
Accommodation: 34 en suite ★★★

TRURO,
Oliver's Restaurant

Yellow walls, dark blue tablecloths and plain white tableware bring hints of the Mediterranean to this brasserie below the Wig and Pen Inn, a listed building dating back to 1820. Hints of the Mediterranean may show up on the plate too, in a filo tart of ratatouille, but the thrust of the menu is British through and through: pan-fried pheasant with blackcurrant reduction on a compote of fruit, baked guinea fowl with braised bacon and mushrooms in a tarragon and white wine sauce, or succulent pork stuffed with apples and oranges on red onion confit with red wine sauce. Fish is a strength too, as in a starter of crab pancake on a lemon and orange salad, or 'delicious'

Castle Street TR1 3DP
Map 2: SW84
Tel/Fax: 01872 273028
Chef: Colin Hankins
Owners: David & Serena London
Cost: *Alc* £21.50, set-price D £20. ☺ H/wine £8.95
Times: Noon-2pm/7-9.30pm. Closed Sun, 26 Dec, 1 Jan
Additional: Bar food; Children welcome; ◑ dishes
Seats: 32
Smoking: No smoking in dining room

seafood and saffron cassolette. Stalwarts of bread-and-butter pudding with caramel ice cream, or a duo of white chocolate mousse and strawberry parfait with chocolate sauce, all tasting as good as they look, end meals on an upbeat note. Chocolate and fruity petits fours are served with coffee, and wines by the glass include a great-value Australian Chenin Blanc.

Directions: Below Law Courts in the city centre

VERYAN, Nare Hotel

One hotel, two restaurants, pleasant service. As well as the main dining-room, light lunches and suppers can be taken in the conservatory-style Gwendra Room overlooking the outdoor pool and terrace. Seafood and fish are delivered daily, high quality meat comes from local sources and an imaginative pastry chef produces a fine selection of desserts. Hors d'oeuvre from the trolley makes a splendid and, these days, rarely sighted first course; alternatively there may be duck liver parfait with Armagnac and Cumberland sauce or home-made soup of the day. Both honey-roast best end of English lamb with creamed celeriac and simply presented, beautifully cooked steamed fillet of bass with balsamic jus and deep-fried leeks showed skill and careful preparation. Locally caught lobster is cooked to your choice, as is whole Dover sole. Our summer pudding with clotted cream was blissfully juicy and fresh – just perfect.

Directions: Through village passing New Inn on L, continue 1 mile to sea

Carne Beach TR2 5PF
Map 2: SW93
Tel: 01872 501279
Fax: 01872 501856
Chef: Malcolm Sparks
Owner: Mrs T N Gray
Cost: *Alc* £34, set-price L £13/D £31 (5 courses). H/wine £12
Times: Noon-2pm/7.15-9.30pm. Closed 3 Jan-1 Feb
Additional: Bar food L; Sunday L; Children welcome; ◑ dishes
Smoking: No smoking in dining room. Jacket & tie preferred at D
Accommodation: 40 en suite ★ ★ ★ ★

CUMBRIA

ALSTON,

Lovelady Shield Hotel

CA9 3LF
Map 12: NY74
Tel: 01434 381203
Fax: 01434 381515
Chef: Barrie Garton
Owners: Peter & Marie Haynes
Cost: Set-price D £29.50 (4 courses). H/wine £9.95

Appealing bar, opulent lounge and well-stocked library capture the rural charm of the house. Local and regional produce dictates the daily changing, set-price menu. Summer Isles smoked duck breast and smoked pork loin complemented by a salad of carrot, raisin and toasted pine kernels tossed in a

roasted sesame oil dressing, and grilled Northumberland lamb leg steak with savoury butter, for example. Desserts include such delights as pistachio-stuffed pear poached in an elderflower syrup with a sweetened cinnamon yogurt, with local English cheeses bringing up the rear.

Directions: Off A689, 2.5 miles from Alston; signposted at the end of drive

Times: D only, 7.30-8.30pm. Closed Jan
Additional: Bar food L; Sunday L by arrangement; Children 7+
Seats: 30. Private dining room 10
Smoking: No smoking in dining room
Accommodation: 12 en suite ★★

AMBLESIDE,
Drunken Duck Inn NEW

Barngates LA22 0NG
Map 7: NY30
Tel: 015394 36347
Fax: 015394 36781
Cost: Alc £18.50. ☺ H/wine £9.80
Times: Noon-2.30pm/6-9pm
Additional: Bar food; Children welcome; ✤ dishes
Smoking: No smoking in dining room
Accommodation: 10 en suite

Directions: Take A592 from Kendal, follow signs for Hawkshead, in 2.5m sign for inn on R. 1m up hill

Four-hundred year-old hostelry that's going from strength to strength. New blood in the kitchen has introduced a contemporary spin to trad pub staples. Fish and chips is beer battered cod with pont neuf potatoes and beurre blanc, grilled black pudding comes with dauphinoise. Great.

AMBLESIDE, Fisherbeck Hotel

Using a high proportion of good local produce, the kitchen creates modish dishes for a menu that is full of interest. Breast of Lunedale duckling on citrus rösti with Puy lentils and spinach with gin, plum and lime glaze shows the style.

Smoking: No smoking in dining room
Accommodation: 18 en suite ★★

Directions: Telephone for directions

Lake Road LA22 0DH
Map 7: NY30
Tel: 015394 33215
Fax: 015394 33600
Cost: Set-price D £18.95 (5 courses). ☺ H/wine £7.95
Times: D only, 7-8.30pm. Closed 26 Dec-15 Jan
Additional: Bar food; Children 5+; ✤ dishes

AMBLESIDE,
The Glass House

The converted mill offers stripped pine by the acre with some liberal sprinkling of halogen downlights to sharpen the style. On the whole, the three split-levels work well although, when busy (as the place often is), trying to attract a waiter can present a problem. The lunch menu is a mix of fashionable snacks complemented by some sturdier dishes and our lunch showed the style admirably: leek and potato soup; pasta with Cumbrian pancetta, rocket sauce and Parmesan; rich chocolate tart. The dinner menu is lengthier, coupled with a more formal style of service. Thus Singapore-style chicken, peanuts and

Rydal Road LA22 9AN
Map 7: NY30
Tel: 015394 32137
Fax: 015394 31139
Chef: Stuart Birkett
Owner: Adrian Sankey
Cost: Alc £20, set-price L £8 (2 courses)/D £9.95 (2 courses). ☺ H/wine £9.95
Times: Noon-10pm. Closed 25 Dec
Additional: Bar food L; Sunday L; Children welcome; ✤ dishes

The Glass House

Seats: 80. Private dining room 40
Smoking: No smoking in dining room

Directions: Telephone for directions

chilli sauce, then chargrilled tuna, sweet potato and roasted pepper salad, tapenade fritter, and roasted stone fruits, clotted cream and shortbread, raise the standards a notch or two.

AMBLESIDE,
Nanny Brow Country House

An idyllic country house with great views of the River Brathey and the Langdale Valley beyond. Don't be fooled by the hotel's curious name, instead expect adventurous modern dishes along the lines of prime Scottish sirloin rolled with a spicy caper farce. Our late summer meal kicked off with 'super' canapés: chicken liver parfait on toasted brioche, salmon mousseline in a puff pastry lattice, and a tiny, subtle, Stilton quiche. Then chicken fillets coated in sesame seeds and served with an almond, apple and olive salad. Between this and the main course of squid, lobster and sea scallop fricassée, came an 'excellent' beetroot and chicken soup. Hot peppermint and chocolate soufflé, and some 'delightful' rum and raisin fudge petits fours served with coffee made a splendid finish.

Directions: One mile from Ambleside on A593 to Coniston

Clappersgate LA22 9NF
Map 7: NY30
Tel: 015394 32036
Fax: 015394 32450
Chef: Mark Joyce
Owners: Michael & Carol Fletcher
Cost: *Alc* £19.99, set-price D £27.50
(5 courses). ☺ H/wine £12.99
Times: D only, 7.30-9.45pm
Additional: Children 12+; ✿ dishes
Seats: 36. Private dining room 10.
Jacket & tie preferred
Smoking: No smoking in dining room
Accommodation: 17 en suite ★ ★

AMBLESIDE, **Rothay Manor**

Regency-style hotel where the elegant dining room makes the perfect setting for a short but carefully chosen menu and a serious selection of wines.

Smoking: No smoking in dining room; Air conditioning
Accommodation: 18 en suite ★ ★ ★

Directions: Quarter of a mile out of Ambleside on the Coniston road

Rothay Bridge LA22 0EH
Map 7: NY30
Tel: 015394 33605
Fax: 015394 33607
Cost: *Alc* £14. ☺ H/wine £12
Times: 12.30-2pm (1.30pm Sun)/7.45-9pm. Closed Jan
Additional: Bar Food L; Sunday L; Children 10+ at D; ✿ menu

AMBLESIDE, **Wateredge Hotel**

Delightful hotel (a 17th-century fisherman's cottage houses the restaurant) with gardens sweeping down to Lake Windermere. Grilled fillet of red sea bream, noisettes of lamb with braised red cabbage, and roast breast of Barbary duck set the pace.

Borrans Road Waterhead
LA22 0EP
Map 7: NY30
Tel: 015394 32332
Fax: 015394 31878
Cost: Set-price D £29.50 (5 courses).
H/wine £12.50

Wateredge Hotel

Times: D only, 7-8.30pm. Closed mid Dec-mid Jan
Additional: Children 7+
Smoking: No smoking in dining room
Accommodation: 23 en suite ★ ★ ★

Directions: From A591 N to Ambleside, fork L at traffic lights after Ambleside sign. Skirt lake for few hundred yards, hotel is on L

APPLEBY-IN-WESTMORLAND,
Appleby Manor ✿

Roman Road CA16 6JB
Map 12: NY62
Tel: 017683 51571
Fax: 017683 52888
Cost: *Alc* £23. ☺ H/wine £13.50
Times: Noon-2pm/7-9pm
Additional: Bar food; Sunday L; Children welcome; ✤ dishes
Smoking: No smoking in dining room
Accommodation: 30 en suite ★ ★ ★

Directions: From N: M6/J40, then A66 (Brough), take Appleby turning. Turn R continue for 0.5 mile. From S: M6/J38 then B6260 (Appleby), through town to T junction, L then 1st R and follow road for 0.75 mile

Victorian mansion with panoramic views of the valley and Appleby castle. Dinner brings baked escalopes of suckling pig in lemon pastry, and chargrilled Irish skate with dill cream sauce. An impressive range of malt whiskies.

APPLEBY-IN-WESTMORLAND,
Tufton Arms Hotel ✿

Market Square CA16 6XA
Map 12: NY62
Tel: 017683 51593
Fax: 017683 52761
Cost: *Alc* £18, set-price D £23. ☺ H/wine £9.50
Times: Noon-2pm/7-9pm
Additional: Bar food; Sunday L; Children welcome; ✤ dishes
Accommodation: 23 en suite ★ ★ ★

Directions: In centre of Appleby on B6260, 12 miles from M6/J38

Centrally located Victorian coaching inn offering good food. Carpaccio of beef, sautéed pigeon breast with rösti potatoes and summer pudding with iced nougat parfait show both a cosmopolitan outlook and an incisive approach.

BASSENTHWAITE,
Armathwaite Hall

Keswick CA12 4RE
Map 11: NY23
Tel: 017687 76551
Fax: 017687 76220
Cost: Set-price L £14.95 (4 courses)/D £33.95 (6 courses). H/wine £12.95
Times: 12.30-1.45pm/7.30-9.30pm
Additional: Bar food L; Sunday L; Children welcome; 🍃 dishes
Smoking: No smoking in dining room
Accommodation: 43 en suite ★★★★

Grand, imposing hotel with service to match. Fresh seasonal cooking provides the stamp of quality. Lunches tend to be lighter than dinner, but at each cooking is ambitious, with classical and modern influences. Our test meal included sauté tiger prawns flashed with sesame seeds and accompanied by a light salad, and 'gorgeous' chicken and leek sausage with mashed potato and onion jus. Do leave room for dessert, perhaps lemon tart with fresh summer fruits, and a platter of chocolate truffles is served with coffee.

Directions: From M6/J40 take A66 to Keswick then A591 towards Carlisle. Turn L by Castle Inn, 8m to hotel

BASSENTHWAITE,
Overwater Hall Hotel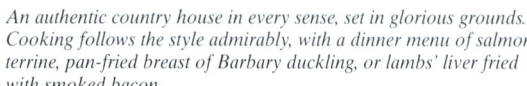

An authentic country house in every sense, set in glorious grounds. Cooking follows the style admirably, with a dinner menu of salmon terrine, pan-fried breast of Barbary duckling, or lambs' liver fried with smoked bacon.

Accommodation: 12 en suite ★★

Directions: Take A591 from Keswick to Carlisle, after 6 miles, turn R at the Castle Inn. Hotel is signposted after 2 miles

Ireby CA5 1HH
Map 11: NY23
Tel/Fax: 017687 76566
Cost: Set-price D £24 (5 courses). ☺ H/wine £9.25
Times: D only, 7-8.30pm
Additional: Sunday L (12.30-1.30pm); Children 5+; 🍃 dishes
Smoking: No smoking in dining room

BORROWDALE,
Borrowdale Gates Hotel

Friendly family-run hotel with stunning views of Borrowdale valley. As the nights draw in, log fires are lit to warm guests as they return from exploring the Dales. Dinner is taken in the stylish open-plan restaurant, which aptly overlooks the Jaws of Borrowdale. Starters range from a pressing of Tuscan vegetables, goats' cheese and seared tuna fish, to Waberthwaite ham and asparagus strudel with sherry jus. Main courses are along the lines of baked fillet of hake on a confit of roast tomatoes, and roast breast of Abbeystead grouse with game chips and bread sauce. Prune and port frangipane tart, and

Grange-in-Borrowdale Keswick CA12 5UQ
Map 11: NY21
Tel: 017687 77204
Fax: 017687 77254
Chef: Wendy Lindars
Owners: Terry & Christine Parkinson
Cost: Set-price D £27.25 (5 courses). H/wine £11.75
Times: 12.15-1.30pm/7-8.45pm. Closed Jan

maple syrup cheesecake with pecan ice cream feature amongst the desserts. For those with a hearty appetite, the selection of farmhouse cheeses can be taken as an extra course.

Directions: B5289 from Keswick. After 4 miles turn R over double humpback bridge to Grange village. Hotel 400yds through village on R

BRAMPTON, Farlam Hall Hotel

High standards at this 16th-century house surrounded by landscaped grounds that take in an ornamental lake and stream. The restaurant provides that timeless sense of well-being that comes with soft lighting, well-spaced polished antique tables and discreet staff. The four-course dinner menu offers three choices at each stage – quality not quantity prevails – and reflects a focused and balanced approach by the kitchen; the style is predominantly British with a slight French accent. Our own meal took in a cool lobster and herb mousse with marinated cucumber, sautéed guinea fowl with spiced couscous, a selection of British cheeses (a Ribblesdale goats' cheese was particularly impressive), and a chocolate and pecan pie.

Hallbankgate CA8 2NG
Map 12: NY56
Tel: 016977 46234
Fax: 016977 46683
Chef: Barry Quinion
Owners: Quinion & Stevenson families
Cost: Set-price D £30 (4 courses). H/wine £13.50
Times: D only, 8 for 8.30pm. Closed 25-30 Dec
Additional: Children 5+; dishes
Seats: 40. Private dining room 20. Jacket & tie preferred
Smoking: No pipes & cigars
Accommodation: 12 en suite ★ ★ ★

Directions: On the A689 Brampton to Alston road. Not in Farlam Village

CARLISLE, Crosby Lodge Hotel

A hotel that portrays traditionalism at it's best in terms of service and food. The extensive menu makes good use of local game and fish, there's a laden sweet trolley, and all dishes are thoughtfully prepared.

High Crosby Crosby-on-Eden CA6 4QZ
Map 11: NY35
Tel: 01228 573618
Fax: 01228 573428
Cost: Alc £30, set-price L £16.50/D £29 (4 courses). ☺ H/wine £12.50
Times: 12.15-1.30pm/7.15-8.45pm. Closed D Sun, 24 Dec-mid Jan
Additional: Bar food L; Sunday L; Children welcome; dishes
Smoking: No smoking in dining room. Jacket & tie preferred
Accommodation: 11 en suite ★ ★ ★

Directions: 3 miles from M6/J44 on A689 towards Carlisle Airport/Brampton. R at Low/High Crosby sign, 1 mile on R
Shortlisted for AA Wine Award – see page 16

Additional: Bar food L; Sunday L; Children 7+ at D
Seats: 60. Jacket & tie preferred
Smoking: No smoking in dining room
Accommodation: 29 en suite ★ ★ ★

CARLISLE, **Magenta's**

What a find! Entry is down a side alley, descending to a smartly converted cellar with white-washed brick, archways and stout pillars. The bistro-style and modern furnishings lend themselves to the casual approach at lunch and the more intimate expectations of dinner. Brothers Paul and Chris Taylor have worked at Heathcotes, Northcote Manor, The Greenhouse as well as Gleneagles and this background is very evident in the food. Gravad lax with mixed leaves and balsamic dressing showed good technique, and shellfish risotto (prawns, squid, shrimp) with spring greens and a Parmesan disc was fresh tasting and cooked to perfection. Hot chocolate pudding with pistachio ice cream was excellent. Attention to lesser details is impressive, with some of the best own-baked bread we've tried in a long time

Times: Noon-2.30pm/7-9.30pm. closed L Sat, all Sun, Bhs
Additional: Children welcome; 🍷 dishes
Seats: 32
Smoking: No-smoking area; No pipes & cigars

Fisher Street
Map 11: NY35
Tel: 01228 546363
Chefs: Chris & Paul Taylor
Owners: Chris & Paul Taylor, Alison Watkin
Cost: Alc £24. ☺ H/wine £12.95

CARTMEL,

Aynsome Manor Hotel

A 16th-century manor house run with relaxed hospitality by the Varley family. Dinner, which has a sense of occasion without being stuffy, brings soundly cooked dishes such as salmon with lemon, tarragon and vermouth sauce, or beef Wellington.

Smoking: No smoking in dining room
Accommodation: 12 en suite ★★

Directions: Leave A590 signed Cartmel. Hotel is 0.5 mile N of Cartmel village on R

Grange-over-Sands LA11 6HH
Map 7: SD37
Tel: 015395 36653
Fax: 015395 36016
Cost: Set-price D £16.50. ☺ H/wine £10
Times: D only, 7-8.30pm. Closed D Sun, Jan
Additional: Sunday L for 1pm; Children 5+ at D; 🍷 dishes

CARTMEL, **Uplands Hotel**

Tom and Diana Peter have been here for many years and the style has not changed in all that time. It is perhaps a little dated now and has shades of the old Miller Howe/John Tovey experience still showing. This is especially so in main courses where vegetables are in high numbers and all are served with 'something else', giving too many flavours over all. That said, the quality of the cooking is still good and the use of prime fresh produce laudable. At our test meal, monkfish was very fresh with the bacon, shallot and white wine sauce a great match. But the star of the meal was the soup – a wonderful combination of pea, watercress and pear with each flavour standing up and being counted. The large tureen was left on the table to help oneself, and the accompanying bread was excellent, being a wholemeal loaf, also left on the table. A real taste of summer came through in dessert, a simple combination of coffee meringue mixed with strawberries, raspberries and cream: simple but effective.

Directions: 1 mile up road signed Grange opposite the Pig & Whistle pub in Cartmel

Haggs Lane Grange-over-Sands LA11 6HD
Map 7: SD37
Tel: 015395 36248
Fax: 015395 36848
Chef: Tom Peter
Owners: Tom & Diana Peter
Cost: Set-price L £15/D £28 (4 courses). H/wine £10.50
Times: 12.30 for 1pm/7.30 for 8pm. Closed all Mon, L Tue & Wed, Jan, Feb
Smoking: No smoking in dining room
Seats: 28
Accommodation: 5 en suite

COCKERMOUTH,
The Trout Hotel

Crown Street CA13 0EJ
Map 11: NY13
Tel: 01900 823591
Fax: 01900 827514

Smart, traditional hotel by the banks of the River Derwent. Chicken cannelloni, poached pavé of fresh sea trout, and a rich chocolate tart show ambition and imagination.

Cost: *Alc* £30, set-price L £11.95 (4 courses)/D £20.45 (4 courses). ☺
H/wine £6.45
Times: Noon-2pm/7-9.30pm

Smoking: No smoking in dining room
Accommodation: 31 en suite ★ ★ ★

Additional: Bar food; Sunday L; Children welcome; ✤ dishes

Directions: A66 from J40 of M6, or A595 W from Carlisle. Hotel is by the river

CROOKLANDS, **Crooklands Hotel**

Milnthorpe nr Kendal LA7 7NW
Map 7: SD58
Tel: 015395 67432
Fax: 015395 67525
Cost: *Alc* £25. ☺ H/wine £8.95
Times: D only, 7-9pm. Closed Sun, Mon
Additional: Bar food; ✤ dishes
Smoking: No-smoking area; Air conditioning
Accommodation: 30 en suite ★ ★ ★

Farmhouse hotel with an authentic rural theme: The Hayloft restaurant is filled with farming memorabilia. Expect ragout of ocean fish in a spicy tomato and basil sauce, and medallions of pork cooked with paprika and Greenland prawns.

Directions: 1.5 miles from M6/J36; 4 miles from Kendal A65

CROSTHWAITE, **The Punchbowl**

Kendal LA8 8HQ
Map 11: SD49
Tel: 015395 68237
Fax: 015395 68875
Owner: Steven Doherty
Cost: *Alc* £15. ☺ H/wine £12
Times: Noon-2pm/6-9pm (9.30pm Sat). Closed 2 wks Nov
Additional: Sunday L; ✤ dishes
Smoking: No smoking in dining room
Accommodation: 3 en suite

Relaxed friendly atmosphere and attentive service within a traditional Lakeland inn. Despite the pub trappings, the real emphasis is on the food and busy, smart staff in polo shirts optimise an unusual blend of trendy, cosmopolitan food. Modern cooking reflects the influence of Steven Doherty whose pedigree shows in his direct, straightforward style with its emphasis on quality and clarity of flavours. Various meals this year have produced glowing endorsements for roasted Barbary duck breast, carrot and coriander mash, sauté potatoes and creamed leeks, roast cod fillet with deep-fried sage and silky fennel purée, chocolate nemesis with vanilla ice cream, and a classic Roux Brothers lemon tart with a simple raspberry coulis.

Directions: M6/J36 (Kendal). L onto A540 (Barrow). R at Jaguar dealership and follow A5074 until Crosthwaite sign. Top of lane on L next to church

GRANGE-OVER-SANDS,

Clare House

Traditional Lakeland courtesies at a family-run hotel overlooking Morecambe Bay. Five-course dinners feature roast fillet of beef with Yorkshire pud, and breast of guinea fowl wrapped in pancetta and Savoy cabbage.

Accommodation: 17 rooms (16 en suite) ★

Directions: From M6 take A590 then B5277 to Grange-over-Sands. Park Road follows the shore line. Hotel on L

Park Road LA11 7HQ
Map 7: SD47
Tel: 015395 33026/34253
Cost: Set-price D £22 (5 courses). ☺
H/wine £9
Times: D only, 6.45-7.15pm
Smoking: No smoking in dining room
Credit cards: None

GRASMERE, **Gold Rill Hotel**

Repeat visitors testify to the popularity of this relaxed hotel. Traditional dishes get a modern make-over with good soups and puddings. Roast beef with Yorkshire pud is offset by a battered sea bass with hollandaise sauce.

Additional: Bar food L; Children welcome; ◑ dishes
Smoking: No smoking in dining room; Air conditioning
Accommodation: 28 en suite ★ ★ ★

Directions: M6/J36 then A590/591: Red Bank Road in centre of village opposite St Oswalds Church. Hotel 200yds on L

Red Bank Road LA22 9PU
Map 11: NY30
Tel/Fax: 015394 35486
Cost: Alc £25, set-price D £19.50. ☺
H/wine £10.40
Times: D only, 7.30-8.30pm.
Closed Jan

GRASMERE, **Grasmere Hotel** ✿

Broadgate LA22 9TA
Map 11: NY30
Tel/Fax: 015394 35277
Cost: Set-price D £20 (5 courses). ☺
H/wine £12
Times: D only, 7-8pm. Closed Jan
Additional: Children 12+; ◑ dishes
Smoking: No smoking in dining room
Accommodation: 12 en suite ★ ★

Directions: Off A591, a short distance from the village centre, by the river

The River Rothay runs through the garden of this small Victorian country house on the edge of the village. Dinner might offer local lamb with garlic and rosemary, or guinea fowl with wild mushroom and Madeira sauce.

GRASMERE,

Michael's Nook ✿✿✿✿

How does Reg Gifford do it? Another change in the kitchen brings Michael Wignall (formerly Waldo's Cliveden) to the stove with a change in style but no shift in the standards of excellence set by his predecessors. The cooking is just one element in the make up of a very special country house. The restaurant, like the rest of the hotel, is resplendent with

Ambleside LA22 9RP
Map 11: NY30
Tel: 015394 35496
Fax: 015394 35645
Chef: Michael Wignall
Owner: Reg Gifford
Cost: Set-price L £34.50/D £45
(5 courses). H/wine £16.50

Michael's Nook

Times: 12.30-1pm/7.30-8.30pm
Additional: Children 7+
Seats: 50. Private dining room 35.
Jacket & tie preferred
Smoking: No smoking in dining room
Accommodation: 14 en suite ★ ★ ★

majestic furnishings and eclectic artworks but, once the dishes begin to arrive, one's attention is not likely to be diverted from the plate. At this level the cooking can be distinguished by a variety of outstanding characteristics – with Michael Wignall it is depth of flavour and impeccable balance that sets him apart from the crowd. It's a trademark that runs and builds through the courses from canapés to petits fours. Thus a starter of quail comes with a bird of buttery milk-white flesh and accompanied by gently steamed cabbage and an intelligently restrained sauce. Next might be a cappuccino of mushrooms, aromatic and teasingly understated as an excellently judged precursor to heavyweight main courses such as a brilliantly intense assiette of lamb with foie gras and rosemary jus. Desserts need to punch their weight in this company and there was no lack of presence in one inspector's Bramley apple mousse with a vanilla foam, apple sorbet and a magical apple crisp. Petits fours are little delights of flavour, likely to prove irresistible. More great cooking at Grasmere's finest: there must be something in the water. The wine list matches the depth of the cooking, exploring lesser wine producing countries with as much curiosity as the depth of knowledge shown in the major areas. The list invites experimentation and there is much to suit all pockets.

Directions: On N side of Grasmere. From A591, turn uphill at The Swan, bear L for 400yds.

GRASMERE,

Rothay Garden Hotel ❀❀

Westmorland lamb with dauphinoise potatoes and rosemary jus demonstrates that good ingredients need no further complications. Red snapper with prawn risotto, leeks and ginger adds an adventurous touch. Lakeland's most famous pud, sticky toffee, gets its own interpretation.

Accommodation: 26 en suite ★ ★ ★

Directions: Turn off A591, opp Swan Hotel, into Grasmere, 300yds on L

Broadgate LA22 9RJ
Map 7: NY30
Tel: 015394 35334
Fax: 015394 35723
Cost: Set-price L £10.50/D £22 (5 courses). ☺ H/wine £11.50
Times: Noon-1.45pm/7.30-9pm/last D 9pm. Closed 3 Jan-5 Feb
Additional: Bar food L; Sunday L; Children 5+; ❹ dishes
Smoking: No smoking in dining room

GRASMERE, **The Swan**

Ambleside LA22 9RF
Map 11: NY30
Tel: 015394 35551
Fax: 015394 35741
Telephone for further details

Directions: On A591

A charming 300-year-old inn with splendid views of the surrounding fells, The Swan was mentioned by Wordsworth in his poem 'The Waggoner'. Try shortcrust steak and kidney pie, or monkfish with prawn sauce, and oven-baked leg of lamb with herb jus.

GRASMERE,
White Moss House

Traditional country hotel that retains air of an intimate family atmosphere. The house was once owned by William Wordsworth (he wrote poetry in the porch) and makes a peaceful get away. Indeed, the setting overlooking Rydal Water is stunning and the comforts of the house seductive. Food is good too. The sourcing is impeccable with much use made of local and organic produce. Peter Dixon adopts a classical approach, underwritten by a creative streak that he expresses through a five-course, set-menu. One spring dinner ran along these lines: woodland mushroom, marjoram and Madeira soup; a duo of salmon, Shetland poached with Sancerre and dill, and River Eden smoked with oak and bracken; rack of Westmorland Mansergh Hall organic lamb roasted with a herb-crust of parsley, sage, rosemary and thyme; Mrs Beeton's chocolate pudding with chocolate sauce; British cheeses. The fabulous wine list further underlines why so many guests regularly return.

Rydal Water Ambleside LA22 9SE
Map 11: NY30
Tel: 015394 35295
Fax: 015394 35516
Chefs: Peter Dixon, Robert Simpson
Owners: Sue & Peter Dixon
Cost: Set-price D £28 (5 courses).
H/wine £10.50
Times: D only, at 8pm. Closed Sun,
Dec-Feb
Seats: 18
Smoking: No smoking in dining room
Accommodation: 8 en suite ★

Directions: On A591 between
Grasmere and Ambleside opposite
Rydal Water

GRASMERE, **Wordsworth Hotel**

Ambleside LA22 9SW
Map 11: NY30
Tel: 015394 35592
Fax: 015394 35765
Chef: Bernard Warne
Owner: Mr R Gifford
Cost: *Alc* £18.50, set-price L
£12.50/D £32.50 (4 courses). H/wine
£13.75
Times: 12.30-1.45pm/7-9pm (Fri, Sat
9.15pm)
Additional: Bar food L; Sunday L;
Children welcome; ✿ dishes
Seats: 60. Private rooms 16-80. Jacket
& tie preferred
Smoking: No smoking in dining room;
Air conditioning

The hotel is next to the churchyard where Lakeland's most famous poet is buried, but sits in its own two acres of landscaped grounds. Once an old coaching inn, it has been totally refurbished, and light, lemon colours and large conservatory windows fill the dining-room with light. The cooking places an emphasis on seasonal produce. Typical dishes include chartreuse of pigeon with a red wine sauce; a warm salad of west coast scallops with raspberry vinegar dressing and glazed baby vegetables; summer pudding. The wine list includes familiar favourites, some pleasantly surprising 'finds' and a fine selection of clarets and Burgundies.

Accommodation: 37 en suite ★ ★ ★ ★

Directions: In the village centre next to the church

Wordsworth Hotel

HAWKSHEAD,
Highfield House Hotel ✿ NEW

Elegant Victorian house with a growing reputation for simple, honest cooking. Good use of local produce. Expect chicken livers laced with a sherry dressing, prime pavé of hake with a hint of vermouth, and a zesty lemon tart.

Accommodation: 11 en suite ★ ★

Directions: From Ambleside take A593 south and turn L at Clappersgate onto B5286 towards Hawkshead. Turn R onto B5285, hotel up hill on L

Hawkshead Hill LA22 0PN
Map 7: SD39
Tel: 015394 36344
Fax: 015394 36793
Cost: Set-price D £19 (4 courses). ☺
H/wine £9.30
Times: Noon-2pm/7.30-8.30pm.
Closed Xmas, Jan
Additional: Bar food L; Children welcome; ✿ dishes
Smoking: No smoking in dining room

HOWTOWN, **Sharrow Bay** ✿✿✿

The spirit and example of the late Francis Coulson survive, which may be a mixed blessing. Management and kitchen are showing signs of uncertainty, not sure if they should follow the Coulson philosophy of old fashioned country-house cooking in hugely generous helpings, or if the time is right for a change to modern cooking and lighter touches. For the moment the food combines both styles. However, service remains as attentive as ever, Brian Sack does the tour that Francis used to do, and it is still obligatory to gasp at the dessert table before being seated. The lovely setting can never change, and the views from the dining room are stunning. The formula has not changed either

Sharrow Bay Penrith
CA10 2LZ
Map 12: NY41
Tel: 017684 86301
Fax: 017684 86349
Chefs: Juan Martin, Colin Akrigg
Owner: Brian Sack
Cost: Set-price L £35.25 (4 courses)/D £46.25 (5 courses). H/wine £14.95
Times: 1-1.30pm/8-8.30pm. Closed end Nov-mid Feb
Additional: Sunday L; Children 13+; ✿ dishes
Seats: 65. Jacket and tie preferred

with orders taken in the lounges and all seated in the dining room before 8.30pm. This is how our meal went. Canapés took in a warm tartlet of livers with herb crust, smoked salmon roulade on toast, fishy tempura; good bread rolls, home-made brown and white with an unusual sliced orange bread. Then excellent plump scallops and a perfectly dressed salad came with great pesto, but begged the question – why add a thick and substantial slice of smoked salmon? The fish course was a brilliant sole, accompanied by a good scallop mousseline with balanced mustard butter sauce, and slight overkill – leek risotto. The sorbet was a sweet and too intensely lemon. The centrepiece of the meal was a very well marinated noisette of venison served pink with a corn mousseline on a curried noodle cake, fried red and green peppers, chateau potatoes, carrots, and a juniper and dill sauce. Dessert was a great banana and butterscotch tart, really well made, with toffee banana garnish.

Smoking: No smoking in dining room; Air conditioning
Accommodation: 26 rooms (24 en suite) ★ ★ ★

Directions: Turn off A592 through Pooley Bridge, turn R (signed to Howtown), hotel 2 miles

KENDAL, Castle Green Hotel

Commanding stunning views of distant fells, this new hotel has been created from former offices. Expect an eclectic range of dishes such as Dublin Bay prawns with tomato and basil cream, and venison with pan jus and wild mushrooms.

Directions: M6/J36 to Kendal. Take Kendal S, 1st R at the 1st traffic lights, L to K Shoes, then R into Parkside Rd. 0.75 mile, hotel on R

LA9 6RG
Map 7: SD59
Tel: 01539 734000
Fax: 01539 735522
Cost: *Alc* £25. ☺ H/wine £9.95
Times: Noon-10pm (Sat 11pm)
Additional: Children welcome; ✔ dishes
Smoking: No smoking in dining room
Accommodation: 65 en suite ★ ★ ★

KENDAL, Crooklands Hotel

See Crooklands, Cumbria

KESWICK, Dale Head Hall

The Lowe family offer exceptional hospitality. The rear of the house, which includes the dining room and several bedrooms, dates from the 16th century and oak beams, original woodwork and natural stone provide character features. Dinner brings a short-choice, set-menu that reflect modern British styles but is rooted in classic France. A duo of duck and pheasant breasts, wrapped in puff pastry with a wild mushroom farce, a juniper and gin sauce and kumquat and lemon compote, or Atlantic turbot fillets, steamed with a salmon and chive soufflé mousse with a watercress velouté, and pineapple and nectarine Florentine, spun with chocolate and served with a raspberry coulis are typical of the repertoire. The extensive wine list is listed according to colour and taste rather than by region.

Lake Thirlmere CA12 4TN
Map 11: NY22
Tel: 017687 72478
Fax: 017687 71070
Chef: Caroline Bonkenburg
Owners: Mr & Mrs A Lowe
Cost: Set-price D £27.50 (5 courses)
Times: D only, 7.30-8pm
Additional: Children 12+; ✔ dishes
Seats: 18
Smoking: No smoking in dining room
Accommodation: 9 en suite ★ ★

Directions: 12 miles from M6/J40, between Keswick & Grasmere.

KESWICK, Thwaite Howe Hotel

Friendly Victorian hotel enjoying wonderful views across the Derwent Valley. A typical five-course dinner might include fish soup with home-baked bread, aromatic chicken with orange and sage, and local cheeses.

Accommodation: 8 en suite ★ ★

Directions: From A66 W of Keswick, follow signs to Thornthwaite Gallery. Hotel signed from there.

Thornthwaite CA12 5SA
Map 11: NY22
Tel: 017687 78281
Fax: 017687 78529
Cost: Set-price D £17.50 (5 courses). ☺ H/wine £8.95
Times: D only at 7pm. Closed Nov-Feb
Additional: Children 12+
Smoking: No smoking in dining room

KESWICK, **Underscar Manor** ✿✿✿

Applethwaite CA12 4PH
Map 11: NY22
Tel: 017687 75000
Fax: 017687 74904

Chef: Robert Thornton
Owners: Pauline & Derek Harrison, Gordon Evans
Cost: *Alc* £38, set-price L £25 (5 courses)/D £30 (6 courses). H/wine £13
Additional: Sunday L; Children 12+; ✿ dishes
Seats: 50. Jacket & tie preferred
Smoking: No smoking in dining room
Accommodation: 11 en suite

Built in 1856, Underscar is a solid Italianate manor in 40 acres of grounds. The main restaurant is in a Victorian conservatory with outstanding views over Derwent Water and the Borrowdale fells. Red squirrels running about the lawns might be the evening's entertainment too, and if you don't glimpse the odd guinea fowl you could well see the same bird on the menu, its breast roasted and served with a red wine and grain mustard sauce. The kitchen mixes and matches with confidence, working along the lines of sea bass with king prawns accompanied by caramelised banana, basmati rice and a delicately spiced cream sauce, or an interesting twist of an old classic in the form of roasted Barbary duck – 'sweet and juicy, so tender and just oozing flavour' with orange and juniper sauce, a Malaysian popiah (a pancake stuffed with Chinese vegetables) giving contrast. Starters could run to a cheese soufflé, tasting strongly of Cheddar, expertly timed, with 'no sign at all of sinking', and might come on julienned vegetables hinting of sesame oil, or warm chicken mousse with asparagus and morel sauce. A soufflé might be among desserts too – apple, say, with almond ice cream – with another option being super-smooth orange and Grand Marnier parfait with an orange sorbet centre and a topping of amaretti.

Directions: From M6/J40, A66 Keswick/Workington for 17miles. At large roundabout take 3rd exit. Turn immediate R at signpost for Underscar; hotel 0.75 mile on R.

MUNGRISDALE, **The Mill Hotel** ✿

Former miller's cottage set amidst terrific mountain scenery. Typical dishes might include American red bean soup with baked soda bread, and honey-glazed breast of Barbary duck with a port, red onion and cranberry sauce.

Penrith CA11 0XR
Map 11: NY33
Tel: 017687 79659
Fax: 017687 79155

Cost: Set-price D £27.50 (5 courses). ☺ H/wine £7.50
Times: D only at 7pm. Closed Nov-Feb
Additional: Children welcome; ✿ dishes
Smoking: No smoking in dining room
Accommodation: 7 rooms ★
Credit cards: None

Directions: Mungrisdale is signed on A66 midway between Penrith & Keswick. Hotel 2 miles N of A66

NETHER WASDALE,

Low Wood Hall Hotel

Victorian building decorated to reflect that age's love of colonisation and travel. North African influences are particularly notable in the restaurant, where strong colours combined with stunning fell views are backed up by staff who are are delightful, informal, chatty. The menu is a short, punchy, daily changing set affair which leaves one in no doubt that the chef is switched into modern contemporary methods; he also makes good use of local game and fish. Canapés of warm tartlets filled with Brie, sun-dried tomatoes and pine kernels kick in with a background sweet-and-sour effect. Guinea fowl terrine with beetroot, an intermediary course of celeriac and Bramley apple soup, pan-fried medallions of pork with shallot purée, roasted root vegetables and sage polenta, and iced Grand Marnier parfait with a light tuile filled with red soft summer fruits, all revealed good depth of flavour and sound, focused skills.

Directions: Exit A595 at Gosforth & bear L for Wasdale, after 3 miles turn R for Nether Wasdale

CA20 1ET
Map 6: NY10
Tel: 019467 26100
Fax: 019467 26111
Chef: Alan Skivington
Owner: Geraldine Turner
Cost: Set-price D £27.50 (5 courses). H/wine £14.95
Times: D only 7.30-8.45pm. Closed Sun, early Jan
Additional: Children 12+
Seats: 28
Smoking: No smoking in dining room
Accommodation: 14 rooms (13 en suite) ★ ★

NEWBY BRIDGE,

Lakeside Hotel

Ulverston LA12 8AT
Map 7: SD38
Tel: 015395 31207
Fax: 015395 31699
Chefs: Robert Marshall-Slater, Paul Waring
Owner: Neville R Talbot
Cost: *Alc* £32.50, set-price L £16 (2 courses)/D £35 (5 courses). ☺ H/wine £14
Times: Noon-3pm/7-9.30pm
Additional: Bar food; Sunday L; Children welcome; ⚫ dishes
Seats: 70. Private room 30
Smoking: No smoking in dining room; Air conditioning
Accommodation: 80 en suite ★ ★ ★ ★

Diners are spoilt for choice: two splendidly furnished restaurants and one delightful conservatory with a fine view of the lake, for afternoon teas and light lunches. Located next to the popular steamer pier and steam railway terminus, the stylish and spacious hotel is well served by its friendly staff who are attentive but discreet. The stately, panelled 'Lakeview' Restaurant is for fine dining, whilst 'Ruskins' Brasserie offers a more cosmopolitan style of cookery. At the former, the menu provides six choices at each course with a good showing of local produce. A summer meal featured pan-fried scallops with a light ginger salad, smoked haddock broth, and roasted chicken with Puy lentils, sautéed foie gras and Madeira jus.

Directions: M6/J36 follow A590 to Newby Bridge, R over bridge, follow Hawkshead Road for 1 mile

PENRITH, **A Bit on the Side**

Stylish split-level restaurant in character barn conversion. Modern dishes such as pan-fried breast of pheasant with a rich game sauce, and filo parcel of goats' cheese and creamed leek with red pepper sauce set the pace.

Additional: Children 7+; dishes
Smoking: No smoking in dining room

Directions: Follow town centre signs from M6 J40. Brunswick Sq is opposite Bluebell Lane car park

Brunswick Square CA11 7LG
Map 12: NY53
Tel: 01768 892526
Cost: *Alc* £20, set-price L £10.95/D £15.95. ☺ H/wine £8.95
Times: Noon-1.30pm/6.30-9pm. Closed L Sat & Mon, all Sun

RAVENSTONEDALE,
Black Swan Hotel

Friendly hotel in a sleepy village just ten minutes from the M6. This is a place that attracts people who love the outdoors: there's plenty of good walking and fishing to be done, and spectacular birdlife to observe. Huge oil paintings adorn the walls of the classical dining room – here sound traditional cooking is served by attentive staff. A winter meal might kick off with a platter of smoked duck, chicken and Cumberland sausage, served on dressed leaves with a warm Farthinghoe sauce. Follow this with supreme of corn-fed guinea fowl with winter truffles and scallion, or oven-baked rainbow trout with herbs and white wine. A choice of home-made desserts is offered, followed by coffee and mints.

Directions: M6/J38/A685 (Brough). Through Kirkby Stephen, then to Ravenstonedale

Nr Kirkby Stephen CA17 4NG
Map 12: NY70
Tel: 015396 23204
Fax: 015396 23604
Chef: Bryan Parsons
Owners: Mr & Mrs G Stuart
Cost: *Alc* £15, set-price L £9.75/D £23 (5 courses). ☺ H/wine £9
Times: Noon-1.30pm/7-9pm
Additional: Bar food; Sunday L; Children welcome; ⚫ dishes
Smoking: No smoking in dining room
Accommodation: 18 en suite ★★

TEBAY, **Westmorland Hotel**

Orton Penrith CA10 3SB
Map 7: NY60
Tel: 015396 24351
Fax: 015396 24354
Cost: *Alc* £23, set-price L £15/D £21 (4 courses). ☺ H/wine £11
Times: Noon-2.30pm/7-9pm
Additional: Bar food L; Children welcome; ⚫ dishes
Smoking: No smoking in dining room; Air conditioning
Accommodation: 53 en suite ★★★

Family-owned hotel set well back from the north-bound Westmorland Service Area on the M6. Stunning views are complemented by skilled cooking with special praise for chicken liver parfait, oven-fresh breads and the assiette of chocolate.

Directions: Next to Westmorland's Tebay Services on M6, easily reached from S-bound carriageway by using rd linking the 2 service areas

TEMPLE SOWERBY,
Temple Sowerby House Hotel ✤

Near Penrith CA10 1RZ
Map 12: NY62
Tel: 017683 61578
Fax: 017683 61958
Cost: *Alc* £29. ☺ H/wine £10.25
Times: Noon-2pm/7-8.45pm
Additional: Bar food L; Children welcome; ✤ dishes

Terrine of goose breast and foie gras with Cumberland sauce really works well, or go for the excellent corn-fed chicken with langoustine tails, pilaff and saffron cream sauce. Good vegetarian choice.

Smoking: No smoking in dining room
Accommodation: 13 en suite ★ ★ ★

Directions: On A66 5 miles E of Penrith in village centre

TROUTBECK,
Queen's Head Hotel ✤✤

Town Head nr Windermere
LA23 1PW
Map 7: SD49
Tel: 015394 32174
Fax: 015394 31938
Chef: Wallace Drumond
Owners: Mark Stewardson, Joanne Sherratt
Cost: *Alc* £15.50. ☺ H/wine £9.50
Times: Noon-2pm/6.30-9pm. Closed 25 Dec
Additional: Children welcome; ✤ dishes
Seats: 120. Private dining room 40
Smoking: No-smoking area
Accommodation: 9 en suite

17th-century coaching inn with oak beams, flagged floors, log fires and views of the Garburn Pass. Eat in the bar or the Mayor's Parlour (used for the past 200 or so years for the annual mayor-making ceremony). If steak, ale and mushroom cobbler, and lamb shank braised with red wine and rosemary sound as red-bloodedly English as the surroundings, there's also cod fillet wrapped in pancetta on spinach mash, and chicken breast marinated in lemon, soy and coriander on crispy beansprouts. You could start with deeply flavoured, nourishing cauliflower soup redolent of cheese with a hunk of herby bread, or a warm salad of duck confit and chorizo with tomato marmalade, go on to the clean and fresh flavours of langoustines cooked in lemongrass and coriander, and finish with blackberry and Cassis parfait with rich mixed-fruit coulis. Vegetarians are well catered for, children have their own menu, and an enterprising wine list runs to 30 bottles.

Directions: On the A592, approx 2 miles from Windermere

ULVERSTON,
Bay Horse Hotel ✤✤

LA12 9EL
Map 7: SD27
Tel: 01229 583972
Fax: 01229 580502
Chef: Robert Lyons
Owners: John J Tovey, Robert Lyons
Cost: *Alc* £25, set-price L £16.75. H/wine £13.95

A fine traditional inn with a cosmopolitan attitude. The spectacular position with a stunning panoramic view right across the Leven estuary to Ulverston is part of the draw, but the heart of this operation is the skilled and dedicated cooking of chef-patron Robert Lyons. His weekly menus encompass simple descriptions of dishes that make good use of hearty, rustic English ingredients. Without breaking the bounds of convention, there is a lightness of touch that pleases in dishes such as poached fillets of lemon sole filled with prawn mousse and served with a Noilly Prat and chive cream sauce, and rack of Lakeland lamb roasted with red onions and sun-dried tomatoes with a white wine and redcurrant glaze. This version of modern British cooking has many successes, not least the banana fritters with cinnamon sugar and rum and raisin ice cream.

Directions: From A590 on entering Ulverston follow signs for Canal Foot

Times: Noon-1.30pm/7.30-8pm. Closed L Sun & Mon
Additional: Bar food L; Children 12+; ❀ dishes
Seats: 50.
Smoking: No smoking in dining room
Accommodation: 7 en suite ★ ★

WATERMILLOCK,
Leeming House ❀

Penrith CA11 0JJ
Map 12: NY42
Tel: 017684 86622
Fax: 017684 86443
Cost: Set-price L £13.95/D £23.50. H/wine £14.95
Times: Noon-2pm/7-9pm
Additional: Bar food; Sunday L; Children welcome; ❀ dishes
Smoking: No smoking in dining room
Accommodation: 40 en suite ★ ★ ★

Directions: 8 miles from M6 J40; 8 miles from Penrith

Delightful hotel that combines a peaceful setting, stunning scenery and comfort. The four-course dinner menu mixes luxury items such as foie gras, Goosnargh chicken, Kyle of Lochalsh scallops with the likes of Cumberland ham, ox tongue and roast beef salads.

WATERMILLOCK,
Old Church Hotel ❀

Old Church Bay CA11 0JN
Map 12: NY42
Tel: 017684 86204
Fax: 017684 86368
Cost: *Alc* £25. ☺ H/wine £11.50
Times: D only, 7.45-8.15pm. Closed Sun
Additional: Children 8+
Smoking: No smoking in dining room
Accommodation: 10 en suite ★

Directions: M6 J40 then take A592 and continue for 2.5 miles SW of Pooley Bridge

Charming lakeside hotel with stunning views. There is an admirable emphasis on fresh ingredients, simply cooked. Rack of lamb with a rosemary and port jus, for example, or chicken with lemon and chives.

WATERMILLOCK,

Rampsbeck Hotel ❀❀❀

Penrith CA11 0LP
Map 12: NY42
Tel: 017684 86442
Fax: 017684 86688
Chef: Andrew McGeorge
Owners: T I & M M Gibb,
Mrs M J MacDowall
Cost: *Alc* £36, set-price L £25/D £26.
H/wine £11.25
Times: L by prior arrangement (ex
Sun)/D 7-8pm. Closed Jan-mid Feb
Additional: Bar food L; Sunday L
(noon-1pm); Children 8+; 🍲 dishes
Seats: 40. Private dining room 12
Smoking: No smoking in dining room
Accommodation: 20 en suite ★ ★ ★

Grand Edwardian residence with much to commend it. The
lakeside setting, acres of grounds, stunning views, are backed
up by wonderful, unobtrusive service. Andrew McGeorge's
cooking lives up to the impressive surroundings. Skill, sound
technique and a cosmopolitan approach are all apparent. His
menu rolls out luxury ingredients on the *carte* – red mullet
lasagne, for example, with roasted squat lobster, or a
sumptuous foie gras terrine with confit of duck, prunes
d'Agen and caramelised apples – balanced by a more
straightforward but equally accomplished roasted best end of
lamb with potato and garlic rösti, glazed shallots and lamb jus
on the table d'hôte. There's complete confidence shown in the
likes of sea bass with a basil purée and brochette of
langoustine. That dish came with the addition of sautéed
spinach and a light tomato jus, was 'fresh with dynamic
flavours', and 'cooked to perfection. Dessert, too, can be
extraordinary. The assiette of chocolate is a stunning
collection of extravagance 'only for those with an extra
unused notch on their belt': iced white chocolate sorbet
wrapped in a bitter chocolate tear; warm bitter chocolate and
orange fondant; chocolate and raisin bread-and butter
pudding; raspberry and chocolate mousse; milk and white
chocolate iced bombe. Bread, canapés and petits fours
maintain the same high standards. The wine list provides an
accomplished selection, although some of the sharper
Bordeaux are less suited to the subtle but multi-faceted
aspects of the food.

Directions: M6/J40, follow signs to Ullswater on A592, turn R at
lake's edge. Hotel 1.25 miles along lake shore

WINDERMERE,

Beech Hill Hotel ❀❀

***Hotel with plenty of facilities, including a heated swimming
pool.*** The views over the lake and the hills beyond to the Old
Man of Coniston are a memorable aspect of Beech Hill. Where
better to enjoy the sunset over the lake than from the
comfortable dining-chairs in the restaurant, with its oak
panelling and shades of burgundy? A warm mousseline of
smoked salmon and lobster, larded with halibut and baby

Newby Bridge Road Cartmel Fell
LA23 3LR
Map 7: SD49
Tel: 015394 42137
Fax: 015394 43745
Chef: Adrian Law
Owner: E K Richardson
Cost: *Alc* £27.50, set-price L & D
£27.50 (5 courses). H/wine £11.75

Beech Hill Hotel

Times: 11.30am-2.30pm/7-9.15pm
Additional: Bar food L; Sunday L;
Children welcome;
🍴 dishes
Seats: 110. Private dining room 80.
Jacket & tie preferred
Smoking: No smoking in dining room,
Air conditioning
Accommodation: 57 en suite ★ ★ ★

leeks, could be one of the starters on the set-price four-course menu, followed by white onion soup. Fillet of Aberdeen Angus, wrapped in smoked bacon and grilled, could crop up among main courses alongside saddle of Lakeland lamb, or seared escalope of Scottish salmon on a crab potato cake with saffron butter. Baked apple is made into a treat with the addition of Drambuie-soaked fruits and apricot ice cream. Staff are vigilant and on the ball and the wine list should have something for everyone.

Directions: On A592, Newby Bridge 4 miles from Windermere

WINDERMERE,

Burn How Garden House

Back Belsfield Road Bowness
LA23 3HH
Map 7: SD49
Tel: 015394 46226
Fax: 015394 47000
Cost: Set-price D £17.50. 😊 H/wine
£13.50
Times: Noon-1.45pm/7-8.30pm
Additional: Bar food L; Children
welcome; 🍴 dishes
Smoking: No smoking in dining room
Accommodation: 26 en suite ★ ★ ★

A traditional hotel where adventurous food and attentive service have been drawing those in the know for years. Skilful cooking is epitomised by our stunning salmon with a red wine reduction, and sea bass on a sweet pepper risotto.

Directions: Exit 36 of M6, 200 yds from Bowness Bay on Windermere

WINDERMERE,
Fayrer Garden House ✤

Lyth Valley Road
Bowness-on-Windermere LA23 3JP
Map 7: SD49
Tel: 015394 88195
Fax: 015394 45986
Cost: Set-price D £25 (5 courses). ☺
H/wine £10.95
Times: D only, 7.15-8.30pm
Additional: Bar food L; Children 5+;
🍲 dishes
Smoking: No smoking in dining room;
Air conditioning
Accommodation: 18 en suite ★ ★

Directions: On A5074 1 mile from
town centre

*A stately example of Victorian architecture with the conservatory
restaurant giving the best views over Lake Windermere. Daily
changing menu takes in the likes of smoked Windermere eel with
fresh crayfish tails, or calves' liver with a deep red wine jus.*

WINDERMERE,
Gilpin Lodge Hotel

Crook Road LA23 3NE
Map 7: SD49
Tel: 015394 88818
Fax: 015394 88058
Chefs: Christopher Davies &
Christine Cunliffe
Owners: John & Christine Cunliffe
Cost: *Alc* (L only Mon-Sat) £19, set-
price D £29.50 (5 courses). H/wine
£12.50
Times: Noon-2.30pm/7-9pm
Additional: Bar food L; Sunday L;
Children 7+; 🍲 dishes

No rosettes this year for this three AA Rosetted
establishment. As we went to press we learnt that changes in
the kitchen made our current assessment invalid.

Seats: 55. Private dining rooms 15, 28
Smoking: No smoking in dining room ★ ★ ★
Accommodation: 14 en suite

Directions: M6/J36 & A590/(Kendal), then B5284 for 5 miles

WINDERMERE,
Holbeck Ghyll ❀❀❀

Holbeck Lane LA23 1LU
Map 7: SD49
Tel: 015394 32375
Fax: 015394 34743
Chef: Stephen Smith
Owners: David & Patricia Nicholson
Cost: Set-price L £17.95/D £32.50.
H/wine £13.95
Times: 12.30-2pm/7-9pm
Additional: Bar food L; Sunday L;
Children 8+; ⚘ dishes
Seats: 50. Private dining room 14
Smoking: No smoking in dining room
Accommodation: 20 en suite ★ ★ ★

Directions: 3 miles N of Windermere
on A591. Turn R into Holbeck Lane.
Hotel is 0.5 mile on L

Few hotels in the country can boast such dramatic views.
Sipping drinks while taking in the views across the lawn and
lake to the distant Langdale Peaks (with perhaps a stunning
sunset thrown in at dinner), is a typical way to start a meal
here. Fans of Holbeck Ghyll will be relieved to hear that
Stephen Smith has proved a worthy successor to Jake Watkins,
and our initial report suggests a seamless take-over. Smith's
menu brings together classic combinations and modern
cooking styles, so that lightness and flavour are very much to
the fore. This was clearly seen in a dish of roast sea scallops,
Jerusalem artichoke purée, truffle vinaigrette and, more
emphatically, in braised ox cheek bourguignon 'very tender,
full of flavour' with parsnip purée. Dessert maintained
standards with a very accomplished warm bitter chocolate tart
with Madeira sorbet. The style of service might be formal, but
broad smiles from the pleasant staff create a lighter
atmosphere. The wine list remains largely unchanged with an
excellent range, but some of the clarets would grate against the
light style of cooking.

WINDERMERE, **Jerichos** ❀❀

Birch Street LA23 1EG
Map 7: SD49
Tel/Fax: 015394 42522
Chefs: Chris Blaydes, Sarah Connolly
Owners: Chris & Joanne Blaydes
Cost: *Alc* £24. ☺ H/wine £10.75
Times: D only, 6.45-9.45pm. Closed
Mon, 25, 26 Dec, 1 Jan
Additional: Children 12+; ⚘ dishes
Seats: 36. Private dining room 22
Smoking: No smoking in dining room

Directions: In town centre

***Restaurant bringing modern clean lines, low-voltage lighting
and an open-plan kitchen to Cumbria.*** Jerichos couldn't come
as more of an antithesis to most other Lakeland eating venues,
so it might be something of a surprise to find that Chris
Blaydes cut his teeth at Miller Howe (see entry). He brings his
own style to the menus, too, which offer a handful of choices at
each course. Pan-fried crusted salmon on sweet-and-sour onion
with tomato and basil sauce, 'cooked and seasoned to
perfection', shows a kitchen well in control of flavours, and the
same cooking process could be applied to marinated turkey
liver on orange-spiced red cabbage in red wine sauce. Curried,
herbed butter gives a new dimension to chargrilled fillet steak,
and a subtle red wine sauce with seared rack of lamb with
kidneys, all exceptionally tender, lets the flavours shine from
both the meats and the hints of honey and chilli in roasted
vegetables. Bitter chocolate and ginger mousse on a sponge
base has been described as 'sinful', its orange sauce providing
good contrast. The wine list has been extended since the place
opened in spring 1998.

WINDERMERE, Lindeth Fell Hotel

Lyth Valley Road Bowness LA23 3JP
Map 7: SD49
Tel: 015394 43286
Fax: 015394 47455
Cost: Set-price D £19 (5 courses). ☺
H/wine £8.95
Times: D only, 7.30-8.30pm. Closed
4 Jan-10 Feb
Additional: Bar Food L; Sunday L
(noon-1.30pm); Children 7+ at D;
🌢 dishes
Smoking: No smoking in dining room
Accommodation: 15 en suite ★ ★

Directions: 1 mile S of Bowness on
A5074 Lyth Valley Road

*Exciting modern cooking served in the sunny dining rooms of this
large Edwardian house, with magnificent views of the lake and
mountains.*

WINDERMERE,
Lindeth Howe Country House

Longtail Hill Bowness-on-Windermere
LA23 3JF
Map 7: SD49
Tel: 015394 45759
Fax: 015394 46368
Cost: Set-price D £21.95 (4 courses).
☺ H/wine £9.95
Times: D only, 7-8.30pm
Additional: Bar food L; Sunday L
(12.30-2pm); Children 7+, 🌢 dishes
Smoking: No smoking in dining room
Accommodation: 37 en suite ★ ★

Directions: On B5284, 1 mile south
of Bowness

*The former home of Beatrix Potter enjoys wonderful views of Lake
Windermere and the distant fells beyond. Expect modern British
cooking along the lines of best end of Herdwick lamb with rosemary
jus, and fried fillet of plaice sliced onto watercress and saffron sauce.*

WINDERMERE,
Linthwaite House Hotel

Crook Road Bowness LA23 3JA
Map 7: SD49
Tel: 015394 88600
Fax: 015394 88601
Chef: Ian Bravey
Owner: Mike Bevans
Cost: Set-price D £35 (4 courses).
H/wine £14
Times: D only, 7.15-9pm
Additional: Bar food L; Sunday L
(12.30-1.30pm); Children 7+;
🌢 dishes
Seats: 45. Private dining room 18
Smoking: No smoking in dining room

*A superb location, breathtaking views of the lake and a
terrace in summer that is just made for alfresco dining and
cocktails.* All that plus excellent cuisine in portions ample
enough to satisfy appetites whetted by the fresh Lakeland air.
The cooking style is upmarket: warm mousseline of chicken
and thyme with pickled red cabbage and glazed thyme sauce is
a typical starter. Main courses tend to the rich and creamy,
along the lines perhaps of breast of guinea fowl with shallots
and morels baked with Madeira and double cream, or grilled
escalope of salmon served on a bed of deep-fried spinach with
a Chardonnay butter sauce. Desserts are models of technical
accomplishment. Choose between a crisp tear of two

chocolates filled with milk chocolate and cognac mousse complemented by white chocolate sauce or iced parfait of passion fruit with warm chargrilled oranges and Drambuie caramel.

Linthwaite House Hotel

Accommodation: 26 en suite ★ ★ ★

Directions: Take 1st L off A591 at roundabout NW of Kendal (B5284). Follow for 6 miles, hotel is 1 mile after Windermere Golf Club on L

WINDERMERE,

Low Wood Hotel

NEW

Popular hotel with excellent leisure and conference facilities. Good cooking too, as we found in our meal of warm carpaccio of tuna, cod in crispy pancetta with gazpacho beurre blanc, and dark chocolate tart.

Directions: M6 J36, A590 then A591 to Ambleside. Hotel on R

LA23 1LP
Map 7: SD49
Tel: 015394 33338
Fax: 015394 34072
Telephone for further details

WINDERMERE,

Miller Howe Hotel

Well-established lakeside hotel with stunning views from the lounges, dining room and bedrooms. Former newspaper editor Charles Garside has introduced a small number of changes to Miller Howe. Founded in 1971 by John Tovey (who remains as 'food consultant') a meal at the hotel was always a theatrical affair with much raising and dimming of lights: the no choice set-menu encouraged diners to 'experience tastes they might otherwise not have chosen'. That tradition continues, but now there's a *carte* of alternative 'Editions'. Starters range from

Rayrigg Road LA23 1EY
Map 7: SD49
Tel: 015394 42536
Fax: 015394 45664
Chef: Susan Elliott
Owners: Charles & Iain Garside
Cost: *Alc* £15, set-price L £15/D £35 (5 courses). H/wine £17.50
Times: 12.15-1.15pm/D at 8pm. Closed 3 Jan-11 Feb
Additional: Sunday L; Children 8+; ⓭ dishes
Seats: 68. Private room 30. Jacket & tie preferred
Smoking: No smoking in dining room; Air conditioning
Accommodation: 12 en suite ★ ★

Directions: On A592 between Windermere and Bowness

flash-fried scallops on shredded mange-tout to warm foie gras and caramelised apple galette, while typical main courses include roast rack of lamb with juniper-scented Savoy cabbage, and roasted butternut squash with toasted sunflower seeds and Pecorino tossed with walnut oil. Desserts include Armagnac parfait with warm brandy prunes, and sticky toffee sponge.

WINDERMERE, **The Old England**

Georgian country house with lovely views over Lake Windermere. The restaurant offers sound cooking from a daily menu; on some evenings a pianist entertains.

Smoking: No smoking in dining room
Accommodation: 76 en suite ★ ★ ★

Directions: M6/J36, W on A592, hotel is behind St Martins Church at Bowness Bay

Church Street Bowness LA23 3DF
Map 7: SD49
Tel: 015394 42444
Fax: 015394 43432
Cost: *Alc* £25, set-price D £20. ☺
H/wine £13.45
Times: D only, 6.30-9.15pm
Additional: Bar food L; Sunday L (12.30-2.15pm); Children welcome; ✤ dishes

WINDERMERE,
Quarry Garth Hotel

Charming Edwardian country house with open log fires and antique furniture and brilliant service. Anglo-French cooking takes in oven-roasted loin of venison sliced onto a rich forest mushroom and blueberry jus.

Smoking: No smoking in dining room
Accommodation: 14 en suite ★ ★

Directions: On A591

Troutbeck Bridge LA23 1LF
Map 7: SD49
Tel: 015394 88282
Fax: 015394 46584
Cost: *Alc* £26, set-price D £25.95 (5 courses). ☺ H/wine £12.95
Times: D only, 6.30-8.45pm
Additional: Sunday L (noon-2.15pm); Children welcome; ✤ dishes

WINDERMERE,
Storrs Hall Hotel

Georgian mansion with breathtaking views across landscaped grounds and Lake Windermere. We enjoyed some ambitious ham and foie gras terrine, sea bass with tomato and basil coulis and cherry tart with beer ice cream.

Smoking: No smoking in dining room
Accommodation: 18 en suite ★ ★ ★

Directions: On A592, 2 miles S of Bowness on the Newby Bridge Road

Storrs Park Bowness-on-Windermere LA23 3LG
Map 7: SD49
Tel: 015394 47111
Fax: 015394 47555
Cost: Set-price L £15/D £32 (5 courses). H/wine £12
Times: Noon-1.45pm/7.15-8.30pm
Additional: Bar food L; Sunday L; Children 10 +; ✤ dishes

WINDERMERE,
Wild Boar Hotel

Smart, traditional coaching inn run by an eager team. Quality is assured in dishes such as duck and foie gras terrine with Cumberland sauce, and sea bass with white wine cream and tomato confit.

Directions: 2.5m S of Windermere take B5284 towards Crook. 3.5m Hotel on R

Crook LA23 3NF
Map 7: SD49
Tel: 015394 45225
Fax: 015394 42498
Telephone for further details

WITHERSLACK,
Old Vicarage Hotel

Church Road
Grange-over-Sands
LA11 6RS
Map 7: SD48
Tel: 015395 52381
Fax: 015395 52373
Chef: James Brown
Owners: Reeve & Brown families
Cost: Set-price D £29.50 (4 courses)
Times: D only, 7-9pm
Additional: Sunday L (1pm); Children welcome; 🍴 dishes
Seats: 40. Private dining room 10
Smoking: No smoking in dining room
Accommodation: 14 en suite ★

Georgian vicarage offering peace and tranquillity. The dining-room is a bistro-cum-Victoriana cross, featuring wicker furniture, stylish paintings and intimate lighting. Welcoming and friendly staff help by being fully clued up on the menu, putting everyone at their ease with good-humoured chat. Pride in local ingredients is evident in dishes such as Waberthwaite ham mousse terrine, Morecambe bay shrimps potted in a light crème fraîche with grain mustard, and Westmorland curd tart with damson sauce. Otherwise there's whole baked sea bass on courgette cassoulet with curried mussel broth or grilled breast of Gressingham duck with creamed polenta and ratatouille of Mediterranean vegetables, broccoli and apple gravy. Crumbles and hot puddings are offered alongside more sophisticated desserts such as chocolate and prune tartlet with dark chocolate and orange sauces. An excellent wine list includes plenty of choice for those on a budget.

Directions: From M6/J36 take A590 to Barrow. Sign for Witherslack on R. In village take 1st L signed to church

DERBYSHIRE

ASHBOURNE, ## Callow Hall

Impressive country house with all the trappings. The grey-stone Victorian pile is the business, complete with tall chimneys and a turret, plus 42 acres overlooking Bentley Brook and the Dove Valley. Within, high ceilings, ornate plasterwork and antiques make it all as elegant and calming as you could wish. Dinner, taken in the red dining room (although the yellow room may also be called into service), with its hand-printed William Morris wallpaper and candlelight, is a set-price affair with around a handful of choices at each course. Pot-roast quail, pink and succulent, come served on braised chicory with a rich Madeira sauce, or there's fresh, meaty scallops on spinach with a port and lime butter sauce, and medallions of local venison with wild mushrooms in a rich red wine sauce . There could also be a

Mappleton Road
DE6 2AA
Map 7: SK14
Tel: 01335 343403
Fax: 01335 343624
Chefs: David & Anthony Spencer
Owners: David, Dorothy & Anthony Spencer
Cost: D £37 (5 courses). H/wine £10.25
Times: D only, 7.30-9.30pm. Closed D Sun except for residents, 25, 26 Dec
Additional: Sunday L (12.30-1.30pm); Children welcome; 🍴 dishes
Seats: 60. Private dining room 30

Callow Hall

Smoking: No smoking in dining room
Accommodation: 16 en suite ★ ★ ★

soup to start, leek or celeriac, say, and hot chocolate fondant cake, well worth the 15-minute wait. The wine list extends to over 100 bins.

Directions: 0.75 mile from Ashbourne; A515 (Buxton), sharp L by Bowling Green Pub, 1st R Mappleton Road

Shortlisted for AA Wine Award – see page 16

ASHFORD-IN-THE-WATER,

Riverside House Hotel

Fennel Street Bakewell
DE45 1QF
Map 7: SK17
Tel: 01629 814275
Fax: 01629 812873
Chef: John Whelan
Owner: Penelope Thornton Hotels Ltd
Cost: Set-price D £40 (5 courses). H/wine £13.75
Times: Noon-2pm/7-9.30pm
Additional: Bar food L; Sunday L; Children 10+; ✿ dishes
Seats: 40. Private dining room 20
Smoking: No smoking in dining room
Accommodation: 15 en suite ★ ★ ★

The graceful Georgian house sits on the banks of the river Wye in its own exquisite gardens. The Modern British menu changes regularly and is in tune with urban fashion. Flavoured oil and jus give interest to dishes such as pan-fried sea scallops, apple and ginger mousse and beetroot oil, and roast sea bass fillet with spinach, crushed potatoes, baby leeks and vanilla jus. The cooking looks beyond conventional techniques with an unusual steamed corn-fed chicken breast with confit potatoes and roasted root vegetables. Combinations are inspired: roasted lamb's kidney with white bean purée and saffron oil; terrine of confit pheasant and game with kumquat and quince chutney; bitter chocolate tart with pistachio ice-cream. As well as a warm cheese course, blue cheese and pear beignet, perhaps, there is a fine, annotated list of artisan cheeses.

Directions: 2 miles from centre of Bakewell on A6 (Buxton). In Ashford village next to Sheepwash Bridge

BAKEWELL, Croft Hotel

Victorian-built hotel where everyone sits down to dinner at the same time. The four-course menu offers choices only of starters and puddings. Chicken breast with a creamy whisky sauce, or noisettes of lamb with balsamic dressing, show the style.

Accommodation: 9 en suite ★★

Directions: A6 from Bakewell towards Buxton, 1.7 miles turn R (A6020). After 0.75 mile turn L signed Great Longstone. Hotel on R in village

Great Longstone DE45 1TF
Map 8: SK26
Tel: 01629 640278
Cost: Set-price D £24.50 (4 courses).
☺ H/wine £8.75
Times: D only, at 7.30pm. Closed
1 Jan-10 Feb
Additional: Children 10+; ✦ dishes
Smoking: No smoking in dining room

BAKEWELL,
Renaissance Restaurant

A tasteful barn conversion forms the heart of this quiet, inviting restaurant overlooking a small walled garden. The menu reveals a strong French bias with duck galantine and fig sauce and paupiette of turbot with wild mushrooms and Normandy sauce setting the pace.

Smoking: No smoking in dining room

Directions: From Bakewell roundabout in town centre take A6 Buxton exit. 1st R into Bath Street (one-way)

Bath Street DE45 1BX
Map 8: SK26
Tel: 01629 812687
Cost: *Alc* £21.45, set-price L & D
£19.95. ☺ H/wine £9.99
Times: Noon-1.30pm/7-9.30pm.
Closed D Sun, all Mon, 1st 2 wks Jan,
1st 2 wks Aug
Additional: Bar food L; Sunday L;
Children welcome; ✦ dishes.

BAKEWELL, Rutland Arms

Historic hotel in the heart of Bakewell. Typical dishes include fillet steak topped with Brie, and baked aubergine glazed with goats' cheese on a bed of curried vegetables. Desserts include lemon parfait and, of course, Bakewell pudding.

Smoking: No smoking in dining room
Accommodation: 35 en suite ★★★

Directions: On A6 between Matlock/Manchester. In main square

The Square DE45 1BT
Map 8: SK26
Tel: 01629 812812
Fax: 01629 812309
Cost: *Alc* £17.95, set-price D £21 (4 courses). ☺ H/wine £9.25
Times: Noon-2pm/7-9pm
Additional: Bar food; Sunday L;
Children welcome; ✦ dishes

BASLOW, Cavendish Hotel

Country house hotel on the edge of the Chatsworth estate with wonderful old-fashioned standards of service. Both Mediterranean and oriental influences permeate the menu with tempura of red mullet with a potato salad, sweetcorn salsa and sweet pepper purée offset, for example, by ravioli of cream cheese, crayfish and rocket with lemon oil and tomatoes. Or baked fillet of sea bass on a ragout of fennel and celeriac with a ginger and lemon sauce topped with crispy noodles, sits next to pan-seared pigeon breasts on a truffle risotto and a sauce made from the essence, with trumpet mushrooms and deep-fried leeks. Desserts are more straight forward, perhaps a classic lemon tart with Mascarpone cheese and plum salad, or a prune and Armagnac sponge pudding with crème anglaise and vanilla ice cream.

Directions: In the centre of Baslow village

Bakewell DE45 1SP
Map 8: SK27
Tel: 01246 582311
Fax: 01246 582312
Chef: Nick Buckingham
Owner: Eric Marsh
Cost: Set-price L £25/D £37. H/wine
£17.50
Times: D only 7-10pm.
Additional: Sunday L (12.30-2pm);
Children welcome; ✦ dishes
Seats: 40. Private dining room 10
Smoking: No smoking in dining room
Accommodation: 23 en suite ★★★

BASLOW,
Fischer's Baslow Hall ✿✿✿

Calver Road DE45 1RR
Map 8: SK27
Tel: 01246 583259
Fax: 01246 583818
Chef: Max Fischer
Owners: Max & Susan Fischer
Cost: Set-price L £24/D £45 (4 courses). H/wine £13
Times: Noon-1.30pm/7-9.30pm. Closed L Sat, D Sun (ex residents), 25-26 Dec
Additional: Café Max L & D; Sunday L; Children 12+ at D
Seats: 40. Private dining rooms 12-24. Jacket & tie preferred
Smoking: No smoking in dining room
Accommodation: 6 en suite ★ ★

Traditional country house dining room with service by friendly and efficient local girls. Max and Susan Fischer run their Derbyshire manor house on the edge of the Chatsworth estate with great style. The heart of the operation remains the kitchen, where Max cooks with panache. His menus have a cosmopolitan ring, with the likes of pigs' trotters with pommes purée and morel mushrooms, lots of game along the lines of roast rabbit saddle with baby leeks and mustard sauce, and a signature civet of wild hare with chestnuts. Canapés, then chef's freebie, a coffee cup of warm vichyssoise of excellent taste, opened our test meal. Then came morel tartlet with beurre blanc sauce, followed by roast saddle of spring Derbyshire lamb, cooked beautiful pink and teamed with rösti potato and a restrained tarragon sauce with a melange of roasted peppers and courgettes. A dessert of chocolate and raspberry soufflé was perfectly risen and came with a tiny brandy snap filled with raspberry sorbet.
Signature dishes: scallops on black pudding with broad bean purée and white truffle oil; pan-fried turbot on basil risotto and spinach purée; a trio of Yorkshire forced rhubarb with strudel, brûlée and sorbet with prune fritter.

Directions: From Baslow on A623 towards Calver. Hotel on R

Shortlisted for AA Wine Awards – see page 16

BELPER, # Makeney Hall Hotel ✿

Milford DE56 0RS
Map 8: SK34
Tel: 01332 842999
Fax: 01332 842777
Cost: *Alc* £24, set-price L £13.50/D £18.50. ☺ H/wine £11
Times: Noon-2.30pm/7-9.30pm
Additional: Bar Food; Sunday L; Children welcome; 🍴 dishes
Smoking: No smoking in dining room
Accommodation: 45 en suite ★ ★ ★

Directions: Join A6 N of Derby & turn R into Milford. Hotel is 0.25 mile, just past Garden Centre

Oak-panelled restaurant with large windows affording superb views of the gardens and Derwent Valley. The menu offers a good choice of interesting and unusual dishes.

BUXTON,

Best Western
Lee Wood Hotel ❀❀

The Park SK17 6TQ
Map 7: SK07
Tel: 01298 23002
Fax: 01298 23228
Chef: Chris Bates
Owner: John C Millican
Cost: *Alc* £15, set-price D £23.50. ☺
H/wine £12
Times: 12.15pm-2pm/7.15-9.30pm
Additional: Bar food; Sunday L;
Children welcome; ❦ dishes
Seats: 80. Private dining room 20
Smoking: No smoking in dining room
Accommodation: 37 en suite ★ ★ ★

Sturdy, stone-built mansion. The Garden Restaurant,
complete with piped 'jungle' sounds, overlooks the landscaped
grounds and is light and airy in the day, pleasing at night. A
vast international menu works hard to make an impact with
fancy sounding dishes such as 'oysters rolled in smoked bacon
roasted in chilli and basil oil edged with roasted red pepper
sauce and a ratatouille of vegetables' and 'breast of French
duckling cooked in fennel seed, ginger and garlic nestled on a
ruby grapefruit garnished with fresh figs'. But our sample leg
of lamb with tomato and rosemary sauces was far from tender,
although it was served with excellent vegetables. There is also
plenty of vegetarian choice, uncomplicated steaks and
expensive lobster dishes.

Directions: Follow A5004 Long Hill to Whaley Bridge. Hotel
300 metres beyond the Devonshire Royal Hospital

DARLEY ABBEY,

Darleys Restaurant ❀❀

Darley Abbey Mill DE22 1DZ
Map 8: SK33
Tel: 01332 364987
Fax: 01332 541356
Chef: Ian Wilson
Owner: David Pinchbeck

*Former canteen for the adjoining cotton mill, the restaurant
overlooks the River Derwent – particularly dramatic if in full
flood.* Tables have been carefully placed to give everyone a

good view of the river and resident wild fowl. The menu is not over large, yet contains enough innovation and choice to please most palates. Starters include soufflé of Parmesan and ratatouille or ham hock and Agen prune terrine, but we opted for a well-flavoured asparagus mousseline with apple and tomato sorbet mille-feuille. Roast rump of new season lamb was cooked pink, tender and full of flavour, accompanied by excellent celeriac mash and cep jus. Other choices might be rosemary infused venison loin with red onion tartlet, or sautéed kidneys and mustard velouté. Look out for Gloucestershire Old Spot Sausages on the lunch menu. It was worth waiting for a cooked to order caramelised pear Tatin with butterscotch sauce.

Directions: From Derby take A6 N. Darley Abbey is signed on R. Restaurant is adjacent to river over a single lane bridge

Cost: *Alc* £28.50, set-price L £12.50 (2 courses)/D £22. ☺ H/wine £13
Times: Noon-2pm/7-10pm. Closed D Sun, Bhs
Additional: Sunday L; Children welcome; 🍴 dishes
Seats: 70
Smoking: No smoking in dining room; Air conditioning

DERBY, **Mickleover Court Hotel**

Etwall Road Mickleover DE3 5XX
Map 8: SK33
Tel: 01332 521234
Fax: 01332 521238
Cost: *Alc* £20. ☺ H/wine £11.50
Times: 12.30-2.30pm/7-10pm
Additional: Bar food; Sunday L; Children welcome; 🍴 dishes
Smoking: No-smoking area; Air conditioning
Accommodation: 80 en suite ★ ★ ★ ★

Directions: From Mickleover take A516 (Uttoxeter) hotel is L of 1st roundabout

Smartly-appointed modern hotel on the outskirts of Derby. A wide choice of brasserie-style dishes includes breast of duck with a shallot and green peppercorn sauce, or grilled Dover sole with lemon and watercress.

DOVERIDGE,
The Beeches Farmhouse Hotel

DE6 5LR
Map 7: SK13
Tel: 01889 590288
Fax: 01889 590559
Chef: Barbara Tunnicliffe
Owners: Barbara & Paul Tunnicliffe

18th-century farmhouse close to Alton Towers. The restaurant features a small bar with a roaring open fire and rough-hewn tables and smart, intimate dining areas with traditional table

settings, all given character by quarry tiles, polished floorboards, rugs and low beams. The menu combines a feel for the country as well as some more modern ideas. A terrine of chicken with wild mushrooms and duck livers, wrapped in spinach and served with home-made orange marmalade is as popular as prawns in a cream and mustard sauce with a crisp cheese topping. Main courses can include a commendable dish of organically fed duck breasts glazed with honey and crushed peppercorns, teamed with fried mash and bacon and served with a blackberry sauce, or roast suckling pig with Savoy cabbage and smoky bacon as well as sage and onion chutney.

Directions: From A50 take exit signposted Doveridge and follow signs for Waldley. At grass triangle turn R; hotel is 1st L

Cost: Alc £25, set-price L £13.95. ☺
H/wine £9.95
Times: Noon-2pm/7-9pm. Closed 24-26 Dec
Additional: Sunday L; Children welcome; 🌢 dishes
Seats: 65
Smoking: No smoking in dining room
Accommodation: 10 en suite

HATHERSAGE, George Hotel

15th-century stone coaching inn surrounded by stunning Peak District scenery. Dinner in the cosy restaurant will feature traditional and innovative dishes: look out for smoked salmon fishcakes with sweet pepper relish.

Smoking: No smoking in dining room
Accommodation: 19 en suite ★★★

Directions: In village centre on A625

Main Road S32 1BB
Map 8: SK28
Tel: 01433 650436
Fax: 01433 650099
Cost: Alc £30, set-price L £14.95/D £19.95. ☺ H/wine £13.50
Times: Noon-3pm/7-10pm
Additional: Bar food; Sunday L; Children welcome; 🌢 dishes

HATHERSAGE, Hathersage Inn NEW

Traditional country inn with a smartly refurbished restaurant. Recommended are savoury salmon custard, chicken breast with oyster mushroom fricassée, and chocolate sponge pudding.

Smoking: No-smoking area
Accommodation: 15 en suite ★★★

Directions: In village centre on A625

Main Road S32 1BB
Map 8: SK28
Tel: 01433 650259
Cost: Alc £20, set-price L £10/D £16.50. ☺ H/wine £9
Times: D only, 7-9.30pm
Additional: Bar food; Sunday L (12.30-2pm); 🌢 dishes

MATLOCK, Riber Hall ✿✿

Tansley DE4 5JU
Map 8: SK35
Tel: 01629 582795
Fax: 01629 580475
Chef: John Bradshaw
Owner: Alex Biggin
Cost: Set-price L £16/D £32. H/wine £14.75
Times: Noon-1.30pm/7-9.30pm
Additional: Children welcome
Smoking: No smoking in dining room
Accommodation: 14 en suite ★★★

Directions: One mile up Alders Lane and Carr Lane off A615 at Tansley

Historic building, peaceful setting, old-fashioned service.
Looking at the lovingly maintained Elizabethan manor house it is hard to imagine it was in a near-derelict condition until painstakingly restored some 30 years ago. The grounds are a

particular joy, especially the walled garden and the tranquil conservatory. The set-price menu offers real quality and interest. Boneless quail with flavour-packed Madeira dressing, served sliced with a herb and garlic stuffing was well balanced and constructed, whilst the breast of duck that followed was 'one of the plumpest and tastiest I have had, moist and exceptionally tender, this was an absolute delight; even managing to keep the skin crisp while providing pink meat. The accompanying sauce and cassoulet of lentil du pays was very well matched'. A hot rhubarb soufflé with a creamy brandy sauce hit just the right balance between acidity and sweetness. Fresh, mellow coffee comes with delicate, home-made petits fours.

MELBOURNE, The Bay Tree

17th-century coaching inn, now a smart restaurant with beamed dining room. Expect traditional dishes with a twist: rich foie gras and chicken liver parfait studded with marinated raisins, followed by carved rack of Moroccan lamb served with spicy 'Casablanca' couscous and olives.

4 Potter Street DE73 1DW
Map 8: SK32
Tel: 01332 863358
Fax: 01332 865545
Telephone for further details

Directions: Town centre

RIDGEWAY,
The Old Vicarage

Relaxing setting and attentive, professional service. Set amidst tranquil countryside, with pretty lounges, a dining room with starched white cloths and Wedgwood and silver candelabra, Tessa Bramley's stylish restaurant offers a distinct, very feminine style that has many supporters. The menu changes every six weeks or so in order to remain seasonal, and the clear emphasis is on traditional, simple, tried-and-tested concepts. Our summer inspection was a huge success. Hot canapés of corn and chilli cake, tiny shepherd's pies and crab beginners, were followed by an *amuse-bouche* of lemon-baked cod with tomato chutney. A starter of Bridlington crab with smoked salmon, rösti and mango salsa was a refreshing summer dish, and a main course of fillet of lamb with pommes Anna, courgette in lemon thyme, carrots with sesame seeds, and strawberry and mint compote was simply 'super'. Typical of desserts was an unusual and well-liked praline basket of woodruff ice cream with mango and cardamom peach schnapps. A good selection of British cheeses is also on offer. Own-baked breads and petits fours are superior versions. The wine list is fairly modest but adequately suits both the menu and customer budgets.

Ridgeway Moor S12 3XW
Map 8: SK48
Tel: 0114 2475814
Fax: 0114 2477079
Chefs: Tessa Bramley, Nathan Smith, Andrew Gilbert
Owner: Tessa Bramley
Times: 12.30-2.30pm/7-10.30pm.
Closed L Sat, D Sun, all Mon, 26 Dec, 31 Dec, 1 Jan
Additional: Sunday L; Children welcome; 🍴 dishes
Seats: 50. Private dining room 28
Smoking: No smoking in dining room

Directions: SE of Sheffield off A616 on B6054; follow signs for Ridgeway Cottage Industries. Restaurant is 300yds on L

RISLEY, Risley Hall Hotel

Impressive Victorian manor house set midst beautiful gardens. With a new chef has come a less exotic and more consistent style of cooking. Highlights of our most recent meal included a creamy crab and coriander fishcake enlivened by a spring onion and chilli salsa, an outstanding sauce accompanying a lamb pot-roast, and a rich, chocolate tart. Pan-fried scallops with saffron noodles and a lightly spiced tomato oil, and breast of Barbary duck with a confit of the leg, honey

Derby Road DE72 3SS
Map 8: SK43
Tel: 01159 399000
Fax: 01159 397766
Chef: John Molnar
Owner: Mrs Isobel Crosbie
Cost: *Alc* £26. ☺ H/wine £10.50
Times: Noon-2.30pm/7-9.30pm.
Closed D Sun, D 25 Dec & 1 Jan
Additional: Bar Food L; Sunday L;

roast parsnips and cider sauce are other offerings from a well-balanced *carte* that includes several interesting vegetarian options.

Directions: From M1/J25 take road signposted Risley. Up to crossroads, turn R. Hotel is 0.75 mile on R past garage.

Children welcome; 🍴 dishes
Seats: 80. Private dining rooms 14 & 18. Jacket & tie preferred at D
Smoking: No smoking in dining room
Accommodation: 16 en suite ★ ★ ★

ROWSLEY, East Lodge Hotel

Tastefully refurbished Victorian lodge with traditional and modern British cooking based on good local produce. Warm lentil salad with walnuts and Stilton, shank of lamb and warm pumpkin pie are typical of the weekly-changing, set-priced menu.

Smoking: No smoking in dining room
Accommodation: 15 en suite ★ ★ ★

Directions: Hotel drive access on A6, 5 miles from Matlock and 3 miles from Bakewell

DE4 2EF
Map 8: SK26
Tel: 01629 734474
Fax: 01629 733949
Cost: Set-price D £25 (4 courses). ☺
H/wine £9.75
Times: Noon-2pm/7-9pm
Additional: Bar food; Sunday L;
Children welcome; 🍴 dishes

SOUTH NORMANTON,
Swallow Hotel

Modern low-rise hotel with well-equipped conference and banqueting centre. Dine in the Pavilion restaurant, where the menu includes the likes of tomato tart pistou, and confit of duck with red wine jus.

Directions: From M1/J28 – A38 (signed Mansfield). At 100 yards 1st L into car park

Carter Lane East DE55 2EH
Map 8: SK45
Tel: 01773 812000
Fax: 01773 580032
Telephone for further details

THORPE,
Izaak Walton Hotel ✿

Ashbourne DE6 2AY
Map 7: SK15
Tel: 01335 350555
Fax: 01335 350539
Cost: Set-price D £23.50 (4 courses).
☺ H/wine £10.25
Times: D only, 7.30-9.15pm
Additional: Bar food; Sunday L (noon-2pm); Children welcome; 🍴 dishes
Smoking: No smoking in dining room
Accommodation: 30 en suite ★ ★ ★

17th-century hotel with breathtaking views of the Dovedale Valley where guests can enjoy a spot of fishing on the meandering river. Top dishes include fillet of pork wrapped in smoked bacon and glazed with honey and ginger, and grilled plaice with lemon and asparagus butter.

Directions: One mile W of Thorpe on the Ilam road

DEVON

ASHBURTON,
Holne Chase Hotel ❀❀❀

Two Bridges Road Newton Abbot
TQ13 7NS
Map 3: SX77
Tel: 01364 631471
Fax: 01364 631453
Chef: Jake Watkins
Owners: Sebastian & Philippa Hughes
Cost: Set-price D £28.50 (4 courses).
H/wine £11.50
Times: Noon-2pm/7.15-8.45pm
Additional: Bar food L; Sunday L;
Children 10+
Seats: 45. Private dining room 12
Smoking: No smoking in dining room
Accommodation: 17 en suite ★ ★ ★

Family-owned hotel, a former hunting lodge set in an idyllic wooded landscape. The daily-changing menus are rooted in English tradition, with influences from the Mediterranean grafted on as inspiration. The seasons and the availability of local produce dictate. Ballantine of salmon with sauce vierge, gazpacho of crab and coriander, rabbit cooked two ways with pearl barley and wild mushrooms, smoked haddock risotto with poached egg and hollandaise, hazelnut pyramid, are typical of the repertoire. The kitchen can also do a good shank of lamb, served with Savoy cabbage and mashed potato. The recipes are fairly conventional, but are executed with enough variation in detail to make them work.

Directions: Travelling N&E, take 2nd Asburton turning off A38. 2 miles to Holne Bridge, hotel is 0.25 mile on R. From Plymouth take 1st Ashburton turn

ASHWATER,
Blagdon Manor ❀❀   NEW

EX21 5DF
Map 2: SX39
Tel: 01409 211224
Fax: 01409 211634
Cost: Set-price D £23. ☺
Times: D only, at 8pm
Additional: Children 12+
Seats: 14. Private dining room 6
Smoking: No smoking in dining room
Accommodation: 7 en suite ★ ★

A delightful retreat dating from the 16th-century, set in rolling Devonshire countryside. Dinner is served 'en famille' at 8 o'clock – the magnificent table seats just fourteen, so it's best to stay at the hotel or phone in advance. The style is modern British with the likes of wild mushroom risotto, or a toasted English goats' cheese with a chicory, walnut and orange salad on the menu. We visited in November, when the set menu kicked off with a simple pasta and asparagus with tomato concasse topped with shavings of Parmesan, a good quality fillet of salmon atop a bed of buttery mash and crowned with nicely crisped onion. Marinated autumn fruits with zabaglione for dessert had 'nice flavours'.

Directions: From Launceston take A388 N towards Holdsworthy. Turn R at 2nd sign for Ashwater, then 1st R; hotel on R

AXMINSTER, **Lea Hill**

*Delightful 14th-century thatched hotel bursting with rural charm.
The short menu takes in modern ideas such as roasted breast of
chicken with home-made basil tagliatelle, and seared yellow-fin tuna
with mango salsa.*

Accommodation: 11 en suite ★★

Directions: From Axminster take A358 towards Chard. 2m L to
Smallridge, follow signs to Membury. 0.5m on R after village

Membury EX13 7AQ
Map 3: SY29
Tel: 01404 881881
Fax: 01404 881890
Cost: Set-price D £22.95. ☺ H/wine
£9.95
Times: Noon-1.45pm/7-8.45pm.
Closed D Sun, 3 Jan-28 Feb
Additional: Bar food L; Children 12+;
☙ dishes
Smoking: No smoking in dining room

BAMPTON, **Bark House Hotel**

Cosy, cottagey hotel of great charm where you feel at home.
Alastair Kameen cooks with flair and passion, albeit in a
simple way. The menu is limited with only a choice of two
dishes per course but you can rest assured that everything is
cooked to order – so expect a wait. Canapés give a clue to the
ambition and dedication in the kitchen – at our test meal wild
mushroom tartlet, small pizza, and a meaty rissole. We also
enjoyed an excellent fillet of beef with a sauce of mushroom
and Madeira, plus fresh asparagus, carrots with tarragon, purée
of parsnip and dauphinoise potatoes, and a beautifully tangy
lemon cream with raspberry coulis to finish.

Directions: 9 miles N of Tiverton on A396

Oakford Bridge Tiverton EX16 9HZ
Map 3: SS92
Tel: 01398 351236
Chef/Owner: Alastair Kameen
Cost: Set-price L £14.50/D £19.95. ☺
H/wine £8.50
Times: 12.30-1.30pm/7.30-9pm.
Closed 1 wk April, restricted service
Nov-Easter
Additional: Bar food L; Sunday L;
Children 5+; ☙ dishes
Seats: 14
Smoking: No smoking in dining room
Accommodation: 5 rooms (4 en suite)
★★
Credit cards: None

BARNSTAPLE,
Halmpstone Manor ✿✿

Hotel set in its own grounds amid a working farm.
Halmpstone Manor has an air of peace and tranquillity to it.
Have an aperitif in the well-stocked bar and relax after your
meal in front of the log fire in the comfortable lounge. The
dining room, panelled and candlelit, is the setting for a five-
course, no-choice dinner of perhaps caviar tart, or smoked
salmon with Parmesan, then a fish course of, say, crevettes
grilled in garlic served with aïoli, or roasted fillet of monkfish
with a mustard and tarragon sauce. Main courses might be a
trio of fillets of pork, lamb and beef, each in its own sauce, or
roasted local duckling with apple sauce. A selection of cheeses
comes next, preceding a choice of desserts.

Directions: From Barnstaple take A377 to Bishop's Tawton. At
end of village turn L for Cobbaton; sign on R

Bishop's Tawton EX32 0EA
Map 2: SS53
Tel: 01271 830321
Fax: 01271 830826
Chef: Jane Stanbury
Owners: Mr & Mrs C Stanbury
Cost: Set-price D £35 (5 courses).
H/wine £10
Times: D only, 7-9pm. Closed Sun,
Nov-Jan
Additional: ☙ dishes
Seats: 24. Jacket & tie preferred
Smoking: No smoking in dining room
Accommodation: 5 en suite ★★

BARNSTAPLE,
Royal & Fortescue, The Bank ✿

*A former coaching inn with a smart restaurant and informal bistro.
The Bank bistro serves both meals and snacks, many influenced by
Mexican cooking, so look out for hot nachos tempered by generous
quantities of soured cream, salsa, and guacamole.*

Directions: A361 into Barnstaple, along Barbican Rd signposted
town centre; turn R into Queen St & L (one way) Boutport St.
Hotel on L

Boutport Street
EX31 1HG
Map 2: SS53
Tel/Fax: 01271 42289
Telephone for further details

BEER, Old Steam Bakery

Quite simple and seems to have been done on a budget.
Informal and friendly 30-seater eaterie, well-used by locals
who have taken to the informal stripped pine and brightly
coloured walls as much as the Pacific Rim cuisine (Michael
Stride is from Australia, Sarah Stride from New Zealand). The
blackboard menu changes nightly, puts an emphasis on local
fish and presentation is simple rather than elaborate. We loved
it all, the superb black olive bread, mussels steamed with chilli
and soy sauce, the fat skate and scallop spring roll, locally
caught lobster, pan-fried with lime and butter ('worth every
penny'), grey mullet with tomato and black olive concasse, and
champagne sorbet layered with strawberries.

Directions: Turn off A3052 (Exeter to Lyme Regis). Beer is 2
miles from Seaton

Fore Street EX12 3JJ
Map 3: SY28
Tel: 01297 22040
Fax: 01297 625886
Chef: Michael Stride
Owners: Michael Stride, Sarah Doak-
Stride
Cost: *Alc* £28, set-price L £15.50. ☺
H/wine £10.50
Times: Noon-2.30pm/7-10.30pm.
Closed Tue, limited openings during
winter
Additional: Children welcome,
🐟 dishes
Seats: 38

BIDEFORD, Yeoldon Hotel

*Ivy-clad Victorian hotel overlooking the River Torridge. The menu
features innovative dishes, perhaps grilled fillet of salmon in
coriander, garlic and chilli marinade or butternut squash and fennel
risotto. For dessert try hot sticky toffee and date pudding, with
'lashings' of rich toffee sauce.*

Directions: From Barnstaple take A39 towards Bideford. At
Torridge Bridge roundabout take A386 to Northam. Take 3rd R
into Durrant Lane. Hotel 0.25m

Durrant Lane Northam EX39 2RL
Map 2: SS42
Tel: 01237 474400
Fax: 01237 476618
Cost: *Alc* £26, set price D £20. ☺
H/wine £10.25
Times: D only, 7-8.30pm
Additional: Sunday L (noon-1.30pm);
Children welcome; 🐟 dishes
Smoking: No smoking in dining room
Accommodation: 10 en suite ★★

BOVEY TRACEY, Edgemoor Hotel

Haytor Road
Lowerdown Cross
TQ13 9LE
Map 3: SX87
Tel: 01626 832466
Fax: 01626 834760
Chef: Edward Elliott
Owners: Pat & Rod Day
Cost: Set-price L £16.95/D £23.95. ☺
H/wine £8.95.
Times: Noon-1.45pm/7pm-9pm.
Closed 1 wk at New Year
Additional: Sunday L; Children 8+;
🐟 dishes
Seats: 35. Private dining room 60
Smoking: No smoking in dining room

A backdrop of mature trees frames the beautiful gardens.
Inside, lacy cloths, pastel shades and candlelight give a
romantic air to the dining-room, where a good selection of
modern and not so modern British dishes are served. There is
a touch of nostalgia in starters such as beer-battered button
mushrooms, stuffed with garlic cream cheese, and smoked
chicken and oyster mushrooms with white wine sauce served
in a savoury eclair. Regional ingredients feature in green-
lipped mussels with smoked bacon, Somerset Brie and a light
tarragon sauce, and also in a roast half guinea fowl with strips
of Denhay air-dried smoked ham in an aromatic cream sauce.
Local venison is cooked in a ragout with a rich red wine
sauce with prunes and black mushrooms, served with a

timbale of wild and basmati rice. Fish dishes change daily, as do desserts.

Directions: From A38 take A382 (Drumbridges). Cross first mini roundabout & turn L at 2nd roundabout. Bear L towards Haytor. Hotel 0.25 mile on R

BRANSCOMBE, **The Masons Arms**

Picture book old inn, idyllic village. Bar and restaurant menus offer choice and quality. Some traditional dishes (lamb's liver with back bacon, sweet onions and mustard gravy), others with a Mediterranean influence.

Accommodation: 18 rooms (most en suite) ★ ★

Directions: Turn off A3052 and follow road through Branscombe

EX12 3DJ
Map 3: SY18
Tel: 01297 680300
Fax: 01297 680500
Cost: Set-price D £22. ☺ H/wine £11
Times: Noon-2.15pm/7-8.45pm
Additional: Bar Food; Children welcome; ◑ dishes
Smoking: No smoking in dining room

BRIXHAM, **Maypool Park Hotel**

Pan-fried Torbay scallops and avocado, chicken and fromage frais gâteau are typical of the cooking at this delightful hotel. An interesting wine list complements the restaurant's innovative menus.

Galmpton TQ5 0ET
Map 3: SX95
Tel: 01803 842442
Fax: 01803 845782
Cost: Set-price D £22 (4 courses). ☺ H/wine £9.50
Times: D only, 7-8.30pm. Closed Mon, Tue, Xmas & New Year, 2 wks Jan, 2 wks Nov
Additional: Sunday L (noon-1.45pm); Children 12+; ◑ dishes
Smoking: No smoking in dining room
Accommodation: 10 en suite ★ ★

Directions: Turn off A3022 at Churston into Manor Vale Road for Maypool, pedestrian ferry and Greenway Quay and continue for 2 miles

BRIXHAM, **Quayside Hotel** **NEW**

Panoramic views of the harbour are just one reason to dine at the Quayside Hotel. The choice of modern British dishes is another. Try pan-fried fillet of halibut with local scallops and brandy sauce, followed by summer pudding.

41-49 King Street TQ5 9TJ
Map 3: SX95
Tel: 01803 855751
Fax: 01803 882733
Cost: *Alc* £25, set-price D £17.50. ☺ H/wine £10
Times: D only, 7-9.30pm
Additional: Children 12+; ◑ dishes
Smoking: No smoking in dining room
Accommodation: 29 en suite ★ ★ ★

Directions: From Exeter take the A380 towards Torquay, then A3022 to Brixham. Hotel overlooks harbour

Accommodation: 17 en suite ★ ★ ★

BROADHEMBURY, **Drewe Arms**

Friendly olde-worlde inn in picturesque village. Good fish cooking – gravlax, fillet of plaice with hollandaise sauce, sea bream with chilli and orange butter. Entertainment by 'bucolic locals'.

Directions: From M5/J28, 5 miles on A373 Cullompton to Honiton. Pub 1 mile NE of Broadhembury turning

EX14 0NF
Map 3: ST10
Tel/Fax: 01404 841267
Cost: *Alc* £22.50, set-price D £22.50.
☺ H/wine £10
Times: Noon-2pm/7-10pm. Closed D Sun
Additional: Bar food; Children welcome

BURRINGTON, **Northcote Manor**

For peace and quiet, head for this secluded 17th-century manor set amid rolling lawns and woodland with views over the countryside. The refurbished dining room is now light, cool and classy, with richly upholstered high-backed chairs giving a hint of the baronial; murals depict the property in former times. The kitchen takes fresh produce and integrates the disparate elements into dishes that are unified yet allow the separate flavours to shine out. Take a starter of seared Brie with potatoes, roast peppers and herbs, showing exactly the right contrast between ingredients, or a pretty-looking main course of roasted cod on herb mash with parsley sauce and a compote of mixed vegetables. Cauliflower purée and chive mayonnaise could come with goujons of Dover sole, and cassoulet of mixed pulses and buttered Savoy cabbage with breast of Trelough duck with a Pithiviers of confit. Skill with sauces is evident in a wild mushroom one with pan-fried fillet of beef and parsnip fondue, and a dab hand with pastry is behind a good crisp tart of 'light and moreish' chocolate partnered by pale and creamy chocolate ice cream. Vanilla pannacotta has been praised, too, and cheeses are all from the West Country. The wine list well suits the style, with some good vintages, although a limited choice by the glass.

Nr Portsmouth Arms Station
Umberleigh EX37 9LZ
Map 3: SS61
Tel: 01769 560501
Fax: 01769 560770
Chef: Chris Dawson
Owner: David Boddy
Cost: Set-price D £29.50 (4 courses). H/wine £12
Times: D only, 7-9pm. Closed Jan
Additional: Sunday L (12.30-1.30pm); Children 10+; ⬤ dishes
Seats: 30. Private dining room 12
Smoking: No smoking in dining room
Accommodation: 11 en suite ★ ★ ★

Directions: A377 Exeter to Barnstaple. 7 miles S of Barnstaple turn into private drive opposite Portsmouth Arms railway station (Don't enter Burrington)

CHAGFORD, **Gidleigh Park**

'I could not have picked a better day; it was gloriously sunny, drinks and coffee [were served] in the garden, with views that are unbeatable anywhere on a day like this.' Inspectors always enthuse about the splendours of Gidleigh, but it was a stroke of good fortune that our latest visit coincided with perfect weather – it showed Paul Henderson's masterpiece of a country hotel at its very best. Michael Caines continues to impress locals and visitors alike with his cooking, and the excellent value set-lunch at £30 for three courses 'and you still

Newton Abbot
TQ13 8HH
Map 3: SX78
Tel: 01647 432367
Fax: 01647 432574
Chef: Michael Caines
Owners: Paul & Kay Henderson
Cost: Set-price D £60 (4 courses). H/wine £21
Times: 12.30pm-2pm/7pm D 9pm

Gidleigh Park

Additional: Bar food L; Sunday L; Children 7+
Seats: 35
Smoking: No smoking in dining room
Accommodation: 14 en suite ★ ★ ★

Directions: In Chagford Square turn R at Lloyds Bank into Mill Street, after 150 yd fork R, straight across crossroads into Holy Street. Restaurant is 1.5 miles

get canapés, *amuse-bouches* and petits fours' is remarkable considering the quality of the cooking and raw materials. From this menu we were delighted with deliciously vibrant terrine of lobster, red mullet, monkfish and scallops with provençale vegetables, and superb roast best end of local lamb accompanied by sweetbreads, a tian of spinach, tomato and aubergine caviar, whole roast garlic, and a fine dice of root vegetables in a light thyme sauce. From the *carte* came tender roast quail teamed with a raviolo stuffed with intensely flavoured spinach and Parmesan, pea purée with braised celery and light quail jus, and little 'nests' of fine fried leek topped with lightly poached quails' eggs. Then top-quality turbot, perfectly timed, with a nicely crisped skin, and set on a full-flavoured ragout with tender langoustines, girolles, tomato concasse and tarragon. For dessert, a light and wonderfully intense passion fruit mousse with a tuile spiral and rice pudding ice cream, all set on a fine dice of mango, pineapple and pawpaw. Canapés (served for both menus) took in first-class goujons of sole with tartare sauce, tiny tender marinated veal kebabs, and wild mushroom soufflé omelette tartlets, the *amuse-bouche* was an intensely flavoured asparagus soup. The wine list is good reading and prices are not scary; a very candid explanation of the pricing structure at the front is impressive and makes the idea of spending a little more quite worthwhile as the policy favours the upper reaches.

CHAGFORD, Mill End Hotel

18th-century water mill with working wheel and six miles of fishing rights on the Teign. The cooking makes a stay here even more enjoyable: pigeon breast wrapped in bacon with red cabbage and brandy cream sauce delivered all the promised flavours; fillets of lemon sole filled with prawns and spinach, served with a saffron sauce, was a delicate, well-balanced dish. Fish comes from Brixham market – a selection may be grilled with black pepper and sesame seeds on a tomato and basil coulis. In season, goose breast is roasted pink and sliced around an onion marmalade with redcurrant and rosemary jus. Freshly brewed coffee is served in the sitting room with a selection of locally produced chocolates. Two special treats, however, are the award-winning cheese selection and the wonderful breakfast buffet.

Directions: From Exeter take A30 to Whiddon Down, turn S on A382 (Moretonhampstead) – don't turn into Chagford at Sandy Park; hotel is at Dogmarsh Bridge

Sandy Park TQ13 8JN
Map 3: SX78
Tel: 01647 432282
Fax: 01647 433106
Chef: Alan Lane
Owner: Keith Green
Cost: *Alc* £25. H/wine £12
Times: Noon-3pm/7-9pm. Closed 3 wks from Jan 1st
Additional: Bar food L; Sunday L; Children welcome; ✆ dishes
Seats: 40
Smoking: No smoking in dining room
Accommodation: 17 en suite ★ ★ ★

CHAGFORD,

22 Mill Street

Shop-front restaurant, intimate with unpretentious air and pleasant service. Amanda Leaman and Duncan Walker enjoy a lively local trade with burgeoning interest from further afield. Good taste dictates the elegant glasses and crockery, the menu is unfussy and devoid of trendy vernacular; it's basically a simple shopping list of ingredients strong on seasonality. A pair of inspectors were impressed by the imagination and the industry of the kitchen in an autumn dinner that satisfied on most counts of taste and presentation. It included scallops poached in pickled ginger, lemongrass and basil consommé, a saffron risotto with rabbit, Parmesan and rosemary, fillet of sea bass with warm potato, mushroom and truffle oil salad, superb sautéed calves' sweetbreads and kidneys, braised cabbage and Madeira, prune and Armagnac soufflé, and a fig and walnut tart with cinnamon ice cream that was an interesting flavour combination. The punchy wine list is tightly banded in price.

Directions: 200 yds on L after turning R out of Chagford Sq

22 Mill Street TQ13 8AW
Map 3: SX78
Tel: 01647 432244
Fax: 01647 433101
Chef: Duncan Walker
Owners: Amanda Leaman, Duncan Walker
Cost: Set-price D £27. H/wine £14.50
Times: 12.15-1.45pm/7.15-9pm. Closed L Mon, all Sun, 2 wks Jan, 1 wk May
Additional: Children 14+
Seats: 30. Private dining room 12
Smoking: No smoking in dining room
Accommodation: 2 en suite

CHITTLEHAMHOLT,

Highbullen Hotel

Victorian Gothic mansion with magnificent views of the surrounding countryside. Eat in the hotel's cellar restaurant and enjoy grilled salmon steak with roasted fennel and shallots, or casseroled local venison with celery, mushrooms, red wine and walnuts.

Accommodation: 40 en suite ★ ★ ★

Directions: From M5/J27 take A361 to South Molton, then B3226 (Crediton rd); after 5.2m turn R to Chittlehamholt. Hotel 0.5 mile beyond village

Umberleigh EX37 9HD
Map 3: SS62
Tel: 01769 540561
Fax: 01769 540492
Cost: Set-price D £20 (4 courses). ☺ H/wine £10
Times: Noon-2pm/7-9pm
Additional: Bar food L; Sunday L; Children 8+; 🍴 dishes
Smoking: No smoking in dining room; Air conditioning

CLOVELLY, **Red Lion Hotel**

Walk down a cobbled street to reach this unique 18th-century quay-side inn. Inside, locals enjoy a pint or two by the open fires in the beamed bar, and there's lively cooking in the restaurant. Typical starters include sautéed chicken with warm potato salad, and lightly-smoked Exmoor trout.

Accommodation: 11 en suite ★ ★

Directions: Leave A39 at Clovelly Cross onto B3237. At bottom of hill take 1st L by white railings to harbour

The Quay EX39 5TF
Map 2: SS32
Tel: 01237 431237
Fax: 01237 431044
Cost: Set-price D £18.50. ☺
Times: D only, 7-8.30pm
Additional: Bar food; Children welcome
Smoking: No smoking in dining room

COLYFORD, **Swallows Eaves**

Wisteria-covered 1920's gentleman's residence with a spacious blue and white dining room. Recommended dishes include sautéed chicken livers, and local beef with grain mustard sauce.

Accommodation: 8 en suite ★ ★

Directions: In the centre of the village on the A3082

Swan Hill Road Colyton EX13 6QJ
Map 3: SY29
Tel: 01297 553184
Fax: 01297 553574
Cost: Set-price D £22.50 (5 courses). ☺ H/wine £9.85
Times: D only, 7- 8.30pm
Smoking: No smoking in dining room

CREDITON,

Coombe House Hotel

Georgian manor praised for meals composed of such dishes as avocado and smoked garlic soup served with memorable home-made breads, and grilled breast of maize-fed chicken in a lightly curried sauce.

Directions: Telephone for directions

Coleford EX17 5BY
Tel: 01363 84487
Fax: 01363 84722
Telephone for further details

CROYDE, **Kittiwell House Hotel**

Charming thatched hotel with a cottage-style atmosphere. The popular restaurant focuses on modern British cooking: try goose liver pâté with strawberry coulis, and poached lemon sole with a white wine and mushroom sauce.

Accommodation: 12 en suite ★★

Directions: From Barnstaple take A361 to Braunton. L at traffic lights. In Croyde R into St Mary's Rd

St Mary's Road EX33 1PG
Map 2: SS43
Tel: 01271 890247
Fax: 01271 890469
Cost: *Alc* £28, set-price D £21.50. ☺
H/wine £10
Times: D only, 7-8.45pm. Closed last 3 wks Jan
Additional: Children 9+; ✤ dishes
Smoking: No smoking in dining room; Jacket & tie preferred

DARTMOUTH, **The Carved Angel**

Celebrated quayside restaurant. However, changes have taken place since our last edition. Both Joyce Molyneaux and Nick Coiley have retired, although Joyce remains as an owner, but the day-to-day running and control of the kitchen is in the hands of David Jones (formerly of Lewtrenchard Manor, Lewdown, see entry). Some revamping and new menus are the result. However, the kitchen remains open-plan and views over the busy Dart still mean there's plenty to catch the eye. There's no questioning the quality of the ingredients and the team's undoubted skills. As you'd expect, fish plays a central role and the kitchen certainly knows what to do with it. Fillet of brill is served with new potatoes, caponata and beurre noisette, spiced sea bass with creamed leeks, spinach and red wine sauce. Meat gets the modern treatment in ideas that show a thorough understanding of metropolitan thinking. Thus squab pigeon comes with broad beans, potato rösti and red wine sauce, but breast of duckling is teamed with pak choi, shiitakes and a chilli and soy dressing. Look out for unusual desserts: deep-fried rice pudding with mango, paw paw and passion fruit, for example, or lemongrass and vanilla ice cream with rhubarb and champagne.

2 South Embankment TQ6 9BH
Map 3: SX85
Tel: 01803 832465
Fax: 01803 835141
Chef: David Jones
Owners: Joyce Molyneux, Meriel Matthews, Zoë Wynne
Cost: Set-price L £27.50/D £45.
H/wine £15
Times: 12.30-2.30pm/7-9.30pm.
Closed D Sun, all Mon, Xmas, 6 wks from 1 Jan
Additional: Sunday L; Children welcome
Seats: 50. Private dining room 20
Smoking: No smoking in dining room

Directions: Dartmouth centre, on the water's edge

DARTMOUTH, **The Exchange** ✿✿

13th-century former mayor's residence occupying two floors. There's a French provincial feel to this architecturally interesting brasserie-style restaurant. It's informal dining with blackboard specials and about six or seven main courses on the carte. The cooking is very much in the modern idiom with polenta, prosciutto, saffron, black pudding and balsamic punctuating the menu. Grilled goats' cheese comes on a bed of mixed leaves and roasted pine nuts, pork tenderloin is oven-baked with a warm dressing of soya sauce, honey and grain mustard, and desserts range from a brilliant St Emilion au chocolat to a traditional bread-and-butter pudding.

Directions: In town centre near parish church

5 Higher Street TQ6 9RB
Map 3: SX85
Tel/Fax: 01803 832022
Chef: Colin Newton
Owner: Sarah Allan
Cost: *Alc* £22, set-price L £9.95. ☺
H/wine £9.95
Times: 12.30-2pm/7-9.30pm. Closed L Sun, all Tue, Xmas, Jan
Additional: Children welcome; ✤ dishes
Seats: 46

EXETER,

Barton Cross Hotel

Huxham Stoke Canon EX5 4EJ
Map 3: SX99
Tel: 01392 841245
Fax: 01392 841942
Chef: Paul George Bending
Owner: B A Hamilton
Cost: *Alc* £25, set-price D £25. ☺
H/wine £9.25
Times: D only, 7-9.30pm. Closed Sun
Additional: Children 5+; ⏺ dishes
Seats: 50. Private dining room 18
Smoking: No smoking in dining room
Accommodation: 9 en suite ★ ★ ★

Directions: 4 miles N of Exeter on
A396. At Stoke Canon, turn R at
church

17th-century thatched charm with up-to-date comforts sums up this hotel set deep in the mid-Devon countryside. The heavily beamed restaurant, with an unusual first-floor gallery and open fire, is decorated in soft pinks and greens, with ladderbacked chairs giving a comfortable rustic look. Dishes can be cooked more plainly on request should the seasonal menu daunt with dishes such as wild mushroom tart topped with foie gras. Guinea fowl and chicken in Riesling (a refined coq au vin) and panaché of sole, salmon and red mullet on roast shallots and asparagus with red wine fumet, set a cosmopolitan tone. More down-to-earth country ones include garden pea and ham terrine layered with chicken, and a spring lamb platter – a big boy's dish of lamb pasty, liver, kidneys, sweetbreads, cutlet, home-made sausage and bubble-and-squeak. Iced banana parfait with passion fruit sauce and caramelised bananas makes an exotic ending.

EXETER, **Buckerell Lodge**

Topsham Road EX2 4SQ
Map 3: SX99
Tel: 01392 221111
Fax: 01392 491111
Chef: Nicholas Mort
Owner: Regal/Corus
Cost: *Alc* £29.95, set-price L
£12.50/D £19.95. ☺ H/wine £10.95
Times: Noon-2pm/7-9.30pm. Closed
L Sat
Additional: Bar food; Sunday L;
Children welcome; ⏺ dishes
Seats: 60. Private dining rooms 30.
Jacket & tie preferred
Smoking: No smoking in dining room
Accommodation: 53 en suite ★ ★ ★

Directions: 5 minutes from M5/J30,
follow signs for Exeter city centre.
Aiport 5 miles, station 2 miles

Five acres of tall pines, broad lawns and serene gardens surround this pretty white hotel on Exeter's outskirts. Dinner is served in Raffles Restaurant. Here, at a late summer meal we enjoyed a 'fabulous' haddock and potato soup served with chive cream and poached egg. This was followed by roasted red snapper on a bed of courgette with lemon and ginger butter sauce, washed down with a 'super' bottle of Chilean red.

For dessert, a light steamed date pudding served with a cherry kirsch sauce and brandy snaps. This is a popular venue for wedding parties, particularly at the weekends, so it's advisable to phone ahead to check arrangements.

EXETER,

Ebford House Hotel ❀❀

Exmouth Road EX3 0QH
Map 3: SX99
Tel: 01392 877658
Fax: 01392 874424
Chef: Paul Bazell
Owners: Mr & Mrs D Horton
Cost: *Alc* £20. ☺ H/wine £8.95
Times: Noon-1.30pm/6.30-9.30pm.
Closed L Sun 25-26 Dec
Additional: Bar food; ❀ dishes
Seats: 50
Smoking: No smoking in dining room
Accommodation: 16 en suite ★ ★ ★

Directions: On A376 Exmouth road near Topsham

There is an engagingly enthusiastic tone to the menu descriptions: a daily 'soup of goodness', 'succulent' pan-fried rabbit and orange salad, 'lots of rough chopped parsley' with scallop and cod Rick Stein-style. An extensive carte broadly divides into two sections, meat and fish. Amongst the former there is Madeira marinated lamb noisettes, pan-fried on a celeriac tower with garlic cream sauce, and beef and ale pie with crusty puff pasty topping. Fish starters include steamed mussels with leek and bacon in a garlic broth, and fillet of Cajun spiced trout with Marie Rose sauce. Follow with chargrilled monkfish fillet with vegetable spaghetti on a rich fish and red wine sauce, or be daring and try the pan-fried shark topped with lime scented foie gras with lime, pepper, chilli and tomato confit.

EXETER, **Lord Haldon Hotel** ❀

Dunchideock EX6 7YF
Map 3: SX99
Tel: 01392 832483
Fax: 01392 833765
Cost: *Alc* £20, set-price L £14.50/D £19.50. ☺ H/wine £8.95
Times: Noon-1.30pm/7-8.30pm
Additional: Bar food; Sunday L; Children welcome; ❀ dishes
Smoking: No smoking in dining room
Accommodation: 22 en suite ★ ★ ★

Directions: Leave M5/J31, take A30 (Okehampton); follow signs to Ide. Through village for 2.5 miles, L after phone box, follow for 0.5 mile; hotelon L after low stone bridge

A spacious hotel with marvellous views of the surrounding countryside. A typical meal in the Chandelier Restaurant could start with pan-fried pigeon breasts in a red wine sauce, followed by grilled noisettes of lamb.

EXETER,

St Olaves Court Hotel

Mary Arches Street EX4 3AZ
Map 3: SX99
Tel: 01392 217736
Fax: 01392 413054
Chef: Robert Drakett
Owners: Raymond & Ute Wyatt,
James Wyatt
Cost: *Alc* £30, set-price L & D
£14.50. ☺ H/wine £10.50
Times: Noon-2pm/6.30-9.30pm.
Closed L Sat & Sun
Additional: Bar food L; Children
welcome; ⌾ dishes
Seats: 50. Private dining rooms 8-14
Smoking: No smoking in dining room
Accommodation: 15 en suite ★ ★ ★

Just a short stroll from Exeter's medieval cathedral, a well-appointed hotel with good service. The intimate surroundings of Golsworthy's Restaurant are enhanced in summer months when the doors are thrown open and guests can enjoy a light lunch or evening meal in the hotel's pretty walled garden. We, however, visited in winter when typical starters included deep-fried crab cakes with spicy tomato and coriander sauce, and terrine of game wrapped in Parma ham with toasted brioche and Cumberland sauce. Main courses of loin of pork braised in beer with deep-fried leeks, or roast breast of goose with crushed peppercorns and honey and desserts of caramelised pears with creamed rice, and 'classic' lemon tart with raspberry coulis, show a kitchen working with modern ideas. There's a simply annotated wine list that features a page of fine bin-end wines at bargain prices.

Directions: Follow signs to city centre, then 'Mary Arches P';
hotel is opposite car park entrance

GULWORTHY,

The Horn of Plenty

Tavistock PL19 8JD
Map 2: SX47
Tel/Fax: 01822 832528
Chef: Peter Gorton
Owners: Paul & Andie Roston
Cost: Set-price D £35. H/wine £14
Times: Noon-2pm/7-9.30pm. Closed
24-26 Dec
Additional: Bar food L; Sunday L;
Children 13+ at D; ⌾ dishes
Seats: 50
Smoking: No smoking in dining room
Accommodation: 8 en suite ★ ★

Beautiful country house with stunning views across Bodmin Moor. New owners have taken over since our last visit, although chef Peter Gorton remains in control of the kitchen.

There is a commitment to maintain the high standards which have made this a special place, and the cooking remains as strong as ever with Gorton's style combining old favourites with more inspirational ideas. Pan-fried breast of duck, for instance, is teamed with sweet potato, bok choi and an orange sauce. Our meal saw much to praise. First a 'serious league starter' of roast quail with a mushroom sauce, which was a mischievously understated description, actually arriving as two plump breasts sitting atop arborio rice and surrounded by a well-judged sauce of wild mushrooms. Then excellent fillet of wild trout served with a swirl of spinach with butter-lemon-wine sauce and a liberal smattering of chives. Dessert was a chocolate tart with a strawberry coulis and a beautiful restrained pear sorbet. The wine list majors in France with a strong selection of classic clarets and Burgundies, but other European and New World producers are explored.

Directions: 3 miles from Tavistock on A390. Turn R at Gulworthy Cross, then signed

The Horn of Plenty

HAYTOR, **Bel Alp House**

Short, set-price menu that hits the spot with carrot and lentil soup, fillet of beef with mushroom and green peppercorn sauce, then cheese, lemon tart, or local strawberries and clotted cream.

Smoking: No smoking in dining room
Accommodation: 8 en suite ★ ★ ★

Directions: 1.5 miles W of Bovey Tracey off B3387 to Haytor

Bovey Tracey TQ13 9XX
Map 3: SX77
Tel: 01364 661217
Fax: 01364 661292
Cost: *Alc* £25, set-price L £9.50 (2 courses)/D £22.50. ☺ H/wine £9
Times: Noon-2pm/7-8.30pm
Additional: Bar food; Children welcome; ❹ dishes

HAYTOR, **Rock Inn**

Food is important at this delightful 16th-century inn set in a tranquil Dartmoor village. Local, often organic, produce is the mainstay of a menu that offers a good choice of honest, satisfying dishes.

Smoking: No smoking in dining room
Accommodation: 9 en suite ★ ★

Directions: In Haytor village on A3387, 3 miles from A382

Haytor Vale Newton Abbot
TQ13 9XP
Map 3: SX77
Tel: 01364 661305
Fax: 01364 661242
Cost: *Alc* £25, set price L £20.95 (2 courses)/D £29.95. ☺ H/wine £8.95
Times: Noon-2.15pm/7-9.45pm
Additional: Bar food; Sunday L; Children welcome; ❹ dishes

HEDDON'S MOUTH,
Heddon's Gate Hotel ✿

Victorian hunting lodge on the edge of Exmoor with great views of Heddon Valley. The 8pm dinner gong sounds for the likes of 'excellent' butternut squash soup, and local lamb with thyme sauce.

Smoking: No smoking in dining room
Accommodation: 14 en suite ★ ★

Directions: A39 from Lynton. After 4m turn R towards Martinhoe/Woody Bay. 1st L after 0.5 mile, follow signs to Hunters Inn/Heddon's Mouth. Hotel on R

Martinhoe Barnstaple EX31 4PZ
Map 3: SX64
Tel: 01598 763313
Fax: 01598 763363
Cost: Set-price D £25 (5 courses). ☺ H/wine £9
Times: D only, at 7.30pm. Closed Nov-Mar
Additional: Children 8+

HONITON,

Combe House Gittisham

Gittisham EX14 0AD
Map 3: SY19
Tel: 01404 540400
Fax: 01404 46004
Cost: Set-price D £27.50 (4 courses).
H/wine £13.50
Times: Noon-2pm/7-9.30pm. Closed
L Mon
Additional: Bar food L; Sunday L;
Children welcome; 🍴 dishes
Smoking: No smoking in dining room
Accommodation: 15 en suite ★ ★ ★

Directions: In Gittisham village off
A30 & A303 south of Honiton

*A mile long drive through meadows and wooded valleys leads to
this splendid Elizabethan mansion, set in its own three thousand
acres. An eclectic mix of global ideas includes hot chicken liver salad
with balsamic dressing, followed by pan-fried skate wing served on a
bed of pasta.*

HONITON, **Home Farm Hotel**

*Thatched 16th-century former farmhouse. Lengthy carte and nightly
changing dinner menu covers all bases; king prawns, rack of lamb,
fillet steak and salmon are the mainstays.*

Smoking: No smoking in dining room
Accommodation: 13 en suite ★ ★

Directions: Three miles E of Honiton in village of Wilmington

Wilmington EX14 9JR
Map 3: ST10
Tel: 01404 831278
Fax: 01404 831411
Cost: *Alc* £21, set-price L&D £14.50.
☺ H/wine £8.95
Times: Noon-2pm/7-9.15pm. Closed
Xmas wk
Additional: Bar meals; Sunday L;
Children welcome; 🍴 dishes

ILSINGTON,

Ilsington Country Hotel

*Suited to both leisure and business travellers, the hotel is situated in
extensive grounds on the southern slopes of Dartmoor. The choice
of food is balanced, varied and interesting.*

Smoking: No smoking in dining room
Accommodation: 25 en suite ★ ★ ★

Directions: From A38 take exit to Newton Abbot/Bovey Tracey.
At Drum Bridges Roundabout take 3rd exit (Ilsington/Liverton).
1st R after 400yds. Continue 3 miles

TQ13 9RR
Map 3: SX77
Tel: 01364 661452
Fax: 01364 661307
Cost: Set-price L £12.50/D £22.50. ☺
H/wine £8.95
Times: Noon-2pm/6.30pm-9pm
Additional: Bar food; Sunday L;
Children welcome; 🍴 dishes

IVYBRIDGE, **Glazebrook House**

*Delightful Georgian house in five acres on the southern edge of
Dartmoor. A typical dinner might take in warm salad of lightly
roasted pigeon breast and wild mushrooms, followed by pan-fried
medallions of beef glazed in Stilton and pear butter.*

Smoking: No smoking in dining room
Accommodation: 11 en suite ★ ★

South Brent
TQ10 9JE
Map 3: SX66
Tel: 01364 73322
Fax: 01364 72350
Cost: *Alc* £38, set-price L & D
£19.50. ☺ H/wine £10
Times: 12.30-1.30pm/7-8.30pm.
Closed Sun

Glazebrook House

Additional: Children welcome;
 dishes

Directions: From A38, between Ivybridge and Buckfastleigh, follow 'Hotel' signs to South Brent

KINGSBRIDGE,

Buckland-Tout-Saints ✿✿

1999 has seen major refurbishment at this 1690-built mansion. The roof has been replaced, the bell tower reinstated, a new function suite (ideal for weddings) has been created, and decor generally has been upgraded. The grounds remain untouched, as does the pine panelling in the restaurant. The set-price dinner menu gives a handful of choices at each course except the second, when a sorbet or soup is served: perhaps flavoursome cauliflower. A terrine of foie gras with Sauternes jelly might come first, although the kitchen seems to excel with fish, as in a 'stunning' tartare of tuna bound with chive mayonnaise, simply constructed and bursting with taste. Main courses could be lamb tenderloin wrapped in a herb pancake with a tarragon-infused casserole of sweetbreads, kale and quenelles of potato and carrots, or baked fillet of monkfish in a dill, mussel and saffron sauce with julienne vegetables. Skills extend into puddings of orange soufflé with blood orange sorbet, and the well-combined flavours of a duo of light and dark chocolate with orange confit.

Goveton TQ7 2DS
Map 3: SX74
Tel: 01548 853055
Fax: 01548 856261
Chef: Jean-Philippe Bidart
Owners: Captain Mark & Mrs Julia Trumble
Cost: Set-price D £30 (4 courses). ☺
H/wine £9.95
Times: Noon-1.45pm/7-9pm
Additional: Bar food L; Sunday L; Children 6+; dishes
Seats: 40. Private dining room 20-150
Smoking: No smoking in dining room
Accommodation: 10 en suite ★ ★ ★

Directions: 2 miles N of Kingsbridge on A381. Through village of Goveton, 500 yds past church

KINGSKERSWELL,

Pitt House Restaurant ✿✿

All very chocolate boxy and picturesque. Intimate, beautifully kept thatched cottage with a tidy, colourful garden and cooking that really stands out in an area that our inspector considers to be something of a culinary desert. We thoroughly enjoyed the homely appeal of fresh crab, leek and mustard crumble, and the lightness of a twice-baked cheese soufflé. Ragout of salmon, brill and prawns with a saffron and dill sauce was also delicious, as was a roast fillet of pork with Madeira sauce. Rich chocolate tart, and traditional summer pudding kept standards high until the end.

2 Church End Road Nr Newton Abbot TQ12 5DS
Map 3: SX86
Tel: 01803 873374
Chef: Miss Vanessa Rogers
Owners: Mr A & Mrs J Rogers
Cost: Set-price D £25. H/wine £10.50
Times: D only, 7-8.30pm. Closed Sun, Mon, 2 wks summer, 2 wks winter
Additional: Children 10+; dishes
Seats: 25. Private dining room 12
Smoking: No smoking in dining room

Directions: Torquay road from Newton Abbot, 1st R, follow road to junction & turn L, parish church on R. Take 1st R, restaurant 50yds on L

LEWDOWN,

Lewtrenchard Manor

Delightful Jacobean manor house with sweeping views across the Lewtrenchard estate and Dartmoor. Inside, the rooms are decorated in warm colours and are rich in ornate ceilings, oak panelling, and granite window frames. New chef Kevin Barron had only been in place for a short time when we visited and was still cooking off the menus devised by the previous incumbent, David Jones, who has departed for the Carved Angel (see entry, Dartmouth). However, we were impressed by both the skill and flavour apparent in that meal: sweet, gently caramelised Cornish scallops with crushed potato and smoked paprika, best end of Devon accompanied by dauphinoise and a sharp, pungent, to the point caper gravy, and a real highlight – chocolate fondant with Malteser ice cream which, encouragingly, was one of Kevin Barron's own dishes. The new menu, we are led to understand, will include plenty of local fare such as loin of Tiverton pork with cider, fondant potatoes, choucroute and a thyme jus. James Murray continues to dispense bonhomie and advice on the extensive wine list which is particularly strong on South African bottles.

Okehampton EX20 4PN
Map 2: SX48
Tel: 01566 783256
Fax: 01566 783332
Chef: Kevin Barron
Owners: Mr & Mrs James Murray
Cost: *Alc* £32, set-price D £32.
H/wine £10
Times: D only, 7-9pm
Additional: Bar food; Sunday L
(12.30-1.30pm); Children 8+;
🍴 dishes
Seats: 40. Private dining room 16.
Jacket & tie preferred
Smoking: No smoking in dining room
Accommodation: 9 en suite ★ ★ ★

Directions: Take A30 for Lewdown, after 6 miles turn L at signpost for Lewtrenchard. Follow signs for 0.75 mile

LIFTON,

Arundell Arms

PL16 0AA
Map 2: SX38
Tel: 01566 784666
Fax: 01566 784494
Chefs: Philip Burgess, Nick Shopland
Owner: Mrs Anne Voss-Bark
Cost: *Alc* £35.50, set-price L £19/D
£28.50 (5 courses). ☺ H/wine £10
Times: 12.30-2pm/7.30-9.30pm
Additional: Bar food; Sunday L;
Children welcome; 🍴 dishes
Seats: 70. Private dining room 20
Smoking: No smoking in dining room
Accommodation: 28 en suite ★ ★ ★

Directions: Just off A30 in village of Lifton

Relaxed with understated style, very much a hotel to use and enjoy. This popular fishing hotel sports a traditional-looking dining room that comes complete with hefty chandelier, clothed tables and warm peach colours; service comes with character. Admiral restraint is the hallmark of the cooking here, with Philip Burgess and Nick Shopland still holding sway in the kitchen, producing a repertoire that ranges from asparagus and thyme soup to spiced fillet of Cornish red mullet with celeriac and basil relish, among starters, main courses of casserole of salmon, sole and red mullet with saffron, dill and cream, or fillet of Gressingham duck with a compote of blueberries and a Madeira glaze; and orange and Grand-Marnier soufflé with a warm compote of raspberries for dessert. To some extent, a meal is only as good as the suppliers and in recognition of this fact, the details of the local suppliers are listed on the front of the menu. Indeed, the highlight of our test meal was certainly the sheer quality of the mignon of Devon beef, sensibly not over-embellished with superfluous

details or flavours, just teamed with some celeriac purée, pan-fried chicken liver and a red wine glaze. A generous slice of lightly grilled smoked salmon with caramelised lime and a toasted hazelnut dressing opened that meal, and a simple, but rich, vanilla and raspberry creme brûlée closed it.

LYDFORD, **Castle Inn Hotel**

Elizabethan inn, full of character, with a 12th-century fireplace in the restaurant. The menu reflects a creative approach to local game and seafood.

Smoking: No-smoking area; No pipes & cigars
Accommodation: 9 en suite

Directions: From A30 take A386 towards Tavistock. Lydford signposted to R after 5 miles

Okehampton EX20 4BH
Map 2: SX58
Tel: 01822 820242
Fax: 01822 820454
Cost: *Alc* £27.30, set-price D £16.95.
☺ H/wine £8.15
Times: D only, 6.30-9.30pm
Additional: Bar food L; Sunday L
(noon-2.30pm); Children 5+; ⬤ dishes

LYMPSTONE,
River House Restaurant

The Strand EX8 5EY
Map 3: SX98
Tel: 01395 265147
Chef: Shirley Wilkes
Owner: Michael Wilkes
Cost: *Alc* £20, set-price L £19/D
£35.50. H/wine £9.95
Times: Noon-1.30pm/7-9.30pm.
Closed Sun, Mon (exc D for
residents), 25-27 Dec, 1-2 Jan, Bhs
Mon
Additional: Children 6+; ⬤ dishes
Smoking: No smoking in dining room
Accommodation: 3 en suite

Directions: In Lower Lympstone,
approx 2 miles off A376 Exeter-
Exmouth road

On the edge of the Exe estuary with wonderful views from its first-floor dining room. Although the style is country house 'the property feels much too comfortable to be like a restaurant', comments an inspector. There's art work for sale, a decidely unstuffy atmosphere and good cooking. The menu lists an impressive mix of English and European dishes – with plenty of Mediterranean and North African influences. Provençale fish soup, or a risotto of mushrooms with roasted Med vegetables, and tagine of lamb stand out. Or there's a classic coq au vin, and closer to home wild dartmoor beef steak served with melted Stilton cheese. Desserts stay in the English mould with sticky toffee pudding and bread-and-butter pudding leading the pack.

LYNMOUTH, **Rising Sun Hotel**

Beamed, oak-panelled and candlelit restaurant with bags of character. Nestling right on the harbour front of historic Lynmouth, the 14th-century former smugglers' inn makes an ideal base from which to explore the stunning countryside of North Devon. The kitchen specialises in local Exmoor game and seafood dishes, along the lines of game terrine with orange

Harbourside EX35 6EQ
Map 3: SS74
Tel: 01598 753223
Fax: 01598 753480
Chef: Patrice Grunenwald
Owner: Hugo Jeune
Cost: *Alc* £30, set-price L £19.50
Times: Noon-1.55pm/7-8.45pm

redcurrant sauce, crab bisque with garlic croûtes, and lemon sole soufflé with linguini nero and saffron sauce. A vibrant pork and Mediterranean vegetable terrine was served, unusually, with marrowfat peas and garlic butter. Careful attention to presentation also distinguished a main course of best end of superbly flavoured lamb with rosemary and bordelaise sauce, served in a large soup bowl with dauphinoise potatoes, fève beans, tomato concasse and finely diced celeriac. To finish, a rich chocolate tart.

Directions: M5/J23 (Minehead). Take A39 to Lynmouth. Opposite the harbour

LYNTON,
Chough's Nest Hotel

Beautiful stone house with spectacular views over Lynmouth Bay – dine at dusk and you could be treated to a famous 'red rocks' sunset. Typical dishes from the daily-changing menu include confit of chicken with roasted red onion and sour cream, and baked fillet of lemon sole with shrimp butter.

Accommodation: 10 en suite ★

Directions: From Lynton Parish Church in centre, turn onto North Walk. Last hotel on L

MARTINHOE,
Old Rectory Hotel

A short walk away from the North Devon Coast Path, this 18th-century rectory provides an ideal base for exploring Exmoor. The kitchen produces the likes of apple, red pepper and sweetcorn soup, and fillet of trout with mushrooms and wine.

Accommodation: 10 en suite ★ ★
Credit cards: None

Directions: M5/J27 onto A361, R onto A399 Blackmore Gate, R onto A39 Parracombe. At Martinhoe Cross, 3rd road on L to Woody Bay/Martinhoe

Rising Sun Hotel

Additional: Bar food L; Sunday L; Children 7+; 🍴 dishes
Seats: 30
Smoking: No smoking in dining room
Accommodation: 16 en suite ★ ★

North Walk EX35 6HJ
Map 3: SS74
Tel: 01598 753315
Cost: Set-price D £19 (4 courses). ☺ H/wine £6.75
Times: Noon-2.30pm/7-9pm. Closed Nov-Jan
Additional: Bar food L; Children 5+; 🍴 dishes
Smoking: No smoking in dining room

Parracombe EX31 4QT
Map 3: SS64
Tel: 01598 763368
Fax: 01598 763567
Cost: Set-price L & D £28.50 (4 courses)
Times: D only at 7.30pm. Closed Nov-Mar
Additional: Children 14+; 🍴 dishes
Smoking: No smoking in dining room

MORETONHAMPSTEAD,
Blackaller Hotel

A small hotel with a restaurant of old pine tables, granite walls, flowers and lots of crafty bits. The kitchen's style is best illustrated by chicken breast in lightly curried mayonnaise with crunchy peanut butter, and duck breast with a sauce of plums, port and honey.

Directions: From M5 – A30 Okehampton Road. Then Marsh Barton sign onto B3212 (Moretonhampstead). Take North Bovey road from there

North Bovey TQ13 8QY
Map 3: SX78
Tel/Fax: 01647 440322
Telephone for further details

MORETONHAMPSTEAD,
Manor House Hotel

A substantial Victorian manor house in quiet grounds. Imaginative dishes are served in the Hambleden Restaurant with typical starters including tomato and roasted pepper soup, and carpaccio of Highland beef.

Smoking: No smoking in dining room
Accommodation: 90 en suite ★ ★ ★ ★

Directions: 2m from Moretonhampstead towards Princetown on B3212

TQ13 8RE
Map 3: SX78
Tel: 01647 440355
Fax: 01647 440961
Cost: *Alc* £25, set-price D £21.50. ☺
H/wine £10.50
Times: D only, 7-9.30pm
Additional: Bar food L; Sunday L (12.30-2pm); Children welcome; ✿ dishes

PARKHAM,
Penhaven Country House

17th-century house with distant views of Exmoor noted for an interesting choice of dishes with the emphasis on locally produced ingredients. Expect fillets of local brill with vodka beurre blanc, and medallions of pork with honey and Devonshire cider sauce.

Smoking: No smoking in dining room
Accommodation: 12 en suite ★ ★ ★

Directions: From A39 at Horns Cross, follow signs to Parkham and turn L after church

Bideford EX39 5PL
Map 2: SS32
Tel: 01237 451711
Fax: 01237 451878
Cost: *Alc* £25, set-price D £14.95. ☺
H/wine £11.95.
Times: D only, 7.15-9pm.
Additional: Sunday L (12.15-1.30pm); Children 10+; ✿ dishes

PLYMOUTH,
Boringdon Hall Hotel

Queen Victoria once stayed at this attractive oak-beamed house, popular nowadays with business guests. The Gallery Restaurant serves pan-fried fillet of wild sea bass, and seared fillet of lamb with red currant jus.

Smoking: No smoking in dining room
Accommodation: 40 en suite ★ ★ ★

Directions: From A38 at Marsh Mills rdbt, follow signs for Plympton along dual carriageway to small island. L over bridge & follow brown tourist signs

Colebrook Plympton PL7 4DP
Map 2: SX45
Tel: 01752 344455
Fax: 01752 346578
Cost: *Alc* £22.95, set-price D £22.95 (4 courses). ☺ H/wine £12.45
Times: Noon-1.45pm/7-9.45pm.
Closed D Wed
Additional: Bar food; Sunday L; Children welcome; ✿ dishes

PLYMOUTH, Chez Nous

13 Frankfort Gate PL1 1QA
Map 2: SX45
Tel/Fax: 01752 266793
Chef: Jacques Marchal
Owners: Jacques & Suzanne Marchal
Cost: *Alc* £34. H/wine £10.50
Times: 12.30-2pm/7-10.30pm. Closed
L Sat, all Sun & Mon, 3 wks Feb, 3
wks Sep
Seats: 28

Directions: Frankfort Gate is a
pedestrianised street between Western
Approach & Market Avenue

*Chez Nous continues to be the flag bearer for food in
Plymouth.* The restaurant is something of an enigma and
certainly does nothing to flaunt itself. Situated in the scruffy
end of a scruffy city, the dishevelled urbanites who skulk
outside can have little idea what happens behind the shuttered
windows. The interior is utterly unpretentious, almost
apologetic, nothing to distract the attention from the food.
Sensibly Jacques Marchal relies upon the inherent strength of
the locale, i.e. fruits of the sea. Although not a place to look
for the latest trends in food fashion, there is an
uncompromising Gallic merit which is rooted in an innate
confidence in ability. Marchal cooks in primary colours with
flavours by the bucketful. Our test meal was a great success.
Straightforward canapés consisted of robust-flavoured salami,
crostini topped with sun-dried tomatoes, olives with garlic and
fennel seeds. A starter of plump, sautéed chicken livers with
pine nuts and port sauce proved a cracking dish, and cod with
tapenade crust surrounded by puréed pepper, tomato and olive
oil was distinguished by the quality of fish and the sensitive
restraint shown to allow the fish to shine. Dark and light
chocolate marble cake surrounded by white and dark
chocolate sauce was light and agreeable.

PLYMOUTH,
Duke of Cornwall

*The setting is Victorian: grand chandelier, marble pillars,
luxurious drapes and seascape oil paintings.* A touch of the
Pacific Rim hoves onto the horizon with dishes along the lines
of shellfish hot-pot with lemongrass, ginger and chillies, and
roasted tail of spiced monkfish on shrimp and lime risotto
drizzled with a Pernod and saffron dressing. Other fusion-style
ideas might pair seared breast of West country chicken with
marinated vegetable couscous and sweet capsicum cream.
Modern British here means using traditional ingredients with
imagination – wild boar cutlet is chargrilled and served on a
sauté of celeriac and apples flavoured with sage and apple
brandy; game terrine en croûte is given piquancy with a
beetroot and horseradish pickle. A more classic combination is
sirloin with green peppercorn and Cognac cream sauce.

Directions: City centre, follow signs 'Pavilions', hotel road is
opposite

Millbay Road PL1 3LG
Map 2: SX45
Tel: 01752 266256
Fax: 01752 600062
Chef: Tim Bailey
Cost: *Alc* £27.50, set-price D £19.50.
☺ H/wine £9.95
Times: D only 7-10pm
Additional: Bar food L; Sunday L
(12.30-1.45pm); Children welcome;
🍴 dishes
Seats: 70. Private dining rooms 30-
280
Smoking: No smoking in dining room
Accommodation: 72 en suite ★★★

PLYMOUTH,

Kitley House Hotel 🏵

Yealmpton PL8 2NW
Map 2: SX45
Tel: 01752 881555
Fax: 01752 881667
Cost: *Alc* £22.50, set-price L £15/D
£22.50. ☺ H/wine £12.95
Times: Noon-2pm/7.30-9.30pm

A mile-long tree-lined drive with a fine Grade I Tudor revival house at the end promises much. Meals in the book-lined dining room are well constructed with a twist of French: fish soups, terrines, and tasty roasted duck with mushrooms and tarragon.

Additional: Bar food; Sunday L; Children welcome; 🍴 dishes
Smoking: No smoking in dining room
Accommodation: 19 en suite ★★★

Directions: From Plymouth take A379 (Kingsbridge). Entrance between villages of Brixton & Yealmpton on R (10 mins)

PLYMOUTH,

Langdon Court Hotel 🏵

Down Thomas PL9 0DY
Map 2: SX45
Tel: 01752 862358
Fax: 01752 863428
Cost: *Alc* £25, set-price D £19.50. ☺
H/wine £7.95
Times: D only, 7-11pm. Closed D
Sun, all Mon

Tudor manor house said to have been used by Edward VII to entertain Lily Langtry. The French-inspired menu includes fresh fish delivered daily from the Barbican fish market. Look out for tempura of monkfish with a bitter orange jus.

Additional: Bar food; Sunday L; Children welcome; 🍴 dishes
Accommodation: 17 en suite ★★

Directions: From A379 at Elburton, follow signs for HMS Cambridge

ROCKBEARE,

The Jack In The Green Inn 🏵🏵

Exeter EX5 2EE
Map 3: SY09
Tel: 01404 822240
Fax: 01404 823445
Chef: Matthew Mason
Owner: Paul Kevin
Cost: Set-price L/D £16.95. ☺ H/wine
£8.95
Times: Noon-1.45pm/6-9.45pm.
Closed 25-26 Dec
Additional: Bar food; Sunday L;
Children 5+; 🍴 dishes
Seats: 60. Private dining room 30
Smoking: No smoking in dining room

Popular roadside pub with friendly, casual service. The quiet façade belies the interior – the place is usually packed with locals enjoying both bar and restaurant food. Staff are young and enthusiastic and the owner very hands-on, ensuring that however busy it gets, waiting is kept to a minimum. An extensive choice of bar snacks takes in supreme of Cajun chicken with spicy peanut dressing, salad and chips, as well as steak and kidney pie. Things go up a notch on the restaurant menu with pan-fried foie gras with fried egg on toasted brioche, oven-roasted cod with sun-dried tomato, tapenade and new potatoes, with rib-eye steak with veal kidney and Meaux mustard sauce and pommes frites for the farming contingent. As well as a fine choice of cheeses, there are sensible puds such as steamed stemmed ginger sponge with rhubarb and strawberry sauce, and lemon curd tart with candied zest.

Directions: 5 miles E of Exeter on the A30

SALCOMBE,
Bolt Head Hotel

South Sands TQ8 8LL
Map 3: SX73
Tel: 01548 843751
Fax: 01548 843061
Cost: Set-price D £25 (5 courses). ☺
H/wine £10
Times: Noon-2.15pm/7-9pm
Additional: Bar food L; Sunday L;
Children welcome; 🍴 dishes
Smoking: No-smoking area
Accommodation: 28 en suite ★ ★ ★
Directions: At Malborough follow
National Trust signs for Sharpitor; the
hotel is above the beach at South
Sands

Attractive restaurant with superb views over the Bay of Salcombe.
Traditional dishes include local crab with pink grapefruit, and
chicken supreme with red wine and mushroom sauce.

SALCOMBE, # Lyndhurst Hotel

Bonaventure Road TQ8 8BG
Tel/Fax: 01548 842481
Telephone for further details

The dining room has wonderful views of the yacht-filled estuary and
rolling countryside. Singled out for praise have been a salad of
coarsely-chopped squid and peppers dotted with squid ink on
polenta, and roasted lamb's liver on mash with caramelised onions
and bacon-flecked gravy.

Directions: Telephone for directions

SALCOMBE,
The Marine Hotel

Cliffe Road TQ8 8JH
Map 3: SX73
Tel: 01548 844444
Fax: 01548 843109
Cost: *Alc* £35, set-price L £12.50/D
£27. H/wine £12.50
Times: 12.30-1.45pm/7.30-9pm
Additional: Bar food; Sunday L;
Children 8+; 🍴 dishes

Splendid hotel with stunning views over the Dart estuary. Classical
French describes the cooking: roast saddle of English lamb with a
woodland mushroom fricassée and roasted cloves of garlic.

Smoking: No smoking in dining room
Accommodation: 51 en suite ★ ★ ★ ★

Directions: From Exeter take A384 to Totnes, then follow A381
to Kingsbridge and Salcombe

SALCOMBE,
Soar Mill Cove Hotel

Soar Mill Cove
Malborough
TQ7 3DS
Map 3: SX73
Tel: 01548 561566
Fax: 01548 561223
Chef: Keith S Makepeace
Owners: The Makepeace Family
Cost: *Alc* L £20, set-price D £34 (5
courses). H/wine £13.50

Re-built, re-modelled and newly refurbished – much has
changed, save for the glorious marine panorama. And the
high standard of cooking. Crab and lobster pots in the
exceptionally clean waters of the cove supply the daily-
changing menus including the popular crab cake appetisers;
the house speciality is lobster cooked with queen scallops in a
light saffron sauce. Organic South Devon lamb can be ordered
in take-home packs; time your visit accurately and you may be

Soar Mill Cove Hotel

Times: Noon-2.30pm/7.15-9pm. Closed end Nov-Feb (excl Xmas & New Year)
Additional: Bar food L; Sunday L; Children welcome; dishes
Seats: 50
Smoking: No smoking in dining room
Accommodation: 21 en suite ★ ★ ★

served 'The First of the Flock', in which the whole lamb is encrusted with herbs, then slowly roasted until very tender. Regional ingredients are given a sophisticated spin in layered terrine of local seafood served with minted yogurt dressing, and marinated pork loin steak with caramelised Bramley apples and a Luscombe cider sauce. The hotel also runs cookery master classes.

Directions: A381 to Salcombe, through village follow signs to sea

SALCOMBE,
Tides Reach Hotel

South Sands TQ8 8LJ
Map 3: SX73
Tel: 01548 843466
Fax: 01548 843954
Chef: Finn Ibsen
Owner: R.R. Edwards
Cost: Set-price D £28 (5 courses). H/wine £11.75
Times: D only, 7-9pm. Closed Dec-Jan
Additional: Bar food L; Children 8+; dishes
Seats: 90
Smoking: No smoking in dining room
Accommodation: 38 en suite ★ ★ ★

Those who like to start at the end of a menu and work backwards will immediately find their eye captured by some deliciously tempting items such as hot apple fritters set on an apricot sauce with clotted cream or rhubarb and ginger fool topped with chocolate shavings – though that's not really the end of the meal, as there's English cheese to follow plus coffee and petits fours served in the lounge and bar. Earlier on in the meal, there are other key choices to be made – is it to be the clam and salmon chowder or the local mussels steamed in white wine with vegetables and garlic, the roast Gressingham duck on egg noodles with honey and soy sauce or the medallions of venison with balsamic vinegar sauce? Vegetarians have a simpler choice – in May it was fresh green asparagus with tomato and basil dressing, tomato and tarragon soup or vegetable curry.

Directions: Take cliff road towards sea and Bolt Head

SIDMOUTH, **Brownlands** ✿

Sid Road EX10 9AG
Map 3: SY18
Tel/Fax: 01395 513053
Cost: Set-price D £19.95 (6 courses). ☺ H/wine £8.90
Times: Noon-1.15pm/7-8pm. Closed Nov-Mar
Additional: Bar food L; Sunday L; Children 8+; dishes

Well-presented dishes served in an elegant panelled dining room. Medallions of pork fillet with crab meat and asparagus spears and a butter, herb and tomato sauce were particularly pleasing.

Smoking: No smoking in dining room
Accommodation: 14 en suite ★ ★
Credit cards: None

Directions: Take A3052 (Exeter – Sidford), turn R at crossroads past Blue Bull Inn onto Fortescue Rd. Hotel in 1 mile

SIDMOUTH,
Riviera Hotel

The Esplanade EX10 8AY
Map 3: SY18
Tel: 01395 515201
Fax: 01395 577775
Cost: *Alc* £24.50, set-price L £16 (5 courses)/D £26 (7 courses). ☺ H/wine £11.70
Times: 12.30-2pm/7-9pm
Additional: Bar food L; Sunday L; Children welcome; ✿ dishes
Smoking: No-smoking area; No pipes & cigars; Air conditioning
Accommodation: 27 en suite ★ ★ ★ ★

Directions: From M5/J30, take A3052 to Sidmouth. In the centre of The Esplanade, overlooking Lyme Bay

The hotel's restaurant offers elegant surroundings and traditional standards of service. Menu choices include roast loin of lamb, and steamed salmon and sole mousse.

SIDMOUTH, Victoria Hotel

Swimming, tennis or snooker are just some of the daytime entertainment; in the evening relax over dinner of scampi and monkfish in puff pastry with white wine and dill sauce, and medallions of local venison with caramelised walnuts.

Directions: At the western end of the esplanade

Esplanade EX10 8RY
Map 3: SY18
Tel: 01395 512651
Fax: 01395 579154
Telephone for further details

SOUTH MOLTON,
Marsh Hall Hotel ✿

Local produce, sensible, straightforward cooking. Try rack of Devon lamb roasted with rosemary and redcurrant sauce, or medallions of Somerset pork pan-fried, served with cream and wholegrain mustard sauce.

Smoking: No smoking in dining room
Accommodation: 7 en suite ★ ★

Directions: Off A361 signed North Molton; first R, then R again

EX36 3HQ
Map 3: SS72
Tel: 01769 572666
Fax: 01769 574230
Cost: Set-price D £20 (4 courses). ☺ H/wine £9
Times: D only, 7-8pm
Additional: Children 12+

SOUTH MOLTON,
Whitechapel Manor ✿✿✿

Grade I listed manor house full of period charm. The setting is remote, on the edge of Exmoor with its own gardens and grounds. Public areas include various lounges, some fine screens, linen-fold panelling, and open fires and it all adds up to a great get-away-from-it-all place. Matt Corner's cooking does not disappoint. His menu is short and simple, but reveals assiduous balance and the food itself is technically assured. In general, the repertoire features a selection from the categories the clientele demands: home-smoked salmon with Sevruga caviar and crème fraîche, grilled lemon sole with a lemon and

EX36 3EG
Map 3: SS72
Tel: 01769 573377
Fax: 01769 573797
Chef: Matt Corner
Owners: Margaret Aris, Charles Brown
Cost: Set-price D £34. H/wine £10.75
Times: D only, 7-8.45pm
Additional: Children 10+
Seats: 24
Smoking: No smoking in dining room

thyme butter. However, the fashion for global influences is not ignored with a roast assiette of fish with bouillabaisse, or fillet of sea bass with chervil risotto and smoked vanilla sauce, duck confit with creamed parsley potatoes and caramelised shallots, or breast of corn-fed chicken with spiced couscous and red pepper coulis showing the range.

Accommodation: 10 en suite ★ ★

Directions: From Tiverton take A361, Whitechapel signed at roundabout. Right after 0.75 mile

STAVERTON,

Sea Trout Inn

TQ9 6PA
Map 3: SX76
Tel: 01803 762274
Fax: 01803 762506
Chef: John Hughes
Owners: Mr & Mrs Andrew Mogford
Cost: Alc £22, set-price D £18.75. ☺
H/wine £6.95
Times: Noon-2pm/7-9.30pm. Closed D 25, 26 Dec
Additional: Bar food; Sunday L; Children welcome; ❹ dishes
Seats: 40. Private dining room 26
Smoking: No-smoking area; No pipes & cigars; Air conditioning
Accommodation: 11 en suite ★ ★

Charming 15th-century inn expanded to a hotel with all of today's standards of comfort. There's a good mix of styles with a something-for-everyone approach: the traditional bar is popular for bar snacks; there's a separate 'village inn' at the end, mainly for locals and darts teams; and the more formal conservatory-style restaurant which overlooks pretty gardens. In the latter the menu concentrates on reworking French/international dishes. Our test meal of chicken liver parfait, breast of duck in a cherry and Kirsch sauce, accompanied by Delmonico potatoes, and rum baba gâteau with clotted cream, shows the style admirably.

Directions: From A38 follow A384 at Buckfastleigh (Dart Bridge) and proceed to Staverton

THURLESTONE,

Heron House Hotel

Fabulous views of the South Devon coast are one reason to visit this family-run hotel. Another is the imaginative British fare: salad of herring marinated with Madeira, and venison sausage with herb mash.

Accommodation: 16 en suite ★ ★

Directions: From A38 between Exeter & Plymouth, take A385 to Totnes. Then A381, through Kingsbridge, towards Salcombe. Take L turn signed Hope Cove. 50yds beyond Galmpton sign take R to Thurlestone Sands

Thurlestone Sands Nr Salcombe
TQ7 3JY
Map 3: SX64
Tel: 01548 561308/561600
Fax: 01548 560180
Cost: Alc £21.95, set-price D £21.95.
H/wine £10.95
Times: Noon-2.30pm/7-8.30pm
Additional: Bar food L; Sunday L; Children welcome; ❹ dishes
Smoking: No smoking in dining room

THURLESTONE, **Thurlestone Hotel**

Kingsbridge TQ7 3NN
Map 3: SX76
Tel: 01548 560382
Fax: 01548 561069
Telephone for furthr details

Directions: A381 (Kingsbridge), then A379 (Churchstow), turn onto B3197, then turn into lane signposted Thurlestone

There's a stylish restaurant and new terrace at this hotel, which affords wonderful views of the Devon coast. Lime crème brûlée was the highlight of a recent meal.

TORQUAY, **The Grand**

Edwardian hotel with fine bay views. Dinner in the formal Gainsborough Restaurant might be carpaccio of smoked sirloin with spring onion and yellow pepper dressing, and grilled breast of mallard duckling with pickled walnut sauce.

Accommodation: 110 en suite ★ ★ ★ ★

Directions: From M5 take A380 to Torquay. At seafront turn 1st R. Hotel on corner 1st on L

Sea Front TQ2 6NT
Map 3: SX96
Tel: 01803 296677
Fax: 01803 231462
Cost: *Alc* £34.35, set-price L £13.50/D £23.50 (4 courses). ☺ H/wine £10.50
Times: 12.15-2pm/7-9.30pm
Additional: Bar food; Sunday L; Children welcome; ✿ dishes
Smoking: No smoking in dining room

TORQUAY, **Grosvenor Hotel**

Belgrave Road TQ2 5HG
Map 3: SX96
Tel: 01803 294373/215515
Fax: 01803 291032
Telephone for further details

Directions: Telephone for directions

Mima's at the Grosvenor is an intimate, romantic restaurant with rustic charm. Highlights of the modern British menu include spicy Thai fish soup, and a dish of liver and bacon served with onion mash and rich onion sauce.

TORQUAY, **Imperial Hotel**

Well-established hotel with fabulous harbour views. Expect high standards of service and fresh-tasting traditional dishes such as seafood ravioli with fennel, and roasted fillet of lamb.

Park Hill Road TQ1 1DG
Map 3: SX96
Tel: 01803 294301
Fax: 01803 298293
Telephone for further details

Imperial Hotel

Directions: M5 to Exeter, A380 then A3022 to Torquay. Park Hill Road is off Torwood Street/Babbacombe Road, just N of new harbour

TORQUAY, Mulberry House

Victorian villa providing a civilised atmosphere for enjoyable cooking. Highly recommended are the marvellous home-made breads and sautéed lambs'kidneys in Marsala with sweetcorn purée.

1 Scarborough Road TQ2 5UJ
Map 3: SX96
Tel: 01803 213639
Cost: *Alc* £16.50, set-price L £7.95. ☺
H/wine £9.50
Times: Noon-1.30pm/7.30-9pm.
Closed D Sun, (all Mon & Tue except residents)
Additional: Sunday L; Children welcome;
🌢 dishes
Smoking: No smoking in dining room
Accommodation: 3 en suite
Credit cards: None

Directions: From the seafront turn up Belgrave Road, then 1st L into Scarborough Road.

TORQUAY, Orestone Manor 🌸🌸

Rockhouse Lane Maidencombe
TQ1 4SX
Map 3: SX96
Tel: 01803 328098
Fax: 01803 328336
Chef: Wayne Pearson
Owners: Bill & Gill Dagworthy
Cost: Set-price D £29.50. H/wine
£11.95

A sense of dedication prevails at Bill and Gill Dagworthy's attractive Georgian hotel. Elegance and comfort ooze, but the big draw is cooking that is very much in the modern mould, with a peppering of influences from the Mediterranean enlivening such dishes as hot scallop mousseline with pesto cream, and breast of Barbary duckling with oyster mushroom risotto. Other interesting ideas include a best end of lamb with rhubarb crumble and roasted red mullet with kedgeree. Desserts range from warm honey and walnut tart with vanilla ice cream to traditional bread-and-butter pudding.

Directions: Off A379 Torquay/Teignmouth coastal road, turn R on Watcombe Hill opposite Brunel Manor.

Times: D only 7-8.45pm. Closed 1st 2 wks Jan
Additional: Children 8+; ⚫ dishes
Seats: 40. Private dining room 12
Smoking: No smoking in dining room
Accommodation: 18 en suite ★ ★ ★

TORQUAY, The Osborne Hotel

Hesketh Crescent Meadfoot TQ1 2LL
Map 3: SX96
Tel: 01803 213311
Fax: 01803 296788
Chef: Neil Fanous
Owners: Caparo Hotels
Cost: *Alc* £25, set-price D £17.95. ☺
H/wine £10.50
Times: D only 7-9.45pm
Additional: Bar food; Sunday L; Children welcome; ⚫ dishes
Seats: 68. Private dining room 30
Smoking: No smoking in dining room
Accommodation: 29 en suite ★ ★ ★

Traditional hotel setting with correct service. The 'Gastronomic' dinner typically starts with double beef consommé with ravioli of wild mushrooms, or buckwheat blini with smoked salmon, sour cream and keta, then a sorbet such as green apple and Calvados. Main courses might include medallions of venison with a casserole of Puy lentils and winter vegetables or chargrilled collops of monkfish with braised fennel and roasted garlic. Finish in style with lemon bavarois with raspberry coulis and spun sugar spirals or warm mulled pear Bakewell tart served with a quenelle of clotted cream and a cinnamon crème anglaise. Local cheeses, with celery, apple and walnuts, include Cornish Yarg, Harbourne Blue and Tiskey Meadow. The good value daily menu does not lack for interest – baked escalope of freshwater pike with spicy Creole sauce and saffron rice made at least one hardened inspector look again with renewed interest.

Directions: Follow A3022 to seafront, turn L towards Harbour. At Clock Tower turn L; at next junction/traffic lights turn R. Over brow of hill and gates of Hesketh Crescent and hotel are opposite.

TORQUAY,
The Table Restaurant

Tiny end-of-terrace Victorian house run with single-handed passion. All the meat and most of the produce is West Country organic – a mark of commitment that exemplifies the kitchen philosophy to uphold high standards without commercial compromise. And all ingredients are freshly procured on the day by Julie Tuckett who also greets, seats, serves and cooks. She specialises in game dishes – usually cooked very pink – such as gamey roast mallard with red cabbage. Other beautifully cooked main courses have included supreme of

135 Babbacombe Road TQ1 3SR
Map 3: SX96
Tel/Fax: 01803 324292
Chef/Owner: Julie Tuckett
Cost: Set-price L £12.85 (2 courses)/D £28.50. H/wine £11
Times: 12.15-1.30pm/7.15-9.30pm. Closed L Fri & Sat, 2 wks early Feb, 2 wks end Mar
Additional: Sunday L; Children 11+; ⚫ dishes

chicken filled with spinach and ricotta cheese, and fillet of Welsh veal with leeks and orange. Fish catch of the day is simply 'very fresh and simply cooked'. Fish soup just burst with flavour, as did perfect risotto with sautéed pigeon breasts, Calvados and herbs. Her special spin on bread-and-butter pudding takes in ginger and orange, whilst the near-legendary 'very serious' chocolate terrine has to be tasted to be believed.

Seats: 16
Smoking: No pipes & cigars

Directions: From Torquay harbour follow signs for Babbacombe (approx 2 miles). Restaurant on L where road flattens after rising

TORQUAY, Toorak Hotel

Well appointed hotel opposite the Riviera Centre offering a fixed-price evening menu with dishes such as pesto-coated fillet of hake, and collops of ostrich with spaghetti of vegetables.

Smoking: No smoking in dining room
Accommodation: 92 en suite ★ ★ ★

Directions: Opposite Riviera Conference Centre

Chestnut Avenue TQ2 5JS
Map 3: SX96
Tel: 01803 400400
Fax: 01803 400140
Cost: Set-price D £16.75 (5 courses). ☺ H/wine £9.95
Times: D only, 7-9pm
Additional: Bar food L; Children welcome; ❹ dishes

TOTNES, Durant Arms

Attractive 18th-century inn offering a good choice of seafood dishes – scallops and monkfish with bacon and cream sauce, or poached halibut with broccoli and cheese sauce. Alternatively, there's rack of lamb in blackberry and apple sauce.

Smoking: No-smoking area; No pipes & cigars
Accommodation: 3 en suite

Directions: Telephone for directions

Ashprington TQ9 7UP
Map 3: SX86
Tel: 01803 732240
Fax: 01803 732471
Cost: *Alc* £18, set-price L&D £6.75 (1 course). ☺ H/wine £8.95
Times: Noon-2pm/6.30-9.15pm
Additional: Bar food; Sunday L; Children welcome; ❹ dishes

TWO BRIDGES,
Prince Hall Hotel

The panoramic view over the West Dart River onto the rolling hills beyond is as magnificent as ever. Inside renovation has greatly enhanced the exposed granite stone walls which are the main feature of the hotel restaurant. Added sophistication has been given by quartz-lit table tops. The Anglo-French carte changes nightly: a February dinner saw game consommé with a dash of port, pan-fried peppered Brixham monkfish with a shellfish sauce, and a brace of boneless quail served on a nest of sweet-and-sour cabbage with raspberry vinegar sauce. Later in the year there were stir-fried shell-on prawns with garlic butter, supreme of chicken Veronique with vermouth cream and asparagus tips, with warm apple and cinnamon pie with vanilla ice cream as an ever-popular dessert. The set dinner also includes a West Country cheese board.

PL20 6SA
Map 2: SX67
Tel: 01822 890403
Fax: 01822 890676
Chefs: Adam Southwell, Les Pratt
Owners: Adam & Carrie Southwell
Cost: Set-price D £25 (4 courses). ☺ H/wine £8.95
Times: D only, 7-8.30pm. Closed Jan
Additional: Children 12+; ❹ dishes
Seats: 26
Smoking: No smoking in dining room
Accommodation: 8 en suite ★ ★

Directions: From Two Bridges take B3357 Dartmeet Road; hotel is hidden 1 mile on R

TWO BRIDGES,
Two Bridges Hotel

Unusual, idiosyncratic Dartmoor hotel. A fascinating history lies behind this delightful Dartmoor hotel which offers the weary traveller a warm and welcoming atmosphere. Huge log fires, enveloping easy chairs, and an eclectic collection of

Dartmoor PL20 6SW
Map 2: SX67
Tel: 01822 890581
Fax: 01822 890575
Chef: Andrew Shortman
Owner: Warm Welcome Hotels

Two Bridges Hotel

Cost: *Alc* £24.95, set-price L £9.95 (2 courses)/D £21.95. ☺ H/wine £9.95
Times: Noon-2.30pm/7-9pm
Additional: Bar food; Sunday L; Children welcome; ✷ dishes
Seats: 100. Private room 26
Smoking: No smoking in dining room; Air conditioning
Accommodation: 29 en suite ★ ★

Directions: From Tavistock take B3357, hotel at junction with B3312

ephemera and artwork all contribute to the individuality and relaxing atmosphere. Traditional bar food is served in the Saracen's Bar, ideally washed down with a pint or two of the locally brewed Jail Ale. The refurbished restaurant now boasts oak panelling, decorative plasterwork and two stunning chandeliers. The *carte* features locally sourced produce such as mousseline of guinea-fowl spiked with duck liver and wild rabbit and served with tropical fruit chutney, plus an interesting spin on a local speciality – a superb darne of River Dart salmon on risotto with bell pepper and basil broth, topped with roasted fennel. Dessert, a pavé of white chocolate with dark chocolate sauce, typified the care and attention which went into the whole meal.

WHIMPLE, Woodhayes Hotel

EX5 2TD
Map 3: SY09
Tel: 01404 822237
Fax: 01404 822337
Cost: Set-price D £30 (5 courses). ☺ H/wine £12.50
Times: D only at 8pm. Closed mid Dec-mid Jan
Additional: Children 12+; ✷ dishes
Smoking: No smoking in dining room
Accommodation: 8 en suite

Directions: On A30 midway Honiton/Exeter. Straight down Whimple Road, first building on R

Gracious Georgian building with a restaurant in gentle shades of peaches and cream. A set five-course dinner of carefully cooked dishes is served on the dot of eight.

WINKLEIGH, Pophams

Small, intimate and popular – an idiosyncratic restaurant.
Melvyn Popham and Dennis Hawkes do it their way and over the years have drawn phenomenal support for an operation that is only open for lunch four day a week and is booked up weeks/months ahead. Originally a deli, the 'shop' remains intact: bay window, two or three tables, and a refrigerated counter holding iced water with lime, and wine which guests must bring themselves. The kitchen is larger than the dining area and air

Castle Street EX19 8HQ
Map 3: SS60
Tel: 01837 83767
Chef: Melvyn Popham
Owners: Melvyn Popham, Dennis Hawkes
Cost: *Alc* £26. Unlicenced (BYO)
Times: L only, noon-1.30pm. Closed Sun, Mon, Tue, Feb
Additional: Children 14+

conditioning keeps the temperature down when the pans are flying. Quality of ingredients is foremost in Melvyn's mind when preparing menus and the strength of his cooking lies in a consistency that never falters. We could not fault our summer meal. Bread came straight from the oven and was offered with local Devon butter. Gazpacho was perfectly balanced, and a simple dish of prawns asparagus and salmon was top-notch in terms of quality and simply dressed with lemon oil with lemon and olive oil added. Both our lamb in pastry with mushroom pâté and red wine jus, and roasted breast of duck marinated in cinnamon, orange and port with Madeira sauce (and accompanied by sautéed apples) could not have been improved. Real skills came through in a rich chocolate charlotte with a lovely white chocolate ice cream and coffee bean sauce, and an orange tart with orange coulis was so good that we could have eaten more. Coffee is made to order, the rich aroma permeates the room, and is served with home-made peppermint creams.

Seats: 10
Smoking: Totally no smoking establishment; Air conditioning

Directions: In village centre, about 9 miles from Okehampton

WOOLACOMBE, Little Beach Hotel

An Edwardian seafront hotel with splendid views over Morte Bay. Wholesome home-cooking is the order of the day: cream of vegetable soup, and steak pie with new potatoes and broccoli.

Directions: Telephone for directions

The Esplanade EX34 7DJ
Tel: 01271 870398
Telephone for further details

WOOLACOMBE, Watersmeet Hotel

High above a rocky inlet with magnificent views across the Bristol Channel. Typical dishes include poached supreme of maize-fed chicken with Pernod sauce, and roast pork with crackling, apple sauce and onion stuffing.

Mortehoe EX34 7EB
Map 2: SS44
Tel: 01271 870333
Fax: 01271 870890
Cost: *Alc* £23.50, set-price D £26.50 (5 courses). ☺ H/wine £9.85
Times: Noon-2pm/7-8.30pm. Closed Dec, Jan
Additional: Children 8+; ❹ dishes
Smoking: No smoking in dining room; Jacket & tie preferred
Accommodation: 24 en suite ★★★

Directions: M5/J27. Follow A361 to Woolacombe, R at beach car park, 300 yds on R

YELVERTON,
Moorland Links Hotel

Spacious restaurant with views over oak-fringed lawns to the Tamar Valley. Fresh local produce features on an imaginative menu, and live music is a weekend feature.

Smoking: No smoking in dining room
Accommodation: 45 en suite ★★★

Directions: On A386, within Dartmoor National Park

PL20 6DA
Map 2: SX56
Tel: 01822 852245
Fax: 01822 855004
Cost: Set-price L & D £21. ☺ H/wine £8.95
Times: 12.30-2pm/7.30-10pm. Closed L Sat, L Bhs
Additional: Bar food; Sunday L; Children welcome; ❹ dishes

DORSET

BEAMINSTER,
Bridge House Hotel

Small country house hotel with long-standing staff, offering something quaint and British. The heart of the property is 13th century, and the small cottagey dining room, although Georgian in character, projects an air of relaxation. The kitchen have the sense to keep things simple, the idea being to serve good food at reasonable prices with a mix of simple dishes for their older clientele mixed in with some more innovative items. Thus gravad lax with a dill and mustard sauce, or a salad of pigeon breast, feta cheese and tomato in balsamic vinegar, could open the set-price dinner. Roasted breast of chicken with thyme and rosemary, or fillet of cod served on provençale vegetables maintain the theme. Desserts include a good caramelised soufflé with walnuts.

Directions: On A3066, 200m down hill from town centre

3 Prout Bridge DT8 3AY
Map 3: ST40
Tel: 01308 862200
Fax: 01308 863700
Chef: Simon Clewlow
Owner: Peter Pinkster
Cost: Set-price L £12/D £25.50 (4 courses). ☺ H/wine £9.50.
Times: Noon-2pm/7-9pm
Additional: Sunday L; Children welcome; 🍴 dishes
Seats: 36. Private dining room 16
Smoking: No smoking in dining room
Accommodation: 14 en suite ★ ★ ★

BLANDFORD FORUM,
Castleman Hotel

In the same family for over 150 years, quirky with bags of character. The building dates from the 16th century and for a small hotel has loads of public areas (two large lounges in addition to the bar). The evening *carte* offers some seven choices at each course, the cooking has a comfortable country feel with sufficient modern touches to retain interest and everything is freshly cooked. Celery and Stilton soup comes with cheese straws, for example, whereas calves' liver, pork and bacon terrine is paired with a bright, breezy butternut squash chutney. Roast duck leg confit is a classic with potato and cabbage pancake and red wine jus, yet haddock fillet is updated with tomato, red pepper, vermouth and basil sauce. Desserts range from the nursery blackberry and apple crumble with clotted cream, to the sophisticated elderflower and lemon sorbet with langues de chat biscuit.

Directions: 1 mile from A354. Hotel is signposted within village

Chettle DT11 8DB
Map 3: ST80
Tel: 01258 830096
Fax: 01258 830051
Chefs: Barbara Garnsworthy, Richard Morris
Owners: Barbara Garnsworthy, Edward Bourke
Cost: *Alc* £22, set-price L £14. ☺ H/wine £9.
Times: D only, 7pm-9.30pm. Closed Feb
Additional: Sunday L (noon-1.30pm); Children welcome; 🍴 dishes
Seats: 40
Smoking: No smoking in dining room
Accommodation: 8 en suite

BOURNEMOUTH,
Bistro on the Beach

Smashing place right on the beach. It's not the most striking of buildings, but that doesn't stop people from flocking here for sound, good value, cooking. Booking is essential if you want to enjoy the likes of cod on a bed of roasted peppers, or pan-fried breast of chicken with grain mustard sauce.

Additional: Children welcome; 🍴 dishes
Smoking: Air conditioning

Directions: Telephone for directions

Solent Promenade Southbourne BH6 4BE
Map 4: SZ09
Tel: 01202 431473
Fax: 01202 252091
Cost: *Alc* £17, set-price D £15.50. ☺ H/wine £8.95
Times: D only, 7-9.30pm. Closed Sun, Mon, Tue, 3wks Nov, 1 wk Xmas, 2 wks Apr

BOURNEMOUTH,

Carlton Hotel

On clear days enjoy magnificent sea views across to the Isle of Wight. Eat in Frederick's Restaurant for the likes of wild mushroom ravioli with creamy tarragon sauce, and risotto of asparagus with black truffle oil and shavings of Parmesan.

Smoking: No smoking in dining room; Air conditioning
Accommodation: 73 en suite ★★★★

Directions: M3/M27, follow A338 (Bournemouth). Follow signs to town centre and East Overcliff. Hotel is on seafront

East Overcliff BH1 3DN
Map 4: SZ09
Tel: 01202 552011
Fax: 01202 299573
Cost: Alc £28.50, set-price L £16.50/D £25. H/wine £13
Times: 12.30-1.45pm/7-9.45pm
Additional: Bar food; Sunday L; Children welcome; dishes

BOURNEMOUTH,

Chine Hotel

Wine is one of the MD's great passions, and his world travels have borne fruit in a fine list with good, skilful cooking to match, served in the richly-coloured 'Sea View' restaurant.

Boscombe Spa Road BH5 1AX
Map 4: SZ09
Tel: 01202 396234
Fax: 01202 391737
Cost: Set-price L £14.50/ D £18.50. ☺ H/wine £10.95
Times: 12.30pm-2pm/7-8.30pm. Closed L Sat
Additional: Bar Food L; Sunday L; Children welcome; menu
Smoking: No smoking in dining room. Jacket & tie required
Accommodation: 92 en suite ★★★

Directions: From M27, A31 and A338 follow signs to Boscombe Pier, Boscombe Spa Road is off Christchurch Road near Boscombe Gardens

BOURNEMOUTH, **Farthings**

Victorian coach house in the town centre with four separate dining areas and al fresco summer eating. Canapés, vegetables or salad, petits fours and coffee are included in the cost of the freshly prepared main courses.

5/7 Grove Road BH1 3AS
Map 4: SZ09
Tel: 01202 558660
Fax: 01202 293766
Cost: Alc £26, set-price L £13/D £23. ☺ H/wine £11
Times: Noon-2pm/7-10pm. Closed D Sun, all Mon, Jan-Mar
Additional: Sunday L; dishes
Smoking: No-smoking area
Accommodation: 5 rooms

Directions: On roundabout, top of hill on Bath Road going from Pier to Lansdowne

BOURNEMOUTH,

Langtry Manor Hotel

Built by Edward VII for Lillie Langtry, the house is perfect for a modern-day romantic break. Staff in period costume provide polished service. Try game soup flamed with brandy, followed by baked Wiltshire pork chop with glazed chestnuts.

Smoking: No smoking in dining room; Jacket & tie preferred
Accommodation: ★ ★ ★

Directions: On the East Cliff, at corner of Derby and Knyveton Roads

26 Derby Road BH1 3QB
Map 4: SZ09
Tel: 01202 553887
Fax: 01202 290115
Cost: *Alc* £24.75, set-price D £21.75 (5 courses). ☺ H/wine £9.95
Times: D only, 7-9pm
Additional: Bar food L; Children welcome

BOURNEMOUTH, **Queens Hotel** ✿

Spacious open-plan hotel restaurant flooded with lots of natural light. A sound choice of dishes might include herb-crusted roast rack of lamb and grilled whole Poole Bay plaice.

Smoking: No smoking in dining room; Air conditioning
Accommodation: 114 en suite ★ ★ ★

Directions: Follow signs to East Cliff, hotel is one road back from seafront

Meyrick Road East Cliff BH1 3DL
Map 4: SZ09
Tel: 01202 554415
Fax: 01202 294810
Cost: *Alc* £20, set-price L £8.95/D £17.95. ☺ H/wine £10.25
Times: 12.30-1.30pm/7-8.30pm
Additional: Bar food; Sunday L; Children welcome; ⁍ dishes

BOURNEMOUTH,

Royal Bath Hotel ✿✿

Hotel restaurant with rich, striking colours and a high level of comfort. Oscar's restaurant has been given a complete makeover as part of an ongoing refurbishment programme. The menus have a distinctly modern feel – note properly cooked fillet of red mullet with saffron risotto, although rather overwhelmed by the addition of an anise dressing, and a terrine of foie gras with apple and pear chutney. Pan-fried calves' liver with bacon, black pudding, caramelised apples and rosemary mash, fillet of sea bass with succulent and sweet roasted peppers, or duck breast with a 'dumpling' of the leg, spicy couscous and a ginger sauce reveal that the kitchen has its finger on the button. A flair for puddings shows up in chocolate tart with orange and Grand Marnier sorbet, and there may even be peach Melba.

Bath Road BH1 2EW
Map 4: SZ09
Tel: 01202 555555
Fax: 01202 554158
Chef: Peter Leyland-Jones
Owner: De Vere Hotels
Cost: *Alc* £35, set-price L £16.50/D £30 (4 courses). H/wine £12.50
Times: 12.30-2pm/7-10pm
Additional: Bar food L; Sunday L; Children welcome; ⁍ dishes
Seats: 48. Private dining rooms 10-400
Smoking: No-smoking area; Air conditioning
Accommodation: 140 en suite
★ ★ ★ ★ ★

Directions: Follow signs for Bournemouth Pier and beaches

BOURNEMOUTH,

Swallow Highcliff Hotel

There's a strong emphasis on fish in the classy-looking Robert Wild Room. Fresh chargrilled tuna, marinated tail of local monkfish and pan-fried sea bass may be amongst dishes prepared to order and presented in rather elaborate style.

Additional: Bar food L; Sunday L; Children welcome; 🌢 dishes
Smoking: No smoking in dining room. Jacket & tie preferred
Accommodation: 157 en suite ★ ★ ★ ★

Directions: Telephone for directions

St Michael's Road West Cliffe
Map 4: SZ09
Tel: 01202 557702
Fax: 01202 292734
Cost: *Alc* £32.50, set-price D £22. ☺
H/wine £12.50
Times: D only, 7-10pm. Closed Sun,
Mon, Xmas

BRIDPORT, **Horseshoes**

Cosy village inn with understated style in the heart of mellow Dorset countryside. Local produce features strongly on the daily-changing blackboard with fish predominating. Try grilled Lyme Bay plaice or turbot fillet with saffron sauce and crispy air-dried ham.

Additional: Bar Food; Sunday L; Children 8+ at D; 🌢 dishes
Smoking: No smoking in dining room

Directions: In the village of Powerstock, 5 miles NE of Bridport, signposted off A3066 Beaminster Road.

Powerstock DT6 3TF
Map 3: SY49
Tel/Fax: 01308 485328
Cost: *Alc* £20. ☺ H/wine £8.75
Times: Noon-2pm (3pm Sat & Sun)/7-9.30pm (10pm Sat)

BRIDPORT,

Riverside Restaurant

West Bay DT6 4EZ
Map 3: SY49
Tel: 01308 422011
Chefs: Mike Mills, Nic Larcombe
Owners: Janet & Arthur Watson
Cost: *Alc* £20. ☺ H/wine £12
Times: Noon-2.15pm/6.30-8.45pm.
Closed D Sun, all Mon (except Bhs),
29 Nov-26 Feb
Additional: Sunday L; Children
welcome; 🌢 dishes
Seats: 70. Private dining room 16
Smoking: No pipes & cigars

Directions: In the centre of West Bay
by the river

Simple seafood restaurant with bare wooden tables, chunky water glasses and background jazz. A small walkway leads to this engaging relaxed place, while views of West Bay and glimpses of the channel beyond set the scene for some fantastic food. The emphasis is on locally-landed fish – the short set menu is backed up by additional blackboard specials which vary according to the state of the sea and the success of the local fishermen. We dined on a mountain of seared scallops, mussels, oysters and warm water prawns – and that was just the starter! This was followed by grilled fillet of brill 'wonderfully fresh', served with crispy spinach and sauce deauvillaise. Desserts are another highlight: try prune and Armagnac tartlet, or crème brûlée.

CHARMOUTH,
Thatch Lodge ✿✿

Charming 14th-century hotel which still has thick cobb walls, oak beams and an inglenook fireplace. Sensitive restoration by current owners, Christopher and Andrea Worsfold, has created a peaceful environment, enhanced by unusual artefacts. They are enthusiastic hosts, with Andrea building her menus around fresh local produce. Expect dishes such as creamy wild mushroom risotto with Parmesan shavings, and fresh mango and fig salad.

Directions: Charmouth, off A35, 2 miles E of Lyme Regis. Hotel on R half way up High Street

The Street DT6 6PQ
Map 3: SY39
Tel/Fax: 01297 560407
Chef: Andrea Ashton-Worsfold
Cost: Set-price D £25 (4 courses). H/wine £10.50
Times: D only at 7.30pm. Closed Sun, Mon, Jan-mid Mar
Seats: 14
Smoking: Totally non-smoking hotel
Accommodation: 7 en suite ★ ★

CHIDEOCK,
Chideock House Hotel ✿

Main Street DT6 6JN
Map 3: SY49
Tel: 01297 489242
Fax: 01297 489184
Cost: *Alc* £25, set-price D £20.
H/wine £9.50
Times: D only, 7-9pm. Closed D Sun & Mon, Jan
Additional: Sunday L (1st Sun of month, noon-2pm); Children welcome
Smoking: No smoking in dining room
Accommodation: 7 en suite ★ ★
Credit cards: None

Directions: 3 miles W of Bridport, fronting onto A35 in centre of village.

Dating from the 15th century, the comfortable dining room has age-darkened beams and a huge inglenook fireplace. The cooking keeps it simple, emphasising quality, and both food and setting are in tune with each other.

CHRISTCHURCH, Avonmouth ✿

Attractive hotel restaurant with a waterside setting alongside Mudeford Quay. The menu is a mixture of classic French and modern British dishes featuring locally supplied fish.

Smoking: No smoking in dining room
Accommodation: 40 en suite ★ ★ ★

Directions: Close to bridge over Avon on A35. Hotel is on the approach to Mudeford Quay

95 Mudeford BH23 3NT
Map 4: SZ19
Tel: 01202 483434
Fax: 01202 479004
Cost: *Alc* £18, set-price L £7.95 (2 courses)/D £20. H/wine £10.95
Times: 12.30-2pm/6.45-8.45pm. Closed L Sat, 24-26, 31 Dec
Additional: Bar Food L; Sunday L; Children welcome; 🍴 dishes

CHRISTCHURCH, Splinters ✿✿

A listed building situated in a cobbled street. Inside, diners have a choice of where to eat: the private cellar room, complete with wine racks; the light, 'modern' blue room; another furnished with intimate pine booths; plus a first-floor drawing room (for coffee after the meal or available as a separate dining room). The menu is appealing and well-

12 Church Street
BH23 1BW
Map 4: SZ19
Tel: 01202 483454
Fax: 01202 480180
Chef: Jason Davenport
Owners: Timothy Lloyd, Robert Wilson

Splinters

Cost: *Alc* £32.50, set-price L £18.50.
H/wine £11.95
Times: Noon-2pm/7-10pm. Closed
Sun, Mon, 26 Dec
Additional: Brasserie; Children
welcome; dishes
Seats: 40. Private dining room 8-22
Smoking: No smoking in dining room

balanced. Describing itself as modern international, and in spite of offering various dishes from other parts of the world, this cuisine owes most to France. A roast loin of lamb with basil couscous and minted béarnaise had a superb appearance, the meat well trimmed, cooked pinkish and thinly sliced, while orange shortbread surrounded by strawberries and a Champagne sabayon was crisp and delicious. Its accompanying vanilla ice cream was home-made, as were excellent walnut and other breads.

Directions: Splinters is directly in front of Priory Gates

CHRISTCHURCH,
Waterford Lodge Hotel ✿

Colourful gardens and ornamental fishpond focus the view from the restaurant, which majors in an equally bright, globally aware style of cooking, say tortellini of Thai spiced prawns scented with lemon grass and lime.

Smoking: No smoking in dining room
Accommodation: 18 en suite ★ ★ ★

Directions: From A35 Somerford roundabout take A337 towards Highcliffe, at next roundabout turn R to Mudeford, hotel on L

87 Bure Lane Friars Cliff Mudeford
BH23 4DN
Map 4: SZ19
Tel: 01425 272948
Fax: 01425 279130
Cost: Set-price D £25.50. H/wine
£11.30
Times: Noon-1.30pm/7-9pm
Additional: Bar food L; Sunday L;
Children welcome; dishes

CORFE CASTLE,
Mortons House Hotel ✿

Time has only improved the Elizabethan manor: deep stone walls provide a cool summer retreat and warm winter haven. The cooking also lifts the spirits, especially cream of white onion and Brie soup and roast loin of lamb with garlic and butter bean stew.

Smoking: No smoking in dining room
Accommodation: 17 en suite ★ ★ ★

Directions: In centre of village on A351

East Street BH20 5EE
Map 3: SY98
Tel: 01929 480988
Fax: 01929 480820
Cost: *Alc* £22, set-price L £12.50/D
£22.50 (6 courses). ☺ H/wine £11
Times: Noon-2pm/7-8.30pm
Additional: Bar food L; Sunday L;
Children welcome; dishes

CRANBORNE,
La Fosse at Cranborne

London House The Square BH21 5PR
Map 4: SU01
Tel: 01725 517604
Fax: 01725 517778
Cost: *Alc* £20, set-price L £6.50 (2 courses)/D £10.95 (2 courses). ☺ H/wine £9.95
Times: Noon-2pm/7-10pm. Closed L Sat, D Sun, all Mon, 26 Dec
Additional: Sunday L; Children welcome; 🌱 dishes
Smoking: No smoking in dining room
Accommodation: 5 en suite

Directions: M27 – W on to A31 to Ringwood, then to Verwood, then Cranborne

Delightful restaurant in a village setting. Recommended dishes include fillet of cod with pesto crust and lobster sauce, and strawberry trifle with Muscat. Lunch is particularly good value.

DORCHESTER, **The Mock Turtle**

Town-centre restaurant on three floors with a relaxed atmosphere and comfy seating. Wonderful crab soup was followed by pan-fried pork tenderloin with lime and green peppercorn sauce.

Additional: 🌱 dishes
Smoking: No smoking in dining room

Directions: Town centre, top of High West Street

34 High West Street DT1 1UP
Map 3: SY69
Tel: 01305 264011
Cost: *Alc* £23, set-price L £15/D £22. ☺ H/wine £8.95
Times: Noon-2pm/7-9.30pm. Closed L Sat & Mon, all Sun, 25-27, 31 Dec

DORCHESTER, **Yarlbury Cottage**

300-year-old thatched cottage with oak beams and inglenooks in both lounge and restaurant. Medallions of venison, and turbot with roasted garlic are typical fare.

Additional: Children welcome; 🌱 dishes
Smoking: No smoking in dining room
Accommodation: 8 en suite

Directions: Two miles east of Dorchester, off A35

Lower Bockhampton DT2 8PZ
Map 3: SY69
Tel: 01305 262382
Fax: 01305 266412
Cost: Set-price D £22. ☺ H/wine £9.50
Times: D only, 7-9pm. Closed 27 Dec-31 Jan

EVERSHOT, **Summer Lodge**

Delightful family-run hotel in a picturesque Dorset village is worth the detour. Our lunch was heralded by a wonderful smell of freshly baked bread, followed by duck liver parfait and Cumberland sauce, then pan-fried fillet of sea bream with chive sauce, leaf spinach, asparagus and home-made tagliatelle, finishing with vanilla crème brûlée. Sunday lunches have a strong following, and need booking well in advance. The evening *carte* is more expensive, but rightly so. Timothy Ford prepares and cooks each dish to order, and although more simply cooked food is available on request, it seems a shame not to sample some fine game cooking in the form of pithiviers of local pheasant and truffle with port wine

DT2 0JR
Map 3: ST50
Tel: 01935 83424
Fax: 01935 83005
Chef: Timothy Ford
Owners: Nigel & Margaret Corbett
Cost: *Alc* £44, set-price L £13.75/D £37.50 (4 courses). ☺ H/wine £11.75
Times: 12.30-2pm/7-9pm
Additional: Bar food L; Sunday L; Children 7+ at D; 🌱 dishes
Seats: 40. Private dining room 20
Smoking: No smoking in dining room
Accommodation: 17 en suite ★ ★ ★

Summer Lodge

sauce, marinated saddle of venison with beetroot purée, and roasted saddle of wild rabbit with risotto of morels and an orange and thyme sauce. Non-game eaters might prefer pan-fried fillets of John Dory on herb risotto with balsamic dressing or Cornish fishcakes with deep-fried vegetables and a lemon butter sauce.

Signature dishes: steamed cutlet of Dorset spring lamb, finished with a tarragon mousse; torte of duck foie gras layered with globe artichoke hearts, served with a summer truffle dressing; pink roasted saddle of Melbury venison with honey glazed chestnuts and quinces; pan-fried fillet of Cornish sea bass served on fennel confit with aubergine caviar.

Directions: 1 mile W off A37, between Dorchester and Yeovil. Entrance in Summer Lane

GILLINGHAM,

Stock Hill Hotel

Stock Hill SP8 5NR
Map 3: ST82
Tel: 01747 823626
Fax: 01747 825628
Chefs: Peter Hauser & Lorna Connor
Owners: Peter & Nita Hauser
Cost: Set-price L £20/D £35 (4 courses). H/wine £16.50
Times: 12.30-1.45pm/ 7.30-8.45pm. Closed L Sat & Mon
Additional: Sunday L; Children 7+; dishes
Seats: 24. Private dining room 12. Jacket & tie preferred
Smoking: No smoking in dining room
Accommodation: 10 en suite ★ ★ ★

One of the country's more attractive hotels with a beech-lined driveway that gives a grand first impression. Peter Hauser cooks in a style that combines modern ideas with traditional Austrian, and the kitchen garden behind the hotel is testimony to the kitchen's requirements for the freshest, highest quality ingredients. The communicative menu describes a remarkable range, with particular attention paid to purchasing, technique, and some excellent flavour combinations. The use of spices is impressive. A quenelle of trout hinted at ginger and 'something a bit spicy possibly allspice and pepper' giving another dimension to the fish, and a fat escalope of pork – tender enough to cut with a fork – was teamed with a light Austrian bread and herb dumpling, steamed until melting (far removed from its fatty English cousin), and served with a creamy brandy mustard sauce just lifted with a hint of juniper. And a highly unusual lemon sorbet with fresh marinated dates owed more to verbena or lemon barley than lemon, but the 'untangyness' of the sorbet did match the giant dates, which were served in a marinade of red wine and cinnamon – the whole thing was a huge success. Breads are outstanding, canapés and petits fours show astonishing attention to detail. The wine list is easy to understand, there's a good selection of half-bottles; obviously, Austrian wines feature.

Directions: 3 miles off A303 on B3081

HIGHCLIFFE,
The Lord Bute Restaurant

Lymington Road BH23 4JS
Map 4: SZ29
Tel: 01425 278884
Fax: 01425 279258
Chef: Christopher Denley
Owners: Simon & Christopher Denley, Stephen Caunter
Cost: *Alc* £25, set-price L £13.95/D £19.95. ☺ H/wine £10.95
Times: Noon-2pm/7-10pm. Closed L Sat, D Sun, all Mon
Additional: Sunday L; Children 12+; ● dishes
Seats: 80
Smoking: No smoking in dining room; Air conditioning
Accommodation: 10 en suite

Formal restaurant with a historical pedigree. The present owners built this restaurant tucked away behind one of a pair of Robert Adam lodges in the same classical style in 1989. (The great house, commissioned by Lord Bute, no longer exists.) An orangery has just been added to create a new bar/lounge area. Looking out across the gardens, the fairly formal restaurant sticks largely to traditional favourites – lobster bisque, beef Wellington, Dover sole (grilled or meunière), and traditionally garnished steaks – along with the likes of asparagus and Brie parcels and warm chicken salad with a lime, cumin and coriander marinade plus a cucumber and dill sauce. At lunchtime there is an additional brasserie menu that ranges from bangers and mash, and grilled sardines to red mullet glazed with caper, lemon and saffron butter.

Directions: Follow A337 to Lymington, situated opposite St Mark's churchyard in Highcliffe

LYME REGIS, ## Kersbrook Hotel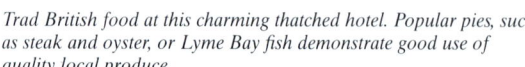

Trad British food at this charming thatched hotel. Popular pies, such as steak and oyster, or Lyme Bay fish demonstrate good use of quality local produce.

Smoking: No-smoking area; No pipes & cigars
Accommodation: 12 en suite ★★

Directions: Town centre – go along main street (Pound Street), turn R at car park into Pound Road, hotel on L

Pound Road DT7 3HX
Map 3: SY39
Tel/Fax: 01297 442596
Cost: *Alc* £16.50, set-price L £8.95/D £16.50 (4 courses). ☺ H/wine £9
Times: 12.30-2pm/7.30-9.30pm. Closed D Sun, L Mon, Fri & Sat
Additional: Bar food L; Sunday L; Children welcome; ● dishes

MAIDEN NEWTON, ## Le Petit Canard

Simple, unfussy decor with spaced tables, lit by candles and tiny white lights, makes for an interesting and easy atmosphere. Jazz plays in the background. The eponymous canard appears in the form of Barbary duck leg, brushed with hoisin, stir-fried and served with peppered Chinese greens and cashews. Creative cooking ideas are highlighted in dishes such as pan-fried red mullet on smoked salmon risotto with crispy leek and watercress oil, and black pepper ice cream and passion fruit sorbet with exotic fruit juice. More classic

Dorchester Road DT2 0BE
Map 3: SY59
Tel/Fax: 01300 320536
Chef: Geoff Chapman
Owners: Lin & Geoff Chapman
Cost: Set-price D £25. H/wine £12
Times: D only, 7.15-8.45pm. Closed Sun & Mon
Additional: Children 9+
Seats: 28
Smoking: No smoking in dining room

combinations are grilled salmon on roasted new potatoes tossed with mustard, dill and chilli crème fraîche, and baked lemon scented chicken breast with coriander pasta. Crème brûlée is given an unusual twist in being served as a torte with rhubarb sorbet and raspberry swirls. Finish with Valrhona chocolate truffles and champagne, or almond-choc chip biscotti with a glass of Muscat.

Directions: In the centre of Maiden Newton 8 miles from Dorchester

POOLE, Haven Hotel

Banks Road BH13 7QL
Map 4: SZ09
Tel: 01202 707333
Fax: 01202 708796
Chef: Karl Heinz Nagler
Owner: FJB Hotels
Cost: *Alc* £30, set-price D £22.50. ☺
H/wine £10.50
Times: D only, 7-9.30pm. Closed Sun, Mon, Xmas, Bhs
Additional: Bar food L; Sunday L; Children welcome; ◕ dishes
Seats: 50. Private room 160
Smoking: No smoking in dining room; Air conditioning
Accommodation: 94 en suite ★★★★

Popular hotel for people of all ages. A stunning water's edge position and fantastic views across Poole Bay say it all. The premier restaurant, La Roche, continues to impress with its modern English dishes. A November meal started with Black Forest ham and grilled asparagus with warm walnut oil dressing. To follow, a 'stunning' terrine of chicken and lobster studded with asparagus and served with braised shallots and a few wild mushrooms. Dessert was a deep-filled citrus tart with a fine layer of caramel and sprinkled with a handful of forest fruits. Lighter meals and snacks are available throughout the day in the conservatory and on the terrace. Wherever you choose to eat however, you can be sure the service will be professional and proper.

Directions: Follow signs to Sandbanks Peninsula; hotel next to Swanage ferry departure point

POOLE, Mansion House Hotel

Smart Georgian hotel, originally built for the mayor in 1779. Tucked away off the Old Quay, this is home to enjoyably honest British food, served up in the hotel's comfortable wood-panelled restaurant. Typical starters (all available as main courses) include grilled scallops with a Thai dressing, twice-baked cheese soufflé, and local mussels cooked with white wine, onions and cream. Our inspector plumped for the home-made soup of the day, which on a chill November evening was a piping hot cream of mushroom. This was followed by calves' liver with bubble-and-squeak, rashers of bacon and a piquant shallot sauce. For dessert, a good hazelnut crème brûlée arrived with a scoop of chocolate ice cream in a tiny brandy snap basket.

Thames Street BH15 1JN
Map 4: SZ09
Tel: 01202 685666
Fax: 01202 665709
Chef: Gerry Godden
Owners: Robert Leonard, Jackie & Gerry Godden
Cost: Set-price L £16.25/D £19.85 (2 courses). ☺ H/wine £12
Times: Noon-2pm/7-9.30pm. Closed L Sat, D Sun, L Bh Mon
Additional: Bar food; Sunday L; Children 5+; ◕ dishes
Seats: 85. Private dining room 32
Smoking: No smoking in dining room; Air conditioning
Accommodation: 32 en suite ★★★

Directions: Follow signs to Channel Ferry/Poole Quay, L at bridge, 1st L is Thames Street

POOLE, **Salterns Hotel**

38 Salterns Way Lilliput BH14 8JR
Map 4: SZ09
Tel: 01202 707321
Fax: 01202 707488
Chef: Nigel Popperwell
Owners: John & Beverley Smith
Cost: *Alc* £30, set-price L £15/D £25.
☺ H/wine £11.50
Times: Noon-1.45pm/7-9.30pm
Additional: Bar food; Sunday L;
Children welcome; ✆ dishes
Seats: 50. Private dining room 50
Smoking: No-smoking area; No pipes
& cigars; Air conditioning
Accommodation: 20 en suite ★ ★ ★

Hotel with glorious views across the harbour to Brownsea Island. Light, modern dishes dominate the cooking. A meal in April took in lemon chicken and tarragon terrine with yellow pepper coulis; pan-fried calves liver with smoked bacon and Puy lentils; and an 'excellent' lime and ginger creme brûlée, rounded off with a 'wonderful' caffeine-injected espresso. The popular Sunday lunch menu has all the usual suspects (wild mushroom and chestnut soup followed by roast beef and Yorkshire pudding) as well as the more adventurous slices of smoked duck with kumquat salad, or fillet of brill with cucumber and crayfish butter sauce. The fairly extensive wine list offers a good number of interesting bottles. There's more casual dining in the pretty bistro.

Directions: From Poole take B3369 for Sandbanks; after 1.5 miles in Lilliput turn R (Salterns Way). Hotel on R at end

POOLE, **Sandbanks Hotel**

15 Banks Road Sandbanks BH13 7PS
Map 4: SZ09
Tel: 01202 707377
Fax: 01202 708885
Cost: Set-price L £14.50/D £18.50. ☺
H/wine £14
Times: 12.30-2pm/7-9pm. Closed L
Sat & all L during peak season
Additional: Sunday L; Children
welcome; ✆ dishes
Smoking: No smoking in dining room;
Air conditioning
Accommodation: 107 en suite ★ ★ ★

Directions: From Poole or
Bournemouth, follow signs to
Sandbanks Peninsula

Comfortable waterside restaurant with views of Poole Bay and the Purbeck Hills. The menu offers a varied choice of interesting dishes using local produce.

SHAFTESBURY, **La Fleur de Lys**

A former coaching inn overlooking Blackmoor Vale. The first-floor restaurant has a friendly, intimate atmosphere – bits and pieces of art contrast nicely with the dark mustard

25 Salisbury Street SP7 8EL
Map 3: ST82
Tel: 01747 853717
Chefs: D Shepherd, M Preston

coloured walls, while green top cloths match the dark green fleur de lys patterned chairs. The menu is modern English with French influences coming through in dishes such as roasted saddle of venison with caramelised pears, shallots and blueberries, and steamed fillets of salmon and lemon sole in a saffron sauce. A meal in early spring got off to a good start with a seafood tartlet of scallops, langoustines and king prawns served with roquette dressed with pesto oil. This was followed by honey roasted breast of guinea fowl sliced onto a bed of freshly-cooked spinach and surrounded by a well-made mustard jus and roasted garlic. Sweets are along the lines of mocha and hazelnut crème brûlée, and lemon ice cream bombe filled with blackcurrant sorbet.

La Fleur de Lys

Owners: D Shepherd, D M Griffin, M Preston
Cost: *Alc* £30, set-price D £23.50. H/wine £11
Times: Noon-2.30pm/7-9.30pm. Closed D Sun, L Mon, 2 wks Jan, all Mon in winter ex Dec
Additional: Sunday L; Children welcome
Seats: 40
Smoking: No smoking before 10pm

Directions: Town centre, near the Post Office, on the main road

SHAFTESBURY, Royal Chase Hotel ✿✿

A former priory located in the heart of Thomas Hardy's Wessex. The well-appointed Byzant restaurant offers an extensive choice of traditional and contemporary dishes. A recent meal started with Portland shellfish bisque – a tasty soup cooked with brandy and Chablis. This was followed by breast of duck filled with kumquat and pinenut stuffing which was colourful and had good flavours. Other main courses could include pot-roasted venison with juniper berries and a rich port wine sauce, and oven-roasted supreme of guinea fowl wrapped in prosciutto. The meal was rounded off with a raspberry crème brûlée, served with a timbale of jellied fruits. Fresh fish is always available: look out for halibut steak served with a cheese, spinach and cream sauce, and steamed fillet of sea bass with a lime, chilli and coriander butter.

Royal Chase Roundabout SP7 8DB
Map 3: ST82
Tel: 01747 853355
Fax: 01747 851969
Chef: Andrew Wheatcroft
Owner: George Hunt
Cost: *Alc* £23.50, set-price L & D £21 (2 courses). ☺ H/wine £11.60
Times: Noon-2pm/7-9pm
Additional: Bar food; Sunday L; Children welcome; 🍴 dishes
Seats: 60. Private dining room 120. Jacket & tie preferred
Smoking: No smoking in dining room
Accommodation: 32 en suite ★ ★ ★

Directions: On roundabout where A350 crosses A30 (avoid town centre)

SHAFTESBURY,
Wayfarers Restaurant ❀❀

Sherborne Causeway SP7 9PX
Map 3: ST82
Tel: 01747 852821
Chef: Mark Newton
Owners: Mark & Clare Newton
Cost: *Alc* £28.80, set-price L & D
£14.95. ☺ H/wine £9.50
Times: Noon-1.30pm/7-9.15pm.
Closed L Sat, D Sun, all Mon, 2 wks
after 25 Dec
Additional: Sunday L (Mar-Sep);
Children 7+; ❹ dishes
Seats: 35. Private room 20

Directions: 2 miles W of Shaftesbury
on main A30 heading towards
Sherborne and Yeovil

Relaxed farmhouse-style restaurant. Bare-stone walls, beamed ceilings and an inglenook with a log fire in cool weather form the backdrop to a somewhat chintzy decor, complete with dried flowers and knick-knacks on wooden shelves. Outside is a courtyard of local stone with apple trees and views of the countryside. The menu defies the surroundings with such starters as confit of duck glazed with hoisin, and main courses of roast fillet of sea bass with pesto and polenta, and roast breast of Barbary duck on creamed spinach with poached pineapple, roast potatoes, and Earl Grey-infused gravy. Care and attention to detail goes into lemon tarte Tatin, an unusual spin on an old favourite, given additional zap with poached strawberries. Bread is said to be very good, petits fours are served with coffee, and the wine list is comprehensive.

SHERBORNE, ## Eastbury Hotel ❀

Enjoy views over the walled gardens from this conservatory restaurant while contemplating choices such as chicken and pistachio mousseline followed by slow-roasted hock of ham.

Smoking: No smoking in dining room
Accommodation: 6 en suite ★ ★ ★

Directions: 800 metres from Abbey

Long Street DT9 3BY
Map 3: ST61
Tel: 01935 813131
Fax: 01935 817296
Cost: *Alc* £19, set-price L £13/D
£16.95. ☺ H/wine £8.45
Times: Noon-2pm/7.30-9.30pm
Additional: Bar Food; Sunday L;
Children welcome; ❹ dishes

SHERBORNE, ## Pheasants Restaurant ❀❀

Restaurant-with-rooms that's popular with parents and visitors to the various boarding schools in the area. This is an extremely comfortable place, a lounge in addition to the bar, and good touches such as exposed stone walls, pale apricot colours, and plenty of space between tables. Local, regional and seasonal produce dictates the menu and in amongst the simpler offerings there's plenty of awareness of what's happening in modern cookery these days. Seared Scottish salmon, for example, is served with a hoisin sauce, sesame seeds and stir-fried vegetables, yet there could also be a classic black pudding and bacon salad with poached egg and raspberry vinegar dressing. Poached halibut with scallops and a butter sauce shows perfect timing, and for meat lovers there's

24 Greenhill DT9 4EW
Map 3: ST61
Tel/Fax: 01935 815252
Chefs: Neil Cadle, Chris Wicks
Owner: Andrew Overhill
Cost: Set-price L £15/D£24. ☺
H/wine £9.50
Times: Noon-1.50pm/6.30-9.50pm.
Closed D Sun, all Mon,
L Tue-Fri, 2 wks mid-Jan
Additional: Sunday L; Children
welcome; ❹ dishes
Seats: 45. Private 12
Smoking: No pipes & cigars
Accommodation: 6 en suite

the perfect combination of lamb noisettes with liver and kidneys, caramelised onions and a lamb jus. Hot buttered fruits with coconut sorbet, and pecan and treacle pie with creamy custard sauce, show sound skills.

Directions: At the top of the High Street, A30 (Salisbury/Yeovil)

STURMINSTER NEWTON,

Plumber Manor ❀❀

Hazelbury Bryan Road
DT10 2AF
Map 3: ST71
Tel: 01258 472507
Fax: 01258 473370
Chef: Brian Prideaux-Brune
Owner: Richard Prideaux-Brune
Cost: *Alc* £23, set-price D £21.50. ☺
H/wine £10
Times: D only 7.30-9pm. Closed Feb
Additional: Sunday L (12.30-1.30pm);
Children welcome; ◑ dishes
Seats: 65. Private dining rooms 26.
Smoking: No smoking in dining room
Accommodation: 16 en suite ★★★

Directions: In Sturminster Newton cross the packhorse bridge, R to Stalbridge (A537). 1st L to Hazelbury Bryan. 2 miles on L opposite Red Lion

A strong country house-style permeates this lovely property, very much run, and advertised, as a restaurant-with-rooms. Careful interpretation of well-tried favourites may be a leitmotif and the cooking is sound, generous and loyal to tradition: witness gravad lax and smoked trout, duck liver pâté with plum relish, lemon sole with smoked haddock mousse, and supreme of chicken with a lemon and tarragon sauce. A juicy, well-hung medallion of beef is served with a Stilton mousse, and vegetables are ample and perfectly cooked. There's an awful lot of mousse-like puddings – chocolate, blackberry, cheesecake – but they are well made.

SWANAGE, Grand Hotel

Burlington Road BH19 1LU
Map 4: SZ07
Tel: 01929 423353
Fax: 01929 427068
Telephone for further details

Wonderful views across Swanage Bay provide a stunning backdrop to dinner at this cliff-top hotel. Kick off with home-made carrot and ginger soup, then loin of pork with sage and lime parfait and a wild mushroom sauce.

Directions: From North Beach end of town into Ulwell Road, 2nd on R

WAREHAM, Kemps Hotel

Modern English cooking offers freshly baked bread served with home-made soup whilst maize-fed chicken supreme comes on a nest of peppered leeks, oyster mushrooms and thyme cream sauce.

Times: Noon-1.30pm/7-9.30pm. Closed L Sat
Additional: Bar food L; Sunday L;
❹ dishes
Smoking: No smoking in dining room
Accommodation: 14 en suite ★ ★

Directions: On A352 midway between Wareham and Wool

East Stoke BH20 6AL
Map 3: SY98
Tel: 01929 462563
Fax: 01929 405287
Cost: *Alc* £22.90, set-price L £9.95/D £20.95 (4 courses). ☺ H/wine £8.95

WAREHAM,

Priory Hotel ❀❀

Delightful 16th-century former priory in an idyllic setting on the banks of the River Frome. Monastic asceticism has given way to sybaritic luxury in the bedrooms and in the vaulted stone cellar which now serves as the main restaurant. Terrine of salmon, crabmeat, asparagus and prawns with saffron and chive dressing indicate a kitchen with a good sense of timing and control of flavours. Accurately roasted breast of chicken stuffed with tomato and Mozzarella mousseline sat on a bed of creamed leeks and chanterelle sauce; accompanying vegetables were sound. For a touch of grandeur, order the fillet of beef Wellington for two, encased in puff pastry, served on a truffled Madeira sauce and carved at the table. Sauces come with a kick – pan-fried calves' liver with crispy pancetta and shallots on a raisin and Brandy sauce; roast breast of duck with braised Puy lentils, caramelised apples and creamy Calvados sauce.

Directions: Town centre between the church and the River Frome

Church Green BH20 4ND
Map 3: SY98
Tel: 01929 551666
Fax: 01929 554519
Chef: Stephen Astley
Owners: Stuart & John Turner
Cost: *Alc* £40.91, set-price L £15.95/D £26.50 (4 courses). H/wine £12.50
Times: 12.30-2pm/7.30-10pm
Additional: Bar food L; Sunday L; Children 8+; ❹ dishes
Seats: 46. Private dining room 22. Jacket & tie preferred
Smoking: No smoking in dining room
Accommodation: 19 en suite ★ ★ ★

WEYMOUTH,

Moonfleet Manor

At the end of a winding country lane with spectacular sea views from the stylish restaurant. Set in front of the hotel like the prow of a ship, it's a restaurant that has plenty going for it – all very much great white hunter goes to the souk, or Terence Conran meets Biba, with Indian artefacts such as carved tables, and the odd tiger skin (actually in the lobby). Chesil Beach is below and the ocean can be seen clearly. Food is sensible, lots of local fish and some decent meat from a local butcher. We tucked into Thai spiced crab cake with sauce Jacqueline, loin of venison on a potato and bacon roulade with glazed chestnuts and port jus, and chocolate mousse with raspberry shortbread and praline.

Fleet DT3 4ED
Map 3: SY67
Tel: 01305 786948
Fax: 01305 774395
Cost: *Alc* £26, set-price L £15.50/D £18.75. ☺ H/wine £11.25
Times: D only, 7-9.30pm
Additional: Sunday L (noon-2pm); Children welcome; ◕ dishes
Smoking: No smoking in dining room
Accommodation: 40 en suite ★ ★ ★

Directions: A354 from Dorchester. R into Weymouth at Manor rdbt. R at next rdbt, L at next rdbt, up hill (B3157) then L, 2 miles towards sea

WEYMOUTH,

Perry's Restaurant

Relaxed, bistro-style restaurant. Marble-topped tables, foodie artwork and cheery painted walls, plus a cosy shop-front feel and blackboard menu spells out the sort of relaxed environment that sees a high level of repeat business. Freshly caught local fish is a speciality (8 choices when we visited), reflecting Perry's great position on the quay ('although murder to park' sighs our reporter). Crab appears in many guises, Portland crab soup, crab gratin, or cracked crab claw salad, or there's grilled whole baby turbot with sea salt and lime, and roast medallions of monkfish with a fricassée of mussels. Meat eaters are not neglected. Crispy confit of duck leg on spring onion mash with a honey and lemon glaze, perhaps, or roast rack of English lamb with gratin daupinoise and red wine sauce. Desserts are comforting ranging from the nursery-style warm apple crumble tart, to the international appeal of brandy snap of home-made banana sorbet with butterscotch sauce.

4 Trinity Road The Old Harbour DT4 8TJ
Map 3: SY67
Tel/Fax: 01305 785799
Chef: Andy Pike
Owners: Raymond, Alan & Vivien Hodder
Cost: *Alc* £23, set-price L £16. ☺ H/wine £8.95
Times: Noon-2pm/7-9.30pm. Closed L Sat & Mon, D Sun Easter-end Aug, 25-27, 31 Dec
Additional: Sunday L; ◕ dishes
Seats: 58. Private dining room 26
Smoking: No-smoking area; No pipes & cigars

Directions: On western side of old harbour – follow signs for Brewers Quay

WEYMOUTH,

The Sea Cow

Quayside restaurant popular with locals and passing tourists. An abundance of local fresh fish and seafood is the draw – look out for wing of Wey Bay skate fried with capers and lemon butter, and whole grilled lemon sole with garlic butter.

7 Custom House Quay DT4 8BE
Map 3: SY67
Tel: 01305 783524
Cost: *Alc* £24.50. ☺ H/wine £10.95
Times: Noon-2pm/7-10.15pm. Closed D Sun in winter, L Mon, 26 Dec-1 Jan
Additional: Sunday L; Children welcome; ◕ dishes

Smoking: No smoking in dining room

Directions: On the quay – park in large car parks near town bridge, 5 mins walk to restaurant

WIMBORNE MINSTER,
Beechleas Hotel ✿✿

17 Poole Road BH21 1QA
Map 4: SZ09
Tel: 01202 841684
Fax: 01202 849344
Cost: Set-price D £21.75. ☺ H/wine
£10.95
Times: D only 7-9pm. Closed Xmas-
New Year
Additional: Children welcome;
🍴 dishes
Smoking: No smoking in dining room
Accommodation: 9 en suite ★ ★

A charming Georgian town house within easy walking distance of the Minster. Our early spring meal of chicken liver parfait with pear and apple chutney, and breast of duck sliced onto a piquant honey sauce with roasted vegetables just hit the spot. A smooth crème brûlée showed desserts were equally on the ball. Breakfast comes with fresh orange juice.

Directions: On A349 at Wimborne

WIMBORNE MINSTER,
Les Bouviers ✿✿

Oakley Hill Merley BH21 1RJ
Map 4: SZ09
Tel/Fax: 01202 889555
Chef/Owner: James Coward
Cost: *Alc* £26.75, set-price L
£12.75/D £23.95 (4 courses). ☺
H/wine £11.50
Times: Noon-2.15pm/7-10pm. Closed
L Sat, D Sun, some Bhs
Additional: Sunday L; Children
welcome; 🍴 dishes
Seats: 40. Private dining rooms 12-30
Smoking: No-smoking area; Air
conditioning

Purple and green might be unusual shades for restaurant decor, but the effect is nonetheless quite charming. The kitchen, too, shows itself to be in tune with its ingredients, and rightly has no qualms in describing the strong but harmonious flavours of the signature hot cheese soufflé with watercress and horseradish sauce as 'renowned'. Technical skill was evident in pan-fried calves' liver on a thin potato rösti enriched with a raspberry scented stock, sliced superbly thin, cooked just pink as requested and given depth by a well balanced sauce. The Menu Surprise offers a chef-selected choice of seven courses, together with four wines served by the glass.

Directions: 0.5 miles south of A31 Wimborne by-pass on A349

DURHAM, COUNTY

BEAMISH, **Beamish Park Hotel**

Well located hotel with a smart, contemporary design. Global
bistro food is served in the conservatory: wok-fried beef fillet
and King prawn Schezuan style with crispy wun-tuns; salmon
and leek rissoles on a whisky and langoustine bisque; slow-
braised brisket in Irish ale with wholegrain mustard mash and
roast parsnip crisps. In the more classically styled dining room,
the cooking goes up a notch with more refined dishes such as
breast of 'maize-fed chicken stuffed with oyster mushroom and
apricot mousseline carved upon roasted pimentos, partnered
with basil, garlic and white wine jus-lie'. They're not too posh,
though, and offer sticky toffee pudding with butterscotch
sauce, but perhaps it's gilding the lily to add both praline ice
cream and compote of winter berries.

Directions: Just off A6076 Newcastle to Stanley road

Beamish Burn Road Marley Hill
NE16 5EG
Map 12: NZ25
Tel: 01207 230666
Fax: 01207 281260
Chef: Steven Justice
Owner: William Walker
Cost: Set-price D £23.50. H/wine
£8.95
Times: Noon-2.15pm/7-9.30pm
Additional: Bar food; Sunday L;
Children welcome; 🥄 dishes
Seats: 40.
Smoking: No smoking in dining room;
Air conditioning
Accommodation: 47 en suite ★★★

CHESTER LE STREET,
Austin's Bar & Bistro

NEW

*Despite the unlikely location of Durham County Cricket Club's
social and sporting premises, the kitchen team know what they are
about. The quality ingredients and accurate flavours of a warm salad
of lightly griddled chicken, and sole filled with salmon mousse on a
butter sauce with blackened scallops, score highly.*

Directions: Off A1M J63. Follow Riverside signs

Durham County Cricket Club County
Ground Riverside DH3 3QR
Map 12: NZ25
Tel: 0191 3874711
Fax: 0191 3874697
Telephone for further details

DARLINGTON, **Hall Garth Hotel**

***Delightful 16th-century manor house with a magnificent
grand hall, rural surroundings and easy access to the A1.***
A golf course and an up-to-date leisure centre are added
attractions. The restaurant offers an excellent choice, with
poached sea bass stuffed with watercress mousse, and sautéed
fillet of pork with braised red cabbage providing a taste of the
lengthy *carte*. Snacks are available in the Stables pub.

Accommodation: 41 en suite ★★★

Directions: A1(M) exit 59 (A167) (Darlington), top of hill turn L
signed Brafferton, hotel 200 yds on R

Coatham Mundeville DL1 3LU
Map 8: NZ21
Tel: 01325 300400
Fax: 01325 310083
Cost: *Alc* £28, set-price D £22.95 (4
courses). ☺ H/wine £11.75
Times: D only, 7-9.45pm
Additional: Bar food; Sunday L
(12.30-2pm); Children welcome;
🥄 dishes
Seats: 50. Private dining room 12
Smoking: No smoking in dining room

DARLINGTON, **Headlam Hall Hotel**

*Impressive Jacobean manor house which has an air of grand
opulence. The modern British menu is stuffed with an abundance of
fresh fish and game: try saddle of venison en daube, or grilled fillet
of salmon with tartare mash.*

Smoking: No-smoking area
Accommodation: 36 en suite ★★★

Directions: 1.5 miles north of Gainford, off A67

Headlam Gainford DL2 3HA
Map 8: NZ21
Tel: 01325 730238
Fax: 01325 730790
Cost: *Alc* £22, set-price L £13. ☺
H/wine £8.50
Times: Noon-2.30pm/7.30-9.30pm.
Closed 25 Dec
Additional: Sunday L; Children 7+;
🥄 dishes

DURHAM, **Bistro 21** ✿

Flagstone floors and stone walls give this former farmhouse an authentic rustic feel. The simple lunch menu offers good value: try slow-cooked knuckle of ham with braised lentils, or roasted cod with saffron mash and sauce bouillabaisse.

Aykley Heads House Aykley Heads DH1 5TS
Map 12: NZ24
Tel: 0191 3844354
Fax: 0191 3841149
Cost: *Alc* £25, set-price L £14.50. ☺ H/wine £9.50
Times: Noon-2pm/6-10.30pm. Closed Sun, Bhs
Additional: Children welcome; dishes
Smoking: No smoking in dining room

Directions: Off B6532 from Durham centre, pass County Hall on R and Dryburn Hospital on L; turn R at double roundabout into Aykley Heads

DURHAM,
Swallow Royal County Hotel ✿✿

Overlooking the River Wear in the heart of Durham, a long-established hotel with a 17th-century heart. Both the *carte* and set menu blend modern and classic English dishes. Medallions of venison, for example are teamed with potato rösti and beetroot, and salmon is done in an oriental fashion with wilted pak choi and deep-fried egg noodles. The highlight of our early summer inspection was a double-baked mature Cheddar soufflé with grain mustard cream, but a generous fillet of salmon, roasted and served with crushed potatoes, spinach and warm ratatouille vinaigrette also got the thumbs up. For dessert – a good apple tarte Tatin with almond ice cream. Service is both friendly and smoothly efficient.

Old Elvet DH1 3JN
Map 12: NZ24
Tel: 0191 3866821
Fax: 0191 3860704
Chef: Ken Thompson
Owner: Swallow Hotel
Cost: *Alc* £33, set-price L £16.50/D £25.50 (4 courses). ☺ H/wine £13
Times: 12.30-2.15pm/7.15-10.15pm
Additional: Bar food L; Sunday L; Children welcome; dishes
Seats: 90. Private dining room 120
Smoking: No-smoking area; No pipes & cigars; Air conditioning
Accommodation: 151 en suite
★ ★ ★ ★

Directions: From A1(M) onto A690. Follow City Centre signs, straight ahead at 1st roundabout, L at 2nd, over bridge, L at lights, hotel on L

HARTLEPOOL,
Krimo's Restaurant ✿

Cheery Med-style restaurant with great sea views. The good-value menu majors on the likes of seared fillet of salmon on a bed of

8 The Front Seaton Carew TS25 1BS
Map 8: NZ53
Tel: 01429 290022
Cost: *Alc* £20, set-price L £6.50/D

linguini, breast of chicken with wild mushrooms, and penne tossed with crisp vegetables and goats' cheese. Set lunch is a bargain.

Additional: Children 10+; 🍴 dishes
Smoking: Air conditioning

Directions: On A178 2 miles from Hartlepool on the seafront

REDWORTH, **Redworth Hall** ❁❁

An imposing Elizabethan mansion, now a hotel and country club. The Conservatory provides wide choice with dishes ranging from spicy vegetable spring rolls, to pork fillet with black pudding risotto, plus grills and a roast of the day. The evening alternative is the elegant dinner-only Blue Room, the original drawing-room of the house, hand-painted by the Cornish artist Lyn le Grice. It is here that the kitchen's skills are given full rein in mosaic of shellfish with marbled herb dressing, and John Dory with lobster risotto and crispy noodles, or loin of veal with a mille-feuille of sweetbreads and Madeira sauce. If you can't decide among the puds go for the grande assiette and get a taste of several.

Directions: From A1(M) take A68. Hotel is on A6072 (off A68) near Newton Aycliffe

£12.95 (both 2 courses). ☺ H/wine £8.90
Times: Noon-1.30pm/7.30-9pm. Closed L Sat, all Sun & Mon, 2 wks Aug

Nr Newton Aycliffe DL5 6NL
Map 8: NZ22
Tel: 01388 772442
Fax: 01388 775112
Chef: Craig Nicholls
Owner: Scottish Highland Hotels
Cost: *Alc* £37.50, set-price D £37.50. H/wine £11.95
Times: D only, 7-10pm. Closed Sun, Xmas
Additional: Children 12+; 🍴 dishes
Seats: 36. Private dining room 20. Jacket & tie preferred
Smoking: No smoking in dining room
Accommodation: 100 en suite
★★★★

ROMALDKIRK,
Rose and Crown Hotel ❁❁

Nr Barnard Castle DL12 9EB
Map 12: NY92
Tel: 01833 650213
Fax: 01833 650828
Chefs: Christopher Davy, Dawn Stephenson
Owners: Christopher & Alison Davy
Cost: Set-price D £24 (4 courses).☺ H/wine £9.50
Times: D only, 7.30-9pm. Closed D Sun, Xmas
Additional: Bar food; Sunday L (noon-1.30pm); Children 6+ at D; 🍴 dishes
Seats: 24
Smoking: No smoking in dining room
Accommodation: 12 en suite ★★

A splendid Jacobean house combining the luxury of a country mansion hotel with the atmosphere of a rambling country inn. For anyone seeking a peaceful yet stylish getaway, as well as good food, then this is the place. Open fires, log beams and comfortable highback dining chairs provide guests with a level of comfort that's hard to beat. As for the food, think traditional English with modern overtones: 'feather-light, smooth' three cheese soufflé topped with a chunk of fresh Gruyère; crisp breast of Norfolk duckling with a compote of preserved fruit on an orange and balsamic sauce, and 'perfect' grouse and almond soup, which tasted of 'desolate, heather-covered moors on a crisp autumn evening' its flavours were so good. Long lists of classical Burgundies and Bordeaux dominate the wine list, although a few light Californian whites and oaky Spanish Riojas are available.

Rose and Crown Hotel

Directions: On B6277 in the centre of the village, near the church

RUSHYFORD,
Swallow Eden Arms Hotel

DL17 0LL
Map 8: NZ22
Tel: 01388 720541
Fax: 01388 721871
Cost: *Alc* £27.94, set-price D £22 (4 courses). ☺ H/wine £12.50
Times: D only, 7-9.30pm
Additional: Sunday L (noon-2pm); Children welcome; ⋓ dishes
Seats: 90. Private room 15-20
Smoking: No smoking in dining room
Accommodation: 45 en suite ★ ★ ★

A former 17th-century coaching inn, now very much up-to-date both in facilities and food. Cosmopolitan themes thread through the value-for-money menus. Expect the likes of pan-fried calves' liver with chunky black pudding and lashings of thyme jus.

Directions: From A1M/J60, follow A689 towards Bishop Auckland for 2 miles. Take 2nd exit at large roundabout, hotel is on L

STOCKTON-ON-TEES,
Parkmore Hotel

Some interesting combinations of flavours and a commitment to local produce are very apparent in the cooking at Reed's at Six Three Six, a restaurant set within a hotel.

Smoking: No smoking in dining room
Accommodation: 56 en suite ★ ★ ★

Directions: On A135 between Yarm and Stockton-on-Tees, almost opposite Eaglescliffe Golf Course

636 Yarm Road Eaglescliffe
TS16 0DH
Map 8: NZ41
Tel: 01642 786815
Fax: 01642 790485
Cost: *Alc* £20. H/wine £8.50
Times: Noon-2pm/6.45-9.30pm
Additional: Bar food; Sunday L; Children welcome; ⋓ dishes

ESSEX

BRENTWOOD,
Marygreen Manor ✿✿

London Road CM14 4NR
Map 5: TQ59
Tel: 01277 225252
Fax: 01277 262809
Chef: Theresa Valentine
Owner: S P Pearson
Cost: *Alc* £31, set-price L £17/D £21.
☺ H/wine £12.50
Times: 12.30-2pm/7.15-10pm
Additional: Bar food; Sunday L;
🍴 dishes
Seats: 80. Private dining room 50.
Jacket & tie preferred
Smoking: No-smoking area; No pipes
& cigars; Air conditioning
Accommodation: 43 en suite ★★★★

Historic baronial hall with eager, attentive service. It may be
just off the A12/M25 interchange, but the setting is all peace
and tranquillity and the house boasts tremendous original
features such as beamed ceilings, carved panelling and a lovely
landscaped courtyard. The cooking lives up to the setting –
sound, reliable, with lots of cosmopolitan influences. Crab and
chive flan, for example, comes with a delicate curry sabyon,
tender calves' liver accompanied by grilled bacon and red
onion sauce. This is also the place for some retro 70s dining:
prepared in the restaurant could be those well-known blasts-
from-the-past-fillet steak with fresh green peppercorns, cream
and brandy (aka steak au poivre) or crêpes Suzette. The wine
list is comprehensive with lots of tasting notes plus a range of
price and variety.

Directions: 1 mile from Brentwood town centre, 0.5 mile from
M25/J28

CHELMSFORD, ## Pontlands Park Hotel ✿

West Hanningfield Road
Great Baddow CM2 8HR
Map 5: TL70
Tel: 01245 476444
Fax: 01245 478393
Telephone for further details

Directions: From M25/J28 take A12
then A130; leave by 1st slip road
(Great Baddow) and take 1st turning L

*Country house hotel on the outskirts of Chelmsford. The bright, airy
restaurant offers Thai-style salmon fishcakes with lemongrass, or
smoked haddock on a bed of spring onion champ.*

COGGESHALL,
Baumann's Brasserie ✿

4-6 Stoneham Street CO6 1TT
Map 5: TL82
Tel: 01376 561453
Fax: 01376 563762
Cost: *Alc* £25, set-price L £12.95/D
£15.50 (both 4 courses). ☺ H/wine
£9.95
Times: 12.15-2pm/7.15-10pm. Closed
L Sat, D Sun, all Mon, 1st 2 wks Jan
Additional: Sunday L; Children
welcome; 🍴 dishes

Vibrant brasserie with a lengthy carte that lists an eclectic mix of modern British ideas. Daily fish specials and a light lunch menu are big hits but look out for wild boar and apple bangers with basil mash.

Smoking: No-smoking area; No cigars & pipes

Directions: In centre of Coggeshall opposite the clock tower

COGGESHALL, White Hart Hotel ✿

Market End CO6 1NH
Map 5: TL82
Tel: 01376 561654
Fax: 01376 561789
Cost: *Alc* £30, set-price L & D
£14.95. ☺ H/wine £10.95
Times: Noon-2pm/7-10pm. Closed D
Sun
Additional: Bar food; Sunday L;
Children welcome; 🍴 dishes
Accommodation: 18 en suite ★★★

Directions: From the A12 towards
Ipswich take the A120, L towards
Braintree; at B1024 crossroads turn L

Historic inn with traditional Italian/continental menu: fritto misto di mare; scampi Newburg; pollo alla Romana – breast of chicken with Parma ham in white wine sauce. Also home-made pastas and risottos.

DEDHAM, Le Talbooth ✿✿

'Super setting and service impeccable', notes one inspector of Gerald and Paul Milsom's striking black-and-white timbered restaurant. Beams predominate, both in the bar and in the restaurant, which also offers stunning river views; in the summer meals are served on the terrace. A new chef has arrived with a style that is now firmly established as modern British. We sampled oriental duck confit with sweet-and-sour cabbage with a hoisin-style plum sauce, a good quality roast

Colchester
CO7 6HP
Map 5: TM03
Tel: 01206 323150
Fax: 01206 322309
Owners: Gerald & Paul Milsom
Cost: *Alc* £35, set-price L £19/D £24.
H/wine £12.50
Times: Noon-2pm/7-9.30pm. Closed
D Sun in winter

Le Talbooth

Additional: Sunday L; Children welcome; 🍴 dishes
Seats: 75. Private dining room 30
Smoking: No pipes & cigars
Accommodation: 10 en suite (Maison Talbooth) ★ ★ ★

fillet of cod with crab and herb crumble, basil-infused noodles and roasted scallops with a lemon and thyme sauce. Dessert was a tarte fine aux pommes with a 'fudgy' caramel sauce and vanilla-pod ice cream. The very good wine list offers some well-priced regional selections as well as *premier crus* and some rarer options and vintages.

Directions: 6 miles from Colchester: follow signs from A12 to Stratford St Mary, restaurant on L before village

FELSTEAD, **Rumbles Cottage**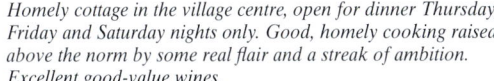

Homely cottage in the village centre, open for dinner Thursday, Friday and Saturday nights only. Good, homely cooking raised above the norm by some real flair and a streak of ambition. Excellent good-value wines.

Directions: In centre of village, approached by A120 or A130. 15/20 minutes' from M11

Braintree Road CM6 3DJ
Map 5: TL62
Tel: 01371 820996
Telephone for further details

GREAT DUNMOW,
Starr Restaurant ✿✿

Market Place CM6 1AX
Map 4: TL62
Tel: 01371 874321
Fax: 01371 876337
Chef: Mark Fisher
Owners: Brian & Vanessa Jones
Cost: *Alc* £32.50, set-price L £24.50/D £32.50. ☺ H/wine £11.95

Behind its Georgian façade this former coaching inn actually dates back to the 15th century. Within, you can choose to eat in the original old beamed area or in an elegant conservatory overlooking the courtyard. Long-serving chef Mark Fisher's menus have a French accent although other

influences are also evident: grilled polenta with roast fillet of English beef; and sage beignets and blackcurrant jus with pan-fried calves' liver. Finish with the likes of chocolate terrine, pear and prune tart or a selection of British and French cheeses. The wine list is worth more than a casual glance; last year it was short listed for the AA Wine Award. Staff are young and helpful.

Directions: M11 exit 8, A120 7 miles eastward towards Colchester. In town centre

Times: Noon-1.30pm/7-9.30pm. Closed D Sun, 1st wk Jan
Additional: Sunday L; Children welcome; ✿ dishes
Seats: 60. Private rooms 12 & 36
Smoking: No smoking in dining room
Accommodation: 8 en suite

GREAT YELDHAM, White Hart

Rustic modernity best describes this 500-year-old country pub set in extensive gardens. Wood floors, old beams and lovely oak panelling are all part of the charm of this Elizabethan black-and-white timber framed building. It's split in two: a casual bar with the more formal restaurant on the other side of the inglenook, although, as with all inns in the Huntsbridge group, you can eat the same menu in either. A starter of baby squid stuffed with saffron rice with stir-fried pak choi and ginger and soy sauce is as up to the minute as dishes come. Wilted rocket, pine nuts, marinated mushrooms and tagliatelle are the components of main-course grilled fillet of sea bass, with coconut and lime couscous and mango salsa served with breast of Deben duck. Add to these a snack menu – from ploughman's to grilled Lincolnshire sausages with mash and gravy – a bargain lunch menu, and puddings ranging from tarte Tatin with 'great' cinnamon ice cream to a selection of unpasteurised cheeses, and it's easy to understand the popularity of the operation. Excellent beers too, though they tend to be knocked into the shadows by the superb wine list, which has plenty by the glass.

Halstead CO9 4HJ
Map 5: TL73
Tel: 01787 237250
Fax: 01787 238044
Chef: Roger Jones
Owner: John Hoskins
Cost: *Alc* £20, set-price L £8.50. ☺
H/wine £9.75
Times: Noon-2pm/6.30-9.30pm.
Closed D 25, 26 Dec, 1 Jan
Additional: Bar food; Sunday L;
Children welcome; ✿ dishes
Seats: 70. Private dining rooms 24-30
Smoking: No smoking in dining room

Directions: On A1017 (old A604)
midway between Braintree &
Haverhill

HARLOW,
Swallow Churchgate Hotel

Churchgate Street Village CM17 0JT
Map 5: TL41
Tel: 01279 420246
Fax: 01279 437720
Cost: *Alc* £25, set-price L £15 (2
courses)/D £20. ☺ H/wine £11.95
Times: 12.30-2pm/7-9.45pm. Closed
L Sat
Additional: Bar food; Sunday L;
Children welcome; ✿ dishes
Smoking: No smoking in dining room
Accommodation: 85 en suite ★ ★ ★

Popular business hotel housed in former Jacobean chantry house. Expect modern British fare along the lines of braised shank of lamb with olive oil mash, grilled pork with honey and lemon, and sautéed tiger prawns and scallops with a crab risotto.

Directions: From M11 J7 take A414 towards harlow. Take B183 at 4th roundabout, then L into village street; hotel past church, at bottom of hill

HARWICH, **Pier at Harwich**

Attentive, reassuringly friendly service surrounded by nautical memorabilia. Seafood is the speciality and restraint in not messing with the natural appeal of simple fish cookery is as much part of the draw as some of the more complex dishes on Chris Oakley's menu. There is the odd ambitious dish and Mediterranean influences are gradually coming through, away from the more traditional cream and butter bases. Dinner in the first-floor Harbourside Restaurant took in Thai fishcakes, served with a searingly hot-and-sour sauce. Fish pie was stuffed with salmon, cod, scampi, scallop and prawn, all in a buttery saffron velouté and topped by a light gratin crust of creamed potato. Dark chocolate parfait was simple but effective. The wine list has good value and quality. The Ha'Penny Pier bistro downstairs is less formal, more family orientated.

The Quay CO12 3HH
Map 5: TM23
Tel: 01255 241212. **Fax:** 01255 551922
Chef: Chris Oakley
Owner: G M W Milsom
Cost: *Alc* £25, set-price L £15 (2 courses)/D £19.50. ☺ H/wine £11.50
Times: Noon-2pm/6-9.30pm. Closed D 25, 26 Dec
Additional: Sunday L; Children welcome; ✤ dishes
Seats: 80. Private dining room 40
Smoking: No-smoking area; No pipes & cigars
Accommodation: 6 en suite ★★

Directions: A12 to Colchester then A120 to Harwich town quay front

MANNINGTREE, **Stour Bay Café**

Bright orange walls contrast well with original 16th-century wooden beams. The menu is billed as global fusion – spiced duck breast with lime and spring onion rice and cranberry jus, and fillet of organic pork with roast Rocha pears and parsnip mash.

39-43 High Street CO11 1AH
Map 5: TM13
Tel: 01206 396687
Fax: 01206 395462
Cost: *Alc* £20, set-price L £8.50. ☺ H/wine £9.75
Times: Noon-2pm/7-9.30pm. Closed L Sat, all Sun, Mon, 2 wks beginning Jan.
Additional: Children welcome; ✤ dishes
Smoking: No-smoking area; No pipes and cigars

Directions: Town centre (A317 from Colchester to Ipswich) – large green building in High Street

ROCHFORD, **Hotel Renouf**

Smart hotel that's family owned and run. Duck is a speciality, including various forms of pressed duck. Other classic choices include lobster Thermidor, bouillabaisse, chicken Calvados and entrecôte au poivre.

Bradley Way SS4 1BU
Map 5: TQ89
Tel: 01702 541334
Fax: 01702 549563
Cost: *Alc* £28.50, set-price L/D £17.50. ☺ H/wine £10.50
Times: Noon-1.45pm/7-9.45pm. Closed L Sat, D Sun (except residents), 27-30 Dec
Additional: Sunday L; Children welcome; ✤ dishes
Smoking: No smoking in dining room; Air conditioning
Accommodation: 23 en suite ★★★

Directions: M25/J29, A127 into Rochford onto B1013

STANSTED,
Whitehall Hotel

Church End Broxted CM6 2BZ
Map 5: TL52
Tel: 01279 850603
Fax: 01279 850385
Cost: *Alc* £35, set-price L & D £20.
H/wine £13.50
Times: 12.30-1.30pm/7.30-9.30pm.
closed L Sat, D Sun, 26-30 Dec
Additional: Sunday L; Children
welcome; ✆ dishes
Smoking: No pipes & cigars
Accommodation: 26 en suite ★ ★ ★

*Simple British dishes are served in the 15th-century timber-vaulted
restaurant overlooking the gardens. Typical starters include smoked
salmon and ricotta tartlet, and stir-fried king scallops with water
chestnuts and ginger.*

Directions: From M11/J8 follow signs for Stansted Airport and
then for Broxted

TOLLESHUNT KNIGHTS,
Five Lakes Hotel

*Medieval-style restaurant in a modern leisure hotel. A typical meal
might start with seared peppered salmon with crisp leaves dressed in
walnut oil, followed by slow-roasted pork with a sage and apple
compote.*

Accommodation: 114 en suite ★ ★ ★ ★

Directions: Kelvedon exit A12 follow signs to Tiptree, over
staggered crossroads past jam factory, take L fork, approx 2
miles turn R at T junction

Colchester Road CM9 8HX
Map 5: TL91
Tel: 01621 868888
Fax: 01621 869696
Cost: *Alc* £30, set-price D £23.50. ☺
H/wine £15.50
Times: D only, 7-10pm. Closed D Sun
Additional: Sunday L (12.30-2.30pm);
Children welcome; ✆ dishes
Smoking: No smoking in dining room;
Air conditioning

WETHERSFIELD,
Dicken's Restaurant ✿✿

***Olde worlde beamed restaurant with various eating areas and
a minstrels' gallery.*** The country decor is not reflected in the
menu which manages a restrained eclecticism, with a variety of
flavours and influences kept in check in almost classical vein.
Thus Mediterranean fish soup, steamed game pudding served
with a fine dice of al dente winter root vegetables, and a
raspberry and coconut tart with raspberry coulis and crème
anglaise, show the range.

Directions: From M11/Stansted Airport take A120, bypass Gt
Dunmow, towards Braintree. Turn L to Gt Saling then R towards
Shalford. Wethersfield is next village

The Green CM7 4BS
Map 5: TL73
Tel/Fax: 01371 850723
Telephone for further details

GLOUCESTERSHIRE

BIBURY, Bibury Court ❀❀

Cirencester GL7 5NT
Map 4: SP10
Tel: 01285 740337
Fax: 01285 740660
Chef: Tom Bridgeman
Owners: Mr & Mrs Johnston,
Miss Collier
Cost: Set-price D £25. ☺ H/wine
£10.95
Times: Noon-2pm/7-9pm. Closed
Xmas & New Year
Additional: Bar food; Sunday L;
Children welcome; ♣ dishes
Seats: 50. Private dining room 30
Smoking: No smoking in dining room
Accommodation: 19 en suite ★ ★ ★

Imposing Tudor mansion with substantial grounds beside the River Colne. Within, roaring log fires, flagstone floors and wood panelling maintain the traditional country house feel. The food, however, is modern with a classic edge, and there are plenty of Mediterranean influences in dishes such as wild mushroom risotto with Reggiano Parmesan, and breast of duck flamed in cognac with green peppercorns and cream. The highlight of our winter meal was a well-judged pigeon salad with lardons and black pudding, while the main course was an excellent paupiette of brill with lobster ravioli and a saffron cream. Desserts tend to be indulgent, and a good walk in the grounds might be needed after tackling sweets such as the rich treacle tart served with clotted cream and passion fruit sauce.

Directions: On B4425 between Cirencester & Burford; hotel lies behind the church

BIBURY, Swan Hotel ❀❀

Cirencester GL7 5NW
Map 4: SP10
Tel: 01285 740695
Fax: 01285 740473
Chef: Stephen Bulmer
Owner: Elizabeth A Rose
Cost: Set-price D £28.50. H/wine £15
Times: D only, 7-9.45pm

Bucolic setting for a surprisingly elegant restaurant (though there's also an informal brasserie). Bibury is a pretty Cotswolds village, and at its heart, facing the river and the bridge over it, is the creeper-clad, long, low building of the Swan. The restaurant boasts sconces on the maroon walls, lavish drapes over the large windows, and white-clothed, well-spaced tables. Here you can expect confit of Gressingham duck with roast shallots and celeriac remoulade, Coln trout plainly grilled with lemon and parsley served with asparagus and mash, and Eastern-influenced pan-fried medallions of monkfish in lemongrass and coriander sauce with crab, ginger and scallop tortellini. Thin apple tart, its pastry light and crisp, hits the button, and hot chocolate fondant with pistachio ice cream is worth the 15-minute wait. Those wanting to push the boat out can choose one of the fine wines from an interesting list that's long enough to give a good choice.

Additional: Sunday L (noon-2.30pm); Children welcome; ✿ dishes
Seats: 60. Private dining room 30. Jacket & tie preferred
Smoking: No smoking in dining room
Accommodation: 18 en suite ★ ★ ★

Directions: On B4425 between Cirencester (7 miles) and Burford (9 miles). Beside bridge in centre of Bibury

BLOCKLEY, **Crown Inn**

Built of mellow Cotswold stone, this 16th-century former coaching inn is full of charm and character. Foodwise there is an extensive range of dishes to be enjoyed either in the bar or brasserie. Good wine list.

Smoking: No smoking in dining room
Accommodation: 21 en suite ★ ★ ★

Directions: A44 W from Moreton-in-Marsh, right on to B4479

High Street GL56 9EX
Map 4: SP13
Tel: 01386 700245
Fax: 01386 700247
Cost: *Alc* £25, set-price D £25. ☺
H/wine £10.95
Times: Noon-2.30pm/7-10pm
Additional: Bar food; Sunday L; Children welcome; ✿ dishes

BOURTON-ON-THE-WATER,

Dial House Hotel

The Chestnuts High Street GL54 2AN
Map 4: SP12
Tel: 01451 822244
Fax: 01451 810126
Chef: Calum Williamson
Owners: Lynn & Peter Boxall
Cost: *Alc* £20, set-price L £7.50 (2 courses). ☺ H/wine £9.95
Times: Noon-2pm/7-9pm
Additional: Bar food L; Sunday L; Children 8+; ✿ dishes
Seats: 30. Private dining room 14
Smoking: No smoking in dining room
Accommodation: 14 en suite ★ ★

Delightful hotel, dating from 1698, that makes an ideal retreat. Log fires burn in the lounge during the winter, and another in the original inglenook in the dining room, which has antique furniture and many period features. Dinner could open with crab and mango gâteau in a lime and ginger dressing, or home-smoked chicken, and go on to roast rack of local lamb with mint rösti and a jus of home-smoked garlic, or pan-fried sea bass on roasted pepper and crab couscous. Finish with something traditional like bread-and-butter pudding with rum-soaked raisins or, not for the faint-hearted, Stinking Bishop, a cheese known for its strong smell. House wines are Australian, and the list has much of interest from the rest of the world.

Directions: In village centre; A436 from Cheltenham, A40-A424 from Oxford

BUCKLAND, **Buckland Manor**

Broadway WR12 7LY
Map 4: SP03
Tel: 01386 852626
Fax: 01386 853557
Chef: Kenneth Wilson
Owners: Roy & Daphne Vaughan
Cost: *Alc* £50, set-price L £28.50.
H/wine £13.50
Times: 12.30-1.45pm/7.30-9pm
Additional: Bar food L; Sunday L;
Children 12+; ❹ dishes
Seats: 34. Jacket & tie preferred
Smoking: No smoking in dining room
Accommodation: 13 en suite ★ ★ ★

Directions: 2 miles SW of Broadway.
Take B4632 signposted Cheltenham,
then take turn for Buckland. Hotel is
through village on R

*Expensive, impeccable, professional and attentive – the
hallmarks an imposing 13th-century manor set on a secluded
hillside.* The interior has a classic country house look with
well-upholstered chintzy chairs, highly polished tables and
large framed portraits. Dinners begin in style with a choice of
canapés – Parma ham roulade on a crisp croûte, prawn
mayonnaise served on a baby endive leaf, spicy beef in a pastry
case – plus a selection of home-made breads. Chef Ken Wilson
knows how to time his dishes to perfection – note a crisp-
skinned fillet of salmon with asparagus, crushed potatoes and
velvety, intensely flavoured langoustine sauce. He also has a
light hand with pastry, and an open tart of onion, olives, duck
confit and goats' cheese with olive vinaigrette was marred only
by an excess of olives in the filling. Coconut milk made an
unusual appearance in a carefully constructed dessert of delice
of chocolate with coconut, macadamia nuts and rum-baked
bananas. The Hawaiian nuts might also feature in ice cream
served with a warm chocolate tart and poached kumquats. The
wine list is an excellent and well-described, if lengthy,
collection of serious, top quality bottles.

CHARINGWORTH,
Charingworth Manor

Chipping Campden GL55 6NS
Map 4: SP13
Tel: 01386 593555
Fax: 01386 593353
Telephone for further details

Directions: From A429 Fosse Way
take B4035 towards Chipping
Campden, hotel is 3 miles on R

Changes in the kitchen occurred as we went to press, too late
for us to assess the new regime. In the past Charingworth
Manor has maintained two AA Rosettes.

CHEDWORTH, **Hare and Hounds**

Rustic stone pub on a remote stretch of the ancient Foss Way, now under the direction of Sonja Kidney and Leo Brooke-Little: that means only one thing to Cotswold gastronomes – decent pub food. Brill with roast fennel, tomatoes, chervil & vanilla sauce, and home-made faggots, red wine, onions & thyme show the range.

Foss Cross GL54 4NN
Tel: 01285 720288
Telephone for further details

Directions:

CHELTENHAM, **The Beaujolais** NEW

Cheerful edge of town bistro serving earthy French dishes with a few Med influences. Try sautéed wild mushrooms followed by pork tenderloin en-croûte with apples and brandy.

Additional: Children 4+; 🍴 dishes

Directions: Telephone for directions

15 Rotunda Terrace Montpellier GL50 1SW
Map 3: SO92
Tel: 01242 525230
Cost: *Alc* £20, set-price L £15.95/D £18.95. ☺ H/wine £9.95
Times: 12.30-2pm/7-10pm. Closed Sun, Mon, Xmas & Easter

CHELTENHAM,

Le Champignon Sauvage

24 Suffolk Road GL50 2AQ
Map 3: SO92
Tel/Fax: 01242 573449
Chef: David Everitt-Matthias
Owners: David & Helen Everitt-Matthias
Cost: Set-price L £18.50/D £35. ☺ H/wine £9.95
Times: 12.30-1.30pm/7.30-9pm. Closed Sun & Mon, 10 days Xmas, 2 wks summer, Easter
Additional: Children welcome
Seats: 28

Directions: South of town centre, near Boys' College on A40 (Oxford). Please phone for exact details

All agree that the Everitt-Matthias' run a super restaurant. 'Helen is a great host and their guests really appreciate the attention,' observed one inspector. The blue and yellow interior is stylish and David's painted cover plates in bold primary colours work well with the decor. Paintings chosen from the local art college reflect a love of jazz and the countryside and all are chosen with a discerning eye. David's cooking is equally enlightened: classic, sassy, and reflecting a love of prime raw materials; sauces are well made and discreet, and the techniques deliver bold flavours, a sense of balance and some dazzling spicing. Thus a lunchtime cauliflower soup is light but given depth with some judicious spicing with cumin, roasted fillet of pork comes flavoured with tea, the braised belly with Chinese spices. Gutsier dishes encompass breast of local wood pigeon partnered by duck gizzards and served with mushy peas, and rabbit ravioli with smoked bacon and flageolet beans. Desserts are equally appealing, and inspired. They extend to mango with Thai-spiced cream, served with mulled red wine, or chilled coconut creamed rice, roasted pineapple and pineapple sorbet. The selection of cheeses are hard to pass up, but then so are the petits fours that arrive with coffee; all signs of the painstaking attention to detail that makes Le Champignon Sauvage a long-standing success.

CHELTENHAM, **The Daffodil** ❀❀

18-20 Suffolk Parade Montpelier
GL50 2AE
Map 3: SO92
Tel: 01242 700055
Fax: 01242 700088
Cost: *Alc* £20, set-price L £12.50. ☺
H/wine £8.95
Times: 11am-3pm,/6.30-10.30pm.
Closed Sun, 25, 26 Dec, 1st wk Jan
Additional: Bar food; Children
welcome; ❹ dishes
Smoking: No-smoking area; No pipes
& cigars; Air conditioning

Directions: S of town centre, just off
Suffolk Rd, nr Cheltenham Boys'
College

The last credits rolled over thirty years ago at this art deco cinema – taking centre stage these days is a kitchen producing modish food, presented in a bright, punchy fashion well suited to the glamorous surroundings. Dishes don't overcomplicate and there is a welcome emphasis on seasonality and freshness in dishes such as the layered provençale tart, which rely for their success on being in tip-top condition. Main courses offer plenty of heavyweight options such as seared calves' liver with bacon, pommes Anna and a super rich Madeira jus. A wealth of fish has included roast fillet of monkfish with saffron and spinach potato. For the indecisive, desserts include the option of a plate of Daffodil desserts which count amongst them a creamy lemon tart with a sharp raspberry and grenadine coulis. In enlightened fashion the entire wine list is available by the glass.

CHELTENHAM, **The Greenway** ❀❀❀

Shurdington GL51 5UG
Map 3: SO92
Tel: 01242 862352
Fax: 01242 862780
Chef: Peter Fairclough
Owners: David & Valerie White
Cost: *Alc* £40, set-price L £19.65/D
£32. H/wine £13.50
Times: 12.30-2pm/7.30-9.30pm.
Closed L Sat, Bhs
Additional: Sunday L; Children 7+;
❹ dishes
Seats: 50. Private dining room 24

Splendid Elizabethan manor house with attentive service. The Greenway makes an ideal base for the Cotswolds: the backdrop of countryside to the rear of the hotel is picture postcard material and the conservatory dining room has views over the sunken garden, terrace and hills beyond. We were particularly impressed by Peter Fairclough's lack of complexity in the execution of dishes, with a back-to-basics approach that really allowed good raw materials to shine through. A squab breast, for example, was cooked to perfection and simply accompanied by red onion marmalade and lots of natural jus

to be soaked up by a 'really herby' mash. First-class sea bass came with a stir-fry of vegetables, and a particularly sound, creamy chocolate parfait and a really fruity banana sorbet both shone through on the dessert list. Oriental influences are threaded throughout the menu, especially first courses, but these are handled with particular restraint. Carpaccio of monkfish with nori parcel and a teriyaki dressing, say, or duck confit spring roll with deep-fried leeks and an oriental dressing. *Signature dishes:* chicken and truffle boudin with creamed leeks and white truffle oil; mussel and saffron soup with cucumber pickle and a potato ravioli; red medallion of Cotswold venison with a leek and smoked bacon pommes Anna and a crème de mûre sauce; seared fillet of red mullet with pesto mash, roasted Provençale vegetables and a tomato fondue.

Smoking: No smoking in dining room
Accommodation: 19 en suite ★ ★ ★

Directions: 2.5 miles S of Cheltenham on A46 (Stroud)

CHELTENHAM, **Le Petit Blanc**

The Cheltenham version of Raymond Blanc's mini-brasserie chain is discreetly located to the side of the Queen's Hotel on the edge of the town centre. Brasserie-style certainly, with benched seating, brushed steel tables and bright, polo-shirted staff, but the menu shows more ambition. Chargrilling and pan-frying are to be expected, but there's also deep-fried crab cakes with green onion risotto and chilli oil dressing, or a tagliatelle of smoked chicken with a chilli cream sauce. Double pork cutlets come with mushroom soya jus and sauté bok choi, and pan-fried black bream with squid and provençale vegetables. Desserts range from the traditional lemon tart to apricot soufflé with chocolate ice cream. Blanc Vite provides a fast-track weekday list of the likes of moules and frites or sausage baguette, and the set price lunch or dinner choice is excellent value.

The Queen's Hotel The Promenade
GL50 1NN
Map 3: SO92
Tel: 01242 266800
Fax: 01242 266801
Chef: Steve Nash
Owner: Raymond Blanc
Cost: *Alc* £35, set-price L & D £15.
☺ H/wine £9.95
Times: Noon-3pm/6-10.30pm. Closed 25 Dec
Additional: Bar food L; Children welcome; 🍴 dishes. **Seats:** 152
Smoking: No smoking in dining room; Air conditioning

Directions: To the side of the Queen's Hotel, town centre

CHELTENHAM,
Restaurant On The Park

Smart town house hotel, comfortable restaurant. Some food marriages are made in heaven. The crusted loin of venison with blueberry and chocolate sauce and red onion tarte Tatin surprised even further with the inclusion of some beetroot in the sauce, but turned out to be one of the *carte's* more successful matches. Enthusiasm certainly is the hallmark of the cooking, but the willingness to mix a myriad of ingredients tends to hide the cooking skills that the kitchen possesses. A scallop salad with black pudding and avocado ravioli, for example, suffered from an excess of elements competing for attention. Pudding was the hit of our visit – bitter chocolate soufflé stylishly served in a small copper pan with vanilla ice and twizzles of brandy snap. The restful restaurant interior has drapes in muted regency stripes of cream and charcoal along with Caesar-like busts and two giant teddy bears.

Hotel on the Park 38 Evesham Road
GL52 2AH
Map 3: SO92
Tel: 01242 518898
Fax: 01242 511526
Chef: Graham Mairs
Owner: D Gregory
Cost: *Alc* £ 29.95, set-price L
£14.25/D £21.50. ☺ H/wine £9.75
Times: Noon-2pm/7-9pm
Additional: Sunday L; Children 8+;
🍴 dishes
Seats: 40. Private room 18
Smoking: No smoking in dining room
Accommodation: 12 en suite ★ ★ ★

Directions: A435 (Evesham) from Cheltenham centre, hotel at 3rd lights opposite Pittville Park

CHELTENHAM,
Hotel Kandinsky NEW

Well-maintained Regency villa within easy reach of the town centre. Dinner only is served in the hotel restaurant, a three-

Bayshill Road Montpellier GL50 3AS
Map 3: SO92
Tel: 01242 527788
Fax: 01242 226412

course set-price affair that reveals modish ideas and a sound buying policy. An autumn meal took in crab cakes bursting with flavour, well matched by a light curry sauce. Oriental-style beef stir-fry was based on good quality beef, sound fresh vegetables and a well-liked oyster sauce. Light open apple tart had a good tangy filling.

Chef: Sally Rathbone
Cost: Set-price D £19.95. ☺ H/wine £12.95
Times: D only, 6.30-9.30pm (8.30pm Sun)
Additional: Children 12+; ❀ dishes
Seats: 35. Private dining room 12
Smoking: No smoking in dining room
Accommodation: 43 en suite ★★★

CHELTENHAM,
Thistle Cheltenham

Gloucester Road GL51 0TS
Map 3: SO92
Tel: 01242 232691
Fax: 01242 221846
Cost: *Alc* £24.85. ☺ H/wine £11.50
Times: 12.30-2pm/7-10pm
Additional: Bar Food; Sunday L; Children welcome; ❀ dishes
Smoking: No-smoking area; No pipes & cigars; Air conditioning
Accommodation: 122 en suite ★★★★

Directions: 2.5 miles from centre of Cheltenham on A40 (Gloucester). 1 mile M5/J11, towards Cheltenham (A40), 2nd exit off 1st roundabout

The popular Burford restaurant offers a balanced range of bright, carefully executed dishes, such as pan-fried razor clams, and loin of tuna with a Mediterranean tomato and chive sauce.

CHIPPING CAMPDEN,
Cotswold House

The Square GL55 6AN
Map 4: SP13
Tel: 01386 840330
Fax: 01386 840310
Chef: David Toon
Owners: C S & L A Forbes
Cost: *Alc* £30, set-price D £22. ☺ H/wine £12
Times: D only
Additional: Brasserie L & D; Sunday L; Children 7+; ❀ dishes
Seats: 42. Private dining room 18
Smoking: No smoking in dining room
Accommodation: 15 en suite ★★★

Directions: 1 mile N of A44 between Moreton-in-Marsh and Broadway on B4081

A classic English dining-room, with marbled pillars and glimpses of an old-fashioned English garden. English cooking, albeit in Euro-guise, takes in roast whole quail filled with spinach mousse on sautéed butter beans and thyme, and roast fillet of beef on beetroot mash with roast artichokes, tapenade and Dijon sauce. A duo of lamb comprises pan-fried lambs' liver with onion confit and roast garlic, plus sautéed lambs' kidneys, fondant potato and peppercorn sauce. A palate of modern flavourings is explored in fillet of brill poached in balsamic with vanilla risotto and peppered fennel, and fillet of salmon in lemongrass broth with herb crème fraîche. Fruity desserts include banana tarte Tatin with plum sauce and vanilla ice cream. Forbes Brasserie has a less informal choice of grills, pastas, salads and main courses such as seared calves' liver on spiced aubergine purée with lime jus.

CHIPPING CAMPDEN,

The Malt House

Broad Campden GL55 6UU
Map 4: SP13
Tel: 01386 840295
Fax: 01386 841334
Chef/Owner: Julian Brown
Cost: *Alc* £30, set-price D £27.50.
H/wine £18
Times: D only, 7.30-8.30pm. Closed Tue, Wed
Additional: Children 8+; 🍃 dishes
Seats: 22. Jacket & tie preferred
Smoking: No smoking in dining room
Accommodation: 8 en suite

Relaxed restaurant-with-rooms with space and warmth. Julian Brown continues to deliver a distinctive brand of modern British cooking to this tastefully appointed Cotswold house. The underlying intention is informality, the atmosphere welcoming, and the menus intrigue without being complicated (although choice is limited). Bold flavours results in dishes like a warm pigeon breast salad with Cassis dressing and roasted black pudding, roast English duck breast with red onion and aubergine marmalade, as well as a warm chocolate tart with coffee ice cream.

Directions: Entering Chipping Campden on A44, turn R for Broad Campden, follow four sharp turns to Malt House

CHIPPING CAMPDEN,

Noel Arms Hotel

High Street GL55 6AT
Map 4: SP13
Tel: 01386 840317
Fax: 01386 841136
Chef: Mark Jenkins
Owner: Cotswold Inns & Hotels Ltd
Cost: *Alc* £22. ☺ H/wine £9.95
Times: D only, 7-9pm
Additional: Bar food; Sunday L (noon-2pm); Children welcome; 🍃 dishes
Seats: 55. Private dining room 12
Smoking: No smoking in dining room
Accommodation: 26 en suite ★ ★ ★

Extensive refurbishment has given the 14th-century Noel Arms a bright new look without losing any of its original character. The popular bar serves a good range of snacks, but the restaurant goes confidently upmarket with dishes such as garden leaf salad with crisp vegetables and Parmesan biscuits, and rillette of poached salmon and crab with aromatic lemon and herb dressing. More herbs feature in a signature dish of roast rack of Cornish lamb with a fresh herb and mustard crust, and sea bass is given the spice treatment with a potato, saffron and tomato broth. Desserts are simple but sophisticated – dark chocolate mousse layered with raspberries and marbled discs, and poached pear in red wine and Cassis served with crème fraîche.

Directions: Town centre

CHIPPING CAMPDEN,

Seymour House Hotel

Country house hotel noted for splendid service. Parts of this lovely Cotswold stone house date back to the early 18th century. The menu has an Italian slant: grilled goats' cheese on a garlic croûte with pesto-dressed rocket salad, or tagliatelle with fresh tomatoes, extra-virgin olive oil and basil. Calves' liver is a popular choice, perhaps served with crispy leeks, laced with gin and lime sauce. There is also a daily fish dish, and the menu denotes healthy eating choices such as supreme of pheasant filled with wild mushrooms, served on spiced cabbage with a Madeira cream. We found the tangy, well-made lemon tart with raspberry coulis rounded the meal off in style. The staff are a credit to the hotel and work hard as a team to ensure everything runs smoothly.

Directions: Town centre

High Street GL55 6AH
Map 4: SP13
Tel: 01386 840429
Fax: 01386 840369
Chef: Toby Bult
Cost: Set-price D £24.95. ☺ H/wine £13.50
Times: Noon-2pm/7-10pm
Additional: Bar food; Sunday L; Children welcome; ⏇ dishes
Seats: 60. Private room 40
Smoking: No smoking in dining room
Accommodation: 15 en suite ★ ★ ★

CHIPPING CAMDEN,

Three Ways House NEW

Home of 'The Pudding Club' where regular meetings are held in appreciation of great British puds. The menu, however, has ambitions beyond dessert with the likes of pan-fried fillet of sea bass with lemongrass and ginger being particularly successful.

Seats: 80. Private dining room 80
Smoking: No smoking in dining room
Accommodation: 41 en suite ★ ★ ★

Directions: On the B4632, in the centre of the village

Mickleton GL55 6SB
Map 3: SO92
Tel: 01386 438429
Fax: 01386 438118
Cost: *Alc* £30, set-price L £13.50/D £21. ☺ H/wine £10.50
Times: 12.30-2.30pm
Additional: Bar food; Sunday L; Children welcome; ⏇ dishes

CIRENCESTER,

Crown of Crucis

A 16th-century Cotswold inn with a newly decorated, contemporary-style restaurant presenting a punchy menu of bright-flavoured favourites.

Directions: 3 miles E of Cirencester on A417 to Lechlade

Ampney Crucis GL7 5RS
Map 3: SP00
Tel: 01285 851806
Fax: 01285 851735
Cost: *Alc* £18, set-price L £11.50/D £17. ☺ H/wine £8.20
Times: Noon-2.30pm/6-10pm. Closed 25 Dec
Additional: Bar Food; Sunday L; Children welcome; ⏇ dishes
Smoking: No-smoking area; No pipes & cigars; Air conditioning
Accommodation: 25 en suite ★ ★ ★

CIRENCESTER, **Harry Hare's**

3 Gosditch Street GL7 2AG
Map 4: SP00
Tel: 01285 652375
Fax: 01285 641691
Telephone for further details

Directions: Opposite Cirencester
Parish Church, in market place at
centre of town

*Bright, upbeat restaurant in a historic 17th-century town house. The
all-day menu includes lots of salads, and plenty of hearty dishes such
as bangers & mash, lobster & chips and salmon kedgeree.*

CIRENCESTER, **Polo Canteen**

29 Sheep Street GL7 1QW
Map 4: SP00
Tel: 01285 650977
Fax: 01285 642777
Cost: *Alc* £25. ☺ H/wine £9.50
Times: Noon-2pm/7-10pm. Closed
Sun, 25-26 Dec
Additional: Children welcome;
🍴 dishes
Smoking: No-smoking area; Air
conditioning

Directions: Just off Cirencester ring
road, opposite Waitrose

*Relaxed brasserie-style operation on the edge of the polo capital of
England. A flavour first approach translates into simple but
eminently effective dishes with the emphasis on fresh local produce.*

CIRENCESTER, **Stratton House Hotel**

Gloucester Road GL7 2LE
Map 3: SP00
Tel: 01285 651761
Fax: 01285 640024
Telephone for further details

*Attractive 17th-century manor house with traditional restaurant
overlooking a pretty walled garden. Much is made of local produce
in dishes such as salmon with lime and coriander.*

CLEARWELL,
Tudor Farmhouse Hotel ✿

Near Coleford GL16 8JS
Map 3: SO50
Tel: 01594 833046
Fax: 01594 837093
Cost: *Alc* £23, set-price D £19.95 (4
courses). ☺ H/wine £8.95
Times: D only, 7-8.45pm. Closed D
Sun, 1 wk Xmas.

*The beamed restaurant of this charming hotel (in part dating back to the
13th century) offers a well-balanced menu and honest, robust cooking.*

Additional: Sunday L; Children welcome; 🍴 dishes
Smoking: No smoking in dining room
Accommodation: 14 en suite ★★

Directions: Leave A466 & follow Clearwell signs

COLN ST ALDWYNS,
New Inn

Cirencester GL7 5AN
Map 4: SP10
Tel: 01285 750651
Fax: 01285 750657
Chef: Stephen Morey
Owners: Mr & Mrs Brian Evans
Cost: Set-price L £15.50/D £26.50.
H/wine £10.50
Times: Noon-2pm/7-9pm (9.30pm Fri)
Additional: Bar food; Sunday L;
Children 10+; dishes
Seats: 36. Private dining room 20
Smoking: No smoking in dining room
Accommodation: 14 en suite ★ ★

Directions: 8 miles E of Cirencester
between Bibury (B4425) and Fairford
(A417)

Built in the 16th century, this creeper-covered building with a dovecote has everything you'd expect of a Cotswold hostelry. Flagged floors, roaring fires, friendly, helpful staff, and a bar serving a broad-ranging menu that takes in kedgeree with a poached egg, fish and chips with peas, and pheasant casserole with smoked bacon and wild mushrooms. Dinner in the cottagey restaurant, with its beams, low ceilings and candlelight, could start with glazed Welsh rarebit with celery and apple salad, or a selection of dim sum (from crab and pepper wun-tun to duck spring roll) with sweet chilli dipping sauce. More mainstream to the kitchen's style is a main course of loin of new season's lamb, cooked pink, on a potato cake with minted pea purée and a 'sparkling' rosemary-scented gravy. Wild mushrooms are used in season: in a sauce with red wine for pan-fried sirloin steak, and as a jus with truffled Savoy cabbage to go with pan-fried sea bass. Expect to close with something like thin apple tart with clotted cream ice cream before good petits fours with coffee.

EWEN, # Wild Duck Inn **NEW**

Drakes Island GL7 6BY
Map 3: SU09
Tel: 01285 770310
Fax: 01285 770924
Cost: *Alc* £20, set-price D £25. ☺
H/wine £8.95
Times: Noon-2pm/6.30-10pm
Additional: Bar food; Sunday L;
Children welcome; dishes
Accommodation: 12 en suite ★ ★

Directions: Telephone for directions

The quintessential English country pub of one's imagination. Straightforward, full-flavoured pub food from a chalked-up menu that applies to both bar and restaurant. Typically, salami and chorizo salad with home-made piccalilli, melting braised knuckle of ham and suitably sharp lemon tart.

FOSSEBRIDGE, **Fossebridge Inn**

Traditional oak-beamed Cotswold inn with open fires. Expect modern English dishes like best end of lamb with roasted vegetables, as well as old favourites such as Jessie Smith's sausages with bubble-and-squeak.

Accommodation: 11 en suite ★ ★

Directions: On A429 between Cirencester and Northleach

Northleach Cheltenham GL54 3JS
Map 4: SP01
Tel: 01285 720721
Fax: 01285 720793
Cost: *Alc* £17. ☺ H/wine £8.95
Times: 12-2.30pm/7-9.30pm
Additional: Bar food; Sunday L;
Children welcome; ♨ dishes
Smoking: No smoking in dining room

FRAMPTON-ON-SEVERN,
Restaurant on the Green

Small, simple village restaurant with a pleasant, informal style. Gill Getvoldsen features a well-tried repertoire of dishes such as goats' cheese and leek soufflé filo tart with a tomato salad, confit of duck with orange and brandy sauce, mushroom Stroganoff with Camargue red rice, and salmon steak with white wine and herb butter. Individual Pavlova filled with banoffee ice cream and banana with butterscotch sauce is popular, as is treacle pear steamed pudding served with golden syrup sauce and cream.

Directions: From M5/J13 take A38 towards Bristol. Turn R at Frampton/Saul signpost, continue for 1 mile, L across village green, restaurant at end, on R

The Green GL2 7DY
Map 3: SO70
Tel: 01452 740077
Chef/Owner: Gill Getvoldsen
Cost: Set-price L £7.50 (2 courses)/D £23.95. H/wine £8.50
Times: Noon-1.30pm/7-9pm. Closed D Sun, all Mon, L Tue, 25 Dec
Additional: Sunday L; Children 10+; ♨ dishes
Seats: 26
Smoking: No smoking in dining room

GLOUCESTER, **Hatton Court**

Beautiful 17th-century Cotswold manor house with spectacular views of the Severn valley. A varied choice of menus bring the likes of pan-fried breast of wood pigeon with pearl barley and lentil risotto, and croustade of goats' cheese and warm woodland mushrooms.

Upton Hill Upton St Leonards GL4 8DE
Map 3: SO81
Tel: 01452 617412
Fax: 01452 612945
Cost: *Alc* £22.50, set-price L £14.50/D £22.50. ☺ H/wine £11.50
Times: 12.30-2pm/7.15-9.30pm
Additional: Bar food; Sunday L;
Children welcome; ♨ dishes
Smoking: No smoking in dining room; Air conditioning
Accommodation: 45 en suite ★ ★ ★

Directions: 3 miles from Gloucester on B4037

LOWER SLAUGHTER,
Lower Slaughter Manor

Splendid country house hotel, equally splendid service.
Excellent Anglo-French cooking shows great attention to detail and service from a highly professional French serving team cannot be faulted. The small dining room is elegantly in

GL54 2HP
Map 4: SP12
Tel: 01451 820456
Fax: 01451 822150
Chef: Dominic Blake
Owners: Roy & Daphne Vaughan

Lower Slaughter Manor

Cost: *Alc* £45, set-price L £19.50
Times: Noon-1.45pm/7.30-9.30pm.
Additional: Sunday L; Children 12+;
🌢 dishes
Seats: 30. Private dining room 22.
Jacket & tie preferred
Smoking: No smoking in dining room
Accommodation: 16 en suite ★ ★ ★

Directions: Off A429, signposted 'The
Slaughters'. 0.5 mile into village on R

keeping with the rest of the listed manor; highly polished
tables sport solid silver cutlery and cut crystal glasses. Dinner
is a grand affair with both canapés and appetisers to be
negotiated before arriving at the first course. A salad of roast
scallops with aubergine caviar and sweet pepper dressing
starred first class diver scallops, cooked to perfection. Saucing
is skilful and correct – excellent, creamy Madeira jus gave
context to a succulent pan-fried veal loin served with wild
mushroom risotto. Grilled fillet of beef is classically served
with roasted artichokes, potatoes and onions and truffle sauce.
Mirroring the pre-starters, there is also a fashionable pre-
dessert – a mini crêpe topped with diced pear and maple syrup.
And that's before you tackle the banana parfait with chocolate
sauce, coffee, truffles and petits fours. An epic wine list is well-
constructed; mark-ups can be high, but there are some good
value bottles as well, plus a commendable listing of Chilean
wines.

LOWER SLAUGHTER,

Washbourne Court

GL54 2HS
Map 4: SP12
Tel: 01451 822143
Fax: 01451 821045
Chef: Chris Short
Owners: Mr & Mrs R Vaughan
Cost: *Alc* £35, set-price L £19.
H/wine £13.50
Times: 12.30-2pm/7.30-9pm
Additional: Bar food L; Sunday L;
Children 12+; 🌢 dishes

*Set next to the River Eye, this 17th-century hotel built in
honey-coloured Cotswold stone is magnificent.* Beamed
ceilings and open log fires set the scene within, and the
spacious dining room enjoys views of the grounds and river
through stone-mullioned windows. The style of cooking,
however, is modern, so expect the likes of pan-fried calves'
liver with bubble-and-squeak, or breast of duck with port and
passion fruit jus. Our early spring inspection meal started with

lavender-smoked rabbit, served with shavings of Parmesan and rocket with a pepper tapenade. Smoked artichokes accompanied the main dish of sea bass, a 'cracking piece of fish' set off well by a light coriander and lemongrass nage. Dessert – a pear and frangipane tart with clotted cream – was followed by excellent tea and well-made petits fours. Service is friendly and highly professional.

Seats: 65. Private dining room 14. Jacket & tie preferred
Smoking: No smoking in dining room
Accommodation: 28 en suite ★ ★ ★

Directions: Off A429 village centre by the river

MORETON-IN-MARSH,

Manor House Hotel

16th-century Cotswold manor house hotel with a relaxed, sometimes jovial feel. There's an inviting lounge and bar with log fires and deep-cushioned sofas, and a pretty walled garden – ideal for drinks in the summer. The restaurant offers a good selection of modern English dishes. Duck liver parfait with red onion marmalade and toasted brioche, for example, or cured salmon with roasted beetroot and watercress dressing. Main dishes tend to be more sturdy fare: expect the likes of medallions of beef with wild mushrooms and sauce béarnaise, steamed fillet of sea bass with roasted asparagus spears and a light tarragon jus, and roast rack of lamb with home-made apple and mint jelly. The reasonable wine list is marked with restraint and offers some decent bottles from around the world.

High Street, GL56 0LJ
Map 4: SP23
Tel: 01608 650501
Fax: 01608 651481
Chef: Richard Smith
Owner: Mr C Joseph
Cost: *Alc* £32, set-price L £12.50/D £24.50. ☺ H/wine £13.50
Times: Noon-2pm/7-9.30pm (9pm Sun)
Additional: Bar food L; Sunday L; Children welcome; 🍴 dishes
Seats: 50. Private dining room 100
Smoking: No smoking in dining room
Accommodation: 39 en suite ★ ★ ★

Directions: On main A429 Stow/Stratford road; at crossroads with A44 Evesham/Oxford road

MORETON-IN-THE-MARSH,

Marsh Goose

Soft hued and welcoming and often buzzing with cheerful conversation. Although the Marsh Goose empire is continuing to expand (the original restaurant and delicatessen have now been supplemented by a new venture – the Churchill Arms at Paxford , see entry), the virtues that have made this one of the most popular Cotswolds restaurants show no sign of dissipating. The atmosphere is unfussy and the cooking just as honest. Much of the emphasis is on the quality of the produce and the combinations are both intelligent and comforting. Typical of the approach would be the spiced pigeon breast with red pepper pesto and herb oil taken as a lunchtime starter, a deeply satisfying beginning to a winter meal. Main courses tend to be similarly hearty with the likes of a 'sublime' chump of lamb accompanied with butter beans, blackpudding and

High Street GL56 0AX
Map 4: SP23
Tel: 01608 653500
Fax: 01608 653510
Chefs: Sonya Kidney, Matthew Laughton
Owners: Sonya Kidney, Leo Brooke-Little, G Campbell Gray
Cost: Set-price D £29.50. H/wine £10
Times: 12.30-2.15pm/7.30-9.15pm. Closed D Sun, all Mon
Additional: Sunday L; Children welcome
Seats: 60
Smoking: No smoking in dining room

Meaux mustard sauce. The robust theme stretches to the desserts, where roasted figs with almonds served with a Mascarpone iced parfait provided a deliciously rewarding end to one inspection meal.

NAILSWORTH, Egypt Mill Hotel

Converted 16th-century mill with a ground floor bistro and comfortable restaurant upstairs. Interesting dishes include Thai fishcakes with plum sauce and an excellent shank of lamb.

Smoking: No smoking in dining room
Accommodation: 18 en suite ★ ★

Directions: On the A46

GL6 0AE
Map 3: ST89
Tel: 01453 833449
Fax: 01453 836098
Cost: *Alc* £20, set-price L £9 (2 courses). ☺ H/wine £9.95
Times: Noon-1.45pm/7-9.45pm. Closed L Sat, D Sun, all Mon
Additional: Bar food; Sunday L; Children welcome; ✿ dishes

NAILSWORTH,
Waterman's Restaurant ✿✿

Old Market GL6 0BX
Map 3: ST89
Tel: 01453 832808
Chef: Sarah Waterman
Owners: John & Sarah Waterman
Cost: *Alc* £22. ☺ H/wine £8.95
Times: D only, 6-9.30pm. Closed Sun, Mon
Additional: Bar food L Sat (10-2pm); Children welcome; ✿ dishes
Seats: 28. Private dining room 10
Smoking: No-smoking area; No pipes & cigars

Directions: Signposted off A46, in the centre of Nailsworth

Nooks and crannies abound in the 16th-century Cotswold stone cottage. Low beams galore in the Garden Room and a walled courtyard garden with lion's head fountain and trout stream are all part of the attraction. Wine books, bottles and magazines (wines are carefully chosen and during the winter there are regular tastings and supper nights), plus antlers and a huge fireplace add to the relaxed atmosphere. Sarah Waterman's cooking is modern but uncluttered: foie gras, bacon and potato cakes topped with a poached egg; hot and spicy pork tenderloin sliced over sweet potato mash with an apricot and ginger butter sauce; and sticky caramel tart with cinnamon cream and oranges poached in Glayva liqueuer are typical of the style. Game, fish and meat are sourced locally and vegetables frequently come from the restaurant's organic allotment.

NEWENT, Three Choirs
Vineyards Restaurant ✿✿

Warm and inviting restaurant, with views over the vineyards and the rolling countryside. Naturally, the wine list is composed mainly of bottles from the estate, with guest wines chosen for their quality and value. A great deal of produce is local: pork is from a breed of Gloucester Old Spots, for

GL18 1LS
Map 3: SO72
Tel: 01531 890223
Fax: 01531 890877
Chef: Antony Warburton
Cost: *Alc* £16, set-price L £10 (2 courses)/D £18.50. ☺ H/wine £7.50

Three Choirs Vineyards Restaurant

Times: Noon-2.30pm/7-9pm. Closed D Sun, all Mon
Additional: Children welcome; dishes
Seats: 50
Smoking: No smoking in dining room

Directions: On B4215, N of Newent

instance, and a lot of the fruit comes from a nearby farm. English goats' cheese on a croûte with walnut salad makes a simple but effective starter, as does a terrine of game and duck liver with damson sauce. A winter main course of a hearty and earthy lamb casserole has been well received, and there might also be calves' liver and bacon with sage and onion jus, or pan-fried fillet of sea bass with roasted red pepper and chorizo. Puddings are from the bread-and-butter and sticky toffee school, although there might be something fruity like pears poached in white wine.

PAINSWICK, **Country Elephant** ✿✿

A small bar area leads into this restaurant, a room full of refreshing fabrics and colours. It's also comfortably furnished, with fresh flowers, a roaring fire in winter. and manages to retain its Cotswold charm. 'A high percentage of our food is organic or free-range,' writes the Elephant, a policy that converts into Hereford snails with scallops in Pernod and herb butter, medallions of Scottish beef with a red onion and port confit, and a selection of British and Irish cheeses. Both *carte* and set-price menu have just three or four choices at each course, another good policy given that this is a one-man band. An inspector was enraptured by a starter of smoked eel with 'bags of flavour' on smooth and creamy potato purée and topped with crisp pancetta and herbs. Honey-roast breast and thigh of guinea fowl came next on a bed of cubed carrot and swede with sautéed wild mushrooms, then a simple but none the less effective dessert of light passion fruit mousse with mango sauce. A number of wines are sold by the glass – another customer-friendly touch.

New Street GL6 6XH
Map 3: SO80
Tel/Fax: 01452 813564
Chef/Owner: Robert Rees
Cost: *Alc* £28, set-price L £13 (2 courses)/D £18 (2 courses). ☺ H/wine £10.80
Times: Noon-2pm/7-10pm. Closed D Sun, all Mon, 1 wk Xmas
Additional: Sunday L; Children welcome; dishes
Seats: 30
Smoking: No smoking in dining room

Directions: On the A46 between Stroud and Cheltenham

PAINSWICK, **Painswick Hotel** ✿✿

Delightful Palladian mansion enjoys calming views of the valley and is a perfect place to relax and unwind. On warm evenings sip an aperitif on the stone balcony or in the well-manicured garden, before moving to the oak-panelled dining room to try some classic French cooking. Our April meal was a joy. A salad of rabbit and mixed leaves with black truffle dressing we found 'full of flavour'. The centrepiece of the meal, however, was an impressive (and large) fresh fillet of Dover sole wrapped around a langoustine tail, set on a bed of thin home-made noodles, deftly flavoured with lemon and herbs, and garnished with oysters, scallops and asparagus.

Kemps Lane GL6 6YB
Map 3: SO80
Tel: 01452 812160
Fax: 01452 814059
Chef: Kenny Coltman
Owners: Helen & Gareth Pugh
Cost: *Alc* £32, set-price L £13 (2 courses)/D £26.50. H/wine £12.50
Times: 12.30-2pm/7.30-9.30pm
Additional: Sunday L; Children welcome; dishes
Seats: 60. Private dining room 16
Smoking: No pipes & cigars

Directions: From Painswick centre turn by the church, continue & turn R by the cross. Hotel 1st turn on R

PAXFORD, **The Churchill Arms**  **NEW**

Sonja Kidney and her husband Leo Brooke-Little have, after years of running a popular and successful country town restaurant (The Marsh Goose, see entry Moreton-in-Marsh), expanded into the pub market (see also Hare and Hounds Chedworth). Keen to find a more informal and flexible set-up, where 'people's expectations are not so rigid' and where 'we have the freedom to experiment', they bought the Churchill Arms, a humble village pub. Expect an eclectic mix of furnishings, a fine inglenook fireplace with woodburning stove, and a corner where the odd table or two are kept for local drinkers, maintaining the traditional village pub atmosphere. Chalkboards provide the twice-daily-changing menu. Dishes listed are modern, occasionally reflecting Sonja's Caribbean roots. We enjoyed freshly-made cheese fritters served on a pool of grain mustard and orange sauce, and red snapper on roasted butternut squash with pesto. In addition, there's local real ales on draught and a good blackboard list of wines.

Painswick Hotel

Accommodation: 19 en suite ★★★

GL55 6XH
Tel: 01386 594000
Telephone for further details

Directions: 2 miles E of Chipping Campden, 4 miles N of Moreton-in-Marsh

RANGEWORTHY,

Rangeworthy Court Hotel

A warm and welcoming atmosphere prevails at this substantial creeper-clad manor house within striking distance of the motorway system. The varied, interesting menu takes in a daily soup and fish dishes.

Church Lane Wotton Road
BS37 7ND
Map 3: ST68
Tel: 01454 228347
Fax: 01454 228945
Cost: *Alc* £24, set-price L £9.95. ☺
H/wine £10.50
Times: Noon-1.45pm/7-9pm (9.30pm Sat)
Additional: Bar food L; Sunday L; Children welcome; ☻ dishes
Smoking: No smoking in dining room
Accommodation: 13 en suite ★★

Directions: Signposted off B4058, down Church Lane

STONEHOUSE,

Stonehouse Court ❀❀

Historic house with resident ghost amid the comfortable trappings. The John Henry Restaurant at this Cotswolds country-house hotel is named after a butler who killed himself after being rejected by the lady of the house, and he is said to haunt older parts of the building (it dates from 1601). Relax in the comfortable panelled lounge, where there's an impressive fireplace, and enjoy a meal in the restaurant. Start with wild mushroom risotto with Parmesan, roasted pine nuts and white truffle oil unusually joined by poached eggs, and go on to sautéed fillet of beef with foie gras and beetroot salad. Vegetarians have a separate menu, and fish-eaters could opt for marinated mackerel fillets with celeriac remoulade and then grilled Dover sole with lemon butter. Finish with an impressive array of English cheeses or something sweeter, like sticky toffee pudding with butterscotch sauce. Helpful tasting notes facilitate choosing a bottle of wine from a fairly lengthy list.

Directions: M5/J13/A419 (Stroud); 1.5 miles from M-way, 1 mile from Stonehouse

Stroud GL10 3RA
Map 3: SO80
Tel: 01453 825155
Fax: 01453 824611
Chef: Ali Hussain
Owner: Pageant Hotels
Cost: *Alc* £30, set-price D £25. ☺
H/wine £10.95
Times: Noon-1.45pm/7-9.45pm.
Closed L Sat
Additional: Bar food L; Sunday L;
Children welcome; ⑤ dishes
Seats: 70. Private room 20
Smoking: No smoking in dining room
Accommodation: 36 en suite ★ ★ ★

STOW-ON-THE-WOLD,

Fosse Manor ❀

Country house-style restaurant combining some modish dishes (snapper with sun-dried tomato and basil sauce) with more traditional elements (plaice with lobster sauce).

Cheltenham GL54 1JX
Map 4: SP12
Tel: 01451 830354
Fax: 01451 832486
Cost: *Alc* £30, set-price L £15.50. ☺
H/wine £11.95
Times: 12.30-2pm/7-9.30pm. Closed
7 days Xmas
Additional: Bar Food; Sunday L;
Children welcome; ⑤ dishes
Smoking: No smoking in dining room;
Air conditioning
Accommodation: 20 rooms, 18 en
suite ★ ★ ★

Directions: One mile S of Stow-on-
the-Wold on the A429 (Cirencester)

STOW-ON-THE-WOLD,

Grapevine Hotel ❀❀

Charming 17th-century town centre hotel. The name comes from the gnarled old Hamburg vine that spreads out under the roof of the hotel's light, airy conservatory restaurant. An informal lunch *carte* (offering the likes of brochette of Brie and pancetta with cranberry and orange confit, and Cajun chicken with French fries and mayonnaise) is replaced at night by a fixed-price menu with about five choices at each stage. Warm crab and ginger strudel with avocado salsa and chilli oil, and a red onion tartlet topped with duck livers typify starters.

Sheep Street GL54 1AU
Map 4: SP12
Tel: 01451 830344
Fax: 01451 832278
Chef: Maria Holley
Owner: Mrs S Elliot
Cost: *Alc* £15.85, set-price D £26 (5
courses). H/wine £10.95
Times: Noon-2.30pm/7-9.15pm
Additional: Bar food L; Sunday L;
Children welcome; ⑤ dishes

Main courses such as seafood fricassée with Pernod cream sauce, honey-baked tenderloin of pork with caramelised apples and cider sauce, and breast of Barbary duck with a wild berry sauce and crispy leeks show a sure hand. Puddings range from rich dark-chocolate and stout cake with Cornish clotted cream, to a selection of farmhouse cheeses served with walnut bread.

Directions: Off Fosseway A429, take A436 Chipping Norton; 150 yards on R facing green

Grapevine Hotel

Seats: 70. Private dining room 20
Smoking: No smoking in dining room
Accommodation: 22 en suite ★ ★ ★

STOW-ON-THE-WOLD,

Old Farmhouse Hotel

16th-century listed manor farm complete with Cotswold stone walls, beams, and oak panelling. This is the place for richly flavoured farmhouse cooking, as well as exploring the extensive range of malt whiskies.

Smoking: No smoking in dining room
Accommodation: 13 rooms, 11 en suite ★ ★

Directions: One mile W of Stow-on-the-Wold, on B4068

Lower Swell GL54 1LF
Map 4: SP12
Tel: 01451 830232
Fax: 01451 870962
Cost: Set-price L £14.50/D £18.75. ☺
H/wine £11.75
Times: Noon-2pm/7-9pm
Additional: Bar food; Sunday L;
Children welcome; ❀ dishes

STOW-ON-THE-WOLD,

Wyck Hill House Hotel

Delightful 18th-century house with acres of grounds and excellent service. The kitchen demonstrates a serious approach to food with a studied menu built on quality produce, much of it local. There's an uncluttered modern British feel to some soundly traditional dishes – a level of well-judged eclecticism and restraint in dishes such as supreme of salmon wrapped in iceberg lettuce leaves ad served with a gratin of mussels, or breast of chicken with a red pepper mousse, grilled ratatouille and a red wine sauce. A typical meal could bring duck and pistachio terrine with an apple and grape chutney, braised shank of lamb with lentils, winter vegetables and a rosemary jus, and a passion fruit mousse with spiced orange syrup.

Directions: A424 (Burford) 1.5 miles from Stow

Burford Road GL54 1HY
Map 4: SP12
Tel: 01451 831936
Fax: 01451 832243
Chef: Ian Smith
Cost: *Alc* £35. H/wine £14.95
Times: 12.30-2pm/7-9.30pm
Additional: Sunday L; Children welcome; ❀ dishes
Seats: 60. Private dining room 24. Jacket & tie preferred
Smoking: No smoking in dining room
Accommodation: 32 en suite ★ ★ ★ ★

STROUD,

Bear of Rodborough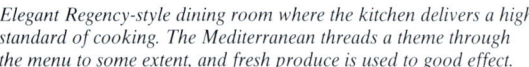

Rodborough Common GL5 5DE
Map 3: SO80
Tel: 01453 878522
Fax: 01453 872523
Cost: *Alc* £22, set-price L £9.75/D £19.95 (4 courses). ☺ H/wine £9.75
Times: 12.30-2.30pm/7-9.30pm
Additional: Bar food; Sunday L; Children welcome; ✿ dishes
Smoking: No smoking in dining room
Accommodation: 46 en suite ★ ★ ★

Directions: From M5 J13 follow signs for Stonehouse then Rodborough

Old coaching inn high above Stroud with stunning views of the Golden Valley. Visitors are drawn by the quality cooking: look out for pan-fried smoked salmon fishcakes, and traditional roast rack of lamb with mint gravy.

STROUD, Burleigh Court

Elegant Regency-style dining room where the kitchen delivers a high standard of cooking. The Mediterranean threads a theme through the menu to some extent, and fresh produce is used to good effect.

Smoking: No smoking in dining room
Accommodation: 17 en suite ★ ★ ★

Directions: 0.75m off A419 E of Stroud

Minchinhampton GL5 2PF
Map 3: SO80
Tel: 01453 883804
Fax: 01453 886870
Cost: *Alc* £17.50, set-price D £22.50. ☺ H/wine £11
Times: Noon-1.45pm/7-8.45pm
Additional: Bar food; Sunday L; Children welcome; ✿ dishes

STROUD, Fischers

Fischers is an intimate, warm restaurant in what used to be a school house. The good-value set lunch menus might see sautéed duck livers with a poached egg on a potato cake, followed by fillets of lemon sole with spinach and deep-fried leeks, then British cheeses. Dinner sets the kitchen running to the full extent of its capabilities, with the same duck livers turning up in a starter alongside partridge breast and poached quails' eggs, and turning out ambitious main courses of fillet of sea bass with olive potatoes, mussel tarte Tatin and tomato cannelloni, pan-fried fillet of beef with cheese tortellini, seared marinated foie gras and red wine jus, and carved loin of lamb with baby leeks, caramelised turnips and juniper sauce. Puddings show no less skill and imagination, either, in a trio of lemon desserts tart, sorbet and mousse – or caramel crème brûlée with pear and apple cake.

169 Slad Road GL5 1RG
Map 3: SO80
Tel: 01453 759950
Chef: Ben Glassonbury
Owners: Stephen & Jacqueline Fischer
Cost: *Alc* £28, set-price L £15/D £17.50. ☺ H/wine £10
Times: Noon-2.30pm/7-10pm. Closed D Sun, all Mon
Additional: Sunday L; Children 4+; ✿ dishes
Seats: 30
Smoking: No smoking in dining room

Directions: From M5 J13 take Stroud ring road towards Cheltenham. At last roundabout turn R, then 1st L into Slad Rd

TETBURY, Calcot Manor

Traditional country house, smart yet unstuffy. The Conservatory restaurant has a bright cheery informality about

Calcot GL8 8YJ
Map 3: ST89
Tel: 01666 890391
Fax: 01666 890394

Calcot Manor

Chef: Michael Croft
Owner: Richard Ball
Cost: Set-price L £13.50 (2 courses)
Times: Noon-2.30pm/7-9.30pm
Additional: Bar food; Sunday L;
Children welcome; 🍴 dishes
Smoking: No smoking in dining room
Accommodation: 27 en suite ★★★

Directions: 4 miles W of Tetbury on
A4135 close to intersection with A45

it; good quality table linen and fresh flowers help create the sense of being at a posh garden party. Service is well-handled and dispensed by mainly French staff in relaxed bistro-style. The menu is reminiscent of the River Café, a style that appealed to our inspector who found herself completely spoilt for choice. In the end she ate, with relish, pappardelle with roasted butternut squash, Mozzarella and pine nuts, with pesto, Parmesan, spinach and roasted peppers (memorable for clarity of flavours and simplicity), slow-cooked crispy pork served in a deep bowl with Chinese-style vegetables (pronounced 'earthy' and a good modern British version of a Chinese classic), and banana toffee crumble tart with vanilla ice cream. The wine list has around 100 offerings.

TETBURY,

The Close Hotel ✿✿✿

Taking the helm at a restaurant with an established reputation must engender mixed feelings in a relatively unknown chef. On the one hand, it must be a marvellous opportunity, on the other, the challenge of maintaining standards makes it something of a sink or swim situation. Happily, we can report that Daren Bale is comfortably afloat and making something of a name for himself in an area not short of serious restaurants. A glance at the menu reveals plenty of the country house style to be found elsewhere in the region. The heart of the cooking though, is an intelligent approach that sees quality of produce and depth of flavour well to the fore. Canapés, appetisers and petits fours can be something of an afterthought, but here the kitchen uses them as an extra chance to impress with, for instance, a witty teaspoon of 'steak and chips' being the star of the pre-dinner offerings. That kind of wry style adds an extra edge to a menu that has also included an inspired remake of fish, chips and mushy peas with a fillet of Whitby cod, purée of green pea and crisp lemon potato taking the principal parts, and a welcome slab of foie gras as the special guest star. The cooking has resulted in some fine balancing of flavours: pan-roasted chump of lamb, for example, is able to co-exist with delicately truffle-scented green beans and a lavender and horseradish jus. The dexterity extends to the desserts with a top-notch pineapple tarte Tatin with fromage frais ice cream being a notable success. The wine list is of manageable length, well sourced and not outrageous in its pricing.

8 Long Street GL8 8AQ
Map 3: ST89
Tel: 01666 502272
Fax: 01666 504401
Chef: Daren Bale
Owner: Old English Inns
Cost: *Alc* £35, set-price L £16/D
£29.50. ☺ H/wine £14.50
Times: Noon-2pm/D from 7.30pm
Additional: Sunday L; 🍴 dishes
Seats: 20. Private dining room 18.
Jacket & tie required
Smoking: No smoking in dining room
Accommodation: 15 en suite ★★★

Directions: From M4 J17 onto A429
to Malmesbury. From M5 J14 onto
B4509

TETBURY, **Snooty Fox**

Market Place GL8 8DD
Map 3: ST89
Tel: 01666 502436
Fax: 01666 503479
Cost: *Alc* £20. ☺ H/wine £11.95
Times: Noon-2pm/7-9.45pm
Additional: Bar food; Sunday L;
Children welcome; 🍴 dishes
Smoking: No smoking in dining room
Accommodation: 12 en suite ★ ★ ★

Directions: Town centre opposite the
Market Place

*Despite the name, there's nothing snooty at the Fox. The atmosphere
is warm, service is attentive, and the food unpretentious. Try seared
salmon on pepper and tomato salsa, or home-made faggots with
mushy pea mash.*

THORNBURY, **Thornbury Castle**

Castle Street BS35 1HH
Map 3: ST69
Tel: 01454 281182
Fax: 01454 416188
Chef: Stephan Oppenhagen
Owner: The Baron of Portlethen
Cost: Set-price D £39.50. H/wine £12
Times: Noon-2pm/7-10pm. Closed 4
days Jan from 1st Sun
Additional: Sunday L; Children
welcome; 🍴 dishes
Seats: 60. Private dining rooms 14.
Jacket & tie preferred
Smoking: No smoking in dining room
Accommodation: 20 en suite ★ ★ ★

Directions: At bottom of High Street
turn left into Castle Street. The
entrance is to left of St. Mary's
Church

***Steeped in history and still as much a castle as when building
commenced in 1511.*** Recent years have seen Thornbury
transformed into a fine country house hotel with the restoration
handled sympathetically and both public and bedrooms remain
true to the character of the original building. Cooking is a
strength, with Stephan Oppenhagen bringing some Scandinavian
influences to a menu that generally runs along modern British
lines. A meal in May produced vegetable terrine oriental served
with ginger, soy and lemongrass marinade, roasted rack of lamb
with parsley and cheese crust, garlic confit, tomato, aubergine
and ravioli, and assiette of citrus fruits. The grounds include
classical gardens and a vineyard producing Müller-Thurgau
wines, which are available in the hotel.

UPPER SLAUGHTER,
Lords of the Manor

GL54 2JD
Map 4: SP12
Tel: 01451 820243
Fax: 01451 820696
Chef: John Campbell

***One of the finest country house hotels with exemplary
service.*** The setting is quintessentially English, and the mellow
former rectory in lovingly tended gardens lends itself to the

Lords of the Manor

Cost: *Alc* £42, set-price L £19.50/D
£32.50. H/wine £14.95
Times: Noon-2.30pm/7-9.30pm
Additional: Bar food L; Sunday L;
Children 7+; ◑ dishes
Seats: 55. Private dining room 9
Smoking: No smoking in dining room
Accommodation: 27 en suite ★ ★ ★

Directions: Follow sign towards The
Slaughters off A429. The restaurant is
in centre of Upper Slaughter

pursuit of peace and relaxation. Service remains at all times a
highly polished formal display, yet very attentive. John
Campbell's cooking is a major draw. Exciting and memorable
in places, his terse menus, really no more than a
straightforward list of ingredients, belie the skill and talent
required to produce them. Dishes are prepared with precision,
accuracy is a keyword. Our inspector's superlative strewn
report took in a superb *amuse-bouche* of breaded soft
poached quail's egg with asparagus tips and a little truffled
dressing; a terrine of pressed chicken and foie gras layered
with slender cabbage leaves, tiny mushrooms and pine nuts, as
well as a little more truffle flavour over green beans salad; sea
bass set on fine-cut ratatouille with a delicate ravioli of lobster
meat and mousseline topped with a lovely frothy lobster
essence; and an assiette of desserts which started with a
tumbler of pannacotta topped with raspberry jelly, was
followed by banana soufflé, champagne and rhubarb jelly,
then a multi-layered ice cream separated by crisp wafer-thin
apple slices; and finished with a melting chocolate fondant.
The big wine list is a quality tome, offering choice and depth
and requires time to do it justice. Do ask the advice of Tibet
Kamel, the exceptionally friendly and helpful sommelier, you
will not be disappointed.

WINCHCOMBE, **Wesley House** ✿✿

High Street GL54 5LT
Map 4: SP02
Tel: 01242 602366
Fax: 01242 602405
Chef: Jonathan Lewis
Owners: Jonathan Lewis,
Matthew Brown

Restaurant with rooms that's the epitome of comfort. If more
evidence is needed of good things coming in small packages
then Wesley House is it. The high street frontage is almost
dolls house in scale, but gives way to a long lounge and dining

area laid out in elegant but relatively informal style. The cooking is more modish and metropolitan than might be expected in this location and the menu is awash with sturdy flavours together with liberal oriental influences. Amongst the starters, Thai vegetable soup with noodles, lemon grass and enoki wun-tuns has featured alongside marinated fillets of red mullet with warm potato and truffle salad. Fish is well sourced and judiciously cooked with a fat chunk of monkfish, for instance, being accompanied by chilli noodles. Desserts are handled with dexterity and have included an accurate lemon tart and wild strawberry delice. A shortened lunchtime menu offers particularly good value.

Cost: *Alc* £28.50, set-price L £8.95 (2 courses)/D £15.50 (2 courses). ☺ H/wine £11.50
Times: Noon-2pm/7-9pm. Closed D Sun, 2 wks Jan
Additional: Bar food L; Sunday L; Children welcome; ✿ dishes
Seats: 50
Smoking: No-smoking area; No pipes & cigars
Accommodation: 5 en suite

Directions: In the centre of Winchcombe on the main road

GREATER MANCHESTER

ALTRINCHAM, **Juniper**

21 The Downs WA14 2QD
Map 7: SJ78
Tel: 0161 9294008
Fax: 0161 9294009
Chef: Paul Kitching
Owner: Mrs Miles
Cost: *Alc* £32, set-price L £18/D £36. H/wine £14
Times: Noon-2.30pm/7-10pm. Closed L Sat & Mon, all Sun
Additional: Children welcome
Seats: 48. Private dining room 12
Smoking: No pipes & cigars; Air conditioning

High-flying Cheshire restaurant that pulls out all the stops.
When French cooking meets Italianate decor, the result is lift-off, especially when powered by the passion Paul Kitching puts into every dish that comes out of his tiny kitchen. The menu is impressive and includes some exciting concepts. Dishes have a deceptive simplicity of construction, are dependent on the best and freshest of seasonal ingredients and frequently show the touch of magic only certain chefs can produce to bring it all together. Carrot, foie gras and wild mushroom pressing with saffron glaze was a triumph of subtle flavour, superb presentation and spot-on seasoning. This is high wire with other dishes in the Kitching repertoire including a fabulous creamy winter soup of parsnip and sauté foie gras, and breast of duck with black pudding and mustard seed sauce. Signature soufflés, such as rice pudding with rosemary ice cream, have pride of place on the dessert menu. Such stylish cooking does not come cheap, but the restaurant has built a strong following among the well-heeled, well-travelled residents of North Cheshire.

Directions: A556 Chester-Manchester Rd

FROM 2009   NOW THE BOWDON HOTEL & LEISURE CLUB

ALTRINCHAM,

Quality Hotel Altrincham

Stylish black and gold decor, alcoves and pillars set the tone for careful cooking that takes in modern English and Mediterranean ideas. Popular, extended hotel within easy reach of the motorway system and airport.

Langham Road Bowdon
WA14 2HT
Map 7: SJ78
Tel: 0161 9287121
Fax: 0161 9277560
Cost: *Alc* £23, set-price L £9.40/D £17.95. H/wine £10.95
Times: Noon-2pm/7-9.45pm. Closed L Sat
Additional: Bar food; Sunday L; Children welcome; dishes
Smoking: No-smoking area; No pipes & cigars; Air conditioning
Accommodation: 89 en suite ★ ★ ★

Directions: Leave M56/J7 (Altrincham). At large roundabout take 3rd exit (Altrincham); at next traffic lights turn R into Park Rd. Hotel 1 mile on R

ALTRINCHAM,

Woodland Park Hotel

Privately owned hotel where carefully prepared four-course meals are professionally served in the Terrace restaurant. Well reported dishes include seared ginger scallops and supreme of chicken.

Wellington Road Timperley
WA15 7RG
Map 7: SJ78
Tel: 0161 9288631 ✗
Fax: 0161 9412821
Cost: *Alc* £24, set-price L £12.95/D £15.95 (2 courses). ☺ H/wine £10.95
Times: 10am-2pm/7-10pm. Closed L Sat
Additional: Bar Food L; Children welcome; dishes
Smoking: No smoking in dining room; Air conditioning
Accommodation: 46 en suite ★ ★ ★

Directions: 300 yds from Metro-Link Station – Navigation Road

BURY, # Normandie Hotel

High on a hill at the end of a steep country lane, yet surprisingly close to the motorway network, the hotel enjoys far-reaching views over Greater Manchester to the Pennines beyond. An enthusiastic team offer warm hospitality and professional service in the small and friendly restaurant decorated in acid-bright tones. The style of cooking is based on classical Anglo-French foundations with a happy emphasis on the careful cooking of good raw materials. An excellent piece of brill, perfectly cooked, was the centrepiece of one inspection dish that also combined some sweet, crunchy langoustine with Alsace sauce. Starters have included a seasonal salad of asparagus with tomato and broad bean vinaigrette and well-

Elbut Lane Birtle BL9 6UT
Map 7: SD81
Tel: 0161 7643869/1170
Fax: 0161 7644866
Chef: Paul Bellingham
Owners: Max & Susan Moussa
Cost: *Alc* £25, set-price L £12.50/D £15. ☺ H/wine £9.95.
Times: Noon-2pm/7-9.30pm. Closed L Sat, all Sun, 1 wk Easter, last wk Dec, 1st wk Jan
Additional: Children welcome; dishes
Seats: 50

executed soups, often with an interesting twist. On the dessert front, there are plenty of familiar favourites including poached caramelised pears with chocolate sauce. The wine list is full of character and mark-ups are sensible.

Smoking: No pipes & cigars
Accommodation: 23 en suite ★ ★ ★

Directions: From M66/J2, take A58 – Bury. After 100yds turn R into Wash Lane, then 1st R into Willow Street, R at B6222. After 1 mile L into Elbut Lane, then up hill 1 mile

---

MANCHESTER,

Copthorne Manchester

Clippers Quay Salford Quays M5 2XP
Map 7: SJ89
Tel: 0161 8737321
Fax: 0161 8737318
Telephone for further details

Set next to Salford Quays, this modern brick-built hotel offers fine dining in Chandlers Restaurant. Typical dishes include escabeche of red mullet with salsa verde, and medallions of venison with grilled polenta and roasted shallots.

Directions: Close to M602

MANCHESTER, **Little Yang Sing**

17 George Street M1 4HE
Map 7: SJ89
Tel: 0161 2287722
Fax: 0161 2379257
Cost: *Alc* £17, set-price L £9/D £15.
☺ H/wine £10
Times: Noon-11.15pm. Closed 25 Dec

Basement restaurant, part of a listed building in the heart of Chinatown, which, despite its bright modern decor, retains an authentic Cantonese atmosphere.

Additional: Sunday L; Children welcome; 🐟 dishes
Smoking: Air conditioning

Directions: Behind Piccadilly Plaza on the corner of George & Charlotte Street, on Metrolink route

---

MANCHESTER,

Market Restaurant

104 High Street M4 1HQ
Map 7: SJ89
Tel/Fax: 0161 8343743
Chefs: Mary-Rose Edgecombe, Paul Mertz, Dawn Wellens
Owners: Peter O'Grady, Anne O'Grady, Mary-Rose Edgecombe
Cost: *Alc* £25. ☺ H/wine £6.95
Times: D only, 6-9.30pm. Closed Sun, Mon, Tue, 1 wk Xmas/Spring, most of Aug
Additional: Children welcome; 🐟 dishes
Seats: 46.
Smoking: Air conditioning

Directions: On the corner of Edge St and High St, close to Craft Village. Nearest Metro station – High St

Bright, breezy, refreshing restaurant with a cluttered bric à brac look. This totally unpretentious place is run as a sideline by partners working full-time elsewhere, hence no lunches and only open four evenings a week. The menu roams all over the world with dishes such as the Indonesian salad gado gado, potage garbanzos, or afelia (pork fillet marinated in red wine and coriander seeds). Blasts-from-the-past include fillet of beef stuffed with Stilton and wrapped in smoked bacon with red wine gravy, and Eton Mess (crushed meringues, strawberries, Kirsch, and whipped jersey cream). Vegetarians are well looked after with imaginative ideas such as Gruyère cheese and chive roulade with leek filling and herb sauce. Dessert lovers should enquire when the next Pudding Club convenes: one savoury course and five puddings.

MANCHESTER,

Marriot Manchester Hotel

Worsley Park Walkden Road Worsley M28 2QT
Map 7: SJ89
Tel: 0161 9752000
Fax: 0161 7996341
Cost: *Alc* £28, set-price L £15/D £18. ☺ H/wine £11.95
Times: Noon-2pm/7-10pm. Closed L Sat, 31 Dec

Farming implements displayed in Brindleys restaurant reflect the modern hotel's origins as a farm. A short but varied carte offers an interesting range of seasonal dishes.

Additional: Sunday L; Children welcome; ✦ dishes
Smoking: No-smoking area; Air conditioning
Accommodation: 159 en suite ★★★★

Directions: From M60 J13 take A575. Hotel on L

MANCHESTER, **Mash & Air**

40 Chorlton Street M1 3HW
Map 7: SJ89
Tel: 0161 6616161
Fax: 0161 6616060
Chef: Jason Whitelock
Owner: Oliver Peyton
Cost: *Alc* £30, set-price L £13. ☺ H/wine £12.50
Times: Noon-3pm/5-11pm, (Air D Thu-Sat only). Closed Sun
Additional: Bar food; Sunday Brunch; Children welcome; ✦ dishes
Seats: 120. Private dining room 10
Smoking: Air conditioning

Directions: City centre on corner of Chorlton Street/Canal Street

The name is taken from a stage in the brewing process, appropriate given that this converted mill is built around a microbrewery. Mash, composed of ground-floor bar and first-floor eating area, concentrates on such things as pizzas from the wood-fired oven, salads and sandwiches, Air is a smart, modernist restaurant with floor-to ceiling windows. In here you can expect to find modish tuna spring roll with an oriental dressing, ginger crisps and wasabi. A starter of tomato tarte Tatin has been praised for its pastrywork and flavour, and a main course of roasted sea bass on a tomato and vanilla emulsion is surprisingly well-partnered by a delicate mixture of crab and scallops. Nougatine parfait, crunchily studded with pistachios on a moreish caramel cream, comes recommended too. The adventurous could try one of the house beers, or go for something from the eclectic wine list, where many are sold by the glass.

MANCHESTER,

Le Meridien Victoria & Albert

Water Street M60 9EA
Map 7: SJ89
Tel: 0161 8321188
Fax: 0161 8342484
Chef: Paul Patterson
Cost: *Alc* £35, set-price D £25. ☺ H/wine £13
Times: D only, 7-10pm. Closed Sun, Mon, Bhs
Additional: Bar food; Children welcome; ✦ menu
Seats: 50. Private dining room 60. Jacket & tie preferred
Smoking: No-smoking area; No pipes & cigars; Air conditioning
Accommodation: 156 en suite ★★★★

Plush hotel converted from a bonded warehouse. Of the Coronation Street residents, possibly only Mike Baldwin would be likely to frequent The Sherlock Holmes restaurant. Not unusual though to see the actors here, as this is just a stone's throw from the Granada Studios. In actual fact, the atmosphere is far from rarefied and staff offer a relatively relaxed service. Paul Patterson continues to mix from a palette that offers Mediterranean and Oriental influences as well as some British classics. Of the latter, simply grilled Dover sole has been distinguished by spot-on timing and the use of excellent fish. Classic French styles are often the most successful here with roasted Bresse pigeon being the highlight of one inspector's meal. Desserts are generally variations on well known themes such as crème brûlée with rhubarb sorbet.

Directions: Head for city centre and follow signs for Granada Studio Tours. Hotel is opposite

MANCHESTER,
Moss Nook Restaurant ❀❀

Ringway Road M22 5WD
Map 7: SJ89
Tel: 0161 4374778
Fax: 0161 4988089
Chef: Kevin Lofthouse
Owners: Derek & Pauline Harrison
Cost: *Alc* £40, set-price L £18.50 (5 courses)/D £31.50 (7 courses). H/wine £9.95
Times: Noon-1.30pm/7-9.30pm. Closed L Sat, all Sun & Mon, 2 wks Xmas
Seats: 65. Jacket & tie preferred

Restaurant of long standing, hard by Manchester Airport.
Red dominates the interior, with its old clocks, lace cloths, cream napkins and crystal glassware. The kitchen might not follow the latest fads in food fashion, but it buys the best ingredients and cooks them carefully. Both the 'surprise' and 'tasting' menus are popular choices, while from the *carte* you could order a starter of chicken mousse with black pudding, the whole dish lifted by a tarragon sauce, or a luxurious plate of grilled lobster on baby vegetables surrounded by pan-seared scallops. Medallions of venison with green peppercorn sauce satisfied an inspector for their pronounced flavour and tenderness, with toùrnedos Rossini or grilled Dover sole meunière among other options. Chocolate and chestnut parfait, rich and perfectly smooth, lightened by mint cream, makes a satisfying pudding.

Directions: Close to Manchester Airport – at junction of Ringway with B5166

MANCHESTER, # New Emperor ❀

52-56 George Street M1 4HF
Map 7: SJ89
Tel: 0161 2282883
Fax: 0161 2286620
Cost: *Alc* £10, set-price L £3.80 (2 courses)/D £15.50. ☺ H/wine £10
Times: Noon-11.45pm
Additional: Children welcome; ✿ dishes
Smoking: Air conditioning

Large modern Cantonese restaurant popular with local Chinese. A good choice of dim sum was complemented by casseroled bean curd served with shredded red cooked pork.

Directions: Heart of Chinatown, near Manchester Piccadilly

MANCHESTER,
Rhodes & Co

Waters Reach Trafford Park
Map 7: SJ89
Tel: 0161 8681900
Fax: 0161 8681901
Cost: *Alc* £25, set-price L £11.50. ☺
H/wine £12
Times: Noon-2.30pm/6.30-9.45pm.
Closed Sat & Sun L (restaurant only),
25 Dec, New Year

No doubt the denizens of the Stretford Road end will be queueing for their post-match cod and chips outside the Man United fan's latest venture. Gary Rhodes (for it is he) is on target with simple, direct food and decor. Look for confit of duck, and red wine risotto with wild mushrooms and Mozzarella.

Additional: Bar food; Children welcome; 🍃 dishes
Smoking: Air conditioning

Directions: Opposite Old Trafford Football Ground, off A5081

MANCHESTER, **Simply Heathcotes**

Jacksons Row Deansgate M2 3WD
Map 7: SJ89
Tel: 0161 8353536
Fax: 0161 8353534
Chef: James Gingell
Owner: Paul Heathcote
Cost: *Alc* £25, set-price L&D £12.50.
☺ H/wine £11.50
Times: 11.45am-2.30pm/6-11pm.
Closed Bhs
Additional: Bar food L; Children
welcome; 🍃 dishes
Seats: 160. Private dining room 45
Smoking: No pipes & cigars; Air
conditioning

Sharp design defines this modern brasserie. Simply Heathcotes manages the design feat of feeling light and airy, part in thanks to the high ceilings, but also to one completely mirrored wall and the white walls, enlivened by splashes of bold primary colours. Our meal started with baked terrine of smoked chicken, surprisingly subtle in flavour, varied in texture and well contrasted with a spicy olive oil dressing. Cod fillet on bubble-and-squeak came in a dangerous-looking tower block format that also included a poached egg and piquant tartare butter. But regional references remain a distinguishing feature of the *carte* with, for example, roast lobster with Morecambe bay shrimp chowder, and roast breast of Goosnargh duckling with sweet pea purée and foie gras butter. Local tastes are also turned on their head. Note the piccalilli and ham hock soup, mild 'curry' risotto with onion bhaji and mint raita, and 'Northern Smoothie' of iced beer parfait with peanut brittle.

Directions: M62/J17. Restaurant at the top end of Deansgate

MANCHESTER, **Thistle Manchester**

3-5 Portland Street Piccadilly Gardens
M1 6DP
Map 7: SJ89
Tel: 0161 2283400
Fax: 0161 2286347
Cost: *Alc* £25, set-price L £16.45/D
£21.45. ☺ H/wine £11.50
Times: Noon-1.50pm/6.30-10.20pm
Additional: Bar food L; Sunday L;
Children welcome; 🍃 dishes

An intimate restaurant with book-lined walls set in a large hotel in the centre of the city. The brasserie menu and carte offer an interesting and varied choice of dishes.

Smoking: No-smoking area; No pipes & cigars;
Air conditioning
Accommodation: 205 en suite ★ ★ ★

Directions: Opposite Piccadilly Gardens

MANCHESTER, Yang Sing

At the time of writing Manchester's foremost Chinese restaurant, Yang Sing, was still operating out of temporary premises at 3 Charlotte Street after the disastrous fire that destroyed the Princess Street site in late 1997. However, Yang Sing hope to be back in their completely redesigned, refurbished Princess Street restaurant in the autumn of 1999 with an updated Cantonese menu (although some popular dishes will remain).

Directions: Telephone for directions

34 Princess Street M1 4JY
Map 7: SJ89
Tel: 0161 2362200
Fax: 0161 2365934
Chef: Harry Yeung
Owners: Yang Sing Restaurants
Cost: *Alc* £19.50, set-price D £22 (5 courses). ☺ H/wine £9.95
Times: Noon-11pm. Closed 25 Dec
Additional: Children welcome; ✤ dishes
Seats: 140. Private dining rooms 30, 70, 200
Smoking: Air conditioning

MANCHESTER AIRPORT,
Etrop Grange Hotel

Extended Grade II-listed Georgian mansion retains the aura of a stylish comfortable hotel. The attractively appointed Coach House Restaurant, with a veranda, has been built on to the front of the hotel, and although within sight of the airport, noise levels are low. The menus offer plenty of choice, from tender pan-fried escalopes of pork on a Madeira and peppercorn sauce served with a duxelle-stuffed baby aubergine to steamed fillet of sea bass with spring onions, lemongrass and horseradish. A starter of smoked salmon and crab mousse, with a delicate sauce of sour cream and chives, has been described as excellent, and a terrine of pressed ham, Dijon mustard and parsley is no more likely to disappoint. A broad choice of British farmhouse cheeses is a strong point among the desserts, and those hankering for nursery food could go for steamed lemon sponge with custard. The well-chosen wine list ranges from good vintage clarets to more modest house wines.

Thorley Lane M90 4EG
Map 7: SJ88
Tel: 0161 4990500
Fax: 0161 4990790
Chef: Hamish Deas
Owner: Regal Hotels
Cost: Set-price L £16.50/D £28.95. H/wine £13.95
Times: Noon-2pm/7-10pm. Closed L Sat
Additional: Bar food; Sunday L; Children welcome; ✤ dishes
Seats: 45. Private dining room 50
Smoking: No smoking in dining room
Accommodation: 64 en suite ★★★

Directions: Off M56/J5. At main airport roundabout, take 1st L (to Terminal 2), then 1st R (Thorley Lane), 200yds on R

MANCHESTER AIRPORT,
Quality Hotel Altrincham

See under Altrincham

OLDHAM, Avant Hotel

Smart purpose-built hotel with panoramic views. Expect fresh sea scallops lightly grilled with a smooth saffron cream, followed by

Windsor Road Manchester Street
OL8 4AS
Map 7: SD90
Tel: 0161 6275500

pan-fried breast of chicken with a rich Madeira sauce, or perhaps a Chinese stir-fry with oyster sauce.

Smoking: No smoking in dining room; Air conditioning
Accommodation: 103 en suite ★★★

Directions: From M62/J20 take A627(M) towards Oldham, then A62 Manchester Street. Hotel on L

Fax: 0161 6275896
Cost: Set-price L £9.50 (4 courses)/D £16.75 (4 courses). ☺ H/wine £9.95
Times: Noon-1.45pm/7-9.45pm
Additional: Bar food; Sunday L; Children welcome; ● dishes

OLDHAM, Hotel Smokies Park ❀

Anglo-Italian cooking in a modern hotel complex, midway between Ashton and Oldham. Long menu supplemented by market specials.

Additional: Sunday L; Children welcome; ● dishes
Smoking: Air conditioning. **Accommodation:** 47 en suite ★★★

Directions: On A627 between Oldham and Ashton-under-Lyne

Ashton Road Bardsley OL8 3HX
Map 7: SD90
Tel: 0161 6243405
Fax: 0161 6275262
Cost: *Alc* 20, set-price L £5.95/D £14.95. ☺ H/wine £9.95
Times: Noon-2pm (3pm Sun)/6-11pm. Closed L Sat

OLDHAM, White Hart Inn ❀❀

Solid stone building that's a local, a popular brasserie, and a smart restaurant. The brasserie menu is extensive: terrine of home-made pork pie with home-made chutney; seared king scallops and sweetbreads with linguine pasta, basil oil and sautéed spinach; tempura of cod with tarragon peas and fried potatoes (fish and chips revisited?). Upstairs, the monthly changing restaurant menu goes in for more refinement, offering the likes of salad of warm wood pigeon with poached quails' eggs and Caesar salad, or roast loin of lamb with vegetable ratatouille and pesto tortellini; mango tart with lime sorbet and butterscotch sauce. The place is lively, bustling, very warm and welcoming.

Directions: From M62/J20 take A627M to Oldham Mumps – A669 Lees Road through Lees & Grotton. Turn R at disused petrol station (A6050). The White Hart is on L, opp. church

51 Stockport Road Lydgate OL4 4JJ
Map 7: SD90
Tel: 01457 872566
Fax: 01457 875190
Chef: John Rudden
Owners: Charles Brierley, John Rudden
Cost: Set price L £16/D £24.75 (4 courses). ☺ H/wine £13.50
Times: D only, 6.15-9.30pm. Closed D Sun, all Mon
Additional: Bar food; Sunday L (Noon-2.45pm)/; Children welcome; ● dishes
Seats: 56. Private dining room 35
Smoking: No smoking in dining room; Air conditioning
Accommodation: 5 en suite

RAMSBOTTOM, The Village Restaurant ❀

16-18 Market Place BL0 9HT
Map 7: SD71
Tel: 01706 825070
Fax: 01706 822005

Chef: Ros Hunter
Owners: Ros Hunter, Chris Johnson
Cost: Fixed-price L £9.50/D £19.50 (4 courses). ☺ H/wine £9
Times: L at 12.45pm (Sat at noon & 2pm)/D at 8pm. Closed D Sun, all Mon, Tue
Additional: Sunday L at 1pm & 3pm
Smoking: No smoking in dining room

Directions: From M66 northbound take J1 and follow signs to Ramsbottom. Restaurant in centre of village

Plain honest food tasting as it should at this tiny terraced restaurant set above one of the best delicatessens in the country. There's a strong organic philosophy, seen in organic vegetable soup, but also Mozzarella 'caprese', Pennine-reared beef, and superb bread are just some of the treats. Make a detour if you must, but go.

ROCHDALE, **Nutter's**

Edenfield Road Cheesden Norden
OL12 7TY
Map 7: SD81
Tel/Fax: 01706 650167
Chef: Andrew Nutter
Owners: Rodney, Jean & Andrew Nutter
Cost: *Alc* £29, set-price L £19.95 (4 courses)/D £29.95 (6 courses). ☺
H/wine £10.50
Times: Noon-2pm (5pm Sun)/6.45-9.30pm (9pm Sun). Closed Tue, 1st 2 wks Aug
Additional: Sunday L; Children welcome; ✿ menu
Seats: 52. Private dining room 50
Smoking: No smoking in dining room

Utter Nutter let loose in the kitchen. 'Flash! Bang! Wallop!' shrieks the menu, 'Nutter's been let loose in the kitchen again.' Yes, it's celebrity chef Andrew Nutter, cooking up a storm in this former pub high on the moors. There's nothing shy or retiring about the man, the menu or the dishes: flamboyant, cock-sure and demanding. Nutter mixes and matches vibrant flavours and quality ingredients – our intrepid reporter described his starter as 'a cacophony of flavours'. Concentration is needed to fully enjoy the variety of flavours in dishes such as roasted cod with shrimp and coriander mash, say, and sesame seared fillet of salmon spiced up with a ginger and orange sauce, or even nutty chocolate torte with a wattleseed and Cointreau coulis. You have been warned!

Directions: On the A680 between Rochdale and Edenfield

WIGAN, **Kilhey Court Hotel** ✓

Chorley Road Standish WN1 2XN
Map 7: SD51
Tel: 01257 472100
Fax: 01257 422401
Cost: *Alc* £24.95, set-price L £13.95/D £24.95 (4 courses). ☺
H/wine £11.95
Times: 12.30-2pm/7-9.30pm. Closed L Sat
Additional: Sunday L; Children welcome; ✿ dishes
Smoking: No smoking in dining room
Accommodation: 62 en suite ★ ★ ★ ★

Directions: On A5106 1.5m N of A49/A5106 junction

The Laureate Restaurant is situated in a split level Victorian conservatory overlooking the grounds and Worthington lakes. Choice of menus which reflect French and Modern British styles.

WIGAN, **Wrightington Hotel**

See Wrightington, Lancashire

HAMPSHIRE

ALRESFORD, **Hunters**

Cosy high street restaurant with a carte supported by chalked-up specials. We sampled a good duck breast with sage, bacon, crispy cabbage and red berry sauce.

Smoking: No-smoking area; No pipes & cigars
Accommodation: 3 en suite

Directions: Off A31 – in centre of Alresford

32 Broad Street SO24 9AQ
Map 4: SU53
Tel/Fax: 01962 732468
Cost: *Alc* D £30, set-price L & D £15.
☺ H/wine £9.95
Times: Noon-2pm/7-9.30pm. Closed D Sun, Xmas
Additional: Sunday L; Children welcome; ☕ dishes

ALTON, **Alton Grange Hotel** NEW

Well-handled Modern English cooking, note roast cod fillet with herb crust, curry oil and minted couscous. Vegetable tempura with plum and ginger sauce and sushi for starters show a kitchen also looking beyond the horizon.

Smoking: No-smoking area; No pipes & cigars
Accommodation: 30 en suite ★★★

Directions: Situated midway between Guildford & Winchester, 300 yds from A31 on A339 into Alton

London Road GU34 4EG
Map 4: SU73
Tel: 01420 86565
Fax: 01420 541346
Cost: *Alc* £25. ☺ H/wine £10.95
Times: Noon-2.30pm/7-9.30pm.
Closed L Sat
Additional: Bar food; Sunday L; Children 4+; ☕ dishes

ANDOVER,
Esseborne Manor

Hurstbourne Tarrant SP11 0ER
Map 4: SU34
Tel: 01264 736444
Fax: 01264 736725
Cost: *Alc* £28, set-price L £13/D £18.
☺ H/wine £13
Times: Noon-2.30pm/7-9.30pm
Additional: Bar food L; Sunday L; Children welcome; ☕ dishes
Smoking: No-smoking area
Accommodation: 15 en suite ★★★

Country house dining room with a relaxed style. Esseborne Manor is a great place, the dining room boasts lots of light and super views over the surrounding countryside, and there are several comfy lounges for pre drinks and coffee. The kitchen shows an intelligence in its menu planning and sound skills in execution. The highlight of our latest test meal was thick juicy cuts of roasted tenderloin of pork accompanied by a tian of hazelnuts and apples. However, a chicken liver pithiviers with caramelised shallots, and a white chocolate and mint cheesecake with chocolate sorbet were greatly enjoyed.

Directions: Between Andover & Newbury on A343, just N of Hurstbourne Tarrant

BASINGSTOKE,
Audleys Wood

Alton Road RG25 2JT
Map 4: SU65
Tel: 01256 817555
Fax: 01256 817500
Chef: Ronnie Wyatt-Goodwin
Cost: *Alc* £36.90, set-price L £20/D £26. H/wine £15
Times: Noon-1.45pm/7-9.45pm. Closed Xmas-New Year, L Bhs
Additional: Sunday L; Children welcome; ❹ dishes
Seats: 70. Private room 14.
Smoking: No smoking in dining room
Accommodation: 71 en suite ★ ★ ★ ★

Gothic-Renaissance style residence in a discreet setting. Bars and lounges have real character but reserve your oohs and aahs for the high-vaulted ceiling in the restaurant. The *carte* changes seasonally, the set lunch every two days. The kitchen split their allegiance between classic French and modern British cookery. Glazed pigeon breast, red berry rösti and a port and red currant jus, and a rabbit and guinea fowl terrine with grain mustard sauce and toasted blinis are typical starters, while main courses may range from boudin of sole with salmon and lobster with fish risotto and beurre blanc and keta to a trio of lamb cutlets topped with truffle and mushroom mousse. Crème de menthe parfait with rich chocolate sauce is a typical dessert.

Directions: M3/J6 & A339 (Alton). Hotel entrance is on R 0.5 mile S of Basingstoke towards Alton

BASINGSTOKE,
Basingstoke Country Hotel

Popular business hotel with a sophisticated menu. Oak-smoked sea scallops served warm with crisp pancetta and mixed herb salad perhaps, or breast of wild Hampshire mallard pan-fried with juniper berries and well paired with a celeriac and fresh horseradish dauphinoise.

Smoking: No-smoking area; Air conditioning
Accommodation: 100 en suite ★ ★ ★

Directions: On A30 between Nately Scures and Hook

Nately Scures Hook RG27 9JS
Map 4: SU65
Tel: 01256 764161
Fax: 01256 768341
Cost: *Alc* £26.50, set-price L £15.25/D £18.50. ☺ H/wine £12.95
Times: 12.30-1.45pm/7-9.45pm. Closed L Sat, D Sun
Additional: Bar food; Sunday L; Children 12+; ❹ dishes

BEAULIEU, # Beaulieu Hotel

Hotel restaurant with lovely forest views. The daily menu provides an interesting choice of dishes, such as wild mushroom risotto, roast leg of lamb, and summer pudding.

Directions: On B3056 between Lyndhurst and Beaulieu, opposite railway station

Beaulieu Road Lyndhurst SO42 7YQ
Map 4: SU30
Tel: 01703 293344
Fax: 01703 292729
Telephone for further details

BISHOP'S WALTHAM, **Banks Bistro**

Change of name and ownership at this restaurant, a beamed former granary. Fish fritters, crispy confit of duck, and a delicious raspberry cheesecake made for an enjoyable inspection meal.

Additional: Bar food L; Children welcome; ⑤ dishes
Smoking: No-smoking area

The Old Granary Bank Street
SO32 1AE
Map 4: SU51
Tel: 01489 896352
Fax: 01489 896288
Cost: *Alc* £18.50, set-price L £9.95.
☺ H/wine £8.50
Times: Noon-2pm/7-10pm. Closed
Sun, Bhs

BISHOP'S WALTHAM,
Cobblers Restaurant

The Square SO32 1AR
Map 4: SU51
Tel: 01489 891515
Fax: 01489 891577
Chef: David Heywood
Owner: Andrew Cobb
Cost: *Alc* £20, set-price L £13.99/D
£20.95. ☺ H/wine £9.45
Times: 11.45am-2pm/6.45-9.30pm.
Closed Sun, Mon
Additional: Bar food L; Children
welcome; ⑤ dishes
Smoking: No-smoking area; No pipes
& cigars

Directions: Bishop's Waltham is on
B2177, midway between Winchester
& Portsmouth/Southampton

Smart restaurant in a Georgian townhouse right in the centre of the village. Attractively decorated in Mediterranean colours with a number of old shoes on the walls, the whole place is overseen by owner Andrew Cobb who, with his smart young team, provides good, efficient service. We enjoyed home-smoked duck breast on a bed of salad leaves with fresh figs, roast lamb fillet on a bed of wild mushrooms, aubergine caviar and freshly cooked spinach, and endorse strongly the light marmalade pudding with home-made brown bread ice cream. Bread is home-made.

BROCKENHURST, **Carey's Manor**

SO42 7RH
Map 4: SU30
Tel: 01590 623551
Fax: 01590 622799
Cost: *Alc* £35, set-price L £15.75/D
£24.50. H/wine £11.95
Times: Noon-1.45pm/7-9.45pm.
Closed L Sat
Additional: Sunday L; Children 7+;
⑤ dishes
Smoking: No smoking in dining room
Accommodation: 79 en suite ★ ★ ★

Directions: M27/J1, follow signs for
Lyndhurst and Lymington A337.
Railway station 5 minutes from hotel

A variety of dishes is offered from a choice of menus at this country house hotel. Examples are terrine of salmon and sole, followed by saddle of venison with polenta and Madeira.

BROCKENHURST,

Forest Park Hotel

*Friendly, informally run hotel in the heart of the New Forest,
popular for weekend breaks. Country house cooking is along the
lines of spicy tomato soup and breast of chicken in white wine,
cream and dill.*

Smoking: No smoking in dining room
Accommodation: 38 en suite ★ ★ ★

Directions: From A337 to Brockenhurst turn into Meerut Road,
follow road through Waters Green; at T junction turn R into
Rhinefield Road

Rhinefield Road SO42 7ZG
Map 4: SU30
Tel: 01590 622844
Fax: 01590 623948
Cost: Set-price L £9.95/D £19.95. ☺
H/wine £9.95
Times: 12.30-2pm/7-9.45pm
Additional: Bar food; Sunday L;
Children welcome; ✿ dishes

BROCKENHURST,

New Park Manor

*New Park was Charles II's favourite hunting lodge, and there's a
strong game theme to the hotel's menus. Roast breast of squab
pigeon with a casserole of curried lentils, perhaps, followed by
medallions of pork tenderloin topped with a Stilton mousse.*

Lyndhurst Road SO42 7QH
Map 4: SU30
Tel: 01590 623467
Fax: 01590 622268
Cost: Alc £37, set-price L £14.95/D
£27. H/wine £12.95
Times: Noon-2pm/7.30-9.30pm
Additional: Bar food L; Sunday L;
Children 7+; ✿ dishes
Smoking: No smoking in dining room;
Jacket & tie preferred
Accommodation: 24 en suite ★ ★ ★

Directions: Turn off A337 between
Lyndhurst and Brockenhurst and
follow the hotel signs

BROCKENHURST,

Le Poussin Restaurant

**Small, smart, attractive restaurant, hidden in a courtyard
behind the shops in the village centre, has a 'chicken' theme
evident in small ways.** Alex Aitken has built up a reputation
for using locally sourced, seasonal produce, much of it organic.
Mushrooms from the New Forest might go into a salad of
lightly chargrilled pigeon breast on a bed of lentils, or sautéed
with bacon to accompany creamy white sausage in rosemary
sauce, and the same forest might have been home to venison,
cooked rare and accompanied by a reduced port sauce. The set-
price menus give three choices at each course. Chicken
mousseline in an intense crayfish sauce, followed by a fish
course: skate with scallops ('perfect') in chive sauce, say. Main
courses could extend to well-executed guinea fowl with morels
and Muscat sauce. A brandy snap of sharp lime sorbet comes
with creamy lemon tart tasting as good as it should, and passion
fruit soufflé is the house speciality. The serious wine list is a 30-
page document with a handful of bottles sold by the glass.

The Courtyard Brookley Road
SO42 7RB
Map 4: SU30
Tel: 01590 623063
Fax: 01590 623144
Chef: Alexander Aitken
Owners: Alexander & Caroline Aitken
Cost: Alc £32.50, set-price L £15 (2
courses)/D £22.50 (2 courses). H/wine
£16
Times: Noon-1.30pm/7-9pm. Closed
Mon, Tue
Additional: Sunday L; Children
welcome
Seats: 25
Smoking: No smoking in dining room

Directions: Village centre through an
archway between two shops

BROCKENHURST,
Rhinefield House

Rhinefield Road SO42 7QB
Map 4: SU30
Tel: 01590 622922
Fax: 01590 622800
Telephone for further details

Directions: From M27/J1 follow signs
to Lyndhurst, then take A35 to
Christchurch. After 3 miles turn L to
Rhinefield. Hotel approx 2 miles on R

A 19th-century mock Elizabethan mansion in the heart of the New Forest. The menu offers a good choice with vegetarian, gluten-free and healthy option dishes denoted.

BROCKENHURST,
Thatched Cottage Hotel ❀❀

Small hotel of great charm and character. The main feature of the dining room is the open-to-view kitchen with 'chefs-on-show'. Here, Martin Matysik continues his stint at the stoves, imparting welcome steadiness with his strong support of organic produce. The menu is a lively read with the litany of accompaniments adding extra interest. Feuillantine of rock lobster, for example, is teamed with sweet potato purée and beetroot chips, and three foie gras terrine combinations are served with confit of aubergine, young leek and Périgord truffle and a salad of apple, mushroom and celery tossed in white truffle vinaigrette. Main courses bring a cannon fillet of Welsh lamb with baby spinach and deep-fried walnuts, a haricot bean tart and Gewürztraminer white wine sauce. A light passion fruit soufflé with honey avocado sauce, and a goats' cheese baked in a puff pastry cushion with crème fraîche and quince Turkish delight are intriguing desserts.

Directions: On A337 in Brockenhurst, turning before level crossing

16 Brookley Road SO42 7RR
Map 4: SU30
Tel: 01590 623090
Fax: 01590 623479
Chef: Martin Matysik
Owners: The Matysik Family
Cost: Set-price L £25 (2 courses)/D £35. H/wine £12.50
Times: 12.30-2pm/7.30-9.30pm. Closed D Sun, all Mon, Jan
Additional: Sunday L; Children 12+
Seats: 20
Smoking: No smoking in dining room
Accommodation: 5 en suite

BROCKENHURST,
Whitley Ridge Hotel ❀❀

The kitchen aims to please at this former royal hunting lodge set in five acres of New Forest seclusion. With a little notice, they will prepare any dish enjoyed on a previous occasion or serve any item on the *carte* or set menu without sauce or garnish. Home-smoked items are something of a speciality – trout with creamed dill sauce is a classic combination; goose breast is more unusually paired with prune and Earl Grey syrup. The cooking is rooted in traditional home recipes – breast of duck with caramelised orange and rich Cointreau sauce – with grilled Thai supreme of chicken indicative of a

Beaulieu Road SO4 7QL
Map 4: SU30
Tel: 01590 622354
Fax: 01590 622856
Chef: Gary Moore
Owner: Rennie Law
Cost: *Alc* £24, set-price D £21.50. ☺ H/wine £9.50
Times: D only, 6.30-9pm
Additional: Bar food L; Sunday L (Noon-2pm); Children welcome; ❀ dishes

Whitley Ridge Hotel

Seats: 34. Private dining room 20.
Jacket & tie preferred
Smoking: No smoking in dining room
Accommodation: 14 en suite ★★★

new style of British home cooking. Iced lime parfait with
passion fruit sauce or chocolate and port fondant are followed
by coffee and handmade chocolates from Beaulieu.

Directions: A337 (from Lyndhurst) turn L towards Beaulieu on
B3055, approx 1 mile

BROOK, **Bell Inn** ✿

*Popular golfing hotel where a strict dress code applies. The cooking
shows less constraint – calves' liver was given an exotic touch with
mango and grain mustard sauce, and Thai saucing spiced up
carefully cooked seafish tempura. Classic desserts.*

Lyndhurst SO43 7HE
Map 4: SU21
Tel: 01703 812214
Fax: 01703 813958
Cost: Set-price D £26.50 (4 courses).
H/wine £13.50.
Times: L all day/D from 7.30-9.30pm
Additional: Bar food; Sunday L;
Children welcome; ⚫ dishes
Smoking: No smoking in dining room
Accommodation: 25 en suite ★★★

Directions: M27/J1 (Cadnam) 3rd exit
on to B3078, signed Brook, 0.5 mile

BUCKLERS HARD, **Master Builders House Hotel** ✿✿

NEW

***18th-century building featuring a light airy restaurant
overlooking the River Beaulieu.*** Once the home of the master
shipbuilder who oversaw the construction of the Navy's fleet
during the great age of sail. Here, guests can enjoy well-
prepared food with a modern edge. Expect the likes of roast
breast of chicken with polenta and grain mustard sauce, mille-
feuille of lemon sole with sweet peppers and basil sauce, and
roast breast of pheasant with braised turnips and red wine
sauce. A mid-winter meal started with wild mushroom risotto
topped with shavings of Parmesan. This was followed by a
'perfectly fresh' sea bass which rested on a base of crushed
potatoes with herbs, surrounded by olives. Dessert was

Brockenhurst SO42 7XB
Map 4: SU40
Tel: 01590 616253
Fax: 01590 616297
Chef: Denis Rhoden
Owners: Jeremy Willcock, John Illsley
Cost: *Alc* £26, set-price L £16.95. ☺
H/wine £11.50
Times: Noon-2.30pm/7-9.30pm.
Closed D Sun
Additional: Sunday L; Children
welcome; ⚫ dishes
Seats: 60 Private dining room 50
Accommodation: 25 en suite ★★★

poached pear with smooth cinnamon ice cream. Less formal meals can be enjoyed in the Yachtsman's bar and gallery. The wine list is ordered according to price.

Directions: Follow signs to Beaulieu off M27/J2. Turn L onto B3056. 1st L and hotel in 2 miles

CADNAM, Bartley Lodge

Former hunting lodge, ideally located for exploring the New Forest. The dining room has a comfortable feel and boasts lovely green vistas – all gardens and forest. On the night we visited the place was packed 'all tucking into the most lovingly prepared food'. Most dishes are interesting but with familiar ingredients, 'there's no truck with fusion here'. A terrine of duck, caramelised onion and potato had been constructed with precision and temperature and taste were perfect. Paupiettes of lemon sole with salmon and dill mousseline was all trembling texture and fresh flavours, and a Neapolitan parfait was bursting with the flavours of passion fruit, strawberry and lime.

Lyndhurst Road SO40 2NR
Map 4: SU31
Tel: 01703 812248
Fax: 01703 812075
Cost: *Alc* £28.50, set-price D £20.50.
☺ H/wine £9.95
Times: D only, 7-9pm
Additional: Bar food L; Children welcome; 🐟 dishes
Smoking: No smoking in dining room
Accommodation: 31 en suite ★ ★ ★

Directions: Telephone for directions

CRAWLEY, Vistro Restaurant

Each dish at the pretty blue and yellow French restaurant is matched with recommendations by the glass from the extensive, well-chosen wine list. Try goats' cheese soufflé with walnut oil sausage or fillet of venison with red wine sauce, bitter chocolate and raspberry.

Additional: Sunday L; Children 7+; 🐟 dishes
Smoking: No-smoking area; No pipes & cigars

Shortlisted for AA Wine Award – see page 16

Nr Winchester SO21 2PR
Map 4: SU43
Tel: 01962 776285
Fax: 01962 776005
Cost: *Alc* £30, set-price L £15.95/D £17.95. ☺ H/wine £10.95
Times: 12.15-2.15pm/7.15-9.30pm. Closed D Sun, all Mon, 2 wks Aug, 1 wk Xmas

CLOSED

DENMEAD, Barnard's Restaurant

Charming, small high street restaurant. The style is modern British: twice-baked Swiss cheese soufflé, and grilled mushrooms and snails with garlic butter are typical, with desserts including fresh apple rings cooked in butter and honey, served warm with vanilla ice cream.

Smoking: No-smoking area; No pipes & cigars

Directions: Opposite village church, from A3M/J3 then B2150 (Waterlooville)

Hambledon Road Nr Waterlooville PO7 6NU
Map 4: SU61
Tel/Fax: 01705 257788
Cost: *Alc* £25.60, set-price L £12.50/D £19.50. ☺ H/wine £10
Times: Noon-1.30pm/7-9.30pm. Closed L Sat, all Sun & Mon, 2 wks Aug, 1 wk Dec
Additional: Children welcome; 🐟 dishes

EMSWORTH, Julies

Tiny restaurant – only 8 tables – strong on service. If you read the menu backwards, starting at the sweets, then you will know to pace yourself for treats ahead. Crêpes come oozing with butter and liqueur and icky sticky toffee pudding laced with melted toffee sauce. Seasonally changing dishes have some intriguing combinations. Crispy monkfish with orange and parsley butter, lightly spiced and topped with slices of pan-fried foie gras proved a well thought out balance of flavours, and Aylesbury duck with stewed blackberries, sorrel, figs, smoked bacon and truffle cream came through its paces successfully. Excellent home-made bread, petits fours and freshly ground coffee add an extra layer of pleasure.

Directions: In town centre, 1st R after Emsworth Sq 100 yds towards the Quay. Restaurant on L

30 South Street PO10 7EH
Map 4: SU70
Tel: 01243 377914
Chef/Owner: Kevin Hartley
Cost: Set-price L/D £24.95. ☺ H/wine £9.95
Times: Noon-2.30pm/7-9.30pm. Closed Sun, Mon, 1-2 wks Jan
Additional: Children 10+; 🐟 dishes
Seats: 28. Private dining room 18
Smoking: No smoking in dining room

EMSWORTH, Spencers

Popular restaurant run on friendly, informal lines. Gas lighting and racks of books give this popular first-floor restaurant a cosy, congenial atmosphere. An impressive array of fish, as well as a sound clutch of modern British brasserie-style dishes, means there's always something to tickle your fancy. We plumped for an 'exceptionally good' starter of chicken liver, black pudding and apple salad, followed by cod steak stuffed with fresh crab and asparagus and baked in a light, crisp filo pastry. There's also a good selection of salads, which come either as a starter or main course. Try the warm smoked chicken and mango salad, or the fresh crab salad, served with smoked paprika and garlic mayonnaise.

Directions: Follow A259 to Emsworth roundabout, turn L into North Street, restaurant is 0.5 mile on L

36 North Street PO10 7DG
Map 4: SU70
Tel/Fax: 01243 372744
Chef: Denis Spencer
Owners: Denis & Lesley Spencer
Cost: Alc £19. ☺
Times: D only, 7.30-10.30pm. Closed Sun, Mon, 24-26 Dec
Additional: Children welcome; ✪ dishes
Seats: 34. Private dining room 10
Smoking: No-smoking area; No pipes & cigars; Air conditioning

EMSWORTH,
36 On The Quay

A serious operation, now beginning to attract wider interest. The pale blue and yellow decor has a strong Mediterranean-provençale feel and, with just 30 tables and a tiny courtyard garden for fair-weather drinks, it is very peaceful. Views take in Chichester Harbour and the graveyard at nearby Bosham, which allegedly has the grave of King Canute. Our lunch was a mere sampling of well-executed dishes showing the skills and passion for food that Ramon Farthing so clearly has, and was a real bargain for the quality of the food. The thinnest, crispest cheese straws and olives go with drinks, followed by a chef's 'freebie' of artichoke soup with truffles – 'perfectly smooth and well-balanced and could have made a whole meal out of it'. Then came a perfect Tatin of duck confit and wild mushrooms served with roasted duck liver, caramelised ginger, apples and sherry vinegar sauce, followed by fillet of sea bass, pan-fried with a layer of crispy potato placed on aubergine and basil and complemented by a dressing of tomatoes, courgettes, peppers and olives. Dessert was caramelised pears with caramel ice cream and caramel sauce. Three types of coffee, six or so of tea, and petits fours show as much care and attention as the main meal – we particularly enjoyed the creamy fudge and the sesame and poppy seed tuile. Karen Farthing runs front-of-house, assisted by a young and very competent team. The wine list is a selection from the world over, some from the renowned cellars of the White Horse at Chilgrove, but half-bottles are pricy.

Directions: Last building on R in South Street, which runs from the Square in the centre of Emsworth

47 South Street PO10 7EG
Map 4: SU70
Tel: 01243 375592
Fax: 01243 375593
Chef: Ramon Farthing
Owners: Ramon & Karen Farthing
Cost: Alc £34.70, set-price L £19/D £37.50 (6 courses). H/wine £13.50
Times: Noon-1.45pm/7-9.15pm. Closed L Sat & Mon, all Sun, 1-18 Jan, 4-11 Oct
Additional: Children welcome; ✪ dishes
Seats: 30. Private dining room 10
Smoking: No smoking in dining room

AA Wine Award-see page 16
Shortlisted for

EVERSLEY, New Mill

Until the beginning of this century, farmers brought their grist to this mill on the bank of the River Blackwater. Converted into a restaurant in the early 1970s, it retains much of its character, a cosy feel engendered by log fires in winter, with spacious gardens (complete with ducks) making a relaxing place for a stroll in summer. The Grill Room, in the oldest part of the mill, has a patio for alfresco dining, while the Riverside

New Mill Road Hook RG27 0RA
Map 4: SU76
Tel: 0118 9732277
Fax: 0118 9328780
Chef: Simon Smith
Cost: Alc £30, set-price L £12.50/D £19.50. ☺ H/wine £11
Times: Noon-2pm/7-10pm. Closed L Sat

New Mill

Additional: Bar food; Sunday L;
Children welcome; dishes
Seats: 100. Private dining rooms 12,
40
Smoking: No pipes & cigars

Restaurant is the place to come to for its views. Game terrine
(quail, partridge, rabbit and venison) with fennel confit, or
dived scallops with lemon butter, a dish of 'excellent flavour',
followed by cannon of lamb glazed with red wine on thyme
couscous, calves' liver with onion and sage marmalade, or roast
turbot in a cracked wheat crust on citrus butter sauce are the
types of dishes the kitchen produces. Lemon tart with passion
fruit coulis, or rich chocolate bombe might be among the
desserts, and around a dozen well-chosen house wines head up
an international list.

Directions: From Eversley take A327 (Reading), cross river, turn
L at cross roads into New Mill Road

FAREHAM,
Lysses House Hotel

51 High Street PO16 7BQ
Map 4: SU50
Tel: 01329 822622
Fax: 01329 822762
Cost: *Alc* £23.70, set-price L
£13.95/D £18.50. H/wine £9.50
Times: Noon-1.45pm/7.30-9.45pm.
Closed L Sat, all Sun, 24 Dec-2 Jan,
Bhs

*Bold combinations such as smoked haddock with Jerusalem
artichokes and mustard sauce sit alongside more conventional steaks
and salmon at this elegant Georgian establishment.*

Additional: Bar food; Children welcome; dishes
Smoking: No smoking in dining room; Air conditioning
Accommodation: 21 en suite ★ ★ ★

Directions: From M27 J11 follow signs to Fareham town centre;
hotel is at top of High Street

FAREHAM, Solent Hotel

Rookery Avenue Whiteley PO15 7AJ
Map 4: SU50
Tel: 01489 880000
Fax: 01489 880007
Cost: *Alc* £26, set-price L £18.50/D
£23. ☺ H/wine £11.45
Times: 12.15-1.45pm/7.15-10.45pm.
Closed L Sat & Sun, Bhs

*Smart, purpose-built hotel with a lively menu that takes in ginger
crab cakes on mixed leaves with red pepper chilli jam – though it's
often hard to beat a good chargrilled sirloin with Café de Paris
butter, salad and fries.*

Additional: Bar food; Children welcome; dishes
Smoking: No smoking in dining room; Air conditioning
Accommodation: 117 en suite ★ ★ ★ ★

Directions: From M27/J9, follow signs to Solent Business Park &
Whiteley. At roundabout 1st L, then R at mini-roundabout

FLEET,

The Gurkha Square

Exciting Nepalese cooking on Fleet's high street. Try kukhara swadilo – boneless chicken cooked in a mild nutty sauce, or khashi rashilo – an exotic Khatmandu dish of diced lamb and spiced sauce.

327 Fleet Road GU13 8BU
Map 4: SU85
Tel: 01252 811588
Fax: 01252 810101
Cost: *Alc* £17.50, set-price L £10.99/D £16.99. ☺ H/wine £9.50
Times: Noon-2pm/6-10.30pm
Additional: Children 12+, ✿ dishes
Smoking: Air conditioning

Directions: Telephone for directions

FORDINGBRIDGE, **Ashburn Hotel**

Traditional family-run hotel on the edge of the village. A choice of menus is offered in the dining room, which offers wonderful views across the garden to the New Forest.

Directions: On B3078

Station Road SP6 1JP
Map 4: SU11
Tel: 01425 652060
Fax: 01425 652150
Telephone for further details

FORDINGBRIDGE, **Hour Glass**

Painstaking cooking of fresh ingredients results in consistently good cooking – hock of lamb braised for eight hours with tomatoes, garlic and rosemary, and crab ravioli with shellfish sauce.

Directions: On A338 (Salisbury/Ringwood road) just outside Fordingbridge

Burgate SP6 1LX
Map 4: SU11
Tel/Fax: 01425 652348
Cost: *Alc* £19.95
Times: Noon-1.45pm/6.45-9.30pm. Closed 2 wks Feb, 1 wk Nov
Additional: Sunday L; Children 10 +; ✿ dishes
Smoking: No-smoking area

FORDINGBRIDGE,

The Three Lions

A farmhouse converted into a pub in 1901. An open fireplace, pine tables and chairs, and plants on window ledges, backed up by a simply written blackboard menu ('squab lobster and mussels', for instance), provide a low-key, unpretentious background that might lead people to underestimate the power of the kitchen until the food arrives. Then impressions switch to the kitchen's attention to detail minus gravity-defying garnishes and to quote an inspector 'twiddly bits of nothing'. What is baldly described as 'galette of smoked haddock' has its origins in Yorkshire pudding crossed with an egg custard smoky from the haddock, on a rich wild mushroom sauce with tiny dots of chives, black olives and sun-dried tomatoes. Stunning. New Forest mushroom might also go into main courses of lasagne or chicken breast, while fish might be represented by fillet of brill with saffron sauce, intense of both

Stuckton SP6 2HF
Map 4: SU11
Tel: 01425 652489
Fax: 01425 656144
Chef: M Womersley
Owners: Mr & Mrs M Womersley
Cost: *Alc* £27.50, set-price L £13.50 (2 courses). ☺ H/wine £11.75
Times: Noon-2pm/7-9.30pm. Closed D Sun, all Mon, mid Jan-early Feb
Additional: Sunday L; Children welcome; ✿ dishes
Seats: 55. Private dining room 25
Smoking: No smoking in dining room
Accommodation: 3 en suite

taste and colour, with a separate plate of garden-fresh vegetables, the carrots 'as sweet as sugar with nothing added'. A 'pastry star' is responsible for treacle tart, its sweetness cut with lemon, with vanilla ice cream. Coffee and truffles ended what, to an inspector, was 'a real meal'.

Directions: In the village of Stuckton, near Fordingbridge, 0.5m off A338

HIGHCLERE,

Hollington Country House

Woolton Hill Newbury RG20 9XA
Map 4: SU45
Tel: 01635 255100
Fax: 01635 255075
Chef: Yves Girard
Owners: John & Penny Guy
Cost: *Alc* £40. H/wine £18
Times: Noon-2pm/7-9.30pm
Additional: Sunday L; Children welcome; ✿ dishes
Seats: 50. Private dining rooms 12-60
Smoking: No smoking in dining room
Accommodation: 21 en suite ★ ★ ★

Directions: Take A343 (Andover) from Newbury. Follow signs for Hollington Herb Garden, hotel is next door.

Relaxing, comfortable surroundings in a charming setting. John and Penny Guy never stand still in their search for improvements at their country house hotel set in the heart of parkland and woodland. One of the strengths of the place is the high standard of service, and the notable enthusiasm and professionalism of the young team. Yves Girard has taken over the kitchens, with a menu that leaves no doubt as to the classic French influence, but with enough modern British references to keep it up to date. Papillote of frogs' legs is served with herb-flavoured risotto, tian of scallops with a light ginger-infused fish sauce. Cannon of lamb is set on rösti and served with aubergine gâteau and a roast garlic creamy sauce. Vegetarians are not neglected: a roasted globe artichoke filled with mixed vegetables and set on a bed of spinach, with cumin and tomato coulis makes an interesting choice. Chilled parfait of chestnut served with almond-infused milk and iced tiramisu accompanied by coffee-flavoured anglaise sauce are typical of desserts.

LIPHOOK, **Nippon-Kan**

The authentic Japanese eating option within the Japanese-owned Old Thorns Hotel. Nippon Kan has a lacquer-box red interior with lovely varnished woods making up the tables, chairs and bars. The teppanyaki tables (where diners sit and watch the chef griddle various meats, fish and vegetables with theatrical dexterity) are a popular choice but there's also a *carte* with all the usual Japanese choices described in clear English. Also note the bento boxes (a complete meal served in a compartmentalised lacquered box) and special sushi for children. Presentation is exquisite and the quality and freshness of the raw materials of the very best as exemplified by the wafer thin slices of highly marbled beef used in our shabu shabu (a beef and vegetable fondue with noodles), a dish named after the way the ingredients sound as they are swished about.

Griggs Green GU30 7PE
Map 4: SU83
Tel: 01428 724555
Fax: 01428 725036
Chef: T Suzuki
Owner: London Kosaido Co Ltd
Cost: *Alc* £17.30, set-price L £10.50 (2 courses)/D £22 (4 courses). ☺ H/wine £12
Times: Noon-2pm/6.30-9.30pm. Closed Mon, D Bhs + day after
Additional: Children welcome; ✿ dishes. **Seats:** 36
Smoking: No pipes & cigars
Accommodation: 33 en suite ★ ★ ★

Directions: See following entry

LIPHOOK, Old Thorns Hotel, Thorns Restaurant ✿

Griggs Green GU30 7PE
Map 4: SU83
Tel: 01428 724555
Fax: 01428 725036
Cost: Alc £20. ☺ H/wine £12
Times: D only, 7-9.30pm
Additional: Bar food; Sunday L
(12.15-2.30pm); Children welcome;
♨ dishes
Smoking: No smoking in dining room
Accommodation: 33 en suite ★ ★ ★

Directions: Approx 500 yds from
Griggs Green exit off A3

Country house-style restaurant, part of a hotel complex (see entry above), with garden views and patio doors leading to the terrace. A wide choice of modern inspired dishes is offered from an extensive carte.

LYMINGTON,
Gordleton Mill ✿✿

Silver Street Hordle SO41 6DJ
Map 4: SZ39
Tel: 01590 682219
Fax: 01590 683073
Chef: Alan Dann
Owner: W F Stone
Cost: Alc £27, set-price L £9.50 (2
courses)/D £45 (6 courses). H/wine
£13.80
Times: Noon-2pm/7-9.30pm. Closed
D Sun, all Mon, Jan
Additional: Sunday L; Children 3+;
♨ dishes
Seats: 35
Smoking: No smoking in dining room;
Air conditioning
Accommodation: 8 en suite ★ ★

Directions: Take A337 to Lymington,
at railway bridge mini-roundabout go
straight on then 1st R 1.5 miles

Lovely 17th-century watermill set on the banks of the River Avon in picturesque grounds. Some big hitters have made their names at Gordleton Mill, but a tumultuous few months in the wake of an aborted sale in the spring of 1999 have left the place reeling. Mr Stone remains as owner, with Alan Dann, formerly of Lower Slaughter Manor (see entry, Lower Slaughter, Gloucestershire), where he achieved three AA Rosettes, taking over in the kitchens. It was early days when we visited, to find Dann working alone with the help of two commis chefs and in the process of building up his brigade. The menu had been adapted, naturally enough, to reflect this. However, our meal was good, Dann's style of cooking is straightforward with the emphasis on simple creations with robust flavours, and we were left with the strong impression that, as the team builds, things can only get better. Our meal took in crab and scallop salad, lamb chop and lamb confit with a white bean and tarragon purée, and hot chocolate fondant.

LYMINGTON,
Stanwell House Hotel

High Street SO41 9AA
Map 4: SZ39
Tel: 01590 677123
Fax: 01590 677756
Cost: *Alc* £26.45, set-price D £20. ☺
H/wine £12
Times: Noon-2pm/7-9.30pm
Additional: Bar food L; Sunday L;
Children welcome; ⚫ dishes
Smoking: No smoking in dining room
Accommodation: 31 en suite ★ ★ ★

Privately owned Georgian hotel. The bistro serves modern brasserie food, perhaps medallions of beef fillet with black pudding mousse and French-fried onions, with lighter meals in the bar.

Directions: 2 miles from M27/J1. Take A337 through the New Forest to the coast

LYNDHURST, **Crown Hotel**

High Street SO43 7NF
Map 4: SU30
Tel: 01703 282922
Fax: 01703 282751
Cost: *Alc* £30, set-price D £18. ☺
H/wine £9.95
Times: D only, 7-9.30pm
Additional: Bar food; Sunday L
(12.30-2pm); Children welcome;
⚫ dishes
Smoking: No smoking in dining room
Accommodation: 39 en suite ★ ★ ★

Traditional hotel dining in the heart of the New Forest. Expect pan-fried calves' liver with smoked bacon and red onions, and poached fillet of salmon with sea asparagus and a smoked salmon cream.

Directions: Top end of Lyndhurst High Street, opposite church

LYNDHURST, **Parkhill Hotel** ✿✿

Comfortable country house hotel with elegant restaurant. The venison loin that appears on the plate, rolled in garden herbs on a fricassee of wild mushrooms, garlic and shallots with pommes Anna, could hardly have been sourced more locally. There are fine views from the restaurant, and New Forest deer can sometimes be seen grazing beyond the lawns. Much care goes into the construction and presentation of dishes; a typical dinner might comprise a trio of smoked salmon, marinated salmon and smoked halibut with asparagus and truffle dressing, followed by honey roasted whole duckling carved

Beaulieu Road SO43 7FZ
Map 4: SU30
Tel: 01703 282944
Chef: Darren Whiffen
Owners: Mr & Mrs Topham
Cost: Set-price D £27. H/wine £12
Times: Noon-2pm/7-9pm
Additional: Bar food L; Sunday L;
Children welcome; ⚫ dishes
Seats: 80. Private dining room 50
Smoking: No smoking in dining room;
Jacket & tie preferred

Parkhill Hotel

Accommodation: 19 en suite ★ ★ ★

onto a compote of apricot and apples with rosemary jus, with dark chocolate tart flavoured with raspberry and wild berry compote for dessert. An interesting gastronomic footnote: carved stone pineapples decorate the Georgian house which, legend has it, was once the home of the gentleman who introduced the fruit to England.

Directions: On entering Lyndhurst from M27 at Cadnam, take the A35 towards Southampton. Immediately after turning for Lyndhurst Park Hotel take the next R towards Beaulieu, B3056. Hotel 1 mile on R

MIDDLE WALLOP,

Fifehead Manor

Stockbridge SO20 8EG
Map 4: SU23
Tel: 01264 781565
Fax: 01264 781400
Chef: Simon Garbutt
Owners: Colin Dabin, Christopher Paul
Cost: *Alc* £35, set-price L & D £25. H/wine £10.95
Times: Noon-2pm/7-9.30pm
Additional: Bar food; Sunday L; Children welcome; dishes
Seats: 40. Private dining room 20
Smoking: No smoking in dining room. Jacket & tie preferred
Accommodation: 17 en suite ★ ★ ★

Directions: On A343, 5 miles S of Andover

11th-century manor with character, history and attentive service. Fifehead Manor was under siege from builders when our inspector called with completion too close for deadlines for us to be able to make any comment on the food. However, Simon Garbutt remains as head chef, offering a variety of set menus, a *carte* and speciality dishes. Simply described, in a style best known as modern British, there is watercress soup, roast marinated rump of lamb with garlic and thyme, and chocolate and walnut tart with clotted cream offered on the set menu, or pressed ham hock and parsley terrine with pea and mint tartlet, a steamed fillet of wild sea bass, saffron mash, spinach and roast cherry tomatoes and, for dessert, pashka, Russian cheesecake with pistachio nut biscotti on the ambitious *carte;* seared yellow fin tuna niçoise is listed as a speciality.

MILFORD ON SEA,
South Lawn Hotel ❀

Lymington Road SO41 0RF
Map 4: SZ29
Tel: 01590 643911
Fax: 01590 644820
Cost: *Alc* £25, set-price D £19.75.
☺ H/wine £10
Times: Noon-1.45pm/7-8.30pm.
Closed L Mon, Xmas & New Year
Additional: Bar food L; Sunday L;
Children 7+; ✍ dishes
Smoking: No smoking in dining room;
Air conditioning
Accommodation: 24 en suite ★★★

*Charming country house hotel. Fresh flowers fill the dining room
and locally caught fish is a feature of the menu. The sweet trolley has
its moments too, especially the traditional sherry trifle.*

Directions: A337 from Lymington, L after 3 miles onto B3058;
hotel 1 mile on R

MILFORD ON SEA,
Westover Hall Hotel ❀❀

Park Lane SO41 0PT
Map 4: SZ29
Tel: 01590 643044
Fax: 01590 644490
Chef: Neil Johnson
Owners: Stewart Mechem,
Nicola Musetti
Cost: Set-price D £25. H/wine £11.95
Times: Noon-2pm/7-8.45pm
Additional: Bar food L; Sunday L;
Children 7+; ✍ dishes
Seats: 37. Private dining room 12
Smoking: No smoking in dining room
Accommodation: 13 en suite ★★★

Grand, late Victorian mansion with country house style.
Retaining many original features, including a superb galleried
entrance hall and some striking stained glass windows, this
pleasant hotel has a fine marine location on the edge of the
New Forest. From the oak-panelled restaurant enjoy fine views
across the Solent to the Isle of Wight. There's an Italian slant
to the cooking. Cappuccino of haricot beans with white truffle
oil, smoked duck breast with red onion marmalade and
ciabatta wafers, and fillet of Cornish cod with a warm vanilla
and tomato dressing are typical of the offerings. Try polenta
cake with fresh raspberries and passion fruit sauce or the
classic tiramisu for dessert. Good coffee and excellent truffles
round things off.

Directions: From M27/J1 take A337 then B3058. Hotel is
situated just out of Milford centre, towards clifftop

NEW MILTON,

Chewton Glen Hotel ❀❀❀

Christchurch Road BH25 6QS
Map 4: SZ29
Tel: 01425 275341
Fax: 01425 272310
Chef: Pierre Chevillard
Owners: Mr & Mrs Skan
Cost: Set-price L £18.50/D £45.
H/wine £17.25
Times: 12.30-1.45pm/7.30-9.30pm.
Closed L Mon
Additional: Sunday L; Children 7+;
❀ dishes
Seats: 120. Several private dining
rooms. Jacket & tie preferred at D
Smoking: No smoking in dining room;
Air conditioning
Accommodation: 53 en suite
★ ★ ★ ★ ★

Grand-scale country house in the New Forest with lots of attentive service. Luxuries abound, not least in the health and leisure centre with its expansive pool and wide range of facilities. For the less driven, an appetite can be worked up via a gentle 20 minute stroll down to the sea. Pierre Chevillard's cooking has many fine qualities of accuracy and discretion; indeed, the repertoire seeks no grand gestures of brash or over-bold flavours and ingredients work in harmony with each other. One late winter dinner produced chargrilled escalope of tuna served with new potatoes, red pepper confit, black olives and sauce anchois, pan-fried fillet of peppered venison with braised quince and cinnamon, caramelised onions and a peppercorn and game sauce, and Grand Marnier cream-filled pancakes with Suzette sauce. Fish is recommended, for instance baked noisette of monkfish in a light curry and mussel bouillon. Desserts carry on the good work, whether a bread-and-butter pudding to a baby pineapple filled with exotic sorbets and baked in meringue, and each comes with its own recommended dessert wine. The wine list has immense breadth and offers a balanced global selection, ranging from plenty of expensive French first growths to reasonably priced wines from South Africa, Chile, Australia and the USA.

Signature dishes: double-baked Emmental soufflé served with a fondue sauce; pan-fried loin of veal topped with tomato, glazed with Parmesan and served with a white wine and sage jus; braised fillet of sea bass with shiitake mushrooms and bean sprouts flavoured with ginger and lemon grass.

Directions: On A35 (Lyndhurst) turn
R through Walkford, then 2nd left into
Chewton Farm Road

**Shortlisted for AA Wine Award – see
page 16**

RINGWOOD,

Moortown Lodge Hotel ❀❀

A small, comfortable hotel to the south of Ringwood. The set-price dinner menus are hand-written each day and offer a choice of three starters and the same number of main courses. New Forest mushrooms might be laced with sour cream and tarragon and served as a starter, and Somerset goats' cheese, perhaps grilled and served on a bed of mixed leaves or made into a warm tartlet, and potted fish (a mixture of smoked salmon, trout and mackerel) could also make an appearance. Main courses – noisettes of local lamb with an unusual orange, port and mint sauce, lightly baked salmon fillet marinated in

244 Christchurch Road BH24 3AS
Map 4: SU10
Tel: 01425 471404
Fax: 01425 476052
Chef: Jilly Burrows-Jones
Owners: Jilly & Bob Burrows-Jones
Cost: Set-price D £18.95. ☺ H/wine
£8.95
Times: D only, 7-8.30pm. Closed Sun
(non-residents), 24 Dec-mid Jan
Additional: Children welcome;
❀ dishes

ginger and lime, or chicken breast with scallops and mushrooms on a creamy curry sauce – are notable for their good, clean flavours and are accompanied by correctly cooked vegetables. Puddings might run to a yummy sherry trifle, cheeses are British, and the wine list centres on France but extends to the New World, with some other European bottles and a good range of halves.

ROMSEY, Bertie's

Restaurant housed in a former women's workhouse, built some 250 years ago. The ambience has a contemporary feel with walls that are painted dark pink and cream and offset by large floral arrangements. The lunch menu offers a mix of dishes and luxury sandwiches, but at dinner a more formal menu is provided of some six starters, main courses and desserts. Seared scallops, 'succulent and full of flavour', served with crisp onions and basil oil, seared breast of duck, served on a bed of red cabbage, buttered baby fennel and a light lavender jus were both excellent. However, dessert was disappointing; a shame as, generally, the food is well judged and competently prepared. The wine list is interesting, and predominantly French.

Seats: 24
Smoking: No smoking in dining room
Accommodation: 6 rooms ★ ★

Directions: From Ringwood town centre take B3347 towards Christchurch for about 1.5 miles

80 The Hundred SO51 8BX
Map 4: SU32
Tel/Fax: 01794 830708
Chef: Michael Weir
Owner: David Birmingham
Cost: Alc £25. ☺ H/wine £9.75
Times: Noon-2pm/6.30-10pm. Closed Sun, 25-30 Dec
Additional: Bar food L; Children welcome; ☙ dishes. **Seats:** 46
Smoking: No-smoking area
Accommodation: 5 en suite

Directions: 200m from Broadlands' gate in the centre of town

ROMSEY, Old Manor House

21 Palmerston Street SO51 8GF
Map 4: SU32
Tel: 01794 517353
Chef: Mauro Bregoli
Owners: Mauro & Esther Bregoli
Cost: Alc £28. H/wine £11.50
Times: Noon-2pm/7-9.30pm. Closed D Sun, all Mon
Additional: Sunday L; Children welcome
Seats: 20
Smoking: No pipes & cigars

Directions: Opposite the entrance to Broadlands Estate

Mauro Bregoli understands the quality of ingredients and need for clarity of flavours. He describes his cooking as peasant food, and while it does have a certain simplicity and directness, it is a gilt-edged rusticity. The Italian connection is evident from the choice of home-smoked salamis, olive oil, abundance of herbs and marvellous white Italian bread. Coppa, home-cured neck of pork is served on a bed of winter salad, hot cotechino with lentils. Other first courses might include Tuscan bean soup with olive oil and Parmesan or seared scallops with broad bean purée and tomato confit, a simple but great combination especially with the addition of chargrilled baby leeks. Steamed monkfish is served on a squid ink sauce, and celeriac purée provides an interesting backdrop for grilled fillets of red mullet with rocket and pine nuts. Roe deer is given the Italian treatment, marinated in olive oil, fresh herbs and garlic and served with onion confit and spiced fruit. Porchetta arrosto is a memorable dish of roast piglet, boned and stuffed with wild fennel, thyme and sage, especially if there's also some delicious quince jam to go with it.

ROTHERWICK, Tylney Hall ❁❁

Rotherwick Hook RG27 9AZ
Map 4: SU75
Tel: 01256 764881
Fax: 01256 768141
Chef: Stephen Hine
Cost: *Alc* £42.50, set-price L £15 (2 courses)/D £23 (2 courses). H/wine £15.50
Times: 12.30-2pm/7.30-9.30pm
Additional: Bar food ; Sunday L; Children welcome; ❁ dishes
Seats: 80. Private dining room 14
Smoking: No smoking in dining room
Accommodation: 110 en suite
★ ★ ★ ★

Crisp white linen, silver cloches and lots of waiting staff in an oak-panelled dining-room with open fires and hand-painted Spanish leather. The setting signals serious eating. Canapés are taken in the bar, the *amuse bouche* at table, say a mini game terrine with peach chutney. The expensive Anglo-French *carte* takes a classical line with lots of luxury ingredients along the lines of a warm mousse of lobster with poached chicken, tomato and basil butter, or fillet of beef roasted with foie gras pâté and confit of shallots. Roast monkfish is wrapped in Parma ham and served with minestrone risotto, and partridge paired with bacon, onion, cabbage, lentils and thyme. Desserts include some tempting concepts, Earl Grey parfait with liquorice and apricot compote for example, but there's also a fine selection of British farmhouse cheeses.

Directions: M3/J5 take A287 (Newnham). From M4/J11 take B3349 (Hook), at sharp bend L (Rotherwick), L again and L in village (Newnham), 1 mile on R

SILCHESTER, Romans Hotel ❁

Little London Road
RG7 2PN
Map 4: SU66
Tel: 01189 700421
Fax: 01189 700691
Cost: *Alc* £26.50, set-price L&D £16.
☺ H/wine £11.50
Times: Noon-2pm/7-9.30pm. Closed L Sat, 26-30 Dec
Additional: Bar food; Sunday L; Children welcome; ❁ dishes
Smoking: No smoking in dining room
Accommodation: 25 en suite ★ ★ ★

Terrine of quail with a compote of grapes, garnished with fresh herbs from the garden is a speciality. Other fine choices from the traditional French menu might be duck breast with raspberry vinegar, and pistachio crème brûlée.

Directions: Signposted on the A340 between Basingstoke and Tadley

SOUTHAMPTON,
Botleigh Grange Hotel ❀❀

Hedge End SO30 2GA
Map 4: SU41
Tel: 01489 787700
Fax: 01489 788535
Chef: Edward Denovan
Owners: The Plumpton Family
Cost: *Alc* £22.50, set-price L
£16.50/D £19.50. ☺ H/wine £10.95
Times: Noon-1.45pm/7-9.45pm.
Closed L Sat
Additional: Bar food; Sunday L;
Children welcome; ❁ dishes
Seats: 70. Private dining room 26
Smoking: No smoking in dining room
Accommodation: 59 en suite ★★★

A much extended mansion with a spacious, light and airy
dining-room. A classically orientated menu – well, as much as
smoked salmon chow mein spring roll with mango salsa and
minted yogurt sauce can be counted as classical, vies with
dishes of a more French pedigree such as roast breast of
pigeon with celeriac purée, Puy lentils, confit of red onion and
rosemary oil. The exact nature of a black pudding salsa which
accompanied roast breast of duck, sage dumplings and red
wine sauce flavoured with apple and ginger jelly remains,
however, a global conundrum. Desserts have value-added
flavourings – chocolate fondant with lime ice-cream, warm
apricot and almond flan with basil ice cream.

Directions: On A334, 1.5 miles from M27 J7

SOUTHAMPTON,
Woodlands Lodge Hotel ❀

18th-century New Forest hunting lodge, stylishly converted into a
small hotel. The food is up to date with plenty of quality; local
ingredients are favoured. Crab, cod and dill fishcakes, rack of lamb
with Puy lentils and chocolate tart show the range.

Smoking: No smoking in dining room
Accommodation: 16 en suite ★★★

Directions: Telephone for directions

Bartley Road Woodlands SO40 7GN
Map 4: SU41
Tel: 01703 292257
Fax: 01703 293090
Cost: *Alc* £25, set-price L £11.95/D
£25 (4 courses). H/wine £11.95
Times: D only, 7-8.45pm
Additional: Bar food L; Sunday L
(noon-1.45pm); Children welcome;
❁ dishes

SOUTHSEA, # Queens Hotel ❀

Stately Edwardian hotel with magnificent views across the Solent.
Anglo/French dishes such as cannon of lamb with red wine jus, and
pan-fried minute steak filled with Stilton are recommended.

Additional: Bar food; Sunday L; Children welcome; ❁ dishes
Smoking: No-smoking area; No pipes & cigars
Accommodation: 75 en suite ★★★

Directions: From M27/J12 take M275 & follow signs for
Southsea seafront. Hotel opposite Hovercraft terminal

Clarence Parade PO5 3LJ
Map 4: SZ69
Tel: 01705 822466
Fax: 01705 821901
Cost: *Alc* £25, set-price L £14.75/D
£17.95 (4 courses). ☺ H/wine £11.45
Times: 12.30-2pm/7-9.45pm

SWAY, **String of Horses**

Small hotel in a peaceful New Forest location. A candlelit meal in the low-beamed restaurant might start with a dish of fresh asparagus tips cooked with fondue butter, and be followed by fillet mignon of beef topped with prosciutto and Mozzarella.

Smoking: No smoking in dining room
Accommodation: 8 en suite ★ ★

Directions: From B3055 turn R over station bridge, 2nd L into Mead End Road, 350 yds on L

Mead End Road SO41 6EH
Map 4: SZ29
Tel: 01590 682631
Fax: 01590 682911
Cost: *Alc* £23.50, set-price L & D £22 (4 courses). H/wine £11.90
Times: D only, 7-9.30pm. Closed D Sun
Additional: Bar food; Sunday L (noon-1.45pm); Children welcome; ⬗ dishes

WICKHAM, **Old House Hotel**

There has been a change of ownership at this small Georgian townhouse hotel since our last edition of The Restaurant Guide. Nicolas Ruthven-Stuart is the new chef-patron and those familiar with his former restaurant, The Old Chesil Rectory in Winchester, will know to expect some thoroughly enjoyable cooking from a menu with strong French roots. Starters such as foie gras parfait with Sauternes jelly and toasted brioche and crispy duck, bacon and lentil salad lead on to the likes of mixed fish fricasée with curried coriander sauce and couscous, and crepinette of braised oxtail with red wine fumet and carrot and parsnip purée. The pudding menu might include a caramelised bread-and-butter pudding, or our good chocolate marquise along with a selection of pasteurised and unpasteurised cheeses. Wines, on the balanced, fairly-priced list, are usefully arranged by style.

Directions: In the centre of Wickham, 3 miles N of Fareham at junction of A32/B2177

The Square PO17 5JG
Map 4: SU51
Tel: 01329 833049
Fax: 01329 833672
Chef: Nicholas A Ruthven-Stuart
Owners: Nicholas & Christina Ruthven-Stuart
Cost: *Alc* £32, set-price L £17.50/D £24.50. ☺ H/wine £10.95
Times: Noon-2pm/7-9.30pm. Closed L Mon, D Sun, 2 wks after Xmas, 2 wks Aug
Additional: Sunday L; Children welcome; ⬗ dishes
Seats: 36. Private dining room 14
Smoking: No pipes & cigars
Accommodation: 8 en suite ★ ★

WINCHESTER,
Hotel du Vin & Bistro

It avoids stuffiness while remaining elegant. The centrally located townhouse has become something of an institution; indeed, Robin Hutson and Gerard Basset are replicating the style – last year, successfully in Tunbridge Wells (see entry, Kent), another to open in Bristol as we go to press. The core of the operation, which includes bedrooms sponsored by a different wine producer, is the informal bistro and its imaginative menu built around British dishes with a world-wide slant. Here the kitchen's natural style of cooking puts the emphasis on the materials themselves and enlivens them with herbs and spices. Mediterranean vegetable terrine with basil vinaigrette, and oriental crab spring roll with a sweet chilli sauce, are examples of their production. Another is a marinated pavé of salmon with sweet potato purée, Thai asparagus and Asian pesto. Tempura of skate with pommes frites and aïoli is a modern twist on an old standby. To finish, queen of puddings and hot chocolate fondant with pistachio sauce are the things to go for. The wine selection is intelligently balanced and has no truck with rubbish.

Directions: M3 J11, follow signs for Winchester. Hotel on L just before town centre

14 Southgate Street SO23 9EF
Map 4: SU42
Tel: 01962 841414
Fax: 01962 842458
Chef: Andy Clark
Owners: Robin Hutson, Gerard Basset
Cost: *Alc* £25. ☺ H/wine £10.50
Times: Noon-1.45pm/7-9.45pm
Additional: Sunday L; Children welcome; ⬗ dishes
Seats: 65. Private dining rooms 12-48
Smoking: No pipes & cigars
Accommodation: 23 en suite ★ ★ ★ ★

WINCHESTER, **Hunters**

Casual in style, with original murals and collages, and a short menu that feature modern British food with a twist on old favourites. Thus Cumberland sausage with mash and cider sauce and comforting Arborio rice pudding with poached quince.

Smoking: No-smoking area

Directions: Towards top of the City just off High Street, 200 yards from Theatre Royal & Library car park

5 Jewry Street SO23 8RZ
Map 4: SU42
Tel: 01962 860006
Cost: *Alc* £25, set-price D
£12.95. ☺ H/wine £9.95
Times: Noon-2pm/6.30-10pm. Closed
Sun, Bhs
Additional: Children welcome;
🥕 dishes

WINCHESTER,
Lainston House Hotel ✿✿

A country house hotel that embodies the fine traditions of the genre. The restaurant provides a stately setting, heavily oak panelled with deeply comfortable seats and is supported by a loyal following. There is an evergreen quality about the food here. Frederich Litty has been at Lainston for many years but his ability to follow culinary fashion is to be applauded. Witness red mullet with stuffed salmon soufflé and lime dressing, or a mille-feuille of quails with veal jus. Main courses include beef fillet baked in brioche with a chive mash and morel sauce, and desserts take in a stunning passion fruit and chocolate delice.

Sparsholt SO21 2LT
Map 4: SU42
Tel: 01962 863588
Fax: 01962 776672
Chef: Frederich Litty
Owner: G Peccorelli
Cost: *Alc* £45.50, set-price L
£17.50/D £37. H/wine £17.
Times: 12.30-2.20pm/7-9.50pm
Additional: Bar food L; Sunday L;
Children welcome; 🥕 dishes
Seats: 55. Private dining room 18.
Jacket & tie preferred
Smoking: No smoking in dining room
Accommodation: 38 en suite ★★★★

Directions: 3 miles from Winchester,
off A272 to Stockbridge. Signposted

WINCHESTER, **Nine The Square** ✿✿

City centre hot spot offering both a formal and informal ambience. Even on wet, dreary winter days this town centre restaurant – just opposite the splendid Norman cathedral – has a buzz about it. Downstairs, there's a wine bar feel, while upstairs is more formal (and only open in the evenings). The menu is influenced by Italy with the likes of risotto, polenta and four types of home-made pasta. Salmon and crab roulade set on a bed of roasted fennel and beetroot, and charred duck breast with orange and apricot risotto, served with a side order of cabbage and pancetta, has been well reported. For dessert, try a caramelised pear mille-feuille – a simple dish with layers of filo pastry, sweetened cream and slices of pear. The compact wine list is well balanced, and offers a good selection by the glass.

Directions: In the main square, just outside the cathedral grounds and opposite the museum

The Square SO23 9HA
Map 4: SU42
Tel: 01962 864004
Fax: 01962 879586
Chef: David Bennett
Owners: David & Debra Bennett
Cost: *Alc* £25, set price L £5.95 (2
courses). ☺ H/wine £ 11.25
Times: Noon-2pm, 6-10pm. Closed
Sun, 1 wk Dec
Additional: Children welcome;
🥕 dishes
Seats: 45. Private room 20
Smoking: Air conditioning

WINCHESTER,
Old Chesil Rectory ✿✿

The former sous chef, Philip Storey, took over the business from the Ruthven-Stuarts last year. Reports suggest no dramatic changes in the quality of the food. Menus are short and quite simple with daily specials listed on a blackboard. The Mediterranean is obviously an inspiration with the repertoire taking in risottos, sauce vierge, and the likes of langoustine bisque with rouille and Gruyère croûtes. The dessert list runs from crème brûlée to chocolate mousse and passion fruit sorbet. The wine list is divided by style – light, medium, full-bodied – and offers good variety in both the old and New World. Prices are reasonable.

1 Chesil Street SO23 8HU
Map 4: SU42
Tel: 01962 851555
Fax: 01962 869704
Chef/Owner: Philip Storey
Telephone for further details

Directions: From King Alfred's statue (bottom of The Broadway), cross small bridge turn R; restaurant is to the R, just off mini roundabout

WINCHESTER, # Royal Hotel ✿

Conservatory restaurant attached to a building dating from 1540. Typical dishes include champagne risotto scented with truffles, and Aberdeen Angus steak from the charcoal grill.

St Peter Street SO23 8BS
Map 4: SU42
Tel: 01962 840840
Fax: 01962 841582
Cost: *Alc* £25, set-price L £9.50 (2 courses)/D £18.50. ☺ H/wine £11.50
Times: Noon-2.15pm/7-9.30pm
Additional: Bar Food L; Sunday L; Children welcome; 🍴 dishes
Smoking: No smoking in dining room; Air conditioning
Accommodation: 75 en suite ★ ★ ★

Directions: Take one-way system through Winchester, turn R off St George's Street into St Peter Street. Hotel on R

WINCHESTER,
Wykeham Arms ✿

250-year-old inn sandwiched between the College and Cathedral. The modern menu lists Med-influenced fare: mushrooms in red wine and garlic, and roasted chicken breast with creamy mushroom risotto. Very good wine list with a preference for Burgundy.

Smoking: No-smoking area; Air conditioning
Accommodation: 13 en suite

Directions: S out of city along Southgate Street. Take 3rd turning L into Canon Street, inn on R at end

75 Kingsgate Street SO23 9PE
Map 4: SU42
Tel: 01962 853834
Fax: 01962 854411
Cost: *Alc* £20. ☺
H/wine £10.95
Times: D only, 6.30-9pm. Closed Sun, 25 Dec
Additional: Bar food L; Children 14+; 🍴 dishes

HEREFORDSHIRE

HEREFORD, Ancient Camp Inn

Nr Eaton Bishop HR2 9QX
Map 3: SO53
Tel: 01981 250449
Fax: 01981 251581
Chef: Jason Eland
Owners: Jason & Lisa Eland
Cost: *Alc* £22.50, set-price L £15/D
£22.50. ☺ H/wine £8.95
Times: Noon-2pm/7-9pm. Closed D
Sun, all Mon, 1st 2wks Jan
Additional: Sunday L; Children 10+;
❹ dishes
Seats: 25. Private dining room 8
Smoking: No smoking in dining room
Accommodation: 5 en suite ★★

Country riverside inn and restaurant built on the grounds of an old fort high above the River Wye. The premises were originally intended as a shop, then used as a forge and later as a cider house. The restaurant retains the flagstone floor, oak beams and uses the old cider tables. The setting is relaxed, rustic and full of unpretentious charm. The menu reflects these virtues with a direct and uncluttered cooking style that relies on the excellent local produce. Six starters and six main courses are offered on the *carte*. The approach is fairly summed up by a main course of loin of Gloucestershire Old Spot pork roasted with honey and accompanied by a sage and garlic jus. Desserts remain a strength, particularly a warm sticky lime pudding served with cinnamon and clove syrup. Since the last entry, this establishment is under new ownership. Jason and Lisa Eland are building on the former owners' reputation.

Directions: Take A465 (Abergavenny road) from Hereford. Turn R to Ruckhall and Belmont Abbey; inn is 2.5 miles along road

LEDBURY, Feathers Hotel

High Street HR8 1DS
Map 3: SO73
Tel: 01531 635266
Fax: 01531 638955
Cost: *Alc* £20, set-price D £20. ☺
H/wine £8.75
Additional: Bar food; Sunday L;
Children welcome; ❹ dishes
Accommodation: 19 en suite ★★★

Directions: Ledbury is on
A449/A438/A417, and the hotel is
prominent on the main street

Fuggles is the main restaurant at this striking, black-and-white timbered hotel. The carte, supported by blackboard specials, provides a good choice of soundly prepared dishes.

ROSS-ON-WYE, **Chase Hotel**

Gloucester Road HR9 5LH
Map 3: SO52
Tel: 01989 763161
Fax: 01989 768330
Chef: Ian Beale
Cost: *Alc* £25, set-price L & D £17.
☺ H/wine £9.50
Times: Noon-1.45pm/7-9.45pm.
Closed 26 Dec
Additional: Bar food; Sunday L;
Children 12+; ✿ dishes
Seats: 50
Smoking: No smoking in dining room
Accommodation: 38 en suite ★★★

Directions: From town centre follow
B4260 towards Gloucester, hotel
200yds on R

*Georgian country-house hotel producing a calming
atmosphere.* Indeed the restaurant has a gentle colour scheme
of warm peach and beige. Dishes vary from the robust - terrine
of rabbit, quail and pigeon with redcurrant and port sauce,
collops of venison on a cabbage and smoked bacon cake with
juniper and Madeira sauce, and deep-fried apple fritters with
prune and Armagnac ice cream - to classics of shellfish bisque,
baked salmon with hollandaise, and crème brûlée. We chose
tomato and pepper tarte Tatin with Mozzarella and basil and
found it 'like a pizza, only with light, flaky pastry', an
enjoyable dish no less accomplished than the main course of
saffron-infused cassolette of grey mullet and mussels
accompanied by a selection of vegetables that included a
sorrel-stuffed tomato. Crêpe soufflé was a bit of a poser,
turning out to be a novel combination of two desserts: light
pancakes folded around a nicely risen soufflé served with a
good, rich custard.

ROSS-ON-WYE, **Glewstone Court**

*Lively country house hotel full of eclectic antiques and curios.
Expect some crisp, country cooking from a diverse menu that
ranges from warm crab, leek and lemongrass cheesecake to grilled
fillet of Hereford beef with green peppercorn cream.*

Accommodation: 7 en suite ★★

Directions: From Ross Market Place take A40/A49
(Monmouth/Hereford) over Wilton Bridge. At roundabout L onto
A40 (Monmouth/S Wales), after 1 mile R for Glewstone

Glewstone HR9 6AW
Map 3: SO52
Tel: 01989 770367
Fax: 01989 770282
Cost: Set-price L £15/D £27 (4
courses). H/wine £10
Times: Noon-2pm/7-9.30pm. Closed
25-27 Dec
Additional: Bar food; Sunday L;
Children welcome; ✿ dishes
Smoking: No pipes & cigars

ROSS-ON-WYE,
Hunsdon Manor Hotel

*Sandstone manor house dating back to Elizabethan times. A meal
here might take in the home-made soup, and chicken breast cooked
with Stilton. Fresh seafood is a strong point.*

Smoking: No pipes & cigars
Accommodation: 24 en suite ★★★

Directions: On A40 2 miles E of Ross-on-Wye

Gloucester Road
Weston under Penyard
HR9 7PE
Map 3: SO52
Tel: 01989 563376
Fax: 01989 768348
Cost: *Alc* £25, set-price D £18. ☺
H/wine £12.50
Times: Noon-2pm/7-9.30pm
Additional: Children 8+; ✿ dishes

ROSS-ON-WYE,
Pencraig Court Hotel ✿

Large Georgian house with impressive views of the River Wye. Dinner starts with a selection of home-made breads (try olive and walnut), followed by the likes of casserole of pheasant in a wine and mustard sauce.

Smoking: No smoking in dining room
Accommodation: 11 en suite ★ ★ ★

Directions: Approximately 3 miles S of Ross-on-Wye on A40

Pencraig HR9 6HR
Map 3: SO52
Tel: 01989 770306
Fax: 01989 770040
Cost: Set-price D £23 (4 courses). ☺
H/wine £9.50
Times: 12.30-2pm/7.30-9pm
Additional: Sunday L; Children welcome; ✿ dishes

ROSS-ON-WYE,
Pengethley Manor

Georgian mansion that's the business with a high standard of service. The restaurant maintains the Georgian style with soft blues and beige colours, large mirrors and oil paintings. Ferdinand van de Knaap's carte and set-price menus continue to offer a sound choice: bread, canapés and petits fours are made in-house, Wye salmon, Herefordshire beef and Welsh lamb dictate the menus and herbs are grown in the garden. Flavours are as intense and powerful as ever, as could be seen in a beautifully tender lamb marinated in apricot conserve and encrusted in breadcrumbs, pungent oregano and rosemary.

Pengethley Park HR9 6LL
Map 3: SO52
Tel: 01989 730211
Fax: 01989 730238
Chef: Fred van der Knaap
Owners: Patrick & Geraldine Wisker
Cost: *Alc* £40, set-price L £16/D £25 (4 courses). H/wine £13.85
Times: Noon-1.45pm/7-9.15pm
Additional: Bar food L; Sunday L; Children 8+; ✿ dishes
Seats: 50. Private dining room 28. Jacket & tie preferred
Smoking: No smoking in dining room
Accommodation: 25 en suite ★ ★ ★

Directions: 4m N on A49 Hereford road

ULLINGSWICK, **The Steppes**

Personally run 17th-century house with 14th-century origins. Tricia and Henry Howland have won hearts and minds over the years with their willingness to please and their determination to produce good food, and they play the hosts with enthusiasm. The cooking is quite simple based on recognisable materials in familiar forms - pork leg forestière, boeuf bourgignon - but grasps current fashion for dishes such as Thai seafood dim-sum and kiln-roasted chunky smoked salmon with cracked pepper. Vegetables are good and plentiful. Desserts call variously on Kirsch, for griottines cherries, and rose water to flavour ice cream to serve with lychees.

Directions: Off A417 Gloucester to Leominster road

Nr Hereford HR1 3JG
Map 3: SO54
Tel: 01432 820424
Fax: 01432 820042
Chef: Tricia Howland
Owners: Henry & Tricia Howland
Cost: Set-price D £26 (4 courses). H/wine £7.50
Times: D only, 7.30-9pm.
Additional: Children 10+; ✿ dishes
Seats: 12. Jacket & tie preferred
Smoking: No smoking in dining room
Accommodation: 6 en suite ★ ★

WEOBLEY, The Salutation Inn

Market Pitch HR4 8SJ
Map 3: SO45
Tel: 01544 318443
Fax: 01544 318216
Chef: Graham Leaveasley
Owners: Mr & Mrs Christopher
Anthony
Cost: *Alc* £24. ☺ H/wine £8.75
Times: Noon-2pm/7-9pm. Closed D
Sun, L Mon, 25 Dec
Additional: Bar food; Sunday L;
🍲 dishes
Seats: 38.
Smoking: No smoking in dining room
Accommodation: 4 en suite ★★

Directions: Down hill into village,
take 1st R, then 2nd R

Ancient inn noted for warmth of service. Weobley is a
quintessentially English village, with medieval buildings, a
church almost as old as the millennium, and this old timber-
framed hostelry, with large stone fireplaces in both bar and
restaurant. In the latter, you could start with terrine of smoked
duck with redcurrant and onion relish, or delicately flavoured
asparagus soup, 'thick, hot and good'. Rack of lamb marinated
in tomato, basil and garlic, nicely pink, on rösti with a rich dark
sauce, makes a distinctive main course, and there might be
fillet of sole with lemon sauce infused with thyme. Vegetarians
have their own menu. Good old bread-and-butter pudding, this
one with apricot purée, is on the list of desserts.

HERTFORDSHIRE

ELSTREE,
Edgwarebury Hotel

Barnet Lane WD6 3RE
Map 4: TQ19
Tel: 0181 9538227
Fax: 0181 2073668
Chef: Chris Fisher
Owner: Corus Hotels
Cost: *Alc* £27.90, set-price L & D
£29.50. ☺ H/wine £11.50
Times: 12.30-2.15pm/7-9.45pm.
Closed L Sat
Additional: Sunday L; Children
welcome; 🍲 dishes
Seats: 60. Private rooms 40, 18
Smoking: No smoking in dining room
Accommodation: 47 en suite ★★★

Directions: Access from M1 J4 & 5,
M25 J19 & 23, Barnet Lane is signed
Elstree & Aldenham

*The 'Plain and Simple' menu will strike a chord with anyone
sick of the sight of sun-dried tomatoes.* Whole grilled
Brixham plaice with parsley and lemon and roast breast of
chicken with creamed leeks and bacon are just the thing for
jaded palates and finicky eaters. But Chris Fisher can do a
whole lot more than roast rump of English lamb with red
cabbage and creamed potatoes, however comforting. Some of

his most stylish dishes include tian of Orkney scallops with spinach, deep-fried sharia pastry and lemongrass butter sauce, and grilled fillet of sea bass with a shellfish broth, rouille and tarragon. He also gives a makeover to, of all things, pot-roasted rabbit faggot with maple-glazed parsnips and shallot gravy. Haggis, too, makes an unexpected appearance in a confit of skate wing and garlic with pommes Anna and chicken stock. A whimsical note is struck in the menu description 'calves' liver with breakfast mash, celeriac chips, and once an onion sauce', whatever that means. Desserts are inventive but less puzzlingly described – warm savarin of Agen prunes with Armagnac, crème fraîche ice and dried apple crisps; rosewater gratin of blood oranges with rhubarb ice and cinnamon.

HADLEY WOOD,
West Lodge Park Hotel

Impressive William IV mansion surrounded by beautiful rolling countryside. The hotel has thirty-five acres of grounds, from which trees were felled to provide timber for the ships of the Royal Navy after the Battle of Trafalgar. Almost two centuries later, visitors to West Lodge Park can work up an appetite by strolling round the Beale Arboretum – filled with examples of trees from all over the world. The kitchen shows ambition, as was evident at our test meal taken in early winter: duck rillettes, served with good home-made brioche, and an excellent fillet of beef served with pan-fried foie gras and haricots vert.

Directions: 1 mile S of M25/J24 on the A111; 1 mile from Cockfosters & Hadley Wood stations

Cockfosters Road Barnet EN4 0PY
Map GtL: C5
Tel: 0181 2163900
Fax: 0181 2163937
Chef: Peter Leggat
Owners: Beale's Group
Cost: *Alc* £22.95, set-price L £19.95 (2 courses)/D £26.95. ☺ H/wine £13.25
Times: 12.30-2pm/7.15-9.30pm
Additional: Sunday L; Children welcome; ✿ dishes
Seats: 80. Private dining room/conference
Smoking: No smoking in dining room
Accommodation: 55 en suite

HEMEL HEMPSTEAD,
Watermill Hotel

Hotel in a village setting by the river, with the Grand Union Canal to the rear. The Riverside Restaurant offers an interesting range of dishes from a choice of menus.

Directions: From M1/J8 follow signs to and join A41 (Aylesbury), then A4251 to Bourne End

London Road Bourne End HP1 2RJ
Map 4: TL00
Tel: 01442 349955
Fax: 01442 866130
Telephone for further details

SAWBRIDGEWORTH, **The Shoes**

A bustling little town with a narrow high street and the restaurant at the end on the crossroads – a good place to watch life go by. Midweek lunchtimes can be quiet but the place livens up in the evenings, and service is friendly. The restaurant's ambience fits well with the style of cooking: bright and modern, sometimes inventive, coupled with a strong vein of classicism. For starters, a version of cannelloni of lobster and salmon with a Muscat butter sauce sits happily next to roasted pigeon breast on a compote of red onions and blackcurrants. Main-course corn-fed chicken breast with roasted parsnip purée and smoked garlic sauce is equally at home with marinated venison steak with confited Savoy cabbage and a rich red wine finished with a hint of bitter chocolate, or pan-

52 Bell Street CM21 9AN
Map 4: TL41
Tel: 01279 722554
Fax: 01279 832494
Chef: Mark Green
Owners: Lyndon Wootton, Peter & Doreen Gowan
Cost: *Alc* £30, set-price L £16.25. H/wine £10.95
Times: Noon-1.30pm/7-9.30pm. Closed L Sat & Mon, all Sun, 2 wks after Xmas, last 2 wks Aug
Additional: Children welcome; ✿ dishes
Seats: 60. Private room 20

The Shoes

Smoking: No-smoking area; Air conditioning

Directions: From M11 J7 take A414 (Harlow); continue as road becomes A1186 (Bishop's Stortford). Sawbridgeworth is midway between Harlow and Bishop's Stortford

fried fillets of grey mullet served on a Thai fishcake with red curry sauce and deep-fried basil. Desserts of the order of white chocolate and fresh egg custard tartlet with a compote of Kirsch and cherries, or apple and cinnamon tarte Tatin with a mixed spice syllabub are intriguing.

ST ALBANS, **St Michael's Manor**

16th-century town house set in five acres of grounds, complete with lake and river. Cooking runs along the lines of oven-roasted breast of chicken with fondant potatoes, and grilled fillet of sea bass with a prawn butter and saffron sauce.

Smoking: No pipes & cigars
Accommodation: 23 en suite ★ ★ ★

Directions: At the Tudor Tavern in High Street turn into George Street. After Abbey & Boys' school on L, road continues into Fishpool Street. Hotel 1 mile on L

Fishpool Street AL3 4RY
Map 4: TL10
Tel: 01727 864444
Fax: 01727 848909
Cost: Set-price L £19.75/D £29.50.
H/wine £13.95
Times: 12.30-2pm/7-9.30pm (10pm Sat/9pm Sun)
Additional: Bar food L; Sunday L; Children welcome; dishes

ST ALBANS,
Sopwell House Hotel ✿✿

A combination of hotel, leisure complex and conference centre, with a hall of fame dedicated to football clubs. Not surprisingly there's a range of eating options with the Magnolia Restaurant, built around a live tree being the most formal. Little nooks and crannies give intimacy, but the main floor is

Cottonmill Lane Sopwell AL1 2HQ
Map 4: TL10
Tel: 01727 864477
Fax: 01727 844741
Chef: Warren Jones
Owner: Abraham Bejerano
Cost: *Alc* £40, set-price L £16.95/D £24.50. ☺ H/wine £13.50
Times: 12.30-2.30pm (3pm Sun)/7.30-9.45pm. Closed L Sat, D Sun
Additional: Sunday L; Children welcome; ✆ dishes
Seats: 90. Private dining rooms 300
Smoking: No smoking in dining room
Accommodation: 92 en suite ★ ★ ★ ★

Directions: On London Road from St Albans follow signs to Sopwell, over mini-roundabout, hotel on L

the place to be seen. Interesting breads make a promising beginning to dinner. Fish plays a leading role among the starters, from perhaps escabèche of red mullet with pickled fennel and a tomato broth, to traditional smoked salmon with horseradish, lemon and capers, and comes highly praised in the shape of a main course 'superb fresh salmon grilled to perfection' with a chowder of mussels and coriander, or there might be roasted fillet of beef on creamed cabbage with parsnip fondant and Parmentier potatoes. Rich and flavourful bitter chocolate marquise with poached kumquats makes a luxurious pudding. The wine list is a mixture of classic labels and bottles from the New World.

ST ALBANS, **Thistle St Albans**

Watford Road AL2 3DS
Map 4: TL10
Tel: 01727 854252
Fax: 01727 841906
Cost: *Alc* £40, set-price L £19.50/D £25. H/wine £11.75
Times: 12.30-1.45pm/7-9.45pm. Closed L Sat, L Bhs
Additional: Sunday L; Children welcome; 🍴 dishes
Smoking: No smoking in dining room; Air conditioning
Accommodation: 111 en suite
★ ★ ★ ★

Country house hotel with modern British food: try salmon parcel filled with lobster mousse, or medallions of monkfish flamed with whisky and served with a couscous and nut timbale.

Directions: On A405, Watford road. From M25/J21A, 1st roundabout, turn L

TRING, **Pendley Manor**

Cow Lane HP23 5QY
Map 4: SP91
Tel: 01442 891891
Fax: 01442 890687
Cost: *Alc* £29.50, set-price L & D £23 (4 courses). ☺ H/wine £13
Times: 12.30-2.30pm/7-9.30pm
Additional: Bar food; Sunday L; Children welcome; 🍴 dishes
Smoking: No smoking in dining room
Accommodation: 74 en suite ★ ★ ★ ★

Impressive Victorian mansion in extensive grounds. Seasonal menus from an ambitious kitchen has ham, fennel and wild mushroom risotto, and pigeon breast with sage mousse wrapped in Parma ham, with red onion comfit and Madeira sauce scoring points.

Directions: Tring exit from A41, follow sign for Berkhamsted, 1st L, R after Rugby Club

WARE,
Marriott Hanbury Manor

Thundridge SG12 0SD
Map 5: TL31
Tel: 01920 487722
Fax: 01920 487692
Chef: Robert Gleeson
Cost: *Alc* £35, set-price L £25/D £33.
H/wine £19.50
Times: 12.30-2pm/7.30-10pm. Closed
1 Jan
Additional: Sunday L; Children 12+;
❦ dishes
Seats: 50. Private dining room 20.
Jacket & tie preferred
Smoking: No smoking in dining room;
Air conditioning
Accommodation: 96 en suite
★ ★ ★ ★ ★

A large Jacobean-style property with extensive public rooms.
All feature fine wooden panelling, crystal chandeliers, antique
furniture and open fires. There are 200 acres outside too, a golf
course among them. The Zodiac Restaurant is the apple of the
hotel's eye. This used to be the Hanbury family's summer
drawing room, and magnificent surroundings it provides:
stuccoed walls, barrel-vaulted ceiling, grand dark wooden
carver chairs, gleaming silver and glassware, and white linen.
Anglo-French spiked with oriental touches is the idiom,
although the kitchen enriches many dishes with classical
butter-based sauces, often over-gilding the lily in the process:
citrus butter for cannelloni of Cornish crab with ginger and
preserved peaches, turmeric butter with fillet of Aberdeen
Angus with wild mushrooms and a potato and rosemary
galette. Lobster turns up in a salad with mango dressed with
lime and coriander, or in tortellini along with chilli and
coconut nage to accompany main-course roasted monkfish, but
the kitchen also mines an earthier seam in dishes like stuffed
pig's trotters with morels, and roast saddle of hare with
juniper-scented jus. The grandiose-sounding chocolate
indulgent pyramid lives up to its name: fine chocolate sponge
containing creamy orange mousse with an 'excellent' vanilla
sabayon sprinkled with pistachio praline. Incidentals like
breads get the thumbs up, while the wine list is a tome: most
people should find something on a page of bottles also sold by
the glass and around a further dozen recommended by the
sommelier.
Signature dishes: torte of rabbit and duck confit with braised
endive, spinach and cep sabayon; loin of English lamb wrapped
in truffle-scented potato and a herb crust with port jus; warm
cinnamon pear and pistachio financier with vanilla and rum
sorbet.

Directions: On A10, 12 miles N of
M25 J25

WELWYN, ## Auberge du Lac ❦❦

Lakeside setting for the restaurant of Brocket Hall. The
former 17th-century hunting lodge is sited on the bank of the
Broadwater. The conservatory-style restaurant has additional
tables on the patio to make the most of the setting, weather
permitting. The very French service matches classic French
cooking that has been updated by Asian influences. This
translates as marinated Cornish scallops 'lightly salted with

Brocket Hall AL8 7XG
Map 4: TL21
Tel: 01707 368888
Fax: 01707 368898
Chef: Paul Hackett
Cost: *Alc* £38, set-price L £22.50.
H/wine £16
Times: Noon-2.30pm/7-10.30pm.
Closed D Sun, all Mon

chilli, lime and coriander', and the likes of breast of guinea fowl, boudin blanc and leek sauce being served with a tempura of vegetables 'somewhat out of place', but nevertheless showing good skill. Presentation is a strong point, a bitter chocolate mille-feuille looked stunning on the plate. Hard work and good intent sums up the kitchen.

Directions: Telephone for directions

Additional: Sunday L; Children 5+; dishes
Seats: 65. Private dining rooms 2-14. Jacket & tie preferred
Smoking: No pipes & cigars; Air conditioning
Accommodation: 16 en suite

KENT

ASHFORD, **Eastwell Manor** ❀❀❀

The slightly oppressive tastes of the Victorians linger – much panelling, wooden ceilings, leather Chesterfields, baronial-style stone fireplaces and leaded windows. But Queen Victoria clearly felt that this Jacobean-style manor in 3,000 acres was sufficiently noble for her to pay a visit, and a queen of Romania was born here. Ian Mansfield has departed to the Swallow, Birmingham (see entry), and Steven Black now heads the kitchen. Perhaps the kitchen's style is best defined by roasted, boned quail on Savoy cabbage with cep juices, 'great' roasted king scallops with spicy couscous, and main courses of fillet of Aberdeen Angus with watercress purée, and grilled Dover sole, filleted at the table and served with parsley butter. Luxuries – lobster, foie gras, caviar, quails' eggs – rub shoulders with pan-fried lambs' kidneys and sweetbreads on rösti, and smoked haddock risotto with a poached egg. Lamb is a favoured main course, braised leg with black pudding and thyme mash receiving plaudits of 'excellent', 'full of flavour and cooked correctly'. Truffles give a lift to another main course, of braised pork cheek and roasted pork fillet in marjoram-scented juices with boulangère potatoes, while rarely-seen conger eel steak is pan-fried and served with sauce vierge. A pudding of dark chocolate brûlée with passion fruit sorbet has been endorsed for the contrast between the tart sorbet and the richness of the chocolate, and there might be tarte Tatin with vanilla ice cream.

Signature dishes: lobster with linguine, spinach purée, asparagus and garlic froth; loin of lamb with sweetbreads and kidney, provençale vegetables and dauphinoise potatoes; poached pear in red wine, comice pear sorbet and poire William soufflé.

Eastwell Park Boughton Lees TN25 4HR
Map 5: TR04
Tel: 01233 213000
Fax: 01233 635530
Chef: Steven Black
Owner: Turrloo F Parrett
Cost: *Alc* £42.50, set-price L £10 (2 courses)/D £30. H/wine £15.50
Times: Noon-2pm/7-10pm
Additional: Bar food; Sunday L; Children welcome; dishes
Seats: 80. Private dining room 80. Jacket & tie preferred
Smoking: No smoking in dining room
Accommodation: 61 en suite ★ ★ ★ ★

Directions: M20/J9 follow A251 Faversham, hotel on L after Kennington. From Canterbury, A28 to Ashford L turn to Boughton Lees

BEARSTED,

Le Soufflé ❀❀

The 16th-century building is a forest of exposed timbers, but has been given an upmarket look with white cloths and candles. Nick Evenden, has returned to his home county and injected a fresh infusion of life and talent into this well-established restaurant. A good, straight-to-the-point menu reflects time he spent in London with Marco Pierre White. Fish is a strong point. Sea bass, for example, may be roasted and served with langoustine ravioli and coriander sauce, or seared with chorizo sausage, mashed potato and spring onion. Sweet, pan-fried scallops are given balance by meaty black pudding set on rich creamed potatoes, olive oil hollandaise and vibrantly green parsley sauce. Alternatively, there's pressed cassoulet terrine with mustard vinaigrette or breast of Gressingham duck with limes and soy scented sauce. From a choice of desserts along the lines of rhubarb crème brûlée, Grand Marnier parfait, comes a startlingly refreshing terrine of fruit set in a passion fruit jelly.

31 The Green Maidstone ME14 4DN
Map 5: TQ85
Tel/Fax: 01622 737065
Chef: Nick Evenden
Owners: Nick & Karen Evenden
Cost: *Alc* £30, set-price L £22. ☺
H/wine £10.95
Times: Noon-2pm/7-9.30pm. Closed L Sat, D Sun, all Mon
Additional: Sunday L; Children welcome; ⬤ dishes
Seats: 40. Private dining room 30
Smoking: No pipes & cigars

Directions: Telephone for directions

BIDDENDEN,

West House Restaurant ❀❀

Country restaurant with relaxed, well-paced service. This is a lovely room, beamed, bare boards, bare wooden tables set with brass candlesticks, a stove in a huge inglenook. Nice decorative touches that pick up on the age of the place that is the setting for the second career for former futures traders David and Susan Cunningham – he out front, she slaving over a hot stove. They only open for dinner, bookings on the six tables are staggered so as not to compromise the quality of the food, and the result is a proper country restaurant with first-class cooking. Strong Mediterranean influences, a love of colour and presentation and an emphasis on flavour distinguish Susan's style. Heavily endorsed dishes this year have been starters of warm blue cheese, pear and rosemary tart, tuna fish cake with sweetcorn relish, and Mozzarella wrapped in Parma ham on chargrilled focaccia with a tomato pesto dressing, and main courses of fillet of red mullet with ratatouille and new potatoes, and noisette of lamb with apricot and nut stuffing, pea mash and tomato compote. Puddings include a gooey, fondant and very grown-up chocolate pudding with passion fruit ice cream, and a sound coconut crème brûlée. A great find.

28 High Street TN27 8AH
Map 5: TQ83
Tel/Fax: 01580 291341
Chef: Susan Cunningham
Owners: David & Susan Cunningham
Cost: Set-price D £22.50. ☺ H/wine
£10.50
Times: D only, 7-9.30pm. Closed Sun, Mon, Tue, 1st 2 wks Jan, 2 wks autumn, Xmas, 1 Jan
Additional: Children welcome; ⬤ dishes
Seats: 20
Smoking: No pipes & cigars

Directions: Junction of A2862 and A274. 14 miles S of Maidstone

BRANDS HATCH,

Brandshatch Place ❀❀

Peaceful Georgian county house set in its own extensive gardens despite being close to the famous racing circuit and the M20. Facilities at the hotel include an excellent leisure club and a wide range of meeting rooms, yet the setting remains cosy and country-style. The kitchen adopts a serious approach to food, and the menu hints at dishes that allow ingredients to come through. There's not too much complication and the *carte* is supplemented by a daily changing set menu. Pressed ham and chicken terrine with

Fawkham DA3 8NQ
Map 5: TQ56
Tel: 01474 872239
Fax: 01474 879652
Chef: Aimé Zbinden
Owners: Arcadian Hotels
Cost: *Alc* £40, set-price L £16.95/D £21.95. ☺ H/wine £12.95
Times: Noon-2.30pm/7-9.30pm
Additional: Bar food; Sunday L; Children welcome; ⬤ dishes

balsamic vinegar and basil oil, followed by simply baked cod atop a rösti with a red pepper sauce, with mango Tatin and mango sorbet to finish, formed the components of our most recent meal.

Directions: Off A20, M25/J3, follow signs for Circuit then Fawkham; 2nd turn R after motorway bridge

BROMLEY, **Chapter One**

See London

CANTERBURY,
Canterbury Hotel

Sturdy provincial hotel with a strong French influence. Classic French cuisine can be enjoyed in the bright, vibrant yellow and orange restaurant. Jazz music plays in the background as guests tuck into starters such as hare and hazelnut terrine, smoked duck breast with citrus fruit salad, and scallops and langoustines with tomato, garlic and mushroom sauce. A summer meal might start with lobster gratin, served with a white wine cream sauce. To follow, perhaps cutlet of veal with morel sauce, or roast John Dory fillet with green lentils and foie gras jus. Desserts come in all shapes and sizes: why not try apple and pear tarte Tatin with Calvados sorbet, or the selection of fine French cheeses? The compact wine list is notable for its use of small growers.

Brandshatch Place

Seats: 60. Private dining room 120
Smoking: No smoking in dining room
Accommodation: 41 en suite ★★★

71 New Dover Road CT1 3DZ
Map 5: TR15
Tel: 01227 450551
Fax: 01227 780145
Chef: Jean-Luc Jouvente
Owners: Mr & Mrs F Bevan
Cost: *Alc* £24, set-price L & D £15.95. ☺ H/wine £9.50
Times: Noon-1.45pm/7-9.45pm
Additional: Children welcome; 🍽 dishes
Seats: 45. Private dining room 20. Jacket & tie preferred
Smoking: No smoking in dining rom
Accommodation: 25 en suite ★★

Directions: On A2, Dover road

CHATHAM,

Bridgewood Manor Hotel

Modern, fully leisure-equipped hotel, but traditional service and hospitality. Proximity to Rochester and easy access to the motorway network ensures a fair proportion of corporate business, lured as much by the extensive leisure facilities (including a heated indoor pool and full-size snooker table), as by Jean-Claude MacFarlane's modernish menu. The style is an understated neo-classicism that maintains proper regard for prime materials. Rabbit and green olive terrine, for example, is paired with a lemon-thyme sauce, roast Barbary duck with a rich fruit sauce, and pan-fried fillets of sea bass with vegetable ribbons and a vanilla jus. Desserts can range from a traditional apple pie and vanilla ice cream to a more intense hot passion fruit soufflé with Grand Marnier and passion fruit coulis.

Directions: Adjacent to roundabout on A229

Bridgewood Roundabout
Walderslade Woods
ME5 9AX
Map 5: TQ76
Tel: 01634 201333
Fax: 01634 201330
Chef: Jean-Claude MacFarlane
Owner: Marston Hotels
Cost: *Alc* £31.50, set-price L £18/D £26. H/wine £13.75
Times: 12.30-1.45pm/7-9.45pm. Closed L Sat
Additional: Bar food; Sunday L; Children welcome; 🍴 dishes
Seats: 80. Private dining room 24
Smoking: No smoking in dining room; Air conditioning
Accommodation: 100 en suite
★ ★ ★ ★

CRANBROOK,

Kennel Holt Hotel

Goudhurst Road TN17 2PT
Map 5:TQ73
Tel: 01580 712032
Fax: 01580 715495
Chef: Neil Chalmers
Owners: Neil & Sally Chalmers
Cost: Set-price D £27.50. H/wine £12.50
Times: D only, 7.30-9pm. Closed D Sun, Mon, 3 wks Jan
Additional: Sunday L (mid Sep-mid Apr); Children 10+; 🍴 dishes
Seats: 25. Private dining room 18
Smoking: No smoking in dining room
Accommodation: 10 en suite ★ ★

A charming Elizabethan manor house with immaculately kept gardens. The restaurant has a charming rustic appeal, with the cooking noted for bold flavours. Gutsy dishes include pheasant breast with gingered pear and creamy white wine sauce, and calves' liver with a Cassis and pancetta sauce. We kicked off a meal in April with tuna spring rolls with spicy tomato sauce, and followed it with a boudin of chicken and foie gras with tagliatelle and wild mushroom sauce. A talented pastry cook is at work here, our bread-and-butter pudding was outstanding, and we found the bread and petits fours from the same hand equally irresistible. The wine list leans heavily towards Bordeaux, but there should be something to suit most tastes and pockets.

Directions: On A262 1 mile from A229 crossroads, 3 miles from Goudhurst towards Cranbrook

CRANBROOK,

Soho South

23 Stone Street TN17 3HF
Map 5: TQ73
Tel: 01580 714666
Fax: 01580 715653
Chef: Nigel Tarr
Owners: Nigel & Linnea Tarr
Cost: *Alc* £24. ☺ H/wine £8.90
Times: 11am-2.30pm/6.30-9.30pm.
Closed Sun, Mon, Tue, 1 wk end May
Additional: Children 8+; ✿ dishes
Seats: 30
Smoking: No pipes & cigars

Directions: In town centre, opposite Barclays Bank, 50 metres from Tourist Information Centre & church

A casual and friendly atmosphere, with pleasant young staff, runs through this bistro-style operation. Pine furniture, bare wood floors, and walls displaying dried herbs and flowers reinforce the relaxed atmosphere. The wide-ranging influences on the kitchen are shown by Thai-style crab and salmon fishcakes, Italian pork sausages with olive oil mash and butterbeans, and confit of Barbary duck on Puy lentils with red cabbage and apples. Wild mushrooms could appear with chargrilled fillet steak or as a starter, stuffed with spinach and gratinated, and shellfish might turn up as pan-fried Rye Bay scallops with tagliatelle. Leg of lamb is marinated in lime, yogurt and turmeric, and mullet gets the traditional treatment, deep-fried, its cider-flavoured batter light and crisp, served with chips. Warm chocolate and coconut cake has been described as 'delicious', its chocolate sauce equally good. House wines are from Georges Duboeuf.

DARGATE, **The Dove** **NEW**

The sort of country pub you dream of as your local. Roses round the door, a simple interior with wood floor, plain tables and hop-garlanded bar, cheerful, prompt service and astonishingly good food sum up this very rurally situated pub. Nigel Morris is another of those chefs who has got sick of the grand kitchen environment (he held three AA Rosettes at Llangoed Hall) and has bought his own pub. Food is simply described on a series of blackboard menus, runs with the seasons, and reflects the proximity of both the sea and the surrounding countryside: fish is delivered from Hythe, game in season comes from local shoots. Lunchtime snacks could run to potted shrimp and salmon with a tomato and onion salad, or a stunning warm marinated chicken salad, aromatic with basil and given extra lift with the subtle hit of curry oil. From a fuller menu, salad of duck confit with green beans is a sound dish, well constructed and full of flavour, while baked fillet of cod impresses with its freshness and accompanying vibrant-tasting tomato and basil sauce. Desserts such as lemon tart are classics: here was fine pastry with the filling offset by a quenelle of soured cream that gave acidic balance to the sweetness. Splendid sheltered garden for summer meals. This is some of the best food in the area.

Plumpudding Lane Canterbury ME13 9HB
Map 5: TR06
Tel: 01227 751360
Chef: Nigel Morris
Owners: Nigel & Bridget Morris
Cost: *Alc* £18. ☺ H/wine £8
Times: Noon-2pm/7-9pm. Closed D Sun, all Mon
Additional: Bar food L; Sunday L; Children welcome; ✿ dishes
Seats: 20

Directions: Telephone for directions

DEAL, **Dunkerley's of Deal** ✿

19 Beach Street CT14 7AH
Map 5: TR35
Tel: 01304 375016
Fax: 01304 380187
Cost: *Alc* £30, set-price L £10.
☺ H/wine £8.95
Times: Noon-2.30pm/6-9.45pm.
Closed Mon
Additional: Bar food; Sunday L;
Children welcome; ✆ dishes
Smoking: No-smoking area; Air
conditioning
Accommodation: 16 en suite ★ ★ ★

Seafront hotel restaurant with a Victorian feel. Fresh fish is the
speciality with caramelised scallops with Vermouth butter, or gâteau
of crab with tarragon and tomato coulis, showing the style
admirably. Meat eaters are not ignored.

Directions: Turn off A2 onto A258 to Deal – 100 yds before
Deal Pier

DOVER, **Wallett's Court** ✿✿

West Cliffe St Margarets-at-Cliffe
CT15 6EW
Map 5: TR34
Tel: 01304 852424
Fax: 01304 853430
Chef: Steven Harvey
Owners: The Oakley Family
Cost: *Alc* £32.50, set-price L
£17.50/D £25. ☺ H/wine £14
Times: Noon-2pm/7-9pm. Closed 31
Dec
Additional: Bar food; Sunday L;
Children welcome; ✆ dishes
Seats: 60. Private dining room 40
Smoking: No smoking in dining room
Accommodation: 16 en suite ★ ★

Personally run country house hotel with a relaxed style.
When the Oakley family discovered Wallett's Court in 1975,
the Jacobean farmhouse was in a near derelict state.
Painstakingly, they built the place up, retaining many original
features and injecting a warm and welcoming atmosphere.
Recent developments include four more sumptuous rooms
and a striking leisure club. The monthly changing menu
reveals the best of regional produce, cooked in a reassuringly
traditional style. Two-game terrine, for example, comes with a
well-made Cumberland sauce, and pan-fried medallions of
pork fillet, served with Stilton and spring onion chiffonade,
caramelised apples and sage dumplings, is about as satisfying
as country cooking can get. Lemon tart got the thumbs up
too.

Directions: From A2 take A258 (Dover/Deal) 1st R to St
Margarets, hotel on R

EDENBRIDGE,
Haxted Mill

Feast on fruits de mer in a converted barn adjacent to the old mill. Baked whole fish flamed in Pernod and sautéed tenderloin of pork with cumin and coriander also sound good. Extensive summer menu.

Haxted Road TN8 6PU
Map 5: TQ44
Tel: 01732 862914
Cost: *Alc* £25, set-price L (winter only) £10 (2 courses). ☺ H/wine £10.75
Times: Noon-2pm/7-9pm (6.30-10pm Thu-Sat in summer). Closed D Sun, all Mon
Additional: Sunday L; Children 8+; 🌢 dishes
Smoking: No smoking in dining room

Directions: Telephone for directions

EDENBRIDGE, **Honours Mill**

18th-century watermill where, in summer, a balcony overlooking the mill pond comes into its own. Modern Anglo-French cooking is detailed in a short carte that might include cassoulet toulousaine, or fillet of beef with Madeira and foie gras sauce.

Additional: Sunday L; Children welcome; 🌢 dishes

Directions: Town centre, southern end of High Street, just N of the bridge

87 High Street TN8 5AU
Map 5: TQ44
Tel: 01732 866757
Cost: *Alc* £32.75, set-price L £15.50/D £19.95. ☺ H/wine £10.15
Times: 12.15-2pm/7.15-10pm. Closed L Sat, D Sun, all Mon, 1 wk Xmas, Good Friday

---

FAVERSHAM, **Read's**

Long-standing restaurant where service is solidly professional. David Pitchford has been in the business a long time (23 years, but who's counting), but has lost none of his enthusiasm and ability to train up young new chefs and launch them into the London firmament. Assured and confident, fresh flavours remain the keynote, underpinned by sound techniques. One of the most admirable aspects is the commitment to sourcing of raw materials, especially of local produce. A fillet of Whitstable turbot on parsley mashed potato with red wine sauce and home-made potted shrimps was an exquisite dish – the shrimps sweet and fresh, the fish exactly timed and the mash and sauce individual enough to contribute flavour to the end. A generous serving of omelette Arnold Bennett was superb, light and fluffy with undyed smoked haddock and a delicate Reggiano Parmesan cheese sauce. The end of the meal made equal impact with Kentish pear and frangipane tart with a quince jelly glaze, vanilla ice cream and separately served butterscotch sauce. The interior of the restaurant carries the air of a solid, provincial French restaurant, with plush curtains and sofas, discreet water colours and exceedingly well-spaced and spacious tables, a look that fits the cooking.

Mummery Court Painters Forstal
ME13 0EE
Map 5: TR06
Tel: 01795 535344
Fax: 01795 591200
Chef: David Pitchford
Owners: Rona & David Pitchford
Cost: *Alc* £37, set-price L £18.50/D £22. ☺ H/wine £14
Times: Noon-2pm/7-9.30pm. Closed Sun, Mon
Additional: Children welcome; 🌢 dishes
Seats: 40. Private dining room 20
Smoking: No pipes & cigars

Directions: M2/J6, turn L onto A2, then L into Brogdale Road, signposted Painters Forstal 1.5 miles S of Faversham

FOLKESTONE,
Sandgate Hotel, La Terrasse ❀❀❀

You can tell the high calibre of the operation by the seriousness of the wine list and the professionalism of the service. The restaurant at this seaside hotel rising above a pebbled beach is done out in yellow and blue. The silver and porcelain are French and oil paintings of the Loire Valley give more than a hint of Samuel Gicqueau's homeland. Predictably, fish is a strong suit, the kitchen overlaying a modern spin on the classical French repertoire to produce starters of pan-fried scallops on purée potatoes with black truffles, or langoustines with artichoke hearts in a punchy glazed sauce of Pineau des Charentes and peppermint. Escalope of warm duck foie gras with a pear and kumquat confit might be a meat option, with main courses of perhaps fillet of Aberdeen Angus layered with foie gras and served with wild mushrooms and red wine sauce, with lobster marinière, or pan-fried fillet of sea bass with celeriac mousseline and a Chardonnay and truffle oil vinegar among more mainstream items. A Valrhona chocolate dessert with an almond cream and roasted coffee ice cream 'delivered all flavours with knobs on'. Canapés are great and are followed at table by an *amuse-gueule*, perhaps frothy Jerusalem artichoke soup ('subtle and very creamy'), and breads are baked fresh each morning.
   Signature dishes: fillets of sole on a bed of tomatoes glazed with a white wine sauce and home-made pasta; turbot roasted on the bone with girolles; gratin of woodland strawberries.

The Esplanade CT20 3DY
Map 5: TR23
Tel: 01303 220444
Fax: 01303 220496
Chef: Samuel Gicqueau
Owners: Samuel & Zara Gicqueau
Cost: *Alc* £40, set-price L & D £20.50. ☺ H/wine £13.50
Times: 12.15-1.30pm/7.15-9.30pm. Closed D Sun, all Mon, 4 wks Jan, 1st wk Oct
Additional: Sunday L; Children welcome
Seats: 22
Smoking: No smoking in dining room
Accommodation: 15 en suite ★ ★

Directions: On A259 coastal road in Sandgate, between Hythe and Folkestone

Shortlisted for AA Wine Award – see page 16

HYTHE, # Hythe Imperial Hotel ❀

A magnificent seafront hotel. Typical starters from the Anglo/French menu include warm salad of wild mushrooms drizzled with tarragon oil, and smoked salmon with mixed leaves.

Smoking: No smoking in dining room
Accommodation: 100 en suite ★ ★ ★ ★

Directions: M20/J11/A261 to Hythe; follow signs to Folkestone, turn R into Twiss Rd opposite Bell Inn towards seafront

Princes Parade CT21 6AE
Map 5: TR13
Tel: 01303 267441
Fax: 01303 264610
Cost: *Alc* £30, set-price L £17/D £24. ☺ H/wine £12.50
Times: 12.30-2pm/7-9.30pm. Closed L Sat
Additional: Bar food L; Sunday L; Children welcome; ✿ dishes

HYTHE, # Stade Court Hotel ❀

Just a few steps away from the shingle strand and sparkling sea. The kitchen offers modern British fare along the lines of roasted whole partridge with a bacon, walnut and red wine sauce.

Smoking: No smoking in dining room
Accommodation: 42 en suite ★ ★ ★

Directions: M20 J11 then A261 to Hythe

West Parade CT21 6DT
Map 5: TR13
Tel: 01303 268263
Fax: 01303 261803
Cost: *Alc* £27, set-price D £19.50. ☺ H/wine £11.40
Times: D only, 6.30-9pm
Additional: Bar food; Sunday L (12.30-2pm); Children welcome; ✿ dishes

LENHAM, # Chilston Park ❀❀

Mildly eccentric hotel with candles, dark drapes, a vast array of knick-knacks and paintings on display and staff wearing period dress. The menu tries to match its baroque setting. A *carte* (supplemented menu), table d'hôte (market menu) and a

Sandway ME17 2BE
Map 5: TQ85
Tel: 01622 859803
Fax: 01622 858588
Chef: Stephan Santin
Owners: Arcadian

vegetarian menu are offered. A starter and main course of sardines rillettes with aïoli and gazpacho emulsion, and lamb and cep steamed pudding with honey-glazed parsnips and turnips paid too much attention to the appearance. However the simpler dishes are executed with skill. All the main courses come with vegetables. The desserts are good; coffee is served with home-made petits fours.

Directions: Telephone for directions

LENHAM, **The Lime Tree**

Atmospheric 14th-century beamed restaurant with ambition. Modish menu of smoked sea bass terrine, and calves' liver with blackcurrant reduction, dauphinoise potatoes and fresh vegetables shows imagination and effort.

Directions: Off the A20. 5 miles from M20

ROYAL TUNBRIDGE WELLS,
Hotel du Vin & Bistro ❀❀

Reminiscent of a French bistro with courteous French staff.
The Kent branch of Hotel du Vin (see entry, Winchester, Hampshire) runs to the same formula of imaginative menu (without being over ambitious) and a wine list that is chosen with knowledge and a sense of adventure, offering a good range of styles and flavours from around the world. Prices are

---

Chilston Park

Cost: Set-price L £17.50/D £29.95. H/wine £14.25
Times: Noon-2.15pm/7-9.30pm
Additional: Sunday L; Children welcome; ❹ dishes
Seats: 36. Private dining rooms 6-20
Smoking: No smoking in dining room
Accommodation: 53 en suite ★ ★ ★ ★

8-10 The Limes The Square ME17 2PL
Map 5: TQ85
Tel: 01622 859509
Fax: 01622 850096
Telephone for further details

Crescent Road TN1 2LY
Map 5: TQ53
Tel: 01892 526455
Fax: 01892 512044
Chef: Sam Mahoney
Cost: *Alc* £30, set-price D £27.50. H/wine £12
Times: Noon-1.30pm/7-9.30pm. Closed 2 days btween Xmas and New Year
Additional: Sunday L; Children welcome; ❹ dishes
Seats: 70. Private dining rooms 14-70
Smoking: No pipes & cigars
Accommodation: 32 en suite ★ ★ ★ ★

Directions: Telephone for directions

reasonably and choice from the Mediterranean-inspired carte runs from grilled smoked salmon with new potato artichoke salad, to goats' cheese, sage and hazelnut risotto with poached egg, and pan-fried halibut with marinated fennel and saffron orange broth, to loin of pork stuffed with prunes, parsley mash and mustard jus. Vanilla poached figs with mascarpone cream and red wine syrup catches the eye on the dessert list.

ROYAL TUNBRIDGE WELLS,

Royal Wells Inn

Mount Ephraim TN4 8BE
Map 5: TQ53
Tel: 01892 511188
Fax: 01892 511908
Chef: Robert Sloan
Owners: David & Robert Sloan
Cost: *Alc* £29, set-price L £10.50 (2 courses). H/wine £9.95
Times: 12.30-2.15pm/7.30-9.30pm. Closed Sun, Mon, 25-26 Dec, 1 Jan
Additional: Bar food; Sunday L (Wells Brasserie); Children welcome; dishes
Seats: 35. Private dining room 18
Accommodation: 18 en suite ★★★

Family-run hotel once popular with the young Queen Victoria. Enjoy stunning views across the common- the best view is from the first floor conservatory restaurant where an equally eye-catching menu of British and French dishes is offered. Typical dishes include pan-fried tenderloin of pork with balsamic figs and mash, confit of Scotch salmon with caramelised shallots, black olives and capers, and flash-fried calves' liver with bacon. Hints of the East are evident in the likes of tempura of tiger prawns with sweet chilli dipping sauce, and pan-fried skate and king scallops in sesame oil and Indonesian soy sauce. Sweets range from lemon pie to prune and Armagnac tart with English custard. The well-chosen wine list offers something to suit most tastes and pockets.

Directions: Situated 75 yards from the junction of the A21 and A264

ROYAL TUNBRIDGE WELLS,

Signor Franco

A stylish first-floor restaurant serving traditional Italian fare: insalata tricolore, pastas, main courses of chargrilled mixed fish (prawn, monkfish, cod and swordfish) with salsa verde, or baked rabbit with polenta, and pannacotta.

Additional: Children welcome; dishes
Smoking: Air conditioning

Directions: Near Tunbridge Wells train station

5a High Street TN1 1UL
Map 5: TQ53
Tel: 01892 549199
Fax: 01892 541378
Cost: *Alc* £28. ☺ H/wine £11.80
Times: Noon-2.45pm/6.45-10.45pm. Closed Sun

ROYAL TUNBRIDGE WELLS,

The Spa Hotel

The restaurant of this 18th-century house is named after some magnificent chandeliers that really set the tone. The extensive menu has a traditional feel with grills and whole fish filleted at the table.

Additional: Bar food; Sunday L; Children welcome; 🍃 dishes
Smoking: No-smoking area
Accommodation: 71 en suite ★★★

Directions: On A264 leaving Tunbridge Wells towards East Grinstead

Mount Ephraim TN4 8XJ
Map 5: TQ53
Tel: 01892 520331
Fax: 01892 510575
Cost: *Alc* £26, set-price L & D £19.
☺ H/wine £11.75
Times: 12.30-2pm/7-9.30pm. Closed L Sat

ROYAL TUNBRIDGE WELLS,

The Tagore

As we went to press we learned that The Tagore had moved from Welling to Tunbridge Wells. The team remains the same, especially in the kitchen, and the following is how we found our last meal in the old restaurant.
    Start with one of the kebabs – kabargha, say (tender grilled lamb with a hit of chilli), or king prawns in a cheese sauce with herbs and cashew nuts, and then try one of the simmered dishes – murgh Afghani lababdar (boneless chicken slowly cooked with peppers, tomatoes and onions), a lamb masala, or something from the earthen oven, like whole pomfret marinated in coriander and mint. Okra, unusually cooked crisp, and a spicy purée of potato and aubergine make fine accompaniments, and the kitchen shows the same care and attention with naan and basmati rice. Finish with kulfi or sorbets.

Directions: Telephone for directions

4 Neville Street TN2 5SA
Map 5: TQ53
Tel: 01892 549877
Fax: 0181 3045363
Chef: Rajendra Balmiki
Owner: Nur Monie
Telephone for further details

ROYAL TUNBRIDGE WELLS,

Thackeray's House Restaurant

The former home of William Makepeace Thackeray is a covetable tile-hung 17th-century property that stands out at the corner of a small, pretty green tucked below the London Road. The restaurant appears to have grown into the house rather than been converted: it is charmingly worn, comfortably appointed, with well-spaced tables and solicitous service. Bruce Wass's classically based cooking does not neglect modern trends – lime and chilli marinated monkfish, squid and tiger prawn tempura salad, for example – but one is left with the impression that he does not follow fashion for fashions sake. His repertoire marches with the seasons and there is a loyal following for the likes of a spot-on spring lunch that offered asparagus soup, artichoke and herb risotto, rump of lamb with garlic sauce and chickpea cake, and île flottante.

Directions: At corner of London Road/Mount Ephraim Road overlooking Common, 2 mins from hospital

85 London Road TN1 1EA
Map 5: TQ53
Tel/Fax: 01892 511921
Chef/Owner: Bruce Wass
Cost: Set-price D £23.50 (2 courses).
H/wine £12.85
Times: 12.30-2pm/7-10pm. Closed D Sun, all Mon, 5 days Xmas
Additional: Sunday L; Children welcome; 🍃 dishes
Seats: 50. Private dining room 20
Smoking: No-smoking area; No pipes & cigars

SEVENOAKS, **Royal Oak Hotel**

17th-century flint-fronted hotel with a breezy, modern brasserie-style restaurant. We were impressed by chicken and smoked duck terrine, seared red snapper on black ink linguini, and warm walnut tart with passion fruit sorbet.

Directions: M25/J5; at far end of High Street, opposite Sevenoaks school, walking distance from the town centre

Upper High Street TN13 1HY
Map 5: TQ55
Tel: 01732 451109
Fax: 01732 740187
Telephone for further details

SISSINGHURST, **Rankins**

Lovingly worn cottagey restaurant run simply but effectively. The Rankins – he in the kitchen, she out front – know what they are doing. A short, eclectic and seasonally inspired menu draws a loyal following. Raw ingredients are locally sourced and built around a style that is light and fresh offering, perhaps, braised lamb fillets with cumin-flavoured red wine sauce, apricots and fresh mint, or pan-fried pheasant breast and roast leg, with a light curry sauce and apples. A stunning roast red pepper terrine with artichoke and frisée salad and basil dressing is a popular starter, as is Rankin's smokie: a pot of smoked haddock baked in a creamy lemon sauce with a Cheddar topping. Desserts are good. Chocolate nemesis is a must try, but then so is coffee fudge pudding. The wine list is keenly priced, short with a good range of half-bottles.

The Street TN17 2JH
Map 5: TQ73
Tel: 01580 713964
Chef: Hugh Rankin
Owners: Hugh & Leonora Rankin
Cost: Set-price D £25.50. H/wine £8.50
Times: D only, 7.30-9pm. Closed D Sun, all Mon & Tue, Bhs
Additional: Sunday L (12.30-1.30pm)
Seats: 24
Smoking: No smoking in dining room

Directions: Village centre, on A262 (Ashford)

SITTINGBOURNE, **Hempstead House Country Hotel**

Strong country house feel – lots of family possesions – plus a homely, conservatory-style restaurant that's proving popular with locals. The kitchen shows ambition in dishes such as steamed brill with saffron vegetables and dill cream sauce.

Accommodation: 13 en suite

Directions: On A2, 1.5 miles east of Sittingbourne

London Road Bapchild ME99 9PP
Map 5: TQ96
Tel: 01795 428020
Fax: 01795 436362
Cost: Alc £29.50, set-price L £15.50/D £19.50. ☺ H/wine £13.50
Times: Noon-2pm/7-9.45pm
Additional: Bar food; Sunday L; Children welcome; ✦ dishes
Smoking: No smoking in dining room

WESTERHAM, **Kings Arms Hotel**

Market Square TN16 1AN
Map 5: TQ45
Tel: 01959 562990
Fax: 01959 561240
Telephone for further details

Directions: On A25, in the centre of Westerham

Attractive Georgian hotel in the centre of the town. The Conservatory Restaurant offers an imaginative menu and enjoys a loyal local following.

WHITSTABLE,
Whitstable Oyster Fisher Co, Hotel Continental

A converted boathouse and oyster store looking onto the North Sea, complete with old worn floors and rough white walls; it's a quirky place well known for its fantastic fresh fish. Keep it simple with half-a-dozen plump oysters, then a great take on an English classic – roast codling with chunky home-made chips. Alternatively, the Hotel Continental, at 29 Beach Walk, tel 01227 280280, from the same stable, is a stylishly converted 1930s seafront hotel with a great-value menu of moules marinière, steak and frites, chargrilled chicken, and hake with parsley sauce.

Directions: On High Street, follow one-way then 1st L

Horsebridge Beach CT5 1BU
Map 5: TR16
Tel: 01227 276856
Fax: 01227 770666
Cost: *Alc* £20
Times: Noon-2pm/7-9.30pm. Closed D Sun & all Mon in winter
Additional: Sunday L; Children welcome; dishes
Accommodation: 32 en suite

WYE, ## Wife of Bath

Lovely house, a former doctor's residence, in a pretty village. Cooking is good and represents excellent value for money, especially at lunch. Enjoy the likes of French onion and thyme tart or roast rack of lamb.

4 Upper Bridge Street TN25 5AW
Map 5: TR04
Tel: 01233 812540
Fax: 01233 813630
Cost: *Alc* £22, set-price L £10 (2 courses)/D £23.75. ☺ H/wine £12.50
Times: Noon-2pm/7-10pm. Closed Sun, Mon, 1 wk from 25 Dec
Additional: Children welcome; dishes
Smoking: No-smoking area; No pipes or cigars
Accommodation: 6 rooms, 5 en suite

Directions: Just off A28 Ashford to Canterbury Road

LANCASHIRE

ACCRINGTON,
Dunkenhalgh Hotel

NEW

Seven hundred-year-old manor house with period decor. An interesting menu takes in risotto of cod, and roast breast and leg of guinea fowl with herb farce and Madeira jus.

Smoking: No smoking in dining room: Air conditioning
Accommodation: 121 en suite ★★★★

Directions: Adjacent to M65/J7

Blackburn Road Clayton-le-Moors BB5 5JP
Map 7: SD72
Tel: 01254 398021
Fax: 01254 872230
Cost: Set-price D £25. H/wine £10.75
Times: 12.30-2pm/7-9.50pm
Additional: Bar food; Sunday L; Children 12+; dishes

BLACKBURN,
Clarion Hotel & Suites Foxfields

Whalley Road Billington BB7 9HY
Map 7: SD62
Tel: 01254 822556
Fax: 01254 824613
Cost: *Alc* £23, set-price L £7.50 (2 courses)/D £18.95. ☺ H/wine £11.95
Times: Noon-2pm/7-9.30pm. Closed L Sat
Additional: Bar food L; Sunday L; Children 1+; ♨ menu
Smoking: No smoking in dining room; Air conditioning
Accommodation: 44 en suite ★ ★ ★ ★

Modern hotel in a rural location. The carte might offer trio of smoked salmon, halibut and trout, roasted rack of Bowland lamb, and chocolate and pecan soufflé.

Directions: From A59 follow sign for Whalley, hotel is 0.5 mile on R

BLACKBURN, **Millstone Hotel**

Church Lane Mellor BB2 7JR
Map 7: SD62
Tel: 01254 813333
Fax: 01254 812628
Telephone for further details

Stone-built coaching inn offering an inviting range of dishes in the bar (popular locally) or the rich, wood-panelled restaurant. Scallops were fresh, calves' liver and bacon got the thumbs up, and chocolate and Grand Marnier mousse was sound.

Directions: M6 J31, follow A677 (Blackburn) for 2 miles. Turn L (Mellor), follow road to top of hill, hotel is on R

BLACKPOOL, **De Vere Hotel** **NEW**

Business is brisk and guests advised to book at the smart new restaurant – run under TV chef Andrew Nutter's consultative eye. Salmon fish cakes with lemon butter sauce, tournedos of beef with smoked bacon and pork show the style.

East Park Drive FY3 8LL
Map 7: SD33
Tel: 01253 838866
Fax: 01253 798800
Telephone for further details

Directions: M6 J32/M55 J4, A583. At 4th traffic lights turn R & follow signs for Zoo. Hotel on R

CHIPPING, **Gibbon Bridge Hotel**

Fine views of Longridge Fells. An inspection meal started with a feta cheese tartlet with excellent pastry and crunchy pesto, went on to tender fillet of beef on sweet potatoes with mustard jus and ended with iced Amaretto parfait.

Smoking: No smoking in dining room; Air conditioning
Accommodation: 29 en suite ★★★★

Directions: In village turn R at T junction for Clitheroe, hotel at 0.75 mile

Forest of Bowland Preston PR3 2TQ
Map 7: SD64
Tel: 01995 61456
Fax: 01995 61277
Cost: *Alc* £25, set-price L £13/D £20.
☺ H/wine £11.25
Times: 12.30-1.30pm/7-9pm
Additional: Bar food; Sunday L;
Children welcome; ✿ dishes

LANGHO,
Northcote Manor ✿✿✿

Northcote Road Nr Blackburn
BB6 8BE
Map 7: SD73
Tel: 01254 240555
Fax: 01254 246568
Chef: Nigel Haworth
Owners: Nigel Haworth,
Craig Bancroft
Cost: *Alc* £40, set-price L £16/D £37
(5 courses). H/wine £12.90
Times: Noon-1.30pm (2pm Sun)/7-
9.30pm (9pm Sun). Closed L Sat, 25
Dec, 1 Jan
Additional: Sunday L; Children
welcome; ✿ dishes
Seats: 60. Private dining room 30;
Jacket & tie preferred
Smoking: No smoking in dining room
Accommodation: 14 en suite ★★★

Small country-house hotel on the edge of the Ribble Valley.
Refurbishment has brought cool lemon walls to the restaurant, a light and airy room overlooking the gardens, and paintings dot the walls. Many of the salad leaves and vegetables are organically grown in the grounds, and Nigel Haworth believes firmly in his roots, so Morecambe Bay shrimps, corn-fed Goosnargh duckling with an open ravioli of mulled pears and onion jam, and Eccles cake might all make an appearance, with Lancashire cheese ice cream accompanying apple crumble soufflé. But the appeal is much broader than this, with starters of game terrine with beetroot 'carpaccio', pan-roast foie gras with black pea and bacon purée, and a 'classy dish' of chicken and tarragon ravioli on ribboned vegetables. Excellent saucing shows up in a red wine jus with lambs' liver, roast shallots and thyme mash, and in a foie gras jus with seasonal roast wild partridge with a gratin of vegetables and hash browns, while fish – codling, perhaps – may be plainly roasted and served with lemon and parsley butter. Rhubarb and frangipane turnover with custard makes a patriotic pudding, and there might also be prune and walnut tartlet with buttermilk ice cream. Four house wines kick off a catholic list that runs to 15 pages.

Directions: From M6 J31 take A59, follow signs for Clitheroe. At first traffic lights L onto Skipton/Clitheroe Rd for 9 miles. L into Northcote Rd. Hotel on R

Shortlisted for
AA Wine Award-see page 16

LONGRIDGE,
Paul Heathcotes Restaurant

104-106 Higher Road PR3 3SY
Map 7: SD63
Tel: 01772 784969
Fax: 01772 785713
Chefs: Paul Heathcote, Steven Forgie
Owner: Paul Heathcote
Cost: *Alc* £45, set-price L £22.50 (4 courses)/D £55 (10 courses). H/wine £13.50
Times: Noon-2pm (Fri & Sun only)/7-9.30pm. Closed Mon
Additional: Sunday L; Children 5+; dishes
Seats: 60. Private dining room 18
Smoking: No smoking in dining room

Directions: Follow signs for Golf Club & Jeffrey Hill. Higher Road is beside White Bull Pub in Longridge

Paul Heathcote has long championed sourcing from local producers, as his book **Rhubarb and Black Pudding** *celebrates.* His cooking is rooted in regional ingredients and traditions, crisp fillet of cod with warm potted shrimps or roast rack of lamb with hot-pot potatoes and stockpot vegetables, for example, but elevated by sophisticated technique. As Heathcote's celebrity has increased (note the signed menus on sale at £5 each), so have his range of other interests, from satellite restaurants to outside catering – arguably, the result is he has spread himself too thinly and fails to reach the heights he once so easily occupied. Nonetheless, it's still worth the treck to the cottagey blue and yellow restaurant, if only for a big-spend special occasion. The best dish sampled, on our visit was a herb and broad bean risotto. However, beetroot borscht terrine was stunning in colour, and slow-roasted pork shoulder was meltingly tender with a slice of crispy skin on top and powerfully sauced. Certain 'signatures' such as bread-and-butter pudding are permanent fixtures; other desserts might include pistachio soufflé with chocolate sorbet or tarte Tatin of pineapple.

LYTHAM ST ANNE'S,
Qbrasserie

You could almost be on the Fulham Road at this stylish modern brasserie where quality prevails, from walnut bread, through olives, to sticky chocolate pudding with Chantilly cream. In between comes grilled goats' cheese with caramelised onions, Chinese-style plum sauce and ciabatta, and roast duck breast with orange and ginger sauce.

Directions: Town Centre

5 Henry Street FY8 5LE
Map 7: SD32
Tel: 01253 733124
Cost: *Alc* £20.17, set-price L £6.50 (2 courses)/D £15.50. ☺ H/wine £8.95
Times: Noon-2.30pm/6-11pm. Closed Sun, 25, 26 Dec, 1 Jan
Additional: Children welcome; dishes

PRESTON,
Heathcote's Brasserie

Minimalist chic for this cutting edge brasserie. Although Heathcote signature ingredients – Goosnargh duck, black pudding and so on – still feature on the menu, dishes are evolving as the kitchen starts to chart its own course. Two

23 Winckley Square PR1 3JJ
Map 7: SD52
Tel: 01772 252732
Fax: 01772 203433
Chef: Jamie Holland
Owner: Paul Heathcote

Heathcote's Brasserie

Cost: *Alc* £21, set-price L&D £12.50.
☺ H/wine £11.50
Times: Noon-2.30pm/7-10.30pm
(open 5pm Sat). Closed Bhs
Additional: Bar food; Sunday L;
Children welcome; ✦ dishes
Seats: 90. Private dining room 85
Smoking: No pipes & cigars; Air
conditioning

Directions: Town centre

which stood out in terms of depth of flavour, balance and technical skill were baked fillet of cod on Swiss chard with balsamic dressing, and chargrilled pork loin on black pudding mash with caramelised apples. Amongst the starters, a confit duck terrine was given a lift by the inclusion of some carrot and horseradish; smoked haddock fishcakes were nicely crisped and the proportion of potato to fish just right. Depending on the season, there may be iced cherry parfait (the marinated fruit packing an alcoholic punch) or pear and damson crumble with honey ice cream. Downstairs on the Square offers spit-roasted chicken, Lancashire hotpot with pickled red cabbage, and an excellent choice of sandwiches.

SAWLEY,

Spread Eagle Inn ❀❀ NEW

Spacious restaurant and bar in a 16th-century inn done with a deft, modern touch. It brings a touch of the metropolitan brasserie to the hillside. Real ales are on tap, a blackboard lists wines by the glass (with the full list on the reverse of the menu), and friendly, helpful staff cope well with the bustle. In the split-level restaurant, it's worth asking for a window table for the view over the Ribble and its birdlife. Good, honest cooking of brasserie favourites with some surprises is the magnet: chicken liver parfait, or filo tart of caramelised red onions, sun-dried tomatoes, Lancashire cheese and pesto to start, then grilled fillet of lamb on ratatouille with rosemary jus, or sliced grilled duck breast with Chinese-style five-spice sauce served with noodles and oyster mushrooms. Fish ranges from seared tuna fillet topped with zingy sesame seeds in a soy and ginger dressing with spring onions to a main course of good and fresh fillet of cod under a rich herb and cheese crust with herb butter on mashed potatoes. What better way to finish than with floating islands, tarte Tatin, or lemon crème brûlée?

BB7 4NH
Map 7: SD74
Tel: 01200 441202
Fax: 01200 441973
Chefs: Steven Doherty, Greig Barnes
Owners: Steven Doherty,
Lionel Yates, Alan Bell
Cost: *Alc* £16, set-price L (Mon-Fri)
£9.50. ☺ H/wine £9.25
Times: Noon-2pm/6-9pm. Closed 2
wks Nov
Additional: Sunday L; Children
welcome; ✦ dishes
Seats: 80. Private dining room 80
Smoking: No smoking in dining room
Accommodation: 8 en suite

Directions: Telephone for directions

SLAIDBURN, **Parrock Head** ❀

Farmhouse-style restaurant – located in a former milking parlour – where local produce influences the menu (plus herbs from the garden). Nothing pretentious, just good home cooking along the lines of tangy onion and Stilton tart, and delicately cooked salmon.

Nr Clitheroe BB7 3AH
Map 7: SD75
Tel: 01200 446614
Fax: 01200 446313
Telephone for further details

Directions: Take B6478 to Slaidburn; L by village pub up Woodehouse Lane, hotel drive 1 mile on L

UPHOLLAND, **Holland Hall Hotel**

6 Lafford Lane Skelmersdale
WN8 0QZ
Map 7: SD50
Tel: 01695 624426
Fax: 01695 622433
Chef: Tony Chaya
Owners: Tom & Lorraine Rathbone
Cost: *Alc* £26.50, set-price L £12.50.
☺ H/wine £11.95
Times: Noon-1.45pm (Sun & Wed
only)/6-9.45pm. Closed L Mon, Tue,
Thu-Sat, D Sun, Bhs
Additional: Bar food; Sunday L;
Children welcome; ✿ dishes
Seats: 55. Private dining room 24
Smoking: No-smoking area; Air
conditioning
Accommodation: 34 en suite ★ ★ ★

Country house hotel with slick service. The deeply
comfortable, dark-coloured Churchill's Restaurant is very
popular. The kitchen produces a modern menu with a lot of
nods to regional cooking and Lancashire specialities. Thus ham
hock terrine comes with piccalilli and mustard dressing, and
sirloin steak is served on a bed of horseradish mash, stuffed
tomato, black pudding and poached egg. Even classic fish and
chips gets the treatment with a light batter, home-made fries
and mushy peas, but the team is just as comfortable with the
likes of honey-glazed confit of duck leg, salad leaves and
balsamic dressing, or a chargrilled chicken breast served with
Mediterranean vegetables and pesto dressing.

Directions: 2 minutes drive from M6 J26. Take A577
(Upholland), turn R into Lafford Lane

WRIGHTINGTON, **High Moor Inn** ☺

High Moor Lane WN6 9QA
Map 7: SD51
Tel: 01257 252364
Fax: 01257 255120
Cost: *Alc* £21.95, set-price L & D
£13. ☺ H/wine £9.95
Times: Noon-2pm/5.30-10pm
Additional: Bar Food L; Sunday L;
Children welcome; ✿ dishes

Directions: M6 J27, follow sign to
Parbold, after hospital turn R into
Robin Hood Lane, 1st L into High
Moor Lane

*Moorland inn with a cosy beamed restaurant. A selection from the
extensive menu could include chicken livers in puff pastry, salmon
fillet with a herb crust, and iced satsuma mousse.*

WRIGHTINGTON,
Wrightington Hotel ✿✿

*A modern hotel set in open countryside with easy access to
the M6.* Modern describes the style in the Snape & Nugent

Moss Lane Standish WN6 9PB
Map 7: SD51
Tel: 01257 425803
Fax: 01257 425830

Restaurant (where the eponymous chefs whip up dishes with a certain amount of flair). Typical starters include carrot and Gruyère cheese gâteau, pressed terrine of duck and vegetables wrapped in cured ham, and pan-fried black pudding with a Pommery mustard sauce. However, we chose a light and delicately flavoured smoked salmon mousse served with buttered courgettes and topped with a beautifully seared scallop. Pot-roasted shoulder of lamb followed, carved onto a delicious mustard seed mash surrounded by a rich dark red wine sauce. Desserts range from steamed vanilla and pistachio nut pudding to blueberry and maple syrup pancakes, but we plumped for a freshly-baked rhubarb pie with creamy Anglaise sauce and didn't regret it.

Directions: From M6 J27, drive 0.25 mile towards Parbold. 200yds past church, fork R. Hotel is 100yds on R

Chefs: Ian Snape, Jeff Nugent
Owner: Barry Aspinall
Cost: *Alc* £18.50, set-price D £18.50.
☺ H/wine £8.95
Times: D only, 7-9.30pm. Closed Sun, 1 Jan
Additional: Children welcome; ✤ dishes
Seats: 80
Smoking: No pipes & cigars
Accommodation: 47 en suite ★ ★ ★

LEICESTERSHIRE

CASTLE DONINGTON,
The Priest House on the River

A long lane through thick woods leads to this former working mill on the River Trent. Expect imaginative British cooking along the lines of marinated marlin steak in oyster sauce, and supreme of chicken with wild mushroom and garlic sauce.

Kings Mills DE74 2RR
Map 8: SK42
Tel: 01332 810649
Fax: 01332 811141
Cost: *Alc* £30, set-price L £15.50/D £24.50. ☺ H/wine £11.95
Times: 12.30-2pm/7-9.30pm. Closed L Sat
Additional: Bar food; Sunday L; Children welcome; ✤ dishes
Smoking: No smoking in dining room
Accommodation: 45 en suite ★ ★ ★

Directions: In Castle Donington turn L at 1st traffic lights and follow to river

EAST MIDLANDS AIRPORT,
Thistle East Midlands Airport

Large modern hotel in a remarkably peaceful setting with a good local reputation: baked fillets of haddock, and roast ribeye of beef with Yorkshire pudding are typical of the carte. For dessert there's Swiss chocolate soufflé.

Smoking: No smoking in dining room
Accommodation: 110 en suite ★ ★ ★ ★

Directions: At East Midlands International Airport, 1 mile from M1 J23A/24 and A42(M) Birmingham link road

Derby DE74 2SH
Map 8: SK42
Tel: 01332 850700
Fax: 01332 850823
Cost: *Alc* £25, set-price L £15/D £21. ☺ H/wine £11.45
Times: 12.30-2pm/7-10pm. Closed L Sat
Additional: Sunday L; Children welcome; ✤ dishes

HINCKLEY,
Sketchley Grange Hotel

Sketchley Lane Burbage LE10 3HU
Map 4: SP49
Tel: 01455 251133
Fax: 01455 631384
Chef: John Bacon
Owner: Nigel I Downes
Cost: Alc £25, set-price L £13.95/ D
£19.95 (5 courses). H/wine £10.95
Times: Noon-1.45pm/7-9.45pm.
Closed L Sat, D Sun, Bhs
Additional: Bar food; Sunday L;
Children welcome; ⬤ dishes
Seats: 100. Private dining room 250
Smoking: No smoking in dining room;
Air conditioning
Accommodation: 55 en suite ★ ★ ★

Directions: From M69 J1 take B4109,
at mini roundabout turn L, then 1st R

Extended country house in its own quiet landscaped gardens,
yet just minutes from the M69. Visitors can eat in the lively
Terrace Bistro or the more formal Willow Restaurant. In the
latter, the style is set by a starter of duck confit with red
onion jam and truffle dressing, main courses of braised shin
of veal on saffron risotto with gremolata, or fillet of turbot
glazed with mustard and pan-fried with button onions in red
wine. At inspection, shellfish consommé with scallops and a
hint of smoked bacon was judged a successful dish, as was
tender, pink quail stuffed with chicken mousseline on an
exemplary red wine jus. Creamy crème brûlée
counterbalanced by the tartness of raspberries provided the
finale to the meal. Service, from a smartly presented brigade
of staff, is attentive.

LEICESTER, **Belmont House**

De Montfort Street LE1 7GR
Map 4: SK50
Tel: 0116 2544773
Fax: 0116 2470804
Cost: Set-price D £18.50. ☺ H/wine
£10
Times: 12.30-2pm/7-10pm. Closed L
Sat, D Sun, Bhs
Additional: Sunday L; ⬤ dishes
Smoking: No-smoking area
Accommodation: 75 en suite ★ ★ ★

Directions: From railway station, first
R off A6 southbound

At the time of writing, the restaurant was due to undergo a
makeover, but the well-located hotel, near the station and town
centre, continues to be popular with both midweek business and
weekend leisure guests.

LEICESTER, **The Tiffin**

Popular up-market tandoori serving traditional north Indian cuisine.
Sizzling lamb boti kebabs with yogurt and mint dressing, and

1 De Montfort Street LE1 7GE
Map 4: SK50
Tel: 0116 2470420/2553737
Fax: 0116 2625125

The Tiffin

Cost: *Alc* £18, set-price D £18.
H/wine £14
Times: Noon-1.45pm/6-10.45pm.
Closed L Sat, all Sun, Xmas
Additional: Children welcome;
❹ dishes
Smoking: No-smoking area; Air
conditioning

Directions: Near railway station on
the corner of De Montfort Street and
London Road (A6)

*creamy chicken korma with mushroom and cauliflower bhaji have
been endorsed.*

LEICESTER, **Time Out Hotel**

*Small hotel on the outskirts of the city with a smart colonial-style
restaurant. Med-influenced dishes include braised rump of lamb
with olive mash and parsnip crisps, and darne of halibut with a
ragout of prawn and leek.*

Smoking: No pipes & cigars; Air conditioning
Accommodation: 48 en suite ★ ★ ★

Directions: Off A426, 3 miles S of Leicester

Enderby Road Blaby LE8 4GD
Map 4: SK50
Tel: 0116 2787898
Fax: 0116 2781974
Cost: *Alc* £24.50, set-price L £11.95
(2 courses)/D £18.95. ☺
Times: Noon-2pm/7-9.45pm. Closed
L Sat
Additional: Bar food; Sunday L;
Children welcome; ❹ dishes

MARKET HARBOROUGH,
Three Swans Hotel

*Variations on a traditional theme include chicken Cordova-chicken
with spinach, shallots, tarragon and white wine cream sauce, and
Cod Sargasso – fillet of cod baked with a saffron broth with roasted
tomatoes and mustard mash.*

Smoking: No-smoking area; No pipes & cigars; Air conditioning
Accommodation: 49 en suite ★ ★ ★

Directions: Follow High Street S through town centre; hotel is
on R at traffic lights

21 High Street LE16 7NJ
Map 4: SP78
Tel: 01858 466644
Fax: 01858 434633
Cost: *Alc* £30, set-price L £13.95/D
£21.95 (4 courses). ☺ H/wine £10.95
Times: Noon-2.15pm/7-10pm. Closed
D Sun
Additional: Bar food; Sunday L;
Children welcome; ❹ dishes

MELTON MOWBRAY,
Stapleford Park

**Quite a stately home surrounded by woods, parkland, lake,
stables, church and garden.** The hotel surroundings may be
opulent but the atmosphere is relaxed with high-quality service
that's there for the asking. Rooms are sumptuous: all polished
mahogany panelling, rich damask, squashy sofas. Grinling
Gibbons carvings feature in the dining room, a splendid
backdrop to the short, daily changing menu which always
contains one 'adult nursery dish', steak and chips, say. Roasted
tomato and Mozzarella tart was well made, tenderloin of pork
caramelised (good flavour and well-timed), served with a
mushroom risotto was so far so good, but the addition of

Stapleford LE14 2EF
Map 8: SK71
Tel: 01572 787522
Fax: 01572 787651
Chef: Geoff Balharrie
Cost: *Alc* £25, set-price D £39.50.
H/wine £18
Times: Noon-2.30pm/7.30-9.45pm
Additional: Bar food ; Sunday L;
Children 12+; ❹ dishes
Seats: 50. Private dining rooms 12-26
Smoking: No smoking in dining room
Accommodation: 51 en suite ★ ★ ★ ★

Yorkshire pudding, a black pudding and a rich sauce flavoured with Calvados and cream nearly finished our inspector off. Clafoutis was not like anything she had ever had (or made) before: it looked like lemon tart set in a good pastry case with a creamy filling under a layer of rhubarb with very good stem ginger ice cream (she enjoyed it – 'but it was not clafoutis'). Breads and petits fours are good too.

Directions: Follow Melton ring road A607 (Grantham) onto B676, 4 miles turn R signed Stapleford

QUORN,

Quorn Country Hotel

Charnwood House Leicester Road
LE12 8BB
Map 8: SK51
Tel: 01509 415050
Fax: 01509 415557
Chef: David Wilkinson
Owner: Liam Walshe
Cost: *Alc* £27, set-price L £ 17 (2 courses)/D £21. ☺ H/wine £10.75
Times: Noon-2.30pm/7-9.30pm. Closed L Sat
Seats: 60. Private dining room 80
Accommodation: 23 en suite ★★★★

Ditherers beware: there are two dining venues to choose from, the alcoved Shires, with a beamed ceiling and intimate atmosphere, and the light, bright Orangery, with its fountain and hand-painted mural. Menus tend towards the traditional, with some modern touches overlaid. We started our meal with goose liver pâté and went on to pink and tender breast of mallard, a dense and rich game sausage alongside with a sauce of its cooking juices laced with Grand Marnier – a bit of a culinary cliché but in this case it worked well. Alternatively, there might be fillet of red mullet on a tomato and basil tart, and braised lamb shank with a bacon and mustard sauce. Plum compote with rice-pudding ice cream ('excellent, lovely flavour') makes a grand finale. Work off any unwanted calories with a walk through the grounds to the River Soar.

Directions: Off A6 in village centre

LINCOLNSHIRE

BELTON, **Belton Woods Hotel**

A good choice of dishes is offered in the Manor Restaurant. The style tends towards the traditional, although cosmopolitan influences are evident. Service is attentive and friendly.

Smoking: No smoking in dining room
Accommodation: 136 en suite ★★★★

Directions: 2 miles on A1 to Grantham, then A607 to Belton

Grantham NG32 2LN
Map 8: SK93
Tel: 01476 593200
Fax: 01476 574547
Cost: *Alc* £35, set-price D £24.95. ☺ H/wine £14.50
Times: D only, 7-9.30pm. Closed Sun
Additional: Children 4+; ☻ dishes

BOURNE, **Black Horse Inn**

Grimsthorpe PE10 0LY
Map 8: TF02
Tel: 01778 591247
Fax: 01778 591373
Chef: Brian Rey
Owner: Elaine Rey
Cost: *Alc* £23, set-price L £12.50. ☺
H/wine £9.80
Times: Noon-2pm/7-9.30pm
Additional: Bar food; Sunday L;
Children 14+; ⌀ dishes
Seats: 48. Private dining room 12
Smoking: No smoking in dining room
Accommodation: 6 en suite ★ ★

Directions: Follow A151 for 4 miles,
west towards Grantham

It may look like a small country pub, but both the bar food and the restaurant have big ambitions. The former is pub-grub-meets-brasserie with Lincoln red sausage and horseradish mash, seafood Mornay, meat and potato pie, and sea bass with mushroom risotto. The restaurant aims even higher with a wide choice: roasted corn-fed chicken supreme, spinach and bacon couscous, sauce foie gras; medallions of monkfish with squid ink and saffron noodles with saffron-infused mussel emulsion. Rare breed organic meats are much favoured. We looked forward to the prospect of herb crusted confit (roasted loin, really) of Gloucester Old Spot with Mediterranean vegetables and aged balsamic sauce, and only the crackling let down what was an otherwise cracking dish. 'A Chocolate Present', twinned chocolate and coffee mousse in a sculpted teardrop of chocolate, suggested a kitchen that, in some respects at least, needs to walk before it runs so fast.

CLEETHORPES, **Kingsway Hotel**

Traditional, family-run, seafront hotel. Alongside the classic deep-fried scampi tartare and roast beef with Yorkshire pud, there are now more adventurous dishes such as Lapsang Souchong smoked poached chicken supreme with spring onion, coriander, sesame and rice wine soup.

Additional: Bar food L; Sunday L; Children 5+; ⌀ dishes
Accommodation: 50 en suite ★ ★ ★

Directions: At junction of A1098 and sea front

Kingsway DN35 0AE
Map 8: TA30
Tel: 01472 601122
Fax: 01472 601381
Cost: *Alc* £26.50, set-price L £12.50
(2 courses)/D £17.95. ☺ H/wine
£10.75
Times: 12.30-1.45pm/7-9pm Closed
25-26 Dec

GRANTHAM, **Harry's Place**

Everything's on a small scale at this Georgian-fronted listed building in the high street. The warm, dark-pink-walled dining room, with its antiques and collection of china, seats just ten, and the menu runs to no more than two choices at each course, with a wine list of some dozen bottles. Harry Hallam chooses raw materials that are second to none – meats are organic, all fish is wild, grouse arrive in feather from Yorkshire, as do teal from the Wash – translating into clear, identifiable flavours on the plate. Herbs are used judiciously, as in a shiny sauce of red wine, Madeira, sage and tarragon, all components clearly identifiable, to match fillet of Cornish beef with wild and dried

17 High Street Great Gonerby
NG31 8JS
Map 8: SK93
Tel: 01476 561780
Chef: Harry Hallam
Owners: Harry & Caroline Hallam
Cost: *Alc* £46. H/wine £20
Times: 12.30-2pm/7-9.30pm. Closed
Sun & Mon, 25-26 Dec, Bhs
Additional: Children 5+
Seats: 10
Smoking: No smoking in dining room

mushrooms. Another main course, of perfectly cooked scallops from Orkney, has come with a 'delightful, creamy, light yet rich' chive hollandaise, the taste of the herbs shining through; together with fettucine tossed in olive oil with Parmesan, wilted baby spinach and a light chutney, 'all aspects of this dish were perfect'. The same respect and understanding of ingredients is apparent in starters: sautéed chicken livers are set in a sherry and black pepper jelly, full of rich tastes, accompanied by Cumberland sauce, the earthy flavours of watercress dressed in truffle oil adding another dimension. Puddings could run to crisp-topped caramel mousse brûlée, raspberries at their peak breaking up the sweetness of the caramel, or hot gooseberry soufflé.

Signature dishes: wild Scottish salmon with champagne beurre blanc, basil and fennel; filleted loin of roe deer with a sauce of white wine, Madeira, shallots and tarragon; young rhubarb soufflé.

Directions: On B1174 2 miles NW of Grantham

HORNCASTLE,

Magpies Restaurant

A cottage-style restaurant with a relaxed and family-friendly feel. Canapés are served in the lounge bar where a lovely open fire roars away during winter months, much appreciated when we inspected one day in late November. That welcome hearty meal opened with a really enjoyable rich fish soup, built around fillets of red mullet, and was followed by pan-fried breast of duck, cooked pink with crisp skin, and sliced over a bed of apple, Savoy cabbage and strips of bacon, accompanied by a Calvados sauce. The extensive wine list includes bottles from around the world.

Directions: 0.5 mile from Horncastle on A158 towards Skegness

71-75 East Street LN9 6AA
Map 8: TF26
Tel: 01507 527004
Fax: 01507 524064
Chefs: Matthew Lee, Simon Lee
Owners: The Lee Family
Cost: *Alc* £25, set-price D £25.
H/wine £10
Times: D only, 7.15-9.45pm. Closed D Sun & Mon, 2 wks Aug
Additional: Sunday L (12.30-2.30pm); Children welcome
Seats: 40. Private dining room 10
Smoking: No smoking in dining room

LINCOLN, **Castle Hotel**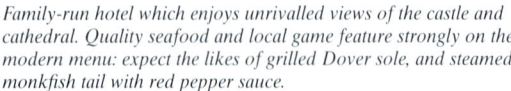

Family-run hotel which enjoys unrivalled views of the castle and cathedral. Quality seafood and local game feature strongly on the modern menu: expect the likes of grilled Dover sole, and steamed monkfish tail with red pepper sauce.

Smoking: No smoking in dining rom
Accommodation: 20 en suite ★ ★

Directions: Hotel is opposite Lincoln Castle, at E end of Westgate

Westgate LN1 3AS
Map 8: SK97
Tel: 01522 538801
Fax: 01522 575457
Cost: *Alc* £17. ☺ H/wine £8.95
Times: D only, 7-9.30pm. Closed D 25 Dec
Additional: Bar food; Children 10+; ❸ dishes

LINCOLN, **The Jew's House**

Built in the 12th century at the bottom of Steep Hill, the idiom here is Anglo-French: moules marinière, grilled goats' cheese with aubergine and pesto, chicken risotto with a rich tomato and red pepper sauce, or duck breast with beetroot, then lemon tart or Grand Marnier soufflé.

Smoking: No smoking in dining room

Directions: Telephone for directions

15 The Strait LN2 1JD
Map 8: SK97
Tel: 01522 524851
Fax: 01522 520084
Cost: *Alc* £25, set-price L £7.50/D £25 (5 courses). ☺ H/wine £10
Times: Noon-1.30pm/6.45-9pm. Closed Sun, Mon
Additional: Children welcome; ❸ dishes

LINCOLN, **Washingborough Hall Hotel** ❀❀

Church Hill, Washingborough
LN4 1BE
Map 8: SK97
Tel: 01522 790340
Fax: 01522 792936
Chef: Derek Bell
Owners: David Hill &
Margaret Broddle
Cost: Alc £27, set-price L £11.25/D
£19.75. ☺ H/wine £9.95
Times: 12.30-2.30pm/7-9.30pm.
Closed L Sat, 26-30 Dec
Additional: Sunday L; Children 15+;
❹ dishes
Seats: 40. Private dining room 40
Smoking: No smoking in dining room
Accommodation: 14 en suite ★★★

A listed Georgian manor in its own grounds. The Wedgwood
Dining Room, with a fine fireplace and views out of bay
windows over the gardens, is a high-ceilinged room decorated
in greens in the formal style of its namesake. Fillet of beef on
rösti with a rich mushroom sauce, or pink and tender pot-roast
shank of lamb with redcurrant sauce atop herbed mash and
chargrilled root vegetables, are the sorts of main courses the
kitchen delivers. Salmon fillet topped with white fish
mousseline then wrapped in filo and baked and served with a
light butter sauce shows the attention to detail that goes into
fish options. These could be preceded by tiger prawns pan-fried
with coriander, or a good, meaty game terrine with a
contrasting jam of cranberries and juniper berries. Tangy
lemon tart, or rich, light-textured vanilla cheesecake with a tart
topping of seasonal berries deliver the goods. A lengthy wine
list has two pages of 'Owners' Selection' of mainly New World
wines, although France tops the list.

Directions: From B1188 onto B1190 Church Hill, after 2 miles
turn R opposite Methodist church

LINCOLN, **Wig & Mitre** ❀

*The restaurant has moved in to larger premises next door but the
format remains the same, a twice daily menu of modern British
cooking supplemented by a seasonal selection.*

Directions: Close to cathedral, castle and car park at top of
Steep Hill

30 Steep Hill LN2 1TL
Map 8: SK97
Tel: 01522 535190
Fax: 01522 532402
Cost: Alc £20. ☺ H/wine £10.25
Times: 8am-11pm
Additional: Bar Food; Sunday L;
Children welcome; ❹ dishes

LOUTH, **Beaumont Hotel** ❀

*Late Victorian building with a warm, cosy atmosphere. Fresh
seafood salad, could be followed by gammon steak Hawaiian,
topped with tomato and cheese, or poached salmon steak with a
watercress and avocado sauce.*

Smoking: No-smoking area; No pipes & cigars
Accommodation: 17 en suite ★★★

Directions: Telephone for directions

66 Victoria Road LN11 0BX
Map 8: TF38
Tel: 01507 605005
Fax: 01507 607768
Cost: Alc £19, set-price L £9 (2
courses)/D £12.75. ☺ H/wine £7.50
Times: Noon-1.30pm/6-9.30pm.
Closed L Sun
Additional: Bar food; Children
welcome; ❹ dishes

LOUTH, **Kenwick Park Hotel**

Extended Georgian house with many acres and full leisure facilities. 'There's no doubting the quality of the produce used', noted an inspector of a meal taken in the depths of winter; overall freshness and balance of flavours were keynotes. 'Delightfully fresh' king scallops came set on a bed of deep-fried leeks as well as a cider and white wine dressing that cut through the richness of the shellfish. Chump of lamb followed, tender, pink with good natural flavour, accompanied by an onion and sage rösti and a nicely reduced red wine jus. Pistachio and hazelnut tart was very fresh 'made just before service?' and was complemented by a generous scoop of luscious home-made toffee ice cream.

Directions: Take A631 from Market Rasen

Kenwick Park LN11 8NR
Map 8: TF38
Tel: 01507 608806
Fax: 01507 608027
Chef: Paul Harvey
Owner: S D Flynn
Cost: *Alc* £26.95, set-price L & D £19.95 (4 courses). ☺ H/wine £12.95
Times: Noon-1.45pm/7-9.15pm
Additional: Bar food; Sunday L; Children welcome; 🍽 dishes
Seats: 44. Private dining room 22. Jacket & tie preferred
Smoking: No smoking in dining room
Accommodation: 24 en suite ★ ★ ★

SCUNTHORPE, **Briggate Lodge Inn**

Modern hotel with a championship golf course and an ambitious kitchen. Smoked haddock risotto, roast venison loin with ragout of mushrooms and fettucine, and raspberry flan set the pace.

Ermine Street Broughton DN20 0AQ
Tel: 01652 650770
Fax: 01652 650495
Telephone for further details

Directions: Telephone for directions

STALLINGBOROUGH, **Stallingborough Grange**

The 18th-century thatched house is quiet and secluded, with a fine, panelled dining-room. The kitchen remains in reliable and capable hands, and meals are of a consistently high standard. The style varies: caramelised breast of duckling with oyster mushrooms, parsnip crisps and a pink peppercorn and tarragon essence; steamed skate and vegetable parcel, olive crushed new potatoes and tapenade butter; ragout of pork fillet and grilled provençale vegetables dressed with pesto. However, the set-menus and *carte* are well constructed and balanced. Warm haricot bean and parsley salad served with a sauté of mange-tout, and ox tongue dressed with a chilli-garlic oil, is typical of an especially imaginative choice of starters. Amongst the desserts, coconut and rum bread-and-butter pudding is a clever variation on a theme. Afterwards, choose from a selection of fresh cafetière coffees – an idea that deserves to be more widely copied.

Riby Road DN41 8BU
Map 8: TA11
Tel: 01469 561302
Fax: 01469 561338
Chef: Neal Birtwell
Owners: Mr & Mrs G W Feeney
Cost: *Alc* £23, set-price D £21.95. ☺ H/wine £8.90
Times: D only, 6.30-10pm. Closed D Sun
Additional: Bar food; Sunday L (noon-2pm); Children welcome; 🍽 dishes
Seats: 42. Jacket & tie preferred
Smoking: No smoking in dining room
Accommodation: 32 en suite ★ ★ ★

Directions: On A1173 between Riby crossroads and Stallingborough village

STAMFORD, **George of Stamford**

This bastion of genteel hospitality and tradition has flourished for centuries. The Garden Room is open all day for light dishes; the more formal restaurant offers both traditional roasts and imaginative modern cooking using good local ingredients.

Accommodation: 47 en suite ★ ★ ★

Directions: From A1 take B1081 to Stamford. Follow road to traffic lights, hotel on L

71 St Martins PE9 2LB
Map 8: TF00
Tel: 01780 750750
Fax: 01780 750701
Cost: *Alc* £34.50, set-price L £14.50-£16.50 (2 courses). H/wine £9.95
Times: Noon-11pm
Additional: Bar food; Sunday L; Children welcome; 🍴 dishes

SUTTON-ON-SEA,
Grange & Links Hotel

Friendly seaside hotel where popular home cooking is the norm. Home-made terrine, seafood and steaks meet local demands, with lobster at 24-hours' notice.

Sea Lane Sandilands LN12 2RA
Map 9: TF58
Tel: 01507 441334
Fax: 01507 443033
Cost: *Alc* £22, set-price L £13.50. ☺ H/wine £9.50
Times: D only, 7-9.30pm
Additional: Sunday L (noon-1.30pm); Children welcome; 🍴 dishes
Accommodation: 24 en suite ★ ★ ★

Directions: Follow signs to Sandilands from Sutton-on-Sea

WINTERINGHAM,
Winteringham Fields ✿✿✿✿

The remote restaurant-with-rooms has a slightly magical, quite captivating air of total comfort and genuine hospitality. Current pride and joy is the lovingly tended potager and garden, an enviable source of organic produce including rare varieties. That the whole place runs as smoothly as a well-oiled watch from Germain's native Switzerland, is a tribute to total

DN15 9PF
Map 8: SE92
Tel: 01724 733096
Fax: 01724 733898
Chef: Germain Schwab
Owners: Germain & Annie Schwab
Cost: *Alc* £56, set-price L £20/D £29. H/wine £13.50

professionalism, unceasing hard work and the loyalty the Schwabs deservedly inspire. The 16th-century building is furnished in period style – Victoriana predominates and the small sitting rooms are a treasure trove of collectibles. The L-shaped dining-room has a slightly more modern look, and now boasts a newly laid marble floor. The food's the thing, though, and Germain Schwab has a rare talent. His cooking is predicated on fresh local ingredients, with superb flavours, endless ideas and a technique which is at times dazzling. For example, lightly oak-smoked skate wing and pike mousse served with dry cider sauce, or fillet of Shetland lamb crusted with beetroot, liquorice and Merlot sauce. Germain still loves to cook country dishes which remind him of his Jura farming childhood, but transformed into ones which could take any capital city by storm: pig's trotters are stuffed with veal sweetbreads and chicken mousse, served with a red wine glazed sauce, and crepinettes of pork and guinea fowl are carefully partnered with champ potato and wild mushrooms (probably gathered by Germain that morning). Good cooking never stands still, though, and new directions are signalled by exciting ideas such as tuna marinated in grapefruit juice, almond oil and Caribbean spices on an aspic of ruby grapefruit. Presentation is always spectacular, often witty, especially the desserts -a dome of orange chocolate was described as a match made in heaven. The cheese trolley is a star turn that regulars await with relish. The lengthy wine list complements the menus well, with great bottles listed alongside a reassuring majority of realistic and well-chosen offerings.

Times: Noon-1.30pm/7-9.30pm. Closed Sun, Mon, 2 wks Xmas, 1st full wk Mar & Aug
Additional: Children welcome; dishes
Seats: 46. Private dining room 10
Smoking: No smoking in dining room
Accommodation: 10 en suite ★ ★

Directions: Village centre, off the A1077, 4 miles S of Humber Bridge

AA Shortlisted for Wine Award-see page16

MERSEYSIDE

BIRKENHEAD, **Capitol** ❀

24 Argyle Street Hamilton Square L41 6AE
Map 7: SJ38
Tel: 0151 6479212
Fax: 0151 6473793
Cost: *Alc* £18, set-price L £7/D £17 (5 courses). ☺ H/wine £10
Times: 11.30am-1.45pm/6-11.15pm. Closed L Sat & Sun, 25, 26 Dec
Additional: Children welcome; dishes
Smoking: No pipes & cigars; Air conditioning

Directions: Town centre, at the corner of Hamilton Square

It's almost like a Chinese art gallery with the amount of original paintings and artefacts on the walls, but this is a popular restaurant offering familiar dishes such as tender beef with ginger and spring onions, and chicken with cashews and yellow bean sauce.

LIVERPOOL, **Becher's Brook** ❀❀

Friendly restaurant located near the city's two cathedrals and the university. Becher's Brook is decorated with a mixture of old English furniture and native Canadian artwork (the chef/proprietor is from Canada). The seasonally changing *carte*

29a Hope Street L1 9BQ
Map 7: SJ39
Tel: 0151 7070005
Fax: 0151 7087011
Chefs: Donna Cooke, Gerard Hogan
Owners: David & Donna Cooke

has an international twist, and three types of home-made bread start things off very nicely. How about daube of pig's cheek with straw potatoes and beetroot relish, followed by grilled sea bream on a mousse of broccoli and Parmesan, with a tomato, caper and olive compote and mussels? Puddings are well-presented, even running to spun sugar confections, as in a mille-feuille of summer berries and white chocolate mousse accompanied by a tasty orange yogurt and basil ice cream. The staff are friendly and more than happy to offer advice on food and wines (there are nearly 100 bottles to choose from), and the atmosphere is pleasant and warm.

Directions: From M62 follow signs for City Centre and Catholic Cathedral. L into Mount Pleasant Rd, then L again into Hope St. Restaurant is 100yds on L

Cost: *Alc* £29, set-price L £17.50. ☺
H/wine £11.50
Times: Noon-2.30pm/5-10pm. Closed L Sat, all Sun, 31 Dec, Bhs
Additional: Children 7+; dishes
Seats: 40
Smoking: No smoking in dining room

LIVERPOOL, Swallow Hotel

Modern hotel sited in the newly developed Queen Square area. Olivier's Restaurant emphasises modern trends with ambitious cooking of the likes of roasted turbot with roast garlic on a creamy brandade with red wine jus.

Directions: Telephone for directions

1 Queen Square L1 1RH
Map 7: SJ39
Tel: 0151 476 8000
Fax: 0151 474 5000
Telephone for further details

SOUTHPORT, Royal Clifton Hotel

Victorian hotel on the promenade. Typical dishes in the Pavilion restaurant are baked chicken supreme filled with crabmeat, or chargrilled pork fillet with pulses and chorizo sausage.

Smoking: No-smoking area; No pipes & cigars
Accommodation: 107 en suite ★ ★ ★

Directions: M6 J26, take M58 (Southport), exit at J3. Follow A570 through Ormskirk – hotel on Southport promenade

Promenade PR8 1RB
Map 7: SD31
Tel: 01704 533771
Fax: 01704 500657
Cost: *Alc* £24, set-price D £17. ☺
H/wine £9.50
Times: D only, 6.30-9.30pm
Additional: Bar food; Sunday L (12.30-3pm); Children welcome; dishes

THORNTON HOUGH,
Thornton Hall Hotel ✿✿

Neston Road Wirral L63 1JF
Map 7: SJ38
Tel: 0151 3363938
Fax: 0151 3367864
Chef: Mark Dallas
Owners: C D Thompson (Hotels) Ltd

The restaurant at this country house hotel has an unusual, perhaps even unique, mother-of-pearl and leather ceiling, installed when the house was built, along with the original

carved fireplace. A seasonally changing menu operates alongside a daily changing one, so there's plenty of choice, from noisettes of Welsh lamb with a redcurrant reduction, through grilled steaks with all the trimmings, to marinated pork tenderloin with a mille-feuille of apples and creamed leeks. Sausages are a favourite: seafood (salmon, sole and scallops) with smoked bacon cream, or chicken and wild mushrooms with a rich red onion confit as starters, and game, sitting on truffle-infused champ, as a main course. Finish with moist pear and frangipane gâteau, or traditional egg custard with nutmeg and cinnamon ice cream. Two Vins de Pays d'Oc head up the wine list.

Directions: M53 J4 onto B5151. Turn R at first crossroads – B5136 (Thornton Hough). Hotel just past village centre on L

Cost: *Alc* £30, set-price L £11.50/D £22. ☺ H/wine £11.50
Times: 12.30-1.45pm/7-9.30pm. Closed L Sat
Additional: Bar food; Sunday L; Children welcome; ☙ menu
Seats: 45. Private dining room 22
Smoking: No pipes & cigars
Accommodation: 63 en suite ★ ★ ★

NORFOLK

BLAKENEY,
Morston Hall ❁❁❁

Very special country house hotel with dedicated staff. It is a lovely 17th-century house, tucked away in a small coastal village and shielded from the reality of late twentieth-century existence by mature trees and acres of garden. The interior is elegant without seeming stuffy; it is all very gracious and civilised. Dinner menus are four-course, no-choice affairs, prepared by Galton Blackiston with accuracy and dedication. His enthusiasm comes through in dishes such as pan-fried calves' liver on olive oil and spring onion mashed potato with beef jus, and pot-roast best end of lamb on cocotte potatoes and roasted niçoise vegetables, or even classic lemon tart with red fruit ice cream. The produce, much of it local, is incredibly fresh and of the highest quality. Proximity to the sea means that fish is, of course, excellent, whether steamed halibut on chargrilled courgettes with a tarragon nage, or a simple crab salad served with avocado and tomato vinaigrette. Keenly priced wines of the month are also featured, designed to complement the food and can be sampled by the bottle or glass.

Morston NR25 7AA
Map 9: TG04
Tel: 01263 741041
Fax: 01263 740419
Chef: Galton Blackiston
Owner: Galton & Tracy Blackiston, Justin Fraser
Cost: D £32 (4 courses). H/wine £10.50
Times: 7.30-8pm. Closed 3 wks Jan
Additional: Sunday L (12.30-1pm); Children welcome; ☙ dishes
Seats: 35
Smoking: No smoking in dining room
Accommodation: 6 en suite ★ ★

Directions: On A149 (King's Lynn/Cromer) 2 miles W of Blakeney in the village of Morston

BURNHAM MARKET,
Hoste Arms ❁❁

Dedicated owner Paul Whittome has painstakingly transformed this 16th-century former coaching inn into one of the finest inns in the country. In keeping with its setting, overlooking the green of a well-heeled village , it is upmarket and stylish in appearance, yet manages to achieve the rare and successful combination of village pub, hotel and restaurant offering fine ale and wines and some eclectic and vibrant cooking. Quality ingredients are sourced from within a 20-mile radius and the wide-ranging menu could offer seared king scallops on black pasta with Szechuan and lemongrass dressing, and salmon and chilli fishcake with sweet-and-salt spinach keta and soy sauce. Expect excellent fish such as sea bass with roasted vegetable gateaux and pesto dressing, alongside lambs'

The Green Nr. King's Lynn PE31 8HD
Map 9: TF84
Tel: 01328 738777
Fax: 01328 730103
Chef: Stephen David
Owner: Paul Whittome
Cost: *Alc* £18.50
Times: Noon-2.15pm/7-9.15pm
Additional: Sunday L; ☙ dishes
Seats: 170. Private dining room 16
Smoking: No-smoking area; No pipes & cigars
Accommodation: 28 en suite ★ ★

Hoste Arms

Directions: In the centre of the village

liver and kidney with saffron mash and chargrilled fillet steak with rösti and glazed onions. Finish with a memorable hot orange soufflé with chocolate sauce and fruit salsa.

DISS, Salisbury House

84 Victoria Road IP22 3JG
Map 5: TM18
Tel/Fax: 01379 644738
Chef: Barry Davies
Owners: Mr & Mrs Barry Davies
Cost: Set-price D £24.95. ☺ H/wine £7.90
Times: D only (L Tue-Fri by arrangement), 7.15-8.45pm. Closed Sun, Mon, 2 wks summer, 1 wk Xmas
Additional: Children welcome; ❹ dishes
Seats: 36. Private dining room 20
Smoking: No smoking in dining room
Accommodation: 3 rooms, 2 en suite

Relaxed country house hotel. The building is mainly Victorian, formerly the local miller's house; there's an old mill at the bottom of the garden. Two eating choices brings the formal restaurant, plushly decorated and carpeted with neat, well-set tables, or the more casual bistro sporting bare polished floorboards and pastel colours. The monthly-changing menu in the latter could run from avocado filled with piquant fish salad, through roasted breast of pheasant with a creamy ginger sauce, to strawberry omelette. However, the restaurant moves up a notch with set three to five courses of good country house cooking with coffee and home-made petits fours thrown in. Game terrine with a purée of port and apples, a combination felt to work well, chargrilled salmon finished with lime, herbs and butter, and nicely tender pork fillet satay with wild rice illustrate the kitchen's versatility. An interesting approach to puddings shows up in pear and Stilton pie.

Directions: On A1066 (Thetford/Scole) 0.25 mile E of Diss town centre

ERPINGHAM, Ark Restaurant

The Street Norwich NR11 7QB
Map 5: TG13
Tel/Fax: 01263 761535
Chef: Sheila Kidd
Owners: Sheila & Michael Kidd
Cost: *Alc* £26.50. H/wine £10.50
Times: D only, 7-9.30pm. Closed D Sun, all Mon, D Tue-Wed in winter, part Oct, part Jan
Additional: Sunday L (12.30-2pm); Children welcome; ❹ dishes
Seats: 26. Private dining room 8
Smoking: No smoking in dining room
Accommodation: 3 rooms (2 en suite)
Credit cards: None

At first glance looks like a pretty, cottagey private house. However, within, the outline of a restaurant is discernible: a small lounge-bar and a comfortable 30-seater restaurant with good views over the garden. Sheila Kidd is an industrious cook. Her style is influenced by local raw materials and is interpreted in an unpretentious country way with lots of traditional English feel to the food; but there's a strong awareness of modern trends too. Great, fresh-baked bread opens dinner, and we went on to a simple but very enjoyable wild mushroom feuilleté. Although tempted by sea bass with sorrel sauce, we were delighted by our roast loin of spring lamb with tomato and cream gratin and selection of new potatoes, mange-tout, carrots and broccoli. Dessert presented a problem too. Caramelised apple tart with home-made caramel ice cream sounded good, but was reluctantly passed over for a rich, creamy white and bitter chocolate pavé. The wine list may be small but it is certainly well chosen.

Directions: Off A140 4 miles N of Aylsham

GREAT YARMOUTH, **Imperial Hotel** ❀

North Drive NR30 1EQ
Map 5: TG50
Tel: 01493 851113
Fax: 01493 852229
Cost: *Alc* £23, set-price L £13.50 (2 courses)/D £20. ☺ H/wine £11
Times: Noon-2pm/7-10pm. Closed L Sat
Additional: Bar food; Sunday L; Children welcome; 🍴 dishes
Smoking: No-smoking area; Air conditioning
Accommodation: 39 en suite ★ ★ ★

Directions: On the seafront 100 yards N of Britannia Pier

Located in the basement, the informal Rambouillet Restaurant offers an uncomplicated menu with a French brasserie feel. Main courses may include wing of Longshore skate, escalope of turkey Holstein, pancake provençale, and omelette 'Arnold Bennett'.

GRIMSTON, **Congham Hall** ❀❀

Georgian country retreat, secluded and elegant. The real talking point at Congham Hall must be the huge herb garden which is a real labour of love for Christine and Trevor Forecast. The Orangery Restaurant overlooks the garden and offers a menu that favours roasting and mixes classic technique with modern ideas. Tortellini of crab, spring onions and ginger with a lemongrass and coriander cream, oven-roasted partridge with fondant potatoes, roasted vegetables and juniper with Gewürztraminer juices, and praline mille-feuille with caramelised pears and an espresso anglaise show the range. A test meal highlighted sound terrine of ham knuckle and foie gras with pease pudding, and roast rump of spring lamb with herb-roasted sweetbreads, braised onion and tarragon jus. There's a good, separate vegetarian menu, and lunch is a bargain.

Lynn Road King's Lynn PE32 1AH
Map 9: TF72
Tel: 01485 600250
Fax: 01485 601191
Owners: Christine & Trevor Forecast
Cost: *Alc* £34, set-price L £13.50/D £34. H/wine £13.25
Times: 12.30-2pm/7.30-9.30pm
Additional: Bar food; Sunday L; Children 12+; 🍴 dishes
Seats: 50. Private dining room 16. Jacket & tie preferred
Smoking: No smoking in dining room
Accommodation: 14 en suite ★ ★ ★

Directions: From A14, turn toward Grimston. Hotel is 2.5 miles on L; don't go to Longham

HETHERSETT, **Park Farm Hotel** ❀

NR9 3DL
Map 5: TG10
Tel: 01603 810264
Fax: 01603 812104
Cost: *Alc* £25, set-price L £13.75/D £19.50. ☺ H/wine £10.50
Times: Noon-2pm (2.30pm Sun)/7-9.30pm (9pm Sun)
Additional: Bar food; Sunday L; Children welcome; 🍴 dishes
Smoking: No smoking in dining room; Air conditioning
Accommodation: 36 en suite ★ ★ ★

Directions: 5 miles S of Norwich on B1172 (the old A11)

Candlelit restaurant with ivory-coloured linen and quality soft furnishings set in a modern hotel converted from a Georgian farmhouse. An interesting range of dishes is offered to suit most palates.

HOLT, Yetman's

In summer, the two converted cottages look ravishingly pretty with tubs and baskets full of flowers. Rarely do we come across a menu where every single dish appeals to the extent it does here; daily-changing, it is a model of its kind. Sautéed Louisiana crabcakes with red capsicum mayonnaise are deservedly a regular part of the repertoire; other starters include Jerusalem artichoke soup with sautéed fresh scallops, hot gougère with fresh local asparagus and crème fraîche, and deep-fried fresh sardine fillets in Parmesan crumbs. Our main course of roast corn-fed fillet of beef was perfectly cooked, enhanced by a good hollandaise with just the right hint of fennel and orange. Alternatively, there may be roasted apple-fed Hereford duck with Agen prune stuffing and blackberry sauce, or try the perfect marriage of ingredients and technique that is steamed skate wing with warm green salsa. British cheeses are from Neal's Yard Dairy. Blackcurrant and almond tart, fresh rhubarb fool and toasted fresh quince and apple pancakes are amongst the delicious desserts.

37 Norwich Road NR25 6SA
Map 9: TG03
Tel: 01263 713320
Chef: Alison Yetman
Owners: Peter & Alison Yetman
Times: D only, 7.30-9.30pm. Closed D Mon (in winter),Tue, 4 wks Oct-Nov
Additional: Sunday L (12.30-2pm); Children welcome; 🍴 dishes
Seats: 30. Private dining room 10
Smoking: No smoking in dining room

Directions: Village centre

KING'S LYNN, Rococo

Lively, cosmopolitan restaurant set in a 17th-century cottage. Stripped wooden floors, huge abstract paintings on the yellow walls and colourful artwork covering the menus sets the scene for some cracking modern cooking that merges with the Mediterranean. Breads are all home-made, we recommend strongly the unusual poppy and sunflower seed bread with garlic leaves. Follow this with a stylish rocket salad of mustard-scented Finnan haddock sausage – we found it delicate and 'light in flavour'. Then perhaps, roast monkfish with shrimp tortellini, which we thought a 'lovely, tender fish', and was served with a light beurre blanc. Finish the meal off with a rich, sticky banana chocolate pudding or a lively champagne and raspberry mousse cake.

Directions: Follow signs to The Old Town, next to Tourist Information

11 Saturday Market Place PE30 5DQ
Map 9: TF62
Tel/Fax: 01553 771483
Chef: Nick Anderson
Owners: Nick & Anne Anderson
Cost: Set-price L £14.50/D £29.50. H/wine £11.95
Times: Noon-1.30pm/7-10pm. Closed L Mon, all Sun, 24-31 Dec, 1 wk beginning May
Additional: Children welcome; 🍴 dishes
Seats: 40
Smoking: No-smoking area; No pipes & cigars

NORTH WALSHAM, Beechwood Hotel

The interior of the ivy-clad Georgian house has an air of country house seclusion. British based cooking – kidney Turbigo and rack of lamb with shallot and garlic sauce – but there are forays further afield with duck oriental soup and pork in prune and Armagnac sauce.

NR28 0HD
Map 9: TG23
Tel: 01692 403231
Fax: 01692 407284
Cost: Set-price L £11/D £22. ☺ H/wine £12
Times: Noon-1.30pm/7-8.45pm. closed L Sat
Additional: Sunday L; Children 10+; 🍴 dishes
Smoking: No smoking in dining room
Accommodation: 9 en suite ★ ★

Directions: From Norwich take B1150 to North Walsham (13 miles). Turn L at 1st traffic lights and R at next. Hotel 150m on L

NORWICH,

Adlard's Restaurant ❀❀❀

Charming restaurant with attentive service. Situated on the
edge of the town centre in a row of shops in a rather quaint
street (no parking but just a few minutes from an NCP),
Adlard's presents a dark green front and stripped wood floors
inside. Walls are strewn with a diverse selection of painting (all
for sale), there's good linen and an interesting wine list. All in
all, a great place to eat, we loved it. David Adlard describes his
chef Roger Hickman's cooking as 'modern classical French – is
this modern English?', and dishes are offered on short, simply
described menus. Our own meal took in sautéed calves'
sweetbreads, lightly cooked and layered with fine leaves of
parsnip mille-feuille style, and set atop an ambrosia-like
parsnip purée, then first-class pan-fried fillet of turbot with an
accompanying light, creamy mash, herb nage, and fresh baby
vegetables of asparagus, turnips, carrots and leaks. Pineapple
Tatin to finish came with a good creamy pineapple ice cream
and extra caramel sauce. Bread and petits fours maintain the
high standards.
   Signature dishes: roast sweetbreads, onion purée and
pommes-Maxim; steamed partridge with pear boulangère and
roast parsnips; passion fruit soufflé with blood orange sorbet.

Directions: City centre, 200 yards behind City Hall

79 Upper St Giles Street NR2 1AB
Map 5: TG20
Tel: 01603 633522
Fax: 01603 617733
Chef: Roger Hickman
Owner: David Adlard
Cost: Set-price L £19/D £33. H/wine
£12.50
Times: 12.30-1.45pm/7.30-10.30pm.
Closed L Mon, all Sun, 1 wk after
Xmas
Additional: Children welcome;
 dishes
Seats: 40
Smoking: No pipes & cigars; Air
conditioning

AA Wine Shortlisted for
Award-see page 16

NORWICH,

Annesley House Hotel ❀   NEW

*A brand-new conservatory restaurant overlooking the floodlit
landscaped water gardens provides the backdrop for enthusiastic,
eclectic cooking: chicken liver salad with beer damper bread, or
Thai green chicken curry and tomato and chilli jam.*

Smoking: No smoking in dining room
Accommodation: 26 en suite ★★

Directions: On A11 close to city centre

6 Newmarket Road NR2 2LA
Map 5: TG20
Tel: 01603 624553
Fax: 01603 621577
Cost: *Alc* £24, set-price £17.50. ☺
H/wine £8.50
Times: Noon-2.30pm/7-9pm. Closed
4 days Xmas
Additional: Bar food; Sunday L;
 dishes

NORWICH, **Brasted's** ❀❀

**Small restaurant tucked away down a side street in the
ancient city centre.** Floor-to-ceiling drapes in rich, vibrant
colours create an intimate, smart atmosphere, and impressive
napery and place settings complete the picture. Thai crab
cakes, or fillet of beef with coconut milk, lemongrass, lime
leaves and chilli might extend the range of the largely
traditional menu where beef Stroganoff is proclaimed the
house speciality and sautéed lambs' liver with bacon, mash and
onion gravy is typical of the main courses. A dish of sautéed
lambs' sweetbreads has been noteworthy for its delicacy, and a
main course of chicken breast with pesto on a mound of
Biarritz potatoes shows an equally deft hand at the stove. Rice
pudding with blueberry jam and honey ice cream is a
comfortable way to finish. A page of house wines starts off the
wide-ranging list.

8-10 St Andrews Hill NR2 1AD
Map 5: TG20
Tel: 01603 625949
Fax: 01603 766445
Chef: Adrian Clarke
Owner: John Brasted
Cost: *Alc* £27, set-price L £13/D
£14.95. ☺ H/wine £10.85
Times: Noon-2pm/7-10pm. Closed L
Sat, all Sun, Bhs
Additional: Children 10+; ⬤ dishes
Seats: 20
Smoking: No pipes & cigars

Directions: City centre, close to the
Castle & Cathedral, between London
Street and St Andrews Street

NORWICH,

St Benedicts Restaurant

French brasserie-style restaurant in a trader's house with pitch pine and Norfolk brick walls creating a cosy atmosphere. The award winning ladies' loo should not be missed!

Additional: Children welcome; dishes
Smoking: No-smoking area; No pipes & cigars

Directions: At city end of St Benedicts. Nearest car park Duke Street (day), on street (evening)

9 St Benedicts Street NR2 4PE
Map 5: TG20
Tel/Fax: 01603 765377
Cost: *Alc* £15.95. ☺ H/wine £7.95
Times: Noon-2pm/7-10pm. Closed Sun & Mon, 25-31 Dec

NORWICH,

Swallow Sprowston Manor

Striking country house hotel built around a 16th-century manor house and set in attractive parkland. Typical dishes may include roasted king scallops with creamy coriander butter sauce, and brill filled with crab mousseline.

Directions: Take A1151 (Wroxham), follow signs to Sprowston Park

Sprowston Park Wroxham Road NR7 8RP
Map 5: TG20
Tel: 01603 410871
Fax: 01603 423911
Telephone for further details

NORWICH,

The Wildebeest Arms

Simple pub serving good food. The pub decor may be African in inspiration – memorabilia, African motifs, ochre yellow walls – but the food is more provençale than Southern hemisphere. It's a simple concept, good food and wine, no pretensions, real ales on tap, or a reassuring but quite interesting selection of Adnams wine and others. Confit of duck salad with pickled plums and spicy croûtons, or salmon ceviche with charred polenta, dressed leaves and crème fraîche, are typical starters. Main courses run along the lines of marinated lemon chicken, pommes Anna and sweet glazed shallots, or confit of tuna with piperade. A side order of hand-cut chips is recommended.

Directions: A140 (Ipswich), under southern by-pass. Turn L into last exit before Dunston Hall and follow road into Stoke Holy Cross

Norwich Road Stoke Holy Cross NR14 8QJ
Map 5: TG20
Tel: 01508 492497
Chef: Paul Hatch
Owners: Henry Watts, Andrew Wilkins
Cost: *Alc* £28, set-price L £15. ☺ H/wine £9.95
Times: Noon-2pm/7-9.30pm
Additional: Sunday L; Children welcome; dishes
Seats: 66
Smoking: No-smoking area

SWAFFHAM, **Romford House** ✿

Small, friendly restaurant, good for light lunches and dinners. Fish dishes such as fillet of sea bass grilled with prawns, capers and walnuts, and baked lemon sole topped with gherkin and Dijon mustard crust, are a speciality. Fillet steaks come with a choice of sauces.

Seats: 45. Private dining room 25
Smoking: No-smoking area

Directions: 16 miles from Kings Lynn, on the main Market Place

5 London Street PE37 7DD
Map 9: TF80
Tel: 01760 722552
Chef/Owner: Jane Rose
Cost: *Alc* £20.
Times: Noon-2pm/7-late. Closed L Mon, all Sun
Additional: Children welcome; dishes

THORPE MARKET,

Elderton Lodge ✿

Game from adjacent estates and fresh seafood from the nearby North Norfolk coast are the things to go for at this Victorian shooting lodge. Follow Blakeney harbour mussels with roast partridge in smoked bacon and grape sauce.

Gunton Park nr Cromer NR11 8TZ
Map 9: TG23
Tel: 01263 833547
Fax: 01263 834673
Cost: *Alc* £23, set-price L
£14.50. ☺ H/wine £9.50
Times: Noon-2pm/7-9pm. Closed 25-26 Dec
Additional: Sunday L; Children 10+; 🍲 dishes
Smoking: No smoking in dining room
Accommodation: 11 en suite ★★

Directions: On A149 (Cromer/North Walsham rd), 1 mile S of village

TITCHWELL,

Titchwell Manor ✿

Freshly decorated restaurant with cane furniture, white cloths, and views over the walled garden. The food is modern European with a good choice of local seafood.

Brancaster PE31 8BB
Map 9: TF74
Tel: 01485 210221
Fax: 01485 210104
Cost: Set-price D £24. ☺ H/wine £12.50
Times: Noon-2pm/6-9.30pm. Closed last 2 wks Jan
Additional: Bar Food; Sunday L; Children welcome; 🍲 dishes
Smoking: No smoking in dining room
Accommodation: 16 en suite ★★

Directions: On A149 coast road between Brancaster and Thornham

WYMONDHAM,

Number Twenty Four

Refurbished restaurant with imaginative options: roast rack of Indian spiced lamb with aubergine confit, and pan-fried breast and braised leg of local pheasant with winter berries.

Additional: Sunday L; Children welcome; 🍲 dishes
Smoking: No cigars & pipes

Directions: Town centre opposite war memorial

24 Middleton Street NR18 0BH
Map 5: TG10
Tel/Fax: 01953 607750
Cost: *Alc* £25, set-price D £15.95. ☺ H/wine £8.95
Times: Noon-2.30pm/7-9.30pm. Closed D Sun, all Mon, Tue, 25-31 Dec

WYMONDHAM,

Wymondham Consort Hotel

24 Market Street Norwich NR18 0BB
Map 5: TG10
Tel: 01953 606721
Fax: 01953 601361
Cost: *Alc* £25, set-price L £11.95/D £17.95. ☺ H/wine £8.95
Times: Noon-1.45pm/7-9.30pm
Additional: Bar Food; Sunday L; Children 12+; ◑ dishes
Smoking: No smoking in dining room
Accommodation: 20 en suite ★ ★

Directions: Town centre opposite Barclays Bank

Intimate hotel restaurant offering a range of international dishes. Try quail with tarragon mousse and wild mushroom sauce, and a 'saints and sinners' plate of desserts.

NORTHAMPTONSHIRE

CASTLE ASHBY, **Falcon Hotel**

NN7 1LF
Map 4: SP85
Tel: 01604 696200
Fax: 01604 696673
Telephone for further details

Intimate hotel restaurant overlooking the rear garden and terrace. Local produce drives a menu that has a refreshing modern outlook. Quail stuffed with herb mousseline, a nest of fresh quails' eggs and sultana and nettle tea sauce show the imagination at work.

Directions: From A428 (Northampton-Bedford) turn off at Castle Ashby sign, hotel 1.5 miles ahead

DAVENTRY, **Fawsley Hall** **NEW**

Fawsley NN11 3BA
Map 4: SP56
Tel: 01377 892000
Fax: 01327 892001
Chef: James Haywood
Cost: *Alc* £50, set-price L £18.95. H/wine £17.50
Times: Noon-2pm/7-10pm
Additional: Bar food; Sunday L; Children welcome
Seats: 75. Private dining room 24
Smoking: No-smoking area; No pipes & cigars
Accommodation: 30 en suite ★ ★ ★ ★

Directions: From M40 J11 take A361, follow for 12 miles. Turn R towards Fawsley Hall

The hall, in grounds designed by Capability Brown, dates back to Tudor times and has mullioned windows, stone or wooden floors, large fireplaces and tapestries on the walls. Apart from the wealth of history and architectural detail, a major attraction is the sheer peace and tranquillity of the house. The well-planned menus take in the Med (fillet of cod studded with croûtons with bouillabaisse sauce) the modish (aubergine caviar with sliced saddle of lamb) and make the occasional nod towards the East with crispy salmon teriyaki with Oriental sauce. A classical influence is at work behind a starter of remoulade of salt cod, of smooth and creamy texture, given a new dimension with a light topping of roughly textured tapenade, and timing shows to advantage in that rarity of a perfectly poached egg on an excellent fishcake with velvety hollandaise. Crème brûlée – raspberry, perhaps, or strawberry – brings things to a conclusion, along with nougat glacé, 'a rich, nutty, creamy concoction' in a chocolate tuile in a puddle of raspberry coulis. Don't expect any bargains on the wine list.

HELLIDON, **Hellidon Lakes Hotel** 🌸

Surrounded by rolling countryside and a 27-hole golf course. The cherrywood-panelled restaurant is the setting for dishes that range from pan-fried duck livers with pine kernels, to breast of chicken with chilli, coriander and coconut cream sauce. A new evening-only Four Seasons restaurant is planned with magnificent views over lakes.

Smoking: No-smoking area; No pipes & cigars; Air conditioning
Accommodation: 51 en suite ★ ★ ★ ★

Directions: 1.5 miles off A361 at Charwelton, follow signs for Golf Club

Daventry NN11 6LN
Map 4: SP55
Tel: 01327 262550
Fax: 01327 262559
Cost: *Alc* £25, set-price L £12.50/D £22.50. ☺ H/wine £9.75
Times: Noon-3pm/6.30-9.30pm. Closed Xmas
Additional: Bar food; Sunday L; Children 14+; 🍴 dishes

HORTON,
The French
Partridge Restaurant 🌸🌸

David and Mary Partridge have been running their creeper-covered restaurant for over 35 years. The interior is furnished in the style of an exclusive club and has a bit of an Edwardian feel to it, and if the menus themselves feature such timeless classics as gravad lax, chicken Kiev, crispy roast duck with orange sauce, lemon sole meunière, and Bakewell pudding, the kitchen shows it moves with the times in terrine of roast Mediterranean vegetables, grilled swordfish steak with ginger, soy and chilli sauce, and braised young rabbit with cheesy polenta. Our meal started with smoked chicken and bacon terrine with tomato chutney, 'full-flavoured and well-textured', and went on to perfectly baked cod topped with a crust of garlic, coriander and parsley, the *pièce de résistance* being tender and moist roast duck. 'I was tempted to finish with the savoury (mushrooms on toast) but opted for a fresh fruit Pavlova and was not disappointed.' Mrs Partridge oversees the smart, friendly and skilled staff.

Directions: On B526, village centre, 6 miles from Northampton

NN7 2AP
Map 4: SP85
Tel: 01604 870033
Fax: 01604 870032
Chef: David Partridge
Owners: David & Mary Partridge
Cost: Set-price D £28 (4 courses). H/wine £10
Times: D only, 7.30-9pm. Closed Sun, Mon, 2wks Xmas, 2 wks Easter, 3wks Jul/Aug
Additional: 🍴 dishes
Seats: 45
Smoking: No smoking in dining room
Credit cards: None

AA Wine Award–see page 16 Shortlisted for

KETTERING,
Kettering Park Hotel 🌸

Smart, purpose-built hotel with a bright bustling restaurant offering an airy Mediterranean atmosphere. Seared tuna, olives and tomatoes carries the theme, duck confit is more oriental with its fresh ginger and spring onion.

Directions: A14 J9 – hotel on that roundabout

Kettering Parkway NN15 6XT
Map 4: SP87
Tel: 01536 416666
Fax: 01536 416171
Telephone for further details

MARSTON TRUSSELL, **The Sun Inn**

17th-century inn that offers a quietly comfortable restaurant finished in dark greens with muted lighting and good linen and glasses. Sound modern cooking takes in the likes of home-smoked breast of guinea fowl, and roast wild boar.

Smoking: No-smoking area
Accommodation: 19 en suite ★★

Directions: Off A4304, between the villages of Lubenham & Theddingworth

Main Street LE16 9TY
Map 4: SP68
Tel: 01858 465531
Fax: 01858 433155
Cost: *Alc* £20, set-price L £10 (2 courses)/D £22.50 (5 courses). ☺
H/wine £9.95
Times: Noon-2pm/6.30-9.30pm
Additional: Bar food; Sunday L; Children welcome; ◑ dishes

NORTHAMPTON, **Swallow Hotel**

Modern red-brick hotel with excellent facilities for leisure and business guests. The modern menu offers wild mushroom risotto, warm salad of red mullet with lime-scented couscous, and classics such as lobster bisque.

Smoking: No-smoking area; Air conditioning
Accommodation: 120 en suite ★★★★

Directions: M1/J15, follow A508 then A45 (Wellingborough). L at roundabout signposted Delapre Golf Complex. Hotel on R

Eagle Drive NN4 7HW
Map 4: SP76
Tel: 01604 768700
Fax: 01604 769011
Cost: *Alc* £15.75, set-price L £19.75/D £21.75. ☺
Times: Noon-1.30pm/6.30-10.15pm
Additional: Bar food; Sunday L; Children welcome; ◑ dishes

ROADE,

Roade House Restaurant

Period building, modernised and extended, with an oak-beamed dining room. Lightly curried fish stew, and breast and leg of corn-fed chicken on cabbage and chorizo are typical dishes.

Smoking: No smoking in dining room; Air conditioning
Accommodation: 8 en suite

Directions: M1 J15 (A508 Milton Keynes) to Roade, L at mini-roundabout, 500yds on L

16 High Street NN7 2NW
Map 4: SP75
Tel: 01604 863372
Fax: 01604 862421
Cost: *Alc* £27, set-price L £17. ☺
H/wine £10.50
Times: 12.30-1.45pm/7-10pm. Closed L Sat & Mon, D Sun, 1 wk Xmas
Additional: Sunday L; Children 5+

STOKE BRUERNE, **Bruerne's Lock** NEW

The Canalside Towcester NN12 7SB
Map 4: SP74
Tel: 01604 863654
Fax: 01604 863330
Cost: *Alc* £24, set-price L/D £17. ☺
H/wine £11.95
Times: 12.15-2pm/7.15-9.45pm. Closed L Sat, D Sun, all Mon, 1 wk Jan, 2 wks Oct
Additional: Sunday L; Children welcome; ◑ dishes
Smoking: No smoking in dining room

Directions: On A508 between Northampton & Milton Keynes

Modern British fare is the order of the day at this attractive lockside restaurant on the Grand Union Canal. A cellar bar and patio provide for pre-meal drinks and light lunches.

TOWCESTER,

Vine House Restaurant

Built over 300 years ago out of local limestone, great care has gone into preserving the original features and character of the old building. The cooking uses fresh, seasonal ingredients, and traditional dishes are given a modern twist as in the use of sage and onion polenta accompanying roasted blade of beef steak with red wine sauce and garlic butter. Changing modern tastes are reflected in the use of korma curry to spice up fillet of cod with herb crust, red pepper and basil butter. Home-made venison and bacon sausages need no such elaboration, especially when served with bubble-and-squeak and a port, chestnut and button mushroom sauce. Mouth-watering starters include game pâté with walnut oil and home-made chutney, and haddock, smoked bacon and potato terrine with chive pesto. Desserts are predominantly fruity – poached pear with crispy nut filo wafers and chocolate sauce, passion fruit jelly with a minestrone of fresh fruit salad.

Directions: 2 miles S of Towcester, just off A5

100 High Street Paulerspury
NN12 7NA
Map 4: SP64
Tel: 01327 811267
Fax: 01327 811309
Chef: Marcus Springett
Owners: Julie & Marcus Springett
Cost: Set-price D £24.95. ☺ H/wine £11.95
Times: 12.15-1.30pm/D 7.15-9.30pm. Closed L Sat-Wed, all Sun, 24 Dec for 2 wks
Additional: Children welcome
Seats: 45. Private dining room 10
Smoking: No smoking in dining room
Accommodation: 6 en suite

NORTHUMBERLAND

BELLINGHAM,

Riverdale Hall Hotel

There's much to commend, although the cooking tends to the retro – prawn cocktail Marie Rose, steak Diane – in parts. The straightforward style suits the many families who return each year.

Additional: Bar food; Sunday L; Children welcome; 🍴 dishes
Smoking: No pipes & cigars
Accommodation: 20 en suite ★ ★

Directions: Turn off B6320, after bridge, hotel on L

NE48 2JT
Map 12: NY88
Tel: 01434 220254
Fax: 01434 220457
Cost: *Alc* £19, set-price L £9.95 (4 courses)/D £19.50 (5 courses). ☺ H/wine £8.60
Times: Noon-2.30pm/6.45-9.30pm

BERWICK-UPON-TWEED,

Marshall Meadows Hotel

Georgian mansion house hotel offering a varied menu. Dishes might include roast loin of Highland venison with berry and pear compote, and an excellent Irish tipsy bavarois.

Additional: Sunday L; 🍴 dishes
Smoking: No smoking in dining room
Accommodation: 19 en suite ★ ★ ★

Directions: Just off the A1 N of Berwick

TD15 1UT
Map 12: NT95
Tel: 01289 331133
Fax: 01289 331438
Cost: *Alc* £28, set-price L £9/D £20
Times: Noon-2.30pm/6.30-9.30pm

BLANCHLAND,
Lord Crewe Arms Hotel ⊛

Nr Consett DH8 9SP
Map 12: NY95
Tel: 01434 675251
Fax: 01434 675337
Cost: Alc £28, set-price D £28 (4 courses). H/wine £9
Times: D only, 7-9.15pm
Additional: Bar food; Sunday L (noon-2pm); Children welcome; ⬤ dishes

Monks once lodged in this historic building, which features flagstone floors and vaulted ceilings. Now visitors arrive eager to sample decent British fare like loin steak of wild boar with grilled apple rings.

Accommodation: 19 en suite ★★

Directions: 10 miles S of Hexham on B6306

CHOLLERFORD,
Swallow George Hotel ⊛⊛

Hexham NE46 4EW
Map 12: NY96
Tel: 01434 681611
Fax: 01434 681727
Chef: Paul Montgomery
Cost: Alc £30, set-price L £15/D £24 (4 courses). ☺ H/wine £12
Times: Noon-1.45pm/6.30-9.30pm
Additional: Bar food; Sunday L; Children welcome; ⬤ dishes
Seats: 90. Private dining room 40
Smoking: No smoking in dining room
Accommodation: 47 en suite ★★★

The refurbished restaurant overlooks the gardens and the Tyne. Although there are straightforward grills, most of the menu has a more upmarket feel. There is, however, a pleasing brevity to menu descriptions: salad of asparagus and artichoke; grilled goats' cheese with balsamic dressing. Braised brisket of beef with rosemary creamed potato and Madeira jus, and halibut en croûte both depend on kitchen skills which sadly have fallen into disuse in many places. Smart hotel ingredients feature in dishes such as velouté of wild mushroom with foie gras ravioli and warm salad of quail with truffle dressing. Desserts are colour supplement-style: citron tart set on a pool of raspberry sauce; dark chocolate tart served with crème chantilly and mint syrup.

Directions: From A6079 take B6318. 400 yds on opposite side of river

NOTTINGHAMSHIRE

LANGAR, # Langar Hall ⊛

NG13 9HG
Map 8: SK73
Tel: 01949 860559
Fax: 01949 861045
Cost: Alc £30, set-price D £17.50. ☺ H/wine £12.50
Times: 12.30-1.30pm/7-9.30pm
Additional: Bar food L; Sunday L; Children welcome; ⬤ dishes
Smoking: No smoking in dining room
Accommodation: 10 en suite ★★

Directions: Off A46 and A52, in village centre (behind church)

Delightful country hotel and family home close by the village church. Committed cooking and quality ingredients were highlighted for us in a dinner of seared scallops and black pudding, breast of guinea fowl with sage ravioli and girolle nage, and raspberry brûlée.

NETHER LANGWITH,

Goff's Restaurant

Smart dining in an 18th-century mill house. The monthly changing menu is filled with well-focused, modern ideas such as chargrilled loin of wild boar with confit of sage and onion plus red wine and caper sauce.

Additional: Sunday L; Children welcome
Smoking: No smoking in dining room

Directions: Telephone for directions

Langwith Millhouse Mansfield NG20 9JF
Map 8: SK57
Tel: 01623 744538
Fax: 01623 747953
Cost: Set-price L £15.50/D £35. H/wine £9.50
Times: Noon-1.30pm/7-9.30pm. Closed L Sat, D Sun, all Mon

NOTTINGHAM,

Hart's Restaurant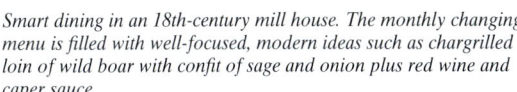

1 Standard Court Park Row NG1 6GN
Map 8: SK53
Tel: 0115 9110666
Fax: 0115 9110611
Chef: Mark Gough
Owner: Tim Hart
Cost: *Alc* £23, set-price L £13. ☺ H/wine £9.50
Times: Noon-2pm/7-10.30pm
Additional: Sunday L; Children welcome; 🍴 dishes
Seats: 90. Private dining room 12
Smoking: No-smoking area; No pipes & cigars; Air conditioning

19th-century building, but a light, pillared room, strong on comfort. One wall is a striking rich blue, the others off-white, hung with paintings by Mrs Hart's father. Tables are spotlit, seating is banquettes or comfortable chairs in a variety of colours, the floor polished wood and there's a real buzz in the air. The modern brasserie-style menu offers the likes of grilled squid with rocket and lemon oil, fricassée of lambs' kidneys with mustard mash, and apple Charlotte. Partridge could also make an appearance in season, roasted with ceps, and pearl barley risotto could turn up alongside roast breast of pheasant. We started, however, with an excellent terrine of partridge, chicken and duck, and went on to what must be something of a signature dish – superbly fresh pan-fried monkfish with tomato and spinach risotto. Puddings end on a high note. Perhaps rich, light hot chocolate pudding, melting within, with pistachio ice cream, or pear tarte Tatin, or Hart's own fruit salad. The wine list befits the style of the place, and Mr Hart and his team are only too happy to advise if asked.

Signature dishes: smoked salmon with poached egg and horseradish hollandaise; baked fillet of cod with basil mash and smoked bacon jus; gratin of summer berries with raspberry sorbet.

Directions: Follow signs for Castle and from Maid Marian Way take last L after Casino into Park Row. At top turn L into site of old General Hospital

NOTTINGHAM,

Merchant's Restaurant

Located in the Lace Market, the inside of the 1812 townhouse is bright and modern, decorated in bold, warm colours. There are stripped wooden floors throughout, and the main dining area is on a raised level off the bar. The exactness of the cooking is helped by the two short but focused menus. Foie gras layered on baby spinach on a sweetcorn pancake was a rich and strongly flavoured starter, although the accompanying Muscat and mace sauce added extra layers of richness. Another heavily reduced sauce underpinned a full-flavoured roast leg of Cornish lamb with turnip gratin and braised lamb faggot. Our dessert had to be ordered with the main course – and seeing the final product, a thin, freshly baked apple tart with sultana and Calvados ice cream plus caramel sauce we could understand why. Professional and attentive service is well-informed on both menu content, dish construction and wines.

Directions: Follow town centre signs for Lace Market. Opposite Galleries of Justice

29-31 High Pavement The Lace Market NG1 1HE
Map 8: SK54
Tel: 0115 9589898
Fax: 0115 9414322
Chef: Clive Dixon
Owners: R Beacham & J Whitehead
Cost: *Alc* £30, set-price L £13.50. ☺
H/wine £10.95
Times: Noon-3pm/7-10.30pm. Closed L Sat, D Sun
Additional: Bar food L; Sunday L; Children welcome; ✿ dishes
Seats: 70. Private dining room 16
Smoking: Air conditioning
Accommodation: 29 en suite

NOTTINGHAM, **Sonny's**

Popular city centre restaurant with bright minimalist decor. A heaving restaurant means a buzzing atmosphere, and the quality of cooking at Sonny's is clearly a major draw. Here, modern British dishes are matched by a lack of frills and a breezy, casual front-of-house style. Confit of chicken proved an interesting and dynamic variation on a familiar theme, delivering not just outstanding flavour, but contrasting crisp skin and tender meat with tomato salsa with a potent kick and a smoothly refreshing guacamole. Roast rack of lamb came with husky butter bean and garlic purée and excellent, moreish frites. An unusual, warm pear and polenta cake ('rather like an upside-down pear cake') finished the meal on a suitably upbeat note.

Directions: City centre, close to Market Square and Victoria Centre

3 Carlton Street Hockley NG1 1NL
Map 8: SK54
Tel: 0115 9473041
Fax: 0115 9507776
Chef: Graeme Watson
Owner: Ms R Mascarenhas
Cost: *Alc* £25, set-price L £13.95. ☺
H/wine £8.95.
Times: Noon-3pm/7-10.30pm. Closed Bhs
Additional: Sunday L; Children welcome; ✿ dishes
Seats: 75
Smoking: No pipes & cigars; Air conditioning

OXFORDSHIRE

BANBURY, **Wroxton House Hotel**

Refurbished restaurant with original beams and inglenook fireplace. Options might include timbale of chicken mousseline, baked sea bass, and ginger and lemon grass soufflé.

Additional: Bar food, Sunday L; Children welcome; ✿ dishes
Smoking: No smoking in dining room
Accommodation: 32 en suite ★ ★ ★

Directions: From M40 J11 take A422 towards Stratford-upon-Avon. Hotel in 3 miles on A422

Wroxton St Mary OX15 6QB
Map 4: SP44
Tel: 01295 730777
Fax: 01295 730800
Cost: *Alc* £34.50, set-price L £15.50/D £24.50 (both 4 courses). ☺
H/wine £9.95
Times: 12.30-2pm/7-9.30pm. Closed L Sat

BLEWBURY,

Blewbury Inn ✿

Modest pub, not smart, but with a homely, welcoming feel. Short menus have a Gallic flavour and show good use of quality ingredients. Expect three fish terrine, and medallions of lamb, aubergine, courgettes, grilled potatoes and a sauce with sun-dried tomatoes and fresh basil.

Accommodation: 2 en suite

Directions: On A417 between Wantage & Reading

London Road Didcot OX11 9PD
Map 4: SU58
Tel: 01235 850496
Cost: *Alc* £22. ☺
Times: Noon-2pm/7-9pm. Closed D Sun, all Mon
Additional: Bar food L; Sunday L; 🍲 dishes
Smoking: No smoking in dining room

BURFORD, **The Bay Tree** ✿

12-14 Sheep Street OX18 4LW
Map 4: SP21
Tel: 01993 822791
Fax: 01993 823008
Telephone for further details

Directions: Off main street in centre of Burford

Historic house whose restaurant overlooks a walled garden. The cooking is unfussy, using quality ingredients such as mussels which are steamed in Chablis. Lamb is a sound choice offered throughout the year in a variety of guises.

BURFORD,

Cotswold Gateway Hotel ✿

Friendly hotel offering enjoyable dishes such as darne of salmon florentine and roast rack of lamb, along with a steak selection. Don't miss the delicious home-made puddings.

Smoking: No smoking in dining room; Air conditioning
Accommodation: 20 en suite ★ ★ ★

Directions: On A40 roundabout at Burford

Cheltenham Road OX18 4HX
Map 4: SP21
Tel: 01993 822695
Fax: 01993 823600
Cost: *Alc* £17.95. ☺ H/wine £90
Times: Noon-2.30pm/6.30-9.30pm
Additional: Bar food; Sunday L; Children welcome; 🍲 dishes

BURFORD,

Inn For All Seasons ✿

Traditional 16th-century coaching inn with a log fire in the restaurant. Local game and fresh fish feature in an extensive choice of dishes catering for all tastes and appetites.

Smoking: No pipes & cigars
Accommodation: 10 en suite ★ ★ ★

The Barringtons OX18 4TN
Map 4: SP21
Tel: 01451 844324
Fax: 01451 844375
Cost: *Alc* £17.50, set-price D £17.50.
☺ H/wine £9.95
Times: 11.30-2.30pm/6.30-10pm
Additional: Bar Food; Sunday L; Children welcome; 🍲 dishes

Inn For All Seasons

Directions: On A40 at The Barringtons, 3 miles from Burford & 17 miles from Cheltenham

BURFORD, Lamb Inn

Wonderful old Cotswold stone inn strong on traditional atmosphere. The stone flag floors, log fires and gleaming copper and brass is backed up by the traditional English food served in the pretty dining room. And it is good, as our inspection meal found with some 'succulent and well-flavoured' medallions of veal that came with noodles. Supreme of pheasant filled with venison and chestnut mousse, and pan-fried fillet of sea bass with tomato and ginger sauce show the range. Sunday lunch is popular: for less than £20 enjoy a glass of Bucks Fizz before tucking into cream of mushroom soup, then jugged hare with buttered tagliatelle or supreme of maize-fed chicken filled with goats' cheese.

Directions: 1st L as you descend the High Street

Sheep Street OX18 4LR
Map 4: SP21
Tel: 01993 823155
Fax: 01993 822228
Chef: Pascal Clavaud
Owners: Richard & Caroline de Wolf
Cost: Set-price D £25. H/wine £10
Times: D only, 7-9pm. Closed 25-26 Dec
Additional: Bar food L; Sunday L (12.30-1.45pm); dishes
Seats: 50
Smoking: No smoking in dining room
Accommodation: 15 en suite ★★★

CHALGROVE, Red Lion Inn   NEW

OX44 7SS
Map 4: SU69
Tel: 01865 890625
Telephone for further details

Directions: Telephone for directions

Historic 17th-century inn complete with babbling brook and a good local following for the food. The range suits most appetites, from home-made bar snacks to more substantial fare such as roasted half shoulder of lamb with hoisin sauce and plum compote.

CHINNOR, Sir Charles Napier

Eclectic furnishings with unmatching old chairs and tables, and wonderful sculptures are part of the charm. In summer, lunch is served on the terrace shaded by vines and wisteria overlooking the extensive lawns and herb gardens. In winter

Spriggs Alley OX9 4BX
Map 4: SP70
Tel: 01494 483011
Fax: 01494 485311
Chefs: David Jones & José Cau
Owner: Julie Griffiths

there are huge log fires, and local people may bring in fungi, pigeons, pheasants and berries. A hand-written menu offers a fine choice of modern British dishes – salmon fishcakes with sorrel sauce; crispy Gressingham duck with soy, ginger and papaya salsa; braised shoulder of lamb with cumin, coriander and chive mash. Risotto appears in various guises – minted pea risotto with griddled scallops, basil risotto with baked monkfish and bouillabaisse sauce. Flavoured oils (basil, chilli, truffle) add vibrancy to Cornish baked lobsters, whole steamed crabs, and crostini of pigeon and mushrooms. The chargrill is used for Mediterranean vegetables, tuna and ribeye of beef. Altogether, a super pub-cum-restaurant.

Directions: M40 J6 follow signs to Chinnor. In Chinnor turn R at roundabout. Up hill to Spriggs Alley

Cost: *Alc* £26.50, set-price L & D £15.50 (both 2 courses). ☺ H/wine £11.75
Times: Noon-2.15pm (3.30pm Sun)/6.30-10pm. Closed D Sun, all Mon
Additional: Bar food L ex Sun; Sunday L; Children 7+ at D; ◑ dishes
Seats: 75. Private room 40
Smoking: No-smoking area; Air conditioning

AA Wine Award-see page 16 Shortlisted for

CHIPPING NORTON,
Chavignol

Quite a contrast to the country house style that dominates eating out in the Cotswolds. Chavignol offers a funkier approach that is most evident in the jazzy design of the menu but also pervades the decor and in a more restrained way the cooking itself. The service is as cheerful as the environment with the Maguires offering easy conversation and the whole ambience is pleasingly relaxed. Marcus Ashenford cooking seems similarly at ease with itself. There is a deceptive amount of complexity in the dishes but the overall effect is harmonious and the style is in some ways quite unique. Typical of the witty and intelligent style was a lunchtime starter of celery and walnut quiche which was fresh, crunchy and pretty much amounted to a Waldorf salad turned tartlet. Crisp fruit and vegetables are a feature with John Dory, for instance, coming with sautéed leeks and grapes in an excellent champagne sabayon. There is classic underpinning to dishes such as breast of wood pigeon with sautéed foie gras and crisp potato but vibrancy is added in the form of caramelised apple, braised cabbage and poached beetroot. Punchy desserts have included an extravagant chocolate fondant with plum compote and a flawless passion fruit tart. Wines are offered from an extensive and thoughtful list, bursting with bins of character and quality.

Directions: On Banbury side of main Chipping Norton road

7 Horsefair OX7 5AL
Map 4: SP32
Tel/Fax: 01608 644490
Chef: Marcus Ashenford
Owner: Mark & Donna Maguire
Cost: *Alc* £38, set-price L £26/D £45 (7 courses). H/wine £11
Times: 12.15-2pm/7-9.45pm. Closed Sun, Mon, 2 wks Jan
Additional: Children welcome; ◑ dishes
Seats: 28. Private dining room 8
Smoking: No smoking in dining room

AA Wine Award-see page 16 Shortlisted for

CHIPPING NORTON, **Morel's**

Classical French restaurant, recently redecorated in warm terracotta, with a bar area made of old whisky barrels. Look out for seasonal fish, superb pastry and fine cheeses.

Smoking: No pipes & cigars; Air conditioning

Directions: Immediately before town centre entering on A44 Oxford/Banbury road, on rd to Evesham

2 Horsefair OX7 5AQ
Map 4: SP32
Tel/Fax: 01608 641075
Cost: Set-price L £14.50/D £23. ☺ H/wine £10.50
Times: Noon-1.45pm/7-10pm. Closed Sun, Mon, 1 Jan for 3 wks, 1 wk Sep
Additional: Children 10+; ◑ dishes

CLANFIELD, **Plough at Clanfield**

Archetypal Elizabethan hostelry with mullioned windows and log fires. Cotswold turkey makes a welcome appearance, for once on a non-Christmas menu. The escalope is filled with minced pork, sage and herbs and served with a red pepper sauce. No Brussels sprouts, though, unless you're vegetarian in which case they come as a main course with sweet chestnut and onion risotto cake and brandy and herb butter sauce. Other country ideas include cream of Stilton and celeriac soup, and terrine of braised ham hock, black pudding and cabbage with Puy lentils. Traditional British ingredients are to the fore – oak smoked Scottish salmon, steamed fillets of lemon sole with caramelised red cabbage, fillet of beef with horseradish cream mash and Madeira sauce. Puddings range from pistachio nut parfait with chocolate sauce, to ginger and syrup steamed pudding with crème anglaise. Lunch is an abbreviated version of the dinner *carte.*

Bourton Road OX18 2RB
Map 4: SP20
Tel: 01367 810222
Fax: 01367 810596
Chef: Rosemary Hodges
Owners: Mr & Mrs J C Hodges
Cost: *Alc* £27.50, set-price L £16.75. H/wine £13.50
Times: 12.15-1.45pm/7-9pm. Closed 26 Dec-2 Jan
Additional: Bar food L; Sunday L; Children 12+;🍴 dishes
Seats: 30. Private dining room 10
Smoking: No smoking in dining room
Accommodation: 6 en suite ★ ★ ★

Directions: Village centre, on A4095 between Faringdon & Witney, easy reach of A40 and A420

DEDDINGTON,
Dexters Restaurant

A pretty little place in the centre of an equally pretty village. The daily set lunch and dinner menu is usually composed of three starters, main courses and puddings; the *carte* is hardly extensive, but offers some slightly more complex dishes. Gazpacho was unlike any other tasted but was enjoyable none the less. A fillet of John Dory was well cooked and served on chargrilled aubergines, red and yellow peppers, courgettes and tomato with chervil oil, and topped with finely sliced raw spring onion, and accompanied by really good mash with olive oil. Roast pork fillet was well flavoured and succulent, set on top of grilled polenta. Desserts include a zesty lemon tart and a first class Chocolate St Emilion – 'with a beautiful light texture and fine Amaretti crumbs sprinkled over'. Lots of sensibly-priced regional wines, with sixteen available by the glass.

Market Place OX15 0SE
Map 4: SP43
Tel/Fax: 01869 338813
Chefs: Jamie Dexter Harrison, Brad Morris, Stuart Cox
Owners: Jamie Dexter Harrison, Roger Blackburn
Cost: *Alc* £27, set-price L & D £18. ☺ H/wine £11.50
Times: Noon-2.15pm/7-9.30pm. Closed D Sun, all Mon
Additional: Sunday L; Children 4+; 🍴 dishes
Seats: 70
Smoking: No-smoking area; No pipes & cigars

Directions: Village centre, A4260 from Banbury; L at lights

DEDDINGTON, **Holcombe Hotel**

Traditional beamed restaurant with a menu that takes traditional favourites, adds a new twist and makes good use of local produce. Start with smoked haddock tartlet with poached egg and grain mustard sauce, and go on to roast breast of duck.

High Street OX15 0SL
Map 4: SP43
Tel: 01869 338274
Fax: 01869 337167
Cost: *Alc* £25, set-price L £10 (2 courses)/D £22. ☺ H/wine £11.95
Times: Noon-1.45pm/7-9.30pm. Closed 25 Dec-2 Jan
Additional: Bar meals; Sunday L; Children welcome; 🍴 dishes
Smoking: No-smoking area; No pipes & cigars
Accommodation: 16 en suite ★ ★ ★

Directions: On A4260 between Banbury & Oxford. M40/J11 – follow A4260 (Adderbury) 7 miles, hotel is on R at traffic light

DORCHESTER-ON-THAMES,

George Hotel

The cooking mixes modern and traditional dishes, so will suit all
tastes. Gazpacho with prawns impressed, as did halibut with
pancetta, mustard mash and barigoule sauce. Meals are available in
the beamed restaurant or snug bar.

Additional: Bar food; Sunday L; Children welcome; ⚭ dishes
Smoking: No pipes & cigars
Accommodation: 18 en suite ★★★

High Street OX10 7HH
Map 4: SU59
Tel: 01865 340404
Fax: 01865 341620
Cost: Alc £25. ☺ H/wine £8.70
Times: Noon-2.15pm/7-9.30pm.
Closed Xmas/New Year

Directions: In town centre

DORCHESTER-ON-THAMES,

White Hart Hotel

**Historic timbered 14th-century coaching inn, unmissable in
this trendy Thameside village popular for its winding lanes
and antique shops.** Within, open fires and exposed stone walls
create a cosy atmosphere. The cooking runs to such dishes as
smoked chicken and spiced mango salad, and chilled wild
mushroom and basil risotto. Home-made pasta with a choice of
sauces is popular amongst regulars, but for something more
adventurous, dip into the *carte*. We tried a rustic gazpacho,
followed by loin of lamb wrapped in bacon served with
excellent dauphinoise potatoes and rosemary mousse. The
wine list is commendable for its realistic prices.

Directions: In village centre

High Street OX10 7HN
Map 4: SU59
Tel: 01865 340074
Fax: 01865 341082
Chef: Gary Palmer
Cost: Alc £20, set-price L £17.50. ☺
H/wine £7.95
Times: Noon-2pm/7-9.30pm (9pm
Sun)
Additional: Bar food; Sunday L;
Children welcome; ⚭ dishes
Seats: 50. Private dining room 10
Smoking: No-smoking area
Accommodation: 20 en suite ★★

FARINGDON,

The Lamb at Buckland

Elegant country pub with an oak-beamed restaurant. Typical dishes
include warm pheasant mousse with wild mushroom sauce,
monkfish ragout, and orange and cardamom tart.

Smoking: No smoking in dining room
Accommodation: 4 en suite

Directions: On A420, 4 miles E of Faringdon

Buckland SN7 8QN
Map 4: SU29
Tel: 01367 870484
Fax: 01367 870675
Cost: Alc £20. ☺ H/wine £9.25
Times: Noon-2pm/6.30-9.30pm.
Closed 25, 26 Dec
Additional: Bar food; Sunday L;
Children welcome; ⚭ dishes

GORING, **The Leatherne Bottel**

**Spring nettles, pea asparagus, broad-bean flowers, dandelion
leaves, chickweed and purple orach – the menu reads like a
herbalist's dream.** Much produce is home-grown and local,
top-quality ingredients are matched with a high standard of
cooking and exciting ideas that emphasise strong and clear
flavours. Smoked wood-pigeon breasts are quickly pan-fried
with cowparsley and hawthorn chutney and served with home-
pickled walnuts and deep-fried wild rocket leaves; marinated
and roasted spring lamb chump comes with apple mint, spring
onion, roasted hedge garlic and sweet potato. Influences are
free-ranging: hot fresh smoked salmon, for example, is
combined with dandelion leaves, roasted jumping rice, 'bloody
Mary' ice cream and basil olive oil. Techniques can be
painstaking, combinations eye-opening – glazed wild duck leg

RG8 0HS
Map 4: SU68
Tel: 01491 872667
Fax: 01491 875308
Chefs: Keith Read, Julia Storey
Owner: Keith Read
Cost: Alc £30, set-price D £19.50. ☺
H/wine £14.50
Times: 12.15-2.30pm(3.30pm Sun)/
7.15-9.30pm. Closed D Sun, 25 Dec
Additional: ⚭ dishes

is braised for a 'very, very long time' and served with caramelised vegetables and blackened sesame seed, bok choi, piquello yogurt and harissa crisps. Phew!

Directions: M4 J12 or M40 J6, signed off B4009 Goring-Wallingford

GREAT MILTON,

Le Manoir aux
Quat' Saisons ✿✿✿✿✿

Raymond Blanc's 15th-century manor house has seen an impressive rebuilding programme with seemingly no expense spared in terms of luxury and style. This extends to the restaurant, in part, a bright conservatory decorated in the palest vanilla creams with an airy feel brought about by views of perfectly manicured gardens. Lunch is busy, with no hushed whispers or awkward silences – staff have the formality without the fuss – and aperitifs in the garden or the sumptuous lounges are, of course, a must. Canapés give way to an *amuse-bouche* (perhaps extremely tender suckling pig morsels served embedded in a slice with a little aspic), and the bread is heavenly. The highlight of our meal was a strikingly simple starter of warm, tiny fillets of John Dory, red mullet and a fat scallop, all perfectly timed, each set on its own bed of marinated vegetables – the thinnest slices of carrot, and courgette – with a drizzle of deep coriander dressing along each side. Other dishes enjoyed ranged from mille-feuille of asparagus and risotto that was layered with Parma ham and offset by a really vibrant parsley jus; sea bream on a fricassée of squid; a perfectly baked fat squab in a salt crust (which was carved to the oohs and aahs of the nearest tables) needing little more than a good slab of tender foie gras to set it all off. Some stunning desserts included a delicate lemon parfait topped with sharp strips of orgeat encased within a tuile-textured parcel 'wrapped' with piped chocolate ribbon. Only Le Manoir could get away with two wines by the glass amidst an extensive 36 page French-biased (but by no means exclusively so) list, yet both, needless to say, are well chosen and versatile.

Directions: From M40 J7 follow A329 towards Wallingford. After 1 mile turn R, signposted Great Milton Manor

The Leatherne Bottel

Seats: 60. Private dining room 20
Smoking: Air conditioning

Church Road OX44 7PD
Map 4: SP60
Tel: 01844 278881
Fax: 01844 278847
Chef/Owner: Raymond Blanc
Cost: *Alc* £80, set-price L £32/D £72
(7 courses). H/wine £20
Times: 12.15-2.15pm/7.15-9.45pm
Additional: Children welcome;
🍴 dishes
Seats: 120. Private dining room 55.
Jacket & tie preferred
Smoking: No smoking in dining room;
Air conditioning
Accommodation: 32 en suite ★ ★ ★ ★

HENLEY-ON-THAMES,
Red Lion Hotel

Red-brick former coaching inn, dating from the 16th century, right on the Thames. Inside are wood panelling and floors of flagstones or bare boards, while the restaurant is done out in shades of mustard yellow, with floral curtains and candle-style lamps. A short *carte* offers a handful of choices at each course, perhaps goats' cheese soufflé with rocket and walnuts, then chicken breast with wild mushroom risotto. An inspector was impressed by a main course of attractively presented guinea fowl with chive pasta and girolles but felt that the highlight of the meal was pudding: three chocolate desserts of intensely flavoured sorbet, rich mousse and chewy and nutty brownie. A set-price lunch menu is served in both the bar and the restaurant. The wine list runs to 40 or so bottles.

Hart Street RG9 2AR
Map 4: SU78
Tel: 01491 572161
Fax: 01491 410039
Owners: The Miller family
Cost: *Alc* £21, set-prive L & D £16.
☺ H/wine £12
Times: Noon-2pm/7-9.45pm
Additional: Bar food L; Sunday L;
Children welcome; ✆ dishes
Seats: 35. Private dining room 8-80
Smoking: No pipes & cigars
Accommodation: 26 en suite ★ ★ ★

Directions: On the right when entering Henley by the bridge

HORTON-CUM-STUDLEY,
Kings Arms Hotel NEW

Mr Bumbles Restaurant features a vast collection of honey pots. Good use is made of seasonal produce to create both modern and traditional dishes with a leaning toward French classics.

Smoking: No-smoking area; No pipes & cigars
Accommodation: 18 en suite ★ ★

Directions: From M40/J8 take A40 towards Oxford. Then R on B4027. Follow signs for Horton-cum-Studley on R

Horton Hill OX33 1AY
Map 4: SP51
Tel: 01865 351235
Fax: 01865 351721
Cost: *Alc* £16.50, set-price D £7.95.
☺ H/wine £ 8.50
Times: D only, 6-9pm
Additional: Bar food L; Sunday L
(noon-2pm); Children welcome;
✆ dishes

HORTON-CUM-STUDLEY,
Studley Priory Hotel

Nr Oxford OX33 1AZ
Map 4: SP51
Tel: 01865 351203
Fax: 01865 351613
Chef: Peter Hewitt
Owner: Mr J Parke
Cost: *Alc* £27.50, set-price L £15 (2 courses). H/wine £15
Times: 12.30-1.45pm/7.30-9.15pm
Additional: Bar Food L; Sunday L;
Children 5+; ✆ dishes
Seats: 50. Private dining room 30

Set in extensive grounds, a haven of peace and tranquillity yet only six miles from the bustle of Oxford city centre. Originally a 15th-century Benedictine nunnery, the building was extended and turned into the present impressive manor house at the time of the dissolution of the monasteries. The restaurant, overlooking the gardens, has a beamed ceiling and stone mullioned windows. In contrast to the setting, the well-judged menu speaks of restrained modernity. This is exemplified in dishes such as a risotto of ceps and confit tomatoes with

Parmesan crisp and chive dressing, or a breast of free-range chicken with wild mushrooms, truffle noodles and cream sauce, and braised fillet of John Dory with baby fennel, tomatoes and black olives. Finish with farmhouse cheeses or such desserts as hot raspberry soufflé and passion fruit tart. Good canapés and petits fours complete the picture.

Smoking: No smoking in dining room
Accommodation: 18 en suite ★★★

Directions: At top of hill in the village

KINGHAM,
The Mill House Hotel

Chipping Norton OX7 6UH
Map 4: SP22
Tel: 01608 658188
Fax: 01608 658492
Cost: *Alc* £30, set-price L £13.95/D £22.75 (both 4 courses). ☺
H/wine £10.70
Times: Noon-2pm/7-9pm
Additional: Bar food L; Sunday L; Children welcome; ✿ dishes
Smoking: No smoking in dining room
Accommodation: 23 en suite ★★★

Cotswold stone mill house that was first recorded in the Doomsday Book of 1086. Fresh flowers and candles adorn the tables. Dishes are carefully prepared from first-class local produce.

Directions: On B4450, on southern outskirts of Kingham village

KINGSTON BAGPUIZE,
Fallowfields
Country House Hotel

Faringdon Road Nr Oxford OX13 5BH
Map 4: SU49
Tel: 01865 820416
Fax: 01865 821275
Cost: *Alc* £29, set-price L £22.50 (2 courses). H/wine £13.75
Times: Noon-2pm/7-9.30pm. Closed Sun, Mon
Additional: Bar food; Children 10+; ✿ dishes
Smoking: No smoking in dining room. Jacket & tie preferred
Accommodation: 10 en suite

Elegant 17th-century house with intimate dining room. Guests are introduced to each other before sitting down to some serious cooking based on local and home-grown produce.

Directions: From A34 at Abingdon take A415 (Witney). At mini-roundabout in Kingston Bagpuize turn L. Fallowfields is 1 mile on L

MIDDLETON STONEY,
Jersey Arms Hotel ✻

Bicester OX6 8SE
Map 4: SP52
Tel: 01869 343234
Fax: 01869 343565
Cost: *Alc* £26
Times: Noon-2.15pm/6.30-9.30pm
Smoking: No smoking in dining room
Accommodation: 16 en suite ★★

One extensive menu is available in the bar or restaurant supplemented by blackboard specials. Old favourites such as fish pie run alongside more modern chicken wings and vegetarian lasagne.

Directions: On B430, 3 miles from Bicester, 10 miles N of Oxford

MILTON COMMON,
The Oxford Belfry ✻

Nr Thame OX9 2JW
Map 4: SP60
Tel: 01844 279381
Fax: 01844 279624
Cost: *Alc* £37, set-price L £17/D £25. H/wine £12.40
Times: 12.30-2pm/7-9.30pm (10pm Sat). Closed L Sat
Additional: Bar food; Sunday L; Children welcome; ✦ dishes

Smart modern hotel with an ash-panelled restaurant. Typical dishes are ragout of scallops with home-made black pasta, and pan-fried breast of guinea fowl with Calvados cream sauce.

Smoking: No smoking in dining room
Accommodation: 131 en suite ★★★

Directions: From S: M40/J7. A329 towards Thame. Cross motorway, turn L (A40) for 300yds, hotel on R. From N: M40/J8. Follow A418 (Aylesbury). Turn R onto A40 (A329). Hotel 1.5 miles on L

MOULSFORD,
Beetle and Wedge Hotel ✻✻✻

Ferry Lane Wallingford OX10 9JF
Map 4: SU58
Tel: 01491 651381
Fax: 01491 651376
Chef: Richard Smith
Owners: Richard & Kate Smith
Cost: *Alc* £30 (Boathouse), Set-price L £27.50/D £35 (Dining Room). H/wine £13.50
Times: 12.30-2pm/7.30-10pm. Closed D Sun, Mon (Dining room only)
Additional: Bar food (Boathouse); Sunday L; Children welcome; ✦ dishes
Seats: 30 (Dining Room) 65 (Boathouse). Private dining room 64

Fine Thames-side hotel that sets high standards. The former home of Jerome K Jerome is part of a collection of historic buildings that have been brought together to create a homogenous whole. Good taste is evident throughout and almost all rooms enjoy river views. Oliver Bouet, under the guidance of Richard Smith, serves the same high standards of cooking in both the relaxed-brasserie style Boathouse, and the more formally appointed Dining Room, only the style varies. The kitchen also takes every care and effort in sourcing produce – most items are grown locally and are often organic, thus menus are changed in some way each day to allow flexibility in market availability and variation. Our meal in The Boathouse opened with rustic bread and canapés of gravad lax on toast. Good quality scallops served with a well-flavoured tomato salsa, and a caramelised onion tart topped with a slice of seared foie gras with a rich truffle sauce were promising starters. Tronçon of turbot simply served on a bed of spinach with béarnaise sauce, and fillet of excellent beef with a rich cream sauce of morels and wild mushrooms came next, followed by beignets soufflé with fresh lemon curd, and roast plums set on an almond sponge and topped with a brandy snap, vanilla ice cream and served with a warm plum sauce and a caramel sauce. The wine list is worth exploring, particularly the special recommendations, and since there is no obligation to drink a whole bottle, a dipstick system operates.

Directions: In the village, turn towards the river via Ferry Lane.

OXFORD,
Bath Place Hotel

A change of name, and a change of identity. The hotel's restaurant 'Il Cortile' (The Courtyard) has reinvented itself and now serves classical Italian food, using fresh Italian and local produce, cooked by real Italian chefs. Both cappelletti in brodo, light chicken broth, flavoured with cep mushrooms, served with fresh pasta parcels filled with veal ragout, and 'Sartu di Riso', oven-baked risotto bound with Mozzarella, salami and hard-boiled eggs served with crispy Parma ham and tomato and basil coulis, are rarely found outside Italy. Another famous dish is roasted wild duck flavoured with citrus fruits and honey glazed shallots; but there is also fillet of veal Rossini for the firmly unreconstructed. Amongst an intriguing list of desserts, deep-fried aubergines coated in cinnamon and sugar, bound with ricotta cheese and candied fruit and served with a white chocolate sauce, takes pole position.

Directions: City centre, opposite Holywell Music Room, between Hertford & New College

OXFORD, **Bistro 20**

NEW

Situated in the vaults under the Randolph hotel, but surprisingly bright with sunshine yellow, aquamarines, and deep reds. Brasserie-style menu offers carpaccio of tuna, saffron risotto, great salmon fishcake, ribeye, spicy braised lamb, and side dishes of mash, spinach, chips and salads. One to watch.

Directions: Telephone for directions

Smoking: No smoking in dining room
Accommodation: 10 en suite ★ ★

4/5 Bath Place Holywell Street
OX1 3SU
Map 4: SP50
Tel: 01865 791812
Fax: 01865 791834
Chef: Pasquale Amico
Owners: Kathleen & Yolanda Fawsitt
Cost: Alc £35, set-price L £19.50/D £25. H/wine £11.95
Times: Noon-2pm. Closed Sun, Mon
Additional: Children 8+; ◔ menu
Seats: 30
Smoking: No smoking in dining room; Air conditioning
Accommodation: 10 en suite

20 Magdalen Street OX1 3AE
Map 4: SP50
Tel: 01865 246555
Fax: 01865 204333
Telephone for further details

OXFORD,

Cotswold Lodge Hotel ✿

66a Banbury Road OX2 6JP
Map 4: SP50
Tel: 01865 512121
Fax: 01865 512490
Telephone for further details

Family-run hotel, popular for conferences and banquets. The traditional-style restaurant offers a menu that leans towards modern trends with good quality ingredients such as scallops and calves' liver carefully put together.

Directions: Take A4165 (Banbury Road) off A40 ring road, hotel 1.5m on left

OXFORD, **Lemon Tree** ✿✿

268 Woodstock Road OX2 7NW
Map 4: SP50
Tel/Fax: 01865 311936
Chef: Robert Ingleston
Owner: Clinton Pugh
Cost: *Alc* £30. ☺ H/wine £9.95
Times: Noon-11pm. Closed 24-26 Dec
Additional: Children welcome; ✿ dishes
Seats: 90

What a refreshing place; the perfect setting to recapture that Mediterranean holiday atmosphere. The restaurant is owned by interior designers so there are lots of fascinating, quirky ideas: huge mirrors, ochre colour-washed walls, large abstract paintings in earthy colours, twisted metal light fittings, plus lots of plants give a bright, airy feel. The place opens at 11am for coffee, noon for food, and the menu is served straight through till 11pm. We were impressed with the cooking. Good olives and delicious breads really set the standard. Thai prawns were large, tender and spicy, foie gras and duck confit, served simply with preserved baby figs, was very well made. A main course of confit of knuckle of lamb proved to be a good rustic dish, beautifully tender served on a borlotti bean 'stew', with small dice of chorizo and a lightly creamy sauce with cider, rosemary and garlic, and its counterpart, a blue nose bass was good, well-timed and served on Puy lentils with roasted cherry tomatoes, red onions and balsamic dressing. Dessert was an intriguing pineapple Tatin with good pastry and decent vanilla ice cream. The wine list represents the New World and Europe with most bottles under £20.

Directions: From M40 J8 take A40 towards Oxford. At 3rd rdbt turn L into Woodstock Rd. Restaurant 0.75m on L

OXFORD, **Liaison** ✿

29 Castle Street OX1 1LJ
Map 4: SP50
Tel: 01865 242944/251481
Telephone for further details

At the back of Westgate shopping centre, Liaison keeps the oriental culinary flag flying. The lunchtime dim sum menu is recommended. In the evening a five-page menu offers some adventurous choices. Noted for good quality.

Directions: Behind main shopping centre

OXFORD, **Munchy Munchy**

Hand-painted murals adorn this long, narrow restaurant with its plain wooden floors, tables and chairs. The cooking style is a remarkable interpretation South East Asian and Indonesian cuisines.

Smoking: No-smoking area; No pipes & cigars

Directions: W of city centre, between Nuffield College & the railway station

6 Park End Street OX1 1HH
Map 4: SP50
Tel: 01865 245710
Fax: 01865 792880
Cost: *Alc* £15
Times: Noon-1.50pm/5.30-9.45pm. Closed Sun, Mon, 3 wks Aug/Sep, 3 wks Dec/Jan

OXFORD, **Le Petit Blanc**

71-72 Walton Street OX2 6AG
Map 4: SP50
Tel: 01865 510999
Fax: 01865 510700
Chef: Stuart Lyall
Owner: Raymond Blanc
Cost: *Alc* £25, set-price L & D £15 (6-7pm only). ☺ H/wine £9.95
Times: Noon-2.45pm (Sat, Sun till 3.30pm)/6-10.45pm (Sun 6.30-10pm). Closed 25 Dec
Additional: Children welcome; ☙ dishes
Seats: 120. Private dining room 18
Smoking: No-smoking area; Air conditioning

Design by Terence Conran, food by Raymond Blanc. The bright, open-plan eating house is stylish, with a punchy, good-value modern menu (including one for children, and afternoon tea). No wonder the place is packed most days with punters as impressed by the high standards of the service as by the cooking. Classics such as Mediterranean fish soup with rouille and ragout of Burgundy snails with garlic and parsley butter sit side by side with the more upbeat twice-baked goats' cheese with thyme soufflé and piperade on the list of starters. Main courses range from peppered Aberdeen Angus pavé rump steak with béarnaise sauce to slow-roast pork belly with egg noodles, spring onion and coriander broth. Fish also features, whether moules marinière (with frites, of course) or grilled brill with pommes Pont Neuf and sauce gribiche. Side orders of chips are a must.

Directions: From centre of Oxford, N up St Giles, L down Little Clarendon St and R at end into Walton Street

OXFORD, **The Randolph**

Landmark hotel with splendid views over the city from Spires Restaurant. Expect the likes of chargrilled guinea fowl with leek risotto cakes, and baked halibut on saffron mash.

Additional: Bar food; Sunday L; Children welcome; ☙ dishes
Smoking: No smoking in dining room
Accommodation: 119 en suite ★ ★ ★ ★

Directions: At corner of Beaumont St and Magdalen St, opposite Ashmolean Museum

Beaumont Street OX1 2LN
Map 4: SP50
Tel: 01865 247481
Fax: 01865 791678
Cost: *Alc* £27, set-price L £10 (2 courses)/D £27. H/wine £15
Times: 12.30-2pm/7-9.45pm

SHIPTON-UNDER-WYCHWOOD,
Lamb Inn

Lovely 17th-century Cotswold pub just off the main street. The menu ranges from game terrine with plum chutney, and smoked haddock tartlets to roast leg of lamb, duck with cranberry and ginger, and steak with peppercorn sauce.

Smoking: No smoking in dining room
Accommodation: 5 en suite

Directions: In village centre

High Street OX7 6DQ
Map 4: SP21
Tel: 01993 830465
Fax: 01993 832025
Cost: Alc £25. ☺ H/wine £9.95
Times: Noon-2pm/7-9.15pm
Additional: Bar food; Sunday L; Children welcome

SHIPTON-UNDER-WYCHWOOD,
Shaven Crown Hotel

Historic former hospice dating from the 14th century. A good range of traditional food is served in both the bar and the restaurant. Home-made soups and pies are particular favourites, and there are plain grilled meat and fish dishes for the health conscious.

Directions: On A361, village centre, 4 miles N of Burford

OX7 6BA
Map 4: SP21
Tel: 01993 830330
Fax: 01993 832136
Telephone for further details

STADHAMPTON, The Crazy Bear

Bear Lane OX44 7UR
Map 4: SU69
Tel: 01865 890714
Fax: 01865 400481
Chef: Graham Beltcher
Owner: Jason Hunt
Cost: Alc £22, set-price L £14.95. ☺ H/wine £ 11.95
Times: Noon-3pm/6-10pm
Additional: Bar food; Sunday L; Children welcome; ❹ dishes
Seats: 50. Private dining room 22
Smoking: No pipes & cigars; Air conditioning
Accommodation: 10 en suite

From the outside looks like your average 16th-century pub, the flamboyance of the interior tells a different story. The bar boasts draught champagne (accompanied by fresh Galway oysters if you like), exotically flavoured home-made vodkas and a selection of world beers along with the real ales. In the kitchen however, the commitment to good food is serious, as we discovered with our super shallot tarte Tatin topped with a generous slice of perfectly seared foie gras, and the well-conceived dish of calves' liver with white truffle mash and robust Pommery mustard sauce. Other choices from a menu that mixes both contemporary and classic dishes might include provençale fish soup, tournedos Rossini, duck confit with honey-roast parsnips, shallot cake and thyme jus, and seared tuna with tempura vegetables. Chocolate crème brûlée, sticky toffee pudding and chocolate marquise typify the desserts.

Directions: From London leave M40/J7, L onto A329, continue for 5 miles, L after petrol station & L again into Bear Lane

STEEPLE ASTON,
The Holt Hotel ✿

OX6 3QQ
Map 4: SP42
Tel: 01869 340259
Fax: 01869 340865
Cost: *Alc* £26, set-price D £22. ☺
H/wine £10.50
Times: Noon-2pm/7-9.30pm
Additional: Bar food; Sunday L;
Children welcome
Smoking: No smoking in dining room
Accommodation: 82 en suite ★ ★ ★

Formerly Hopcrofts Holt. Carefully prepared dishes, such as chicken liver parfait, and steamed fillet of sea bass with quails' eggs and coriander butter sauce, are offered from a short set-price dinner menu.

Directions: Follow A426 through Kidlington towards Deddington. Hotel on R at traffic lights

STONOR, **Stonor Arms** ✿✿

Nr Henley-on-Thames RG9 6HE
Map 4: SU78
Tel: 01491 638866
Fax: 01491 638863
Chef: Steven Morris
Cost: *Alc* £30, set-price L £21. ☺
H/wine £11.50
Times: Noon-2pm/7-9.30pm
Additional: Bar food; Sunday L;
Children 12+; ❹ dishes
Seats: 50. Private dining room 24
Smoking: No smoking in dining room
Accommodation: 10 en suite ★ ★ ★

Picturesque scenery and a pretty village set the scene for this small hotel with plenty of historic charm. Enjoy a drink in Blades – the informal bar filled with rowing memorabilia – before settling down to a meal in the elegant dining room or airy conservatory restaurant overlooking the walled garden. The well-presented menus list an extensive choice. On a bright spring day we were tempted by flavours of the Mediterranean in a dish of marinated peppers and warm goats' cheese. Pan-fried chicken followed, topped with deep-fried carrot slivers and served with a dark fruity butter sauce. Desserts include passion fruit tart, chocolate and hazelnut soufflé, and an excellent choice of regional cheeses.

Directions: In centre of village

THAME, **Spread Eagle Hotel** ❀

A local tradition since the 1920s. Food styles may have changed, but the original recipe for Chocolate Mud remains on the menu. There are more sophisticated choices, but steak and kidney pie was declared a winner on a recent inspection.

Smoking: No-smoking area; Air conditioning
Accommodation: 33 en suite ★ ★ ★

Directions: M40/J6 from S (J8 from N). Town centre on A418 Oxford to Aylesbury road

Cornmarket OX9 2BW
Map 4: SP70
Tel: 01844 213661
Fax: 01844 261380
Cost: *Alc* £23.95, set-price L £17.95/D £21.95. ☺ H/wine £10.35
Times: 12.30-2pm/7-10pm (9pm Sun). Closed 28-30 Dec, Bh Mon L
Additional: Bar food; Sunday L; Children welcome; ♨ dishes

WALLINGFORD,
Shillingford Bridge Hotel ❀

Parts of the hotel date from the 1700s and the beamed restaurant offers views of the Thames. Peppered medallions of monkfish and rack of lamb with lavender crust are typical fare.

Smoking: No smoking in dining room
Accommodation: 42 en suite ★ ★ ★

Directions: From S – M4 J12, A340 through Wallingford towards Oxford. Hotel 1.5 miles on L

Shillingford OX10 8LZ
Map 4: SU68
Tel: 01865 858567
Fax: 01865 858636
Cost: *Alc* £20, set-price L & D £17.95. ☺ H/wine £8.85
Times: 12.30-2pm/7.30-10pm
Additional: Bar food; Sunday L; Children welcome; ♨ dishes

WALLINGFORD, **Springs Hotel** ❀❀

Victorian Tudor-style country house, set in 30 acres of gardens, edged by woods. The restaurant looks out onto the swan-and-duck-filled lake. The clubhouse, adjacent to the main hotel, offers light meals and snacks, while the Lakeside Restaurant provides a set-menu plus an evening *carte* . Good gazpacho came with pieces of deep fried basil leaf, then we sampled halibut with a fresh five spice coating and served with plenty of cucumber spaghetti plus a carrot and ginger sauce, but of particular note was an excellent spinach salad, that came with an olive oil dressing and Parmesan shavings. Our nougatine parfait had all the right ingredients: almonds, glacé cherry, honey and pistachios, and was not too sweet. A longish wine list includes twelve half-bottles, all good quality. Staff are attentive and friendly.

Directions: From A4130 to Wallingford take A4074 (Reading); over first roundabout, turn R on B4009 (Goring). Hotel 1 mile on R

Wallingford Road North Stoke OX10 6BE
Map 4: SU68
Tel: 01491 836687
Fax: 01491 836877
Chef: Stephen Roberts
Cost: *Alc* £31, set-price L £15.50/D £27 (4 courses). H/wine £12
Times: 12.15-2pm/7-9.30pm
Additional: Sunday L; Children welcome; ♨ dishes
Seats: 60. Private dining room 35
Smoking: No smoking in dining room
Accommodation: 31 en suite ★ ★ ★

WESTON-ON-THE-GREEN,
Weston Manor Hotel ❀

A baronial hall with linen-fold panels and minstrels' gallery provides the setting for some traditional dishes with a modern twist at this impressive manor house hotel.

Smoking: No smoking in dining room
Accommodation: 36 en suite ★ ★ ★

Directions: 2 mins from M40 J9 via A34 (Oxford) to Weston-on-the-Green; hotel in village centre

Oxford OX6 8QL
Map 4: SP51
Tel: 01869 350621
Fax: 01869 350901
Cost: *Alc* £35
Times: Noon-1.45pm/7-9.30pm. Closed L Sat & Sun
Additional: Bar food; Children welcome; ♨ dishes

WOODSTOCK,

The Bear Hotel

Park Street OX20 1SZ
Map 4: SP41
Tel: 01993 811511
Fax: 01993 813380
Chef: Simon Bull
Owner: Forte Hotels
Cost: *Alc* D £23. ☺ H/wine £15
Times: 12.30-2pm/7-10pm
Additional: Bar food L; Sunday L;
Children welcome; ❹ dishes
Seats: 80. Private dining room 30
Smoking: No smoking in dining room
Accommodation: 44 en suite ★ ★ ★

Directions: Town centre, facing the
market square

Ancient inn with warm hospitality. The exposed stone walls
and heavy beamed ceilings of this 13th-century coaching inn
are as much a part of the experience of eating at the Bear
Hotel as the food. We visited on a cold evening in February
when crackling log fires provided extra comfort. The lengthy
carte offers the likes of game terrine with truffles and orange
marmalade and pan-fried breast of chicken stuffed with crab
meat, prawns and coriander. We, however, chose finely sliced
duck rillettes served with a pile of corn salad, good buttery
brioche, and a decent fig chutney, then smoked haddock served
on top of a rich kedgeree with creamy mustard sauce.

WOODSTOCK, **Chef Imperial**

22 High Street OX20 1TF
Map 4: SP41
Tel: 01993 813593
Fax: 01993 813591
Cost: *Alc* £16, set-price L £5.95/D
£15. ☺ H/wine £8.50
Times: Noon-2.25pm/6-11.55pm.
Closed 25, 26 Dec

*Shop-fronted Chinese restaurant with a stylish interior in bright
yellow and blue. There is a vast carte of Peking and Szechuan
dishes, plus set meals for two, three, four or eight.*

Additional: Sunday L; Children welcome; ❹ dishes
Smoking: No-smoking area; Air conditioning

Directions: From Oxford take A44, following signs
Woodstock/Blenheim Palace. Restaurant in centre of Woodstock
by back entrance to Palace

WOODSTOCK,

Feathers Hotel

Market Street OX20 1SX
Map 4: SP41
Tel: 01993 812291
Fax: 01993 813158
Chef: Mark Treasure
Owners: Messrs Leeman, Lowe &
Malin
Cost: *Alc* £45, set-price L £21/D £44
(6 courses tasting). H/wine £11.95
Times: 12.30-2.15pm/7.30-9.15pm.
Closed D 25 Dec (ex residents)
Additional: Bar food L (D Mon-Fri
only); Sunday L; Children welcome;
❹ dishes

*The feathers here belong to the garrulous African Grey parrot
that stands sentry at the reception of this easygoing country-
town hotel.* The bird offers plausible imitations of meowing
cats, ringing phones and reversing trucks in a repertoire that is
almost as extensive as that of chef Mark Treasure and his
team. In no sense is this copycat cooking though. The
judgement, technical skill and understanding of flavours has
few peers and our inspectors have been impressed by the sheer
consistency of the quality. The menu is wide-ranging and bang
up to date with the emphasis on the use of top-notch
ingredients. Most striking is the lightness of touch, with rarely
a flavour out of place. A summer menu seemed perfectly

Feathers Hotel

Seats: 60. Private dining room 20
Smoking: No smoking in dining room;
Air conditioning
Accommodation: 22 en suite ★ ★ ★

pitched for a sultry June evening with an excellent demi-tasse of gazpacho the ideal *amuse-gueule*. A starter of scallops (diver caught, of course) was as saline sweet as one could hope for with an unobtrusive purée of haricots blanc and salsify the accompaniments. Fish is something of a strength but the same care is evident in the weightier meat dishes such as a punchy best end of lamb with minted peas, crushed new potatoes and sun-dried tomatoes, or saddle of rabbit pot-roasted with mild mushrooms, shallot mousseline and pancetta. The dessert *carte* is along familiar lines (brûlées, chocolate marquise, parfait etc.) but the execution sets it apart with a pear and almond tart with honey ice cream being described by one inspector as a benchmark example.

Directions: Town centre

WOODSTOCK,
Kings Head Inn ✿

Chapel Hill Wootton OX20 1DX
Map 4: SP41
Tel/Fax: 01993 811340
Cost: *Alc* £27.50. ☺ H/wine £10.95
Times: Noon-2pm/7-9pm. Closed D Sun
Additional: Sunday L; Children 12+ at D; 🍴 dishes
Smoking: No smoking in dining room
Accommodation: 3 en suite

Pretty inn with a village setting. Quality ingredients are imaginatively employed in a style described as New World/Mediterranean fusion, ably demonstrated by a richly flavoured fish stew.

Directions: On A44 2 miles N of Woodstock turn R to Wootton. The Inn is located near church on Chapel Hill

RUTLAND

OAKHAM, **Barnsdale Lodge**

The Avenue
Rutland Water LE15 8AH
Map 8: SK80
Tel: 01572 724678
Fax: 01572 724961
Cost: Set-price L £16.95. ☺ H/wine
£9.95
Times: Noon-2.15pm/7-9.45pm
Additional: Bar food; Sunday L;
Children welcome; ✤ dishes
Smoking: No-smoking area; No pipes
& cigars
Accommodation: 45 en suite ★ ★ ★

Directions: Telephone for directions

*Dine in a series of intimate Edwardian rooms within a 17th-century
farmhouse. The carte of predominantly classical British dishes is
based on high quality local produce. Good vegetarian and, for once,
diabetic choices.*

OAKHAM, **The Boultons Hotel**

*Next to the Rutland Museum in quiet residential surroundings, this is
a much extended cottage. A wide array of modern British cooking
appeals.*

4 Catmose Street LE15 6HW
Map 8: SK80
Tel: 01572 722844
Fax: 01572 724473
Telephone for further details

Directions: Town centre

OAKHAM, **Hambleton Hall** ✤✤✤✤

Hambleton LE15 8TH
Map 8: SK80
Tel: 01572 756991
Fax: 01572 724721
Chef: Aaron Patterson
Owners: Tim & Stefa Hart
Cost: *Alc* £55, set-price L £14.50/D
£35. H/wine £16
Times: Noon-2.30pm/7.30-9.30pm
Additional: Sunday L; Children
welcome; ✤ dishes
Smoking: No smoking in dining room

The epitome of an English country house hotel. Surrounded
by wonderfully landscaped gardens and set against the
backdrop of Rutland Water, the setting is idyllic. Individually
decorated bedrooms are an exercise in taste and style and owe
much to the initial imput of designer Nina Campbell, although
proprietors Tim and Stefa Hart have stamped their own
personalities on the house. Aaron Patterson continues to run
the kitchens, offering a truly seasonal menu based on the best
raw materials and considerable talent. Indeed, our inspector

writes the sort of report that brooks no argument. Canapés in the lounge were inventive, especially a tiny Florentine tartlet of spinach topped with a quail egg, and there was a notable mini beef kebab, then an *amuse-bouche* – a chilled essence of tomato so vibrantly flavoured and finished with just the right amount of acidity. A first-course red mullet niçoise was basically a simple construction but first-class quality, ditto the breast of Goosnargh duck, honey roasted, set on some onion marmalade with just the hint of orange, and served with a confit of the leg in a tiny tartlet 'pie' topped with hollandaise. An accompanying sauce was light but well-flavoured with the subtle hint of ginger. Dessert was an exemplary prune and passion fruit soufflé and, even after all that the chessboard proved irresistible – about twenty in tip-top condition (and staff knew them all). And just as we thought it was all over, a vast array of outstanding petits fours came with coffee. The wine list is a tour de force and requires time to do justice to it. However, 'Wines of the Moment', three pages of some 30 wines that are drinking particularly well, are worth checking out – both range of choice and price are sound. Also, the sommelier's advice is worth taking.

Seats: 60. Private dining room 20; Jacket & tie preferred
Accommodation: 15 en suite ★ ★ ★

Directions: From A1 – A606 Oakham. After 8.4 miles take turning signed Hambleton/Egleton only. Hotel on R in main street of Hambleton village

OAKHAM, Whipper-in Hotel

A 17th-century coaching inn set in the market square. An interesting choice of modern British dishes ranges from Rutland sausage and mash to sea bass with lime and ginger butter.

Smoking: No smoking in dining room
Accommodation: 24 en suite ★ ★ ★

Directions: In the market place, town centre

The Market Place LE15 6DT
Map 8: SK80
Tel: 01572 756971
Fax: 01572 757759
Cost: *Alc* £22, set-price L £12.95/D £18.50. ☺ H/wine £9.95
Additional: Bar food; Sunday L; Children welcome; ♠ dishes

STRETTON, Ram Jam Inn

Landmark pit stop on the A1. It has an informal, stylish ambience which distinguishes it from other places along the route. Very much like a café bar and bistro with rooms.

Directions: From A1 exit Oakham B668, follow signs to inn

Great North Road LE15 7QX
Map 8: SK91
Tel: 01780 410776
Fax: 01780 410361
Telephone for further details

UPPINGHAM,
Lake Isle Hotel

High Street East LE15 9PZ
Map 4: SP89

Restaurant located in a row of original shops in a pretty market town. It's an informal rustic room with wood-panelling, dark green blinds, pine tables, chairs and a period piece Welsh dresser. Set-menus at lunch (2 or 3 courses) and dinner (3 or 5 courses) are written in English but the dishes have strong French accents. An *amuse-bouche* of salmon and sole terrine served with a lime and spinach sauce was an even combination of flavours, but the highlight of our meal was a warm breast of pigeon, served sliced and wrapped in bacon in a ham mousseline . However, a breast of Barbary duck was carefully cooked, well-matched by apple and prunes flavoured with Armagnac. The straightforward desserts are good. Coffee comes with home-made chocolates and mint.

Directions: Town centre, on foot via Reeves Yard; via Queen Street by car

Lake Isle Hotel

Tel/Fax: 01572 822951
Chef: David Whitfield
Owners: David & Claire Whitfield
Cost: Set-price L £10.50 (2 courses)/D £23.50. ☺ H/wine £9.75
Times: 12.30pm-1.45pm/7.30pm-9.30pm. Closed L Mon
Additional: Sunday L; Children welcome; ◑ dishes
Seats: 40. Private dining room 10
Smoking: No smoking in dining room; Air conditioning
Accommodation: 12 en suite ★★

SHROPSHIRE

CHURCH STRETTON,
Stretton Hall Hotel

NEW

Imposing Georgian residence, where the restaurant has been recreated in striking yellows. Typical dishes are ravioli of lobster, and tuna steak au poivre with lemongrass risotto.

Smoking: No smoking in dining room
Accommodation: 12 en suite ★★★

Directions: Off A49 Ludlow to Shrewsbury road, in village of Stretton

All Stretton SY6 6HG
Map 7: SO49
Tel: 01694 723224
Fax: 01694 724365
Cost: *Alc* £19, set-price L & D £15.50. ☺ H/wine £9.95
Times: 12.30-2pm/7-9.30pm
Additional: Bar food; Sunday L; Children welcome; ◑ dishes

CHURCH STRETTON,
The Studio

NEW

Small High Street restaurant, originally an old coaching inn. Classical European cooking includes smoked haddock fishcakes with horseradish cream and warm Dutch apple tart (a speciality of the Dutch chef/patron).

SY6 6BV
Map 7: SO49
Tel/Fax: 01694 722672
Cost: *Alc* £20, set-price L £10.95. ☺ H/wine £8.50
Times: Noon-2pm/7-10pm. Closed D Sun, all Mon, Xmas
Additional: Sunday L; Children welcome; ◑ dishes
Smoking: No smoking in dining room

Directions: From A49 into village. L at crossroads into High Street

CLEOBURY MORTIMER,
Redfern Hotel

*Delightful, friendly small hotel with some tempting local recipes
such as Shropshire chicken (stuffed with Shropshire Blue cheese)
and rabbit and liver casserole in Murphy's Ale. Home-cured hams
hang from the beams of the relaxed bistro-style restaurant.*

Accommodation: 11 en suite ★ ★ ★

Directions: On A4117 midway between Kidderminster and
Ludlow. For Kidderminster leave at M5/J3

DY14 8AA
Map 7: SO67
Tel: 01299 270395
Fax: 01299 271011
Cost: *Alc* £18.50, set-price L £5.55/D
£17.50 (5 courses). ☺ H/wine £7.50
Times: Noon-2pm/7.30-9.30pm
Additional: Bar food L; Sunday L;
Children 7+; ♨ dishes
Smoking: No smoking in dining room

DORRINGTON,
Country Friends Restaurant

*Ancient building, replete with old beams, antique furniture
and an inglenook fireplace.* For the last 15 years this has been
home to Charles Whittaker's sound modern British cooking.
The menu (priced for two, three or four courses) offers half-a-
dozen choices at each stage beginning with the likes of tomato,
red pepper and pesto soufflé, or confit of duck, then breast of
Trelough duck with oriental sauce, or venison on celeriac purée
with sloe gin sauce, and ricotta and spinach gnocchi with sage
and walnut pesto. From a list of desserts that included
chocolate tart with pistachio ice cream, and baked lemon
cream, we enjoyed a beautiful queen of puddings. The good list
of dessert wines is also worthy of note.

Directions: On A49 in centre of village, 6 miles S of
Shrewsbury

Shrewsbury SY5 7JD
Map 7: SJ40
Tel: 01743 718707
Chef: Charles Whittaker
Owners: Charles & Pauline Whittaker
Cost: Set-price L £27 (2 courses)/D
£29.50. H/wine £11.95
Times: Noon-2pm/7-9pm. Closed
Sun, Mon, 2 wks mid July
Additional: Bar food L; Children
welcome; ♨ dishes
Seats: 40
Smoking: No smoking in dining room
Accommodation: 3 rooms

LUDLOW, The Cookhouse

*Ultra-modern roadside inn yet with the look of the farmhouse
it once was.* There's a stylish café open for breakfast and
lunches – bangers and mash, steak and kidney pie, BLT
baguette – that transmogrifies into a bistro after the 7pm
watershed, when you can expect Stilton mousse with a berry
sauce, fricassée of chicken with saffron rice, or Cajun-spiced
salmon with honey and orange dressing, and rhubarb and
apple crumble with ice cream. Alongside all this is a restaurant
serving an in-and-out lunch menu (for those who need to be
fed and watered within an hour) and an evening *carte* that
takes in Mediterranean fish soup, sautéed breast of corn-fed
chicken in white wine sauce with wild mushrooms, and lemon
tart. The kitchen might not stray into uncharted territory, but
what it does it does well, from grilling (halibut, with chive
butter sauce) to roasting (pork fillet, stuffed with prunes).
Vegetarians are not overlooked even at Sunday lunchtime,
when roasted pepper tart with spring vegetables might be one
of the options, and wine drinkers will find a good variety of
styles on the short list.

Bromfield SY7 8LR
Map 7: SO57
Tel: 01584 856565
Fax: 01584 856661
Chef: Peter Gartell
Owner: Norman Swallow
Cost: *Alc* £22, set-price L £9.50 (2
courses)/D £14.75. ☺ H/wine £8.75
Times: 12.30-2.15pm/7.30-9.45pm.
Closed D 25 Dec
Additional: Bar food L; Sunday L;
Children welcome; ♨ dishes
Seats: 40. Private dining room 40
Smoking: No-smoking area; No pipes
& cigars

Directions: 1 mile north of Ludlow on
A49 to Shrewsbury

LUDLOW, The Courtyard **NEW**

*A warm, jolly restaurant with dark pine furniture and sandy/ochre
Paul Klee prints. The modern British menu includes 'excellent' fillet*

Quality Square SY8 1AR
Map 7: SO57
Tel: 01584 878080
Cost: *Alc* £19. ☺ H/wine £9.50

of brill with mussels, leeks and saffron sauce, and beef fillet with Shropshire blue cheese and bubble-and-squeak. Finish off with a brilliant rice pudding.

Smoking: No-smoking area; No pipes & cigars; Air conditioning

Directions: Town centre, off Market Place

LUDLOW, Dinham Hall ❀❀ MAR 2010

A lovely old house set in an attractive garden just opposite Ludlow Castle. Large floral displays, pastel colours and atmospheric gas lighting create a suitable setting for classical French cooking. Four course dinners start with home-made soup such as spicy lamb and vegetable. Then home-made terrine of foie gras on a bed of red onion and fig marmalade, followed by pan-fried beef fillet with sarladaise potatoes and sweet peppercorn sauce. The French flavour also appears in the dessert list; choose from strawberry and Grand Marnier crème brûlée, apple tarte Tatin and hot chocolate pudding with aniseed ice cream and pistachio sauce.

Directions: Town centre, off Market Place

Times: L only, noon-2pm. Closed Sun, 25, 26 Dec, 1 Jan, May Day Bh
Additional: Bar food L; Children welcome; dishes

By The Castle SY8 1EJ
Map 7: SO57
Tel: 01584 876464
Fax: 01584 876019
Chef: Oliver Bossut
Owner: Mr J P Mifsud
Cost: *Alc* £22, set-price L & D £22. ☺ H/wine £11.50
Times: Noon-2pm/7-9pm
Additional: Bar food L; Sunday L; Children welcome; dishes.
Seats: 30. Private dining room 26
Smoking: No smoking in dining room
Accommodation: 14 en suite ★★★

LUDLOW, The Merchant House ❀❀❀

62 Lower Corve Street SY8 1DU
Map 7: SO57
Tel: 01584 875438
Fax: 01584 876927
Chef: Shaun Hill
Owners: Shaun & Anja Hill
Cost: Set-price D £28.50. H/wine £13.50
Times: 12.30-2pm (Fri-Sat only)/7-9.30pm. Closed Sun, Mon
Seats: 22
Smoking: No smoking in dining room

Directions: Town centre, next to Unicorn pub

It would be unfair to call Merchant House a one-man-band, (wife Anja runs front of house) but Sean Hill's solo style in the kitchen does dictate the tone for the whole operation. As it turns out this is undoubtedly a good thing. One side effect is a guaranteed warm welcome for our inspectors (it means an interruption to the washing-up), but the main beneficiary is the cooking which is necessarily no-nonsense and concentrates on the essentials rather than the frivolous. There are rarely more than three or four components to any dish and it is the flavours of the main elements that are encouraged to shine through. Superbly timed scallops for instance with a judiciously spiced lentil and coriander sauce or similarly well-judged monkfish with mustard and cucumber are staples of the menu and typical of the style. Hill is adept at obtaining every nuance of flavour, as with a squab pigeon served with wild mushrooms and an intense jus and the crunchiest of spring greens. Desserts perhaps sum up the style best: apricot tart, for instance, may sound pretty prosaic, but in Mr Hill's hands we are talking about 'the best fruit tart I've ever come across'. All in all a very special place, and in is simplicity and lack of pretension an example to others.

LUDLOW, Mr Underhills

Dinham Weir SY8 1EH
Map 7: SO57
Tel: 01584 874431
Chef: Christopher Bradley
Owners: Christopher & Judy Bradley
Cost: Set D £25. H/wine £12.50
Times: L by arrangement/7.15-
8.30pm. Closed Tue
Additional: dishes by arrangement
Seats: 24. Private parties 24
Smoking: No smoking in dining room
Accommodation: 6 en suite

Directions: From Castle Square: with
castle in front turn immediately L,
proceed round castle, turn R before
bridge, restaurant on L

Reminiscent of a French auberge, tucked under Ludlow Castle with the river right outside. The long, low dining-room is simple in style and hung with modern prints with French windows opening onto the garden, terrace and weir. Dinner is a no-choice set-menu until dessert, but guests are asked in advance for dislikes and special needs. This is a tried-and-tested formula that works well, maximising freshness and focusing the kitchen. Menu balance is spot-on and, the night of our visit, a starter of first-rate marinated salmon with a bright, fresh tasting gazpacho was a perfect foil to a main course of delicate, superbly flavoured braised duck in a filo parcel served with top-notch vegetables that took in excellent French beans and celeriac purée. Both cheese and dessert are offered - a hard choice when the lemon tart comes with 'loads of citrus flavour' and superb pastry. The wine list is wide ranging with sensible mark ups.

LUDLOW, Oaks Restaurant

17 Corve Street SY8 1DA
Map 7: SO57
Tel: 01584 872325
Fax: 01568 874024

Chef/Owner: Kenneth Adams
Cost: Set-price L £24 (Fri & Sat only)/D £24. H/wine £12.90
Times: Noon-1.30pm (Fri & Sat only)/7-9.30pm. Closed Sun, Mon, 1 wk spring, 1-2 wks autumn
Additional: Children 8+
Seats: 30. Private dining room 14
Smoking: No smoking in dining room; Air conditioning

Directions: Town centre, bottom of hill below Feathers Hotel

Civility as well as comfort sums up this restaurant in a former 17th-century coaching inn. Original features such as the oak panelling from which the restaurant derives its name, the warm tones of the wood complemented by gold brocade-covered chairs and buttermilk table cloths, forms a backdrop to Ken Adams sharply observed interpretation of modern English cooking. He's an industrious chef, growing his own vegetables and herbs, smoking his own seafood, and sourcing raw materials with incredible care, using local small producers and organic farms where possible; all suppliers are listed on the menu. This translates as both classic combinations and more cutting edge ideas handled with a sense of balance, restraint and skill. Ravioli of crab and Dover sole, minced fennel and sauce vierge combine in a stunning first-course. Breast of Trelough duck is poached then grilled and teamed with celeriac and carrot 'julien' and a wild mushroom sauce, or a sautéed cannon of lamb is accompanied by tomato and basil risotto, grilled Mediterranean vegetables and artichoke tortellini. Prime condition, unpasteurised British and French cheeses come with superb 'moreish' bread. Desserts are stunning, whether an unusual white pepper crème brûlée with pink grapefruit salad on a strawberry syrup, to a more recognisably reworking of an English classic – warm rhubarb and ginger pudding with marmalade ice cream. If you feel like a change from coffee, the list of Russian speciality teas is worth exploring. The wine list blends value-for-money with some considered choices that are varied and interesting.

Signature dishes: sauté loin of rabbit on tarragon mayonnaise with beetroot terrine and warm pistachio dressing; breast of squab pigeon stuffed with foie gras on potato rösti with grenadine apple and Hereford cider brandy sauce; roast fillet of sea bass on tomato confit with reduced tomato consommé and watercress tortellini.

LUDLOW, **Overton Grange**

Hereford Road SY8 4AD
Map 7: SO57
Tel: 01584 873500
Fax: 01584 873524
Chef: Claude Bosi
Owner: Grange Hotels Ltd
Cost: *Alc* £25, set-price L £20/D £30. ☺ H/wine £12
Times: 12.30-2.30pm/7.15-9.30pm. Closed L Sat, 9-21 Jan
Additional: Sunday L; Children welcome; ❹ dishes
Seats: 35. Private dining room 20
Smoking: No smoking in the dining room
Accommodation: 14 en suite ★ ★ ★

Directions: On B4361 off A49

Overton Grange has all the relaxing atmosphere and appeal of a country-house hotel, which is exactly what it is. Sit amid the oak panelling in the restaurant and brush up your French with the menu (although subtitles are provided for those who'd rather not). 'Classical modern French cuisine' is the self-described style, so expect to find morel velouté with asparagus ravioli and Parmesan, then saddle of lamb with ginger, salsify and horseradish. Excellent breads, including treacle, and an appetiser of perhaps squid with chilli set the scene for starters of Aberdeen Angus steak tartare or terrine of foie gras with artichoke, baby spinach and pears. Berkshire pork chop studded with truffle might follow, in a butter-thickened stock along with perfectly cooked lyonnaise potatoes, baby leeks and onion confit, or lobster, roasted with butter and served with peas. Cheeses, both British and French, come with home-made chutney bread or biscuits, and fruit might appear among desserts in the shape of strawberries with black pepper ice cream, or raspberries made into a classic tart, with chocolate mille-feuille for the sweet of tooth. Service is enthusiastic, and even Uruguay and Canada are represented on the round-the-world wine list.

Signature dishes: langoustines dusted with a light Thai curry with celeriac and Granny Smiths; suckling pig scented with orange; avocado soufflé with chocolate ice cream.

LUDLOW, **Roebuck Inn Restaurant**

Popular village inn with convivial interior, friendly service and good food. Fresh fish and local game stand out on a tempting seasonal menu, supplemented by daily specials such as grilled Cornish lobster with garlic and shallot butter.

Accommodation: 3 en suite

Directions: Just off A49, halfway btw Ludlow & Leominster

Brimfield SY8 4NE
Map 7: SO57
Tel: 01584 711230
Fax: 01584 711654
Cost: *Alc* £20. ☺ H/wine £9.95
Times: Noon-2.30pm/7-9.30pm
Additional: Bar food; Sunday L; Children welcome; ❹ dishes
Smoking: No smoking in dining room

MARKET DRAYTON, **Goldstone Hall**

Goldstone TF9 2NA
Map 7: SJ63
Tel: 01630 661202
Fax: 01630 661585
Chef: Carl Fitzgerald-Bloomer
Owners: John Cushing, Helen Ward
Cost: *Alc* £25, set-price L £15. ☺
H/wine £9.65
Times: Noon-2.30pm/7.30-10.30pm
Additional: Sunday L; Children
welcome; 🌢 dishes
Seats: 40. Private dining room 40
Smoking: No cigars & pipes
Accommodation: 8 en suite ★ ★ ★

Directions: From A529, 4 miles S of
Market Drayton, follow signs for
Goldstone Hall Gardens

A charming old house with walled gardens and views over the countryside. There's a billiard room for a leisurely after-dinner game, a croquet lawn, and even a lobster pool (one of the creatures may be plainly grilled and served with garlic and herb butter). Starters range from the simple langoustine and mussels in black butter to the more complicated whole roast local quail stuffed with a quail's egg, foie gras and Parma ham, plated on celeriac rösti with crab cakes and a pawpaw and mango salsa somewhere in between. Vegetables are well-reported, accompanying perhaps roast local lamb, grilled fillet of beef with a casserole of Puy lentils and port, or fried salmon escalopes with Noilly Prat sauce. Desserts are strong on ice creams and sorbets, or there might be plum and almond tart, with good crisp pastry, or densely flavoured caramel cheesecake. Colourful tasting notes bring life to the wine list, where around a dozen halves will be found.

MUCH WENLOCK, **Raven Hotel**

Barrow Street TF13 6EN
Map 7: SO69
Tel: 01952 727251
Fax: 01952 728416
Chef: Ernst Van Haldren
Cost: *Alc* £27, set-price L £15.
H/wine £12
Times: Noon-2pm/7-9.15pm. Closed
25 Dec
Additional: Bar food L; Sunday L;
🌢 dishes
Seats: 40

The founders of the modern Olympic Games met at the Raven in the 1890s, which accounts for the prints and other memorabilia on the restaurant walls. The core of this operation is a 17th-century coaching inn, the restaurant itself in what were this historical town's ancient almshouses. But don't expect dyed-in-the-wool tradition here. Good canapés come with aperitifs, breads are made in-house, and much use is made of local produce, as in ravioli of asparagus with Shropshire blue cheese. An impressive start to a meal might be light and fluffy, distinctively flavoured yet delicate salt-cod cake well complemented by black-eyed beans and spinach pesto and a whole tiger prawn. A main course of fillet of beef has been accompanied by rich and creamy red wine risotto, rosemary jus adding another dimension, and a decent selection of properly cooked vegetables. Crème brûlée – perhaps honey and pistachio – is a favoured dessert. The wine list covers most countries, with half-bottles well represented.

Smoking: No smoking in dining room
Accommodation: 15 en suite ★ ★ ★

Directions: Town centre

OSWESTRY, The Old Mill Inn

Popular former watermill with a lengthy carte, bar meals and blackboard specials. Appealing dishes, using quality fresh produce, include black pudding Glencoe and seafood rendezvous.

Accommodation: 5 rooms

Directions: From A5 follow B4579 signed Trefonen & Llansilin; after Ashfield take 1st R towards Llansilin then 1st R again down hill

Candy SY10 9AZ
Map 7: SJ22
Tel/Fax: 01691 657058
Cost: Alc £11. ☺ H/wine £8.25
Times: Noon-2.30pm/6-9.30pm. Closed Tue
Additional: Bar food; Sunday L; Children welcome; ✤ dishes
Smoking: No smoking in dining room

OSWESTRY, Pen-y-Dyffryn Hotel

Charming old rectory run with old-fashioned courtesy and service. Surrounded by spectacular scenery and tranquil grounds, welcoming fires burn in the restaurant, lounge and bar, reflecting the warmth and hospitality of the staff. The short, set-price menu shows flare and imagination and changes frequently to take account of seasonally fresh produce, much of which comes from local suppliers. Steamed mussels, leek and saffron broth was a Borders version of moules marinière and main courses tempt with casserole of corn-fed chicken legs with roast shallots, green lentils and meat jus (hurrah for breast haters!), or baked John Dory with truffle risotto, petit pois and white wine sauce. Sign off with exemplary glazed lemon tart and raspberry coulis plus a pot of good strong coffee.

Rhydcroesau SY10 7JD
Map 7: SJ22
Tel/Fax: 01691 653700
Chef: Paul Thomasson
Owner: Miles Hunter
Cost: Set-price D £19.50. ☺ H/wine £9
Times: D only, 7-9pm
Additional: Children welcome; ✤ dishes
Seats: 25
Smoking: No smoking in dining room
Accommodation: 10 en suite ★ ★ ★

Directions: Leave A5 at Oswestry, follow signs to Llansilin through town. Hotel is 3 miles W of Oswestry on B4580 Llansilin Road

OSWESTRY, Wynnstay Hotel ✤

Church Street SY11 2SZ
Map 7: SJ22
Tel: 01691 655261
Fax: 01691 670606
Cost: Alc £22, set-price L £10.50 (2 courses)/D £16.95. ☺ H/wine £8.75
Times: Noon-2pm/7-9.30pm. Closed D Sun
Additional: Bar food; Sunday L; Children welcome; ✤ dishes
Smoking: No pipes & cigars; Air conditioning
Accommodation: 29 en suite ★ ★ ★

Directions: In centre of town, opposite church

Hotel restaurant serving Italian food that ranges from mussels with shallots, sun-dried tomatoes, wine and cream, to braised lamb shank with mustard crust and red onion sauce.

SHIFNAL, **Park House Hotel**

Imposing high ceilings and chandeliers are reminders of a bygone age when this hotel was two individual houses. The Silvermere Restaurant is a comfortable room with views over the garden. Canapés raise expectations: tiny shepherds' pies, packed full of flavour 'really moreish,' and a tasty dip of feta, sun-dried tomatoes and pink peppercorns. Starters could run from a well-executed confit of duck terrine with artichokes and chutney, to a beautifully presented, light and fluffy twice-baked Roquefort soufflé with spiced pears. Main courses include cannon of local lamb with celeriac purée and apple and grape chutney, and grilled darne of wild Scottish salmon in a herb dressing. Vegetables are well-reported, and presentation reaches new heights with puddings involving spun sugar spirals or a cage of caramel. Glazed lime tart with vanilla ice cream sounds more pedestrian but is equally well thought of.

Park Street TF11 9BA
Map 7: SJ70
Tel: 01952 460128
Fax: 01952 461658
Chef: Graeme Shaw
Cost: *Alc* £33, set-price L £13.95/D £23.50 (4 courses). ☺ H/wine £12.50
Times: 12.30-2pm/7-9.30pm. Closed L Sat
Additional: Bar food; Sunday L; Children welcome; 🍽 dishes
Seats: 50. Private dining room 10-200
Smoking: No smoking in dining room
Accommodation: 54 en suite ★★★★

Directions: M54 J4, A464 through Shifnal; hotel 200yds after rail bridge

SHREWSBURY,
Albright Hussey Hotel

Ellesmere Road SY4 3AF
Map 7: SJ41
Tel: 01939 290571/290523
Fax: 01939 291143
Chef: Brian McKenna
Owners: Franco, Vera & Paul Subbiani
Cost: *Alc* £28.50, set-price L £12.50 (4 courses)/D £24.50 (5 courses). ☺ H/wine £9.75.
Times: Noon-2.15pm/7-10pm
Additional: Sunday L; Children 4+; 🍽 dishes
Seats: 80. Private dining room 50. Jacket & tie preferred
Smoking: No smoking in dining room
Accommodation: 14 en suite ★★★

Timber-framed Tudor house with extensive banqueting and conference facilities. The striking 16th-century moated manor house stands in four acres of mature landscaped gardens. Bedrooms in the older parts of the house are the most lavishly furnished; more modern rooms in a new wing are superbly equipped. The beamed, panelled dining room is the core of the hotel where a modish menu is offered, built around fresh regional and local produce. Menu buzz words such as lamb shank, rocket, chargrilled tuna, sea bass, reveal a kitchen with an eye for modern trends.

Directions: On A528, 2 miles from centre of Shrewsbury

SHREWSBURY,
Sol Restaurant

However inclement the weather in Shrewsbury a little sunshine is guaranteed at Sol. The optimistic yellows and oranges of the decor might have been inherited from the

82 Wyle Cop SY1 1UT
Map 7: SJ41
Tel: 01743 340560
Fax: 01743 340552
Chef: John Williams

building's previous life as a tapas bar, but it's an appropriately upbeat setting for John William's punchy style of cooking. Some of the Mediterranean feel appears to have rubbed off on the kitchen too; a spring inspection began with an appetiser of a demi-tasse of gazpacho that was a good indicator of the light but well-defined flavours to come. Produce is well chosen and the cooking is sensitive, resulting in dishes such as a top-notch ballotine of foie gras presented with a remarkably intense tomato and basil gelée. There is a great deal of emphasis on accuracy of cooking, with texture and taste the beneficiary of the studied approach. Fish, such as the John Dory and sea bass, served with summer greens, are therefore an excellent choice and there is also a lightness of touch to the saucing (in this case saffron and chive cream), which ensures key flavours are not overwhelmed. Desserts tend to the classic and are none the worse for that. Expect elegantly presented versions of, for instance, rhubarb crème brûlée and chocolate fondant with mint ice cream.

Sol Restaurant

Owners: John & Debbie Williams, Simon Cousins, Clare Cadwallader
Cost: Set-price D £27.50/£35 (5 courses). H/wine £9.95
Times: 12.30-2pm/7-9.30pm. Closed Sun, Mon, 1 wk winter, 1 wk summer
Additional: Children welcome; 🕮 dishes
Seats: 45. Private dining room 20
Smoking: No smoking in dining room

Directions: From A5 by-pass follow town centre signs, cross English Bridge & restaurant is at top of hill on L after Lion Hotel. Best to park at bottom and walk up

TELFORD,
Clarion Hotel Madeley Court 🌸 NEW

The restaurant was once the great hall of a 13th-century priory. Typical dishes include spiced roast fillet of monkfish, and medallions of beef fillet with a haggis mousse.

Smoking: No smoking in dining room
Accommodation: 47 en suite ★★★

Directions: M54/J4 then A4169 to Telford. Take A442 at 2nd roundabout towards Kidderminster. 1st L at roundabout

Castlefields Way Madeley TF7 5DW
Map 7: SJ60
Tel: 01952 680068
Fax: 01952 684275
Cost: *Alc* £28, set-price D £19.50. ☺ H/wine £12.25
Times: D only, 7-9.30pm
Additional: Bar food; Sunday L (noon-2pm); Children 12+; 🕮 dishes

TELFORD, **Valley Hotel** 🌸

Situated in the World Heritage site of Ironbridge, the hotel's Chez Maw restaurant (home of the distinguished tile-maker) offers a wide range of dishes with healthy/vegetarian options.

Additional: Bar food L; Sunday L; Children welcome; 🕮 dishes
Smoking: No smoking in dining room
Accommodation: 35 en suite ★★★

Directions: Follow signs to Ironbridge Gorge. At mini roundabout at bottom turn L, hotel 200yds on L

Ironbridge TF8 7DW
Map 7: SJ60
Tel: 01952 432247
Fax: 01952 432308
Cost: *Alc* £25, set-price L & D £19.75 (4 courses). ☺ H/wine £8.95
Times: Noon-2pm/7-9.30pm

WORFIELD,
Old Vicarage Hotel ❀❀❀

Bridgnorth WV15 5JZ
Map 7: SO79
Tel: 01746 716497
Fax: 01746 716552
Chefs: Blaine Reed, Richard Arnold
Owners: Peter & Christine Iles
Cost: Set-price L £17.50/D £25.
H/wine £14
Times: D only, 7-9pm
Additional: Sunday L (noon-2pm);
Children welcome; ❀ dishes
Seats: 40. Private dining room 14-40
Smoking: No smoking in dining room
Accommodation: 14 en suite ★ ★ ★

Directions: From Wolverhampton
take A454 Bridgnorth road; from M54
J4 take A442 towards Kidderminster

*Delightful hotel created from an imposing early Edwardian
vicarage.* There may be easy access to the motorway network
but the fast-paced life does not intrude and the commitment of
Peter and Christine Iles to their guests' comfort is impressive.
The whole enterprise is a model of its kind. The kitchen, under
the eye of executive chef Richard Arnold and headed by
Blaine Reed, offers straightforward but clear-headed cooking.
There's a sense of adventure, as when hot chicken and shiitake
mousse is paired with sweet-and-sour pak choi, and creamy
organic watercress and lime soup with curry cream, but on the
whole modern ideas are built on a classic French base and are
more restrained. Glazed breast of Gressingham duck with
creamed cabbage, Madeira sauce and rösti is a case in point.
Desserts such as iced lime parfait with dark chocolate mousse
are well composed. Local and regional produce brings local
game, Shropshire lamb, and prime condition cheeses such as
Shropshire Blue and a West Midlands full-fat ewes' milk
cheese – Berkswell. The kitchen is certainly industrious: black
pudding is home-made, as is bread, and petits fours are good.
The wine list is a serious tome and stands out as much for a
succinct no-fuss approach – presented with an informed but
unpompous enthusiasm – as for the quality of the bottles and
the carefully chosen halves. Extraordinarily catholic in range,
oenophiles are warned to allow time for study.
　Signature dishes: home-made black pudding with
sweetbreads and swede and rosemary galette; Shropshire
rabbit loin, pan-fried and confit leg with shallot marmalade
and wholegrain mustard sauce; fresh blackberry jelly, pumpkin
and ginger ice cream and apple parfait.

SOMERSET

AXBRIDGE, # Oak House Hotel ❀

The Square BS26 2AP
Map 3: ST45
Tel: 01934 732444
Fax: 01934 733112
Telephone for further details

*17th-century building in the main square of a delightful old village
offering British bistro-type dishes along the lines of broccoli and
Stilton soup, and crispy-skinned duck breast with sweet-and-sour
plum and ginger sauce.*

Directions: On E side of town square

BATH,

Bath Priory ❀❀❀

Georgian building, carefully extended to incorporate a smart new leisure centre where the pool is themed on the Roman baths. Guests of a less energetic nature can enjoy the comfort of two elegant sitting rooms and the intimate and clubby atmosphere of the restaurant, whose walls are covered in a collection of 18th-century paintings. The kitchen, though, keeps a weather eye on the modern, producing menus that run from pan-fried scallops with a mixed herb and Parmesan salad to sautéed loin of lamb in an olive and thyme jus with roasted provençale vegetables. An appetiser, of perhaps pan-fried goose liver with caramelised pink grapefruit, makes a promising start, which we followed with 'exquisite' ravioli of smoked haddock with creamy fish sauce. 'Beautifully tender' roast breast of Deben duck came next, with a 'superbly done' reduction of its cooking juices infused with sage and accompanied by wild mushroom risotto. Alternative main courses could include rump of veal roasted with shallots in Madeira sauce, or caramelised monkfish with crushed potatoes and a chive velouté. The assiette of desserts gets a standing ovation: it includes lemon tart ('one of the best I've ever tasted'), mango and passion fruit sorbet, a fruit crumble and warm chocolate fondant.

Weston Road BA1 2XT
Map 3: ST76
Tel: 01225 331922
Chef: Robert Clayton
Owner: Andrew Brownsword
Cost: *Alc* £37.50, set-price L £15 (2 courses)/D £35. H/wine £15
Times: Noon-1.45pm/7-9.45pm
Additional: Sunday L; Children welcome; ✿ dishes
Seats: 28. Private dining room 30
Smoking: No smoking in dining room
Accommodation: 28 en suite ★ ★ ★ ★

Directions: At the top of Park Lane, on W side of Victoria Park, turn L into Weston Rd; 300 yds on L

BATH, # Bath Spa ❀❀

Set amidst ancient cedars, the Grecian façade and Georgian portico conceal a fine interior with two very different styles of restaurant. In the Alfresco Restaurant, distinctive murals and exotic plants create an informal and vibrant atmosphere. The cooking style is eclectic, anything from parfait of foie gras and chicken livers with shallot relish and toasted brioche to Thai green chicken and tiger prawn curry with haricot vert, rice and crispy noodles. The Vellore Restaurant, however, is the heart of the house and the revitalised ballroom has its own elegant style. Dinner menus might comprise black mushroom, rosemary and garlic soup, followed by loin of English lamb, shallot purée honey and thyme jus, and iced chocolate St Emilion with espresso sauce. Alternatively, the selection might be baked brill in filo with tomato, aubergine and basil, breast of chicken wrapped in basil and Parma ham with tomato and shallot salsa, and warm apricot and almond tart with Amaretto sauce.

Sydney Road BA2 6JF
Map 3: ST76
Tel: 01225 444424
Fax: 01225 444006
Chef: Jonathan Fraser
Cost: *Alc* £25, set-price L £12.50 (2 courses). ☺ H/wine £13.25
Times: Noon-2pm/6.15-10pm
Additional: Sunday L; Children welcome; ✿ dishes
Seats: 42
Smoking: No smoking in dining room; Air conditioning
Accommodation: 98 en suite
★ ★ ★ ★ ★

Directions: From A4 turn L onto A36 Warminster, R at mini roundabout and pass fire station, turn L into Sydney Place

BATH, Cliffe Hotel

Regency country house situated in terraced grounds overlooking the Avon Valley. A good choice of dishes might include cannon of lamb, breast of duck, and leek and Stilton tartlet.

Additional: Bar food; Sunday L; Children welcome; ✿ dishes
Smoking: No smoking in dining room
Accommodation: 11 en suite ★ ★ ★

Directions: From A36 take B3108 (Bradford-on-Avon), turn R before rail bridge, to Limpley Stoke. Hotel on brow of hill

Crowe Hill Limpley Stoke BA3 6HY
Map 3: ST76
Tel: 01225 723226
Fax: 01225 723871
Cost: *Alc* £25, set-price L £12.75. ☺
H/wine £12.50
Times: Noon-2pm/7-9.30pm

BATH, Clos du Roy ✿✿

1 Seven Dials Saw Close BA1 2EN
Map 3: ST76
Tel: 01225 444450
Fax: 01225 404044
Chef: Simon King
Owners: Emma & Philippe Roy
Cost: *Alc* £22, set-price D £19.50. ☺
H/wine £9.95
Times: Noon-2.15pm/6-10pm
Additional: Sunday L; Children 5+;
✿ dishes
Seats: 80
Smoking: No pipes & cigars

High standards and infusions of fresh kitchen talent make this long-established restaurant evergreen. Wednesday lunches, when it's matinée day at the nearby theatre, are particularly popular, and not only because the *menus du jour* are jolly good value. The cooking is an amalgam of French and modern British – fresh crab cheesecake is served with dill creamed sauce, and salad of pigeon breast with citrus fruit vinaigrette. Classic tastes are catered for with duck and wild mushroom parfait with toasted brioche and pan-fried fillet of Scottish beef with deep-fried julienne of leek and Stilton sauce; a lightly spiced oriental seafood hotpot with cumin risotto, however, demonstrates a lively streak of independence from the conventions. Desserts also span the styles – coconut and fresh mango crème brûlée on the one hand, iced nougat terrine with raspberry coulis on the other.

Directions: Next to Theatre Royal

BATH,
Combe Grove Manor

Georgian manor with stylish cooking, interesting ingredients and great views. Purée of roasted Jerusalem artichokes is topped with aromatic chillies, and chargrilled Angus steak comes with morel and purple truffle mash.

Smoking: No smoking in dining room
Accommodation: 40 en suite ★ ★ ★ ★

Brassknocker Hill Monkton Combe
BA2 7HS
Map 3: ST76
Tel: 01225 834644
Fax: 01255 834961
Cost: *Alc* £30, set-price D £25.
H/wine £12.20
Times: D only 7-9.30pm
Additional: Children 14+; ✿ dishes;
Jacket & tie preferred

Combe Grove Manor

Directions: A4 from Bristol to roundabout (Newton St Loe), 2nd exit for Combe Down (5 miles). At Combe Down continue for 1.5 miles, hotel entrance on R

BATH, **The Francis** NEW

Large, spacious hotel restaurant overlooking Queen Square. Straight-forward cooking with the food matched by a wide range of wines.

Smoking: No smoking in dining room
Accommodation: 95 en suite ★ ★ ★

Directions: Telephone for directions

Queen Square BA1 2HH
Map 3: ST76
Tel: 01225 424257
Fax: 01225 319715
Cost: *Alc* £24, set-price L £12.50/D £19.95. ☺ H/wine £ 14
Times: D only, 6.30-10pm
Additional: Bar food; Sunday L (noon-3pm); Children welcome; ◑ dishes

BATH, **The Moody Goose**

7A Kingsmead Square BA1 2AB
Map 3: ST76
Tel/Fax: 01225 466688
Chef: Stephen Shore
Owners: Stephen & Victoria Shore
Cost: *Alc* £29, set-price L £10 (2 courses)/D £20. ☺ H/wine £11
Times: Noon-2pm/6-9.30pm (10pm Sat). Closed Sun & Mon, 1st 2 wks Jan, Xmas
Additional: Children 7+; ◑ dishes
Seats: 30. Private dining room 8
Smoking: No smoking in dining room

Directions: Telephone for directions

Georgian terrace basement restaurant in the heart of the city.
The Moody Goose is a light and airy room simply but elegantly decorated, with splashes of colour provided by cushions and French water-colours on the walls. There's a small, comfortable bar, tables are of a good size, and the eponymous goose keeps its beady eyes on proceedings. This is cooking of the modern British school, which means that innovation is never far away, the kitchen turning its hand to Brixham crab with crisp pancetta and tarragon mayonnaise, roast breast of guinea fowl with smoked chicken ravioli, and pan-fried beef fillet with crepinette of oxtail, smoked garlic and Madeira sauce. Seasonality is a linchpin, with game prominent in winter: tender and succulent roasted partridge with parsnip cream, say, or gamey-flavoured pan-fried saddle of venison with port sauce and glazed oranges. The kitchen spends a lot of time caramelising: bananas, with toffee cream and chocolate sauce, rice pudding with glazed pears, and a light and crisp tarte Tatin with vanilla ice cream.

BATH, **No 5 Bistro** ❀❀

Warm, welcoming bistro just by Poultney Bridge and the River Avon. The cooking style is right up to date with hints of oriental and European influences. Although the highlight of a recent meal was a warm chicken and tarragon mousse, baked in puff pastry, an innovative dish of roasted duck breast with lemongrass, lime and coconut cream was also a hit. For dessert the steamed chocolate sponge arrived with a dark bitter chocolate sauce which was complemented by a rich vanilla ice cream. With your meal ask for the local Batheaston white wine, admired for its big nose and fruity flavour, or one of the interesting bottled beers. On Monday and Tuesday evenings you're invited to bring your own wine – no corkage charged. Reservations are strongly recommended.

Directions: 30 yds from Poultney Bridge towards Laura Place

5 Argyle Street BA2 4BA
Map 3: ST76
Tel: 01225 444499
Fax: 01225 318668
Chefs: Stephen Smith, Paul Hearne, Sarah Grantins
Owners: Stephen Smith, Charles Home
Cost: *Alc* £23. ☺ H/wine £8.95.
Times: Noon-2.20pm/6.30-9.50pm (10.30 Fri,11 Sat). Closed Sun, L Mon, 1 wk Xmas
Additional: Children welcome, dishes
Seats: 35
Smoking: No smoking in dining room

BATH, **The Olive Tree at The Queensberry Hotel** ❀❀

Russel Street BA1 2QF
Map 3: ST76
Tel: 01225 447928
Fax: 01225 446065
Chef: Mathew Prowse
Owners: Stephen & Penny Ross
Cost: *Alc* £30, set-price L £14.50/D £21. ☺ H/wine £11.50
Times: Noon-2pm/7-10pm. Closed L Sun, New Year
Additional: Children welcome; dishes
Seats: 50. Private dining room 35
Smoking: No smoking in dining room; Air conditioning
Accommodation: 29 en suite ★ ★ ★

Lovingly restored Georgian town house, not far from the city centre. The restaurant is more up-market Tuscan in style with rug-strewn tiled floor and foodie pictures on the walls. There's a strong Mediterranean influence to the cooking too: Provençale fish soup; sea bass with couscous, chilli and grilled fennel, and pesto and cannellini beans with the Aberdeen Angus rump steak. A more eclectic choice might be scallops and squid poached in coconut milk with lime and lemongrass. Finish with the likes of lemon curd tart with confit of lemons, chocolate pavé with raspberry sorbet or warm black cherry strudel with mulled-wine ice cream. Fudge and mince pies accompanied the good strong coffee at our last test meal. The popularity of the restaurant is such that both residents and non-residents alike are advised to book.

Directions: 100 yds north of Assembly Rooms in Lower Lansdown

BATH, **Restaurant Lettonie** ❀❀❀❀

The Blunos family are well settled into their Georgian restaurant-with-rooms, and it runs like a well oiled machine. There are fabulous views from the appropriately

35 Kelston Road BA1 3QH
Map 3: ST76
Tel: 01225 446676
Fax: 01225 447541
Chef: Martin Blunos

elegant restaurant – pictures on the walls are of Latvian country scenes, courtesy of Martin's uncle who teaches art in Riga. Other personal touches include a liberal smattering of family photos to emphasise the fact that this also doubles as a home . We dined on a night that saw a 'good mix of clientele who appeared to be eating here for all the right reasons – lots of complimentary remarks moving through the restaurant like a Mexican wave'. Dishes are delivered with pride, a two-man job from tray holder to table server with Martin's food still hitting all the right notes. His menus are an interesting fusion of ideas, with Eastern European ethnic touches combined with a French classic repertoire, resulting in such wonderful ensembles as a signature scrambled duck egg topped with Sevruga caviar served with blinis pancakes and a glass of iced vodka'. An *amuse-bouche* of fish soup topped with puff pastry opened our meal. Unusual kipper tortellini with scallops and tomato in a Sauternes cream sauce came next, followed by excellent roast calves' sweetbreads glazed with Pineau des Charentes and almonds. Pre-dessert was another famous Blunos touch – an egg shell filled with vanilla cream and topped with mango purée and biscuit soldiers; salt and pepper was provided by way of chocolate and sugar! Bitter chocolate pudding with marinated strawberries and Mascarpone was nothing more than 'stylishly simple and utterly enjoyable'. The wine list is serious with a good selection of half-bottles

Owners: Siân & Martin Blunos
Cost: Set-price L £25/D £44.50
Times: Noon-2pm/7-9.30pm. Closed Sun & Mon, 2 wks Jan, 2 wks Aug
Additional: Children welcome
Seats: 38. Private dining room 8
Smoking: No smoking in dining room
Accommodation: 4 en suite

Directions: 2 miles from Bath on A431 Bilton Road

BATH,
Royal Crescent Hotel, Pimpernel's, The Brasserie ❀❀❀

Bang at the centre of Bath's most famous crescent, this prestigious hotel has two highly rated restaurants.
Pimpernel's, crisp and light and of simple design inspired by the Regency period, marries modern English cooking to the East: tiger prawns with Thai curry cream, or Szechuan-style foie gras, then squab pigeon with lime sauce and a ginger dressing, or beef with noodles. A decent selection of notable breads makes the rounds before starters of, say, baked codling in a punchy marinade of tomatoes and garlic, chargrilled asparagus with Parmesan, or marinated quail in a ginger dressing with stir-fried vegetables. Beautifully tender, succulent and flavoursome beef fillet makes a memorable main course, perhaps wrapped in Parma ham on a bed of pea purée in sherry vinegar jus coupled with a pungent confit of red cabbage and onion. Roast sea bass might be there too, with rocket salad, tomato dressing and basil oil, or Bresse chicken with wilted greens, tarragon and mushrooms. 'Really most enjoyable' apricot and almond feuilleté with Amaretto ice cream brings up the rear, with pistachio soufflé with raspberry ice cream another success. The Brasserie, in the garden in the Dower House, decorated with hand-painted 18th-century wall hangings, brings an up-to-date slant to the classical repertoire, from beef broth with cheese straws to guinea fowl with rosemary jus.
Signature dishes: braised lamb shank with minted jus; scallops with pancetta and curry oil; chocolate and cherry mousse with cherry compote.

16 Royal Crescent BA1 2LS
Map 3: ST76
Tel: 01225 823333
Fax: 01225 339401
Chef: Steven Blake
Owner: Cliveden Ltd
Cost: *Alc* £37.25, set-price L £19.50/D £31. H/wine £16
Times: 12.30-2pm/7-10.30pm
Additional: Sunday L; Children welcome; ❀ dishes
Seats: 46. Private dining room 70. Jacket & tie preferred
Smoking: No smoking in dining room; Air conditioning
Accommodation: 45 en suite
★★★★★

Directions: In city centre follow signs to Royal Crescent

BATH,
Woods Restaurant

Three inter-connecting dining rooms with an informal café-bar at one end, wood floors, high ceilings, smallish tables and wicker-backed chairs sums up Woods Restaurant neatly. A short, well-balanced menu (a bargain at lunch 'and not skimpy portions either') offers the likes of rare pigeon breast salad, and timbale of crab, as starters, with red sea bream with a sauce of Pernod, herbs and cream amongst main courses. Desserts include apple and blueberry tart and hot chocolate pudding with a mint crème anglaise.

Directions: Opposite the Assembly Rooms

9-13 Alfred Street BA1 2QX
Map 3: ST76
Tel: 01225 314812
Fax: 01225 443146
Chef: David Price
Owners: David & Claude Price
Cost: Alc £16.50, set-price L £7 (2 courses)/D £12.25 (2 courses). H/wine £10
Times: Noon-3pm/6-11pm. Closed Sun, 25-26 Dec
Additional: Children welcome; ✿ dishes
Seats: 100. Private dining room 40
Smoking: No pipes & cigars

BECKINGTON, **Woolpack Inn**

Old coaching inn complete with open fires, beams and flagstones. Eat at the bar or have a full meal in one of the comfortable, welcoming dining rooms: the Garden Room, smart and up to date and leading on to a courtyard, or the Oak Room, more intimate, with high-backed upholstered chairs. This might be Somerset, but the kitchen has an eye on the rest of the world, turning out crab cakes with carrot and coriander salad and red Thai curry sauce, as well as pan-fried scallops with sun-dried tomato risotto and Parmesan shavings. Otherwise, there might be an exemplary tart of smoked chicken and Stilton, or a creamy soup of mussels, cockles and saffron, then roast fillet of sea bass of tremendous flavour (fish is delivered daily from Brixham) on a bed of braised squid with Parma ham. Puddings, from lemon tart to chocolate and rum truffle cake with coffee-bean sauce, are successful and beautifully presented, vegetables are well-reported, and good wines are sold by the glass.

Bath BA3 6SP
Map 3: ST85
Tel: 01373 831244
Fax: 01373 831223
Chefs: Ashley James, Francois Gardillon
Owner: Old English Country Inns & Hotels
Cost: Alc £25. ☺ H/wine £9.95
Times: Noon-2.30pm/7-9.30pm
Additional: Bar food L; Sunday L; Children welcome; ✿ dishes
Seats: 50. Private dining room 20
Smoking: No-smoking area; No pipes & cigars
Accommodation: 12 en suite ★★

Directions: Village centre. On A36 (Bath – Southampton) near junction with A361.

BRENT KNOLL, **Woodlands Hotel**

A family-run hotel in four acres with country views. Expect roasted Somerset Brie with smoked ham and apricot coulis, salmon with lemon butter, and crème brûlée with strawberries stewed with brandy.

Directions: From A38 take 1st turn L into village, then 5th turn R into Church Lane, 1st L into Hill Lane; hotel on R at 250yds

Hill Lane TA9 4DF
Map 3: ST35
Tel/Fax: 01278 760232
Telephone for further details

BRUTON, **Truffles Restaurant**

Enterprising restaurant with a regular programme of gourmet events and wine tastings. Monthly changing menus are skilful and varied. Winter pheasant and wild mushroom pâté is given zest with lightly pickled red cabbage, and a warm tomato salsa with olives and capers adds a sunny note to fillet of pan-fried monkfish. Medallions of pork fillet with caramelised apples and Calvados sauce are a classic combination, as are lamb cutlets topped with a mushroom duxelle wrapped in filo pastry, oven-baked and served with a sherry and tarragon sauce. There are some delightful puddings – hot ginger sponge with red wine and ginger spicy sauce, and passion fruit and orange torte with bramble apple juice sauce. An imaginative vegetarian menu might include oriental vegetable wun-tuns with home-made chilli jam. The midweek supper menu offers exceptionally good value.

95 High Street BA10 0AR
Map 3: ST63
Tel/Fax: 01749 812255
Chef: Martin Bottrill
Owners: Denise & Martin Bottrill
Cost: Set-price L £13.95/D £22.95. ☺
H/wine £10.95.
Times: D only, 7-9pm. Closed D Sun, all Mon, 2wks Feb
Additional: Sunday L (noon-2pm); Children 6+; ✦ dishes
Seats: 20
Smoking: No pipes & cigars

Directions: Bruton centre, at start of one-way system, on L

CASTLE CARY, **The George Hotel**

Market Place BA7 7AH
Map 3: ST63
Tel: 01963 350761
Fax: 01963 350035
Telephone for further details

Directions: From A303 take A371 at Wincanton to Castle Cary. Centre of town

Thatched roof, bay windows – this 15th-century building is a magnet for tourists. Fresh produce enlivens a menu that punches flavour with dishes such as Barbary duck terrine, and pork tenderloin with a sauce of quince and apple brandy.

DULVERTON, **Ashwick House**

Edwardian residence with a south facing restaurant opening onto a large terrace overlooking the grounds. Skilful cooking of quality ingredients is offered from a short four-course menu.

Accommodation: 6 en suite ★★   **Credit cards:** None

Directions: From M5 J27 follow signs to Dulverton, then take B3223 Lynton road and turn L after second cattle grid

TA22 9QD
Map 3: SS92
Tel/Fax: 01398 323868
Cost: Set-price D £19.75 (4 courses).
☺ H/wine £10.25
Times: D only, 7.15-8.30pm
Additional: Sunday L (12.30-1.45pm); Children 8+
Smoking: No smoking in dining room

EXFORD, **Crown Hotel**

Country hotel strong on comfort and style. Exford is a picturesque village at the heart of Exmoor National Park, and the Crown is the perfect base from which to explore the area. There's a comfortable lounge with an open fire, a bar with a blackboard menu, and a spacious, tranquil restaurant overlooking the garden. The kitchen makes the most of local produce and turns out some boldly flavoured dishes: langoustine

Park Street TA24 7PP
Map 3: SS83
Tel: 01643 831554/5
Fax: 01643 831665
Chef: Eric Bouchet
Owners: Michael Bradley, John Atkin
Cost: Set-price D £27.50. H/wine £10.50

Crown Hotel

Times: Noon-2pm (bar only)/7-9.30pm
Additional: Bar food; Sunday L; Children welcome; ✤ dishes
Seats: 30. Private room 16
Smoking: No-smoking area
Accommodation: 17 en suite ★ ★ ★

Directions: Village centre facing the green

tails go into a pouch of pastry served on Pernod cream with fennel fondue, and noisettes of venison receive a raspberry vinegar and chocolate sauce and potato and apple galette. A coarse pâté of wood pigeon and wild mushrooms, with Cumberland sauce and sun-dried tomato brioche, makes a hearty starter, followed perhaps by fillet of sea bass, cooked on the skin, in tapenade sauce, with aubergine caviar and tomato concasse. Cheeses, all West Country, are copious in quantity goats', ewes', cows', smoked and blue, all in their prime – and served at room temperature, and visual effects are striking in puddings of fine apple tart with cinnamon ice cream and vanilla sauce.

FARRINGTON GURNEY,

Country Ways Hotel ✿

Cosy little hotel where the proprietor is responsible for freshly prepared dishes, such as goujons of lemon sole with tarragon and lime mayonnaise, and lamb steaks with sage and sherry sauce.

Accommodation: 6 en suite ★ ★

Directions: From village take A362 to Midsomer Norton, then 1st R into Marsh Lane. Hotel next to Farrington Golf Club

Marsh Lane BS39 6TT
Map 3: ST65
Tel: 01761 452449
Fax: 01761 452706
Cost: *Alc* £21.50. ☺ H/wine £9.50
Times: D only, 7-8.45pm. Closed Sun, Xmas & New Year
Additional: ✤ dishes
Smoking: No smoking in dining room

FROME, **Talbot Inn Restaurant** ✿

A 15th-century inn with stone floors, log fires, beams and large wooden tables. Options include daily fish dishes, saddle of Somerset deer, and lamb cutlets with tarragon mousse.

Mells BA11 3PN
Map 3: ST74
Tel: 01373 812254
Fax: 01373 813599
Cost: *Alc* £16. ☺ H/wine £7.50
Times: Noon-2pm/7-9.30pm. Closed 25, 26 Dec
Additional: Bar food L; Sunday L; Children welcome; ✤ dishes
Smoking: No-smoking area
Accommodation: 7 en suite

Directions: From M5/J23, follow Wells & Shepton Mallet towards Frome. Before Frome turn L to Mells

HINTON CHARTERHOUSE,
Homewood Park

Relaxing surroundings yet still maintaining high standards of professionalism. The Georgian house is quite impressive, reached via a long drive, and it makes an eminently comfortable, elegant country retreat. The sense of space, combined with discreetly supervised Anglo-French staff, are all part of the experience. Number two in the kitchen, Andrew Hamer, took over from Gary Jones too late for us to assess his cooking in the last edition of *Best Restaurants.* Reports this year have confirmed the promise Hamer showed as sous chef and the incumbent now well settled in with a style that encompasses classic French and modern British influences. The approach is direct and to the point and shows a great deal of flair and dedication. A test meal in March highlighted ravioli of spinach and Parmesan with tiny leeks and wild mushrooms that delivered all the promised flavours, and tender west country lamb with spring vegetables, sweetbreads, kidney and parsley. Caramel and walnut mousse with caramel ice cream was as imaginative as it was intensely flavoured. Breads, canapés, *amuse-bouche*, pre-dessert, and petits fours reveal an industrious kitchen with an eye for the smallest detail. The wine list is comprehensive, although it majors in France.

Bath BA3 6BB
Map 3: ST75
Tel: 01225 723731
Fax: 01225 723820
Chef: Andrew Hamer
Owner: Alan Moxon
Cost: *Alc* £45, set-price L £20.
H/wine £16
Times: Noon-1.45pm/7-9.30pm
Additional: Bar food L; Sunday L;
Children welcome; ✿ dishes
Seats: 50. Private dining room 40
Smoking: No smoking in dining room
Accommodation: 19 en suite ★ ★ ★

Directions: 5 miles SE of Bath off
A36, turning marked Sharpstone

HOLFORD, Combe House Hotel

Country restaurant with polished wooden tables in a converted 17th-century tannery. Typical options from the short menu include trout meunière, roast leg of pork, and stuffed pepper.

Smoking: No smoking in dining room
Accommodation: 16 en suite ★ ★

Directions: M5/J24 (A39 Bridgwater) towards Minehead. Turn L up lane between Holford Garage and Plough Inn

Nr Bridgwater TA5 1RZ
Map 3: ST14
Tel: 01278 741382
Fax: 01278 741322
Cost: Set-price D £18.75 (4 courses).
☺ H/wine £7.95
Times: D only, 7.30-8.30pm
Additional: Bar food L; Children welcome

HUNSTRETE,
Hunstrete House Hotel

Pensford BS39 4NS
Map 3: ST66
Tel: 01761 490490
Fax: 01761 490732
Chef: Stewart Eddy
Cost: *Alc* £50, set-price L £19.95/D
£29.50. H/wine £14.95
Times: Noon-2pm/7-9.30pm
Additional: Bar food L; Sunday L;
Children welcome; ✿ dishes
Seats: 35. Private dining room 30
Smoking: No smoking in dining room
Accommodation: 23 en suite ★ ★ ★

Wonderful setting surrounded by 90 acres of gardens and deer park. The dining room is formal but not uncomfortably starchy and service shows similar adherence to tradition but tempered by the youthfulness (and Gallic charm) of the staff. Stewart Eddy continues to cook confidently with clear indication of an innate faith in his own abilities and confidence in quality of produce. This includes close attention to detail in the likes of canapés of, say, a delicate quenelle of chicken liver and foie gras en croûte, impressive flavoured breads, and a simple, but effective *amuse-bouche* of garden vegetable broth. Our summer meal took off with a classy but simple opening salvo: an accomplished warm quail and grape salad – the eggs deep-fried and with a restrained sherry vinegar sauce. Sea bass on a tomato and basil tart with ratatouille and pesto showed the importance of texture and ability to sensitively translate and re-interpret ideas and flavours with impressive restraint. Banana parfait with caramel sauce and ginger ice cream was spot on. The handsome wine list has a number of hefty bins and wide-ranging prices – £300 plus, downwards to £14.50.

Signature dishes: a potage of mussels, oysters and cockles with fines herbs and Sevruga caviar; local pheasant and black pudding with a bouillon of winter vegetables and chestnuts, scented with Madeira; pistachio crème brûlée with a hot chocolate fondant and pistachio ice cream.

Hunstrete House Hotel

Directions: On A368 – 8 miles from Bath

MINEHEAD, Periton Park Hotel

An interesting carte and an extensive wine list provide plenty of choice at this restaurant, located in the former billiard room. Dishes are based on the best from Exmoor's larder.

Middlecombe TA24 8SN
Map 3: SS94
Tel/Fax: 01643 706885
Cost: Set-price D £23.50. ☺ H/wine £8.95
Times: D only, 7-9pm. Closed Jan
Additional: Children 12+; ◑ dishes
Smoking: No smoking in dining room
Accommodation: 8 en suite ★★

Directions: Off A39 signposted Porlock & Lynmouth. Hotel about 1 mile on L

NUNNEY, The George at Nunney

Cask-conditioned ales and speciality whiskies plus great steaks from the chargrill, salmon and halibut en croûte, or chef's 'Devil Breath' chicken piri piri supreme.

Smoking: No smoking in dining room
Accommodation: 9 en suite ★★

Directions: Take A361 Frome to Shepton Mallet road and turn off in village centre, opposite medieval castle

11 Church Street BA11 4LW
Map 3: ST74
Tel: 01373 836458
Fax: 01373 836565
Cost: *Alc* £18, set-price L £5.50 (2 courses). ☺ H/wine £9.75
Times: Noon-2pm/7-9pm
Additional: Bar food; Sunday L; Children welcome; ◑ dishes

PORLOCK, The Oaks Hotel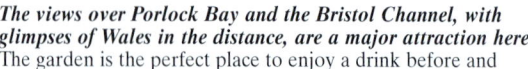

The views over Porlock Bay and the Bristol Channel, with glimpses of Wales in the distance, are a major attraction here. The garden is the perfect place to enjoy a drink before and

Doverhaye TA24 8ES
Map 3: SS84
Tel/Fax: 01643 862265
Chef: Anne Riley
Owners: Tim & Anne Riley

after dinner. This is a four-course business (with the option of extending it to five with the addition of cheese), the second course normally fish: perhaps perfectly poached salmon in a delicately flavoured cream-based tomato sauce, or grilled lemon sole with Muscadet. A soup, pear and watercress, say, or something like prawn and spinach roulade are normally found among the starters, with main courses running to calves' liver, accurately cooked, with a restrained hand behind an orange and Dubonnet sauce, or roast fillet of Exmoor venison with a port and redcurrant sauce. In season, English strawberries are combined with feather-light hazelnut meringue to produce a 'well-judged balancing act' of a gâteau, and in winter treacle tart with marmalade ice cream could appear. Be prepared for lots of conversation between guests and a surprisingly upbeat wine list with a decent showing of halves.

Cost: Set-price D £25 (4 courses). H/wine £9.50
Times: D only, 7-8.30pm. Closed Nov-Mar
Additional: Children 8+
Seats: 22
Smoking: No smoking in dining room
Accommodation: 9 en suite ★★

Directions: At bottom of Dunstersteepe Road, on L, on entering Porlock from Minehead

SHEPTON MALLET, Bowlish House ❀❀

Bowlish BA4 5JD
Map 3: ST64
Tel/Fax: 01749 342022
Chef: Linda Morley
Owners: Bob & Linda Morley
Cost: Set-price D £22.50. H/wine £9.95
Times: D only, 7-9pm. Closed 1 wk autumn, 1 wk spring
Additional: Sunday L (1st Sun of month); Children welcome
Seats: 24
Smoking: No smoking in dining room
Accommodation: 3 en suite

Imposing 18th century house set on the outskirts of Shepton Mallet. Hoorah for the clearly annotated cheese list and the supplier's credit. It's a sign of a kitchen that cares about quality ingredients and careful sourcing. Local Denhay air-dried ham is another product that deserves promotion, and that needs no further enhancing than a salad of dressed leaves and Parmesan shavings. More labour intensive starters include garlic mushroom soufflé glazed with cheese and cream, and smoked salmon mousse with watercress and avocado cream. Main courses keep things on an even wicket with saddle of lamb roasted with parsley, roasted red onions and pesto sauce, and fillet of turbot with saffron and fresh chervil velouté. We felt we suddenly slipped into a nouvelle cuisine timewarp, however, on sighting honey-glazed duck breast on strawberry and pink peppercorn sauce. Not something you could say, happily, about sticky toffee pudding with butterscotch sauce and cream.

Directions: 0.25 mile from town centre on A371 Wells road

SHEPTON MALLET,
Charlton House Hotel ❀❀❀

Charlton Road BA4 4PR
Map 3: ST64
Tel: 01749 342008
Fax: 01749 346362
Chef: Adam Fellows
Owners: Mr & Mrs Roger Saul
Cost: Alc £38, set-price L £14.50/D £35. H/wine £15
Times: 12.30-2pm/7.30-9.30pm
Additional: Bar food L; Sunday L; Children welcome
Seats: 84. Private dining rooms 24-30
Smoking: No smoking in dining room
Accommodation: 16 en suite ★★★

Directions: M4 J17, follow A350 S. At Trowbridge join A361. Hotel is located 1 mile before Shepton Mallet on L

Just outside the town in eight acres of landscaped grounds, Charlton House is owned by the founders of Mulberry and provides a showcase for the company's fabrics, furnishings and curios. Rugs on polished floorboards, antiques, richly decorated walls and a restaurant with tassel-backed upholstered chairs are the setting for a relaxed and unstuffy atmosphere, with staff bright and amenable, a description that could equally apply to Adam Fellows' cooking. Lightness of touch characterises the style, although deftness is accompanied by flavours as incisive as one could wish for. A starter of scallops steamed with lemon balm and coriander in a light curry sauce with caramelised apples is at one end of the spectrum, with a main course of pan-seared veal sweetbreads with truffle-scented mash and sherry vinaigrette at the other, while fillet of beef with leek fondue, onion soubise and beetroot jus is as colourful as the surroundings. An inspector was in raptures over sea bass in tapenade with baby artichokes and sauce vierge, while shredded duck confit with Parmesan, frisée and truffle oil dressing delivered the goods too. Vegetarians are taken seriously, and puddings reach a crescendo: wild strawberry soup with excellent fromage frais sorbet, or méli-mélo of red berries with pistachio ice cream. An intelligent, sensibly priced wine list completes the rosy picture.

SHIPHAM,
Daneswood House Hotel ❀❀

Elegant Edwardian house on the edge of the Mendip Hills, with spectacular views over the Severn Estuary. Furnishings reflect the style and age of the hotel, but dinners hit a more modern note (shame, we would have enjoyed some game consommé and mutton chops). Many dishes, nonetheless, have an identifiable lineage which puts the cooking in context: pressed ham knuckle and foie gras terrine with red onion salad and green bean chutney; roasted white onion and leek soup with dark truffle oil and chives; pot-roast saddle of lamb, minted mash potatoes, red wine and onion gravy; old fashioned fruit pudding with orange sauce and brandy cream. Other dishes are a mix of French, Mediterranean and more exotic influences, such as sweet potato and walnut risotto, and a white chocolate and coconut crème brûlée. There is a selection of excellent English cheese.

Cuck Hill Winscombe BS25 1RD
Map 3: ST45
Tel: 01934 843145
Fax: 01934 843824
Chefs: Julian Prosser, Heather Matthews
Owners: David & Elise Hodges
Cost: Set-price L £ 15.95/D £29.95. H/wine £10.95
Times: Noon-2pm/7-9.30pm. Closed L Sat, 26 Dec-4 Jan
Additional: Sunday L; Children welcome; ❀ dishes
Seats: 50. Private dining room 8-30
Smoking: No smoking in dining room
Accommodation: 12 en suite ★ ★ ★

Directions: From Bristol take A38 towards Bridgwater. Shipham on L. (Hotel on Cheddar side of the village)

SIMONSBATH,
Simonsbath House Hotel ❀

Comfortable but formal dining room elegantly situated in an attractive 350-year-old house. Traditional country house cooking is given an imaginative spin and served at tables set with silver, crystal, fresh flowers and candles.

Accommodation: 7 en suite ★ ★

Directions: Situated on B3223 in the village

Minehead TA24 7SH
Map 3: SS73
Tel: 01643 831259
Fax: 01643 831557
Cost: Set-price D £20 (5 courses). H/wine £8.25
Times: D only, 7- 8.30pm. Closed Dec-Jan
Additional: Children 10+
Smoking: No smoking in dining room

STON EASTON, **Ston Easton Park**

The painstakingly restored Palladian mansion is majestically framed by the classical parkland. Consistency is the key word here, with good quality market ingredients used in both traditional and modern dishes; it's good to see old favourites such as split-pea and mint soup, steak and kidney pudding, and

Bath BA3 4DF
Map 3: ST65
Tel: 01761 241631
Fax: 01761 241377
Chef: Mark Harrington
Owners: Mr & Mrs P L Smedley
Cost: *Alc* £49, set-price L £16/D

Ston Easton Park

£39.50 (4 courses). H/wine £15.50
Times: Noon-2pm/7-9.30pm
Additional: Sunday L; Children 7+;
🌢 dishes
Seats: 40. Private dining room 26.
Jacket & tie preferred
Smoking: No smoking in dining room
Accommodation: 21 en suite ★ ★ ★ ★

Directions: On A37 from Bristol to
Shepton Mallet, about 6 miles from
Wells

treacle and lemon sponge with custard, sitting alongside more
Mediterranean-influenced onion tart and warm marinated goats'
cheese with saffron and black pepper. Other dishes which have
impressed include wild mushroom risotto, tournedos Rossini
with foie gras, truffle and Madeira-flavoured sauce, and tarte
Tatin with crème anglaise. Fish dishes include skate meunière
with capers, anchovies, parsley and lemon, and roast loin of
monkfish with oyster mushrooms and a crispy noodle pancake.
Excellent breakfast croissants and afternoon teas.

TAUNTON, Brazz NEW

Castle Bow TA1 1NF
Map 3: ST22
Tel/Fax: 01823 252000
Cost: *Alc* £20. ☺
Additional: Bar food L; Sunday L;
Children welcome; 🌢 dishes
Times: Noon-3pm/6.30-10.30pm
(11pm Fri & Sat)
Smoking: Air conditioning

Directions: Follow signs to town
centre, castle & museum

*Stylish brasserie from the owners of the Castle Hotel (see entry),
with 25ft zinc bar, 6ft aquarium filled with silver dollar fish and a
vast dome lit by fibre optic stars. The menu is designed to appeal to a
diverse clientele.*

TAUNTON, Castle Hotel

Castle Green TA1 1NF
Map 3: ST22
Tel: 01823 272671
Fax: 01823 336066
Owners: The Chapman Family
Cost: *Alc* £38. set-price L £20/D
£27.50. H/wine £11.50
Times: 12.30-2pm/7.30-9pm
Additional: Bar food; Sunday L;
Children welcome; 🌢 dishes
Seats: 60. Private dining room 80
Smoking: No smoking in dining room
Accommodation: 44 en suite ★ ★ ★

Alas, no rosettes can be awarded this year for as we went to
press we learnt that Phil Vickery, who had achieved four AA
Rosettes here, had left the Castle Hotel. However, our last
inspection found the Castle wearing well – good housekeeping
sees to that. It's been a hotel for 300 years (and before that
was a fortress from the time of the Conquest, with a Norman
garden to substantiate the fact), but rather than old-world
boards and beams its atmosphere today is one of elegance,
comfort and good taste.

Directions: Town centre follow directions for Castle & Museum

TAUNTON, **Farthings Hotel**

An elegant Georgian country hotel with a relaxed, convivial atmosphere where we enjoyed terrine of salmon and sole, and a sound fillet of beef with garlic, ginger and sesame seeds. Service is relaxed but efficient.

Smoking: No smoking in dining room
Accommodation: 9 en suite ★★

Directions: Village centre, just off A358 between Taunton (M5/J25) & Ilminster

Hatch Beauchamp TA3 6SG
Map 3: ST22
Tel: 01823 480664
Fax: 01823 481118
Cost: Set-price D £19.95. ☺
H/wine £9.95
Times: D only. Closed D Sun
Additional: Bar food D; Sunday L;
🍃 dishes

TAUNTON, **Meryan House Hotel**

Period dining room with large inglenook fireplace and ceiling beams. Dishes include fillet of wild Scottish salmon with asparagus, and rack of lamb with a honey and mustard crust.

Smoking: No smoking in dining room
Accommodation: 12 en suite

Directions: From Taunton/A38 direction Wellington. After 1 mile take 1st R (past crematorium) signed Bishops Hull Rd. Hotel is 600yds

Bishops Hull TA1 5EG
Map 3: ST22
Tel: 01823 337445
Fax: 01823 322355
Cost: Alc £18, set-price D £12.
☺ H/wine £9
Times: D only, 7-8.30pm. Closed Sun
Additional: Children welcome;
🍃 dishes

TAUNTON,
Mount Somerset Hotel

Splendid Georgian house enjoying wrap-around views of the Somerset countryside. Crispy duck leg and truffled pomme purée, and pan-fried pavé of sea bass with spinach and nutmeg purée, show the style.

Henlade TA3 5NB
Map 3: ST22
Tel: 01823 442500
Fax: 01823 442900
Cost: Set-price L £16.95/D £24.50.
H/wine £11.50
Times: Noon-2pm/7-9.30pm
Additional: Sunday L; Children welcome
Smoking: No smoking in dining room
Accommodation: 11 en suite ★★★

Directions: 3 miles SE of Taunton. From M5 J25 take A358 (Chard), turn R in Henlade (Stoke St Mary), then L at T-junction, hotel entrance 400yds R

WELLINGTON, **Bindon House**

The carte is the same price as the set-dinner, except every dish carries a supplement. Once you've worked that out, you can think about choosing between pan-fried sea bass, baby spinach, roasted scallops and a fish velouté, or roasted guinea fowl with wild mushroom ravioli and tarragon infusion – and that's only for starters. Main course dishes include grilled red mullet with pasta, baby vegetables and balsamic dressing, and beef Wellington with sarladaise potato, turned vegetables and

Langford Budville TA21 0RU
Map 3: ST12
Tel: 01823 400070
Fax: 01823 400071
Chef: Patrick Robert
Owners: Mark & Lynn Jaffa
Cost: Alc £40, set-price L £14.95 (2 courses)/D £29.50 (4 courses). H/wine £12.50
Times: Noon-2pm/7.30-9pm

Bindon House

Additional: Sunday L; Children 14+ at
D; 🍴 dishes
Seats: 32. Private dining room 12
Smoking: No smoking in dining room
Accommodation: 12 en suite ★★★

thyme sauce. For dessert, there's either variations on a set
theme – raspberry (mille-feuille, clafoutis, sorbet) or orange
(soufflé, sorbet, tart), or a 'trilogy' of Bindon chocolate, which
we take to mean a trio unless it comes consecutively rather
than concurrently. We should be told.

Directions: From Wellington B3187 to Langville Budville,
through village & R towards Wiveliscombe, R at jct, past Bindon
Farm, R after 450yds

WELLS,
Ancient Gate House Hotel

20 Sadler Street BA5 2RR
Map 3: ST54
Tel: 01749 672029
Fax: 01749 670319
Cost: *Alc* £22.70, set-price L £5.90/D
£14.50. ☺ H/wine £8.90
Times: Noon-2pm/7-10pm. Closed
25, 26 Dec
Additional: Bar food L; Sunday L;
Children welcome
Smoking: No pipes & cigars
Accommodation: 9 rooms
(7 en suite) ★

Directions: The corner of Cathedral
Green and Sadler Street

*A 14th-century inn overlooking the cathedral. The hotel's Italian
restaurant, popular among locals and tourists alike, provides silver
service of a wide choice of dishes.*

WELLS,
The Market Place Hotel

Ancient building with a modern outlook. When you get
wattleseed ice cream in Wells, then you know something
interesting is going on. The hotel, in the lee of the Cathedral,
might be over 500 years old, but is now a fascinating blend of
unique original features cleverly interwoven with uncluttered
modern styling, with cooking to match. An inner courtyard is
ideal for al fresco dining, and the busy bar and restaurant is
always buzzing. The dinner menu changes daily – impressive

One Market Place
BA5 2RW
Map 3: ST54
Tel: 01749 672616
Fax: 01749 679670
Chef: Paul Mingo-West
Owner: Christopher Chapman
Cost: *Alc* £25. ☺ H/wine £10.50
Times: Noon-2pm/7-9.30pm. Closed
L Sun, 28 Dec-2 Jan

The Market Place Hotel

Additional: Bar food L; Children welcome; 🌢 dishes
Seats: 50
Smoking: No smoking in dining room
Accommodation: 34 en suite ★ ★ ★

given the choice. Terrine of pressed ham hocks with apricot chutney showed a proper balance of sweet and sharp flavours; grilled supreme of salmon with sautéed spinach and a soft poached egg hollandaise arrived cooked exactly right with a deliciously fresh flavour. To finish, iced banana mousse with toffee sauce, but the choice might have been the equally racy dark chocolate torte with white chocolate sorbet and peppermint syrup. A simpler lunch menu changes seasonally.

Directions: A39 – A371. In centre of town, down one-way system. Directly in front of Conduit in Market Square

WILLITON, Curdon Mill ✤

Vellow TA4 4LS
Map 3: ST04
Tel: 01984 656522
Fax: 01984 656197
Cost: *Alc* £10, set-price L £14/D £22.50. ☺ H/wine £8.45
Times: Noon-2pm/6-8.30pm. Closed L Sat & Mon, all Sun
Additional: Sunday L; Children 8+
Smoking: No smoking in dining room
Accommodation: 8 en suite ★ ★

Directions: From A358 take Vellow/Stogumber road. Hotel 1 mile on L

Cosy first-floor restaurant in a converted mill with wonderful views of the Quantock Hills. Dishes from the short monthly menu reflect quality local produce and continental influences.

WILLITON,
White House Hotel ✤✤✤

The nicest of hotels tend to have the nicest of owners, and this is no exception. The house has a slightly bohemian air, albeit a rather smart boho, and Dick and Kay Smith go to a lot of trouble to make guests feel welcome and create a wonderfully relaxed and easygoing atmosphere. Fresh fish from Brixham and local game, is hard to beat and the delicious desserts (particularly Mrs Smith's chocolate pudding) are quite irresistible. Some of the most popular dishes have a provençale

Long Street TA4 4QW
Map 3: ST04
Tel: 01984 632306
Chef: Dick Smith
Owners: Dick & Kay Smith
Cost: Set-price D £31.50 (4 courses). H/wine £10
Times: D only, 7.30-8.30pm. Closed early Nov-mid May
Additional: Children welcome

White House Hotel

Smoking: No smoking in dining room
Accommodation: 10 en suite ★ ★
Credit cards: None

Directions: On A39 in the centre of village

touch, such as tartlet of smoked haddock brandade, and grilled sea bass on honey and wine vinegar with marinated aubergine in a light tomato jus. Another 'signature' dish is chargrilled breast of wood pigeon with fresh thyme and marjoram, thinly sliced and served rare on a hot beetroot and soured cream 'salad'. Local cheese is served with home-made oatcakes.

WINCANTON,

Holbrook House Hotel

Country house hotel set in pretty grounds; within log fires and deep armchairs. Canapés of mini croquette of smoked haddock, croûton topped with Mediterranean vegetables, mini beef kebab, and an *amuse-bouche* of salmon croquette, mini salad and balsamic dressing, started our test meal on a high note that never faltered. Confit of duck leg with five spice glaze came next, matched by aromatic couscous and oriental dressing. Marinated rump of lamb with ratatouille, confit of garlic and a Puy lentil, red wine jus was a delicious combination, as was the hot chocolate fondant with a honeycomb and praline ice cream. Espresso gave just the right hit of caffeine, petits fours showed that attention to lesser detail was exact. Comprehensive wine list.

Holbrook BA9 8BS
Tel: 01963 32377
Fax: 01963 32681
Telephone for further details

Directions: From A303 at Wincanton, L onto A371 towards Castle Cary & Shepton Mallet

WINSFORD,

Savery's at Karslake House

Former a 15th-century malt house, now a peaceful, welcoming hotel. A pleasant base from which to explore the surrounding Exmoor National Park. Another big attraction is John Savery's cooking with its emphasis on good locally sourced produce. The result is classic dishes given a modern twist: marinated salmon and prawns, for example, with a crème fraîche and horseradish dressing, or a foie gras parfait served with Cumberland sauce. Guinea fowl comes with bacon, cherry tomatoes and a light Pernod butter sauce, whilst lamb fillet gets spring onion mash on a mint and caper sauce. Desserts range from sticky toffee pudding and a delightfully presented individual rice pudding with caramelised bananas and Drambuie, to home-made ice creams (the Amaretto was superb) and sorbets. Partner Patricia Carpenter oversees service in a charming manner that is classy but unstuffy.

Halse Lane TA24 7JE
Map 3: SS93
Tel/Fax: 01643 851242
Chef: John Savery
Owners: Patricia Carpenter, John Savery
Cost: *Alc* £30, set-price D £27.50. H/wine £12.50
Times: D only, 7-9pm. Closed Feb
Additional: Children 15+; ✿ dishes
Seats: 28
Smoking: No smoking in dining room
Accommodation: 7 rooms

Directions: From A396 follow signs to Winsford and Exford. Enter Winsford and turn L at garage. On R past the Royal Oak Inn

WITHYPOOL, Royal Oak Inn ✿

Exmoor National Park TA24 7QP
Map 3: SS93
Tel: 01643 831506
Fax: 01643 831659
Cost: *Alc* £25, set-price D £19.50. ☺
H/wine £10
Times: D only, 7-9pm
Additional: Bar food; Sunday L (noon-1.30pm); Children 14+; ✿ dishes
Smoking: No smoking in dining room
Accommodation: 8 rooms (7 en suite)
★ ★

Directions: From M5 J27 take A396 (Minehead) 20 miles turn L to Winsford, then L in village

Village inn with a charming restaurant in the heart of Exmoor National Park. Dishes include rack of lamb with rosemary and redcurrant, and fillet of brill with fennel and Pernod.

WIVELISCOMBE,
Langley House ✿✿

The elegant dining-room is beamed, but instead of dark, heavy wood, pastel paintwork artfully co-ordinates with chintz fabric and light stencilled walls. Four-course dinners are based on prime quality cuts of meat, fish fresh from Brixham, and freshly harvested herbs and vegetables, many from their own kitchen garden. There is no choice until the dessert, but it would be hard to be displeased with a sample Saturday dinner that started with roasted cod with pine nut crust on a bed of lemon pearl barley with beurre blanc, followed by mignons of Somerset lamb (cut from the saddle) with a mint topping, onion and Cassis purée and a reduction of sherry vinegar, redcurrant and mint. After local cheese with walnut and banana bread, there was clementine and Cointreau syllabub, bread-and butter-pudding or a galette of fresh Tamar strawberries.

Langley Marsh TA4 2UF
Map 3: ST02
Tel: 01984 623318
Fax: 01984 624573
Chef: Peter Wilson
Owners: Peter & Anne Wilson
Cost: Set-price D £27.50. H/wine £12.50
Times: D only, 7.30-8.30pm
Additional: Children 7+; ✿ dishes
Seats: 18. Private dining room 18
Smoking: No smoking in dining room
Accommodation: 8 en suite ★ ★

Directions: Off B3277 0.5 mile from Wiveliscombe on Langley Marsh Rd

WOOKEY HOLE, Glencot House ✿

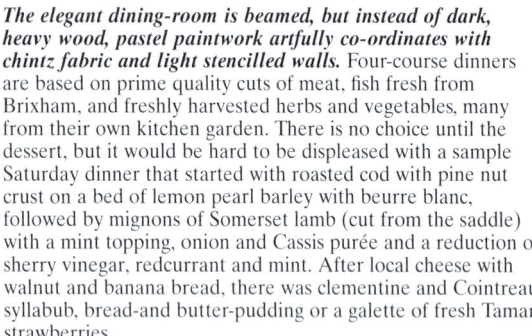

Glencot Lane BA5 1BH
Map 3: ST54
Tel: 01749 677160
Fax: 01749 670210
Cost: Set-price D £25.50. H/wine £9.95
Times: D only, 7-8.30pm
Additional: Bar food D; Children welcome; ✿ dishes
Smoking: No smoking in dining room
Accommodation: 13 en suite ★ ★

Directions: In village, turn L at sign for hotel after pink cottage on hill brow

An elegant riverside mansion set in 18 acres of peaceful grounds. In the oak-panelled dining room expect the likes of fillet of salmon with fettucine and crab meat, and cream of carrot and coriander soup.

WOOLVERTON,
Woolverton House Hotel

Stone-built period property retaining its panelling and stone fireplaces. Centimes restaurant offers a weekly fixed-price menu of dishes prepared by the French chef-proprietor.

Accommodation: 12 en suite ★★

Directions: On A36, 7 miles SE of Bath

Bath BA3 6QS
Map 3: ST75
Tel: 01373 830415
Fax: 01373 831243
Cost: *Alc* £15, set-price D £13.95. ☺
H/wine £9.95
Times: D only, 7.30-9.30pm. Closed Sun
Additional: dishes
Smoking: No smoking in dining room

YEOVIL, **Little Barwick House**

The Colley family have run this charming country hotel for twenty years. The unpretentious surroundings are matched by warm hospitality. Veronica Colley builds her menus around quality raw ingredients and her undoubted skill in the pastry/bread department. Combined with simple presentation on the menu and the plate – with freshness a major player – it is no wonder that the place was packed when our inspector called. That May dinner produced tomato soup with basil oil and garlic crostini, confit of duck on noodles with five-spice marinated breast, and lemon tart.

Barwick Village BA22 9TD
Map 3: ST51
Tel: 01935 423902
Fax: 01935 420908
Chef: Veronica Colley
Owners: Veronica & Christopher Colley
Cost: Set-price D £27.90 (4 courses). H/wine £10.90
Times: D only, 7-9pm. Closed Sun (ex residents)
Additional: Children welcome; dishes
Seats: 40. Private dining room 16
Smoking: No smoking in dining room; Air conditioning
Accommodation: 6 en suite ★

Directions: Turn off A371 Yeovil/Dorchester opposite Red House pub, 0.25 mile on L

YEOVIL, **Yeovil Court Hotel**

Family-run hotel on the outskirts of town. The popular bar leads into the Regency-striped restaurant; roast Gressingham duck with honey and orange sauce and ribeye steak with home-cut fries are good bets.

West Coker Road BA20 2NE
Map 3: ST51
Tel: 01935 863746
Fax: 01935 863990
Cost: *Alc* £18. ☺ H/wine £8.90
Times: Noon-1.45pm/7-9.45pm Closed L Sat, D Sun
Additional: Bar food; Sunday L; Children welcome; dishes
Smoking: No smoking in dining room
Accommodation: 26 en suite ★★★

Directions: On A30, 2.5 miles W of town centre

STAFFORDSHIRE

ACTON TRUSSELL,

Moat House

ST17 0RJ
Map 7: SJ91
Tel: 01785 712217
Fax: 01785 715344
Cost: *Alc* £30, set-price L £14.95/D
£21.95. ☺ H/wine £11.50
Times: Noon-2pm/7-10pm. Closed
26 Dec
Additional: Bar food; Sunday L;
Children welcome; 🍃 dishes
Smoking: No smoking in dining room;
Air conditioning
Accommodation: 21 en suite ★ ★ ★

Directions: M6 J13 head towards
Stafford, 1st R to Acton Trussell; Moat
House by church

*At the heart of this much expanded hotel complex is a 16th
Century inn which gives way to a spanking new conservatory
restaurant.* Families of ducks may well trundle past as you sit
at your table and the barges of the adjacent canal are often in
view. Matthew Davies and his team have worked hard to
reach a consistent standard with an intelligently conceived
menu that these days has a distinctly Mediterranean bent.
Fish is often well handled with some excellent sea-bass, for
instance, coming with langoustine, white beans and sauce
vierge in a light and aromatic combination. The style is fairly
direct, but there is plenty of technical skill apparent in dishes
such as poached quail with celeriac remoulade and onion
marmalade. Desserts are variations on some well known
themes with a lemon grass and tarragon crème brûlée having
been a particular success.

ECCLESHALL,

Julians Restaurant

NEW

21 High Street ST21 6BW
Map 7: SJ82
Tel: 01785 851200
Fax: 01785 859097
Cost: *Alc* £25, set-price L £11.95
(4 courses). ☺ H/wine £8.95
Times: Noon-2.30pm/7-9.30pm.
Closed Mon, Bh Mon
Additional: Sunday L; Children
welcome; 🍃 dishes
Smoking: No smoking in dining room

Directions: M6 J14 – A5013 to
Eccleshall 6-7 miles

*Open all day, the menu expands from coffee shop to restaurant as
day moves into night. Food is honest, soundly prepared and good
value; service is informal and friendly.*

STOKE-ON-TRENT,
George Hotel

Black Forest gâteau may be alive and well, but the cooking is sound and we had no complaints about a dinner of house pâté with Cumberland sauce, paupiettes of beef, and fresh fruit crumble with sauce anglaise.

Smoking: No pipes & cigars
Accommodation: 39 en suite ★★★

Directions: M6 J15 or 16 onto A500. Exit A53 towards Leek. Turn L onto A50 (Burslem)

Swan Square Burslem ST6 2AE
Map 7: SJ84
Tel: 01782 577544
Fax: 01782 837496
Cost: *Alc* £21, set-price L £10.95/D £15.95. ☺ H/wine £9.50
Times: Noon-2pm/7-9pm. Closed 25 Dec
Additional: Bar food; Sunday L; Children 12+ at D; ♨ dishes

SUFFOLK

ALDEBURGH,
Regatta Restaurant

Just the spot for a day at the coast. Bright bistro with nautical murals, pine floor and tables. Good fish dishes include breaded cod fillet Kiev with tomato tartare sauce, but there's also confit of duck with minty mushy peas and hand-cut chunky chips. Child-friendly.

Smoking: No-smoking area

Directions: Town centre

171 High Street IP15 5AN
Map 5: TM45
Tel/Fax: 01728 452011
Cost: *Alc* £18, set-price L & D £10. ☺ H/wine £9.50
Times: Noon-2pm/6-10pm. Closed Weds Nov-April
Additional: Sunday L; Children welcome; ♨ dishes

BECCLES, Randalls

18 Ballygate NR34 9NA
Map 5: TM48
Tel: 01502 716100
Cost: Set-price L £9.95/D £22.95. ☺ H/wine £8.50
Times: Noon-2pm/7-9pm. Closed D Sun, all Mon, 1 wk after Xmas, 2 wks Sep
Additional: Sunday L; Children 12+; ♨ dishes
Smoking: No smoking in dining room

Dating from the Middle Ages, decorated in soothing yellows and whites, open timbers as partitions, with the terraced garden to the rear an added attraction. Expect to find chicken liver parfait with light grape chutney, and pan-fried sea bass on fennel and leeks with a rich purée of plum tomatoes.

Directions: 200 yds from church in town centre

BECCLES, Swan House

By the Tower NR34 9HE
Map 5: TM48
Tel: 01502 7133474
Fax: 01502 716400
Cost: *Alc* £22, set-price L & D
£14.50. ☺ H/wine £8.80
Times: Noon-2.15pm/6.45-9.30pm
Additional: Children 14+; ✿ dishes
Smoking: No pipes & cigars

Directions: Next to church tower in
Market Place

*Built in the 16th century as a coaching inn. Free-range meats are a
strong suit: fillet steak, served with Stilton sauce, or duck, as confit
with rosemary and redcurrant jelly jus, preceded perhaps by Cromer
crab with lemon mayonnaise, and followed by bread-and-butter
pudding.*

BURY ST EDMUNDS, Angel Hotel

Angel Hill IP33 1LT
Map 5: TL86
Tel: 01284 753926
Fax: 01284 750092
Telephone for further details

Directions: Town centre, close to
Tourist Information

*Charles Dickens stayed at this ancient market square hotel. Today,
there's a choice of eating venues: the formal Abbeygate Restaurant
(original Georgian features complemented by a vivid Eastern
colonial look), or lighter meals in the brasserie-styled 12th-century
Vaults.*

BURY ST EDMUNDS,

The Priory Hotel ✿

*A fine Georgian house, popular with business and leisure guests.
The ambitious carte offers chargrilled chorizo and poached quails'
egg salad, or terrine of pink chicken livers and smoked bacon. For
dessert try lemon and ginger parfait with red berry coulis.*

Smoking: No-smoking area
Accommodation: 27 en suite ★ ★ ★

Directions: Leave A14 at exit for Bury St Edmunds West. Turn L
and after 1 mile turn R at 1st mini roundabout, hotel entrance
on R

Tollgate IP32 6EH
Map 5: TL86
Tel: 01284 766181
Fax: 01284 767604
Cost: *Alc* £30, set-price L £12 (2
courses)/D £22. ☺ H/wine £12.95
Times: Noon-2pm,/7-10pm. Closed L
Sat & Sun
Additional: Children welcome;
✿ dishes

BURY ST EDMUNDS,

Ravenwood Hall

An ornate interior brings reminders of the building's early Tudor history. Most dishes have a contemporary edge with fish and poultry smoked on the premises – it's worth trying oak-smoked breast of duck with apple and Calvados jus.

Seats: 50. Private dining room 50
Smoking: No smoking in dining room
Accommodation: 14 en suite ★ ★ ★

Directions: 3 miles E of Bury on A14, signposted to Rougham

Rougham IP30 9JA
Map 5: TL86
Tel: 01359 270345
Fax: 01359 270788
Chef: Annette Sherman
Owner: Craig Jarvis
Cost: *Alc* £27.95, set-price L
£18.95/D £27.95. ☺ H/wine £9.95
Times: Noon-2pm/7-9.30pm
Additional: Bar food; Sunday L;
Children welcome; ◑ dishes

FRESSINGFIELD,

Fox and Goose

In winter months open fires blaze in this olde worlde beamed inn, overlooking the graveyard. Most nights the atmospheric bar is filled with locals enjoying a pint, while diners tuck into some upbeat gutsy cooking in the bright, pretty dining room next door. We enjoyed seared chump of tender lamb with bacon, 'velvety' thyme mash and chunky battered onion rings but could have chosen equally tempting escalope of salmon with ginger butter, or pan-fried lambs' liver and mushrooms with tumeric rice. Desserts range from a 'creamy concoction' of apricot and Amaretto trifle with crushed toasted almonds, to sticky toffee pudding with toffee sauce.

Directions: A140 & B1118 (Stradbroke) L after 6 miles – in village centre by church

Nr Diss IP21 5PB
Map 5: TM27
Tel: 01379 586247
Fax: 01379 586688
Chef: Maxwell Dougal
Owners: Tim and Pauline O'Leary
Cost: *Alc* £25, set-price L £9.50 (2
courses)/D £17.50. ☺ H/wine £13.50
Times: Noon-2pm, 7-9pm
Additional: Bar food; Sunday L;
Children welcome: ◑ dishes
Seats: 40. Private dining room 20
Smoking: No smoking in dining room

HINTLESHAM,

Hintlesham Hall

IP8 3NS
Map 5: TM04
Tel: 01473 652268
Fax: 01473 652463
Chef: Alan Ford
Owner: David Allan
Cost: Set-price L £19.59/D £26.
H/wine £12.90
Times: Noon-1.45pm/7-9.30pm.
Closed L Sat

Fine example of a country house hotel with polished service.
The magnificent Georgian façade belies the Tudor origins of the house (parts date from 1570) and people applaud it for atmosphere and elegance. Although a pine-panelled parlour is sometimes called into use as a second dining room, the Salon is the real seat of action. It's a grand, elegant room with high ceilings, a fine setting for Alan Ford whose cooking is well able

to cope with every kitchen skill. However, this year unevenness has been coming through in reports. None the less, plaudits have been given for scallops with deep-fried salsify and orange marmalade, smoked chicken tomato and new potato terrine, and cod with oyster mushrooms and asparagus. There's a sense of style in dishes such as rosettes of red mullet and salmon with smoked eel kedgeree, or breast of pheasant served with wild mushrooms, pearl barley and foie gras chipolatas. Details – canapés and appetisers, petits fours – are all to the point. The wine list is good with plenty of curiosity here and a fair pricing policy. Three pages of house recommendations show careful selection. There's a decent selection of halves.

Signature dishes: double-baked crab and smoked salmon soufflé with cucumber chutney and asparagus salad; pot-roasted breast of maize-fed chicken with Parma ham and tiger prawns served in a red wine and lemongrass reduction; caramelised thin pineapple tart served with green peppercorn ice cream.

Directions: 5 miles west of Ipswich on the A1071 Hadleigh road

Additional: Sunday L; Children 10+ at D; ✿ dishes
Seats: 100. Private rooms 16, 40, 80. Jacket and tie preferred
Smoking: No smoking in dining room
Accommodation: 33 en suite ★ ★ ★ ★

AA Wine Award-see page 16
Shortlisted for

IPSWICH,

Marlborough Hotel ✿✿

Henley Road IP1 3SP
Map 5: TM14
Tel: 01473 257677
Fax: 01473 226927
Chef: Simon Barker
Owner: Robert Gough
Cost: *Alc* £29.50, set-price L £16/D £19.85. ☺ H/wine £9.85
Times: 12.30-2pm/7.30-9.30pm. Closed L Sat
Additional: Bar food; Sunday L; Children welcome; ✿ dishes
Seats: 50. Private dining rooms 30
Smoking: No smoking in dining room; Air conditioning
Accommodation: 22 en suite ★ ★ ★

Country house style in a quiet, residential setting. Polished and professional service paves the way for a style of cooking that is admirably varied and interesting within the context of a short *carte*. Freshly prepared pan-fried fillets of red mullet on fettucine with creamy rosemary sauce, and a warm salad of duck breast and Toulouse sausage dressed with truffle oil and balsamic vinegar are upbeat starters. The pace is maintained with fillets of turbot with filo parcels of lobster meat and king prawns with a delicate ginger sauce, and calves' liver with lardons of pancetta, creamy mash and beetroot chips with a port wine sauce. Vegetarian choice includes deep-fried Somerset brie with caramelised apples, and roasted Mediterranean vegetables in a provençale sauce with spätzle. There is a varying selection of cheeses, home-made sweets and petits fours.

Directions: Take A1156 from A14, or A1214 from A12. Turn R at Henley Road/A1214 crossroads

IPSWICH, **Scott's Brasserie**

Smart brasserie with a short carte strong on regional ingredients. Expect Cromer crab cakes with roasted vine tomato and basil dressing, and braised Norfolk lamb shank with roasted root vegetables, port and redcurrant sauce.

Smoking: No-smoking area; No pipes & cigars

Directions: Near Buttermarket shopping centre, close to Cox Lane and Foundation Street car parks

4a Orwell Place IP4 1BB
Map 5: TM14
Tel: 01473 230254
Fax: 01473 218851
Cost: Set-price L £12.95/D £17.95. ☺
H/wine £9.95
Times: Noon-2.30pm/6.30-9.45pm.
Closed L Sat, all Sun
Additional: Children 14+; ✦ dishes

IPSWICH,
Swallow Belstead Brook Hotel

Hotel with great leisure facilities, peaceful grounds and ambitious cooking. The menu yields some vibrant flavours packaged in a reassuring country-house style. Useful, well chosen wine list.

Belstead Brook Park Belstead Road
IP2 9HB
Map 5: TM14
Tel: 01473 684241
Fax: 01473 681249
Telephone for further details

Directions: Take A1214 exit at main
A12/A14 interchange then 3rd exit at
1st roundabout; after bridge take 1st L

IXWORTH,
Theobalds Restaurant

68 High Street Nr Bury St Edmunds
IP31 2HJ
Map 5: TL97
Tel/Fax: 01359 231707
Chef/Owner: Simon Theobald
Cost: *Alc* £30. H/wine £13.25
Times: 12.15-1.30pm/7.15-9.15pm.
Closed L Sat, D Sun, all Mon, 2 wks
Aug

Smart, upmarket restaurant, housed in a 16th-century building in the heart of the village. The seasonal menu is as elegant in its composition as the interior. In winter, choose roast skate wing with buttered white port and mustard seed sauce, or roast breast and braised leg of wild duckling on Savoy cabbage with port wine sauce (for two). Tournedos of hare are served on croûtons with bacon, wild mushrooms and Madeira sauce. Saucing skills are prominent: later in the year there may be roast lobster on tagliatelle with saffron and Noilly Prat sauce, or grilled fillet of brill on a bed of candied aubergines with a fresh tomato juice and herb sauce. Tantalising dishes include steamed globe artichokes with toasted walnuts and hollandaise sauce. Caramelised lemon and lime tart with lemon and lime sorbet is worthy of serious consideration.

Additional: Sunday L; Children 8+ at D; 🍴 dishes
Seats: 45. Private dining room 16. Jacket & tie preferred
Smoking: No smoking in dining room

Directions: 7 miles from Bury St Edmunds on A143 Bury/Diss road

LAVENHAM, Angel Hotel ✿

15th-century coaching inn at the centre of the fine medieval village with lots of beams and inglenook fireplaces. An appealing menu is based around traditional home-made fare.

Market Place CO10 9QZ
Map 5: TL94
Tel: 01787 247388
Fax: 01787 248344
Cost: *Alc* £17. ☺ H/wine £7.95
Times: Noon-2.15pm/6.45-9.15pm. Closed 25, 26 Dec
Additional: Bar food; Sunday L; Children welcome; 🍴 dishes
Smoking: No-smoking area; No pipes & cigars
Accommodation: 8 en suite ★ ★

Directions: Take A143 from Bury St Edmunds and turn onto A1141 after 4 miles; hotel is on Market Place, off High Street

LAVENHAM, The Great House ✿

There's a strong French feel to this restaurant-with-rooms overlooking the market square. Sample delicately sautéed sweetbreads on a warm potato and coriander salad topped with a poached egg; finish with a slice of rich chocolate terrine with orange coulis.

Market Place CO10 9QZ
Map 5: TL94
Tel: 01787 247431
Fax: 01787 248007
Cost: *Alc* D £33, set-price L £11.95 (2 courses)/D £18.95. ☺ H/wine £10.20
Times: Noon-2.30pm/7-9.30pm. Closed D Sun, all Mon (ex residents & Bhs at D), 3 wks Jan
Additional: Bar food L; Sunday L; Children welcome; 🍴 dishes
Smoking: No smoking in dining room
Accommodation: 5 en suite

Directions: In Market Place (turn into Market Lane from High Street)

LONG MELFORD,
Chimneys Restaurant ✿✿

There's a butcher, a baker and even a candlestick maker in the longest main street in the land. And even Lovejoy was here – the centre of East Anglia's antique trade, the

Hall Street CO10 9JR
Map 5: TL84
Tel: 01787 379806
Fax: 01787 312294
Chef: Wayne Messenger

Chimneys Restaurant

Owners: Sam & Zena Chalmers
Cost: *Alc* £29.50
Times: Noon-2pm/7-9.30pm. Closed Sun
Additional: Children welcome; ✿ dishes
Seats: 45

Directions: On main street of Long Melford village

picturesque and bustling village was the natural location for filming the TV series. The 16th-century beamed restaurant is light and airy, filled with pictures, prints and fresh floral arrangements. If at first sight the menu seems to lack challenge, it is worth remembering that little can beat traditional British dishes such as cream of mushroom soup, braised lamb shank with red onion and rosemary, and bread-and-butter pudding with fresh egg custard, when they are done as well as they are here. Other dishes are more European in style – warm salad of duck confit and orange; breast of chicken filled with Mozzarella and pesto on fresh tomato and basil sauce; tarte au citron.

LONG MELFORD,

The Countrymen

Well-established hotel on the village green, with a candlelit restaurant offering a set-price dinner menu with Mediterranean influences and a gastronomic menu including wines.

The Green CO10 9DN
Map 5: TL84
Tel: 01787 312356
Fax: 01787 374557
Cost: Set-price L £15.75/D £20.75 (4 courses). ☺ H/wine £10
Times: Noon-1.45pm/7-9pm. Closed D Sun, all Mon
Additional: Bar food L; Sunday L; Children welcome; ✿ dishes
Smoking: No smoking in dining room
Accommodation: 9 en suite ★★

Directions: On the village green in Long Melford

LONG MELFORD,

Scutchers Restaurant

It's not hard to see why this bright and busy bistro, decorated in primary colours with pine tables and chairs, is so popular.
The menu romps through a good cross-section of mod Brit dishes, and delivers them freshly cooked with a fair degree of panache. To start, there's wafers of Parma ham with

Westgate Street CO10 9DP
Map 5: TL84
Tel: 07000 728824
Fax: 07000 785443
Chef: Nicholas Barrett
Owners: Nicholas & Diane Barrett
Cost: *Alc* £22.50. ☺ H/wine £9.20

Parmesan, artichokes and rocket salad or sautéed foie gras on rösti with pea purée and port jus. Roasted fillet of halibut on a lobster and tarragon risotto, and roasted fillet of lamb with celeriac dauphinoise and Madeira jus are amongst the main courses, but grilled sirloin steaks with chasseur sauce are always a popular choice. Farmhouse Cheddar and Stilton with toasted crumpets and onion chutney stirs memories of high tea; otherwise there's iced tiramisu with a compote of raspberries or good old spotted dick with fudge sauce and vanilla custard.

Times: Noon-2pm/7-9.30pm. Closed Sun, Mon, 1st wk Jan, last wk Aug
Additional: Children welcome; 🍴 dishes
Seats: 75
Smoking: No pipes & cigars

Directions: About a mile from Long Melford on the road to Clare

LOWESTOFT,
Ivy House Farm

Ivy Lane Oulton Broad NR33 8HY
Map 5: TM59
Tel: 01502 501353/588144
Fax: 01502 501539
Cost: *Alc* £24.30. ☺ H/wine £9.50
Times: Noon-1.45pm/7-9.30pm
Additional: Bar food; 🍴 dishes
Smoking: No smoking in dining room
Accommodation: 13 en suite ★★★

Directions: From Lowestoft – follow A146 (Norwich). Hotel approx 0.25 mile after junction to A1117 (Ipswich), over small railway bridge

The restaurant is in an 18th-century barn, heavily beamed and thatched. The menu offers a good choice of ambitious modern European dishes with vibrant flavours.

MILDENHALL,
Riverside Hotel ✿

Mill Street IP28 7DP
Map 5: TL77
Tel: 01638 717274
Fax: 01638 715997
Telephone for further details

An imposing 18th-century, red-brick house situated on the banks of the River Lark. Facing the gardens and river, the hotel's restaurant offers a wide-ranging selection of dishes, with Thai chicken brochette, and duck breast en croûte featuring at inspection.

Directions: Leave M11/J9, then take A1101 from A11. L at mini roundabout along High St. Hotel is last building on L before bridge

NAYLAND, **White Hart Inn**

High Street CO6 4JF
Map 5: TL93
Tel: 01206 263382
Fax: 01206 263638
Cost: Set price L £17.70/D£23. H/wine £10
Times: Noon-2pm/6.30-9.30pm. Closed Mon, 26 Dec-3 Jan
Accommodation: 6 rooms

Directions: In the centre of village

Civilised inn that does everything with great style and panache. However, when our inspector called major changes were afoot, with the White Hart about to close for total refurbishment, to re-open in the autumn of 1999. In the kitchen chef Mark Precott was also leaving, making our current assessment invalid. But an inn under the watchful eye of Michel Roux, with a good wine list and a dedication to first-class quality produce and service, is one to take seriously; we expect the new-style White Hart to at least maintain its previous two AA Rosettes.

NEWMARKET,
Bedford Lodge Hotel

18th-century former hunting lodge that follows a racing theme throughout the hotel. The menu in the Godolphin restaurant offers a wide choice; the kitchen shows ambition and an awareness of modern trends.

Directions: From town centre follow A1303 towards Bury St Edmunds for half a mile

Bury Road CB8 7BX
Map 5: TL66
Tel: 01638 663175
Fax: 01638 667391
Telephone for further details

POLSTEAD, **Cock Inn**

Rural village pub overlooking the green. Vibrant cooking offers a global selection: tempura of seafood with red chilli and onion pickle, followed perhaps by Cajun spiced sirloin steak with roasted vegetables and straw potatoes.

Smoking: No-smoking area; Air conditioning

Directions: From Colchester take A134 towards Sudbury, then R to Stoke-by-Nayland. L at Angel Inn & follow signs for Polstead

The Green CO6 5AL
Map 5: TM14
Tel: 01206 263150
Fax: 01206 263950
Cost: *Alc* £25. ☺ H/wine £9.50
Times: 11am-2.30pm/6-9pm. Closed D Sun, all Mon
Additional: Bar food L; Sunday L; Children welcome; ◑ dishes

SOUTHWOLD, **Crown at Southwold**

Adnams-owned hotel-cum-restaurant-cum-bar renowned for its wine list. An assured, cosmopolitan kitchen produces smoked haddock fishcake with a light, herby chive sauce and pink lamb fillets glazed with chilli sauce, minted couscous and cucumber and yogurt dressing.

Directions: Take A1095 from A12; hotel at top of High Street, just before Market Place

90 High Street IP18 6DP
Map 5: TM57
Tel: 01502 722275
Fax: 01502 727263
Telephone for further details

SOUTHWOLD, **Swan Hotel**

Adnam's flagship hotel backing onto the brewery. Diners can mix-and-match from a choice of three interesting menus: The Classics, The Market Choice and the Swan Dinner.

Smoking: No smoking in dining room
Accommodation: 43 en suite ★★★

Directions: Take A1095 off A12; follow High Street into Market Place, hotel on L

Market Place IP18 6EG
Map 5: TM57
Tel: 01502 722186
Fax: 01502 724800
Cost: Set-price L £18/D £25. ☺ H/wine £8
Times: Noon-1.30pm/7-9.30pm. Closed L Nov-Mar exc Xmas
Additional: Bar food L; Sunday L; Children 5+; ◑ dishes

STOWMARKET, **Tot Hill House** ✿ **NEW**

An elegant calm prevails at this old beamed building, despite the proximity of the A14. An appetiser of a mini portion of fish and chips starts things off with a bang before, say, deep-fried goats' cheese with avocado and pecan nuts, then roast sea bass with truffled mash and chillied tomato compote.

Smoking: No smoking in dining room

Directions: On eastbound carriageway of A14 midway between Ipswich & Bury St Edmunds

IP14 3QH
Map 5: TM05
Tel/Fax: 01449 673375
Cost: *Alc* £27.95, set-price L £15.95. ☺ H/wine £13.50
Times: Noon-1.30pm/7-9.30pm. Closed D Sun, all Mon & Tue, L Sat, 1st 2 wks Jan, 2 wks end Aug-Sep
Additional: Sunday L; Children welcome; ◑ dishes

SUDBURY, Brasserie Four Seven

At one end of the town square, this popular bistro-style restaurant is a good place for a leisurely dinner or a speedy bite at lunch. An appealing, wide-ranging menu offers differing tastes and blackboard specials give extra choice.

Directions: 150 yards from Market Hill, next to Gainsborough House Museum

47 Gainsborough Street CO10 6ET
Map 5: TL84
Tel/Fax: 01787 374298
Telephone for further details

SUDBURY, Red Onion Bistro

Converted meeting hall with a café atmosphere. There's a daily set-lunch and dinner menu and a fortnightly evening carte, plus self-selection of wine from a large display.

Additional: Children welcome; ❸ dishes
Smoking: No pipes & cigars

Directions: On A131 Chelmsford road out of Sudbury

57 Ballingdon Street CO10 6DA
Map 5: TL84
Tel: 01787 376777
Fax: 01787 883156
Cost: Alc £16, set-price L £8.10/D £10.25. ☺ H/wine £7.75
Times: Noon-2pm/6.30-9.30pm. Closed Sun, Bh Mon, 25, 26 Dec

WOODBRIDGE, Captain's Table

Natural wood and pale yellow decor give an up-to-date look to the historic beamed cottage. The menu cleverly plots a course that will please both the gastronomically challenged and the adventurous foodie, without losing quality or integrity. As well as fresh melon with ginger and home-made pork pie with cucumber and onion pickle, there is layered red pepper, aubergine and courgette with tapenade dressing, although chargrilled tuna steak with salsa is about as exotic as it gets. Most dishes are as simple and direct as their descriptions – slow-roasted duck leg with cabbage; smoked haddock and salmon fishcake with lemon butter sauce; braised lamb shank and red wine sauce. Desserts are in the same vein (hot toffee pudding, vanilla crème brûlée), though for our money, freshly churned marmalade and Cointreau ice cream is the one that gets the taste buds going. Daily blackboard specials.

Directions: From A12, pass garden centre on L. Quay St is opposite station & theatre; restaurant 100 yds on L

3 Quay Street IP12 1BX
Map 5: TM24
Tel: 01394 383145
Fax: 01394 388508
Chef: Pascal Pommier
Owners: Jo Moussa, Pascal Pommier
Cost: Alc £17. ☺ H/wine £8.95
Times: Noon-2pm (3pm Sun)/6.30pm-9.30pm (10pm Fri, Sat). Closed D Sun, all Mon (ex Bhs)
Additional: Children welcome; ❸ dishes
Seats: 50. Private dining room 24
Smoking: No-smoking area

WOODBRIDGE,
Seckford Hall Hotel

Elizabethan manor house with magnificent panelled lounge and courtyard brasserie. The elegant restaurant serves poached sea bass on a warm vinaigrette of asparagus, tomato and artichoke or pan-fried venison with pickled red cabbage and mulberry sauce. Well-chosen wine list.

Additional: Bar food L (Bistro); Sunday L; Children welcome; ❸ dishes
Smoking: No smoking in dining room; Air conditioning
Accommodation: 32 en suite ★★★

Directions: Signposted on A12 (Woodbridge by-pass). Do not follow signs for town centre

IP13 6NU
Map 5: TM24
Tel: 01394 385678
Fax: 01394 380610
Cost: Alc £27.50, set-price L £13.50. H/wine £10.25
Times: 12.30-1.45pm/7.30-9.30pm. Closed 31 Dec

YAXLEY, The Bull Auberge

Ipswich Road Nr Eye IP23 8BZ
Map 5: TM17
Tel/Fax: 01379 783604
Cost: *Alc* £22, set-price L £10 (2
courses)/D £15.50. ☺ H/wine £9.20
Times: Noon-2pm/7-9pm. Closed D
Mon, all Sun
Additional: Bar food L; Children
welcome; ✦ dishes
Smoking: No-smoking area; Air
conditioning
Accommodation: 1 en suite

Directions: Adjacent to A140
(Norwich to Ipswich) on junction
B1117 to Eye

Small carte with a French feel and oriental influences at this 15th-century inn. Best dishes were Thai crab cakes, and roast fillet of beef with peppercorn and mustard sauce.

YOXFORD, Satis House Hotel

East meets West in decor and cuisine at this English country house. A wide choice of Malaysian dishes is offered and the chef's Malaysian Kenduri banquet is recommended.

Smoking: No smoking in dining room
Accommodation: 8 en suite ★★

Directions: On A12 just N of village

IP17 3EX
Map 5: TM36
Tel: 01728 668418
Fax: 01728 668640
Cost: *Alc* £22, set-price L £15 (4
courses)/D £22.50 (7 courses). ☺
H/wine £9.95
Times: D only, 7-9.30pm. Closed Sun
ex Bhs
Additional: Children 7+; ✦ dishes

SURREY

BAGSHOT, Pennyhill Park ✿✿✿

London Road GU19 5ET
Map 4: SU96
Tel: 01276 471774
Fax: 01276 473217
Chef: Karl Edmunds
Owners: Exclusive Hotels
Cost: *Alc* £55, set-price L £26/D £35.
H/wine £18.50
Times: 12.30-2.30pm/7-10pm. Closed
L Sat

The ornate italic print of the menu is in keeping with the mock Tudor dining room, heavily beamed and ornate with plaster relief rosettes. Part of the original, creeper-clad, Victorian house, now much extended, it looks out on beautiful formal gardens and flagged terraces used, under covers, for summer dining. The style of cooking is best described as modern English with French influences, typified by ballotine of salmon with herbs, langoustines and crème fraîche, and roasted sea bass on beetroot and horseradish risotto with star anise-infused Zinfandel jus. Ingredients are carefully sourced – La Ratte potatoes, for example, with sweet mustard dressing make an interesting accompaniment to a pressed terrine of foie gras. The latter is used unstintingly (reflected in the top-drawer prices), topping fillet of beef on a gâteau of spinach and wild mushrooms, or used as stuffing in breast of wild duck with truffled cabbage. Exotic fruit consommé with passion fruit Mascarpone cream, and hot liquorice and caramel soufflé with sharp lemon sorbet are desserts that manage to be both fashionable and alluring.

Additional: Bar food; Sunday L; Children welcome; 🍴 dishes
Seats: 32. Private dining room 20. Jacket & tie preferred
Smoking: No smoking in dining room; Air conditioning
Accommodation: 114 en suite
★ ★ ★ ★ ★

Directions: On A30 between Bagshot and Camberley

CLAYGATE,

Le Petit Pierrot Restaurant

Popular French restaurant with a lively atmosphere, decorated in shades of pink and grey. Set-lunch and dinner menus offer the same choice of dishes but vary in terms of number of courses taken. The menu is written in French with English explanation. First courses include traditional favourites such as terrine of duck livers with port wine, served with toasted rosemary brioche, and cream of Jerusalem artichoke soup with chervil, croûtons and crispy bacon. A more modern approach shows in marinated salmon with citrus fruits and dill chicory salad, and lobster salad with mango and turmeric flavoured sauce. The repertoire of main course dishes includes both sautéed calves' liver with sage and lime, or roast rack of lamb with tarragon jus, and steamed stuffed fillet of lemon sole, served with a ragout of squid. Crème caramel is a classic of its kind.

4 The Parade KT10 0NU
Map 4: TQ16
Tel: 01372 465105
Fax: 01372 467642
Chef: Jean-Pierre Brichot
Owners: Jean-Pierre & Annie Brichot
Cost: Set-price L £11.25 (2 courses)/D £22.50. 😊 H/wine £10.25
Times: 12.15-2.15pm/7.15-9.30pm. Closed L Sat, all Sun, 1 wk Xmas, Bhs
Additional: Children 9+; 🍴 dishes
Seats: 32
Smoking: No cigars; Air conditioning

Directions: Telephone for directions

EGHAM, **Runnymede Hotel**

Windsor Road TW20 0AG
Map 4: TQ07
Tel: 01784 436171
Fax: 01784 436340
Chef: Laurence Curtis
Owner: Ralph Trustees Ltd
Cost: H/wine £13.95
Times: 12.15-2.15pm/7-10.15pm. Closed L Sat, D Sun
Additional: Sunday L (12.15-3pm); Children welcome; 🍴 dishes
Seats: 150. Private rooms 10-350
Smoking: No-smoking area; Air conditioning

Large business hotel next to the Thames and handy for the M25. The stylish Left Bank restaurant has a contemporary aquatic decor, views of the river and an open-view kitchen. The quality of ingredients is important with locally grown vegetables and herbs in season and organic meats coming from a farm near Swindon. There's a distinctly fishy slant to the menu with such dishes as Loch Fyne scallops with roasted tomato, garlic and thyme, and monkfish with braised fennel and vanilla sauce. Or there might be roast chicken with root vegetables and tarragon jus, and calves' liver with shallot chutney and raisin jus. Even the vegetables are interesting with the likes of warm wood-roasted vegetable salad with Parmesan, and Dijon mustard sauce enlivening bubble and squeak. There is also a Seafood Bar with oysters, lobster mayonnaise and seafood platter. Pretty desserts.

Directions: On A308 Windsor road from M25 J3

Accommodation: 180 en suite
★ ★ ★ ★

EPSOM, Le Raj ✿

Bangladeshi restaurant with contemporary decor and soft lighting. Specialities such as freshwater fish with herbs sit alongside the more usual tikkas and dhansaks. Breads are a must.

Additional: Sunday L; Children welcome; 🍴 dishes
Smoking: No-smoking area; No pipes & cigars; Air conditioning

Directions: Off A217, near the racecourse

211 Firtree Road
KT17 3LB
Map 4: TQ26
Tel: 01737 371371/371064
Fax: 01737 211903
Cost: *Alc* £30, set-price L £9.99 (2 courses)/D £18. ☺ H/wine £10.95
Times: Noon-2pm/6-10.30pm. Closed 25, 26 Dec

EWELL, C'est la Vie ✿

French music puts you in the mood at this popular local restaurant, housed in a listed 16th-century building, where the seats are comfortable and the wine glasses large.

17 High Street KT17 1SB
Map 4: TQ26
Tel: 0181 3942933
Fax: 0181 7867123
Cost: *Alc* £24, set-price L £8.95/D £16.95 (4 courses). ☺ H/wine £9.75
Times: Noon-2pm/7-9.30pm
Additional: Sunday L; Children welcome; 🍴 dishes
Smoking: No-smoking area; Air conditioning

Directions: Village 1 mile from Epsom towards Kingston. Restaurant is 5 mins walk from rail station

FARNHAM, Bishop's Table Hotel ✿✿

Personally run Georgian town house hotel noted for attentive service. There's a delightful walled garden, and inside the place has been decorated tastefully with light pink walls and

27 West Street GU9 7DR
Map 4: SU84
Tel: 01252 710222
Fax: 01252 733494
Chef: Nicholas Reeves
Owner: Mr K Verjee
Cost: Set-price L&D £21. ☺ H/wine £10.50
Times: 12.30-1.45pm/7.30-9.30pm. Closed L Sat, 26 Dec-2 Jan
Additional: Sunday L; Children 10+; 🍴 menu
Seats: 50. Private dining room 18
Smoking: No smoking in dining room
Accommodation: 17 en suite ★ ★ ★

Directions: In the centre of the town

terracotta velvet chairs. Choose from three different menus, including a particularly strong vegetarian selection. Expect dishes along the lines of chargrilled breast of chicken with mushroom and lentil ice cream, roast fillet of cod with panaché of winter vegetables, and whole roast wood pigeon with port wine sauce. Desserts range from light mango mousse with Morello cherry ice cream, to white and dark chocolate truffles with Seville marmalade ice cream. The wine list includes some useful minor bottles at realistic prices.

GUILDFORD,
The Angel Posting House

91 High Street GU1 3DP
Map 4: SU94
Tel: 01483 564555
Fax: 01483 533770
Telephone for further details

Directions: In town centre (one way street)

Historic coaching inn where standards of service are high.
The town centre location means parking can be impossible at times – the hotel's valet parking service to the nearest car park is a bonus. Characterful old beams are part and parcel of the decor here, with the odd Jacobean fireplace and a 17th-century parliament clock thrown in for good measure, but the restaurant, located in the 13th-century stone-vaulted Crypt Restaurant, takes the prize for atmosphere. The kitchen, however, is rooted in the present day, and provide interesting dishes based on sound raw materials.

HERSHAM, Dining Room

10 & 12 Queens Road KT12 5LS
Map 4: TQ16
Tel: 01932 231686
Cost: *Alc* £17.50, set-price L/D £12.75 (2 courses). ☺ H/wine £10.50
Times: Noon-2pm/7-10.30pm. Closed L Sat, D Sun, 24 Dec-3 Jan, Bh Mon
Additional: Sunday L; Children welcome; ❹ dishes
Smoking: No-smoking area; No cigars & pipes; Air conditioning

Directions: From A3 at Esher take A244 (Walton-on-Thames); turn L into Hersham at Barley Mow pub/roundabout; restaurant just beyond village green

Cottagey, easy-going restaurant where British stalwarts such as steak and kidney pudding and spotted Dick share the menu with more innovative ideas like tomato and basil summer pudding.

HORLEY,

Langshott Manor

Elizabethan manor with a beamed dining room decorated in dark blue and gold. Dishes such as hogs pudding and roast duckling reflect good use of fresh produce and sound cooking skills.

Smoking: No smoking in dining room
Accommodation: 15 en suite ★★

Directions: From A23 Horley, take Ladbroke Road turning off Chequers Hotel roundabout, 0.75 mile on R

Ladbroke Road RH6 9LN
Map 4: TQ24
Tel: 01293 786680
Fax: 01293 783905
Cost: Set-price L £24.95/D £35. H/wine £17
Times: Noon-2pm/7-9.30pm
Additional: Bar food; Sunday L; Children welcome; ❹ dishes

KINGSTON-UPON-THAMES,

Ayudhya Thai Restaurant

14 Kingston Hill KT2 7NH
Map GtL: B2
Tel/Fax: 0181 5495984/5465878
Chef/Owner: Somjai Thanpho
Cost: *Alc* £19. ☺ H/wine £8.75
Times: Noon-2.30pm/6.30-11pm. Closed Mon, 25, 26 Dec, Bhs
Additional: Children welcome; ❹ dishes
Seats: 82. Private dining room 22
Smoking: No-smoking area

Teak-panelled restaurant, very atmospheric with wood carving, artefacts, a small temple shrine and many (Thai) royal portraits. The menu is a large affair, but is lifted above the average by authentic, quality ingredients and clarity of flavours. Tried and tested starters include chicken marinated in screwpine leaves, and minced pork with coriander, garlic and soy sauce, wrapped in a thin pancake and deep-fried. Hot-and-sour prawn soup delivers expected fire, backed up by the slow release of subtle flavours of lemongrass, galangal, kaffir and spring onions. Good spicing and coconut creaminess was properly balanced in a classic green chicken curry which got full marks for meat that had actually been poached in the stock. There are a few traditional desserts on offer, mostly coconut and egg custard-based, but whilst good to see, in reality these are something of an acquired taste.

Directions: 0.5 mile from Kingston town centre on A308, and 2.5 miles from Robin Hood Roundabout at the junction of A3

KINGSTON-UPON-THAMES,

Frère Jacques

With its bustling atmosphere, French staff and menus, you could well be across the Channel, tucking into fish soup, moules, chargrilled

10-12 Riverside Walk off Bishops Hall KT1 1QN
Map GtL: B2
Tel: 0181 5461332

steak with frites, or confit of duck. Another branch is located at 136 Upper Richmond Road, Putney SW15, Tel 0181 7883900.

Frère Jacques

Fax: 0181 5461956
Cost: *Alc* £18.50, set-price L £7.50 (2 courses)/D £16.50. ☺ H/wine £10.90
Times: Noon-11pm. Closed 25, 26 Dec, 1 Jan
Additional: Sunday L; Children welcome; ✿ dishes
Smoking: No-smoking area; Air conditioning

Directions: 50 metres S of the Kingston side of Kingston Bridge. By the river

OCKLEY,

Bryce's Seafood Restaurant

Lively British fish and seafood restaurant with a menu to gladden the hearts of fishmongers everywhere. There's Thai-style fish stew, spiced sesame crusted tuna, roasted monkfish in Cajun spices and lots more along the same upbeat lines.

Additional: Bar food; Sunday L; Children welcome; ✿ dishes
Smoking: No smoking in dining room

Directions: 8 miles south of Dorking on A29

RH5 5TH
Map 4: TQ14
Tel: 01306 627430
Fax: 01306 628274
Cost: Set-price L £17.50 (2 courses)/D £23.50. ☺ H/wine £9.75
Times: Noon-2.30pm/7-9.30pm. Closed D Sun Nov, Jan, Feb, 25-26 Dec, 1 Jan

REDHILL, **Nutfield Priory**

Nutfield RH1 4EL
Map 4: TQ35
Tel: 01737 824400
Fax: 01737 823321
Chef: David Rees
Owners: Arcadian Hotels
Cost: *Alc* £35, set-price L £16/D £24.50. ☺ H/wine £12.50
Times: Noon-2pm/7-10pm. Closed L Sat, 26-29 Dec
Additional: Bar food; Sunday L; Children welcome; ✿ dishes
Seats: 65. Private dining room 6-100
Smoking: No smoking in dining room

The huge Gothic-style house is modelled on the Palace of Westminster. It is set in extensive grounds and the stone-cloistered dining-room has spectacular views through arched windows over the Sussex and Surrey countryside. The *carte* is an impressive affair with a good range of modern British dishes. All the expected elements are there – ravioli with cappuccino, pesto, Balsamic dressing, saffron mash, lemongrass – but for the main part, execution lifts them a cut above the norm. Both hand-dived scallops with rösti potato, baby spinach, crème fraîche and caviar, and breast of mallard with confit of leg, roast pear and Amontillado sauce owed much of

their success to high quality ingredients. Passion fruit tart with caramel ice cream also delivered all the expected flavours. Given this was on the menu, however, it was a mite careless to have a sorbet course also flavoured with – yes, you've guessed it – passion fruit!

REIGATE, **Bridge House Hotel**

High on Reigate Hill with panoramic views over the surrounding countryside, this well-established hotel offers a good standard of cooking with a strong Mediterranean accent. Live music and dancing are featured on most nights.

Directions: M25/J8 (Reigate), A217 under footbridge and then on R

Accommodation: 60 en suite ★ ★ ★ ★

Directions: On A25 1 mile E of Redhill

Reigate Hill RH2 9RP
Map 4: TQ25
Tel: 01737 246801/244821
Fax: 01737 223756
Telephone for further details

REIGATE, **The Dining Room**

Smart, modern restaurant decorated with still life prints.
Media star Tony Tobin heads the brigade and weaves a streak of clever innovation through the *carte*. Warm salad of calves' liver, Jerusalem artichokes, rocket and Balsamic dressing, for example, or roasted breast of guinea fowl with shiitake lasagne. The daily lunch menu offers a good choice – a sample menu featured ragout of mussels and saffron with potatoes and asparagus, plus braised shin of beef in red wine with little thyme dumplings. Simplicity won the day in a dessert of summer pudding with raspberry coulis and clotted cream, though honeycomb, caramel and bitter chocolate ice cream sandwich with chocolate florentines sounds interesting.

Directions: First floor restaurant on Reigate High Street

59a High Street RH2 9AE
Map 4: TQ25
Tel/Fax: 01737 226650
Chef: Tony Tobin
Owner: Paul Montalto Elite Restaurants Ltd
Cost: *Alc* £35, set-price L £10 (2 courses)/D £16.95 (2 courses). ☺
H/wine £9.50
Times: Noon-2.30pm/7-10pm. Closed L Sat, D Sun
Additional: Sunday L; Children welcome; ✤ dishes
Seats: 50
Smoking: No smoking in dining room; Air conditioning

RIPLEY,
Michels' Restaurant

13 High Street GU23 6AQ
Map 4: TQ05
Tel: 01483 224777
Fax: 01483 222940
Chef: Erik Michel
Owners: Erik & Karen Michel
Cost: *Alc* £45, set-price L £18/D £30 (4 courses). H/wine £14.50
Times: 12.30-1.30pm/7.30-9pm (7-9.30pm Sat). Closed L Sat, D Sun, all Mon, beginning of Jan, 2 wks Aug
Additional: Sunday L; Children welcome
Seats: 50. Private dining room 12
Smoking: No pipes & cigars

Push open the front door (the place might actually look closed). Have a drink in a 'squishy' armchair in the seating area, then take a place at one of the high-backed chairs in the buttermilk-walled restaurant, with its paintings, objets d'art, peach tablecloths and napkins folded in a bow shape. This is the setting for some gutsy cooking: chunky brandade of salmon and potato sandwiched between two crisp croûtons with a caper and parsley sauce, or pan-fried boar in black pepper jus with purée chestnuts, watercress and spätzle. The kitchen's labour-intensive philosophy is well exemplified by pork crepinette, a cut of shoulder soaked in brine for a couple of days, poached in a spiced and herbed liquor, then shredded and wrapped in caul, arriving on the plate with creamy mash, lentils and crunchy sauerkraut – all 'thoroughly enjoyed'. A taster of farmhouse cheese is served before puddings, the kitchen's skills shining through a 'floaty' baba soaked in spiced rum syrup with fresh fruit salad. Breads are good, as are petits fours, and eight reasonably priced house wines, from France, Spain and Chile, head up the wine list.

Directions: Take M25 J10 towards Guildford. First exit to Ripley just past lights on R

SHERE, Kinghams

Gomshall Lane GU5 9HE
Map 4: TQ04
Tel: 01483 202168
Chef/Owner: Paul Baker
Cost: *Alc* £30, set-price L £10.95/D £12.50 (both 2 courses). ☺ H/wine £10.95
Times: Noon-2pm/7-9.30pm. Closed D Sun, all Mon, 25 Dec-2 Jan
Additional: Sunday L; Children welcome; ✿ dishes
Seats: 46. Private dining room 26
Smoking: No smoking in dining room

Rambling roses, bronze statues and fountains, a picture-book house in a best kept village. Kinghams simply couldn't have a more delightful setting. The kitchen, however, explores pastures new with dishes such as pan-fried fillet of ostrich marinated in lemon, orange and ginger with cranberry and port dressing, or tian of fresh white crabmeat and papaya with melon and basil dressing. A more conventional note is struck in main course dishes: tenderloin of pork wrapped in spinach and smoked bacon, glazed with brie on wholegrain mustard; roast best end of lamb with an apricot crust on a minted lamb jus. Daily fish dishes are highlighted on the fish board. Side dishes might include baby roast or creamy mashed potatoes. Desserts sound positively yummy – pineapple treacle tart with clotted cream, and gooey chocolate pudding served with orange scented anglaise. The English cheeseboard includes Cornish Yarg and Shropshire Blue.

Directions: From Dorking follow A25; from Guildford follow A246 then A25

SOUTH GODSTONE,
Tu Tu L'Auberge Restaurant ❁

Restaurant with a country house outlook but radically modern aspects to its interior. Up-to-date ideas include polenta and mascarpone tart and pan-fried fillet of sea bream with confit of aubergine.

Tilburstow Hill
RH9 8JY
Map 5: TQ35
Tel: 01342 892318
Fax: 01342 893435

Tu Tu L'Auberge Restaurant

Cost: *Alc* £29, set-price L & D £16.50. ☺ H/wine £12.75
Times: Noon-1.45pm/7-9.45pm. Closed D Sun, all Mon, 26-30 Dec
Additional: Sunday L; Children welcome; 🍴 dishes
Smoking: No pipes & cigars

Directions: M25 J6 – A22 (Godstone) turn right after Bell pub

STOKE D'ABERNON, Woodlands Park

Woodlands Lane KT11 3QB
Map 4: TQ15
Tel: 01372 843933
Fax: 01372 842704
Chef: James Chapman
Owners: Arcadian Hotels
Cost: *Alc* £40, set-price D £25.50. H/wine £11.95
Times: 12.30-1.45pm/7-9.30pm. Closed D Sun, 25 Dec
Additional: Sunday L; Children welcome; 🍴 dishes
Seats: 35. Private dining room 2-300
Smoking: No smoking in dining room
Accommodation: 59 en suite ★ ★ ★ ★

Directions: On A245 between Leatherhead and Cobham, close to M25 J10

The Bryant and May fortune was founded on a simple, everyday necessity. Millions of matches bought them a Victorian mansion set in its own parkland (now conveniently close to the motorway network). The hotel offers modern British cooking in the traditional setting of the Oak Room, with a *carte* that is focused and carefully thought out with well-matched ingredients. Breast of Debben duck with braised duck leg is accompanied by creamed potatoes, white bean and choucroute; grilled calves' liver is given extra interest by braised Baby Gem lettuce with roast carrots, caper and onion mash and a peppered sauce. Fish such as roast sea bass on confit fennel with niçoise garnish is generally simply handled, although starters such as carpaccio of tuna with rocket salad, deep-fried parsnip and ginger syrup, or seared red snapper with asparagus and watercress dressing make a good alternative to white bean soup with truffle oil, or warm quail salad with quails' eggs and balsamic potatoes.

TADWORTH, Gemini

28 Station Approach KT20 5AH
Map 4: TQ25
Tel: 01737 812179
Cost: Set-price L £15.50/D £28.50. H/wine £9.50
Times: Noon-2.30pm/7-9.30pm. Closed L Sat, D Sun, all Mon, 2 wks Xmas & summer
Additional: Sunday L; Children welcome L only; 🍴 dishes

Confidently prepared classical dishes at this semi-rural restaurant, with the likes of fresh mussels steamed with cider and lime leaves, and saddle of wild roe venison with roast pears.

Smoking: No smoking in dining room

Directions: M25 J8, on roundabout turn R to Sutton, on 3rd roundabout take 2nd exit to Tadworth. At traffic lights turn R, restaurant is on L

THAMES DITTON, Avant Garde

Snails and frogs legs, duck magret and fish soup – no prizes for guessing the national affiliation of this blue-and-white bistro. The first two ingredients are served in 'cassolettes', the *specialité de la maison,* cooked in a cream of garlic sauce with julienne of leeks and wild mushrooms. Queen scallops are served in the same style. There is a good choice of fish dishes within the short menu, such as roasted sea bass with red wine butter sauce, fennel fondue, vegetables and new potatoes, or seafood medley cooked in a mushroom sauce, served in a puff pastry and accompanied by a salad. Roasted rack of lamb on grain mustard sauce, decorated with fried basil, with courgettes, tomatoes and potato gratin, keeps to a typical cuisine bourgeois style. Try the home-made chocolate gâteau served warm with vanilla ice cream and whipped cream for dessert.

75 High Street KT7 0SF
Map GtL: B1
Tel/Fax: 0181 398 5540
Chef/Owner: Frederic Dervin
Cost: *Alc* £25, set-price L £12/D £16.50. ☺ H/wine £11.95
Times: Noon-2pm/7-10pm. Closed Sun
Additional: Children 6+; 🍲 dishes
Seats: 44. Private dining room 12

Directions: 5 mins from Hampton Court Palace

WEYBRIDGE,
Oatlands Park Hotel

Elegant restaurant with lake views, recapturing an age when people had time for the finer things in life. Seasonal menu featuring fresh fish and game, with a sensational dessert trolley.

Accommodation: 134 en suite ★★★★

Directions: Through town, up Monument Hill, L into Oatlands Drive. Hotel on L

146 Oatlands Drive KT13 9HB
Map 4: TQ06
Tel: 01932 847242
Fax: 01932 842252
Cost: *Alc* £35, set-price L £19/D £24. ☺ H/wine £12.25
Times: 12.30-2pm/7-9.45pm
Additional: Bar food; Sunday L; Children welcome; 🍲 dishes
Smoking: No-smoking area; No pipes & cigars

SUSSEX
EAST

ALFRISTON,
Moonraker's Restaurant

Attractive 16th-century cottage restaurant with lots of beams and white-painted walls. An interesting and well-balanced menu is complemented by a good wine list.

Smoking: No-smoking area; No pipes & cigars

Directions: Signposted from A27 between Brighton & Eastbourne

High Street BN26 5TD
Map 5: TQ50
Tel: 01323 870472
Cost: *Alc* £23, set-price D £15.95. ☺ H/wine £9.50
Times: D only, 7-10pm. Closed D Sun, 1st wk Jan
Additional: Sunday L; Children 8+; 🍲 dishes

BATTLE, Netherfield Place

Georgian-style country house, with a beautiful wood-panelled restaurant that overlooks delightful formal gardens. The kitchen garden provides most of the vegetables and herbs, the restaurant has both a *carte* and table d'hôte menus, and there is good bread, canapés and petits fours. This is a formal restaurant offering many well-known dishes: chicken liver parfait; tartlet of wild mushrooms; oven-roasted fillet of sea bass topped with a black olive crust and set on a spicy tomato fondue; and nougat parfait glacé with raspberry coulis. Unfortunately the kitchen doesn't always reach the high

Netherfield TN33 9PP
Map 5: TQ71
Tel: 01424 774455
Fax: 01424 774024
Chef: Anton Goodwin
Owner: Michael Collier
Cost: *Alc* £32, set-price L £16.95/D £27.50. H/wine £11.95
Times: 12.30-2pm/7-9.30pm (9pm Sun). Closed Xmas, New Year
Additional: Bar food; Sunday L; Children welcome; 🍲 dishes

Netherfield Place

Seats: 50. Private dining room 4-40
Smoking: No pipes & cigars
Accommodation: 14 en suite ★ ★ ★

standards it aspires to, which is a shame as the service and setting are both first class

Directions: M25 J5 – A21 (Hastings) to A2100 for Netherfield; hotel is on L after 1.5 miles

BRIGHTON, **Black Chapati** ✿✿

Decor is an exercise in shabby minimalism on a shoestring – black, white and stark lighting – you are here for the food.
Indomitable proprietor Stephen Funnell can claim to be the father of fusion cooking in this country – he was doing it long before the term was coined and is one of the few chefs in Britain who actually understands what the term and concept mean. So he continues to do his own thing, woefully under appreciated, producing food that is generically Asian, but even then not slavishly so. Chinese, Japanese, Thai, Indian and South East Asian ingredients are given an excellent twist, French classics are examined too, and even the odd Moroccan-inspired dish might crop up on the menu. Flavours and combinations are intelligently thought through and pairings can be inspired. Sri Lankan lamb patties with vibrant fresh chutneys are a marvellous reworking of the samosa, or there could be pan-fried Cornish scallops with glass noodles. For main course grilled chicken with lemongrass and coconut, sticky steamed rice and Malaysian pickles, could be offset by a more classic crispy roast duck leg, spring onion mash, shallot sauce and preserved greens. Desserts are Europe-based, occasionally with a twist – cardamom crème brûlée, walnut toffee tart, or lemongrass and banana ice cream. The booze offered is sourced cleverly: raw Breton cider is a good accompaniment, as is Czech Budweiser, but the short, well-chosen wine list slightly misses the point – you need to quaff wine here, not sip daintily.

12 Circus Parade New England Road
BN1 4GW
Map 4: TQ30
Tel: 01273 699011
Chef: Stephen Funnell
Owners: Stephen Funnell, Lauren Alker
Cost: *Alc* £20.50. ☺ H/wine £9.95
Additional: Children welcome; ⌬ dishes
Times: D only 7-10.30pm (from 6.30pm Sat). Closed Sun, Mon, 2 wks Xmas, 2 wks Jul
Seats: 32
Smoking: No pipes & cigars

Directions: Directions are complex. Readers are advised to use a local map

BRIGHTON, **La Marinade** ✿

Intimate split-level restaurant with late 70's decor. Typical dishes are Dover sole gratinée 'Bonne Femme', red mullet fillets with basil and olive oil, and crêpes Suzette with Grand Marnier.

Smoking: No-smoking area; Air conditioning

Directions: From Palace Pier take direction of Marina, turn L at Royal Sussex Hospital sign, then first L

77 St George Road Kemp Town
BN2 1EF
Map 4: TQ30
Tel/Fax: 01273 600992
Cost: Set-price L £14/D £19. ☺ H/wine £9.80
Times: Noon-2pm/7-10pm. Closed D Sun, all Mon
Additional: Sunday L; Children welcome; ⌬ dishes

BRIGHTON,
One Paston Place ❀❀

Light, airy restaurant with striking decor. The Emmersons
have been very successful at creating a bright, warm
atmosphere, and they play the consummate hosts: Nicole
mothers her guests ever so slightly in a delightfully endearing
way; Mark cooks 'some of the best food in Brighton'. He offers
roast scallops with pancetta and green bean purée, warm lentil
salad with foie gras and sweetbreads and a beetroot
vinaigrette, squab pigeon glazed with lemon and star anise, and
pavé of wild boar, horseradish and capers. Fish is good,
especially given the location, with red mullet served as a soup
with rosemary, sea bass 'au pistou', and brill with girolles.
Desserts are imaginative. Vanilla and rice pudding crème
brûlée, and banana tarte Tatin with tamarind and nutmeg ice
cream are two begging to be tried.

Directions: Just off the seafront about halfway between the
Palace Pier and the Marina

1 Paston Place BN2 1HA
Map 4: TQ30
Tel: 01273 606933
Fax: 01273 675686
Chef: Mark Emmerson
Owners: Mark & Nicole Emmerson
Cost: *Alc* £32, set-price L £16.50/D
£38 (5 courses). H/wine £11
Times: 12.30-2pm/7.30-10pm. Closed
Sun, Mon, 1st 2 wks Jan & Aug
Additional: Children 5+
Seats: 45
Smoking: No pipes & cigars; Air
conditioning

BRIGHTON, **Terre à Terre** ❀

*Wittily styled, global modern vegetarian food in a colourful,
contemporary setting. Great sushi starters, followed by smoked
Cheddar soufflé, chocolate and Amaretto mousse and super espresso
added up to an experience well worth a return visit.*

71 East Street BN1 1HQ
Map 4: TQ30
Tel: 01273 729051
Fax: 01273 327561
Cost: *Alc* £18. ☺ H/wine £9.75
Times: Noon-5.30pm/6-10.30pm.
Closed L Mon, 25-26 Dec, 1 Jan
Additional: Children welcome;
🍽 dishes
Smoking: No-smoking area; No pipes
& cigars; Air conditioning

Directions: Town centre near Cannon
cinema, close to Palace Pier

BRIGHTON, **Whytes** ❀❀

***A small, cosy restaurant, just off the seafront, with
interesting pictures on plain walls, banquette seating, closely
set tables and a friendly atmosphere.*** Special themed nights
are something of an occasion – a gourmet night of game
terrine, pigeon sausages, guinea fowl then pudding, say – but
otherwise the short, sharp menu sticks to starters like beef
carpaccio with Parmesan shavings and basil, then roast saddle
of rabbit with a sauce of roasted pepper, garlic and tarragon
hinting of chilli. The daily fish dish might be a medley that
includes brill, turbot and lemon sole, all moist and full of
flavour, on couscous with a light thyme sauce, and among
interesting vegetarian options could be roasted vegetable
gâteau on rösti and sun-dried tomato dressing. Round things
off with apple crumble with banana ice cream and vanilla
sauce.

33 Western Street BN1 2PG
Map 4: TQ30
Tel/Fax: 01273 776618
Chef: Ian Whyte
Owners: Ian & Jane Whyte
Cost: Set-price D £21. ☺ H/wine
£9.40
Times: D only, 7-9.30pm. Closed
Sun, Mon, last 2wks Feb
Additional: 🍽 dishes
Seats: 36. Private dining room 12
Smoking: No pipes & cigars

Directions: On the Brighton-Hove
border, Western St is off the seafront,
1st R after the Norfolk Resort Hotel

CROWBOROUGH,
Winston Manor Hotel ❁❁

Traditional country house hotel with enthusiastic, charming staff. Dinner is a real treat with modern British cooking to the fore, and some stunning pastry work to boot. We started our test meal with pan-fried scallops topped with some intense tomato fondue and raw salsa of courgettes, peppers, tomatoes and olive oil – nice clean flavours throughout. Main course was a confit and breast of duck on sweet garlic mash teamed with Puy lentils and a really clean tasting, rich claret-based duck jus. Pudding produced three superbly executed chocolate puddings: a white chocolate ganache mille-feuille; a stunning chocolate torte; and a chocolate and Bailey's assemblage. Good canapés and petits fours, great breads. A place to watch.

Directions: Midway between Tunbridge Wells and Uckfield on A26

Beacon Road TN6 1AD
Map 5: TQ53
Tel: 01892 652772
Fax: 01892 665537
Chefs: Jason Kilby, Andy Owen
Cost: *Alc* £32, set-price D £21.50. ☺
H/wine £10.50
Times: D only, 7-9.15pm. Closed Xmas
Additional: Bar food; Sunday L (noon-2.30pm); Children welcome; ✿ dishes
Seats: 50. Private dining room 25
Smoking: No smoking in dining room
Accommodation: 51 en suite ★ ★ ★

EASTBOURNE, **Grand Hotel – Mirabelle**

Impressive Victorian hotel at the western end of the seafront before the steep ascent to Beachy Head. Major transformation equals change and as we went to press the two AA Rosette restaurant Mirabelle was closed for refurbishment and a replacement being sought for head chef Simon Hulstone (although executive chef Keith Mitchell remains). The restaurant will be expanded to incorporate a larger bar area.

Smoking: No pipes & cigars; Air conditioning
Accommodation: 152 en suite ★ ★ ★ ★ ★

Directions: At the western end of the seafront

King Edward's Parade BN21 4EQ
Map 5: TV69
Tel: 01323 412345
Fax: 01323 412233
Cost: *Alc* £40, set-price L £19.50/D £32. H/wine £12.95
Times: 12.30-2pm/7-9.30pm. Closed Sun, Mon, 1st 2 wks Jan, 1st 2wks Aug
Additional: Children welcome; ✿ dishes
Seats: 50. Private dining rooms up to 250. Jacket & tie preferred

FOREST ROW,
Ashdown Park Hotel ❁❁

Wych Cross RH18 5JR
Map 5: TQ43
Tel: 01342 824988
Fax: 01342 826206
Chef: John McManus
Cost: *Alc* £40, set-price L £21/D £33 (4 courses). ☺ H/wine £13.25
Times: 12.30-2pm/7.30-10pm
Additional: Bar food L; Sunday L;

Not many restaurants can boast such wonderful views over lake, park and woodland beyond. Ashdown Park has also mastered the art of balancing the needs of corporate as well as private guests – the latter get the better views in the dining room – and service is genuinely helpful without being arrogant and pretentious. John McManus can cook. His menus are simple and to the point with the emphasis on accuracy of technique and flavour. Seared tuna with crispy squid and tomato salsa, or venison, pigeon and smoked bacon terrine with kumquat and pistachio marmalade, are typical starters. Main courses bring medley of seafood with mussel risotto and saffron bouillon, or breast of corn-fed chicken glazed with creamed leeks and truffles. Desserts range from warm pecan pie with clotted cream to passion fruit delice. The wine list is both informed and informative, sources are eminently respectable and prices are sensible.

Directions: From A22 at Wych Cross take Hartfield turning, hotel is 0.75 mile on R

Children welcome; ✿ dishes.
Seats: 100. Private dining room up to 150. Jacket & tie preferred
Smoking: No smoking in dining room
Accommodation: 95 en suite ★ ★ ★ ★

AA Wine Award-see page 16 Shortlisted for

HAILSHAM, **Boship Farm Hotel** ✿

A 17th-century farmhouse set in 17 acres. Trio of venison sausages with onion gravy and chive mash, and salmon and broccoli tagliatelle are typical fare in Cromwells Restaurant.

Smoking: No smoking in dining room
Accommodation: 47 en suite ★ ★ ★

Directions: On A22 at Boship; junction of A22/A267/A271

Lower Dicker BN27 4AT
Map 5: TQ50
Tel: 01323 844826
Fax: 01323 843945
Cost: Set-price D £18. ☺ H/wine £8.85
Times: D only, 7-10pm
Additional: Bar food; Sunday L (noon-2.30pm); Children welcome; ✿ dishes

HASTINGS & ST LEONARD'S,
Beauport Park ✿

Georgian building with a stylish restaurant overlooking floodlit gardens. There is a fixed-price menu and an extensive carte, with flambé dishes, grills and a vegetarian selection.

Accommodation: 25 en suite ★ ★ ★

Directions: On main A2100, 3 miles from both Hastings and Battle

Battle Road TN38 8EA
Map 5: TQ80
Tel: 01424 851222
Fax: 01424 852465
Cost: Alc £25, set-price L £15.50/D £21. ☺ H/wine £9.95
Times: 12.30-2pm/7-9.30pm
Additional: Bar food; Sunday L; Children welcome; ✿ dishes
Smoking: No smoking in dining room

HASTINGS & ST LEONARD'S,
Röser's Restaurant ✿✿✿

A hugely likeable restaurant despite an excessive amount of chintz, stripped wood, banquette seating and frilly lampshades. The point though is that Gerald Röser can really cook and his wife Jenny is a delightful presence running front of house. Details count, and it is not often that an inspector asks for and receives seconds, especially of the *amuse-bouche* – in this case, an intensely flavoured mallard consommé with Madeira and chives with enough impact 'to make a cynical foodie take notice'. The meal proper started with a dish of spot-on and perfectly timed pike soufflé, just as it was described, although it was more like classic quenelles de brochet with a smoked salmon and dill sauce. In the main course dish of roast goose breast with five spice sauce and pickled plums, Röser showed his remarkable skill at using the

64 Eversfield Place
TN37 6DB
Map 5: TQ80
Tel/Fax: 01424 712218
Chef: Gerald Röser
Owners: Gerald & Jenny Röser
Cost: Alc £35, set-price L £19.95/D £22.95. ☺ H/wine £11.50
Times: Noon-2pm/7-10pm. Closed L Sat, all Sun & Mon, 1st 2 wks Jan, 2nd 2 wks Jun
Additional: Children welcome; ✿ dishes
Seats: 26. Private dining room 30
Smoking: No pipes & cigars

Röser's Restaurant

Directions: On the seafront, opposite Hastings pier

kind of sweet spices not widely found in France or Britain, and although the sauce sounded Chinese in origin, it was much more Germanic in feel, with a great balance of sweet-and-sour flavours. Desserts include high-class chocolate mousse, crème brûlée and classic nougat parfait with raspberry coulis.

HERSTMONCEUX,

Sundial Restaurant

Auberge-style restaurant still going strong after more than three decades. Enthusiastic and serious about good food, Guiseppe and Laure Bertoli's menus of classical French dishes with Italian overtones are as tempting as ever. Sliced smoked goose marinated in olive oil and chives, and prime Scotch fillet steak with peppercorn sauce are typical of the style. Fish and seafood dominate the menu though: quality langoustine lightly sautéed and served with sugar snap peas and asparagus spears, or a great, simple starter of sliced roasted salmon topped with two perfectly poached eggs. There's a good wine list to complement the food – classic clarets and Burgundies are worth a try and a good showing from the rest of the world should mean there's something for every taste.

Directions: In centre of village, on A271

Hailsham BN27 4LA
Map 5: TQ61
Tel: 01323 832217
Chef: Giuseppe Bertoli
Owners: Mr G & Mrs L Bertoli
Cost: *Alc* £35, set-price L £19.50/D £27.50. H/wine £13.25
Times: Noon-2.30pm/7pm-9.30pm. Closed D Sun, all Mon, from 1st wk Aug – end Aug
Additional: Sunday L; Children welcome; ❹ dishes
Seats: 50. Private dining room 25
Smoking: No smoking in dining room

HOVE, **Quentin's**

Idiosyncratic restaurant run with panache. The foodie pictures and reliefs around the vivid orange walls of this popular restaurant tell of Quentin Fitch's culinary enthusiasm. The floor is of worn boards with mismatched old pine tables and schoolroom chairs the simple furnishings. The menu is in touch with current trends and dishes rework modern/classic combinations with a personal twist. For example, a home-smoked salmon fishcake was studded with sun-dried tomato and basil, served with a chive cream and a delicious salad flavoured with lemongrass and kaffir lime leaves. Other dishes might include goats' cheese soufflé with fig and walnut jam, and best end of lamb on couscous with an aromatic cumin sauce. Apple pie with lavender ice cream and chocolate bombe with griottine cherries typify the desserts.

Directions: On the south side of Western Road between Brunswick Square and Palmeira Square

42 Western Road BN3 1JD
Map 4: TQ20
Tel/Fax: 01273 822734
Chef: Quentin Fitch
Owners: Quentin & Candy Fitch
Cost: *Alc* £20.45, set-price L & D £18.95. ☺ H/wine £9.95
Times: Noon-2pm/7-9.30pm. Closed L Sat, all Sun, Mon, 1 wk Xmas, 2 wks Aug
Additional: Children welcome; ❹ dishes
Seats: 28. Private dining room 20
Smoking: No pipes & cigars; Air conditioning

JEVINGTON, **Hungry Monk**

Polegate nr Eastbourne BN26 5QF
Map 4: TQ50
Tel/Fax: 01323 482178
Chef: Sharon Poulton
Owners: Nigel & Sue Mackenzie
Cost: Set-price D £24.95. H/wine £11
Times: D only, 7-10pm. Closed Bh
Mon, 24-26 Dec
Additional: Sunday L (noon-2.30pm);
Children 3+; ✿ dishes
Seats: 38. Private dining rooms 4-16
Smoking: No smoking in dining room;
Air conditioning
Credit cards: Amex only

Homely, ancient cottage restaurant. Once a monastic retreat, the Mackenzie's charming 14th-century flint cottage comes complete with antiques, candlelight, log fires and original oil paintings. French country cooking merges with British and Mediterranean touches on a menu that ranges from loin of organic pork with cassoulet beans, via breast of pheasant with bacon pudding and sloe gin sauce, to char-roasted vegetable and polenta tart. As originators of the now ubiquitous banoffee pie it is appropriate that the 'Original Hungry Monk' version should head a list of desserts that might also include cappuccino brûlée, chocker bocker glory, and a Victorian sherry trifle.

Directions: Follow A22 towards Eastbourne. Turn R on to B2105. The restaurant is between Polegate and Friston

LEWES, **The Shelleys**

High Street BN7 1XS
Map 5: TQ41
Tel: 01273 472361
Fax: 01273 483152
Chef: Roy Askew
Cost: *Alc* £25, set-price D £26.
H/wine £12.50
Times: 12.30-2pm/7-9.15pm
Additional: Bar food; Sunday L;
Children welcome; ✿ dishes
Seats: 60. Private dining room 50
Smoking: No smoking in dining room
Accommodation: 19 en suite ★ ★ ★

Directions: Town centre

Dating from the 17th century and retaining much of the feel of a Georgian manor house, beginning with the flagstoned entrance hall. A sophisticated menu is served in the elegant dining room overlooking the peaceful garden. The menu, the night of our visit, showed a tendency to overdo the wild mushrooms, but a sample menu some months later included them in only one dish – pan-fried fillet of Scotch beef on rösti potato with morels and Madeira wine and cream sauce. There are some interesting ideas: fillet of smoked haddock tartare is served with pickled cucumbers and rock oysters; steaming adds a light touch to monkfish cutlet with coriander, ginger and butter. Good desserts include raspberry crème brûlée and iced coconut terrine with rum-scented crème anglaise, or else there's Long Clawson Stilton with oatcakes and celery.

NEWICK, **Newick Park**

An example of the grand country house dining room with superb decor, great plasterwork and fine paintings. Tables, chairs, linen, crockery and silver are all appropriately impressive. Although service is formal, as befits a Grade II listed Georgian house set in 250 acres of parkland, the atmosphere is not aloof. The menu is short and precisely worded – sautéed breast of pigeon on spiced lentils with deep-fried garlic chips or seared beef fillet with foie gras and morels. There's a nod to an East-West idiom with such dishes as pan-fried crispy squid with pak choi and chilli oil, but on the whole the repertoire treads a modern classic path with the likes of pan-fried loin of lamb, shallot purée, buttered spinach and thyme jus. A selection of British cheeses is served with home-made hazelnut bread. Don't pass up on the undyed smoked haddock served at breakfast.

BN8 4SB
Map 5: TQ42
Tel: 01825 723633
Fax: 01825 723969
Chef: Tim Neil
Owners: Michael & Virginia Childs
Cost: *Alc* £32.50, set-price L £19.50/ D £32.50 (4 courses). H/wine £9.75
Times: Noon-2.15pm/7-10pm
Additional: Bar food; Sunday L; Children welcome; 🍴 dishes
Seats: 40. Private dining room 40. Jacket & tie preferred
Smoking: No smoking in dining room
Accommodation: 16 en suite ★ ★ ★

Directions: From Newick on A272 between Haywards Heath/Uckfield, turn S on Church Road, at end of road turn L. Hotel 0.25 mile on R

PEASMARSH,
Flackley Ash Hotel 🏵

A cosy dining room and friendly service create a pleasant atmosphere for a daily set-price dinner menu, with dishes such as roast Romney lamb, chicken tagine and pan-fried sea bass.

Rye TN31 6YH
Map 5: TQ82
Tel: 01797 230651
Fax: 01797 230510
Cost: Set-price D £22.50. ☺ H/wine £10.95
Times: 12.30-1.45pm/7-9.30pm
Additional: Bar food; Sunday L; Children welcome; 🍴 dishes
Smoking: No smoking in dining room
Accommodation: 42 en suite ★ ★ ★

Directions: From M25 J5, take A21 (Flimwell), turn L onto A268 (Peasmarsh)

RYE, **Landgate Bistro** ❀

Honest cooking and casual but attentive service are keynotes at this popular bistro sited in one of Rye's lovely narrow streets. Mushroom risotto, lamb with mint and tomato sauce are just two of the dishes offered. Good-value wines.

Directions: From the High Street head towards the Landgate. The bistro is in a row of shops on L

5-6 Landgate TN31 7LH
Map 5: TQ92
Tel: 01797 222829
Telephone for further details

RYE, **The Mermaid Inn** ❀

Steeped in history with brooding oils of Tudor and Restoration worthies, ancient beams, linen-fold panelling, ghosts. Dinner in the dining room is very up to date: deep-fried salmon and smoked haddock parcel; succulent fillet of beef with anchovy and sun-dried tomato butter.

Directions: Town centre. Car park through archway

Mermaid Street TN31 7EU
Map 5: TQ92
Tel: 01797 223065
Fax: 01797 225069
Telephone for further details

SEAFORD, **Quincy's** ❀❀

A bit of a gem in a place where you wouldn't expect it.
Seaford is perhaps not the most happening of places, and Quincy's presents such a discreet front that it could be missed easily. Ian Dowding cooks well from menus that change seasonally and offer traditional dishes with a twist, as well as some more altogether unusual ones such as terrine of beetroot with orange and cranberry. Fresh fish features in the likes of brill, monkfish and gurnard in a cream and vermouth sauce, and in our very fresh cod with pesto crust. For our main course we chose an excellent breast of duck with sweet-and-sour plum sauce and braised red cabbage, and followed it with a very well-liked raspberry and Kirsch crème brûlée. The wine list is quite large with mainly French offerings, but some English, and New World including Lebanon, as well as a good selection of half-bottles and wines by the glass.

42 High Street BN25 1PL
Map 5: TV49
Tel: 01323 895490
Chef: Ian Dowding
Owners: Ian & Dawn Dowding
Cost: Set-price D £24. H/wine £9.25
Times: D only, 7-10pm. Closed D Sun, all Mon, 1st wk Jan
Additional: Sunday L (noon-2pm); Children welcome; ⓓ dishes
Seats: 30
Smoking: No smoking in dining room

Directions: From A259 turn into Broad Street (opposite Caffyns Garage) then L into old High Street. Restaurant is 50 metres on R

UCKFIELD,
Buxted Park ❀❀

The restaurant is in the original conservatory of a Georgian mansion. The kitchen plunders the world for dishes such as starters of wild mushroom cappuccini, and scallop lasagne with orange vanilla sauce, and main courses of lamb chump with couscous and harissa vegetables, or lobster basmati, and monkfish with flat parlsey risotto and lobster sauce.

Directions: Turn off A22 Uckfield bypass (London-Eastbourne road), then take A272 to Buxted. Cross set of traffic lights, entrance to hotel is 1 mile on R

Buxted TN22 4AY
Map 5: TQ42
Tel: 01825 732711
Fax: 01825 732770
Chef: Valentine Rodriquez
Cost: Alc £25, set-price L £14.95
Times: Noon-2pm/7-10pm. Closed L Sat
Additional: Bar food; Sunday L; Children welcome; ⓓ dishes
Seats: 65. Private dining room 12-120
Smoking: No smoking in dining room
Accommodation: 44 en suite ★ ★ ★ ★

UCKFIELD, **Horsted Place** ❀❀

Horsted Place is a Victorian (Gothic revivalist) pile built by George Myers and later augmented by Augustus Pugin. The restaurant is small and intimate and suits the business

Little Horsted TN22 5TS
Map 5: TQ42
Tel: 01825 750581
Fax: 01825 750459
Chef: Allan Garth

fraternity and those who wish to use the East Sussex National Golf Course. The kitchen uses quality fresh ingredients and scores heavily on presentation. *Carte*, table d'hôte and chef's seasonal signature dishes and vegetarian menus are offered with brief descriptions and take in cannon of lamb, and almond and chocolate tart with chocolate chip ice cream in tuile basket. There is an extensive wine list including wines from Austria, Oregon and Portugal and a number of half-bottles of champagnes.

Directions: Two miles South of Uckfield on A26

Owner: Grenfel Holdings
Cost: *Alc* £35, set-price L £14 (2 courses)/D £32. H/wine £14.25
Times: Noon-1.45pm/7-9.30pm
Additional: Sunday L; Children 7+; dishes
Seats: 40. Private dining room 10-100. Jacket & tie preferred
Smoking: No smoking in dining room
Accommodation: 17 en suite ★ ★ ★

WILMINGTON, **Crossways Hotel** ❀❀

Small country hotel of considerable charm. Crossways is a very relaxed place that attracts a strong following with people returning regularly. Menus change by the month and are set-price to include four courses and coffee. There are the usual traditional country-house dishes with local asparagus with hollandaise, and roast rack of lamb with mint on the menu when we visited, but more unusual combinations include duck with grapefruit and elderflower. We enjoyed seafood pancake, vegetable soup, calves' liver and bacon with onion gravy, and iced white chocolate mousse with raspberry coulis. The industrious kitchen is happy to make bread, canapés and petits fours, as well as home-made ice creams such as marmalade, and strawberry jelly made with whole fruit and dessert wine. The wine list covers much ground and there are a few English wines available.

Directions: A27, 2 miles W of Polegate

Nr Polegate BN26 5SG
Map 4: TQ50
Tel: 01323 482455
Fax: 01323 487811
Chefs: David Stott & Juliet Anderson
Owners: David Stott & Clive James
Cost: Set-price D £28 (4 courses). H/wine £10.95
Times: D only, 7.30-8.45pm. Closed Sun, Mon, Jan
Additional: Children 12+; dishes
Seats: 24
Smoking: No smoking in dining room
Accommodation: 7 en suite

SUSSEX WEST

AMBERLEY, **Amberley Castle** ❀❀

Arundel BN18 9ND
Map 4: TQ01
Tel: 01798 831992
Fax: 01798 831998
Chef: Sam Mahoney
Owners: M G & J E Cummings
Cost: Set-price L £12.50 (2 courses)/D £35 (6 courses). H/wine £13.95

It's the real thing! An 11th-century castle complete with massive gate-house (with working portcullis) and high curtain walls concealing delightful grounds. However, Amberley Castle is now a luxury hotel with reassuring modern comforts; even the antique-dotted public rooms are cosy despite the odd suit of armour and racks of pikes. Menus include a simple set-price lunch offering the likes of Mascarpone, blue cheese and basil tart with creamed leeks and chive butter, and grilled red mullet with parsley potato purée. 'Castle Cuisine', however, comes into its own in the evening when the kitchen offers a list of carefully researched old English recipes such as pike in water souchy sauce, quince and gin water ice, wild rabbit marjoram dumplings, and Sussex pond pudding to finish. More up-to-date offerings include pan-fried pigeon supreme with mille-feuille of potato and chestnut and wild mushroom sauce, and pan-fried black bream with smoky soy broth, Chinese greens, lemon noodles and braised vegetables.

Times: Noon-2pm/7-9.30pm
Additional: Sunday L; Children 12+; 🍴 dishes
Seats: 38. Private dining room 12, 48. Jacket & tie preferred
Smoking: No smoking in dining room
Accommodation: 15 en suite ★ ★ ★

Directions: Off B2139 between Amberley and Houghton

ARUNDEL,
The Arundel Swan Hotel

Hotel in the heart of Arundel offering a good choice of dishes in its Victorian-style restaurant. Typical examples are Magret duck breast with blueberry sauce, and pork fillet oriental.

Smoking: No smoking in dining room; Air conditioning
Accommodation: 15 en suite ★ ★ ★

Directions: Town centre

27-29 High Street BN18 9AG
Map 4: TQ00
Tel: 01903 882314
Fax: 01903 883759
Cost: Alc £25, set-price L & D £14.95. ☺ H/wine £8.40
Times: Noon-2.30pm/6.30-9.30pm
Additional: Bar Food; Sunday L; Children welcome; 🍴 dishes

ARUNDEL,
Burpham Country House Hotel

A combination of English and Swiss cuisine reflects the nationalities of the proprietors. Dishes from the daily menu are mostly light and fresh, perhaps halibut with lime and coriander sauce.

Old Down Burpham BN18 9RJ
Map 4: TQ00
Tel: 01903 882160
Fax: 01903 884627
Cost: Set-price D £23.50. ☺ H/wine £9.80
Times: D only, 7.30-8.45pm. Closed Mon, early Jan
Additional: Children 10+; 🍴 dishes
Smoking: No smoking in dining room
Accommodation: 10 en suite ★ ★

Directions: 3 miles NE of Arundel, off A27

ARUNDEL, George & Dragon

Pub-turned-restaurant serving modern English cooking. Expect risotto of local game, noisettes of venison on mulled wine and blackberry sauce, and the contrasting, sweet-sour flavours of grilled duck breast with caramelised pineapple and sweet cinnamon coulis.

Smoking: No pipes & cigars

Directions: 2.5m up no-through road signed Burpham off A27

Burpham BN18 9RR
Map 4: TQ00
Tel: 01903 883131
Cost: Alc £21
Times: D only, 7.15-9.30pm. Closed D Sun, 25 Dec
Additional: Bar food; Sunday L (12.15-1.45pm); 🍴 dishes

ARUNDEL, **Norfolk Arms Hotel**

Georgian coaching inn offering an extensive menu, which might include supreme of Sussex chicken filled with mushroom and garlic duxelle, or roasted fillet of salmon with pepper coulis.

Smoking: No smoking in dining room
Accommodation: 34 en suite ★ ★ ★

Directions: In Arundel High St

High Street BN18 9AD
Map 4: TQ00
Tel: 01903 882101
Cost: Set-price L £9.95/D £17.95. ☺
H/wine £9.95
Times: 12.30-2pm/7-9pm
Additional: Bar food L; Sunday L;
Children welcome; ✦ dishes

BOSHAM, **Millstream Hotel**

Bosham Lane PO18 8HL
Map 4: SU80
Tel: 01243 573234
Fax: 01243 573459
Cost: Set-price D £20. ☺ H/wine
£9.75
Times: 12.30-2pm/7-9.30pm
Additional: Bar food L; Sunday L;
Children welcome; ✦ dishes
Smoking: No smoking in dining room;
Air conditioning
Accommodation: 33 en suite ★ ★ ★

Directions: Take A259 exit from
Chichester roundabout and in village
follow signs for quay

In a pretty spot with the water flowing past outside. Smoked duck with wild mushroom pâté, a medley of quail, venison and pigeon, and roast lamb with commendably cooked vegetables have all received endorsements.

BRACKLESHAM,
Cliffords Cottage Restaurant

16th-century building with a low beamed ceiling, horse brasses and, in winter, an open log fire creating a cosy atmosphere. It all might sound an implausible setting for a menu straight out of the old French school: magret de canard (with blackcurrant sauce), lobster Thermidor, and sole grillé (with tartare sauce). The set-price menu provides an antithesis in the form of, perhaps, carrot and parsnip soup, and baked monkfish in bacon on creamed leeks. Fruits de mer au safran scampi – succulent scallops, prawns and lemon sole cooked with Noilly-Prat and saffron makes a good starter – and mignons de boeuf forestière is mentioned in dispatches for its tender meat and well-made sauce of wild mushrooms and Madeira, and for the selection of vegetables that came with it. Bread-and-butter pudding, light and creamy and counterpoised by lemon coulis, is a popular way to finish.

Bracklesham Lane PO20 8JA
Map 4: SZ89
Tel: 01243 670250
Chef: Tony Shanahan
Owners: Tony & Brenda Shanahan
Cost: Alc £25, set-price D £20. ☺
H/wine £8.95
Times: D only, 7-9pm. Closed D Sun,
Mon
Additional: Sunday L (12.30-1.30pm);
Children 5+; ✦ dishes
Seats: 28. Jacket & tie preferred
Smoking: No-smoking area; No pipes
& cigars; Air conditioning

Directions: On B2179
Birdham/Bracklesham road

CHICHESTER, **Comme Ça**

Tastefully decorated restaurant with rich, bold colours, garlands of dried flowers and hops hanging from ceiling beams. A place that comes into its own in summer, when the doors in the garden room are thrown open on to the patio and garden beyond. In winter, a log fire in the inglenook blazes

67 Broyle Road
PO19 4BD
Map 4: SU80
Tel: 01243 788724
Fax: 01243 530052
Chefs: Michel Navet,
Olivier Vennetier

away in the bar. A first glance at the French menu shows where the kitchen's heart lies, although dishes here are by no means stuck in a time warp. Thus, wild Scottish salmon smoked in oak leaves served with frisée contrasts with a dish that shows the kitchen's Normandy roots: chicken liver pâté flavoured with Armagnac and presented with apple jelly, a combination that works well. Salmon also pops up among the main courses, this time an accurately roasted fillet on basil risotto with a deep-flavoured red wine sauce. More mainstream, perhaps, is wild rabbit braised with mushrooms, baby onions and bacon in a creamy Calvados sauce. Simple-sounding chocolate mousse turns out to be layers of mousse between moist almond sponge, an orange sauce providing sharp contrast. The wine list has been assembled with care.

Owners: Michel Navet, Jane Owen-Navet
Cost: *Alc* £23, set-price L £17.75. ☺
H/wine £9.95
Times: Noon-1.45pm/6-10.30pm.
Closed D Sun, all Mon, 25-26 Dec, 1 Jan
Additional: Bar food L; Sunday L; Children welcome; ✿ dishes
Seats: 80. Private dining room 40
Smoking: No smoking in dining room

Directions: On A286 near Festival Theatre

CHICHESTER, **Crouchers Bottom** ✿

Family-run hotel that is going from strength to strength. The simple but attractive dining room offers some first-class cooking along the lines of foie gras parfait with truffle dressing, confit of ducks, and a rich chocolate tart.

Smoking: No smoking in dining room
Accommodation: 16 en suite ★ ★ ★

Directions: Telephone for directions

Birdham Road PO20 7EH
Map 4: SU80
Tel: 01243 784995
Fax: 01243 539797
Cost: *Alc* £25, set-price D £23.50.
H/wine £10.95
Times: D only, 7-10pm
Additional: Sunday L (1-2.30pm);
Children welcome; ✿ dishes

CHICHESTER, **The Ship Hotel** ✿

Well-presented Georgian hotel once home to Admiral Murray, one of Nelson's right-hand men. Enjoy modern British cooking along the lines of roast chump of lamb with thyme and orange, and pan-fried fillet of cod with fresh mussels and monkfish.

Accommodation: 35 en suite ★ ★ ★

Directions: From the inner ring road at large Northgate roundabout turn L into North St; hotel on L

North Street PO19 1NH
Map 4: SU80
Tel: 01243 778000
Fax: 01243 788000
Cost: *Alc* £28, set-price L £13.95 (2 courses)/D £18.95. ☺ H/wine £9.65
Times: Noon-2pm/7.15-9.30pm
Additional: Bar food; Sunday L; Children welcome; ✿ dishes
Smoking: No smoking in dining room

CHILGROVE, **White Horse Inn** ✿

Chichester PO18 9HX
Map 4: SU81
Tel: 01243 535219
Fax: 01243 535301
Cost: Set-price L & D £24.50. H/wine £17
Times: Noon-2pm/7-10pm. Closed D Sun, all Mon except Bhs
Additional: Bar food; Sunday L; Children welcome; ✿ dishes
Smoking: No smoking in dining room; Air conditioning

Directions: On the B2141 between Chichester and Petersfield

New owners at this oak-beamed and thatched 17th-century coaching inn, renowned for its wide-ranging, in-depth wine list. Trade mark specials include foie gras and oysters, together with robust cooking that matches the spirit of the wines.

CLIMPING, **Bailiffscourt Hotel**

Littlehampton BN17 5RW
Map 4: SU90
Tel: 01903 723511
Fax: 01903 723107
Chef: Frank Eckermann
Owners: Sandy & Anne Goodman
Cost: *Alc* £39, set-price L £19.50/D
£32.5. H/wine £14
Times: 12.30-2.15pm/7-9.30pm
Additional: Bar food L (not Sun);
Sunday L; Children welcome;
🍽 dishes
Seats: 55. Private dining room 40
Smoking: No smoking in dining room
Accommodation: 32 en suite ★ ★ ★

Directions: W of Littlehampton off the
A259, signposted Bailiffscourt

A unique 'medieval' hotel created in the 1930s from original 13th-century building materials. The result is quite delightful: old stone windows, heavy iron-studded doors, and ancient arches. The beamed restaurant, with its hanging tapestries and vaulted ceiling, provides a suitable setting for the sound cooking of Frank Eckermann. His *carte* is a mix of classical and modern styles – grilled goats' cheese on brioche with roasted garlic and rosemary marinade, followed perhaps by roast sirloin of Aberdeen Angus with red wine and shallot gravy. Our test meal took in fricassée of noodles with smoked halibut, salmon and tiger prawns, fillet of beef with forest mushrooms and a port glaze. Both dishes were competent and full of flavour. The fairly substantial wine list features bottles from the old world, but there are a number of prize vintages from elsewhere.

COPTHORNE,
Copthorne London Gatwick

Copthorne Way RH10 3PG
Map 5: TQ33
Tel: 01342 714971
Fax: 01342 717375
Chef: Richard Duckworth
Owner: Millennium & Copthorne
Hotels
Cost: *Alc* £25, set-price L £18.50/D
£22.50. ☺ H/wine £12.95
Times: Noon-2pm/7-9.45pm. Closed
L Sat, all Sun

The average airport hotel is unlikely to boast the 100 acres of gardens and woodlands that belong to this much extended 16th-century farmhouse. It also makes this a popular venue for business conferences and weddings. The glass-partitioned Lion d'Or restaurant is traditional in style with exposed beams, cosy corners and crisp linen. Our meal, chosen from the *carte*, started with minestrone soup that was just the business – a hearty tomato base, plenty of vegetables and broken spaghetti and a heady topping of grated Parmesan. Poached trout fillet with butter, lemon and caper sauce was simple but precisely cooked, as were the accompanying vegetables. A last gasp of summer, strawberry charlotte, was equally exact. Strudel of vegetables on a garlic and potato cream sauce, and saffron ravioli of morels, chanterelles and spring onions are amongst vegetarian choices. Espresso is still served Turkish style in a glass beaker – be warned, it's a potent brew.

Directions: From M23 J10 follow A264 signed East Grinstead; take 3rd exit off 1st roundabout

Additional: Bar food; Sunday L (Brasserie); Children welcome; 🐟 dishes
Seats: 50. Private dining room 10. Jacket & tie preferred
Smoking: Air conditioning
Accommodation: 227 en suite
★ ★ ★ ★

CUCKFIELD, Ockenden Manor

Ockenden Lane RH17 5LD
Map 4: TQ32
Tel: 01444 416111
Fax: 01444 415549
Chef: Geoff Welch
Owners: Mr & Mrs Sandy Goodman
Cost: *Alc* £45.50, set-price L £18.50/D £32.50. H/wine £14.50
Times: 12.30-2pm/7.30-9.30pm
Additional: Bar food; Sunday L; Children welcome; 🐟 dishes
Seats: 45. Private dining room 75. Jacket & tie preferred
Smoking: No smoking in dining room
Accommodation: 22 en suite ★ ★ ★

Directions: Village Centre, off main street

Charming 16th-century hotel set in its own peaceful, mature grounds. Overlooking the South Downs, yet in the centre of the village, the hotel boasts a particularly handsome dining-room with oak panelling, historic stained glass windows and an ornate hand-painted ceiling. The special shellfish menu features the likes of creamed Jerusalem artichoke, leek and potato soup with sliced Selsey scallops, and a selection of Cornish crab, langoustine, Norwegian prawns, rock oysters, cockles, mussels and brown shrimps served in the shell with dressed salad and lemon mayonnaise. Alternatively, choose a terrine such as Sussex game studded with pistachio nuts, orange segments and Cumberland sauce, or a brace of quail roasted and served with rösti potatoes, Madeira wine and truffle sauce. Finish, as our inspector did, with the highly satisfactory combination of caramelised rice tart, glazed apples and vanilla ice cream.

EAST GRINSTEAD,
Gravetye Manor Hotel

RH19 4LJ
Map 5: TQ33
Tel: 01342 810567
Fax: 01342 810080
Chef: Mark Raffan
Owners: The Herbert Family
Cost: *Alc* £47, set-price L £29/D £38. H/wine £18
Times: 12.30-2pm/7.30-9.30pm. Closed 25 Dec D (non-residents)
Additional: Children 7+; 🐟 dishes

Elizabethan stone manor house set in 1000 acres that includes William Robinson's famous English garden. Created by Peter Herbert in 1958, Gravetye was one of the first country house hotels and remains one of the finest in Britain today. In the kitchen, Mark Raffan builds imaginative menus around top quality produce, including that grown in the hotel's own walled kitchen garden. An early spring lunch produced some skilled cooking. Braised ham hock terrine was a masterpiece: pieces of ham set with leeks, mustard seeds and herbs in a light aspic lined with a thin layer of cured ham. Fillet of west coast brill

Gravetye Manor Hotel

Seats: 40. Private dining room 16.
Jacket & tie preferred at D
Smoking: No smoking in dining room
Accommodation: 18 en suite ★ ★ ★

Directions: From M23 J10 take A264
towards East Grinstead. After 2 miles
take B2028 (signposted Haywards
Heath/Brighton)

with foie gras produced a great combination of flavours, from
the super piece of fish, exactly timed, to the equally spot-on
pan-fried piece of foie gras. An underlying sweetness was
provided by a rich reduced jus flavoured with Pineau des
Charentes, and all was offset by the earthy tang of spinach.
Dessert kept up the pace of the other two dishes. A simple but
effective mille-feuille of crisp nougatine with lime cream
accompanied by a light, clear fruit jelly and some raspberry
coulis. Canapés, breads and petits fours show that the eye for
detail never falters. The wine list, as one might expect, is well
chosen (with Bill Baker as the consultant). It features some
great Australians and New Zealanders. Italy is well
represented and it is here you should look for bottles under
£30, not in the classy, in-depth French list.

FINDON, **Findon Manor Hotel**

High Street BN14 0TA
Map 4: TQ10
Tel: 01903 872733
Fax: 01903 877473
Chef: Stanley Ball
Owners: Mike & Jan Parker-Hare
Cost: Set-price L £17.95/D £19.50. ☺
H/wine £11.50
Times: Noon-2pm/7-9pm. Closed D
25 Dec
Additional: Bar food; Sunday L;
Children 5+; ✇ dishes
Seats: 50. Private dining room 28
Smoking: No smoking in dining room
Accommodation: 11 en suite ★ ★ ★

Former rectory dating from the 16th century. The menu may
be elaborate in terms of description but the kitchen knows
what it is about. Get past the subtitled menu-speak, curried
risotto of Selsey crab enhanced with ginger and coriander
(lightly curry-scented crab risotto flavoured with ginger and
coriander) for example, and you have prime raw materials
carefully prepared with a strong emphasis on flavour. This is
decidedly modern cooking with red snapper glazed with honey
and mustard seeds and served with a saffron and lime fumet,
or braised shank of lamb accompanied by a light tomato and
tarragon dressing showing the range.

Directions: Just off A24 in Findon, 3 miles N of Worthing

GOODWOOD,

Marriott
Goodwood Park Hotel

Close to the racecourse and part of the Goodwood Estate, the hotel is well located for punters, bookies and owners (sans horses). The dining-room, with its high roof and stencilled beams, feels a touch English medieval. Professional service comes from a French team who are friendly without being overbearing. The cooking, however, fell at a few fences; the quality of seared sea scallops with creamed celeriac and red wine dressing was wasted by poor timing, and hot lemon soufflé with vanilla sauce, despite a good, clear zesty flavour, suffered from excess of egg white and lack of body. Quality English lamb came with good vegetables and rosemary jus. Other typical dishes might include seared salmon with mussel and leek risotto and caviar sauce, plus a straightforward selection from the grill.

Directions: 3 miles NE of Chichester. From Portsmouth head E along A27, staying S of Chichester. Signposted within area

Chichester PO18 0QB
Map 4: SU80
Tel: 01243 775537
Fax: 01243 520120
Chef: Phillip Edwards
Cost: *Alc* £30, set-price L/D £22.95. ☺ H/wine £11.95
Times: Noon-2pm/7-9.30pm. Closed L Sat
Additional: Sunday L; Children welcome; ✿ dishes
Seats: 100. Private dining room 120
Smoking: No smoking in dining room
Accommodation: 94 en suite ★ ★ ★ ★

HENFIELD,

Tottington Manor Hotel

16th-century manor house overlooking the South Downs. A typical meal might start with sun-dried tomato and ricotta tart with a salad of mixed leaves, followed by roast medallions of venison with honey roast parsnips.

Additional: Sunday L; Children 5+; ✿ dishes
Smoking: No-smoking area; No pipes & cigars
Accommodation: 6 en suite ★ ★

Directions: Turn off B2037 between Upper Beeding and Small Dole, hotel 0.25m on L

Edburton BN5 9LJ
Map 4: TQ21
Tel: 01903 815757
Fax: 01903 879331
Cost: *Alc* £25, set-price L £12.50 (2 courses)/D £28.50. ☺ H/wine £11.50
Times: Noon-1.45pm/7-8.45pm. Closed D Sun

HORSHAM,

Random Hall Hotel

The Tapestry Restaurant serves some modern British cooking, although the setting is a 16th-century former farmhouse featuring traditional tapestries, flagstone floors and open fires.

Additional: Bar Food; Sunday L; Children 10+; ✿ dishes
Smoking: No smoking in dining room
Accommodation: 15 en suite ★ ★ ★

Directions: 4 miles W of Horsham, 15 miles SW of Gatwick Airport

Stane Street Slinfold RH13 7QX
Map 4: TQ13
Tel: 01403 790558
Fax: 01403 791046
Cost: Set-price L £16 (4 courses)/D £23. ☺ H/wine £11
Times: Noon-2pm/7-10pm. Closed 2 wks from 27 Dec

HURSTPIERPOINT, **Boles**

Beamed restaurant with a walled garden for summer meals. Typical dishes are marinated prawns with guacamole and sour cream, and Barbary duck breast with lemon jasmine jus.

117 High Street BN6 9PU
Map 4: TQ21
Tel: 01273 833452
Cost: *Alc* £23, set-price D £18.95. ☺ H/wine £8.50

Boles

Times: D only, 7.30-10pm. Closed D Sun, all Mon, Bhs, some evenings Jan
Additional: Sunday L (12.30-2pm); Children welcome; dishes
Smoking: No-smoking area

Directions: In town centre, half way along High Street

LICKFOLD, **Lickfold Inn** **NEW**

Nr Petworth GU28 9EY
Map 4: SU92
Tel: 01798 861285
Fax: 01798 861342
Cost: *Alc* £25, set-price L £25
Times: Noon-2.30pm/7-9.30pm
Additional: Bar food; Sunday L; Children welcome; dishes

15th-century timber-framed inn nestling with beams, huge log fires and a first-floor restaurant complete with wood-fired oven. Chargrilled scallops with pesto and Tuscan toast, oak-roasted lamb with rosemary potatoes, and strawberry and mascarpone cheesecake are typical choices.

Directions: NE of Midhurst, Lickfold signed from A286

LOWER BEEDING,
Jeremy's at the Crabtree

Brighton Road RH13 6PT
Map 4: TQ22
Tel: 01403 891257
Fax: 01403 891606
Cost: *Alc* £20, set-price L £10.50 (2 courses)/D £25. ☺ H/wine £11
Times: 12.30-2pm/6-9.30pm. Closed D Sun, 25 Dec
Additional: Bar Food (except D Fri, Sat); Sunday L; Children welcome; dishes

A foody pub with some excellent cooking that takes in mod Med references. It has more of the feel of a new-wave London gastropub than a Sussex country inn and is usually packed, so reservations are essential.

Smoking: No-smoking area

Directions: 4 miles SE of Horsham on A281 Brighton road

LOWER BEEDING,
South Lodge Hotel ✿✿✿

Brighton Road Horsham RH13 6PS
Map 4: TQ22
Tel: 01403 891711
Fax: 01403 891766
Chef: Lewis Hamblet

An imposing pile, parts covered in creepers with professional but friendly staff. South Lodge was built in 1883 in a prime site looking over the South Downs for Frederick Godman, a noted botanist (which accounts for the hundreds of camellias and rhododendrons in the surrounding parkland). The kitchen uses vegetables from the garden and shows a commitment to local supplies, many of them organic, turning them into a menu of traditionally English cuisine with Mediterranean and broader influences. Thus, diver-caught scallops with rocket and pesto risotto might show among starters, with pan-fried organic beef fillet with a potato and onion cake and confit of root vegetables among main courses. Our meal started with 'beautifully seared' fillet of red mullet on a bed of vegetables stir-fried in a sauce of Eastern spices, sesame seeds and soy, went on to pink roast South Downs lamb on olive potatoes with tapenade jus, and finished with a 'delightfully thin, crisp' tart with a rich filling of Belgian chocolate and a small tuile of spot-on milk chocolate ice cream. Classic pear Belle Hélène may be there too, along with an array of British and Irish farmhouse cheeses. Incidentals of appetisers, breads and petits fours all add to the appeal, and the serious wine list is notable for its range sold by the glass.

Owner: Mr G Pecorelli
Cost: Alc £50, set-price L £18.50/D £35 (5 courses). H/wine £16.50
Times: 12.30-2.30pm (3pm Sun)/7.30-10pm (7-10.30pm Fri & Sat)
Additional: Bar food; Sunday L; Children welcome; 🍴 dishes
Seats: 40. Private dining rooms 2/80. Jacket & tie preferred
Smoking: No smoking in dining room
Accommodation: 39 en suite ★ ★ ★ ★

Directions: At junction of A279 (Horsham) and A281, turn onto the Cowfold/Brighton road. Hotel is 0.5 mile on R

MIDHURST, Angel Hotel ❀❀

North Street GU29 9DN
Map 4: SU82
Tel: 01730 812421
Fax: 01730 815928
Chef: Martin Furlong
Owners: Nicholas Davies & Peter Crawford-Rolt
Cost: Alc £30, set-price L £12.50 (2 courses)/D £21. ☺ H/wine £11.50
Times: Noon-2.30pm/7-10pm
Additional: Bar food; Sunday L; Children welcome; 🍴 dishes
Seats: 50. Private dining rooms 40 & 60
Smoking: No pipes & cigars
Accommodation: 28 en suite ★ ★ ★

Directions: Town centre, junction of A286 and A2721

A fine old market town building, used as a courthouse until the late 19th century. While the restaurant is Georgian in style, the cooking takes a more modern approach: expect the likes of chargrilled breast of chicken with pearl barley, lemon and tarragon risotto, and medallions of monkfish with roasted peppers and garlic. Desserts are inventive with rhubarb and ginger creme brûlée, and gratin of orange, chocolate bread-and-butter pudding catching the eye. The wine list offers a choice of serious wines, as well as a good house selection by the glass. As well as the elegant Cowdray room, visitors can eat in the more informal brasserie. Here, typical dishes include stuffed fillet of Devon brill with sorrel and saffron sauce, penne pasta with pumpkin cream, and cannon of Southdown lamb with tarragon mousse.

MIDHURST, Southdowns Hotel ❀❀

Attractive hotel in its own grounds amid the peace of the countryside. The beamed Tudor Bar, where a log fire burns in winter, is an informal place for drinks or light meals, the main action taking place in the Country Restaurant. The kitchen has a propensity for bold combinations of flavours, so chicken

Trotton GU31 5JN
Map 4: SU82
Tel: 01730 821521
Fax: 01730 821790
Chefs: A Bale, William Jack
Owners: R Lion, D Vedovato
Cost: Alc £25. H/wine £10.95

Southdowns Hotel

Times: Noon-2pm/7-9.30pm
Additional: Bar food; Sunday L;
🍷 dishes
Seats: 70. Private dining room 20
Smoking: No-smoking area; Air
conditioning
Accommodation: 20 en suite ★ ★ ★

Directions: 1 mile off A272
Petersfield Road

livers could be made into a parfait with smoked paprika and
served with onion confit and spiced plum sauce, and a main-
course breast of duckling coated with peppers and served with
poached tamarillo and a Cassis reduction. Wok-fried
caramelised king prawns might come with preserved lemons
and roasted sweet potatoes, and collops of Scottish fillet steak
plated on wild mushrooms with a pickled walnut dressing and
anchovy oil. Coconut, Malibu and lime parfait shows the same
Eastern influence at work among the puddings, as does
macerated Pacific fruits with mango sorbet.

MIDHURST,

Spread Eagle Hotel ✿✿

South Street GU29 9NH
Map 4: SU82
Tel: 01730 816911
Fax: 01730 815668
Chef: Stephen Crane
Owners: Mr & Mrs Goodman
Cost: Alc £38. Set-price L £30/D
£32.50. H/wine £12.95
Times: 12.30-2pm/7.30-9.30pm
Additional: Sunday L; Children
welcome; 🍷 dishes
Seats: 55. Private dining room 20
Smoking: No smoking in dining room
Accommodation: 39 en suite ★ ★ ★

Directions: Town centre

*Character hotel with sloping floors, ancient beams and
inglenook fireplaces.* A new leisure centre with pool, gym and
beauty treatments brings the facilities bang up to date.
Changes in the kitchen too, with a new chef bringing a modern,
unfussy style of cooking. Lunch could take in fresh pasta with
broad beans, artichoke and an olive oil sauce, or fish risotto
with fresh herbs and Parmesan, while the style moves up a
notch for dinner with the likes of starters such as seared king
scallops wrapped in smoked salmon with crispy potatoes and
caviar or chicken and foie gras ravioli with morels. Main
courses are strong on fish, perhaps pan-fried John Dory with
olive cakes and a shallot vinaigrette, but a meaty option could
be honey-roast duck breast with a crispy confit duck leg and
Sauternes sauce. Classic desserts include caramelised lemon
tart and warm chocolate mousse with pistachio ice cream.

PULBOROUGH,
Chequers Hotel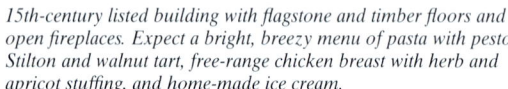

Small, charming hotel with sound, old fashioned standards of service. Menus rely heavily on local produce with the likes of pan-fried breast of Sussex chicken with egg noodles and rosemary jus, or a casserole of wild mushrooms flavoured with garden herbs. This is good, sound country cooking strong on old favourites such as pan-fried rainbow trout with soft roes and toasted almonds, or grilled Scotch sirloin steak en croûte with pâté maison and a course grain mustard sauce. John Searancke has been running his hotel for over thirty years and his strong commitment to quality is to be applauded.

Directions: On A29 just N of Pulborough, turn R opposite the church

Church Place RH20 1AD
Map 4: TQ01
Tel: 01798 872486
Fax: 01798 872715
Chef: Paul Lowis
Owner: John Searancke
Cost: Set-price L £12.50/D £22.95 (4 courses). ☺ H/wine £10.95
Times: Noon-1.45pm/D from 7pm
Additional: Bar food L; Sunday L; Children welcome; ♨ dishes
Seats: 26
Smoking: No smoking in dining room
Accommodation: 11 rooms (10 en suite) ★ ★

ROWHOOK, **The Chequers Inn**

15th-century listed building with flagstone and timber floors and open fireplaces. Expect a bright, breezy menu of pasta with pesto, Stilton and walnut tart, free-range chicken breast with herb and apricot stuffing, and home-made ice cream.

Smoking: No pipes & cigars

Directions: Telephone for directions

Nr Horsham RH12 3PY
Map 4: TQ13
Tel/Fax: 01403 790480
Cost: *Alc* £20. ☺ H/wine £8.50
Times: Noon-2.15pm/7-9.15pm. Closed D Sun, all Mon
Additional: Bar food; Sunday L; Children 12+; ♨ dishes

STORRINGTON, **Fleur de Sel**

At the beginning of 1999 Michel Perraud moved Fleur de Sel from its home in Haslemere to Storrington. The new restaurant, previously known as Manleys, offers a striking blue-and-yellow colour scheme which gives the place a pleasant, warm atmosphere; there's also a small bar area at the entrance. Service, from a French team , is highly attentive, while the set-price menu, in both French and English, is based on classic French cooking. Both warm Cornish crab cake with hazelnut and roast Gressingham duck are specialities, and have received sound endorsements on previous visits, but for our spring inspection meal we ordered a carefully cooked asparagus in puff pastry with an orange and chive cream sauce, enjoyed a top-class celeriac purée that came with sea bass set on a bed of squid with a light red wine sauce, (a dish that admirably illustrated the consistently high quality of the ingredients used), and went overboard for a warm chocolate cake 'with a delightful runny ganache centre' teamed with an excellent vanilla ice cream. Good canapés and petits fours too.

Manleys Hill RH20 4BT
Map 4: TQ01
Tel: 01903 742331
Fax: 01903 740649
Chef: Michel Perraud
Owners: Michel & Bernadette Perraud
Cost: *Alc* £33.50, set-price L £16.50/D £20.50. ☺ H/wine £12.50
Times: Noon-2pm/7-10pm. Closed L Sat, D Sun, all Mon, 1st 2 wks Jan
Additional: Sunday L; Children welcome; ♨ dishes
Seats: 50. Private dining room 16
Smoking: No pipes & cigars
Accommodation: 1 en suite

Directions: On A283, off A24, just E of Storrington

STORRINGTON, **Old Forge**

Service, like the restaurant, is informal yet efficient. Tables are nicely spaced to give some privacy and ample leg room and the proprietor's interest in cricket is shown by the many pictures and memorabilia on the walls. The *carte* is understated, but concepts excite – seared monkfish is served with pea purée and mint vinaigrette; calves' kidney and rocket tart with Vermouth sauce. It's hard to think of anything new to

6 Church Street RH20 4LA
Map 4: TQ01
Tel: 01903 743402
Fax: 01903 742540
Chef: Clive Roberts
Owners: Cathy & Clive Roberts
Cost: *Alc* £28, set-price D £23. ☺ H/wine £11.75
Times: 12.15-1.15pm/7.15-9pm.

Old Forge

Closed L Sat, D Sun, all Mon, Tue, 2
wks spring, 2 wks autumn
Additional: Sunday L; Children
welcome
Seats: 34. Private room 12
Smoking: No smoking in dining room

Directions: On a side street in the
village centre

do with crème brûlée, but here it is given an original lemon
and fennel flavouring. Both buttermilk pudding with
caramelised orange salad and fruit minestrone with
Mascarpone sorbet are fresh ideas worth applauding. A starter
of chilled salmon lasagne with dill cream was flavoursome and
well prepared, followed by excellent roast supreme of goose
with cassoulet sauce. Other unusual seasonal offerings are
woodpigeon and butterbean soup, and roast duck magret,
pearl barley and pancetta. The place comprises three cosy
rooms with low, beamed ceilings and white painted walls.

TURNERS HILL,

Alexander House

East Street RH10 4QD
Map 4: TQ33
Tel: 01342 714914
Fax: 01342 717328
Chef: Neil Wiggins
Owner: International Hotels
Cost: Alc £50, set-price L £24/D £32.
H/wine £15.25
Times: 12.30-2pm/7-10pm
Additional: Bar food; Sunday L;
Children 7+; ✿ dishes
Seats: 60. Private dining room 25
Smoking: No smoking in dining room
Accommodation: 15 en suite ★ ★ ★

*Particularly fine 17th-century mansion set in some hundred
acres of well-tended gardens.* A splendid place offering both a
sunny south-facing drawing room, or the oak-panelled library –
complete with roaring fire – for pre-prandial drinks served by
impressively polished tail-coated waiters. Expect to be
pampered. The classic French cooking with its modern English
accent complements the elegant surroundings exactly. Our
inspection meal got off to a good start with breast of Balcombe
wood pigeon topped with a pan-fried sliver of foie gras and
accompanied by creamed cabbage. Then gratin of turbot
followed, served on a bed of seasoned spinach with noodles,
crab and lemon bisque, with dessert a 'very competent'
chocolate and raspberry gâteau.

Directions: 1.5 mile east of Turners Hill on B2110

WORTHING, Ardington Hotel

Fourth generation owners continue to ensure guests well-being. At dinner, choose from a short, freshly cooked range of dishes: venison terrine with home-made chutney; traditional steak and kidney pie with Guinness; grilled local turbot with lime butter.

Additional: Bar food L; Children welcome; 🌢 dishes
Accommodation: 45 en suite ★ ★ ★

Directions: Central Worthing

Steyne Gardens BN11 3DZ
Map 4: TQ10
Tel: 01903 230451
Fax: 01903 526526
Cost: Alc £25, set-price D £19.50. ☺
H/wine £11.50
Times: D only, 7-8.45pm. Closed 24 Dec-5 Jan

TYNE & WEAR

BOLDON,
Forsters Restaurant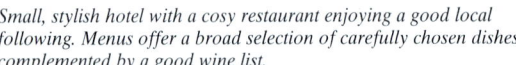

Former shop in a suburban village, now quietly stylish within, with designer prints on the walls. Classic dishes straight out of the old French school – moules marinière, steak au poivre – mingle with such items as grilled Finnan haddock with Welsh rarebit (and that's just a starter!), an antipasto of Parma ham, salami, baby artichokes, sun-dried tomatoes and Parmesan, and main courses of roast pheasant breast with crispy bacon, spring greens and Calvados cream sauce, and sirloin steak with spicy garlic, parsley and mustard butter. Ice creams and sorbets are made in-house, or go for indulgent tiramisu or crème brûlée. Service is friendly and attentive, and the wine list centres on France.

Directions: In village of East Boldon, off A184 Newcastle/Sunderland rd

2 St Bedes Station Road NE36 0LE
Map 12: NZ36
Tel: 0191 5190929
Chef: Barry Forster
Owners: Barry & Sue Forster
Cost: Alc £25, set-price D £17.50. ☺
H/wine £8.50
Times: D only, 7-9.30pm. Closed Sun, Mon, 1 wk spring, 2 wks summer, Bhs
Additional: Children 7+; 🌢 dishes
Seats: 28
Smoking: No smoking in dining room

GATESHEAD,
Eslington Villa Hotel

Small, stylish hotel with a cosy restaurant enjoying a good local following. Menus offer a broad selection of carefully chosen dishes complemented by a good wine list.

Directions: Off A1(M) along Teme Valley, turn R at Eastern Avenue, then L into Station Road

8 Station Road Low Fell
NE9 6DR
Map 12: NZ26
Tel: 0191 4876017
Fax: 0191 4200667
Telephone for further details

NEWCASTLE UPON TYNE,
Blackgate Restaurant ✤

A comfortable restaurant presenting well-balanced and uncomplicated dishes made from fresh local produce. Smoked salmon fillet, grilled chicken breast with spicy peppers and a basil and tomato fondue are typical of the range.

Directions: 2 mins walk from Newcastle Central Station. Situated behind St Nicholas Cathedral, opposite Castle Keep

The Side NE1 3JE
Map 12: NZ26
Tel: 0191 2617356
Telephone for further details

NEWCASTLE UPON TYNE, Café 21

35 The Broadway Darras Hall
Ponteland NE20 9PW
Map 12: NZ26
Tel/Fax: 01661 820357
Cost: *Alc* £25, set-price L £10.50 (2
courses)/ D £12.50. ☺ H/wine £9.50
Times: D only, 5.30-10.30pm. Closed
Sun, Bhs
Additional: Saturday L; Children
welcome; ✿ dishes
Smoking: No-smoking area; No pipes
& cigars

*Modern, upbeat café from the Terry Laybourne stable, offering
Caesar salad, seared sea scallops with black bean vinaigrette,
smoked pork knuckle with braised haricot beans, and spotted dick
with custard sauce.*

Directions: From A696, follow signs for Darras Hall, L at mini-
roundabout, 200yds to restaurant

NEWCASTLE UPON TYNE,
The Copthorne Newcastle

The Close Quayside NE1 3RT
Map 12: NZ26
Tel: 0191 2230333 (Le
Rivage)/2220333 (Harry's)
Fax: 0191 2301111
Cost: *Alc* £32.50 (Le Rivage) £21.50
(Harry's). H/wine £11.75
Times: D only, 7.30-10.15pm. Closed
Sun
Additional: Bar food; Sunday L;
Children welcome; ✿ dishes
Smoking: No-smoking area; Air
conditioning
Accommodation: 156 en suite
★★★★

*Hotel overlooking the Tyne offering the popular, informal Harry's
with a brasserie-style menu and, in the evening, Le Rivage with a
more refined choice of Anglo-French cooking in a stylish setting.*

Directions: From S cross Redheugh
Bridge, turn L at B1600 for Quayside,
hotel on R

NEWCASTLE UPON TYNE,
Courtneys

*A stylish yet cosy split-level restaurant close to the quay serving
modern British food with a global influence: roasted haloumi with
tomatoes and pine kernels, beef fillet with a herby polenta croûton
and a morel and red wine jus, and apricot sponge with chocolate and
orange sauce.*

Smoking: No-smoking area; No pipes & cigars; Air conditioning

Directions: Bottom of Dean St on R before roundabout at
Quayside

5-7 The Side NE1 3JE
Map 12: NZ26
Tel: 0191 2325537
Fax: 0191 2211745
Cost: *Alc* £30, set-price L £16.95. ☺
H/wine £12.95
Times: Noon-2pm/6-10.30pm. Closed
L Sat, all Sun, 1st wk Jan
Additional: Children welcome;
✿ dishes

NEWCASTLE UPON TYNE,

Fisherman's Lodge

Jesmond Dene Jesmond NE7 7BQ
Map 12: NZ26
Tel: 0191 2813281
Fax: 0191 2816410
Chefs: Steven Jobson, Paul Amer
Owners: Franco & Pamela Cetoloni
Cost: *Alc* £35, set-price L £17.80/D
£29.50. H/wine £12.50
Times: Noon-2pm/7-11pm. Closed L
Sat, all Sun, Bhs
Additional: Children 9+ at D;
🍃 dishes
Seats: 60. Private dining rooms 14-43
Smoking: No smoking in dining room

Restaurant noted for formal service and tranquil park setting.
Seafood is what this restaurant does best. Lobsters, grilled with
garlic butter, or cold in a salad, remain one of the pillars of the
carte, or there could be deep-fried monkfish with garlic
mayonnaise, and seared peppered salmon with spicy cucumber
pickle. Three varieties of fishcakes – salt cod with garlic,
seafood with Thai dressing, and smoked and fresh salmon
worked well together; interesting sea and mountain combos
might include sea bass with duck confit, as well as classic surf
'n' turf. There is plenty of meat choice, however, along the
lines of braised lamb shank with pepper and garlic mash with
rosemary sauce. It's a welcome retreat from the hurly-burly of
the city centre.

Directions: 2.5 miles from City centre, off A1058 (Tynemouth)
road at Benton Bank, middle of Jesmond Dene Park

NEWCASTLE UPON TYNE,

The Magpie Room Restaurant

St James Park NE1 4ST
Map 12: NZ26
Tel: 0191 2018439
Fax: 0191 2018611
Owners: Newcastle United F C
Cost: *Alc* £25, set-price L £13. 😊
H/wine £10.95

*You don't have to be a Newcastle FC supporter or ticket
holder to eat here.* This is no pie and Bovril eatery behind the
stand, but a smart, executive-style restaurant within a state-of-
the-art soccer stadium, home of Newcastle United. Reached
by glass-windowed lift and set high up behind one of the

stands, the restaurant offers views of the stadium and the pitch; they put the lights on in the evening for effect, and Sunday lunch includes a tour of the stadium. Alas, you can't enjoy a match and the food at the same time – the restaurant is closed during fixtures. The cooking is good – terrine of foie gras and chicken with sauce gribiche, seared salmon with nage of clams, mussels and baby leeks, and a dessert of baked vanilla cream with macerated fruits, gives a good idea of the style. Quietly attentive service.

Directions: From the south, follow Gateshead A1 signs, then A692 over Redheugh Bridge, Blenheim St & then L on Bath Lane

Times: Noon-2.30pm/7-10pm. Closed L Sat, D Sun, all Mon, 25 Dec, match days
Additional: Sunday L; Children welcome; ❹ dishes
Seats: 149. Private dining room 10. Jacket & tie preferred
Smoking: Air conditioning

NEWCASTLE UPON TYNE,
Malmaison Hotel ❀

Quayside NE1 3DX
Map 12: NZ26
Tel: 0191 2455000
Fax: 0191 2450566
Telephone for further details

Part of the fashionable redeveloped quayside, Malmaison is something of a celebrity watering hole. A meal may consist of roast courgette and rocket salad, confit of duck on garlic and parsley mash, and chocolate brownie with vanilla ice.

Directions: Telephone for directions

NEWCASTLE UPON TYNE,
Swallow Gosforth Park Hotel ❀❀

Purpose-built hotel matched by excellent service. The Brandling Restaurant is where the main action is, offering a sharply focused menu of French-inspired cooking. Classic starters such as rich chicken consommé en croûte, or pressed foie gras terrine with Madeira jelly, are off set by the more modern ideas seen in braised stuffed quail with forest mushroom salad and mango vinaigrette, and confit of duck with rosemary pomme purée. Main courses are more adept at blending the classic and the modern on one plate, as can be seen in cutlets of venison with cinnamon poached pear and rich Burgundy wine sauce, and roast supreme of halibut with foie gras rösti, pearl onion, forest mushroom, smoked bacon and lobster gravy. The Conservatory Restaurant offers a less formal setting and choice.

Directions: 2 mins from A1

High Gosforth Park NE3 5HN
Map 12: NZ26
Tel: 0191 2364111
Fax: 0191 2368192
Chef: Simon Devine
Owner: Swallow Hotels
Cost: Alc £35, set-price L £20/D £25. ☺ H/wine £13
Times: 12.30-2.30pm/7-10pm
Additional: Bar food; Sunday L; Children welcome; ❹ dishes
Seats: 130. Private dining room 40
Smoking: No-smoking area; No pipes & cigars; Air conditioning
Accommodation: 178 en suite
★ ★ ★ ★

NEWCASTLE UPON TYNE,

Taylor's Wharf

There has been a change of emphasis at this popular restaurant, formerly Fisherman's Wharf. Alan Taylor has taken over, put in a new chef and placed an even greater emphasis on seafood (which Mr Taylor's company continues to supply). A new, stylish look too, which adds to the vibrancy of the otherwise traditional ambience. Service remains formal, but is attentive and not at all stuffy. The *carte* and set-price menus are supplemented by chalkboard specials. We found the cooking good. Seared tuna marinated in ginger and spring onion worked well, and was teamed with warm spinach and wild mushrooms, monkfish cooked in butter with onion and tarragon Pernod was equally successful, and the avocado-style mango accompaniment and some smashing seared scallops enhanced the dish greatly. Bread-and-butter pudding made a good finish.

15 The Side NE1 3JE
Map 12: NZ26
Tel: 0191 2321057
Fax: 0191 2320496
Owner: Alan E Taylor
Telephone for further details

Directions: From N side of Tyne Bridge, turn L into Mosley Street, L into Dean Street and L again into The Side

NEWCASTLE UPON TYNE,

21 Queen Street

21 Queen Street Quayside NE1 3UG
Map 12: NZ26
Tel: 0191 2220755
Fax: 0191 2210761
Chef: Terence Laybourne
Owners: Terence & Susan Laybourne
Cost: *Alc* £34.60, set-price L £17.50
Times: Noon-2pm/7-10.30pm. Closed L Sat, all Sun, Bhs
Additional: Children welcome
Seats: 70
Smoking: No pipes

Directions: Queen Street runs parallel to and just behind Newcastle Quay – almost under the Tyne Bridge on N side of the river

21 Queen Street continues to reflect cutting-edge restaurant design. A bare wooden floor, modern tan-coloured chairs, much white, with good use of pastel, earth shades of greens, yellows and reds, and abstracts on the walls have a fresh modern look. Terence Laybourne has been at the stoves for over 10 years now and shows no sign of flagging, his cooking continuing to keep smiles on faces. Luxury ingredients there may be linguine (made in-house, of course) with lobster 'bolognese', for instance, or potato salad with caviar and chives in oyster sauce – but the same understanding of how the components of a dish interact also shows up in the vibrant flavours of a tart of spring leeks, potatoes and bacon. Technical accomplishments and the quality of ingredients can be taken as read – perfectly cooked turbot roasted in meat juices served with an onion compote and wild mushrooms, for example – and seasonality is at the core, producing spring starters of herb soup with soft-boiled quails' egg, or crab salad with asparagus and Italian parsley juice, and a main course of new season's lamb with pearl barley and fried new potatoes. Arctic roll didn't go down with the Titanic – it appears here in a double chocolate version – and baked rhubarb with a crumble of hazelnut macaroon may also present itself. A handful of wines by the glass are recommended on the set-price dinner menu, the full list, with a good range of halves, concentrating on France. Switched-on staff all contribute to the enjoyment.

NEWCASTLE UPON TYNE,
Vermont Hotel ❀❀

Previously the city's County Hall, now a fine hotel with great views across the Tyne. The Blue Room is the more formal of the various restaurants and bars. Our test meal revealed a kitchen well up on modern ideas. That meal opened with steamed scallops wrapped in lettuce and leek with caviar cream, then a mango gratinée as a palate cleanser, followed by honey-glazed best end of lamb with spices served with French and flageolet beans, and toasted sesame seed and caramel iced soufflé with a slice of roast orange marinated in cardamom syrup. Breads and petits fours are home-made. The Brasserie is open for lighter meals all day, as well as in the evening

Castle Garth NE1 1RQ
Map 12: NZ26
Tel: 0191 2331010
Fax: 0191 2331234
Chef: Thierry Billot
Owners: Lincoln Group
Cost: *Alc* £38
Times: D only, 6.30-10.15pm. Closed D Sun, 1-14 Aug
Additional: Bar food; Sunday L (brasserie); Children welcome; ❹ dishes
Seats: 80. Jacket & tie preferred
Smoking: No-smoking area
Accommodation: 101 en suite
★ ★ ★ ★

Directions: City centre, by the Castle and swing bridge

SUNDERLAND, **Brasserie 21** ❀

The third of Terry Laybourne's brasserie-style eateries, providing sound contemporary cooking in stylish surroundings. The striking quayside warehouse setting is complemented by seared scallops with tomato and red onion salsa, and robust lamb shank and chick pea purée.

Wylam Worth Low Street SR1 2AD
Tel: 0191 5676594
Owner: Terry Laybourne
Telephone for further details

Directions: Telephone for directions

SUNDERLAND, **Swallow Hotel** ❀

Occupying a seafront location, the Promenade is a classically-styled restaurant with a bandstand centre-piece and pianist. Expect roast loin of lamb with couscous, and seared crispy chicken with black pudding farce.

Queen's Parade Seaburn SR6 8DB
Map 12: NZ35
Tel: 0191 5292041
Fax: 0191 5294227
Telephone for further details

Directions: On A184 (Boldon): at roundabout after Boldon turn L, then 1st R to Seaburn. L at next roundabout, follow road to coast. Turn R; hotel is 100m on R

WARWICKSHIRE

ABBOT'S SALFORD,

Salford Hall Hotel

A beautifully restored 15th-century manor house, retaining many charming features, including exposed beams, stonework and open fireplaces. The oak-panelled dining room has large mullioned windows and is housed in a wing that was added in the 17th century. Canapés precede a four-course table d'hôte (no choice). Pan-seared Cornish scallops were fresh and had good flavour, braised blade of Aberdeenshire beef, served on a bed of rosemary-scented Savoy cabbage, topped with a good grain mustard-flavoured mash, a baby turnip, baby carrot and bay leek, was 'melt-in-the-mouth tender'. Baked apple tarte Tatin tasted freshly made, and came with a good puff pastry, a sharp but not too tart filling, and a rich, dark caramel sauce. Home-made fudge is served with the coffee.

Directions: On A439 8 miles W of Stratford-upon-Avon

Evesham WR11 5UT
Map 4: SP05
Tel: 01386 871300
Fax: 01386 871301
Chef: Robert Bean
Owner: Charter Hotels Ltd
Cost: Set-price L £15.25/D £25. ☺
H/wine £11.75
Times: 12.30-1.30pm/7-9.30pm.
Closed L Sat, Xmas
Additional: Bar food L; Sunday L;
Children welcome; ♨ dishes
Seats: 50. Private dining room 50
Smoking: No smoking in dining room
Accommodation: 34 en suite ★ ★ ★

ALDERMINSTER,

Ettington Park Hotel

Stratford-upon-Avon CV37 8BU
Map 4: SP24
Tel: 01789 450123
Fax: 01789 450472
Chef: Chris Hudson
Owners: Arcadian Hotels
Cost: *Alc* £35, set-price L £17.50/D
£30.50. ☺ H/wine £16
Additional: Bar food; Sunday L;
Children 5+; ♨ dishes
Seats: 45. Private dining room 80.
Jacket & tie preferred
Smoking: No smoking in dining room
Accommodation: 48 en suite ★ ★ ★ ★

Gothic grandeur gives great atmosphere. The Oak Room Restaurant features 19th-century family crests and a Rococo ceiling, plus original paintings, antiques and magnificent stained glass windows. This could be quite intimidating, but the atmosphere is unexpectedly comfortable and intimate. Fine produce and a simple approach help. Amongst the starters are chicken and Madeira boudin with creamed leeks and cep mushroom sauce, and seared sea scallops with tagliolini pasta and fresh herb velouté. A good choice of main courses takes in seared calves' liver with curried potato, glazed apples and kumquats with mango and chutney sauce, as well as lemon sole fillets on oriental vegetable stir-fry with ginger and saffron velouté. If we have any criticisms, it is in a certain repetition of menu descriptions.

Directions: 5 miles S of Stratford

ATHERSTONE,
Chapel House Hotel ✿✿

Friar's Gate CV9 1EY
Map 4: SP39
Tel: 01827 718949
Fax: 01827 717702
Chef: Adam Bennett
Owner: David Arnold
Cost: *Alc* £24, set-price L £16.95. ☺
H/wine £10
Times: D only, 7-9.30pm. Closed D
Sun, 24-26 Dec, 1 Jan, Bh Mon
Additional: Sunday L (noon-2.30pm);
Children 10+; ✿ dishes
Seats: 50. Private dining room 26.
Jacket & tie preferred
Smoking: No smoking in dining room
Accommodation: 13 en suite ★ ★

'An oasis of hospitality' from this 18th-century former dower house located next to the church in the Market Square. Nicely varied canapés and petits fours top-and-tail a monthly-changing dinner menu that has a solidly classical foundation. Starters might include rillettes de canard with green peppercorn sauce or our well-balanced salt cod and haricot bean broth, while main courses range from breast of guinea fowl (with a faggot of the leg, Puy lentils and Madeira jus), to grilled monkfish on a smoked haddock brandade. Do leave room for one of the delicious desserts such as the exemplary chocolate, rum and raisin brulée that we ordered. Occasional themed events include wine-tasting dinners and 'Befores and Afters' meals consisting of starters and desserts.

Directions: Town centre

CLAVERDON,
Ardencote Manor Hotel ✿

Lye Green Road CV35 8LS
Map 4: SP16
Tel: 01926 843111
Fax: 01926 842646
Cost: Set-price D £24.95. ☺ H/wine
£10.95
Times: D only, 7-9.30pm.
Additional: Bar food; Sunday L
(12.30-2pm); Children 12+; ✿ dishes

Small hotel with a big heart, offering a varied choice of eateries. Formal meals in the Oak Room bring ravioli of scallops with Thai-scented broth, pan-fried sea bass and champagne sauce, and apple Charlotte.

Smoking: No smoking in dining room; Air conditioning
Accommodation: 18 en suite ★ ★ ★

Directions: From A4189 in Claverdon follow signs for Shrewley. Hotel 0.5 mile on R

KENILWORTH,
Restaurant Bosquet ✿✿

97a Warwick Road
CV8 1HP
Map 4: SP27
Tel: 01926 852463
Chef: Bernard Lignier
Owners: B & J Lignier
Cost: *Alc* £30, set-price L & D £25.
☺ H/wine £12

Charming 'front-room'-style restaurant. Mrs Lignier is in charge front of house and her husband Bernard runs the kitchen, offering a repertoire that is based squarely on traditional French cuisine. Thus, a typical set-price menu (not available on Saturdays) might run from parfait de foie de canard et foie gras to selle d'agneau en croûte de fines herbes and finish with fromages de France. But the kitchen has a confident touch in playing around with ingredients, deftly combining flavours and textures in starters of perhaps watercress soup with a mousse of pike filled with crayfish and frogs' legs. Accurate timing shows up in main courses of sea bass on roasted tomatoes in a light saffron sauce with squid ink, and in pastry work: a croustade normande was an 'absolutely delish' tart of spicy, buttery apples in crisp, glazed filo pastry, served with vanilla ice cream and 'scrummy' caramel sauce. Canapés and home-made bread rolls are highly regarded, and petits fours end things on a high note.

Times: Noon-2pm/7-10pm. Closed L Sat, all Sun, Mon, 25 Dec-2 Jan, 7-31 Aug
Additional: Children welcome; ⏺ dishes
Seats: 30
Smoking: No pipes & cigars

Directions: In main street of Kenilworth

KENILWORTH,
Simpson's

Bright, attractive restaurant in a good position on the main street. Green wicker chairs, bold prints and stripped-wood floor create a French café feel; there's a great atmosphere and it's perfect for enjoying light lunches as well as full-blown dinners. Our lunch was impressive. Home-marinated olives and excellent ciabatta, then a 'stunning, perfectly cooked' seared foie gras set on grilled endive with caramelised oranges. 'Top-notch' monkfish with basil risotto followed, a 'well-timed dish' with 'good spicy seasoning', finished off with drizzles of chorizo oil and balsamic. Finally 'superb' apple tarte Tatin, backed up real cappuccino, which brought lunch to a stylish close.

Directions: In main street

Warwick Road CV8 1HL
Map 4: SP27
Tel: 01926 864567
Fax: 01926 864510
Chefs: Andreas Antona, Andrew Waters, Luke Tipping
Owner: Andreas Antona
Cost: *Alc* £28.45, set-price D £26.95. H/wine £11.50
Times: 12.30-1.45pm/7-9.45pm. Closed Sun, 24, 26, 27, 31 Dec, 1 Jan, Bhs
Additional: Children welcome; ⏺ dishes
Smoking: No-smoking area; Air conditioning

LEAMINGTON SPA,
Lansdowne Hotel

Delightful Regency hotel where the daily menu might offer prime Aberdeen Angus steaks, salmon with seafood and caper sauce, and buckwheat blinis with Mediterranean vegetables.

Additional: Children 5+; ⏺ dishes
Smoking: No smoking in dining room
Accommodation: 14 en suite ★

Directions: Town centre, crossroads of Warwick Street and Clarendon Street

87 Clarendon Street CV32 4PF
Map 4: SP36
Tel: 01926 450505
Fax: 01926 421313
Cost: *Alc* £18.95. ☺ H/wine £8.95
Times: D only, 6.30-8.30pm. Closed D Sun (exc residents), 25-26 Dec

---

LEAMINGTON SPA,
Leamington Hotel

The Bistro at this stylish Victorian town house offers a combination of modern British and traditional French cuisine: braised pheasant, Cumberland sausage, and prime fillet of salmon.

Additional: Sunday L; Children welcome; ⏺ dishes
Smoking: No pipes & cigars
Accommodation: 30 en suite ★ ★ ★

Directions: Along Newbold Terrace, turn L at lights. Hotel on right-hand corner of Willes Road & Upper Holly Walk

64 Upper Holly Walk CV32 4JL
Map 4: SP36
Tel: 01926 883777
Fax: 01926 330467
Cost: *Alc* £18, set-price L £9. ☺ H/wine £8.75
Times: Noon-1.30pm/7-9.30pm

LEAMINGTON SPA, **Mallory Court** ✿✿✿

Harbury Lane Bishop's Tachbrook
CV33 9QB
Map 4: SP36
Tel: 01926 330214
Fax: 01926 451714
Chef: Allan Holland
Owners: Allan Holland, Jeremy Mort
Cost: *Alc* £55, set-price L £30/D £38.
H/wine £16
Times: Noon-2pm/7-10pm
Additional: Sunday L; Children 9+;
✿ dishes
Seats: 50. Private dining room 20
Smoking: No smoking in dining room
Accommodation: 18 en suite ★ ★ ★

Beautifully restored country house with acreage without,
splendid service within. This is a real country house with a
chintzy lounge, a baby grand in one corner, and things like fine
Waldorf salad in vol au vent served as canapés before dinner.
Allan Holland offers a synthesis of craft and brisk modernity
in a repertoire that is based on ingredients that are of the
freshest and finest. He understands the need for balance, and
that everyone wants an old favourite once in a while. Thus
starters range from a classic terrine of foie gras with Sauternes
jelly to a dressed Cornish crab with celeriac remoulade, or a
more upbeat boudin blanc with spinach and apple sauce. The
freshest fish requires only the simplest treatment and here
grilled Cornish lobster is partnered by garlic butter, Dover sole
with herb butter, and that philosophy can extend to
Chateaubriand with béarnaise sauce. Pan-fried calves' liver
with Italian bacon, braised Little Gem lettuce and sage is a
modern reworking of a great brasserie dish, while aubergine
and buffalo Mozzarella beignet with salsify and balsamic is
enough to make vegetarians of us all. Chocolate nemesis and
glazed lemon tart are first-rate desserts, but Sauternes custard
with Armagnac prunes stands out.

Directions: From M40 J13
(northbound) take A452 (signed
Leamington Spa), next L into Oakley
Wood Rd (B4087). R into Harbury Ln.
Hotel on R. From M40/J14/A452 into
Mallory Rd, then B4087

STRATFORD-UPON-AVON,

Alveston Manor ✿

Clopton Bridge CV37 7HP
Map 4: SP25
Tel: 01789 204581
Fax: 01789 414095
Telephone for further details

Directions: Take A46 towards
Stratford, then A439 to town centre;
hotel is on S side of river

The hotel, a 16th-century manor, offers a grill menu during the week
with a popular choice of individually priced dishes, and a set-price
menu at weekends.

STRATFORD-UPON-AVON,
Billesley Manor Hotel

The manor dates from the 16th century, and is surrounded by peaceful grounds and parkland yet within striking distance of the town centre. Despite refurbishment, the public rooms retain a period feel, helped no doubt by oak panelling and magnificent fireplaces. Both a *carte* and a set-price menu are available in the restaurant, candlelit at night. Bread rolls are described as 'really good', and at inspection a starter of chicken liver parfait with brioche and onion marmalade was well liked, uncomplicated, smooth, with good depth of flavour. Properly cooked red mullet with crispy noodles and red wine sauce was felt to be an unlikely combination that worked well, and care had been taken with the vegetables too. White chocolate torte – really more like a cheesecake – with strawberry sauce ended the meal. A limited choice of wines are sold by the glass from the large list.

Directions: On the A46, 3 miles west of Stratford-upon-Avon

Billesley Alcester B49 6NF
Map 4: SP25
Tel: 01789 279955
Fax: 01789 764145
Chef: Adrian Kirkman
Owners: Queens Moat House
Cost: *Alc* £25, set-price D £19.95 (4 courses). ☺ H/wine £12.50
Times: 12.30-2pm/7.30-9.15pm. Closed L Sat
Additional: Bar food L; Sunday L; Children welcome; 🍴 dishes
Seats: 40. Private dining room 30
Smoking: No smoking in dining room
Accommodation: 41 en suite ★★★★

STRATFORD-UPON-AVON,
The Boathouse

Swan's Nest Lane CV37 7LS
Map 4: SP25
Tel/Fax: 01789 297733
Chef: Patrick Robiquet
Owners: Ms M Brebner, William Meredith-Owen
Cost: *Alc* £22, set-price L £14.95. ☺ H/wine £11.75
Times: Noon-2pm/6-9.45pm. Closed L Sat, Mon, & Tue, all Sun, 25, 26 Dec, 1 Jan
Additional: Children welcome; 🍴 dishes
Seats: 90
Smoking: No pipes & cigars

Above a picturesque working boathouse alongside the river, just a short walk from the Stratford theatres. The restaurant boasts polished wood floors, old oak timbers and a good deal of rope in a pleasing decor that also features a balcony that opens up in the summer. Our last test lunch started with a simple but effective squid risotto enlivened with chilli oil, then went on to a crusted roast cod on herb mash with an artichoke ratatouille – a super lunchtime dish. Other offerings might include carpaccio of tuna with Parmesan salad and wasabi dressing, or duck confit on lightly curried salad. Our sweet conclusion was a 'trio of citrus' comprising a good lime bavarois, orange sorbet and a lemon curd-filled tuile basket.

Directions: From town centre, cross river by Clopton Bridge towards Oxford and Banbury, then double back around roundabout 50 yards on, then 1st L

STRATFORD-UPON-AVON,

Desports

13-14 Meer Street CV37 6QB
Map 4: SP25
Tel/Fax: 01789 269304
Chef: Paul Desport
Owners: Julie & Paul Desport
Cost: Set-price L £14. H/wine £10.25
Times: Noon-2pm/6-11pm. Closed
Sun, Mon, Jan
Additional: Children welcome;
🍴 dishes
Seats: 50
Smoking: No-smoking area; No pipes
& cigars

Directions: In town centre between
Market Place and Shakespeare Centre

Desports is above Desports Bistro in a delightful 16th-century building. Climb the stairs to a bright yellow room with a profusion of exposed beams, bare boards, and a mass of wrought iron. Menus are interesting, tend to be understated, but the cooking is very much in the modern style with a variety of influences ranging from the Mediterranean to Asia. The format allows many dishes to be taken as starters or main courses. Seared scallops flavoured with Indian spices, golden mango chilli salsa and coriander oil, saddle of rabbit with chorizo, prunes and Calvados on a white pudding sauce, mille-feuille of polenta with Parmesan, aubergine caviar, forest mushrooms with tapenade, and bitter chocolate and cherry Kirsch pudding with cardamom ice cream show the range.

STRATFORD-UPON-AVON,

Grosvenor Hotel

Warwick Road CU37 6YT
Map 4: SP25
Tel: 01789 269213
Fax: 01789 266087
Telephone for further details

At this distinctive Grade II listed Georgian hotel, the Garden Restaurant opens onto a colourfully planted courtyard. Modern menus include some interesting dishes, including smoked haddock ravioli, and lamb fillet and spinach in filo pastry with port wine jus.

Directions: Telephone for directions

STRATFORD-UPON-AVON,

Lambs of Sheep Street

12 Sheep Street CV37 6EF
Map 4: SP25
Tel/Fax: 01789 292554
Cost: *Alc* £17.50, set-price L
£12.95/D £17.50. ☺ H/wine £8.50
Times: Noon-1.45pm/5.30-10.30pm
Additional: 🍴 dishes

A 16th-century building housing a lively restaurant frequented by theatre-goers. Expect the likes of moules marinière, spinach and ricotta crêpes, fillet steak, and saltimbocca alla Romana.

Smoking: No pipes & cigars

Directions: From Stratford town centre, head towards 'Waterside' and 'Royal Shakespeare Theatre'. Sheep Street is 1st R on Waterside

STRATFORD-UPON-AVON,

The Shakespeare

Chapel Street CV37 6ER
Map 4: SP25
Tel: 01789 294771
Fax: 01789 415411
Telephone for further details

Directions: Follow signs to town
centre. Go round one-way system up
Bridge Street. At roundabout turn L.
Hotel is 200yds on L

Elizabethan landmark hotel in the town centre. The classic and
modern British carte is supplemented by daily specials. Dinner could
include a confit of duck, with a main course of chicken breast with a
charcuterie faggot.

STRATFORD-UPON-AVON,

Thistle Stratford-on-Avon

Waterside CV37 6BA
Map 4: SP25
Tel: 01789 294949
Fax: 01789 415874
Cost: *Alc* £35. H/wine £9.95
Times: Noon-2pm/5.45-9.30pm
Additional: Bar food; Sunday L;
Children welcome; ⬧ dishes
Smoking: No smoking in dining room;
Air conditioning
Accommodation: 62 en suite ★★★

Directions: On Waterside, opposite
Royal Shakespeare and Swan Theatres

Traditional hotel on the water's edge, overlooking the Royal
Shakespeare and Swan theatres. The menus have an olde English
feel, but modern trends are evident in dishes such as roasted sea bass
on dill mash, and poached supreme of chicken on Parmesan
tagliatelle.

STRATFORD-UPON-AVON,

Welcombe Hotel

Jacobean-style Victorian manor run by a friendly team
steeped in the traditions of good service. Part of the 800 acres
of landscaped parkland was once owned by William
Shakespeare; incongruously, the place is but a mile from the
town centre. The food here is ambitious and thoroughly up-to-
date, although it is based on a sound classical background.
Thus poached supreme of Cornish turbot is served with a
salmon mousseline and asparagus fondue, and loin of local

Warwick Road
CV37 0NR
Map 4: SP25
Tel: 01789 295252
Fax: 01789 414666
Chef: Mark Naylor
Cost: *Alc* £45, set-price L £19.50/D
£37 (4 courses). H/wine £16
Times: Noon-2pm/7-9.30pm. Closed
L Sat, 1st wk in Jan

venison comes with layered caramelised mango and lime with a juniper-scented sauce. The modern, as in roasted sweet pepper and fennel terrine with a saffron and ratatouille dressing, is offset by the traditional: the silver carving trolley offers a daily roast. desserts take in crêpes Suzette, flambéed at table, and passion fruit ganache with coconut mousse. The wine list is well balanced, offers some good older vintages as well as a fair selection of halves.

Directions: On A439 1 mile from town centre

Welcombe Hotel

Additional: Bar food; Sunday L; Children welcome; ✍ dishes
Seats: 50. Private dining room 120. Jacket & tie preferred
Smoking: No smoking in dining room
Accommodation: 64 en suite ★ ★ ★ ★

WISHAW, **The Belfry**

Busy resort hotel geared up for top-level golfing, leisure pursuits, and international conferences. While all that's going on, check out the menu in the intimate, cottage-style French restaurant. It's here that guests can unwind and enjoy well-prepared dishes along the lines of fillet of halibut with scallops and mussels, and grilled calves' liver with bacon and caramelised shallots. We kicked off a November meal with a traditional confit of duck, which came perfectly partnered with a 'lip-smacking' Savoy cabbage and chorizo mix. Then 'perfectly tender' roast loin of lamb wrapped in chicken mousse and a thin layer of spinach, accompanied by a selection of fresh vegetables: roasted carrots, minted mash and asparagus. A well-made vanilla crème brûlée and good espresso rounded things off.

Directions: At junction of A446 & A4091, 1 mile NW of M42/J9

Sutton Coldfield B76 9PR
Map 7: SP19
Tel: 01675 470301
Fax: 01675 470256
Chef: Eric Bruce
Owner: Greenalls Hotels & Leisure
Cost: *Alc* £37.50, set-price L £16.95/D £29.95. ☺ H/wine £14.95
Times: 12.30-2pm/6.30-10pm
Additional: Bar food; Sunday L; Children welcome; ✍ dishes
Seats: 175. Private dining room 300
Smoking: No smoking in dining room; Air conditioning
Accommodation: 324 en suite ★ ★ ★ ★

WEST MIDLANDS

BALSALL COMMON, Haigs Hotel ❀❀

Kenilworth Road CV7 7EL
Map 7: SP27
Tel: 01676 533004
Fax: 01676 535132
Chef: Paul Hartup
Owners: Alan & Hester Harris
Cost: *Alc* £26, set-price D £22. ☺
H/wine £10.25
Times: D only, 7.30-9.30pm
Additional: Sunday L (12.30-2pm);
Children welcome; ⚘ dishes
Seats: 60. Private dining room 28
Accommodation: 23 en suite ★★

Directions: On A452, 4 miles N of
NEC/Airport, on L before village
centre

The main road and residential surroundings belie the charm of this lovely, well-run hotel. Poppy's Restaurant is appropriately styled with a floral theme in the airy, bright dining room. Much technical prowess goes into the Anglo-French repertoire: Parmesan soufflé beignet; game pressed terrine; baked fillet of lamb wrapped in basil mousse and filo pastry with orange sauce. Sautéed breast of squab pigeon, served with a leg mousseline and Savoy cabbage on pigeon jus, shows a kitchen that cares about the quality of its ingredients. Veal is given welcome billing, either pan-fried with peppercorn sauce or on a celeriac fritter with chive sauce. Snails and sweetbreads have also been spotted. Modern ideas are not neglected in the form of chargrilled cod with wilted spinach and basil oil, and roast Gressingham duck with beetroot purée and Cassis. Desserts are classic – marjolaine, fresh fruit salad, iced rum and raisin parfait.

BALSALL COMMON,
Nailcote Hall ❀❀

Nailcote Lane Berkswell CV7 7DE
Map 7: SP27
Tel: 01203 466174
Fax: 01203 470720
Telephone for further details

Elizabethan manor steeped in the history of Cromwell and the Civil War. Indeed, the house remains largely unspoilt and is stylishly furbished with contemporary wall coverings and fabrics that accentuate the heavy timbers and open fires. The Oak room was the formal setting for our inspection meal, although the Mediterranean-style annexe offers an informal eaterie in Rick's Garden Café and Bar. The kitchen is benefiting from some new blood, and there's ambition at work in that area. We tried tiger prawns and scallops in Thai-flavoured broth, fillet of venison served with broad beans, scallions and baby vegetables, and marinated peach flan.

Nailcote Hall

Directions: On B4101
(Balsall/Coventry), 10 mins from
NEC/Birmingham Airport

BIRMINGHAM,

Chung Ying Garden

17 Thorp Street B5 4AT
Map 7: SP08
Tel: 0121 6666622
Fax: 0121 6225860
Telephone for further details

Directions: City centre, off Hurst
Street, nr Hippodrome Theatre

Large Chinatown restaurant with a predominantly Cantonese menu offering a bewildering choice of dishes, all carefully prepared and served in generous portions.

BIRMINGHAM,

Copthorne Birmingham

There's a choice of dining between Goldies Brasserie and the more formal Goldsmiths Restaurant, where you might eat crab chowder, flamed medallions of beef, and lemon posset.

Smoking: Air conditioning
Accommodation: 212 en suite ★ ★ ★ ★

Directions: City centre

Paradise Circus B3 3HJ
Map 7: SP08
Tel: 0121 2002727
Fax: 0121 2001195
Cost: *Alc* £26.95, set-price D £26.95
Times: D only, 7-10pm. Closed Sun,
Bhs
Additional: Bar food; Sunday L;
Children welcome; 🍃 dishes

BIRMINGHAM,

Lombard Room Restaurant

Although a hotel, the restaurant is separate from the bedroom block. The Lombard Room has been carved out of a former paper mill (with adjoining conservatory-style bar), and proffers an elegant look with well-spaced tables. Menus change monthly and the kitchen is well-acquainted with modern ideas. Sauté of wild mushrooms in a herb muffin with tarragon cream, baked Cornish hake topped with a horseradish and herb crust with fresh tomato sauce and truffle oil, or pot-roast chump of lamb with green peppercorns, rosemary and wild honey, and baked passion fruit tart with blackcurrant sorbet, is typical of the range. The wine list is notable, with a good range

180 Lifford Lane Kings Norton
B30 3NT
Map 7: SP08
Tel: 0121 4595800
Fax: 0121 4598553
Chef: Anthony Morgan
Owners: Anthony Morgan,
Antony Davis
Cost: Set-price L £17.85/D £26.
H/wine £13.85
Times: Noon-2.30pm/7-9.30pm.
Closed L Sat, D Sun, 1st 2 wks Jan,
Bhs

of options, mainly concentrated on France, with lots of champagne and a large list of half-bottles.

Directions: From city centre take A441 (Pershore road) until Stirchley. Turn L at Breadon Bar, hotel is 1 mile on R

BIRMINGHAM,
Restaurant Gilmore ✿✿

In the heart of the Jewellery Quarter, the former industrial building has been carefully converted. The long, narrow dining area with its exposed brick lining, large cast-iron stove and girders has an atmosphere good for both lunchtime and evening eating. Chef/owner Paul Gilmore used to be a specialist food supplier, so not only are his dishes both imaginative and consistently well cooked, he chooses his ingredients with the greatest care. After a well-balanced starter of roasted sweet peppers with avocado mousse, wild sea bass with garlic potatoes proved a great choice. Roast fillet of turbot with vanilla seed risotto and porcini cappuccino puts a vibrant spin on a fish which can tend to blandness. Pot-roasting gives pork fillet with apple and sage noodles depth of flavour, and lively spicing lifts vegetarian dishes such as lemon roasted fennel with minted couscous, pickled ginger and sesame oil. Bread-and-butter pudding does not disappoint.

Directions: In 'Jewellery Quarter' 1 mile N of city centre

BIRMINGHAM, Shimla Pinks ✿

Large restaurant with striking modern decor. Much effort is made to recreate the authentic flavour of the Punjab. Look out for the reasonably priced set lunch and evening 'banquets'.

Directions: In city centre, opposite Novotel and near the ICC

BIRMINGHAM, Swallow Hotel

No Rosettes awarded this year, for as we went to press changes occurred in the kitchen. Three AA Rosetted chef Jonathan Harrison left to open his own business, The Sandpiper Inn, Leyburn, Yorkshire, and Ian Mansfield, a three AA Rosetted chef from Eastwell Manor in Kent (see entry)

Lombard Room Restaurant

Additional: Bar food L; Sunday L; Children welcome; 🍴 dishes
Seats: 80. Private dining room 50
Smoking: No smoking in dining room; Air conditioning
Accommodation: 9 en suite ★★★

27 Warstone Lane B18 6JQ
Map 7: SP08
Tel: 0121 2333655
Fax: 01543 415511
Chef: Paul Gilmore
Owners: Paul & Dee Gilmore
Cost: Set-price L £15.50/D £21.50. ☺ H/wine £12.50
Times: Noon-2pm/7-9.30pm. Closed L Sat, all Sun & Mon, 1 wk Jan, 1 wk Easter, 2 wks Aug, all Bhs + Tue following Bh Mon
Additional: Children welcome; 🍴 dishes
Smoking: No-smoking area; Air conditioning

214 Broad Street B15 1AY
Map 7: SP08
Tel: 0121 6330366
Fax: 0121 6436383
Telephone for further details

12 Hagley Road Five Ways B16 8SJ
Map 7: SP08
Tel: 0121 4521144
Fax: 0121 4563442
Chef: Ian Mansfield
Cost: Alc £40, set-price L £21.50/D £33.50 (4 courses). H/wine £16.50

Times: 12.30-2.30pm/7.30-10.30pm.
Closed L Sat
Additional: Sunday L; Children
welcome; ❹ dishes
Seats: 60. Private dining rooms 20

arrived to head the kitchen too late for us to make a proper
assessment.

Smoking: No-smoking area; Air conditioning
Accommodation: 98 en suite ★ ★ ★ ★ ★

Directions: City end of the A546, at the Five Ways roundabout

COVENTRY,

Brooklands Grange Hotel

Smart business hotel on the outskirts of Coventry. The rural
origins of this converted 16th-century farmhouse are still
evident, although the dining room is now richly decorated and
is the ideal venue for modern international dishes like salmon
and crab ravioli and crispy roast duck with red pepper sauce. A
typical lunch might begin with a starter of warm goats' cheese
and grilled vegetables, or deep-fried baby aubergine in cider
batter. Then one might try breast of chicken served with wild
mushrooms and Madeira sauce, or the roast cod with parsley
crust. Dessert might be steamed lemon sponge pudding or
indulgent profiteroles with hot chocolate sauce.

Directions: On A4144; on right at Allesley roundabout

Holyhead Road CV5 8HX
Map 4: SP37
Tel: 01203 601601
Fax: 01203 601277
Chef: Regina Kemp
Cost: *Alc* £22.85, set-price L £10.95
(2 courses). H/wine £10.95
Times: Noon-2pm/7-10pm. Closed L
Sat, 26 Dec, 1 Jan
Additional: Bar food; Sunday L;
Children welcome; ❹ dishes
Seats: 60. Private dining room 14
Smoking: No-smoking area; No pipes
& cigars
Accommodation: 31 en suite ★ ★ ★

COVENTRY, Hyland's Hotel

*Modern in appearance, convenient for both the railway
station and the city centre, yet enjoys an outlook over an
attractive park.* Hylands Hotel's Restaurant 153 has been
designed around the clean and simple principles of Philippe
Starck, although the staff create a relaxing and welcoming
atmosphere amid the strong visual impact of their
surroundings. A tart of red and yellow cherry tomatoes has
been commended for its sweet, concentrated flavours well-
complemented by the sharpness of melted goats' cheese, with a
main course of grilled salmon with caper cream, tagliatelle,
crispy Parma ham and a poached egg showing the kitchen's
confident handling of ingredients and flavours. Traditional
bubble-and-squeak and rosemary jus might accompany pinkly
cooked lamb fillet, and baby spinach and chive butter sauce a
Cajun-spiced fishcake. Vanilla crème brûlée is creamy and
thick, as it should be, or go for white chocolate mousse with
dark chocolate and mint sauce.

Warwick Road CV3 6AU
Map 4: SP37
Tel: 01203 502501
Fax: 01203 501027
Chef: Darrion Smethurst
Owner: Salim Moloo
Cost: *Alc* £18.95, set-price L
£13.75/D £15.95. ☺ H/wine £10.95
Times: Noon-2pm/7-10pm. Closed L
Sat, L Sun
Additional: Bar food L; Children
welcome; ❹ dishes
Seats: 80. Private room 40
Smoking: Air conditioning
Accommodation: 61 en suite ★ ★ ★

Directions: Telephone for directions

HOCKLEY HEATH,

Nuthurst Grange Hotel ❀❀

Nuthurst Grange Lane Solihull
B94 5NL
Map 7: SP17
Tel: 01564 783972
Fax: 01564 783919
Chef/Owner: David L Randolph
Cost: *Alc* L £19, set-price D from
£29.50. H/wine £13.50
Times: Noon-2pm/7-9.30pm. Closed
L Sat
Additional: Sunday L; Children
welcome; ◉ dishes
Seats: 50. Private dining rooms 10-90
Smoking: No smoking in dining room
Accommodation: 15 en suite ★ ★ ★

*A wonderfully secluded location, set within seven acres of
landscaped gardens and woodlands, approached via a long
avenue drive.* A formal set menu includes 'highly flavoured'
canapés, *amuse-bouches* of lambs' liver wrapped in bacon, and
petits fours at the end of the meal. Overall, the menu seems
dated, but some good dishes are to be found: a galantine of quail
and foie gras with truffle oil and balsamic vinegar was delicately
flavoured, and grilled monkfish and sea bass, thin medallions of
the former, fillets of the latter were set on a very soft bed of
braised fennel and accompanied by a cream Pernod sauce;
indeed the kitchen clearly favours cream sauces. The highlight
among the mostly old-fashioned desserts is a top class crème
brûlée, 'thin properly caramelised topping, thick creamy filling'.

Directions: Off A3400, half mile S of Hockley Heath, turning at
notice board into Nuthurst Grange Lane

MERIDEN, **Manor Hotel** ❀❀

Main Road CV7 7NH
Map 4: SP28
Tel: 01676 522735
Fax: 01676 522186
Chef: Peter Griffiths
Cost: *Alc* £26, set-price D £19.95. ☺
H/wine £12.95
Times: 12.30-1.45pm/7-9.45pm.
Closed L Sat
Additional: Bar food; Sunday L;
Children welcome; ◉ dishes
Seats: 160. Private dining room 8-200
Smoking: No smoking in dining room;
Air conditioning
Accommodation: 112 en suite ★ ★ ★

Directions: From M42 J6 take A45
towards Coventry. 0.5m after fly-over,
turn R across dual carriageway onto
B4104. Over mini-roundabout. Hotel
on L

Smart hotel dating from 1745. The Regency Restaurant
occupies a central position, a vast room, light and airy and
elegantly decorated in greens and golds; staff are generally
young, cheerful and competent. Start with something traditional
like chicken liver parfait with port and redcurrant sauce; more
exotic tastes could go for fillet of red mullet pan-fried with fennel
confit and accompanied by mango salsa and curry oil. Roast cod,

well-timed, might come under a thick pesto crust and plated over a well-judged bed of horseradish mash with a red pepper sauce, while meat-lovers could opt perhaps for lamb shank with bubble-and-squeak and a mint jus, or good old-fashioned roast duck with orange sauce. Chocolate crème brûlée is a creamy affair, but more praise is piled on the petits fours served with coffee: chocolate truffle, coconut ice and a tiny caramel tart.

MERIDEN,

Marriott Forest of Arden Hotel

Maxstoke Lane CV7 7HR
Map 4: SP28

Impressive modern hotel in a rural setting. The attractive, split-level restaurant offers the likes of tender, well-cooked pigeon with sherry vinaigrette, braised knuckle of lamb, and raspberries crème brûlée.

Tel: 01676 522335
Fax: 01676 523711
Cost: *Alc* £25, set-price L £16.50/D £22.50. ☺ H/wine £12.75

Smoking: No smoking in dining room; Air conditioning
Accommodation: 215 en suite ★★★★

Times: Noon-2pm/7-10pm. Closed D 26 Dec
Additional: Bar food L; Sunday L; Children welcome; ✿ dishes

Directions: From M42 J6, take A45 (Coventry) after Stonebridge island, then L (Shepherds Lane), 1.5 miles on L

SOLIHULL, Solihull Moat House ✿

61 Homer Road B91 3QD
Map 7: SP17

The stylish Brookes Restaurant is in keeping with the hotel's attractive contemporary atmosphere. Our meal included crab flakes with lemon grass and ginger, and duck with oranges and chestnut.

Tel: 0121 6239988
Fax: 0121 7112696
Telephone for further details

Directions: Follow signs to Town Centre and Conference Centre, 3rd turn at roundabout (Homer Road)

SUTTON COLDFIELD, New Hall

Walmley Road B76 1QX
Map 7: SP19
Tel: 0121 3782442
Fax: 0121 3784637
Cost: *Alc* £40.75, set-price L £10 (2 courses)/D £26.50. H/wine £15.50
Times: Noon-2pm/7-9.30pm. Closed L Sat
Additional: Bar food L; Sunday L; Children 8+; ✿ dishes
Seats: 60. Private dining room 50. Jacket & tie preferred
Smoking: No smoking in dining room
Accommodation: 60 en suite ★★★★

The New Hall has all the ingredients for a serious county house hotel cosseting bar, formal, knowledgeable service, wood-panelled restaurant. However, changes in the kitchen occurred just as we went to press, making it impossible for us to access the new regime. In the past, New Hall has maintained two AA Rosettes.

Directions: On B4148 E of Sutton Coldfield, close to M6/M42

WALSALL,

The Fairlawns at Aldridge

Comfortable country house, pleasant, airy dining room with patio views. Although much extended, Fairlawns retains the charm of the original red-brick building. The modern British *carte* is supplemented by a daily choice of fish dishes such as pan-fried scallops with leeks and chive sauce. Our inspector, however, went for an Arnold Bennett-style omelette, followed by roasted 'bullet' of Scottish beef fillet. The former was fluffy, light, well filled with smoked haddock and, together with a rich and creamy sauce, proved a satisfying and substantial starter. The beef was tender and served with chicken liver pâté croûtons, roast shallots and a rich claret sauce. To finish there is old-fashioned English custard tart with poached raspberries, savouries and a selection of artisan British cheeses.

178 Little Aston Road Aldridge
WS9 0NU
Map 7: SP09
Tel: 01922 455122
Fax: 01922 743210
Chef: Todd Hubble
Owners: John & Tammy Pette
Cost: *Alc* £28, set-price L £16.95/D £22.95 (5 courses). ☺ H/wine £10.95
Times: Noon-2.30pm/7-10.30pm. Closed L Sat, Bhs
Additional: Bar Food; Sunday L; Children welcome; ⓭ dishes
Seats: 70. Private dining room 8-80
Smoking: Air conditioning
Accommodation: 46 en suite ★ ★ ★

Directions: Outskirts of Aldridge, 400 yards from crossroads of A452 (Chester Road) & A454 (Little Aston Road)

WIGHT, ISLE OF

GODSHILL, **Cask & Taverners**

17th-century pub with a restaurant that has a beamed, cottagey feel. One well reported meal took in a smooth smoked mackerel mousse, accurately cooked chicken breast, and a light baked orange sponge.

Additional: Bar food; Sunday L; Children welcome; ⓭ menu
Smoking: No smoking in dining room

Directions: From Shanklin take A3020 3 miles into Godshill

High Street PO38 3HZ
Map 4: SZ58
Tel: 01983 840707
Fax: 01983 840861
Cost: *Alc* £22, set-price L £9.75 (4 courses)/D £15.75 (5 courses). ☺ H/wine £7.90
Times: Noon-2.30pm/7-9.30pm

RYDE, **Biskra House Beach Hotel**   NEW

Take pre-prandial drinks on the waterside garden terrace before retiring to a colonial-style restaurant where the contemporary menu makes good use of quality produce. Belly of pork in teriyaki sauce, or Scottish sirloin with haggis mash potato demonstrates the range.

Smoking: No-smoking area; No pipes & cigars
Accommodation: 14 en suite ★ ★

17 St Thomas's Street PO33 2DL
Map:
Tel: 01983 567913
Fax: 01983 616976
Cost: £25-£30. ☺ H/wine £8.95
Times: Noon-2pm/7-10pm. Closed 25-27 Dec
Additional: Bar food; Sunday L; Children welcome; ⓭ dishes

SEAVIEW,

Priory Bay

Priory Drive PO34 5BU
Map 4: SZ69
Tel: 01983 613146
Fax: 01983 616539
Cost: *Alc* £23, set-price D £23.
H/wine £13
Times: 12.30-2.30pm/7.30-9.15pm
Additional: Bar food L; Children
welcome; ✿ dishes

Steeped in history, sympathetically restored, this country hotel comes complete with its own beach. A promising meal featured superb Roquefort soufflé, tender cannon of lamb with smoked garlic jus, and lemon tart with delicious strawberry ice cream.

Smoking: No-smoking area; No pipes & cigars
Accommodation: 18 en suite ★ ★ ★

Directions: On B3330 to Nettlestone, half mile from St Helens

SEAVIEW,

Seaview Hotel & Restaurant

High Street PO34 5EX
Map 4: SZ69
Tel: 01983 612711
Fax: 01983 613729
Chefs: Charles Bartlett,
Bob Rodwell, Tom White
Owners: Nicholas & Nicola Hayward
Cost: *Alc* £21.50. ☺ H/wine £8.95
Times: Closed D Bh Sun
Additional: Bar food; Sunday L;
Children 5+ at D; ✿ dishes
Seats: 80. Private dining room 16
Smoking: One no-smoking dining
room; No pipes; Air conditioning
Accommodation: 16 en suite ★ ★ ★

Directions: In High Street, near
seafront, 3 miles E of Ryde

Seaview is an unassuming Victorian resort, the eponymous hotel a little gem. The nautical theme of the two bars runs into the two dining rooms, with model ships and clean blue and white decor in one, the other more traditional, with ships' gauges, clocks and original watercolours. The same menu is served in each, with the island's produce arriving in the shape of plaice plainly grilled on the bone served with parsley butter, and pheasant with apple bubble-and-squeak. Samphire accompanies roasted salmon with a warm balsamic and horseradish vinaigrette, and the range might extend to Cajun chicken and prawns with noodles. These are preceded by imaginative starters of perhaps a pâté of wild mushrooms and liver served with gherkins and green peppercorn chutney, a cocktail of prawns, Pernod and celeriac, and hot goats' cheese and spinach mousse. Rich, sweet puddings of chocolate marquise with coffee cream round things off. Wines by the glass are from Corney & Barrow, and there's also a sparkling rosé.

VENTNOR, **The Royal**

Belgrave Road PO38 1JJ
Map 4: SZ57
Tel: 01983 852186
Fax: 01983 855395
Chef: Alan Staley
Owner: William Bailey
Cost: Set-price D £22 (4 courses). ☺
H/wine £10
Times: D only, 7-9pm.

Queen Victoria apparently used this beautiful honey-coloured stone hotel as an annexe to Osborne House for some of her eminent visitors. In recent years the place has been generously restored and refurbished. The attractive dining room provides an excellent setting for some good contemporary cooking. The menu changes daily; the evening table d'hôte comprises six starters and main courses, plus a few dishes with supplementary charges. Some tempura-fried tiger prawns were very good in themselves, although the sweet chilli dressing was nearer a ratatouille than anything oriental. Sea bass with a cream sauce was well cooked but the vegetables were dull. (Most of the main courses may be served plain without sauces.) The puddings include a tuile basket of fresh fruit, a home-made orange and Grand Marnier sorbet and a 'stunning' crème caramel.

Directions: On main A3055 coastal road

YARMOUTH, George Hotel

Built in 1670 as a private house for the island's governor, now a stylish hotel. There's a popular terrace, a clubby panelled bar, and a light, fun brasserie serving the likes of pan-roasted cod with a salad of green beans, lentils and bacon, braised ox cheek with wild mushrooms, and seafood cassoulet with a herb sausage. The restaurant is notable for its dark, rich colours of maroon and green, smart table appointments and staff who are chatty and approachable but not familiar. The kitchen works in contemporary mode, often using luxury ingredients as a clever backup to complement the main component: truffle spaghetti with assiette of rabbit, langoustine risotto with pan-fried John Dory, for instance. A wee piece of 'excellent' pan-fried foie gras on sultanas marinated in sweet wine is one element in a trio of duck, the others being duck rillettes, crisp outside, smooth inside, and a good, thin single raviolo filled with minced duck leg, a tasty starter, prettily presented, that shows immaculate precision. Evidence of the thought that goes into each dish is evidenced by a main course of pan-fried red mullet with baby squid, baby carrots and broad beans in a mint-flavoured 'cappuccino', its individual parts merging into a unified whole, and a 'resourceful' sausage of lamb and black olives accompanying loin of lamb with a rich stock-based jus and glazed winter vegetables. Puddings are impressive, not least rich Valrhona chocolate balls deep-fried in coconut-based pastry served with orange chocolate ganache, which 'worked superbly'.

Additional: Bar food L; Children 5+; 🍶 dishes
Seats: 100. Private dining room 40. Jacket & tie preferred
Smoking: No smoking in dining room
Accommodation: 55 en suite ★★★★

Quay Street PO41 0PE
Map 4: SZ38
Tel: 01983 760331
Fax: 01983 760425
Chef: Kevin Mangeolles
Owners: Jeremy & Amy Willcock, John Illsley
Cost: Set-price D £38.75. H/wine £12.50
Times: D only (restaurant) 7-10pm. Closed Sun, Mon
Additional: Children 8+
Seats: 35. Private dining room 20
Smoking: No smoking in dining room; Air conditioning
Accommodation: 17 en suite ★★★

Directions: Ferry from Lymington. Hotel visible from ferry between castle and pier

WILTSHIRE

ALDBOURNE, Raffles Restaurant

The bar and restaurant are part of an old cottage just off the village green; the sort of place where, were it not for the views of newly built houses, one would think old-fashioned village life still exists. Dark oak, silver and candles give credence to the overall effect. The menu, however, is a lot more up to date. Pan-fried blue cheese polenta with warm salsa verde, or vegetable gâteau with aubergine, courgette, tomato, and served with a tomato and basil sauce are typical starters. Main courses bring braised fillet of red mullet with a confit of white cabbage and saffron sauce, or noisettes of venison with redcurrant enriched game sauce and chestnuts. Keenly priced wines are served by the bottle or glass and represent a fair selection from around the world.

The Green SN8 2BW
Map 4: SU27
Tel: 01672 540700
Fax: 01672 540038
Chef: James Hannan
Owners: James & Mary Hannan
Cost: Alc £19.50, set-price L £10.50. ☺ H/wine £8.60
Times: 12.30-2pm/7-10 pm. Closed L Sat, D Sun, all Mon, Bhs (ex 25 Dec)
Additional: Sunday L; Children welcome L only; 🍶 dishes
Seats: 36. Private dining room 45
Smoking: No smoking in dining room; Air conditioning

Directions: On B4192 between M4 J14 & 15

AMESBURY, **Antrobus Arms Hotel**

Elegant 17th-century building, convenient for Stonehenge and Salisbury, featuring a walled Victorian garden and fountain. The panelled Fountain Restaurant is the main dining option.

Directions: In town centre

15 Church Street SP4 7EU
Map 4: SU14
Tel: 01980 623163
Fax: 01980 622112
Telephone for further details

BRADFORD-ON-AVON,
Georgian Lodge

The sort of historic-looking place that impresses American visitors. The Stotts continue to delight a loyal brigade of visitors. The atmosphere is peaceful and unhurried, service is invariably attentive and friendly. The kitchen is industrious, with Peter Stott making his own bread (crunchy date and walnut, or a white with sun-dried tomatoes), and delivers a repertoire that is classically entrenched but spiked with touches of modernism. Visual appeal is an important as freshness of produce and fresh mussels with Indian spices, or a soup of celery and tomato with orange are typical starters. An unusual smoked haddock rarebit listed amongst main courses has a simple visual appeal. Desserts range from caramelised pineapple in vanilla syrup to chocolate almond marquise. The wine list includes an above average selection by the glass.

25 Bridge Street BA15 1BY
Map 3: ST86
Tel: 01225 862268
Fax: 01225 862218
Chef: Peter Stott
Owner: Peter & Elizabeth Stott
Telephone for further details

Directions: Town centre, off Silver Street, S of River Avon

BRADFORD-ON-AVON,
Woolley Grange

Children are made to feel welcome at this splendid Jacobean manor house built in the early 17th century. A nursery and a special 'den' for the over eights should keep them occupied for part of the day, while at meal times kids can have their own lunch and tea. Grown-up meals are served in either the formal dining room or the Victorian conservatory – it's also possible to eat alfresco on the terrace or around the pool. The cooking is splendid, based on a firm classic foundation of technique with a modish outlook. This translates as pan-fried chicken with butterbeans and garlic, or fillet of brill with braised lentil chowder. The highlight of our inspection meal in early autumn was an excellently flavoured goats' cheese soufflé with hazelnut crust, served with roasted vine tomatoes.

Woolley Green BA15 1TX
Map 3: ST86
Tel: 01225 864705
Fax: 01225 864059
Chef: Phil Rimmer
Owners: Nigel & Heather Chapman
Cost: *Alc* £34.50, set-price L £15.50 (2 courses)/D £34.50. H/wine £10.50
Times: 12.30-2pm/7.30-9.30pm
Additional: Sunday L; Children welcome; ✦ dishes
Seats: 80. Private dining room 22
Smoking: No smoking in dining room
Accommodation: 23 en suite ★ ★ ★

Directions: On B105 at Woolley Green, 1 mile NE of Bradford, 20 mins from M4 J17

CASTLE COMBE,

Castle Inn ✿

Chippenham SN14 7HN
Map 3: ST87
Tel: 01249 783030
Fax: 01249 782315
Cost: *Alc* £20. ☺ H/wine £11.25
Times: Noon-2pm/7-9.30pm (9pm Sun)
Additional: Bar food; Sunday L; Children 5+; ✿ dishes
Smoking: No smoking in dining room
Accommodation: 11 en suite ★★★

A famous hostelry that can trace its origins back to the 12th century. Eat in either the restaurant, bar or conservatory and take your pick from a tried and tested menu. Don't miss delicious puddings such as rhubarb cheesecake and poached pear and fruit crumble.

Directions: In village centre, M4 J17

CASTLE COMBE,

Manor House Hotel ✿✿✿

Chippenham SN14 7HR
Map 3: ST87
Tel: 01249 782206
Fax: 01249 782159
Chef: Mark Taylor
Cost: *Alc* £45, set-price L £18.95/D £35 (4 courses). H/wine £16.50
Times: Noon-2pm/7-9.30pm
Additional: Bar food; Sunday L; Children welcome; ✿ dishes
Seats: 95. Private dining rooms up to 30. Jacket & tie preferred
Smoking: No smoking in dining room
Accommodation: 45 en suite ★★★★

14th-century house that has been sympathetically extended – a great place to relax. The estate takes in some 26 acres of grounds and includes an Italian garden as well as an 18-hole championship golf course. Mark Taylor's cooking is just as much a draw as the facilities; his menus a thoughtful balance of interesting combinations and more straightforward dishes. Thus starters range from gravad lax of halibut with seared scallops, orange vanilla and cardamom, to boudin of organic chicken with truffle and roast parsnip purée. Main courses show considerable imagination. Take roast fillet of turbot, crab risotto, rouille juices and herb oil, for example, or milk-fed pigeon, honey-roasted turnips and garlic chips. Desserts include some lively reworking of traditional dishes: rice pudding is served with mulled fruits and cinnamon ice cream, or there could be warm chocolate fritters with pear purée. The wine list is comprehensive and nicely annotated with a reasonable selection of halves.

Signature dishes: soup of Jersey royal, young leeks, smoked salmon parsley oil; red mullet, sardine tart; loin of lamb, tomato confit, aubergine hollandaise; apple fritter, caramel syrup, clotted cream ice cream

Directions: Off B4039 near centre of village, R immediately after the bridge

COLERNE,

Luncknam Park ✿✿✿

Chippenham SN14 8AZ
Map 3: ST87
Tel: 01225 742777
Fax: 01225 743536
Chef: Paul Collins
Cost: *Alc* £59, set-price D £40. H/wine £16
Times: D only 7.30-9.30pm (7-10pm Fri & Sat)
Additional: Bar food (leisure spa); Sunday L (12.30-2.30pm); Children 12+ at D; ◑ dishes
Seats: 80. Private room 80. Jacket & tie preferred
Smoking: No smoking in dining room
Accommodation: 41 en suite ★ ★ ★ ★

Approached along a beech-lined avenue, this 1720-built mansion makes a striking impression. Privately owned until the late 1980s, it's been converted with consummate care. An elegant bow-fronted drawing room, wood-panelled library, 24-hour room service, a dining room that was originally the ballroom, with hand-painted ceiling and crystal chandeliers, and discreet, professional staff create a cosseting atmosphere – at a price, of course. Dining off the set-price menu may bring roast fillet of beef with crushed garlic potatoes and spinach purée, with a supplement charged for Trelough duck roasted with honey and ginger in red wine sauce. But it's the *carte* that lets the kitchen express the full range of its abilities. Items might seem understated – risotto of ceps and truffles, or confit of duck salad, the latter arriving, stunningly presented, with a few salad leaves in an orange and cardamom dressing – but the kitchen certainly delivers the goods. Roast loin of lamb 'full of superb spring lamb flavour', partnered by couscous, spinach and roasted garlic, is finished with an intense jus flavoured with finely diced anchovies. Those seeking luxuries will find them in foie gras terrine with Muscat jelly, fillet of brill braised in a langoustine and coriander bouillon, or Chateaubriand with béarnaise sauce. A spot-on pastry chef is behind a round of crisp apple tart with a scoop of rum and raisin ice cream drizzled with rum-flavoured caramel sauce. The wine list centres on France, with some distinguished producers and vintages, although there's plenty of quality drinking elsewhere.
Signature dishes: fillet of sea trout filled with langoustines served with asparagus and tarragon butter sauce; pot-roast partridge with wild mushroom ravioli and thyme; chocolate fondant with pistachio ice cream.

Directions: Turn off A4 2 miles from Bath for Batheaston and L for Colerne, L again at crossroad, entrance 0.25 mile on L

FORD, **White Hart Inn** ❀

Chippenham SN14 8RP
Map 3: ST87
Tel: 01249 782213
Fax: 01249 783075
Cost: *Alc* £18.95. ☺ H/wine £10.95
Times: Noon-2pm/7-9.30pm
Additional: Bar Food L; Sunday L;
Children welcome; ✿ dishes
Smoking: No pipes & cigars
Accommodation: 11 en suite

Directions: M4 J17 or 18, 10 minutes
drive on A420 Colerne road

*Delightful Cotswold stone inn set beside a trout stream. Enjoyable
dishes include timbale of crab and smoked salmon – full of natural
flavours – and onion tart with grilled goats' cheese.*

HINDON, **Grosvenor Arms**

**Long, flagstone-floored dining room with lowish lighting
and high-backed wicker chairs, gleaming cutlery and large
glasses brightening up the tables.** The room might be a bit
barn-like, but the view into the glass-fronted, theatre-style
kitchen at the end gives a modern feel to the place. Friendly,
efficient staff are on hand to pour wines by the glass and
serve the food. Start with a tian of roasted vegetables topped
with melting Mozzarella and an intense tomato compote,
balsamic dressing drizzled trendily around the plate. Perfectly
cooked, crisply skinned red mullet with plum tomato salad
makes an impressive main course, and marinated loin of pork
with Thai-flavoured couscous and coriander sauce illustrates
the kitchen's fondness for fusing elements of different
cuisines. Poached pear with warm caramel sauce and nuts and
a dollop of cinnamon ice cream is an enjoyable way to end a
meal.

High Street Salisbury SP3 6DJ
Map 3: ST93
Tel: 01747 820696
Fax: 01747 820869
Chef: Paul Suter
Owner: West Country Village Inns
Cost: *Alc* £22. ☺ H/wine £9.95
Times: Noon-2pm/7-9.30pm
Additional: Bar food; Sunday L;
Children 5+; ✿ dishes
Seats: 40 + 20 bar
Smoking: No smoking in dining room
Accommodation: 7 en suite ★★

Directions: 1 mile from both the
A350 & A303

HINDON, **Lamb at Hindon** ❀

Salisbury SP3 6DP
Map 3: ST93
Tel: 01747 820573
Fax: 01747 820605
Cost: £18, set-price D £18.95. ☺
H/wine £8.95
Times: Noon-2pm/7-9.30pm. Closed
25-26 Dec
Additional: Bar food; Sunday L;
Children welcome; ✿ dishes
Smoking: No smoking in dining room
Accommodation: 14 en suite ★★

Directions: In village centre, 1 mile
off A303 & A350

*Sophisticated bar meals plus a more formal restaurant menu lift the
cosy, stone-built free house above the norm. Dinner might include
coriander and carrot soup, pan-fried guinea fowl with wild
mushroom sauce and apricot and almond tart.*

INGLESHAM, **Inglesham Forge**

Converted 15th-century forge that's now a popular restaurant.
The menu may lack the current culinary buzz words, but it
does concentrate on traditional dishes cooked correctly. These
may include seafood Breton, a traditional seafood gratinée, or
baked scampi in garlic butter. Steaks take star billing when it
comes to main courses, whether that classic blast-from-the-past
fillet steak au poivre, or beef Stroganoff. However, there's also
poached salmon with hollandaise sauce, and breast of duck
with Morello cherries.

Directions: In hamlet just off A361 midway between Highworth
and Lechlade

Lechlade Swindon SN6 7QY
Map 4: SU29
Tel: 01367 252298
Chef/Owner: Manuel Gomez
Cost: *Alc* £23. ☺ H/wine £9.95
Times: Noon-1.45pm/7-9.30pm.
Closed L Sat & Mon, all Sun, Bhs
Additional: Children welcome;
🍴 dishes
Seats: 30
Smoking: No pipes & cigars

LITTLE BEDWYN, **Harrow Inn**

Nr Marlborough SN8 3JP
Map 4: SU26
Tel/Fax: 01672 870871
Chef: Roger Jones
Owners: Roger & Sue Jones
Cost: *Alc* £30. ☺ H/wine £12
Times: Noon-2pm/7-9.30pm. Closed
D Sun, all Mon, Aug
Additional: Sunday L; Children 10+
Seats: 34. Private dining room 20
(terrace)
Smoking: No smoking in dining room

Directions: Take Marlborough Road
from Hungerford, after 2 miles Little
Bedwyn signposted

A converted Victorian pub, with a cosy area for drinking. The
smart interior includes crisp table linen and designer plates.
Menus change daily, sometimes twice, and fish features strongly,
with at least nine fish dishes. Our langoustine risotto, 'moist,
nutty texture, good fresh flavours came with grated Parmesan
and shelled broad beans'. The menu description of the Aberdeen
Angus beef includes the animal's registered number, date of
birth and slaughter together with the farmer's name. New season
lamb fillet came with provençale vegetables, 'moist slices of fillet
was beautifully cooked', sitting on some halved cherry tomatoes
and tiny parisienne potatoes. The kitchen uses top quality dark
chocolate for its rich chocolate terrine with berry sauce. Other
desserts include compote of red fruits, garnished with
strawberries and cape gooseberries and dusted with icing sugar.
The short wine list is well conceived but as stocks are kept to a
minimum, the list is changed on a rolling basis.

MALMESBURY,

The Horse and Groom

*Set in the village centre, this small Cotswold pub and restaurant
serves from a seasonally changing menu. A sample includes salmon
tagliatelle, roast loin of lamb served on a potato cake, and a dessert
of glazed lemon tart.*

Directions: M4 J17, take 2nd roundabout exit, B4040
(Cricklade). 2 miles to Charlton, pub on L

The Street Charlton SN16 9DL
Map 4: ST98
Tel: 01666 823904
Fax: 01666 823390
Telephone for further details

MALMESBURY, Knoll House Hotel

Built as a family home in Victorian times, Knoll House, on the outskirts of England's oldest borough, is a comfortable place, an outdoor swimming pool one of its attractions. Large windows in the dining room give views on to a cedar tree at the bottom of the garden. Breads are first-rate, and the kitchen puts a lot of work into even simple-sounding dishes: mussel broth is served with crab dumplings, for instance, and asparagus with Parmesan shavings come on gnocchi with lemon hollandaise. Main-course fillet of lamb is wrapped in a basil mousse, sauced with Madeira jus and plated on celeriac rösti alongside spinach and forest mushrooms, and seared fillets of red snapper in lemon and saffron butter are set on a spaghetti of vegetables. Warm lemon sponge makes a traditional end to a meal, here served with condensed milk ice cream cut with blackcurrant sauce, or there may be raspberry ripple cheesecake with a pair of fruit coulis.

Swindon Road SN16 9LU
Map 3: ST98
Tel: 01666 823114
Fax: 01666 823897
Chef: Mark Miller
Cost: *Alc* £25
Times: Noon-1.45pm/7-9pm. Closed 27-29 Dec
Additional: Bar food; Sunday L; Children welcome; ✿ dishes
Seats: 30. Private dining room 14
Smoking: No smoking in dining room
Accommodation: 22 en suite ★ ★ ★

Directions: From M4 J17 take A429 (Cirencester); turn onto B4042 (Swindon); hotel is 500 yards on L

MALMESBURY,
Mayfield House Hotel

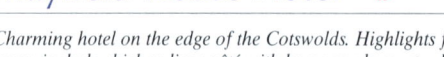

Charming hotel on the edge of the Cotswolds. Highlights from the menu include chicken liver pâté with home-made mustard pickle, and pan-roasted Barbary duck with plum and blackberry sauce. Good wine list.

Smoking: No smoking in dining room
Accommodation: 23 en suite ★ ★

Directions: 10 minutes from M4 J17. On A429 in village centre between Malmesbury and Cirencester

Crudwell SN16 9EW
Map 3: ST98
Tel: 01666 577409
Fax: 01666 577977
Cost: Set-price D £17.95. ☺ H/wine £8.50
Times: D only, 6.30-8.45pm
Additional: Bar food; Sunday L (noon-2pm); Children welcome; ✿ dishes

MALMESBURY, Old Bell Hotel

Abbey Row SN16 0AG
Map 3: ST98
Tel: 01666 822344
Fax: 01666 825145
Chef: Michael Benjamin
Owners: Nicholas Dickinson, Nigel Chapman
Cost: *Alc* £26, set-price L £15/D £19.75. ☺ H/wine £11.75
Times: 12.30-2pm/7.30-9.30pm.
Additional: Sunday L; Children welcome; ✿ dishes

Claims to be the oldest inn in the country. The Grade I listed building cannot fail to please visitors wanting to sample a bit of history. The Edwardian period dictates the style of the restaurant, a comfortable room with well-spaced tables, but the kitchen is up to date, producing food that is very much in the modern idiom. Steamed skate wing with a Chinese flavoured broth and coriander, or Gruyère tart with a salad of Provençale olives could open a meal. Daube of beef with sweet potato mash and Dijon mustard sauce, or roasted salmon with a crust of cabbage and cumin, with cream polenta and white wine sauce, are typical of main courses. Caramelised lemon tart with red berry sorbet is the star of the dessert list.

Directions: In centre of town

Seats: 80. Private dining room 27
Smoking: No smoking in dining room
Accommodation: 32 en suite ★ ★ ★

MALMESBURY, **Whatley Manor**

Nr Easton Grey SN16 0RB
Map 3: ST98
Tel: 01666 822888
Fax: 01666 826120
Cost: Set-price L £15.50/D £29.50.
H/wine £13.50
Times: 12.30-2pm/7.30-9pm.
Additional: Bar food; Sunday L;
Children welcome; 🍴 dishes
Smoking: No pipes & cigars
Accommodation: 29 en suite ★ ★ ★

Directions: 3 miles W of Malmesbury
on B4040. 15 mins from M4/J17 or
J18

Cooking of a high standard, with fine flavour and textures defining a supreme of duck, cooked to order, with orange liqueur sauce. Lamb en croûte is served with Madeira sauce and Dover sole grilled à la meunière.

MARLBOROUGH, **Ivy House Hotel** 🌸

High Street SN8 1HJ
Map 4: SU16
Tel: 01672 515333
Fax: 01672 515338
Cost: *Alc* £30, set-price L 13.50. ☺
H/wine £12
Times: Noon-2pm/7-9.30pm
Additional: Bar food L; Sunday L;
Children welcome; 🍴 dishes
Smoking: No smoking in dining room
Accommodation: 30 en suite ★ ★ ★

Directions: Town centre in main
street

The elegant restaurant at this 1707-built, ivy-covered hotel is a popular place for such dishes as smoked salmon parcel filled with guacamole, pan-fried marinated venison with plum sauce, then cherry clafoutis.

MELKSHAM, **Shaw Country Hotel**

The Mulberry Restaurant offers a choice of menus, with dishes such as roast loin of lamb with lentil and shallot casserole, and steamed fillet of lemon sole with a light shellfish sauce.

Smoking: No smoking in dining room
Accommodation: 13 en suite ★ ★

Directions: 1 mile NW of Melksham on A365, from M4/J17 or J18

Bath Road Shaw SN12 8EF
Map 3: ST96
Tel: 01225 702836
Fax: 01225 790275
Cost: *Alc* £17.95, set-price L
£12/£17.95. ☺ H/wine £8.50
Times: Noon-1.30pm/7-9pm. Closed
D Sun, 26-28 Dec
Additional: Bar Food; Sunday L;
Children welcome; 🍴 dishes

MELKSHAM, **Toxique**

Despite the name, a vicarage-type property down a country lane where one always thinks the wrong turn has been taken. Roses and cottage garden plants give the usual picture postcard effect, and tables and chairs appear in the garden when the weather permits. Within is far less traditional: one dining room is coloured aubergine and midnight blue, the other 'banana' room is, well, guess the colour. Paintings adorn the walls, bright splashy affairs painted by the owner Peter Jewkes. Home-made bread is a of the brown dense variety, flavoured with fennel and poppy seeds 'one always feels healthy when eating stuff like this'. Goats' cheese tart with a courgette and chive salad, could be followed by pan-fried salmon with juniper, rock-salt glazed onions and mustard mash. Puddings take in lemon Mascarpone mousse, and a prune and almond tart with crème fraîche.

187 Woodrow Road SN12 7AY
Map 3: ST96
Tel: 01225 702129
Fax: 01225 742773
Chef: Helen Bartlett
Owner: Helen Bartlett, Peter Jewkes
Cost: Set-price D £31. H/wine £12.50
Times: D only 7.30-10pm. Closed Sun-Tue
Additional: Children welcome; 🍴 dishes
Seats: 40. Private dining rooms
Smoking: No smoking in dining room
Accommodation: 5 en suite

Directions: Take Calne road from Melksham centre, 0.3 mile turn into Forest Road. Restaurant is on L after 0.75 mile

NOMANSLAND, **Les Mirabelles**

A very French restaurant. If details like the red-check tablecloths do not give a clue then the French menu with English translations will. Expect monkfish with tarragon sauce, feuilleté of quail with foie gras and cognac, and Chateaubriand with a choice of béarnaise, poivre and moutarde sauces.

Directions: A36 (Salisbury-Southampton); turn R into New Road (signposted Nomansland); straight ahead at crossroads and over cattle grid. Within a mile restaurant on R by church

Forest Edge Road nr Salisbury SP5 2BN
Map 4: SU22
Tel/Fax: 01794 390205
Cost: Alc £27.50. ☺ H/wine £9.50
Times: Noon-2pm/7-9.30pm. Closed D Sun, all Mon, 1st 2wks Jan, last wk May
Additional: Sunday L; Children welcome; 🍴 dishes
Smoking: Air conditioning

PEWSEY,
London House Restaurant

Queen Anne house with very slick appointments and staff: a restaurant that could be straight out of Kensington and Chelsea. Pewsey is a pleasant if unremarkable Wiltshire village; its inhabitants must count themselves lucky to have such a sophisticated restaurant in their midst. Several inspectors have returned with glowing reports on Peter Quinion's cooking, which reveals a strong sense of season based on a firm foundation of good local raw materials, but also takes in an evolving appreciation of modern French cooking. An appetiser of tartlet of crayfish with wild asparagus and a dribble of butter sauce, buttered gnocchi with more asparagus, morels, vermouth

Market Place SN9 5AB
Map 4: SU16
Tel: 01672 564775
Fax: 01672 564785
Chef: Peter Quinion
Owner: David J Gerhardt
Cost: Alc £30, set-price L & D £21. H/wine £12
Times: Noon-2pm/7-10pm. Closed L Mon, all Sun, 25-28 Dec, 3-10 Jan, 2-8 Aug, 17-20 Sep
Additional: Children 10+; 🍴 dishes
Seats: 30. Private dining rooms 30

London House Restaurant

Smoking: No smoking in dining room

Directions: Telephone for directions

cream sauce and grated black truffles, roast chump of lamb stuffed with lots of garlic, rosemary, pancetta and wrapped in caul, and hazelnut mille-feuille with poached peaches and ginger mousse, have all been singled out for flavour and accuracy of cooking. Even a separate vegetarian menu shows imagination in dishes such as tempura of vegetables with soy, ginger and tarragon butter sauce, or mille-feuille of spinach, artichokes, and wild mushrooms with a herb and white wine cream sauce. Attention to small details shows the kitchen never falters: bread is excellent, and petits fours are on a grand scale.

PURTON, The Pear Tree at Purton ✿✿

Church End SN5 9ED
Map 4: SU08
Tel: 01793 772100
Fax: 01793 772369
Chef: Alan Postill
Owners: Francis & Anne Young
Cost: Set-price L £17.50/D £29.50 (4 courses). H/wine £12
Times: Noon-2pm/7-9.15pm. Closed L Sat, 26-30 Dec
Additional: Sunday L; Children welcome; ✿ dishes
Seats: 60. Private dining room 50
Smoking: No-smoking area; No pipes & cigars
Accommodation: 18 en suite ★ ★ ★

Former Cotswold stone vicarage, now an elegant country retreat. The pretty conservatory restaurant overlooks the gardens which act as a fitting backdrop for a menu that is built around home-grown herbs and local produce. Delicious canapés of tartare of salmon tartlet and grilled goats' cheese with sun-dried tomato opened our inspection dinner on a positive note that never faltered. Terrine of confit of guinea fowl and foie gras proved to be a clever combination of flavours and textures, especially when offset by a white onion marmalade, and steamed supreme of halibut was well-matched by a fresh lobster sabayon. Dessert was a dariole of well-flavoured coffee mousse with a tuile basket containing a scoop of quality dark chocolate sorbet. The wine list, ordered by type, is well balanced and includes a few half-bottles.

Directions: From M4 J16 follow signs to Purton. Turn right at Spa shop, hotel 0.25 mile on right

REDLYNCH,

Langley Wood Restaurant ❀

Salisbury SP5 2PB
Map 4: SU22
Tel: 01794 390348
Cost: *Alc* £21. ☺ H/wine £10.25
Times: 12.30-2pm/7-10.30pm. Closed
L Sat, D Sun, all Mon & Tue
Additional: Sunday L; Children
welcome; ❀ dishes
Smoking: No smoking in dining room
Accommodation: 3 rooms

Directions: In village, between
Downton (on A338 Salisbury to
Bournemouth) & Landford (A36
Salisbury)

Comfortable surroundings are offered at this 17th-century country
house set in wooded grounds. Dishes might include devilled kidneys
or roast leg of lamb with spiced aubergine.

ROWDE,

George & Dragon ❀❀

Informality is the keynote at this village pub dating from
1675. A beamed ceiling, red woodwork, simple tables and a
mixture of chairs provide the backdrop for a cosmopolitan
menu that ranges from goose and pork rillettes to Thai fish
curry. A classic starter of chicken liver pâté, complemented by
spicy pickled orange, has been praised for its flavour and
consistency, while crab pancakes come bursting with fresh,
mainly white crabmeat. Fish and shellfish are the main business
here – skate with capers and black butter, say, or sea bass
steamed with ginger, soy and spring onions – although
dedicated meat-eaters could choose perhaps lambs' kidneys
with mushrooms in sherry vinegar followed by ribeye steak
with garlic butter. Lemon curd tart or sticky toffee pudding
round things off nicely. There are wines aplenty on this
splendid list, range is eclectic with good growers.

Additional: Bar food; Children welcome; ❀ dishes
Seats: 35
Smoking: No smoking in dining room

Directions: On A342 Devizes-Chippenham road

High Street SN10 2PN
Map 3: ST96
Tel: 01380 723053
Fax: 01380 724738
Chefs: Tim Withers, Hannah Seal,
Kate Phillips
Owners: Tim & Helen Withers
Cost: *Alc* £25, set-price L £10. ☺
H/wine £9.50
Times: Noon-2pm/7-10pm. Closed
Sun & Mon, Xmas, 1 Jan

Shortlisted for
AA Wine Award-see page 16

SALISBURY,

Howard's House Hotel ❀❀❀

Charming country house hotel. A log fire in the sunflower
yellow lounge offers a cosy touch, before giving way to the long
oblong of light green that is the refurbished dining room; a
massive floral decoration at one end seems to bring the garden
into the room. The intention of the cooking is to allow the
flavour of ingredients to speak for themselves, and the simplicity
of presentation is the result of much hard work. We started with
a sweet-and-sour tomato soup garnished with torn basil; other

Teffont Evias SP3 5RJ
Map 4: SU12
Tel: 01722 716392/716821
Fax: 01722 716820
Chef: Paul Firmin
Owners: Paul Firmin, Jonathan Ford
Cost: Set-price D £25. H/wine £9.95
Times: D only, 7.30-9.30pm
Additional: Sunday L (12.30-2pm);
Children welcome

Howard's House Hotel

Seats: 30
Smoking: No smoking in dining room
Accommodation: 9 en suite ★ ★

Directions: A36/A30 from Salisbury,
turn onto B3089, 5 miles W of
Wilton, 9 miles W of Salisbury

first courses included quail breasts on mushroom risotto and (the popular choice of the night) crab ravioli with spinach and lobster sauce. Main courses steer a confident line between the conventional and the contemporary. Breast of pheasant is given the lightest of spins with cranberry pomme anna, honeyed cabbage and Calvados jus, for example, whilst caramelised red mullet with Thai style stir-fried noodles opens up the menu. Loin of venison, cooked within a crisp pastry case with apple and wild mushroom stuffing and redcurrant jus was tender and full of flavour. Vegetables arrived in a self-service manner, with enough on offer for one to feed a family of four. Classic lemon tart with kumquat sorbet and orange sauce vied with warm chocolate and rum flan with vanilla custard in popularity.

SALISBURY, Milford Hall Hotel

206 Castle Street SP1 3TE
Map 4: SU12
Tel: 01722 417411
Fax: 01722 419444
Telephone for further details

Directions: At junction of Castle
Street, A30 ring rd & A345
(Amesbury), less than 0.5 mile from
Market Square

Set in an extended Georgian mansion, the hotel's restaurant offers freshly prepared food. Particular favourites include rack of lamb on rosemary and garlic purée and fresh fish, perhaps roasted halibut with shellfish sauce.

SWINDON, Blunsdon House Hotel

Blunsdon SN2 4AD
Map 4: SU18
Tel: 01793 721701
Fax: 01793 721056
Telephone for further details

A family-run hotel with all the facilities of a smart establishment but without the corporate feel. Choose from a varied menu which includes hot Stilton soufflé, fresh chargrilled fish, loin of lamb with port and redcurrant, and a wide dessert selection.

Directions: 3 miles N of town centre. From A419 take turning signposted Broad Blunsdon, then first L

SWINDON,

Chiseldon House Hotel

New Road Chiseldon SN4 0NE
Map 4: SU18
Tel: 01793 741010
Fax: 01793 741059
Telephone for further details

Directions: M4 J15 & 16, on B4006.
Short distance from Swindon town
centre

Traditional country house popular for weddings and small conferences. The Orangery Restaurant has a summery feel, is light and bright. Menu descriptions tend to be on the flowery style but are kept sensibly short and the kitchen does show admirable ambition and talent. A modern English slant is taken in dishes such as chicken mousse and spinach terrine, and mille-feuille of salmon, cabbage and leek. The wine list is reasonably priced with examples from around the globe, plus a good selection of celebration wines.

SWINDON, **Parklands Hotel**

Ogbourne St George SN8 1SL
Map 4: SU18
Tel: 01672 841555
Fax: 01672 841533
Cost: Set-price D £17. ☺ H/wine
£8.95
Times: D only, 7.30-9.30. Closed Sun
Additional: ❹ dishes
Smoking: No smoking in dining room

A cosy dining room, popular with residents and locals in the know. Dishes sampled included duck breast with stir-fried oriental vegetables, followed by scallops with aubergine tian.

Accommodation: 10 en suite

Directions: From M4 J15 take A346 towards Marlborough, pass Ogbourne Golf Club on L. Take next slip road. R at T junction, and R again after 100yds

WARMINSTER, **Bishopstrow House**

BA12 9HH
Map 3: ST84
Tel: 01985 212312
Fax: 01985 216769
Chef: Chris Suter
Owners: Simon Lowe,
Andrew Leeman, Howard Malin
Cost: Set-price D£35. H/wine £13.50
Times: 12.30-2pm/7.30-9pm (9.30pm
Fri, Sat)
Additional: Bar food; Sunday L;
Children welcome; ❹ dishes
Seats: 70. Private dining room 23
Smoking: No smoking in dining room
Accommodation: 32 en suite ★ ★ ★ ★

Directions: From Warminster take
B3414 (Salisbury). Hotel is signposted

Fine example of Georgian architecture with grand design within. Pass through the porticoed front door and enter the country-house world of well-proportioned rooms, antiques, heavily draped windows and open fires. The menu highlights dishes low in cholesterol and low in fat – tuna carpaccio with soy mustard dressing, grilled sea bass with spinach, saffron and tomatoes – leaving the virtuous to pig out on sticky toffee pudding with butterscotch sauce and clotted cream. Locally sourced raw materials are used to good effect: wild mushrooms go into risotto, or partner roast turbot with garlic confit, Quantock duck is made into a crispy confit with chilli, lentils and coriander, and organic watercress is paired with rocket for a simply dressed salad with Parmesan shavings. Caramelised foie gras, with spicy pear and prune compote is here for the self-indulgent, who can finish with chocolate tart with cappuccino ice cream, or poached rhubarb with a matching sorbet for the health-conscious. The wine list is strong in France and surprisingly wide-roaming, with house wines from Chile.

WORCESTERSHIRE

ABBERLEY, The Elms ❀❀

Fine Queen Anne mansion with warm hospitality and professional service. The high ceilings and wealth of antiques ensure that the period feel is retained in the spacious public rooms. The restaurant overlooks the landscaped gardens and, despite the idiosyncratic English setting, offers a menu with a strong French bias but with some English presence of mind. Thus duck foie gras terrine is served with turnip chutney, and seared sea bream with a clementine and dill sauce and fennel and parsley casserole. First-class seared tuna with a simple dressed citrus salad, opened our inspection meal and was the undoubted highlight. Salad of venison was picked up by nicely sweetened and spiced red cabbage, but let down by undercooked baby root vegetables. Apple Pithiviers came with a home-made vanilla ice cream served with plums and a compote which worked well.

Directions: 15 minutes from M5 J5. 10 miles from Worcester

WR6 6AT
Map 3: SO76
Tel: 01299 896666
Fax: 01299 896804
Chef: Olivier Bichard
Owners: Roy & Daphne Vaughan
Cost: Set-price L £19.50/D £30.50.
H/wine £16
Times: 12.30-2pm/7.30-9.45pm
Additional: Bar food; Sunday L;
Children welcome; ⓭ dishes
Seats: 40. Private dining rooms 32/60.
Jacket & tie preferred
Smoking: No smoking in dining room
Accommodation: 16 en suite ★ ★ ★

BROADWAY,
Collin House Hotel ❀

Candlelit dinners are served in the beamed restaurant. The food is traditional English, with options such as lemon sole and braised pheasant casserole.

Smoking: No smoking in dining room
Accommodation: 7 rooms ★ ★

Directions: 1m NW of Broadway. Hotel is signposted from roundabout on A44

WR12 7PB
Map 4: SP03
Tel: 01386 858354
Fax: 01386 858697
Cost: Alc £24, set-price L £16.50. ☺
H/wine £9.85
Times: Noon-2pm/7-9pm. Closed 5 days Xmas
Additional: Bar Food; Sunday L;
Children 5+; ⓭ dishes

BROADWAY,
Dormy House Hotel ❀❀

Willersey Hill WR12 7LF
Map 4: SP03
Tel: 01386 852711
Fax: 01386 858636
Chef: Alan Cutler
Owner: J Philip-Sorensen

Honey-coloured stone walls and oak beams are de rigueur in this part of the world. The restaurant, decorated in shades of coral and soft green, with tapestries hanging on the walls, is set

in the old farmhouse which is the core of this largely modern development (many bedrooms are in separate cottage-style buildings). Choose between the *carte* or a set-price, five-course 'gourmet' menu, perusing the long wine list at leisure, perhaps, over a drink in the bar. The kitchen's a hive of industry, smoking its own venison to go with baby pears and redcurrant sauce, producing a coriander and lime butter sauce and a seafood samosa to accompany baked supreme of Cornish sea bass, and making cinnamon-scented ice cream before flambéing crêpes. At inspection, an appetiser of chicken liver parfait was a good augur for what followed: fricassée of turbot, scallops and asparagus in a tasty lentil and coriander sauce, then 'beautifully tender' rare fillet of beef thinly sliced over rösti with a rich red wine sauce, and finally creamy brown-bread ice cream on warm chocolate fudge sauce.

Directions: Take Saintbury turn, off A44, after 1 mile bear L at staggered crossroads

Cost: *Alc* £40, set-price D £30.50 (4 courses). H/wine £12.75
Times: 12.30-2pm/7-9.30pm (9pm Sun). Closed L Sat, 24-27 Dec
Additional: Bar food; Sunday L; Children welcome before 7.30pm; ✆ dishes
Seats: 70. Private dining room 40. Jacket & tie preferred
Smoking: No-smoking area; Air conditioning
Accommodation: 48 en suite ★ ★ ★

BROADWAY, Lygon Arms

A 16th-century coaching inn that has had the deluxe Savoy Group treatment. Both Charles I and Oliver Cromwell were amongst its earliest guests and the latter's name lives on in Oliver's Brasserie. the main restaurant occupies the great hall, a reproduction of an Elizabethan banqueting hall, stuffed with coats of arms, suits of armour and deer heads. An extensive menu, orchestrated by chef Graeme Nesbitt, has a suitably deluxe feel and there's no stinting on the truffles and foie gras. Top quality ingredients defined a signature first course of baby squid stuffed with saffron and trompette risotto, the whole dish brought together by a well-tempered sweet chilli sauce and grilled scallops. Poaching resulted in a flavour-full breast of maize-fed chicken stuffed with truffle and foie gras farce with roast cherry tomatoes – again the whole thing was underpinned by a fine, rich and creamy morel sauce. Sauce-free main courses such as grilled Dover sole and milk-fed English lamb cutlets are also available. The lemon flavour could have been more pronounced in a dessert of blackcurrant and lemon parfait with warm apple compote, but it was a small quibble in the context of the overall success of our visit.
   Signature dishes: roast loin of venison with a white sausage and plum mille-feuille, baby fondant potatoes and cracked pepper sauce; Mirabelle plum soufflé with gingerbread ice cream.

WR12 7DU
Map 4: SP03
Tel: 01386 852255
Fax: 01386 858611
Chef: Graeme Nesbitt
Owner: Savoy Group
Cost: *Alc* £47.50, set-price L £24.50/D £39.50. H/wine £15.50
Times: Noon-2.15pm/7.30-9.15pm
Additional: Bar food L; Sunday L; Children 8+ at D; ✆ dishes
Seats: 90. Private room 70
Smoking: No smoking in dining room
Accommodation: 65 en suite ★ ★ ★ ★

Directions: In the centre of the High Street

BROMSGROVE,
Grafton Manor

Six acres surround this 1727 manor house and the interior doesn't disappoint either. It's a quintessentially English setting for a kitchen with a passion for all things Indian. The only hint of this may be in one of the breads, made with fenugreek, mustard seeds and cumin, although Indian dishes might crop up on the four-course dinner menu: a starter of aromatic beef kofta with a clove and cardamom dressing, followed by lamb cooked with coconut milk and curry leaves served with spicy basmati rice. Otherwise, modern European is the tone – ballotine of cod in sun-dried tomato dressing with anchovies, Parmesan and tomatoes, then crisp duck confit with Puy lentil

Grafton Lane B61 7HA
Map 7: SO97
Tel: 01527 579007
Fax: 01527 575221
Chefs: Simon Morris, William Henderson
Owners: The Morris Family
Cost: *Alc* £27.85, set-price L £20.50/D £32.50. ☺ H/wine £11.75
Times: 12.30-1.30pm/7.30-9pm. Closed L Sat
Additional: Sunday L; Children welcome; ✆ dishes

sauce, fondant potatoes and sauerkraut – although traditional British elements surface in ham hock terrine with mushy peas, and main-course roast pork with a meaty gravy, crunchy carrots and a purée of broad beans and lovage (herbs are from the garden). Finish perhaps with crème brûlée, served in a pool of mint syrup with poached oranges.

Seats: 60. Private dining room 30
Smoking: No smoking in dining room. Jacket & tie preferred
Accommodation: 9 en suite

Directions: M5 J5, off B4091, 1.5 miles S of Bromsgrove

BROMSGROVE,

Pine Lodge Hotel 🌸🌸

Kidderminster Road B61 9AB
Map 7: SO97
Tel: 01527 576600
Fax: 01527 878981
Chef: Mark Higgins
Owner: Andrew Weir Hotels
Cost: *Alc* £35, set-price L £16/D £18.50. ☺ H/wine £10.50
Times: Noon-2pm/7-9.45pm. Closed L Sat
Additional: Bar food; Sunday L; Children welcome; 🍴 dishes
Seats: 100. Private dining room 180
Smoking: No-smoking area; Air conditioning
Accommodation: 114 en suite ★ ★ ★

Directions: On A448 Kidderminster road 1 mile W of Bromsgrove centre

Large, modern purpose-built hotel with a Spanish architectural theme. The Parador restaurant offers classic dishes with a modern twist. This translates as wild boar terrine with sweet Chinese apples, marinated figs and a pepper coulis, French onion and smoked garlic soup, Dover sole with a lemon-butter meunière sauce, or honey-glazed wild duck with turnip and celeriac mash with a sherry and walnut sauce.

CHADDESLEY CORBETT,

Brockencote Hall 🌸🌸🌸

Kidderminster DY10 4PY
Map 7: SO87
Tel: 01562 777876
Fax: 01562 777872
Chef: Didier Philipot
Owners: Mr & Mrs Joseph Petitjean
Cost: *Alc* £45, set-price L £19.50/D £24.50. ☺ H/wine £12.80
Times: Noon-1.30pm/7-9.30pm. Closed L Sat
Additional: Sunday L; Children welcome; 🍴 dishes
Seats: 50. Private room 30
Smoking: No smoking in dining room
Accommodation: 17 en suite ★ ★ ★

Directions: On A448, just outside village, btw Kidderminster & Bromsgrove (M5 J5, M42 J1)

English country house with a French emphasis. The setting is quintessentially English: glorious countryside surrounding 70 acres of landscaped grounds that take in a dovecote and lake. Yet the cooking is classical French, service is from a French team and Alison Petitijean is much in evidence. The menu is basically a dual table d'hôte which guests can mix-and-match.

Didier Philipot works with quality ingredients and precise cooking skills to produce food that has a simple directness and works to good effect. Indeed, an early spring meal opened with encouraging signs of an industrious kitchen: canapés of rabbit tartlet, aubergine caviar, a mini omelette kebab and Parmesan crisps, a good selection of breads including a brioche, and bacon, cheese and onion, and an *amuse-bouche* of crab between two thin crisps with a light butter sauce. That early promise continued with veal sweetbreads with honey vinegar, French bean salad and truffle oil (clear flavours and good sweet-sour contrasts revealing a sound understanding of balance), and a duo of John Dory and scallops with an apple and celeriac rösti, served with a light, frothy nage well suited to the concept of the dish. Dessert was a top-class fruit terrine with crystallised coriander and lemon and basil sorbet. The wine list is heavily based in France with New World offerings.

CORSE LAWN,

Corse Lawn House Hotel

Extended Queen Anne building that's a fine country-house hotel. However, the restaurant menu is less than typical of the genre, with a hot crab sausage with shellfish sauce and chickpeas followed perhaps by marinated loin of pork with provençale vegetables and pesto, making a contemporary point. Seafood features strongly – a selection of grilled shellfish may crop up among both starters and main courses and the style ranges from chargrilled squid with rocket and chilli oil, or chunky and delicately spiced Thai fishcakes, to pan-fried guinea fowl with yellow split peas and white pudding. Pastry work is a high point throughout, not least in a lemon tart served with lemon ice cream. The wine list is thoughtful, full of character and sensibly priced.

Directions: Village centre, on B4211, 5 miles SW of Tewkesbury

GL19 4LZ
Map 3: SO83
Tel: 01452 780771
Fax: 01452 780840
Chef: Baba Hine
Owners: The Hine Family
Cost: *Alc* £34.50, set-price L £16.95/D £25. H/wine £9.95
Times: Noon-2pm/7-9.30pm. Closed 24-26 Dec
Additional: Bar food; Sunday L; Children welcome; ✿ dishes
Seats: 50. Private dining rooms 16, 30
Smoking: No smoking in dining room
Accommodation: 19 en suite ★ ★ ★

Shortlisted for AA Wine Award – see page 16

EVESHAM, **The Evesham Hotel**

Just a few minutes walk from the busy market town of Evesham, this well-run hotel is set in three acres of peaceful grounds. An autumn meal might start with hot chestnut soup, followed by tender fillets of beef with sweet onion sauce.

Additional: Sunday L; Children welcome; ✿ dishes
Smoking: No smoking in the dining room
Accommodation: 39 en suite ★ ★ ★

Directions: Coopers Lane is off road alongside River Avon

Coopers Lane, off Waterside
WR11 6DA
Map 4: SP04
Tel: 01386 765566
Fax: 01386 765443
Cost: *Alc* £22. ☺ H/wine £10.50
Times: 12.30-2pm/7-9.30pm Closed 25, 26 Dec

EVESHAM,

The Mill at Harvington

The Mill, in wooded parkland with willows shading its Avon frontage, has served time as both a malting and bread mill. Today it's something of a rural haven, sunny in summer, cosy fires lit in winter, of appeal to nature-lovers (look out for

Anchor Lane Harvington
WR11 5NR
Map 4: SP04
Tel/Fax: 01386 870688
Chef: Jane Greenhalgh
Owners: Simon & Jane Greenhalgh

The Mill at Harvington

Cost: *Alc* £22, set-price L £13.95/D
£22. ☺ H/wine £10.25
Times: Noon-1.45pm/7-8.45pm.
Closed 24-28 Dec
Additional: Bar food L; Sunday L;
Children welcome; ♨ dishes
Seats: 40. Private dining room 16
Smoking: No smoking in dining room
Accommodation: 19 en suite ★ ★

Directions: Turn S off B439, opposite
Harvington village, down Anchor
Lane

herons, kingfishers and partridges) and foodies alike, while
sportier types can have a swim or play tennis. Game turns up
in season, as in pheasant braised in red wine with mushrooms
and bacon, with perhaps fillet of pork stuffed with apricot and
sage among other meat dishes. They might be preceded by a
delicate timbale of crab with white fish and a creamy dill and
chervil sauce, while fish main courses could run to monkfish
coated in peppercorns and served with a red pepper sauce. In
summer, enjoy a terrine of seasonal fruits set in rosé wine jelly,
full of refreshing sharp flavours. The wine list is notable for its
showing of half-bottles.

EVESHAM, Riverside Hotel

The Parks Offenham Road WR11 5JP
Map 4: SP04
Tel: 01386 446200
Fax: 01386 40021
Chef: Rosemary Willmott
Owners: Vincent & Rosemary
Willmott
Cost: Set-price L £16.95/D £26.95 (4
courses). H/wine £11.50
Times: 12.30-1.45pm/7.30-9pm.
Closed D Sun, all Mon, 1st 2 wks Jan
(ex weekends)
Additional: Bar food L; Sunday L;
Children welcome
Seats: 48
Smoking: No smoking in dining room
Accommodation: 7 en suite ★ ★

*The restaurant of this family-run hotel is comparatively
formal, with some tables offering fine views across the River
Avon.* A daily-changing menu offers nine starters and main
courses. The cooking describes itself as English, French and
Middle Eastern, though there appear to be few Middle Eastern
influences. The 'assiette de crudités' were generous and included
eggs with garlic mayonnaise. Thai fishcakes were 'light and had
good delicate flavour enhanced by lemongrass, ginger and chilli',
the roast rack of lamb was high quality, 'tender and cooked nice
and pink', on a creamy garlic mash, accompanied by roast
parsnips. The hot apple syrup, cinnamon and lemon pancake
was light with a good and sharp filling'. Choice of coffees
included a good espresso, but surprisingly no petits fours.

Directions: 2 miles from town centre on B4510 (Offenham). At
end of narrow lane marked 'The Park'

EVESHAM,
Wood Norton Hall ❀❀

Wood Norton WR11 4YB
Map 4: SP04
Tel: 01386 420605
Fax: 01386 420190
Chef: Steve Waites
Owners: BBC
Cost: Set-price D £32.50 (4 courses).
H/wine £14
Times: 12.30-2pm/7.30-9.30pm.
Closed L Sat
Additional: Bar food; Sunday L;
Children welcome; 🍴 dishes
Seats: 70. Private dining room 35
Smoking: No-smoking area; No pipes
& cigars
Accommodation: 45 en suite ★ ★ ★ ★

Directions: 2 miles NW of Evesham
on A4538. Hotel is 0.5 mile on R

An impressive Victorian hall, with magnificent carved oak panelling and ornate fireplaces, standing in a large estate just north-west of Evesham. Given the location, it is only fitting the greenhouse should supply the kitchen with salads and herbs during the summer. All dishes are beautifully presented, and a luxurious note is struck in the seasonal, modern French menu with foie gras seared with shallot marmalade and butter broiche, and home-smoked salmon, 'gazpaccio' and Beluga caviar, followed by roasted partridge with purée of potato, button sprouts, juniper and red currant jus or smoked fillet of beef wrapped in pancetta with mushroom purée, smoked garlic and pommes Pont-Neuf. Home-smoking skills are also displayed in cold chicken breast with mushroom beignet and roast garlic vinaigrette. Hot fig tarte Tatin with marshmallow ice cream cleverly rings the changes on a familiar method.

MALVERN,
Colwall Park Hotel ❀❀

Walwyn Road Colwall WR13 6QG
Map 3: SO74
Tel: 01684 540206
Fax: 01684 540847
Chef: Peter Botterill
Owners: Clive & Heather Sturman
Cost: *Alc* £30, set-price L £12.50/D
£25. ☺ H/wine £14
Times: Noon-2pm/7-9pm

Colwall Park was purpose-built as a hotel at the turn of the century, to serve the local railway station from which trains still run to London. The restaurant is warmly furnished in Edwardian style with wood panelling and rich, patterned fabrics. There are good home-made canapés before dinner starts with a choice, amongst others, of rich rabbit and prune terrine, mille-feuille of sautéed king scallops and carrot spaghetti, or paupiettes of lemon sole with a crab and ginger farce. We were attracted by the sophisticated simplicity of lobster bisque, and it did not disappoint, with good rich colour and true distinctive flavour. Tender Chateaubriand of Scottish beef was classically accompanied by grilled beef tomato and béarnaise sauce. Fanned breast of guinea fowl with light truffle pomme purée and a rich Madeira sauce is a signature dish, as is warm poached Conference pear presented in a puff pastry sauté pan and drizzled with an Armagnac sauce. Passion fruit soufflé with warm passion fruit and orange sauce, displayed all the true qualities of the dish, and was well risen, light and moist.

Additional: Bar food; Sunday L; Children welcome; ⬤ dishes
Seats: 35. Private dining room 8
Smoking: No smoking in dining room
Accommodation: 23 en suite ★ ★ ★

Directions: On B4218 between Ledbury and Malvern

MALVERN,

The Cottage in the Wood

Holywell Road Malvern Wells WR14 4LG
Map 3: SO74
Tel: 01684 575859
Fax: 01684 560662
Cost: *Alc* £30, set-price L £14. H/wine £13.50
Times: 12.30-1.45pm/7-9pm

Once the home of Sir Edward Elgar, this delightful hotel enjoys magnificent views across the Severn Valley. A typical meal might start with some good home-made bread, thick slices of wholemeal perhaps, then crab cakes stuffed with tasty meat and served with a vibrant chilli jam. Our confit of lamb shoulder was perfect, served with mushrooms, and walnut and whisky tart made a great dessert in our opinion. Vegetarian dishes are interesting – note roast parsnip crumble with a port and cranberry sauce. The wine list encompasses a big range of flavours and some fine makers.

Additional: Sunday L; Children welcome; ⬤ dishes
Smoking: No smoking in dining room; Air conditioning
Accommodation: 20 en suite ★ ★ ★

Directions: 3 miles S of Great Malvern off A449. 300yds N of B4209 turning on opposite side of road

Shortlisted for AA Wine Award-see page 16

MALVERN,

Croque-en-Bouche 🌸🌸🌸

221 Wells Road WR14 4HF
Map 3: SO74
Tel: 01684 565612
Chef: Marion Jones
Owners: Marion & Robin Jones
Cost: Set-price D £25 (Thu only), £35 (4 courses). H/wine £10

Now in their 21st year, Robin and Marion Jones have really perfected a simple, successful formula. The set-up is remarkable – he is out front, she cooks, and timing is everything: all bookings are carefully staggered. The menu is necessarily simple but offers up to six courses and is great value for money. Pistachios, olives and savoury strudel are served as nibbles, then each table gets a terrine of soup; on our visit a deeply satisfying fish and herb soup served with the traditional accompaniments of croûtes, Gruyère and a delightful pungent rouille. A crab croustade proved to be a perfect light pastry parcel with a vibrant filling of spinach, Newlyn crab and lobster, partnered by a rich chive beurre blanc. The main course was Cotswold spring lamb that had been marinated in herbs, roasted and stuffed with garlic, aubergine and spinach and accompanied by a claret-based sauce flavoured with thyme. A fresh green salad consisted of some home-grown leaves and herbs and thinly sliced cucumber, all tossed in sesame oil and a Japanese peanut sauce. A selection of British cheeses were in top condition, including an oozing Bath soft, Cerney goats', double Worcester, and Cornish yarg, served with home-made bread. Finally a stunning, refreshing sorbet terrine made up of different flavours including pink grapefruit, mango, passion fruit and melon. Wine is a very important element here, with Robin running a successful wine business. The list is legendary, huge, with separate books for each colour; for a wine lover this place is paradise (with very fair mark-ups throughout). A good selection is also offered by the glass.

Times: D only, 7.30-9.30pm. Closed Sun-Wed
Additional: Children welcome
Seats: 22. Private dining room 6
Smoking: No smoking in dining room

Directions: 2 miles S of Gt Malvern on A449

MALVERN,

Foley Arms Hotel

14 Worcester Road WR14 4QS
Map 3: SO74
Tel: 01684 573397
Fax: 01684 569665
Cost: *Alc* £26, set-price L £8.95 (2 courses)/D £19.50. ☺ H/wine £8.95
Times: Noon-2pm/7-9.15pm. Closed L Sat, 25 Dec, 31 Dec
Additional: Bar meals; Sunday L; Children welcome; 🍴 dishes
Smoking: No smoking in dining room
Accommodation: 28 en suite ★ ★ ★

Directions: Telephone for details

This lovely old Georgian property commands wonderful views across the Severn Valley. Good ingredients are evident in skilfully prepared dishes such as wild mushroom and aubergine risotto and casserole of seafood in saffron cream sauce.

MALVERN,

Holdfast Cottage 🏵🏵

Charming 17th-century oak-beamed hotel with impressive views of the Malvern hills. The pretty dining room overlooks the hotel's gardens and wisteria-clad terrace. Our mid-winter inspection started with a robust smoked fish chowder, and was followed by good quality lamb cutlets cooked 'nice and pink', served on a sweet potato rösti with rosemary-flavoured roasted baby onions and a selection of vegetables (mashed carrot, fine crisp beans, dauphinoise potatoes). Dessert was a little spiced raisin pudding served with a 'delicious and distinct' tangy

Little Malvern WR13 6NA
Map 3: SO74
Tel: 01684 310288
Fax: 01684 311117
Cost: Set-price D £25 (4 courses). ☺ H/wine £10.50
Times: D only, 7-8.45pm. Closed D Sun, Xmas, 1st 2 wks Jan
Additional: Children 8+; 🍴 dishes
Seats: 24. Private dining room 14
Smoking: No smoking in dining room

Holdfast Cottage

Accommodation: 8 en suite ★★

Directions: On A4104 midway between Welland and Little Malvern

lemon sauce. The reasonably-priced wine list takes an international approach with bottles from England, South Africa and Chile alongside favourites from continental Europe.

OMBERSLEY,
The Venture In Restaurant ✿✿ **NEW**

Main Road WR9 0EW
Map 3: SO86
Tel: 01905 620552
Chef/Owner: Toby William Fletcher
Cost: Set-price L £15.95/D £25.95. H/wine £9
Times: Noon-2pm/7-9.45pm. Closed D Sun, all Mon, 2wks winter & summer, Bhs
Additional: Sunday L; Children welcome; ❧ dishes
Seats: 32
Smoking: No smoking in dining room; Air conditioning

Directions: Head N out of Worcester towards Kidderminster – A449 (approx 5 miles). Turn L at Ombersley turning – 0.75 miles on R

Ancient building with olde worlde charm in spades. A resident ghost is said to inhabit the old black-and-white timbered High Street residence. The olde-worlde interior is suitably quaint and full of character with an inglenook fireplace and exposed timbers. By contrast, the menu is modern world with an up-to-date mix of ingredients and styles typified in a celeriac soup with Roquefort ravioli, or a barley and cream risotto with wild mushrooms. Rich saucing underpinned both rib-eye beef with wild mushrooms with Madeira sauce, and superbly flavoured duck breasts with coriander sauce served on a bed of pickled red cabbage and apple. White chocolate mousse and a fruit sundae were both enjoyed. Do, as they say – venture in.

PERSHORE, Epicurean Restaurant **NEW**

76 High Street WR10 1DU
Map 3: SO94
Tel: 01386 555576
Fax: 01386 555572
Chef: Patrick McDonald
Owners: Patrick & Claire McDonald
Cost: Set-price D £27.50 (5 courses).

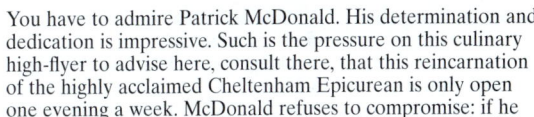

You have to admire Patrick McDonald. His determination and dedication is impressive. Such is the pressure on this culinary high-flyer to advise here, consult there, that this reincarnation of the highly acclaimed Cheltenham Epicurean is only open one evening a week. McDonald refuses to compromise: if he can't be present in the kitchen to cook for his customers than he can't be open, so Friday evening is devoted to loyal customers - booking in advance is recommended. As we went to press, plans were afoot to open at other times, perhaps a lunch as well as another dinner, so it is well worth telephoning to check. What you can expect is a five or six-course, no-choice menu of stunning accuracy. A superlative-strewn late report (not enough meals taken to award Rosettes this year) praised fresh garden pea soup with lobster and basil ravioli; pressed terrine of pork knuckle with foie gras; tian of avocado and salmon tartare; roast squab pigeon, broad beans, tomato, morels and jus of summer truffles; prime cheeses with a warm almond and poire William tartlet; and lime tart. A novel idea is to offer wines by the glass, chosen to complement the dishes, but there's also an impressive, wide-ranging wine list.

H/wine £10.50
Times: Fri D only from 7.30pm. Other times by appointment
Seats: 24. Private dining room 12-24
Smoking: No pipes & cigars
Credit cards: None

Directions: On High Street

SEVERN STOKE, Old Schoolhouse

Until its conversion into a hotel, this 17th-century, timber-framed former farmhouse was the village school. Your meal may include salmon and sole terrine, or medallions of beef in a mushroom, onion and red wine sauce.

Directions: Telephone for directions

WR8 9JA
Map 3: SO85
Tel: 01905 371368
Fax: 01905 371591
Telephone for further details

STOURPORT-ON SEVERN,
Stourport Manor

NEW

The former home of Prime Minister Sir Stanley Baldwin, now a modernised hotel with good corporate facilities. Ambition and motivation is evident in the kitchen and our meal showed talent at work. Chicken truffle and ham roulade with a saffron dressing and shallot and onion marmalade, oven-baked fillet of beef topped with an onion soufflé, and summer pudding with crème fraîche were all much enjoyed. A separate vegetarian menu offers the likes of avocado and fresh coriander quesadillas with a fresh chilli salsa, and chargrilled tower of courgette, aubergine and beef tomato with a pesto and basil dressing. The wine list ofers a keenly priced, wide-ranging selection with plenty of halves and quite a few available by the glass.

Hartlebury Road DY13 9LT
Map 7: SO87
Tel: 01299 289955
Fax: 01299 878520
Chef: John Trueman
Owner: Menzies Hotels & Leisure
Cost: Alc £24.50, set-price L £8.95/D £19.95. ☺ H/wine £11.95
Additional: Bar food; Sunday L; Children welcome; ☒ dishes
Seats: 100. Private dining room to 300
Smoking: No-smoking area
Accommodation: 68 en suite ★ ★ ★ ★

Directions: Telephone for directions

WORCESTER, Brown's Restaurant

Former converted grain mill, now an airy, high-ceilinged restaurant. Enjoying an idyllic location alongside the River Severn yet only a short walk from the city centre; picture windows make the best of the river view. The set-price menu offers about half-a-dozen simply described choices at each stage: smoked haddock fishcakes with red onion and caper salsa, and warm salad of grilled foie gras, and roast breast of pheasant with apple and sage sauce, or charcoal grilled fillet of Scotch beef. Desserts might include a little pot of rich dark chocolate, treacle tart with vanilla ice cream and our good ginger meringue glacé. Staff, smartly turned out in dark green aprons, are professional and attentive.

Directions: City centre, along river bank, car park opposite

The Old Cornmill
South Quay WR1 2JJ
Map 3: SO85
Tel: 01905 26263
Fax: 01905 25768
Chefs: W R Tansley & Lee Jones
Owners: W R & P M Tansley
Cost: Set-price L £18.50 (4 courses)/D £34.50 (5 courses). H/wine £11.95
Times: 12.30-1.45pm/7.30-9.45pm. Closed L Sat, D Sun, all Mon, 24-31 Dec
Additional: Sunday L; Children 8+; ☒ dishes. **Seats:** 80
Smoking: No-smoking area; No cigars & pipes

YORKSHIRE EAST RIDING

BEVERLEY, The Manor House

Northlands Walkington HU17 8RT
Map 8: TA03
Tel: 01482 881645
Fax: 01482 866501
Chef: Derek Baugh
Owners: Derek & Lee Baugh
Cost: Set-price D £30 (4 courses). ☺
H/wine £11.95
Times: D only, 7-9.15pm. Closed
Sun, 25, 26 Dec
Additional: Children 12+; ⚬ dishes
Seats: 55. Private dining room 24
Smoking: No pipes and cigars
Accommodation: 7 en suite ★★

Splendidly run country house hotel in the heart of open countryside. Derek Baugh's cooking provides the goods admirably; his is a straightforward style with the added attraction of adherence to the use of prime local ingredients. Menus, more a list of ingredients, have impact. A soft poached egg on a galette of black pudding and bacon with a chive béarnaise, for example, or sizzled duck livers with a cracked pepper sauce and beetroot crisps, are typical starters. Main courses run along similar lines with roasted rack of lamb served with an onion and mint marmalade, and roasted quail with seared foie gras, Puy lentils and sloe gin sauce.

Directions: 4 miles SW off B1230

BEVERLEY, Tickton Grange Hotel

Charming Georgian house set in four acres of grounds. Dishes that have impressed include a nicely balanced seafood timbale with tomato and dill sauce, and a tender, full flavoured, duck with cherry brandy sauce.

Accommodation: 17 en suite ★★★

Directions: From Beverley take A1035 towards Bridlington. Hotel on L, after 3 miles, just past village of Tickton

Tickton HU17 9SH
Map 8: TA03
Tel: 01964 543666
Fax: 01964 542556
Cost: *Alc* £30, set-price L £15.95/D
£25 (4 courses). ☺ H/wine £10.75
Times: Noon-2pm/7-9.30pm
Additional: Bar food L; Sunday L;
Children welcome; ⚬ dishes
Smoking: No smoking in dining room

MARKET WEIGHTON,
Londesborough Arms Hotel

Restored Georgian hotel reflecting high standards of decor and service. The restaurant is stylish with thick marble pillars and tablecloths 'so immaculately crisp and long that you could take away the tables from underneath them and continue eating. The menu is simply structured to avoid over stuffiness with modern techniques built up from a classical base. This is a very busy restaurant.

44 High Street YO4 3AH
Map 8: SE84
Tel: 01430 872214
Telephone for further details

Willerby Manor Hotel

The hotel's restaurant overlooks three acres of lovely gardens. Dishes include 'Duck Ballantine' with guinea fowl and prune farce, grilled fillet of sea bream, and roast loin of lamb.

Additional: Bar food; Sunday L; Children welcome; ● dishes
Smoking: No-smoking area; Air conditioning
Accommodation: 51 en suite ★ ★ ★

Directions: Off A1105 W of Hull, just off main street of Willerby

Well Lane HU10 6ER
Map 8: TA03
Tel: 01482 652616
Fax: 01482 653901
Cost: *Alc* £24, set-price L £14.50/D £17.25. ☺ H/wine £9.75
Times: Noon-2pm/7-9.30pm. Closed L Sat, D Sun, 25 Dec, Millennium

YORKSHIRE NORTH

Amerdale House Hotel

A small hotel in a small village at the end of a small dale. The style is country house, but without any sense of tweeness; service is very friendly and natural. The short, hand-written menu changes daily and features four starters, a middle course, two main courses (plus a vegetarian option), with dishes built around local ingredients plus some vegetables from the hotel's own kitchen garden. We enjoyed some very good apricot and walnut bread, a mushroom tart lifted by the heady flavour of truffle oil, delicate spinach and ricotta ravioli with a sweet tomato sauce, pan-fried fillet of sea bass with smoky-flavoured Mediterranean vegetables, and a gentle elderflower sorbet served with crisp almond tuiles.

Directions: On edge of village

Littondale Skipton BD23 5QE
Map 7: SD97
Tel/Fax: 01756 770250
Chef: Nigel Crapper
Owners: Paula & Nigel Crapper
Cost: Set-price £29 (4 courses). H/wine £12.50
Times: D only, 7.30-8.30pm. Closed mid Nov-mid Mar
Additional: ● dishes
Seats: 24
Smoking: No smoking in dining room
Accommodation: 11 en suite ★ ★

Crab & Lobster

Chock-full of antiques, bygones and curios, this friendly 16th-century thatched pub provides a unique setting. First things first. The emphasis is on seafood with crab-stuffed fillets of lemon sole with lobster sauce, sea bass on basil and scallop risotto, and a 'hunk' of halibut with wild mushroom sauté and Beaujolais sauce demonstrating the style. Carnivores are not forgotten however, and can tuck into beef fillet with bacon rolls and horseradish mash, or roast venison with pears, chocolate and figs. Starters range from mussels marinière, to king scallops with oriental stir-fry, crab and Gruyère soufflé. Our last meal ended with a 'hot and sticky and very yummy' pear tarte Tatin. Good coffee and home-made petits fours.

Directions: Leave A1 for A19 at Dishforth, 3 miles turn L for Asenby

Dishforth Road YO7 3QL
Map 8: SE37
Tel: 01845 577286
Fax: 01845 577109
Chefs: David Barnard, Steven Dean
Owners: David & Jackie Barnard
Cost: *Alc* £26, set-price L £14.95/D £19.95. ☺ H/wine £10.50
Times: 11.30am-2.30pm/6-10pm
Additional: Bar food; Sunday L; Children welcome; ● dishes
Seats: 65. Private dining rooms 6-25
Smoking: No smoking in dining room
Accommodation: 10 en suite

ASKRIGG, **King's Arms Hotel**

Famous character inn dating from the 18th century. The public rooms retain much of their old charm, especially the original bars and there is a good choice of eating options: simply in the bars, informally in the brasserie-styled Silkroom, formally in the Clubroom. In the latter an imaginative, short-choice menu offers some interesting combinations: roast woodpigeon on a croûton with marbled Cassis and pistachio nut dressing, for example, or maize-fed chicken supreme with a blue Wensleydale cheese filling, wrapped in Parma ham with a sage, red onion and pink grapefruit dressing. Cheeses are local, from Wensleydale and Swaledale, served with home-baked date and walnut bread.

Directions: 0.5 mile off A684 from A1 (Leeming Bar); in centre of village

Market Place Leyburn DL8 3HQ
Map 7: SD99
Tel: 01969 650258
Fax: 01969 650635
Chef: Campbell Cameron
Owners: Elizabeth & Raymond Hopwood
Cost: Alc £25, set-price L £12.50. ☺
H/wine £9
Times: Noon-2pm/6.30-9pm
Additional: Bar food; Sunday L; Children 10+ at D; ✿ dishes
Seats: 28. Private dining room 10. Jacket & tie preferred
Smoking: No smoking in dining room.
Accommodation: 11 en suite ★★

BUCKDEN, **Buck Inn**

Former coaching inn with lively public bar and more formal restaurant. The glorious Dales scenery serves to sharpen the appetite for satisfying cooking that uses local fresh ingredients wherever possible. Originally a coaching inn, the restaurant is in the former courtyard where in olden days local wool auctions were held. Today it is the setting for dishes such as chicken liver and foie gras parfait with toasted brioche and sautéed fillet of pork medallion served with a rosemary fondant potato, honey and mead sauce. Apple surprise, to our pleasure, turned out to be a rich bread pudding, filled with grated apple, nutmeg and plump dried fruit – substantial and rich on a gale-swept autumn evening, and served with a Calvados sauce that should have had a Government health warning for alcohol content! The popular public bar serves a similar menu as well as a selection of light snacks including 'risotto of whatever'.

Directions: In centre of village

Near Skipton BD23 5JA
Map 7: SD97
Tel: 01756 760228
Fax: 01756 760227
Chef: Jonathan Chapman
Owners: R & M Hayton
Cost: Set-price D £23.95. ☺
H/wine £13
Times: Open daily for L & D
Additional: Bar food; Sunday L; Children 6+ in restaurant; ✿ dishes
Seats: 40. Private dining room 40
Smoking: No smoking in dining room
Accommodation: 14 en suite ★★

BURNSALL, **Red Lion**

Welcoming 16th-century ferrymen's inn on the banks of the River Wharf. The restaurant offers a varied range of modern dishes built around locally sourced ingredients, together with a comprehensive wine list.

By the Bridge BD23 6BU
Map 7: SE06
Tel: 01756 720204
Fax: 01756 720292
Cost: D £23.95. ☺ H/wine £9.95
Times: D only, 7-9.30pm
Additional: Bar food; Sunday L (Noon-2.45pm); Children welcome; ✿ dishes
Smoking: No smoking in dining room
Accommodation: 11 en suite ★★

Directions: On B6160 between Bolton Abbey (A59) & Grassington

CRATHORNE, **Crathorne Hall**

Grand Edwardian country house hotel. The formal dining room, oak panelled, with an ornate ceiling, serves classical dishes with a modern spin. Simple ones work best: roasted Whitby cod, a full flavoured cannon of Welsh lamb with caramelised shallots, and gnocchi cooked with Yorkshire blue cheese. Items are listed with symbols to indicate healthy options, vegetarian (3 choices), and those suitable for coeliacs. Desserts are sometimes too elaborate, but the chocolate and Grand Marnier torte is sensational. A long wine list – 25 pages – includes wines from all around the world, but only lists whether they are from the old or New World and what grape variety they are. A welcome selection of half bottles is available.

Directions: From A19, take junction signposted Crathorne and follow the signs. Hotel entrance is to the L on way into village

Yarm TS15 0AR
Map 8: NZ40
Tel: 01642 700398
Fax: 01642 700814
Chef: David Spencer
Cost: *Alc* £30, set-price D £25.
H/wine £14.50
Times: Noon-2pm/7-9.45pm
Additional: Bar food; Sunday L;
Children 12+ ; ✆ dishes
Seats: 45. Private dining room 120
Smoking: No smoking in dining room
Accommodation: 37 en suite ★ ★ ★ ★

EASINGTON, **Grinkle Park Hotel**

Good cooking, local produce and an elegant setting are the order of the day here. Roast cod was straight off the Whitby boat, served with sweet-and-sour sauce. 'Scoundrel's steak' is fillet with wild mushrooms, herbs, brandy and cream.

Additional: Bar food; Sunday L; Children welcome; ✆ dishes
Smoking: No cigars & pipes
Accommodation: 20 en suite ★ ★ ★

Directions: 9 miles from Guisborough, signed L off main A171 Guisborough-Whitby road

Saltburn-by-the-Sea TS13 4UB
Map 8: NZ71
Tel: 01287 640515
Fax: 01287 641278
Cost: *Alc* £25, set-price L £13.50/D
£20. ☺ H/wine £10
Times: 12.15-2pm/7.15-9pm

ESCRICK, **The Parsonage Hotel**

Early 19th-century former parsonage with charming country-house atmosphere and caring professional staff. In the kitchen things are going from strength to strength. Good home-baked breads come with various additions (including mint and almond, and smoked cheese at our last visit) and the up-to-date menu is equally adventurous. A starter of couscous and cod cake with croissant crumbs, tiger prawns and a honey and chive dressing and fillet steak accompanied by a wild mushroom and ginger risotto and crispy wun-tun exemplify the style. More mainstream offerings include salmon with a basil and black olive crust, and saddle of rabbit with ratatouille and rosemary jus. Desserts like white chocolate tart and iced lemon soufflé are followed by home-made petits fours.

Directions: From York head S on A19, Parsonage on R, 4 miles out of town in Escrick village

Main Street YO19 6LF
Map 8: SE64
Tel: 01904 728111
Fax: 01904 728151
Chef: Kenny Noble
Owner: Mrs K Ridley
Cost: *Alc* £24, set-price L £12/D
£24.50. ☺ H/wine £9.95
Times: 12-2pm/7-9.30pm
Additional: Bar food L; Sunday L;
Children welcome; ✆ dishes
Seats: 28. Private dining room 16.
Jacket & tie preferred
Smoking: No smoking in dining room
Accommodation: 21 en suite ★ ★ ★

GRASSINGTON,
Grassington House

Bustling little hotel standing in the centre of the town's cobbled square. Expect friendly service. Typical dishes include chicken liver

5 The Square BD23 5AQ
Map 7: SE06
Tel: 01756 752406
Fax: 01756 752135

parfait with Cumberland sauce, duck with red onion marmalade, and chocolate and ginger cheesecake.

Accommodation: 9 en suite ★★

Directions: From Skipton bypass take B6265 to Grassington

Cost: *Alc* £16. ☺ H/wine £7.95
Times: Noon-2pm/6.30-9pm
Additional: Bar food; Sunday L;
Children welcome; 🍽 dishes
Smoking: No smoking in dining room

HACKNESS,

Hackness Grange

NEW

The restaurant overlooks acres of parkland and a lake full of ducks. High ceilings and oil paintings bring out the Regency origins of the house. A modern English menu shows a wide variety of influences, but local roots are not forgotten in dishes such as steamed natural-smoked haddock with new potatoes, buttered spinach, poached egg and grain mustard sauce, as well as twice-baked Wensleydale and walnut soufflé, and pressing of ham knuckle and root vegetables with pease pudding and walnut dressing. Amongst dishes sampled, beignets of monkfish with crab butter sauce were fresh and crunchy, and loin steaks of pork with tomato compote and a Parmesan sabayon were full of flavour. Dessert was a treat, a melting chocolate fondant with butterscotch sauce that had the texture of a soufflé but the flavour of a cake. Considerate staff keep everything running smoothly.

North Yorkshire National Park
Scarborough YO13 0JW
Map 8: SE99
Tel: 01723 882345
Fax: 01723 882391
Chef: David Chambers
Owners: English Rose Hotels
Cost: *Alc* £27.50, set-price L
£12.50/D £27.50. H/wine £12.95
Times: Noon-1.45pm/7-9pm
Additional: Bar food L; Sunday L;
Children welcome; 🍽 dishes
Seats: 50
Smoking: No smoking in dining room
Accommodation: 28 en suite ★★★

Directions: A64 to Scarborough, then
A171 towards Whitby. Follow signs to
Hackness/Forge Valley National Park.
Hotel through hackness on L

HARROGATE, **The Bistro**

Set in a quiet corner of Harrogate, in an attractive mews surrounded by quality shops. This restaurant has a strong Mediterranean-Italian feel , from the yellow and cream walls and blue-checked cloths to the wood-block flooring and raffia seating. The menu follows suit: a Mediterranean fish soup, toasted Tuscan bread salad, risotto of walnut pesto and main courses of tagliatelle of wild mushrooms. The food is well-presented and our goats' cheese crostini came with a good selection of leaves, a shank of lamb just fell from the bone and was 'lovely and sticky – just how it should be'. A light and extremely tangy lemon tart came with a raspberry coulis. Coffee is excellent, service friendly and relaxed.

1 Montpellier Mews HG1 2TG
Map 8: SE35
Tel: 01423 530708
Chef: Marc Papon
Owner: Maurizio Capurro
Cost: *Alc* £21.50. ☺ H/wine £10.95
Times: Noon-2pm/7-10pm. Closed
Sun & Mon, 10 days Xmas
Additional: Children welcome;
🍽 dishes
Seats: 32
Smoking: No pipes & cigars

Directions: Town centre. Just W of Parliament St, near the
Cenotaph

HARROGATE,

Boar's Head Hotel

Ripley Castle Estate HG3 3AY
Map 8: SE35
Tel: 01423 771888
Fax: 01423 771509
Chef: Steve Chesnutt
Owners: Sir Thomas & Lady Ingilby
Cost: *Alc* £30, set-price L £13.50 (2
courses)/D £30 (5 courses). ☺ H/wine
£12
Times: Noon-2pm/7-9.30pm
Additional: Bar food; Sunday L;
Children welcome; 🌶 dishes
Seats: 40
Smoking: No pipes and cigars. Jacket
& tie preferred
Accommodation: 25 en suite ★ ★ ★

*Traditional hostelry, built as a coaching inn on the London
to Edinburgh road, in a charming, unspoiled village.* Strong,
rich reds fill the dining room, along with paintings from Ripley
Castle (hotel and castle have the same owners, and, indeed, the
whole village is part of the castle's estate), service is French
and friendly, the global wine list is a long one, and the menu
combines tradition with more adventurous dishes. Chargrilled
calves' liver with excellent bacon, mustard mash and a red
wine gravy hinting of rosemary, and carbonnade of prime beef
with Ripley ale, chestnuts and wild mushrooms might share
main-course billing with confit of salmon on a crab and caper
cake with a sauce of shallots, orange and star anise. These
could be preceded by a strongly flavoured terrine of goats'
cheese and cured venison (from the estate) in peppered
strawberry vinaigrette, spinach and walnut gnocchi, or a
layered terrine of smoked fish, and followed by perhaps
raspberry bavarois with a warm compote of berries.

Directions: On A61, 3 miles N of Harrogate

HARROGATE,

Dusty Miller ❀❀

Low-Laithe Summerbridge HG3 4BU
Map 8: SE35
Tel: 01423 780837
Chef: Brian Dennison
Owners: Brian & Elizabeth Dennison
Cost: *Alc* £32.20, set-price D £24. ☺
H/wine £9.90
Times: D only, 7-11pm. Closed Sun,
Mon, 2 wks in Aug or Sep
Additional: Children 9+
Seats: 28. Private dining room 14

Former pub, which retains its bar. Open fires, lots of candles
and fresh flowers, antique furniture, friendly service and a
series of three cosy rooms all create the atmosphere of a
homely cottage. The short, snappy menu concentrates on
seafood and locally sourced meat: Whitby crab salad, rack of
Nidderdale lamb with rosemary jus, then, in season, summer
pudding with ice cream. Lobster – perhaps in a salad with
prawns and mayonnaise – and oysters are normally available,
crisply roast duckling is so popular it's never been off the
menu, and baked turbot might be offered with seared scallops
on a bed of fresh spinach with mash and a herby beurre blanc.
Finish with light lemon mousse, or tarte Tatin with Calvados.
The wine list, almost entirely French, holds plenty of interest,
not least for those here for a celebration.

Directions: Situated on B6165, 10 miles from Harrogate

HARROGATE,

Harrogate Brasserie Hotel

Along with a distinctly continental operation, this lively town-centre hotel offers live jazz and blues at weekends. We enjoyed chicken liver and smoked duck pâté with Cumberland sauce, rack of lamb with boulangère potatoes, and light, fruit-filled pancake.

Directions: In town centre, 500m from railway station, behind theatre

28-30 Cheltenham Parade
HG1 1DB
Map 8: SE35
Tel: 01423 505041
Fax: 01423 530920
Telephone for further details

HARROGATE, **Olivers 24** NEW

The stark, stone exterior contrasts with the soft pastel interior of this terraced Victorian house. Imagination, skill and consistency mark out this Harrogate newcomer. The short lunch menu offers excellent value, and a special budget menu is available for pre-theatre dinner. Our lunch started with a 'super' terrine of ham hock, foie gras and smoked duck, went on to calves' liver with a robust red wine sauce, perfect mash and baby onions, and finished with a traditional creme brûlée and excellent espresso. Other top notch dishes we can recommend include seared monkfish and pancetta with tomato and olive risotto, and salt roast cod with parsley mash.

Directions: Telephone for directions

24 Kings Road HG1 5JW
Map 8: SE35
Tel: 01423 568600
Fax: 01423 531838
Chefs: Dean Sowden, Jamie Dilasser
Owners: James & Sandy Greetham
Cost: *Alc* £19.50, set-price £10. ☺
H/wine £9.50
Times: Noon-2pm/6-10pm. Closed Sun, L Mon, 25-26 Dec, 1 Jan
Additional: Bar food; Children welcome; dishes
Seats: 110. Private dining room 50
Smoking: No pipes & cigars; Air conditioning

HARROGATE, **Rudding Park House** ✿✿

Follifoot HG3 1JH
Map 8: SE35
Tel: 01423 871350
Fax: 01423 872286
Chef: Jason Wardill
Owner: Simon Mackaness
Cost: *Alc* £25, set-price L £13.95/D £25. ☺ H/wine £12.50
Times: 12.30-2pm/7-9.30pm (10pm weekends)
Additional: Bar food; Sunday L; Children welcome; ● dishes
Seats: 90. Private dining rooms 6-250
Smoking: No pipes and cigars; Air conditioning
Accommodation: 50 en suite ★ ★ ★ ★

Directions: 3 miles S of Harrogate, just off A658 linking A61 from Leeds to A59 York road

The refurbished Clocktower Bar and Brasserie may have doubled in size but the restaurant retains a more traditional look, although it has a modern feel (green walls, tartan curtains, red and green chairs and large food-inspired pictures of chillies). The menus reflect Mediterranean and Asian influences. Our chicken liver parfait was 'the best ever', and chicken breast was 'moist and caramelised', set on honey parsnips served with a rich Cabernet Sauvignon jus, split with a herb purée. The set-menu also features confit of duck on crispy greens, bean sprouts, sesame seeds with lime and sweet soy dressing. Fillet of salmon on fresh lemon and saffron noodles was served with baby leeks, oyster mushrooms and a spicy tom-yum liqueur. Desserts include an orange tiramisu in a creamy Mascarpone brûlée-style custard with coffee-soaked sponge.

HARROGATE,
Studley Hotel ✿

Swan Road HG1 2SE
Map 8: SE35
Tel: 01423 560425
Fax: 01423 530967
Telephone for further details

Directions: Close to Conference
Centre, near the entrance to Valley
Gardens

*An interesting mix of classical and charcoal-cooked dishes is served
in this Mediterranean style restaurant. Look out for sauté lamb's
kidney with bacon, shallots and mushrooms, and chargrilled
noisettes of lamb with garlic and rosemary jus.*

HARROGATE,
The White House ✿✿

10 Park Parade HG1 5AH
Map 8: SE35
Tel: 01423 501388
Fax: 01423 527973

Chef/Owner: Jennie Forster
Cost: *Alc* £28, set-price L £16.50/D
£14.95 (2 courses). ☺ H/wine £12.95
Times: 12.30-2pm/7-9pm. Closed Sun
Additional: Children welcome;
🍴 dishes
Seats: 30. Private dining room 10
Smoking: No smoking in dining room
Accommodation: 10 en suite ★ ★ ★

**The White House was inspired by a Venetian villa and built
in 1836.** However, there's nothing remotely Venetian about
the cooking which is best described as modern English. The
carte is supplemented by a 'Chef's Dinner' aimed at diners
wanting something more straightforward. Yorkshire pudding
with home-made raspberry vinegar, black risotto with prawns
and squid and baby haggis feature on the five choice of
starters. A good quality loin of pork was small and tender,
flavoured with tea soaked in raisins. That dish came with
shredded courgettes, light mash with black pepper, Belle de
Fontenay potatoes, carrot batons and green beans, all well-
cooked and properly seasoned. Desserts are English classics
such as poached pears, creamed rice pudding, and summer
pudding with raspberry sauce.

Directions: Opposite Christchurch, parallel with A59 close to
Wetherby/Skipton junction

HAWES, Simonstone Hall

Delightful Jacobean hunting lodge with stunning views of the upper Wensleydale Valley. After a day exploring the Yorkshire moors, return to a warm welcome and roaring fires. For dinner expect simple but creative dishes that make the most of local game and fish.

Accommodation: 18 en suite ★★

Directions: 1.5m N of Hawes on road signed to Muker & Buttertubs

Simonstone DL8 3LY
Map 7: SD88
Tel: 01969 667255
Fax: 01969 667741
Cost: *Alc* £25, set-price L £13 (4 courses)/D £22.50 (4 courses). ☺ H/wine £12.95
Times: D only 7-9pm
Additional: Bar food; Sunday L (12.30-2pm); Children 10+; 🍽 dishes
Smoking: No smoking in dining room

HAZLEWOOD, Hazlewood Castle

'Surroundings are modern baronial, if that makes sense, very dramatic,' remarks an inspector. The combination of grand-scale castle and John Benson Smith's cooking style (a chef who believes that more is more with the menu verging on the gimmicky) has clearly hit the spot with most of Yorkshire, who all seemed to be eating there on the various nights we visited. In a style reminiscent of John Tovey, ingredients slug it out on the plate, trying to grab your attention. A rabbit terrine, for example, was excellent 'if not knowing when to stop', delivering not only rillettes-style smooth liver and Parma wrap with chutney but also hazelnuts, redcurrant, shallot dressing and crispy pear slice, and an open pie of very good local pigeon breasts (two and perfectly pink) and red cabbage had to make room for some confit of duck and rather overdosed on the fowl in the bargain. Red snapper, on the other hand was simpler in conception, it came crisp-skinned with a caramel and lime dressing (which worked).

Paradise Lane LS24 9NJ
Tel: 01937 535353
Fax: 01937 530630
Telephone for further details

Directions: Telephone for directions

HELMSLEY, The Black Swan

Set in an enviable position overlooking the square, this historic hotel has a very elegant restaurant. The menu may include smoked mackerel pâté in a pastry case, and calves' liver with truffle jus on an onion mash.

Directions: Take A170 from Scarborough or Thirsk; Black Swan is in centre of village, at top end of Market Place

Market Place YO6 5BJ
Map 8: SE68
Tel: 01439 770466
Fax: 01439 770174
Telephone for further details

HELMSLEY, Feversham Arms Hotel

A warm atmosphere, candlelit, with mahogany furniture, shield chairs, and Goya prints on the walls. The menu has a Spanish tilt too, with tapas and zarzuela (fish stew) among broccoli and Stilton soup, moules marinière, steak, and braised saddle of rabbit.

Accommodation: 18 en suite ★★★

Directions: 200 yds N of Market Place

1 High Street YO62 5AG
Map 8: SE68
Tel: 01439 770766
Fax: 01439 770346
Cost: *Alc* £20, set-price L £15/D £20 (4 courses). ☺ H/wine £10
Times: Noon-1.30pm/7-9pm
Additional: Bar food; Sunday L; Children 7+; 🍽 dishes
Smoking: No smoking in dining room

HELMSLEY, Star Inn

14th-century thatched pub with a traditional atmosphere and charming service. The pubby look that comes with open log fires, hunting trophies, old photos of cricket teams, and hand-crafted oak bar furniture, is offset by Andrew Pern's cooking which takes a fresh, modern look at traditional favourites.

Harome YO6 5JE
Map 8: SE68
Tel: 01439 770397
Fax: 01439 771833
Chef: Andrew Pern
Owners: Andrew & Jacquie Pern
Cost: *Alc* £20. ☺

Star Inn

Times: 11.30-2pm/6.30-9.30pm (Sun noon-6pm). Closed D Sun, all Mon, 2 wks Jan
Additional: Bar food; Sunday L; Children welcome; 🍴 dishes
Seats: 32. Private room 10
Smoking: No smoking in dining room

Directions: 3 miles SE of A170, first building in village

Thus, beef bourguignon comes with olive mash, seared supreme of salmon with potted shrimps, and roast loin of suckling pig gets an unusual black pudding risotto. We were tempted by grilled Queenies in a sauce of creamed leeks and strong Lancashire cheese, a rustic portion of pork and apple casserole with sage mash, and rhubarb trifle, although there was strong competition from chocolate indulgence and fresh lemon tart. The well-annotated wine list is another Star attraction.

HETTON, Angel Inn ❁❁

Skipton BD23 6LT
Map 7: SD95
Tel: 01756 730263
Fax: 01756 730363
Chefs: Denis Watkins, John Topham, Richard Smith
Owners: Denis Watkins, John Topham, Julie Watkins
Cost: Alc £30, set-price L £20/D £30. ☺ H/wine £10.95
Times: D only, 6-9pm. Closed D Sun, 1 wk Jan
Additional: Sunday L (noon-2pm); Children welcome
Seats: 56
Smoking: No-smoking area; No pipes & cigars

Directions: In village centre, B6265 (Rylestone) from Skipton by-pass

A 400-year-old inn, all oak beams and open fires, in the Yorkshire Dales National Park. This is very much an inn with a difference, with an excellent range of up-to-the-minute bar food (terrine of parsleyed ham shank and foie gras with grape chutney and Puy lentils, or West Coast smoked cod with a poached egg, black pudding, mash and grain mustard sauce), and a first-class wine list that includes over 20 by the glass. Eating in the two connecting dining rooms – more beams, exposed stonework and a fireplace – is a comfortable and inviting experience, with service friendly but quite formal. An *amuse-bouche* of smoked haddock fishcake with aïoli gets the appetite going, followed perhaps by oysters wrapped in smoked salmon glazed with hollandaise, then full-flavoured, tender breast of mallard sliced over wilted spinach with a confit of the leg. Much is made of game in season, as in traditional roast pheasant with a wild boar sausage, truffle-infused bread sauce and game chips. Finish with rich and smooth chocolate tart, or go for a plate of English farmhouse cheeses.

HOVINGHAM,
Worsley Arms Hotel ✿✿

YO62 4LA
Tel: 01653 628234
Fax: 01653 628130
Map 8: SE67
Chef: Andrew Jones
Owner: Euan Rodger
Cost: *Alc* £20 (Bistro)/set-price D £25
(Restaurant). ☺ H/wine £11.50
Times: Noon-2pm (Bistro only)/7-
9.30pm
Additional: Bar food; Sunday L (noon-
2pm); Children welcome; ✿ dishes
Seats: 30 (Bistro), 60 (Restaurant).
Private dining room 30.
Smoking: No smoking in restaurant
Accommodation: 18 en suite ★★★

Forming the focal point of an attractive village this
charming hotel offers a comfortable, relaxing environment.
Choice is a problem here: whether to dine in the formal
restaurant or eat more casually in the separate Cricketers
Bistro, both have excellent food based on modern ideas and
sound technique. In the latter, for example, terrine of
Goosnargh chicken, girolles and Perigord foie gras, chestnut
and sultana salad and toasted brioche, or there could be a
small honey-roast lamb joint with minted chick pea, with a
broth of butter beans, bacon and Parmesan potato, as well as
sandwiches and salads. In the restaurant the set-dinner menu
could bring a terrine of Goosnargh chicken, duck confit and
smoked salmon, pan-fried sea bass, fennel confit and mussels
and tiger prawn broth, and finish with hot mango tart with
Cornish clotted cream.

Directions: On B1257

KNARESBOROUGH,
Dower House Hotel ✿

Bond End HG5 9AL
Map 8: SE35
Tel: 01423 863302
Fax: 01423 867665
Cost: *Alc* £22, set-price L £11.75 (4
courses)/D £21.50 (5 courses). ☺
H/wine £8.95
Times: D only, 7-9.30pm. Closed Sat
Additional: Bar food; Sunday L (noon-
1.45pm); Children welcome; ✿ dishes
Smoking: No smoking in dining room
Accommodation: 32 en suite ★★★

Candlelit tables provide an intimate setting for dinner, and the
carefully prepared dishes feature much local produce. A test meal
produced a rich and full flavoured lobster bisque.

Directions: At Harrogate end of Knaresborough High Street

KNARESBOROUGH,

General Tarleton Inn ❀❀

Boroughbridge Road Ferrensby
HG5 0QB
Map 8: SE35
Tel: 01423 340284
Fax: 01423 340288
Chef: John Topham
Owners: Denis & Juliet Watkins,
John Topham
Cost: Set-price D £25. ☺ H/wine
£9.95
Times: D only, 6-9.30pm. Closed 25
Dec
Additional: Bar food; Sunday L
(Noon-2pm); Children welcome;
🍴 dishes
Seats: 65
Smoking: No smoking in dining room
Accommodation: 14 en suite ★★★

**Popular foodie pub with an informal but welcoming
approach.** Sister restaurant to The Angel at Hetton and the
same solid brand of good modern British cooking in an
informal setting. Regional produce is featured in soufflé of
Yorkshire Blue ewes' cheese with poached pear salad and roast
Vale of York wood pigeon carved onto a potato and mushroom
galette with girolle mushroom sauce. As well as a fresh fish dish
of the day, there are 'exotics' such as shiitake mushroom spring
rolls, plus some lovely old English revivals along the lines of
slow-cooked salt beef brisket with winter roots, pearl barley
broth and spinach dumplings. Melting chocolate pudding with
vanilla ice-cream, and rhubarb and custard – sorbet, compote
and deep-fried custard – feature amongst a strong dessert
menu. A good-value 'Early Bird' menu caters for all tastes with
terrine of ham shank and foie gras with Cumberland sauce and
West coast fish and chips with mushy peas.

Directions: A1M/Boroughbridge Junction. Follow A6065
(Knaresborough) for 3 miles to Ferrensby

LEYBURN, Foresters Arms ❀

*Flagstone floors, low creaking beams and roaring fires are part and
parcel of this delightful Yorkshire inn. So too is the high standard of
food: dishes such as crab pancakes with oyster sauce and breast of
chicken with pancetta and mushrooms. Desserts are sumptuous.*

Smoking: No-smoking area. **Accommodation:** 3 en suite

Directions: Off A684, 5 miles S of Leyburn

Carlton-in-Coverdale
DL8 4BB
Map 7: SE19
Tel/Fax: 01969 640272
Cost: *Alc* £23.50. ☺ H/wine £9.60
Times: Noon-2pm/7-9.30pm. Closed
D Sun, all Mon, Jan
Additional: Bar food L; Sunday L;
Children welcome; 🍴 dishes

MALTON, Burythorpe House Hotel ❀

*The restaurant offers plenty of choice from two menus. Good use is
made of local produce and fish features prominently. Fillet of turbot
on red onion salsa was a highlight.*

Smoking: No smoking in dining room
Accommodation: 11 en suite ★★★

Directions: Edge of Burythorpe village, 4 miles S of Malton

Burythorpe YO17 9LB
Map 8: SE77
Tel: 01653 658200
Fax: 01653 658204
Cost: *Alc* £20, set-price L £12.75/D
£17.50. ☺ H/wine £9.20
Times: Noon-1.15pm/7-9.30pm
(Reservations only)
Additional: Sunday L; Children 7+;
🍴 dishes

MARKINGTON,
Hob Green Hotel

Country house-style restaurant with a patio overlooking the valley. Fish is well represented on the two menus and a Thai herb-smoked salmon is recommended.

Smoking: No smoking in dining room
Accommodation: 12 en suite ★ ★ ★

Directions: One mile W of village off A61

Harrogate HG3 3PJ
Map 8: SE26
Tel: 01423 770031
Fax: 01423 771589
Cost: *Alc* £28, fixed price L £14.95/D £21.50. ☺ H/wine £10.95
Times: Noon-1.30pm/7-9.30pm
Additional: Bar Food L; Sunday L; Children welcome; 🍃 dishes

MIDDLEHAM,
Millers House Hotel

Sea bass with zingy couscous and lemon pepper sauce, or guinea fowl with whisky and walnut sauce, are some lively ideas that lift the cooking above the norm. Confidently prepared desserts include classics such as lemon tart and banana parfait.

Accommodation: 6 en suite ★ ★

Directions: A1 & A684 (Bedale & Leyburn). At Leyburn turn L to Middleham

DL8 4NR
Map 7: SE18
Tel: 01969 622630
Fax: 01969 623570
Cost: Set-price D £20.50. ☺ H/wine £5
Times: D only, 7-8.30pm. Closed Jan
Additional: Children 10+; 🍃 dishes
Smoking: No smoking in dining room

MIDDLEHAM, # Waterford House

Kirkgate DL8 4PG
Map 7: SE18
Tel: 01969 622090
Fax: 01969 624020
Chef: Everyl M Madell
Owners: Everyl & Brian Madell
Cost: *Alc* £27, set-price L £19.50/D £22.50 (both 4 courses). ☺ H/wine £9.50
Times: L by prior arrangement/7-10pm
Additional: Sunday L; Children welcome; 🍃 dishes
Seats: 20
Smoking: No smoking in dining room
Accommodation: 5 en suite ★

Historic restaurant-with rooms just off the village square.
The house may present a modest façade, but within it is a veritable Aladdin's cave of posh bijouterie with vast amounts of highly polished silver and a collection of every conceivable device for opening, handling. pouring or decanting wine: with a list of over 1,000 classical wines, impeccably catalogued, Mr Madell marks himself as a wine lover and will happily open most bottles for one glass. Mrs Madell has many fans for her sound country cooking and her short five-course menus offer the likes of deep-fried seafood platter with aïoli, casserole of local pheasant in a cream and Calvados sauce, or fillet of salmon and halibut with olive mash and beurre blanc sauce with ginger. The size of the dining room reflects its previous use, as a lounge, and has a cosy, intimate feel.

Directions: Just off Market Square

MIDDLESBROUGH,
The Purple Onion

Influenced by the brasseries of Les Halles in Paris, with bits of New York and San Francisco thrown in. This busy, bustling establishment is full of interest; gilded mirrors, Tiffany lamps, ornate brass ceiling fans, parlour palms and even a 30-foot long zinc bar. While the atmosphere is informal, the kitchen takes its job seriously. Our most recent meal began with a soup of the day that was 'a superb concoction of tomato and roast pepper with deep colour and full flavour' and finished with a 'delightful' ginger and banana terrine wrapped with molasses sponge on a coffee bean sauce. Other offerings included a sweet potato, vanilla and marjoram risotto from the pasta and risotto section (offered either as first or main courses), a range of vegetarian dishes, chargrilled steaks and the likes of rack of lamb on pea purée with Poire William and juniper berry sauce. Boards list the day's fish dishes.

Directions: Exit A66 at Hospitality Inn near Riverside Football Stadium. Restaurant centrally located nr Law Courts/Odeon Cinema

80 Corporation Road TS1 2RF
Map 8: NZ41
Tel: 01642 222250
Fax: 01642 248088
Chefs: Graeme Benn, Bruno McCoy, Tony Chapman
Owners: Bruno & John McCoy
Times: Noon-2.30pm/6-10.30pm. Closed D Sun, 25 Dec
Additional: Bar food L; Sunday L; Children welcome; 🍴 dishes
Seats: 80
Smoking: No-smoking area; Air conditioning

MOULTON, **Black Bull Inn** 🌸

Dine in the traditional bar, colonial conservatory or a 1932 Pullman coach from the Brighton Belle and enjoy sound cooking with an emphasis on quality fresh fish, game and offal.

Additional: Bar food L; Children 7+; 🍴 dishes
Smoking: Air conditioning

Directions: Off A1M, 1 mile S of Scotch Corner

Richmond DL10 6QJ
Map 8: NZ20
Tel: 01325 377289
Fax: 01325 377422
Cost: *Alc* £25, set-price L £14.95. H/wine £8.50
Times: Noon-2pm/6-10.15pm Closed Sun, 24-26 Dec

PICKERING, **Fox & Hounds** 🌸

Traditional coaching inn with a menu of familiar favourites such as home-made steak and Guinness pie, battered Whitby scampi, mixed grill and vanilla cheesecake with toffee brandy sauce.

Additional: Bar food; Sunday L; Children 5+; 🍴 dishes
Smoking: No smoking in dining room
Accommodation: 10 en suite ★ ★

Directions: In centre of Sinnington, 300 yards off A170 between Pickering and Helmsley

Main Street Sinnington York YO62 6SQ
Map 8: SE78
Tel: 01751 431577
Fax: 01751 432791
Cost: *Alc* £20. H/wine £9.95
Times: Noon-2pm/6.30-8.45pm. Closed D 25-26 Dec

PICKERING, **White Swan** 🌸

Early 16th-century coaching inn offering a good range of well-prepared food (including bar meals). The restaurant carte may list halibut with truffle mousse and lemon butter sauce, and confit of duck and white bean cassoulet.

Additional: Sunday L; Children welcome; 🍴 dishes
Smoking: No smoking in dining room
Accommodation: 12 en suite ★ ★

Directions: Between the church and steam railway station

Market Place YO18 7AA
Map 8: SE78
Tel: 01751 472288
Fax: 01751 475554
Cost: *Alc* £20. ☺ H/wine £11.95
Times: Noon-2pm/7-9pm

RAMSGILL,

Yorke Arms

Heritage building keeping up great traditions. Pewter, beams, open fires, antique furniture: what could be more appropriate for a stone-built creeper-covered building that has been an inn for over 150 years and before that was a shooting lodge owned by the Yorke family? The menus manage successfully to combine the metropolitan with tradition, so Thai-spiced fishcakes, pasta with chilli could be listed alongside game pie with mash and greens. Or you could start with Swiss potato cake with smoked bacon and Parmesan, go on to venison steak in port sauce with celeriac and wild mushrooms, and end with Yorkshire curd tart with rum custard, while the savoury-toothed could try Welsh rarebit or a glass of port with a selection of Yorkshire cheese. Breads are made in-house (try a bacon and tomato bap), as are ice creams and sorbets, and you can pop in for home-made cake and biscuits for afternoon tea.

Directions: Take B6265 from Ripon. Turn R in Pateley Bridge for Ramsgill

Pateley Bridge HG3 5RL
Map 7: SE17
Tel: 01423 755243
Fax: 01423 755330
Chef: Mrs Frances Atkins
Owners: Gerald & Frances Atkins
Cost: *Alc* £25. ☺ H/wine £11
Times: Noon-1.45pm/7-8.45pm.
Closed D Sun (to non-residents)
Additional: Bar food; Sunday L;
Children welcome; ⏛ dishes
Seats: 70. Private dining room 20
Smoking: No smoking in dining room
Accommodation: 13 en suite ★ ★

ROSEDALE ABBEY,

Milburn Arms

Pickering YO18 8RA
Map 8: SE79
Tel/Fax: 01751 417312
Chef: Stephen Turner
Owners: Terry & Joan Bentley
Cost: *Alc* £24. ☺ H/wine £8.95
Times: D only, 7-9.30pm. Closed 25,
26 Dec
Additional: Bar food; Sunday L (noon-
2.15pm); Children 8+; ⏛ dishes
Seats: 60
Smoking: No smoking in dining room
Accommodation: 11 en suite ★ ★

Charming hotel (with parts dating from the 15th century) that has the atmosphere of a village inn. Rosedale Abbey features only the ruined bell tower of a priory these days, but its peaceful setting, tucked in a fold of the dramatic North Yorkshire Moors, makes this heart-of-the-village hotel overlooking the green a popular weekend retreat. Dinner in the split-level restaurant is a smart affair. Begin, perhaps with wood pigeon and foie gras ravioli with baby leeks and roasted garlic jus. Main courses are equally inventive: roast mullet with olive crust, potato and basil purée and roasted sweet peppers, for example, or seared fillet of beef with calves' liver and red onion on horseradish jus. Sticky toffee pudding with caramel sauce gets back to basics nicely. Lengthy wine list that keeps a keen eye on price; reasonable selection by the glass and half-bottle.

Directions: In village centre, 3 miles W of A170 at Pickering

SCARBOROUGH, Wrea Head Hotel

Scalby YO13 0PB
Map 8: TA08
Tel: 01723 378211
Fax: 01723 355936
Cost: *Alc* £17.50, set-price L
£12.50/D £25 (4 courses). H/wine
£11.95
Times: Noon-1.45pm/7-9.15pm
Additional: Bar food L; Sunday L;
Children welcome; 🍴 dishes
Smoking: No smoking in dining room
Accommodation: 20 en suite ★ ★ ★

Directions: Take A171 N from
Scarborough, past Scalby village until
hotel is signposted

*Country house hotel with an elegant dining room. Aubergine and
pepper terrine with local feta cheese, and noisettes of lamb with an
apricot and olive stuffing have both been well reported.*

SKIPTON, Devonshire Arms

**Country house hotel that takes its name from the Dukes of
Devonshire, who own the Wharfedale estate on which it was
built as a coaching inn.** Many items of furniture and paintings
have been provided by the present Duke and Duchess, which
gives some indication of the style and quality to expect. Eating
in the brasserie is a relaxed affair where you can mix and
match, while the Burlington Restaurant is an altogether more
refined experience. The kitchen abounds with ideas, from a
starter of ravioli of monkfish and mussels with tomato coulis
and tapenade to main courses of breast of guinea fowl with a
confit of the leg with cep risotto, wilted greens and Parmesan
cream, or anise-marinated salmon served with lemongrass,
scented rice and ginger beurre blanc. Plums could surface in a
pudding of tarte Tatin with vanilla ice cream, with warm
chocolate fondant maybe an alternative.

Bolton Abbey BD23 6AJ
Map 7: SD95
Tel: 01756 710441
Fax: 01756 710564
Chef: Andrew Nicholson
Owners: The Duke & Duchess of
Devonshire
Cost: Set-price L £18.95/D £37 (5
courses). H/wine £14.25
Times: D only, 7-10pm. Closed Xmas
Additional: Bar food; Sunday L (noon-
2.30pm); Children welcome; 🍴 dishes
Seats: 70. Private dining room 100.
Jacket & tie preferred
Smoking: No smoking in dining room
Accommodation: 41 en suite ★ ★ ★

Directions: On B6160 to Bolton Abbey, 250 yards N of A59
roundabout junction

SKIPTON,
Hanover International Hotel

*Set beside a canal and overlooking gentle hills, the Waterside
Restaurant serves from a short but varied menu: leek and potato
soup, perhaps or escalopes of salmon on flash-fried tomato, and
tournedos of beef on wild mushrooms.*

Keighley Road Snaygill
BD23 2TA
Map 7: SD95
Tel: 01756 700100
Fax: 01756 700107
Telephone for further details

Directions: From M62 J26 onto M606, follow signs for A650
(Keighley), then A629 (Skipton). Hotel 1 mile S of town centre

STADDLEBRIDGE,
McCoys (Tontine Inn)

**An excellent place for bistro-style food in idiosyncratic
surroundings.** There's a colonial French feel to eating in the

Northallerton DL6 3JB
Map 8: SE49
Tel: 01609 882671
Fax: 01609 882660

atmospheric basement bistro: thirties accordion tunes provide background and the heady smell of cooking wafts in from the kitchen. The menu provides an extensive choice of dishes. Our inspection got off to a good start with a toasted muffin topped with an excellent combination of poached egg and chorizo. Then a 'fresh-flavoured' tuna steak, served 'deliciously pink', with roasted aubergines, sweet peppers and sun-dried tomatoes. For dessert, a 'superb' blackcurrant Bakewell tart came with bitter-sweet marmalade ice cream. Our verdict – the food is excellent. The wonderfully distinctive restaurant is open for dinner on Friday and Saturday only.

Directions: At the junction of A19 & A172

Chef: Marcus Bennett
Owners: McCoy Brothers
Cost: Alc £28
Times: Bistro noon-2pm, 7-9.30pm (earlybird menu 6.45-8pm).
Restaurant D only, 7-9.30pm, Fri, Sat only
Additional: Children welcome; dishes
Seats: 30. Private dining room 25
Smoking: Air conditioning
Accommodation: 6 en suite

WEST WITTON,
Wensleydale Heifer Inn ✥

Traditional inn with upbeat menu. Goats' cheese and red onion tart, calves' liver and bacon with a sage butter, and chocolate mousse with crisp almond tuile set a cracking pace.

Additional: Bar food; Sunday L; Children welcome; dishes
Accommodation: 15 en suite ★ ★

Directions: From Leyburn take A684 towards Hawes. 4 miles to West Witton, inn on R

Wensleydale DL8 4LS
Map 8: SE08
Tel: 01969 622322
Fax: 01969 624183
Cost: Set-price L £14.50/D £23.50. ☺
H/wine £9.25
Times: Noon-2pm/6.30-9.30pm

WHITBY, # Lavinia House ✥   NEW

The dining room of this Victorian guest house has been transformed into an intimate restaurant and attracts a loyal local following. Vegetarian dishes are a strong feature.

Smoking: No smoking in dining room
Accommodation: 5 rooms

Directions: Telephone for directions

3 East Crescent YO21 3HD
Map 8: NZ81
Tel: 01947 602945/820656
Cost: Set-price D £21 (4 courses). ☺
H/wine £7.50
Times: D only, 7.30-8.30pm. Closed Sun, Mon, Thu
Additional: Children 14+; dishes

YARM, # Judges Hotel ✥

Kirklevington TS15 9LW
Map 8: NZ41
Tel: 01642 789000
Fax: 01642 782878
Telephone for further details

Directions: From A69 take A67 towards Kirklevington, hotel 1.5 miles on left.

Set among beautiful gardens and parkland, this former judges' lodging has been restored to its former glory. In the restaurant you may sample asparagus with caraway and nutmeg porridge, chicken breast coq au vin, and soufflé with ice cream and pistachio nuts.

YORK, Ambassador ❀

125 The Mount YO2 2DA
Map 8: SE65
Tel: 01904 641316
Fax: 01904 640259
Cost: *Alc* £25, set-price L £10.50/D
£19.50. ☺ H/wine £9.50
Times: 12.30-2pm/6.30pm-9.30pm
Additional: Children welcome;
🍴 dishes
Smoking: No smoking in dining room
Accommodation: 25 en suite ★ ★ ★

Directions: 5 minutes walk from city
centre, near junction of A1036 and
A59

*Spacious, elegant setting (grand piano included) for interesting
contemporary cooking. Deep-fried crab parcel wrapped in seaweed
and pan-fried marlin on noodles with minestrone sauce may be
among the more unusual choices.*

YORK, Dean Court Hotel ❀

Duncombe Place YO1 7EF
Map 8: SE65
Tel: 01904 625082
Fax: 01904 620305
Cost: *Alc* £28, set-price L £11 (2
courses)/D £23.50. ☺ H/wine £10.65
Times: 12.30-2pm/7-9.30pm
Additional: Bar food; Sunday L;
Children 6+ at D; 🍴 dishes
Smoking: No smoking in dining room
Accommodation: 39 en suite ★ ★ ★

Directions: City centre, directly
opposite York Minster

*Victorian hotel standing in the shadow of York Minster. Expect a
seasonally-changing menu which may feature seafood chowder,
lamb cutlets with roast garlic, and baked chocolate fondant.*

YORK, The Grange Hotel ❀❀

1 Clifton YO30 6AA
Map 8: SE65

Bustling city hotel furnished in country-house style. Public
areas include a sunny morning room, an attractive first-floor
drawing room and library, a seafood bar with a mural of York
racecourse, a popular brasserie in the brick-vaulted cellars, and
the elegant Ivy Restaurant. Here you can order from the set-
price menus or from the *carte:* intensely flavoured and
brilliantly clear tomato consommé with avocado and cherry
tomatoes, or Caesar salad, 'one of the best I've sampled this
year, 'then a well flavoured rack of lamb with a polenta cake
and ratatouille, or seared sea bass with olive oil mash and sauce
vierge. To finish, there might be sweet and sticky banana tarte
Tatin with rum and raisin sauce, or steamed chocolate pudding
with a gooey centre. Petits fours are served with coffee, and the
wine list is a comprehensive collection from around the world.

The Grange Hotel

Tel: 01904 644744
Fax: 01904 612453
Chef: David Bates
Owner: Mr J Cassel
Cost: *Alc* £29, set-price L £11.50/D £25. H/wine £10
Times: Noon-2pm/7-10pm. Closed L Sat, L Sun
Additional: Children welcome; dishes
Seats: 35. Private dining room 60
Smoking: No pipes & cigars
Accommodation: 30 en suite ★ ★ ★

Directions: 400 yds to N of city walls on A19

YORK,

Knavesmire Manor Hotel

The brasserie provides the perfect setting for some lively food at this popular hotel overlooking the racecourse. Lamb shank, tender and full of flavour, was an inspection highlight.

Additional: Sunday L (noon-2.30pm); Children welcome; dishes
Smoking: No smoking in dining room
Accommodation: 21 en suite ★ ★

302 Tadcaster Road YO2 2HE
Map 8: SE65
Tel: 01904 702941
Fax: 01904 709274
Cost: Set-price D £15. ☺ H/wine £9.50
Times: D only, 6-15pm.

Directions: A64 to York, then A1036 York-Bishopthorpe leads on to Tadcaster Rd. Hotel on left overlooking racecourse

YORK, Melton's Restaurant

7 Scarcroft Road YO23 1ND
Map 8: SE65
Tel: 01904 634341
Fax: 01904 635115
Chefs: Michael Hjort, Adam Holliday
Owners: Michael & Lucy Hjort
Cost: *Alc* £24, set-price L £15/D £19.50. ☺ H/wine £11.50
Times: Noon-2pm/5.30-10pm. Closed L Mon, D Sun, 1 wk Aug, 3 wks Xmas

An inviting, personally run shop-fronted restaurant in an attractive Victorian terraces. Colourful prints by local artists adorn the deep coral pink walls, giving the restaurant a bright, friendly feel. The style of cooking is best described as Anglo/French, so expect dishes along the lines of medley of seafish with garlic and rosemary. Our meal hit the spot with a coarse ham and tongue terrine served with a salad verde and a bowl of roughly-cut home-made bread, a perfectly roasted 'bright white' halibut served on a five spice and sweet pepper vinaigrette ('which gave the whole dish a very fresh Mediterranean feel'). To finish, a 'brilliant' apple and Calvados soufflé 'cooked to perfection'. A discount is offered to early evening diners who don't mind leaving by 7.45pm. The wine list is wide-ranging and keenly priced – mark-ups are limited to a maximum of £10 making the more expensive wines the better deal.

Directions: From centre head south across Skeldergate Bridge, restaurant opposite Bishopthorpe Road car park

Additional: Sunday L; Children welcome; ✿ dishes
Seats: 30. Private dining room 16
Smoking: No-smoking area

AA Wine Award-see page 16 Shortlisted for

YORK,

Middlethorpe Hall ✿✿✿

Bishopthorpe Road Middlethorpe
YO23 2GB
Map 8: SE65
Tel: 01904 641241
Fax: 01904 620176
Chef: Martin Barker
Owner: Historic House Hotels
Cost: Set-price L £17.50/D £32. H/wine £13
Times: 12.30-1.45pm/7-9.45pm. Closed 25 Dec (non-residents)
Additional: Sunday L; Children 8+; ✿ dishes
Seats: 60. Private room 50. Jacket & tie preferred
Smoking: No smoking in dining room
Accommodation: 30 en suite ★ ★ ★

Built in 1699 – a splendid country house whose restored parkland includes a white garden, ha-has and a small lake. There's much to admire inside, too, not least an oak-panelled dining room looking over the gardens. Traditional elements surface on the menus – roast fillet of beef with creamed spinach and wild mushrooms, and roast breast of Goosnargh duck with a confit of the leg and glazed turnips – but the kitchen is equally confident with the mores of the day, as in a starter of pan-fried red mullet with a saffron and mussel risotto and pesto, or a main-course roast fillet of pork with cep polenta. As an inspector was dithering over which bread to go for, an *amuse-bouche* arrived: 'beautifully cooked' cod fillet, the fish 'as fresh as a daisy', on stir-fried vegetables. A starter of roast sweetbreads – delicate and tender – wrapped in prosciutto, topped with a slice of black truffle, and on crushed new potatoes and peeled broad beans, was followed by sautéed fillets of dorado on red pepper risotto, the fish properly cooked and well matched by the richness of the rice, a slice of roasted aubergine under the fish to give extra texture. The finale was intensely flavoured signature roast pineapple filled with unctuous coconut crème brûlée, passion fruit sauce mixing deliciously with the filling. The wine list is a master of its type, helpfully annotated, with a page of sommelier's choices and a handful of house wines.

Signature dishes: mille-feuille of roast scallops and foie gras with baby leeks and an apple bouillon; roast turbot with a purée of Puy lentils, confit garlic and cep sauce.

Directions: 1.5 miles S of York, next to the racecourse

YORK,

Mount Royale Hotel

Delightfully furnished restaurant offering a wide choice of dishes featuring plenty of local produce. The highlight of a recent meal was a deeply flavoured lobster bisque.

The Mount YO2 2DA
Map 8: SE65
Tel: 01904 628856
Fax: 01904 611171
Telephone for further details

Directions: On The Mount (A1036) leading SW out of the city

YORK,

York Pavilion Hotel

45 Main Street Fulford YO1 4PJ
Map 8: SE65
Tel: 01904 622099
Fax: 01904 626939
Chef: David Spencer
Owners: Andrew & Irene Cossins
Cost: Alc £30, set-price L £30. ☺
H/wine £12
Times: Noon-2pm/6.30-9.30pm
Additional: Sunday L; Children 12+;
🍴 dishes
Seats: 80. Private dining rooms 2/150
Smoking: No-smoking area; No pipes
& cigars
Accommodation: 44 en suite ★★★

Brasserie-style restaurant in an attractive Georgian hotel.
The menu changes every six weeks and includes daily market specials. The chef has a spring in his step, judging by an upbeat inspection dinner that began with crab and ginger spring rolls, notable for excellent filo and the depth of flavour with just the right hint of ginger. This was followed by bright white monkfish on lemony mash served with seared Parma ham and a light gazpacho dressing, plus a good plate of steaming vegetables. Super banana tarte Tatin with caramel sauce and nutmeg ice cream sent our inspector happily up the apples and pears to bed.

Directions: From York city centre head S on A19 (Selby), hotel 2 miles on L

YORKSHIRE SOUTH

BARNSLEY, Armstrongs

102 Dodworth Road S70 6HL
Map 8: SE30
Tel: 01226 240113
Chef: Nick Pound
Owners: Nick Pound & Deborah Swift
Cost: Set-price D £30 (4 courses). H/wine £12.50
Times: D only, 7-9.30pm. Closed Sun, Mon, 2 wks summer
Additional: Children welcome; ♨ dishes
Seats: 50
Smoking: No pipes & cigars

The detached Victorian house has been effectively updated in pale yellow with charcoal and indigo striped drapes and parquet flooring. This light informality is reflected in the cooking – seared king scallops with saffron sauce, and tempura of monkfish with salad leaves and chilli coriander dressing are modern-look starters. Simplicity rules the day and dishes such as free-range Bresse chicken with pancetta, and noisettes of lamb with garlic sauté potatoes and sauce nivernaise make a virtue out of good ingredients. An interesting, almost renaissance twist is given to roast haunch of venison by serving it with sweet'n'sour Sicilian aubergine, spinach, fried onion and carrot crisps. Desserts allow the kitchen's imagination to take wing – caramelised Italian rice cake with boozy fruit compote and hazelnut crème fraîche draws the eye irresistibly. And how about tequila orange segments with chocolate chilli ice-cream and 'jalebis'? At least they're daring to be different.

Directions: 1 mile from M1 J37. Take A625 towards Barnsley, on R

CHAPELTOWN, Greenhead House

84 Burncross Road Sheffield S35 1SF
Map 8: SK39
Tel/Fax: 0114 2469004
Cost: Alc £30, set-price L £12. H/wine £11
Times: Noon-1pm/7-9pm. Closed Sun-Wed, L Sat, Xmas & New Year, 2 wks Easter, 2 wks mid Aug

A 300-year-old stone-built house with a delightful walled garden in a Sheffield suburb. Enjoyable dishes include tender veal with potato rösti, and crème brûlée with pistachio nuts.

Additional: Children 7+
Smoking: No smoking in dining room

Directions: M1 J35 follow signs to Chapeltown, straight across 2 roundabouts onto Burncross Rd. Restaurant is on R, 200m

ROTHERHAM, Swallow Hotel

West Bawtry Road S60 4NA
Map 8: SK49
Tel: 01709 830630
Fax: 01709 830549
Cost: Alc £24, set-price L £12.50/D £19 (4 courses). ☺ H/wine £12
Times: Noon-1.45pm/6.30-9.30pm. Closed L Sat

Modern restaurant in contemporary colours. The new concept menu has a Mediterranean feel with a choice of portion size, while traditional favourites are retained on the daily set menu.

Additional: Bar food L; Sunday L; Children welcome; ♨ dishes
Smoking: No smoking in dining room; Air conditioning
Accommodation: 100 en suite ★ ★ ★

Directions: From the M1 J37; the hotel stands on A630, 2 miles from Rotherham centre

SHEFFIELD, Charnwood Hotel

10 Sharrow Lane S11 8AA
Map 8: SK38
Tel: 0114 2589411
Fax: 0114 2555107
Telephone for further details

Leo's Brasserie is the informal restaurant at the Charnwood, once the home of a Georgian master cutler. Knives and forks at the ready for potato and goats' cheese brûlée, poached sea bass with baby leeks and scallops, and chocolate pineapple upside-down cake.

Directions: M1 J33 & A621. 1.5 miles SW of city centre, off London Road

SHEFFIELD, **Harley Hotel**

Redbrick townhouse situated close to the city centre and university campus. A recent meal included fettucine of sea scallops, pan-fried chicken livers, marinated fillet of brill baked in spiced yoghurt, and blackberry Bakewell with vanilla ice cream.

Directions: In University and Teaching Hospitals campus, 0.5 mile from centre on junction of West Street (A57) and Hanover Street (Inner City Ring Road)

334 Glossop Road S10 2HW
Map 8: SK38
Tel: 01142 752288
Fax: 01142 722383
Telephone for further details

SHEFFIELD, **Milano Restaurant**

NEW

Originally a park keeper's Lodge, this Grade II listed building now houses a restaurant whose cooking aims to be at the cutting edge. Much attention has gone into the interior design which, with its polished metal, light wood surfaces and stone murals, has the feel and atmosphere of a trendy London brasserie. The menu comprises a set-menu and a *carte*, the latter includes seven starters and eight main courses, in addition to a plateau de fruits de mer. The kitchen tries hard, but perhaps some of the combinations are a step too far. Nettle and potato soup was a thick purée and rough in texture but had a good peppery flavour. King prawn jambalaya served with soft salt cod, tiny shrimps, chorizo and unpeeled peppers was disappointing. Caramel mousse was technically sound and came with a well-made poppy seed tuile. The wine list offers plenty of reasonably-priced bottles.

Directions: Telephone for directions

Archer Road Millhouses S8 0LA
Map 8: SK38
Tel: 0114 2353080
Fax: 0114 2353010
Chef: Jason Fretwell
Owners: Bohan/Brady Parnership Ltd
Cost: *Alc* £30, set-price D £19.95. ☺ H/wine £9.75
Times: Noon-2.30pm/7-10pm. Closed D Sun
Additional: ⏺ dishes
Seats: 60. Private dining room 30
Smoking: No smoking in dining room; Air conditioning

SHEFFIELD, **Mosborough Hall Hotel**

Fine 16th-century manor house within easy reach of the city centre and M1 J30. Seasonal menus offer the likes of chargrilled scallops with herb salad, and pheasant with beetroot and shallot confit.

Additional: Bar food; Sunday L; Children welcome; ⏺ dishes
Smoking: No-smoking area
Accommodation: 24 en suite ★ ★ ★

Directions: Hotel on A616, 5 miles from M1 J30

High Street S20 5EA
Map 8: SK38
Tel: 0114 2484353
Fax: 0114 2477042
Cost: *Alc* £27, set-price L £11/D £17. ☺ H/wine £9.75
Times: Noon-1.30pm/7.30-9.30pm. Closed L Sat, D Sun

SHEFFIELD, **Rafters Restaurant**

All the food is home-made here, including the bread and ice cream. A particularly popular dish is Bosworths baked apple bread-and-butter pudding with sticky toffee sauce.

Smoking: No pipes & cigars
Credit cards: Amex only

Directions: Telephone for directions

220 Oakbrook Road Nethergreen S11 7ED
Map 8: SK38
Tel: 0114 2304819
Cost: Set-price D £23.95. H/wine £8.90
Times: D only, 7-10pm. Closed Sun, Tue, 1 wk Jan, 1 wk Aug, Bhs
Additional: Children 5+; ⏺ dishes

SHEFFIELD,
Smith's of Sheffield ❀❀❀

34 Sandygate Road S10 5RY
Map 8: SK38
Tel: 0114 2666096
Chef: Richard Smith
Owners: Richard & Victoria Smith,
John & Sallie Tetchner
Cost: *Alc* £25, set-price D £18.50. ☺
H/wine £9.50
Times: D only, 6.30-9.30pm. Closed
Sun, Mon
Additional: Children welcome;
🍴 dishes
Seats: 45. Private dining room 20
Smoking: No smoking in dining room

*Richard Smith is a conscientious, skilled chef and his wife
Victoria has a natural charm well suited to running front of
house.* Part of Richard's success is his use of prime quality
produce, taking it one step further by using rare breed meat
where the flavours are so much more evident. We found a foie
gras and chicken liver parfait to be very successful, freshly
made, a lovely pink colour and with superb texture. Flavours
were well balanced and the use of balsamic and white truffle
oil dressing on accompanying salad leaves gave the dish a lift
and bite, with a touch of sweetness reintroduced through a
good caramelised onion. A very generous portion of sweet
tender lamb shank came next, glazed with honey and studded
with rosemary, good lamb flavours were enhanced by a rich
cooking jus that had the right amount of rosemary flavouring.
Creamy garlic mash teamed with an earthy ragout of Puy
lentils shared the cooking jus. White chocolate brioche bread
pudding was 'a real killer' – a really rich dish, with a velvety
hot chocolate fudge sauce.

Directions: From Sheffield centre take A57; at Crosspool turn R
onto Sandygate Road. 100 yds on R

SHEFFIELD,
Staindrop Hotel ❀

*Delightful family-run hotel offers two short menus both with an
interesting choice. Our latest meal highlighted scallops with orange
and mange-tout salad, veal and calves' liver with a rich sherry sauce,
and bread-and-butter pudding.*

Smoking: No smoking in dining room
Accommodation: 15 en suite ★ ★ ★

Directions: From M1 J35 follow signs to Chapeltown and
Huddersfield; go over 1st roundabout, R at 2nd and hotel is 0.5
mile on R

Lane End S35 3UH
Map 8: SK38
Tel: 0114 2846727
Fax: 0114 2846783
Cost: *Alc* £19, set-price L £9 (2
courses)/D £15 (4 courses). ☺ H/wine
£10
Times: Noon-2.30pm/7-10pm. Closed
D Sun
Additional: Sunday L; Children
welcome; 🍴 dishes

YORKSHIRE
WEST

BRADFORD,

The Quality Hotel Bradford

Bridge Street BD1 1JX
Map 7: SE13
Tel: 01274 728706
Fax: 01274 736358

Refurbished former Victorian railway hotel retaining a wealth of period detail. The informal Vic and Bert's Brasserie offers soundly cooked food. Expect king prawns with sweet chilli oil, and duck with caramelised onions.

Cost: *Alc* £21.30, set-price L £11.50/D £14.50. ☺ H/wine £8.75
Times: Noon-2pm/7-10pm. Closed L Sat & Sun, 26 Dec-2 Jan

Additional: Bar food; Children welcome; ⏻ dishes
Smoking: No-smoking area
Accommodation: 60 en suite ★ ★ ★

Directions: From M606 take 3rd turn at roundabout (A6177). Next roundabout R (A641). End of dual carriageway R at roundabout (Hallings). R at next traffic lights; hotel on L

BRADFORD,

Restaurant Nineteen

19 North Park Road Heaton BD9 4NT
Map 7: SE13
Tel: 01274 492559
Fax: 01274 483827
Chef: Stephen Smith
Owner: John Holland
Cost: *Alc* £28.50, set-price D £12.95. ☺ H/wine £12.50
Times: D only, 7-9.30pm. Closed Sun, Mon
Additional: Children welcome; ⏻ dishes
Seats: 36
Smoking: No pipes & cigars
Accommodation: 4 en suite

Located in an old detached town house in a tree lined avenue in a suburb of Bradford. Five starters, main courses and desserts are on offer, inspired mainly by the Modern British school, including quail with pancetta, apple and spinach, a goats' cheese mousse with tapenade and herb leaf salad, and seared tuna served on hot asparagus, with Jersey Royals in a light poultry jus and a cold salad niçoise on top . Best of all are simple dishes such as the chocolate and pear tart, 'crisp pastry, pears simply poached and unadulterated,' served with a dollop of whipped cream. The wine list has a wide range of decently-priced bottles, some excellent budget choices, as well as some well-established, pricier offerings.

Directions: Take A650 (Manningham Lane) from Bradford. L at Manningham Park gates, then 1st R onto North Park Road

DEWSBURY,
Healds Hall Hotel ✵

A strong local following for dishes such as roast loin of venison with choucroute, juniper berry and port sauce, or grilled sirloin steak with Dijon and peppercorn sauce. Excellent cheeseboard.

Leeds Road Liversedge WF15 6JA
Map 8: SE22
Tel: 01924 409112
Fax: 01924 401895
Cost: *Alc* £22.65, set-price L £12/D £18.50. ☺ H/wine £8.50
Times: Noon-2pm/6.30-9.30pm; Closed L Sat, D Sun, 1 Jan, Bhs
Additional: Bar food L; Sunday L; Children welcome; 🍴 dishes
Smoking: No smoking in dining room; Air conditioning
Accommodation: 25 en suite ★★

Directions: On A62 Leeds/Huddersfield road near M1 J40 and M62 J26-27 (turn right at Swan pub)

HALIFAX,
The Design House ✵

Listed former textile mill with a stylish modern interior. Short menus offer the likes of ham and parsley terrine, and roast corn-fed chicken with chorizo, chickpeas and potatoes.

Smoking: No pipes & cigars; Air conditioning

Directions: From M62 follow signs to Halifax, Dean Clough is signposted (approx 0.5 mile from town centre)

Dean Clough HX3 5AX
Map 7: SE02
Tel: 01422 383242
Fax: 01422 322732
Cost: *Alc* £25, set-price L £12.95/D £14.95. ☺
Times: Noon-2pm/6-10pm. Closed L Sat, D Sun & Mon
Additional: 🍴 dishes

HALIFAX, # Holdsworth House ✵✵

Holdsworth HX2 9TG
Map 7: SE02
Tel: 01422 240024
Fax: 01422 245174
Chef: Garry Saunders
Owners: Gail Moss, Kim Pearson
Cost: *Alc* £25, set-price L £13. ☺ H/wine £10.25
Times: Noon-1.45pm/7-9.30pm. Closed L Sat & Sun, Xmas

Jacobean manor with period features and sympathetic extension; popular for both conferences and weddings. The two dining rooms have a lot of charm with open fireplaces, wood-panelled walls, antique tables and high-backed chairs and the place attracts a good loyal following. Menus are short and are priced at two, three and four courses. Braised duck with lentil terrine, Jerusalem artichoke and thyme soup, butter-grilled turbot with roasted onion and fennel purée, and banana and toffee crumble with honey and vanilla ice cream show the range admirably.

Directions: From Halifax take A629 (Keighley), 2 miles turn R at garage to Holmfield, hotel 1.5 miles on R

Additional: Children welcome; dishes
Seats: 70. Private dining rooms 130. Jacket & tie preferred
Smoking: No smoking in dining room
Accommodation: 40 en suite ★ ★ ★

HAWORTH, Weavers Restaurant

A trio of weavers' cottages with period charm, space, clutter and comfort. The description of the setting reads like the old Hovis ad: a cobbled street in the heart of a hilltop village; the close proximity of the Brontë museum is an added bonus. Colin and Jane Rushworth run a friendly, down-to-earth sort of restaurant and produce satisfying food, much of it sourced locally, which they describe as 'modern and traditional British'. The latter category brings Whitby fisherman's pie that's stuffed with haddock, prawns, cream and lots of rich mashed potato, game pie, or Cumberland sausage with mash and onion gravy. Aubergine soufflé with roast vegetable salad, and local calves' liver with colcannon, crisp bacon and a sharp sauce shows an awareness of metropolitan trends, and an understanding of a lighter approach. Bread is home-baked, puddings take in the likes of bread-and-butter pudding, and their own ice cream.

15 West Lane BD22 8DU
Map 7: SE03
Tel: 01535 643822
Fax: 01535 644832
Chefs/Owners: Jane & Colin Rushworth
Cost: *Alc* £22.50, set-price D £13.50 (not Sat). ☺ H/wine £9.95
Times: D only, 6.30-9pm. Closed Sun & Mon, 1 wk Xmas. 1 wk late June
Seats: 60. Private dining room 15
Smoking: No smoking in dining room; Air conditioning
Accommodation: 3 en suite

Directions: Haworth centre, by Brontë Museum car park

HUDDERSFIELD, The Lodge Hotel

Art nouveau interior meets modish Euro cooking with the likes of roast medallion of Scottish roe deer with rösti potato, port and sultana jus, or sea bass, red mullet and turbot with linguine nero and crayfish butter sauce.

Accommodation: 13 en suite ★ ★

Directions: M62 J24 (Huddersfield), L at 1st lights (Birkby Road) then A629, R after Nuffield Hospital (Birkby Lodge Road), 100 yds on L

48 Birkby Lodge Road Birkby HD2 2BG
Map 7: SE11
Tel: 01484 431001
Fax: 01484 421590
Cost: Set-price L £13.95/D £25 (4 courses). ☺ H/wine £10.95
Times: Noon-1.45pm/7.30-9.45pm. Closed L Sat, D Sun, 26 Dec, 1 Jan
Additional: Sunday L; Children welcome; dishes
Smoking: No smoking in dining room

HUDDERSFIELD, Weavers Shed Restaurant

Former mill with bar lounge extended into the mill owner's house, offering spacious, comfortable surroundings. Stone walls come crammed with loads of framed menu covers from everywhere and there's a whole library of cookery books – Stephen Jackson's passion for food is evident. However, the head chef is Ian McGunnigle, with Jackson acting as pastry chef. Local ingredients play a huge part in the composition of the menu, as can be seen with the inclusion of roast loin of old breed pork (either Tamworth or Gloucester Old Spot according to season) or roast breast of Lunesdale duckling. The restaurant's own kitchen garden provides some vegetables and herbs, and other suppliers get prominent billing on the menu. A modern twist is given to such dishes as steamed Cornish crab dumplings with French beans and ginger soy dressing, or braised lamb shank with wild mushrooms, mashed roots and parsnip crisps. The wine list features some good dessert wines.

Directions: Haworth centre, by Brontë Museum car park

Acre Mills Knowl Road Golcar HD7 4AN
Map 7: SE03
Tel: 01484 654284
Fax: 01484 650980
Chefs: Ian McGunnigle, Robert Jones, Stephen Jackson
Owner: Stephen Jackson
Cost: *Alc* £35, set-price L £13.95 (2 courses). ☺ H/wine £12.95
Times: Noon-2pm/7-10pm. Closed Sun, Mon, 25 Dec, 31 Dec, 1 Jan, Bhs
Additional: Children welcome; dishes
Seats: 40. Private dining room 30
Smoking: No pipes & cigars
Accommodation: 5 en suite

ILKLEY,

Box Tree Restaurant 🏵🏵🏵

35-37 Church Street LS29 9DR
Map 7: SE14
Tel: 01943 608484
Fax: 01943 607186
Chef: Thierry LePrêtre-Granet
Owner: The Box Tree Restaurant
(Ilkley) Ltd
Cost: *Alc* £25, set-price L & D £19.50
(2 courses). ☺ H/wine £14
Times: Noon-2.30pm/7-9.30pm.
Closed D Sun, all Mon, Xmas-New
Year, last 2 wks Jan
Additional: Children welcome;
🍴 dishes
Seats: 50. Private dining room 16
Smoking: No smoking in dining room

Famous restaurant still living up to its reputation. The white-fronted house comes with a pretty front garden and stained glass windows. Within, the colours are rich (burgundy predominates), and the style quite opulent – paintings cover the wall 'even in the ladies', and tables are set with solid silver and Riedel glasses. Proprietor Mrs Avis is also passionate about organic food, everything is carefully sourced, is of the highest quality and ably interpreted by her chef Thierry LePrêtre-Granet who reveals great respect for his materials. Our inspector was full of praise for a perfectly executed terrine of duck foie gras with prunes, for roasted sea bass that was well-timed and crisp-skinned, served on top of wild mushrooms with steamed potatoes and fresh English asparagus, and for a clafoutis of cherries accompanied by a chocolate sorbet and vanilla ice cream. Everything the kitchen undertakes is done very well, as can be witnessed by breads – white, brown and walnut – straight from the oven, excellent canapés and chocolate truffles served with coffee (seven varieties of beans all ground to order). The wine list is extensive with over 800 bins. Mrs Avis is not only a fanatic on the subject but very knowledgeable.

Signature dishes: sautéed Cornish scallops served with fruit chutney and lemongrass; cutlet of lamb with sweetbread farce, potato galette and tomato and rosemary sauce; dark chocolate cone with crunchy sesame tuile and passion fruit coulis.

Directions: On A65, on the Skipton side of Ilkley near the church

ILKLEY,

Rombalds Hotel 🏵🏵

Elegant Georgian terrace hotel on the edge of Ilkley Moor with high standards of hospitality. Past promise in the kitchen has been fully realised this year. A feel for modern trends and a commitment to fresh produce was evident in an early spring meal. 'Delightful' home-made vol-au-vents filled with an excellent parfait and salmon mousse were served in the bar, and an appetiser of deep-fried potato cake with cheese and leeks, served at table, opened proceedings on a high note. Tender breast of pigeon marinated in lime and coriander and

11 West View Wells Road
LS29 9JG
Map 7: SE14
Tel: 01943 603201
Fax: 01943 816586
Chef: Andrew Davey
Owners: Colin & Jo Clarkson
Cost: *Alc* £24, set-price L £9.95/D
£12.95. ☺ H/wine £9.75
Times: Noon-2pm/6.30-9.30pm.
Closed 27-31 Dec

Rombalds Hotel

Additional: Bar food; Sunday L; Children welcome; 🍴 dishes
Seats: 35. Private dining room 50
Smoking: No smoking in dining room
Accommodation: 15 en suite ★ ★ ★

Directions: From A65 traffic lights in town, turn up Brook Street, cross The Grove to Wells Road and hotel is 600 yds on L

served on garlic and tomato polenta scored points for presentation as well as flavour. Fresh roasted halibut was outstanding, served with a linguini of oyster mushrooms and tarragon – well chosen ingredients that went well together. A good Key lime pie with a deep-fried vanilla ice cream kept the standard high to the end.

LEEDS,

Brasserie Forty Four 🌸🌸

44 The Calls LS2 7EW
Map 8: SE23
Tel: 0113 2343232
Fax: 0113 2343332
Chef: Jeff Baker
Owner: Michael Gill
Cost: *Alc* £22, set-price L & D £12.95. ☺ H/wine £9.90
Times: Noon-2pm/6.30-10.30pm (11pm Fri, Sat). Closed L Sat, all Sun, Bhs
Additional: Children welcome; 🍴 dishes
Seats: 110. Private dining room 45
Smoking: No pipes & cigars; Air conditioning

Converted grain store in the rejuvenated canal quarter is home to this lively brasserie. The food, a fashionably eclectic mix, covers a good deal of ground as evidenced by deep-fried duck wun-tuns with plum sauce, Turkish spiced aubergines with minted yogurt and coriander, and pork and Bury black pudding terrine with Granny Smith's apple chutney. Main courses are no less diverse: hand-made pizza, Whitby cod on a white bean casserole, paella, and a 'posh pastie' (potted duck and foe gras with Agen prunes and truffled Madeira sauce). Side orders include skin-on fries, olive oil mash and carrot and swede purée. Desserts range from steamed marmalade sponge with English custard to iced banana and rum parfait. The Evening Early Bird menu (order before 7.15pm, vacate table by 8.15pm) and lunchtime specials offer exceptional value.

Directions: From Crown Point Bridge, L past Church, L into High Court Road. On the riverside

LEEDS,
The Fourth Floor Café at Harvey Nichols ✿

107/111 Briggate LS1 6AZ
Map 8: SE23
Tel: 0113 2048000
Fax: 0113 2048080
Cost: *Alc* £25, set-price L £17.50/D £16.50. H/wine £11.95
Times: Noon-3pm/6-10pm (from 7pm Sat). Closed D Mon-Wed, all Sun, 25, 26 Dec, 1 Jan
Additional: ✤ dishes
Smoking: No-smoking area; Air conditioning

Directions: In Harvey Nichols department store

Stylish café and terrace offering stunning views over the rooftops of Leeds. Stylish cooking too. We loved our smooth chicken liver parfait, followed by wonderfully fresh cod with a wild mushroom and herb crust.

LEEDS, # Haley's Hotel ✿✿

Shire Oak Road Headingley LS6 2DE
Map 8: SE23
Tel: 0113 2784446
Fax: 0113 2753342
Chef: Jon Vennell
Owner: John J Appleyard
Cost: *Alc* £26. ☺ H/wine £12.25
Times: D only, 7.15-9.45 pm. Closed D Sun (except residents), 26 Dec-4 Jan
Additional: Sunday L (12.15pm-2pm); Children welcome; ✤ dishes
Seats: 52. Private dining room 24
Smoking: No smoking in dining room; Air conditioning
Accommodation: 29 en suite ★ ★ ★

Directions: On A660 (Leeds/Otley) in Headingley between Yorkshire & HSBC banks

Elegance of a country house plus the range of services required of a modern city hotel. The stone-built Victorian house presides over a quiet, tree-lined cul-de-sac and, what's more, it's nowt but a wicket away from the county cricket ground. Yorkshire's most famous dish, Yorkshire pudding, might appear along with foie gras, aubergine wafers and Guinness sauce to fancy up a grilled fillet of beef, but otherwise the cooking runs along well-polished modern British lines. There is usually a terrine amongst the starters; rabbit and duck confit, perhaps, as well as a salad such as spinach, beetroot and pine nuts with balsamic vinaigrette. A main course of duck breast came with interesting cashew nut dumplings, turned apples and cider-scented jus, and an excellent banana and chocolate pudding with a 'gravy boat' of lovely toffee sauce ensured our meal finished on a winning streak.

LEEDS, **Leeds Marriott**

Dysons Restaurant, a former jewellers, retains the shop counter and many clocks in cases. An extensive range of dishes includes scallops with lentils du pay, and duckling with juniper jus.

Directions: From M1 or M62 follow signs to City Centre, turn into Sovereign St, L at lights, R into NCP car park adjacent to hotel

LS1 6ET
Map 8: SE23
Tel: 0113 2366444
Fax: 0113 2366367
Telephone for further details

LEEDS, **Oulton Hall Hotel**

Seared scallops with red mullet in a citrus jus, and chicken with roasted chestnuts, followed perhaps by sticky toffee apple pudding formed one well-reported meal in the elegantly styled Brontë Restaurant.

Rothwell Lane Oulton LS26 8HN
Map 8: SE23
Tel: 0113 2821000
Fax: 0113 2828066
Cost: *Alc* £32, set-price L £15 (4 courses)/D £23 (4 courses). ☺
Times: 12.30-2pm/7-9.45pm. Closed L Sat
Additional: Sunday L; Children welcome; ✦ dishes
Smoking: No smoking in dining room
Accommodation: 152 en suite
★★★★★

Directions: M62 J30, follow signs to Rothwell

LEEDS,
Pool Court at 42 ✿✿✿

44 The Calls LS2 7EW
Map 8: SE23
Tel: 0113 2444242
Fax: 0113 2343332
Chef: Jeff Baker
Owner: Michael Gill
Cost: Set-price L £19/D £35. H/wine £12.95
Times: Noon-2pm/7-10pm (10.30pm Fri/Sat). Closed L Sat, all Sun, Bhs
Additional: Children welcome; ✦ dishes.

Sophisticated restaurant adjoining the hotel, 42 The Calls.
Although adjoining a hotel, the restaurant is run as a separate entity by Michael Gill. The cool, sophisticated decor of deep blue and white – long blue dress tablecloths overlaid by crisp white linen – with lots of silver and pewter decorative ice buckets, gives way to comfy seating and friendly but very professional staff. There's a French classicism to Jeff Baker's menu, overlaid with modern English ideas, so that a signature 'nage ' of native shellfish might be served with baby bok choi,

root ginger and coriander leaves, or peppered loin of venison accompanied by caramelised shallot soufflé, baby turnips and an aged sherry sauce. There is an easy assurance to much of the cooking, as was noted at our inspection lunch. That meal took in tartare of scallops and salmon with avocado and Oscietra caviar, chargrilled mignon of veal with glazed sweetbreads and saffron risotto, and an assiette of desserts: dark chocolate and Amaretto tart, orange brûlée, fruit parfait, raspberry shortcake, vanilla ice cream.

Signature dishes: 'pot au feu' of Bresse pigeon with potato and foie gras ravioli, fumet of celeriac and thyme; roast partridge on creamed Savoy cabbage with broken chestnuts, potato and truffle beignets and a rich game sauce; spiced winter fruit frangipane, served warm on a mulled wine syrup with a full cream vanilla ice.

Seats: 38
Smoking: No pipes & cigars; Air conditioning

Directions: From M1 follow A61 (Harrogate) into city centre, cross River Aire via Crown Point Bridge. 2nd L at roundabout on to Maude St and you arrive at The Calls

LEEDS, Rascasse

Canal Wharf Water Lane LS11 5BB
Map 8: SE23
Tel: 0113 2446611
Fax: 0113 2440736
Chef: Simon Gueller
Owners: Simon Gueller, Nigel Jolliffe
Cost: *Alc* £28.50, set-price L & early D £17. ☺ H/wine £12
Times: Noon-2pm/6.30-10pm (10.30pm Fri/Sat). Closed L Sat, all Sun, 1 wk after Xmas, Bhs Mon
Additional: Children welcome; ✆ dishes
Seats: 100
Smoking: No pipes & cigars; Air conditioning

Canal-side restaurant with smart, well-trained, knowledgeable staff. Big glass doors open into the restaurant and the first impression is of being on a yacht: polished wood floors, a curved staircase winding up to the bar (with its light snacks menu), a slightly raised level separated by a glass and chrome rail screen. The window tables, which appear to overhang the canal, are always popular. Lemon napery, chairs of cobalt and amethyst fabric, and stunning modern flower displays complete the picture. The regularly changing *carte* marries classic French technique (terrine, ballotine, velouté) with big Mediterranean flavours (saffron risotto, sauce gazpacho, tapenade) backed-up by a pacy lunchtime/early weekday evening fast-track menu. Our inspector, however, opted for the leisurely pace set by first-class risotto of English lobster, breast of chicken -succulent and full of flavour – that had been rolled in powdered morels giving a rich, almost aromatic flavour, and set on top of a silky, fine celeriac cream. To finish, raspberry soufflé came with a good, tart raspberry sauce. 'I really liked this place and would certainly use it if I lived here,' was a heartfelt conclusion. There's a splendid selection of half-bottles and plenty by the glass on a well annotated wine list that takes in most of the wine producing countries of the world. Prices are keen.

Directions: 0.5 mile from M621 J3; follow signs to City Centre, turn L Water Lane, then R on Canal Wharf. On Canal Basin. 4 min walk from railway station

LEEDS, **Shear's Yard** ✤

The Calls LS2 7EY
Map 8: SE23
Tel: 0113 2444144
Fax: 0113 2448102
Cost: *Alc* £20. ☺ H/wine £9.95
Times: Noon-2.30pm/6-10.30pm.
Closed Sun, Bh Mon, 1 wk Xmas
Additional: Bar food; Children
welcome; ❹ dishes
Smoking: No-smoking area; No pipes
& cigars; Air conditioning

Dine alfresco on the terrace, perhaps listening to live jazz, or in the light and spacious interior of this former sheep shearing shed. A fun place to eat with some sound cooking too, ranging from good-value tapas to rack of lamb with rosemary jus, or confit of duck with creamy mash and Madeira sauce.

Directions: From M1 follow A61 (Harrogate) into city centre, cross Crown Point Bridge then L onto inner city loop. At J14 restaurant is on R

RIPPONDEN,
Over the Bridge Restaurant ✤

Millfold HX6 4DJ
Map 8: SE23
Tel: 01422 823722
Fax: 01422 824810
Cost: *Alc* £24.50. ☺ H/wine £12.50
Times: D only, 7.30-9.30pm. Closed
Sun, Mon, Bhs
Additional: Children 10+; ❹ dishes
Smoking: No pipes & cigars

The kitchen at this well-established village restaurant continues to produce good, honest dishes using prime ingredients: soufflé of the day – courgette, say, on creamy cheese sauce – tender rack of local lamb with a red onion and rosemary gravy, and chocolate tart with Amaretto cream.

Directions: M62 J22(E)/J24(W), A58 from Halifax, in village centre by church

WENTBRIDGE,

Wentbridge House Hotel ✿

WF8 3JJ
Map 8: SE41
Tel: 01977 620444
Fax: 01977 620148
Cost: *Alc* £29, set-price L
£14.50/D £21. ☺ H/wine £12.50
Times: 12.30-2pm/7.30-9.30pm.
Closed D 25 Dec
Additional: Sunday L; Children
welcome; ♨ dishes
Smoking: No pipes in dining room
Accommodation: 19 en suite ★ ★ ★

Directions: 0.5 mile off the A1, 4
miles S of M62/A1 interchange

*The Fleur de Lys restaurant, as it name suggests, offers classical
French cooking (confit of duck, halibut with lobster sauce;
individual apple tart) in keeping with the wood-panelled decor and
formal polished service.*

WETHERBY, **Wood Hall Hotel**

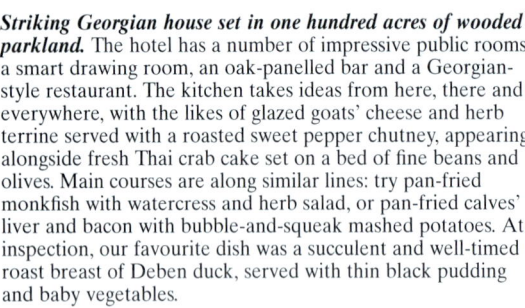

Trip Lane Linton LS22 4JA
Map 8: SE44
Tel: 01937 587271
Fax: 01937 584353
Chef: Phillip Pomfret
Cost: Set-price L £15.95/D £29.95.
H/wine £11.95
Times: Noon-2pm/7-10pm. Closed
L Sat
Additional: Bar food; Sunday L;
Children welcome; ♨ dishes
Seats: 35. Private dining rooms 25
Smoking: No smoking in dining room
Accommodation: 43 en suite ★ ★ ★

Directions: In town, take turning
opposite Windmill pub signed Wood
Hall and Linton

**Striking Georgian house set in one hundred acres of wooded
parkland.** The hotel has a number of impressive public rooms:
a smart drawing room, an oak-panelled bar and a Georgian-
style restaurant. The kitchen takes ideas from here, there and
everywhere, with the likes of glazed goats' cheese and herb
terrine served with a roasted sweet pepper chutney, appearing
alongside fresh Thai crab cake set on a bed of fine beans and
olives. Main courses are along similar lines: try pan-fried
monkfish with watercress and herb salad, or pan-fried calves'
liver and bacon with bubble-and-squeak mashed potatoes. At
inspection, our favourite dish was a succulent and well-timed
roast breast of Deben duck, served with thin black pudding
and baby vegetables.

CHANNEL ISLANDS
GUERNSEY

CATEL, **Cobo Bay Hotel**

Popular family-run hotel overlooking Cobo Bay on the glorious west coast of Guernsey. Guests return year after year to watch spectacular sunsets from their balconies, and to enjoy modern European cooking in the candlelit dining room. A mid-winter meal kicked off with salmon tartare with thin slices of beetroot drizzled with balsamic vinegar. Roast breast of fresh goose followed, carved onto an apple and prune compote and served with a rich ruby port jus. Desserts are from the trolley and could include rosewater meringue or apricot and sultana steamed pudding. The short wine list is mainly French, with an emphasis on well-known brands.

Directions: First turn L from hotel, approximately 3 miles to St Peter Port

Cobo GY5 7HB
Map: 16
Tel: 01481 57102
Fax: 01481 54542
Chef: John Chapman
Owner: David Nussbaumer
Cost: *Alc* £20, set-price D £18.95 (4 courses). ☺ H/wine £7.95
Times: D only, 7-9.30pm
Additional: Bar food; Sunday L (noon-2pm); Children welcome; 🍴 dishes
Seats: 110. Private dining room 30
Smoking: No pipes & cigars; Air conditioning
Accommodation: 36 en suite ★★★

CATEL, **La Grand Mare Hotel**

Modern, purpose-built hotel set in extensive grounds with views over the Atlantic. Light lunches are served in the conservatory but the main action is in the restaurant where classic French cooking is tempered with some modern British ideas. A warm salad of scallops wrapped in Black Forest ham and served with a cracked pepper sauce sits happily next to rose of cantaloupe and galia melons with an apple and orange chutney. Or main courses of the likes of marinated supreme of duck with stir-fried vegetables and a soy and lime dressing act as a foil to flambé dishes (meats named after golf stars) and the chargrilled T bone steaks served with a choice of creamy garlic butter of sauce béarnaise.

Directions: 15 min from both St Peter Port and the airport. Hotel is opposite Vazon Bay

The Coast Road Vazon Bay GY5 7LL
Map: 16
Tel: 01481 256576
Fax: 01481 256532
Chef: Fergus Mackay
Owners: The Vermeulen Family
Cost: *Alc* £24, set-price L £12.45/D £17.95. ☺ H/wine £7.95
Times: Noon-2pm/7-9.30pm
Additional: Bar food L; Sunday L; Children welcome; 🍴 dishes
Seats: 120. Private dining room 40
Smoking: No-smoking area
Accommodation: 35 en suite

PERELLE, **L'Atlantique Hotel**

'Try a sunset,' extols *L'Atlantique.* And why not? There can be no better place to do so than from a hotel on the island's

Perelle Bay St Saviours GY7 9NA
Map: 16
Tel: 01481 264056
Fax: 01481 263800

west coast looking over the Bay of Perelle. You can eat in the popular Victorianas Bar or have a drink on the terrace of the more elegant Cocktail Bar before moving on to dinner in the restaurant. As you'd expect, seafood plays a significant role: lobster and crab ravioli with seared scallops, wilted spinach and tomato essence as a starter, baked fillet of brill under a crust of sun-dried tomato and herbs, or grilled sea bass with honey-roasted vegetables and a sweet pepper reduction as main courses. On the other hand, home-smoked venison is there, too, along with medallions of Scottish fillet steak pan-fried with pancetta and served with mustard mash and a whisky glaze. Risk-takers could try 'Comatosed by Chocolate' – a selection of Valrhona chocolate desserts – a healthier option is a spicy compote of winter fruits.

Directions: On west coast road overlooking Perelle Bay

Chef: John Tonge
Owner: Michael Lindley
Cost: *Alc* £24, set-price D £17 (5 courses). ☺ H/wine £8.40
Times: D only, 6.30-9.30pm. Closed Jan, Feb
Additional: Bar food; Sunday L (noon-2pm); Children welcome; ⏹ dishes
Seats: 50. Jacket & tie preferred
Smoking: No-smoking area; No pipes & cigars; Air conditioning
Accommodation: 23 en suite ★ ★ ★

ST MARTIN, La Barbarie

Granite-built former priory with a beamed restaurant boasting a conservatory section. A wide choice of dishes is offered with local fish featuring strongly.

Smoking: No-smoking area ★ ★ ★
Accommodation: 23 en suite

Directions: At traffic lights in St Martin take road to Saints Bay – hotel is on R at end of Saints Road

Saints Road Saints Bay GY4 6ES
Map: 16
Tel: 01481 235217
Fax: 01481 235208
Cost: *Alc* £22, set-price D £14.95 (5 courses). ☺ H/wine £7.95
Times: Noon-1.45pm/6.15-9.15pm
Additional: Bar Food L; Sunday L; Children welcome; ⏹ dishes

ST MARTIN, Hotel Bon Port

The hotel's restaurant manages to be smart without appearing stuffy. Within, it is decorated in rich reds, blues and greens, tables are well-spaced and decked out in blue and white linen. The windows overlook Moulin Huet Bay, offering wonderful views of the famous Pea Stacks and the Isle of Jersey. It seems popular with both residents and non-residents of the hotel. The cooking is mostly classic French; in the evening both a *carte* and set-menus are offered, while lighter dishes are provided at lunch (including sandwiches and salads). Delicious canapés and four types of bread come with pesto and tomato butters alongside tiny pots of pesto and sun-dried tomato paste. A starter of lobster and salmon terrine, served with two dressings had 'distinctive and well-matched flavours'. A fillet of beef with braised ox tail was 'well-executed, if a little over the top, though the quality of the beef was excellent'. The highlight was a perfect hot chocolate soufflé with home-made vanilla ice cream served in a thin tuile basket garnished with white chocolate wafers.

Moulin Huet Bay GY4 6EW
Map: 16
Tel: 01481 39249
Fax: 01481 39596
Chef: Robert McKillop
Owner: Lenard Shaw
Cost: *Alc* £30, set-price L £12.50 (4 courses)/D £18.50 (5 courses). ☺ H/wine £10
Times: Noon-2pm/7pm-9.30pm
Additional: Bar food; Sunday L; Children welcome; ⏹ dishes
Seats: 60
Smoking: No smoking in dining room
Accommodation: 18 en suite ★ ★ ★

Directions: Follow road from airport into St Martin. At last traffic lights turn R and follow signs

ST MARTIN, Hotel Jerbourg

Light conservatory restaurant overlooking cliffs and sea towards the neighbouring islands and France. The carte and daily fixed-price menus offer a good choice of modern British dishes.

Smoking: No-smoking area; No pipes & cigars; Air conditioning
Accommodation: 32 en suite ★ ★ ★

Directions: 5 mins drive from St Peter Port on main road

Jerbourg Point GY4 6BJ
Map: 16
Tel: 01481 238826
Fax: 01481 238238
Cost: *Alc* £23, set-price L £10.50/D £15.95 (5 courses). ☺ H/wine £8.50
Times: Noon-2.30pm/6.30-9.30pm
Additional: Bar food; Sunday L; Children welcome; ⏹ dishes

ST MARTIN, **Idlerocks Hotel**

*Stunning panorama over neighbouring islands to the French coast.
Prime raw materials appear in terrine of lobster and leeks, calves'
liver with rosemary jus, brill with crab sauce, and strawberry
bavarois.*

Directions: 5 mins drive from St Peter Port on main road

Jerbourg Point GY4 6BJ
Map: 16
Tel: 01481 37711
Fax: 01481 35592
Telephone for further details

ST MARTIN, **St Margaret's Lodge**

*Hotel restaurant overlooking the garden. The menu offers a good
choice of dishes, and is particularly good for local seafood. There is
also a vegetarian selection.*

Directions: Out of airport, turn L. Follow road for 1.5 miles.
Hotel on L

Forest Road GY4 6UE
Map: 16
Tel: 01481 35757
Fax: 01481 37594
Telephone for further details

ST PETER PORT, **The Absolute End**

Longstore GY1 2BG
Map: 16
Tel: 01481 723822
Fax: 01481 729129
Cost: *Alc* £22, set-price L £11. ☺
H/wine £8
Times: Noon-2pm/7-10pm. Closed
Sun, 26 Dec, Jan
Additional: Children 12+; ✿ dishes
Smoking: No pipes & cigars

Directions: Less than 1 mile from
town centre, going N on seafront road
to St Sampson

*Aptly named converted fisherman's cottage with a loyal following.
As well as an extensive fish and seafood menu (brill with mussels
and prawns, crab salad), there are meat and vegetarian dishes.
Lemon tart and sticky toffee pud are perennial favourites.*

ST PETER PORT, **Battens** **NEW**

1 Fountain Street GY1 1DA
Map: 16
Tel: 01481 729939
Fax: 01481 729938
Chef: James Scowen

*An elegant, comfortable, spacious restaurant and cheerful
modern brasserie with super harbour views to the outer*

islands. The kitchen shows serious intent as our March inspection revealed. The Mediterranean infuses the menu, note fillet of sea bass with aubergine caviar and roasted cherry tomato vinaigrette, and seared scallops with mizuna salad, sauce nero and watercress dressing. However, we enjoyed a ham, parsley and potato terrine with toasted home-made bread and sultana chutney, followed by pan-fried breast of chicken served with a sweetcorn risotto and red wine sauce. The wine list is reasonably priced and has a good selection by the glass.

Owners: Peter & Janice Batten
Cost: Alc £30, set-price L £10.50/D £25. ☺ H/wine £8.50
Times: Noon-2.30pm/6-11pm. Closed Sun, 25-26 Dec
Additional: Bar food L; Children 7+; 🐟 dishes
Seats: 30
Smoking: No pipes & cigars; Air conditioning

Directions: In the centre of St Peter Port

ST PETER PORT, Da Nello's ✿ NEW

A 500-year-old granite house with a glass-covered courtyard decorated in Mediterranean style, specialising in Italian and other Continental dishes, with fish a strong point. Chargrilled brill smeared with tomato and garlic salsa has been endorsed.

46 La Pollet GY1 1WF
Map: 16
Tel: 01481 712552
Fax: 01481 724235
Cost: Alc £25, set-price L £9.50/D £15.90. ☺ H/wine £7.95
Times: Noon-2pm/6.30-10.30pm

Addtional: Children welcome; 🐟 dishes
Smoking: No-smoking area; Air conditioning

Directions: In town centre, 100yds from North Beach car park

ST PETER PORT,

La Frégate ✿✿

Les Cotils GY1 1UT
Map: 16
Tel: 01481 724624
Fax: 01481 720443
Chef: Günter Botzenhardt
Owner: Guernsey Summer Holidays Ltd
Cost: Alc £20, set-price L £13.50/D £20 (both 4 courses). ☺ H/wine £8.50
Times: 12.30-1.45pm/7-9.45pm
Additional: Sunday L; Children 12+; 🐟 dishes
Seats: 70. Jacket & tie preferred
Smoking: No pipes & cigars; Air conditioned
Accommodation: 13 en suite ★★★

Originally built as a Manor House, La Frégate sits on a hillside overlooking St Peter's Port. This is an established hotel with a traditional restaurant, especially popular with the Guernsey locals. The *carte* mixes traditional and modern dishes: avocado vinaigrette, prawn cocktail, goujons of sole and coquilles St Jacques – some work better than others. The set-menus demonstrate the kitchen's strengths, and may offer a better bet, such as a delicious crab gazpacho, or a super piece of fresh turbot, which came with an assortment of herbed vegetables, all sliced paper-thin. Desserts are good and include chocolate sorbet. The chef has a passion for petits fours, which arrive on a silver platter: chocolate, coconut and lemon truffles, plus tiny Austrian pastries. The service is friendly and attentive.

Directions: Town centre, above St Julian's Avenue

ST PETER PORT,

Le Nautique Restaurant

A 400-year-old warehouse on two floors overlooking the harbour. Fresh fish served in a number of traditional ways, or classics such as roast duck are mainstays of the menu.

Additional: Children 5+; 🍴 dishes
Smoking: No pipes & cigars

Directions: Sea front opposite Harbour and Victoria Marina

Quay Steps GY1 2LE
Map: 16
Tel: 01481 721714
Fax: 01481 721786
Cost: *Alc* £22.50, set-price L £11.50 (2 courses). H/wine £8.60
Times: Noon-2pm/6.30-9.45pm. Closed L Sat, all Sun, 25 Dec-15 Jan

ST PETER PORT, **Old Government House Hotel** NEW

The hotel restaurant's giant windows overlook the town and harbour. Choose from one of two menus, both featuring quality ingredients such as local scallops with tomato salsa and rack of Welsh lamb with thyme jus.

Directions: Telephone for directions

GY1 4AZ
Map: 16
Tel: 01481 724921
Fax: 01481 724429
Telephone for further details

ST PETER PORT,

St Pierre Park Hotel

Rohais GY1 1FD
Map: 16
Tel: 01481 728282
Fax: 01481 712041
Chef: John Hitchen
Cost: *Alc* £25, set-price L £14.50/D £19.95 (5 courses). H/wine £10.75
Times: Noon-2.15pm/7-10pm. Closed L Sat, D Sun
Additional: Children welcome; 🍴 dishes
Seats: 55
Smoking: No-smoking area
Accommodation: 132 en suite
★ ★ ★ ★

Close to St Peter Port, a purpose-built hotel set in 45 acres of mature parkland. There's a choice of restaurants: Café Renoir, an all-day brasserie, and the more formal Victor Hugo Restaurant which offers a stylish setting to match the kitchen's serious approach. Seafood plays a leading role be it in a starter like warm monkfish terrine with grilled asparagus and mussel casserole or a main dish such as panaché of shellfish with crab bavarois, green asparagus, roasted tomatoes and tarragon cream. The day's catch can also be ordered 'free style' – cooked according to taste with a choice of sauces. Even meat dishes often have a fishy component – glazed lobster topping poached fillet of veal, for example or a crab Thermidor glaze to a dish of beef medallions.

Directions: 1 mile from town centre on route to west coast

VALE, Pembroke Bay Hotel

The hotel is situated near to a popular beach and boasts a spacious restaurant. Not surprisingly fresh local fish is a speciality of the menu, which offers an interesting selection of dishes.

Directions: Next to Royal Guernsey Golf Club

Pembroke Bay GY3 5BY
Map: 16
Tel: 01481 41175
Fax: 01481 48838
Telephone for further details

JERSEY

L'ETACQ, Lobster Pot Hotel

Sympathetically restored terrace of fishermen's cottages overlooking St Ouens Bay. Local seafood, especially lobster, stars on a menu which offers a wide choice from steak and kidney pudding to sole Veronique.

Smoking: No smoking in dining room; Air conditioning
Accommodation: 12 en suite ★★★

JE3 2FB
Map: 16
Tel: 01534 482888
Fax: 01534 485584
Cost: *Alc* £30, set-price L £12.95. ☺
H/wine £9.99
Times: Noon-2pm/7-9.30pm
Additional: Bar food L; Sunday L;
Children welcome; 🌢 dishes

GOREY,
Jersey Pottery Restaurant

Conservatory-like restaurant with plenty of natural light.
Grape vines grow overhead, there's lots of greenery, pottery, and the place is packed with punters. The high-octane atmosphere with everyone in view tucking into seafood platters piled higher than they are testifies to the continuing success of the Jersey Pottery. The formula is tried and tested: breads comes as plain, olive and brown, with Jersey butter and olives, puddings are displayed on a central table: fruit salad (both berries and tropical) almond and prune tart, mille-feuille of raspberries, chocolate slice. In between there's mussels steamed in Jersey cider, or squid with garlic, parsley and balsamic dressing, and duck spring rolls with tomato salsa, with main courses running along the lines of crab cakes and sweet chilli sauce, lobster with pesto, assorted fish grills. Wines by the glass are plentiful, staff are happy to recommend.

Gorey Village JE3 9EP
Map: 16
Tel: 01534 851119
Fax: 01534 856403
Chef: Tony Dorris
Owner: The Jones Family
Cost: *Alc* £26. H/wine £13
Times: L only, noon-5pm. Closed Sun
Additional: Children welcome;
🌢 dishes
Seats: 150
Smoking: No-smoking area

Directions: In Gorey village, well signposted from main coast road

GOREY, Suma's

Modern, white-walled restaurant with fantastic harbour views. Suma's hit the ground running when it opened in 1997. It's now established a reputation for strong cooking, with visitors returning to enjoy up-to-date cooking with Mediterranean flair. One test meal took in risotto of butternut squash and sweet potato, topped with shavings of Parmesan and thinly sliced spring onions, roast rump of lamb with ratatouille and sweetcorn fritters, and banana and chocolate wun-tun with ginger sauce. Baba ganoush, shouting loudly of cumin, tadzaki and served with a small dollop of coriander, tomato salad and hot flat bread, and calves' liver, creamy potato purée cabbage and apple bound in a light cream with a black pudding on top, have also been endorsed. The wine list is compact but is well-balanced and offers great value for money.

Gorey Hill St Martins JE3 6ET
Map: 16

Suma's

Tel: 01534 853291
Fax: 01534 851913
Chef: Mark Anderson
Owners: Susan Duffy, Malcom Lewis
Cost: Alc £23, set-price L £13.75
Times: Noon-3pm/6.30-10.30pm.
Closed D Sun, 22 Dec-22 Jan

AA Shortlisted for Wine Award-see page 16

Additional: Sunday L; Children welcome; ✿ dishes
Seats: 40
Smoking: Air conditioning

Directions: Take A3 E from St Helier to Gorey. Restaurant is 100yds before harbour on L

GOREY, **The Village Bistro** ✿✿

Gorey Village JE3
Map: 16
Tel: 01534 853429
Chef: David Cameron
Owners: David Cameron,
Sandra Daziel
Cost: Alc £25, set-price L £13.50.
H/wine £7.50
Times: Noon-2pm/7-10pm (9.30pm
Sun). Closed all Mon, L Tue-Thu, last
2 wks Oct
Additional: Sunday L; Children
welcome; ✿ dishes
Seats: 40
Smoking: No pipes & cigars

A charming conversion from what was once a church. The restaurant is painted in rich blues and decorated with a sun and moon theme. There is a small terrace outside where meals can be taken, weather permitting. Of the various menus, there is one at lunch (four options on a three course menu), an extensive *carte*, and two blackboards – the first offering vegetarian dishes, the second offering specials of the day. What could be described as predominantly modern cooking, there is also a hint of Asian influence to be found in such dishes as a wun-tun soup, and a 'perfectly cooked' fillet of cod with pak choi, lardons and garlic-infused mash. A 'well-executed' woodland risotto included shiitake, trompettes and oyster mushrooms. A refreshing dessert of grapefruit and orange jelly was served with a small brandy snap basket with granita and some passion fruit purée drizzled around the edge of the plate. The wine list is fair with some good quality bottles listed.

Directions: Village centre

ROZEL BAY,
Château La Chaire ❀❀

JE3 6AJ
Map: 16
Tel: 01534 863354
Fax: 01534 865137
Chef: Simon Walker
Owners: Hatton Hotels Ltd
Cost: *Alc* £26.50. ☺ H/wine £10.25
Times: Noon-2pm/7-9.45pm
Additional: Bar food L; Sunday L;
Children welcome; ♨ dishes
Seats: 65. Private dining room 20
Smoking: No-smoking area; No pipes
& cigars
Accommodation: 14 en suite ★ ★ ★

Château la Chaire has changed emphasis, simplified the
lunch menu and seen a huge increase in trade. Simple fish
dishes are served with salads and 'lip smacking' lobster and
ribeye steak are sold together as 'surf n turf'. The set-menu
offered in the evening is more formal and interesting, includes
nine starters and mains and chef's specials, some of which
include a supplement . Start with leek and asparagus soup with
truffle oil, go on to halibut with wok-fried vegetables, or Thai
pork with black onion and chilli marmalade. Mains include
fillet of cod with peas, asparagus and mint, or fillet of lamb
with honey and rosemary jus, and confit of duck with jasmine
jus. Desserts include chocolate marquise with coffee bean
sauce, home-made coconut ice cream with tropical fruits, and a
good selection of cheeses.

Directions: From St Helier NE towards Five Oaks, Maufant, then
St Martin's Church & Rozel; 1st L in village, hotel 100m

ST BRELADE, **The Atlantic Hotel** ❀❀

Mont de la Pulente
JE3 8HE
Map: 16
Tel: 01534 744101
Fax: 01534 744102
Chef: Ken Healy
Owners: Patrick Burke & family
Cost: *Alc* £33, set-price L £16/D
£24.50 (4 course). ☺ H/wine £10

Well-established, modern hotel in a superb location. Set on a
headland overlooking both the sea and La Moye golf course,
guests can relax in the elegant public rooms, take advantage of
the good range of leisure facilities, as well as eat in the smart,
fairly spacious restaurant overlooking the outdoor swimming-
pool. A tasty appetiser of a small croque-monsieur sets the

tone. Then you could start with a mosaic of foie gras, duck and pickled wild mushrooms with prunes and pistachios, and go on to tender duck breast with stir-fried pak choi in a sauce of five spice and plums. Otherwise go for one of the many seafood offerings: sautéed local lobster and scallops in a Thai curry sauce, then poached fillet of sea bass and mussels with griddled Parma ham. Hazelnut tart with honey ice cream has been endorsed, too. Breads are excellent – try the black pudding variety. The wine list is well-balanced with some depth in the claret and Burgundy sections.

Directions: From St Brelade take the road to Petit Port, turn into Rue de Sergente and R again, signed to hotel

Times: 12.45-2.15pm/7.30-9.30pm. Closed Jan-Feb
Additional: Sunday L; Children welcome; 🍴 dishes
Seats: 80. Private dining room 24. Jacket & tie preferred
Smoking: No pipes or cigars
Accommodation: 50 en suite ★★★★

ST BRELADE, **Hotel L'Horizon**

St Brelade's Bay JE3 8EF
Map: 16
Tel: 01534 43101
Fax: 01534 46269
Chef: Paul Wells
Owner: Arcadian Hotels
Cost: *Alc* £28, set-price L £17/D £25 (4 courses). ☺ H/wine £11.50
Times: 12.30-2.30pm/7.30-10pm. Closed L Sun & Mon
Additional: Bar food; Sunday L; Children welcome; 🍴 dishes
Seats: 60. Jacket & tie preferred
Smoking: Air conditioning
Accommodation: 107 en suite ★★★★

What a setting! Right on the beach looking south over St Brelade's Bay. The informal Brasserie, near the leisure club, is open throughout the day for light meals, or go to the more traditional Crystal Room. The Grill, decorated in art deco style, is what earns the hotel its two rosettes, and it's here that the chef makes particularly good use of the island's fish and seafood: ravioli of lobster and pan-seared scallops, say, or an adventurous-sounding dish of scallops with black pudding, carrot and parsnip purée and pancetta, followed by fillet of red mullet with Dublin Bay prawns, roasted fennel heart and anise sauce. Meat-lovers could decide on a terrine of smoked chicken and foie gras with pomegranate vinaigrette, then well-reported breast of Gressingham duck with red cabbage, roast pear and blueberry jus. You could end a meal with crème brûlée, or mango parfait with a compote of the same fruit.

Directions: Overlooking St Brelade's Bay

ST BRELADE, **Hotel la Place**

A fire in the beamed lounge in winter, a pool-side palm-dotted terrace in summer, and Knights restaurant bedecked in medieval style, with shields and tapestries much in evidence: all are found at this hotel complex based around an 18th-century farmhouse. Well-spaced tables mean you're unlikely to jog your neighbour's elbow as you study the oversized menu and decide on a wine from a list centred squarely on France. The table space may be taken up by staff cooking sirloin steak flamed in brandy, carving the likes of Chateaubriand, and

Route du Coin La Haule JE3 8BT
Map: 16
Tel: 01534 744261
Fax: 01534 745164
Chef: Neil Graham
Cost: *Alc* £30, set-price D £24.50. ☺ H/wine £10.75
Times: D only, 7.30-9.30pm
Additional: Bar food L; Sunday L (noon-2pm); Children welcome; 🍴 dishes

Hotel la Place

Seats: 80. Private dining room 50
Smoking: No-smoking area; No pipes
& cigars
Accommodation: 42 en suite ★ ★ ★ ★

boning Dover sole. Otherwise, expect roast breast of
Aylesbury duck with a confit of shallots and cabbage, sautéed
rump of lamb with roasted garlic, and fillet of red mullet with
tapenade sauce. Finish with lemon tart, or poached pear with
pannacotta.

Directions: Before St Aubin turn up La Haule Hill by La Haule
Manor Hotel, then L at sign towards red houses, hotel 400yds
on R

ST CLEMENT,
Green Island Restaurant ❀

*Beachside restaurant with a Mediterranean mood – the terrace
overlooking the sea comes with an outdoor heater. Local seafood is
a speciality, we found the scallops first rate.*

Additional: Sunday L; Children welcome; ❹ dishes

Directions: Telephone for directions

JE2 6LS
Map: 16
Tel: 01534 857787
Fax: 01534 619309
Cost: *Alc* £20, set-price L £10.95. ☺
H/wine £9
Times: Noon-2.30pm/7-9.30pm.
Closed D Sun, all Mon, Xmas week,
2 wks Nov, 2 wks Mar

ST HELIER, The Grand Hotel ❀❀

The Esplanade JE4 8WD
Map: 16
Tel: 01534 722301
Fax: 01534 37815
Chef: Calum Watson
Owners: De Vere Hotels
Cost: *Alc* £30, set-price L £15.50 (4
courses)/D £23.50 (5 courses). ☺
H/wine £10.50
Times: 12.30-2.15pm/7-10pm. Closed
D Sun
Additional: Bar food; Sunday L;
Children welcome; ❹ dishes
Seats: 140. Private dining room 22.
Jacket & tie preferred
Smoking: No-smoking area; Air
conditioning
Accommodation: 114 en suite
★ ★ ★ ★

Prominent, busy seafront hotel. The world's their oyster – the
carte at the hotel's premier restaurant demonstrates an
approach to global fusion that would put the United Nations to
shame. Twice cooked belly of pork with honey-roasted
butternut squash, minted flageolet bean purée and spiced

Directions: On outskirts of town,
overlooking Victoria Park

redcurrant sauce, perhaps braised duck leg filled with black olives and woodland mushroom risotto on choucroute with truffle vinegar jus-lie, for example, or griddled thyme flavoured polenta with buttered leek, caramelised 'chickory' and basil cappuccino froth are typical dishes. There's also a wide choice of dishes on offer at The Regency Restaurant, the hotel's second dining room.

ST HELIER, Pomme d'Or Hotel

Liberation Square JE2 3NF
Map: 16
Tel: 01534 880110
Fax: 01534 737781
Chef: Steve Le Corre
Owner: Seymour Hotels
Cost: *Alc* £25, set-price L £15 (5 courses)/D £17.50 (5 courses). ☺
H/wine £7.50
Times: 12.30-2pm/7-10pm. Closed L Sat, all Sun
Additional: Bar food; Sunday L; Children welcome; ♨ dishes
Seats: 45. Private dining rooms 200
Smoking: No-smoking area; Air conditioning
Accommodation: 141 en suite ★★★

Extensive conference facilities make this a popular business hotel. La Petite Pomme is the hotel's premier restaurant, a smart dining room with well-spaced tables. It's considered a special occasion restaurant by locals – dishes flambéd at table are a speciality. The choice is extensive, perhaps confusingly so, with a lengthy *carte* of some fifteen choices at each course, as well as a set-menu. Classic France dictates (there are English subtitles), examples include mousseline of sole and lobster, and supreme de volaille. However some exoticism creeps in with the likes of king prawns coated in breadcrumbs and served with a marmalade, chilli, passion fruit and sesame glaze.

Directions: Opposite Harbour and Marina

ST SAVIOUR, Longueville Manor

JE2 7WF
Map: 16
Tel: 01534 725501
Fax: 01534 731613
Chef: Andrew Baird

Dating in part from the 13th century and set in 17 acres of well-kept grounds. Fine specimen trees, a lake and an extensive kitchen garden are all part of the attraction. The latter provides the kitchens with a wealth of fresh produce to be transformed into high-class, sophisticated cuisine. There are twin dining-rooms, one venerable with ancient, heavily carved oak panelling and an austere dresser, the other with a lighter and more contemporary feel and views over the gardens. Conscientious, friendly staff guide you through the menu and wine list with informed skill. Seemingly laser-cut parfait of foie gras with celeriac and citrus salad was technically faultless, served with excellent brioche. A main course salad of poached salmon, Jersey lobster and a warm salad of Jersey royals was a showcase of the best of the island on a plate, made memorable by lobster meat 'as fresh as I have ever tasted, really sweet and moreish'. Pear and almond tart with caramel ice-cream was spot-on for flavour and texture. As well as the carte, there are two Degustation Menus, to be taken by the whole table (to remind us of the proximity of French shores) in which individual dishes have been matched with accompanying wines.

Owners: Malcom Lewis & Sue Dufty
Cost: *Alc* £42, set-price L £20/D £35 (4 courses). H/wine £9
Times: 12.30-2pm/7.30-9.30pm
Additional: Bar food; Sunday L; Children welcome; ◑ dishes
Seats: 65. Private dining room 20
Smoking: No-smoking area
Accommodation: 32 en suite ★ ★ ★ ★

Directions: From St Helier take A3 to Gorey, hotel 0.75 mile on L

SARK

SARK,

La Sablonnerie

This is a charming 16th-century converted farmhouse that is set in extensive secluded gardens in a wonderfully tranquil setting. There are roaring log fires in the colder months but alas, the hotel only opens from Easter to the beginning of October. La Sablonnerie has been owned by the same family for over fifty years and is largely self-supporting with most of the meat, dairy foods, vegetables, and fruit being produced from its own farm and gardens. The restaurant prides itself on the French menu, which changes daily, of two starters, three or four main courses and desserts. Dishes include a parfait of duck livers, a savarin of fresh salmon, pan-fried beef fillet with soubise glaze, a fricassée of wild mushrooms and shallots with a Burgundy jus. Desserts are classics such as chilled nougatine of roasted hazelnuts, caramel ice cream and coffee bean sauce, and poached snow eggs on a Sablonnerie biscuit.

Directions: On southern part of island

GY9 0SD
Map: 16
Tel: 01481 832061
Fax: 01481 832408
Chef: Colin Day
Owner: Miss Elizabeth Perrée
Cost: *Alc* £19.80, set-price L £24.50/D £26.50 (both 5 courses). ☺ H/wine £6.80
Times: Noon-2.30pm/7-9.30pm. Closed mid Oct-Easter
Additional: Bar food; Sunday L; Children welcome; ◑ dishes
Seats: 39. Private dining room 12
Smoking: No-smoking area; No pipes & cigars
Accommodation: 22 rooms

MAN, ISLE OF

CASTLETOWN,
The Chablis Cellar

*The refurbished premises occupy the ground floor of a large
house, overlooking Castletown harbour.* There are separate
dining rooms, each one elegantly decorated in period style –
tables are laid with crisp linen, individual candle lamps and
fresh flowers. The kitchen prepares a good, varied choice of
dishes, taking into account the available seasonal produce
(some locally produced) on both the *carte* and set-price menu.
Fresh Manx queen scallops, for example, baked in filo parcel
and accompanied by a rich saffron cream, followed by roulade
of pork stuffed with spinach leaves and complemented by
fresh, lightly cooked vegetables show the style. Amber of apple
and cinnamon makes a well-endorsed pudding, especially when
accompanied by a fabulous Armagnac sorbet. The service is
charming and friendly.

Directions: Telephone for directions

21 Bank Street IM9 1AT
Tel: 01624 823527
Telephone for further details

CASTLETOWN,
Keys Restaurant

*Basement restaurant in an 18th-century building with exposed stone
walls and original beams. Dishes are modern and take full account
of fresh local produce, including fish.*

Additional: Children 12+; ✿ dishes
Smoking: No smoking in dining room

Directions: Opposite Castle Rushen

Parliament Square IM9 1LA
Map 6: SC26
Tel: 01624 824000
Cost: *Alc* £22, set-price L £15.50/D
£22. ☺ H/wine £9
Times: Noon-2pm/7-9pm. Closed L
Sat, D Tue, all Sun, Feb

DOUGLAS,
Waterfront Restaurant

*Cosy restaurant on the first floor of a stone building overlooking
Douglas Harbour. Home-made breads, delicious oak-smoked
haddock with Welsh rarebit and tomato and basil confit, good
sausages with creamy mash and caramelised red onion gravy, set
the pace.*

Directions: Telephone for directions

North Quay IM1 4LE
Map: 6
Tel: 01624 673222
Fax: 01624 673145
Telephone for further details

SCOTLAND
ABERDEEN CITY

ABERDEEN, Ardoe Hotel

Lofty turrets, towers and spires mark out this impressive baronial mansion. The hotel's elevated position gives magnificent views of the River Dee and forms quite an impression on visitors. As does the cooking, which mixes the traditional with the modern, relies firmly on sound local produce and occasionally dips its toes in the Mediterranean – grilled provençale vegetables glazed with goats' cheese, for example. A typical meal, however, might start with cream of woodland mushroom and Arran mustard soup, followed by lightly steamed fillet of turbot on a bed of potato mash, topped with crispy spaghetti of vegetables laced with mussels. Glazed lemon tart with mango and papaya ice cream, or a selection of good condition Scottish cheeses with apple chutney and wheat wafers round things off nicely. The wine list offers an extensive range of good vintages from around the world.

Directions: 3 miles from Aberdeen on B9077, on L

South Deeside Road Blairs AB12 5YP
Map 15: NJ90
Tel: 01224 867355
Fax: 01224 861283
Chef: Ivor Clark
Owner: Macdonald Hotels plc
Cost: *Alc* £30, set-price L £15/D £27.50. H/wine £14.50
Times: Noon-2pm/6.30-9.45pm. Closed L Sat
Additional: Bar food; Sunday L; Children welcome; 🍽 dishes
Seats: 60. Private dining room 200. Jacket & tie preferred
Smoking: No smoking in dining room; Air conditioning
Accommodation: 71 en suite ★★★★

ABERDEEN,
Copthorne Aberdeen

Poachers restaurant has been redesigned to reflect the traditional style throughout the hotel. Food is emphatically Scottish and makes good use of Grampian produce.

Additional: Bar food; Children welcome; 🍽 dishes
Smoking: No-smoking area; Air conditioning
Accommodation: 89 en suite ★★★★

Directions: Telephone for directions

122 Huntly Street AB10 1SU
Map 15: NJ90
Tel: 01224 630404
Fax: 01224 640573
Cost: *Alc* £24, set-price L £9.95 (2 courses)/D £18.50. ☺ H/wine £11
Times: Noon-2pm/7-10pm. Closed L Sat & Sun

ABERDEEN,
Maryculter House

A popular hotel on the south banks of the River Dee. The Priory Restaurant's six-course menu features prime beef, fish and game, with dishes such as apricot and date stuffed breast of pheasant wrapped in bacon with tarragon cream sauce.

Directions: 8 miles west of Aberdeen off A93 or B9077

South Deeside Road AB1 6BB
Map 15: NJ90
Tel: 01224 732124
Fax: 01224 733510
Telephone for further details

ABERDEEN, Norwood Hall

Stately Victorian mansion set in seven acres of wooded grounds. A reasonable selection of dishes awaits guests, including an impressive rose of salmon and halibut with a basil and shellfish sauce, as well as traditional sticky toffee pudding.

Directions: Off A92, at 1st roundabout, turn L & continue to hotel sign

Garthdee Road Cults AB15 9FX
Map 15: NJ90
Tel: 01224 868951
Fax: 01224 869868
Telephone for further details

ABERDEEN, **Patio Hotel** ✿

Beach Boulevard AB24 5EF
Map 15: NJ90
Tel: 01224 633339
Fax: 01224 638833
Cost: *Alc* £25, set-price L £9.50. ☺
H/wine £10.95
Times: Noon-1.45pm/7-10.30pm
Additional: Bar food L; Sunday L;
Children welcome; ✿ dishes
Smoking: No-smoking area;
Air conditioning
Accommodation: 124 en suite
★ ★ ★ ★

*Hotel with two different restaurant styles. The airy, modern
conservatory offers a comprehensive menu of international and
Scottish fare, while Footdee's specialises in seafood and steak.*

Directions: From Union St turn onto King St; at 1st traffic
lights turn R onto East North St; at next roundabout 2nd exit.
Hotel on L

ABERDEEN, **Simpsons Hotel** ✿

59 Queens Road AB15 4YP
Map 15: NJ90
Tel: 01224 327777
Fax: 01224 327700
Cost: *Alc* £23. ☺ H/wine £10.50
Times: Noon-2pm/6.30-9.45pm
Additional: Bar food L; Sunday L;
Children welcome; ✿ dishes
Smoking: No-smoking area;
Air conditioning
Accommodation: 37 en suite ★ ★ ★

*Although a relative newcomer, already firmly established as part of
the Granite City's restaurant scene. A solid townhouse exterior
conceals a smart split-level Mediterranean-themed brasserie with
monthly-changing menus.*

Directions: Please telephone for directions

ABERDEENSHIRE

ABOYNE,
White Cottage Restaurant ✿✿

*Expect a friendly welcome from Laurie and Josephine Mill
who have run the restaurant for the past 14 years.* It's a small
granite-walled cottage with one long room featuring pine
floors, panelled walls, open fires and rear conservatory

AB34 5BP
Map 15: NO59
Tel/Fax: 013398 86265
Chef: Laurie Mill
Owners: Laurie & Josephine Mill

overlooking a landscaped garden and Deeside farmland, and attracts a loyal following for the sensibly short, daily-changing hand-written menus. Lunch tends to be a lighter affair, while the set-dinner menu begins with canapés (smoked fish and Parmesan tart) in the conservatory, prior to pan-fried rösti crab sea-cakes with ceviche of prawn and salmon flavoured with tarragon, or mango, carrot and cardamom soup. Then, perhaps, herb-crusted halibut on leek confit with a light vanilla butter sauce, or rack of lamb with rosemary and tomato jus and roasted organic roots, could be followed by golden passion fruit tart, or apple and sultana charlotte with caramel sauce.

Directions: On A93 between Aboyne and Kincardine O'Neil

Cost: *Alc* £24.75, set-price D £29.50.
☺ H/wine £12.80
Times: 11.30am-2.45pm/7-9pm.
Closed Sun, Mon, 25-29 Dec, 1 wk after Easter, 1 wk in summer, 1 wk Oct
Additional: Bar food;
Children welcome; ✍ dishes
Seats: 40. Private dining room 20.
Jacket & tie preferred at D
Smoking: No smoking in dining room
Accommodation: 1 en suite

BALLATER,

Balgonie House Hotel ❀❀

Exceptional hospitality is high on the list of attractions at this small country house set in four acres of mature grounds. From the restaurant you can enjoy views of the Glenmuick Hills. French inspired dishes from the set four-course dinner menu offer limited choice – some three dishes at each stage except the second – but the overall quality of the cooking is high. A typical dinner takes in chicken liver terrine with Cumberland sauce or green pea with yogurt soup, loin of lamb with redcurrant jus, or halibut with asparagus and tomato confit and sauce vierge. There's pecan and treacle tart with crème anglaise, or rice pudding with plum compote for dessert. Good cafetière coffee and petits fours are served in several lounges.

Directions: On outskirts of Ballater, signposted off A93 (Ballater-Perth)

Braemar Place AB35 5NQ
Map 15: NO39
Tel/Fax: 013397 55482
Chef: John Finnie
Owners: John & Priscilla Finnie
Cost: Set-price L £17.50/D £29.50 (4 courses). H/wine £17.50
Times: 12.30-2pm (by reservation only)/7-9pm. Closed 5 Jan-7 Feb
Additional: Sunday L;
Children welcome; ✍ dishes
Seats: 30
Smoking: No smoking in dining room
Accommodation: 9 en suite ★ ★

BALLATER,

Darroch Learg Hotel ❀❀❀

The pink granite house perches high above the village of Ballater on 'the hill of oaks'. The blue and beige conservatory dining room has views south over the River Dee to the Grampians. Lamb, venison and Aberdeen Angus are regular features of David Mutter's modern Scottish menu, and home-smoked salmon makes a classy starter when served with a free-range poached egg, Oscetra caviar and chive velouté. Combinations aim high – foie gras and Parma ham make a deluxe stuffing for ravioli with onion jam, crispy potatoes and Parmesan cream; foie gras also appears in a waist-expanding dish of big flavours that takes in beef fillet, braised shin, confit of celeriac and morel mushroom sauce. Not everything is so muscular – fillet of halibut with basil and olive crust with tapenade is fashionably paired with fried squid and avocado salsa, while haricots blanc, asparagus and truffle cream make an elegant base for breast of Gressingham duck. The assiette of house desserts is served with crème fraîche ice cream, or else stick with the classic simplicity of lemon tart. A serious quaffer has compiled the wine list, extensively annotated in terms of history, background and tasting notes. Prices are remarkably fair, given the excellence of some of the producers.

Directions: On A93 at the W end of village

Braemar Road AB35 5UX
Map 15: NO39
Tel: 013397 55443
Fax: 013397 55252
Chef: David Mutter
Owner: Nigel Franks
Cost: *Alc* £36.50, set-price D £31.50. H/wine £14.50
Times: 12.30-2pm/7-9pm.
Closed Xmas, last 3 wks Jan
Additional: Bar food L; Sunday L; Children welcome
Seats: 48
Smoking: No smoking in dining room
Accommodation: 18 en suite ★ ★ ★

BALLATER,

Glen Lui Hotel

Invercauld Road AB35 5RP
Map 15: NO39
Tel: 013397 55402
Fax: 013397 55545
Cost: *Alc* £18. ☺ H/wine £8.30
Times: Noon-2pm/6-9pm
Additional: Sunday L;
Children welcome; ☙ dishes
Smoking: No smoking in dining room
Accommodation: 19 en suite

With views over Ballater golf course towards the mountain of Lochnagar, this small hotel provides sound cooking. Chicken liver parfait, turbot with an asparagus and dill sauce, and cappuccino creme brûlée show the style.

Directions: Please telephone for directions

BALLATER, **Green Inn**

9 Victoria Road AB35 5QQ
Map 15: NO39
Tel/Fax: 013397 55701
Chef: Jeff Purves
Owners: Mr & Mrs J J Purves
Cost: *Alc* £29.50, set-price D £25 (2 courses). H/wine £12.50
Times: D only, 7-9pm.
Closed 2 wks Oct, 1 wk Xmas
Additional: Children welcome; ☙ dishes
Seats: 32
Smoking: Air conditioning
Accommodation: 3 en suite.

The Green Inn is situated in an attractive village, set in the hills of Royal Deeside. The menu changes four to five times a year and offers five starters, mains and desserts, supplemented by a few daily specials. The cooking is impressive. Home-made breads of walnut, black olive, and sun-dried tomato are delicious. A starter of a twice-baked cheese soufflé on a thin oatcake with salad laced with dried apricots and a Strathdon blue cheese dressing, was excellent – 'the highlight'. A main course of salmon trout was 'cooked to perfection', sea bass, however, accompanied by a rich langoustine sauce, topped by fresh asparagus, was a shade dry. Puddings include golden apple and sultana tart with Mascarpone and lemon cream, a terrine of Valrhona chocolate with Agen prunes soaked in malt whisky and a raspberry brûlée. The wine list is extensive with a particularly notable claret section.

Directions: On A93 in centre of Ballater on the green

BANCHORY,

Raemoir House Hotel ❀❀

AB31 4ED
Map 15: NO69
Tel: 01330 824884
Fax: 01330 822171
Chef: Stuart Doust
Owners: Roy & Lesley Bishop-Milnes
Cost: *Alc* £26.50, set-price L £15.50.
☺ H/wine £13.40
Times: Noon-2pm/7-9pm
Additional: Bar food; Sunday L;
Children welcome; ◑ dishes
Seats: 30. Private dining room 30
Smoking: No smoking in dining room
Accommodation: 20 en suite ★★★

Grand Scottish baronial hotel in a magnificent setting. A new
chef has brought changes and, in place of the *carte,* dinner now
comprises a short, daily-changing set price menu. The idiom is
modern Scottish: seared scallops, langoustine and monkfish
with a gâteau of vegetables and sauce vert; roast saddle of
venison with quail mousseline, Jerusalem artichoke mousse,
braised red cabbage and juniper jus. An enjoyable pressed
game terrine, laced with pistachios, came with shallot confit and
beetroot sauce, and a main course of lightly grilled fresh turbot
arrived moist and tender, with thinly sliced boiled potatoes and
quite delicious wood blewits (wild mushrooms), young braised
leeks and a chive velouté. Rich chocolate marquise with coffee
bean sauce is typical of the suave style of desserts. Good
cheeses are served with biscuits, celery and grapes.

Directions: A93 to Banchory then A980, hotel at crossroads in
2.5 miles

BANCHORY,

Tor-Na-Coille Hotel ❀   NEW

AB31 4AB
Map 15: NO69
Tel: 01330 822242
Fax: 01330 824012
Cost: Set-price L £15.75/D £26.50.
H/wine £12.75
Times: 6.30-10pm. Closed 25-28 Dec
Additional: Bar food; Sunday L;
Children welcome; ◑ dishes
Smoking: No-smoking area; No pipes
& cigars
Accommodation: 23 en suite ★★★

*Ivy-clad Victorian mansion serving Taste of Scotland dishes such as
roast pork fillet on wholegrain mustard mash finished with leeks in a
Dunsyre Blue cheese and double cream sauce.*

Directions: From Aberdeen take A93 (18 miles)

BRIDGE OF MARNOCH,

The Old Manse of Marnoch

By Huntly AB54 7RS
Map 15: NJ55
Tel/Fax: 01466 780873
Chef: Keren Carter
Owners: Patrick & Keren Carter
Cost: Set-price D £27 (4 courses).
H/wine £9
Times: D only, 7-9pm. Closed 2 wks
Nov, Xmas, New Year
Additional: Children 12+
Seats: 26
Smoking: No smoking in dining room
Accommodation: 8 en suite ★ ★

Directions: On B9117 just off A97
Huntly/Banff road

Patrick and Keren Carter have created a stylish country house hotel through the sympathetic conversion of a former Georgian manse. The building stands peacefully beside the River Deveron in four acres of carefully tended gardens. In keeping with the setting, the interior has been beautifully furnished featuring hand-crafted pieces, fine antiques and, in the lounge, mementoes of the owners' extensive travels. The dining room has a nautical theme and provides a striking backdrop for Keren's cooking, which utilises the best local produce – some from the hotel's own gardens. A typical set dinner may begin with smoked Lorne beef with horseradish cream, or twice-baked cheese and herb soufflé, followed by pork tenderloin with pears and Pernod and, to finish, lemon tart or toffee sponge pudding with caramel sauce. Good choice of wines and single malt whiskies.

INVERURIE, **Thainstone House**

AB51 5NT
Map 15: NJ72
Tel: 01467 621643
Fax: 01467 625084
Chef: Martin Ward
Owner: Macdonald Hotels
Cost: Set-price L £16/D £29.95 (4
courses). H/wine £14
Times: Noon-2.30pm/7-9.30pm
Additional: Bar food; Sunday L;
Children welcome; 🍴 dishes.

A palatial Scottish mansion combing classical elegance with modern day comforts. With easy access the airport, the hotel's forty acres of parkland provide a relaxing setting for a weekend break. In the Georgian-style restaurant prime local beef, game and seafood feature strongly. Note our January meal that comprised an excellent tomato and basil consommé garnished with crab, pan-fried loin of venison with winter cabbage, roasted shallots and baked baby apples and a 'seductive' chocolate tart with pistachio ice cream and strawberries for dessert.

Directions: 2 miles from Inverurie on the A96 Aberdeen road

Seats: 55
Smoking: No smoking in dining room
Accommodation: 48 en suite ★ ★ ★ ★

KILDRUMMY, Kildrummy Castle

AB33 8RA
Map 15: NJ41
Tel: 019755 71288
Fax: 019755 71345
Cost: *Alc* £30, set-price L £16.50/D £30 (4 courses). ☺ H/wine £12
Times: 12.30-1.45pm/7-9pm. Closed Jan
Additional: Sunday L; Children welcome; ✿ dishes
Smoking: No smoking in dining room
Accommodation: 16 en suite ★ ★ ★

Directions: Off A97 Huntly/Ballater Road 35 miles W of Aberdeen

Splendid, atmospheric Victorian mansion overlooking the ruins of the 13th-century castle. Traditional Scottish cooking features seafood, game and local Aberdeen Angus beef.

NEWBURGH, Udny Arms Hotel

Main Street Ellon AB41 6BL
Map 15: NJ92
Tel: 01358 789444
Telephone for further details

Directions: Village centre – A92 Aberdeen/Peterhead, turn right to Newburgh

Comfortable village hotel with views over the Ythan Estuary. The split-level bistro is noted for its quality raw ingredients and local seafood, including pan-seared scallops on a bed of wilted spinach with a saffron butter sauce.

PETERHEAD, Waterside Inn ✿

Large restaurant popular with both visitors and locals. Fresh fish from Peterhead and Scottish game are featured, with wild goose as a special when we visited.

Additional: Bar Food; Sunday L; Children welcome; ✿ dishes
Smoking: No smoking in dining room
Accommodation: 109 en suite ★ ★ ★ ★

Directions: Follow A90 (A952) to roundabout on outskirts of Peterhead; turn L for Fraserburgh

Fraserburgh Road AB42 1BN
Map 15: NK14
Tel: 01779 471121
Fax: 01779 470670
Cost: *Alc* £25, set-price L £10/D £21. ☺ H/wine £13
Times: 12.30-2pm/7-9.45pm

ANGUS

AUCHTERHOUSE,
Old Mansion House Hotel

A 16th-century building with Jacobean ceilings and an exquisite fireplace provide elegant surroundings for a choice of international dishes featuring fine Scottish produce.

Smoking: No smoking in dining room
Accommodation: 8 en suite ★ ★ ★

Directions: From Dundee take A923, then B954 for 2 miles. Hotel on L

DD3 0QN
Map 11: NO33
Tel: 01382 320366
Fax: 01382 320400
Cost: *Alc* £15, set-price D £26. ☺
H/wine £12.50
Times: Noon-2pm/7-9.30pm
Additional: Bar Food; Sunday L;
Children welcome; ❹ dishes

BRIDGEND OF LINRATHEN,
Lochside Lodge

Honest country restaurant that is firmly establishing itself as a serious place to eat locally. Set in a converted farm in a rural village deep in the beautiful Angus Glens, loyal regulars are attracted by the good-value, daily-changing menus which incorporate the finest local produce. Menus are sensibly short with the lunchtime *carte* being available in both the bar and restaurant. At inspection, a competent and well-flavoured chicken liver pâté came with a light clove, thyme and cranberry sauce. To follow, tender, crisp-skinned local duck was complemented by a spicy bean, tomato and lentil sauce and served with good vegetables, notably a mound of puréed carrot with a herb crust. The whole meal was rounded off with a light textured crème caramel with a maple syrup sauce laced with strawberries.

Directions: From Kirriemuir take B591 Glenisla Rd for 6 miles. Turn L at Lintrathen sign

By Kirriemuir DD8 5JJ
Map 15: NO25
Tel: 01575 560340
Fax: 01575 560202
Chef: Stephen Robertson
Owners: Stephen & Jackie Robertson
Cost: *Alc* L £15/D £23. ☺
H/wine £10.50
Times: Noon-1.45pm/6-9pm.
Closed Mon
Additional: Children 12+; ❹ menu
Seats: 32
Smoking: No smoking in dining room
Accommodation: 2 rooms

CARNOUSTIE, 11 Park Avenue

Warmly decorated restaurant in reds and oranges with green woodwork. It is popular locally, offering modern Scottish cooking and a comprehensive wine list.

Directions: From Dundee take A92 N (Arbroath). After 10-12 miles turn R to Carnoustie; at crossroads L, then R at mini-roundabout. Restaurant on L

11 Park Avenue DD7 7JA
Map 12: NO53
Tel/Fax: 01241 853336
Cost: *Alc* £25, set-price L £15/D
£18.50. ☺ H/wine £10.50
Times: Noon-2pm/7-9.30pm.
Closed Sun, Mon, 1st wk Jan
Additional: Children 10+; ❹ dishes
Smoking: No smoking in dining room

GLAMIS,
Castleton House Hotel

Delightful Victorian house set in its own grounds along the A94. Sound Scottish cooking is served in the informal conservatory restaurant and the elegant dining room, the latter offering an imaginative set-price menu.

Directions: W of Glamis on A94, between Forfar and Coupar

Forfar DD8 1SJ
Map 15: NO34
Tel: 01307 840340
Fax: 01307 840506
Telephone for further details

INVERKEILOR,
Gordon's Restaurant ❀❀

Civilised little family restaurant where everything focuses on the merits of the kitchen. The menu is short, the repertoire well up to date with modern kitchen practice and takes note of the season. A typical meal could be ceviche of hot-smoked salmon with spiced tabouleh, lime crème fraîche with herb oils and a light saffron vinaigrette, medallion of Angus fillet topped with a Stilton mousse soufflé with celeriac rösti and claret essence, and lemon and ginger pudding served with lemon curd ice cream and raspberry coulis or Scottish farmhouse cheeses. The food is carefully cooked and naturally served.

Directions: Just off A92 (Arbroath to Montrose)

Main Street by Arbroath DD11 5RN
Map 15: NO64
Tel: 01241 830364
Chef: Gordon Watson
Owners: Gordon & Maria Watson
Cost: *Alc* £25, set-price L £14. ☺
H/wine £9.60
Times: Noon-2pm/7-9pm.
Closed Mon, L Sat, last 2 wks Jan
Additional: Sunday L; Children welcome
Seats: 24
Smoking: No smoking in dining room
Accommodation: 2 en suite

ARGYLL & BUTE

ARDBEG, ## Ardmory House Hotel ❀

Light and airy restaurant with views across Rothesay Bay and the Firth of Clyde. Dishes range from king prawn tails with tiger prawn sushi to pan-fried brace of pork chops.

Ardmory Road Isle of Bute PA20 0PG
Map 10: NS06
Tel: 01700 502346
Fax: 01700 505596
Cost: *Alc* £20.25, set-price L £7.50 (2 courses)/D £17.50 (4 courses). ☺
H/wine £8.90
Times: D only, 7- 9pm
Additional: Bar food; Sunday L (noon-1.30pm); Children welcome; ❦ dishes
Smoking: No smoking in dining room
Accommodation: 5 en suite ★★

Directions: N from Rothesay on A844. 1m turn L up Ardmory road. 300 metres on left

ARDUAINE, ## Loch Melfort Hotel ❀❀

Well-run hotel offering genuine hospitality and a superb setting

Oban PA34 4XG
Map 10: NM71
Tel: 01852 200233
Fax: 01852 200214
Chef: Philip Lewis
Owners: Philip & Rosalind Lewis
Cost: Set-price D £29.50 (5 courses).
H/wine £12.50
Times: D only, 7.30-9pm
Additional: Bar food; Children welcome; ❦ dishes
Seats: 80. Private dining room 25
Smoking: No smoking in dining room
Accommodation: 26 en suite ★★★

Directions: From Oban, 20 miles S on the A816; from Lochgilphead, 19 miles N on A816

beside the National Trust of Scotland's Arduaine Gardens.
Glorious views over Asknish Bay to the islands of Shuna,
Scarba and Jura are all part of the appeal. And, as you'd
expect in a restaurant looking over the sea, the kitchen makes
the most of fish and seafood, from light twice-baked crab
soufflé with richly flavoured shellfish sauce, to a 'rosette' of
Dover sole with Loch Etive trout in champagne sauce. Oysters
are from the Isle of Seil, scallops from Islay and lobster from
Luing. Meat-eaters might prefer to start with bresaola with
Parmesan and go on to chargrilled Aberdeen Angus sirloin
steak with parsley butter, or roast gigot of pork with crackling,
baked apple, roast potatoes and Calvados gravy. Lightly
textured lemon and mango mousse might bring up the rear,
and there's a good selection of well-kept Scottish cheeses.

BRIDGE OF ORCHY,
Bridge of Orchy Hotel ✿   NEW

PA36 4AD
Map 10: NN23
Tel: 01838 400208
Fax: 01838 400313
Cost: *Alc* £20. ☺ H/wine £8.95
Times: D only, 7-8.30pm
Additional: Bar food;
Children welcome; 🍴 dishes
Smoking: No smoking in dining room
Accommodation: 10 en suite ★★

Directions: On A82, 6 miles N of
Tyndrum on main Glasgow to Skye
road

*Travellers – by road and those walking the West Highland Way –
will find a haven of warmth and comfort. Feast in the bar or dining
room on smoked venison with Cumberland sauce, grilled fillet of
salmon, and hearty bread-and-butter pudding with custard.*

BUNESSAN, ISLE OF MULL,
Assapol House

*Old manse with views over Loch Assapol. The decor has a Chinese
theme but not the food, when you consider dishes such as roast fillet
of Mull beef with roast vegetables and Madeira jus.*

Accommodation: 5 en suite ★★

Directions: Turn off A849 just after Bunessan School and follow
sign for 1m on minor road

PA67 6DW
Map 10: NM32
Tel: 01681 700258
Fax: 01681 700445
Cost: Set-price D £25 (4 courses).
H/wine £8.50
Times: D only, at 6.30pm
Additional: Children 10+
Smoking: No smoking in dining room

CLACHAN-SEIL, ISLE OF SEIL,
Willowburn Hotel ✿✿

**Tranquil waterside views set the tone at this pretty cottage
hotel.** The restaurant, in particular offers fine views down the
garden and over the Sound of Seil. Food is a passion here,
sourced form local suppliers, and a good proportion is organic.

By Oban PA34 4TJ
Map 10: NM71
Tel: 01852 300276
Fax: 01852 300597
Chef: Chris Mitchell
Owners: Chris Mitchell, Jan Wolfe

Willowburn Hotel

Cost: Set-price D £25 (5 courses).
H/wine £10.50
Times: D only, 7- 8.30pm.
Closed Jan-Feb
Additional: Children welcome;
 dishes
Seats: 24
Smoking: No smoking in dining room
Accommodation: 7 en suite ★ ★

Directions: 11 miles S of Oban via
A816 and B844 (Easdale) over
Atlantic Bridge

Simple treatment allows the wonderful ingredients to speak for themselves with medallion of pan-fried mountain venison requiring little more than a marinade of oak leaf wine and thyme pan-frying and a bitter-sweet sauce. Fish features prominently, whether as baked crab-stuffed mushrooms, or as fresh turbot grilled with prawn butter and served with lemon sauce and samphire. Desserts follow a Scottish theme with heather honey ice with Hebridean liqueur and fresh raspberries, and there are hand-made Scottish cheeses. House wines are excellent, for price, choice and quality.

DERVAIG, ISLE OF MULL,

Druimard Hotel ❁❁

Attractive Victorian country house in a quiet hamlet on the north-west of the island. Superb views over the glen and the River Bellart form the backdrop for the smart but unstuffy restaurant. The five-course dinner menus offer no choice until pudding: monkfish fritters with roast tomato relish, or wild mushroom pastry with herb sauce to start, then a soup – courgette and mint, say – or a lemon or lime sorbet. A main course of fillet of Aberdeen Angus on a bed of celeriac with baby spinach, wild mushrooms and a sauce of red wine and braised shallots has been much appreciated, or there might be a medley of local fish with champagne and chive sauce. Champagne could be used again in a jelly to accompany passion fruit and citrus salad, and the kitchen shows a fondness for mousses, fools and tarts among other puddings, producing nationalist-sounding whisky, honey and oatmeal ice cream for a walnut and whisky tart.

PA75 6QW
Map 13: NM45
Tel: 01688 400345/400291
Fax: 01688 400345
Chef: Wendy Hubbard
Owners: Haydn & Wendy Hubbard
Cost: Set-price D £26.50 (5 courses).
H/wine £9.25
Times: D only, 6.30-8.30pm.
Closed Nov-Mar
Additional: Bar food (residents only);
Children welcome
Seats: 24
Smoking: No smoking in dining room
Accommodation: 7 en suite ★ ★

Directions: From the Craignure ferry turn R to Tobermory. Go through Salen, turn L at Aros, signposted Dervaig, hotel on right-hand side before village

DUNOON, Chatters

A converted cottage in the town centre makes an informal little restaurant offering coffees, teas, good home baking. There's a more serious approach to dinner when dishes like fettucine of scallops and mussels, spiced pork fillet with Calvados jus, or monkfish with spinach and red wine sauce come into their own.

Smoking: No smoking in the dining room

58 John Street PA23 8BJ
Map 10: NS17
Tel/Fax: 01369 706402
Cost: Alc £25. ☺ H/wine £10.95
Times: Noon-3pm/6-9pm.
Closed Sun, Mon, Tue, Jan, Feb
Additional: Bar food;
Children welcome; ✿ dishes

DUNOON, **Enmore Hotel**

Friendly seafront hotel with wonderful views of the Firth of Clyde. Natural flavours come through in simple dishes such as chicken terrine with Cumberland sauce, seared fresh scallops in a light Pernod sauce, and rhubarb crumble with a hint of ginger.

Accommodation: 10 en suite ★★

Directions: From Glasgow M8/A8 (Greenock) & ferry, or via Loch Lomond, A815 to Dunoon. Hotel on promenade btw 2 ferry terminals, 1 mile N of Dunoon

Marine Parade Kirn PA23 8HH
Map 10: NS17
Tel: 01369 702230
Fax: 01369 702148
Cost: Alc £25, D £25 (5 courses). ☺
H/wine £13.50
Times: D only, 6-9.30pm (booking essential off season)
Additional: Bar food; Sunday L; Children welcome; ✦ dishes
Smoking: No smoking in dining room

ERISKA, **Isle of Eriska**

Approached over a bridge, Eriska is a nature-lover's dream, offering access to beaches, woodlands and moors. The Victorian granite building is furnished with style and comfort foremost, and the Buchanan-Smiths excel in standards of service and hospitality. People appreciate the attentive and well-paced service in the dining-room too, with its bare polished tables, silver and sparkling glassware. The kitchen takes top-quality ingredients and treats them with respect, combining them with expertly made sauces to produce well-balanced meals. As you'd expect from the setting, the sea plays a significant role in the repertoire, as in a luxurious crab bisque with squat lobster dumplings, although land-based supply lines might produce best end of local lamb with foie gras and truffle jus on a confit of onion and thyme. The set dinner could typically start with langoustine salad with baby fennel and roasted beetroot in a lemon and caviar dressing, continue with a main course of breast of duck, pink and tender, with foie gras, mounted on potato slices and peppery black pudding with a well-judged jus of thyme and sloes. In between might come something fishy, pan-fried fillet of red mullet with herbs, or meaty wild rabbit and roe deer with pieces of turnip in a creamy velouté with Puy lentils. Scotland's best turn up on the cheeseboard, and puddings could extend to cherry soufflé, well-risen and nicely textured, with vanilla sauce poured in. Canapés are first-rate and the wine list is notable for its breadth and fair prices.

Ledaig by Oban PA37 1SD
Map 10: NM94
Tel: 01631 720371
Fax: 01631 720531
Chef: Robert MacPherson
Owners: The Buchanan-Smith Family
Cost: Set-price D £37.50 (6 courses).
H/wine £8.50
Times: D only, 8-9pm. Closed Jan
Additional: Bar food L; Children welcome; ✦ dishes
Seats: 40. Jacket & tie preferred
Smoking: No smoking in dining room
Accommodation: 17 en suite ★★★★

Directions: On a private island with vehicular access to mainland

KILCHRENAN,
Taychreggan Hotel

Former drovers' inn with friendly service and a relaxed atmosphere. Although this is a former drovers' inn right on the shores of Loch Awe the house, set around a cobbled courtyard, has extensions more reminiscent of a continental villa. Nonetheless the public rooms are delightful. Food is an important element in the mix, and the short but carefully chosen menu changes daily. The bitter chocolate tart adorned with spun sugar wand and spiral lattice baton of white and dark chocolate rather dominated our inspector's thoughts, such was its perfection in texture and depth of flavour. However, medley of west-coast shellfish in an open ravioli with a plum tomato butter sauce was also highly commended. This was followed by a pan-fried fillet of Aberdeen Angus beef with caramelised shallots, roast pimentos, blush tomatoes and port wine and truffle jus, and a blueberry sorbet to finish.

Taynuilt PA35 1HQ
Map 10: NN02
Tel: 01866 833211/833366
Fax: 01866 833244
Chef: Scott Dickson
Owner: Mrs Annie Paul
Cost: Set-price L £17/D £30 (5 courses). H/wine £9.95
Times: 12.30-2pm/7.30-8.45pm
Additional: Bar food L; Sunday L; Children 14+; ✦ dishes
Seats: 45. Private dining room 24
Smoking: No smoking in dining room
Accommodation: 19 en suite ★★★

Directions: One mile before Taynuilt, turn L onto B845 and follow signs to loch side

KILFINAN, **Kilfinan Hotel**

PA21 2EP
Map 10: NR97
Tel: 01700 821201
Fax: 01700 821205
Chef: Rolf Mueller
Owner: N K S Wills
Cost: Set-price D £28 (4 courses). ☺ H/wine £12
Times: D only, 7.30-9pm. Closed Feb
Additional: (Bistro-Bar food L; Sunday L); Children 12+
Seats: 22. Private dining room 20
Smoking: No smoking in dining room
Accommodation: 11 en suite ★ ★

Directions: On B8000 between Tighnabruaich and Otter ferry

Improvements include a new bistro, designed sympathetically to retain the atmosphere and character of the original 17th-century building. The public areas are cosy and inviting, with log fires blazing in cooler weather, and the two dining areas, candlelit at night, provide a focal point. The number of choices per course on the set-price menu varies with the seasons – perhaps two in spring, three in summer – because the kitchen relies on local supply lines. Dinner might start with terrine of woodcock on port jelly, with fillet of halibut spiked with pancetta in a light chervil and Vermouth sauce among main-course options. Alternatively, pan-fried langoustines and scallops on a bed of spinach in a delicate sauce of saffron and chives in an artistic puff pastry shell 'delicious', as our inspector noted, could be followed by a main course of pink, succulent cannon of Scottish lamb with morels and a thyme jus, a combination that couldn't be bettered. Vegetables get the thumbs up in the form of a potato lattice holding carrots, asparagus and courgettes, with a separate plate of exemplary rösti. In between comes a soup – courgette with pesto, perhaps, or barley and diced vegetables, with smoked venison giving it an 'unbelievable flavour'. Desserts are superb, especially a light and tangy mandarin bavarois in a thin, dark chocolate cup topped with whipped cream and red berries, the plate decorated with chocolate and raspberry coulis. Cabernet-Syrah and Chardonnay Vin de Pays D'Oc kick off the wine list.

KILLIECHRONAN, ISLE OF MULL,
Killiechronan House

PA72 6JU
Map 10: NM53
Tel: 01680 300403
Fax: 01680 300463
Cost: Set-price D £27 (5 courses). H/wine £12
Times: D only, 7-8.30pm. Closed Nov-Feb
Additional: Sunday L (noon-1.45pm); Children 10+; ✿ dishes
Smoking: No smoking in dining room. Jacket & tie preferred
Accommodation: 6 en suite ★ ★

Directions: Leaving ferry turn R to Tobermory (A849), in Salen (12 miles) turn L to B8035, after 2 miles turn R to Ulva ferry (B8073). Killiechronan on R

Delightful country house hotel close to the shore of Loch na Keal. Tempting five-course dinners of up-to-date Scottish food are served in either of the two elegant dining rooms.

KILMARTIN, **Cairn Restaurant**

Lochgilphead PA31 8RQ
Map 10: NR89
Tel: 01546 510254
Cost: Alc £20. ☺ H/wine £9.50
Times: Noon-3pm/6.30-10pm. Closed Tue, 25 Dec, 1Jan
Additional: Bar food; Sunday L; Children 10+ after 8pm; ✿ dishes

Reliable, friendly, enjoyable and affordable describe this bistro-style operation where menus are as unpretentious as the surroundings: chicken liver pâté, pan-fried scallops 'done to perfection', chocolate whisky cake, and a short list of popular wines encapsulate the style.

Smoking: Air conditioning

Directions: On A816 Lochgilphead-Oban road

LUSS,

The Lodge on Loch Lomond

By Alexandria G83 8PA
Map 10: NS39
Tel: 01436 860201
Fax: 01436 860203
Cost: *Alc*: £17
Times: Noon-2.45pm/6-9.30pm
Additional: Bar food; Sunday L;
Children welcome; ✦ dishes
Smoking: No smoking in dining room
Accommodation: 29 en suite ★ ★ ★

Directions: From Glasgow take A82
(follow signs for Erskine Bridge) then
N to Luss

*An idyllic lochside hotel offering innovative Scottish fare in peaceful
surroundings. Our March meal started with a field mushroom risotto
with green salsa oil, while the main course of pan-fried venison loin
came with an irresistible haggis skirlie. The wine list offers many
New World wines.*

OBAN, Dungallan House Hotel

*Taste of Scotland dishes prepared from local produce are on offer at
this Victorian villa. Expect house pâtés, Highland beef with
mushroom and Drambuie sauce, and strawberry cranachan.*

Smoking: No smoking in dining room; Air conditioning
Accommodation: 13 (11 en suite) ★ ★

Directions: From Argyll Square in Oban follow signs for
Gallanach. Approx 0.5 miles from Square

Gallanach Road PA34 4PD
Map 10: NM82
Tel: 01631 563799
Fax: 01631 566711
Cost: *Alc* £25, set-price L £15/
D £25. ☺ H/wine £8.75
Times: 12.30-1.45pm/7.30-8.15pm.
Reservations only
Additional: Bar Food L; Sunday L;
Children welcome; ✦ dishes

OBAN, Manor House Hotel

Gallanach Road PA34 4LS
Map 10: NM82
Tel: 01631 562087
Fax: 01631 563053
Chef: Neil O'Brien
Cost: Set-price L £18.90/D £25.90 (5
courses). H/wine £13
Times: Noon-2pm/6.45-9pm.
Closed D Sun, all Mon, L Tue Nov-
Feb
Additional: Bar food L; Sunday L;
Children 12+; ✦ dishes
Seats: 30
Smoking: No smoking in dining room
Accommodation: 11 en suite ★ ★

Directions: 300 metres past Oban
ferry terminal

***Charming small hotel noted for welcoming atmosphere and
enthusiastic staff.*** In the elegant dark-green and panelled
dining room of the former Georgian dower house overlooking
Oban Bay, the atmosphere is highly civilised but unstuffy.
Good quality Scottish ingredients, particularly fish and game,
go into the daily-changing set-price menu. Our inspection meal

began with a wonderful shellfish and tomato broth, lovely and rich in both colour and flavour. Spanking fresh scallops, lightly seared and encased in smoked bacon, shone with honest flavour. You can't visit the Highlands without sampling venison – here it may come as collops with apple and black pudding with redcurrant and rosemary glaze. Then there's sticky toffee pudding with butterscotch sauce or a selection of Scottish and continental cheeses. Plan the next day's activities over strong cafetière coffee and chocolate mints.

PORT APPIN, Airds Hotel

Built as a ferry inn, looking over the waters of Loch Linnhe to Lismore Island and the hills of Morvern beyond. A glassed-in conservatory faces the loch, there are two sitting rooms to relax in (the excellent canapés are served here: chicken pâté in pastry, say, and sun-dried tomato and pesto on a crisp croûton), and the dining room is comfortable, nicely furnished and well maintained – although few will notice, given the views. Dinner orders are asked for in advance from a menu that offers three or four starters and main courses, with a soup in between – pea and mint, or tomato and basil – with half-a-dozen puddings. Shellfish is a favoured opener, perhaps west coast lobster with avocado salad and gazpacho dressing, or roasted langoustines accompanied by small squares of red mullet and aubergine caviar, all brought together by a lively herb salad and a light, mildly chillied tomato salsa. Chicken liver terrine also shows up regularly, alongside breast of wood pigeon on a potato pancake with wild mushrooms. The quality of ingredients speaks for itself: roast fillet of Aberdeen Angus in a restrained Burgundy sauce with earthy-tasting truffled leeks, or fillet of salmon with crisp pancetta, fennel and asparagus salad and lemon butter. Perfectly smooth chocolate parfait comes with orange sauce to cut the bitter-rich chocolate, and orange and grapefruit in Grand Marnier jelly is a popular alternative. The same high standards extend to the wine list too, with unfaltering good judgement behind every bin.

Appin PA38 4DF
Map 14: NM94
Tel: 01631 730236
Fax: 01631 730535
Chefs: Graeme Allen, Steve McCullum
Owners: The Allen Family
Cost: Set-price D £40 (4 courses). H/wine £14
Times: D only, 7.30-8.30pm. Closed 20-27 Dec, 6-29 Jan
Additional: Children 8+; ☺ dishes
Seats: 36
Smoking: No smoking in dining room
Accommodation: 16 en suite ★ ★ ★

Directions: Leave A828 at Appin, hotel is 2.5 miles between Ballachulish and Cannel

SCALASAIG, Colonsay Hotel

Island hotel in an 18th-century building overlooking the gardens to the sea. Local and regional produce dictate the menu, which is set, with a French theme running through the very sound cooking.

Smoking: No smoking in dining room
Accommodation: 11 rooms ★ ★

Directions: 400 yards west of Colonsay pier

Isle of Colonsay PA61 7YP
Map 10: NR39
Tel: 01951 200316
Fax: 01951 200353
Cost: Set-price L £4 (2 courses)/D £25 (4 courses). H/wine £10
Times: Noon-2pm/7.30 for 8pm
Additional: Bar food; Children welcome

STRACHUR, Creggans Inn

Candlelit restaurant with fabulous views over the loch. Innovative dishes are based on fine Scottish produce. Expect dishes such as roast salmon with smoked haddock, potato and fried parsnip.

Directions: From Glasgow A82, along Loch Lomond, then W on A83 (through Arrochar/Rest and be Thankful) onto A815 to Strachur. Or by car ferry from Gourock to Dunoon onto A815 to Strachur

PA27 8BX
Map 10: NN00
Tel: 01369 860279
Fax: 01369 860637
Cost: Set-price D £22.50. ☺ H/wine £10.95
Times: D only, 7-9.30pm
Additional: Bar food; Children welcome; ☺ dishes
Smoking: No smoking in dining room
Accommodation: 17 en suite ★ ★ ★

TOBERMORY, ISLE OF MULL,

Highland Cottage

A new building designed in traditional style offering a high level of personal attention and considerable cooking skills. Navarin of seafood, ginger and French bean stew, and baked spiced breast of Barbary duck, suggest this is one small hotel likely to build a large following.

Smoking: No smoking in dining room
Accommodation: 6 en suite ★ ★

Directions: Opposite fire station. From Main Street proceed up Back Brae, turn L at top by White House and below Arts Centre. Follow road round to R, L at next junction

Breadalbane Street PA75 6PD
Map 13: NM55
Tel: 01688 302030
Fax: 01688 302727
Cost: Set-price D £19.50 (4 courses).
☺ H/wine £10.50
Times: D only, 7-9pm.
Closed 14 Oct-6 Nov
Additional: Children welcome;
🍴 dishes

AYRSHIRE, EAST

DARVEL,

Scoretulloch House

Massive ceiling beams and half-panelling make an appropriate setting for a restaurant, accompanied by a handful of letting bedrooms, in a 500-year-old building. The set-price four-course dinner menu gives a good choice at each course, perhaps kicking off with carpaccio of prime Scottish beef with Parmesan, Aga-dried tomatoes and a rocket and basil salad, or roasted West Coast scallops with leek purée and mint-infused olive oil. Highland venison is roasted and served with garlic fondant potatoes and rosemary gravy, or there are simply grilled steaks for traditionalists. A strong hand with fruit shows up in desserts – a brandy snap basket filled with wild berries, say, or poached figs and air-dried plums served with a Madeira and citrus essence – and the cheeseboard is exclusively Scottish. House wines from Australia head up a list of 50 or so bins.

Directions: Take M74/J8 for A71. Hotel is clearly signed 1 mile S of A71 (Strathaven-Kilmarnock), just E of Darvel

KA17 0LR
Map 11: NS53
Tel: 01560 323331
Fax: 01560 323441
Chef: Kevin Dalgleish
Owners: Don & Annie Smith
Cost: Set-price D £29.50 (4 courses).
H/wine £12
Times: Noon-2.15pm/7-9.15pm
Additional: Sunday L; Children 12+;
🍴 dishes
Seats: 75
Smoking: No smoking in dining room
Accommodation: 4 en suite

FENWICK,

Fenwick Hotel

Newly expanded hotel with a warm Scottish feel from natural wood and tartan furnishings. Seafood and game feature regularly on the reasonably priced carte, supported by daily specials. The cooking is as refreshingly honest as the hospitality.

Smoking: No-smoking area; No pipes & cigars
Accommodation: 31 en suite ★ ★ ★

Directions: Telephone for directions

KA3 6AU
Map 11: NS44
Tel: 01560 600478
Fax: 01560 600334
Cost: Alc £20. ☺ H/wine £10.90
Times: Noon-2pm/6-9.30pm
Additional: Bar food; Sunday L;
Children welcome; 🍴 dishes

AYRSHIRE, NORTH

BRODICK, **Auchrannie Hotel**

Genuine hospitality together with extensive leisure facilities and some sound cooking are all part of the appeal of this renovated Victorian mansion set in extensive landscaped grounds. The formal Garden Restaurant with its airy conservatory extension continues to showcase the best of Scotland's larder on its daily-changing, set-price dinner menu of two, three or four courses. A contemporary twist is given to traditional Scottish dishes, for example oven-baked Kilmory lamb is served with Puy lentils, saffron potatoes and Madeira jus, and grilled local salmon appears with squid ink noodles, steamed cockles and mussels and an Arran mustard cream sauce. Starters may include cold dressed hors d'oeuvre, game terrine and smoked salmon with exotic fruits, and mackerel with caper and lemon butter, with the intermediate soup course possibly featuring cream of winter vegetable. Finish with a home-made dessert. Bramble Bistro offers a more informal atmosphere.

Isle of Arran KA27 8BZ
Map 10: NS03
Tel: 01770 302234
Fax: 01770 302812
Chef: Andy Yuill
Owner: Iain Johnston
Cost: Set-price D £24 (4-courses). ☺
H/wine £11.95
Times: D only, 7-9pm
Additional: Children welcome;
🍴 dishes
Seats: 60. Private dining room 24
Smoking: No smoking in dining room
Accommodation: 28 en suite ★ ★ ★

Directions: From ferry terminal turn R and follow coast road through Brodick village, then take second L past golf club

BRODICK, **Kilmichael Hotel**

Visitors return year after year to this comfortable country house hotel (believed to be the oldest house on the island). Highlights of our meal were the own-baked breads, a soup of creamed sage, and a steamed orange sponge with whisky ice cream.

Directions: Follow Shore Road to golf course, turn L inland at sharp bend. Past church to road end

Glen Cloy Isle of Arran KA27 8BY
Map 10: NS03
Tel: 01770 302219
Fax: 01770 302068
Telephone for further details

DALRY, **Braidwoods** ✿✿

Charming, cosy little restaurant looking to all intents and purposes like someone's home. The small whitewashed 200-year-old cottage is set well back from the road. The set-price three or four-course menus offer around a trio of choices at each course. A smooth parfait of chicken liver and foie gras with gooseberry chutney and sultana brioche, for example, might be among the starters. Lightly curried pea and lettuce soup could follow, and main courses are described as an object lesson on how an excellent dish doesn't need to be fussy and

Drumastle Mill Cottage KA24 4LN
Map 10: NS24
Tel: 01294 833544
Fax: 01294 833553
Chef: Keith Braidwood
Owners: Keith & Nicola Braidwood
Cost: Set-price L £16/D £27.50.
H/wine £11.95
Times: Noon-1.45pm/7-9pm.
Closed D Sun, all Mon, L Tue,
1st 3 wks Jan, 2 wks Sep/Oct

complicated: perfectly baked fillet of Shetland salmon with an Arbroath smokie and saffron sauce served with leek risotto, or honey-glazed breast of Gressingham duck with a confit of its leg and rosemary essence. Add excellent British farmhouse cheeses, rolls made in-house, and service that is friendly and charming, and you have the perfect restaurant.

Directions: 1 mile from Dalry on the Saltcoats Road

KILWINNING, Montgreenan Mansion House Hotel

Imposing 19th-century mansion set in 48 acres of park and woodland. The extensive six-course dinner menu is supported by a short carte and a good wine list.

Directions: 4 miles N of Irvine, & 19 miles S of Glasgow on A736

Montgreenan Estate KA13 7QZ
Map 10: NS34
Tel: 01294 557733
Fax: 01294 850397
Telephone for further details

LOCHRANZA, Harold's Restaurant NEW

Situated on the first floor of the Visitor Centre to Scotland's newest distillery, this contemporary all day eaterie (light lunches and teas) takes a serious approach to food in the evening. A short carte based on fresh ingredients sourced across the island takes in the likes of lobster and crab timbale, and venison with brandy-scented jus.

Smoking: No-smoking area

Directions: Telephone for directions

Isle of Arran Distillery KA27 8HJ
Map 10: NR95
Tel: 01770 830264
Fax: 01770 830364
Cost: *Alc* £23. ☺ H/wine £7.99
Times: 12.30-2.30pm/7-9pm.
Closed D Wed, Jan-Mar
Additional: Children welcome;
🍴 dishes

Additional: Sunday L;
Children welcome
Seats: 24
Smoking: No smoking in dining room

Winner of the AA Restaurant of the Year Award (see p20)

AYRSHIRE, SOUTH

AYR, Fairfield House Hotel ✿✿

Victorian Glasgow tea merchant's house, which enjoys uninterrupted views of the Firth of Clyde. There is a choice of dining with an all-day conservatory brasserie supplementing the elegant dinner-only Fleur de Lys restaurant. The latter offers about half-a-dozen choices at each stage beginning with the likes of twice-baked smoked haddock and chive soufflé, quail galantine and goats' cheese and spinach soup before such dishes as hot-smoked loin of lamb en croûte, halibut on saffron noodles with a shellfish and coriander essence and duck with rum, lime and ginger on bok choi. Desserts range from warm apple tart with honey-glazed Calvados ice cream to iced banana and mango soufflé. Good canapés and petits fours are all made in-house, as are the cheese biscuits. Expansive wine list and notable selection of single malts including many from distilleries that are now closed.

Directions: Town centre, down Miller Rd to T junction with traffic lights, filter L, immediately R into Fairfield Rd

12 Fairfield Road KA7 2AR
Map 10: NS32
Tel: 01292 267461
Fax: 01292 261456
Chef: Adi Schmidt
Owners: Mr & Mrs G Martin
Cost: *Alc* £22, set-price L £9.50. ☺
H/wine £10.95
Times: Noon-2pm/6-9pm
Additional: Sunday L; Children welcome; 🍴 dishes
Seats: 24. Private dining room. Jacket & tie preferred
Smoking: No smoking in dining room
Accommodation: 36 en suite ★★★★

AYR, **Fouters Bistro** ❀❀

**Well-regarded restaurant that's been going strong for a
quarter of a century.** A tribute to the freshness of the food and
the consistency of the cooking. Fisherman's soup is almost a
meal in itself, piled high with mussels, salmon, mullet, haddock,
cod and aïoli croûtons. Another substantial starter, crisp roast
duck confit, was partnered by some great pearl barley risotto
with red wine jus. Loin fillet of Carrick Hill lamb with stem
ginger, honey and Crabbes wine added to the jus, plus fresh
leaf spinach, confounded expectations by coming together
beautifully when combined in one forkful. A combo of
precisely cooked Shetland salmon and Norwegian red fish
made an interesting contrast, with a chive cream sauce kept
deliberately simple. Chargrilled quality Scotch steaks live up to
the house reputation. Desserts stay within well charted
territory – bread-and-butter pudding, crème brûlée and
chocolate terrine with almond cream sauce.

2A Academy Street KA7 1HS
Map 10: NS32
Tel: 01292 261391
Fax: 01292 619323
Chef: Laurie Black
Owners: Fran & Laurie Black
Cost: *Alc* £21.50. ☺ H/wine £12.50
Times: Noon-2pm/6.30-10pm. Closed
Sun, Mon, 25-27 Dec, 1-3 Jan
Additional: Children welcome;
❸ dishes
Seats: 38
Smoking: No-smoking area; No pipes
& cigars; Air conditioning

Directions: Town centre, opposite
Town Hall, down Cobblestone Lane

GIRVAN, **Wildings** ❀

*Popular and good of its type – that's Wildings. Although meat and
game feature, fish and seafood are its specialities, much of which is
landed at the local harbour, enabling chef/proprietor Brian Sage to
offer a weighty selection of most species.*

Montgomerie Street KA26 9HE
Map 10: NX19
Tel: 01465 713481
Telephone for further details

Directions: Just off A77 at the north end of village

MAYBOLE, **Ladyburn** ❀ NEW

*Warm and welcoming country house set in attactive gardens. Guests
are well looked after, with a set three course dinner taking into
account individual preferences. Expect home-cooking with firm
favourites like soups, roasts and sorbets.*

KA19 7SG
Tel: 01655 740585
Fax: 01655 740580
Telephone for further details

Directions: Telephone for directions

TROON, **Highgrove House** ❀❀

**Smart country house built in the 1920s run by a smart,
attentive team.** The restaurant is popular and very well-known
locally, offering a sophisticated dinner menu supplemented by
brasserie dishes in a wide-ranging repertoire. Skill and
presentation are good, with bread, canapés and petits fours all
made in house. Fish features as in west coast seafood chowder,
mussels in white wine, but meatier dishes range from best end
of lamb to plainly grilled steaks. Booking is essential. Lunch is
good value.

Loans Road KA10 7HL
Map 10: NS33
Tel: 01292 312511
Fax: 01292 318228
Telephone for further details

Directions: A77 from Ayr (Glasgow),
L at Prestwick Airport, first R to Old
Irvine. First L to Loans, R at mini
roundabout to Highgrove

TROON,
Lochgreen House ❀❀❀

**The country house is adjacent to the fairways of Royal Troon
Golf Course.** The dining-room looks out over sixteen-acres of
woodland and immaculately groomed gardens. Here, Andrew
Costley's classic French techniques meet good Scottish
ingredients, especially seafood, meat, game and cheeses.
Scallop and sole terrine is served with a salad of fresh herbs

Monktonhill Road Southwood
KA10 7EN
Map 10: NS33
Tel: 01292 313343
Fax: 01292 318661
Chef: Andrew Costley
Cost: Set-price L £18.95/D £29.95 (4
courses). ☺ H/wine £14.50

and a citrus and heather honey dressing; poaching gives the lightest of touches to halibut on a mussel and fennel stew with saffron potatoes and chives. Barley comes out of store-cupboard obscurity to be puréed and served with confit leg of duckling wrapped in pancetta with rocket and thyme vinaigrette. Sweet-and-sour ratatouille adds an unusual note to rosettes of Ayrshire lamb with roasted mint potatoes and red wine sauce. For dessert there are some luscious hot puddings such as mocha chocolate steamed sponge with coffee bean sauce. Bordeaux, Burgundy and other French appellations make a strong showing in the well-chosen list which also includes a wide selection of wines by the glass and half-bottle.

Times: Noon-2pm/7-9pm
Additional: Sunday L; Children 14+ at D; 🍴 dishes
Seats: 60. Private dining rooms 16-30
Smoking: No smoking in dining room
Accommodation: 15 en suite ★ ★ ★

Directions: Off A77 (Prestwick Airport) onto B749, SE of Troon

TROON, Marine Highland Hotel

Split-level restaurant with views of the fairway, Firth of Clyde and Isle of Arran. Classic Scottish dishes are given a modern treatment and come beautifully presented.

Smoking: No-smoking area; Air conditioning
Accommodation: 74 en suite ★ ★ ★ ★

Directions: Take A77 from Glasgow (following signs for Prestwick Airport) and turn onto B789 – hotel overlooks 18th fairway of Royal Troon Golf Course

KA10 6HE
Map 10: NS33
Tel: 01292 314444
Fax: 01292 316922
Cost: *Alc* £15, set-price D £25 (4 courses). ☺ H/wine £11.05
Times: 12.30-2pm/7-9.30pm
Additional: Sunday L; Children welcome; 🍴 dishes

TROON,

Piersland House Hotel

Craigend Road KA10 6HD
Map 10: NS33
Tel: 01292 314747
Fax: 01292 315613
Chef: John Rae
Owner: J A Brown
Cost: *Alc* £22.50, set-price L £12.95/D £22.50 (4 courses). ☺ H/wine £11.95
Times: Noon-2.15pm/6.45-9.45pm
Additional: Children 6+; 🍴 dishes
Seats: 42. Private dining room 94
Smoking: No smoking in dining room
Accommodation: 28 en suite ★ ★ ★

Directions: Opposite Royal Troon Golf Club

Close to the championship golf course, this stylish, carefully extended mansion was built in the 1890s for the grandson of whisky king Johnnie Walker. In addition to a lounge bar menu, the hotel offers an extensive modern brasserie menu in the elegant Red Bowl Restaurant. Fresh raw ingredients, in particular fish and seafood, are competently handled and well executed dishes may include fish chowder, or king scallops, black pudding and potato rösti with piquant pimento sauce, and game terrine with mixed leaves and balsamic dressing. For main course try, perhaps, roast halibut with baby leek mash, tapenade sauce and fennel confit, or peppered duck breast with cherry and Merlot sauce. Puddings come in the shape of prune and Armagnac parfait with tea syrup, and glazed lemon tart with crushed meringue ice.

TURNBERRY, Malin Court ❀❀

KA26 9PB
Map 10: NS20
Tel: 01655 331457
Fax: 01655 331072
Chef: Andrea Beach
Cost: Set-price D £21.95 (4 courses).
☺ H/wine £11.95
Times: 12.30-2pm/7.30-9pm
Additional: Bar food L; Sunday L;
Children welcome; ✿ dishes
Seats: 120. Private dining rooms 16,
70
Accommodation: 18 en suite ★ ★ ★

Directions: On A719 one mile from
A77 on N side of village

Lovely hotel, great location, exemplary service. From the
well-prepared canapés to the home-made petits fours, there is
no doubting the imagination and flair that goes into the
preparation and presentation of good ingredients. A warm
terrine of guinea fowl with red onion and prune confit was
tender, moist and full of flavour; spinach soup refreshing and
light. A trio of beef, venison and lamb, bound with bacon and
served on top of a celeriac rösti and a rosehip jus was a
creative concept and beautifully delivered. Praise too, for a
light chocolate sponge 'and it was', coated with rich dark
chocolate and served with a home-made Drambuie ice cream.
One of the great strengths of this very comfortable hotel
overlooking the Firth of Clyde and Turnberry is the staff; they
should all stand up and take a bow.

TURNBERRY, Turnberry Hotel ❀❀

KA26 9LT
Map 10: NS20
Tel: 01655 331000
Fax: 01655 331706
Chef: D S Cameron
Owner: Starwood Hotels & Resorts
Worldwide Inc
Cost: *Alc* £50, set-price D £48.
H/wine £21.75
Times: D only, 7.30-9.30pm
Additional: Bar food L (Clubhouse);
Sunday L (12.30-2.30pm); Children
welcome; ✿ dishes
Seats: 180. Private dining room 16.

*This famous hotel enjoys tremendous views over the Isle of
Arran, the Mull of Kintyre and Ailsa Craig, as well as of the
golf courses which have been home to the Open
Championship on a number of occasions.* There are three
restaurants: the main Turnberry Restaurant is laid out in
traditional grand hotel style; the Bay Restaurant is
Mediterranean in style; and there's the Tappie Toorie Grill – a
coffee shop-cum-grill. The Turnberry offers both *carte* and set-
menus, built around a classical style brought up to date with a
smattering of rocket, polenta, balsamic vinegar and the like.
It's strengths are to be found in the local produce such as

smoked Scottish salmon, Loch Fyne oysters, some seared west coast scallops, that were simply cooked and presented, and meats served from the carving trolley. The prices are high; the wine list is competent if somewhat safe.

Directions: From A77 to Turnberry. Hotel 0.5 mile on R

Jacket & tie preferred
Accommodation: 132 en suite
★ ★ ★ ★ ★

DUMFRIES & GALLOWAY

CASTLE DOUGLAS,
Plumed Horse Restaurant

Dumfries & Galloway can now vaunt the talents of chef/proprietor Tony Borthwick. It's a small village setting, and the elegantly appointed restaurant has made a promising start. Quality is the keynote here, from the tasteful, warm yellow decor and fine table appointments, to the modern menu which has roots in classical French cooking, and makes good use of luxury ingredients such as foie gras, sweetbreads and wild mushrooms. At inspection, both the atmosphere and the food impressed. Lobster, scallop and langoustine sausage delivered flavour and the accompanying rich Nantua sauce showed skill. Stuffed leg of chicken with a farce of sweetbreads and foie gras was full of flavour and offset by smooth celeriac purée and well-executed rösti. A well made bread-and-butter pudding with crème anglaise and Drambuie caramel followed. Excellent freshly baked bread as well as a short, well-balanced wine list offering both old and New World selections.

Directions: On A713 towards Ayr, 3 miles from Castle Douglas

Main Street by Castle Douglas
DG7 3AU
Map 11: NX76
Tel: 01556 670333
Fax: 01556 670302
Chef: Tony Borthwick
Owners: Tony Borthwick,
Charles Kirkbride
Cost: *Alc* £25.50, set-price L £14.50.
☺ H/wine £9.99
Times: 12.30-1.30pm/7-9.30pm.
Closed Mon
Additional: Sunday L; Children welcome; ◑ dishes
Seats: 30. Private dining room 18
Smoking: No-smoking area; No pipes & cigars; Air conditioning

GATEHOUSE OF FLEET,
Cally Palace Hotel

Georgian mansion with an elegant dining room overlooking the grounds. Smoked salmon and dill mousse might be followed by chicken breast with thyme mash and lemon cream sauce.

Smoking: No smoking in dining room
Accommodation: 56 en suite ★ ★ ★ ★

Directions: From A74(M) take A75, through Dumfries towards Newton Stewart. Take B727 to Gatehouse

DG7 2DL
Map 11: NX55
Tel: 01557 814341
Fax: 01557 814522
Cost: *Alc* £24, set-price L £13/D £24
(both 4 courses). ☺ H/wine £12.10
Times: 1-2pm/6.45-9.15pm. Closed 3
Jan-5 Feb, Mon-Fri in Feb
Additional: Bar food L; Children welcome; ◑ dishes

KIRKCUDBRIGHT,
Selkirk Arms Hotel

Innovative Scottish cooking in a 200 year old inn with Robbie Burns connections. Home-made breads, fresh local fish and Galloway beef are served in the elegant restaurant overlooking the garden.

Smoking: No smoking in dining room
Accommodation: 16 en suite ★ ★ ★

Directions: 5 miles S of A75 junction with A711

Old High Street DG6 4JG
Map 11: NX65
Tel: 01557 330402
Fax: 01557 331639
Cost: Set-price D £21. ☺
H/wine £8.50
Times: Noon-2pm/7-9.30pm
Additional: Bar food; Sunday L;
Children welcome; ◑ dishes

LOCKERBIE, Dryfesdale Hotel

DG11 2SF
Map 11: NY18
Tel: 01576 202427
Fax: 01576 204187
Cost: £25, set-price L £10.95 (4
courses)/D £19.95 (5 courses). ☺
H/wine £13
Times: Noon-2pm/6.30-9pm.
Closed 26 Dec
Additional: Bar Food; Sunday L;
Children welcome; ✿ dishes
Smoking: No smoking in dining room
Accommodation: 15 en suite ★ ★ ★

Directions: M74 J17 to Lockerbie

*From the pillared dining room look out past the terrace to lawns and
distant hills. A peaceful setting for a menu with a modern Scottish
and international flavour.*

MOFFAT, Beechwood Hotel

Harthope Place DG10 9RS
Map 11: NT00
Tel: 01683 220210
Fax: 01683 220889
Cost: Set-price D £23.50 (6 courses).
☺ H/wine £10
Times: Noon-2pm/7-8.45pm.
Closed L Mon-Thu, 2 Jan-19 Feb
Additional: Sunday L; Children
welcome; ✿ dishes
Smoking: No smoking in dining room
Accommodation: 7 en suite ★ ★

Directions: At N end of High Street
turn R into Harthope Place (hotel
signed)

*Traditional-style Scottish country house dining with the ingredients
for the frequently changing five-course menu of fine cooking
sourced as locally as possible.*

MOFFAT,
Well View Hotel

Ballplay Road DG10 9JU
Map 11: NT00
Tel: 01683 220184
Fax: 01683 220088
Chef: Janet Schuckardt
Owners: Janet & John Schuckardt
Cost: Set-price D £28 (6 courses).
H/wine £12
Times: 12.15-1.15pm/6.30-8.30pm.
Closed L Sat
Additional: Sunday L; Children 5+
Seats: 20. Private dining room 6.
Jacket & tie preferred
Smoking: No smoking in dining room
Accommodation: 6 en suite ★

Owned and run by the Schuckardt family, this delightful Victorian house has a well-deserved reputation for good food. Janet's six-course dinner menu displays sound cooking skills and good use of quality local ingredients, as well as imaginative presentation. Preceded by canapés, a meal here is good value and includes home-made sorbet and a selection of fine, mainly Scottish cheeses. Highlights of a recent inspection meal were a tender beef fillet served on roasted vegetables with a whisky and mustard cream sauce, and the ripe condition of the cheeses. Further courses may include a warm tart of bacon, mushrooms and smoked Orkney Cheddar, followed by seared cod with balsamic and tomato jus and, for pudding, a brandy snap basket filled with marinated black cherry and Amaretti trifle topped with Marscarpone. A nice touch is a selection of wines on the menu that have been chosen to complement the food.

Well View Hotel

Directions: From Moffat take A708 (Selkirk); L after fire station in Ballplay Road. 300 yds to hotel

NEWTON STEWART,
Creebridge House Hotel

DG8 6NP
Map 10: NX46
Tel: 01671 402121
Fax: 01671 403258
Cost: *Alc* £28, set-price D £21 (4 courses). ☺ H/wine £9.95
Times: Noon-2pm/6-9pm
Additional: Bar food, Sunday L; Children welcome; ☘ dishes
Smoking: No smoking in dining room
Accommodation: 19 en suite ★★

Directions: Telephone for directions

Award-winning lamb dishes are hard to pass up, but there are also excellent fish and seafood ones at the Garden Restaurant and in the more informal Bridges Brasserie. Home-made sweets include the delicious Ecclefechan butter tart.

NEWTON STEWART,
Kirroughtree House

Built in the early 18th century, with rococo furnishings to match. Kirroughtree House is set in eight acres of rolling forestry and landscaped gardens. Moulded ceilings, heavily draped windows, patterned carpets and white-clothed tables provide the backdrops for menus that run from Thai chicken salad with straw potatoes, through cannon of Scottish lamb niçoise with tapenade sauce garnished with tomato petals, courgettes, couscous and aubergine crisps, to Scottish farmhouse cheeses with home-made bannocks. A terrine of coarse pork knuckle and delicately textured foie gras, all suspended in aspic, with sharp home-made piccalilli is a starter 'bursting with flavour', the product of a kitchen in command of both texture and tastes. Tournedos of milk-fed veal comes with a Madeira sauce showing a deft hand and contributes to the

Minnigaff DG8 6AN
Map 10: NX46
Tel: 01671 402141
Fax: 01671 402425
Chef: Ian Bennett
Owner: Douglas McMillan
Cost: *Alc* £18, set-price L £14/D £30 (4 courses). H/wine £14.50
Times: Noon-1.30pm/7-9pm. Closed 3 Jan-11 Feb
Additional: Sunday L; Children 10+; ☘ dishes
Seats: 50. Jacket & tie preferred
Smoking: No smoking in dining room
Accommodation: 17 en suite ★★★

Kirroughtree House

Directions: From A75 turn left into A712 (New Galloway), hotel entrance 300yds on left

'lovely flavours' of a dish combined with spinach, wild mushrooms, asparagus tips and gratin dauphinoise. Finish with chocolate marquise with white chocolate sorbet, or prune and almond tart with vanilla ice cream. The wine list runs the gamut of house wines to rare vintages.

PORTPATRICK, Fernhill Hotel NEW

DG9 8TD
Map 10: NW95
Tel: 01776 810220
Fax: 01776 810596
Cost: *Alc* £21.50, set-price D £22.50 (4 courses). ☺ H/wine £9.35
Times: Noon-1.45pm/6-9.30pm
Additional: Bar food; Sunday L; Children welcome; ⚫ dishes

Restaurant with spectacular views of the picturesque village, Portpatrick Harbour and beyond to the Irish Sea. A speciality menu of hand-picked Mull of Galloway lobsters is a feature.

Smoking: No-smoking area; Air conditioning
Accommodation: 20 en suite ★ ★ ★

Directions: A77 from Stranraer. R before war memorial. Hotel 1st L

PORTPATRICK,
Knockinaam Lodge

Stranraer DG9 9AD
Map 10: NW95
Tel: 01776 810471
Fax: 01776 810435
Chef: Tony Pierce
Owners: Michael Bricker, Pauline Ashworth
Cost: Set-price L £27 (4 courses)/D £38 (4 courses). H/wine £12
Times: Noon-2.30pm/7.30-9.30pm

Approached along a quiet winding road, this Victorian lodge is surrounded on three sides by wooded hills, the fourth consisting of lawns rolling down to a private beach. Plump green olives and crisps with a drink in the bar should keep people going after an afternoon in the sea air, and dinner, a lengthy set-meal of four courses, will satisfy the sharpest appetite. There's no choice until dessert, although alternatives for vegetarians are clearly available, and the menus show a good sense of balance. A modern approach is brought to prime Scottish produce (rabbit, roe deer, salmon, Galloway lamb), so a menu could start with a risotto of native lobster with sauce nero and feature a main course of lightly grilled Drummore codling (from the southern end of the peninsula) in a lemon and olive oil dressing with baby vegetables. The intermediate course might be a tower of plum tomatoes and asparagus dressed with pesto, and the finale brings a decision: cheeses with honey and sultana bread, or warm chocolate tart with coffee custard. We started with beautifully juicy seared scallops surrounded by yellow pepper gazpacho, then came well-timed fillet of sea bass with samphire and a delicate cardamom froth, and then new season's lamb, just pink, its sweetness complemented by a rich port-based sauce. Lemon tart, smooth and soft, given a lift by a matching sorbet, ended the meal. The wine list, over 30 pages long, has some classy producers and vintages, and you can retire to the bar after dinner for a single-malt whisky – there are over 100 to chose from.

Additional: Bar food L; Sunday L; Children 12+ at D; 🍴 dishes
Seats: 30. Private dining room 10
Smoking: No smoking in dining room
Accommodation: 10 en suite ★ ★

AA Shortlisted for
AA Wine Award-see page16

Directions: A77 or A75 to Stranarer. Then A77 towards Portpatrick. W of Lochans watch for Colfin Smokehouse & hotel signs

---

STRANRAER,

North West Castle Hotel ✿ NEW

An elegant dining room with a pianist playing is the relaxing setting for a short four-course menu of traditional dishes given a contemporary slant.

Smoking: No pipes & cigars; Air conditioning
Accommodation: 73 en suite ★ ★ ★ ★

Directions: Town Centre

DG9 8EH
Map 10: NX06
Tel: 01776 704413
Fax: 01776 702646
Cost: Set-price D £23 (5 courses). ☺
H/wine £12.50
Times: Noon-2pm/7-9.30pm
Additional: Bar Food L; Sunday L; Children welcome; 🍴 dishes

DUNBARTONSHIRE, WEST

BALLOCH,

Cameron House Hotel ✿✿✿

Noble mansion, stylishly extended to include a leisure centre. The hotel is magnificently set in 100 acres of woodland on the

Loch Lomond G83 8QZ
Map 10: NS38
Tel: 01389 755565
Fax: 01389 759522
Chef: Peter Fleming
Cost: Alc £45, set-price L £21/D £38.50 (4 courses). H/wine £13.50
Times: Noon-1.45pm/7-9.45pm. Closed L Sat & Sun, 26 Dec
Additional: Children 14+; 🍴 dishes
Seats: 45. Jacket & tie preferred at D
Smoking: No smoking in dining room; Air conditioning
Accommodation: 96 en suite
★ ★ ★ ★ ★

southern shore of Loch Lomond, with an outlook across the water to distant peaks beyond. There are three eating options to choose from, but the rosettes go to the Georgian Room. Adding some twists and turns to the classic French repertoire, the kitchen delivered at inspection a fine starter of saffron pasta with crab, with a first-class consommé of tomato, olive and leek, and langoustine tails. Pot-roast squab and venison, with a jus of port and elderflower and Parmentier potatoes and roast garlic, was described as 'tender, rich and flavoursome', and other prime Scottish produce turns up in a starter of wild mushroom tart, a dab hand responsible for its pastry, and in main courses of roast saddle of lamb, and confit of turbot flavoured with five spice with fennel boulangère and green vegetables. Dessert-lovers will have a field day with the grande assiette: glazed banana, three fruit sorbets, a huge petit pain au chocolat with a lovely liquid centre, raspberry parfait, a miniature raspberry tartlet, and a dense chocolate pyramid.

Signature dishes: pan-fried foie gras with baby spinach, croustillant potato and a jus of sherry and shallots; casserole of lobster and Mull scallops with ink tortellini; passion fruit soufflé with exotic fruit sorbet.

Directions: M8/A82 to Dumbarton: take road to Luss, hotel signed 1 mile past Balloch on R

CLYDEBANK, **Beardmore Hotel**

Beardmore Street G81 4SA
Map 11: NS56
Tel: 0141 9516000
Fax: 0141 9516018
Chef: Mark Knowles
Cost: *Alc* £26, set-price L £16.50. ☺
H/wine £13.50
Times: Noon-1.45pm/7-9.45pm.
Closed L Sat, 26 Dec
Additional: Bar food; Sunday L;
Children welcome; ☻ dishes
Seats: 60. Private dining room 16
Smoking: No smoking in dining room;
Air conditioning
Accommodation: 168 en suite
★ ★ ★ ★

An impressive sandstone hotel on the banks of the Clyde near the Erskine Bridge. Popular with both business travellers and tourists heading towards Loch Lomond and Argyllshire, the Beardmore boasts modern facilities and a great line in modern British cooking with a strong Mediterranean bias. Citrus, the hotel's vibrantly decorated restaurant, offers the likes of butterbean soup with Mozzarella and garlic croûtons, and roasted monkfish with chorizo and cod brandade. We played it simple however, with a 'smooth and light' wild mushroom soup, baked fillet of cod given extra bite with a Swiss cheese crust (which worked well with the firm, moist fish), and a smooth and distinctive cappuccino torte with rich sweet chocolate sauce.

Directions: M8 J19, follow signs for Clydeside Expressway to Glasgow Rd, then Dumbarton Rd (A814), then signs for Clydebank Business Park. Hotel on L within HCI International Medical Centre complex

DUNDEE CITY

DUNDEE, Sandford Hotel

Set in extensive grounds, this fine listed building boasts a minstrels' gallery and oak bar. Pittenweem and Neuk o' Fife fish are features of the menu, along with sirloin of Angus beef.

Smoking: No smoking in dining room
Accommodation: 16 en suite ★ ★ ★

Directions: 4 miles south of Tay Bridge at jctn of A92 and B946

Newport Hill Wormit DD6 8RG
Map 11: NO43
Tel: 01382 541802
Fax: 01382 542136
Cost: *Alc* £24, set-price L £22/D £24.
☺ H/wine £9.80
Times: Noon-2.30pm/7-9.30pm
Additional: Bar food; Sunday L;
Children welcome; ◑ dishes

EDINBURGH, CITY OF

EDINBURGH, Atrium

10 Cambridge Street EH1 2ED
Map 11: NT27
Tel: 0131 2288882
Fax: 0131 2288808
Chef: Alan Mathieson
Owners: Andrew & Lisa Radford
Cost: *Alc* £30. H/wine £11.50
Times: Noon-2.30pm/6-10.30pm.
Closed L Sat, all Sun, 24 Dec-2 Jan
Additional: Children welcome;
◑ dishes
Seats: 70
Smoking: Air conditioning

Directions: From Princes Street, turn into Lothian Road, 2nd L and 1st R, by the Traverse Theatre

'Design is minimalist yet rustic and atmospheric'. Canvas sailcloth stretched halfway across the ceiling, tables of railway sleepers, low light levels and twisted willow arrangements gave one inspector the impression that this was a set from Macbeth; also, the lack of windows can make the place feel like a casino at lunchtime. But there's nothing but praise for the clearly defined flavours that jump off the plate and for a long wine list that shows discernment on every page, with over 20 sold by the glass. The kitchen translates the Mediterranean style in its own way, so the menu might take in a tart, its pastry light and cheesy, of Mozzarella dressed in pesto with baby spinach, black olives and plum tomatoes, the whole lot dotted with balsamic vinegar and basil oil, or bresaola with potato and basil salad. A thoroughly enjoyable main course has been crispy-skinned pan-fried chicken breast, attractively topped with baby carrots, green beans and roasted garlic, on roast potatoes with caramelised shallots. Vanilla and blueberry mousse is a picture and tastes as good as it looks, and fruitier types could opt for glazed pineapple and banana tart, or pears poached in red wine served with cinnamon ice cream.
   Signature dishes: pan-fried carpaccio of beef fillet with garlic mash and chilli oil; roasted sea bass with pancetta, celeriac, baby spinach, potato cake, oyster and baby fennel; raspberry pannacotta with apricot compote and mango coulis.

EDINBURGH, Balmoral Hotel, Number One ✿✿

1 Princes Street EH2 2EQ
Map 11: NT27
Tel: 0131 5576727
Fax: 0131 5578740
Chef: Jeff Bland
Owner: Rocco Forte
Cost: *Alc* £47, set-price L £18/D
£33.50. H/wine £16
Times: Noon-2.30pm/6.30-10.30pm
Additional: Sunday L;
Children welcome; ❹ dishes
Seats: 45. Private dining room 30
Smoking: No-smoking area; Air
conditioning
Accommodation: 186 en suite
★ ★ ★ ★ ★

Grand, hugely imposing hotel. No 1 restaurant, despite the rather Maoist sounding name and Eastern touches in the contemporary decor, is dedicated to the art of serious European eating. Luxury ingredients, such as the foie gras in morel consommé with sautéed spinach or the roast Bresse pigeon with crisp leaves and rich Madeira dressing are presented with considerable panache alongside fine regional ones such as monkfish from the Isle of Skye, pan-seared and served with saffron mussel broth. Ideas are bold and confident – roulade of French chicken and sweetbread with leek and truffle ravioli plus garlic and wine jus, could pave the way for a hot dark chocolate soufflé with vanilla ice cream. A touch of nostalgia for the hotel's Edwardian heyday is reflected in the inclusion in the *carte* of Roquefort and Parmesan soufflé as a savoury.

Directions: Hotel at east end of Princes Street; hotel is next to Waverley Station

EDINBURGH, Balmoral Hotel, Hadrian's ✿

NEW

1 Princes Street EH2 2EQ
Map 11: NT27
Tel: 0131 5576727
Fax: 0131 5578740
See entry above

Ambitious second restaurant within Edinburgh's Balmoral Hotel. Hadrian's strives towards desirable dishes such as saddle and leg of farmed rabbit with creamed parsley, sweetcorn and tarragon farci, and tarte Tatin of pears and spices.

EDINBURGH, Bonars ✿✿

56 St Mary's Street EH1 1SX
Map 11: NT27
Tel: 0131 5565888
Fax: 0131 5562588
Chef/Owner: Douglas Bonar
Cost: *Alc* £27, set-price L £11 (2
courses)/D £22.95. ☺ H/wine £12.50
Times: Noon-2pm/5pm-10pm
Additional: Sunday L;
Children welcome; ❹ dishes
Seats: 40. Private dining room 30

Popular restaurant tucked one street away from the Royal Mile and within walking distance of Waverley Station and Princes Street. The vermilion and deep sea-green colour scheme within contrasts with the traditional exterior of the building and the restaurant has a particularly formal feel to it with cut crystal glasses, crisp linen and attentive service. The set-lunch menu is a simple affair, offering five choices at each stage; however, the evening *carte* racks the standard up a notch or two with a more refined and adventurous approach. Witness our test meal that opened with seafood soup with garlic and roasted tomatoes 'full of tasty morsels'. Our roulade of salmon and langoustine with a wild mushroom and truffle ravioli was notable for the wonderfully fresh fish. Desserts include an ambitious pear and lime charlotte with lime cigar biscuits – topped with spun sugar.

EDINBURGH, **The Bonham**

A Georgian town house on the edge of the city's New Town. Striking brasserie-style restaurant offers a catchy menu with adventurous dishes like grilled halibut with cucumber noodles, and breast of chicken with black pudding mash.

Smoking: No-smoking area; Air conditioning

Directions: City centre off Royal Mile

35 Drumsheugh Gardens EH3 7RN
Map 11: NT27
Tel: 0131 6239319
Fax: 0131 2266080
Cost: *Alc* £12.50, set-price L £11.50.
☺ H/wine £13
Times: Noon-2.30pm/6.30-9.30
(10pm Fri & Sat). Closed L 25-28 Dec
Additional: Sunday L; Children
welcome; ◑ dishes
Smoking: No-smoking area;
No pipes & cigars
Accommodation: 48 en suite ★ ★ ★ ★

Directions: Located close to west end of Princes St

EDINBURGH,
Bruntsfield House NEW

Enjoy a Taste of Scotland at the Potting Shed Restaurant, overlooking Bruntsfield Links. Try pan-roast rack of hill lamb on black pudding mash with thyme and redcurrant jus. Cheeses come from the excellent Ian Mellis.

Smoking: No-smoking area; No pipes & cigars
Accommodation: 50 en suite ★ ★ ★

Directions: Opposite Bruntsfield Links

69-74 Bruntsfield Place EH10 4HH
Map 11: NT27
Tel: 0131 2291393
Fax: 0131 2295634
Cost: *Alc* £25, set-price L £7.50 (2
courses)/D £18.50. ☺ H/wine £10
Times: Noon-2pm/6.30-9.30pm
Additional: Sunday L;
Children welcome; ◑ dishes

EDINBURGH,
Caledonian Hotel

This hotel has a prime position at the bottom of Princes Street, with fabulous views of the old castle. The 'Calley', as it is affectionately known by locals and regulars, failed for many years to live up to the high standard this fine Victorian building deserved. But recently, a major investment programme including considerable refurbishment was completed, and there are now two reputable restaurants. The first, Chisholms, offers informal service in attractive and contemporary surroundings, while the The Pompadour is more formal and luxurious. The latter is open in the evenings only and guests are entertained by a pianist. The restaurant had only just re-opened when we went to press but initial reports are positive.

Directions: At western end of Princes Street

Princes Street EH1 2AB
Map 11: NT27
Tel: 0131 4599988
Fax: 0131 2256632
Telephone for further details

EDINBURGH,

Carlton Highland Hotel

Large city-centre hotel with prime position close to the Royal Mile.
Quills Restaurant provides a cosy library setting in which to enjoy
fine Scottish food: ballantine of roe deer, loin of highland venison,
and wild berry cranachan gâteau.

North Bridge EH1 1SD
Map 11: NT27
Tel: 0131 4723000
Fax: 0131 5562691
Telephone for further details

Directions: Turn R onto North Bridge at E/end of Princes St

EDINBURGH, **Channings**

South Learmonth Gardens EH4 1EZ
Map 11: NT27
Tel: 0131 3152225/6
Fax: 0131 3329631
Chef: Richard Glennie
Owner: Peter J Taylor
Cost: Set-price L £16/D £27.
H/wine £13
Times: 12.30-2pm/6.30-10pm. Closed
L Sun, 26-29 Dec
Additional: Bar food L;
Children welcome; 🌡 dishes
Seats: 100. Private dining room 18.
Jacket & tie preferred
Smoking: No smoking in dining room
Accommodation: 48 en suite ★ ★ ★

**The brasserie, in the hotel's basement, is an attractive and
comfortably furnished spot, with log fires and a welcoming
ambience.** Some of the tables, however, are a little cramped.
The lunch time set-menu is simpler and cheaper than in the
evening. Local produce is used to produce dishes from all
round the world: a risotto of smoked red pimentos with seared
scallop and spring onions, for example, or caramelised duck
breast with dauphinoise potatoes and Puy lentils. Cumin-
scented cod is served on a pomme fondant with red wine and
wild mushroom jus. Of five desserts offered the banana tarte
Tatin with banana ice cream and fudge sauce was excellent,
with 'light and crunchy' pastry. An orange bavarois with
candied kumquats was also very good. Coffee comes with
petits fours and the wine list is varied with a sensible selection
of countries and regions. Service is attentive and friendly.

Directions: From Princes St follow signs to Forth Bridge (A90),
cross Dean Bridge and take 4th R into South Learmonth Ave.
Follow road to R at bottom of hill

EDINBURGH,

Duck's at Le Marché Noir

Fresh linen and candle-lit tables set the scene for the Franco-Scottish
cuisine – baked haggis in filo, grilled black bream with couscous,
and crème brûlée with strawberry compote.

Smoking: No-smoking area

Directions: Follow the 'Mound' across Princes Street, George
Street, Queen Street to bottom of Dundas Street

2/4 Eyre Place EH3 5EP
Map 11: NT27
Tel: 0131 5581608
Fax: 0131 4677230
Cost: Alc L £15/D £25. ☺ H/wine £9.50
Times: Noon-2.30pm/5-10.30pm.
Closed L Sat, all Sun, Mon, 25, 26
Dec
Additional: Children welcome;
🌡 dishes

EDINBURGH,

George Inter-Continental

19-21 George Street EH2 2PB
Map 11: NT27
Tel: 0131 2251251
Fax: 0131 2265644
Cost: *Alc* £18.95, set-price L £15.95
(2 courses)/D £18.95. ☺
H/wine £12.95
Times: 12.30-2pm/7-10pm.
Closed L Sat, all Sun, Xmas, New
Year, Bhs
Additional: Bar food; Sunday L;
Children 12+; ♦ dishes
Smoking: No-smoking area;
Air conditioning
Accommodation: 195 en suite
★★★★

Directions: At E end of George St,
nr St Andrew's Square

Le Chambertin reflects the grand scale of the hotel, but manages to balance this with an intimate, comfortable atmosphere. Lengthy menu of traditional 'international' offerings: snails in garlic butter, gazpacho, Dover sole with parsley butter, steaks and grills, plus more modish offerings.

EDINBURGH,

Haldanes   NEW

39a Albany Street EH1 3QY
Map 11: NT27
Tel: 0131 5568407
Fax: 0131 5572662
Chef: George Kelso
Owners: George & Michelle Kelso
Cost: *Alc* £27, set-price L £15 (2
courses). H/wine £12.75
Times: Noon-1.45pm/6-10pm.
Closed L Sat & Sun
Additional: Children 1+; ♦ dishes
Seats: 40. Private dining room 18

An elegant basement restaurant in one of Edinburgh's stylish Georgian town house. Expect modern Scottish cooking: dishes such as saddle of Scottish lamb with braised shallots and a port wine sauce, and baked fillet of west coast halibut topped with a crab and spring onion mousse, are typical of the fixed-price menu. Our inspector visited in the depths of winter and found heart-warming flavours in dishes such as terrine of smoked chicken, leeks and bacon with orange and grain mustard dressing, and baked fillet of salmon with a light, spritzy white wine and leek sauce. Desserts are equally innovative, especially the creamy bread-and-butter pudding with poached apricots and warm chocolate sauce. The wine list is well sourced, and there is a good selection of half-bottles.

Directions: Telephone for directions

EDINBURGH, Iggs

Elegant Victorian-style room with friendly staff informally dressed in 'Iggs' emblazoned pink polo shirts. Andrew McQueen is a young chef with a strong pedigree, and our test meal raised hopes for greater things to come. His menus are strong on good contemporary concepts and the emphasis is certainly on simplicity – this come across well. Raw ingredients are well sourced giving impact to fresh flavours. We were particularly impressed by an exact loin of veal on a truffle and Gruyère risotto with a light but purposeful Madeira sauce. Hand-dived scallops served with a cod brandade showed skill, as did a trio of chocolate indulgence with passion fruit sauce.

15 Jeffrey Street EH1 1DR
Map 11: NT27
Tel: 0131 5578184
Fax: 0131 4417111
Chef: Andy McQueen
Owner: Ignacio Campos
Cost: Alc £27.50, set-price L £12.50/D £21 (both 2 courses). H/wine £11
Times: Noon-2.30pm/6-10.30pm. Closed Sun
Additional: Children welcome; dishes
Seats: 40. Private dining room 20
Smoking: No-smoking area; Air conditioning

Directions: At the heart of Edinburgh's Old Town, just off the Royal Mile

EDINBURGH,
Jacksons

Versatile basement restaurant that provides value-for-money lunches. In the evening the tempo moves up a notch and diners can expect more challenging skills from the kitchen. Good use of fresh local produce.

209 High Street EH1 1PZ
Map 11: NT27
Tel: 0131 225 1793
Fax: 0131 220 0620
Cost: Alc £30, set-price L £9.
H/wine £11.95
Times: Noon-2.20pm/6-10.30pm. Closed 25, 26 Dec
Additional: Sunday L, Children welcome; dishes
Smoking: Air conditioning

Directions: On Royal Mile, near St Giles Cathedral

EDINBURGH,
Malmaison Hotel

Stylish hotel just a stone's throw from Leith's waterfront. A short and snappy Mediterranean menu is available in the trendy brasserie:

One Tower Place Leith EH6 7DB
Map 11: NT27
Tel: 0131 4685001
Fax: 0131 4685002

typical dishes include seared salmon with grilled aubergines and olive caviar, and slow-roasted chicken wrapped in prosciutto on polenta.

Malmaison Hotel

Cost: *Alc* £24, set-price L £12.50/D £14.50. ☺ H/wine £13.95
Times: Noon-2.15pm/6-10.15pm
Additional: Bar food; Sunday L; Children welcome; ⚫ dishes
Accommodation: 60 en suite ★ ★ ★

Directions: From the city centre follow Leith Docklands, through 3 sets of lights and L into Tower Street

EDINBURGH, The Marque NEW

The boldness of the cooking is matched by that of the decor.
Striking yellow walls are offset by a large-squared black-and-white chessboard floor. However, seating is mercifully conventional, with just the odd church pew thrown in and there's a cosy alcove at a higher level. Cooking is contemporary, offering classy appetisers of spicy Thai soup, and reflecting the élan of the Atrium, from which the founding team originated. We enjoyed a first-class chicken and foie gras terrine with a perfect onion jam, chargrilled tuna, red pesto, ratatouille cake and balsamic potato, and rhubarb crumble with tamarind ice cream. The wine list is carefully sourced to give global appeal and there's a good balance between old and New World, with classic, popular and lesser known wines all represented. Good halves and wines by the glass are competitively priced.

Directions: Telephone for directions

19-21 Causewayside EH9 1QF
Map 11: NT27
Tel: 0131 4666660
Fax: 0131 4666661
Chefs: John Rutter, Glyn Stevens
Owners: Lara Kearney, John Rutter, Glyn Stevens
Cost: *Alc* £25, set-price L + pre & post theatre £10 (2 courses). ☺ H/wine £11.25
Times: 11.45-2pm (12.30-2pm Sat/Sun), 5.45-10pm (11pm Fri/Sat). Closed Mon
Additional: Sunday L; Children welcome; ⚫ dishes
Seats: 50. Private dining room 6
Smoking: No smoking in dining room; Air conditioning

EDINBURGH, Marriott Dalmahoy

Adam-designed mansion brimming with glorious fresh flowers. The restaurant of this recently refurbished hotel and country club looks out onto expansive grounds, with the Pentland Hills to one side, and the 18th hole of one of two golf courses and a fine lake to the other. The food served in this formal restaurant is worthy of praise. Inspection produced fabulously fresh langoustines served with paper-thin root vegetable ravioli; guinea fowl complemented by a well-judged sauce and delicately cooked sweetbreads. However, dessert, which included a pear tarte Tatin, did not live up to heights of the previous courses. The wine list is comprehensive and listed alphabetically.

Kirknewton EH27 8EB
Map 11: NT27
Tel: 0131 3331845
Fax: 0131 3331433
Telephone for further details

Directions: On A71, 3 miles from Calder roundabout, opposite Ratho turn off

EDINBURGH, Martin's Restaurant

Urban restaurant that has the requisite contemporary features. Bright green and white walls, fresh flowers, narrow spot lighting and some modern prints sum it all up. This is a popular restaurant, to be found in a back street location. The

70 Rose Street North Lane EH2 3DX
Map 11: NT27
Tel: 0131 2253106
Fax: 0131 2203403
Chef: David Romanis
Owners: Martin & Gay Irons

attractive hand-written *carte* changes for lunch and dinner, with six starters and main courses at lunchtimes; two more than at dinner. The breads are exceptional, wholemeal was 'a light crusted loaf, had great texture, smell and flavour', and the cooking in general strives to reach high standards. Our test meal included seared' scallops with two garlic langoustines served with a soupy risotto, well-cooked turbot on a mound of buttered spring cabbage with herbed passatta, and poached pears with banana parfait and sweet chilli syrup. There is a great cheese board.

Directions: North Lane is off Rose Street which runs parallel to and behind Princes Street

Cost: *Alc* L £20/D £34. H/wine £11.80
Times: Noon-2pm/7-10pm. Closed L Sat, all Sun, Mon, 24 Dec-20 Jan, 1 wk May-Jun, 1 wk Oct
Additional: Children 8+
Seats: 28. Private dining rooms 8-16
Smoking: No smoking in dining room

EDINBURGH,
Norton House Hotel

Extended Victorian mansion peacefully set amid over 50 acres of parkland yet convenient for both transport and the city centre. The Gathering, as its name suggests, is a popular meeting place for an informal meal, but the Conservatory restaurant is the flagship. The kitchen takes a modern approach to traditional, sound ingredients, as in the likes of home-smoked pheasant with caramelised apples and chestnuts. Caramelising might also be applied to scallops served alongside spot-on baked sea bass with ginger and spring onion sauce and a julienne of red peppers. Saddle of venison turns up with beetroot and horseradish timbale, sweet potato purée and thyme-flavoured courgettes, and salmon is seared and topped with 'scales' of potatoes and ribboned, chervil-scented vegetables. Eve's pudding makes a welcome comeback among desserts, sharing the billing with perhaps raspberry soufflé with orange curd ice cream. There's a fair showing of wines by the glass.

Ingliston EH28 8LX
Map 11: NT27
Tel: 0131 3331275
Fax: 0131 3335305
Chef: John Newton
Owner: Virgin Hotels
Cost: *Alc* £33, set-price L £15.50/D £26. ☺ H/wine £13
Times: Noon-2pm/7-10pm. Closed L Sat
Additional: Sunday L; Children welcome; ✿ dishes
Seats: 80. Private dining room 50
Smoking: No-smoking area
Accommodation: 47 en suite ★ ★ ★

Directions: M8 J2, off A8, 0.5 mile past Edinburgh Airport

EDINBURGH,
Sheraton Grand Hotel

The Terrace Restaurant at this striking building is an airy conservatory-style room overlooking the square. The daily-changing hot and cold buffet menu features, for example, Cullen skink, smoked trout with potato and spring onion salad, roast ribeye of beef with port sauce, and monkfish, mussels and prawns casseroled with saffron. The Grill Room, warm and

1 Festival Square EH3 9SR
Map 11: NT27
Tel: 0131 2216422 (Grill Room) 2216423 (Terrace)
Fax: 0131 2296254
Chef: Nicolas Laurent
Cost: *Alc* £35, set-price L £29.50/D £39.50 (4 courses). H/wine £16
Times: Noon-2.30pm/7-10.30pm. Closed L Sat, all Sun
Additional: Sunday L (Terrace Rest); Children 12+ ; ✿ dishes
Seats: 45. Private dining room 20
Smoking: No-smoking area; Air conditioning
Accommodation: 261 en suite ★ ★ ★ ★ ★

Directions: Off Lothian Road

elegant and popular with businessmen at lunchtimes, turns out such dishes as pan-fried seafood – crab, langoustine, squid, sole and monkfish – an impressively well-balanced dish served with delicately flavoured couscous, while deep-fried polenta gnocchi, crunchy on the outside, and perfectly cooked miniature vegetables add dimension to maize-fed chicken with a deeply flavoured wild mushroom sauce. Roasted pineapple and almond macaroon – with a 'sumptuous texture' of crispy outside and chewy inside – sandwiched with Mascarpone and passion fruit sorbet kept up the standards. Tablet and truffles come with first-class espresso.

EDINBURGH, 36

36 Great King Street EH3 6QH
Map 11: NT27
Tel: 0131 3363636
Fax: 0131 3363663
Chef: Malcolm Warham
Owner: Peter Taylor
Cost: *Alc* £16, set-price L £14/D £20. ☺ H/wine £12
Times: Noon-2.30pm (2pm Sun)/7-10pm (9.30pm Sun). Closed L Sat, L on 25-28 Dec
Additional: Sunday L; Children welcome; ✦ dishes
Seats: 60. Private dining room 20
Smoking: No smoking in dining room; Air conditioning
Accommodation: 15 en suite ★ ★ ★ ★

Grand hotel run on a grand scale. Don't be deceived by the sumptuous furnishings and ornate chandeliers of The Howard, the splendid, central hotel within which 36 is located. The restaurant is all minimalist white walls with abstract canvases, jewel-coloured chairs, and tiny spotlights casting pools of indigo and magenta. The menu itself has the number '36' depicted to look like the Loch Ness monster surfacing. So the hints are there that this is Modern with a capital M, which in turn translates as fusion food, combining elements of the world's cuisines to produce the likes of brown lentil soup with Thai spices, and baked fillet of salmon with a goats' cheese crumb and sweet-and-sour sauce. Some dishes work well as in a crab and vegetable ravioli with delicately spiced Thai sauce, others less so. Witness a main course of seared tuna topped with a quenelle of guacamole, plated on Puy lentils and surrounded by a vibrant coriander dressing, where all the components seemed to lose touch with each other. Tarte Tatin, on the other hand, is good and caramelly.

Directions: Turn off Princes St into Frederick St for 0.5 mile and turn R into Great King St. Past traffic lights, hotel on L

EDINBURGH, Tower Restaurant NEW

Smart and sophisticated brasserie-style restaurant occupying the roof-top floor of the Museum of Scotland. Dishes mirror the Mediterranean with seafood, salads and such dishes as confit of salmon and cauliflower cream, and lamb with minted couscous. Open all day.

Smoking: No smoking in dining room

Directions: Level 5 of Museum of Scotland

Museum of Scotland Chambers Street EH1 1JF
Map 11: NT27
Tel: 0131 2253003
Fax: 0130 2474220
Cost: *Alc* £30. ☺ H/wine £9.95
Times: Noon-11pm. Closed 25 Dec
Additional: Children welcome; ✦ dishes

EDINBURGH, **The Vintners Room**

*Raw materials are put to good use at this striking candlelit (at night)
Leith eaterie. We enjoyed some good scallops and a lovely cut of
venison. The wine list rewards serious study; great wines by the glass.*

Seats: 60. Private dining room 36
Smoking: No-smoking area

Directions: At end of Leith Walk; L into Great Junction Street, R
into Henderson Street. Restaurant is in old warehouse on R

The Vaults 87 Giles Street
Leith EH6 6BZ
Map 11: NT27
Tel: 0131 5546767
Fax: 0131 4677130
Cost: *Alc* £31, set-price L £11.50 (2
courses). H/wine £12
Times: Noon-2pm/6.30-10pm.
Closed Sun, 2 wks Xmas
Additional: Children welcome;
❹ dishes

EDINBURGH, **Winter Glen**

*Stylish basement restaurant with exposed stone walls and ample
table space. Contemporary Scottish cuisine informs the menu, and
diners can enjoy such dishes as game terrine with plum confit, and
cassoulet of salmon, monkfish and mussels.*

Directions: Telephone for directions

3A1 Dundas Street EH3 6QG
Map 11: NT27
Tel: 0131 4777060
Fax: 0131 6247087
Telephone for further details

EDINBURGH,
Witchery by the Castle

*Located within an historic 16th-century building close to the
gates of Edinburgh castle.* The Witchery offers two elegant
dining rooms that are candlelit in the evenings. Both rooms are
adorned with gilded heraldic ceilings, hung with tapestries, and
leather and wood panels which create a beguiling atmosphere.
Amidst classics such as foie gras with brioche toast the kitchen
uses various ingredients with great confidence and, usually,
success. A main course of sea bass, with creamed mizumu and
salsify white wine cream looked uninspiring, but tasted superb,
and a side order of Jersey potatoes sautéed in truffle oil was
utterly delicious .Peanut butter mousse with glass biscuits and
maple syrup was interesting. The tome of a wine list is chosen
intelligently with an eye for consistent quality across the
splendid and catholic range.

Additional: Sunday L; Children 12+ at D; ❹ dishes
Seats: 120
Smoking: No pipes
Accommodation: 3 en suite

Directions: At the entrance to Edinburgh Castle at the very top
of the Royal Mile

Castle Hill EH2 1NE
Map 11: NT27
Tel: 0131 2255613
Fax: 0131 2204392
Chef: Douglas Roberts
Owner: James Thomson
Cost: *Alc* £35. H/wine £13.50
Times: Noon-4pm/5.30-11.30pm.
Closed 25, 26 Dec

AA Wine Award-see page 16 Shortlisted for

FALKIRK

GRANGEMOUTH,
Grange Manor Hotel

*Former manor house where modern ideas feature the best of
Scotland's produce: west coast mussels in coriander cream, for*

Glensburgh FK3 8XJ
Map 11: NS98
Tel: 01324 474836
Fax: 01324 665861

Grange Manor Hotel

Cost: *Alc* £27, set-price L £9.50 (2 courses)/D £21.50. ☺ H/wine £10.25
Times: Noon-2pm/7-9.30pm.
Closed 26 Dec, 1, 2 Jan
Additional: Sunday L;
Children welcome; dishes
Smoking: No-smoking area
Accommodation: 37 en suite ★★★

Directions: M9 J6 200m on right, M9 J5 A905 2 miles

example, or roast saddle of venison with a pickled walnut and lavender reduction.

POLMONT, Inchyra Grange

The hotel's Priory Restaurant has been extended, incorporating the fabric of the original building. Dishes include a roast carved at the table, and perhaps grilled sea bass with baby vegetables.

Smoking: No smoking in dining room
Accommodation: 109 en suite ★★★★

Directions: M9 J4 or 5. In Polmont, nr BP social club

Grange Road FK2 0YB
Map 11: NS97
Tel: 01324 711911
Fax: 01324 716134
Cost: *Alc* £30, set-price L £12.95.
H/wine £14
Times: Noon-2pm/7-9.30pm.
Closed L Sat
Additional: Sunday L; Children welcome; dishes

FIFE

ANSTRUTHER,

Cellar Restaurant ✿✿✿

An old merchant's house, so called the Cellar for the ambience created from candles everywhere, rough stone walls, tiled floor and dark oak furniture. 'It's a moody effect, but softened by a few adornments, plus very welcome blazing fires' reports an inspector who arrived on a wild, stormy spring night to find the place packed. That dinner was a classic example of fresh is best and let's not mess with it. Peter Jukes revolves his menu around seafood – 'is fish organic', he enquires of our theme this year – and the quality is unquestionable. This is how our inspector's meal progressed. Quiche, which was donated with compliments of the chef, had all one expects of a quiche but never gets: smooth custard trembling to the touch, containing smoked salmon and haddock, encased in a buttery, crisp pastry shell. The first course could have been a great let down in lesser hands: new season's crab had been separated into white and dark meat, carefully placed in the shell, with lemon, home-made granary toast and lemon mayonnaise the only accompaniments, plus a small morsel of dressed salad. 'Super, real crab taste, I urge anyone who has not tasted crab to try one here for the real thing.' The centrepiece of the meal had quality ingredients shouting from the plate. Monkfish on the bone with a light crust of garlicky butter, scallops that were crisp on the outside, smooth-soft within, and sweet pepper risotto that

24 East Green KY10 3AA
Map 12: NO50
Tel: 01333 310378
Fax: 01333 312544
Chef/Owner: Peter Jukes
Cost: Set-price D £28.50.
H/wine £13.50
Times: 12.30-1.30pm/7-9.30pm.
Closed all Sun, L Mon-Thu, Xmas
Additional: Children 8+
Seats: 35
Smoking: No smoking in dining room

Directions: Behind the Scottish Fisheries Museum

punched plenty of flavour. There was little else on the plate apart from some perfectly cooked dauphinoise potatoes. For dessert, triple chocolate terrine with a small pool of vanilla anglaise and some orange coulis. All in all it was a memorable meal. The wine list is vast and complements the food well.

CUPAR, **Eden House Hotel** ✿

2 Pitscottie Road KY15 4HF
Map 11: NO31
Tel: 01334 652510
Fax: 01334 652277
Cost: *Alc* £25, set-price L & D £19.
☺ H/wine £10
Times: Noon-2pm/6.30-9pm.
Closed L Sun
Additional: Bar Food; Children welcome; ✿ dishes
Smoking: No smoking in dining room
Accommodation: 11 en suite ★ ★

Directions: Turn R after railway bridge in Cupar. Hotel is 100 yds to R

There is a freshness and honesty to the carefully prepared dishes served from a choice of menus at this traditionally styled conservatory restaurant.

CUPAR,
Ostlers Close Restaurant ✿✿✿

Bonnygate KY15 4BU
Map 11: NO31
Tel: 01334 655574

Fax: 01334 654036
Chef: James Graham
Owners: James & Amanda Graham
Cost: H/wine £10.50
Times: Closed L Wed & Thu, all Sun & Mon
Additional: Children 6+ at D; ✿ dishes
Seats: 26

Directions: In small lane off main street (A91) of Cupar

Charming, personally run cottage-style restaurant. The series of small rooms that make up this little restaurant, tucked away in an alley, is evidence that it was converted from cottages dating from the 17th century. Flower displays ranging from the first snowdrops to autumnal foliage, come from the proprietors' garden and ingredients are impeccably sourced – vegetables, salad leaves and herbs from an organic farm, game from local estates – and, writes Mrs Graham, 'lobsters and crabs arrive at the kitchen door according to the tides'. Lobster might appear in a salad with a tomato and basil vinaigrette, while game might appear as roast breast of grouse – with wild mushrooms (hand-picked) and bacon in game sauce. Duck is a favoured meat, its breast and confit of its leg in red wine sauce with oriental-flavoured Puy lentils. An impressive array of vegetables – among them perhaps a 'lovely' tart of sliced potato, butternut squash hinting of orange, and pak choi with shallots, tomato and coriander – get the thumbs-up, as do puddings of, say, steamed apricot and syrup sponge, or a trio of chocolate desserts of a good, thin pastry tart, thick mousse and an expertly made sorbet.

DUNFERMLINE,
Keavil House Hotel

Conservatory restaurant with a grand piano and views over extensive hotel gardens. Fresh local produce is used to good effect in Taste of Scotland specialities.

Smoking: No smoking in dining room
Accommodation: 47 en suite ★★★

Directions: M90 J3, 7 miles from Forth Road Bridge, take A985, turning R after bridge. From Dunfermline, 2 miles W on A994

Crossford KY12 8QW
Map 11: NT08
Tel: 01383 736258
Fax: 01383 621600
Cost: *Alc* £25.75, set-price L £17/D £19.95. ☺ H/wine £9.95
Times: Noon-2pm/7-9pm.
Closed 31 Dec, 1 Jan
Additional: Sunday L;
Children welcome; ✤ dishes

ELIE,
Bouquet Garni Restaurant

Cosy, countrified restaurant in the village centre. Fresh local seafood features prominently on both lunch and dinner menus. Enjoy pre-prandial drinks in the pretty bar/lounge with its deep sofas and paintings by local artists. Quality produce is sourced from nearby markets and suppliers. Meat dishes do make an appearance, perhaps in the form of beef fillet served on a leek, onion and potato rösti with an aubergine and sweet pepper cake and a rich game jus. Fish fanciers will not be disappointed with halibut and Finnan haddock chowder, monkfish and scallops with tomato, garlic and walnut oil dressing, or halibut with basil mash and Thai vinaigrette. Puddings may include sticky toffee pudding with butterscotch sauce and warm pear and frangipane tart with cinnamon ice cream. The wine list offers a good balance between French and New World bottles.

51 High Street KY9 1BZ
Map 12: NO40
Tel/Fax: 01333 330374
Owner: Norah Keracher
Cost: *Alc* £16, set-price D £25. ☺ H/wine £12.90
Times: Noon-1.30pm/7-10pm.
Closed Sun, Mon, 3rd wk Nov, 2nd & 3rd wks Jan
Additional: Children 12+; ✤ dishes
Seats: 30. Private dining room 12
Smoking: No smoking in dining room

Directions: 12 miles from St Andrews. Village centre: from A915 (St Andrews) take A917 to Elie

KINCARDINE-ON-FORTH,
Unicorn Inn

Tucked away down a back street in this small, unassuming town, the Unicorn is an unlikely place in which to find some Mediterranean-style atmosphere and an imaginative choice of dishes featuring plenty of olive oil, garlic, herbs and tomato. Service is informal, as one would expect, and both the wine list and the daily-changing blackboard listing are strongly influenced by Mediterranean countries. The kitchen's repertoire encompasses substantial tapas dishes at lunchtime, alongside a good-value two-course lunch menu, and an evening *carte* that may include Andalusian tomato and rice broth and Spanish black pudding on red onion and rosemary marmalade. For main course there could be tuna with sweet chilli and tomato salsa, or pot-roasted pigeon. The dessert menu lists Italian lemon, almond and raspberry trifle or more traditional sweets like sticky toffee pudding.

15 Excise Street FK10 4LN
Map 11: NS98
Tel: 01259 730704
Fax: 01259 731567
Chef: John McQueen
Owner: Mrs Lesley-Ann Mitch
Cost: *Alc* £18, set-price L £7.95 (2 courses). ☺ H/wine £9.95
Times: Noon-2pm/D from 6.30pm.
Closed Sun, Mon
Additional: Children welcome; ✤ dishes
Seats: 60. Private dining room 25
Smoking: No pipes & cigars

Directions: From S, cross Kincardine Bridge, take 1st L, L again, 1st R

LUNDIN LINKS,

Old Manor Hotel ✿✿

Leven Road Nr St Andrews KY8 6AJ
Map 12: NO40
Tel: 01333 320368
Fax: 01333 320911
Chef: Alan Brunt
Owners: The Clark Family
Cost: *Alc* £26.50, set-price D £29.50
(4 courses). ☺ H/wine £10.95
Times: D only, 7- 9.30pm
Additional: Bar food L; Children 5+;
🍴 dishes
Seats: 36. Private dining room 60.
Jacket or tie preferred
Smoking: No smoking in dining room
Accommodation: 24 en suite ★★★

Directions: On A915 Leven-St
Andrews road in the village

Lovely edge of village setting looking over two golf courses and the Firth of Forth beyond. Take in the view from the south-facing terrace as you sip an aperitif, or relax in the bar and nibble canapés of cream cheese and Parma ham roulade, smoked salmon, and a tiny pastry case of chicken liver pâté. Eating in the Coachman's Bistro makes a more casual alternative to the Aithernie Restaurant, where dinner is a fixed-price menu with a decent choice at each course. Local crab goes into a cake served under a light tomato salsa, or there might be roast breast of marinated pigeon with a potato and thyme gâteau. Mouth-melting king scallops (fish and shellfish are the house specialities) with a delicate pesto sauce and a julienne of carrots is a well-presented main course, with perhaps pan-fried loin of venison with saffron and tomato mash and bramble jus among meat options. Finish with Amaretto crème brûlée topped with cherries.

MARKINCH,

Balbirnie House ✿✿

Balbirnie Park KY7 6NE
Map 11: NO20
Tel: 01592 610066
Fax: 01592 610529
Chef: Alan Gibb
Owners: The Russell Family
Cost: Set-price L £13.45/D £29.50 (4
courses). H/wine £13.50

A luxury hotel with high standards of service. In the heart of the Kingdom of Fife, the lovingly restored Balbirnie House provides both exemplary personal attention and a genuine warmth of hospitality. The cooking scores highly for consistency and clarity of flavour. Scallops make regular appearances, seared and served perhaps with a risotto such as mushroom and artichoke. Soup, say white onion and apple or prawn, coconut and rocket is served in a china cup. Prime Scottish steaks are served with chips and béarnaise sauce, though chargrilled breast of maize-fed chicken is given a more upmarket treatment with sauerkraut, mashed potatoes and foie gras scented jus. After desserts such as pear feuilleté with pear ice cream, cafetière coffee is served with tablet.

Directions: M90 J3, follow signs to Glenrothes & Tay Bridge, turn R onto B9130 to Markinch & Balbirnie Park

Times: Noon-2.30pm/7-9.30pm
Additional: Bar food L; Sunday L; Children welcome; ✪ dishes
Seats: 40. Private dining room to 40
Smoking: No smoking in dining room
Accommodation: 30 en suite ★ ★ ★ ★

PEAT INN, The Peat Inn ✿✿✿

Created from the original coaching inn, a most charming restaurant with rooms dedicated to the art of fine dining. Dedicated owners David and Patricia Wilson have painstakingly built up over the past 27 years an enviable reputation for the excellence of their kitchen. The back of the restaurant has picture windows from which the local countryside forms a changing picture to be contemplated between courses and mouthfuls. David Wilson is a legendary name in modern Scottish cooking; his menus draw on regional produce, but the style reflects many classical French techniques. Crab cake with lemon vinaigrette based on basil oil was a true example of what a crab cake can be when the crustacean is unencumbered with extraneous additions. More soup than stew, and a distant cousin of a Scotch broth, cassoulet of lamb, pork and duck with flageolet beans was rich and well-flavoured (and included identifiable items). Breast of pheasant with truffle sauce brought our inspector out in a rash of superlatives: 'the most tender, succulent piece of pheasant ever tasted'. A hard act to follow, but caramelised apple with cinnamon ice cream and caramel sauce did the job well. All the staff are genuinely hospitable and very knowledgeable.

Cupar KY15 5LH
Map 12: NO40
Tel: 01334 840206
Fax: 01334 840530
Chef: David Wilson
Owners: David & Patricia Wilson
Cost: Alc £34, set-price L £19.50/D £28. H/wine £14
Times: 12.30 for 1pm/7-9.30pm. Closed Sun, Mon, 25 Dec, 1 Jan
Additional: Children welcome; ✪ dishes
Seats: 48. Private dining rooms 12 & 24
Smoking: No smoking in dining room
Accommodation: 8 en suite ★ ★

Directions: At junction of B940/B941, 6 miles SW of St Andrews

ST ANDREWS,
The Old Course Hotel ✿✿

The setting beside the 17th hole of this famous championship course is a great attraction for golfers and tourists from all over the world. The hotel has an impressive reception area, and on the fourth floor there is a cocktail bar offering an excellent selection of single malts. The popular new Sands Brasserie

KY16 9SP
Map 12: NO51
Tel: 01334 474371
Fax: 01334 477668
Chef: Mark Barker
Cost: Alc £39, set-price L £15.50/D £38.50 (5 courses). H/wine £18.50

serves a variety of Mediterranean and Pacific rim dishes that cater to a wide variety of tastes. The food at the Road Hole Grill describes itself as modern Scottish, but the undertones are unquestionably French. The *carte* features local produce, including salmon, beef and game. Our rustic pork terrine was nicely larded, had a good texture and composition, a fillet of Angus beef was served with a truffle hollandaise, foie gras, polenta and port wine sauce. From the dessert menu, came apple and almond tart 'crisp with a thick paste tasting of frangipane', with a creamy pistachio ice cream, although a selection of all six desserts can be ordered as an assiette for £13..

Directions: Situated close to A91 on city outskirts

Times: 12.30-2pm/7-10pm. Closed Xmas
Additional: Bar food L; Sunday L; Children welcome; ✿ dishes
Seats: 90. Private dining rooms 16-160
Smoking: No-smoking area; No pipes and cigars; Air conditioning
Accommodation: 125 en suite
★★★★★

ST ANDREWS,
Parkland Hotel

Straightforward with a regional flavour describes fresh smoked haddock Cullen skink or traditional haggis, neeps 'n' tatties. Follow with pan-seared Shetland salmon on leaf spinach with a rich lobster sauce.

Additional: Sunday L; Children welcome
Smoking: No smoking in dining room
Accommodation: 9 rooms ★★

Directions: West of town centre, opposite Kinburn Park

Kinburn Castle Double Dykes Road KY16 9DS
Map 12: NO51
Tel/Fax: 01334 473620
Cost: Set-price D £21. ☺
H/wine £8.50
Times: 12.30-2pm/7-8.30pm. Closed D Sun, all Mon, 2 days Xmas, New Year

ST ANDREWS, Rufflets Hotel

Strathkinness Low Road KY16 9TX
Map 12: NO51
Tel: 01334 472594
Fax: 01334 478703
Chef: Robert Grindle
Owner: Ann Russell
Cost: Set-price L £17/D £30. H/wine £13
Times: 12.30-2pm/7-9.30pm. Closed L Mon-Fri, 1st wk Jan
Additional: Bar food L; Sunday L; Children 14+; ✿ dishes
Seats: 80. Private dining room 24
Smoking: No smoking in dining room
Accommodation: 27 en suite ★★★

One of Scotland's oldest established country house hotels, personally run by Ann Russell. The Garden Restaurant provides an appropriately civilised setting for the well-rounded cooking that is built around the best local produce. Imagination and ambition comes through in the daily changing set-menu. Kiln-roasted smoked salmon is paired with chargrilled vegetables, and lemon and thyme roasted breast of duckling arrives with glazed apple and aubergine. In more traditional vein there could be leek and potato soup, and grilled noisettes of Rannoch venison with red cabbage. Dessert could include the intriguing warm pistachio and apricot pie with coddled cream or a rich chocolate and mocha torte.

Directions: On B939 1.5 miles W of St Andrews

ST ANDREWS, **Rusacks Hotel**

Pilmour Links KY16 9JQ
Map 12: NO51
Tel: 01334 474321
Fax: 01334 477896
Cost: *Alc* £28. ☺ H/wine £12.95
Times: D only, 7-10pm
Additional: Bar Food; Sunday L
(12.30-6pm); Children welcome;
🍴 dishes
Smoking: No smoking in dining room
Accommodation: 48 en suite ★ ★ ★ ★

Directions: From M90 J8 take A91 to
St Andrews. Hotel on L on entering
the town

*The restaurant overlooks the first tee and 18th green of the Old
Course. Cheerful staff assist with menu choices, which may include
game terrine, local scallops and chocolate whisky torte.*

ST ANDREWS,
St Andrews Golf Hotel

40 The Scores KY16 9AS
Map 12: NO51
Tel: 01334 472611
Fax: 01334 472188
Chef: Colin Masson
Owners: The Hughes Family
Cost: *Alc* £30, set-price L £15.95. ☺
H/wine £12
Times: 12.30-2.30pm/7-9.30pm
Additional: Bar food L; Sunday L;
Children welcome; 🍴 dishes
Seats: 55. Private dining room 14
Smoking: No smoking in dining room
Accommodation: 22 en suite ★ ★ ★

Golfing hotel with fine standards of service. See if you can
recognise world-famous golfers from their photographs in the
bar, or perhaps sit opposite one as you relax with a magazine in
the lounge. Alternatively, enjoy the views over the bay from the
elegant and comfortable restaurant, with its old oak panelling,
candlelight, silver and crystal. Choose a wine by the glass as you
decide what to eat from a fairly extensive menu. Lasagne of
seared salmon with spinach in a light, creamy fish sauce starts
things off nicely, or there could be Roquefort soufflé. A main
course of roast rack of Perthshire lamb well-balanced by an
Arran mustard sauce has been endorsed for its 'delicious,
succulent' flavour. Vegetarians have a decent choice, too, from
herby risotto of Mediterranean vegetables to a tart of red
onions, tomato and goats' cheese with pesto dressing. A good
choice of farmhouse cheeses will appeal to savoury-lovers, while
the sweet of tooth could go for pear crème brûlée or steamed
Drambuie pudding with raspberry compote and custard.

Directions: Enter town on A91, cross both mini-roundabouts,
turn L at Golf Place and first R into The Scores. Hotel 200 yards
on R

The Seafood Restaurant

With a new name since our last edition (formerly Ichthus), this harbourside restaurant gains a second Rosette this year. From an airy, conservatory style interior you can enjoy a panoramic view across the Forth of Firth along with some good modern seafood cookery. A simple dish of langoustine tails with garlic-butter dressed salad and cherry tomatoes made a good start to a recent meal that continued to impress with a moist fillet of pan-fried halibut drizzled with lemongrass and chilli vinaigrette on a bed of chive mash. Desserts range from crème brûlée with a petit panier de fruit to chocolate torte with pistachio sauce anglaise. In summer a simpler menu, served out on the terrace, supplements the set-price lunch.

Directions: Take A959 from St Andrews to Anstruther, then head west on A917 through Pittenweem. In St Monans go down to harbour then R

16 West End KY10 2BX
Map 12: NO50
Tel/Fax: 01333 730327
Chef: Craig Millar
Owners: The Butler Family
Cost: *Alc* £25, set-price L & D £17.
☺ H/wine £10
Times: Noon-2.30pm/6.30-9.30pm.
Closed Mon, 25 Dec
Additional: Bar food L
Seats: 36
Smoking: No smoking in dining room

GLASGOW, CITY OF

Buttery Restaurant

One of Glasgow's oldest and most popular restaurants. The Buttery continues to impress with its modern take on traditional Scottish cooking. Typical of this approach are starters such as home-cured salmon with Parmesan tart and fresh spinach, or seared scallops and mussels with home-made tomato and basil pasta. Main courses continue the theme. Try fresh tortellini and langoustine with potato and pancetta sauce, or perhaps steamed halibut and chervil with a champagne sauce. Dessert encompass the likes of orange and chocolate soufflé with almond biscuits, as well as pastry parcels of warm apple and cinnamon pears. Downstairs, the Belfry Bistro caters for lighter, more informal meals.

Seats: 50. Private room 10. Jacket & tie preferred
Smoking: No pipes & cigars; Air conditioning

Directions: City centre

652 Argyle Street G3 8UF
Map 11: NS56
Tel: 0141 2218188
Fax: 0141 2044639
Chef: Ian Fleming
Owner: Allied Domecq
Cost: *Alc* £35, set-price L £16.85.
H/wine £12.50
Times: Noon-2.30pm/7-10.30pm.
Closed L Sat, all Sun, 25, 26 Dec,
1, 2 Jan
Additional: Bar food L; ✿ dishes

Devonshire Hotel

Intimate modern dining room in a Victorian town house with original stained glass. Expect the likes of warm seafood collection, roast loin of Ayrshire lamb, and raspberry crannachan.

Smoking: No smoking in dining room
Accommodation: 14 en suite ★ ★ ★

Directions: On Great Western Road turn L at lights towards Hyndland, 200 yards turn R and R again

5 Devonshire Gardens
G12 0UX
Map 11: NS56
Tel: 0141 3397878
Fax: 0141 3393980
Cost: *Alc* £29.50, set-price L £19.50.
☺ H/wine £10.95
Times: 12.30-2.30pm/7-9.45pm
Additional: Bar food; Children welcome; ✿ dishes

GLASGOW, Gamba

225a West George Street G2 2ND
Map 11: NS56
Tel: 0141 5720899
Fax: 0141 5720896
Cost: *Alc* £25, set-price L £10.95
(2 courses). ☺ H/wine £11.95
Times: Noon-2.30pm/5-10.30pm.
Closed Sun, Xmas, New Year,
Bh Mon
Additional: Children 14+; 🍂 dishes
Smoking: Air conditioning

Directions: Nr Blythswood Square

*New basement restaurant with a Mediterranean feel and a striking
seafish mural. Scottish seafood is the speciality, with options such as
sushi plate, and turbot on mulligatawny prawns.*

GLASGOW, Glasgow Moat House

Congress Road G3 8QT
Map 11: NS56
Tel: 0141 3069988
Fax: 0141 2212022
Cost: *Alc* £24.95, set-price D £24.95.
☺ H/wine £12.55
Times: D only, 7-10.30pm. Closed
Sun, Mon, Xmas wk-early Jan
Additional: Children welcome;
🍂 dishes.
Smoking: No-smoking area;
Air conditioning
Accommodation: 283 en suite
★★★★

Directions: Adjacent to Scottish
Exhibition & Conference Centre,
follow signs

*Hotel built on the old Queens Docks. Two restaurants, but Mariners,
the more formal option, has our rosette award.*

GLASGOW, Malmaison Hotel

278 West George Street G2 4LL
Map 11: NS56
Tel: 0141 5721001
Fax: 0141 5721002
Cost: *Alc* £22, set-price L
£12.50/D £14.50. ☺ H/wine £13.95
Times: Noon-2.30pm/6-11pm.
Closed L Sat
Additional: Sunday L;
Children welcome; 🍂 dishes
Accommodation: 72 en suite ★★★

Directions: From George Square take
Vincent Street to Pitt Street – hotel is
on corner of this and West George
Street

*Popular French-style brasserie. Dishes include grilled liver and bacon
with creamed potatoes, butternut squash risotto with Parmesan
shavings, and the ever-popular steak frites with garlic butter.*

GLASGOW, **Nairns** ❀❀

13 Woodside Crescent G3 7UP
Map 11: NS56
Tel: 0141 3530707
Fax: 0141 3311684
Chef: Neil Forbes
Owners: Nick & Christopher Nairn
Cost: Set-price D £25. H/wine £14.50
Times: Noon-2pm/6-10pm. Closed
25, 26 Dec, 1, 2 Jan
Additional: Sunday L; Children
welcome; ❹ dishes
Seats: 80
Smoking: No pipes & cigars
Accommodation: 4 en suite

Smart Georgian town house combining original features with contemporary style. 'It's all very smart and trendy', as one inspector commented, and the service is equally sharp. Menus follow a set-price formula, with around half-a-dozen choices at each course and give a familiar spin to the Mediterranean with the likes of fish soup, and baked fillet of cod in a tapenade crust with creamed polenta and sorrel beurre blanc. Alternatively, start with artichoke Wellington and go on to loin of hare with shiitaki and a port jus, or a broth of chicken, smoked pork belly and red lentils with braised leeks and new potatoes. Pear tarte Tatin with prune and Armagnac ice cream is typical of puddings – and what better accompaniment can there be but an Australian dessert wine from Vasse Felix?

Directions: Telephone for directions

GLASGOW,
One Devonshire Gardens ❀❀❀

1 Devonshire Gardens G12 0UX
Map 11: NS56
Tel: 0141 3392001
Fax: 0141 3371663
Chef: Andrew Fairlie
Cost: *Alc* £40, set-price L £27.50
Times: Noon-2.15pm/7.15-10pm.
Closed L Sat
Additional: Sunday L;
Children welcome; ❹ dishes
Seats: 35. Private dining rooms 10, 14

They know the golden rule at this discreet hotel – keep it simple. The dining-room has been totally refurbished and although it still has dark-wood half-panelling, the general effect is much lighter with Picasso prints to add streaks of bold, vivid colour. Andrew Fairlie's cooking follows similar simple-but-bold principles. He uses the best ingredients to ensure quality, combines them with accurate cooking and shows restraint both on the plate and in the menu. Roasted king scallops with sun-dried tomato risotto with crisp Parmesan is one of the lengthier descriptions, but is all that's needed to herald superb, plump diver-caught scallops, flash cooked with a touch of outside colour, pearly white and succulent inside. Main course roasted duck confit achieved the double whammy of succulent but dry meat with no hint of fattiness, served on an onion marmalade mixed with fresh orange juice and cloves, with a slice of pink foie gras oozing its juices onto a bed of fondant potato. Other Scottish-French dishes include cutlet of veal with pommes daupinoise and morel jus, and grilled John Dory with roasted aubergine purée and sauce vierge. The dessert trolley has been rescued from gastronomic oblivion, with hot puddings also available in the evening. Bitter chocolate tart with raspberries will not disappoint.

Smoking: No smoking in dining room
Accommodation: 27 en suite ★ ★ ★

Directions: On Great Western Road turn L at lights towards Hyndland, 200 yards turn R and R again

GLASGOW, La Parmigiana

447 Great Western Road
G12 8HH
Map 11: NS56
Tel: 0141 3340686
Fax: 0141 3323533
Cost: *Alc* £18, set-price L £8.30
Times: Noon-2.30pm/6-11pm.
Closed Sun
Additional: Children welcome;
🍴 dishes
Smoking: No pipes; Air conditioning

Directions: Close to Kelvinbridge underground station

Popular, family-run Italian in the city with a bright, Milanese-style interior. Sample venison with porcini with Italian sausage ragout and a polenta croûton, or trusted favourites like veal with Parma ham, Mozzarella and tomato, and tiramisu. Good value set lunch menu.

GLASGOW,

Puppet Theatre

One of the city's more distinctive restaurants tucked away down a narrow lane opposite Hillhead Metro station. Among its four idiosyncratic dining rooms, you may choose to eat in the plant-filled conservatory or in the dark green, candlelit Altar Room. Wherever you sit expect the service to be attentive yet unhurried, and the food an interesting blend of modern Scottish and Mediterranean cooking. Set-price two or three-course menus change monthly and are devised around quality ingredients. Dinner may commence with Arbroath smokie Cullen skink with potato gnocchi, or a tian of Mediterranean vegetables with black olive and basil tapenade. Main courses include imaginative vegetarian dishes such as vegetable cassoulet with herb and horseradish dumplings and goulash cream, and may feature sea bass with mussel, tomato and fennel compote. Desserts are good, perhaps dark chocolate truffle cake with rum sabayon, and raspberry, vanilla and peach cheesecake with pineapple coulis.

11 Ruthven Lane G12 9BG
Map 11: NS56
Tel: 0141 3398444
Fax: 0141 3397666
Chef: James Boyd
Owners: Ron McCulloch,
George Swanson
Cost: Set-price D £28. H/wine £13
Times: Noon-2.30pm/7-10.30pm.
Closed L Sat, all Mon, 1-2 Jan
Additional: Sunday L; Children 12+;
🍴 dishes
Seats: 65. Private dining room 10-26
Smoking: No-smoking area; Air conditioning

Directions: Just off Byres Road

GLASGOW, Rogano

Designed in the 30s, at the same time as the Queen Mary was being built on the Clyde, accounts for the Art Deco style. (And possibly for the seafaring connections on a menu given over largely to fish.) Half a lobster, sea bass with herby beurre blanc, grilled halibut fillet with Guinness and grain mustard sauce, show the range.

Smoking: No pipes & cigars; Air conditioning

Directions: City centre between Buchanan Street & Royal Exchange Square

11 Exchange Place G1 3AN
Map 11: NS56
Tel: 0141 2484055
Fax: 0141 2482608
Cost: Alc £33.50, set-price L £16.50.
H/wine £10.95
Times: Noon-2.30pm/6.30-10.30pm.
Closed 25 Dec, 1 Jan
Additional: Bar food; Sunday L;
✦ dishes
Seats: 60. Private dining room 16

GLASGOW, Stravaigin ❀❀

'**Not so much designed as evolved**'. A basement room with hard benches, raffia chairs, and murals and prints on the walls, 'fusing Glasgow hospitality with international modernism' explains the restaurant. This translates as the kitchen transforming Scotland's produce into dishes picked up around the world. How about Chilean broth of chicken, coriander and cornmeal with Stornaway black pudding, or roast breast of Perthshire pheasant with basil and Parmesan risotto and caramelised pecans? From closer to home, chicken liver pâté redolent of garlic and Armagnac comes well-reported, as does seared salmon, well-timed and of up-to-the-minute freshness served with velvety watercress sauce, or a tender chicken breast atop a stew of borlotti beans and crispy bacon with a garlicky meat jus. Vietnamese tart – thin pastry with pineapple purée stacked with fresh coconut – is topped with a syrup of sweet ginger and lemongrass.

Directions: Next to Glasgow University. 200 yds from Kelvinbridge underground

30 Gibson Street G12 8NX
Map 11: NS56
Tel: 0141 3342665
Fax: 0141 3344099
Chef/Owner: Colin Clydesdale
Cost: Set-price D £23.95. ☺
H/wine £11.15
Times: Noon-2.30pm/5-11pm.
Closed L Sun, 25, 26 Dec, 1, 2 Jan
Additional: Bar food; Children welcome; ✦ dishes
Seats: 75
Smoking: No pipes & cigars;
Air conditioning

GLASGOW,
Ubiquitous Chip

Well established Glasgow eaterie in the fashionable West End. Dishes include Troon landed cod with tapenade mash, and Howtowdie chicken breast with skirlie, glazed shallots and a quail's egg.

Additional: Bar food; Sunday L; Children welcome; ✦ dishes
Smoking: No-smoking area

Directions: Telephone for directions

12 Ashton Lane G12 8SJ
Map 11: NS56
Tel: 0141 3345007
Fax: 0141 3371302
Cost: Alc £23.95, set-price L
£23.95/D £32.95. H/wine £11.95
Times: Noon-2.30pm/5.50-11pm.
Closed 25 Dec, 1 Jan, Hogmanay

GLASGOW, Yes ❀❀

Cosmopolitan style and swagger for a restaurant that attracts a celebrity crowd. The young team running front of house are enthusiastic and keen to please. In the kitchen, good use is made of prime raw materials, although some of the more adventurous ideas reflect the chefs ambition to add his own spin to current fashions and flavour trends/combinations. Our test meal included a restrained but soundly prepared terrine of chicken and vegetables wrapped in crisp bacon and

22 West Nile Street G1 2PW
Map 11: NS56
Tel: 0141 2218044
Fax: 0141 2489159
Chef: Steven Caputa
Owner: Ferrier Richardson
Cost: Alc £31, set-price L £16.95/D
£28.50. H/wine £13.95
Times: Noon-2.30pm/7-11pm.
Closed Sun, 25-26 Dec, 1-2 Jan, Bhs

Yes

Additional: Children welcome;
🍷 dishes
Seats: 100. Private dining room 22

Directions: City centre. M8 exit for
George Sq. Turn L at 2nd lights into
Port Dundas Rd, which joins West
Nile St

accompanied by marinated baby onions with a sherry and
walnut dressing, and a perfect seared fillet of salmon set on an
olive mash and surrounded by a ragout of vegetables. Dessert
showed the greatest innovation – a baked cappuccino pudding
with a warm chocolate centre offset by pistachio ice cream.

HIGHLAND

ARISAIG,

Arisaig House ❀❀❀

Style and comfort in a glorious setting. The splendid Scottish
mansion stands peacefully amid extensive woodland and
carefully tended gardens with azaleas, rhododendrons and
roses providing breathtaking colour displays in season. The
panelled dining room provides an appropriately civilised
setting for the creative modern cooking of the kitchen team
headed up by Duncan Gibson (and now augmented by the
arrival of a French pastry chef). The set four-course menu
contains some exciting prospects: roast squab pigeon with a
cassoulette of root vegetables and a light Madeira jus; terrine
of lamb sweetbreads with a gribiche dressing; grilled king
scallops on a bay leaf skewer with fennel and bell peppers.
Poaching and braising are welcome additions to the usual

Beasdale PH39 4NR
Map 13: NM68
Tel: 01687 450622
Fax: 01687 450626
Chef: Duncan Gibson
Owners: Ruth, John & Andrew
Smither, Alison Wilkinson
Cost: Set-price D £39.50 (4 courses).
H/wine £14.50
Times: 12.30-2pm/7.30-8.30pm.
Closed Nov-Easter
Additional: Bar food L; Children 10+;
🍷 dishes
Seats: 32. Jacket & tie preferred
Smoking: No smoking in dining room
Accommodation: 12 en suite ★ ★ ★

Directions: On A830 Fort William to
Mallaig road, 3 miles east of Arisaig
village

repertoire of techniques – monkfish is poached in a nage of young vegetables and star anise bouillon, and braised supreme of guinea fowl given depth with sauerkraut and smoked bacon jus. A clever combination of styles produced crispy wun-tun Mallaig prawns drizzled with superb, fresh basil pesto. Horn of Plenty – a brandysnap horn filled with white chocolate mousse and served with sliced fruit and compote of warm, fresh prunes – lived up to its promise.

BRORA,

Royal Marine Hotel ✸

Elegant dining room designed by Sir Robert Lorimer, architect of the original country house. Brora fish terrine, Skye scallop timbale, and tangy lemon tart have all been endorsed.

Additional: Bar food; Sunday L; Children welcome; 🍴 dishes
Smoking: No smoking in dining room
Accommodation: 22 en suite ★ ★ ★

Directions: Turn off A9 in village toward beach and golf course

Golf Road KW9 6QS
Map 14: NC90
Tel: 01408 621252
Fax: 01408 621181
Cost: *Alc* £24, set-price L £15. ☺ H/wine £10
Times: Noon-2pm/6.30-9pm

COLBOST,

Three Chimneys Restaurant ✸✸

Charming stone crofter's cottage, in the middle of rugged countryside enjoying views of the sea and distant mountains.
New additions this year include a bar area and lovely bedrooms with a breakfast room looking straight onto the sea. The restaurant is patronised by a steadily growing following who enjoy the stunningly fresh seafood and honest approach evident in the cooking. There is both a *carte* and a set-menu at lunch-times but only a set-menu in the evening. The repertoire is successful, a tried-and -tested formula that requires no embellishments as the quality of local and regional ingredients is a keynote here; portions are ample with lots of gorgeous dressed organic salads (grown locally). Our test meal was superb: cheese sablé canapés were melt-in-the-mouth; the quality and freshness of the lobster with vanilla was 'top drawer', as was the delectable lemon rice; and dessert of a delicious white chocolate pavé with crushed raspberry sauce was a stellar production. An interesting wine list includes a good selection of half-bottles.

Dunvegan Isle of Skye IV55 8ZT
Map 13: NG24
Tel: 01470 511258
Fax: 01470 511358
Chef: Shirley Spear
Owners: Eddie & Shirley Spear
Cost: *Alc* £30, set-price L £11.95/D £22.50 (both 2 courses). H/wine £12.95
Times: 12.30-2.30pm/6.30-9.30pm. Closed L Sun, mid Jan-mid Feb
Additional: Children 8+ at D
Seats: 30. Private dining room 18
Smoking: No smoking in dining room
Accommodation: 6 en suite

Directions: From Dungevan take B884 to Glendale. Restaurant is at Colbost 4.5 miles from main road

CONTIN, **Coul House**

By Strathpeffer IV14 9EY
Map 14: NH45
Tel: 01997 421487
Fax: 01997 421945
Cost: *Alc* £24.50, set-price D £28.50
(6 courses). ☺ H/wine £14.94
Times: Noon-2pm/7-9pm
Additional: Bar food; Sunday L;
Children welcome; ♨ dishes
Smoking: No smoking in dining room
Accommodation: 20 en suite ★ ★ ★

Directions: A9 and A385 to Contin.
Half-mile up private drive on R

Candlelit restaurant with views to the mountains of Wester Ross.
Taste of Scotland dishes include smoked venison and 'croft and
creel' sirloin steak filled with West Coast mussels.

DINGWALL, **Kinkell House**

Honest, direct flavours from good ingredients are sensibly given the
minimum of embellishment on the short dinner carte. Local lamb,
fish and pork dishes all feature; leave room for the home-made
puddings.

Smoking: No smoking in dining room
Accommodation: 9 en suite ★ ★

Directions: On B9169 10 miles N of Inverness, 1 mile from A9
& A835

Easter Kinkell IV7 8HY
Map 14: NH55
Tel: 01349 861270
Fax: 01349 865902
Cost: *Alc* £22.50, set-price L £12.50.
☺ H/wine £10
Times: 12.30-2.15pm/7-8.30pm.
Closed L Sat
Additional: Bar food; Sunday L;
Children welcome; ♨ dishes

DULNAIN BRIDGE,
Muckrach Lodge Hotel ✿

Former Victorian shooting lodge transformed into welcoming hotel.
Obliging staff coupled with a talented kitchen team ensure a
memorable visit. Technical skill is evident, with careful treatment of
seared scallops on a celeriac purée with a citrus butter sauce.

Directions: On A938, 0.5 mile from Dulnain Bridge

PH26 3LY
Map 14: NH92
Tel: 01479 851257
Fax: 01479 851325
Telephone for further details

DUNDONNELL,
Dundonnell Hotel ✿✿

A hospitable family-run Highland hotel, situated at the head
of Little Loch Broom. Thirty years ago this was a small inn
with four rooms available for passing travellers. Now the hotel
boasts twenty-eight rooms and provides excellent food for
visitors keen to explore the hills and beaches of Wester Ross.
A typical four-course autumn meal might kick off with a light
dish of pan-fried pigeon breast with Puy lentils and raspberry
vinegar jus, followed by a choice of soups (cream of
mushroom or mussel and saffron, perhaps). Then, from a
handful of main courses, there could be roast saddle of
Highland venison with baked beetroot and parsnips, or

Little Loch Broom Nr Ullapool
IV23 2QS
Map 14: NH08
Tel: 01854 633204
Fax: 01854 633366
Chefs: Mrs I Bellshaw, Joseph McAtier
Owners: Selbie & Flora Florence
Cost: Set-price D £26 (4 courses). ☺
H/wine £9
Times: Noon-2.15pm/7-8.30pm.
Closed Jan-mid Feb
Additional: Bar food;
Children welcome; ♨ dishes

Dundonnell Hotel

Seats: 70
Smoking: No smoking in dining room
Accommodation: 28 en suite ★ ★ ★

poached fillet of sole with scallop mousse and spinach. Desserts are simple and along the lines of Muscat brûlée and home-made ice cream.

Directions: On A832 Ullapool/Gairloch road, 14 miles from Braemore junction

FORT WILLIAM,

Inverlochy Castle

Torlundy PH33 6SN
Map 14: NN17
Tel: 01397 702177
Fax: 01397 702953
Chef: Simon Haigh
Cost: Set-price L £30/D £55 (4 courses). H/wine £16
Times: 12.30-1.45pm/7.15-9.15pm
Additional: Sunday L; Children 12+; 🍴 dishes
Seats: 36. Private dining room 14. Jacket & tie preferred
Smoking: No smoking in dining room
Accommodation: 17 en suite ★ ★ ★ ★

Directions: 3 miles N of Fort William on A82, just past the Golf Club

Inverlochy remains one of the most impressive destination hotels in the region. The Great Hall sets the tone of Victorian grandeur; the three elegant dining rooms, each decorated with elaborate furniture presented as gifts from the King of Norway, have fine views over the gardens and loch stocked with brown trout. Simon Haigh has an inventive mind and passion for interesting ingredients – rich, smooth ballotine of foie gras is given unusual depth with a (lightly) wood-smoked apple purée and dried, pungent apple slices, while fresher-than-fresh turbot with roasted scallops may be served braised on a bed of vegetables that includes samphire, asparagus, fennel and artichoke fonds. There is some lack of restraint in such multi-element compositions, but on this occasion they were brought together by a delicate chive jus. Celebrate the hotel's thirty years of hospitality with a typical dinner of salad of roasted squab with crispy goats' cheese ravioli and spears of asparagus, followed by chicken consommé scented with thyme, roast best end of Scottish lamb with a herb and mustard crust and tapenade jus, and a hot raspberry soufflé with its own sorbet.

Signature dishes: Isle of Skye crab with potato tuiles and horseradish potatoes; roast loin of Scottish brown hare wrapped in cured ham with a peppery port sauce; whole roasted white peach with a warm raspberry coulis and nougatine parfait.

FORT WILLIAM,

Moorings Hotel ✿

Banavie PH33 7LY
Map 14: NN17
Tel: 01397 772797
Fax: 01397 772441
Cost: Set-price D £26 (4 courses). ☺
H/wine £10.35
Times: D only, 7-9.30pm
Additional: Children welcome;
❹ dishes
Smoking: No smoking in dining room
Accommodation: 20 en suite ★★★

Directions: From A82 take A830 W 1 mile. 1st R over Caledonian Canal on B8004

Jacobean-style dining room in a modern hotel. Full use is made of prime locally sourced produce in dishes enhanced by the judicious use of herbs and flavoured oils.

FORT WILLIAM,

No 4 Cameron Square ✿ NEW

"A most pleasant wee place' – a cottage-style restaurant providing sound modern cooking. Hot-smoked salmon with roasted fennel, and loin of tuna with chilli jam, coriander and lemon grass say it all. Reasonably priced selection of wines.

Additional: Children welcome; dishes
Smoking: No-smoking area; Air conditioning

Directions: Just off pedestrianised High St next to Tourist Information Office

4 Cameron Square PH33 6AJ
Map 14: NN17
Tel: 01397 704222
Fax: 01397 704448
Cost: *Alc* £25, set-price L £11.95/D £18.50. ☺ H/wine £11.95
Times: Noon-2.30pm/6.30-9.30pm. Closed Sun

GLENFINNAN,

The Prince's House ✿

Genuine hospitality and good food are part of the attraction of this hotel on the 'Road to the Isles'. Flora's Restaurant offers the likes of pan-fried pigeon and pheasant breast with rösti and cider cream sauce, and herb-crusted lamb chops with red wine and rosemary gravy.

Additional: Bar food; Children 5+; dishes
Smoking: No smoking in dining room
Accommodation: 9 en suite ★★

Directions: Take A830 NW of Fort William, continue for approx 15 miles

PH37 4LT
Map 14: NM98
Tel: 01397 722246
Fax: 01397 722307
Cost: Set-price D £27 (4 courses). H/wine £9.50
Times: D only, 7-8.30pm. Closed Xmas, New Year, Jan

HALKIRK,
Ulbster Arms Hotel

Bridge Street KW12 6XY
Tel/Fax: 01847 831206
Telephone for further details

Popular sporting hotel offering a set four-course dinner in a rather formal setting. Loin of lamb with thyme and garlic with a gateau of aubergine and ratatouille and a selection of vegetables shows the style. Bar meals are also popular.

Directions: Halkirk off A9, 3m N of Spittal

HARLOSH, **Harlosh House**

Isle of Skye IV55 8ZG
Map 13: NG24
Tel/Fax: 01470 521367
Chef/Owner: Peter Elford
Cost: Set-price D £27.50. ☺
H/wine £12.50
Times: D only, 7-8.30pm.
Closed Oct-Easter
Additional: Children 8+
Seats: 16
Smoking: No smoking in dining room
Accommodation: 6 en suite ★

Built as a tackman's house in 1755, this restaurant still retains some of the original features, including lovely timber beams. This is a small, intimate restaurant that serves a four-course set menu, with no choice except for the desserts. The local seafood is particularly worth a mention. A typical menu might include a simple starter of sweet langoustines served with a well-made garlic mayonnaise and a cucumber/ red onion relish, followed by a salad made from wild herbs. The main course might be pan-fried cod fillet on a Jersey Royal and leek mash, or perhaps some steamed fillet of turbot served on a bed of crisp mange-tout, fine beans and asparagus with a ring of crushed potatoes mixed with fennel. Desserts include a choice of Scottish cheeses, a trio of sorbets and a choice of tarts, parfaits and puddings.

Directions: 4 miles S of Dunvegan, turn R off A863, signed Harlosh

INVERMORISTON,
Glenmoriston Arms Hotel

IV3 6YA
Tel: 01320 351206
Fax: 01320 351308
Telephone for further details

This well-established and friendly family-run holiday and sporting hotel is situated close to Loch Ness. There are a number of eateries to choose from, each offering something different: informal meals at the bar and in the bistro, while in the evening more formal meals are to be found in the dining room. Here, home-made breads are delicious and accompany a variety of starters. Tartare of salmon, perhaps, well-marinated with spices and herbs, and served with yogurt, crisp shredded lettuce and lemon. Then picatta of very tneder pork with pistachio nuts in a garlic, cream and fresh chive sauce and accompanied by roast potatoes, red cabbage and broccoli. We found the generous portion of bread-and-butter pudding to have just the correct degree of crustiness. Lovers of single malt whisky should take note: the Moriston bar is well worth a visit before or after dinner, as it stocks around a hundred of them.

Directions: At the junction of A82/A877

INVERNESS,
Bunchrew House Hotel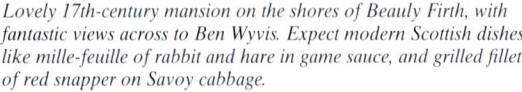

Bunchrew IV3 6TA
Map 14: NH64
Tel: 01463 234917
Fax: 01463 710620
Cost: *Alc* L £25. ☺ H/wine £12.50
Times: 12.30-2pm/7-9pm
Additional: Bar food L; Children welcome; ✦ dishes

Lovely 17th-century mansion on the shores of Beauly Firth, with fantastic views across to Ben Wyvis. Expect modern Scottish dishes like mille-feuille of rabbit and hare in game sauce, and grilled fillet of red snapper on Savoy cabbage.

Smoking: No smoking in dining room
Accommodation: 11 en suite ★ ★ ★

Directions: 2.5 miles from Inverness on A862 towards Beauly

INVERNESS,

Culloden House Hotel

Culloden IV2 7BZ
Map 14: NH64
Tel: 01463 790461
Fax: 01463 792181
Chef: Michael Simpson
Cost: *Alc* £22.50, set-price D £35
(6 courses). H/wine £12.60
Times: 12.30-2.15pm/7-8.45pm
Additional: Children 12+; ❹ dishes
Smoking: No smoking in dining room
Accommodation: 28 en suite ★ ★ ★ ★

Historic building with an atmosphere of refinement and comfort. It was from this Georgian mansion that Bonnie Prince Charlie left for the Battle of Culloden in 1746. Today, marble fireplaces, chandeliers and plasterwork are testament to the period of the building, while the restaurant, designed by Robert Adam, features an 18-foot-high ceiling, wall medallions, mirror and fireplace, and four classical pillars. The set-price, six-course 'Tastes from Scotland' menu at dinner remains loyal to its roots: perhaps West Coast kiln-smoked salmon, a timbale of haggis, neeps and tatties, and then collops of beef with sautéed wild mushrooms. Using the same prime local ingredients for the alternative dinner menu, the kitchen shows skill and innovation in producing a starter of perhaps marinated scallops and smoked salmon baked in filo accompanied by rich langoustine sauce, and a main course of saddle of venison with black pudding and apricot mousse served with a beetroot and potato cake. Atholl brose and Scottish cheeses are apt ways to finish. An interesting wine list features many fine French bottles.

Directions: From Inverness take A96 (Airport road), R at sign "Culloden". After 1.2 miles L at dovecote after 2 sets of traffic lights

INVERNESS,

La Riviera at the Glenmoriston Town House ❀

Classic Italian cuisine is the order of the day. Try a range of specialities including Tuscan pasta and bean soup, beef fillet with pesto, and sautéed Oriental vegetables and beetroot. Decent wines with an Italian bias.

20 Ness Bank IV2 4SF
Map 14: NH64
Tel: 01463 223777
Fax: 01463 712378
Cost: *Alc* £28, set-price L £12/D £24.
☺ H/wine £10.50
Times: Noon-2.30pm/6-9.30pm

Additional: Bar food L; Sunday L; Children welcome; ❹ dishes
Smoking: No-smoking area; No pipes & cigars
Accommodation: 15 en suite ★ ★ ★

Directions: 5 mins from town centre, on river opposite the theatre

ISLE ORNSAY,

Hotel Eilean Iarmain ✦

Stunning location overlooking the Sound of Sleat for a traditional inn noted for hospitality and innovative Scottish cooking. Typical choices may include parsnip and cinnamon soup, venison with rowan and juniper jus, and dark chocolate and ginger marquise.

Isle of Skye IV43 8QR
Map 13: NG71
Tel: 01471 833332
Fax: 01471 833275
Cost: Set-price L £19.50 (4 courses)/D £33 (5 courses). H/wine £14
Times: 12.30-1.45pm/7.30-8.45pm
Additional: Bar food; Sunday L (pre-booking essential); Children welcome; ✦ dishes
Smoking: No smoking in dining room. Jacket & tie preferred
Accommodation: 12 en suite ★ ★

Directions: Cross bridge at Kyle of Lochalsh and take A850 then A851 to Eilean Iarmain/Isle Ornsay sign & turn L. Hotel on harbour

ISLE ORNSAY,

Kinloch Lodge ✦✦

Isle of Skye IV43 8QY
Map 13: NG71
Tel: 01471 833214
Fax: 01471 833277
Chefs: Lady Macdonald, Peter Macpherson
Owners: Lord & Lady Macdonald
Cost: Set-price D £35 (5 courses)
Times: D only at 8pm.
Closed 22-29 Dec
Additional: Children 8+
Seats: 35
Smoking: No smoking in dining room
Accommodation: 15 en suite ★ ★

Directions: 1 mile off main road, 6 miles S of Broadford on A851, 10 miles N of Armadale

Lord and Lady Macdonald's secluded home dates from 1540 and lies at the end of a forest track with splendid views over Loch Na Dal. Although a comfortable country house hotel, it retains the atmosphere of a private home with open fires, drawing rooms filled with antiques and an elegant dining room adorned with family portraits and silver. Dinner is served at 8pm and guests can enjoy Lady Macdonald's set-price dinners which show a refreshing simplicity and feature the best of island produce and good use of spices and herbs. A typical five-course meal may begin with roast red pepper mousse with black olive relish, followed by a soup, perhaps spicy tomato, and a choice of main courses, maybe duck with port ginger and green peppercorn sauce, or baked halibut with lemon butter sauce. Finish with Seville orange and pistachio meringue pie and, if you have room, with fruit and a selection of Scottish cheeses.

KENTALLEN,

Holly Tree Hotel

Edwardian railway station converted to art noveau-style hotel in a stunning setting on the shore of Loch Linnhe. Seafood and game are specialities but other tastes are catered for.

Additional: Sunday L; Children welcome; dishes
Smoking: No smoking in dining room
Accommodation: 10 en suite ★ ★

Directions: 3m S of Ballachulish on A828

Kentallen Pier PA38 4BY
Map 14: NN05
Tel: 01631 740292
Fax: 01631 740345
Cost: *Alc* £25, set-price L £6 (2 courses). ☺ H/wine £12.50
Times: Noon-2pm/7-9.30pm

KINGUSSIE, **The Cross**

Charming small hotel noted for high standards. Reports on the Hadley's civilised converted tweed mill focus on the merits of the kitchen. Ruth Hadley's five-course dinners display quality, intelligence, and a modern edge that take meticulous note of the seasons. The emphasis, of course, is on local produce, whether it be seafood, meat or vegetables – 'by the very nature of wild food it tends to be organic, i.e. venison, pike, mountain hare, scallops etc.', writes Tony Hadley. A typical dinner may run through west coast scallops with asparagus and Thai-dressed noodles, capsicum soup, fishcakes made with salmon, lemongrass, and leeks and served with sweetcorn salsa, fillet of prime Scottish beef, pan-fried with a grain mustard and red wine sauce, and apple tarte Tatin. A passion for fine wine distinguishes the wine list, especially the carefully chosen list of fine vintages from around the world; Tony Hadley will always give advice where needed.

Signature dishes: boudin of local pike; hake with groundnut and capsicum; venison 'Francatelli'; baked lime cheesecake with blackcurrant foil.

Tweed Mill Brae
Ardbroilach Road PH21 1TC
Map 14: NH70
Tel: 01540 661166
Fax: 01540 661080
Chef: Ruth Hadley
Owners: AP & R Hadley
Cost: Set-price D £35 (5 courses). H/wine from £12.50
Times: D only, 7-8.30pm.
Closed Tue, 1 Dec-1 Mar
Additional: Children 12+
Seats: 28
Smoking: No smoking in dining room
Accommodation: 9 en suite ★ ★

Directions: Town centre, 300m uphill from lights along Ardroilach Road & turn left onto Tweed Mill Brae

---

KINGUSSIE, **Osprey Hotel**

Charming hotel in the heart of the Spey valley. Tempting dishes include home-made smoked mackerel pâté, and fillet of rainbow trout topped with finely chopped vegetables and feta cheese.

Additional: Children 10+
Smoking: No smoking in dining room
Accommodation: 8 en suite ★ ★

Directions: South end of High Street off A9

Ruthven Road PH21 1EN
Map 14: NH70
Tel/Fax: 01540 661510
Cost: Set-price D £22 (4 courses). ☺ H/wine £8
Times: D only, 7.30-8.30pm

KINGUSSIE,

The Scot House Hotel

Wholesome Scottish fare is offered from a choice of menus. Recommended are local haggis, monkfish royale, and home-made profiteroles with a 'wicked' chocolate sauce.

Smoking: No smoking in dining room
Accommodation: 9 en suite ★ ★

Directions: South end of main village street

Newtonmore Road PH21 1HE
Map 14: NH70
Tel: 01540 661351
Fax: 01540 661111
Cost: *Alc* £24, set-price D £19 (4 courses). ☺ H/wine £9.50
Times: Noon-2pm/7-8.45pm.
Closed 25, 26 Dec
Additional: Bar Food; Children 10+

LOCHINVER, **Lochinver Larder**

The pretty Riverside Bistro looks over the River Inver where it enters the sea and locally landed seafood is a feature of the dinner menu. Home-made pies are another speciality, and sirloin steaks are well hung.

Directions: Approaching Lochinver on A837, 2nd property on R

Main Street IV27 4JY
Map 14: NC02
Tel: 01571 844356
Fax: 01571 844688
Telephone for further details

MUIR OF ORD, **The Dower House**

Lovingly run by Robyn and Mena Aitchison, this delightful small hotel is set in four acres of mature grounds and offers a quiet and relaxing atmosphere. A country house in every sense, it was built around 1800 and is full of interesting and thoughtful touches, including fresh flowers, log fires and antiques. Robyn's no-choice, set dinners are based on modern British cooking and display good use of fresh herbs from the garden and first-rate seasonal produce. Skilfully cooked dishes may include red wine risotto with asparagus and Parma ham or chicken liver salad, followed by lamb with Marsala sauce or scallops with black spaghetti. Dessert, perhaps warm chocolate soufflé, or Scottish cheese is followed by coffee and home-made chocolate truffles. The excellent wine list is very reasonably priced.

Directions: A862 N from Muir of Ord 1m, L at double bend

Highfield IV6 7XN
Map 14: NH55
Tel/Fax: 01463 870090
Chef: Robyn Aitchison
Owners: Robyn & Mena Aitchison
Cost: Set-price D £25. H/wine £13
Times: L by arrangement/7.30-9.30pm. Closed 25 Dec
Additional: Children 7+; ✿ dishes
Seats: 26
Smoking: No smoking in dining room
Accommodation: 5 en suite ★

NAIRN, **The Boath House**

A house has stood on the site since the 16th century, but the current building dates from 1825. It's a splendid place, decorated with antiques and the restaurant is totally candlelit at night. Local ingredients with a sound organic showing dictate the short, daily *carte*. A Scottish classic – soup and dumplings – is updated in cream of spiced parsnip soup served with chicken dumplings and a coriander crème fraîche. Or there could be seared fillet of salmon and king scallops, served with a simple garlic and herb risotto and a vermouth and carrot cream. Beef is Aberdeen Angus, and game in season could take in roasted grey-legged partridge with a ragout of red cabbage and onion, boudin blanc and a port wine and rosemary jus. Cheeses are Scottish, naturally, and a lemon bramble crème brûlée served with a red berry sorbet showcases first-class ingredients admirably.

Directions: 2m E of Nairn on A96, signposted

Auldearn IV12 5TE
Map 14: NH85
Tel: 01667 454896
Fax: 01667 455469
Chef: Charles Lockley
Owners: Don & Wendy Matheson
Cost: Alc £30, set-price L & D £17.50. H/wine £11
Times: Noon-2pm/7-9pm. Closed L Wed, all Mon, Tue
Additional: Sunday L; Children welcome; ✿ dishes
Seats: 30. Private dining room 8
Smoking: No smoking in dining room
Accommodation: 7 en suite ★★★

NAIRN, **Golf View Hotel** NEW

Expect a short menu in the wood-panelled dining-room and supplementary steak dishes at an additional charge. A simpler, more focused approach has paid dividends in dishes such as medallions of Sutherland venison with peppery shallot marmalade and blackberry and sage sauce.

Accommodation: 47 en suite ★★★★

Directions: 15 miles SE of Inverness, 7 miles from airport on A96. In Nairn turn L at parish church and continue to end of Seabank Road

Seabank Road IV 12 4HD
Map 14: NH85
Tel: 01667 452301
Fax: 01667 455267
Cost: Set-price D £24. ☺
H/wine £10.95
Times: Noon-2pm/7-9pm
Additional: Bar food; Sunday L; Children welcome; ✿ dishes
Smoking: No smoking in dining room; Air conditioning

NAIRN,

Newton Hotel

Inverness Road IV12 4RX
Map 14: NH85
Tel: 01667 453144
Fax: 01667 454026
Cost: Set-price D £23. ☺
H/wine £10.95
Times: Noon-2pm/7-9pm
Additional: Bar food; Sunday L;
Children welcome; ✦ dishes
Accommodation: 57 en suite ★ ★ ★ ★

Directions: West of the town centre

Once favoured by the Chaplins, the well-established hotel boasts an impressive combination of Georgian and Scottish Baronial architecture. The modern Scottish cooking uses high quality meat and game plus freshly caught fish from the Moray Firth and local rivers.

ONICH,

Allt-nan-Ros Hotel ✿✿

PH33 6RY
Map 14: NN06
Tel: 01855 821210
Fax: 01855 821462
Chef: Mark Walker
Owners: Mr & Mrs J MacLeod
Cost: Set-price D £28 (4 courses). ☺
H/wine £11.95
Times: 12.30-1.45pm/7-8.30pm.
Closed mid Nov for 6 wks
Additional: Bar food L; Sunday L;
Children welcome; ✦ dishes
Seats: 50
Smoking: No smoking in dining room
Accommodation: 20 en suite ★ ★ ★

Victorian country house that is now an hospitable family hotel. Set alongside Loch Linnhe, Allt-Nan-Ros translates from the Gaelic as the burn of roses. In the dining room the view across landscaped gardens to the moody loch and rugged hills beyond competes for attention with a four-course dinner menu featuring Scottish produce. A typical evening's main course choices might comprise seared Campbeltown scallops scented with lemon and tarragon with rösti potato, chive mousseline-filled breast of chicken on herb cream with an apple and Savoy cabbage parcel, and roast Aberdeen Angus beef with a duo of sauces and onion and bacon confit. Finish with the likes of chocolate tart with butterscotch ice cream or Scottish cheeses served with oatcakes and fresh fruit.

Directions: On the shores of Loch Linnhe, 10 miles S of Fort William on A82

PORTREE, **Bosville Hotel** ✿

Bosville Terrace Isle of Skye
IV51 9DG
Map 13: NG44
Tel: 01478 612846
Fax: 01478 613434
Cost: *Alc* £22.50, set-price D £20. ☺
H/wine £9.50
Times: 11am-10pm
Additional: Bar Food; Sunday L;
Children welcome; ✦ dishes
Smoking: No smoking in dining room
Accommodation: 15 en suite ★★

Directions: In centre of Portree

Well-established hotel where new blood in the kitchen is producing some interesting food. Seafood is a speciality: langoustine tails in Thermidor sauce; king scallops with green garlic butter with crispy bacon.

PORTREE, **Cuillin Hills Hotel** ✿

Isle of Skye IV51 9QU
Map 13: NG44
Tel: 01478 612003
Fax: 01478 613092
Cost: *Alc* £26, set-price D £26 (4
courses). ☺ H/wine £10.50
Times: D only, 6.30-9pm
Additional: Bar Food; Sunday L
(12.30-2pm); Children welcome;
✦ dishes
Smoking: No smoking in dining room
Accommodation: 30 en suite ★★★

Directions: Signed to right 0.25 miles
from Portree on A855 north

Smart hotel with superb views over Portree Bay to the Cuillins beyond. Modern cooking features fresh local produce, with some traditional favourites and Highland specialities.

PORTREE, **Rosedale Hotel** ✿

Isle of Skye IV51 9DB
Map 13: NG44
Tel: 01478 613131
Fax: 01478 612531
Cost: *Alc* £21, set-price D £25 (5
courses). ☺ H/wine £9.35
Times: 12.30-2.30pm/7-8.30pm
Additional: Bar food;
Children welcome
Smoking: No smoking in dining room
Accommodation: 23 en suite ★★

Directions: Centrally located on
waterfront in Portree

Welcoming holiday hotel ingeniously converted from three 19th-century harbour-front buildings. Expect the hotel's own gravad lax,

broccoli and almond soup, lamb with couscous and red pepper
chutney, as well as glazed lemon tart.

SHIELDAIG,
Tigh an Eilean Hotel

The hotel stands at the water's edge, and local seafood is the
speciality of the house. Try the scallops or lobster Marie-Rose,
followed by poached salmon or turbot Waleska.

Additional: Bar food; Children welcome; ➍ dishes
Smoking: Air conditioning; Jacket & tie preferred
Accommodation: 11 en suite ★

Directions: In centre of Shieldaig, at water's edge

Strathcarron IV54 8XN
Map 14: NG85
Tel: 01520 755251
Fax: 01520 755321
Cost: Set-price D £26.15. ☺
Times: D only, 7-8.30pm

SPEAN BRIDGE,
Old Pines Restaurant with Rooms ✿✿

Superb little pine cabin in the middle of nowhere. What a
delightful haven. Basically, it's slap bang in some of the UK's
most dramatic and yet desolate scenery. Nonetheless, guests
travel from far and wide to sample the excellent Scottish
regional cooking, sharing tables and experiences. The set five-
course menu changes daily and uses much home-grown
produce such as vegetables, herbs and flowers. The honest,
straightforward cooking needs no frills: warm smoked-haddock
mousse with spinach and a lemon and fennel sauce had superb
flavour, a smooth consistency and was light as a feather. A flat
mushroom and cep soup with chicken livers and port and
thyme was a rustic affair yet so delicious. The main course,
breast of duck with Madeira, Seville oranges, garlic and
coriander with a fried parsnip galette again was memorable for
flavour and balance. Vegetables such as creamed potatoes with
leek and cauliflower with wholegrain mustard sauce are served
'family-style'.

Directions: A82, 1 mile N of Spean Bridge take B8004 next to
Commando Memorial towards Gairlochy. 300 yds on R

NEW

By Fort William PH34 4EG
Map 14: NN28
Tel: 01397 712324
Fax: 01397 712433
Chef: Sukie Barber
Owners: Bill & Sukie Barber
Cost: Alc D £23.50, set-price D
£27.50 (5 courses). ☺ H/wine £10
Times: L served all day, D from 8pm.
(closed D Sun except residents May-
Sep)
Additional: Children welcome;
➍ dishes
Seats: 30
Smoking: No smoking in dining room
Accommodation: 8 en suite

SPEAN BRIDGE,
Old Station Restaurant

Worth more than a brief encounter – the fine old Victorian station
has been fully restored to create an attractive restaurant (with
appropriate railway memorabilia), and straightforward modern
Scottish cooking. It's still a working station, so you can arrive and
depart by train.

Additional: Children welcome; ➍ dishes
Smoking: No-smoking area

Directions: Approximately 10 miles N of Fort William, in centre
of village (follow signs for BR station)

Station Road PH34 4EP
Map 14: NN28
Tel: 01397 712535
Cost: Alc £21. ☺ H/wine £10.50
Times: D only, 6-9pm.
Closed Mon, end Oct-beg Apr

STRONTIAN,
Kilcamb Lodge Hotel

Nestling below a wooded hill and fronting half a mile of shoreline to Loch Sunart and the Strontian river, this is a nature-lover's idyll. Deer, golden eagles, wildcat, seals and sea otters, and wild orchids could all be glimpsed in this lovely spot. Dinner from the set-price menu offers plenty of choice at each course except soup. Confit of duck leg seems to be a favoured starter, cropping up with a mushroom risotto one night, beetroot and tarragon risotto another. Or there might be pan-fried langoustine tails with rocket and Parmesan. Among main courses, loin of Argyll venison with game and chocolate sauce comes with rösti of Mozzarella, potato and spinach, and pink, tender best end of Highland lamb is served with a neat gâteau of provençale vegetables. Finish with lemon tart and raspberry sorbet, or a selection of Scottish cheeses.

Directions: Take the Corran ferry off A82. Follow A861 to Strontian. First L over bridge in centre of village

Acharacle PH36 4HY
Map 14: NM86
Tel: 01967 402257
Fax: 01967 402041
Chef: Neil Mellis
Owners: Peter & Anne Blakeway
Cost: Set-price D £29.50 (4 courses). ☺ H/wine £10
Times: Noon-1.30pm/D at 7.30pm
Additional: Bar food L; Children 6+
Seats: 28
Smoking: No smoking in dining room
Accommodation: 11 en suite ★★

TAIN, Mansfield House

An impressive, stone-built Victorian mansion set in its own grounds opposite the Royal Academy. The food is as robust as the architecture, strong on Scottish flair and imagination. Our inspection meal kicked off with good canapés: a tasty round of pumpernickel topped with smoked chicken and fresh asparagus, and small new potatoes filled with goats' cheese. The meal proper started with a red onion and leak risotto on top of which slices of rabbit rested. Venison was excellent, its good gamey taste mixing well with the authentic flavours of the baked forest mushroom duxelle, and with the sloe gin sauce that accompanied it. Finally, a trio of sweets: crème brûlée, mint sorbet and dark chocolate mousse. The wine list has a good range of bottles, with house wines also served by the glass.

Directions: From S on A9, ignore 1st turning to Tain and after 0.5m turn R at sign for police station

Scotsburn Road IV19 1PR
Map 14: NH78
Tel: 01862 892052
Fax: 01862 892260
Chef: David Lauritsen
Owners: Norman, Norma & David Lauritsen
Cost: Alc £30, set-price D £25 (4 courses). ☺ H/wine £12
Times: Noon-2pm/7-9pm. Closed 1st wk Jan
Additional: Bar food; Sunday L; Children welcome; ✤ dishes
Seats: 45. Private dining room 20
Smoking: No smoking in dining room
Accommodation: 18 en suite ★★★

TONGUE, Ben Loyal Hotel

There are splendid views of the Kyle of Tongue and the ruins of Varrich Castle from the hotel, particularly from the attractive dining room, which offers modern Scottish cooking.

IV27 4XE
Map 14: NC55
Tel: 01847 611216
Fax: 01847 611212
Cost: Set-price D £25 (4 courses). ☺ H/wine £12.50
Times: Noon-1.50pm/7-8.30pm
Additional: Bar food; Children welcome; ✤ dishes
Smoking: No smoking in dining room
Accommodation: 11 en suite ★★

Directions: Village centre at A836/A838 junction

TORRIDON, **Loch Torridon Hotel** ❀❀

Achnasheen IV22 2EY
Map 14: NG95
Tel: 01445 791242
Fax: 01445 791296
Chef: Ross Duncan
Owners: David & Geraldine Gregory
Cost: Set-price D £38 (4 courses).
H/wine £14
Times: Noon-2pm/7-8.30pm
Additional: Bar food;
Children welcome; ✿ dishes
Seats: 40. Private dining room 15.
Jacket & tie preferred
Smoking: No smoking in dining room
Accommodation: 20 en suite ★ ★ ★

Directions: From Inverness, follow
signs to Ullapool (A835).
At Garve take A832 to Kinlochewe;
take A896 to Torridon. Don't turn off
to Torridon village – hotel is one mile
on L

*Once a grand shooting lodge built for the first Earl of Lovelace
in 1887.* The hotel enjoys an impressive coastal setting; within,
the wood-panelled dining room still has the original Latin
inscription dedicated to Queen Victoria. The kitchen uses
Scottish ingredients liberally and well. Our meal opened with
canapés of chicken parfait, smoked salmon mousse with chopped
tomato and dill, an *amuse bouche* – of leek and venison ravioli
with curry cream, then confit of duck on thyme mash with sun-
dried tomato dressing, and a fat fillet of John Dory served with
fine beans and baby corn, a single asparagus spear and a cream
white wine sauce. Dessert was a tangy lemon tart.

UIG, **Uig Hotel** ❀ NEW

Isle of Skye IV51 9YE
Map 13: NG36
Tel: 01470 542205
Fax: 01470 542308
Telephone for further details

*Family-run country hotel with fine views across Uig Bay. Locally
sourced produce is prepared with enthusiasm, notably home-smoked
chicken salad, Loch Etive oysters, full-flavoured lamb and lentil
broth, and succulent scallops cooked with garlic butter and bacon.*

Directions: From Skye Bridge take A87 via Portree to Uig

ULLAPOOL,
Altnaharrie Inn ❀❀❀❀❀

IV26 2SS
Map 14: NH19
Tel: 01854 633230
Chef: Gunn Eriksen
Owners: Gunn Eriksen, Fred Brown
Cost: Set-price D £75 (5 courses).
H/wine £11
Times: D only, at 8pm.
Closed early Nov-Easter
Additional: Children 8+; ✿ dishes
Seats: 18
Smoking: No smoking in dining room
Accommodation: 8 en suite

Directions: Telephone from Ullapool
for instructions on ferry

*The setting could not be more exquisite – a lochside croft with
private beach.* Simply furnished with open fires and stark

white walls, plus Indian rugs, tapestries and wall hangings to add a touch of ethnicity wth candles and flowers everywhere, some of which are art works in their own right. The dining-room is small and intimate, guests mingle and chat, mainly to eulogise on Gunn Eriksen's food. In terms of technical accomplishment, quality of produce and overwhelmingly accurate flavours, this is indeed a stunning experience. The only problem is that, if you are lucky enough to go here more than once, the no-choice menu might duplicate meals from earlier visits. On the other hand, gamy tender squab breasts and a crispier leg, set on a sliver of whiter-than-white foie gras, with fungi, kohlrabi and an awesome red wine and rowan jus, is a dish only those tired of life could not enjoy forever. Our dinner started with a dramatic flourish – two langoustine tails presented in the base of the shell on a square black plate with sour cream flavoured with pungent herbs and spices. Lobster salad does not convey the simple perfection of the crustacean with two sauces, a pale vegetable based cream with champagne, and coloured coral from the lobster juices. To make the whole thing even more ambrosial, there were summer truffles, caviar and a droplet of oil. A middle course of scallop soup was constructed in ever deepening ripples of flavour from scallop mousseline to an almost still translucent king scallop to an intense, sweet fine cream broth. Three puddings are listed on the hand-written menu, and three are served – our treats were plum tart with peach liqueur, warm chocolate cake with a soft, runny centre and two chocolate ices, and a caramel cream and ice cream in a web of spun sugar. Wines are well sourced and wide ranging.

WHITEBRIDGE,
Knockie Lodge Hotel ❀❀

IV1 2UP
Map 14: NH41
Tel: 01456 486276
Fax: 01456 486389
Chef: Mark Dexter
Owners: Nicholas Bean, Louise Dawson
Cost: Set-price D £37.50 (5 courses). H/wine £12
Times: D only, 8 for 8.30pm. Closed 1 Nov-30 Apr
Additional: L by arrangement; Children 10+; ❹ dishes
Seats: 30. Private dining room 10. Jacket & tie preferred

Former 200-year-old shooting lodge enjoying a glorious setting high above Loch Nan Lann. Run by enthusiastic owners it is a haven of peace and quiet, maintaining a civilised atmosphere and a high level of hospitality. After an exhilarating day outdoors visitors can relax and enjoy the set, no-choice (except dessert) five-course dinner, served in the panelled dining room. Cooking is accomplished and shows good creative and technical skills, especially in the preparation of canapés. Menus successfully blend the simple with the more elaborate, for example crab terrine wrapped in Parma ham with rose water dressing may be followed by wild nettle soup with Thai basil and Cheddar cheese straws, and a platter of Isle

of Skye shellfish with sweet basil vinaigrette. An excellent cheeseboard precedes pudding which may feature caramelised rice pudding, and white chocolate tart with fresh berries.

Directions: On B862 8 miles north of Fort Augustus

Smoking: No smoking in dining room
Accommodation: 10 en suite ★ ★

LANARKSHIRE, NORTH

CUMBERNAULD,
Westerwood Hotel ✿

The Tipsy Laird restaurant on the first floor of the hotel offers a modern international menu with choices such as crab and scallop pithiviers, blackened Cajun salmon, and Chateaubriand.

1 St Andrews Drive Westerwood
G68 0EW
Map 11: NS77
Tel: 01236 457171
Fax: 01236 738478
Cost: *Alc* £22, set-price L £9.95/D £16.50. ☺ H/wine £11.25
Times: Noon-1.45pm/6.45-9.45pm. Closed L Sat, 24 Dec
Additional: Bar food; Sunday L; Children welcome; ⚫ dishes
Smoking: Air conditioning
Accommodation: 49 en suite ★ ★ ★ ★

Directions: Take exit from A80 signposted Ward Park. At mini roundabout take 1st L, at 2nd roundabout turn R, leads into St Andrews Drive

LANARKSHIRE, SOUTH

BIGGAR, ## Shieldhill Hotel ✿✿

A fortified mansion surrounded by lawns and woodlands currently celebrating its 800th year. The oak-panelled lounge looks out onto the gardens, and in winter makes guests feel cosy with a blazing fire. Best suited for casual meals, the Gun Room menu includes pies, casseroles, steaks and burgers. The Chancellor Restaurant is furnished in a baronial style and offers a daily dinner menu. The dishes are interesting and superbly presented. Four starters and five main courses on the *carte* include poached lobster and salmon ravioli, with prawn and coriander cream sauce topped with deep-fried spinach, and loin of Shieldhill lamb wrapped in crepinette with a chicken & lamb mousseline, on a couscous salad, finished with a thyme & red wine jus. Over the years the wine list has gained in stature. It will please Burgundy and claret drinkers with its good range, fair prices and talented producers, but there are also good choices from Australia, USA and Italy, not to mention South Africa and Chile, to counter any charges of French chauvinism.

Quothquan ML12 6NA
Map 11: NT03
Tel: 01899 220035
Fax: 01899 221092
Chef: Trevor Williams
Owners: Bob & Christina Lamb
Cost: *Alc* £30, set-price L £17.50/D £30 (4 courses). ☺ H/wine £11.50
Times: Noon-1.45pm/7-8.30pm
Additional: Bar food; Sunday L; Children welcome; ⚫ dishes
Seats: 34. Private dining room 24
Smoking: No smoking in dining room
Accommodation: 16 en suite ★ ★ ★

Directions: Off B7016 (Carnwath), turn L, 2 miles from centre of Biggar

BIGGAR,
Toftcombs Country House

Peebles Road ML12 6QX
Map 11: NT03
Tel: 01899 220142
Fax: 01899 221771
Cost: *Alc* £18, set-price L & D £9. ☺
H/wine £8.50
Times: Noon-2.30pm/6.30-9.30pm
Additional: Bar food; Sunday L;
Children welcome; ◑ dishes
Smoking: No smoking in dining room
Accommodation: 4 en suite

Directions: On A702 N of Biggar

Beautifully restored Victorian mansion with relaxed country pub atmosphere. Expect hearty portions of modern British fare – start with seafood chowder, followed by Barbary duck with redcurrant sauce.

EAST KILBRIDE,
Crutherland Hotel

Behind the Georgian façade is a comfortable modern hotel, all set in 37 acres of landscaped grounds. Try home-baked breads, duck liver parfait with lime marmalade, and Med-style seared cod tapenade with piperade and chorizo oil.

Strathaven Road G75 0QZ
Map 11: NS65
Tel: 01355 577000
Fax: 01355 220855
Telephone for further details

Directions: From E Kilbride take A726 towards Strathaven.
1.5 miles, & beyond Torrance roundabout, hotel on L

LOTHIAN, EAST

DIRLETON, **Open Arms Hotel**

Picturesque setting close to the village green, overlooking Dirleton Castle. The original dining room has been replaced by a smart brasserie and an intimate restaurant serving Scottish dishes such as pan-fried pigeon breasts on bubble-and-squeak mash, and roast rack of lamb with roasted peppers, olives and cherry tomatoes. When our inspector visited in late summer, he was impressed by a starter of wild mushrooms cooked in Glenkinchie malt whisky and served on toasted potato cake. Steamed fillet of halibut followed, layered with crab meat and flavoured with lemon juice and dill. For dessert the likes of treacle and walnut sponge, and chocolate marquise with raspberry glaze, competed for attention, but in the end traditional toasted Scotch pancakes, served with bramble and cinnamon and cream cheese ganache won the toss. The decent wine list concentrates on the New World.

EH39 5EG
Map 12: NT58
Tel: 01620 850241
Fax: 01620 850570
Chef: John Kay
Owners: Tom & Emma Hill
Cost: Set-price L £15.50/D £27.50 (4 courses). ☺ H/wine £10.95
Times: Noon-2.30pm/7-9.30pm
Additional: Bar food (Deveau's Brasserie); Sunday L; Children welcome; ◑ dishes
Seats: 35
Smoking: No smoking in dining room; Air conditioning
Accommodation: 10 en suite ★★★

Directions: From A1 (S) take A198 to North Berwick, then follow signs for Dirleton. From Edinburgh take A6137/A198

GULLANE, **Greywalls Hotel**

This Edwardian house overlooking Muirfield golf course was designed by Sir Edwin Lutyens, with beautiful gardens created by Gertrude Jekyll. Furnished mainly in period style with many antiques, the day rooms in this magnificent country house are adorned with the family heirlooms. The formal dining room (where jacket and tie is preferred), has taken a new direction, offering a simpler style than previously. The four-course set-menu might begin with pavé of sole and bok choi with saffron emulsion, then fresh pea soup followed by seared North Berwick turbot on foie gras, or loin of Scottish lamb on Puy lentils and roast mushrooms. Three fairly traditional desserts, Welsh rarebit and Scottish farmhouse cheeses precede hand-made chocolates with coffee. The wine list is splendid; indeed it would be hard to better such a well-informed, keenly priced selection.

Additional: Bar food L; Sunday L; Children welcome
Seats: 45. Private dining room 20. Jacket & tie preferred
Smoking: No smoking in dining room
Accommodation: 23 en suite ★ ★ ★

Directions: From Edinburgh take A1 to North Berwick slip road, then follow A198 along coast to far end of Gullane – Greywalls is up last road on L

Muirfield EH31 2EG
Map 12: NT48
Tel: 01620 842144
Fax: 01620 842241
Chef: Simon Burns
Owners: Ros & Giles Weaver
Cost: *Alc* £20, set-price L £17.50/D £35 (4 courses). H/wine £14
Times: 12.30-1.45pm/7.30-9.15pm. Closed Nov-Mar

AA Shortlisted for Wine Award-see page 16

GULLANE, **La Potinière**

Consistently accomplished food in a rather homely dining room. The menu is written in French, uncompromisingly with no translation. In many ways the simplest things stand out most in the memory – sensational, freshly picked salad or a pannacotta of true excellence. The no-choice, four-course lunches served only on Thursdays and Sundays, and five-course dinners served only on Friday and Saturday (at 1pm and 8pm respectively), usually start with a soup, say cream of sweet peppers, for example, followed by a fish course such as salmon with fennel and vanilla sauce, or mousseline of sole with basil. Pigeon with honey and thyme, venison with Puy lentils and morels, and guinea fowl with cabbage are typical of the French influences that shape the cooking. As ever, the cheese course is a slice of Brie de Meaux. David Brown serves the food, whilst Hilary Brown is fully occupied in the kitchen, although she does make an appearance later on. Given the high standards and labour intensive nature of the cooking, dinner is good value, and booking remains essential.

Main Street EH31 2AA
Map 12: NT48
Tel/Fax: 01620 843214
Chef: Hilary Brown
Owners: David & Hilary Brown
Cost: Set-price L £21.50 (4 courses)/D £32.50 (5 courses). H/wine £13.75
Times: L at 1pm/D at 8pm. Open L Sun & Thu/D Fri & Sat. Closed 1 wk Jun, all Oct
Additional: Sunday L; Children welcome
Seats: 26
Smoking: No smoking in dining room
Credit cards: None

Directions: Village centre

LOTHIAN, WEST

LINLITHGOW, **Champany Inn**

The old farm buildings that make up Champany Inn date from the 16th century and the time of Mary, Queen of Scots. Added to this is an annexed wing of smart, purpose-built bedrooms. The restaurant remains elegant and sophisticated, with service to match. The menu has hardly changed over the years and is well-suited for those who like first-class Aberdeen

EH49 7LU
Map 11: NS97
Tel: 01506 834532
Fax: 01506 834302
Chefs: Clive Davidson, David Gibson, Kevin Hope
Owners: Clive & Anne Davidson

Angus beef. Three soups and eight starters feature on the *carte* and, in addition to the various cuts of beef are four fish dishes and three poultry. Breast of Gressingham duck, for example, its skin crisp and the meat pink and succulent, is served with green lentils; vegetables are selected from a basket and cooked to order. Desserts include blueberry delice with lime and yogurt sauce. There is a new wine cellar (with tasting facilities) which houses an impressive wine list.

Directions: 2 miles NE of Linlithgow at junction of A904 & A803

Cost: *Alc* £55, set-price L £16.75 (2 courses). H/wine £12.50
Times: 12.30-2pm/7-10pm. Closed L Sat, all Sun, 24-26 Dec
Additional: Chop & Ale House for – Bar food & Sunday L; Children welcome; 🍴 dishes
Seats: 50. Private dining room 32. Jacket & tie preferred
Accommodation: 16 en suite

LINLITHGOW,
Livingston's Restaurant 🍴🍴

52 High Street EH49 7AE
Map 11: NS97
Tel: 01506 846565
Chef: David Williams
Owners: Ronald & Christine Livingston
Cost: *Alc* £29.50, set-price L £12.99 (2 courses)/D £25.50 (2 courses). H/wine £11.50
Times: Noon-2.30pm/6-9pm. Closed Sun, Mon, 1st 2wks Jan, 1 wk Jun, 1 wk Oct
Additional: Children 8+; 🍴 dishes
Seats: 40
Smoking: No-smoking area; Air conditioning

Directions: Opposite Post Office

Little cottage-style restaurant, converted from old stables, tucked off the main street. The interior is all sandstone walls and Black Watch tartan carpet, candles lit at night, with the lower level of the dining areas a small conservatory. Deliciously moreish brown and white bread sets the ball rolling, to be followed perhaps by an accomplished risotto of bacon, roast red peppers and apples, or pan-fried pigeon breast with braised Puy lentils. That the kitchen is happy working with up to date ideas is evident in a main course of saddle of venison with Cassis sauce and a cassoulet of butter beans and glazed shallots. Old-fashioned treacle tart, or apple and raisin Charlotte topped with a pat of ice cream might mingle with other puddings or perhaps a chilled soup of strawberries and champagne served with chocolate mousse. The New World shines through the wine list, where there's an unusual dessert wine from the Chiltern Valley.

UPHALL,
Houstoun House Hotel 🍴🍴

Broxburn EH52 6JS
Map 11: NT07
Tel: 01506 853831
Fax: 01506 854220
Chef: David Murray
Owner: MacDonald Hotels plc
Cost: *Alc* £44, set-price L £16.50/D £32.50 (4 courses). H/wine £14
Times: Noon-2.30pm/7-9.30pm. Closed L Sat

A smart business and leisure hotel. The three separate dining rooms which make up this restaurant remain unchanged, despite the hotel's improvements and extensions (built sympathetically around a 17th-century house). Stone stairs lead from the vaulted cocktail bar with its large open fire, up to elegant dining rooms. The four-course set-price dinner menu changes weekly – a *carte* is offered at lunch. Dishes come accompanied by oils (crayfish), dressings (raspberry), coulis (pepper), and presentation, as in a well-reported chicken and pimento roulade, sliced and stacked into three towers and served on a stir-fry of vegetables is impressive. Oven-baked breast of chicken coated in an Arran mustard café au lait was also a success – the chicken tender, carefully carved and served with a beef stock-based sauce containing hints of cream and Cognac. There is an impressive wine list which was in the process of being re-vamped as we went to press. A note should also be made of the very attentive service.

Additional: Bar food L; Sunday L; Children welcome; ✿ dishes
Seats: 70. Private dining room 8-30. Jacket & tie preferred
Smoking: No smoking in dining room
Accommodation: 75 en suite ★ ★ ★ ★

Directions: At junction between A89 and A899

MORAY

ARCHIESTOWN,

Archiestown Hotel

Aberlour AB38 7QL
Map 15: NJ24
Tel: 01340 810218
Fax: 01340 810239
Chef: Judith Bulger
Owners: Judith & Michael Bulger
Cost: Alc £25
Times: 12.30-2pm/6.30-8.30pm. Closed 1 Oct-9 Feb
Additional: Bar food; Sunday L; Children welcome
Seats: 30. Private dining room 15
Accommodation: 8 rooms ★ ★

Directions: Turn off A95 onto B9102 at Craigellachie

A tried-and-tested formula that has stood this Victorian hotel in good stead for many years. However, the main point is that the cooking is refreshingly uncomplicated, everything is cooked to order and is based on quality raw ingredients. Specialities are, of course, fish and shellfish, ranging from moules marinière to halibut with a simple white butter sauce, or there could be game in the form of classic roast grouse of partridge, or pigeon casserole with cabbage and apple. Portions are generous, something which suits the sporting (fishing) clientele down to the ground. Most regulars prefer to eat in the completely informal atmosphere of the bistro/bar, which has a tiled floor, solid wood tables, and is crammed with the most amazing collection of bric-a-brac – known affectionately as 'Michael's junk'. Tremendous atmosphere. A separate room is available for customers who wish to dine in a more formal atmosphere – but not many regulars do.

CRAIGELLACHIE,

Craigellachie Hotel

AB38 9SR
Map 15: NJ24
Tel: 01340 881204
Fax: 01340 881253
Chef: David Kinnes
Cost: Alc £27.50, set-price L £13.95/D £27.50. H/wine £12.95

Impressive Victorian hotel with a cosmopolitan clientele. The Quaich Bar is famed for its collection of some 300 single malt whiskies, but the real action is seen in the Ben Aigan restaurant where modish cooking showcases some prime local produce. Home-smoked venison with spiced fruit compote, red pepper oil and herb salad, for example, followed perhaps by grilled fillet of salmon, capsicum risotto, glazed shallots and hollandaise sauce. Steaks are a feature, all prime Aberdeen Angus served with hand-cut chips. For dessert, hot raspberry soufflé is well worth the £1.25 supplement on the daily set menu, but honey and pear tart with crème anglaise comes a close second.

Times: Noon-2pm/6-10pm
Additional: Bar food L; Sunday L; Children welcome; ❹ dishes
Seats: 30. Private dining rooms 8-40
Smoking: No smoking in dining room
Accommodation: 26 en suite ★ ★ ★

Directions: In the village centre

DRYBRIDGE, Old Monastery Restaurant ❀❀

Buckie AB56 5JB
Map 15: NJ46
Tel/Fax: 01542 832660
Chefs: Sarah McIntosh, Keith Mitchell
Owners: Calum & Valerie Buchanan
Cost: Alc £30, set-price L £12.95 (2 courses). H/wine £12
Times: Noon-1.40pm/6.45-9pm. Closed Sun, Mon, 2 wks Nov, 3 wks Jan
Additional: Children 8+; ❹ dishes
Seats: 42
Smoking: No smoking in dining room

Directions: Leave A98 at Buckie junction on to Drybridge Road for 2.5 miles; don't turn into Drybridge village

Charming converted Benedictine monastery. Booking is advisable for lunch – and essential for dinner, such is the reputation of this splendid restaurant. Although under new ownership, the cooking remains reliable and thoughtfully composed, defined by quality ingredients, such as the best Scottish beef used for the base stock of a traditional French onion soup. Neat, imaginative touches lift to the familiar – parsnip and potato rösti, for example, with prime fillet and chasseur sauce, or gooseberry and mint jelly with venison and pheasant terrine. Tender chicken livers were given contrast by a crunchy croûton and sliced balsamic roast tomatoes. There is some awareness of contemporary trends – a skewer of king prawns and bacon-wrapped scallops with flavoursome tomato risotto and a lime dressing – but the kitchen demonstrates sensible discretion. Marbled raspberry and Amaretto cheesecake drizzled with raspberry coulis, and warm apple toffee crumble topped with apple and Calvados sorbet with cinnamon sauce are guaranteed a popular following.

ELGIN,
Mansion House Hotel ❀

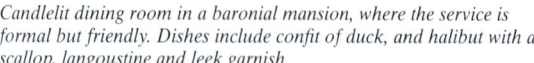

Candlelit dining room in a baronial mansion, where the service is formal but friendly. Dishes include confit of duck, and halibut with a scallop, langoustine and leek garnish.

Smoking: No smoking in dining room
Accommodation: 23 en suite ★ ★ ★

Directions: In Elgin turn off the A96 into Haugh Road; hotel is at the end of the road by the river

The Haugh IV30 1AW
Map 15: NJ26
Tel: 01343 548811
Fax: 01343 547916
Cost: Alc £25, set-price L £15.50/D £27 (4 courses). ☺ H/wine £11
Times: Noon-2pm/7- 9pm
Additional: Sunday L; Children welcome; ❹ dishes

FORRES,
Knockomie Hotel ❀❀

Grantown Road IV36 2SG
Map 14: NJ05
Tel: 01309 673146
Fax: 01309 673290
Chef: Thierry Fournot
Owner: Gavin Ellis
Cost: *Alc* £26, set-price D £28 (4 courses). ☺ H/wine £11.95
Times: D only, 7-9pm. Closed 25, 26 Dec
Additional: Bar food (bistro); Children welcome; ⏺ dishes
Seats: 30. Private dining room 10-30
Smoking: No smoking in dining room
Accommodation: 15 en suite ★ ★ ★

Directions: On A940 1 mile S of Forres

Charming country house that stands in four acres of grounds to the south of the town. The restaurant has an Arabic theme, complemented by a collection of paintings by David Shepherd. There is a bistro, a restaurant and, new this year, a cheerily bright Party Room for additional informal dining. The food owes most to the French repertoire and is generally pretty good. Hospitality is superb. The *carte* includes French onion soup, terrine of duck, followed perhaps by chicken supreme, or lamb fillet on a duxelles of mushrooms, and there's a selection of Scottish cuts of steak. The four-course set-menu offers a choice for the starters, main and desserts. Items tasted included a crayfish terrine followed by confit of duck and braised red cabbage – both 'good value and tasty'.

ORKNEY

ST MARGARET'S HOPE,
Creel Restaurant ❀❀

Simple restaurant, bang on the seafront of a quiet, timeless village. There's a rustic feel to the dining room with its Windsor chairs and original artwork (mostly by local artists and not for sale). The kitchen uses the best local produce and turns out dishes notable for their flavours – even plainly boiled new potatoes with melted butter have been described as 'none better'. Cockles and mussels might go into a soup, salted cod into fishcakes, and queen scallops are baked in the shell with garlic butter. Orcadian fish stew is the house speciality, with pot-roast North Ronaldsay lamb (actually mutton, whose diet of seaweed gives the meat a unique flavour) with baby haggis, pearl barley and caper sauce among the meat options. Lemon tart with strongly-flavoured orange sorbet makes a refreshing finale. The wine list is sensibly short, with house wines sold by the glass.

Front Road KW17 2SL
Map 16: ND49
Tel: 01856 831311
Chef: Alan Craigie
Owners: Alan and Joyce Craigie
Cost: *Alc* £26.50. H/wine £9.60
Times: D only, 7-9.30pm. Closed Jan-Feb, 2 wks Oct
Additional: Children welcome
Seats: 36
Smoking: No smoking in dining room
Accommodation: 3 en suite

Directions: 13 miles S of Kirkwall on the A961, crossing the 4 Churchill barriers

PERTH & KINROSS

ABERFELDY,

Guinach House Hotel ❀❀

'By the Birks' Urlar Road
PH15 2ET
Map 14: NN84
Tel: 01887 820251
Fax: 01887 829607
Chef/Owner: Albert Mackay
Cost: Set-price D £25 (4 courses).
H/wine £9.95
Times: D only, 7-9.30pm. Closed 4
days Xmas
Additional: Children welcome
Seats: 20
Smoking: No smoking in dining room
Accommodation: 7 en suite ★ ★

Directions: From Aberfeldy: A826
(Crieff) hotel is on R

Popular country hotel with a warm, pleasant welcome. The
elegant style of cooking at this delightful small hotel near the
famous Birks of Aberfeldy depends on high quality raw
ingredients – many vegetables come from their own garden. The
menu changes daily and choice is never easy. Our inspector
finally made up his mind and started with a light crab mousse,
encased in smoked salmon, 'bound' by thin strips of leek and
dressed with a tomato vinaigrette, before proceeding onto a good
cream of asparagus soup, and rosette of beef, pink, moist and
tender, capped with chicken mousseline and served with a real
ale sauce. Good crunchy vegetables are served separately. To
finish, there was a superb raspberry mousse with a hint of Glayva
and a matching coulis. The large volume of repeat trade the hotel
attracts is largely down to the food – so non-resident diners are
well advised to book in advance to avoid disappointment.

AUCHTERARDER,

Auchterarder House ❀❀

PH3 1DZ
Map 11: NN91
Tel: 01764 663646
Fax: 01764 662939
Chef: Willie Deans
Owner: The Wrens Hotel Group
Cost: Set-price L £16.50/D £39.50 (5
courses). H/wine £16.50
Times: 12.30-1.30pm/7-9pm
Additional: Sunday L; Children 12+;
❀ dishes
Seats: 36. Private dining room 24.
Jacket & tie preferred
Smoking: No smoking in dining room
Accommodation: 15 en suite ★ ★ ★

Directions: 1.5 miles N of
Auchterarder on B8062

*Handsome Victorian mansion set amidst 17 acres of wooded
and landscaped grounds.* The drawing room is a beautiful
room, part panelled, with an ornate ceiling, two bay windows

with some stained glass. In the dining room a set-menu has replaced the previous menus, offering a better, more interesting choice of dishes built around some good local and regional produce. We were impressed with our first course of foie gras terrine – pink and very smooth in texture, it was served with thin crisp pain de musila, a truffle essence, and a crisp salad garnish. Then came Shetland salmon, served on a bed of fine noodles with a shellfish and lobster bisque. Dessert, a malt whisky liquor parfait was well-flavoured. The wine list has been reduced, but is still interesting and comprehensive.

AUCHTERARDER, Cairn Lodge

Attractive turreted house on the edge of the village. The elegant Capercaillie Restaurant offers tartan drapes and a dark green ceiling with a few pictures and figures of various game birds to give you the total Scottish experience. Sound cooking with a menu based on quality ingredients can range from a steak section (from the finest herds) to sound Med-inspired dishes such as tomato and aubergine cake with yellow pepper coulis. A popular choice is the beef fries – chipped potatoes poached in beef stock and then fried like chips. Otherwise begin with fish soup or game terrine, then oven-baked sea bass with saffron sauce or lamb with port sauce, dauphinoise potatoes and spinach, and finish with an excellent steamed chocolate sponge pudding with chocolate orange sauce. Staff are genuinely down-to-earth and friendly. Wines by the glass are in big quantities.

Orchil Road PH3 1LX
Map 11: NN91
Tel: 01764 662634
Fax: 01764 664866
Cost: *Alc* £25. ☺ H/wine £12.50
Times: Noon-2pm/6.30-10pm
Additional: Bar food L; Sunday L; Children welcome; ✿ dishes
Smoking: No smoking in dining room
Accommodation: 7 en suite ★ ★

Directions: From A9 take A824 (Auchterader). Hotel at S end of town, on road to Gleneagles

AUCHTERARDER,
The Gleneagles Hotel

Renowned world-wide, Gleneagles is a top class international resort hotel. Set in beautiful countryside, and surrounded by its famous golf courses and extensive grounds, this is the business. The drawing room serves its famous afternoon teas – the smart cocktail bar is the centrepiece – but the elegant Strathearn Restaurant is the place for dinner. The service is skilled and friendly but some may find the atmosphere austere. The menus are grand, in the classic style, offering such signature dishes as west coast langoustine bisque with crab and lemon soufflé. Our meal consisted of pressed maize-fed chicken with red peppers, basil and goats' cheese, roast salmon stuffed with mushrooms, pine nuts and braised lettuce, and a parfait of praline, apricot and nougat with poached strawberries. There are various other menus, including several for children of all ages and an extensive and international wine list.

PH3 1NF
Map 11: NN91
Tel: 01764 662231
Fax: 01764 662134
Chef: Mike Picken
Cost: *Alc* £49, set-price L £27.50/D £41. H/wine £17.50
Times: D only, 7-10pm
Additional: Sunday L (12.30-2pm); Children welcome; ✿ dishes
Seats: 175. Private dining rooms
Smoking: No-smoking area; No pipes; Air conditioning
Accommodation: 219 en suite ★ ★ ★ ★ ★

Directions: Just off A9, well signposted

BLAIR ATHOLL,
The Loft Restaurant

Housed in a converted hay loft behind the Tilt Hotel. This is a sophisticated small country restaurant, characterised by twisted beams, stone walls, oak floors, plenty of fresh flowers and a warm provençale decor. Recent additions include an airy conservatory that has direct access to a splendid roof terrace (and is where lighter meals are served) . Style of cooking throughout is modern with a slight French influence, with the restaurant's dinner menu being more adventurous than the

River Tilt Park PH18 5TE
Map 14: NN86
Tel: 01738 481377
Fax: 01738 481511
Chef: Kevin Graham
Owner: Mrs P M Richardson
Times: Noon-2.30pm/6.30-9pm (10am till late from 1 Apr). Closed Jan, Tue-Wed in winter

fairly simplistic lunch which offers options of either two or three courses. Our inspection dinner featured quality home-baked brown bread, honest-flavoured crispy duck with good salad garnish and a delicious orange sauce, accurately cooked escalope of salmon, and a warm treacle tart with vanilla sauce.

Directions: Off A9, N of Pitlochry. In village L at Tilt Hotel

Additional: Bar food; Sunday L; Children welcome; ✿ dishes
Seats: 34. Private dining room 24
Smoking: No smoking in dining room; Air conditioning

BLAIRGOWRIE, Altamount Hotel

Georgian mansion with fine panelling, wooden flooring and Adam fireplaces. A choice of menus offers a tempting range of Scottish specialities featuring game, prime beef and seafood.

Accommodation: 7 en suite ★ ★

Directions: On entering town from A93 take 1st R into Golf Course Rd. Continue for 1.5 miles then L at T junction. Hotel 1 mile on L

Coupar Angus Road PH10 6JN
Map 15: NO14
Tel: 01250 873512
Fax: 01250 876200
Cost: Set-price D £22.50. ☺ H/wine £10.50
Times: Noon-2pm/7-9pm. Closed 1st 2 wks Jan
Additional: Bar ffood; Sunday L; Children welcome; ✿ dishes
Smoking: No smoking in dining room

BLAIRGOWRIE,
Kinloch House Hotel ✿✿✿

PH10 6SG
Map 15: NO14
Tel: 01250 884237
Fax: 01250 884333
Chef: Bill McNicoll
Owners: David & Sarah Shentall
Cost: Set-price L £16.95/D £32 (4 courses). H/wine £15.70
Times: 12.30-2pm/7-9.15pm. Closed 18-30 Dec
Additional: Bar food L; Sunday L; Children 7+; ✿ dishes

Built in 1840, extended in 1911 and run by Mr and Mrs Shentall since 1981. Kinloch House is set in 25 acres of parkland and woods with views to the south over Loch Maree and the Sidlaw Hills beyond. It's an industrious place: all fruit and vegetables are organically grown in the grounds, the kitchen does its own smoking, and sausages, preserves and breads are made in-house.The set-price menus offer decent choice, with a page listing substitutes at an extra charge. Steaks (all from Aberdeen Angus cattle) and lobster are house specialities – the latter might be turned into a mousseline and served with finely chopped leeks and bacon with caviar butter sauce. Loin of venison makes a successful main course, perhaps wrapped in Parma ham then pheasant mousseline, its garnish of parsnips topped with crunchy herb crust acting as a good foil for the tender meat and its port and rosemary jus. The kitchen shows the same ease in handling fish, supreme of halibut, say, with grilled scallops and crisp fried Parma ham with herby butter sauce, or pan-fried cod with ratatouille. We ended our meal with a 'super' dessert of poached pear with rice pudding and Marsala ice cream but could have gone for a savoury instead – maybe creamed smoked haddock with

Shortlisted for AA Wine Award-see page 16

scrambled eggs – and a glass of vintage port. It's best to allow plenty of time to go through the superb wine list.

Signature dishes: Locally caught pike with ratatouille and herb breadcrumb crust with tomato and garlic sauce; partridge and cabbage salad with foie gras; chocolate and crème de menthe soufflé.

Seats: 50. Private dining room 20.
Jacket & tie preferred
Smoking: No smoking in dining room
Accommodation: 21 en suite ★★★

Directions: Three miles W of Blairgowrie on A923

COUPAR ANGUS,

Moorfield House Hotel

Small country hotel in lovely landscaped grounds. Stained glass, panelling and open fires are the sorts of features one would expect to find in a house like this, and the public rooms don't disappoint for their comforts and elegance. You can eat in the bar, a popular venue, or in the restaurant, where dinner is a set affair with a handful of choices at each course (second course is always a sorbet or soup). Pan-fried sirloin steak is a favourite, perhaps with caramelised onions and roasted vegetables, or there might be medallions of salmon and monkfish on chive mash. Desserts of, say, steamed butterscotch pudding, or Pavlova of kiwi fruit, orange and strawberry are followed by cheese and then coffee with petits fours. House wines are from Chile and South Africa.

Directions: On the A923 halfway between Coupar Angus and Blairgowrie

Myreriggs Road By Blairgowrie
PH13 9HS
Map 11: NO23
Tel: 01828 627303
Fax: 01828 627339
Chef: Angela Tannahill
Owners: Jayne & Paul Bjormark
Cost: Set-price D £27.50 (4 courses).
☺ H/wine £9.95
Times: Noon-2.15pm/7-9pm.
Closed L Sat, Xmas, New Year
Additional: Bar food; Sunday L;
Children welcome; ✪ dishes
Seats: 30
Smoking: No smoking in dining room
Accommodation: 12 en suite ★★★

DUNKELD, **Atholl Arms**

Popular Tayside hotel in the centre of the village with a traditional-style restaurant. The menu offers a variety of dishes, with local produce used wherever possible.

Accommodation: 14 en suite ★★

Directions: A9 & A923 (Blairgowrie) to Dunkeld, 1st building on R

Bridgehead PH8 0AQ
Map 11: NO04
Tel/Fax: 01350 727219
Cost: *Alc* £16.50. ☺ H/wine £9
Times: Noon-1.45pm/6-8.45pm
Additional: Bar Food; Sunday L;
Children 8+ after 6pm; ✪ dishes
Smoking: No smoking in dining room

DUNKELD, **Kinnaird**

Kinnaird Estate PH8 0LB
Map 11: NO04
Tel: 01796 482440
Fax: 01796 482289
Chef: Trevor Brooks
Owner: Mrs Constance Ward
Cost: Set-price L £24/D £39.50.
H/wine £18
Times: 12.30-1.45pm/7-9.30pm.
Closed Mon-Wed in Jan & Feb
Additional: Sunday L; Children 12+
Seats: 45. Private dining room 20.
Jacket & tie preferred
Smoking: No smoking in dining room
Accommodation: 9 en suite ★★★

Kinnaird, high in the wooded Tay Valley, is, put simply, a mansion. Built in Edwardian times (although parts date from the 1770s) and now furnished almost entirely with fine antique furniture, paintings and china, Kinnaird manages to feel lived-in and comfortable, with deep sofas and armchairs, open fires and family mementoes, including cases of salmon caught on the Kinnaird beat. Hand-painted Italian frescoes, an elaborately corniced ceiling, drapes on windows that give glimpses of the gardens and valley create a soothing setting for menus that feature the best Scottish produce. Isle of Skye scallops (wrapped in home-smoked salmon), wood pigeon (in an open raviolo with mushrooms and baby leeks) might be just some of the starters, and Aberdeen Angus fillet (in a spicy red wine sauce with spinach and rösti), saddle of venison (in a Burgundy sauce), might appear among main courses. Rack of Perthshire lamb ('nothing short of excellent'), served simply in its own juices, with pancetta, roasted cauliflower and straw potatoes, might be preceded by a ballotine of small chunks of guinea fowl and contrastingly smooth foie gras. Puddings can vary from the wicked rich dark chocolate mousse topped with pistachio ice cream to the more fruity, as in lemon tart with poached rhubarb. Winner of the AA Wine Award for Scotland last year, some of the bottles on the wine list run into three figures, while a page of house suggestions has its feet firmly on the ground.

Kinnaird

Directions: From A9 north take B898 Dalguise/Kinnaird/Balnaguard road for approx 4.5 miles. Hotel gates on R

KILLIECRANKIE,

Killiecrankie Hotel

An inviting hotel with an elegant, tastefully appointed restaurant. The short menu changes daily, and the kitchen uses good local produce. You can't get much more Scottish than a terrine of Arbroath smokie and smoked salmon with oatcakes, or casserole of venison, hare and rabbit with onion skirlie and herb mash. Another terrine – perhaps salmon, sweet potato and rocket with herb mayonnaise may turn up another day, followed by medallions of local beef in a rich red wine sauce with rösti and caramelised shallots. Steamed fillet of halibut with a mussel sauce has appeared among fish dishes. You might have to decide between baked peaches in pistachio caramel sauce and lemon tart before going on to a plate of Scottish and Irish cheeses. The carefully chosen wine list has something for all tastes and pockets. Historical note: Killiecrankie, midway between Pitlochry and Blair Atholl, was the site of the 1689 battle when the Jacobites vanquished the English.

Directions: From A9 take B8079 for Killiecrankie, hotel on R just past village signpost

Pitlochry PH16 5LG
Map 14: NN96
Tel: 01796 473220
Fax: 01796 472451
Chef: Mark Easton
Owners: Colin & Carole Anderson
Cost: Set-price D £31 (4 courses).
H/wine £10.60
Times: D only, 7-8.30pm.
Closed 10 days pre-Xmas, Jan-Feb
Additional: Children 5+
Seats: 34
Smoking: No smoking in dining room
Accommodation: ★ ★

KINCLAVEN,

Ballathie House Hotel ❀❀

Set on a 1,500 acre estate, and enjoying a wonderfully peaceful setting by the banks of the River Tay, Ballathie is an impressive Scottish mansion. The hotel has its own fishing rights and attracts many sporting enthusiasts. The restaurant has a tried-and-tested formula which works well. The kitchen relies on local produce and are industrious in their handling of it: curing their own smoked salmon, for example. Shetland salmon is chargrilled with fennel, chive hollandaise and lemon, and lightly seared Skye scallops are set on a decent risotto with a hint of lemon and adorned with shavings of Parmesan and a

Stanley PH1 4QN
Map 11: NO13
Tel: 01250 883268
Fax: 01250 883396
Chef: Kevin MacGillivray
Owner: Ballathie House Hotel Co Ltd
Cost: Set-price L £17.50/D £33 (4 courses). H/wine £10.50
Times: Noon-2pm/7-9pm
Additional: Bar food L; Sunday L; Children welcome

Ballathie House Hotel

Seats: 60. Private dining room 32.
Jacket and tie preferred
Smoking: No smoking in dining room
Accommodation: 27 en suite ★ ★ ★

light basil and pesto sauce. Desserts include a wonderful
strawberry brûlée 'a good crisp top and nicely flavoured filling
laced with chunks of strawberries' – accompanied by light
home-made shortbread rounds. Good bread rolls are baked on
the premises

Directions: Off A93 at Beech Hedges, follow signs for
Kinclaven, approx 2 miles

KINNESSWOOD,

Lomond Country Inn

*Grilled noisettes of lamb with red wine sauce, filo pastry parcel of
Tay salmon with white wine and dill, and apple and bramble pie
typify the wholesome, uncomplicated Scottish cooking on offer at
this welcoming country inn.*

Additional: Bar food; Sunday L; Children welcome; ⏺ dishes
Accommodation: 12 en suite ★ ★

Directions: On A911, 10 mins from M90 J5 (Glenrothes) or J7
(Milnathort)

KY13 7HN
Map 11: NO10
Tel: 01592 840253
Fax: 01592 840693
Cost: *Alc* £18.50, set-price L/D £10.
☺ H/wine £8.50
Times: Noon-2pm/6-9pm

KINROSS,

Croft Bank

*Exciting things have been happening at this restaurant-with-
rooms since our last visit.* The elegant, formal, dinner-only
dining area remains (as does chef-patron Bill Kerr's assured
hand in the kitchen) but eating choices have been extended
with the opening of the less formal Backroom Brasserie. Set in
a large timber-clad room to the rear of the house (hence the
name), offerings such as moules marinière, cheese-glazed
mushrooms in garlic, cream and white wine sauce, a traditional
beef and mushroom pie, and filo-wrapped salmon and spinach
with lemon and chive butter sauce have quickly gained a
strong local following. In the more formal restaurant dishes
might include Shetland salmon with lemon chive butter sauce,
breast of Barbary duck with Puy lentils and a port bramble jus,
and Scotch ribeye steak with pink and green peppercorn
sauce.

Directions: Just off M90 J6 towards Kinross

KY13 8TG
Map 11: NO10
Tel/Fax: 01577 863819
Chef: Bill Kerr
Owners: Bill & Diane Kerr
Cost: *Alc* £23, set-price L £13.95. ☺
H/wine £9.95
Times: Noon-1.45pm/6.30-9pm.
Closed D Sun, all Mon,
2 wks Sep, 1 wk Mar
Additional: Bar food L (brasserie);
Sunday L; Children 5+; ⏺ dishes
Seats: 48. Private dining room 16
Smoking: No smoking in dining room
Accommodation: 3 en suite

PERTH, **Huntingtower Hotel**

Delightful Edwardian house set in landscaped grounds just west of Perth. Traditional Scottish dishes are served in the Oak Restaurant – look out for top dishes such as pan-seared red snapper on roasted fennel, and charred haunch of venison with juniper jus.

Crieff Road Almondbank PH1 3JT
Map 11: NO12
Tel: 01738 583771
Fax: 01738 583777
Cost: *Alc* £18.95, set-price L £11.95/D £19.95 (4 courses). ☺
H/wine £9.95
Times: Noon-2.30pm/7-9.30pm
Additional: Bar food; Sunday L; Children welcome; ✿ dishes
Smoking: No pipes & cigars
Accommodation: 35 en suite ★ ★ ★

Directions: 5 mins from Perth, on A85 Crieff/Crianlarich Road. Just off A9

PERTH, **Kerachers Restaurant & Oyster Bar** NEW

Smart, minimalist-looking restaurant. The look is as fresh and uncomplicated as the fine choice of seafood, all freshly prepared and cooked to order. The family origins of the place are evident in the retail fish counter alongside the oyster bar. Upstairs in the dining-room, the cooking takes in both classic and modern techniques: lobster bisque and mussels poached with shallots, garlic, white wine and cream; red snapper, pan-fried and served with a garlic and coriander cream sauce; and fillet of North sea cod is given a makeover with toasted sesame oil, shiitake mushrooms and game jus. There's token fillet of Aberdeen Angus beef if you must, but why choose that when there's just-caught whole trimmed lemon sole served on the bone with lemon juice and butter sauce to be had?

Directions: Telephone for directions

168 South Street PH2 8NY
Map 11: NO12
Tel: 01738 449777
Chef: Andrew Thomson Keracher
Owners: Andrew, Peter, James Keracher
Cost: *Alc* £16.50, set-price D £7.90 (2 courses). ☺ H/wine £10.90
Times: Noon-2pm/6-10pm.
Closed Sun, 1st 2 wks Jan
Additional: Children welcome; ✿ dishes
Seats: 60. Private dining room 24
Smoking: No-smoking area

PERTH, **Kinfauns Castle**

Grand castle with grand service. It's a splendid experience to dine in the stately oak-panelled dining-room of a grand castle. The menu is short but precise, the choice limited but tempting. A sample dinner menu might run thus: Kinfauns terrine with home-made chutney or monkfish wrapped in Parma ham with saffron risotto and herb oil, followed by a soup, perhaps leek and pumpkin. Main courses could bring a choice of roast rump of black-faced lamb with provençal vegetables and tomato and basil jus, or crisp fillet of halibut with buttered noodles, stir-fried vegetables, chilli and soy dressing. A selection of cheese precedes dessert of, say, a warm soft chocolate cake with coffee anglaise. Round things off in style with coffee or tea and castle-made truffles and tablet.

Directions: Two miles beyond Perth on A90 Dundee road; turn L at sign for Kinfauns Castle

Kinfauns PH2 7JZ
Map 11: NO12
Tel: 01738 620777
Fax: 01738 620778
Chef: Jeremy Wares
Owners: Mr & Mrs James A Smith
Cost: Set price L £18.50/D £32. H/wine £13.95
Times: Noon-1.30pm/7-8.30pm.
Closed 3 wks Jan
Additional: Sunday L; Children 10+; ✿ dishes
Seats: 50. Private dining room 12; Jacket & tie preferred
Smoking: No smoking in dining room
Accommodation: 16 en suite ★ ★ ★

PERTH, Let's Eat ❀❀

Restaurant housed in what was once a theatre, then an antique shop, with a relaxed, friendly feel. Honest cooking with lots of good flavours and innovative twists continues to be the hallmark of the bistro-style menus. Our inspection meal opened with a creamy wild mushroom risotto flavoured with aromatic truffle oil and freshly sliced Parmesan, but it was the seared fillet of halibut that was a 'winner'. Served on a stir-fry of squat lobsters and local sea kale, it was 'delicate' and had a real, fresh taste of the sea. Meat eaters are catered for with the likes of chargrilled Scotch ribeye steak with sautéed mushrooms. Desserts include a light bread-and-butter pudding with a rich, smooth caramel sauce and plenty of sultanas. The short wine list is entirely in keeping with the style. Another branch, Let's Eat Again has opened in Perth at 33 George Street, PH1 5LA, tel: 01738 633771, a more informal, slightly cheaper bistro with vibrant decor. The menu changes slightly, with home-made sausages and fishcakes at lunchtime being replaced by braised lamb shank at dinner.

77/79 Kinnoull Street PH1 5EZ
Map 11: NO12
Tel: 01738 643377
Fax: 01738 621464
Chef: Tony Heath
Owners: Tony Heath, Shona Drysdale
Cost: *Alc* £18.95. ☺ H/wine £10.50
Times: Noon-2pm/6.30-9.45pm.
Closed Sun, Mon, 2 wks Jan,
2 wks Jul
Additional: Children welcome;
🍴 dishes
Seats: 65
Smoking: No smoking in dining room

Directions: On corner of Kinnoull Street and Atholl Street, close to North Inch

PERTH, Murrayshall Hotel ❀❀

New Scone PH2 7PH
Map 11: NO12
Tel: 01738 551171
Fax: 01738 552595
Chef: Clive Lamb
Cost: *Alc* £23.50, set-price D £21. ☺
H/wine £12.50
Times: D only, 7-9.45pm.
Closed 26 Dec
Additional: Sunday L (12.30-1.45pm);
Children 2+; 🍴 dishes
Seats: 45. Private dining room 25.
Jacket & tie preferred
Smoking: No smoking in dining room;
Air conditioning
Accommodation: 28 en suite ★★★

Guests return time and again to enjoy the relaxing setting – and the eighteen-hole golf course. Set amidst three hundred acres of beautiful parkland, this popular mansion house hotel boasts magnificent views of the Grampian Highlands. The best of Scotland's larder is used in innovative Scottish dishes with a Euro-twist: pan-fried fillet of beef with wild mushrooms and pancetta, or roast saddle of venison with garlic and parsley mash. We visited in October and enjoyed pressed lobster and langoustine terrine with avocado and rocket salad, delicious seared scallops served with tomato and avocado salsa and topped with deep-fried aubergine shavings. Dessert was a wonderful warm blackcurrant soufflé with star anise.

Directions: From Perth A94 R signed Murrayshall

PITLOCHRY, Green Park Hotel ❀

The hotel dining room looks out across gardens to Loch Faskally. A short, daily-changing menu provides traditional dishes such as roast lamb with rosemary mousse and roast garlic jus, or pan-fried chicken with black pudding, glazed poached pear and mustard cream.

Clunie Bridge Road PH16 5JY
Map 14: NN95
Tel: 01796 473248
Fax: 01796 473520
Telephone for further details

Directions: Off A9 at Pitlochry, follow signs

PITLOCHRY,

Knockendarroch House Hotel

Enjoy extensive views of the Tummel Valley at this Victorian
mansion which sits high above Pitlochry. Modern British cooking is
offered on the daily-changing set-price menu.

Smoking: No-smoking area; No pipes & cigars
Accommodation: 12 en suite ★★

Directions: On entering town from Perth 1st R (East Moulin
Road) after railway bridge, then 2nd L, last hotel on L

Higher Oakfield PH16 5HT
Map 14: NN95
Tel: 01796 473473
Fax: 01796 474068
Cost: Set-price D £21 (5 courses). ☺
H/wine £8.90
Times: D only
Additional: Children 10+; 🍴 dishes

PITLOCHRY, # Pine Trees Hotel

Lovely old mansion house, where the Garden Restaurant provides a
tempting range of Scottish dishes, including supreme of Orkney
salmon and loin of Perthshire venison.

Smoking: No smoking in dining room
Accommodation: 19 en suite ★★★

Directions: Signed at N end of town

Strathview Terrace PH16 5QR
Map 14: NN95
Tel: 01796 472121
Fax: 01796 472460
Cost: Alc £27, set-price L £9.75 (2
courses)/D £20 (4 courses). ☺
H/wine £12.75
Times: Noon-2pm/7-9pm
Additional: Bar food; Sunday L;
Children welcome; 🍴 dishes

SPITTAL OF GLENSHEE,

Dalmunzie House

Turreted baronial house surrounded by a 6,500 acre mountain estate.
Traditional Scottish meals are served in the Highland dining room:
try broccoli soup followed by fillet of grey mullet with mange-tout.

Smoking: No smoking in dining room
Accommodation: 17 en suite ★★

Directions: Turn off A93 at Spittal of Glenshee, hotel 200yds
on L

Blairgowrie PH10 7QG
Map 15: NO17
Tel: 01250 885224
Fax: 01250 885225
Cost: Alc £15, set-price D £24. ☺
H/wine £10
Times: 12.30-5pm/7.30-8.30pm.
Closed 1-27 Dec
Additional: Bar food L;
Children welcome; 🍴 dishes

ST FILLANS,

The Four Seasons Hotel

**On the shore of Loch Earn, The Four Season Hotel affords
wonderful views throughout the year.** The restaurant (now
called Meall Reamhar) takes advantage of the picturesque
setting with most of its crisp linen-covered tables overlooking
the Loch. Under the new ownership of Andrew Low, the
restaurant relies on local produce, and aspires to a
contemporary Scottish style of cooking. However, with its
liberal use of mousseline sauces, tarragon, Calvados and jus,
the results seem more French. A starter of ducks' liver parfait
with Cognac was refreshingly uncomplicated, allowing the
natural flavours to come through well. Likewise the loin of
Perthshire lamb. The restaurant offers both a *carte* and daily
set-price four-course menu. The wine list is predominantly
French, but includes some well-known New World wines.

Directions: From Perth take A85 W, through Crieff & Comrie.
Hotel at west end of village

Loch Earn Crieff PH6 2NF
Map 11: NN62
Tel: 01764 685333
Fax: 01764 685444
Chef: Brian Murphy
Owner: Andrew Low
Cost: Alc £25.50, set-price D £23.95
(4 courses). ☺ H/wine £11
Times: 12.30-2.30pm/6-9.30pm
Additional: Bar food; Sunday L;
Children welcome
Seats: 40. Private dining room 20
Smoking: No smoking in dining room
Accommodation: 12 en suite ★★★

RENFREWSHIRE

LANGBANK,

Gleddoch House Hotel

An impressive mansion in its own estate. An equestrian centre, clay-pigeon shooting, and an 18-hole golf course, with a professional in residence, are just some of the amenities, with panoramic views over the Clyde to the hills of Loch Lomond to boot. If a pre-dinner stroll sounds seductive, there are formal gardens to explore, with a club-style bar to tempt afterwards. Dinner could start with smoothly textured parfait of duck, chicken livers and foie gras with Cumberland sauce, or goats' cheese with caramelised apples in filo, go on to lightly seared scallops on caramelised leeks, and then main courses of perhaps grilled halibut on creamed spinach, or Scottish beef tournedos glazed with herb hollandaise served with wild mushroom duxelle and a Madeira-flavoured Arran mustard sauce. Raspberry crème brûlée, lemon tart with Cointreau syrup, or light banana cheesecake make fruity conclusions.

Directions: From Glasgow take M8 (Greenock) then B789 Houston/ Langbank exit. Follow signs to hotel

PA14 6YE
Map 10: NS37
Tel: 01475 540711
Fax: 01475 540201
Chef: Brian Graham
Cost: *Alc* £38, set-price L £19.50/D £33.95 (4 courses). H/wine £12.50
Times: 12.30-2pm/7.30-9pm
Additional: Sunday L; ⬤ dishes
Seats: 70. Private room 28. Jacket & tie preferred
Smoking: Air conditioning
Accommodation: 38 en suite ★ ★ ★ ★

SCOTTISH BORDERS

JEDBURGH,

Jedforest Hotel NEW

Sturdy country house off the beaten track seven miles north of the Border, which claims to be the first hotel in Scotland. Appetites can be worked up in the surrounding thirty-five acres of grounds or with the private fishing on Jed Water. All guests can look forward to modern ideas from the kitchen. Our early spring dinner opened with a tart of Mediterranean vegetables (a mixture of courgettes, aubergines and tomatoes, topped with a 'dariole' of cheddar), followed by roast monkfish sliced onto little mounds of fried leek, served with carrot butter sauce. For dessert, a dense, sticky caramel mousse came with grapefruit segments and a good cardamom sauce.

Camptown TD8 6PJ
Map 12: NT62
Tel: 01835 840222
Fax: 01835 840226
Chef: Patrick Bardoulet
Owner: George W Cochrane
Cost: *Alc* £24, set-price L £12.50/D £19.50. ☺ H/wine £9.95
Times: 12.15-2pm/7.15-9pm
Additional: Sunday L; Children 9+ (no children at D); ⬤ dishes
Seats: 42. Jacket & tie preferred for D
Smoking: No smoking in dining room; Air conditioning
Accommodation: 8 en suite ★ ★ ★

Directions: Just off A68, 3 miles south of Jedburgh

KELSO, The Roxburghe Hotel

Heiton TD5 8JZ
Map 12: NT73
Tel: 01573 450331
Fax: 01573 450611
Chef: Keith Short
Owners: The Duke & Duchess of Roxburghe
Cost: *Alc* £34.50, set-price L £11.50/D £28.50. H/wine £14
Times: 12.30-2pm/7.30-9.30pm. Closed 23-29 Dec
Additional: Bar food L; Sunday L; 🌣 dishes
Seats: 35. Private dining room 16
Smoking: No smoking in dining room
Accommodation: 22 en suite ★ ★ ★

An imposing Jacobean-style mansion (built in 1853 and formerly known as Sunlaws House Hotel) popular with shooting parties, fishermen and golfers. The hotel is owned by the Duke of Roxburghe, and in season the Roxburghe estate provides much of the game and Tweed salmon served in the splendid, classically-styled dining room. However, the cooking is resolutely modern, and the kitchen puts a lot of emphasis on flavour. Our March meal took in baked goats' cheese with rocket, pasta ribbons and chilli oil, and a tender grilled chump of lamb, cooked pink, and sliced onto fresh spinach and mash with a 'rich and intense' garlic and sage sauce. A traditional sticky toffee pudding, moated with butterscotch sauce, rounded the meal off nicely.

Directions: On A698, 3 miles S of Kelso in Heiton village

MELROSE, Burts Hotel

The Square TD6 9PN
Map 12: NT53
Tel: 01896 822285
Fax: 01896 822870
Chef: Gary Moore
Owner: Graham D Henderson
Cost: *Alc* £32, set-price D £19.50/D £26.50. H/wine £11.90
Times: 12.30-1.45pm/7-9.15pm. Closed 26 Dec
Additional: Sunday L; Children 10+; 🌣 dishes
Seats: 46. Private dining room 24

Popular family-run former coaching inn with something for everyone. Built in 1722 for a local dignitary, Burts is in the picturesque market square of this historical town. The bar, with its open fire, is a popular meeting place and food is available both at lunchtime and in the evening. The elegant and well-appointed restaurant – green striped decor, crisp linen and candles on the tables – has a country sports theme, with rods and prints of salmon fishing and game shooting. Game could turn up on the menu in the form of potted venison and pigeon, or an interesting and successful combination of superbly flavoured

pheasant terrine with diced banana and pear. Border lamb could make a showing too, perhaps cannon sliced on black pudding with roast tomatoes and balls of beetroot with Drambuie sauce, or chops with traditional mint sauce and redcurrant jelly. Selkirk Bannock – like a fruity dumpling, served with cinnamon custard and caramel ice cream, and topped with a spun sugar basket – is a 'rather wicked' way to end things. As well as the wine list, there's a wide choice of malt whiskies.

Smoking: No smoking in dining room
Accommodation: 20 en suite ★ ★ ★

Directions: Centre of Melrose

PEEBLES, Cringletie House

EH45 8PL
Map 11: NT24
Tel: 01721 730233
Fax: 01721 730244
Cost: Set-price L £14.95/D £32.50 (4 courses). H/wine £12
Times: 12.30-2pm/7-9pm.
Additional: Sunday L; Children welcome; ✿ dishes
Smoking: No smoking in dining room. Jacket & tie preferred
Accommodation: 13 en suite ★ ★ ★

Directions: 2.5 miles N of Peebles on A703

Turreted baronial mansion set in 28 acres of wooded grounds. A set-price four-course dinner might include local game terrine, and fillet of beef with wild mushroom crumble.

SWINTON, Wheatsheaf Restaurant with Rooms

Small hotel overlooking the village green. The daily-changing carte and blackboard menus offer a good range of Scottish dishes. Try fillet of salmon with lemon butter sauce, or ostrich, pigeon and venison casserole.

Accommodation: 5 rooms

Directions: B6461 – half-way between Kelso and Berwick-upon-Tweed; A6112 – half-way between Duns and Coldstream

Main Street TD11 3JJ
Map 12: NT84
Tel: 01890 860257
Fax: 01890 860688
Cost: *Alc* £24. ☺ H/wine £9.85
Times: 11.45-2pm/6-9.30pm.
Closed D Sun, all Mon, last wk Oct, 2 wks Jan
Additional: Bar food; Sunday L; Children welcome; ✿ dishes
Smoking: No smoking in dining room

SHETLAND

LERWICK, Shetland Hotel ✿

Formal restaurant in a modern hotel opposite the ferry terminal. Local produce is given imaginative treatment, and there is an interesting range of puddings.

Smoking: No smoking in dining room
Accommodation: 64 en suite ★ ★ ★

Directions: Opposite ferry terminal, on main road N from town centre

Holmsgarth Road ZE1 0PW
Map 16: HU44
Tel: 01595 695515
Fax: 01595 695828
Cost: Set-price D £23.50. ☺ H/wine £8.95
Times: D only, 7-9.15pm.
Closed 25, 26 Dec, 1, 2 Jan
Additional: Children welcome; ✿ dishes

STIRLING

BALQUHIDDER, **Monachyle Mhor**

Lochearnhead FK19 8PQ
Map 11: NN52
Tel: 01877 384622
Fax: 01877 384305
Chef: Tom Lewis
Owners: Jean, Rob & Tom Lewis
Cost: *Alc* £25, set-price L £19/D £29.
☺ H/wine £10.50
Times: Noon-2pm/7-8.45pm
Additional: Bar food L; Sunday L;
Children 12+; ✿ dishes
Seats: 26. Private dining room 14
Smoking: No smoking in dining room
Accommodation: 10 en suite ★ ★

Directions: On A84, 11 miles N of
Callander turn R at Kingshouse Hotel.
Monachyle Mhor 6 miles

*Set amidst 2000 acres of tranquil farmland at the lochhead of
a beautiful glen, this converted farmhouse is full of rustic
charm and character.* The attractive dining room occupies a
front extension and overlooks Lochs Voile and Donie. The
kitchen offers some exemplary cooking based on well-sourced
ingredients. Tom Lewis has natural talent, his interesting four-
course lunch and dinner menus feature simply cooked dishes
yet natural flavours are enhanced by a careful blend of herbs,
fruit and vegetables. Dinner may begin with home-baked
breads, Jerusalem artichoke and rosemary soup, or calves' liver
on balsamic red onions with a pear, lime and thyme sauce,
Follow with seared west coast scallops on steamed bok choi
with Italian parsley and wasabi hollandaise, or venison with
juniper and coriander game stock. Round off with a selection
of farmhouse cheeses or a sublime dessert, perhaps hot bread-
and-butter soufflé.

BRIDGE OF ALLAN, **Royal Hotel** ✿

Henderson Street FK9 4HG
Map 11: NS79
Tel: 01786 832284
Fax: 01786 834377
Telephone for further details

*The Royal Hotel's restaurant proffers an assortment of dishes. Try
perhaps the grilled goats' cheese on a toasted brioche with citrus
beurre blanc and coffee parfait with fruits of the forest coulis.*

Directions: Telephone for directions

CALLANDER,

Roman Camp Hotel ✿✿✿

FK17 8BG
Map 11: NN60
Tel: 01877 330003
Fax: 01877 331533
Chef: Ian McNaught
Owners: Eric & Marion Brown
Cost: *Alc* £50, set-price L £18/D £34
(4 courses). H/wine £15
Times: Noon-2pm/7-9pm
Additional: Sunday L; Children 3+;
✿ dishes
Seats: 55. Private dining room 40

*Peaceful country retreat built in 1625 as a hunting lodge for
the Dukes of Perth.* Set in its own extensive grounds (the
walled garden provides the kitchen with herbs and vegetables),
Roman Camp has its own private fishing beat on the River
Teith. The restaurant is a light, warm, spacious room with
tapestries, an open fire and views over the gardens. An *amuse-
bouche* shows the commitment of the kitchen: perhaps a
perfect square of pressed ham knuckle surrounded by tomato
concasse in a light vinaigrette. Widgeon breast, cooked rare
and tender enough to be cut with a fork, marinated in soy and

Roman Camp Hotel

Smoking: No smoking in dining room;
Air conditioning
Accommodation: 14 en suite ★★★

Directions: Turn L into driveway at
east end of Callander main street

honey, partnered with pak choi and needle-thin noodles, might
show up among starters, and those eating off the tasting menu
can expect the likes of a haricot blanc cappuccino with
powdered morels and chunks of duck confit – 'a super
combination'. Plainly steamed sea bass wrapped around sweet
scallop mousse and set on a red pepper essence with saffron
risotto and baby fennel has been praised, or there might be
breast of guinea fowl poached in asparagus bouillon with leek
and chervil dumplings. A pre-dessert could be an egg cup of
the lightest of orange jellies, the finale perhaps sliced pineapple
with coriander syrup, lemon sorbet and a mango tuile. The
kitchen's industry extends to notable breads and petits fours,
and the six-page wine list includes a page of half-bottles.

DUNBLANE,
Cromlix House Hotel ❀❀

Kinbuck By Dunblane FK15 9JT
Map 11: NN70
Tel: 01786 822125
Fax: 01786 825450
Chef: Paul Devonshire
Owners: David & Ailsa Assenti
Cost: Set-price D £39 (5 courses).
H/wine £13.50
Times: 12.30-1.15pm/7-8.30pm.
Closed 30 Dec-mid Jan
Additional: Sunday L;
Children welcome; ❀ menu
Seats: 42. Private dining rooms 4-42
Smoking: No smoking in dining room
Accommodation: 14 en suite ★★★

*Charming Edwardian mansion with a reputation for high
standards of service.* Roaring log fires ensure that the impressive
public rooms are kept warm in winter, while in the summer
months guests can enjoy a game of croquet or tennis (or perhaps
a spot of trout and salmon fishing), within the hotel's three
thousand acre estate. Two elegant dining rooms filled with
gleaming silver and burning candles, set the scene for some
innovative cooking. Although short, the *carte* has some difficult
choices. Our inspector was impressed by pressed foie gras edged
with Parma ham, and by lightly pan-fried fillets of halibut, served
with asparagus, pak choi and a delicate prawn sauce. Dessert was
a made-to-order dark chocolate fondant that 'melted in the

mouth'. The carefully-chosen wine list is extensive, and offers an interesting selection from around the world.

PORT OF MENTEITH,
Lake of Menteith Hotel ❀❀

Charming hotel with magnificent views over the waters of the Lake of Menteith. While the kitchen uses the best ingredients Scotland has to offer, it also uses imagination to turn them into interesting ideas. Salmon is given the escabèche treatment and served with a confit of vegetables, a crisp risotto cake and fresh mussels, while roast fillet of Aberdeen Angus comes with sautéed woodland mushrooms and truffled potato purée. Salmon could crop up among the starters too, oak-smoked, made into a mousse and partnered by saffron potato salad, to be followed by roast breast of local pheasant garnished with lardons and a crisp garlic confit. A fondness for fruit shows up in puddings of apple and almond crumble with butterscotch sauce, or poached prunes in an Earl Grey syrup with a light vanilla cream.

Directions: On A873 in Port of Menteith

Directions: From A9 take B8033 (Kinbuck), through village, 2nd L after small bridge

Stirling FK8 3RA
Map 11: NN50
Tel: 01877 385258
Fax: 01877 385671
Chef: Jonathon Brown
Owner: The Leroy Family
Cost: Set-price L £13.50 (4 courses)/D £27.50 (5 courses). H/wine £10.50
Times: Noon-2pm/7-8.30pm
Additional: Sunday L; Children 12+; 🍽 dishes
Seats: 34. Jacket & tie preferred
Smoking: No smoking in dining room; Air conditioning
Accommodation: 16 en suite ★★

STIRLING, River House ❀

Innovatively designed restaurant combining a wooden stilted structure with modern decor. Uniquely, a children's playroom is provided. Dishes have a Mediterranean flavour.

Castle Business Park Craigforth SK9 4TW
Map 11: NS79
Tel: 01786 465577
Fax: 01786 462255
Cost: *Alc* £17.95, set-price L £5.95 (2 courses)
Times: Noon-2.45pm/6-9.45pm. Closed 25, 26 Dec, 1, 2 Jan
Additional: Children welcome; 🍽 dishes
Smoking: No-smoking area; No pipes & cigars

Directions: 3 mins from J10 of M9. Follow signs for Stirling ring road and Castle Business Park

STIRLING, Stirling Highland

Spittal Street FK8 1DU
Map 11: NS79
Tel: 01786 475444
Fax: 01786 462929
Chef: Paul Cook
Owner: Scottish Highland Hotels plc
Cost: A/c £30, set-price L £12 (2 courses)/D £19.95. ☺ H/wine £11.75
Times: Noon-2pm/7-10pm.
Closed L Sat
Additional: Sunday L; Children welcome; 🍴 dishes
Seats: 75. Private dining rooms 10-100
Smoking: No smoking in dining room
Accommodation: 78 en suite ★ ★ ★ ★

Directions: In the road leading to Stirling Castle – follow Castle signs

An interesting hotel created from a former high school – it still retains many original features. Meeting rooms are named after classrooms, drinks are served in the 'Headmaster's Study', and carefully-prepared meals can be had in the high-ceilinged Scholars Restaurant upstairs, while downstairs is Rizzios, a more informal Italian restaurant. The Scholars' menu is subtitled 'Scottish larder dinner menu', but still manages to include such un-Scottish items as Brie and Galia melon. The evening set-menu is littered with supplements which makes it read as an à la carte. The cooking is generally very good, but let down by the par-baked breads and standard vegetables. Pan-fried cod on salad leaves was 'superbly cooked, flaky, almost silky, contrasting well with crisp leaves,' duck breast in a red wine sauce had 'nicely charred skin and was still pink and juicy in the middle.' An iced hazelnut parfait was good and served with a well-made soft fruit coulis.

STRATHBLANE, Country Club Hotel

Milngavie Road G63 9AH
Map 11: NS56
Tel: 01360 770491
Fax: 01360 770345
Telephone for further details

The main dining room of this pleasant hotel is classically formal in style with service by smartly dressed staff. The set-price menu is very much in the modern idiom and has sufficient items at each course to make the correct choice a challenge.

Directions: Telephone for directions

STRATHYRE, Creagan House

Callander FK18 8ND
Map 11: NN51
Tel: 01877 384638
Fax: 01877 384319
Chef: Gordon A Gunn
Owners: Gordon & Cherry Gunn
Cost: Set-price D £22.50. ☺
H/wine £9.50
Times: D only, 7.30-8.30pm.
Closed all Feb, 1 wk Oct
Additional: Children 10+
Seats: 15. Private dining room 6 (functions 35)
Smoking: No smoking in dining room.
Jacket & tie preferred
Accommodation: 5 en suite ★

Warm, welcoming farmhouse restaurant-with-rooms. The dining room, in faux baronial style with a grand open fireplace, polished wood tables and exclusively designed Isle of Skye pottery, is the setting for fresh produce that is grown specifically for Creagan House in organic smallholdings. 'Smokie in a pokie' is intriguingly listed on the menu alongside more readily understandable dishes such as breast of Barbary duck lightly cooked with a burger of celeriac and oatmeal in a port wine and redcurrant sauce; fruity saucing is a kitchen favourite. The most impressive dish we sampled was a warm seafood pâté of crab and scallops with a sauce made from the coral, though a tutti-frutti steamed pudding, rich with candied and preserved fruits, was pretty memorable as well.

Directions: Lies 0.25 miles N of village off A84

WALES
ANGLESEY, ISLE OF

BEAUMARIS,

Ye Olde Bulls Head Inn

Castle Street LL58 8AP
Map 6: SH67
Tel: 01248 810329
Fax: 01248 811294
Chef: Keith Rothwell
Owners: Keith Rothwell,
David Robertson
Cost: *Alc* £29.50, set-price D £27.50.
H/wine £13.95
Times: D only, 7-9.30pm.
Closed Sun, 25, 26 Dec
Additional: Children 7+; dishes
Seats: 45. Private dining room 16
Smoking: No smoking in dining room
Accommodation: 15 en suite ★★

Characterful inn undergoing a complete refurbishment when we visited. As part of this development a new brasserie has been opened below the oak-beamed restaurant which is decorated with copper pots and guns. The kitchen relies heavily on local produce building a menu around such starters as fresh crab with a salad of asparagus and mixed leaves, delicately drizzled with olive oil and balsamic vinegar. A main course of whole, tender pigeon with a chicken and cep sausage was accompanied by decent broccoli, carrots, green beans and saffron potatoes. Desserts include rhubarb and stem ginger tiramsu – a dariole of rhubarb sponge with stem ginger on top and a rhubarb coulis on the side. There is a long, predominantly French, wine list. The staff are both knowledgeable and friendly.

Directions: Town centre, main street

BRIDGEND

BRIDGEND,

Coed-y-Mwstwr

Oak-panelled restaurant in a handsome Victorian mansion. Typical dishes are seared sea scallops, roast chump of Welsh salt-marsh lamb, and dark chocolate marquise.

Smoking: No-smoking area; No pipes & cigars
Accommodation: 23 en suite ★★★

Directions: M4 J35, A473 (Bridgend) into Coychurch, R at petrol station and up hill for 1 mile

Coychurch CF35 6AF
Map 3: SS97
Tel: 01656 860621
Fax: 01656 863122
Cost: *Alc* £26.50, set-price D £24. ☺
H/wine £10.75
Times: Noon-2pm/7-10pm
Additional: Bar food; Sunday L;
Children welcome; dishes

BRIDGEND, **The Great House**

Fresh flowers and crisp white linen characterise the restaurant at this hospitable manor house hotel. Fine local produce is used to great effect on a short, well chosen carte.

Smoking: No smoking in dining room; Air conditioning
Accommodation: 16 en suite ★ ★ ★

Directions: M4 J35, A473/A48 (Porthcawl and Laleston)

Laleston CF32 0HP
Map 3: SS97
Tel: 01656 657644
Fax: 01656 668892
Cost: *Alc* £31.05, set-price L
£11.95/D £21.50. ☺ H/wine £10.75
Times: Noon-2pm/7-9.30pm.
Closed 25-26 Dec, Bhs
Additional: Bar food L, Sunday L,
Children welcome, ◗ dishes

CARDIFF

CARDIFF, **La Brasseria, Champers, Le Monde**

At the station end of the city centre, these three pillars of the Benigno Martinez empire are all marked by bustling informality and Spanish influenced cooking using the freshest produce.

Directions: Telephone for directions

60 St Mary Street
Cardiff CF1 1FE
Map 3: ST17
Tel: 01222 372164
Telephone for further details

CARDIFF, **Cardiff Bay Hotel**

Former mid-Victorian fruit and vegetable warehouse in heart of Cardiff's waterside development area. Halyard's Restaurant offers the likes of crispy spring roll of duck and ginger with Oriental dressing, tuna with red pepper sauce and ratatouille cake, or prime fillet steak with Madeira sauce.

Accommodation: 156 en suite ★ ★ ★ ★

Directions: From A48M follow 'Docks & Cardiff E'. L at r/bout, R fork onto flyover. At 3rd r/bout take 2nd exit (Ocean Way – Atlantic Wharf). L at r/bout (Penarth). Over next r/bout, under flyover, L at 1st lights; hotel on R

Schooner Way Atlantic Wharf
CF1 5RT
Map 3: ST17
Tel: 01222 475000
Fax: 01222 481491
Cost: *Alc* £27, set-price L £10.95/D
£18.50. ☺ H/wine £10.50
Times: Noon-2pm/7-9.45pm.
Closed L Sat, L Bhs
Additional: Bar food L; Sunday L;
Children 3+; ◗ dishes
Smoking: Air conditioning; Jacket &
tie preferred

CARDIFF, **Le Cassoulet**

5 Romilly Crescent Canton
CF1 9NP
Map 3: ST17
Tel/Fax: 01222 221905
Cost: *Alc* £27.50, set-price L £15. ☺
H/wine £10.95
Times: Noon-2pm/7-10pm.
Closed Sun, Mon, 1 wk Xmas,
3 wks Aug
Additional: Children welcome;
◗ dishes
Smoking: No pipes & cigars

Directions: From M4 follow B4267
Canton. Restaurant is next to Post
Office

There's a modern feel to this popular, long-standing bistro. The cooking specialises in robust French provincial classics, notably from south-west France, such as cassoulet toulousain, duck confit, lamb shank cooked in straw, and foie gras. The proprietor has his roots firmly proclaimed in the photos of the Toulouse rugby team, and by his wine list, of which many choices are brought over specially by the restaurant. Note that house champagne by the glass is a bargain. We enjoyed diced vegetables in courgette mousse wrapped and steamed in cabbage leaf, duck leg stuffed with chicken mousseline and served with wild mushrooms and baby onions, and fruits with champagne sabayon for dessert.

CARDIFF, Chikako's Japanese Restaurant

Japanese outpost in city centre offering graceful service and a wide range of authentic dishes. Enterprising newcomers would do well to sample the clean flavours of good sashimi and sushi, although there are plenty of options of the tempura and teriyaki variety for those able to resist raw fish.

10-11 Mill Lane CF1 1FL
Map 3: ST17
Tel/Fax: 01222 665279
Telephone for further details

Directions: Opp Marriott Hotel, in 'The Hayes' café quarter

CARDIFF, Copthorne Cardiff-Caerdydd

Raglan's Restaurant, with views over the lakes, serves dishes based on fresh Welsh ingredients. Chicken and duck terrine might be followed by tender lamb shank with polenta and port jus.

Copthorne Way Culverhouse Cross CF5 6XJ
Map 3: ST17
Tel: 01222 599100
Fax: 01222 599080
Telephone for further details

Directions: M4 J33 – A4232 (Cardiff West); 3 miles onto A48

CARDIFF, Le Gallois NEW

6-8 Romilly Crescent CF11 9NR
Map 3: ST17
Tel: 01222 341264
Fax: 01222 237911
Chef: Padrig Jones
Owners: Graham & Anne Jones
Cost: *Alc* £25, set-price L £10.95/D £25 (4 courses). ☺ H/wine £9.50
Times: Noon-2.30pm/6.30-10.30pm. Closed Sun, Mon, Xmas, 3 wks Aug
Additional: Children welcome; No pipes & cigars; ◑ dishes
Seats: 50
Smoking: No-smoking area; Air conditioning

Directions: Telephone for directions

'*A sparkling addition to the Welsh capital's eating scene*', enthused one inspector of this edge of city restaurant. The name may emphasise the French connections of the owners, but a glance at the menu reveals influences closer to home. Chef/patron Padrig Jones has served his apprenticeship in some high profile kitchens and the influence of Marco Pierre White is clearly discernible in such offerings as ribeye steak with béarnaise and pommes frites. As might be hoped, it is depth of flavour and uncompromising choice of produce that shines through. Meats are top notch, the power of the aforementioned beef matched by 'knockout' rump of salt marsh lamb delivered with fondant potatoes and grilled provençale vegetables. Fish too is carefully procured and steamed sea bass with crab, rocket and a chilli salsa was judged a beautifully balanced combination. Winner of the AA Restaurant of the Year Award for Wales (see p20).

CARDIFF, Gilby's Restaurant

Popular, lively place with punters flocking for the seafood – lobster, oysters, Pembroke crab. But Welsh lamb takes pride of place too with roast rack of salt-marsh rump offered with butternut squash and chanterelles. Good wine list.

Old Port Road Culverhouse Cross CF5 6DN
Map 3: ST17
Tel: 01222 670800
Fax: 01222 594437
Cost: *Alc* £25, set-price L £7.95 (2 courses)/D £11.95 (6-7pm only). ☺ H/wine £10.95
Times: Noon-2.30pm/6-10.30pm. Closed D Sun, all Mon, 25, 26 Dec, 1 Jan
Additional: Sunday L; Children 7+ ; ⓭ dishes
Smoking: No pipes & cigars

Directions: From M4 J33 follow signs for Airport/Cardiff West. Take A4050 Barry/Airport road and R at 1st mini roundabout

CARDIFF, Manor Parc Hotel

Country house hotel with a distinct Italian flavour that extends to the food. In addition to pasta, expect plenty of rich sauces, fresh fish and, perhaps, veal with mushroom and cream sauce. Lavish desserts from the trolley.

Accommodation: 12 en suite ★★★

Directions: N of Cardiff on A469

Thornhill Road CF4 5UA
Map 3: ST17
Tel: 01222 693723
Fax: 01222 614624
Cost: *Alc* £35. ☺ H/wine £10.50
Times: Noon-1.45pm/7-9.45pm. Closed D Sun, 25 Dec
Additional: Sunday L; Children welcome; ⓭ dishes
Smoking: No pipes & cigars

CARDIFF,
Metropolis Restaurant & Bar

Metropolitan chic hits Cardiff. A stylish bar offers abbreviated menus targeted at grazers, while the mezzanine restaurant provides more formal surroundings with a similarly breezy style of cooking.

60 Charles Street CF1 4EG
Map 3: ST17
Tel: 01222 344300
Fax: 01222 666602
Cost: *Alc* £25, set-price L £8.90/D £12.95. ☺ H/wine £9.95
Times: Noon-11pm. Closed D Sun, 25, 26 Dec
Additional: Bar Food; Sunday L; Children welcome; ⓭ dishes
Smoking: Air conditioning

Directions: In city centre, off Queen Street

CARDIFF,

New House Hotel

On a clear day enjoy panoramic views across the capital to
the North Devon coast from the restaurant of this impressive
Georgian mansion. An ambitiously long menu is handled with
relative ease in the busy kitchen. Consistency is the key to the
success of the cooking here. Imaginative dishes make good use
of quality ingredients and are carefully prepared and artfully
presented in a fashionable, modern style. A typical meal may
begin with bouillabaisse with saffron potato dumplings, or
seared scallops of monkfish on crispy rice noodles with
tarragon mustard sauce. Main course options range from
salmon with chervil butter, to spinach and Brie stuffed chicken
served on smoked bacon, parsley and broad bean gratin. To
finish, there may be summer fruit pudding with red fruit coulis,
warm apple pie, or a good selection of Welsh cheeses.

Thornhill CF4 5UA
Map 3: ST17
Tel: 01222 520280
Fax: 01222 520324
Chef: Ian Black
Owner: Julian Hitchcock
Cost: *Alc* £30, set-price L £15.50/D
£18.50. ☺ H/wine £11.75
Times: Noon-2pm/7-9.45pm
Additional: Bar food; Sunday L;
Children welcome; ✿ dishes
Seats: 40. Private dining room 75.
Jacket & tie preferred
Smoking: No smoking in dining room
Accommodation: 33 en suite ★ ★ ★

Directions: Take A469 to the north of city. Entrance on L shortly
after crossing M4 flyover

CARDIFF,

St David's Hotel

Wales first five star hotel has arrived on the waterfront.
Classical cuisine comes to Cardiff in the shape of Martin
Green. As apprenticeships go, eleven years under Michel
Bourdin at the Connaught must rate as immaculate grooming
and the pedigree is evident in the depth of flavour, quality of
the saucing and accuracy of technique being offered in Tides
Restaurant. It would be wrong, though, to give the impression
that there was anything dull or staid about the cooking here.
There are plenty of twist and turns to a menu that offers its
share of Mediterranean and regional French stylings, but the
foundations are always intelligent and well conceived. A
starter of pan-fried foie gras served with caramelised endive,
sauce 'aigre-doux' and a witty little savoury Welsh-cake was a
heavyweight success at the start of one inspection meal, but a
much simpler squid-ink risotto with roast squid and herb oil
was an equally creditable alternative at a later meal. Martin
Green has been quick to recognise the strengths of the best of
the native produce with a marvellous ribeye of Welsh Black
beef served with sauce Bercy, roasted root vegetables and
parsley mash, and fillet of lamb teamed with aubergine caviar,
roasted shallots and tarragon sauce, as typical examples.
Amongst the desserts a dark and remarkably intense chocolate
tart has won plaudits, with the accompanying lemongrass ice-
cream being a real triumph. The wine list offers the kind of
depth and quality not often seen in these parts.

Havannah Street CF10 6SD
Map 3: ST17
Tel: 029 20454045
Fax: 029 20487056
Chef: Martin Green
Owner: Rocco Forte Hotels
Cost: *Alc* £32, set-price L £19.50.
H/wine £24
Times: 12.30-2.30pm/6.30-10.30pm
Additonal: Bar food; Sunday L;
Children welcome; ✿ dishes
Seats: 115. Private dining rooms
Smoking: No smoking in dining room
Accommodation: 136 en suite
★ ★ ★ ★ ★

Directions: From M4 take A432 to Cardiff Bay where hotel is
signposted

CREIGIAU,

Caesars Arms

It is the abundant selection of fresh fish and shellfish that catches the
eye, cramming the glass counter from which customers can select

Cardiff Road CF4 8NN
Map 3: ST08
Tel: 01222 890486
Fax: 01222 892176

Caesars Arms

Cost: *Alc* £15, set-price L £5 (1
course). ☺ H/wine £9.45
Times: Noon-2.30pm/7-10.30pm.
Closed D Sun, 25 Dec
Additional: Sunday L;
Children welcome; ◑ dishes
Smoking: Air conditioning

Directions: From M4 J34 take A4119
(Cardiff). Turn L at Creigiau

*their choice. The cooking is admirably simple, with bass baked in
rock salt being something of a signature dish. Also good meat and
game dishes.*

CARMARTHENSHIRE

BRECHFA,
Tŷ Mawr Country Hotel

*Attractive country house hotel with a reputation for warm hospitality
and good food. The short fixed-price menu might offer Welsh beef,
Welsh lamb or lemon sole.*

Additional: Bar food L; Sunday L; Children welcome; ◑ dishes
Smoking: No smoking in dining room
Accommodation: 5 rooms, 4 en suite ★★

Directions: Off B4310, village centre

SA32 7RA
Map 2: SN53
Tel: 01267 202332
Fax: 01267 202437
Cost: *Alc* £23, set-price L £13/D £23
(4 courses). ☺ H/wine £9.25
Times: Noon-1.30pm/7.30-10pm.
Closed L Tue, 2nd wk Nov, 3 wks Feb

CARMARTHEN, **Falcon Hotel** **NEW**

*Attractive town-centre restaurant with eye-catching beams and
copper pots. Good use is made of local produce; the small set-price
menu revealing choices such as competently cooked lamb kebab
with leek and mint salad.*

Directions: In town centre, opposite monument

Lammas Street SA31 3AP
Tel: 01267 234959
Fax: 01267 221277
Telephone for further details

CARMARTHEN,
The Four Seasons

*Quality ingredients are evident in the well constructed dishes at this
farmhouse-style restaurant, where locally smoked salmon, salt marsh
lamb and black beef are complemented by home-grown herbs.*

Additional: Children welcome; ◑ dishes
Accommodation: 5 en suite

Directions: From A40 turn onto B4310 at Nantgaredig; L up
hill, 0.25 mile on R

Nantgaredig SA32 7NY
Map 2: SN42
Tel: 01267 290238
Fax: 01267 290808
Cost: Set-price D £22.50 (4 courses).
☺ H/wine £9.50
Times: D only, 7.30-9.30pm.
Closed Sun, Mon, Xmas

LAUGHARNE, Cors Restaurant

Newbridge Road SA33 4SH
Map 2: SN31
Tel: 01994 427219
Chef/Owner: Nick Priestland
Telephone for further details

Beautiful former vicarage set in exceptional gardens with striking interior design. Nick Priestland is an artist-cum-horticulturist-cum chef. His cooking is simple but carefully composed without shortcuts, and is based on an Ital-Med style that fits his vibrant, exuberant decor well. Such bold simplicity demands a well-chosen palette of ingredients and some of the best local bounty is employed to good effect, There is a slight bohemian edge and this extends to the generous spirit of the service; Priestland likes to mingle front-of—house throughout the evening whilst still being kingpin in the kitchen. Those used to more Mussolini-style metropolitan service will do well to chill out and take the evening (or lunchtime) as it comes. This is what to expect: gazpacho, a garrulous version with no stinting on the variety of recently sprung vegetables, potato and dill pancake with locally smoked salmon and crème fraîche, chargrilled cutlets of Welsh spring lamb with a rosemary Parmesan crust and minted aïoli, and a sharp, fresh rhubarb fool. The wine list is New World and new wave.

LLANDEILO,
Cawdor Arms Hotel

Rhosmaen Street SA19 6EN
Map 3: SN62
Tel: 01558 823500
Fax: 01558 822399
Chef: Rod Peterson
Owners: John, Sylvia & Jane Silver
Cost: Set-price L £13.50/D £20. ☺
H/wine £9.90
Times: Noon-2pm/7.30-9pm
Additional: Bar food L; Sunday L; Children welcome; ◑ dishes
Seats: 50. Private dining rooms 16 & 28
Smoking: No smoking in dining room
Accommodation: 17 en suite ★ ★ ★

A warm welcome is to be expected at this impressive Georgian hotel in the centre of Llandeilo. The kitchen is ambitious and delivers a gutsy menu that packs plenty of punch. Note dishes built on robust flavours such as grilled fillet of Welsh beef with a goats' cheese and parsley crust served on roasted shallots and woodland mushrooms. A February inspection meal showed that the kitchen can deliver. Canapés of salmon tartlets and liver pâté en croûte were good, then came a sound rillette of lamb with sweet potato. But the main course had the most impact – chargrilled breast of duck, served with spring onion mash, bean sprouts and a honey jus was infused with evocative oriental flavours. For dessert, passion fruit syrup added extra sparkle to a dark chocolate and coconut mousse.

Directions: Large Georgian building in town centre

CEREDIGION

ABERPORTH,
Penbontbren Farm Hotel

Glynarthen Cardigan SA44 6PE
Map 2: SN25
Tel: 01239 810248
Fax: 01239 811129
Cost: *Alc* £18.90. ☺ H/wine £9
Times: D only, 7-8.30pm
Additional: Children welcome; ◑ dishes

Traditional Welsh fare is offered at this friendly restaurant, housed in a converted farm building. Try cawl soup for starters, followed by lamb cutlets with port sauce.

Smoking: No smoking in dining room; Air conditioning
Accommodation: 10 en suite ★ ★

Directions: E from Cardigan on A487 to Tanygroes. 1 mile after Tanygroes take 2nd R signposted Penbontbren

ABERYSTWYTH,

Belle Vue Royal Hotel

Right on the seafront, the dining-room of the family-run hotel has been freshly updated. Local produce features, as in locally made sausages and leek mash, herb-crusted rack of Welsh lamb and Welsh sirloin steaks plus Welsh and Border cheeses.

Marine Terrace
SY23 2BA
Map 6: SN58
Tel: 01970 617558
Fax: 01970 612190
Cost: *Alc* £19.50, set-price L
£13.50/D £23 (4 courses). ☺
H/wine £9
Times: 12.30-1.45pm/6.30-9.15pm.
Closed D 25 Dec
Additional: Bar food L; Sunday L;
Children welcome; ✿ dishes
Smoking: No pipes & cigars;
Air conditioning
Accommodation: 37 en suite ★ ★ ★

Directions: Overlooking Cardigan
Bay

ABERYSTWYTH, ## Conrah Hotel ✿✿

Personally run country house hotel with conference and leisure facilities. Major pluses are the location – set in 22 acres of mature grounds with spectacular views to the Cambrian mountains – and the fact that food is taken seriously; a good proportion of the fresh ingredients used are produced locally. Our own test meal highlighted home-made bread, a fillet of Black Welsh Mountain beef of excellent quality, served with a good rich red wine sauce, and a decent lemon tart.

Directions: On A487, 3 miles S of Aberystwyth

Ffosrhydygaled Chancery SY23 4DF
Map 6: SN58
Tel: 01970 617941
Fax: 01970 624546
Chef: Stephen West
Owners: Mr & Mrs F J Heading
Cost: Set-price L £12.50 (2 courses)/D
£26. H/wine £11
Times: Noon-2pm/7-9pm.
Closed Xmas wk
Additional: Bar food L; Sunday L;
Children 5+; ✿ dishes. **Seats:** 50
Smoking: No smoking in dining room
Accommodation: 19 en suite ★ ★ ★

ABERYSTWYTH, ## Groves Hotel

Town-centre hotel restaurant with a set-price menu of two or three courses offering the likes of home-made vegetable soup, roast lamb, and strawberry cheesecake.

Directions: Town centre, take road opposite station & 2nd R

44-46 North Parade SY23 2NF
Map 6: SN58
Tel: 01970 617623
Fax: 01970 627068
Telephone for further details

ABERYSTWYTH, **Nanteos**

Rhydyfelin SY23 4LQ
Map 6: SN58
Tel: 01970 624363
Fax: 01970 626332
Cost: Set-price D £22.50. ☺
H/wine £8.50
Times: D only, 7-9. Closed D Sun,
all Mon, Tue, Jan
Additional: Bar food L; Sunday L (by
pior arrangement); Children 12+;
❹ dishes
Smoking: No smoking in dining room
Accommodation: 6 en suite

Directions: Take B4340 to Trawscoed
south of Aberystwyth. Nanteos on L,
signposted

An impressive Georgian house in seventy acres of parkland – a popular venue for weddings. The old wood-panelled library is now the restaurant and offers the likes of pan-fried pigeon breast with basil polenta and brandy jus, or smoked mackerel with horseradish. Try spiced poached pear with chocolate sauce for dessert.

EGLWYSFACH, **Ynyshir Hall**

Machynlleth SY20 8TA
Map 6: SN69
Tel: 01654 781209
Fax: 01654 781366
Chef: Chris Colmer
Owners: Rob & Joan Reen
Cost: Set-price L £21/D £35 (4
courses). H/wine £15
Times: 12.30-1.30pm/7-9pm
Additional: Bar food L; Sunday L;
Children 9+; ❹ dishes
Seats: 28. Private dining room 18
Smoking: No smoking in dining room
Accommodation: 10 en suite ★ ★ ★

Directions: On the A487, 6 miles
from Machynlleth & 11 miles from
Aberystwyth

Discreet country house hotel for a quiet get away. Don't be deceived by the setting. With its virginal white exterior, well-tended gardens and bird sanctuary neighbour, Ynyshir Hall is a picture of tranquillity. Inside, relaxed and attentive service only adds to the sense of calm and well being. Admittedly, owner Rob Reen's striking paintings contribute some sparkle to the walls, but the real fireworks are to be found in the kitchen. If Chris Colmer were a snooker player he'd be much more of a Jimmy White than a Steve Davis: the style is ambitious and sometimes risky, but when it works (and increasingly often it does), the results can be spellbinding. Something of a specialist in attention-grabbing appetisers, Colmer's offerings this year have included a super-intense cappuccino of cauliflower broth with truffle oil, which set the tone for one well-received inspection meal. This is the kind of cooking that offers surprises, an unexpected twist or an extra dimension of flavour guaranteed to provoke an excited response. Witness, for instance, a boudin of scallops that succeeded in distilling a shocking amount of shellfish flavour in the mousse. For invention though, nothing could challenge the fat fillet of roast cod which bore an unexploded parcel of lemon pickle and garlic butter ready to discharge its contents over the fish. Desserts can be a triumph too: a hot lime soufflé with a white chocolate and citronelle sorbet is presentationally stunning but the substance was there too in the form of a perfectly executed soufflé and, once again, marvellous depth of flavour. The wine list is moving forward with a serious range of both clarets and Burgundies.

LAMPETER,
Falcondale Mansion

A delightful mansion house set in 14 acres of grounds. An extensive range of dishes is offered, making good use of local produce, especially top quality Welsh beef.

Smoking: No smoking in dining room
Accommodation: 20 en suite ★ ★ ★

Directions: From High Street turn R up South Drive

SA48 7RX
Map 2: SN54
Tel: 01570 422910
Fax: 01570 423559
Cost: *Alc* £22.50, set-price D £19.50.
☺ H/wine £8.95
Times: D only, 7-9.30pm.
Closed 2nd & 3rd wk Jan
Additional: Bar food; Sunday L (noon-1.45pm); Children welcome; ✿ dishes

CONWY

ABERGELE, Kinmel Arms

St George LL22 9BP
Map 6: SH97
Tel/Fax: 01745 832207
Chef: Gary Edwards
Owners: Gary Edwards & Dermot McGee
Cost: *Alc* £17, set-price L & D £12.95. ☺ H/wine £8.95
Times: Noon-2.30pm/7-9pm.
Closed D Mon, 25 Dec
Additional: Bar food; Sunday L; Children 4+; ✿ dishes
Seats: 32. Private dining room 20
Smoking: No smoking in dining room

A neat, well-appointed restaurant and an informal atmosphere. Set on the edge of the historic Kinmel Estate, this former 17th-century coaching inn boasts a neo-classical style with renaissance sculptures and prints as well as a cosy cottagey bar. In addition to some good bar food, the short *carte* features locally caught fish, prime Welsh lamb and beef and estate game. Begin with a light chicken liver parfait with home-made spiced onion marmalade, or try the smoked haddock and leek tart, then choose, perhaps, sirloin of beef with red wine, bacon and shallot sauce, pork with prune and Armagnac sauce, or a speciality goats' cheese dish served on chargrilled polenta and pimento. Round off with an excellent lemon tart with raspberry coulis or the chocolate marquise with orange sabayon.

Directions: Take A55 towards Conwy; L turn signed 'St George'; L at top of hill and inn on L

BETWS-Y-COED,
Tan-y-Foel Hotel ❀❀❀

Capel Garmon LL26 0RE
Map 6: SH75
Tel: 01690 710507
Fax: 01690 710681
Chef: Janet Pitman
Owners: Mr & Mrs JC Pitman
Cost: Set-price D £23.50 (2 courses).
H/wine £11
Times: D only, 7.45-8.15pm.
Closed Dec including Xmas &
New Year
Additional: Children 7+
Seats: 16
Smoking: No smoking establishment
Accommodation: 7 en suite ★ ★

Directions: A5 onto A470; 2 miles N
towards Llanrwst, then turning for
Capel Garmon. Hotel on L before
village

Viewers of BBC 2 Wales last year will have seen Janet Pitman
prepare her signature dish of Celtic pancakes with Carmarthen
ham, pork and sage and apple purée, but much of her
inspiration comes from outside the Principality. The set dinner
is priced per course, with a limited choice only, but the cooking
is never less than highly focused and expertly delivered. A
typical menu might start with tempura of mixed vegetables with
mustard sauce, or seared fillet of halibut set on spinach risotto
with tomato passata and olive oil dressing (optional as a main
course), followed by loin of pork with apple purée, crisp Parma
ham, boxty potato cakes, seasonal vegetables and an apple wine
jus. For dessert, there may be pear and ginger tart with crème
anglaise, fresh fruit platter, or a selection of Welsh cheeses with
biscuits and celery. The dining room of the beautifully
maintained, old manor house has been transformed using
vibrant modern paint techniques, and also has a glazed
conservatory overlooking a mature rockery.

COLWYN BAY, Café Niçoise ❀❀

Simple, friendly restaurant that offers a warm welcome.
Wooden floors, terracotta walls, well-co-ordinated, friendly
staff and a pleasant atmosphere are the first impressions
people get here. It's small and there's no bar, so go straight to
a table and choose from around half a dozen dishes at each
course. Onion and cider soup with Mozzarella gives a novel
twist to a classic, and there might be – you've guessed – salade
niçoise. The kitchen makes the most of prime local lamb and
beef and, in season, game – perhaps roast pheasant with salsify
and braised red cabbage, while from the sea comes grilled sea
bass with saffron and a shellfish sauce, or an assiette of mixed
fish (fillets of cod, salmon, red mullet and brill) with spinach on
a saffron sauce, all of excellent flavour and delicately
presented. For dessert we went for yummy chocolate pudding
with custard and a brandy snap of vanilla ice cream and didn't
regret it. The wine list has a good selection of countries and
regions.

124 Abergele Road LL29 7PS
Map 6: SH87
Tel: 01492 531555
Chef: Carl Swift
Owners: Carl & Lynne Swift
Cost: Alc £23.95, set-price L £14.95
Times: Noon-2pm/7-10pm.
Closed Sun, L Mon & Tue, 1 wk Jan,
1 wk Jun
Additional: Children 7+ at D;
❋ dishes
Seats: 32
Smoking: No-smoking area

Directions: From A55 take Old
Colwyn exit, L at slip road, R at mini-
roundabout, R towards Bay; restaurant
is on L

CONWY, Lodge Hotel ❀

See *Tal-y-Bont*

CONWY, The Old Rectory

Llanrwst Road
Llansanffraid Glan Conwy LL28 5LF
Map 6: SH77
Tel: 01492 580611
Fax: 01492 584555
Chef: Wendy Vaughan
Owners: Michael & Wendy Vaughan
Cost: Set-price D £29.90.
H/wine £14.90
Times: D only at 8pm.
Closed 20 Oct-1 Feb
Additional: Children 5+
Seats: 16
Smoking: No smoking in dining room
Accommodation: 6 en suite ★ ★

Spectacular uninterrupted vistas from Conwy Castle to Snowdonia plus equally memorable dinners cooked by Wendy Vaughan. The no choice menu (discuss likes and dislikes when booking) uses local produce whenever possible; the freshly caught fish is unbeatable and only locally reared hormone-free Welsh Black beef and Welsh mountain lamb are served (as the menu bi-lingually states). Typically, there may be fillet of cod with Camarthen ham and a herb crust and puréed fennel, followed by roast loin of Conwy lamb with spinach parcels. Another night, the menu might be walnut-crusted goats' cheese with sauté potatoes and spring onions, then roast breast of duck with Puy lentils, hotpot potatoes and crispy Camarthen ham. There is a choice of desserts, perhaps chocolate mousse tart, home-made ice cream or fruit sorbet. Welsh farmhouse cheeses or a savoury of grilled goats' cheese can be taken as an extra course. The wine list is well chosen, with some depth and interest and offers a good balance between the down-to-earth and the special occasion bottles. Michael Vaughan paces the service well in the elegantly styled dining-room.

Directions: On A470, 0.5 mile S of junction with A55

LLANDUDNO,
Bodysgallen Hall Hotel

17th-century country house with stunning gardens set against the superb backdrop of Conwy Castle and Snowdonia.

LL30 1RS
Map 6: SH78
Tel: 01492 584466
Fax: 01492 582519
Chef: Mike Penny
Owner: Historic House Hotels
Cost: *Alc* £32.50, set-price L £16.50.
H/wine £11.75
Times: 12.30pm-1.45pm/7.30-9.30pm
Additional: Bar food L; Sunday L;
Children 8+; ◑ dishes
Seats: 60. Private dining room 40.
Jacket & tie preferred
Smoking: No smoking in dining room;
Air conditioning
Accommodation: 35 en suite ★ ★ ★

Directions: From A55 take A470
(Llandudno). Hotel 1 mile on R

Wood-panelled walls, old oil paintings and open fires add to the atmosphere. Ambitious dinners include some interesting ideas – roast local grey mullet with a lemongrass and crayfish broth; saddle of rabbit filled with prunes on an onion marmalade; breast of Hereford duck with artichokes and a cider and shallot dressing. Fashion dictates the inclusion of certain items such as rocket, potato cakes, carpaccio, couscous and sun-dried tomato polenta, but the most attractive-sounding dishes are often the simplest, witness salad of home-smoked seafood rillette with avocado, or roast loin of venison with a wild mushroom potato purée and baby leeks, as well as loin of pan-fried British veal on home-made pesto noodles. Desserts include Bodsygallen apple tarte Tatin with apple ice cream and caramel sauce, and iced coffee parfait cup on a saucer of bitter chocolate with griottine cherries. A vegetarian menu is available on request.

Bodysgallen Hall Hotel

LLANDUDNO,
Empire Hotel ✿

Leading Llandudno hotel, traditionally run, with an elegant restaurant. Chicken parfait, and loin of pork with hazelnut and apricot stuffing made an enjoyable meal, followed by rich sticky toffee pudding.

Church Walks LL30 2HE
Map 6: SH78
Tel: 01492 860555
Fax: 01492 860791
Cost: Set-price L £14.50 (4 courses)/D £25 (5 courses). H/wine £12.95
Times: 12.30-2pm/6.45-9.30pm. Closed L Mon-Fri, 19-29 Dec
Additional: Bar food; Sunday L; Children welcome; ✿ dishes
Smoking: No-smoking area; No pipes & cigars; Air conditioning
Accommodation: 58 en suite ★ ★ ★

Directions: From A55 take A470 to Llandudno. Proceed along the main street (Mostyn Street/Upper Mostyn Street). Hotel at end and facing town

LLANDUDNO,
Imperial Hotel ✿

Traditional seaside hotel on a grand scale, dominating the imposing Victorian seafront. Chantrey restaurant offers a set-price, monthly-changing menu which is built around local and regional produce.

Smoking: No smoking in dining room
Accommodation: 100 en suite ★ ★ ★

The Promenade LL30 1AP
Map 6: SH78
Tel: 01492 877466
Fax: 01492 878043
Cost: Alc £20, set-price D £20. H/wine £10
Times: D only 6.30-9.30pm

LLANDUDNO, Martins Hotel & Restaurant ✿✿

NEW

Candles and fresh flowers adorn Martin James's attractive little restaurant set in an Edwardian townhouse close to the seafront. Popular with theatre goers (early set-dinners), business suits and tourists alike, Martins is a cut above the

11 Mostyn Avenue Craig Y Don LL30 1YS
Map 6: SH78
Tel: 01492 870070
Fax: 01492 876661
Chef: Martin James

average neighbourhood restaurant, offering excellent home-made breads and petits fours either side of an imaginative 'bill of fare' that features some accomplished cooking. Dedication in the kitchen and use of the finest Welsh produce impressed our inspector, who enjoyed chicken liver terrine with Cumberland sauce, steamed fillet of halibut filled with a creamy crab and smoked haddock mousse, and a hot almond gâteau with raspberry coulis. Alternatives may include fish mousse with scallops and lemon butter sauce, rack of lamb with onion marmalade and red wine jus, and hot apple flan with Calvados ice cream. Interesting and varied list of wines.

Owners: Martin James & Jan Williams
Cost: Alc £25, set-price L £9.95 (2 courses)/D £16.95. ☺ H/wine £10.50
Times: Noon-2pm/6-10pm.
Closed Sun, 2 wks Jan
Seats: 30. Private dining room 20
Smoking: No-smoking area
Accommodation: 4 en suite

Directions: Telephone for directions

LLANDUDNO,

St Tudno Hotel

Promenade LL30 2LP
Map 6: SH78
Tel: 01492 874411
Fax: 01492 860407
Chef: David Harding
Owners: Martin & Janette Bland
Cost: Set-price L £16.50/D £32.50 (5 courses). H/wine £9.50
Times: 12.30-1.45pm/7-9.30pm
Additional: Bar food L; Sunday L; Children 8+ in restaurant; ⚫ dishes
Seats: 60

Charming Victorian, terraced seafront hotel, with connections to Alice (of Wonderland fame). The decor of the Garden Room Restaurant is striking – greens and yellows with lime-green cane-backed chairs, Chinese Chippendale-style painted panels and dramatic green trellis paper (the latter hand-printed in New York). Hanging baskets of ivy and corner baskets of flowers help the restaurant live up to its name. David Harding's signature dishes include terrine of smoked chicken and foie gras with apricot chutney, and saddle of Welsh lamb with a chive potato cake, roasted garlic and lemon sauce. Local seafood is given due prominence: fish soup with fennel and a liaison of garlic and herbs; Conwy mussel risotto with saffron; grilled fillet of sea bass with spicy crab cake, noisette potatoes and French beans. There's a taste of Wales in the popular bara brith-and-butter pudding with Can-y-Delyn ice cream, and it's a national battle between farmhouse Celtic cheeses and English Stilton. Vegetarian dish of the day may be goats' cheese and leek tartlet with tomato compote. The wine list has plenty of interesting drinking at keen prices. This is a hotel restaurant with a strong reputation, booking is advisable.

Smoking: No smoking in dining room; Air conditioning
Accommodation: 20 en suite ★ ★

Directions: Town centre, on Promenade opposite the pier entrance

AA Shortlisted for Wine Award-see page 16

TREFRIW,
Princes Arms Hotel

LL27 0JP
Map 6: SH76
Tel: 01492 640592
Fax: 01492 640559
Cost: *Alc* £22.50, set-price L
£12.50/D £17.50. ☺ H/wine £9
Times: Noon-2.15pm/6-9pm
Additional: Bar food; Sunday L;
Children welcome; ✿ dishes
Smoking: No smoking in dining room
Accommodation: 14 en suite ★★

Directions: At far end of village on L

*Newly refurbished hotel in the lovely Conwy Valley. Good choice of
honest, accurate cooking (plus tasty home-made bread). Try chicken
breast stuffed with red peppers and herbs with a cider and Calvados
sauce. Affable service.*

DENBIGHSHIRE

LLANDEGLA,
Bodidris Hall

Wrexham LL11 3AL
Map 7: SJ25
Tel: 01978 790434
Fax: 01978 790335
Telephone for further details

*In spite of its remote location, this impressively beamed
restaurant remains popular.* There is a set-price menu with
intermediate courses costing extra. Home-made canapés are
served in the bar and include very light cheese puffs and
cheese beignets with chorizzo. The kitchen relies on local and
home-grown produce and produces the likes of delicious salads
packed with local wild herbs, and some excellent courgette
flowers stuffed with salmon mousse and teamed with seared
scallops and black olive oil vinaigrette. Main courses could
include slices of charred peppered duck breast served with
lime, an apple and cranberry compote, fondant potatoes,
cauliflower, mange-touts, asparagus and carrots. A light
chocolate and orange parfait served with crème anglaise is
recommended. The wine list is comprehensive and the service
charmingly directed by the proprietor.

Directions: Llandegla is on A525
(Wrexham-Ruthin). In village (from
Wrexham direction) turn R onto
A5104. Hotel is signed 1 mile on L

LLANDRILLO,
Tyddyn Llan Hotel

Corwen
LL21 0ST
Map 6: SJ03
Tel: 01490 440264
Fax: 01490 440414
Chef: Jason Hornbuckle
Owners: Peter & Bridget Kindred
Cost: *Alc* £17.50, set-price L £15/D
£27. H/wine £13.50

*Built as a hunting lodge around 250 years ago, Tyddyn Llan
is in landscaped gardens among fine scenery.* Log fires burn in
winter, and a fountain tinkles away outside. The hotel has its
own stretch of fishing on the Dee, and salmon might turn up
on the menu too, perhaps with braised fennel, couscous and
gazpacho sauce, or smoked and seared and served with spicy
avocado salsa and balsamic dressing. The kitchen hangs on to a

Tyddyn Llan Hotel

Times: Noon-2pm/7-9pm.
Closed L Mon, 2 wks Jan
Additional: Bar food L; Sunday L;
Children welcome; 🌢 dishes
Seats: 60. Private dining room 30
Smoking: No smoking in dining room
Accommodation: 10 en suite ★ ★

Directions: Take B4401 from Corwen
to Llandrillo. Restaurant on R leaving
village

sense of tradition, so alongside trendy ingredients of pesto, pea risotto, pancetta and sun-dried tomatoes might be a starter of pressed tongue with mustard mayonnaise and Madeira sauce, and a main course of grilled ribeye of local Black beef in red wine sauce with gratin dauphinoise and parsnip purée. Seasonality is at the core: Welsh lamb is stuffed and rolled and served with a walnut-infused jus, breast of guinea fowl is roasted and accompanied by black pudding and a morel sauce. A savoury, such as Welsh rarebit with anchovies and pickled tomatoes, normally appears to round things off, together with sweeteners of perhaps mango crème brûlée with lime sorbet. The solid wine list has much of interest.

LLANGOLLEN,
Bryn Howel Hotel

Carefully extended 19th-century house with magnificent views across the Vale of Llangollen. The Cedar Tree Restaurant features myriad home-made breads and dishes such as delice of salmon topped with fillet of plaice and a fennel purée in filo pastry.

Directions: Two miles east of Llangollen on A539

LL20 7UW
Map 7: SJ24
Tel: 01978 860331
Fax: 01978 860119
Telephone for further details

RUTHIN, Ye Olde Anchor ✿

Rhos Street LL15 1DX
Map 6: SJ15
Tel: 01824 702813
Fax: 01824 703050
Telephone for further details

Directions: Situated in Ruthin at the
junction of A525 & A494

Old world dining room complete with oak beams and wooden tables and adjoining the bar. The menu specialises in steaks and chicken with a separate list of fish and some special dishes.

FLINTSHIRE

EWLOE, St David's Park

St David's Park CH5 3YB
Map 7: SJ36
Tel: 01244 520800
Fax: 01244 520930
Cost: *Alc* £35, set-price L £13.95 (2 courses)/D £19.50. ☺ H/wine £12.95
Times: Noon-2.30pm/7-10pm
Additional: Bar food; Sunday L; Children welcome; ✿ dishes
Smoking: No smoking in dining room; Air conditioning
Accommodation: 145 en suite
★ ★ ★ ★

A fine hotel with a spacious restaurant and a fine wine list. The food takes a modern view along the lines of feuilleté of bass and mullet layered between slices of aubergine and drizzled with chilli oil, and breast of chicken stuffed with asparagus.

Directions: A494 Queensferry to Mold for 4 miles, then B5127 towards Buckley

Shortlisted for
AA Wine Award-see page 16

NORTHOP, Soughton Hall Hotel ✿✿

Soughton Hall, its mellow stone façade covered in creeper, was built in the early 18th century along the lines of a French château. First impressions, as you drive along a lime-lined avenue, are not let down by the interior: antiques, Persian carpets, impressive flower arrangements, although the atmosphere is unstuffy and relaxed. You can eat (and drink real ales) in the ex-stables amid cartwheel-hung bare-brick walls, where fish and steaks are the order of the day, and in the restaurant, with its formal place settings on polished wooden tables. Dinner here is a set-price three or four courses with the kitchen concentrating on local produce. River Dee salmon is served as a salad starter with horseradish cream, baby new potatoes and beetroot crisps, Welsh goats' cheese goes into a tian, pan-fried fillet of local beef comes as a main course with wild mushroom ravioli and Puy lentil sauce, while fish could extend to grilled fillets of sea bass with provençale vegetables. Chocoholics will die for the assiette of chocolate.

CH7 6AB
Map 7: SJ26
Tel: 01352 840811
Fax: 01352 840382
Chef: John Holland
Owners: John & Rosemary Rodenhurst
Cost: *Alc* £29.95, set-price L & D £32.90 (5 courses). H/wine £8.50
Times: Noon-1.45pm/7-9.30pm. Closed L Thu, all Sun, Bhs
Additional: Children 15+
Seats: 45. Private dining room 20
Smoking: No smoking in dining room
Accommodation: 12 en suite ★ ★ ★

Directions: Exit A55 at Northrop, follow A5119 towards Mold. 0.5 mile, hotel is signposted on L

GWYNEDD

ABERDYFI, Maybank Hotel

Attractive restaurant with views over the bay. The set choice menu offers honest cooking along the lines of a delicate crab gratinée with ginger and cheese, and fillet of pork with bacon and a light grain mustard sauce.

4 Penhelig Road Penhelig LL35 0PT
Tel: 01654 767500
Telephone for further details

Directions: From E on A483 500yds before village sign

ABERDYFI,
Penhelig Arms

LL35 0LT
Map 6: SN69
Tel: 01654 767215
Fax: 01654 767690
Cost: Set-price D £19.50. ☺
H/wine £9.50
Times: Noon-2pm/7-9pm.
Closed 25 Dec
Additional: Bar food; Sunday L;
Children welcome; ☙ dishes
Smoking: No smoking in dining room
Accommodation: 10 en suite ★ ★

Directions: From Machynlleth take
A439 coastal route (9 miles)

*A 17th-century building with a newly decorated restaurant in Cape
Cod style. Expect the likes of fresh sardines, chargrilled tuna steak,
and lemon and lime soufflé.*

ABERDYFI, Plas Penhelig

LL35 0NA
Map 6: SN69
Tel: 01654 767676
Fax: 01654 767783
Cost: Set-price L £13.50/D £20. ☺
H/wine £10.75
Times: 12.30-1.45pm/7.30-8.45pm.
Closed Jan-Feb

*Classic Edwardian country house hotel where you can work up an
appetite with croquet, and dine well on medallions of pork fillet with
wholegrain mustard sauce, before succumbing to the temptations of
'Wicked Chocolate Pudding'.*

Additional: Bar food L; Sunday L; Children 8+; ☙ dishes
Smoking: No smoking in dining room
Accommodation: 11 en suite ★ ★ ★

Directions: From Machynlleth take A493 coastal route (9 miles)

ABERSOCH, Neigwl Hotel

Lon Sarn Bach Pwllheli LL53 7DY
Map 6: SH32
Tel: 01758 712363
Fax: 01758 712544
Cost: Set-price D £20 (4 courses). ☺
Times: D only, 7-9pm

*Hotel restaurant overlooking Cardigan Bay, offering a four-course
menu using fresh local produce in dishes such as fricassée of
seafood in piquant sauce, and medallions of fillet of lamb.*

Additional: Children welcome; ☙ dishes
Accommodation: 9 en suite ★ ★

Directions: 400 yards through village centre on the L

ABERSOCH,
Porth Tocyn Hotel ✿✿

Bwlch Tocyn Pwllheli LL53 7BU
Map 6: SH32
Tel: 01758 713303
Fax: 01758 713538
Chefs: David Carney,
Louise Fletcher-Brewer
Owners: The Fletcher-Brewer Family
Cost: Set-price D £30 (5 courses).
H/wine £10.95
Times: Noon-1.45pm/7.30-9.30pm.
Closed mid Nov-wk before Easter

***Family hotel enjoying an enviable position high above
Cardigan Bay.*** Run by the Fletcher-Brewer family for over
half a century, this is a quintessential country hotel. The airy,
antique-furnished dining room makes the best of the stunning
panoramic view, extending as far as Snowdonia, and offers a
daily-changing four-course menu. After starters that might
include Welsh rarebit-glazed bubble-and-squeak on roast
tomato sauce, there is always a soup before the five main
course choices. These offer something to suit most tastes be it

Porth Tocyn Hotel

Additional: Bar food L; Sunday L; Children 7+ at D; ☺ dishes
Seats: 50. Jacket and tie preferred
Smoking: No smoking in dining room
Accommodation: 17 en suite ★★★

Directions: 2.5 miles beyond village of Abersoch, through hamlets of Sarn Bach and Bwlch Tocyn. Follow signs marked 'Gwesty/Hotel' and 'Remote Hotel' from Sarn Bach onwards

herb-crusted roast fillet of beef with mustard and thyme cream and shallot confit, delice of plaice with a timbale of lemongrass and saffron rice and green peppercorn sauce, or a vegetarian option such as baked plum tomato tarte Tatin with balsamic and pesto cream. Puddings might include tiramisu and banana fritters with hot butterscotch sauce. A wide-ranging wine list completes the picture.

ABERSOCH,

The White House Hotel ✿

Pwllheli LL53 7AG
Map 6: SH32
Tel: 01758 713427
Fax: 01758 713512
Cost: *Alc* £30, set-price D £21.50. ☺
H/wine £12
Times: D only, 7-8.30pm.
Closed Xmas wk
Additional: Sunday L (noon-1.15pm); Children welcome; ☺ dishes
Smoking: No smoking in dining room
Accommodation: 13 en suite ★★★

Directions: Hotel on A499 Pwllheli/Abersoch Road, on R (from Pwllheli)

There are magnificent views over Cardigan Bay from the elegant, spacious restaurant. Welsh lamb and beef, fresh crab and lobster feature in robust, well-sauced dishes. The extensive carte is supplemented by a nightly dinner menu.

BALA, **Palé Hall** ✿✿

Country house hotel rating high on the luxury scale. Queen Victoria slept here, and the room she occupied is now much in demand. How amused she would have been. There's a fine entrance hall, with vaulted ceiling and galleried oak staircase, a library bar, two elegant lounges and the baronial-style, candlelit dining room with original hand-carved Japanese oak dresser. The short fixed-price menu makes good use of local produce, and the cooking is carefully executed with some unusual combinations – langoustine tails in filo pastry with sweet-and-sour pineapple cream, for example. More straightforward offerings include noisettes of lamb with

Palé Estate Llandderfel LL23 7PS
Map 6: SH93
Tel: 01678 530285
Fax: 01678 530220
Chef: Wendy Phillips
Cost: Set-price L £15.95/D £23.95.
H/wine £9.95
Times: Noon-2pm/7-8.30pm
Additional: Sunday L; ☺ dishes
Smoking: No smoking in dining room
Seats: 40. Private dining room 18.
Jacket & tie preferred
Accommodation: 17 en suite ★★★

Palé Hall

rosemary and garlic-scented mash, garlic confit and sage and onion sauce, and chocolate cappuccino mousse with bitter chocolate sauce. Breakfasts are taken in the old kitchen, alongside the blackened range.

Directions: Just off B4401, 4 miles from Llandrillo

BARMOUTH,

Ty'r Graig Castle Hotel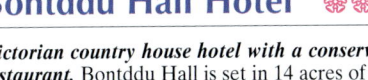

Victorian property built in the shape of a double-barrelled shotgun by Greener the gunsmith. Dishes range from chicken Tahiti to medallions of Welsh beef with tomato couscous.

Smoking: No smoking in dining room
Accommodation: 12 en suite ★ ★

Directions: On coast road 0.75 mile towards Harlech

Llanaber Road LL42 1YN
Map 6: SH61
Tel: 01341 280470
Fax: 01341 281260
Cost: Set-price D £18.50. ☺
H/wine £8.90
Times: 12.30-2pm/7-9pm. Closed Jan
Additional: Bar food L; Sunday L;
Children welcome; ◕ dishes

BARMOUTH,

Wavecrest Hotel ✿

Country cooking using local produce highlights Shelagh Jarman's excellent set-dinner menus at her delightful seafront hotel. Expect a friendly, relaxed atmosphere and dishes like asparagus soup, loin of lamb with redcurrant and rosemary sauce, and Cheshire pudding.

Directions: On seafront, at the centre of the promenade

8 Marine Parade LL42 1NA
Map 6: SH61
Tel/Fax: 01341 280330
Telephone for further details

BONTDDU,

Bontddu Hall Hotel ✿✿

Victorian country house hotel with a conservatory-style restaurant. Bontddu Hall is set in 14 acres of grounds within the Snowdonia National Park. The restaurant affords wonderful views overlooking the Mawddach estuary, the mountains and the sea. There is a light brasserie-style lunch menu and a more formal set-dinner menu in a style of cooking that is described as classical French and British. Local produce such as Ynys Mon mussels are juxtaposed against the pearls of honeydew melon. Rack of Meirionnydd mountain lamb with a

Dolgellau
LL40 2UF
Map 6: SH61
Tel: 01341 430661
Fax: 01341 430284
Chef: David Murphy
Owners: Michael & Margaretta Ball
Cost: *Alc* D £19.50, set-price L £14/D
£25. ☺ H/wine £13
Times: Noon-2pm/7-9.30pm.
Closed Jan, Feb

Bontddu Hall Hotel

Additional: Bar food; Sunday L; Children 3+; ✿ dishes
Seats: 60. Private room 30. Jacket and tie preferred
Smoking: No smoking in dining room
Accommodation: 20 en suite ★ ★ ★

Directions: From A470 1 mile N Dolgellau take A496 to Barmouth, then 4 miles to Bontddu. Hotel on R on entering village

rich plum sauce or tenderloin pork wrapped in bacon roasted and served on a spaghetti of vegetables on orange and coconut cream are good choices. Desserts include classics such as lemon meringue pie, Pavlova and Bakewell tart.

CAERNARFON, **Seiont Manor Hotel** ✿

A splendid hotel set amidst tranquil Welsh countryside close to Snowdon. The highlight of our autumn meal was a 'pristinely fresh' sea bass with spinach and red pesto, but the chocolate tart for dessert was also enjoyed.

Accommodation: 28 en suite ★ ★ ★

Directions: From Bangor follow signs for Caernarfon. Leave Caernarfon on A4086. The hotel is 3 miles on L

Llanrug LL55 2AQ
Map 6: SH46
Tel: 01286 673366
Fax: 01286 672840
Cost: *Alc* £22.80, set-price L £10.50 (2 courses)/D £23.50. ☺ H/wine £10
Times: Noon-2pm/7-10pm
Additional: Bar food; Sunday L; Children welcome; ✿ dishes
Smoking: No smoking in dining room

CAERNARFON, **Ty'n Rhos** ✿✿

The appeal of this peaceful converted farmhouse, other than its idyllic rural setting and views extending to the Isle of Anglesey, lies in the sound cooking. Meticulous shopping for the best local produce and the use of home-grown fruit, herbs and vegetables ensures the quality. Traditional dishes are given a modern twist and those sampled at inspection showed a good degree of technical and presentational skills. Beyond a well-balanced set menu, the *carte* may offer warm smoked haddock and tomato tart with gazpacho dressing , followed by sea bass with Mediterranean-style vegetables and saffron sauce or rack of

Llanddeiniolen LL55 3AE
Map 6: SH56
Tel: 01248 670489
Fax: 01248 670079
Chef: Carys Davies
Owners: Nigel & Lynda Kettle
Cost: *Alc* £27, set-price D £19.50 (4 courses). ☺ H/wine £9.50
Times: D only, 7-9.30pm. Closed D Sun, 1 wk Aug, 1 wk Xmas, 1 wk Jan (restricted service)
Additional: Sunday L (noon-2.30pm); Children 6+; ✿ dishes
Seats: 25. Private dining room 20
Smoking: No smoking in dining room
Accommodation: 14 en suite ★ ★

Directions: In hamlet of Seion between B4366 & B4547

lamb with rosemary and lemon flavoured couscous and red wine sauce. Pear clafoutis tart and Hensir cheese with home-made oatcakes may be offered for dessert. Efficient and friendly staff.

DOLGELLAU, Dolserau Hall

The Victorian conservatory is now the setting for some traditional cooking, perhaps grilled trout with lemon and dill butter sauce, or casserole of venison in red wine sauce and plenty of fresh vegetables.

Accommodation: 15 en suite ★★

Directions: Situated 1.5 miles from Dolgellau on lane between A470 to Dinas Mawddwy and A494 to Bala

LL40 2AG
Map 6: SH71
Tel: 01341 422522
Fax: 01341 422400
Cost: Set-price D £19.95 (4 courses).
☺ H/wine £7.50
Times: D only, 7-8.30pm.
Closed Nov-mid Feb
Additional: Children 6+; ✿ dishes
Smoking: No smoking in dining room

DOLGELLAU, Penmaenuchaf Hall

Penmaenpool LL40 1YB
Map 6: SH71
Tel: 01341 422129
Fax: 01341 422787
Chefs: Wayne Roberts, David Banks
Owners: Mark Watson, Lorraine Fielding
Cost: *Alc* £30, set-price L £14.95/D £26.50 (4 courses). H/wine £11
Times: Noon-2pm/7-9.30pm.
Closed 2nd wk Jan
Additional: Bar food L; Sunday L; Children 6+; ✿ dishes
Seats: 36. Private dining room 16. Jacket & tie preferred
Smoking: No smoking in dining room
Accommodation: 14 en suite ★★★

Welsh slate manor house full of traditional Welsh hospitality. 'Taste the treats of Penmaenpool' advised Gerard Manley Hopkins to those who 'pine for peace and pleasure'. This is indeed a lovely area of mountains and valleys within the Snowdonia National Park. Local produce dots the menu: Menai oysters are poached with smoked ham and red wine dressing; warm fillets of marinated Barmouth mackerel are served with a herb mayonnaise. Local pheasant is given added interest with roast artichokes and pomegranate juices, whilst rib-eye of Bala Black beef is handled classically with local woodland mushrooms and button onions. As an alternative to warm chocolate and hazelnut fondant there's a selection of Welsh cheeses with home-baked bread, celery and grapes.

Directions: From A470, take A493 (Tywyn/Fairbourne), entrance 1.5 miles on L by sign for Penmaenpool

DOLGELLAU, Plas Dolmelynllyn

Old stone-country house hotel with a traditional half-panelled dining room. Bruschetta of roasted goats' cheese might be followed by chargrilled cutlet of salmon and pear tarte Tatin.

Smoking: No smoking in dining room
Accommodation: 10 en suite ★★★

Directions: Village centre on A470, 4 miles N of Dolgellau

Ganllwyd LL40 2HP
Map 6: SH71
Tel: 01341 440273
Fax: 01341 440640
Cost: Set-price D £24.50 (4 courses).
☺
Times: D only, 7-8.30pm.
Closed Nov-Mar
Additional: Bar food L; Children 10+; ✿ dishes

HARLECH, Castle Cottage

Close to Harlech's ancient castle, this quaint 16th-century beamed restaurant has a super atmosphere and a growing reputation for good modern Welsh cooking based on fresh seasonal produce. Chef-patron Glyn Roberts is passionate about his food, so a meal from his sensibly short menu may begin with a rustic terrine with onion marmalade, or Welsh haggis with bashed neeps and whisky gravy. For a main course you may choose herb-crusted rack of lamb with garlic mash and red wine sauce or, perhaps, go for the baked salmon served on herb tagliatelle with a tarragon and white wine cream sauce. Round off with banana and rum strudel or a deliciously light and satisfyingly rich date sponge with butterscotch sauce. Reasonably priced global list of wines.

Directions: Just off High Street (B4573) 100yds from Harlech Castle

Pen Llech LL46 2YL
Map 6: SH53
Tel/Fax: 01766 780479
Chef: Glyn Roberts
Owners: Glyn & Jacqueline Roberts
Cost: Set-price D £22.50. ☺
H/wine £10.50
Times: D only, 7-9.30pm.
Closed 3 wks Jan
Additional: Children welcome;
🍴 dishes
Seats: 45
Smoking: No smoking in dining room
Accommodation: 6 rooms (4 en suite)

LLANBERIS, Y Bistro

Regularly changing menu in Welsh with English translations at this long-standing restaurant, now in its 20th year. Good cooking puts the emphasis on flavour.

Directions: In the centre of the village at the foot of Mount Snowdon by Lake Padarn

43-45 Stryd Fawr (High Street)
LL55 4EU
Map 6: SH56
Tel/Fax: 01286 871278
Telephone for further details

PORTMEIRION,
The Hotel Portmeirion

LL48 6ET
Map 6: SH53
Tel: 01766 770000
Fax: 01766 771331
Chef: Colin Pritchard
Cost: *Alc* £31.50, set-price L
£11.50/D £31.50. H/wine £11
Times: 12.30-2pm/7-9.30pm. Closed
L Mon
Additional: Sunday L;
Children welcome; 🍴 dishes
Seats: 100.
Private dining rooms 12 & 30
Smoking: No smoking in dining room
Accommodation: 40 en suite ★ ★ ★

Directions: Off A487 at Minffordd

The hotel has an idyllic setting near the shore and the restaurant overlooks the Traeth Bach estuary. The hotel is based on the early Victorian villa; the old house was converted into a hotel in 1926. The curvilinear dining room was added in the 1930s and now offers a daily set-price menu using local produce. The cooking, is modern Welsh with many Mediterranean influences: a first coure of fillet of monkfish marinated in lemon juice, dill and olive oil, for example. Of five main courses, shank of Welsh lamb on a bed of creamed leeks with a red wine jus was "excellent". This came with pommes Macaire, broccoli, swede, haricots verts and tomato topped with a garlic crumble. An individual chocolate tart had a light pastry and a good rich filling. There is also an extensive and interesting wine list. Staff are pleasant and helpful.

PWLLHELI, **Plas Bodegroes**

This Georgian manor in tranquil grounds is a Grade II listed building. But there's nothing dated about the restaurant, despite period furnishings, with its restful colour scheme, track lighting, illuminated display cabinets and collection of contemporary Welsh art. Sunday lunch is worth a detour: watercress soup, perhaps, then mushroom-stuffed braised leg of guinea fowl with cabbage and bacon, as well as chocolate mousse with coffee sauce. Good-quality raw materials, most locally sourced, are cooked plainly and honestly and without prissiness and pretension to produce dishes that are often robust of flavour, from roast tomato and garlic soup, to seared fillet of salmon with laverbread and artichoke risotto. A pungent smoked haddock tart with chervil salad with 'excellent' citrus dressing, or warm ballotine of quail with braised vegetables might be among the half-dozen or so starters. Exemplary black beef, paprika-crusted, served with well-matched cep sauce and sour cream mash, or confit and smoked breast of Hereford duck in Madeira sauce with celeriac champ might be featured among the same number of main courses. It's good to see a savoury like Welsh rarebit with walnut and celery salad alongside puddings of a well-balanced gratin of sweet pears with sharper poire William sorbet. The house selection of wines numbers almost 20 bottles, with quality the keynote, although the rest of the list is rewarding too, with some notable producers.

Nefyn Road LL53 5TH
Map 6: SH33
Tel: 01758 612363
Fax: 01758 701247
Chefs: Chris Chown, Shaun Mitchell
Owners: Chris & Gunna Chown
Cost: *Alc* £29.50. ☺ H/wine £12
Times: D only, 7-9pm.
Closed Mon, Dec-Feb
Additional: Sunday L (Noon-2pm)
Seats: 35. Private dining room 16
Smoking: No smoking in dining room
Accommodation: 11 en suite ★★

Directions: On A497, 2 miles NW of Pwllheli

TALSARNAU,
Hotel Maes y Neuadd

Comfortable, welcoming manor sits in its own pretty, well-tended grounds, overlooking the kitchen gardens and the Snowdonia National Park beyond. Given the wealth of home-grown fresh produce (with the gardeners credited on the menu) and regional specialities, the kitchen has plenty of good food with which to work. Dinners are priced according to the number of courses chosen and daily changing dishes might include a salad of pigeon, pine nuts, lentils and a raspberry and mint dressing. Signature dishes include loin of lamb wrapped in apple and black pudding mousse with fondant potatoes, braised shallots and pear chutney. The 'Grande Finale' of cheeses and desserts has become something of a house speciality, much anticipated after a day's rambling. An impressive wine list includes plenty of halves and glasses.

Harlech LL47 6YA
Map 6: SH63
Tel: 01766 780200
Fax: 01766 780211
Chef: Peter Jackson
Owners: June & Michael Slatter, Olive & Malcolm Horsfall
Cost: Set-price L £13.75/D £33 (5 courses). H/wine £12.15
Times: Noon-1.30pm/7-8.45pm
Additional: Bar food L; Sunday L; Children 8+; ◑ dishes
Seats: 50. Private dining room 12
Smoking: No smoking in dining room
Accommodation: 16 en suite ★★

Directions: Off B4573 between Talsarnau & Harlech (sign on corner of unclassified road)

TAL-Y-BONT, **Lodge Hotel** ✿

Peaceful hotel in the Conwy valley. The restaurant makes the most of produce from the hotel's own vegetable garden – try Welsh lamb cutlets glazed with heather honey, or baked trout with a light caper and lemon sauce.

Smoking: No smoking in dining room
Accommodation: 14 en suite ★★

Directions: From Conwy Castle take B5106 to village of Tal-y-Bont. The Lodge is on R, 100yds into village

Conwy LL32 8YX
Map 6: SH67
Tel: 01492 660766
Fax: 01492 660534
Cost: *Alc* £19.50, set-price L £6.95/D £16.95. ☺ H/wine £9.95
Times: Noon-1.45pm(3pm Sun)/7-8.45pm. Closed L Mon, & check winter opening times
Additional: Sunday L; Children welcome; ◑ dishes

MONMOUTHSHIRE

ABERGAVENNY,
Llansantffraed Court Hotel

Llanvihangel Gobion NP7 9BA
Map 3: SO21
Tel: 01873 840678
Fax: 01873 840674
Chef: Didier Bienaimé
Owners: Mike & Heather Morgan
Cost: *Alc* £26, set-price L £14.50/D
£19.50. ☺ H/wine £9.95
Times: Noon-2pm/7.30-9.30pm
Additional: Sunday L; Children
welcome; ⬧ dishes
Seats: 50. Private dining room 26
Smoking: No smoking in dining room
Accommodation: 21 en suite ★ ★ ★

Directions: From Abergavenny take
B4598 signposted Usk towards
Raglan. After 3.5 miles, white gates
on L are hotel entrance

*This imposing red brick mansion, about ten miles from
Abergavenny, is set in its own grounds with a small lake and
fountain.* The interior is Italianate in style, and there is an
outdoor terrace where aperitifs are served. The dining room is
warm and comfortable, decorated with oak beams and oil
paintings. Starters can include a Caesar-style salad with
artichoke hearts in a wholemeal crisp pancake and eight or so
main courses rely on local beef and lamb. Fillet of Welsh beef
crepinette with foie gras and pistachio nut mousse with whisky
and white peppercorn sauce was notable for the good quality
of the beef. Cheeses are Welsh, desserts such as sticky toffee
pudding, and trio of chocolates, are fairly run of the mill.

ABERGAVENNY,
Llanwenarth Arms

*The hotel is set in the shadow of the Sugar Loaf with a restaurant
overlooking the river. An interestling carte, plus daily specials, offers
dishes based on fresh ingredients.*

Directions: On A40 midway between Abergavenny and
Crickhowell

Brecon Road NP8 1EP
Map 3: SO21
Tel: 01873 810550
Fax: 01873 811880
Telephone for further details

CHEPSTOW,
Marriott St Pierre Hotel NEW

*The Orangery is a circular restaurant attached to the 14th-century
manor house. Typical dishes include seared fillet of red snapper,
twice-baked cheese soufflé, and roulade of pork.*

Smoking: No smoking in dining room
Accommodation: 148 en suite ★ ★ ★ ★

Directions: From J2, M48 follow A466 towards Chepstow. Take
3rd exit at 1st roundabout, and at next take A48 signposted to
Caerwent. Hotel 2 miles on L

St Pierre Park NP6 6YA
Map 3: ST59
Tel: 01291 625261
Fax: 01291 629975
Cost: *Alc* £22.50, set-price D £22.50.
☺ H/wine £11.95
Times: D only, 7-10pm
Additional: Sunday L (1-2pm);
Children welcome; ⬧ dishes

CHEPSTOW, **Wye Knot** ❀❀

The Back, NP6 5HH
Map 3: ST59
Tel: 01291 622929
Chef: Kevin Brookes
Owners: Kevin Brookes, Lisa
Mansfield
Cost: *Alc* £30, set-price L £11.95. ☺
H/wine £10
Times: 12.30-2pm/6.30-10pm.
Closed L Sat, D Sun, all Mon
Additional: Sunday L;
Children welcome; ❀ dishes
Seats: 35
Smoking: No smoking in dining room

Directions: From M4 take M48, then
onto Chepstow, following signs for
Chepstow Castle & Riverbank

*Small, cosy, homely restaurant, rather tucked away but right
on the River Wye.* There's a little bar-lounge, mismatched
chairs, white tablecloths and napkins and a blackboard menu
offering the likes of tian of crab with mango and avocado on
chilli and coriander salsa, and grilled goats' cheese with sautéed
chicken livers and baby spinach. Fillet steak in Madeira sauce
on Puy lentils with foie gras ravioli makes a very successful
main course, and there may be prime rump of Welsh lamb in its
own cooking juices with fondant potatoes and root vegetables,
or supreme of salmon with crispy Parma ham. Steamed lemon
sponge with lemon custard and praiseworthy lemon curd ice
cream is a good combination, and summer pudding puts in an
appearance at the right time of year. Miniature Welsh cakes 'an
inspired choice,' are among the petits fours, the home-made
cheese bread is said to be particularly good, and there are some
interesting wines by the glass.

LLANDEWI SKIRRID,

Walnut Tree Inn ❀❀❀

Abergavenny NP7 8AW
Map 3: SO31
Tel: 01873 852797
Chef: Franco Taruschio
Owners: Ann & Franco Taruschio
Times: L Bistro only/D from 7pm.
Closed Sun, Mon
Additional: Children welcome;
❀ dishes
Seats: 46 (60 Bistro)
Smoking: Air conditioning
Credit cards: None

Directions: Three miles NE of
Abergavenny on B4521

'Arriving at noon on the Tuesday after a Bank Holiday and the
place was heaving,' noted an inspector of this pub restaurant
outside Abergavenny. Indeed, people drive for miles for one of
the cramped, close-set tables here, as they've done for over 30
years, in surroundings as unsophisticated as you'd expect for its
bucolic setting. To say that Italian cooking is the attraction is to
oversimplify matters, because the style is unique. There may be
spaghetti with cockle sauce, crab tagliolini, and brodetto, but
Franco Taruschio somehow finds the best and often unusual
ingredients and turns them into his own creations on a menu
that might run to around 15 starters and the same number of
main courses. Game – hare agrodolce, pheasant with cabbage
and quince, roast woodcock – appears alongside fish dishes of
pan-fried sea bass with wild mushrooms and pancetta, cold
crab with lemon dressing, and panaché of steamed mixed fish
with balsamic dressing. Lady Llanover has been immortalised
by her salt duck, here served with preserves, and an 18th-
century recipe is the basis for another starter of vincigrassi
maceratese, a mound of leaves of pasta with porcini, truffles
and Parma ham. The Sicilian Jewish community is evidently
responsible for escalope of salmon with asparagus and a
rhubarb sauce hinting of ginger, and there's a bit of a mixed-
race background to carré of Welsh lamb with borlotti beans

and polenta. Leave room for pudding: a trio of chocolate, say (white chocolate pannacotta, a slice of dark marquise, and a scoop of ice cream, all on crème anglaise), or banana parfait, from a list of around 20. An impressive wine list concentrates on Italy, although France and the New World are well represented too.

LLANGYBI,

Cwrt Bleddyn Hotel

Usk NP5 1PG
Map 3: ST39
Tel: 01633 450521
Fax: 01633 450220
Telephone for further details

Set in parkland in the Welsh borders, Jesters Restaurant offers a wide variety of dishes to suit the mainly corporate mid-weekers and local guests looking for something special.
The bright red and yellow menu is divided thus: the opening act, the missing part, the main scene, supporting acts, the extras and the finale. Local produce is used, though presentation of the food can vary. Excellent quality asparagus was cooked just right and served with a lovely sharp Welsh goats' cheese and was followed by brill stuffed with a shellfish mousseline, chocolate orange tart for dessert was first-class, served with a white chocolate ice cream.

Directions: Near Llangybi village on A449 between Caerleon and Usk

TINTERN,

Parva Farmhouse Hotel

Chepstow NP6 6SQ
Map 3: SO50
Tel: 01291 689411
Fax: 01291 689557
Cost: Set-price D £19.50 (4 courses).
☺ H/wine £8.75
Times: D only, 7-8.30pm
Additional: Children welcome;
🍴 dishes

Sympathetically converted 17th-century farmhouse retaining many period features. The homely dining room is the setting for robust home cooking. Inspection yielded a rich crab pâté, and a good monkfish portugaise.

Smoking: No smoking in dining room
Accommodation: 9 en suite ★ ★

Directions: North end of Tintern on A466 alongside the Wye, 0.75 mile from the Abbey

TINTERN,

Royal George Hotel

Chepstow NP6 6SF
Map 3: SO50
Tel: 01291 689205
Fax: 01291 689448
Telephone for further details

Directions: On A466 between Chepstow & Monmouth, 10 minutes drive from M4 J22

Delightful family-run hotel set in extensive grounds. A flavourful pâté, tender chicken topped with orange flavoured hollandaise, and steamed ginger pudding are menu examples.

USK,
The Bush House at Usk

Intimate little restaurant with simple, traditional furnishings – lots of green and reds, Toulouse Lautrec posters, terracotta pots. Simple, honest cooking with a menu that takes on the world. Expect Thai fishcakes, steak and ale pie, and Welsh lamb with ratatouille and caramelised garlic.

Additional: Bar food L; Sunday L; dishes
Smoking: No-smoking area; No pipes & cigars;
Air conditioning

Directions: Take the Usk exit from A449. Restaurant in centre of town

15 Bridge Street NP5 1BQ
Map 3: SO30
Tel: 01291 672929
Fax: 01291 671215
Cost: *Alc* £18, set-price D £12.95. ☺
H/wine £8.95
Times: Noon-3.30pm/7-9.30pm.
Closed D Sun

USK,
Three Salmons Hotel

Former coaching inn situated in pretty Usk town centre. Here, a long menu offers plenty of choice. Try perhaps the mini beef Wellingtons with smoked salmon and horseradish, followed by the sautéed calves' liver with caramelised onions and mustard mash.

Directions: M4 J24, A449 N, first L A472 to Usk. Hotel in centre of village

Bridge Street NP5 1BQ
Map 3: SO30
Tel: 01291 672133
Fax: 01291 673979
Telephone for further details

WHITEBROOK,
Crown at Whitebrook 🌸🌸🌸

This may be Wales, but it's hard to escape the word 'auberge' in relation to Sandra and Roger Bates' cheerful, unpretentious restaurant-with-rooms and the Gallic leanings of the cooking. Lunch is a particular bargain, only a tad less ambitious than dinner, but compromising not one jot on quality. There is a country earthiness to sautéed lambs kidneys and sausages with rice, or fillet of beef with a black pudding crust, roasted shallots and port wine sauce, whilst French formality shapes a rack of Welsh lamb and lamb farce cooked in a puff pastry trellis on a white onion purée with caper jus. Excellent shellfish and prawn ragout with tomato linguini shows a lighter, more southern influence. Desserts are generally bold and satisfying, along the lines of treacle tart and rhubarb crème brûlée. An excellent wine list offers heaps of well-chosen, characterful bottles and includes some genuine bargains.

Directions: Turn W off A66 immediately S of Bigsweir Bridge (5 miles from Monmouth), 2 miles up this unclassified road

Monmouth NP5 4TX
Map 3: SO50
Tel: 01600 860254
Fax: 01600 860607
Chef: Sandra Bates, Mark Turton
Owners: Roger & Sandra Bates
Cost: *Alc* £29.85, set-price L
£15.95/D £27.95. H/wine 9.95
Times: Noon-1.30pm/7-9pm.
Closed L Mon, D Sun, 2 wks Jan,
2 wks Aug
Additional: Bar food L; Sunday L;
Children welcome; 🍴 dishes
Seats: 20. Private dining room 12
Smoking: No smoking in dining room
Accommodation: 10 en suite ★★

NEATH PORT TALBOT

PORT TALBOT,

Aberavon Beach Hotel ❀

SA12 6QP
Map 3: SS78
Tel: 01639 884949
Fax: 01639 897885
Cost: *Alc* £22, set-price L £12/D £17.
☺ H/wine £8.50
Times: 12.30-1.45pm/7-10pm
Additional: Bar food L; Sunday L;
Children welcome; ❹ dishes
Smoking: No smoking in dining room
Accommodation: 52 en suite ★ ★ ★

Directions: M4 J41 & follow signs for
Aberavon & the beach. Hotel on
seafront

*The Greenhouse Restaurant includes a large conservatory with views
across Swansea Bay to the Gower Peninsular. Food is modern
British with Welsh and French influences.*

NEWPORT

NEWPORT, **Celtic Manor Hotel** ❀❀

*The beautifully restored 19th-century manor house remains the
centrepiece of this impressive hotel and leisure complex.* An
ambitious expansion of accommodation and facilities has been
underway for some years. The choice of dining rooms is ever-
expanding and they now offer guests a good balance of eating
options. The Club Lounge and Hedley's Restaurant have now
been joined by The Olive Tree, a 180 seater (formal) restaurant
which offers Mediterranean dishes, and Owen's, a modern,
stylish restaurant which serves contemporary Welsh cooking
with a continental twist. Hedley's continues to use local produce
in a basically classical repertoire. The *carte* is supplemented with
separate set-lunch and dinner menus. Smoked salmon bavarois
and a mille-feuille of grilled asparagus are listed within a choice
of eight first courses. Nine main courses include roast fillet of
Welsh black beef with shallots, pommes-neuf, roast cherry
tomatoes, fresh asparagus and glazed béarnaise sauce. Soufflés,
parfaits and tarts are offered as desserts.

Coldra Woods NP6 2YA
Map 3: ST38
Tel: 01633 413000
Fax: 01633 412910
Chefs: Peter Fuchs, Trefor Jones
Owner: Terry Matthews
Cost: *Alc* £15.50, set-price L
£15.50/D £18. ☺ H/wine £10.75
Times: L from 12.30pm/D to 10.30pm
Additional: Bar food; Sunday L;
Children welcome; ❹ dishes
Seats: 200. Private dining room 26-30
Smoking: No-smoking area; No pipes
& cigars; Air conditioning
Accommodation: 390 en suite
★ ★ ★ ★

Directions: On A48 just off M4 J24
towards Newport

NEWPORT, **Junction 28** ❀

*The name does refer to the nearby M4 junction, but this is no
motorway service station. Investigation will reveal an incredibly busy
restaurant with a wide ranging brasserie-style menu.*

Smoking: Air conditioning

Directions: M4 J4, follow signs Risca, then L in 0.5m signed
Caerphilly. R at mini-roundabout, then 1st L beyond St Basil's
church

Station Approach Bassaleg NP1 9LD
Map 3: ST38
Tel: 01633 891891
Fax: 01633 895982
Cost: *Alc* £20, set-price D £11.95. ☺
H/wine £11.95
Times: Noon-2pm(4pm Sun)/5.30-
9.30pm. Closed D Sun, 26 Jul-10 Aug
Additional: Sunday L; Children
welcome; ❹ dishes

PEMBROKESHIRE

FISHGUARD, Tregynon Country Farmhouse Hotel ✿

Few hotels have their own smoke-house, so it's worth choosing the oak-smoked fruity-spiced gammon in a sauce of cider, honey, ginger wine and apricots when it's on the nightly changing, rotating menu. Virtually everything is made on the premises, sourced from local ingredients, many organic, including Pembrokeshire beef and lamb.

Accommodation: 6 en suite ★ ★

Directions: Take B4313 towards Fishguard. Take 1st R and 1st R again and follow signs

Gwaun Valley SA65 9TU
Map 2: SM93
Tel: 01239 820531
Fax: 01239 820808
Cost: Alc £24.95, set-price D £22. ☺
H/wine £11
Times: D only, 7.30-8.30pm
Additional: Children 8+; ✿ dishes
Seats: 26. Private dining room 10
Smoking: No smoking in dining room

PEMBROKE, Court Hotel ✿

Georgian mansion with an elegantly traditional restaurant. The menu offers a choice of mainly local produce cooked and served to a notable standard.

Lamphey SA71 5NT
Map 2: SM90
Tel: 01646 672273
Fax: 01646 672480
Cost: Alc £20. ☺ H/wine £9.75
Times: 12.30-1.30pm/7-9.30pm
Additional: Bar food; Sunday L;
Children 6+; ✿ dishes
Smoking: No smoking in dining room
Accommodation: 37 en suite ★ ★ ★

Directions: Hotel signed in Lamphey

ST DAVID'S,
Morgan's Brasserie ✿✿

This brasserie was opened in 1993 and was deemed, at the time, to be the height of 'metropolitan' fashion. The walls are still white, and hung with colourful art. But the point of the whole operation is that the kitchen uses local produce to good effect and the food is always reliable. The carte is supplemented with chef's daily specials. trusted dishes such as confit of duck and grilled goats' cheese salad served on a toasted brioche with blackberry vinaigrette are amongst the six starters. Main courses include roast Gressingham duck supreme and fillet steak Rossini. The kitchen is trying to introduce an emphasis on freshness rather than formality, although the desserts are still pretty traditional, such as a chocolate framboise and a sablé of fresh berries – raspberries, strawberries and blueberries set in sablé pastry with an orange-scented crème pâtissière.

Directions: 60yds off Cross Square

20 Nun Street SA62 6NT
Map 2: SM72
Tel/Fax: 01437 720508
Chef: Ceri Morgan
Owners: Ceri & Elaine Morgan
Cost: Alc £23. ☺ H/wine £10
Times: D only, 6.30-9pm.
Closed Sun, Jan
Additional: Children welcome;
✿ dishes
Seats: 34
Smoking: No smoking in dining room

ST DAVID'S,

St Non's Hotel

Named after the mother of Wales's patron saint, the hotel is situated close to the cathedral and Bishop's Palace. New owners have brought many improvements, and the sunny yellow and blue restaurant offers a range of freshly cooked, appealing dishes.

Additional: Bar food; Children welcome; 🕭 dishes
Smoking: No smoking in dining room
Accommodation: 22 en suite ★★

Directions: Close to Cathedral and St Non's Retreat

Catherine Street SA62 6RJ
Map 2: SM72
Tel: 01437 720239
Fax: 01437 721839
Cost: Set-price D £18.50. ☺
H/wine £9.50
Times: Noon-2pm/7-8.30pm (9pm Fri & Sat). Closed Nov, Dec

ST DAVID'S,

Warpool Court Hotel ✿✿

Looks exactly like it used to be – a school (for the cathedral choir). Subsequently privately owned, one owner was responsible for the thousands of hand-decorated tiles seen throughout the house. Have a drink with canapés – smoked duck goujons, say, or crab tartlets – in the bar and enjoy the views over the gardens to the sea. You could start dinner with a terrine of chicken, quail and pigeon, or home-smoked salmon with a chive sabayon, and then go to spankingly fresh fish – turbot with a herb and Parmesan crust, perhaps, or grilled red mullet with lemon and parsley butter. Best end of lamb is a favoured cut of meat, cooked plainly with herbs and garlic, or with a sauce of mushrooms and garlic. Presentation comes into its own with puddings of a 'heavenly' trio of chocolate desserts, and Tia Maria crème brûlée. Petits fours are home-made, service is attentive and friendly, and the wine list is wide-ranging.

Directions: From Cross Square, left by Midland Bank into Goat St, at fork follow hotel signs

SA62 6BN
Map 2: SM72
Tel: 01437 720300
Fax: 01437 720676
Chef: John Daniels
Owner: Peter Trier
Cost: Set-price L £19.50/D £34.50 (4 courses). H/wine £11.50
Times: Noon-2pm/7-9.15pm. Closed Jan
Additional: Bar food; Sunday L; Children welcome; 🕭 dishes
Seats: 60. Private dining room 24
Smoking: No smoking in dining room
Accommodation: 25 en suite ★★★

TENBY, **Atlantic Hotel**

Hotel set on cliffs overlooking the sea. Local crab and steaks feature, with house specialities such as Pandang chicken and puerco con mango, plus a good vegetarian selection.

Smoking: No-smoking area; No pipes & cigars
Accommodation: 42 en suite ★★★

Directions: Town centre, halfway along The Esplanade on R

The Esplanade SA70 7DU
Map 2: SN10
Tel/Fax: 01834 842881
Cost: Alc £21, set-price L £5.95 (2 courses)/D £19. ☺ H/wine £8.50
Times: Noon-2.30pm/6-10pm. Closed 2-15 Jan
Additional: Bar food; Sunday L; Children 12+ after 6pm; 🕭 dishes

TENBY,

Penally Abbey ✿

A country house-style hotel with many merits, especially a dining room of candlelit elegance serving an unfussy menu. Fish majors in the starters and there's plenty of main course meat choices including Welsh lamb with applemint sauce.

Directions: From Tenby take A4139 to Penally

Penally SA70 7PY
Map 2: SN10
Tel: 01834 843033
Fax: 01834 844714
Telephone for further details

WOLF'S CASTLE,
Wolfscastle Country Hotel ✿

Wholesome Celtic and French cuisine is offered at this country-style hotel, with roast Pembrokeshire duck, grilled Welsh lamb noisettes, and warm lemon tart for example.

Smoking: No smoking in dining room
Accommodation: 20 en suite ★ ★

Directions: On A40, in centre of village

SA62 5LZ
Map 2: SM92
Tel: 01437 741225/741688
Fax: 01437 741383
Cost: *Alc* £21, set-price L £13.50 (2 courses)/D £16.50. ☺ H/wine £7.25
Times: Noon-2pm/7-9pm.
Closed 24-26 Dec
Additional: Bar food; Sunday L; Children 5+; dishes

POWYS

BRECON, # Castle of Brecon Hotel ✿

Friendly hotel adjacent to the castle. Get a window seat if you can and look out over the river and town whilst enjoying the upbeat cooking. Warm chorizo salad with poached egg and in-house gravad lax set the pace.

Smoking: No smoking in dining room
Accommodation: ★ ★

Directions: Follow signs to town centre. Turn opposite Boars Head

Castle Square LD3 9DB
Map 3: SO02
Tel: 01874 624611
Fax: 01874 623737
Cost: *Alc* £25, set-price D £22.90 (4 courses). ☺ H/wine £8.20
Times: D only, 7-8.45pm.
Closed 23-26 Dec
Additional: Bar food; Sunday L (Noon-1.45pm); Children welcome; dishes

BUILTH WELLS,
Caer Beris Manor Hotel ✿

Oak-panelled dining room with a menu featuring fine local produce such as Pencarreg goats' cheese with bitter leaves and sherry vinaigrette, and Welsh lamb with Madeira sauce.

Directions: Off A483 on W side of town

LD2 3NP
Map 3: SO05
Tel: 01982 552601
Fax: 01982 552586
Telephone for further details

CRICKHOWELL, # Bear Hotel ✿✿

NP8 1BW
Map 3: SO21
Tel: 01873 810408
Fax: 01873 811696
Chef: Denver Dodwell

An atmospheric coaching inn dating from 1432. The two dining rooms differ in style: one has oak beams, stone walls

and flagstone floor with rugs, while the other has an intimate atmosphere, with candles, fresh flowers and lace tablecloths. Lighter meals are available at the bar but the restaurant *carte* lists seven starters and eleven main courses. Several dishes from around the world feature, including Thai crab spring rolls with a tomato and coriander salsa. Our rack of lamb, served sliced, with a mustard brioche, herb crumb on a cassoulet of tomato and garlic with mixed beans was 'thoroughly enjoyable', with a lemon crunch cake for dessert noted for its lovely lemony flavour. The wine list is sectioned by type and is sound, if uninspired.

Owners: Mrs J L Hindmarsh & Stephen Hindmarsh
Cost: *Alc* £25. ☺ H/wine £8.50
Times: D only, 7-9.30pm.
Closed D Sun
Additional: Bar food; Sunday L (noon-2pm); Children 7+; ● dishes
Seats: 70. Private dining room 60
Smoking: No pipes & cigars
Accommodation: 36 en suite ★ ★ ★

Directions: Town centre off A40

CRICKHOWELL, Gliffaes Hotel ✿✿

NP8 1RH
Map 3: SO21
Tel: 01874 730371
Fax: 01874 730463
Chef: Justin Howe
Owners: Nicholas & Peta Brabner
Cost: Set-price D £23.30. ☺
H/wine £12
Times: D only, 7.30-9.15pm
Additional: Bar food L; Sunday L (noon-2.15pm); Children welcome; ● dishes
Seats: 70. Private dining room 30.
Jacket and tie preferred
Smoking: No smoking in dining room
Accommodation: 22 en suite ★ ★

19th-century country house hotel with trout fishing on the River Usk. Take a walk in the splendid wooded grounds or stroll along the river before returning for dinner in the hotel's panelled dining room. Good country house cooking was evident at our inspection meal: 'simple but superb' broth of duck confit made with fresh onions, white beans and carrots as well as generous pieces of duck. Smoked haddock brandade followed – a mixture of smoked fish and potato set in a crisp pastry case and topped with Welsh rarebit and white sauce. For dessert, the ubiquitous sticky toffee pudding, surrounded by a pool of caramel sauce. The wine list has some well-chosen bottles at fair prices, as well as some good clarets from the better vintages.

Directions: 1 mile off A40, 2.5 miles W of Crickhowell

CRICKHOWELL,
Manor Hotel ✿

The location is stunning – on a hillside way above the town. Bold modern cooking translates as spicy sweet roasted pork on crisp Caesar salad, and salmon and spinach fishcakes on steamed mangetout and lemon butter sauce.

Smoking: No smoking in dining room
Accommodation: 18 en suite ★ ★ ★

Brecon Road NP8 1SE
Map 3: SO21
Tel: 01873 810212
Fax: 01873 811938
Cost: *Alc* £25. ☺ H/wine £8.25
Times: Noon-2.15pm/7-10pm
Additional: Bar food; Sunday L;
Children welcome; ● dishes

Directions: 0.5 mile W of Crickhowell on A40 Brecon road

CRICKHOWELL,

Nantyffin Cider Mill Inn

Charming 15th-century inn with cider-making machinery in view. In season, local game and fish appear regularly; and items such as Indian spiced marinated monkfish and an unusual lemon posset with almonds and oatmeal satisfy diners.

Additional: Bar food L; Sunday L; Children welcome; 🍴 dishes
Smoking: No smoking in dining room

Directions: 1 mile west of Crickhowell on A40 at junction with A479

Brecon Road NP8 1SG
Map 3: SO21
Tel/Fax: 01873 810775
Cost: *Alc* £19, set-price L £14.95. ☺ H/wine £10.95
Times: Noon-2.30pm/6.30-9.30pm. Closed Mon, 1 wk Jan

HAY-ON-WYE, Kilverts Hotel

Simply decorated restaurant with lively jazz mural on one wall. Imaginative cooking of quality fresh produce includes dishes of Welsh lamb, grilled trout and seven vegetable couscous.

Additional: Bar food; Children welcome; 🍴 dishes
Accommodation: 11 en suite ★★

Directions: Town centre

The Bull Ring HR3 5AG
Map 3: SO24
Tel: 01497 821042
Fax: 01497 821580
Cost: *Alc* £17.50, set-price D £15. ☺ H/wine £8.50
Times: D only, 7-9.30pm.
Closed 25 Dec

HAY-ON-WYE,

Old Black Lion Hotel

26 Lion Street HR3 5AD
Map 3: SO24
Tel: 01497 820841
Chefs: Peter Bridges, Gareth Radcliffe, Carol Hazel
Owners: Mr & Mrs Collins
Cost: *Alc* £20. ☺ H/wine £8.25
Times: Noon-2.30pm/7-9.30pm
Additional: Bar food; Sunday L; Children 5+; 🍴 dishes
Seats: 24
Smoking: No smoking in dining room
Accommodation: 10 en suite ★★

Fine old coaching inn, all low ceilings and exposed beams.
Once occupied by Oliver Cromwell during the siege of nearby Hay castle, the cooking nowadays picks and chooses from a range of global influences, but is honest and plentiful and uses fresh ingredients. The robust approach manifests itself in well-flavoured Thai fishcakes with hot and spicy sauce, or marinated strips of rump steak stir-fried with sweet red peppers, sliced baby corn and tomatoes. A twice daily specials board often features Loch Fyne Seafood, including fresh oysters and langoustines. From a dessert list that might include Tia Maria meringues and profiteroles with chocolate sauce and cream, apple pie and custard proved a sound, if somewhat pedestrian choice.

Directions: Town centre, 100 yards from junction of Brecon Road & Oxford Road

KNIGHTON,
Milebrook House Hotel

Milebrook LD7 1LT
Map 7: SO27
Tel: 01547 528632
Fax: 01547 520509
Cost: *Alc* £20.25, set-price L
£11.75/D £18.75. ☺ H/wine £10.90
Times: Noon-1.30pm/7-8.30pm.
Closed L Mon
Additional: Bar food; Sunday L;
Children 8+; ✿ dishes
Smoking: No smoking in dining room
Accommodation: 10 en suite ★★

An 18th-century dower house with an extended restaurant and terrace area where guests may take a drink or dine. Local produce is a prominent feature of the menus.

Directions: 2 miles E of Knighton on A4113 (Ludlow)

LLANFYLLIN,
Seeds

Short, set-price menu with reliably straightforward cooking and a vegetarian dish on request. The building dates from 1580 and, with slate floors, oak beams, books and puzzles on the table, has a delightfully informal and relaxed atmosphere.

Additional: Bar food L; Sunday L; Children welcome; ✿ dishes
Smoking: No smoking in dining room

Directions: Village centre, on A490 13 miles from Welshpool

5 Penybryn Cottage High Street
SY22 5AP
Map 7: SJ11
Tel: 01691 648604
Cost: *Alc* £15.55 L only, set-price D
£18.95. ☺ H/wine £10
Times: 11am-2.15pm/7-9pm.
Closed D Sun, L Mon, 3 wks Jan/Feb

LLANGAMMARCH WELLS,
Lake Country House ❀❀

The hotel is set in 50 acres of grounds complete with a 3-acre lake, golf course, and river. The dining room is formal and conventionally styled with brocaded curtains, solid cutlery and linen napery. Signature dishes include cannelloni of scallops and poached oyster nage, and pot-roasted duck in marmalade and cracked pepper. Excellent breads are baked on the premises and include bacon with cheese, wholemeal with pistachio and plain white. Our scallops were wonderfully fresh, tasty and sweet – a nice contrast to the bitterness of the accompanying spinach. A saddle of venison, set on mashed potato, was cooked rare and had a robust and gusty flavour, and a walnut crème brûlée had a pleasingly-flavoured cream and a subtle use of walnuts. Hefty and interesting wine list with a French allegiance.

LD4 4BS
Map 3: SN94
Tel: 01591 620202
Fax: 01591 620457
Chef: Jeremy Medley
Owners: Jan & Pierre Mifsud
Cost: Set-price L £17.50 (4 courses)/D
£30 (5 courses) H/wine £9.75
Times: 12.30-1.45pm/7.30-9pm
Additional: Bar food L; Sunday L;
Children 7+; ✿ dishes
Seats: 38. Private dining room 20.
Jacket & tie preferred
Smoking: No smoking in dining room
Accommodation: 19 en suite ★★★

Directions: A483 from Garth, turn L for Llangammarch Wells & follow signs to hotel

LLANWDDYN,

Lake Vyrnwy Hotel ❀❀

Lake Vyrnwy SY10 0LY
Map 6: SJ01
Tel: 01691 870692
Fax: 01691 870259
Chef: Andrew Wood
Cost: Set-price L £15.95/D £25.50.
H/wine £10.95
Times: 12.30-1.45pm/7.30-9.15pm
Additional: Bar food; Sunday L;
Children welcome; ❸ dishes
Seats: 100. Private dining room 100
Smoking: No smoking in dining room
Accommodation: 35 en suite ★ ★ ★

Directions: Follow Tourist signs on
A495/B4393, 200 yards past dam at
Lake Vyrnwy

*Remotely situated hotel – views from the conservatory-style
restaurant are spectacular.* Built at the end of the last century,
the hotel lies in 26,000 acres of mature woodland above the lake
of the same name. The kitchen relies extensively on home-
grown fruit and vegetables, as well as hedgerow wild fruit, field
mushrooms, lake trout and estate game. The set-price menu
changes daily. Typically robust was a starter of crayfish and herb
sausage served with home-cured salmon as well as a dill and
herb dressing. Terrine of Vyrnwy pheasant with pistachios,
trompettes and home-made chutney made imaginative use of a
country staple, whilst pan-fried fillets of Cornish mackerel with
aubergine pâté, red pepper confit and herb sauce proved a
successful summer combination. Tangy lemon tart is given a
modern twist with lemongrass ice cream and blackcurrant sauce.

LLANWRTYD WELLS,

Carlton House ❀❀❀

*It is red kite country around here and an impressive steel
sculpture of the once elusive hawk has recently been placed in
the centre of the town.* Clearly visible from the dining room at
Carlton House, it is tempting to draw parallels between the
larger than life bird and the redoubtable Mary Ann Gilchrist
whose presence in this part of mid-Wales has probably been
responsible for almost as many visitors. The great thing about
the cooking here is that it doesn't stand still; each year our
inspectors find that the style has been developed a little, new
dishes have appeared on the menu and the technique is just a
touch more refined than on the previous visit. A star of a
recent inspection, for instance, was a newly conceived starter
comprising the crunchiest of king prawns with lobster and Thai
rice noodles, dressed in a superbly judged lime and ginger
vinaigrette. If you hit this area at the right time of year, then
the local sewin (sea trout) is a must and the version at Carlton
House, seared with squid-ink pasta and salsa verde has few
peers. On the dessert front the use of some excellent fruits, in
Herefordshire raspberry Pavlova for instance, shows typical
good sense and the offer of a semi-savoury (devils on
horseback) is equally enlightened. Wines are a strength. Good
advice is to make use of Alan Gilchrist's obvious enthusiasm
for his well-chosen list and ask for a recommendation.

Dolycoed Road LD5 4RA
Map 3: SN84
Tel: 01591 610248
Fax: 01591 610242
Chef: Mary Ann Gilchrist
Owners: Dr A J & Mrs M A Gilchrist
Cost: *Alc* £27.50, set-price L £9.95/D
£19.95. ☺ H/wine £9.95
Times: 12.30-1.45pm/7-8.30pm.
Closed L Mon, all Sun
Additional: Children welcome;
❸ dishes
Seats: 14
Smoking: No smoking in dining room
Accommodation: 7 rooms ★ ★

Directions: In the town centre

LLYSWEN,
Griffin Inn ✿

Quintessential country inn, from the log fires to the hearty menu. As well as local game, there may be roast knuckle of lamb with garlic, rosemary and dauphinoise potatoes.

Additional: Bar food; Sunday L; Children welcome; ✿ dishes
Smoking: No smoking in dining room
Accommodation: 7 en suite ★ ★

Directions: On A470 in village

Brecon LD3 0UR
Map 3: SO13
Tel: 01874 754241
Fax: 01874 754592
Cost: *Alc* £21, set-price L £12 (2 courses)/D £17. ☺ H/wine £9.75
Times: Noon-2pm/7-9pm.
Closed D Sun, 25, 26 Dec

LLYSWEN,
Llangoed Hall ✿✿✿

Brecon LD3 0YP
Map 3: SO13
Tel: 01874 754525
Fax: 01874 754545
Chef: Joseph Crone
Owner: Sir Bernard Ashley
Cost: *Alc* £38, set-price L £15 (2 courses)/D £35 (4 courses). H/wine £16.50
Times: 12.15-2pm/7.15-9.30pm

Just prior to going to press a new chef arrived at Llangoed in the form of Joseph Crone (formerly at the Connaught and the Oak Room). When our inspector called, the new regime was still in its infancy but it was already clear that a significant change in direction is underway. As might be expected given the pedigree, the approach is more direct, tending towards the classic with an emphasis on accuracy and top-quality produce. An early set dinner menu displayed much promise with four courses of precise cooking displaying an admirable level of consistency. Typical of the style that can now be expected were a beautifully judged ragout of langoustines, turbot and cucumber preceded by a similarly understated risotto of girolles with chives. A main course of noisettes of lamb with an excellent shallot purée also displayed a welcome concentration on the strength of some excellent meat. This particular meal concluded with a delicate sablé of poached pears served with seasonal red-fruits. Whoever is doing the cooking, Llangoed Hall continues to offer reassuringly high levels of service and a wine list that does justice to any kitchen.

Additional: Sunday L; Children 8+; ✿ dishes
Seats: 50. Private dining room 50. Jacket & tie preferred
Smoking: No smoking in dining room
Accommodation: 23 en suite ★ ★ ★ ★

Directions: On A470, 2 miles from Llyswen heading towards Builth Wells

AA Shortlisted for Wine Award-see page 16

MONTGOMERY, Dragon Hotel

Fine 17th-century former coaching near Montgomery Castle. At inspection a delicious marinière sauce accompanied fresh mussels, and perfectly cooked lamb noisettes were served with a redcurrant and mint jus and decent vegetables.

Directions: Behind the Town Hall

SY15 6PA
Map 7: SO29
Tel: 01686 668359
Fax: 01686 668287
Telephone for further details

NANT-DDU,

Nant Ddu Lodge Hotel

Cwm Taf Nr Merthyr Tydfil
CF48 2HY
Map 3: SO12
Tel: 01685 379111
Fax: 01685 377088
Cost: *Alc* £18. ☺ H/wine £8.95
Times: Noon-2.30pm/6-9.30pm
Additional: Bar food; Sunday L;
Children welcome; ✿ dishes
Smoking: No smoking in dining room
Accommodation: 22 en suite ★★★

Directions: 6 miles N of Merthyr
Tydfil, and 12 miles S of Brecon on
A470

*A bustling bistro in the heart of the Brecon Beacons National Park.
Vibrant colours, original art work and relaxed informal service
create the setting for some robust and enjoyable dishes.*

NEW RADNOR, Red Lion Inn

*Despite its isolated position this unpretentious 16th-century drovers'
inn draws loyal customers from miles around. Expect a bustling
atmosphere, robust cooking using fresh local produce and
blackboard dishes like potted Wye salmon, and Brecon venison with
red wine and chocolate.*

Directions: On N side of A44, 7 miles E of Crossgates and 3
miles W of New Radnor

Llanfihangel-nant-Melan LD8 2TN
Map 3: SO26
Tel/Fax: 01544 350220
Cost: *Alc* £14.50. ☺ H/wine £6.95
Times: D only, 7-9pm.
Closed Tue, 26 Dec, 1 wk Nov
Additional: Sunday L (noon-2pm);
Children welcome; ✿ dishes
Smoking: No-smoking area
Accommodation: 3 en suite

PWLLGLOYW, Seland Newydd

***This 17th century inn has it all: a picturesque setting,
wonderful scenery, and a small village base.*** There's a bar, a
lounge area and a separate restaurant with an open log fire.
Home-made bread is served warm, first courses include a
timbale of smoked salmon and trout with a prawn and
cucumber dressing, and a duck confit, that had 'good depth of
flavour'. Of five main courses, pan-fried breast of chicken on
bed of parsley mash with chicken livers and smoked bacon was
'enjoyable and succulent'. Seven desserts include white
chocolate and passion fruit mousse, and banana and toffee
bread-and-butter pudding, as well as glazed lemon tart with a
honey wafer basket, but you can have these and more on the
so-called 'Full Monty' – a selection of everything. Good,
predominantly French, wine list.

Brecon LD3 9PY
Map 3: SO03
Tel: 01874 690282
Chef: Maynard Harvey
Owners: Maynard & Freya Harvey
Cost: *Alc* £23. ☺ H/wine £8.75
Times: 11am-3pm/6-11pm
Additional: Bar food; Sunday L;
Children welcome; ✿ dishes
Seats: 35. Private room 12

Directions: 4 miles north of Brecon
on B4520

THREE COCKS,

Three Cocks

Unique little 15th-century inn with a Belgian heart. Stone
walls and heavily carved woodwork provide suitably rustic
surroundings in the shadow of the Brecon Beacons. The honest
approach extends to a menu simple in style, but consistently
high in quality. Ardennes smoked ham, salad aveyronnaise and
an excellent list of Belgian beers are testimony to the roots of
the owners and the mid-Wales location is marked by the
presence of local lamb that might come with a vivid ratatouille.
A four-course set-menu begins with a choice of soups that
regularly features a faithful lobster bisque with fiery rouille,
and might extend to grey mullet in a bordelaise-style sauce, or
veal Romanoff. Amongst robust desserts, a hazelnut nougatine
found favour with one inspector and in-house petits fours
accompany coffee. For those not tempted by the range of ales,
there is a thoughtful wine list that offers character and good
value.

Directions: On A438 in the village of Three Cocks, 4 miles from
Hay-on-Wye, 11 miles from Brecon

Brecon LD3 0SL
Map 3: SO13
Tel: 01497 847215
Fax: 01497 847339
Chef: Michael Winstone
Owners: Michael & Marie-Jeanne
Winstone
Cost: Set-price D £27 (5 courses). ☺
H/wine £8.75
Times: D 7-9pm.
Closed Tue, Dec-mid Feb
Additional: Bar food L;
Children welcome
Seats: 30
Smoking: No pipes & cigars
Accommodation: 7 rooms ★★

WELSHPOOL,

Golfa Hall Hotel

*The hotel was originally a farmhouse on the Powis Castle Estate.
In the restaurant the set price menu offers modern cooking
complemented by a decent selection of wines.*

Additional: Bar food; Sunday L; Children welcome; ✤ dishes
Smoking: No smoking in dining room
Accommodation: 14 en suite ★★

Directions: On A458 (Dolgellau), 1.5 miles W of Welshpool
on R

Llanfair Road SY21 9AF
Map 7: SJ20
Tel: 01938 553399
Fax: 01938 554777
Cost: Alc £25, set-price D £17.95. ☺
H/wine £9.95
Times: Noon-2pm/7-9pm

RHONDDA CYNON TAFF

MISKIN, **Miskin Manor Hotel** ✿✿

*Imposing manor house in acres of wooded grounds and
gardens that has been updated to a particularly high
standard.* The dining room has a strong baronial feel, no doubt
due to the heavy oak-panelling and the striking open fire place.
However the cooking follows the modern British course,
offering the likes of bresaola fillet of beef with sea salt and a
salad of beansprouts and watercress, and baked fillet of turbot
with a saffron crumb, fried asparagus tips and chive beurre
blanc.

Seats: 60. Private dining room 60
Smoking: No smoking in dining room
Accommodation: 45 en suite ★★★★

Directions: 8 miles W of Cardiff. M4 J34, follow hotel signs

Groes Faen Pontyclun CF72 8ND
Map 3: ST08
Tel: 01443 224204
Fax: 01443 237606
Chef: Kurt Flemming
Owners: Colin & Leah Rosenberg
Cost: Alc £28, set-price L £16.95 (2
courses)/D £25.95. H/wine £10.95
Times: Noon-2pm/7-9.45pm.
Additional: Bar food L; Sunday L;
Children welcome; ✤ dishes

SWANSEA

LANGLAND,

Langland Court

Langland Court Road SA3 4TD
Map 2: SS68
Tel: 01792 361545
Fax: 01792 362302
Cost: Set-price D £19.95. ☺
H/wine £8.50
Times: D only, 6.30-9.30pm
Additional: Bar food; Sunday L (noon-2pm); Children welcome; ✿ dishes
Smoking: No smoking in dining room
Accommodation: 21 en suite ★ ★ ★

Directions: Take A4067 Swansea-Mumbles road then B4593 (Caswell); turn L at St Peter's Church (hotel signed)

Large Victorian country house with a panelled Oakroom restaurant. Local seafood is a feature of the set-price menu along with home-made desserts from the trolley.

REYNOLDSTON,

Fairyhill ✿✿✿

Owners share a desire to ensure that guests experience unrivalled hospitality. 'Tuesday lunchtime, mid May, and 14 diners, literally in the middle of nowhere', exclaims an inspector, surprised to see anyone after a drive into the heart of the wild, dramatic, but very under populated Gower Peninsula. It says a lot for Andrew Hetherington and Paul Davies that Fairyhill casts such a spell: the setting, the house, the food are all charmed, reflecting a fame that has spread beyond the confines of South Wales. The country house comforts of crackling log fires and deep-cushioned sofas give way to sharp modernity in the dining room, rather three different dining areas with garden views, crisp white cloths and shiny stainless steel. The setting is matched by cooking that owes a lot to local and regional specialities (bar nibbles of deep-fried Penclawdd cockles 'rather tasty', for example) and a thorough appreciation of cosmopolitan trends. Witness our lunch that opened with slow-cooked, spiced belly pork with a warm apple chutney tartlet, went on to an outstanding chump and sausage of Welsh lamb with tapenade jus, set on some creamy mashed potato and oven-roast vegetables, and finished with a 'fabulous, extremely rich' bitter chocolate marquise with orange sauce – a meal that was hard to fault. The extensive wine list is compiled with knowledge and enthusiasm, gives a comprehensive spread and considerable depth. House wines are a bargain, but the section of red and white wines under £20 is worth exploring.

Directions: Just outside Reynoldston, off A4118 from Swansea

SA3 1BS
Map 2: SS48
Tel: 01792 390139
Fax: 01792 391358
Chefs: Paul Davies, Adrian Coulthard
Owners: Paul Davies, Andrew Hetherington, Jane & Peter Camm
Cost: Set-price L £17.50/D £32. H/wine £12.50
Times: 12.30-1.30pm/7.30-9pm. Closed 25 Dec-6 Jan
Additional: Sunday L; Children 8+; ✿ dishes
Seats: 60. Private dining room 40
Smoking: No smoking in dining room
Accommodation: 8 en suite ★ ★

AA Shortlisted for Wine Award-see page 16

SWANSEA, **Windsor Lodge Hotel**

Mount Pleasant SA1 6EG
Map 3: SS69
Tel: 01792 642158/652744
Fax: 01792 648996
Cost: Set-price D £22.50. ☺ H/wine £8.95
Times: L by prior arrangement/7-9.30pm. Closed Sun, 25-26 Dec
Additional: Bar food; Children welcome; 🍴 dishes
Smoking: No smoking in dining room
Accommodation: 19 en suite ★★

Directions: Town centre, L at station, R immediately after 2nd set of lights

Well-furnished hotel close to the town centre that offers good value and friendly, attentive service. Steak and kidney pie and bread-and-butter pudding are popular choices.

VALE OF GLAMORGAN

BARRY, **Egerton Grey Hotel**

Porthkerry CF62 3BZ
Map 3: ST16
Tel: 01446 711666
Fax: 01446 711690
Cost: *Alc* £25, set-price L & D £13.50 (2 courses). ☺ H/wine £10.50
Times: Noon-2pm/7-9.45pm
Additional: Bar food L; Sunday L; Children welcome; 🍴 dishes
Smoking: No smoking in dining room
Accommodation: 10 en suite ★★★

Directions: M4 J33, follow signs for Airport then Porthkerry, & L at hotel sign by thatched cottage

Mahogany-panelled restaurant in a former rectory. The menu offers plenty of choice and typical dishes are duck, venison and hog terrine, and roast breast of pheasant with chestnut stuffing.

WREXHAM

LLANARMON DYFFRYN CEIRIOG, **West Arms Hotel**

NEW

Former farmhouse with characterful, cavernous inglenook fireplaces, massive beams and stone floors. Cornish turbot with garlic and spring onions, and local lamb with wild mushrooms make intelligent use of fine ingredients.

Accommodation: 16 en suite ★★

Directions: Exit A483 (A5) at Chirk and follow signs for Ceiriog Valley (B4500) – 11 miles

Llangollen LL20 7LD
Map 7: SJ13
Tel: 01691 600665
Fax: 01691 600622
Cost: Set-price L £12.50/D £19.50 (5 courses). ☺ H/wine £8.95
Additional: Bar food; Sunday L; Children welcome; 🍴 dishes
Smoking: No smoking in dining room

MARCHWIEL,
Cross Lanes Hotel

Cross Lanes Bangor Road
LL13 0TF
Map 7: SJ35
Tel: 01978 780555
Fax: 01978 780568
Telephone for further details

Directions: 3 miles SE of Wrexham
on A525

*Stone-floored bar/brasserie with views over the lawns and gardens.
The menu is supported by specials on blackboards, and the dishes
are impressively presented.*

ROSSETT,
Llyndir Hall Hotel

*Modern hotel on the English/Welsh border in several acres of
mature grounds. A varied set-price menu and carte offer balanced
flavours: smooth chicken liver pâté with Cumberland sauce, say, and
summer pudding with sauce anglaise.*

LL12 0AY
Map 7: SJ35
Tel: 01244 571648
Fax: 01244 571258
Telephone for further details

Directions: S from Chester on A483 to Wrexham, follow signs
for Pulford/Rossett B5445. Llyndir Hall signed on the R

ROSSETT,
Rossett Hall Hotel ✿

*Elegant Georgian mansion set in mature grounds. The open-all-day
bistro offers snacks, light lunches and a comprehensive menu
featuring lobster and salmon fishcakes with mustard and parsley
sauce, and lamb shank on ratatouille with rosemary and sun-dried
tomato gravy.*

Chester Road LL12 0DE
Map 7: SJ35
Tel: 01244 571000
Fax: 01244 571505
Cost: *Alc* £20. ☺ H/wine £7.95
Times: Noon-9.30pm

Additional: Bar food; Sunday L; Children 7+; ✦ dishes
Smoking: No-smoking area; No pipes & cigars; Air conditioning
Accommodation: 30 en suite ★ ★ ★

Directions: M56, take M53 to Wrexham – becomes A55. Take
A483 Chester/Wrexham exit to Rossett (B5445). Hotel in centre
of village

NORTHERN IRELAND
ANTRIM

LISBURN, Pipers Quay

Newly built riverside bar and restaurant complex with a nautical feel. The food is French with an Irish accent. Try the chicken supreme stuffed with langoustine mousse, paprika and coriander sauce.

Additional: Bar food L; Sunday L; Children welcome; ♨ dishes
Smoking: No-smoking area; No pipes & cigars; Air conditioning

Directions: From M1 take A49 to Lisburn town centre. On L after crossing River Lagan Bridge

88 Bridge Street, BT28 1XX
Map 1: D5
Tel: 01846 628816
Fax: 01846 628863
Cost: *Alc* £25, set-price L £15/D £17.50. ☺ H/wine £8.25
Times: Noon-2.30pm/5-10.30pm.
Closed D Mon

PORTRUSH, Ramore

Appealing, modern restaurant overlooking Portrush harbour. Some 18 years on, and George McAlpin continues to produce reliably good cooking. Our most recent meal began with a well-judged shiitake mushroom tart topped with white truffle mayonnaise (nicely contrasting flavours and very light puff pastry) before an enjoyable rack of lamb (a generous four ribs) with gnocchi, Mediterranean vegetables and pesto. Highlight of the meal though was 'a just about perfect' hot Amaretto soufflé with three separate sauces (chocolate, coffee anglaise and Amaretto cream). Other dishes that caught the eye included spicy monkfish goujons on mango and peanut salad dressed with light curry oil, a fillet of salmon with red pimento and pine nut couscous with aïoli and basil salad, and roast and confit of duck served with an egg noodle pancake, cucumber, spring onion and 'Thai' vinaigrette. Attentive service.

The Harbour BT56 8DF
Map 1: C6
Tel: 01265 824313
Fax: 01265 823194
Chef: George McAlpin
Owners: George & Jane McAlpin
Cost: *Alc* £27.50. ☺ H/wine £9.25
Times: D only, 6.30-10.30pm.
Closed Sun, Mon, 24-26 Dec, 1Jan
Additional: ♨ dishes
Seats: 70
Smoking: Air conditioning

Directions: On the harbour

BELFAST

BELFAST, Culloden House

Elegant baronial mansion offering fine views across the estuary to the city beyond. Modern Irish cooking fancies up good local produce – Mourne lamb, venison and halibut.

Bangor Road BT18 0EX
Map 1: D5
Tel: 01232 425223
Fax: 01232 426777
Cost: *Alc* £28, set-price L £18.50 (2 courses)/D £25.50. H/wine £11
Times: 12.30-2.30pm/7-9.45pm.
Closed L Sat, 24, 25 Dec
Additional: Sunday L; Children 3+; ♨ dishes
Smoking: No-smoking area; No pipes & cigars; Jacket & tie preferred
Accommodation: 79 en suite ★ ★ ★ ★

Directions: From M3 take A3 then A2 (Bangor); hotel is on L just through Holywood

BELFAST,

Deanes

Trend-setting restaurant with cool, modern decor. Both
brasserie and restaurant start from the same principle – to
energise modern British and Irish food with an infusion of
Asian-Pacific rim ideas. They succeed so well because the
multi-faceted cooking is of such a high standard. Start with
Thai-style carpaccio of salmon with sticky rice, cucumber, basil
and curry, or a clear soup of pigeon, parsley and carrot. A
typical main course, might be confit chicken, grilled pancetta
and mushroom risotto with roast foie gras, garlic, shiitake and
truffle oil. Meat predominates, although fillet of salmon is
unusually paired with goats' cheese, pasta, ratatouille and chilli
oil. Desserts promise considerable excitement, exploring
unusual flavour dimensions as in coffee cheesecake, chicory,
peppered plum and apricot. The decor is cooly elegant in
lemon and burgundy, in contrast to the eye-popping brasserie
downstairs, all gilt cherubs and blood red crushed velvet, which
offers a scaled-down version of the repertoire: fried crab and
prawn cakes, spring onion crème fraîche; confit of duck,
haricot blanc hummus, sauce vierge; chargrilled ribeye of beef,
creamed and roast cauliflower, jus of rosemary.

38-40 Howard Street BT1 6PD
Map 1: D5
Tel: 01232 331134
Fax: 01232 560001
Chef: Michael Deane
Owners: Michael Deane,
Brian & Lynda Smyth
Cost: Set-price D £27 (2 courses).
H/wine £15
Times: Noon-2.30pm/5.30-10.30pm
(brasserie), restaurant D only, 7-
9.30pm. Closed Sun (both) & Mon
(restaurant), 1wk Jul, Xmas & New
Year
Seats: 40 (restaurant), 110 (brasserie)
Smoking: No-smoking area; Air
conditioning

Directions: Telephone for directions

BELFAST,

Roscoff

To see and to be seen in. This modern, bright and airy
restaurant remains one of Northern Ireland's most fashionable
and famous venues. Both the *carte* and set-menus are examples
of what is termed modern British cooking with the kitchen
delivering some remarkably competent dishes. Bruschetta of
wild mushrooms with chargrilled radicchio and endive, pan-
fried halibut – 'a lovely piece of fish' served atop simple root
vegetables with seafood ravioli and a frothy shellfish sauce,
were much enjoyed. As was the chocolate pot au crème for
dessert – 'a generous and very rich dish'. The selective wine list
includes Canadian and Mexican options.

Directions: At top of Belfast's 'Golden Mile', Shaftesbury Square
area

7 Lesley House Shaftesbury Square
BT2 7DB
Map 1: D5
Tel: 01232 331532
Fax: 01232 312093
Chefs/Owners: Paul & Jeanne Rankin
Cost: *Alc* £35, set-price L £17.50/D
£25.50 (Mon-Thu only). H/wine £15
Times: 12.30-2.15pm/6.30-10.15pm.
Closed L Sat, all Sun, 25, 26 Dec,
Easter Mon, 12 Jul
Additional: Children welcome;
🍴 dishes
Seats: 70
Smoking: No-smoking area;
Air conditioning

DOWN

BANGOR, # Clandeboye Lodge

*The hotel restaurant has a high ceiling and large Gothic arched
window overlooking the parklands of the Clandeboye estate.
European/Irish dishes are prepared from quality raw ingredients.*

Additional: Bar food; Sunday L; Children welcome; 🍴 dishes.
Smoking: No-smoking area
Accommodation: 43 en suite ★ ★ ★

Directions: Leave A2 at Newtownards sign, 1st junction left,
300 yds

10 Estate Road Clandeboye
BT19 1UR
Map 1: D5
Tel: 01247 852500
Fax: 01247 852772
Cost: Set-price L £11/D £19.50. ☺
H/wine £9
Times: Noon-2.45pm/6.30-9.30pm.
Closed 25-27 Dec

BANGOR, **Royal Hotel** ❀

Seafront BT20 5ED
Map 1: D5
Tel: 01247 271866
Fax: 01247 467810
Telephone for further details

Directions: Take A2 from Belfast.
Through Bangor to seafront. Turn R,
hotel in 300 yards

*Substantial Victorian hotel overlooking the Marina. The serious
eating is done in Quays Restaurant, where only the best raw
ingredients are used in the careful prepared dishes.*

BANGOR, **Shanks** ❀❀❀

*A bar upstairs with the restaurant on the ground floor (where
a terrace can be used for outdoor aperitifs, weather
permitting):* seating and floor of light wood tempered by pastel
shades on walls and in drapes, and a collection of Hockney
prints – it all points to a contemporary setting for a thoroughly
modern menu. Perfectly steamed hake comes as a starter atop
chorizo and saffron risotto, and main-course duck breast is
spiked with Chinese five spice and served with parsnip purée
and honeyed apricots. But the kitchen's equally at home with
more traditional ideas, as in fillet of beef with sauce béarnaise,
or pot-roast free-range chicken with morels, cabbage and
sautéed potatoes. Seasonality and local produce are behind
pheasant tart with wild mushrooms and green peppercorn
cream, and Clandeboye estate venison with red cabbage and
port sauce, as well as 'spring on the plate' in the shape of
meltingly tender new season's lamb with wilted spinach on a
potato galette (cooked in duck fat for extra flavour) that
'combined crunch with substance', the whole dish surrounded
by pea purée scattered with carrots and peas. The list of
puddings may be split into mango soup with light, smooth
lychee ice cream scattered with grated coconut in one corner,
and orange steamed pudding with Grand Marnier sabayon in
the other.
    Signature dishes: spring rolls of duck confit with pineapple,
chilli and mango; roasted squab pigeon and foie gras with a
gratin of lentils, smoked bacon and thyme; lemon and lime tart
with papaya and passion fruit sorbet.

The Blackwood Crawfordsburn Road
BT19 1GB
Map 1: D5

Tel: 01247 853313
Fax: 01247 852493
Chef: Robbie Millar
Owners: Robbie & Shirley Millar
Cost: Set-price L £17.95/D £29.50.
H/wine £12.50
Times: 12.30-2.30pm/7-10pm.
Closed L Sat, all Sun & Mon, 2 wks
Jul
Additional: Children welcome;
❀ dishes
Seats: 60. Private dining room 30
Smoking: No-smoking area;
No pipes & cigars

Directions: From A2 (Belfast-Bangor),
turn R onto Ballysallagh Road 1 mile
before Bangor, 1st L after 0.5 mile
(Crawfordburn Road) to Blackwood
Golf Centre. Shanks is in the grounds

HOLYWOOD,

Rayanne House ❀❀

Victorian house that's superbly run with the emphasis on
attentive service. The restaurant is small and elegant with fresh
flowers and candles. Raymond McClelland does most of the
cooking, but wife Anne is responsible for the puddings. They
run to a tried-and-tested formula which works well, offering a
carte based on local ingredients. There's a certain amount of

60 Desmesne Road
BT18 9EX
Map 1: D5
Tel: 01232 425859
Fax: 01232 423364
Chef: Raymond McClelland
Owners: Raymond & Anne
McClelland

Rayanne House

Cost: Set-price D £27.50 (5 courses).
H/wine £11.50
Times: D only, 7-9pm. Closed Sun,
23 Dec-3 Jan
Additional: Children welcome;
🍽 dishes
Seats: 36. Private dining room 10
Smoking: No smoking in dining room
Accommodation: 9 en suite

flair and innovation to a cooking style that is strong on honest flavours. We enjoyed s confit of duck served with black cherry and Kirsch sauce, a peach sorbet, seafood lasagne (salmon and plaice with fresh spinach), and blackcurrant and port trifle. Booking is essential as this is a popular destination restaurant locally.

Directions: From A2 take Belfast Road into Holywood; immediate R into Jacksons Road leading to Desmesne Road

PORTAFERRY,
Portaferry Hotel   ❀❀

10 The Strand BT22 1PE
Map 1: D5
Tel: 012477 28231
Fax: 012477 28999
Chef: Gerry Manley
Owners: John & Marie Herlihy
Cost: Set-price L £15.75/D £22.50. ☺
H/wine £11.95
Times: 12.30-2.30pm/7-9pm. Closed
24-25 Dec
Additional: Bar food L; Sunday L;
Children welcome; 🍽 dishes
Seats: 80
Smoking: No pipes & cigars
Accommodation: 14 en suite ★ ★ ★

Directions: Opposite Strangford
Lough ferry terminal

This charming hotel enjoys lovely views of the Strangford Lough. Public areas include a choice of inviting lounges, a well-stocked bar, and a smart restaurant. The set-price menu offers a range of imaginative dishes, some with a supplementary charge. The kitchen makes excellent use of Ulster produce, its speciality being the local seafood, and the home-made wheaten bread is impressive. Our salmon and scallop terrine with creamy tarragon and spring onion dressing was 'a most enjoyable start to the meal'. A main course of lightly-grilled escalope of local salmon arrived on a smoked fish risotto, with deep-fried slices of beetroot and a champagne butter sauce, although accompanying vegetables did not need the additional saucing. Desserts included a double chocolate torte with burnt orange sauce, and a Mascarpone cheesecake with strawberries. The wine list is well-chosen with a decent range of half-bottles, and a Connoisseurs Choice for the wine buff.

LONDONDERRY

LIMAVADY, The Lime Tree

Competent modern Irish cooking with a Med twist is proving popular at this small restaurant on tree-lined Catherine Street. Confit of duck, stuffed saddle of rabbit with roasted garlic and wild mushroom sauce, and chocolate and orange torte show the pace. Good-value light lunches.

Smoking: No pipes & cigars

Directions: Entering Limavady from the Derry side, the restaurant is on the right side on a small slip road

60 Catherine Street BT49 9DB
Map 1: C5
Tel: 015047 64300
Cost: Alc L £13/D £20, set-price L £6.95/D £12.95 (not Sat). ☺ H/wine £8.95
Times: Noon-2pm/6-9.30pm. Closed Mon, Tue (except Dec & summer), 1 wk Feb/Mar, 1 wk Jul, 1wk Nov
Additional: Sunday L; Children welcome

LONDONDERRY, Beech Hill Hotel

Impressive 18th-century manor house standing in 32 acres of woodlands. Making the most of the lovely view, the traditional dining room offers modern cooking. Expect clam chowder, olive-crusted sea bass with confit of baby fennel, and coconut parfait with pistachio ice cream.

Smoking: No smoking in dining room
Accommodation: 27 en suite ★ ★ ★

Directions: A6 Londonderry to Belfast road, turn off at Faughan Bridge. 1 mile further to Ardmore Chapel. Hotel entrance is opposite

32 Ardmore Road BT47 3QP
Map 1: C5
Tel: 01504 349279
Fax: 01504 345366
Cost: Alc £27.80, set-price L £15.95 (4 courses)/D £24.95 (5 courses). ☺ H/wine £11.90
Times: Noon-2.30pm/6-9.45pm. Closed 24, 25 Dec
Additional: Bar food; Sunday L; Children 10+; ✦ dishes

LONDONDERRY, Everglades Hotel

Satchmo's Restaurant at the Everglades Hotel implies something of the deep south, but whilst the decor is themed accordingly, the menu has a modern British feel. Robust dishes make the most of Donegal salmon, Ulster beef and Antrim lamb.

Directions: 1 mile from city centre on main Dublin road

Prehen Road BT47 2PA
Map 1: C5
Tel: 01504 346722
Fax: 01504 349200
Telephone for further details

MAGHERAFELT, Trompets

The restaurant's contemporary style is softened by its environs and country-style comfort. Everything from the bold floral arrangements to the graphic-designed menus suggest that the owners are aware of what is going on at the centre of the restaurant world in spite of its distant location. Here they bake their own breads: fruit, soda, treacle – good, but including a plain one would be even better. A *carte* is offered at lunch and in the evening, when there is also a short table d'hôte. Confit of duck with herb polenta, and pan-fried escalope of salmon, truffle pomme purée, wild mushrooms, spinach and cardamom reduction are typical dishes, well-executed and sourced from local ingredients. The wine list is well-thought out and offers some surprisingly interesting examples from around the world.

Directions: On axis of A29 and M2/A6

25 Church Street BT45 6AP
Map 1: C5
Tel: 01648 32257
Fax: 01648 34441
Chef/Owner: Noel McMeel
Cost: Alc £24.95, set-price D £23.95. ☺ H/wine £11.95
Times: Noon-2.30pm/6-9.30pm. Closed D Sun, all Mon
Additional: Sunday L; Children welcome; ✦ dishes
Seats: 55. Private dining room 35
Smoking: No-smoking area; Air conditioning

REPUBLIC OF IRELAND

The Republic of Ireland hotels and restaurants listed below have built their reputations on the quality of their food; all have earned our coveted Rosette award. The information has been supplied by AA Hotel Services, Blackrock, Dublin.

Please note that the area codes for numbers in the Republic of Ireland apply only within the Republic. If dialling from outside you should check the telephone directory. Area codes for numbers in Britain and N. Ireland cannot be used directly from the Republic.

CO CARLOW

Ballykealey House ❀ ★★★

Ballon 0503 59288

Dolmen Hotel ❀ ★★★

Kilkenny Road, Carlow 0503 42002

CO CAVAN

Slieve Russell Hotel ❀ ★★★★

Ballyconnell 049 26444

Kilmore Hotel ❀ ★★★

Cavan 049 32288

Kloisters Bar & Restaurant ❀

Cavan 049 71485

CO CLARE

Gregans Castle ❀❀ ★★★

Ballyvaughan 065 77005

Garvello's Restaurant ❀❀

Clare Abbey, Limerick Rd, Ennis 065 40011

Temple Gate Hotel ❀ ★★★

The Square, Ennis 065 23300

Sheedy's Restaurant & Hotel ❀❀ ★★

Lisdoonvarna 065 74026

Dromoland Castle Hotel ❀❀ ★★★★★

Newmarket-on-Fergus 061 368144

CO CORK

Bay View Hotel ❀❀ ★★★

Ballycotton 021 646746

Sea View Hotel ❀❀ ★★★

Ballylickey 027 50073

Casey's of Baltimore ❀ ★★

Baltimore 028 20197

The Lodge & Spa at Inchydoney Island ❀❀ ★★★★

Clonakilty 023 33143

Arbutus Lodge Hotel ❀❀ ★★★

Middle Glanmire Road, Montenotte, Cork 021 501237

Hayfield Manor ❀ ★★★★

Perrott Avenue, College Road, Cork 021 315600

Courtmacsherry ✤ ★★

Courtmacsherry 023 46198

Garryvoe Hotel ✤ ★★

Garryvoe 021 646718

Inishannon House Hotel ✤✤ ★★★

Inishannon 021 775121

Trident Hotel ✤ ★★★

Worlds End, Kinsale 021 772301

Castle Hotel ✤ ★★

Main Street, Macroom 026 41074

Longueville House Hotel ✤✤✤ ★★★

Mallow 022 47156

Midleton Park ✤✤ ★★★

Midleton 021 631767

Aherne's Seafood Restaurant ✤✤

163 North Main Street, Youghal 024 92424

Devonshire Arms Hotel ✤ ★★

Pearse Square, Youghal 024 92827

CO DONEGAL

Kee's Hotel ✤✤ ★★★

Stranorlar, Ballybofey 074 31018

Harvey's Point Country Hotel ✤✤✤ ★★★

Lough Eske, Donegal 073 22208

Fort Royal Hotel ✤✤ ★★★

Fort Royal, Rathmullan 074 58100

Sand House Hotel ✤✤ ★★★

Rossnowlagh 072 51777

CO DUBLIN

Buswells Hotel ✤ ★★★

23-27 Molesworth Street, Dublin 2 01 6146500

Clarion Stephen's Hall All-Suite Hotel ✤✤ ★★★

The Earlsfort Centre, Lower Leeson Street, Dublin 2 01 6381111

Conrad International Dublin ✤✤ ★★★★

Earlsfort Terrace, Dublin 2 01 6765555

Hibernian Hotel ✤✤✤ ★★★

Eastmoreland Place Ballsbridge, Dublin 4 01 6687666

Kapriol Restaurant ✤

45 Lower Camden Street, Dublin 2 01 4751235

La Stampa ✤✤

35 Dawson Street, Dublin 003531 6778611

Longfield's Hotel ✤✤ ★★★

Fitzwilliam Street, Dublin 2 01 6761367

Marine Hotel ✿✿ ★★★

Sutton Cross, Dublin 13 01 8390000

One Pico Restaurant ✿✿

No 1 Upper Camden Street, Dublin 2 01 4780307

The Plaza Hotel ✿✿ ★★★★

Belgard Road, Tallaght, Dublin 01 4624200

Red Cow Morans Hotel ✿ ★★★★

7 Ballsbridge Terrace, Dublin 4 01 6680623

Roly's Bistro ✿✿

7 Ballsbridge Terrace, Dublin 4 01 6680623

The Clarence ✿✿✿ ★★★★

6-8 Wellington Quay, Dublin 01 6709000

The Commons ✿✿

85-86 Stephen Green, Dublin 003531 4752608

The Merrion Hotel ✿✿✿ ★★★★★

Upper Merrion Street, Dublin 01 6030600

The Schoolhouse Hotel ✿✿ ★★★

2-8 Northumberland Road, Dublin 4 01 6675014

Shelbourne Meridien ✿ ★★★★

St Stephen's Green, Dublin 2 01 6766471

Thornton's Restaurant ✿✿✿✿

1 Portobello Road, Dublin 8 01 4549067
Winner of the AA Restaurant of the Year Award (see p20)

Finnstown Country House Hotel ✿ ★★★

Newcastle Road, Lucan 01 6280644

Portmarnock Hotel ✿✿ ★★★★

Strand Road, Portmarnock 01 8460611

The Red Bank Restaurant ✿

7 Church Street, Skerries 01 8491005

CO GALWAY

Hayden's Hotel ✿ ★★★

Ballinasloe 0905 42347

Ballynahinch Castle ✿✿ ★★★★

Ballynahinch 095 31006

Cashel House Hotel ✿✿ ★★★

Cashel 095 31001

Zetland Country House Hotel ✿✿ ★★★

Cashel Bay, Cashel, Connemara 095 31111

Abbeyglen Castle Hotel ✿ ★★★

Sky Road, Clifden 095 21201

Alcock & Brown Hotel ✿ ★★★

Clifden 095 21206

Ardagh Hotel ✿✿ ★★★

Ballyconneely Road, Clifden 095 21384

Rock Glen Country House Hotel ✿✿ ★★★

Clifden 095 21035

Glenlo Abbey Hotel ✿✿ ★★★★

Bushypark, Galway 091 526666

Westward House ✿✿ ★★★★

Galway 091 521442

Galway Bay Hotel ✿✿ ★★★

Oranmore 091 790500

Ross Lake House Hotel ✿ ★★★

Oughterard 091 550109

Lough Inagh Lodge Hotel ✿✿ ★★★

Inagh Valley, Recess 095 34706

Eldons Hotel ✿ ★★

Roundstone, Connemara 095 35933

CO KERRY

The White Sands Hotel ✿ ★★★

Ballheige 066 33102

Cafe Indigo ✿✿

Kenmare 064 42366

Park Hotel Kenmare ✿✿✿ ★★★★

Kenmare 064 41200

Sheen Falls Lodge ✿✿ ★★★★

Kenmare 064 41600

Aghadoe Heights Hotel ✿✿✿ ★★★

Killarney 064 31766

Arbutus Hotel ✿ ★★

College Street, Killarney 064 31037

Cahernane Hotel ✿✿ ★★★

Muckross Road, Killarney 064 31895

Gleneagle Hotel ✿ ★★★

Killarney 064 31870

Killarney Park Hotel ✿ ★★★★

Kenmare Place, Killarney 064 35555

Muckross Park Hotel ✿ ★★★★

Muckross Village, Killarney 064 31938

Great Southern Hotel ✿ ★★★★

Parknasilla 064 45122

Butler Arms Hotel ✿ ★★★

Waterville 066 74144

CO KILDARE

Leixlip House Hotel ✿✿ ★★★

Captains Hill, Leixlip 01 6242268

Moyglare Manor ✿✿ ★★★

Moyglare, Maynooth 01 6286351

Keadeen Hotel ✿✿ ★★★

Newbridge 045 431666

Barberstown Castle ✿✿ ★★★

Straffan 01 6288157

The Kildare Hotel ✿✿✿ ★★★★★

Straffan 01 6017200

CO KILKENNY

Mount Juliet Hotel ✿✿ ★★★★

Thomastown 056 73000

CO LIMERICK

Dunraven Arms Hotel ✿✿✿ ★★★

Adare 061 396633

Castle Oaks House Hotel ✿ ★★★

Castleconnell 061 377666

Castletroy Park Hotel ✿✿ ★★★★

Dublin Road, Limerick 061 335566

Jurys Hotel ✿✿ ★★★

Ennis Road, Limerick 061 327777

Limerick Ryan Hotel ✿ ★★★

Ennis Road, Limerick 061 453922

CO MAYO

The Kirk Restaurant ✿

Lower Charles Street, Castlebar 094 25066

Belmont Hotel ✿ ★★★

Knock 094 88122

Knockranny House Hotel ✿ ★★★★

Knockranny, Westport 098 28600

The Olde Railway Hotel ✿ ★★

The Mall, Westport 098 25166

CO MONAGHAN

Nuremore Hotel ✿✿ ★★★★

Carrickmacross 042 61438

CO ROSCOMMON

Hodson Bay Hotel ✿✿ ★★★

Hodson Bay, Athlone 0902 92444

CO SLIGO

Markree Castle ✿✿ ★★★

Collooney 071 67800

Silver Swan Hotel ✿ ★★

Sligo 071 43231

CO TIPPERARY

Cahir House Hotel ✿ ★★★

The Square, Cahir 052 42727

Nenagh Abbey Court Hotel ✿ ★★★

Dublin Road, Nenagh 067 41111

Grant's Hotel ✿✿ ★★★

Castle Street, Roscrea 0505 23300

CO WESTMEATH

Prince Of Wales Hotel ✿ ★★★

Athlone 0902 72626

CO WEXFORD

Dunbrody Country House ✿✿ ★★★

Arthurstown 051 389600

Courtown Hotel ✿ ★★

Courtown Harbour 055 25210

Marlfield House Hotel ✿✿ ★★★

Gorey 055 21124

Brandon House Hotel ✿ ★★★

Wexford Road, New Ross 051 421703

Kelly's Resort Hotel ✿✿ ★★★★

Rosslare 053 32114

Ferrycarrig Hotel ✿✿ ★★★

Ferrycarrig, Wexford 053 20999

Talbot Hotel ✿ ★★★

Trinity Street, Wexford 053 22566

Whitford House Hotel ✿ ★★★

New Line Road, Wexford 053 43444

CO WICKLOW

Enniscree Lodge Hotel ✿ ★★

Glencree Valley, Enniskerry 01 2863542

Hunter's Hotel ✿ ★★★

Rathnew 0404 40106

Tinakilly Country House ✿✿ ★★★

Rathnew 0404 69274

Woodenbridge Hotel ✿ ★★★

Wooden Bridge 0402 35146

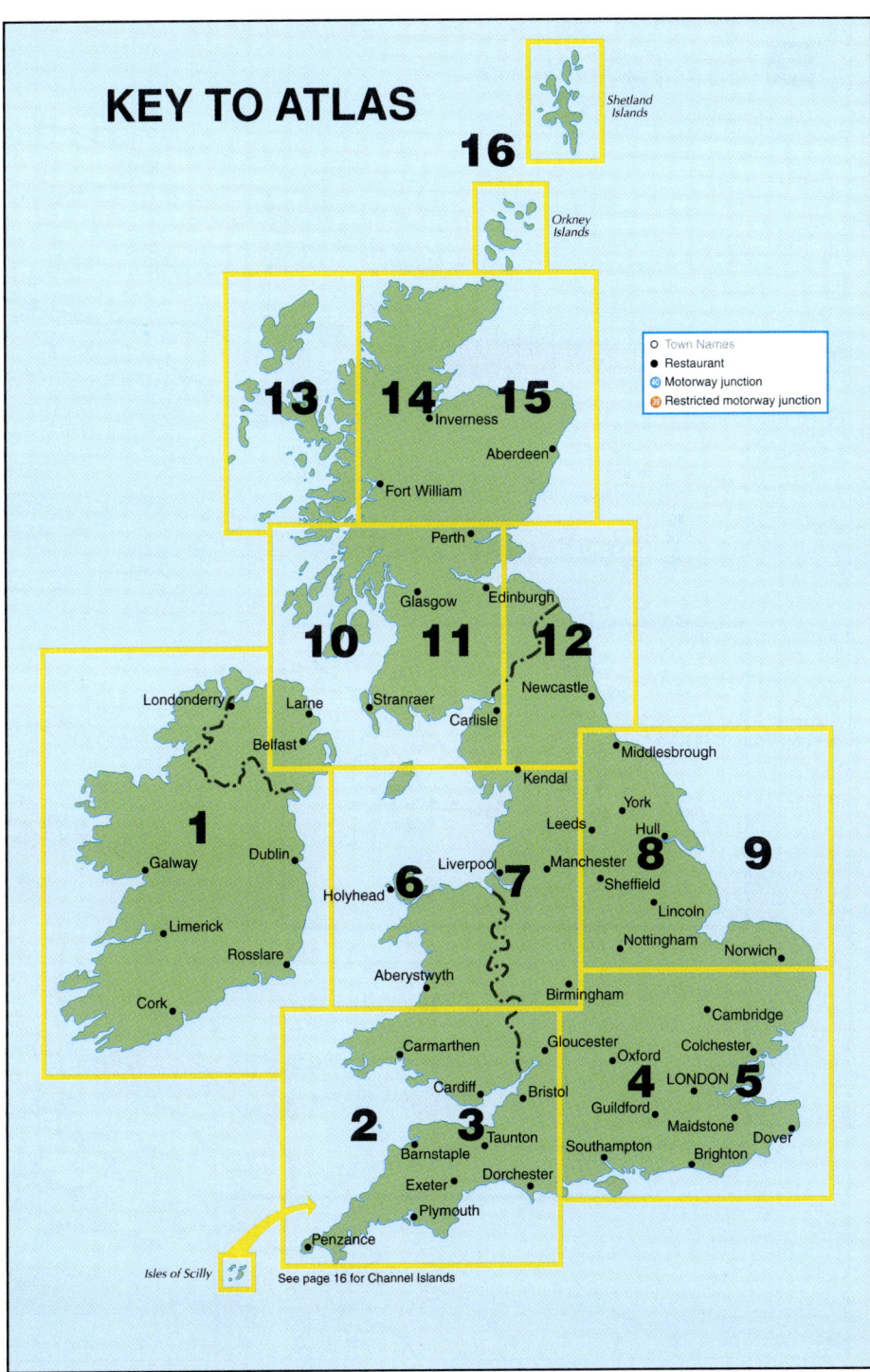

KEY TO ATLAS

16 Shetland Islands

Orkney Islands

Town Names
Restaurant
Motorway junction
Restricted motorway junction

13 **14** **15**
Inverness
Aberdeen
Fort William

10 **11** **12**
Perth
Glasgow Edinburgh
Newcastle
Londonderry Larne Stranraer
Belfast Carlisle
Kendal

1 Middlesbrough
York
Leeds Hull
8 **9**
Galway Dublin Liverpool Manchester
Holyhead **6** **7** Sheffield
Limerick Lincoln
Rosslare Nottingham Norwich
Cork Aberystwyth Birmingham
Cambridge

Gloucester Colchester
Carmarthen Oxford
2 **3** Cardiff Bristol **4** LONDON **5**
Guildford Maidstone Dover
Taunton Southampton Brighton
Barnstaple
Exeter Dorchester
Plymouth
Penzance
Isles of Scilly See page 16 for Channel Islands

© The Automobile Association 1999

2

Aberporth

SN

Cardigan

Strumble Head

SM

Fishguard

St David's
Ramsey
Island
Wolf's Castle

PEMBROKESHIRE

Carmarthen

CARMART

St Brides Bay

Haverfordwest

Skomer Island

Milford
Haven

Laugharne

Skokholm
Island

Pembroke
Dock

Tenby

		Town Names
○		Restaurant
BLAE·G	Blaenau Gwent
BRDGND	Bridgend
MYR TD	Merthyr Tydfil
NEWPT	Newport
RHONDD	Rhondda Cynon Taff
TORFN	Torfaen
V GLAM	Vale of Glamorgan

Pembroke

Caldey
Island

Carmarthen Bay

Reynoldston

Langla
The

SW

ST AUSTELL

Portreath
Truro
St Ives
Ruan High Lanes
Redruth
Veryan
Penzance
Marazion
Portscatho
St Mawes
Constantine
Falmouth
Porthleven
Mawnan Smith
Mousehole
Helston
Gillan

Land's End

Mount's Bay

Lizard Point

SS

Lundy
Woolacombe
Croyde
Barnsta

Hartland Point
Clovelly
Bidefo

Bude

A3072

Ashwater
Okehan

Tintagel
Launceston
Lewo

Land's End

SW

Bryher
St Martin's
Tresco
St Mary's
Isles of Scilly

Polzeath
Port Gaverne
Port Isaac

Altarnun
Lifton
Lydfo

Trevose Head
Constantine Bay

CORNWALL

Padstow
Wadebridge

Bodmin Moor

Gulworthy
Two E

Newquay

St Wenn
Bodmin

Callington
Liskeard
St Mellion

St Keyne

Golant
Fowey
Talland Bay
Polperro

ST AUSTELL

SEE INSET

Dodman Point

SX

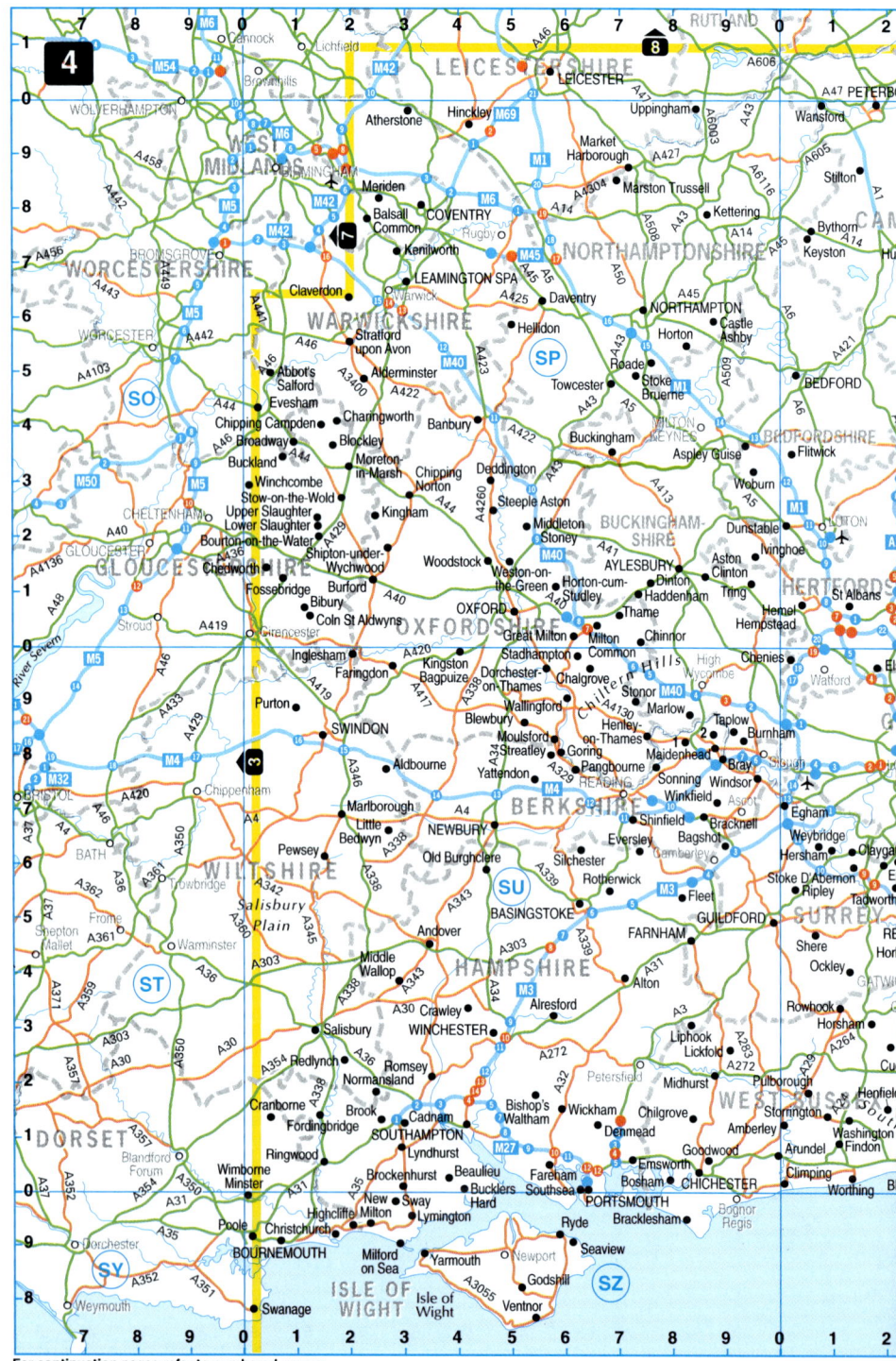

NORFOLK

Wisbech · A47 · Swaffham · NORWICH · GREAT YARMOUTH

Downham Market · Wymondham · Hethersett · A146

Ely · LOWESTOFT

Mildenhall · A143 · Diss · Beccles · BA145

A1066 · Fressingfield · Southwold

SUFFOLK

Newmarket · Ixworth · Yaxley · Yoxford

CAMBRIDGE · BURY ST EDMUNDS · Stowmarket · Aldeburgh

Duxford · Lavenham · Woodbridge · Orford Ness · **TM**

Long Melford · Hintlesham · IPSWICH

Sudbury · Polstead · Felixstowe

Great Yeldham · Nayland · Manningtree

Wethersfield · Dedham · Harwich

Stansted · Great Dunmow · Coggeshall · The Naze

Sawbridgeworth · Felsted · Tolleshunt Knights · COLCHESTER

CHELMSFORD · CLACTON-ON-SEA

ESSEX

BRENTWOOD · Rochford · Foulness Island

Basildon · SOUTHEND-ON-SEA

Tilbury · R.Thames

Isle of Sheppey · Margate

Rochester · Sittingbourne · Whitstable · Ramsgate

Brands Hatch · Chatham · Faversham

Sevenoaks · Bearstead · CANTERBURY

Maidstone · Deal · **TR**

Edenbridge · Lenham · A257

TUNBRIDGE WELLS · Sissinghurst · ASHFORD · Wye · CHANNEL TUNNEL TERMINAL · Dover

Grinstead · Cranbrook · Biddenden · Folkestone

Crowborough · Hythe

Uckfield · Peasmarsh · Rye · Dungeness

Herstmonceux · Battle · **Strait of Dover**

Hailsham · HASTINGS · St Leonards

Wilmington · Jevington

Alfriston · EASTBOURNE

Seaford · Beachy Head · **TV**

1 Burchett's Green
2 Cookham Dean

○ Town Names
● Restaurant

0 · 10 · 20 miles
0 · 10 · 20 · 30 kilometres

5 6 7 8 9 0 1 2 3 4 5 6 7 8 11 9 0 A595

0 · Point of Ayre — A17
Eskd
Gre

9 · Isle of Man — A3 Ramsey
Maughold Head
ISLE
Peel A4 OF
MAN A2

8 · A1
A3 DOUGLAS
A5

7 · Castletown
Dreswick Point

*Irish
Sea*

6

5 · SC

4

3

2

1

0 · M

9 · Carmel Head
Great
Ormes
Head

8 · Holyhead Anglesey Llandudno COLWYN
BAY
Beaumaris
Holy Island A5 Conwy Abergele A55
Tal-y-Bont
7 · ISLE OF CONWY
ANGLESEY Caernarfon Trefriw
A4086 A470
6 · Llanberis
Caernarfon Betws-y-coed
Bay Ru
5 · SH A498 A470 A5
DENBI
A499

4 · A497 A487 A494 Llai
Lleyn Peninsula Portmeirion A4212 Bala
Pwllheli Talsarnau A470
3 · Abersoch Harlech
GWYNEDD
Bardsey A496
2 · Island Bontddu
Barmouth Dolgellau Llanwddyr
A470
1 · A458

0 · ○ Town Names A487 Machynlleth POWYS
● Restaurant Aberdyfi A493 Eglwysfach A470
9 · *Cardigan Bay* Ney
0 10 20 miles
0 10 20 30 kilometres A487 A44 A470
8 · SN Aberystwyth
Llangurig
7 · 2 CEREDIGION A470 Rhayader
5 6 7 8 9 0 1 2 3 4 5 6 7 8 9 0 A485

For continuation pages refer to numbered arrows

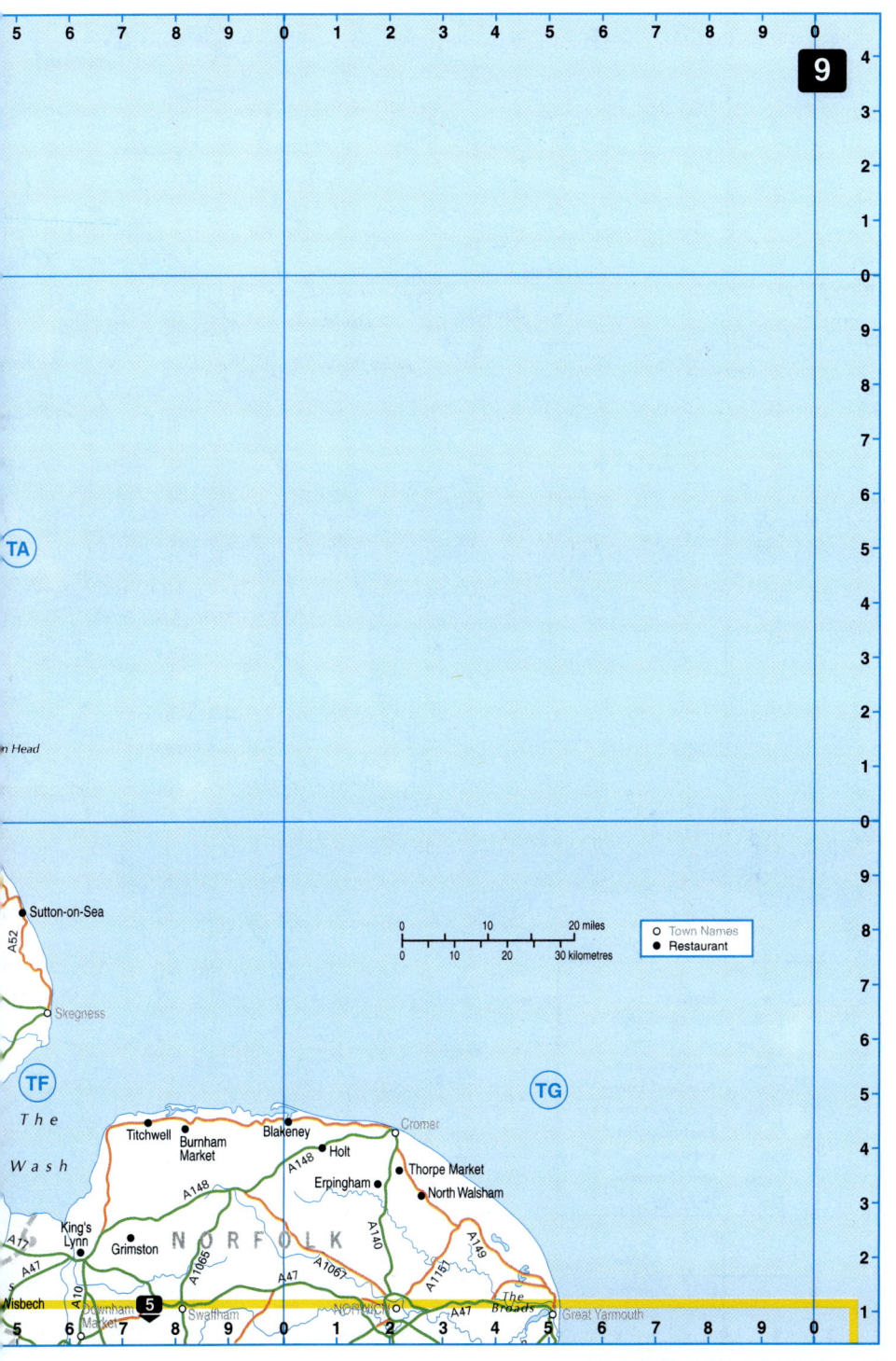

9

4
3
2
1
0
9
8
7
6
5
4
3
2
1
0
9
8
7
6
5
4
3
2
1

5 6 7 8 9 0 1 2 3 4 5 6 7 8 9 0

TA

n Head

Sutton-on-Sea

A52

Skegness

TF   TG

The

Wash

Titchwell   Burnham   Blakeney   Cromer
             Market   Holt
                       A148
                              Erpingham   Thorpe Market
                                           North Walsham

King's   A149
Lynn   Grimston   N O R F O L K
A47   A140
        A1065   A1067
Wisbech   A47   NORWICH   A47   The Broads   Great Yarmouth
        Burnham   5   Swaffham   Broads
        Market

5 6 7 8 9 0 1 2 3 4 5 6 7 8 9 0

| ○ Town Names |
| ● Restaurant |

0   10   20 miles
0   10   20   30 kilometres

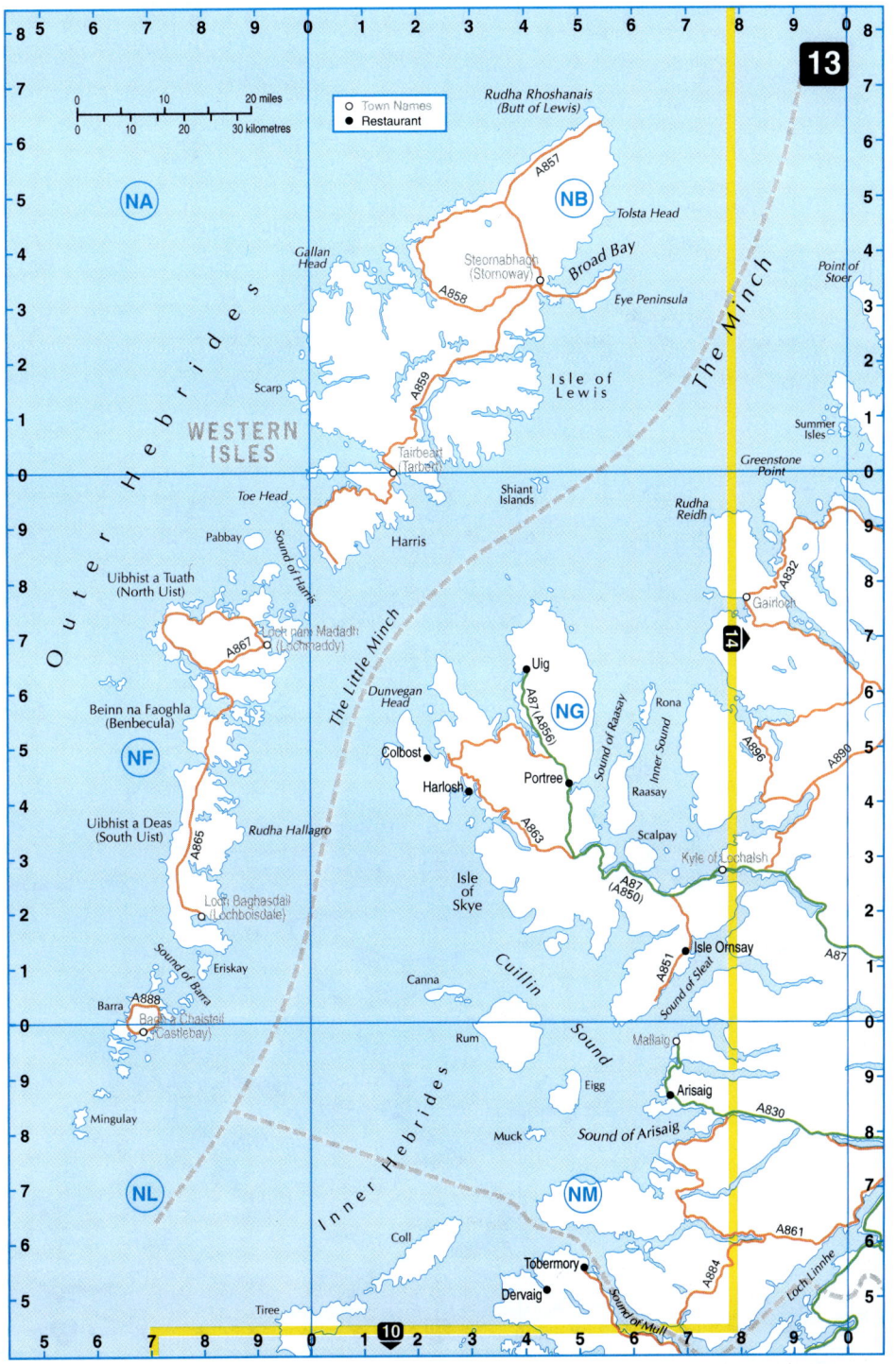

13

Rudha Rhoshanais
(Butt of Lewis)

○ Town Names
● Restaurant

The Minch

NA

A857

NB

Tolsta Head

Gallan
Head

Steornabhagh
(Stornoway)

Broad Bay

A858

Point of
Stoer

Eye Peninsula

Scarp

Isle of
Lewis

A859

WESTERN
ISLES

Summer
Isles

Tairbeart
(Tarbert)

Greenstone
Point

O u t e r   H e b r i d e s

Toe Head

Shiant
Islands

Rudha
Reidh

Pabbay

Sound of Harris

Harris

Uibhist a Tuath
(North Uist)

The Little Minch

A832

Gairloch

Uig

Loch nam Madadh
(Lochmaddy)

A867

Dunvegan
Head

14

Beinn na Faoghla
(Benbecula)

A871(A856)

NG

Rona

Sound of Raasay

Inner Sound

A896

A890

NF

Colbost

Portree

Raasay

Harlosh

Uibhist a Deas
(South Uist)

Rudha Hallagro

A865

A863

Scalpay

Kyle of Lochalsh

Loch Baghasdail
(Lochboisdale)

Isle
of
Skye

A87
(A850)

Sound of Barra

Eriskay

Canna

C u i l l i n

A851

Isle Ornsay

A87

Barra

A888

Sound of Sleat

Bagh a Chaisteil
(Castlebay)

Rum

Mallaig

Mingulay

S o u n d

Eigg

Arisaig

A830

Inner Hebrides

Muck

Sound of Arisaig

A861

NL

NM

Coll

A884

Loch Linnhe

Tobermory

Tiree

Dervaig

Sound of Mull

10

14

Rudha Rhoshanais
(Butt of Lewis)

A857

Tolsta Head

Broad Bay

NB

Steòrnabhagh
(Stornoway)

Eye Peninsula

Isle of
Lewis

Shiant
Islands

The Minch

Greenstone
Point

Rudha
Reidh

A832

Gairloch

A87

Rona

Sound of Raasay

Torridon

Inner Sound

NG

A896

Shieldaig

A890

Portree

Raasay

A863

Scalpay

Isle
of
Skye

A87

Kyle of Lochalsh

13

Cuillin

A851

Sound of Sleat

Rum

Mallaig

Sound

Eigg

Muck

Sound of Arisaig

NM

Tobermory

A884

A861

Strontian

A830

Glenfinnan

Onich

Kentallen

Loch Linnhe

Port Appin

Sound of Mull

Cape Wrath

Whiten
Head

Dumess

Pentland Firth

Strathy
Point

Tongue

A838

A836

Handa Island

A894

NC

A838

A836

A897

Point of
Stoer

A837

Lochinver

Summer
Isles

A835

Ullapool

Dundonnell

A832

A835

A832

A832

Contin

Dingwall

A9

Muir of Ord

INVERNESS

A82

A831

HIGHLAND

North
West
Highlands

Bonar
Bridge

A837

Domoch

Tarbat
Ness

Brora

A9

A839

A836

Tain

Heimsda

A9

Nairn

Fo
A96

Mc

Granto
on-Sp

Dulnain Bridge

A9

A99

Invermoriston

Whitebridge

A887

A87

Kingussie

Newtonmore

Monadliath
Mountains

A9

Spean Bridge

A86

A82

Fort William

NN

A9

Grampian
Mou

Blair Athol

Killiecrankie

Pitlochry

PERTH
AND
KINROSS

Aberfeldy

A82

10

11

ND

NJ

NK

NO

Island of Stroma
Duncansby Head
John O'Groats
A836
rso
A9
Noss Head
A99 (A9)
Wick
A9

ossiemouth
Elgin
Drybridge
Keith
RAY
A941
Bridge of Marnoch
estown
Craigellachie
A920
A941
A97
A96
A920
ABERDEENSHIRE
Kildrummy
A939
A944
A97
A938
A93
A980
A93
Ballater
Aboyne
Banchory
A957
S
ial of Glenshee
ANGUS
A90
Bridgend of Lintrathen
A926
A935
Montrose
A932
Forfar
rie
Glamis
A933
Arbroath

Fraserburgh
A98
A90
A950
A952
A92
A90 (A952)
Peterhead
A90 (A92)
Newburgh
Inverurie
A944
ABERDEEN CITY
ABERDEEN
A90
A92

Lunan Bay

○ Town Names
● Restaurant

0   10   20 miles
0   10   20   30 kilometres

12

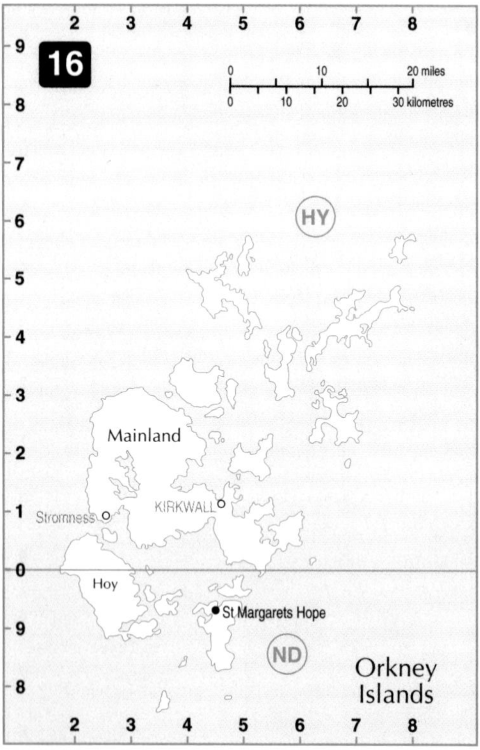
16
0 10 20 miles
0 10 20 30 kilometres
HY
Mainland
Stromness
KIRKWALL
Hoy
St Margarets Hope
ND
Orkney Islands

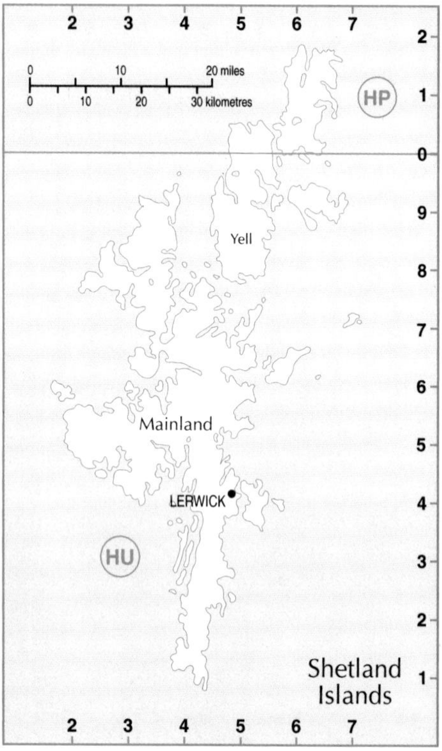
0 10 20 miles
0 10 20 30 kilometres
HP
Yell
Mainland
LERWICK
HU
Shetland Islands

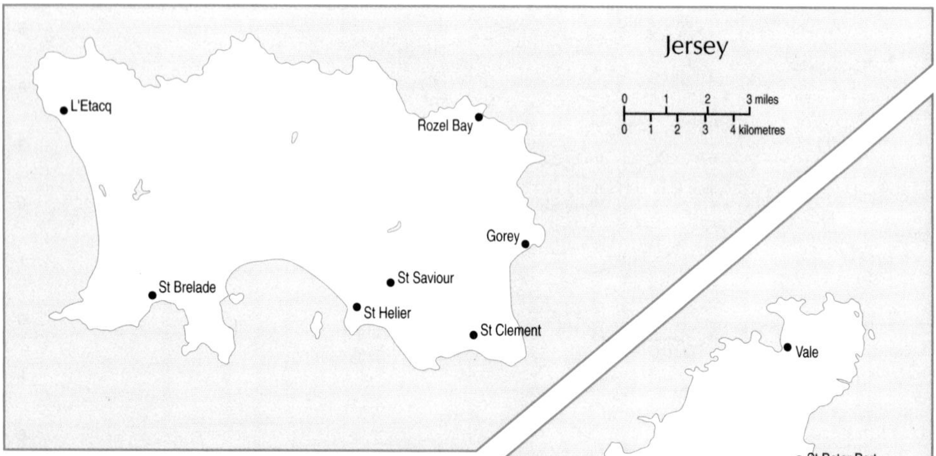
Jersey
0 1 2 3 miles
0 1 2 3 4 kilometres
L'Etacq
Rozel Bay
Gorey
St Saviour
St Brelade
St Helier
St Clement

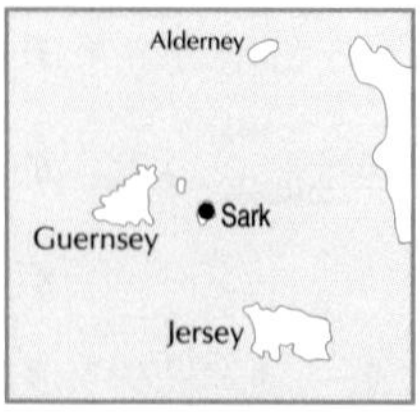
Alderney
Sark
Guernsey
Jersey

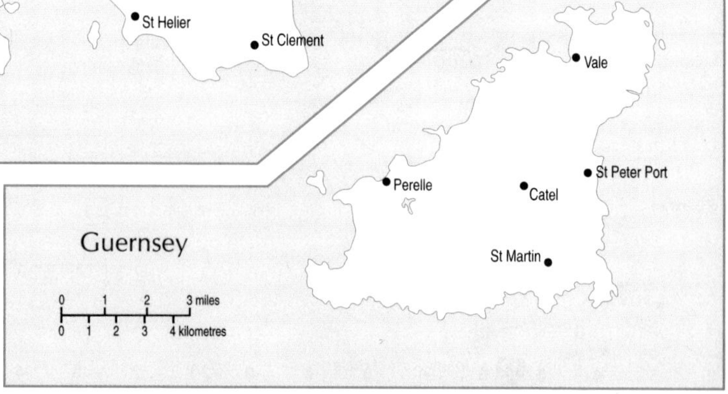
Vale
Perelle
Catel
St Peter Port
Guernsey
St Martin
0 1 2 3 miles
0 1 2 3 4 kilometres

Central London

Regent's Park

Lord's
Cricket
Ground

5

WELLINGTON RD
PRINCE ALBERT RD
ST JOHN'S WOOD RD
PARK ROAD
ALBANY STREET
HAMPSTEAD ROAD
EVERSHOLT STREET
St
Euston
MAIDA VALE

Open Air
Theatre

Euston Square
EUSTON RD
Madame
Tussaud's
Warren
Street
University
College
GOWER
TOTTENHAM COURT
Planetarium
Great
Portland
Street
Marylebone
Baker
Street
Regent's
Park
MARYLEBONE ROAD
EDGWARE ROAD
Edgware
Road
Goodge
Street
PORTLAND PLACE

4 **PADDINGTON**
A40(M) WESTWAY

Wallace
Collection

Tottenha
Court Roa

WESTBOURNE TERRACE
Paddington
SUSSEX GARDENS
EDGWARE ROAD
GLOUCESTER PLACE
BAKER STREET
OXFORD STREET
Oxford Circus
REGENT STREET

BAYSWATER

Marble
Arch
Marble
Arch
Bond
Street
Carnaby
Street
SOH
Trocadero
Centre

Lancaster Gate
BAYSWATER ROAD
Speakers'
Corner
Grosvenor
Square
MAYFAIR
Museum of
Mankind
Piccadilly
Circus

3
Berkeley
Square
Royal
Academy
of Arts
PARK LANE

Hyde Park

Kensington
Gardens

PICCADILLY
Green
Park
ST JAMES'S ST
PALL MALL
St James's
Palace

The Serpentine

Albert
Memorial

Apsley House
(Wellington Museum)

Green Park

St James

KENSINGTON ROAD
Knightsbridge
KNIGHTSBRIDGE
Hyde Park
Corner
Buckingham
Palace
Royal Mews
GROSVENOR PLACE
Guard's
Chapel &
Museum
St

Royal
Albert Hall

2 **KNIGHTSBRIDGE**
Belgrave
Square
WESTMINS

Imperial College
Victoria and
Albert Museum
Harrods
Victoria
Westminster
Cathedral
BROMPTON ROAD
SLOANE STREET
KING'S ROAD
ECCLESTON STREET
VAUXHALL BRIDGE

Science Museum
Natural History
Museum

CROMWELL ROAD

Gloucester
Road
South
Kensington
Sloane
Square
VICTORIA
BELGRAVE ROAD

1
FULHAM ROAD
Chelsea Barracks

**SOUTH
KENSINGTON**
KING'S ROAD
Royal
Hospital
GROSVENOR ROAD

CHELSEA
National Army
Museum

A   B   C   D

King's Cross

PENTONVILLE RD

King's Cross
(Thameslink)

's Cross
'ancras

CITY ROAD

GOSWELL ROAD

ROSEBERY AVENUE

Old Street

CITY ROAD

David
tion of
: Art

Dickens'
House

OLD STREET

Hospitals

CLERKENWELL ROAD

Royal Britain
Exhibition

THEOBALD'S ROAD

Museum of the
Order of St John

ALDERGATE STREET

lle
ersity
ndon

SOUTHAMPTON ROW

Gray's Inn

Barbican

The
Barbican

Liverpool
Street

BISHOPSGATE

JRY

Chancery Leather
Lane   Lane

Farringdon
Central Markets
(Smithfield)

Moorgate

HOLBORN

itish Museum
d Library

HIGH HOLBORN

HOLBORN VIADUCT

St Barts
Hospital

Museum of
London

MOORGATE

HIGH HOLBORN

KINGSWAY

Holborn   Lincoln's Inn

National
Postal
Museum

International
Financial Centre

ter
—

Sir John
Soane's
Museum

City
Thameslink

Old Bailey

Guildhall

Stock
Exchange

Aldgate

Royal Courts
of Justice

St Paul's
Cathedral

St Paul's

Bank of
England

Royal
Opera
House

FLEET STREET

LUDGATE HILL

CHEAPSIDE

Bank

CITY

Lloyd's

Covent
Garden

ALDWYCH

STRAND

Temple

Blackfriars

Mansion
House

Leadenhall
Market

FENCHURCH STREET

Fenchurch
Street

London Transport
Museum

Temple

Cannon
Street

Monument

Tower Gateway (DLR)
Tower Hill

ST MARTIN'S LANE

STRAND

EMBANKMENT

UPPER THAMES STREET

TOWER HILL

Courtauld
Gallery

River   Thames

Custom
House

Tower of
London

nal
ry

Embankment

WATERLOO BRIDGE

Museum of the
Moving Image

Shakespeare
Globe Exhibition

LONDON BRIDGE

HMS
Belfast

TOWER BRIDGE

ar

Charing
Cross

Cleopatra's
Needle

Royal National
Theatre

SOUTHWARK

Southwark
Cathedral

London
Dungeon

Hays
Galleria

admiralty

VICTORIA

Queen
Eliz Hall

Hayward
Gallery

Waterloo
(East)

London
Bridge

Royal Festival
Hall

WHITEHALL

nment
ices

Waterloo

Borough

Guy's
Hospital

Westminster

WATERLOO ROAD

BOROUGH HIGH STREET

LONG LANE

WESTMINSTER
BRIDGE

Lambeth
North

TOWER BRIDGE ROAD

Big Ben

WESTMINSTER BRIDGE RD

BOROUGH RD

nster
ey

Houses of
Parliament

Florence
Nightingale
Museum

ST GEORGE'S RD

GREAT DOVER STREET

Victoria
Tower
Gardens

Lambeth
Palace

KENNINGTON ROAD

Imperial War
Museum

NEW KENT ROAD

OLD KENT ROAD

Museum of
Garden
History

Elephant
and Castle

ate
llery

MILLBANK

F

G

VAUXHALL BRIDGE

ON LANE

KENNINGTON LANE

KEY TO RESTAURANT LOCATIONS

Each restaurant in London has a map reference, eg C2. The letter 'C' refers
to the grid square located at the bottom of the map. The figure '2' refers to
the grid square located at the left hand edge of the map. For example,
where these two intersect, Buckingham Palace can be found.
Due to the scale of the map, only a rough guide to the location of a
restaurant can be given. A more detailed map will be necessary to be
precise.

Vauxhall

D   E   The
Oval

0   ½ mile
0
       ½   1 km

Greater London

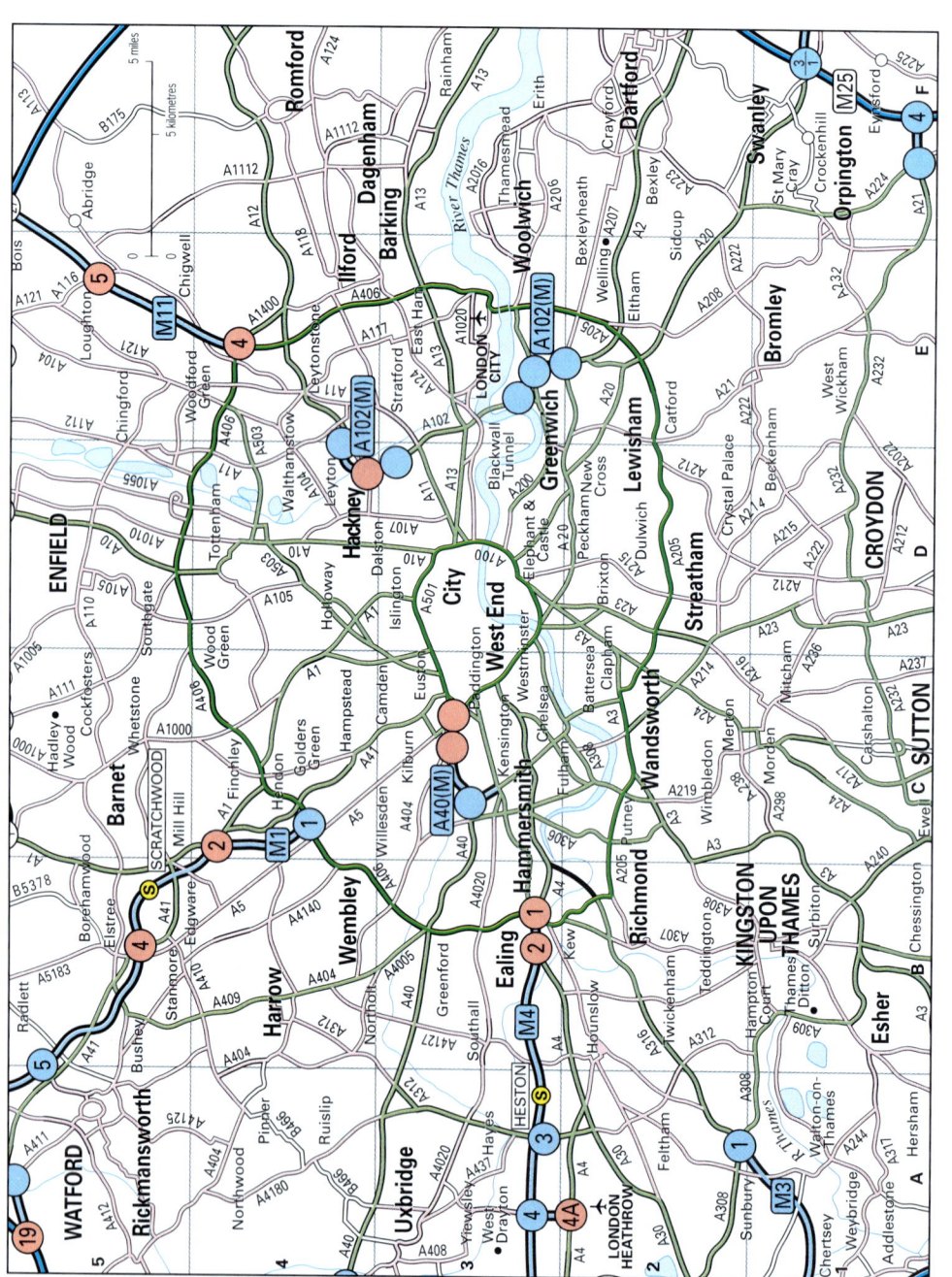

London Postcode Index

Index

Reader's Recommendations

If you have recently eaten well at a restaurant that is not included in this guide, we should be interested to hear about it. Please send this form to Head of Guidebooks, Editorial Department, AA Publishing, Fanum House, Basingstoke RG21 4EA.

Recommendations, and/or any adverse comments will be carefully considered, and passed on to our Hotel & Restaurant inspectors, but the AA cannot guarantee to act on them nor to enter into correspondence about them. Complaints are best brought to the attention to the management of the restaurant at the time, so that they can be dealt with promptly and, it is hoped, to the satisfaction of both parties.

Your name and address

....

....

....

....

....

....

Name and address of the restaurant

....

....

....

....

Was the meal lunch or dinner?

....

....

Approximate cost for two £

....

(continued over)

Type of cuisine English/French/Italian/Thai/Indian/Chinese/Other (please specify)

Comments

Reader's Recommendations

If you have recently eaten well at a restaurant that is not included in this guide, we should be interested to hear about it. Please send this form to Head of Guidebooks, Editorial Department, AA Publishing, Fanum House, Basingstoke RG21 4EA.

Recommendations, and/or any adverse comments will be carefully considered, and passed on to our Hotel & Restaurant inspectors, but the AA cannot guarantee to act on them nor to enter into correspondence about them. Complaints are best brought to the attention to the management of the restaurant at the time, so that they can be dealt with promptly and, it is hoped, to the satisfaction of both parties.

Your name and address

....

....

....

....

....

Name and address of the restaurant

....

....

....

Was the meal lunch or dinner?

....

....

Approximate cost for two £

....

(continued over)

Type of cuisine English/French/Italian/Thai/Indian/Chinese/Other (please specify)

....

....

....

....

Comments

....

....

....

....

....

....

....

....

....

....

....

....

....

....

....

....

....

....

....

....

Reader's Recommendations

If you have recently eaten well at a restaurant that is not included in this guide, we should be interested to hear about it. Please send this form to Head of Guidebooks, Editorial Department, AA Publishing, Fanum House, Basingstoke RG21 4EA.

Recommendations, and/or any adverse comments will be carefully considered, and passed on to our Hotel & Restaurant inspectors, but the AA cannot guarantee to act on them nor to enter into correspondence about them. Complaints are best brought to the attention to the management of the restaurant at the time, so that they can be dealt with promptly and, it is hoped, to the satisfaction of both parties.

Your name and address

Name and address of the restaurant

Was the meal lunch or dinner?

Approximate cost for two £

(continued over)

Type of cuisine English/French/Italian/Thai/Indian/Chinese/Other (please specify)

Comments

Reader's Recommendations

If you have recently eaten well at a restaurant that is not included in this guide, we should be interested to hear about it. Please send this form to Head of Guidebooks, Editorial Department, AA Publishing, Fanum House, Basingstoke RG21 4EA.

Recommendations, and/or any adverse comments will be carefully considered, and passed on to our Hotel & Restaurant inspectors, but the AA cannot guarantee to act on them nor to enter into correspondence about them. Complaints are best brought to the attention to the management of the restaurant at the time, so that they can be dealt with promptly and, it is hoped, to the satisfaction of both parties.

Your name and address

....

....

....

....

....

....

Name and address of the restaurant

....

....

....

....

Was the meal lunch or dinner?

....

....

Approximate cost for two £

....

(continued over)

Type of cuisine English/French/Italian/Thai/Indian/Chinese/Other (please specify)

Comments

Reader's Recommendations

If you have recently eaten well at a restaurant that is not included in this guide, we should be interested to hear about it. Please send this form to Head of Guidebooks, Editorial Department, AA Publishing, Fanum House, Basingstoke RG21 4EA.

Recommendations, and/or any adverse comments will be carefully considered, and passed on to our Hotel & Restaurant inspectors, but the AA cannot guarantee to act on them nor to enter into correspondence about them. Complaints are best brought to the attention to the management of the restaurant at the time, so that they can be dealt with promptly and, it is hoped, to the satisfaction of both parties.

Your name and address

....

....

....

....

....

Name and address of the restaurant

....

....

....

....

Was the meal lunch or dinner?

....

....

Approximate cost for two £

....

(continued over)

Type of cuisine English/French/Italian/Thai/Indian/Chinese/Other (please specify)

Comments